THE PELOPONNESIAN WAR

THUCYDIDES (c.46... ...ocratic Athenian family wh... ...ocratic leader Pericles, but ...himself because of a number of Peric... ...hough not of democracy exc... ...when guided by Pericles. His subject is the Peloponnesian War. This was fought between Athens and Sparta, the two leading powers of fifth-century Greece, and eventually won by Sparta. Thucydides started work at the outset of the war in 431, expecting it to be 'more momentous than any previous conflict'. He served as a general in the war, but was exiled after failing to keep the city of Amphipolis out of Spartan hands in 424/3. He returned to Athens at the end of the war, but although a few sentences refer to later events his surviving narrative breaks off in the autumn of 411. He is more narrowly focused on the war than his predecessor Herodotus (c.485–425) had been on the Persian Wars at the beginning of the fifth century, and his work has great intellectual power: he was energetic and intelligent in establishing the facts and penetrating in his judgement of general issues; he explains events wholly in human terms; the work is skilfully composed, with a blend of plain and vivid narrative passages, and with speeches which often explore the nature of power. Thucydides' history is indeed the 'permanent legacy' which he intended it to be.

MARTIN HAMMOND was born in 1944 and educated at Winchester College and Balliol College, Oxford. He has taught at St Paul's School, Harrow School, and Eton College, where he was Head of Classics from 1974 to 1980, and Master in College from 1980 to 1984. He was Headmaster of the City of London School from 1984 to 1990, and of Tonbridge School from 1990 to his retirement in 2005. He has also translated the *Iliad* (Penguin, 1987), the *Odyssey* (Duckworth, 2000), and the *Meditations* of Marcus Aurelius (Penguin, 2006). He is married, with two children.

P. J. RHODES is Honorary Professor and Emeritus Professor of Ancient History at the University of Durham. He has written widely on Thucydides and ancient Greece; one of his most recent books is *A History of the Classical Greek World 478–323 BC* (2005).

OXFORD WORLD'S CLASSICS

*For over 100 years Oxford World's Classics have brought
readers closer to the world's great literature. Now with over 700
titles—from the 4,000-year-old myths of Mesopotamia to the
twentieth century's greatest novels—the series makes available
lesser-known as well as celebrated writing.*

*The pocket-sized hardbacks of the early years contained
introductions by Virginia Woolf, T. S. Eliot, Graham Greene,
and other literary figures which enriched the experience of reading.
Today the series is recognized for its fine scholarship and
reliability in texts that span world literature, drama and poetry,
religion, philosophy, and politics. Each edition includes perceptive
commentary and essential background information to meet the
changing needs of readers.*

OXFORD WORLD'S CLASSICS

THUCYDIDES

The Peloponnesian War

Translated by
MARTIN HAMMOND

With an Introduction and Notes by
P. J. RHODES

OXFORD
UNIVERSITY PRESS

OXFORD

UNIVERSITY PRESS

Great Clarendon Street, Oxford OX2 6DP

Oxford University Press is a department of the University of Oxford.
It furthers the University's objective of excellence in research, scholarship,
and education by publishing worldwide in

Oxford New York

Auckland Cape Town Dar es Salaam Hong Kong Karachi
Kuala Lumpur Madrid Melbourne Mexico City Nairobi
New Delhi Shanghai Taipei Toronto

With offices in

Argentina Austria Brazil Chile Czech Republic France Greece
Guatemala Hungary Italy Japan Poland Portugal Singapore
South Korea Switzerland Thailand Turkey Ukraine Vietnam

Oxford is a registered trade mark of Oxford University Press
in the UK and in certain other countries

Published in the United States
by Oxford University Press Inc., New York

Translation © Martin Hammond 2009
Editorial material © P. J. Rhodes 2009

British Library Cataloguing in Publication Data

Data available

Library of Congress Cataloging-in-Publication Data

Thucydides.
[History of the Peloponnesian War. English]
The Peloponnesian War / Thucydides; translated by Martin Hammond, with an
introduction and notes by P.J. Rhodes.
p. cm.—(Oxford world classics)
Includes bibliographical references and index.
ISBN 978-0-19-282191-1
1. Greece—History—Peloponnesian War, 431–404 B.C. I. Hammond, Martin, 1944–
II. Rhodes, P. J. (Peter John) III. Title.
DF229.T5H36 2009
938'.05—dc22
2008049469

Typeset by Cepha Imaging Private Ltd., Bangalore, India
Printed in Great Britain by
Clays Ltd., Elcograf S.p.A.

ISBN 978-0-19-282191-1

18

PREFACE

THIS book is a collaboration. It has been a pleasure and a reassurance to work closely with Peter Rhodes on every aspect of the book at every stage. I am responsible for the translation, the index, and (for the most part) the decisions on which reading to adopt in the many places where the Greek text is in doubt: Peter for all the rest of the book. The process has been interactive. In a series of virtually weekly emails we have seen and commented on each other's drafts section by section, and I am gratefully conscious that hardly a page of my translation has not benefited from improvements to my first draft suggested by Peter.

Thucydides admired energy, inventiveness, and intellectual power, and all these qualities are manifest in his own writing. He wrote very difficult Greek, in (as far as we can tell) a highly idiosyncratic style. Narrative sections are brilliantly fast and vivid (e.g. the description of the plague, 2.47–54; the escape from Plataea, 3.20–4; the battle on Epipolae, 7.43–4), but when Thucydides brings his intellect to bear, either authorially or in densely textured speeches given to politicians or military men, on the wider and more permanent issues which interested him (e.g. the nature of power, the self-perpetuating logic of empire, the moral collapse in civil war, the clash of rival political systems, cultures, and ideologies), his thought is complex and compressed, set out in innovative language itself so compressed that regular syntax on occasion buckles under the pressure, and a two- or three-word phrase can need careful and sometimes contentious unpacking. The translator needs all the help he or she can get. In addition to the constant vigilance of Peter Rhodes, I have been very fortunate to benefit from the generosity of Chris Pelling and Simon Hornblower. Chris Pelling, Regius Professor of Greek at Oxford, very kindly read the entire translation in draft, and his comments and suggestions have been gratefully incorporated into the final version, much improving what I had first written. Simon Hornblower, Professor of Classics and Grote Professor of Ancient History at University College London, generously allowed both me and Peter Rhodes photocopies of the typescript of the third and final volume (5.25–end) of his magisterial *Commentary on Thucydides* before its publication by Oxford University Press: this has greatly assisted the second half of the translation.

I owe further debts of gratitude to Judith Luna of Oxford World's Classics for her constant help, encouragement, and guidance: and to Andrew Crawshaw for the loan year after year of his delightful house on the island of Andros, where much of this translation was written.

The representation in English of Greek names (people and places) poses a familiar problem, to which there is no obvious or universally accepted solution. The practice I have adopted in this translation is no more consistent than any other. I broadly Latinize (e.g. -us for -os or -ous, and c for k), but mostly retain -ei- (e.g. Peiraeus, Deceleia), and -ou- where that assists the pronunciation (e.g. Thrasyboulus rather than Thrasybulus) or otherwise has claim on aesthetic or etymological grounds.

Martin Hammond

I add my thanks to Judith Luna, for inviting me to join in this enterprise and for her help on various points; and to Simon Hornblower and the Press, for letting us see in advance the third volume of his *Commentary on Thucydides* and adapt one of his maps. I thank Oxbow Books, as successors to Aris & Phillips, for permission to reuse here, at a different level and in a different way, some material from my editions of Books 2, 3, and 4.1–5.24. Above all I thank Martin Hammond, for being a stimulating, alert, and genial collaborator: my understanding of Thucydides is less inadequate now than it was before we started.

P. J. R.

CONTENTS

Abbreviations   viii

Introduction   ix

Select Bibliography   liv

Summary and Analysis   lviii

THE PELOPONNESIAN WAR   I

Appendix: Weights, Measures, and Distances;
    Money; Calendar   473

Explanatory Notes   475

Notes on the Greek Text   633

Index   644

Maps   709

ABBREVIATIONS

For texts of ancient works, including modern collections of text, and for classical journals, we follow the list of abbreviations in the third edition of the *Oxford Classical Dictionary*. Note also the following:

Barrington Atlas	R. J. A. Talbert (ed.), *Barrington Atlas of the Greek and Roman World* (Princeton University Press, 2000)
Brosius	M. Brosius, *The Persian Empire from Cyrus II to Artaxerxes I*, LACTOR 16 (London Association of Classical Teachers, 2000)
Davies, *APF*	J. K. Davies, *Athenian Propertied Families, 600–300 BC* (Oxford University Press, 1971)
Develin, *AO*	R. Develin, *Athenian Officials, 684–321 BC* (Cambridge University Press, 1989)
Hansen and Nielsen, *Inventory*	M. H. Hansen and T. H. Nielsen (eds.), *An Inventory of Archaic and Classical Poleis* (Oxford University Press, 2004)
Pritchett, *GSW*	W. K. Pritchett, *The Greek State at War* (University of California Press, 1974–91; vol. i originally published as *Ancient Greek Military Practices*, 1971)
RO	P. J. Rhodes and R. Osborne, *Greek Historical Inscriptions, 404–323 BC* (Oxford University Press, 2003; corrected reprint, 2007)

INTRODUCTION

Thucydides and his History of the Peloponnesian War

In the second half of the fifth century BC the two leading powers in Greece were Athens, which was democratic and innovative, and whose navy had built up an empire in the Aegean Sea, and Sparta, which was oligarchic and conservative, and whose army of heavy infantry enabled it to dominate the southern part of the Greek mainland. Athens' continuing expansion threatened Sparta's position in Greece, and, prompted by the complaints from some of its allies, from 431 to 404 Sparta challenged Athens in the Peloponnesian War. A peace-treaty in 421 seemed to acknowledge that Sparta had failed to break the power of Athens; but the peace was inherently unstable, and after Athens had weakened itself in an over-ambitious campaign in Sicily, and had provoked the Persians, the dominant power in the Near East, Sparta managed to obtain Persian support and to continue the war until Athens was defeated.

Writing in prose was still a young art in Greece, and no Greek prose work earlier than the second half of the fifth century survives. The earliest prose work which does survive is the history of Herodotus (who was born in Halicarnassus in Asia Minor, but left his home and travelled extensively). Writing in the third quarter of the century, he produced a wide-ranging work focused on the wars between the Greeks and Persians at the beginning of the century, written in a discursive manner which enabled him to include some earlier history and material of various kinds about many peoples and places.

Thucydides was a member of one of the leading families of Athens: he was born not later than 454 (perhaps c.460), lived through and at least once held a command in the Peloponnesian War, and wrote a history of that war. Book 1 contains introductory material, and the narrative of the war begins in Book 2; the surviving narrative ends in the autumn of 411 but includes some references to the end of the war. He was clearly a man of great intelligence, and great determination to establish and record what happened and why (though today's scholars are more conscious than some of their predecessors that he will have had his own prejudices); he was also a very careful and skilful writer (though the meaning of his Greek is not always easy to tease out). Where Herodotus is discursive, Thucydides is usually narrowly focused; where Herodotus believes in some kind of divine plan, Thucydides explains events wholly in human terms; where Herodotus often records alternative versions of an episode, Thucydides almost always reports simply what he has established as the truth and expects his readers to believe him.

Much of his narrative is written in an austere, matter-of-fact style; but there are episodes which he has selected for extended and vivid treatment (often because they enable him to make general points); and there are speeches (which he claims represent some kind of compromise between what men were known to have said and what he thinks it would have been appropriate for them to say), which explore the nature of Athenian power and other major issues.

He himself thought that 'the lack of a romantic element in [his] history will make it less of a pleasure to the ear'; but he hoped that it would be 'judged useful by those who will want to have a clear understanding of what happened—and, such is the human condition, will happen again at some time in the same or a similar pattern. It was composed as a permanent legacy, not a showpiece for a single hearing' (1.22). What he wrote was conceived not only as an account of a war he believed to be the greatest that had yet occurred but also as a vehicle for making general points, sometimes through the narrative of particular events, sometimes explicitly (as in the remarks on *stasis*, civil conflict, in 3.82–3 which arise out of his narrative of the *stasis* in Corcyra).

Thucydides has always been admired for his artistry and for his penetrating analyses. For much of the nineteenth century and the first half of the twentieth he was placed on a pedestal as the ideal objective and dispassionate historian; current fashion is not inclined to believe in that ideal, but still finds much to admire in his search for the truth, his rational explanations of events, and the skill with which he has woven together plain and vivid narrative, and narrative and explanation.

The Peloponnesian War in Context

The Origins of the War

By the beginning of the fifth century BC Sparta and Athens were the largest and strongest of the many city states into which Greece was divided, and most of the other states in the Peloponnese, the southern part of the Greek mainland, were organized under Sparta's leadership in a league of allies, known to modern scholars as the Peloponnesian League. In the middle of the sixth century Persia had made itself the leading kingdom of the Near East, and its conquests had extended to Asia Minor, including the Greek cities on the Aegean coast. In the 490s those cities had risen against Persia in the Ionian Revolt. They appealed for help to the mainland Greeks, and Sparta declined to help but Athens, regarded as the mother-city of those who belonged to the Ionian strand of the Greek people, did send help (though only for one year), and help was sent also by the Euboean city of Eretria. The revolt was put down, and it gave the Persians the excuse (if they thought they needed one) for trying to extend their conquests to mainland Greece. An invasion in 490 was aimed specifically at Athens and Eretria, and Eretria was overcome but Athens, with help from neighbouring Plataea (promised help from Sparta did not arrive until after the battle), defeated the Persians at Marathon. That added to Persia's desire for revenge. In the 480s the Athenians took advantage of surplus revenue from their silver mines to equip themselves with 200 warships (see 1.14), a much larger navy than any other state possessed. When the Persians embarked on a major invasion, in 480, aiming not only to punish Athens but to conquer the whole of Greece, Sparta was accepted with little dispute as the leader of the loyalist cities, and Athens provided by far the largest contingent in the loyalists' navy (more than half of the total, though not the 'nearly two-thirds' of 1.74). Though successful at first, the Persians were defeated at sea in 480, at Salamis, and on land in 479, at Plataea.

The Persians were never in fact to invade Europe again, but in 479 that could not have been predicted, and it seemed important to strike back at the Persians, in order to obtain revenge and to liberate the Greeks of western Asia Minor, who were still under Persian rule, and also to guard against subsequent Persian attacks. Already in 479 Greek forces landed on Cape Mycale, on the mainland of Asia Minor opposite Samos, and defeated the Persians there; later that year, when the Spartans and some of the allies had returned home, the Athenians led others in capturing Sestos, on the European side of the Hellespont (1.89). In 478 the war continued, still under Spartan leadership; but the Spartan commander Pausanias, who first campaigned in Cyprus and then captured Byzantium, made himself unpopular (1.94–5).

The original anti-Persian alliance was not dissolved, but in the winter of 478/7 a new alliance (with its headquarters on the island of Delos, where there was an important sanctuary of Apollo, so the alliance is known to us as the Delian League) was founded under the leadership of Athens to continue the war against Persia. Sparta and the other Peloponnesian states did not join this league, but did not at first feel threatened by it (1.96–7; and, for the sanctuary on Delos, see 3.104).

The Delian League began as an alliance of free states with a common purpose, in which the executive power was vested in Athens, and those among the members who remembered the Ionian Revolt of the 490s will have realized the need for an acknowledged leader, and may have been more afraid that Athens would lose interest in the war against Persia than that it would abuse its position and infringe their independence. However, though the Athenians probably did not set out with selfish intentions, even in the earliest campaigns of the League they found themselves presented with, and accepted, opportunities to advance the particular interests of Athens. The alliance had been made for all time, but the allies' enthusiasm for an unending war was not so durable, and as the Athenians insisted on the obligations of reluctant allies they became increasingly domineering: in particular, more and more members chose or were required to contribute cash (*phoros*, 'tribute') rather than ships of their own to the League's forces, and in this way they were weakened while Athens was strengthened (see 1.98–101).

After the defeat of the Persian invasion of Greece, the Athenian Themistocles had seen Sparta as a rival of Athens (see 1.90–3, and other stories in which Themistocles is credited with an anti-Spartan stance); but he was on the losing side in Athenian politics, and the League's early campaigns were directed by Cimon, who favoured good relations with Sparta. After an earthquake in 465/4, when they were confronted with a revolt of their subject peoples in Laconia and Messenia, the Spartans appealed for help to all who had been their allies against Persia in 480–478, including Athens, and Cimon took a substantial Athenian army to the Peloponnese. But men associated with Themistocles (who had himself been driven into exile with the Persians) gained the upper hand in Cimon's absence, in 462/1, and achieved a major democratic reform. They had been opposed to the sending of help to Sparta, and the Spartans, distrusting the new regime, dismissed Cimon and his army. The Athenians then broke

off their alliance with Sparta, and joined instead with Sparta's enemies on the Greek mainland (see 1.101–2).

Between 460 and 454 the Athenians continued the war against
Persia, in Cyprus (which was partly Greek) and Egypt (where there
had been Greek settlers for two hundred years), and at the same time
fought to build up a powerful position on the Greek mainland: members of the Delian League were called on to help them, in Greece as
well as against the Persians. However, the Egyptian campaign ended
in disaster, and Cimon was killed in a further campaign in Cyprus,
while Athens' expansion in Greece lost momentum (see 1.103–12).
From inscriptions we learn that in the late 450s and early 440s
Athens had to face a good deal of disaffection from League members,
some of whom had Persian support, and that in dealing with this it
took several further steps along the road which led it from being
leader of an alliance to being ruler of an empire. With the Persians
driven out of the Aegean and Cimon dead, there was no longer
enthusiasm in Athens for continuing war against Persia, and c.450
the war which the League had been founded to fight came to an end
(whether de facto or by a formal treaty). Nevertheless, the League
was not disbanded.

In 447/6 subjects in Greece whom Athens had acquired in the
early 450s rebelled, and a Peloponnesian army commanded by the
Spartan king Pleistoanax invaded Attica. He turned back without
attacking Athens, but the Athenians came to terms. By the Thirty
Years Treaty of 446/5 Athens gave up its possessions on the mainland but its domination of the Aegean through the Delian League
was recognized: Greece was divided into a Spartan-led, land-based
bloc and an Athenian-led, sea-based bloc (see 1.113–115.1). But, if
expansion on the mainland was forbidden, Athens was still interested
in expanding wherever it could: in the years after 446/5 we hear of
colonies founded at Thurii, in southern Italy, at Amphipolis, in
Thrace (4.102–3), and on the shores of the Black Sea. The only episode which Thucydides mentions between the Treaty and the events
leading to the Peloponnesian War is a war between Athens and the
island state of Samos in 440–439, where it appears that Sparta would
have liked to support Samos but Corinth successfully opposed the
plan (1.115.2–117 with 1.40). The equilibrium which the Thirty
Years Treaty sought to establish was unstable.

Thucydides' narrative of the events leading directly to the outbreak of the war (1.24–88, 118–26, 139–46) begins with a war between

Corinth, the most powerful member of the Peloponnesian League after Sparta, and its colony Corcyra, an island state off the northwest coast of Greece which had remained outside both blocs: in 433 each appealed to Athens for support, and in the hope of weakening Corinth but avoiding a direct breach of the Thirty Years Treaty Athens granted limited aid to Corcyra (though it could have remained uninvolved, and have left Corinth and Corcyra to weaken each other). In 433/2 Athens put pressure on Potidaea, in the northeast, which was a member of the Delian League but had strong links with Corinth, and Potidaea revolted: there was a battle in which once more Athenians fought against Corinthians, and Athens began a long and expensive siege of Potidaea, which finally capitulated in 430/29 (2.70). Also trouble arose between Athens and Megara (on the isthmus between Athens and Corinth), on which Athens was imposing economic sanctions in response to a border dispute and the alleged harbouring of runaway slaves; and Aegina (near to Athens in the Saronic Gulf), forced into the Delian League in the 450s, complained that it was being denied the autonomy promised in a treaty. Among the members of the Peloponnesian League, Corinth took the lead in protesting against Athens' conduct and putting pressure on Sparta, and in 432 first Sparta and then the Peloponnesian League formally decided to go to war against Athens, and to try to break the Athenian empire (for this objective see 2.8). Thucydides gives detailed accounts of the episodes involving Corcyra and Potidaea, but devotes much less space to Megara and Aegina: he may in part be reacting against a view prevalent in Athens that Megara was particularly important (cf. Ar., *Ach.* 514–38, *Peace* 605–18), and in part be emphasizing matters in which it was easy to show that Athens was in the right.

Thucydides insists three times that what persuaded the Spartans was their fear of Athens' power, rather than the validity of the particular complaints against Athens (1.23, 88, 118). Technically the Peloponnesians were the aggressors (see 2.2, 10–12, 18–20, and 7.18), and except perhaps in the case of Aegina, whose complaint Thucydides reports without comment (1.67, cf. 1.139, 140), Athens seems to have been careful not to break the letter of the Thirty Years Treaty. Some modern scholars accept that Athens was indeed in the right.[1] However, it can be argued that the Athenians knew that there

[1] e.g. G. E. M. de Ste. Croix, *The Origins of the Peloponnesian War* (London: Duckworth; Cornell University Press, 1972).

was bound to be war with Sparta unless they gave up their ambitions (which of course they could not do), that in the late 430s they took a line which was provocative while remaining technically correct, in order to bring about the inevitable war in circumstances favourable to themselves, and that Thucydides has written not an impartial but a patriotically Athenian account of the causes of the war.[2] For 'the Athenians' we may read 'Pericles'. He was one, but not yet the leading one, of the democrats who triumphed over Cimon in 462/1; and, although he never became the universally accepted leader that Thucydides in 2.65 would have us believe, he became increasingly influential, and for the most part the policies pursued by Athens from *c*.460 to 429 were his policies.

Strategy; the Archidamian War

Sparta was fighting to break the Athenian empire and liberate the Greeks from actual or threatened rule by Athens, so it needed a positive victory; Athens needed only to survive unscathed. Sparta was a land power and Athens was a sea power: we are given figures for Athens' own forces in 2.13, and although we have no comparable figures for Athens' allies or for the Spartan side it is a reasonable assumption that Athens had a 3:1 superiority in ships (and the more skilled sailors) but the Spartans had a 3:1 superiority in heavy infantry (and no other city's soldiers were a match for Sparta's).

Sparta began the war with the traditional Greek strategy of invading the enemy's territory with a large army in the hope that they would come outside their fortifications to fight and be beaten (the invasion of 431, 2.10–23). In 431–428 these invasions were led by the Spartan king Archidamus, and the first phase of the war is known as the Archidamian War. However, the Long Walls built in the middle of the century (1.107) had made a single fortified area of Athens and the harbour town of the Peiraeus, and as long as they controlled the sea and had the money to pay for their purchases (and financially the Athenians were far stronger than their opponents: see 2.13) the Athenians could afford to neglect their farms in Attica. Pericles'

---

[2] See P. J. Rhodes, 'Thucydides on the Causes of the Peloponnesian War', *Hermes*, 115 (1987), 154–65. E. Badian, 'Thucydides and the Outbreak of the Peloponnesian War: A Historian's Brief', in J. W. Allison (ed.), *Conflict, Antithesis and the Ancient Historian* (Ohio State University Press, 1990), 49–91, with 165–81, revised in Badian, *From Plataea to Potidaea* (Johns Hopkins University Press, 1993), 125–62, with 223–36, goes beyond my view of a Thucydides writing with Athenian bias to argue for a Thucydides writing with deliberate dishonesty to justify Athens.

strategy for Athens, which tried the patience of some men, was therefore to stay inside the fortifications and not give the Spartans the infantry-battle they wanted. Beyond that, according to Thucydides, he merely thought that it should maintain its naval strength, keeping a firm grip on the empire it already had but not seeking to extend it (see esp. 2.13, 65).

In fact, in the first two years of the war Athens sent out large-scale, expensive naval expeditions, and if it had continued to operate on that scale it would have exhausted its funds long before the Peace of Nicias brought the war to an apparent end in 421—but Thucydides' narrative of these expeditions in Book 2 is disjointed and perfunctory, implying that they were casual raiding expeditions of no great importance. Almost all commentators have agreed that these expeditions are hard to reconcile with the picture of Periclean strategy painted by Thucydides: my own view is that Thucydides reflects Pericles' public statements and that those were more cautious than Pericles' private hopes (see note to 2.24–32). In 428 Thucydides shows the Athenians' awareness of their financial difficulties (3.19).

The Athenians certainly adhered to the policy of keeping a firm grip on the empire they already had. The cities of the island of Lesbos were among the few which had not been subjected to pressure by Athens and still contributed ships to the Delian League. In 428 the largest city, Mytilene, led most of the island in revolt against Athens. Sparta promised support, but it was unable to gain the co-operation of its allies in an additional invasion of Attica at harvest time, and a naval squadron sent to Lesbos wasted time on the voyage and made enemies rather than friends for Sparta. Mytilene was blockaded during the winter; and in spring 427, when the Spartans failed to arrive and the people were starving, it capitulated to Athens. Athens' original decision, to kill all the men and enslave all the women and children, was superseded by a less extreme but still severe punishment (3.2–6, 8–18, 25, 27–50).

Melos, the one Aegean island which had managed to stay outside the Athenian empire (Thera joined soon after 431), was attacked in 426 but not captured (3.91). It was among the states included in Athens' optimistic tribute assessment list of 425, but inclusion in that list does not prove it had succumbed to Athens, and a record of its contributing to a Spartan war fund is possibly though not certainly to be dated to the 420s (see note to 3.91). As a sequel to Athens' dealings with Lesbos, in winter 425/4 Chios, still a ship-contributing member of the League, attracted suspicion by building a new city wall, was ordered to demolish it, and after obtaining assurances from Athens duly did so (4.51).

In 433, when Athens supported Corcyra against Corinth, it was already possible to envisage a war in which the western Greeks, those living in Sicily and southern Italy, would be involved (1.36, 44). In 433/2 Athens renewed alliances with Leontini in Sicily and Rhegium in the south-west of Italy (see note to 1.32–6); most of the Greeks in the west were of Peloponnesian origin, and from the beginning of the war it was expected that they would support the Spartans against Athens (see 2.7). In fact they remained uninvolved; but in 427 Athens responded to an appeal to send help to Leontini against Syracuse, the most powerful city in Sicily. Thucydides writes of the resulting campaigns in a number of separate, low-key sections (beginning in 3.86), but it is clear that eventually, if not from the beginning, the Athenians committed large forces to the war in the west and, in a departure from the declared policy of Pericles, were hoping to add Sicily to their empire. In 424 fear of Athens led the Sicilian Greeks to make an agreement that they would resolve their disputes on their own, without outside intervention: the Athenian commanders had to accept that, but they were punished (4.58–65), and this was not to be the end of Athens' involvement in Sicily (see 5.4–5, on an episode in 422, and p. xxi, below).

Thucydides treats as the first episode of the war an attack by Thebes on Plataea, in the spring of 431 (2.2–6). Plataea was on the Boeotian side of the mountain range separating Boeotia from Attica, but since the late sixth century had refused to join the Boeotian federation dominated by Thebes, and had been an ally of Athens. In 429 Sparta began a siege of Plataea (2.71–8); in winter 428/7 half of the men in Plataea managed to escape and make their way to Athens (3.20–4); in the summer of 427, with no prospect of help from Athens, the remainder surrendered. They were put to death and the city was destroyed (3.52–68), which was clearly to the advantage of Thebes, and made for easier communications between Thebes and the Peloponnese, but the importance of the destruction of Plataea for the course of the Peloponnesian War does not justify the amount of attention which Thucydides devotes to it (see note to 2.2–6).

The area under Peloponnesian influence which was most vulnerable to an attack by a naval power was north-western Greece, where there were many Corinthian colonies but also some friends of Athens, and this area saw a good deal of activity in the early years of the war.

On the mainland, Athens and Sparta were drawn into conflicts in the north-west, between Corinth's colony Ambracia and Athens' allies the Acarnanians (first in 429: 2.80–2). As a sequel to Athens' support for Corcyra against Corinth in 433, Corinth sent its captives back to Corcyra to try to get control of the city and to bring it over to the Peloponnesian side: the result was a bitter civil war which began in 427, with the democrats supported by Athens and the oligarchs by Sparta: the Spartans were for once victorious in a naval battle, but Athenian reinforcements were on their way and the Spartans did not follow up their victory (3.69–85). The civil war dragged on to 425, and ended with Athens' friends victorious but badly weakened (4.2–5, 46–8). Since 429 Athens had had a naval squadron based on Naupactus, on the north side of the Gulf of Corinth. In 426 Demosthenes, one of the most adventurous Athenian commanders, attempted to march from there in a north-easterly direction, perhaps hoping ultimately to reach Boeotia (in a year in which other Athenian forces attacked Boeotia directly); but he was using hoplites, heavy infantry, in rough country where they were at a disadvantage, and he was trapped and badly defeated by the Aetolians at Aegitium (3.94–8). He learnt from this mistake, and in the following winter helped the Acarnanians to trap and defeat opposing forces near the Gulf of Ambracia. However, the peoples of north-western Greece, like the Sicilian Greeks later, became afraid of Athens and made a treaty of neutrality (3.105–14); and in 424/3 the Athenians were unsuccessful in another multiple attack on Boeotia, in which Demosthenes was again to approach from the west and had help from those in the west who were still well disposed to Athens (4.76–7, 89–101).

The one part of the Athenian empire which could be reached from Greece by a land power was the coast of Macedonia and Thrace: when the war began, Potidaea was under siege and its neighbours were in revolt from Athens and, in the interests of his own security, king Perdiccas of Macedonia wavered between friendship and hostility towards Athens. In 426 Sparta founded a colony at Heracleia in Trachis, near Thermopylae, which could serve as a base or a staging-post for activity in the north-east (3.92–3). Brasidas, the most enterprising of the Spartan commanders in the Archidamian War (first appearance in 431: 2.25), took a small force via Heracleia to Thrace in 424. Support from Sparta was lukewarm, on account of the Athenians' success at Pylos in 425 (see below), but he was so successful in detaching north-eastern cities from their allegiance to Athens that special terms had to be provided for several of them in the Peace of Nicias in 421, and Athens' colony Amphipolis, which should have been returned to Athens, defied the treaty with Spartan acquiescence (4.78–88, 102–32, 5.2–3, 6–13, 18, 21, 35).

Sparta would have hurt Athens more than it did by its annual invasions if it had been able to establish a permanent fortress within Attica as a base from which to attack the Athenians all the year round (for which Thucydides uses the term *epiteichismos*). This possibility is mentioned both by the Corinthians and by Pericles in speeches in Book 1 (122, 142), and in 421 Sparta threatened to build a fort in order to secure Athens' acceptance of the Peace of Nicias (5.17), but it was only in 413, after the Athenians had committed the most flagrant breach of the Peace of Nicias (6.105), and had sent so large a proportion of their manpower to Sicily that the risk seemed worth taking, that the Spartans established a post at Deceleia, in northern Attica (7.18–19, 27–8). Similarly, Athens could most effectively have acted against Sparta by establishing a stronghold in Spartan territory, to interfere with Spartan agriculture and incite disaffection among the Spartans' large subject population of Helots. There is no sign that the Athenians contemplated this when they sent their large naval expeditions round the Peloponnese in the first two years of the war; but in 425 Demosthenes was able to establish an Athenian base at Pylos, on the coast of Messenia, and in the fighting which followed the Athenians captured a number of Spartan citizen soldiers, who became an important bargaining counter (4.3–23, 26–41). In 424 a second Athenian base was added, on the island of Cythera, off the coast of Laconia (4.53–7). Thucydides reports that these caused great fear in Sparta, but does not indicate that the fear was justified by the use which the Athenians made of them (see 4.41, 55, 5.14).

Athens was better prepared than Sparta to endure a long war (2.13; cf. 1.80, 121–2, 141–3). If the war was prolonged, Sparta's best hope of outlasting Athens was to gain access to the comparatively unlimited resources of Persia; and Athens needed, if not to obtain Persian support for itself, at any rate to prevent Sparta from obtaining it (2.7, cf. 1.82). In 430 Peloponnesian envoys to Persia were betrayed to the Athenians in Thrace (2.67); and in 425/4 a Persian envoy to Sparta was captured by the Athenians (4.50). Presumably some Athenian approach to Persia lies behind the mockery of an Athenian deputation in Aristophanes, *Acharnians*, 61–125, of 425. The Athenians sent back the Persian whom they captured with representatives of their own: these turned back on learning of the King's death (4.50); but, although Thucydides does not mention it, other evidence makes it certain that once the new King was securely established Athens did succeed in obtaining a treaty.

In 430 Athens was struck by a plague, which persisted until 426/5, killed about a third of the population, and weakened many others; Thucydides himself was one of those who were infected but survived (2.47–54, cf. 58, 3.87). The effect of this was so demoralizing that in 430 the Athenians attempted to make peace with Sparta and deposed Pericles from the office of general; but Pericles revived their determination to fight, and was re-elected general, though eventually he was one of those killed by the plague (2.59, 65). However, after the capture of their soldiers at Pylos in 425, the Spartans in turn were willing to admit defeat and offered to make peace (4.41; cf. before the final capture 4.15–22). A one-year truce was made in 423 (4.117–19), but failed to hold in the Thracian region; the death of the Spartan Brasidas and the Athenian Cleon in a battle outside Amphipolis in 422 removed the men most strongly opposed to a settlement, and in 421 the Peace of Nicias, attempting with a few exceptions to return to the position of 431, seemed to mark the end of the war (5.14–24).

The Middle of the War

At first sight the Peace of Nicias represented a victory for Athens, in that Sparta's attempt to break the power of Athens had failed. But the Peace quickly proved to be unsatisfactory, and it can be argued that Athens placed itself at a disadvantage by returning the prisoners captured at Pylos without obtaining full implementation of the Peace on the Peloponnesian side. Sparta's allies did not share its reason for wanting peace, and some of them refused to accept the treaty (5.17, 22). Argos, Sparta's chief opponent within the Peloponnese, had been kept out of the Archidamian War by a thirty-year peace treaty, but that expired in 421 (5.14; cf. 5.22). Some of the Peloponnesians, disenchanted with Sparta, joined Argos in an alliance; an attempt to enlarge that alliance caused great confusion, and in 420 Athens, unhappy with Sparta's half-hearted implementation of the Peace of Nicias, made an alliance with Argos and some other Peloponnesian states still opposed to Sparta (5.27–48). This combination offered the chance of a confrontation on land, in the Peloponnese, in which Athens might be victorious; but in fact in 418, after an encounter outside Argos which led to the opposing commanders' making a truce without fighting, the battle of Mantinea was a victory for Sparta and enabled it to re-assert its supremacy in the Peloponnese (5.52–83). In 416/5, without any mention by Thucydides of provocation, the Athenians finally besieged and captured the island of Melos (cf. above, p. xvi): Thucydides gives this episode a detailed treatment, as an instance of the Athenians' unsentimental pursuit of power, and as a trivial success for Athens to be contrasted with the major setback which was to follow (5.84–116).

Most of the Greek cities in Sicily and the far south of Italy had been colonized from the Peloponnese, and at the beginning of the war were reckoned among Sparta's allies, but during the Archidamian War they sent no help to Sparta. Athens' intervention in Sicily to support Leontini against Syracuse, from 427 to 424, had to be abandoned when the Sicilian Greeks agreed to reject all outside interference, and a further attempt to interfere, in 422, met further resistance (see p. xvii above). In 415 Athens accepted another invitation to intervene in Sicily—to support Egesta against Selinus, which had the support of Syracuse, and to reassert the independence of Leontini, which by now had been absorbed by Syracuse. In Athens the intervention was championed by the ambitious Alcibiades and opposed by the cautious Nicias. Large forces were sent and great hopes were invested in them, and the forces and the hopes were made even larger in response to Nicias' attempt to prevent the expedition by arguing that the forces originally proposed were insufficient (6.1–32). Egesta was unable to provide the help which it had offered; as in 422 the Athenians found that they were not widely welcomed; and Alcibiades himself, recalled to stand trial for involvement in religious scandals in Athens, went over to Sparta (6.33–93). Despite an unpromising beginning, in 414 the Athenians established themselves in the great bay and on the plateau outside Syracuse, and started building walls to isolate the city. They came close to capturing the city, and might well have succeeded if Nicias had been more energetic; but support for Syracuse from the Peloponnese, though not on a large scale, arrived just in time to prevent the Athenians from completing their walls and the Syracusans from surrendering to Athens, and in 413, although they themselves received reinforcements, the Athenians were disastrously defeated. This was a great blow to their morale, and the drain on their resources seriously weakened them (6.94–8.1). Meanwhile, in 413 the Spartans established their raiding base at Deceleia (see p. xix above), and by occupying this until the end of the war they kept the Athenians confined to their urban fortifications all the year round.

The End of the War

Although in the late 420s the Athenians had made a treaty with the Persians, about 414 they supported a rebel called Amorges against the Persian King. After this provocation, the Persians were prepared to support the Spartans against Athens; and, although not all Spartans were happy to pay Persia's price (the return of the Asiatic Greeks to Persian rule), Persia's support did eventually enable Sparta to defeat Athens. After Athens' failure at Syracuse, its subjects in the Aegean were less afraid to challenge it. Fighting there began in 412; matters were complicated by Alcibiades' falling out with the Spartans, migrating to the Persian satrap Tissaphernes and suggesting to the Athenians that, if the democracy were replaced by an oligarchy and he were restored to Athens, he could divert Persian support from Sparta to Athens (a hope which some Athenians continued to entertain until 407). Thucydides' narrative takes us to the autumn of 411, by which time the extreme oligarchy of the Four Hundred had been set up in Athens and, later, replaced by an intermediate regime, and the Athenians had begun to win some successes in the Aegean (8.2–109: on the incompleteness of Thucydides' history see pp. xxv–xxviii below).

In 410 the Athenians won a major victory over Sparta at Cyzicus, in the Propontis, and the full democracy was restored. There were times when it looked as if the war might yet be won by Athens, but in 407 the Persians committed themselves more strongly to supporting Sparta; the King's younger son, Cyrus, was sent to the Aegean and established a good relationship with the Spartan Lysander. Lysander was succeeded by Callicratidas, who did not find it easy to cooperate with Cyrus, and in 406 the Athenians defeated him (though expensively) near the Arginusae islands between Chios and the Asiatic mainland. Sparta then contrived to reinstate Lysander. His victory at Aegospotami in the Hellespont in 405 left him in control of the Hellespont and able to cut off Athens' vital imports, and left Athens unable to build, equip, and man another fleet. Athens was blockaded during the winter of 405/4, and capitulated in the spring of 404. It lost its empire (the Asiatic Greeks were claimed by Persia, but in fact they as well as the other members passed, at any rate for a few years, into the hands of Sparta), its Long Walls, and nearly all its navy, and became a subordinate ally of Sparta, ruled by a Spartan-backed oligarchy.

But that was not a final settlement of the affairs of Athens or of the balance of power in Greece. Sparta fulfilled the prediction attributed by Thucydides to the Athenians in 432 (1.76–7), and quickly became more unpopular in the Greek world than Athens had been. Athens recovered its democracy in 403; it soon aspired to an independent foreign policy once more, and in 395 it joined disaffected former allies of Sparta in a new war against Sparta. Unable to oppose both Persia and its enemies in Greece, Sparta finally in 386 returned the Asiatic Greeks to Persia in return for Persia's backing of a 'common peace' treaty by which the remaining Greeks were to be free and independent and Sparta determined what that was to mean in particular cases. Sparta's unpopularity increased, until in 378 Athens founded a new league, of states wishing to defend their independence against Sparta. In 371–369 Sparta suffered at the hands of Thebes defeats on land of a kind which Athens had not been able to inflict on it, and lost much of its power in Greece. Athens tried to keep its new league in being, as in the fifth century it had kept the Delian League in being after giving up regular fighting against Persia, while Thebes tried to win Persian support and to break Athens as it had broken Sparta.

Macedonia, in the north, continued to be an unstable region caught up in the wars between the leading Greek cities, until in Philip II (359–336) it gained a king who built up its military strength and also had great diplomatic skills. The Third and Fourth Sacred Wars for the control of Delphi (for the Second Sacred War, in the 440s, see 1.112) provided him with means of entry into Greek affairs; in 338 he defeated a Greek alliance led by Athens and Thebes at Chaeroneia, in Boeotia, and after that he united the mainland Greeks (except Sparta, which he could afford to ignore) in the League of Corinth, under his own leadership. Already during the Peloponnesian War there had been complaints that the Greeks were providing new opportunities for Persia by fighting amongst themselves, and the return of the Asiatic Greeks to Persia in 386 was regarded as a disgrace, providing ammunition for those who claimed that Greece had been great when it united to fight against the Persians, and to become great again needed to unite and fight against the Persians again. Philip with his League of Corinth planned to undertake such a war, and after his assassination it was undertaken by his son Alexander the Great (336–323). The result of Alexander's conquests was to create a much larger Greek world: after his death his empire split into rival kingdoms, and the old cities of Greece found themselves having to manoeuvre not amongst one another but between the great kings.

Thucydides the Man

Thucydides' Life and Political Stance

Thucydides the Athenian historian tells us that he was the son of Olorus, and had mining interests in Thrace (4.104–5). Since the Miltiades who commanded the Athenians at Marathon in 490 married the daughter of a Thracian king called Olorus,[3] and Thucydides the son of Melesias, who opposed Pericles in the 440s, belonged to that family,[4] it is likely that Thucydides the historian belonged to that family too. The relationships shown in the following table are possible but not certain.

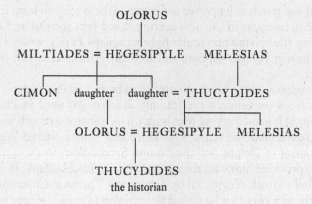

Thucydides served as an Athenian general in 424/3, so if generals had to be at least 30 years old (which is likely but not certain) he was born not later than 454 (perhaps *c*.460).[5] He failed to prevent Amphipolis from falling into the hands of the Spartans, but was in time to save Eïon for Athens (4.104–6). He was exiled for his failure,

---

[3] Hdt. 6.39.
[4] e.g. *Ath. Pol.* 28.2.
[5] C. W. Fornara, 'Thucydides' Birth Date', in *Nomodeiktes: Greek Studies in Honor of M. Ostwald* (University of Michigan Press, 1993), 71–80, argues from 5.26 that he was born before rather than after 460.

and did not return to Athens until an amnesty was proclaimed at the end of the Peloponnesian War, in 404 (5.26).[6] He seems to be particularly well supplied with detailed information from Corinth, and it has been suggested that he spent part of his exile there.[7] It is assumed that he died within a few years of his return: a recent attempt to prolong his life by arguing that the Lichas who was archon in Thasos in 398/7 is the Lichas of Sparta whose death he records in 7.84[8] is unlikely to be correct.

Although he was an aristocrat, from the family which had provided the leading opponents of Pericles in the middle of the century, it is clear that Thucydides became an ardent admirer of Pericles, the aristocrat who presided over the Athenian democracy (see especially 2.65). His admiration seems to have been personal rather than ideological: comments on Sparta and Chios (1.18, 8.24), and on the fickleness of the Athenian assembly and on the regime under which Athens lived in 411/0 (2.65, 8.97), suggest that he was no enthusiast for democracy. He strongly disliked Cleon, the ostentatiously populist politician who dominated Athens in the 420s (e.g. 3.36, 4.3, 21, 27–8, 5.7–10, 16), and Hyperbolus, who tried to succeed to Cleon's position (8.73): Cleon favoured energetic action against Sparta in the north-east, and the statement of an ancient biographer that he was the prosecutor of Thucydides may well be true.[9]

The Composition of his History

Thucydides' history is unfinished. Though he lived beyond the end of the war (cf. p. ix), the text which we have breaks off abruptly in the autumn of 411; and, since Xenophon's *Hellenica* and other histories which have not survived began at that far from obvious point (cf. p. xlvii below), we may safely assume that what we have is, if not all that Thucydides wrote, at any rate all of his writing that was ever made public. Since he started work at the beginning of the war (1.1) and lived beyond the end, we may reasonably wonder about

---

[6] Cf. e.g. Xen., *Hell.* 2.2.20.

[7] R. S. Stroud, 'Thucydides and Corinth', *Chiron*, 24 (1994), 267–304.

[8] J. Pouilloux and F. Salviat, 'Lichas, Lacédémonien, archonte à Thasos, et le livre viii de Thucydide', *CR Acad. Inscr.* (1983), 376–403. S. Flory, 'The Death of Thucydides and the Motif of "Land on Sea"', in *Nomodeiktes . . . M. Ostwald*, 113–23, suggests that Thucydides' work was not cut short by his death but (in the 390s or later) was abandoned in despair; but the usual view is more probably right.

[9] Marcellin., *Life of Thuc.* 46.

the timetable of his work. Did he write up the events of each year or half-year (see note to 2.1) shortly afterwards and then close that section, did he merely make notes during the course of the war, and wait until the war was over to begin composing his history, or did he do something between those two extremes? In any case, we have to assume that when he went into exile he took with him whatever materials he had, added to those materials during his twenty years of exile, and brought back his now larger collection of materials when he returned to Athens. On the normal assumption that his work was ended by his death, somebody must have decided to make public what we now have and to destroy whatever material there was going beyond the end of Book 8 (the division into eight books was made at a later date, and is not the only division that was made in antiquity; and the subdivision of the books into chapters and sections is modern).[10]

The question is complicated by the fact that for some time the Peloponnesian War seemed to have been ended by the Peace of Nicias, in 421: although Athenians and Spartans fought against one another in the intervening years, it was possible to pretend that the Peace was still in force until Athens joined Argos in a raid on Spartan territory, in 414 (6.105, cf. 7.18). When passages in 2.1–5.24 refer to 'this war', it is not always clear whether the Archidamian War of 431–421 or the whole Peloponnesian War is intended (cf. 4.40, 48, with notes). The length of this first phase of the war is discussed in 5.20 in a manner appropriate to the ending of the war; but the chapter ends by referring to 'this first war', and therefore cannot have been written in its present form until Thucydides realized that the Peace of Nicias had not ended the war; 5.24, with another reference to 'the first war', begins Thucydides' eleventh year; 5.25 remarks that even immediately there was not a complete settlement, and the situation worsened until open war resumed; and then in 5.26 we have Thucydides' second preface, which echoes 1.1 and 2.1. In this he says that he continued his history to the dismantling of the Athenian empire and the destruction of the Long

---

[10] In this volume, section numbers are used only (a) where the end and beginning of sections of the Explanatory Notes do not coincide with the end and beginning of chapters, (b) in the Notes on the Greek Text. Because they have been made available to English-language readers, in A. Rengakos and A. Tsakmakis (eds.), *Brill's Companion to Thucydides* (Leiden: Brill, 2006), 3–31, I mention here the (to my mind improbable) views of L. Canfora that Thucydides went into voluntary exile after failing to save Amphipolis from Brasidas, was back in Athens in 411, but left Athens again afterwards; and (prompted by Diog. Laert. 2.57) that Thuc. 5.1–83 and Xen., *Hell.* 1.1.1–2.3.10, are preliminary drafts by Thucydides, edited by Xenophon.

Walls and Peiraeus fortifications (which as far as his published text is concerned is not true), and justifies his decision to treat the whole twenty-seven-year period as a single war.[11]

For most of his narrative of the Peloponnesian War Thucydides follows a strict chronological sequence, year by year, with each year split into a summer of about eight months and a winter of about four (see note to 2.2–6). However, sometimes he steps outside that framework to tell a whole story in one stretch of narrative, or to introduce material needed as background explanation later than the time when it occurred (e.g. 3.34, 3.70, 4.50; and especially 8.45–54); and in the account of the 'Pentecontaetia' in Book 1 we should not assume that each event has been mentioned in order in a single chronological sequence (see note to 1.101–3, for example).

From time to time we find passages which refer to events later than the time of the narrative in which they are set: for instance, the (anticipatory) obituary notice on Pericles in 2.65 mentions events after Pericles' death, including the great Sicilian expedition of 415–413, and the support for Sparta of the Persian prince Cyrus in and after 407. On the other hand, there are passages of a kind which we should not expect to find if the history was written or fully revised after the war had ended: for example, 2.23 writes of 'the Oropians who are subjects of Athens', which ceased to be true in 412/1; a repetition of material from 2.23 in 4.56 would presumably have been tidied up in a final revision.

Therefore neither of the extreme solutions mentioned above is acceptable: throughout the history there are both passages which were written well before the end of the war, and were not revised in the light of subsequent events, and passages which were not written until some time after the events in connection with which we read them, in some cases not until after the war had ended.

---

[11] There was an era when a large proportion of the scholarly work on Thucydides was devoted to the problems of composition, and in the last volume of the *Historical Commentary on Thucydides* begun by A. W. Gomme two appendixes give a detailed and judicious survey (vol. v, app. 1, 'Indications of Incompleteness' (by A. Andrewes: 361–83), and app. 2, 'Strata of Composition' (by K. J. Dover: 384–444)). More recently there has been a fashion, begun by W. R. Connor's *Thucydides* (Princeton University Press, 1984), for stepping aside from these problems, interpreting the text which we have on the assumption that it is the text which Thucydides intended his readers to have, and '[treating] the Separatist hypothesis as the last refuge of the philologist' (p. 19). The questions concerning Thucydides' composition are not nowadays the most fruitful, in that without further evidence it is unlikely that much that is worthwhile can be said about them which has not already been said by somebody; but if we fail to confront them they will not simply disappear.

Moreover, there are internal discrepancies which show that the whole work is not the product of a single spell of thinking. Most strikingly, 2.65 suggests that the Sicilian expedition of 415–413 was not at fault in its conception but failed owing to a lack of proper support from Athens (cf. the remarks on Alcibiades in 6.15); but the narrative of Books 6–7 gives the impression that the expedition was at fault in its conception yet even so short-term success might have been achieved but for the blunders of Nicias.

Chapters 25–83 of Book 5 and the whole of Book 8 are disjointed, with internal inconsistencies, as the rest of the history is not, and it can plausibly be argued that these represent a relatively primitive stage in the process of composition, a first draft which Thucydides hoped to revise later. Book 1, on the greatness of the war and on its causes, is thought by some scholars to betray an attempt to superimpose a later view of the causes on an earlier; I believe, however, that it does not do so, but embodies a carefully worked-out design.[12] It is possible, nevertheless, that the section on Pausanias and Themistocles in 1.128–38 is an early essay, incorporated because Thucydides had written it rather than written in order to be incorporated: the story of Pausanias is relevant to the context in which this section is set, but the story of Themistocles is not, and the justification for its inclusion seems to be that Thucydides regarded him as a forerunner of Pericles.

The number of passages which are demonstrably early or late is not large. It is likely that the account of the years 431–421 was worked up to almost its present form in the years after the Peace of Nicias, when the war seemed to be at an end, and that the accounts of Melos and the Sicilian expedition were similarly worked up soon after the events in question. No section of the history was definitively finished: later events might cause Thucydides to go back and revise a passage which already existed in a polished form, but he never reached the final stage of going through all that he had written to try to bring everything up to date and remove all inconsistencies.

Thucydides the Historian

His History

The writing of historical narrative in prose was a product of the intellectual awakening which seems to have begun among the Greeks

[12] See Rhodes, 'Thucydides on the Causes of the Peloponnesian War'.

living on the west coast of Asia Minor and the offshore islands in the sixth and fifth centuries. The one predecessor of Thucydides whose work survives is Herodotus of Halicarnassus (*c*.485–425), who wrote a history focused on the conflicts between Greeks and Persians at the beginning of the fifth century, in a discursive manner which gave him ample opportunity for digressions on places, peoples, and earlier history. He was an intelligent and energetic enquirer (though some scholars have raised doubts as to whether he visited all the places he claims to have visited and saw all the things he claims to have seen); he had an interest, not totally credulous, in legends of the gods and the remote past, and in his account of events he combined human motivation with a notion of divine justice. His manner was that of a storyteller, and he had the reputation of being 'most Homer-like' (*Homerikotatos*). Thucydides does not mention him by name, but in 1.20 criticizes statements of his.[13]

Other early historians are known only from quotations and allusions by other writers, and many are little more than names to us. Three deserve to be mentioned here. Hecataeus of Miletus, at the beginning of the fifth century, wrote an account of the Mediterranean world, which was used by Herodotus, and a book on families claiming a divine origin. Hellanicus of Lesbos compiled systematized accounts of myths, and works of local history and chronology: Thucydides in 1.97 says that he was the one previous writer to deal with the period between the Persian Wars and the Peloponnesian War, but his account was 'brief and the chronology . . . imprecise' (the reader of 1.89–118 is apt to make the same criticism of that account). The eastern enlightenment quickly spread to the west: Antiochus of Syracuse wrote histories of Sicily and Italy, and his work may be the source of what Thucydides says in 6.2–5 on Greek colonization in Sicily, and of some other western material.

Thucydides states at the outset of his history that he started work on the history of the Peloponnesian War at the beginning of the war, 'reckoning that this would be a major war and more momentous than any previous conflict. . . . This was in fact the greatest disturbance to affect the Greek and a good part of the non-Greek world, one might even say the majority of mankind' (1.1: the whole of Book 1 up to 23.3 is intended to justify this statement). This suggests an objective

---

[13] On Thucydides and Herodotus, see especially S. Hornblower, *A Commentary on Thucydides*, 3 vols. (Oxford University Press, 1991–2008; revised 1997–), ii. 19–38, 122–45.

not unlike that of Herodotus, who had written 'to prevent the traces of human events from being erased by time, and to preserve the fame of the important and remarkable achievements produced by both Greeks and non-Greeks',[14] and had claimed that the force with which the Persians invaded Greece in 480 was greater than any previous force either in the historical period or in the legendary.[15]

Although Thucydides' narrative manner is commonly thought of as matter-of-fact, he can give extremely vivid accounts of exciting episodes (for example, the Theban attack on Plataea in 431: 2.2–6; two campaigns in north-western Greece in 426/5: 3.96–8, 105–14; the episode at Pylos in 425: 4.2–6, 8–23, 26–41), and he seems particularly interested in siege-works (for example, at Plataea, 2.71–8, 3.20–4, at Megara, 4.69). He is also very willing to use superlatives. For instance, at the outbreak of the Peloponnesian War the Greek states were more powerful than ever before (1.1, 3, 18–19, Archidamus' speech, 2.11); never before had there been such destructions of cities, banishment and slaughter of people, earthquakes, eclipses, famine, and diseases (1.23); there had never been such a fatal disease as the plague at Athens (2.47); the losses of Ambracia at Idomene in 426/5 were 'the greatest disaster to befall a single Greek city over so few days in the whole of this war' (3.113); the Athenian success at Pylos in 425 was 'the most surprising event of the whole war' (4.40); when an extreme oligarchy took control of Megara after the Athenians' failure there in 424, 'there was never a change of government effected by so few which lasted for so long a time' (4.74); surprisingly, the Peloponnesian army which did not fight a battle at Argos in 418 was 'the finest Greek army ever raised so far' (5.60); the massacre at Mycalessus in 413 was 'a calamity which, relative to the size of the city, was more pitiable than any other in this war' (7.30); and the disaster suffered by the great Athenian invasion of Sicily was the greatest ever (7.75, 87)—but was followed by yet greater disasters (8.15, 96).

But it is not as a recorder of superlatives that Thucydides is commonly remembered. Most of his narrative is sober and serious in manner, and he has impressed many readers as a man determined to establish the truth. In 1.22 he gives a statement on his method and purpose, which deserves to be taken seriously. It ends with the claim that his history lacks 'a romantic element' and 'was composed as a permanent legacy, not a showpiece for a single hearing' (perhaps

---

[14] Hdt. 1, preface.   [15] Hdt. 7.20.

implying a contrast with Herodotus, who is said to have received an award for a recitation in Athens[16]), that is, that it is intended to be useful (cf. 2.48, on his account of the plague at Athens); and he insists that, although it is hard to get behind the differing accounts of witnesses (cf. 7.44, 71, but he does not often insert such cautionary remarks in his narrative), he has made a great effort to achieve accuracy. He is proud of his achievement, and very willing to criticize those who do not get the facts right (see 1.20, 97, 6.54–5): in 1.23 he states that Sparta's truest reason for going to war against Athens was 'unacknowledged', but he will give a definitive account of the causes of the war; in 2.48 he says he will eschew speculation on the plague and keep to the facts; in 5.68 he complains that it was hard to discover the size of the armies which fought at Mantinea in 418—but he then proceeds to calculate the size of the Spartan army.

For the most part he has relied on oral sources, as he had to do (documents might tell him who commanded the Athenians in a battle and how many soldiers were sent, but they would not give him an account of the course of the battle); and that, and the fact that his history immediately became a classic and that no one else wrote an independent history of the Peloponnesian War, make it very hard for us to check his account. He insists in 1.22 that his 'principle has been not to rely on casual information or [his] own suppositions, but to apply the greatest possible rigour in pursuing every detail both of what [he] saw [himself] and of what [he] heard from others'. Normally he does not, as Herodotus sometimes does, reveal the sources of his information, or give alternative versions before stating which he prefers (there are striking exceptions in 4.122 and 8.87, in 8.94 he reports two versions but prefers the second, and in 2.5 and 6.60 he reports two versions without stating a preference). We know he was aware that witnesses could be biased (1.22), and he tells us that his exile gave him the opportunity to speak to people on the anti-Athenian side (5.26). We know that he made some use of documents: with the treaty quoted in 5.47 we can compare a version inscribed on stone,[17] which differs from his version only in small verbal details; in Book 3 there is a problem about Athens' decisions over Mytilene, since there is a fragmentary document which does not entirely support Thucydides' account and may indicate either that

---

[16] Diyllus *FGrH* 73 F 3; Eusebius, under 446/5 in the Armenian version, under 445/4 in Jerome's version.

[17] *IG* i³ 83 = Tod 72.

his account is misleading or that the original decisions were subsequently modified (see note to 3.50). Documents are directly quoted only in Books 4–5 and 8, but this may be a fact about the writing of his history (and perhaps a sign of experimentation in technique rather than of unfinished work) rather than about the research done for his history.

He explains events entirely in human terms, without any suggestion of intervention by the gods or fulfilment of divine plans (see pp. xlii–xlv below), and his account of what happened and of how and why it happened is almost always credible. (Many, however, have thought that the unexpectedness of the Spartans' encounter with the enemy at Mantinea, on which see 5.66 with note to 5.65, does not make sense unless their view was blocked by a wood whose existence is not mentioned by Thucydides, or by any writer earlier than the traveller Pausanias, in the second century AD).

He reveals more of how he thought one should set about establishing the truth in the passages where he deals with events earlier than the fifth century. In the opening chapters of Book 1 he reviews the growth of power in Greece, to support his claim that the Peloponnesian War was greater than any previous war. The fact that there was no single name for the Greeks, or distinction between Greeks and barbarians, shows that the earliest Greeks were not a united people who engaged in joint actions (1.3). The customs which still prevail in the more primitive parts of Greece show what life used to be like in the parts which are no longer primitive (1.5–6). When corpses were removed from Delos, it was seen that many had been buried in the Carian manner, and this shows that the Aegean islands were once occupied by Carians (1.8). Powerful states do not necessarily leave impressive physical remains: Athens would seem even more powerful than it actually is, but no one would take Sparta to be powerful; so the unimpressiveness of Mycenae does not disprove the tradition that it was once powerful (1.10). Poets are given to exaggeration, but their stories of the past, and even the details in their stories, can be used if they are approached in a rational spirit (1.10).

In a digression in Book 6 on the ending of the Athenian tyranny Thucydides confirms that Hippias was the eldest son of Peisistratus by citing an inscription in which Hippias is the first son to be listed, and the only one to be listed with sons of his own (6.55). He also quotes the couplet recording the younger Peisistratus' dedication of the altar of Apollo (6.54), and puzzles those who have seen the surviving inscription by describing its lettering as faint.[18] Less happily, in telling the dubious story of the Spartan regent Pausanias he quotes not only the boastful couplet which the Spartans deleted from the 'serpent column' (1.132),[19] but also letters allegedly, but hardly in fact, exchanged between Pausanias and the Persian King Xerxes in 478 (1.128–9).

Various statements which Thucydides makes are supported by *tekmeria*, confirmatory pieces of evidence. The fact that originally the city of Athens was on and to the south of the Acropolis is supported by the *tekmerion* that that is where the oldest temples are to be found (2.15). To confirm that birds and animals were vulnerable to the plague at Athens he adduces the *tekmerion* that birds of prey stayed away from the victims and dogs caught the disease from their owners (2.50). A Homeric hymn is cited as providing a *tekmerion* about the festival of Apollo on Delos (3.104: the cognate verb is used after the quotations). He is also prepared to argue from *eikos*, reasonable likelihood. There is no connection (one had perhaps been alleged by a dramatist) between Teres the Thracian, father of Sitalces, and Tereus of Greek legend, the husband of Procne: apart from other arguments, it is likely that an Athenian king would be more interested in a son-in-law from Daulis than in one from distant Thrace (2.29). If Hipparchus had been the reigning tyrant at Athens, it is unlikely that Hippias would have been able to establish himself when Hipparchus was murdered (6.55: in this instance the word *eikos* is not used). Again there is an example at the end of 3.104, where a traditional explanation is said to be a reasonable one.

Thucydides is not infallible. Archaeologists do not now believe that the Aegean islands were once occupied by Carians. He ought not to have been taken in by the letters between Pausanias and Xerxes (there was no time for the exchange of letters while Pausanias was in Byzantium in 478, and the letters seem to improve on a rumour reported by Hdt. 5.32). In 6.54–9 he insists that Hippias as Peisistratus' eldest son was the reigning tyrant, when it may be better to think of joint rule by Peisistratus' sons; and he argues that until 514 the tyranny at Athens was not unpopular, and Harmodius and Aristogeiton murdered Hipparchus for purely personal reasons, yet he gives them some fellow plotters and the hope that when they had struck the first blow the rest of the Athenians would want to reclaim their freedom. His belief

---

[18] *IG* i³ 948 = ML 11, translated Fornara 37.
[19] Cf. ML 27, translated Fornara 59.

that a rational enquirer can extract historical truth from epic poetry is too simple-minded.

Even in the contemporary history which was his main concern we occasionally have reason to think him mistaken on points of detail. An inscription suggests that he is wrong about the commanders of an Athenian expedition in 1.51.[20] Later writers disagreed with 8.67 on the composition of the commission which paved the way for the oligarchy of the Four Hundred in 411, and were probably right to do so.[21] Under the influence of the sophists, the teachers of rhetoric and philosophy who were important in Greek intellectual life in the second half of the fifth century, he was very fond of contrasts such as that between word or surface appearance (*logos*) and deed or underlying reality (*ergon*) (cf. note to 1.22), and we may suspect that sometimes the appearance which he rejects was not wholly false (as in 8.89, where Theramenes and Aristocrates were no doubt personally ambitious but may not have been totally insincere in the arguments which they used against the Four Hundred). Nevertheless, Thucydides' determination to establish the truth, and the range of evidence and arguments which he employed in his investigation of past history, are most impressive.

The statement on method in 1.22, before proceeding to 'the events of the war', begins with 'the various speeches'. Thucydides' history incorporates a considerable number of speeches, and, whereas for the events his 'principle has been not to rely on . . . [his] own suppositions', the speeches represent 'broadly what [he] supposed would have been needed on any given occasion, while keeping as closely as [he] could to the overall intent of what was actually said'. Serious modern historians do not use direct speech except for verbatim quotations, and readers who recognize Thucydides' attitude to historical truth as similar to their own are disturbed to find that in the speeches he confessedly allows himself an element of free composition.[22]

Herodotus earlier had used direct speech, but he made no overt claim to authenticity, and in his case the speeches suit the storytelling manner and have not worried modern readers. Direct speech is used also in the other narrative forms of early Greek literature, epic

[20] *IG* i³ 364 = ML 61, translated Fornara 126.

[21] Androtion *FGrH* 324 F 43 and Philochorus *FGrH* 328 F 136 (the two translated Fornara 148), *Ath. Pol.* 29.2.

[22] Direct speech is lacking from 5.25–83 and from 8 (except 53), but Hornblower (*Commentary*, vol. iii, 32–5), stresses that indirect speech is not. What is said here about speeches presumably applies also to Nicias' letter to Athens, 7.11–15.

and drama, but of course they make no pretence to factual accuracy. With these precedents it is not surprising that Thucydides should have decided to include speeches in his narrative, but he has caused perplexity by professing two apparently conflicting aims, to follow his own judgement of what was appropriate and to adhere to the overall intent of what was actually said. Clearly he was better informed in some cases than in others: he is likely to have heard speeches delivered in Athens before his exile, but he will have had difficulty in finding survivors who had heard and remembered Nicias' speeches in Sicily. Even where he is likely to know what was said in the original speech, he tends to make a speech delivered in one place echo or respond to a speech delivered in another place, as the original cannot have done (compare 1.142, from Pericles' first speech in Athens, with 1.121–2, from the Corinthian speech in the second debate in Sparta in 432; and 2.64, from a speech of Pericles in Athens in 430, with 1.70, from the Corinthian speech in the first debate in Sparta). There are also speeches where what is said is borne out by subsequent events to an extent which suggests hindsight (for example, Nicias' second speech in the debate on the Sicilian expedition, 6.20–3). The similarity of style between speeches makes it clear that the language is on the whole Thucydides' own, though some striking expressions may have been remembered and incorporated from the original speeches (a Spartan speech in 1.86 begins, 'I cannot understand all this talk from the Athenians'; Pericles in 2.62 tells the Athenians to regard their land and houses as 'a back-garden, a mere accessory of wealth'). The kind of argument found in the speeches is appropriate to a generation taught by the sophists, and has parallels in speeches in contemporary drama, but we may suspect that the amount of attention devoted to the nature of Athenian power in Thucydides' speeches reflects his own obsession with the subject rather than the amount of attention devoted to it in speeches actually delivered (cf. pp. xlv–xlvi below).

What room is left for authentic reporting? Most scholars would accept that men did make a speech on occasions when they are said to have done so. (Particular doubts have been raised about speeches to their forces by commanders before a battle: even if such speeches can in principle be accepted, Thucydides' pre-battle speeches sometimes seem to us too intellectual for the occasion, and in any case what is said on such occasions is likely to be less well prepared and less memorable than what is said on more formal occasions, and the need for invention by Thucydides will have been correspondingly greater.) Some scholars resolve the problem of conflicting aims by supposing that the 'overall intent' for which Thucydides claims authenticity is no more than the main point of the speech, for example that at Sparta in 432 king Archidamus was opposed to an immediate declaration of war but the ephor Sthenelaïdas was in favour.[23] However, so small a degree of authenticity is hardly worth claiming, and it is better to think that Thucydides aimed at more than that, and that the general line of argument is the line which the speaker was known to have taken or could reasonably be expected to have taken—though where Thucydides did not know he may have misjudged, and even where he did know his sense of what was appropriate may have led to his giving more or less prominence to particular arguments than the original speaker. The best indication of what Thucydides might have done when he did know what had been said comes from Rome: an inscription records what the emperor Claudius actually said (or at any rate afterwards wanted people to believe he had actually said) in favour of admitting Gauls to the Senate, and Tacitus gives a version of the speech—comprehensively rewritten, but still arguing as Claudius does.[24]

To an unusual extent, parts of the content of Brasidas' speech at Acanthus are confirmed by passages in Thucydides' narrative (see note to 4.84; for another instance see note to 8.52). Thucydidean speakers contradict one another on points of fact and interpretation (notice, for instance, the disagreement between Cleon and Diodotus on whether all the Mytilenaeans had opposed Athens in 428–427: 3.39, 47; the disagreement between Pagondas and Hippocrates on whether the battle of Delium was fought in Athenian or in Boeotian territory: 4.92, 95): it should never be assumed automatically that what a speaker says is true, or is believed by Thucydides to be true.

In the nineteenth and early twentieth centuries total objectivity was often thought to be an aim to which every historian should aspire, and Thucydides was often admired as the ancient historian who aspired most strongly to and most nearly achieved that aim. Nowadays that kind of objectivity is often considered impossible and in any case undesirable, and those who claim to aspire to it are

---

[23] e.g. de Ste. Croix, *Origins of the Peloponnesian War*, 7–16.

[24] *CIL* xiii 1688 = *ILS* 212 = Smallwood, *Docs . . . . Gaius*, 369; Tac., *Ann.* 11.24; Tacitus and inscription translated N. Lewis and M. Reinhold, *Roman Civilization: Selected Readings* (New York: Columbia University Press, ³1990), 52–5.

sometimes considered to be deluded or dishonest, and thus worse than those who admit to their partisan aims (see p. lii below). The tendency of recent scholarship has been not to set Thucydides on a pedestal as a totally accurate and objective historian but to emphasize his partiality[25] and to present him as an 'artful reporter',[26] a writer for whom 'objectivity was . . . not a principle or a goal but an authorial stance',[27] who though his manner is often matter-of-fact has used great artistry in selecting and presenting his material so as to have the desired effect on his readers,[28] and whose family background and involvement in the war make it impossible that his interpretations should be unprejudiced. I still believe, however, that, although Thucydides was human, involved, and prejudiced, he was not dishonest; and, although he did not always succeed in establishing the facts, he did try to do so with exceptional thoroughness and intelligence.[29]

Certainly every historian, however strongly committed to factual accuracy, has to decide which facts to include, which facts to treat prominently and which to treat in passing, and how one fact should be seen in relation to others. There can be no history without selection and interpretation. In the third of a series of brief and disjointed reports of Athenian activity in the west between 427 and 424, which run from the later part of Book 3 to the earlier part of Book 4, with a sequel in 422 at the beginning of Book 5, Thucydides states more explicitly than anywhere else that his narrative is selective (3.90). It is, of course, true that the whole of his narrative is selective. Indeed (as noted above, pp. xvi, xvii) there are affairs which he treats in a low-key manner, such as Athens' naval campaigns of 431 and 430 (which were large and expensive, and of which more may have been hoped than he allows his readers to see: see note to 2.24–32) and this series of campaigns in the west

[25] Perhaps the most extreme attack on his honesty is by Badian, 'Thucydides and the Outbreak of the Peloponnesian War'.

[26] The phrase is borrowed from the title of a book by V. J. Hunter (Toronto: Hakkert, 1973). For an extreme approach to Thucydides' history as a work of literature, noting that he did not always get the facts right and not asking how far he tried to get them right or believed that he had got them right, see A. J. Woodman, *Rhetoric in Classical Historiography* (London and Sydney: Croom Helm; Portland, Ore.: Areopagitica, 1988), 1–69 ch. 1.

[27] Connor, *Thucydides*, 6.

[28] This aspect of early Greek literature is stressed by H. D. F. Kitto in *Poiesis* (Sather Classical Lectures, 36; University of California Press, 1966): he notes that the author 'relies on his reader to read with that degree of imaginative cooperation that makes direct statement unnecessary and the result more effective' (p. 249, referring at that point to Plato).

[29] Cf. P. J. Rhodes, 'In Defence of the Greek Historians', *G&R*[2] 41 (1994), 156–71, at pp. 161–6.

(although in this case Athens' involvement was eventually if not at first on a large scale and with ambitious hopes). There are other affairs, however, of which he gives a vivid and detailed account.

The use of Athens' might to crush Melos, the last island in the Aegean to hold out against it, is written up at length, with a dialogue between representatives of the two sides, at the end of Book 5 (84–116). Immediately afterwards Books 6 and 7 give us a lengthy account of Athens' great expedition to Sicily, which set out with extravagant ambitions but ended in total disaster, while just before the section on Melos Sparta's equally cruel treatment of Hysiae in the Argolid is disposed of in a single sentence (5.83). Thus Athens' treatment of Melos, though neither important for the course of the war nor unparalleled in its cruelty, is used as an opportunity to give the most cynical presentation of Athens' imperialism before it over-reaches itself in the attempt to conquer Sicily. There are detailed passages on Plataea, from the first attack on it by Thebes in 431 to its destruction in 427 (2.2–6, 71–8, 3.20–4, 52–68): this again was not of great significance for the course of the war, but Plataea was near to Athens, so Thucydides could easily obtain detailed information, and the story enabled him to make general points. Another detailed account is devoted to the episode at Pylos in 425 (4.2–6, 8–23, 26–41), and it appears to be a distorted account, attributing the Athenians' success too much to chance and not enough to deliberate planning (see note to 4.2–6): the success was due in part to Cleon, of whom Thucydides disapproved, and the rejection of Spartan peace offers when Athens was in a strong position showed the Athenians departing from Pericles' advice and 'grasping for more'. Sometimes major sections of narrative are interrupted for some very brief reports, for instance in 424/3 on the death of the Thracian ruler Sitalces (4.101.5) and on the Megarians' recovery from Athens and demolition of their long walls (4.109.1).

New approaches to literature in general have encouraged new approaches to some aspects of Thucydides' literary skill: for instance, the investigation of narrative strategies known as 'narratology', applied particularly within classical literature by I. J. F. de Jong to Homer, has been applied profitably to Thucydides by S. Hornblower and T. Rood.[30] This involves, for instance, examining the 'focalization'

---

[30] De Jong, *Narrators and Focalizers: The Presentation of the Story in the Iliad* (Amsterdam: Gruner, 1987; London: Duckworth (Bristol Classical Press, ²2004)), followed by *A Narratological Commentary on the Odyssey* (Cambridge University Press, 2001); Hornblower,

by which material is presented from the viewpoint of different participants, and the planting of 'seeds', early hints of what is to come, which will grow into substantial plants later in the history. We must be cautious, but not overcautious. We have to remember that Thucydides' history is unfinished (cf. pp. xxv–xxviii above), and in a world lacking not only the word-processor and the compact disc, but even the modern form of book, comparison of one passage with another will have been much harder both for author and for readers than it is today. There have been many highly ingenious studies of Thucydides' artistry which have erred no less than those attributing total objectivity to him, by seeing an implausible degree of intention behind every word in the text as it has come down to us.[31] Not everything in Thucydides' writing in which we can find significance was necessarily put there so that we should find that significance; but it is certainly true that he often wrote one passage in full awareness of what he had written in another, and that he has not mechanically compiled a chronicle but has written a well-considered history.

The modern reader may complain of Thucydides' omissions. The problem is not so much that he omits explanations which we need but the first generation of his readers did not. Sometimes he does that, as when he fails to make clear what rights the Athenian generals had with regard to convening the assembly (cf. 2.22 with note, 2.59, 4.118); but he is presumably remembering that not all his readers will be contemporary Athenians when he gives his account of Athens' public funeral for those who died in war (2.34), or writes of 'the territory called the Coastal Region . . . as far as Laureium, the site of the Athenians' silver mines' (2.55). He sometimes but not consistently gives geographical notes, especially for places on the edge of the Greek world (e.g. Cephallenia, 2.30, and Zacynthus, 2.66; Oeniadae and the silting-up of the river Achelous, 2.102; Malea on Lesbos, erroneously, 3.4; Rhegium and Messana, 4.24; Calchedon, 4.75). Occasionally he gives geographical notes on less distant places (e.g. Pylos and Sphacteria, with errors either by Thucydides or by a copyist, 4.8; Cythera, 4.53; the probably not widely known Siphae, 4.76). He frequently indicates the mother-cities of Greek colonies, in the north-east (e.g. 4.7, 84) and elsewhere

---

'Narratology and Narrative Techniques in Thucydides', in Hornblower (ed.), *Greek Historiography* (Oxford University Press, 1994), 131–66, and in his *Commentary*; Rood, *Thucydides: Narrative and Explanation* (Oxford University Press, 1998).

[31] Cf. P. J. Rhodes, ' "Epidamnus is a City": On Not Over-Interpreting Thucydides', *Histos*, 2 (1998).

(e.g. Zacynthus, 2.66; Calchedon, 4.75). On the other hand, he refers to a trophy in Megara and a suburb of Megara as if his readers know them (4.67, 69), and writes as if they know of a portico at Delium but do not know that it had collapsed (4.90).

Nor should we complain too strongly that, by our standards, he takes too narrow a view of what should be included in a history of the Peloponnesian War, that although he devotes a great deal of attention to the morality of the Athenian empire (see pp. xxxv, xlv–xlvi) he devotes very little to its working, that he does not tell us how far the contenders in the war depended on imports for basic materials or how much damage was done to Athenian agriculture by the Peloponnesian invasions (and for Athens' use of Pylos and Cythera see p. xix above): at that level, what he has not done is what no ancient writer would have thought of doing. Modern readers do often complain that, although Thucydides could note occasions when the Athenians were in financial difficulties (3.19), could mention money-collecting expeditions without making their precise status clear (2.69, 3.19, 4.50), and could even mention the change in the Delian League from tribute to a tax on trade, in 413 (7.28), he does not mention the increase in tribute in 425, which we know of from an inscription (see note to 4.50). It has been shown[32] that he is not as neglectful of financial and economic matters as his critics sometimes allege, but it remains true that in this area he omits to mention things which we tend to think he ought to have mentioned.

Other kinds of omission are more irritating. In 433 the Athenians received an appeal from Corcyra for support, and a counter-appeal from Corinth, and the assembly devoted two days to considering these; on the first day they tended to favour Corinth, but on the second they changed their minds and made a limited alliance with Corcyra (1.44)—but how many changed their minds, who spoke on which side, and what was Pericles' position? In Book 2, not every Athenian approves of Pericles' policy of refusing to meet the Peloponnesian invaders in battle, but no opponent is named; in 431 the men of the deme Acharnae collectively are dissatisfied (2.21, cf. 2.20); in 430 'the Athenians' change their mind, attempt to negotiate with Sparta, depose Pericles from his generalship (which Thucydides does not actually state), and fine him, but later re-elect him (2.59, 65). In cases like these it looks as if the artist has got the better of the reporter, and

[32] L. Kallet-Marx, *Money, Expense and Naval Power in Thucydides' History, 1–5.24* (University of California Press, 1993); L. Kallet, *Money and the Corrosion of Power in Thucydides: The Sicilian Expedition and its Aftermath* (University of California Press, 2001).

facts which Thucydides must have known are omitted to show Athens moving towards war in 433, and Pericles towering over the other Athenians in 431 and 430. Thucydides' perfunctory treatment of Athens' campaigns in the west in Books 3–4 is paralleled by his failure to make much of or to make sense of Athens' large-scale naval expeditions around the coasts of Greece in 431 and 430, which has caused great perplexity. There is a particularly vexing omission in connection with the Persians: in Book 4 Thucydides records an episode which ended with the Athenians' sending an embasssy to the Persian court, which turned back on learning of the death of Artaxerxes I, in 424/3 (4.50). He does not mention, but we know from other evidence, that once Dareius II was established as the new King the Athenians sent an embassy to him, and succeeded in making a treaty (see note); and in his text, apart from one sentence in 5.1, the Persians are not mentioned again until 8.5.

There are lesser omissions too, often concerned with the careers of individuals. The last chapter of Book 2 records the return of Phormio from Naupactus to Athens in the spring of 428; a little later, in 3.7, the Athenians send his son to Naupactus since the Acarnanians 'had asked to be sent a son or relative of Phormio to lead them', but Thucydides does not explain why Phormio himself was no longer available (possibly he thought he had explained earlier). The Peloponnesian invasion of Attica in 428, like the previous invasions, was commanded by the Spartan king Archidamus (3.1); that of 427 was commanded by Cleomenes, regent for Pausanias, the son of the exiled king Pleistoanax of the other house (3.26); the abortive invasion of 426 was commanded by king Agis, son of Archidamus (3.89): the illness and death of Archidamus are mentioned nowhere, and the recall from exile of Pleistoanax, apparently in 427/6, is not mentioned until 5.16 (see note). It is likely that Demosthenes was deposed from his generalship after his defeat in Aetolia in 426, but what Thucydides says of him in the remainder of Book 3 does not make his status clear, and it is only in 4.2 that we are told that he is a private citizen (see notes on 3.98, 4.2–6).

His Language and Style

Detailed treatment of Thucydides' language and style would not be appropriate here, but a little may properly be said.[33] In narrative

---

[33] A list of distinctive features of Thucydides' language may be found in K. J. Dover's small editions of Books 6 and 7 (Oxford University Press, 1965), pp. xiii–xviii, xiii–xvii, respectively.

passages his manner is for the most part very straightforward; as noted on p. xxx above, in episodes which he picks out for a detailed narrative it can be extremely vivid. In speeches his style is elaborate and idiosyncratic, making great and sometimes forced use of antithesis, but (unlike his contemporary, the Sicilian orator Gorgias) usually preferring variation in detail to an exact balance between the contrasted elements (but he does sometimes use the latter, for example in the last sentence of 4.61); and it is a compressed style, in which 'he often tries to say too much in too few words',[34] so that the meaning may be hard to fathom.

He sometimes uses, though not as often as Herodotus, the arrangement of material (particularly suited to oral performance) known as ring composition, by which items are presented not in a linear sequence but through rings, and sometimes lesser rings within a greater ring, and the beginning and end of a ring are signalled by the use of similar wording:[35] for instance, in his introduction on the greatness of the Peloponnesian War a ring is opened with observations on the difficulty of ascertaining the truth about past history at the end of 1.1 and closed at the beginning of 1.20. He is fond of abstract concepts, which he expresses sometimes by means of abstract nouns, sometimes by means of a neuter adjective or participle with the definite article; and he is fond of verbs compounded by one or more prefixes, often producing forms which have few or no parallels in surviving classical literature. Though not always perfectly lucid, he was a writer of great skill, at a time when writing in prose was still a young art in Greece. There is little contemporary prose for us to compare with his, but if more existed we should expect to find many features which were distinctively his own: when we look for parallels in surviving texts, we can often find them more easily in contemporary drama than in later prose.[36]

Thucydides' Beliefs

Already by the beginning of the fifth century many Greeks were unhappy with the gods as depicted by Homer, beings who resembled

---

[34] Ibid., pp. xviii and xvi–xvii. Similar criticism was made by ancient writers, such as Cicero and Dionysius of Halicarnassus.

[35] Some Thucydidean rings are set out in Connor, *Thucydides*, apps. 1, 2, 6, 7, 9.

[36] Cf. J. H. Finley, *Three Essays on Thucydides* (Harvard University Press, 1967), 1–117 chs. 1–2.

but surpassed mortals in every respect including their misbehaviour, and some intellectuals, such as Xenophanes and Heracleitus, were prepared to believe in a divine power but complained that human beings create gods in their own image.[37] Among the sophists, Protagoras in the middle of the century proclaimed that man is the measure of all things, and that it is impossible to know whether or not gods exist or what they are like.[38] Critias at the end of the century wrote a play in which one speaker says that originally there were no restraints on human nature; then laws were invented; but men took to breaking the laws when there was no risk of detection, so gods were invented to put a stop to that.[39] Herodotus was prepared to say that a channel was certainly the result of an earthquake, and can be called the work of Poseidon if one likes to attribute earthquakes to him;[40] but he did not deny the existence of the anthropomorphic gods, and he certainly believed in a divine power which punished impiety, was jealous of great human prosperity and had long-term plans which were fulfilled in human affairs, and he believed in the messages conveyed to human beings through oracles.[41]

There is no indication that Thucydides had any religious beliefs. Events are explained in human terms, beyond which there is only the factor which he calls *tyche* (conventionally translated 'chance') or expresses by means of the impersonal verb *xymbainein* (what 'happens'). In some cases these refer to the totality of what happens to a community or individual (e.g. 3.90, 4.14; in 3.89 the opposite of chance is implied when it is stated that a tidal wave would not 'occur', 'happen', without an earthquake). In others they refer to 'chance' in the sense of what cannot be foreseen (e.g. 3.45, or, on the weather, 3.49): in 1.140 Pericles remarks on the habit of blaming *tyche* for what 'happens' contrary to 'our calculation' (*logos*); in 2.61 he classes the plague at Athens among 'events which happen suddenly, unforeseen, and quite beyond any reasonable prediction'. *Tyche* and *xymbainein* are frequent in Thucydides' account of the episode at Pylos, and it is often thought that this is a deliberate device to detract from the Athenians' success (see note to 4.2–6). They are also frequent in his accounts of Brasidas' exploits, but Thucydides clearly admired

[37] Xenophanes, *Vorsokr.* 21 B 11–12, 14–16, 23–6; Heracleitus, *Vorsokr.* 22 B 42, 128.
[38] Protagoras, *Vorsokr.* 80 B 1, 4.
[39] Critias, *Vorsokr.* 88 B 25.
[40] Hdt. 7.129.
[41] See G. E. M. de Ste. Croix, 'Herodotus', *G&R*[2] 24 (1977), 130–48.

Brasidas and will hardly have wished to suggest that his achievements were due to chance.

Religion is a phenomenon which plays a part in the life of some people—but in Pericles' funeral speech festivals have only social value, not religious (2.38), and when the plague strikes Athens the pious are not spared and religious belief does not prevent people from pursuing their immediate advantage by unjust means (2.47, 53); similarly in civil wars oaths were merely gambits to be used against an opponent, and 'neither side observed any religious constraint' (*eusebeia*: 3.82). Religion plays a prominent part in Thucydides' treatment of Brasidas (cf. 4.116, 5.11 with notes), but as usual it is not mentioned in such a way as to suggest that Thucydides was himself a believer. Modern readers are puzzled by his treatment of Nicias in 413: when an eclipse persuades him to delay the Athenians' departure from Syracuse, he is described as 'rather too much inclined to divination and the like', but when he dies in the course of a disastrous failure due to a considerable extent to his own errors he is described as 'of all the Greeks in [Thucydides'] time . . . the least deserving of this depth of misfortune, since he conducted his whole life as a man of principle' (7.50, 86).

Oracles, again, are facts to be taken into account when relevant (e.g. 3.92, 96, and, disparagingly, 3.104): occasionally the rationalist can find in them a sense other than their surface sense (2.17); only with an oracle that the Peloponnesian War was to last thrice nine years does Thucydides seem inclined to go further (5.26). Oracles and the like are mentioned at the beginning of the war, in 2.8; but religious support for the Sicilian expedition of 415–413 is mentioned only in 8.1, when after the defeat the Athenians were angry with those who had given that support. When he uses such expressions as 'enquired of the god' (1.25, 3.92), this is simply using the normal language to report a consultation, and does not imply that he himself believed that a god did receive and respond to the enquiry (cf. the use of such expressions as 'act of God' in insurance policies in the present-day United Kingdom).

Sometimes he suppresses a religious dimension: when the men who escaped from Plataea in 428 did so with their right foot bare, he suggests only a practical reason (3.22 with note); when the Peloponnesian invasion of Attica in 426, and a Spartan attack on Argos in 414, were abandoned because of earthquakes he does not say whether the fear was rationalist or religious (3.89, 6.95). He does not give the reason for Athens' purification of Delos in the same year, which was perhaps to appease Apollo after the plague (3.104); but he does, without comment, give a religious reason for the expulsion of the Delians in 422, and indicates that their restoration in 421 was due to feelings of guilt and to advice from the Delphic oracle (5.1, 32). If men are given appointments because they bear significant names, that is something else which he suppresses (3.92 with note to 3.92–3).

Natural phenomena are just natural phenomena, with no significance for human conduct (e.g. 3.116 on volcanic activity; cf. 3.88, stating of the Islands of Aeolus that 'the people there think' that Hephaestus is at work; 4.52, on a solar eclipse, coinciding with the new moon, and an earthquake; 7.79, on autumn thunderstorms, seen at the time as sinister): 3.89 reaches a rational conclusion on an earthquake and tidal waves, though in 3.87, where earthquakes are mentioned after a recurrence of the plague at Athens, it is possible that the rationalist wavered; otherwise it is exceptional that, at the end of his introduction on the greatness of the Peloponnesian War, Thucydides is tempted to see significance in the earthquakes, eclipses, famines and diseases which accompanied it (1.23).[42]

We have already noticed Thucydides' attitude to Pericles and Periclean democracy (p. xxv above). The nature of Athenian power is a prominent theme in his speeches, and I have suggested that this is because he was obsessed with the subject. Contemporary sophists were fond of the distinction between *physis*, unrestrained nature, and *nomos*, human convention (notice 3.45, from Diodotus' speech in the debate on Mytilene: 'Mistakes, individual or collective, are in human nature [using the verb cognate with *physis*], and no law [*nomos*] will prevent them. . . . In short, when human nature [*anthropeia physis*] is set on a determined course of action, it is impossible—and very naive to think otherwise—to impose any restraint through force of law [*nomoi*] or any other deterrent'). Some men argued that, although laws (*nomoi*) and moral rules were matters of human convention, they were nevertheless desirable;[43] others claimed that they were

---

[42] On the Greeks' interest in recording natural disasters see E. Gabba, 'True History and False History in Classical Antiquity', *JRS* 71 (1981), 50–62, at 56. It is important to notice that Thucydides' attitude to religious matters is not uniformly unbelieving: see S. I. Oost, 'Thucydides and the Irrational: Sunday Passages', *CPhil* 70 (1975), 186–96; N. Marinatos, 'Thucydides and Oracles', *JHS* 101 (1981), 138–40; K. J. Dover, *The Greeks and their Legacy*, Collected Papers, ii: *Prose Literature, History, Society, Transmission, Influence* (Oxford: Blackwell, 1988), 65–73.

[43] e.g. Protagoras in Pl., *Prt.* 320C–322D, 326C–E.

undesirable, as a device to prevent those who were strong by nature (*physis*) from acting as they wished.[44] Plato represents Thrasymachus as claiming that laws are simply rules imposed by the strong, and Callicles as claiming that they are imposed by the weak collectively to restrict the freedom of the strong.[45] It is clear that Thucydides, though he did not believe in divine sanctions for human behaviour, did believe that as far as the conduct of individuals is concerned compliance with moral standards and obedience to law is better than rejection of moral standards and defiance of law (see especially 2.53, in the account of the plague at Athens, 3.82–3, generalizing from the civil war in Corcyra;[46] and compare 2.37, in Pericles' funeral speech).

However, the Athenian empire presented him with a dilemma: as a patriotic Athenian, he was proud of his city's achievement (his admiration of Pericles clearly extends to Pericles' empire: 2.65); yet the means by which the empire was acquired and retained might well be seen as acts of unrestrained *physis*, as rejection of moral standards and defiance of law on the largest scale: the Athenians in 432 say, 'We have done nothing surprising or contrary to human nature [*anthropeios tropos*, literally 'human practice'] . . , It is something worthy of credit when men who follow the natural instinct [*anthropeia physis*] to rule others then show more justice than they need to in their position of strength' (1.76). In his speeches Thucydides represents the Athenians as having no illusions about the nature of their empire: it is described as a tyranny not only by the Corinthians (1.122), and by Cleon, of whom he disapproves (3.37), but also by Pericles, of whom he approves (2.63); cf. also the unknown Euphemus in 6.85. As he suggests that the Athenians naturally exercised their power in their own interests, he suggests that their subjects naturally hated this (for example, the Athenians in 1.75–6, Pericles in 2.63–4, the Mytilenaeans in 3.10–12). I believe that the element of reporting in his speeches is to be taken seriously (cf. pp. xxxiv–xxxvi above): in concentrating on this view of the empire Thucydides may be exaggerating, but he is not fundamentally wrong.[47] And I suspect that he returns to the subject so often because he could not resolve the dilemma to his own satisfaction.

---

[44] e.g. Antiphon the Sophist, *Vorsokr.* 87 B 44. 12–34.

[45] Thrasymachus, Pl., *Resp.* 1.336 B–354 C; Callicles, Pl., *Grg.* 481 B–522 B.

[46] But 3.84 is probably an interpolation (see note).

[47] For the contrary view, see especially G. E. M. de Ste. Croix, 'The Character of the Athenian Empire', *Hist.* 3 (1954–5), 1–41.

After Thucydides

Later Greek Historians

Thucydides' history immediately became a classic: other historians deliberately began their work where his ended (cf. p. xxv above), and as far as we know no one wrote a history of the Peloponnesian War which was essentially independent of his. (There does, however, seem to have been an independent history of Sicily in this period: a fragment from that enables us to supplement Thucydides' account of the campaign of 427–424, at 3.90.)

Some subsequent writers produced general Greek histories, covering a shorter or longer period. Xenophon, an Athenian who spent much of his life as a dependant of Sparta, in his *Hellenica* continued the story from 411 to 362: he was not an energetic enquirer; on many points other sources disagree with him and are sometimes to be preferred to him; he tended to deal with matters which could not be presented in a manner creditable to Sparta by omitting them altogether. He also wrote the *Anabasis*, on an exciting episode in which he was involved, the campaign of the Persian prince Cyrus against his brother Artaxerxes and the journey of Cyrus' mercenaries back to the Greek world; and an account of his hero, the Spartan king Agesilaus. Ephorus, of Cyme in Asia Minor, wrote a general Greek history from the legendary period to the middle of the fourth century, and although that has not survived the section on the fifth and fourth centuries was extensively used in the universal history of Diodorus Siculus (see below): after 411 he is a valuable alternative to Xenophon, but for the earlier part of the Peloponnesian War his account was based on that of Thucydides, with some deviations to the greater glory of Athens from another source or his own invention. Theopompus of Chios wrote *Hellenica*, covering the period 411–394, and *Philippica*, presenting a universal history in a series of digressions from Philip II of Macedonia. All of these were more given than Thucydides to moralizing; Ephorus and Theopompus were both believed to have been pupils of the Athenian orator Isocrates, and Theopompus wrote speeches before he turned to history. Many of the later Greek historians succumbed to rhetorical influence, and were more interested in pleasing their readers and in moralizing than in investigating what had happened and explaining why it had happened.

Those who were still interested in investigation tended to work on a smaller scale, compiling local histories, records of eponymous priests or Olympic victors, and the like: the first to write in this way was Thucydides' older contemporary, Hellanicus of Lesbos (see p. xxix, above). Philistus, a Syracusan historian of the late fifth and early fourth century, was generally considered to be an imitator of Thucydides,[48] and was probably the ultimate source of the account of a plague at Carthage in Diodorus Siculus,[49] clearly based on Thucydides' account of the plague at Athens (2.47–54). In and after the time of Alexander the Great some of the leading generals wrote accounts of the affairs in which they had been involved. Writers such as Nearchus and Ptolemy on Alexander and Hieronymus on the late fourth and early third centuries were at any rate in a position to know much of the truth, and were less given to rhetorical embellishment than the later writers who used them as sources; and it seems that Hieronymus modelled himself on Thucydides in various ways.[50]

The last great Greek historian was another man of affairs, Polybius, who in the second century BC was taken to Rome as a hostage, became an admirer of Rome, and wrote an account of the growth of Rome's empire from 264 to 146. Polybius like Thucydides professed a serious purpose and criticized those who did not come up to his standards. He believed that history should be useful, claiming that he was 'aiming not so much at the pleasure (*terpsis*) of those who will read [his history] as at the benefit (*opheleia*) of those who pay attention to it'.[51] He often protested that history should keep to the truth, of speeches as well as actions: he criticizes Phylarchus for writing history like tragedy, which aims to be plausible and does not mind being false; he criticizes Timaeus for composing rhetorical exercises and passing over the speeches that were actually made.[52] On the causes of wars he perhaps implies criticism of Thucydides (who in 1.118 uses *prophasis*, 'reason', of the immediate grounds for complaint which in 1.23 he called *aitiai*, 'grievances', and distinguished from the true *prophasis*) when he distinguishes between *aitiai*, events prompting the war, *prophasis*, the pretext, and *arche*, the first action of the war itself.[53] The historian needs research in libraries and archives, exploration of the terrain, and personal experience of

---

[48] *FGrH* 556 TT 15–17.
[49] Diod. Sic. 14.70.4–71.
[50] Cf. J. Hornblower, *Hieronymus of Cardia* (Oxford University Press, 1981), 107–8, 122, 138–9, 152.
[51] Polyb. 9.2; and similar remarks elsewhere.
[52] On Phylarchus, Polyb. 2.56; on Timaeus, 12.25[b], cf. 25[i].
[53] Polyb. 22.18, cf. 3.6.

affairs:[54] Polybius' details of the Carthaginian forces at the beginning of the Second Punic War are not plausible invention but are derived from an inscription;[55] other accounts of Hannibal's crossing of the Alps are both false and contradictory, but Polybius credits him with a reasonable plan, and has himself interrogated witnesses and explored the terrain.[56] Two concessions are made: to report miracles is childish credulity, but what will support the piety of the masses can be pardoned as long as it does not go too far;[57] and the historian may yield to patriotic bias as long as it does not lead him into actual falsehood.[58] Polybius, like Thucydides, was human and should not be placed on a pedestal, but he had a sense of the historian's responsibility which was like that of Thucydides and not far from that of a modern historian.

From the time of Polybius the Greek world was part of the Roman, and historians writing in Greek were concerned as much with Rome as with Greece. Diodorus wrote a universal history down to 54 BC: for the most part he followed one main source at a time for each region, rearranging the material in annalistic form (without taking much care to assign events to the correct years) and adding moralizing passages of his own. Appian of Alexandria, in the second century AD, wrote regional histories of the wars through which Rome's empire grew; and Cassius Dio of Bithynia, in the third, rose to be twice consul and wrote a history of Rome. Meanwhile, c. AD 100, Plutarch, of Chaeroneia in Boeotia, wrote parallel Lives to display the characters of famous Greeks and famous Romans, and Thucydides was one of his many sources. In the second century, Arrian, like Dio a man from Bithynia who had a political career under the Romans, wrote histories of Alexander the Great and his successors in which he went back to early and well-informed sources, and paid tribute to Xenophon by giving the title *Anabasis* ('journey up-country') to his work on Alexander. Greek had become the language of educated men throughout the eastern Mediterranean, and histories written in Greek include the *Jewish War* and *Jewish Antiquities* of Josephus (first century AD), who used non-Jewish as well as Jewish sources, and ended his life as a Roman citizen living in Rome. His debt to Thucydides includes the contrast between truth (*aletheia*) and pleasure (*hedone*):[59] for the sentiment, but not expressed in those words, see Thuc. 1.22.

---

[54] Polyb. 12.25ᵉ.   [55] Polyb. 3.33.   [56] Polyb. 3.47–8.
[57] Polyb. 16.12.   [58] Polyb. 16.14.   [59] Joseph., *BJ* 1.30.

The Reception of Thucydides[60]

Thucydides was not as widely read in the fourth century and the hellenistic period as the more obviously attractive Herodotus and Xenophon, but he was far from being totally neglected, and knowledge of him can be found in fourth-century orators and philosophers as well as in historians.[61] One remarkable example is the use by Aeneas Tacticus, in his work on withstanding sieges, written in the mid-fourth century, not only of Thucydides' account of the Theban attack on Plataea in 431 but also of Brasidas' speech before the battle of Amphipolis.[62]

By the first century BC his history was well known in Rome. Lucretius ended his *De Rerum Natura* with an account of the plague at Athens.[63] Cicero commented on Thucydides' history, not recommending it as a model for Roman orators to follow, and seems to have relied on it for his knowledge of fifth-century Athenian oratory.[64] The historian Sallust took Thucydides as a model (*inter alia*, for the debate between Cato and Caesar on the Catilinarians following the debate between Cleon and Diodotus on Mytilene[65]), and his indebtedness to Thucydides was remarked on by Livy and others.[66] Dionysius of Halicarnassus, active in the time of Augustus, wrote essays *About Thucydides* and *About the Distinctive Features of Thucydides*. Quintilian in the first century AD commented on Thucydides' style.[67] Lucian in the second century, in his essay on *How to Write History*, described Thucydides as 'the man who legislated for history'.[68] Much later, in the Byzantine empire, Procopius, the historian of Justinian, was an imitator of Thucydides, and the plague at Athens was pressed into service again when he wrote about the bubonic plague in Constantinople in 542–3.[69]

[60] See in general the last four chapters in Rengakos and Tsakmakis (eds.), *Brill's Companion to Thucydides* (pp. 721–837, by L. Canfora, D. R. Reinsch, M. Pade, and F. M. Pires), to which I owe much of the information in this section.

[61] See Hornblower, 'The Fourth-Century and Hellenistic Reception of Thucydides', *JHS* 115 (1995), 47–68.

[62] Plataea, Aen. Tact. 2.3–6, cf. Thuc. 2.2–6; Amphipolis, Aen. Tact. 32.8, cf. Thuc. 5.9.

[63] Lucr. 6.1090–1286, cf. Thuc. 2.47–54.

[64] Not a model for orators, Cic., *De Or.* 2.56, *Brut.* 287–8, *Orat.* 30–2; source for fifth-century oratory, *De Or.* 2.93, *Brut.* 28–9.

[65] Sall., *Cat.* 50–5, cf. Thuc. 3.36–49.

[66] Livy *ap.* Sen. *Controv.* 9.1.13–14, Vell. Pat. 2.36.2, Quint., *Inst.* 10.1.101, 2.17.

[67] In addition to the passages cited in the previous note, see Quint., *Inst.* 9.4.16, 78, 10.1.33, 73–4.

[68] Lucian, *Hist. Conscr.* 42.

[69] Procop., *De bello Persico*, 2.22–3.

The rediscovery of Thucydides in western Europe began with Juan
Fernández de Heredia, in Rhodes as Master of the Knights Hospitallers
between 1379 and 1382, and by *c*.1400 Thucydides was being read in
Italy. The first Latin translation of Thucydides was made by Lorenzo
Valla, between 1448 and 1452; and the first printed edition of the
Greek text was published by Aldo Manuzio in 1502. Meanwhile, historians of the second half of the fifteenth century, such as Poggio
Bracciolini, claimed to use Thucydides as a model. Because of the
difficulty of his Greek and the lack of moralizing, Thucydides was not
the most popular Greek author in the Renaissance; but in the sixteenth
century at Wittenberg Philipp Melanchthon lectured on and wrote
about him, while in Italy the diplomat Giovanni della Casa translated
many of the speeches and the account of the plague. A landmark in the
development of a scholarly approach to Thucydides, as opposed to the
use of him as a model, came with the editions of Henri Estienne
(Stephanus), first published in 1564 and revised in 1588.

As for political thinkers, there is not much trace of the influence of
Thucydides in Niccolò Machiavelli (late fifteenth–early sixteenth
century); but in Britain in the seventeenth century Thomas Hobbes
was a great admirer of him, and he made a translation (first published
1628), his own first published work, and the first English translation
of Thucydides made directly from the Greek.[70]

It was in nineteenth-century Germany that Thucydides first
came to be praised as the ideal scientific and objective historian.
B. G. Niebuhr, himself often regarded as the first modern historian,
described Thucydides as 'the first real and true historian';[71] and L.
von Ranke, whose 'wie es eigentlich gewesen' (how it actually was)
has been taken as emblematic of the kind of history which claims 'to
let the facts speak for themselves', read Thucydides as a student at
Leipzig, and expressed his admiration in his *Universal History* at the
end of his life.[72] In Britain, meanwhile, T. B. Macaulay admired

[70] De Ste. Croix, *Origins of the Peloponnesian War*, 26–8 with 28 n. 54, found much of
Hobbes's political doctrine distasteful, but suggested that Hobbes may have derived
from Thucydides what de Ste. Croix himself found in Thucydides, 'the belief that a
system of ethics applicable inside a political community can have no relevance in dealings between sovereign States'.

[71] B. G. Niebuhr, *Vorträge über alte Geschichte*, i (Berlin: Reimer, 1847), 205–6 =
Lectures on Ancient History, trans. L. Schmitz, i (London: Taylor, Walton & Maberly,
1852), 169–70.

[72] 'Wie es eigentlich gewesen', L. von Ranke, *Geschichten der romanischen und germani-
schen Völker von 1494 bis 1535* (Leipzig and Berlin: Reimer, 1824), vol. i, p. vi; cf.
p. vii; Thucydides at Leipzig, Ranke, ed. A. W. Dove, *Zur eigenen Lebensgeschichte*

Thucydides for his artistry, at first judged him not 'a really philosophical historian', but eventually came to think of him as 'the greatest historian that ever lived';[73] Thomas Arnold took over the approach of Niebuhr;[74] but George Grote, as a champion of Athenian democracy and democrats, dared to complain that Thucydides was excessively hostile to Cleon.[75] In 1907 F. M. Cornford represented Thucydides as mythical and tragic rather than factual and analytic;[76] but in general the view of Thucydides the scientific historian survived to the middle of the twentieth century, in such scholars as J. H. Finley, jun., J. de Romilly, and H. T. Wade-Gery.[77]

More recently, there has been a tendency to consider objective, scientific history undesirable and impossible. Marxists have claimed that all historians have an agenda, and those who admit it are better than those who do not;[78] 'post-modernists' have argued that a work of history can only be a personal construction, and no one person's construction has greater validity than any other.[79] Recent students of Thucydides have therefore emphasized his personal involvement and prejudices, and his literary artistry, as we have seen above (p. xxxvii).

Thucydides has not only continued to excite admiration through the changes in academic fashion. Outside scholarly circles people have continued to find him 'good to think with'—as he hoped, both

(Leipzig: Duncker & Humblot, 1890), 30; Ranke, *Weltgeschichte*, i. 2 (Leipzig: Duncker & Humblot, ²1881), 42–52, esp. 47–8 = *Universal History* [i], ed. G. W. Prothero (London: Kegan Paul Trench, 1884), i. 314–22, esp. 318.

[73] T. B. Macaulay, *Edinburgh Review*, 94 (May 1828) (published anonymously), 336–42, quoting 341 = *Life and Works of Lord Macaulay*, Edinburgh Edition (London: Longmans, 1897), v. 128–33, quoting 133; letter of 11 February 1835, in *The Letters of T. B. Macaulay*, ed. T. Pinney, iii (Cambridge University Press, 1976), 137; cf. other letters of that year.

[74] T. Arnold, *The History of the Peloponnesian War by Thucydides* (Oxford: Parker, 1830–5), vol. iii, pp. vi–xiv on the 'archaeology' in Book 1, cf. vol. i, pp. xi–xii in praise of Niebuhr.

[75] G. Grote, *History of Greece*, esp. ('new edn.' in 12 vols., 1869/84) vi. 126–30 (on Pylos), 252–5 (on Amphipolis) = ('new edn.' in 10 vols., 1888), v. 264–7, 385–400.

[76] F. M. Cornford, *Thucydides Mythistoricus* (London: Arnold, 1907).

[77] 'An ideal of absolute and rigidly tested truth', Finley, *Thucydides* (Harvard University Press, 1942), 105; 'un soin et une impartialité universellement reconnus', de Romilly, *Histoire et raison chez Thucydide* (Paris: Les Belles Lettres, 1956), 12; 'his singular truthfulness', Wade-Gery, 'Thucydides', *OCD³*, 1516–19 at 1519 (repeated from previous editions).

[78] e.g. J. P. Sullivan, 'Editorial', *Arethusa*, 8 (1975), 6.

[79] e.g. H. V. White, *Metahistory* (Johns Hopkins University Press, 1973); *The Content of the Form: Narrative Discourse and Historical Representation* (Johns Hopkins University Press, 1987).

'useful' and 'a permanent legacy' (1.22)—and relevant to the circumstances of their own time and place. W. R. Connor, himself an academic writing for academics, begins his *Thucydides* with the Vietnam War and an article in the *New Yorker*, whose author in the manner of Thucydides professed 'no wish to pass judgment' but 'merely to record what [he] witnessed'. He ends it with an observation on Thucydides quoted from a book on *Strategy in the Missile Age*, 'that Thucydides was right, that peace is better than war not only in being more agreeable but also in being very much more predictable'.[80] In the First World War quotations from Pericles' funeral oration (2.35–46) were displayed on London buses, including 'The secret of happiness is Liberty, and the secret of Liberty is courage' (2.43).[81] More recently, the 2003 version of the Draft Treaty Establishing a Constitution for Europe began its Preamble by quoting 'Our Constitution . . . is called a democracy because power is in the hands not of a minority but of the greatest number', from the funeral oration (2.37);[82] and in 2006 Sir Ivor Roberts, on retiring as British Ambassador to Italy, in his valedictory telegram quoted 'The strong do what they can: the weak suffer what they must', from the Melian dialogue (5.89).[83] For its combination of the particular and the general, its skilful presentation and its penetrating judgement, Thucydides' history is indeed a permanent legacy.

[80] Connor, *Thucydides*, 6–7, quoting Schell, 'Quang Ngai and Quang Tin', *New Yorker*, 9 March 1968, 37; 250, quoting Brodie, *Strategy in the Missile Age*, 408–9.
[81] G. Wallas, *Our Social Heritage* (London: Allen & Unwin, 1921), 162.
[82] http://european-convention.eu.int/DraftTreaty.asp?
[83] Reported by D. Macintyre, *The Independent*, 27 April 2007, 33.

SELECT BIBLIOGRAPHY

Greek Text

The most recent major editions are:

Alberti, J. B. (Latinized from 'G. B.'), 3 vols. (Rome: Istituto Poligrafico e Zecca dello Stato, 1972–2000).

Romilly, J. de, with R. Weil and L. Bodin (Coll. Budé: with French translation), 6 vols. (Paris: Les Belles Lettres, 1953–72; vol. i² 1958).

Smith, C. F. (Loeb Classical Library: with English translation), 4 vols. (London: Heinemann; Harvard University Press, 1919–23; revised 1928–35); the last volume has a good index.

Stuart Jones, H., with apparatus criticus revised by J. E. Powell (Oxford Classical Texts), 2 vols. (Oxford University Press, 1942; index revised 1963).

English Commentaries

Cartwright, D., A Historical Commentary on Thucydides (based on the Penguin translation) (University of Michigan Press, 1997).

Dover, K. J., editions of Books 6 and 7, with commentary (Oxford University Press, 1965).

Gomme, A. W., Andrewes, A., and Dover, K. J., A Historical Commentary on Thucydides, 5 vols. (Oxford University Press, 1945–81; vol. i corrected 1950).

Hornblower, S., A Commentary on Thucydides, 3 vols. (Oxford University Press, 1991–2008; revised 1997–).

Rhodes, P. J., editions of Books 2, 3, and 4.1–5.24, with translation and commentary (Warminster: Aris & Phillips, 1988, 1994, 1998).

Rusten, J. S., edition of Book 2, with commentary (Cambridge University Press, 1989).

On Thucydides

Badian, E., 'Thucydides and the Outbreak of the Peloponnesian War: A Historian's Brief', in J. W. Allison (ed.), Conflict, Antithesis and the Ancient Historian (Ohio State University Press, 1990), 49–91, with 165–81; revised in Badian, From Plataea to Potidaea (Johns Hopkins University Press, 1993), 125–62, with 223–36.

Bauslaugh, R. A., 'The Text of Thucydides 4.8.6 and the South Channel at Pylos', JHS 99 (1979), 1–6.

Cawkwell, G. L., Thucydides and the Peloponnesian War (London: Routledge, 1997).

Connor, W. R., *Thucydides* (Princeton University Press, 1984).

Cornford, F. M., *Thucydides Mythistoricus* (London: Arnold, 1907).

Dover, K. J., *Thucydides*, Greece & Rome: New Surveys in the Classics, 7 (Oxford University Press, 1973).

Finley, J. H., jun., *Three Essays on Thucydides* (Harvard University Press, 1967).

—— *Thucydides* (Harvard University Press, 1942).

Flory, S., 'The Death of Thucydides and the Motif of "Land on Sea"', in *Nomodeiktes: Greek Studies in Honor of M. Ostwald* (University of Michigan Press, 1993), 113–23.

Fornara, C. W., 'Thucydides' Birth Date', in *Nomodeiktes: Greek Studies in Honor of M. Ostwald* (University of Michigan Press, 1993), 71–80.

Hornblower, S., 'Narratology and Narrative Techniques in Thucydides', in id. (ed.), *Greek Historiography* (Oxford University Press, 1994), 131–66, ch. 5.

—— 'The Fourth-Century and Hellenistic Reception of Thucydides', *JHS* 115 (1995), 47–68.

—— *Thucydides* (London: Duckworth; Johns Hopkins University Press, 1987; revised 1994).

Hunter, V. J., *Thucydides, the Artful Reporter* (Toronto: Hakkert, 1973).

Kallet, L., *Money and the Corrosion of Power in Thucydides: The Sicilian Expedition and its Aftermath* (University of California Press, 2001).

Kallet-Marx, L., *Money, Expense and Naval Power in Thucydides' History, 1–5.24* (University of California Press, 1993).

Kitto, H. D. F., *Poiesis* (on Thucydides, ch. 6), Sather Classical Lectures, 36 (University of California Press, 1966).

Marinatos, N., 'Thucydides and Oracles', *JHS* 101 (1981), 138–40.

Maurer, K., *Interpolation in Thucydides*, Mnemosyne Suppl. 150 (1995).

Oost, S. I., 'Thucydides and the Irrational: Sundry Passages', *CPhil* 70 (1975), 186–96.

Pouilloux, J., and Salviat, F., 'Lichas, Lacédémonien, archonte à Thasos, et le livre viii de Thucydide', *CR Acad. Inscr.* (1983), 376–403.

Rengakos, A., and Tsakmakis, A. (eds.), *Brill's Companion to Thucydides* (Leiden: Brill, 2006).

Rhodes, P. J., '"Epidamnus is a City": On Not Over-Interpreting Thucydides', *Histos*, 2 (1998) (http://www.durham.ac.uk/Classics/histos/1998/rhodes.html).

—— 'In Defence of the Greek Historians', *G&R*² 41 (1994), 156–71.

—— 'Thucydides on the Causes of the Peloponnesian War', *Hermes*, 115 (1987), 154–65.

Romilly, J. de, *Histoire et raison chez Thucydide* (Paris: Les Belles Lettres, 1956).

Rood, T., *Thucydides: Narrative and Explanation* (Oxford University Press, 1998).

Stroud, R. S., 'Thucydides and Corinth', *Chiron*, 24 (1994), 267–304.

Wade-Gery, H. T., 'Thucydides (2)', *OCD*[3] (1996), 1516–19 (repeated from first and second editions).

Woodman, A. J., *Rhetoric in Classical Historiography* (on Thucydides, ch. 1) (London and Sydney: Croom Helm; Portland, Ore.: Areopagitica, 1988).

Zagorin, P., *Thucydides: An Introduction for the Common Reader* (Princeton University Press, 2005).

General

Cambridge Ancient History, vols. ii. 1[3], ii. 2[3], iii. 1[2], iii. 3[2], iv[2], v[2] (Cambridge University Press, 1973, 1975, 1982, 1982, 1988, 1992).

Davies, J. K., *Athenian Propertied Families, 600–300 BC* (Oxford University Press, 1971).

de Ste. Croix, G. E. M., 'Herodotus', *G&R*[2] 24 (1977), 130–48.

—— 'The Character of the Athenian Empire', *Hist.* 3 (1954–5), 1–41.

—— *The Origins of the Peloponnesian War* (London: Duckworth; Cornell University Press, 1972).

Develin, R., *Athenian Officials, 684–321 BC* (Cambridge University Press, 1989).

Dover, K. J., *The Greeks and their Legacy*, Collected Papers, ii: *Prose Literature, History, Society, Transmission, Influence* (Oxford: Blackwell, 1988).

Gabba, E., 'True History and False History in Classical Antiquity', *JRS* 71 (1981), 50–62.

Hall, J., *A History of the Archaic Greek World, ca. 1200–479 BCE* (Oxford: Blackwell, 2007).

Hammond, N. G. L. (ed.), *Atlas of the Greek and Roman World in Antiquity* (Park Ridge, NJ: Noyes, 1981).

Hansen, M. H., and Nielsen, T. H. (eds.), *An Inventory of Archaic and Classical Poleis* (Oxford University Press, 2004).

Hanson, V. D., *A War Like No Other: How the Athenians and Spartans Fought the Peloponnesian War* (London: Methuen; New York: Random House, 2005).

Hornblower, J., *Hieronymus of Cardia* (Oxford University Press, 1981).

Hornblower, S., *The Greek World, 479–323 BC* (London: Routledge, [3]2002).

Jong, I. J. F. de, *A Narratological Commentary on the Odyssey* (Cambridge University Press, 2001).

—— *Narrators and Focalizers: The Presentation of the Story in the Iliad* (Amsterdam: Gruner, 1987; London: Duckworth (Bristol Classical Press), [2]2004).

Kagan, D., *The Archidamian War* (Cornell University Press, 1974).

—— *The Fall of the Athenian Empire* (Cornell University Press, 1987).

—— *The Outbreak of the Peloponnesian War* (Cornell University Press, 1969).

—— *The Peace of Nicias and the Sicilian Expedition* (Cornell University Press, 1981).

—— *The Peloponnesian War* (London: HarperCollins; New York: Viking, 2003).

Lazenby, J. F., *The Peloponnesian War: A Military Study* (London: Routledge, 2004).

Morrison, J. S., Coates, J. F., and Rankov, N. B., *The Athenian Trireme* (Cambridge University Press, ²2000).

Osborne, R., *Greece in the Making, 1200–479 BC* (London: Routledge, 1996).

Pritchett, W. K., *The Greek State at War* (University of California Press, 1974–91; vol. i originally published as *Ancient Greek Military Practices*, 1971).

Rhodes, P. J., *A History of the Classical Greek World, 478–323 BC* (Oxford: Blackwell, 2005 (dated 2006)).

Talbert, R. J. A. (ed.), *Barrington Atlas of the Greek and Roman World* (Princeton University Press, 2000).

Further Reading in Oxford World's Classics

Herodotus, *The Histories*, translated by Robin Waterfield, edited by Carolyn Dewald.

The Homeric Hymns, translated by Michael Crudden.

Plato, *Republic*, translated by Robin Waterfield.

Plutarch, *Greek Lives*, translated by Robin Waterfield, edited by Philip A. Stadter.

Xenophon, *The Expedition of Cyrus*, translated by Robin Waterfield, edited by Tim Rood.

SUMMARY AND ANALYSIS

BOOK ONE

1–23.3	INTRODUCTION
1	Preface: Peloponnesian War greater than any previous war
2–19	'Archaeology': growth of Greek power, to justify that claim
20	Difficulty of getting history right
21	Previous wars not as great as Peloponnesian War
22	How Thucydides has written his history
23.1–3	Greatness of Peloponnesian War
23.4–146	CAUSES OF THE PELOPONNESIAN WAR
23.4–6	Grievances and disputes, real reason
24–55	Corcyra (435–433)
56–66	Potidaea (433–432)
67–88	First meeting in Sparta (432)
88	Repeats real reason more important than grievances
89–118	'Pentecontaetia': growth of Athenian power, to justify that judgement
118	Repeats real reason more important than grievances
119–25	Congress of Peloponnesian League in Sparta (432)
126–38	Digression on past episodes raised in propaganda: Cylon, Pausanias, Themistocles
139–46	Athenian response to Spartan pressure (432)

BOOK TWO

1	FORMAL BEGINNING OF THE WAR
2–32	FIRST SUMMER (431)
2–6	Thebes' attempt to seize Plataea
7–17	Final preparations and resources
18–23	The Peloponnesian invasion of Attica
24–32	Athenian counter-measures
33–46	FIRST WINTER (431/0)
33	A Corinthian campaign in the north-west
34–46	The public funeral in Athens

47–68   SECOND SUMMER (430)
47–54   The plague in Athens
55–8   The summer's campaigns (i)
59–65   Pericles under attack
66–8   The summer's campaigns (ii)

69–70   SECOND WINTER (430/29)
69   Athenian campaigns
70   Capitulation of Potidaea

71–92   THIRD SUMMER (429)
71–8   The siege of Plataea (i)
79   An Athenian campaign in the north-east
80–2   A Spartan campaign in the north-west
83–92   Naval battles in the Gulf of Corinth

93–103   THIRD WINTER (429/8)
93–4   The Peloponnesian fleet
95–101   A campaign by Sitalces the Odrysian
102–3   Phormio in Acarnania

BOOK THREE

1–18   FOURTH SUMMER (428)
1   Peloponnesian invasion of Attica
2–6   Revolt of Mytilene (i)
7   Asopius in the north-west
8–18   Revolt of Mytilene (ii)

19–25   FOURTH WINTER (428/7)
19   Athenian financial difficulties
20–4   The sicge of Plataea (ii): escape of Plataeans
25   Revolt of Mytilene (iii)

26–86   FIFTH SUMMER (427)
26   Peloponnesian invasion of Attica
27–50   Revolt of Mytilene (iv)
51   Minoa
52–68   The siege of Plataea (iii): fall of Plataea
69–85   Civil war in Corcyra (i)
86   Athens and the west (i)

87–8	FIFTH WINTER (427/6)
87	Plague in Athens; earthquakes
88	Athens and the west (ii)
89–102	SIXTH SUMMER (426)
89	Peloponnesian invasion of Attica; earthquakes
90	Athens and the west (iii)
91	Melos and Boeotia
92–3	Spartan colony at Heracleia in Trachis
94–8	Campaigns in north-western Greece (i)
99	Athens and the west (iv)
100–2	Campaigns in north-western Greece (ii)
103–16	SIXTH WINTER (426/5)
103	Athens and the west (v)
104	Athens' purification of Delos
105–14	Campaigns in north-western Greece (iii)
115–16	Athens and the west (vi)

BOOK FOUR

1–49	SEVENTH SUMMER (425)
1	Athens and the west (vii)
2–6	Pylos (i)
7	An episode in the north-east
8–23	Pylos (ii)
24–5	Athens and the west (viii)
26–41	Pylos (iii)
42–5	An Athenian campaign in the Corinthiad
46–48.5	Civil war in Corcyra (ii)
48.6	Athens and the west (ix)
49	A campaign in north-western Greece
50–1	SEVENTH WINTER (425/4)
50	Negotiations with Persia
51	Athenian suspicion of Chios
52–88	EIGHTH SUMMER (424)
52	Eclipse and earthquake; activity of Mytilenaean exiles
53–7	An Athenian campaign against Cythera and Laconia
58–65	Athens and the west (x)
66–74	Athens and Megara (i)

75	The Athenians in the north-east
76–7	Athens and Boeotia (i)
78–88	Brasidas in the north-east (i)

89–116	EIGHTH WINTER (424/3)
89–101.4	Athens and Boeotia (ii)
101.5	The death of Sitalces
102–8	Brasidas in the north-east (ii)
109.1	Athens and Megara (ii)
109.1–116	Brasidas in the north-east (iii)

117–33	NINTH SUMMER (423)
117–19	The year's truce
120–32	Brasidas in the north-east (iv)
133.1–3	Boeotia; Argos
133.4	Brasidas in the north-east (v)

134–5	NINTH WINTER (423/2)
134	Mantinea and Tegea
135	Brasidas in the north-east (vi)

BOOK FIVE

1–12	TENTH SUMMER (422)
1	Delos
2–3	Brasidas in the north-east (vii)
4–5	Athens and the west (xi)
6–12	Brasidas in the north-east (viii)

13–24	TENTH WINTER (422/1)
13	Brasidas in the north-east (postscript)
14–24	The Peace of Nicias

25–35	ELEVENTH SUMMER (421)
25–6	Thucydides' second preface
27–32	Formation of Argive alliance
33–35.1	Summer campaigns
35.2–8	Non-fulfilment of treaty

36–9	ELEVENTH WINTER (421/0)
	Spartan intrigues with Boeotia

40–50   TWELFTH SUMMER (420)
40–8   Various intrigues
49–50   Sparta banned from Olympic games

51   TWELFTH WINTER (420/19)
         Heracleia in Trachis

52–5   THIRTEENTH SUMMER (419)
         Mostly Argos

56   THIRTEENTH WINTER (419/18)
         Argos

57–75   FOURTEENTH SUMMER (418)
57–60   Spartan attack on Argos
61–3   Argive attack on Orchomenus and Tegea
64–75.3 Battle of Mantinea
75.4–6   Epidaurian attack on Argos

76–81   FOURTEENTH WINTER (418/17)
         Peace in Peloponnese

82   FIFTEENTH SUMMER (417)
         Mostly Argos

83   FIFTEENTH WINTER (417/16)
         Mostly Argos

84–115   SIXTEENTH SUMMER (416)
         Mostly Athenian attack on Melos

116   SIXTEENTH WINTER (416/15) (BEGINNING)
         Argos; Melos

BOOK SIX

1–7   SIXTEENTH WINTER (416/15) (CONCLUSION)
1   Athens' Sicilian expedition (i): planning
2–5   Early history of Sicily
6   Athens' Sicilian expedition (ii): planning
7   Various campaigns

8–62   SEVENTEENTH SUMMER (415)
8–26   Athens' Sicilian expedition (iii): preparations
27–9   Religious scandals in Athens (i)

30–52   Athens' Sicilian expedition (iv): voyage to Sicily,
               Syracusan reaction
53.1–2   Religious scandals in Athens (ii): recall of Alcibiades
53.3–59   Harmodius and Aristogeiton (514)
60–1   Religious scandals in Athens (iii): verdicts in Athens,
               flight of Alcibiades
62   Athens' Sicilian expedition (v)

63–93   SEVENTEENTH WINTER (415/14)
63–71   Athens' Sicilian expedition (vi): the Athenians' first
               attempt on Syracuse
72–88.6   Athens' Sicilian expedition (vii): winter preparations
88.7–93   Alcibiades in Sparta

94–105   EIGHTEENTH SUMMER (414) (BEGINNING)
94   Athens' Sicilian expedition (viii): Athenian campaigns
95   Mainland Greece
96–103   Athens' Sicilian expedition (ix): siege of Syracuse begun
104   Athens' Sicilian expedition (x): Gylippus in Italy
105   Mainland Greece

BOOK SEVEN

1–9   EIGHTEENTH SUMMER (414) (CONCLUSION)
1–8   Athens' Sicilian expedition (xi): Gylippus' arrival in
               Syracuse
9   Amphipolis

10–18   EIGHTEENTH WINTER (414/13)
10–17.2   Athens' Sicilian expedition (xii): Nicias' letter to Athens
17.3–18   Preparations of Peloponnesians

19–87   NINETEENTH SUMMER (413) (BEGINNING)
19–20   Mainland Greece, including Deceleia
21–5   Athens' Sicilian expedition (xiii): Plemmyrium, Great
               Harbour
26   Demosthenes' voyage to Sicily (i)
27–30   Mainland Greece: Deceleia, Mycalessus
31   Demosthenes' voyage to Sicily (ii)
32–3   Athens' Sicilian expedition (xiv)
34   Battle in Gulf of Corinth
35   Demosthenes' voyage to Sicily (iii)

36–41   Athens' Sicilian expedition (xv): battle in Great Harbour
42–6   Athens' Sicilian expedition (xvi): arrival of
               Demosthenes, night battle
47–50   Athens' Sicilian expedition (xvii): Athenian withdrawal
               delayed
51–72   Athens' Sicilian expedition (xviii): last battles in Great
               Harbour
73–4   Athens' Sicilian expedition (xix): Athenian withdrawal
               delayed
75–87   Athens' Sicilian expedition (xx): Athenian withdrawal
               and defeat

BOOK EIGHT

1   NINETEENTH SUMMER (413) (CONCLUSION)
           Athens' reaction to defeat in Sicily

2–6   NINETEENTH WINTER (413/12)
           Preparations for war in Greece

7–28   TWENTIETH SUMMER (412)
           Chios leads revolt of Ionia
(18   First Spartan–Persian treaty)

29–60   TWENTIETH WINTER (412/11)
29–44   Campaigns in the Aegean
(37   Second Spartan–Persian treaty)
45–56   Intrigues of Alcibiades
57–9   Third Spartan–Persian treaty
60   Oropus captured from Athens by Boeotians

61–109   TWENTY-FIRST SUMMER (411) (UNFINISHED)
61–63.2   Campaigns in the Aegean
63.3–71   Revolution of the Four Hundred in Athens
72–7   Return to democracy by Athenians at Samos
78–80   Peloponnesian fleet to Hellespont
81–2   Alcibiades joins Athenian fleet at Samos
83–5   Mindarus succeeds Astyochus as Spartan admiral
86   Alcibiades restrains Athenian democrats at Samos
87–8   Tissaphernes goes to Aspendus
89–98   Four Hundred replaced by Five Thousand in Athens
99–109   Campaigns in the Aegean and Hellespont

THE
PELOPONNESIAN WAR

BOOK ONE

Thucydides of Athens wrote this history of the war fought against 1
each other by the Peloponnesians and the Athenians.

He began his work right at the outbreak, reckoning that this would
be a major war and more momentous than any previous conflict.
There were two grounds for this belief: both sides were at the full
height of their power and their resource for war, and he saw the rest
of the Greeks allying with one or the other, either immediately or in
intent.

This was in fact the greatest disturbance to affect the Greek and a
good part of the non-Greek world, one might even say the majority
of mankind. Accurate research into earlier or yet more ancient history was impossible given the great gap of time, but I have enquired
as far into the past as I can, and on the evidence which I can trust
I think there was nothing then on a large scale, either in wars or in
anything else.

It is clear that what is now called Greece was not originally a country 2
of stable settlements. In earlier times there were constant migrations,
any group readily moving on from its present land each time they
were forced out by others who happened to be superior in numbers.
There was no trade, no secure communication with each other by land
or sea. Each group grazed its own land for subsistence, not building
up financial reserves or farming the land, as it was never known when
someone else might attack and take it from them—besides, there
were no walls. In the belief that they could acquire the daily necessities of food anywhere else, it was easy enough for them to uproot.
For that reason they lacked the strength of large cities and all other
kinds of resource. The best land always had the most changes of
population—what is now called Thessaly and Boeotia, most of the
Peloponnese apart from Arcadia, and the finest soil elsewhere. It was
the quality of the earth which led to an imbalance of power and the
resulting internal quarrels which destroyed communities, as well as
the greater risk of aggression from outsiders. Certainly the thin soil
of Attica kept it largely free of such internal strife, so the original
population remained. And here is substantial proof of my argument
that migrations prevented comparable development elsewhere: the

most powerful of those forced out of the rest of Greece by war or civil strife resorted to Athens as a stable society. These new arrivals, admitted to citizenship, directly increased the population of the city from its original size, so that later, with Attica no longer able to support them, colonies were sent out to Ionia.

3   This again I see as significant proof of the weakness of the ancient population: before the Trojan War there is no evidence of any previous enterprise undertaken in common by Greece. Even the very name 'Hellas' was not, I believe, applied to the whole country: and before Hellen the son of Deucalion this appellation did not even exist. Before then the various tribes took their own names, with the Pelasgians the foremost. When Hellen and his sons grew to power in Phthiotis, and were called in as allies to aid the other settlements in the region, these other peoples began one by one to be known as Hellenes, by association: but it was a long time before this name prevailed over all others. The best evidence for this is Homer. He lived much later, born long after the Trojan War, and yet nowhere does he apply this name to the whole Greek force, confining it to Achilles' contingent from Phthiotis, the original Hellenes: in his poems he calls the Greeks Danaans, Argives, or Achaeans. Indeed there is no mention of 'barbarians' either, the reason being, it seems to me, that there had not yet evolved any equivalent generic term for the Greeks. However that may be, these various peoples who came to be called Hellenes—either individually, as understanding of a common language gradually spread from people to people, or, later, collectively—by reason of their weakness and their isolation from each other undertook no combined action before the Trojan War. But they could only make this joint expedition because by now they had acquired greater experience of the sea.

4   Minos is the earliest of those known to tradition who established a navy. He took control of most of what is now called the Hellenic Sea, and ruled over the Cyclades islands, in most of which he founded the first colonies, driving out the Carians and installing his own sons as governors: and naturally he set about clearing the sea of piracy, as far as he could, to protect his own increasing revenues.

5   As soon as traffic in ships developed between them, piracy was the recourse of the ancient Greeks and of the barbarians occupying coastal regions of the mainland and the islands. The leaders were powerful men motivated both by personal gain and by the provision of food for the weak. They fell for their plunder on unwalled communities with

the population scattered in villages, and this was much of their liveli-
hood. Such occupation did not yet carry any stigma: rather it even
brought some glory. Further illustration is given by some of the
mainlanders even now, who take successful piracy as a compliment,
and by the ancient poets: the regular question put to all who arrive
by sea is 'Are you pirates?', with no expectation of denial by the
questioned or criticism from the questioner.

They robbed each other on land also. Even to the present day much
of Greece maintains the old ways—among the Ozolian Locrians, the
Aetolians, the Acarnanians, and the mainland thereabouts. These
mainlanders still retain the habit of bearing arms from the old days
of robbery. There was a time when all of Greece carried arms: with 6
their settlements unprotected and travel dangerous, arms were a
regular part of their lives, as among barbarians now. The fact that
those parts of Greece which I have mentioned still live like this is an
indication of what was once a universal practice.

The Athenians were the first to abandon weapons and relax their
lifestyle into something more luxurious. Affectation lingered long: it
is only recently that older men of the wealthier families stopped
wearing linen tunics and tying their hair in a topknot fastened with
golden cicadas—hence the same fashion which prevailed for some
time among the older of their kinsmen in Ionia. It was then the
Spartans who first adopted simple dress and set the present style: in
other ways also the wealthier among them conformed their habits to
those of the common people. They were the first, too, to strip naked
for the games, to take off their clothes in public and to rub themselves
with oil after exercise. Originally—even in the Olympic games—
contending athletes took part with loincloths covering their genitals,
and it is not many years since this practice ceased. Some barbarians
even now, especially in Asia, hold boxing and wrestling bouts in
which loincloths are worn. There are many other resemblances one
could point to between the old Greek and the present barbarian ways
of life.

The more recent foundations—when navigation was more 7
common and there was greater capital resource—were of cities built
with fortifying walls right on the coast, commanding the isthmuses
in each case both for trade and for defence against neighbouring
peoples. The old cities, both in the islands and on the mainlands,
were established away from the sea because of the prevalence of
piracy—and the pirates plundered not only one another but also any

coastal dwellers who lacked sea power. These cities are still in their inland locations.

8 The islanders were pirates no less. They were Carians and Phoenicians, the peoples who colonized most of the islands. The evidence is that when Delos was purified by the Athenians in the course of this war and all the graves of those buried in the island were opened, over half of the bodies were seen to be Carians—identified by the style of armour buried with them and the method of burial, which is still in use among them.

After Minos had established his navy communication by sea became safer—in the process of colonizing most of the islands he also drove the malefactors out of them. People living by the sea could now build up greater wealth and lead a more secure existence: with their new affluence some even surrounded themselves with walls. Desire for profit was the motivation both for the weaker to tolerate the domination of the stronger and for the more powerful to use their economic advantage for the subjection of lesser cities. This sort of development had progressed some way by the time of the expedition to Troy.

9 I am inclined to think that it was Agamemnon's pre-eminent power at the time which enabled him to raise this fleet, and not so much that he was followed by the suitors of Helen, bound by the oaths they had sworn to Tyndareus. Those who have preserved most clearly the traditional lore of the Peloponnese say that first of all Pelops acquired such power from the vast wealth which he brought with him from Asia to a poor country that the whole land took its name from him, despite his foreign origin. Thereafter his descendants grew yet more prosperous. Eurystheus was killed in Attica by the sons of Heracles, but as he set out on that expedition he had entrusted Mycenae and its rule, out of kinship, to his maternal uncle Atreus, who had been banished by his father for the murder of Chrysippus. When Eurystheus failed to return, at the Mycenaeans' own request (they were frightened of the sons of Heracles) Atreus took over the kingship of Mycenae and all else that Eurystheus had ruled: he had the reputation of a powerful man, and he had cultivated the common people. So it was that the line of Pelops established supremacy over the line of Perseus. This was Agamemnon's inheritance, and, with greater naval power than any other, it seems to me that his gathering of the expeditionary force depended more on fear than on good will. He evidently brought the largest number of ships to Troy and, in addition to his own, provided a fleet for the Arcadians—so

Homer declares, if he is sufficient authority. And in the description of the sceptre he inherited Homer speaks of Agamemnon as 'king over many islands and all of Argos'. Now as a mainland ruler Agamemnon could not have controlled any islands other than the relatively few close by if he did not possess a substantial navy. From this expedition we can make conjectures about the nature of those before it.

The fact that Mycenae was a small place—or that the buildings of 10 any town of that period do not now seem very impressive—would not be a valid argument for doubting the scale of the expedition as related by the poets and maintained in the tradition. For example, if the city of Sparta were to become deserted, with only the temples and the foundations of buildings left to the view, I imagine that with the passage of time future generations would find it very hard to credit its reputed power. And yet the Spartans occupy two-fifths of the Peloponnese and lead the whole, as well as many external allies: but their dispersed settlement, devoid of temples or expensive buildings, more a collection of villages in the old Greek way, would seem rather disappointing. If the same happened to Athens, people would assume from the overt appearance that the city's power was twice what it is. So there is no cause for disbelief, nor should we judge cities by their appearance rather than their power. It is reasonable to think that that Trojan expedition was greater than all in previous history, but still short of the modern scale. If once more we can trust Homer's poems in this respect—and it is likely that, being a poet, he would exaggerate—even so Agamemnon's forces seem less than those of the present day. Homer gives a total of twelve hundred ships, with the Boeotian ships carrying a hundred and twenty men and Philoctetes' ships fifty, thereby indicating, it seems to me, the largest and the smallest: at any rate there is no other mention of complement in the Catalogue of Ships. That all were fighting men as well as rowers is clear from his description of Philoctetes' ships, where he has all those at the oars archers too.

It is unlikely that there were many non-rowing passengers apart from the kings and the highest other commanders, especially since they had to cross the open sea with all their military equipment and in ships without fenced decking, built in the old piratical style. So to take the mean of the largest and the smallest ships the numbers embarked do not seem very great for a combined expedition from the whole of Greece.

The reason was not shortage of men so much as shortage of money. 11 Lack of supplies made them limit the expeditionary force to the number of troops they thought would be able to live off the land they were fighting in: and even when they had secured the initial victory on arrival (clearly—otherwise they would not have been able to fortify their camp), they did not bring to bear their full force, but were diverted to cultivation of the Chersonese and pillage to supply the lack of food. This dispersal of the Greek troops contributed to the Trojans' ability to hold out against them for those ten years—they could match whatever proportion of the Greek army remained in the field. If the Greeks had come with plentiful supplies and prosecuted the war in full numbers without the interruptions of pillage and cultivation, they would easily have prevailed in the field and taken the city, given that even in less than full numbers they could hold the enemy with whatever sections they had at their disposal: and if they had settled down to a siege they could have taken Troy in shorter time and with less difficulty. But the reason was shortage of money, which had kept all previous campaigns small-scale. Even this one, which became the most famous of them all, is seen to be less impressive in fact than in reputation and in the prevailing tradition established by the poets.

12 Even after the Trojan War Greece continued in a state of upheaval and resettlement, with no opportunity for peaceful growth. The long delay of the Greek return from Troy caused many changes: internal strife developed widely in the cities, and those who were driven into exile founded settlements elsewhere. For example, in the sixtieth year after the capture of Troy the present Boeotians were driven out of Arne by the Thessalians and founded what is now Boeotia but was earlier called Cadmeïs (there had been a contingent of them in this country before, which contributed to the Trojan expedition): and in the eightieth year the Dorians occupied the Peloponnese with the descendants of Heracles. After a long period of difficulty Greece eventually reached a stable state of peace, when the shifts of populations ceased and they began to send out colonies. The Athenians colonized Ionia and most of the islands: the Peloponnesians founded the majority of the colonies in Italy and Sicily, and some in other parts of Greece. All these colonies were established after the Trojan War.

13 As Greece became more powerful, and the accumulation of wealth exceeded previous levels, the growth of revenues led in most cities to the establishment of tyrannies in place of the earlier hereditary kingships with fixed prerogatives: and Greece began to fit out navies and make increasing use of the sea. It is said that the Corinthians were the

first to have managed shipbuilding in something close to the present way, and that the first triremes in Greece were built in Corinth. A Corinthian shipbuilder, Ameinocles, is known to have built four ships for the Samians, and his visit to Samos was about three hundred years before the end of this present war. The earliest sea-battle of which we have record was that between the Corinthians and the Corcyraeans about two hundred and sixty years before the same date.

Situated as it is on the Isthmus, the city of Corinth was always, from the very beginning, a commercial centre. In earlier times when traffic was more by land than by sea, the Greeks within and without the Peloponnese had to pass through Corinthian territory to trade with each other, and Corinth was an economic power—witness the epithet 'wealthy' applied to the place by the ancient poets. When the Greeks took more to sea transport, the Corinthians acquired a fleet and set about eliminating piracy: able then to offer commerce on both elements, they kept their city powerful on the revenues thus received.

Later substantial naval power developed among the Ionians. This was in the time of Cyrus, the first King of Persia, and of his son Cambyses, and in war with Cyrus the Ionians controlled for some time the whole of their own sea. Then Polycrates, tyrant of Samos in the time of Cambyses, used his naval strength to subject a number of the islands, including Rheneia, which he captured and dedicated to Delian Apollo. The Phocaeans too, when they were colonizing Massalia, won a sea-battle against the Carthaginians.

These were the most powerful navies of the time. And yet it is 14 clear that, though operating many generations later than the Trojan War, they employed few triremes and were still equipped with the penteconters and long ships of that much earlier age. Shortly before the Persian Wars and the death of Dareius (King of Persia after Cambyses), triremes came to be used in numbers by the Sicilian tyrants and the Corcyraeans: these were the last navies of any significance in Greece before the expedition of Xerxes. The Aeginetans and the Athenians, and a few others, had acquired small fleets, which consisted largely of penteconters. It was only recently, when Athens was at war with Aegina and the barbarian invasion was in prospect, that Themistocles persuaded the Athenians to build the ships in which they subsequently fought their great sea-battle: and even these did not yet have full decking.

Such then was the state of the Greek navies of both earlier and more 15 recent times. Yet those who concentrated on their navies acquired considerable power through financial revenue and the domination of others: islands were subjugated by naval expeditions, especially by those who were short of territory. There was no land war which resulted in any shift of power. Such wars as took place were all local affairs between contiguous states, and the Greeks did not undertake distant expeditions for foreign conquest. The big cities had not yet formed leagues of subject allies, nor did they choose to make common cause in any joint expedition: rather all wars were fought individually between neighbours. The main exception was the war fought long ago between Chalcis and Eretria, when alliance with one side or the other split the rest of Greece.

16   There ensued a range of obstacles to the progress of the various Greek states. The Ionians, for example, had been developing strongly, but then Cyrus and the Persian kingdom destroyed Croesus, invaded the area between the river Halys and the sea, and subjugated the mainland cities—Dareius later doing the same to the islands with the

17 power of his Phoenician fleet. As for the tyrants in the Greek cities, whose only concern was for themselves, for their own physical safety and the aggrandizement of their family, security was as far as possible their greatest political aim, and nothing notable was done by any of them, other than perhaps in a campaign against their neighbours: and in Sicily the tyrants did indeed increase their power greatly in this way. The result was that all over Greece there was a long paralysis preventing any clear common action or individual initiative in the cities.

18   Eventually the Spartans deposed not only the Athenian tyrants but also those in the rest of Greece, which for the most part had fallen under tyrannies earlier than Athens—at least they deposed the majority of them: with the exception of those in Sicily these were the last of the tyrants. Sparta itself, after the arrival of the present Dorian inhabitants, went through the longest period of unrest in recorded history, yet even so its system of good order is very ancient and it has never been subject to tyrants. The Spartan constitution has remained unchanged for somewhat over four hundred years dating to the end of this war—a source of strength, enabling their political intervention in other states.

Not many years after the deposition of the Greek tyrants the battle of Marathon was fought between the Persians and the Athenians. Ten years later the barbarians returned with their huge armament for the subjection of Greece. With great danger impending, the Spartans,

as the leading power, took command of the Greeks allied for the war,
and in the face of the Persian invasion the Athenians decided to
abandon their city: they decamped, took to their ships, and became
sailors. A joint effort had driven away the barbarians, but not long
afterwards the Greeks—both the allied combatants and those who
had revolted from the King of Persia—split into two groups, favouring
either the Athenians or the Spartans. These were now conspicuously
the greatest powers, the one strong on land, the other by sea. The
defensive alliance held for a short while, but then differences broke
out and the Spartans and the Athenians, together with their allies,
were at war with each other—any other Greeks who might have
disputes now joining one side or the other. So from the Persian War
to the present conflict there were alternating periods of truce and
war, either against each other or caused by revolts among their allies.
As a result both sides were well prepared militarily and had acquired
the added experience of drills tested in real danger.

The Spartan hegemony did not involve the imposition of tribute 19
on their allies, but they took care to ensure oligarchic rule exclusively
in their own interest: whereas the Athenians in time came to deprive
all subject cities of their ships and require payment of tribute, with
the exceptions of Chios and Lesbos. The resources of Athens alone
for this present war were greater than those at the height of the
combined power when the alliance against Persia was intact.

Such are my conclusions about the past, though in this investiga- 20
tion it was difficult to rely on every one of a whole series of indications.
All men show the same uncritical acceptance of the oral traditions
handed on to them, even about the history of their own country. Most
Athenians, for example, think that Hipparchus was tyrant of Athens
when he was killed by Harmodius and Aristogeiton: they do not know
that Hippias was the ruler as the eldest of the sons of Peisistratus,
with Hipparchus and Thessalus his younger brothers. In fact on that
very day Harmodius and Aristogeiton had a sudden suspicion that
Hippias had been informed by some of the conspirators: so they kept
clear of Hippias, thinking him forewarned, and, wanting to take their
chances with some bold action before they were arrested, found
Hipparchus organizing the Panathenaic procession by the shrine
called Leocoreium and killed him.

I could point to many other false beliefs—about the contemporary
world, not the long-forgotten past—in the rest of Greece too: for
example, that the Spartan kings do not have one vote each, but two;

and that at Sparta there is a company of troops called 'the Pitana division', which in fact has never existed. This shows how little trouble most people take in their search for the truth—they happily resort to ready-made opinions.

21   Nevertheless anyone accepting the broad facts of my account on the arguments I have adduced will not go wrong. He will put less faith in the glorified tales of the poets and the compilations of the prose chroniclers, whose stories are written more to please the ear than to serve the truth, are incapable of proof, and for the most part, given the lapse of time, have passed into the unreliable realms of romance. He will conclude that my research, using the clearest evidence available, provides a sufficiently accurate account considering the antiquity of the events. As for this present war, although men always think that any war they are engaged in is the greatest of all wars, and then when it is over return to their awe of past conflicts, this war will even so prove itself, to those who examine the pure facts, a greater war than any in previous history.

22   Of the various speeches made either when war was imminent or in the course of the war itself, it has been hard to reproduce the exact words used either when I heard them myself or when they were reported to me by other sources. My method in this book has been to make each speaker say broadly what I supposed would have been needed on any given occasion, while keeping as closely as I could to the overall intent of what was actually said. In recording the events of the war my principle has been not to rely on casual information or my own suppositions, but to apply the greatest possible rigour in pursuing every detail both of what I saw myself and of what I heard from others. It was laborious research, as eyewitnesses on each occasion would give different accounts of the same event, depending on their individual loyalties or memories. It may be that the lack of a romantic element in my history will make it less of a pleasure to the ear: but I shall be content if it is judged useful by those who will want to have a clear understanding of what happened—and, such is the human condition, will happen again at some time in the same or a similar pattern. It was composed as a permanent legacy, not a show-piece for a single hearing.

23   The most extensive action in previous history was the Persian War: yet even that was brought to a swift conclusion by two battles at sea and two on land. This war far exceeded the Persian War in length, and over its course the suffering that resulted for Greece was

unparalleled in such a timescale. Never before were so many cities captured and desolated, some by barbarians, others through internal conflict (and in some a change of population followed their capture); never so many refugees or such slaughter, both in the war itself and as a consequence of civil strife. The phenomena in the old stories, more often told than attested, now became credible fact: earthquakes, which affected large areas with particular intensity; eclipses of the sun, occurring more frequently than in previous memory; major droughts in some parts, followed by famine; and, one of the most destructive causes of widespread death, the infectious plague. All these had their impact along with this war.

The war was begun by the Athenians and Peloponnesians when they broke the Thirty Years Treaty which they had established after the capture of Euboea. I have set out first the grievances and disputes which led to this breach, so that nobody in future will need to look for the immediate cause which brought such a great war on the Greeks. In my view the real reason, true but unacknowledged, which forced the war was the growth of Athenian power and Spartan fear of it: but the openly proclaimed grievances on either side causing the breach of the treaty and the outbreak of war were as follows.

The city of Epidamnus is situated on the right as you sail up the 24 Ionian Gulf: it is bordered by the Taulantians, a barbarian people of Illyrian descent. Epidamnus was colonized by the Corcyraeans, though the founder-colonist was a Corinthian, Phalius the son of Eratocleides, of the Heraclid family: as was the old custom, the founder was invited from the original mother-city. A number of other settlers joined from Corinth and the rest of the Dorian peoples.

As time went on Epidamnus grew in power and population: but then, it is said, after many years of internal strife the Epidamnians were destroyed in a war with their barbarian neighbours and lost most of their power. Most recently, just before this great war, the people of Epidamnus drove out the men in political control: these then joined forces with the barbarians and began to attack the city people in raids by land and sea. When the Epidamnians in the city found themselves beleaguered, they sent representatives to Corcyra, as their mother-city, appealing for intervention: Corcyra should not stand by and see them destroyed, but should broker a settlement with the exiled party and put an end to the war waged by the barbarians. They made this appeal sitting as suppliants in the temple of Hera: but the Corcyraeans rejected their supplication, and sent them away empty-handed.

25   When the Epidamnians learnt that they had no support from
Corcyra they were uncertain how now to proceed. So they sent to
Delphi and enquired of the god whether they should hand over their
city to the Corinthians as the ultimate founders, and try to obtain
some support from them. The god's oracular answer was that they
should hand over their city and make Corinth their champion. The
Epidamnians went to Corinth and handed over the colony as the
oracle had instructed. They pointed out that the founder-colonist
was from Corinth; they revealed the oracular response; and they
appealed for help, asking that Corinth should not stand by and see
them destroyed, but rather come to their aid.

The Corinthians undertook to support their cause, partly in asser-
tion of their own rights, taking the view that Epidamnus was as much
a Corinthian colony as a Corcyraean, and partly also out of antagonism to the Corcyraeans, resentful that their own colony paid them
little regard. In their common festivals Corcyra did not grant the
customary privileges to the founder-city or allow, as the other colonies did, a Corinthian to take the first honour at their sacrifices.
They looked down on the Corinthians: at that time their wealth compared with that of the richest Greek states; in military resources they
were more powerful than Corinth; they would boast of substantial
naval superiority, even basing their claim on the nautical fame of the
island's original inhabitants, the Phaeacians (this did indeed encourage them to build up their fleet, and they were a substantial force: at
the outbreak of the war they had a hundred and twenty triremes).

26   With all these grievances the Corinthians were glad to send help
to Epidamnus. They called for volunteer settlers, and raised supporting troops from Ambracia, Leucas, and Corinth itself. This force
made its way on foot to Apollonia, a Corinthian colony, deterred
from the sea passage by fear of a Corcyraean interception.

When the Corcyraeans learnt of the arrival of settlers and troops at
Epidamnus, and the handover of the colony to Corinth, their reaction
was angry. They immediately set sail with twenty-five ships, and
another fleet soon after. In the most abusive terms they demanded
that the Epidamnians should both reinstate the men driven into exile
(these exiles had come to Corcyra, pointing out their ancestral tombs
and advancing the claim of kinship in their appeal for restoration) and
also dismiss the new settlers and the troops sent by the Corinthians.

The Epidamnians rejected these demands, and the Corcyraeans
then began operations against them with forty ships: with them were

the exiles they intended to restore, and they had also recruited the Illyrians to the cause. They took up position in front of the city, and proclaimed an amnesty allowing any Epidamnian who so wished and all foreigners to leave the city unharmed: if they did not leave, they would be treated as enemies. There was no response, and so the Corcyraeans began a siege of the city—it lies on an isthmus.

When messengers from Epidamnus reached Corinth with the 27 news that their city was under siege, the Corinthians made preparations for an expeditionary force. At the same time they announced a new colony at Epidamnus, with equal rights and shares for all volunteers: those unwilling to join the immediate convoy could still, if they wished, reserve a share in the colony and stay behind, on payment of a deposit of fifty Corinthian drachmas. There were many ready to sail at once: many too paying the deposit. They asked the Megarians to join them with escort ships, in case the Corcyraeans tried to block the convoy. Megara fitted out an escort of eight ships, and Pale in Cephallenia a further four. Similar requests were made of others: Epidaurus provided five ships, Hermione one, Troezen two, Leucas ten, and Ambracia eight. They asked the Thebans and Phliasians for money, and the Eleans for unmanned ships as well as money. The Corinthians themselves equipped a fleet of thirty ships, and three thousand hoplites.

When the Corcyraeans learnt of these preparations, they came to 28 Corinth with spokesmen from Sparta and Sicyon in support, demanding that the Corinthians should withdraw their troops and settlers from Epidamnus, as they had no claim on Epidamnus. Should Corinth dispute this, they were prepared to refer the matter for arbitration by Peloponnesian cities acceptable to both parties, and the colony would belong to whichever side the arbitrators decided. They were also prepared to entrust judgement to the oracle at Delphi. But they cautioned Corinth not to start a war: otherwise, they said, with Corinth forcing the issue they themselves would be obliged in their own best interest to go beyond their present alliances and make friends where they would rather not.

The Corinthians replied that they would hold discussions if the Corcyraeans withdrew their ships and the barbarian forces from Epidamnus: before that it made no sense to go to arbitration with the city still under siege.

The Corcyraeans countered by saying that they would do this if the Corinthians too would withdraw their presence in Epidamnus.

Alternatively, they were willing for both sides to remain in position, with a truce declared pending the result of arbitration.

29   The Corinthians rejected all these proposals. By now their ships were manned and their allies ready, so they sent in advance a herald to declare war on the Corcyraeans, then set off and sailed for Epidamnus with seventy-five ships and two thousand hoplites to confront them in battle. The commanders of the fleet were Aristeus the son of Pellichus, Callicrates the son of Callias, and Timanor the son of Timanthes. In command of the land force were Archetimus the son of Eurytimus and Isarchidas the son of Isarchus.

When they had reached Actium in Anactorian territory at the mouth of the Ambracian Gulf, where there is the temple of Apollo, the Corcyraeans sent over a herald in a small boat with the warning not to sail on against them. At the same time the Corcyraeans were manning their ships: they had braced the old ships to make them seaworthy and fitted out the others. As the herald reported no peaceful intent on the part of the Corinthians, and by then their ships were fully crewed—eighty of them in all (a further forty were engaged in the siege of Epidamnus)—they sailed out for battle, formed line, and engaged. The result was a decisive victory for the Corcyraeans, with fifteen Corinthian ships destroyed. It so happened that on the same day the forces besieging Epidamnus brought the city to surrender. The terms agreed were that the recent arrivals should be sold as slaves, and the Corinthians among them held in prison until a further decision was taken.

30   After the battle the Corcyraeans set up a trophy on Leucimme, a promontory of Corcyra, and executed all the captives they had taken, apart from the Corinthians: they were kept imprisoned.

When the Corinthians and their allies returned home after their naval defeat, they left Corcyra in complete control of the sea in that area: and the Corcyraeans did send a fleet to Leucas which laid waste some of the land in this Corinthian colony, and they set fire to the Eleans' dockyard at Cyllene, as they had supplied ships and money to the Corinthians. So for most of the time after the sea-battle the Corcyraeans, controlling the sea as they did, kept up destructive attacks on the allies of Corinth. These lasted until the beginning of the next summer, when the Corinthians, in response to complaints from their allies, sent out a fleet and troops and took up positions at Actium and around Cheimerium in Thesprotia, for the protection of Leucas and the other states friendly to them. The Corcyraeans took up an opposing position at Leucimme with ships and land forces. Neither fleet made any attack, but they stayed there watching each other throughout this summer, and it was only at the onset of winter that both sides went back home.

There was anger at Corinth over the war with Corcyra. For the 31 whole of the year following the sea-battle, and the year after that, the Corinthians were building ships and making preparations for the strongest possible navy, buying in crews of rowers both from the Peloponnese and from the rest of Greece. News of these preparations alarmed the Corcyraeans. They had no defensive treaty with any other Greek state, and had not enrolled themselves in either the Athenian or the Spartan alliance. They decided therefore to approach the Athenians, to join their alliance and try to secure some assistance from Athens. When the Corinthians learnt of this they too came to Athens to present their case: their fear was that a combination of Athenian and Corcyraean naval power would prevent them from bringing the war to the outcome they desired. An assembly was convened, and the cases argued. The Corcyraeans spoke first, as follows:

'Men of Athens, it is only right that those who come to others 32 asking for their help, as we do now, with no record of major service rendered or existing alliance on which to base their claim, should demonstrate firstly that what they ask is in fact to the others' benefit (or at least not to their harm), and secondly that there will be gratitude expressed in concrete form. If they do not convince on either count, they should not resent the failure of their appeal. The people of Corcyra have sent us here in the confidence that in asking for your alliance they can also offer you firm assurances on both these issues.

'Our past policy has proved doubly unfortunate—inconsistent towards you when we now have need of your support, and against our own interests in our present situation. Having never yet in any previous time made deliberate alliances with anyone, we are now here to ask for outside help as this very policy has left us isolated in our present war with Corinth. What we once thought of as prudent self-containment—not exposing ourselves through any external alliance to the risks of others' policies—has now proved our mistake and our weakness. Yes, we did defeat the Corinthians unaided in the last battle. But now that they are poised to attack us with greater resources drawn from the Peloponnese and the rest of Greece, and we can see no possibility of surviving that attack with only our own forces (but can see the depth of our plight if we go under), we are obliged to ask for assistance, from you or anyone else: and we trust you will understand that this is no faint-heartedness, but rather the acknowledgement of a mistaken policy which emboldens us to go counter to our previous isolationism.

33   'If you accept our case it will prove a good opportunity for you, in many ways to your advantage. First, you will be giving aid to an injured party, not an aggressor; then, in welcoming a people in extreme danger you will establish a debt of gratitude which, more than any other, will be paid in everlasting remembrance; and we have a navy second in size only to yours. And consider this. Could there be any benefit more extraordinary (or less welcome to your enemies) than to have a power which you would have paid much, and grate-fully, to gain on your side offering itself to you voluntarily, without risk or expense? Moreover, this would bring you the admiration of most other people, the gratitude of those you will be helping, and an increase in your own strength. Few indeed, in the whole of history, are those who have been presented with all these opportunities at one and the same time: few too the requests for alliance when the postu-lants come to the state whose help they ask offering as much security and prestige as they will receive.

'We would be useful to you in war. And if any among you do not think that war is coming, they are deceiving themselves. They do not see that fear of your power is fuelling Spartan desire for war, or that the Corinthians, influential in Sparta and hostile to you, are intent on crushing us now with a view to a subsequent attack on you. The Corinthians do not want us to come together in a common stance of hostility to them, nor do they want to lose the advantage they could gain one way or the other—either destroying us or taking over our forces to bolster their own. Our task on this side is to forestall them with our offer and your acceptance of this alliance: then our counter to them can be proactive rather than reactive.

34   'If the Corinthians say that you have no right to extend a welcome to their own colonists, they need to understand that any colony well treated will honour its mother-city, but a colony wronged will look elsewhere. Colonists are sent out on the basis of equality with their fellows left at home, not in subservience to them. That Corinth wronged us is clear. They were invited to arbitration in the matter of Epidamnus, but determined to pursue their complaints by war rather than fair dealing. And this—the way they behave to us, their own kinsmen—should be a warning to you not to be seduced by their

duplicity or give an immediate ear to their demands. Concessions to one's opponents lead to regret: and the fewer regrets, the safer the future.

'A further point is that in accepting us you will not be breaking the 35 treaty with the Spartans. We are not allied to either side: and the treaty states that any Greek city with no alliance elsewhere is free to join whichever side it wishes. It is monstrous if the Corinthians are to be allowed to crew their ships not only from their allies but also from the rest of Greece and not least from your own subjects, and yet will block us from the alliance which is open to us and from help in any other quarter, then claiming it a crime if you accede to our request. In fact it is we who will have the far greater cause for complaint, if we fail to persuade you. We are in danger, we are not enemies of yours, and in rejecting us you will not only be failing to stop those who are your enemies and the aggressors, but also acquiescing in their build-up of power from your own empire. This is not right. You should either put a stop to their recruitment of mercenaries from states in your control, or give us too whatever help you can be persuaded to send: better still to aid our cause by accepting us in open alliance.

'As we suggested at the beginning, we can point to much that serves your own interests. The greatest consideration, and the surest guarantee of our loyalty, is that you and we have the same enemies, and powerful enemies too, quite capable of crushing defectors. And when the alliance offered you is with a naval rather than a land power, the consequences of refusal are quite different. Your ideal, if that were possible, would be to prevent anyone else acquiring a navy: failing that, your best course is to make friends with the strongest other naval power.

'Some of you will recognize the advantages of which we speak, 36 but still fear that acceptance of our case will break the treaty. Such among you should realize that, when you have the added power of an alliance with us, what to you is an anxiety will be a greater source of fear to your enemies, whereas any boldness you might show in refusing our offer will in fact weaken you and make you less of a threat to a strong enemy. You should bear in mind too that your decision affects Athens as much as Corcyra. When all immediate thoughts are on the coming war—a war which is virtually on us now—it is no foresight for Athens' best interests to dither over welcoming to your side a country whose friendship or hostility is fraught with conse-quence. Corcyra lies nicely on the route of the coastal voyage to Italy and Sicily, in a situation to prevent any fleet from there reaching the Peloponnese and to block any convoys in the reverse direction. And there are other major advantages as well.

'To give the briefest summary of the main thrust and the detail of our case, this is what should convince you not to abandon us. There are three significant navies in Greece: yours, ours, and the Corinthians'. If you stand aside to see two of these amalgamated when Corinth takes pre-emptive control of us, you will find yourselves fighting the combined fleets of Corcyra and the Peloponnese. If you accept us, you will enter the contest with our ships added to your own.'

Such was the speech of the Corcyraeans. After them the Corinthians spoke as follows:

37   'The speech of the Corcyraeans here was not confined to the question of your acceptance of their offered alliance, but they also alleged that we are the aggressors and they the victims of an unjust war. Before we move on to our main argument, then, we too must address these two points, to establish beyond doubt in your minds the basis of what we ask from you, and to give you good reason to reject the Corcyraean demand.

'They speak of "prudent self-containment" as the reason for never yet accepting an alliance with others. In truth, the motives for this policy were more sinister than virtuous: they did not want any ally as witness of their crimes, or to embarrass them if called in aid. Moreover the geographical independence of their location, such that the volume of incoming traffic obliged to put in at Corcyra is much greater than their own commerce with their neighbours, allows them to be their own judges in any criminal action rather than submitting to arbitration under treaties. This specious neutrality of theirs is no wish to avoid implication in the misdeeds of others, but rather a pretext for their own unimpeded misdoing—violence where they have the power, cheating if they can get away with it, no shame at any advantage gained. Yet if they were the honourable folk they claim to be, their very immunity to outside influence would have enabled them to give the clearest demonstration of their honesty by inviting the give and take of judicial arbitration.

38   'But they are not honourable either to others or to us. They are our own colonists, but always estranged and now at war with us. They say that they were not sent out to Corcyra to suffer ill-treatment: and we for our part say that we did not settle them there to be abused by

them, but to retain our leadership and their proper respect. Certainly our other colonies show us due honour, and Corinth is held in greater affection by her colonists than any other city. Clearly, then, if the majority are satisfied with us, Corcyra can have no good cause for its unique dissatisfaction: it is clear too that we are not now campaigning against them without reason, without some signal injustice done to us. Even supposing we were at fault, the proper course for them was to concede our anger, and then it would have been wrong for us to answer their conciliation with force. But in their arrogance and the licence they take from their wealth they have constantly offended us, and most particularly over Epidamnus, which is our colony. When it was in trouble they exercised no claim to it, but as soon as we came in support they took it by force and hold it still.

'They say of course that they were willing in the first place to go 39 to arbitration. But arbitration proposed when you have the upper hand and a secure position is an empty pretence: such proposals should be made before hostilities begin, when you can assimilate what you do to what you say. No word of this from the Corcyraeans before they laid siege to Epidamnus: it was only when they realized our likely involvement that they put forward this specious talk of arbitration. They are come here now, culprits themselves in Epidamnus, asking you not so much for an alliance as for complicity in their crimes, and to accept them when they are in dispute with us. They should have approached you when they were at their most secure, not now when we have been wronged and they are in danger, when any help you grant will not be in requital for any previous share of their power, when you took no part in their offences but in our eyes will be held equally responsible. They should have joined their forces with you from the start if they want you to join in the consequences.

'So far we have shown both that we are here before you with 40 genuine grievances and that the Corcyraeans are violent and grasping: now we should explain why you would be wrong to accept them. Although the treaty does make provision for any non-signatory state to join whichever side it wishes, this article of agreement is not there for those whose purpose in alliance is the injury of other states, but for those looking for security who will not be defecting from others, nor likely to bring their sponsors (if they think about it carefully) war rather than peace: and this could now be the consequence for you, if you do not heed what we say. In giving aid to them you would also change your relations with us from treaty partners to enemies: if you join with them we shall be forced to include you in our counter-attack.

'Yet the right course for you is either, and preferably, to take a neutral stance, or else to join us against them instead. You are after all treaty partners with Corinth, but have never had any relations, not even a truce, with Corcyra. And you should not establish the precedent of accepting defectors from other alliances. Neither did we. When the Samians revolted from you we cast our vote in your favour. The other Peloponnesian states were divided on the issue of support for Samos, but we made our opposition plain, arguing the right of the individual state to bring its own allies under control. If you accept and champion malefactors, you will find just as many of your own side coming over to us, and the precedent you set will be more to your detriment than to ours.

41   'These then are the claims of right which we present to you, and according to the accepted Greek norms they are sufficient for our case. Our relations with you are neither hostile to the point of aggression nor friendly enough for easy dealing, but we would add this advisory claim on your gratitude and propose that now is the time for its repayment. When you were short of warships for your war against Aegina, before the Persian invasion, Corinth let you have twenty ships. This service rendered to you, followed by the service we gave over Samos in preventing Peloponnesian aid to the island, gave you the conquest of Aegina and the crushing of the Samian revolt. And this support was given at those critical times when people intent on their enemies are most oblivious of all considerations other than victory: at these times any helper is considered a friend, even if he was an enemy before, and any contrary view, even from friends, is taken as hostility, when the immediate urge to win displaces familiar relations.

42   'Do reflect on these points. The younger among you should ask their elders what we are talking about, and then realize that it is only right to repay us with like treatment: they should not think that, although they see justice in our case, their interests lie elsewhere if they are to be at war. Best interests are consequent on fewest errors of judgement: and the war whose alleged imminence the Corcyraeans use to frighten you into immoral action is still far from certain. It is not worth your while to allow this scare to leave you with the open and immediate hostility of Corinth. Better and wiser is to reduce the pre-existing tension caused by your treatment of Megara—a late but

timely service, small though it may be, can dispel a greater grievance. Nor should you be seduced by their offer of a great naval alliance: fair treatment of your equals is a surer guarantee of power than the opportunistic pursuit of some immediate but risky advantage.

'There is now a reversal of roles. At the congress in Sparta we 43 argued that individual states should have the right to control their own allies, and we now expect you to accord us the same right: our vote helped you then, and your vote should not harm us now. Give us in fairness what we gave you, recognizing that this is one of those critical times when help is friendship and opposition is enmity. Do not ignore our claims and accept these Corcyraeans as allies, and do not assist them in their crimes. To do as we ask is both the right course of action and the best policy in your own interests.'

Such was the speech of the Corinthians in their turn. The Athenians 44 listened to both sides and held two assemblies. At the first assembly the Corinthians' arguments won at least equal favour, but on the next day opinion swung to an alliance with Corcyra: not a full offensive and defensive alliance (which would cause a breach of their treaty with the Peloponnesians, if the Corcyraeans required them to join a naval attack on Corinth), but they did make a purely defensive alliance providing for reciprocal help if any attack was made on Corcyra or Athens or the allies of either. Their thinking was that they would face war with the Peloponnesians in any case, and they did not want Corcyra and its powerful navy to pass to Corinth: rather, they intended to engineer as far as possible a full collision between the two sides, so that, if the need came, they would enter the war with both Corinth and the other naval powers weakened. At the same time they thought that the island of Corcyra lay nicely on the coastal route to Italy and Sicily.

With such thoughts in mind the Athenians concluded an alliance 45 with the Corcyraeans, and, shortly after the Corinthians had left, sent a squadron of ten ships to support Corcyra, under the command of Lacedaemonius the son of Cimon, Diotimus the son of Strombichus, and Proteas the son of Epicles. Their instructions were not to engage with the Corinthians unless they sailed against Corcyra and were about to land on Corcyra itself or any territory belonging to it: in that case they should do what they could to prevent them. The purpose of these instructions was to avoid a breach of the treaty.

So these ships arrived at Corcyra, and when the Corinthians had 46 completed their own preparations they sailed for Corcyra with a hundred and fifty ships. Of these ten came from Elis, twelve from Megara, ten from Leucas, seventeen from Ambracia, and one from Anactorium: Corinth itself sent ninety ships. Each contributory state had its own commander, and the Corinthian contingent was commanded by Xenocleides the son of Euthycles, together with four others.

Sailing on from Leucas the fleet reached the mainland opposite Corcyra, anchoring at Cheimerium in Thesprotia. There is a harbour, and above it, lying some way from the sea, is the town of Ephyre in the Elaean district of Thesprotia. Near Ephyre the Acherousian lake discharges into the sea: it takes its name from the river Acheron, which flows through Thesprotia and feeds this lake. The other river is the Thyamis, which forms the border between Thesprotia and Cestrine. The promontory of Cheimerium juts out between these rivers. It was here that the Corinthians anchored off the mainland and made their encampment.

47   When the Corcyraeans learnt of the approach of the Corinthian fleet, they manned a hundred and ten ships, under the command of Miciades, Aesimides, and Eurybatus, and made camp on one of the pair of islands called Sybota. The ten Athenian ships were with them. Their land forces were positioned on the promontory of Leucimme, with the reinforcement of a thousand hoplites from Zacynthus. The Corinthians too on the mainland had a substantial force of support from the barbarians of that area, who have always been friendly to Corinth.

48   Their preparations complete, the Corinthians took three days' provisions on board and put out for battle from Cheimerium at night. As they sailed on through the dawn they caught sight of the Corcyraean fleet already on the high sea and bearing down on them. At sight of each other both sides formed into battle array. The Athenian ships were on the right of the Corcyraean line, which consisted of their own fleet divided into three squadrons, each under the command of one of the three generals. This then was the Corcyraean formation. On the Corinthian side the ships from Megara and Ambracia occupied the right wing, their other allies were variously ranged in the centre, and the Corinthians themselves took the left wing with their fastest ships, opposite the Athenians and the right wing of the
49   Corcyraeans. Then, signals given on each side, they engaged and began battle, both fleets still employing the old-fashioned and unsophisticated mode of naval warfare, with large numbers of hoplites,

archers, and javelin-throwers on deck. The fighting was fierce but far from skilful, more like a land-battle at sea. Whenever they collided in attack, it was difficult to break free for the very number and close crowding of the ships, and any confidence of victory resided more in the hoplites on the decks, who fought a pitched battle across stalled ships. There were no attempts to break through the enemy's line, and the battle owed less to science than to pure courage and physical strength. It was, then, a disorderly engagement with a great deal of confusion all round. The part played in this by the Athenian ships was to come up in support of the Corcyraeans wherever they were under pressure. This was an effective deterrent to the enemy, but the commanders would not take overtly aggressive action for fear of exceeding the mandate they had been given by the Athenians.

The right wing of the Corinthian line came into severe trouble. A squadron of twenty Corcyraean ships routed them, drove them back scattered to the mainland, then sailed right up to their camp, landed, set fire to the empty tents, and plundered the goods they found. So here, then, the Corinthians and their allies suffered a defeat and the Corcyraeans had the upper hand. But where their own ships were, on the left wing, the Corinthians were having far the better of it, as the Corcyraeans, in any case the smaller fleet, now lacked the twenty ships engaged in the chase to the mainland. Seeing the Corcyraeans in difficulty, the Athenians now began to intervene more openly. At first they held back from any actual ramming: but when a rout was clearly developing as the Corinthians pressed their advantage, it then became a free-for-all with no more distinctions made. And so it came to the point where Corinthians and Athenians were forced to attack each other.

There was indeed a rout. After their victory, instead of towing 50 away the hulls of the ships they had disabled, the Corinthians turned to the men in the water, sailing up and down to kill rather than capture. In this process they unwittingly began killing their own friends, not realizing the defeat on the right wing. With so many ships engaged on each side and covering a wide expanse of sea, it was difficult, once battle was joined, to see clearly who was winning and who was losing. This was in fact, in terms of the number of ships deployed, the greatest sea-battle ever fought up till then by Greeks against Greeks.

When the Corinthians had chased the Corcyraeans back towards land, they turned to the wrecks and their own dead, managing to bring most of them in to Sybota (this Sybota is an uninhabited harbour in Thesprotia, and it was here that the land army of their barbarian allies had been positioned in support). This operation completed, the Corinthians re-formed and sailed out once more to attack the Corcyraeans.

For their part the Corcyraeans, fearful of an attempted landing on their own island, put out to meet them with all ships still seaworthy from the first battle and any others they had left: and the Athenian ships were with them.

It was now late in the day, and the paean for attack had already been sung when suddenly the Corinthians began to back water. They had caught sight of the approach of a further twenty Athenian ships, which the Athenians had sent out subsequently in reinforcement of the original ten, fearing (as proved to be the case) that the Corcyraeans would lose and their own ten ships would be insufficient protection.

51 Seeing these ships in the distance, and supposing that there were yet more ships from Athens than those in sight, the Corinthians began to withdraw. The direction of their approach kept the Athenian ships invisible for a while to the Corcyraeans, so they were amazed to see the Corinthians backing water: but eventually they were sighted and men called out 'Ships approaching over there!' Then the Corcyraeans too began to turn back: it was already growing dark, and the Corinthian retreat had broken off the action. So the two sides parted, and night stopped battle. The Corcyraeans encamped on Leucimme, and shortly after they had been sighted these twenty ships from Athens, under the command of Glaucon the son of Leagrus and Andocides the son of Leogoras, picked their way through the wrecks and corpses and came up to the camp. It was night, and the Corcyraeans feared they were enemy ships: but then they were recognized, and came to anchor.

52 On the next day the thirty Athenian ships and all the Corcyraean ships still seaworthy put out and sailed to the harbour at Sybota where the Corinthians were anchored, to see if they would fight. The Corinthians left shore and ranged their ships in open water, but stayed there without moving. They had no intention of starting battle, when they could see the reinforcement of a fresh fleet from Athens and had many difficulties of their own to contend with— the custody of the prisoners they held on board, and the lack of facilities to repair their ships in such a desolate place. They were yet more exercised by the means of securing their voyage home: they

feared that the Athenians would consider the treaty broken by the fact that they had come into conflict, and would block their departure. So they decided to put some men in a cutter and send it out to the Athenians, without a flag of truce, to test the situation. This is what their emissaries said: 'Athenians, you are at fault in starting a war and breaking the treaty. We are pursuing a grievance against our own enemies, and you have taken arms to stand in our way. If it is your decision to prevent us sailing against Corcyra or anywhere else we may wish, and are thereby breaking the treaty, you should make us here your first prisoners and treat us as enemies.' That was their message, and those in the Corcyraean armament who could hear it shouted back 'Take them now and kill them!' The Athenians, though, replied as follows: 'Peloponnesians, we are not starting a war nor are we breaking the treaty. The Corcyraeans here are our allies, and we have come to help them. If you wish to sail anywhere else we offer no hindrance. But if you sail against Corcyra or to any other place in its control, we shall intervene to our best ability.'

With this reply from the Athenians the Corinthians made preparations to sail home, and set up a trophy in mainland Sybota. The Corcyraeans for their part salvaged the wrecks of their ships and took up their own dead, all that were carried towards them by the current and a wind which got up in the night and scattered everything far and wide. They then set up a rival trophy on the island of Sybota, claiming victory.

The reasons on each side for claiming the victory and setting up a trophy were as follows. The Corinthians had prevailed in the sea-battle until nightfall, with the result that they were able to bring in their dead and most of the wrecks; they held at least a thousand prisoners; and they had disabled about seventy enemy ships. The Corcyraeans had destroyed some thirty ships; after the arrival of the Athenians they had taken up their own dead and salvaged their wrecks; on the previous day the Corinthians had backed water and retreated from them on sight of the Athenian ships; and after the Athenians had arrived, the Corinthians would not sail out of Sybota to face them. So both sides considered they had won.

In the course of their return journey the Corinthians took Anactorium (at the mouth of the Ambracian Gulf) through treachery—Anactorium was a joint Corcyraean and Corinthian foundation. They installed Corinthian settlers there, then left for home. Of their Corcyraean prisoners they sold the eight hundred who were slaves, and kept two hundred and fifty others in custody, taking very good care of them, in the hope that when returned to Corcyra they might bring the island over to their side: and in fact most of these prisoners were leading men of influence in the city.

Corcyra, then, had worsted Corinth in this campaign, and the Athenian ships now left the island. This was the first of the grievances the Corinthians had which made for war with Athens: while the treaty was still in force the Athenians had joined Corcyra in naval battle against them.

56   Immediately after this there arose another dispute contributory to war between the Athenians and the Peloponnesians. It was as follows. With Corinthian policy bent on retaliation against them, the Athenians, wary of this antagonism, took precautionary measures in Potidaea, a city on the Pallene peninsula which was a Corinthian colony but now a tribute-paying member of the Athenian alliance. They required the Potidaeans to demolish the wall on the Pallene side, to provide them with hostages, to expel the Corinthian magistrates and refuse in future to accept the annual replacements sent from Corinth. Their fear was that the combined influence of Perdiccas and the Corinthians might persuade the Potidaeans to revolt, and that this could spark further revolts among their other allies in the Thraceward region.

57   The Athenians planned these precautions at Potidaea directly after the Corcyra battle. The Corinthians were by then openly hostile, and Perdiccas, the son of Alexander and king of Macedonia, who had previously been a friend and ally, was now turned into an enemy of Athens. The reason for this reversal was that the Athenians had made alliance with his brother Philip and with Derdas, who were joined in opposition to him. Alarmed by this, Perdiccas began to negotiate. He sent envoys to Sparta hoping to foster war between the Athenians and the Peloponnesians, and tried to win over the Corinthians to a Potidaean revolt. He made overtures also to the Thraceward Chalcidians and the Bottiaeans, inciting them to join the revolt. His thought was that if he could make allies of these states which bordered his own, he would be better placed for war with their support.

The Athenians heard of his doings, and were keen to forestall the defection of these states. They were just about to send out against

Macedonia a force of thirty ships and a thousand hoplites under the command of Archestratus the son of Lycomedes and two other generals. They now instructed the commanders of this fleet to take hostages from the Potidaeans, to demolish the wall, and to keep watch on the neighbouring cities to prevent their revolt.

The Potidaeans sent representatives to Athens, hoping to per- 58 suade the Athenians not to make any change in their relations. They also went to Sparta with Corinthian delegates to lay the ground for support if that were needed. Since long negotiation produced nothing helpful from Athens, since the ships destined for Macedonia were being sent just as much against themselves, and since the Spartan authorities promised that they would invade Attica if the Athenians attacked Potidaea, they seized the opportunity to revolt, making sworn cause with the Chalcidians and the Bottiaeans.

Now Perdiccas persuaded the Chalcidians to abandon and destroy their towns on the coast, and to move inland to Olynthus, making that a single secure centre of population. To those people who abandoned their towns he gave, for the duration of the war with Athens, a part of his own territory to cultivate, in Mygdonia around lake Bolbe. So they demolished their own towns, moved inland, and prepared for war.

When the thirty Athenian ships arrived in the Thraceward region 59 they found Potidaea and the others already revolted. The command-ers took the view that it was impossible with their present forces to undertake simultaneous warfare against Perdiccas and against the areas combined in revolt, so they turned to Macedonia (the original objective of their expedition), established their base, and began a campaign in conjunction with Philip and the brothers of Derdas, whose army had invaded from the interior.

With Potidaea revolted and the Athenian ships off Macedonia, the 60 Corinthians now feared for the place and saw this as a crisis which struck at their own interests. They therefore sent out a force of vol-unteers from Corinth itself and mercenaries from the rest of the Peloponnese, a total of sixteen hundred hoplites and four hundred light troops. In command was Aristeus the son of Adeimantus, who had always been a good friend to the Potidaeans: and his popularity was in most cases the main reason for the Corinthians volunteering to serve in the expedition he would lead. These troops arrived in the Thraceward region forty days after the revolt of Potidaea.

The Athenians too received immediate intelligence of the revolt of 61 these cities. And when they heard also of the relief troops on their way under Aristeus they sent out their own force against the areas in revolt, two thousand hoplites and forty ships under the command of Callias the son of Calliades and four other generals. Their first destination was Macedonia. On arrival they found that the original force of a thousand troops had just taken Therme and was now besieging Pydna. They joined in the investment of Pydna for a while, until the siege was lifted when the Athenians reached an agreement and made an alliance of convenience with Perdiccas, pressed to this by the urgent need to deal with Potidaea and the arrival there of Aristeus.

They left Macedonia, then, and came to Beroea. From there they went on to Strepsa, and after failing in their initial attempt to take the place they proceeded by land to Potidaea. They had three thousand of their own hoplites, and in addition a good number from their allies and six hundred Macedonian cavalry on the side of Philip and Pausanias. The seventy ships kept pace with them along the coast. In short marches they reached Gigonus on the third day, and made their camp there.

62   Expecting the Athenians, the people of Potidaea and the Peloponnesians under Aristeus had made camp on the Olynthus side of the isthmus and set up a market outside the city to provision the troops. The allies had chosen Aristeus to command all the infantry, and Perdiccas the cavalry (Perdiccas had once again summarily broken with the Athenians and was now siding with Potidaea: he gave the command to Iolaus as his deputy). Aristeus' strategy was to keep his own troops camped on the isthmus in readiness for an Athenian attack, while the Chalcidians, the allies from outside the peninsula, and the two hundred cavalry sent by Perdiccas stayed in Olynthus: then, when the Athenians attacked on the isthmus, these other troops would come in support from the rear, pinning the enemy between two forces. On the other side the Athenian general Callias and his fellow commanders dispatched their Macedonian cavalry and a few allied troops towards Olynthus to block any intervention from there, while they themselves struck camp and marched on Potidaea. When they reached the isthmus and saw the enemy making preparation for battle, they too formed in battle order and shortly thereafter the engagement began. Aristeus' own wing, where he had with him the pick of the Corinthian and the other troops, routed their immediate opposition and followed up in pursuit for some distance. But the rest of the Potidaean and Peloponnesian army was losing to the Athenians, and took refuge behind the city wall.

When Aristeus returned from the pursuit and saw the rest of his 63 forces defeated, he faced a difficult choice, with danger either way: should he make a move towards Olynthus, or into Potidaea? In the end he decided to crowd his troops into the smallest possible space and force his way into Potidaea at the run. With difficulty, and under a constant barrage, he succeeded by going alongside the breakwater and through the sea. He lost a few, but brought most of his men through safely.

As for those troops in Olynthus ready to bring reinforcement to the Potidaeans, they set out in support when the signals were raised at the onset of battle (Potidaea is about seven miles distant, and visible from Olynthus). They were just a short way on their march, and the Macedonian cavalry deployed to stop them, when the signals were lowered after the quick Athenian victory. They then returned to the walls of Olynthus, and the Macedonians went back to join the Athenians. There was no cavalry operation on either side.

After the battle the Athenians set up a trophy and allowed a truce for the Potidaeans to recover their dead. The casualties on the side of Potidaea and its allies were nearly three hundred. The Athenians themselves lost a hundred and fifty, including their commander Callias.

The Athenians immediately built a wall on the isthmus side of 64 Potidaea and kept it under guard. The south side, facing Pallene, was left without a wall. They did not think they had sufficient numbers to maintain their guard on the isthmus while at the same time crossing over to Pallene to build a wall there. Their fear was that such division of their forces would encourage an attack by the Potidaeans and their allies.

When it was learnt in Athens that the Pallene side was unwalled, some time later the Athenians sent out a force of sixteen hundred of their own hoplites with Phormio the son of Asopius as general in command. On his arrival at Pallene Phormio made his base in Aphytis, then advanced his army on Potidaea in short stages, ravaging the land as he went. And as none came out to oppose him in battle he walled off the city on the Pallene side. So Potidaea was now in the grip of a full siege on both sides, and blockaded too by the Athenian ships offshore.

With the city walled off and no hope of rescue, barring some action 65 from the Peloponnese or other unlikely event, Aristeus advised the Potidaeans to evacuate all but five hundred, so that the food would last longer: the others should watch for the right wind and then escape by sea. He himself volunteered to join the group staying behind. They would not follow his advice: so, intent on taking the measures that were now necessary and establishing the best chance of external support, he slipped past the Athenian guard and sailed away from the city. He remained in the area, helping the Chalcidians prosecute the war. In particular he set an ambush near the town of Sermyle which killed a good number of Sermylians. At the same time he was in contact with the Peloponnese, trying to secure some help.

Meanwhile, after completing the investment of Potidaea, Phormio used his sixteen hundred troops to ravage the land in Chalcidice and Bottice: he also took some of the towns.

66   These, then, were the grievances thus far existing between the Athenians and the Peloponnesians. The Corinthians complained that the Athenians were blockading their colony Potidaea, with Corinthians and Peloponnesians caught in the siege. The Athenian grievance against the Peloponnesians was that they had incited the revolt of an allied and tributary city, had arrived in open support of the Potidaeans, and were fighting on their side. This, though, was not yet the outbreak of the war, and they were still in a state of truce. Corinth had so far been acting alone.

67   With Potidaea under siege and some of their own people inside, the Corinthians would not let matters rest: they were fearful now of losing the place. They immediately invited the allies to meet at Sparta, and their own delegation launched an invective against the Athenians, insisting that they had broken the treaty and were committing an offence against the Peloponnese. The Aeginetans did not send envoys openly, for fear of the Athenians, but in secret collaboration with the Corinthians they played a major part in instigating the war, claiming that they had lost the autonomy guaranteed under the treaty. The Spartans extended the invitation to those of their allies and anyone else who alleged mistreatment by the Athenians, and gave them audience at a regular meeting of their own assembly. Several came forward to make their various charges, not least the Megarians: among a good number of other complaints they declared that, in contravention of the treaty, they were being barred from all ports in the Athenian empire and from the Athenian market itself. The Corinthians were the last to come forward. They let the others do the preliminary inciting of the Spartans, then followed with this speech:

'Spartans, the trust you place in your own constitution and society 68
makes you less trusting of others when we have something to say to
you. This character of yours may produce the virtue of restraint, but
it also leaves you largely ignorant in the way you handle external
affairs. Many times we have warned you of the harm we anticipated
from the Athenians, and every time you would not learn from the
lesson we urged on you, but instead you took the suspicious view that
the speakers were simply airing their own grievances, of interest solely
to them. That is why this conference of the allies is too late—you did
not invite us before the harm was done, but only when we are in the
middle of it. We have as much justification to speak as any of the
allies, in that we have the most serious charges to make—aggression
from the Athenians, and neglect from you.

'Yes, if the Athenians were somehow covering up their crimes
against Greece, you might not know of them and we would have to
instruct you. But as it is there is no need for lengthy exposition: you
can see for yourselves that the Athenians have already enslaved some
states, with designs now on others (not least our own allies), and that
they have long laid preparations for eventual war. Why else would
they steal Corcyra and hold it now in defiance of our claims? Why
else would they be besieging Potidaea? Potidaea is the crucial base for
the control of the Thraceward area, and Corcyra could have brought
huge naval power to the Peloponnesians.

'And you are responsible for all this! First you allowed the Athenians 69
to fortify their city after the Persian Wars, and later to build the
Long Walls: and to this very day you have continued denying their
freedom not only to the states already enslaved by Athens, but now
to your own allies also. The true denial of freedom is not that of the
enslaving power, but rather that of the people who have the ability to
end the subjection but choose to do nothing about it—yet more so if
they make a virtue of their reputation as the liberators of Greece.

'So now we are convened at last, and it was not easy. Even now we
have no clear agenda. The time is past for debating whether or not
there is aggression against us: the question now is how to resist it.
Men of action have their plans laid, and if their opponents are still
dithering they move against them without further warning. And we
know the Athenians' way, how they gradually encroach on their
neighbours. While they think they can get away with it because of
your own lack of attention, they proceed rather cautiously: but once
they realize that you know and do not care, they will press on at

full strength. The fact is that of all the Greeks you Spartans are the
only ones who sit quiet and do nothing, with your defence policy not
force but procrastination. You are the only ones who wait for your
enemies' power to double, rather than curbing its initial growth. And
yet you used to be called "reliable"—which turned out to be more
reputation than fact. We all know that the Persians, coming from the
ends of the earth, reached right to the Peloponnese before meeting
any opposition worth the name from you: and now you are choosing
to ignore the Athenians, who are not some distant enemy like the
Persians, but close to home. Rather than take the offensive yourselves, you prefer to defend only when attacked, thus leaving to
chance your eventual conflict with an enemy grown much stronger.
You are well aware that Xerxes' failure was largely his own fault, and
that with these very Athenians what has saved us so far has been for
the most part their own mistakes rather than any support from you.
Indeed one could say that the hopes they placed in you have been the
ruin of several before now, people who trusted in your help and
made no preparations of their own. And please understand that there
is no animosity in what we say to you: it is more by way of remonstration. People remonstrate with friends who are going wrong: animus
is for enemies who have done wrong.

70   'Yet at the same time we consider we have as much right as any to
find fault with our neighbours, especially when there are such profound differences involved, which in our view you do not appreciate.
You have never worked out what sort of people these Athenians are
who you will have to contend with, how far and how completely they
differ from you. They are revolutionaries, quick with new ideas and
quick to put their thoughts into action: you are conservatives, keeping things as they are with no initiative and incapable of action even
on the bare essentials. Again, they will dare beyond their means, take
risks defying judgement, and stay confident in adversity: whereas
your way is to act short of your power, diffident even in the strengths
of your policy, and convinced that there is no escape from adversity.
Further: they are unhesitant, while you are dilatory; they go abroad,
while you stay firmly at home. They think that their ventures away
from home can bring them gain, whereas your view is that any enterprise risks harm to what you already have. In victory they press their
advantage over the enemy as far as they can: in defeat they fall back
as little as they must. And although they give their bodies to the
service of the city as if they were not their own property, their minds

are very much their own and they cultivate them for the civic benefit they can bring. If they set an aim and fail to achieve it, they take that as a personal loss: if they succeed and make a gain, they regard this as only a minor achievement compared with what comes next. And if they do happen to fail in some attempt, another hope is born to fill the gap. For them, uniquely, in any project hoping and having are the same thing, so quickly does action follow thought. This is their lifelong labour, a constant round of work and risk. They have no time to enjoy what they have as they are always acquiring more. Their only idea of holiday is to do what they have to do. For them the quiet of inactivity is a greater affliction than the burden of business. It would be a fair summary to say that it is in their nature to have no quiet themselves and to deny quiet to others.

'Yet faced with the opposition of a city such as this, you Spartans 71 are still hanging back. You do not realize that the most lasting peace and quiet is secured by those who use their power only in a just cause, but clearly demonstrate their resolve not to yield to any injustice. Your notion of a balanced policy is to keep out of harm's way—no provocation of others, and no risk to yourselves even in self-defence. Such a policy would hardly work even with a neighbouring state of like mind: but in the present situation, as we have just pointed out, your ways are old-fashioned compared to the Athenians'. In politics as in technology the new must always prevail over the old. The established traditions may be best in a settled society, but when there is much change demanding a response there must be much innovative thinking also. This is where the Athenians have great experience, and why their systems have undergone more reform than yours.

'So you have been slow long enough: let us here and now have an end of it. To support your allies and especially to redeem your promise to the Potidaeans you must now make all speed to invade Attica. Otherwise you will be abandoning friends and kinsmen to their worst enemies, and forcing the rest of us to turn in desperation to some other alliance. And if we did this it would be no offence in the eyes of the gods who witnessed our oaths or of men who see how things are. Treaties are not broken by abandoned parties who apply elsewhere: they are broken by those who will not help their sworn partners. If you are prepared to commit yourselves we shall stay with you. In that case it would not be right for us to change allegiance, and we would not find other friends as compatible as you.

Think carefully, then, and look to be the leaders of a Peloponnese as great as that which you inherited from your fathers.'

72   Such was the speech of the Corinthians. Now there happened to be a delegation of Athenians already staying in Sparta, come there on other business. When these delegates heard what the Corinthians were saying, they decided that they too should appear before the Spartans, not to make any specific answer to the charges laid against them by the allied cities, but to show why, in the whole context, they should take more time over their deliberations and not rush to a decision. At the same time they wanted to indicate the extent of their own city's power, reminding their older listeners of what they already knew and instructing the younger in matters outside their experience. They thought that what they said would be more likely to incline the Spartans to keeping quiet than to starting war. So they approached the Spartans and said that they too would like to address their assembly, if there was no objection. The Spartans invited them to appear, and the Athenians came forward and spoke as follows:

73   'Our delegation was not sent here to engage in dispute with your allies, but on a separate mission from Athens. Nevertheless we are aware of considerable outcry against us, and we come before you now not to rebut the charges made by your allied cities—neither we nor they have to make forensic speeches as if your assembly were a court of law—but to ensure that you are not too readily influenced by your allies into making a wrong decision on matters of great importance. At the same time, with regard to the general criticism of us now prevalent, we wish to make it clear that the gains we have acquired are rightfully held, and that you need to take account of our city.

'There is no point in speaking of ancient history, for which the only evidence is stories rather than eyewitness among the audience. But we must make mention of the Persian War and other events within your own experience, even if you find this constant rehearsal tedious. In our actions then we faced those dangers for the common good. You had your share in the benefit gained, and we should not be denied all reference to it when that can help our cause. What we shall say now is not an attempt at deflection. It is more a matter of the evidence to show you with what sort of city you will find yourselves in conflict, if you do not take the right decision.

'Our claim is that at Marathon we stood out alone against the barbarians. And when the second invasion came, without sufficient forces to resist on land we took to our ships with our whole citizen body and joined in the battle of Salamis, which prevented the Persians from sailing on against the Peloponnese and destroying it city by city—since you could not have helped each other against that number of ships. The best witness to this is Xerxes himself: once defeated at sea he realized that his power was diminished and quickly retreated with the bulk of his army.

'That outcome happening as it did clearly demonstrated that the 74 fortunes of Greece depended on her navies. And to that outcome we contributed the three most telling factors—the largest number of ships, the ablest commander, and the most fearless determination. We provided nearly two-thirds of the total of four hundred ships, and we provided Themistocles as commander, who was instrumental in ensuring that the battle was fought in the narrows: this without doubt was our salvation, and for this service you gave greater honours to Themistocles than to any other foreigner received in Sparta. As for our determination, this was displayed in the most exceptionally courageous form. When there was no one to help us by land, when all others right up to our borders were already enslaved, we took the decision to leave our city and sacrifice our homes and possessions, determined that even so we should not abandon the common cause of our remaining allies or fail them by our own dispersal, but should take to our ships and risk the fight—and not resent your failure to support us sooner.

'We claim, then, that we did you at least as great a service as we received. Your help was given when you feared more for yourselves than for us: certainly there was no sign of you when we were still intact. You came from cities still inhabited and with the aim of ensuring their continued occupation: we set out from a city which no longer existed, and in fighting for its small hope of survival we saved ourselves and took our part in saving you. If we had gone over to the Persians at the beginning, as others did, out of fear for our land, or if later we had thought ourselves done for and had not found the courage to take to our ships, there would have been no point then in your attempting a sea-battle with your inadequate navy, and Xerxes would have gone on to achieve his object at leisure.

'We put this question to you, Spartans. Given the determination 75 and decisiveness we showed then, do we not deserve better than to be so violently hated by the Greeks for possessing an empire? We did not acquire this empire by force. It came about because you were not prepared to stay on to deal with the remnants of Persian power, and

the allies approached us of their own accord and asked us to become
their leaders. The very fact of this hegemony was the initial spur to
the expansion of the empire to its present extent: the motives driving
us were, first and foremost, fear, then prestige, and later our own
interests. There came a time when we realized that we could not safely
run the risk of letting it go: most of our allies had come to hate us;
some had already revolted and been subdued; your relations with us
were no longer as friendly as they had been, but had turned to suspicion and grievance; and of course any of our subjects defecting from
us would go over to you. No one can be blamed for looking after their
own best interests when the stakes are so high.

76   'Certainly you Spartans have ensured that the Peloponnesian
cities in your own hegemony are governed to suit your interest. And
we have no doubt that if at that time you had stayed on in command
long enough to be resented, as we did and were, you would have
become just as burdensome to the allies and would have been forced
to rule harshly or risk your own security. So too we have done nothing surprising or contrary to human nature in accepting an empire
when it was offered to us and refusing to give it up, under the domination of the three most powerful motives—prestige, fear, and self-
interest. Nor again did we start anything new in this, but it has
always been the way of the world that the weaker is kept down by the
stronger. And we think we are worthy of our power. There was a time
when you thought so too, but now you calculate your own advantage
and talk of right and wrong—a consideration which has never yet
deterred anyone from using force to make a gain when opportunity
presents. It is something worthy of credit when men who follow the
natural instinct to rule others then show more justice than they need
to in their position of strength. Certainly if others were to take our
place we think it would become abundantly clear how moderate we
are. But with us our very fairness has unfairly been turned more to
criticism than to credit.

77   'For example, finding ourselves disadvantaged against our allies in
lawsuits regulated by treaty, we transferred judgement in such cases
to Athens under our own impartial laws—and this is viewed as an
addiction to litigation. None of our critics enquires why this charge
is not laid against other imperial powers elsewhere whose treatment
of their subjects is less moderate than ours. The reason is that those
who can get their way by force have no need for the process of law.
Our subjects, on the other hand, are accustomed to dealing with us

on equal terms, so if any decision or exercise of our ruling power brings them even the slightest disadvantage compared to what they consider their rights, they are not grateful for the limitation of their loss but resent the shortfall yet more than if we had abandoned law and were openly exploiting them. Were that the case even they would not dispute that the weaker must give way to the strong. It seems that men are more angered by injustice than by enforcement: they see the one as advantage taken by an equal, the other as the compulsion of a superior. They had put up with worse treatment under the Persians, and now they regard our rule as oppressive. That is as expected: the present is always the hard time for those subject to others. But without doubt if you were to remove us and make your own empire, you would quickly lose the good will you have gained through others' fear of us, especially if you show the same attitude as you did earlier in your brief command against the Persians. Your own norms are incompatible with those of the outside world: and further, when any of you goes abroad he ignores both your own standards and those observed by the rest of Greece.

'Be slow, then, in reaching a decision: these are matters of 78 great importance. And do not let other people's opinions and complaints persuade you to incur troubles of your own. Give thought now to all the incalculable elements of war before you find yourselves in it. When war is prolonged it tends to become largely a matter of chance, in which we are both equally far from control and both face the danger of an uncertain outcome. And as they enter on their wars men take to action first, which should come later, and only have recourse to words when things go badly for them. Neither we nor you, as far as we can see, are in any danger yet of this mistake. So we urge you now, while we both still have the freedom to make the best decisions, not to break the treaty or contravene your oaths, but to let our differences be resolved by arbitration under the agreement. Otherwise we shall call in witness the gods by whom you swore, and hold you responsible for starting the war. We shall do our best to defend ourselves by matching any offensive you may launch.'

Such was the speech of the Athenians. When the Spartans had 79 heard the allies' charges against the Athenians and the Athenians' response, they required all other parties to withdraw and debated the situation in closed session. The majority tended to the same view, that the Athenians were already guilty and there should be war at once.

But their king Archidamus, who had a reputation as a man of intelligence and good sense, came forward and spoke as follows:

80   'Spartans, I am old enough myself to be experienced in many wars, and I see some of you here of the same age: none of them will share the longing for war felt by most who have never known the reality, nor will they think that there is any virtue or security in war. A sober analysis of the war you are now debating will reveal its potential scale. Against other Peloponnesians and our neighbours our forces are of similar type and can quickly reach any area of conflict. But against Athens we face a distant enemy and moreover a people who have outstanding skill at sea and the best resources in every other way—private and public wealth, ships, horses, armament, and a population greater than in any other single Greek territory: and they have as well numerous allies who pay them tribute. Why then should we lightly undertake a war against these people? What could give us the confidence to plunge into it unprepared? Our navy? We are inferior, and to train and build up to equality will take time. Our finances, then? Here we are yet more deficient, and by some way. There is no money in a common treasury, and we do not readily make contributions from our private means.

81   'Some might take comfort in the superior armour and numbers of our infantry, so we can regularly invade and ravage their land: but they have much other land in their empire, and will be able to import the supplies they need by sea. Then again if we try for a revolt of their allies, we shall have to extend our naval defence to them too, as most of them are islanders. So what sort of war shall we be fighting? If we can neither defeat them at sea nor stop the revenues which sustain their navy, we shall have the worst of it: and that would not even allow us an honourable peace, especially if we are thought the authors rather than the victims of the dispute. At all events we should not entertain the hope that the war will soon be at an end if we devastate their land. My fear is rather that we shall bequeath this war to our children. Such is the Athenians' pride, they are not likely to become slaves to their own land or take fright at war as if they were novices.

82   'Now I am far from asking you to stand by unconcerned, letting them cause harm to our allies and make their designs without fear of detection. My advice is that we should not yet take up arms, but should first send envoys to complain, giving no unambiguous indication either of war or of acquiescence, and in the meantime make our

own preparations. We should look to acquire further allies, Greek or barbarian—wherever they might be—who can supplement our naval or financial resources. Like all others on whom the Athenians have their designs, we cannot be blamed if for our own preservation we bring in help from barbarians as well as Greeks. And at the same time we must build up what we already have. If they pay some heed to our representations, fine and good. If not, in two or three years' time we shall have stronger defences if we then decide to attack them.

'It may well be that they will be more inclined to hold back when they can see our preparations and a diplomatic policy giving the same signals, when their land is still intact and their decision is made in the enjoyment of their present prosperity, rather than after its destruction. You must look on their land simply as a hostage, the more valuable for the care with which it is cultivated: you should spare it for as long as possible, and not stiffen their resistance by driving them to desperation. If we are pressured by our allies' complaints into ravaging Attica before we are ready, you must consider the potential shame and difficulty for the Peloponnese. Complaints can be resolved, whether they are made by cities or by individuals: but a war undertaken by a whole confederacy in pursuit of individual grievances, with the outcome impossible to tell, cannot easily be settled on honourable terms.

'And no one should think it any lack of courage if many confeder- 83 ate states are slow to attack a single city. They too have just as many allies, and their allies bring them revenue: and war is not so much a matter of armament as of the finance which gives effect to that armament, especially when a land power meets a sea power. So let us first see to our finances, and not be carried away in advance of that by our allies' arguments. We shall bear most of the responsibility for the outcome either way, good or ill, so we should take our time over a calm review of the prospects.

'The slowness and delay for which they like to blame us are noth- 84 ing to be ashamed of. If you were to go to war unprepared, a hasty start could mean a drawn-out finish. And the city which we administer has always been free and always held in high regard: so this very slowness could well be called intelligent restraint. This quality has kept us, uniquely, from arrogance in success and from the surrender which others make to adversity. We are not seduced by the pleasant flattery of those who urge us to dangerous action against our judgement, and if anyone tries to provoke us with accusations, this is no more successful—we are not goaded into agreement. Our discipline makes us both brave in war and sensible in policy: brave, because restraint is the greater part of shame, and shame the greater part of courage; sensible, because our tough training leaves us too naive to question the laws and too controlled to disobey them. We are not schooled in that useless over-intelligence which can make a brilliant verbal attack on the enemies' plans but fail to match it in consequent action. Rather we are taught to believe that other people's minds are similar to ours, and that no theory can determine the accidents of chance. It is always our principle to make practical plans on the assumption of an intelligent enemy, and not to let our hopes reside in the likelihood of his mistakes, but in the security of our own pre-cautions. We do not need to suppose that men differ greatly one from another, but we can think that the strongest are those brought up in the hardest school.

85   'These then are the practices which our fathers handed down to us and which we still maintain to our constant benefit. Let us not aban-don them, or be rushed in the brief space of one day to a decision affecting many lives, much expenditure, many cities, and our own reputation. We must be calm about it: and we can afford that, more than the others, because of our strength. And now you should send envoys to Athens to make representations about Potidaea, represen-tations too about the wrongs alleged by our allies. This is the more important in that they have said they are willing to go to arbitration, and when such an offer is given it is not lawful to proceed pre-emptively as if guilt were already established. At the same time you should prepare for war. What I advise will be the best policy in your own interests and also the most intimidating to your enemies.'

Such was the speech of Archidamus. Then finally Sthenelaïdas, one of the ephors at that time, came forward and spoke as follows:

86   'I cannot understand all this talk from the Athenians. They spent a lot of time blowing their own trumpet, but nowhere answered the charge of doing wrong to our allies and the Peloponnese. They may have acquitted themselves well against the Persians in the past, but, if they are now behaving badly to us, they deserve a double penalty for turning from good to bad. But we are the same now as we were then, and if we have any sense we shall not ignore the wrong done to our allies or delay the punishment—they can hardly delay their suffering. Others may have an abundance of money, ships, and horses: but we have good allies who must not be abandoned to the Athenians.

We must not leave it to arguments in law courts to deal with injuries which are unarguably happening. We must punish now, quickly and in full strength. And let no one try to tell us that when we are wronged we should stop to think about it—it is more the intending wrong-doers who should think hard. So, Spartans, vote for war and for the honour of Sparta. Do not allow the Athenians to grow stronger. Let us not abandon our allies, but with the gods' help let us go out and attack the guilty.'

After this speech he himself, in his capacity as ephor, put the 87 question to the Spartan assembly. Their decisions are made by ac-clamation rather than vote, and Sthenelaïdas claimed that he could not tell which side had the louder shout. With the intention of pro-moting the cause of war by making them show their opinions overtly, he said to the Spartans: 'Those of you who think that the treaty has been broken and the Athenians are guilty should stand up and move over here' (pointing to a particular area), 'and those who think otherwise should move over there.' So they stood up and divided, and there was a great majority on the side of those who thought that the treaty had been broken.

The Spartans then recalled the allies to the assembly and told them that they had decided the Athenians were guilty, and that they wanted to call a full conference of all their allies and put it to the vote, so that war, if approved, would be undertaken with common con-sent. This accomplished, the allies returned home, and the Athenian envoys went back later when their specific mission was completed.

This resolution of the Spartan assembly, that the treaty had been broken, was made in the fourteenth year of the duration of the Thirty Years Treaty established after the affair of Euboea.

In voting for war on the grounds of breach of the treaty the Spartans 88 were not so much influenced by the arguments of their allies as by their fear of increasing Athenian power, when they could see much of Greece already subject to Athens.

There follows now an account of how the Athenians reached 89 the position of such growth. When the Persians had retreated from Europe, defeated by the Greeks at sea and on land, and the remnants who fled in their ships to Mycale had been destroyed, Leotychidas, the Spartan king, who had been in command of the Greeks at Mycale, returned home together with the allies from the Peloponnese. But the Athenians and the allies from Ionia and the Hellespont who had now revolted from the King of Persia stayed on and began a siege of Sestos, then still in Persian hands. They overwintered there and finally took the town when the barbarians abandoned it: after that the allies sailed back from the Hellespont to their own homes.

Meanwhile the Athenian people, rid now of the barbarian occupation of their land, immediately began to bring back their children and women and their remaining goods from their places of safe keeping, and set about the rebuilding of the city and its walls. Only a small part of the circuit wall still stood, and most of the houses were in ruins: the few intact houses were those in which the Persian high command had been quartered.

90 The Spartans could see what was coming, and arrived at Athens with a delegation. They themselves would have preferred to see neither the Athenians nor anyone else in possession of fortifications, but they were mainly spurred by the insistence of their allies who were alarmed at the much increased size of the Athenian navy and the bold approach they had taken to the Persian War. The Spartan request was that the Athenians should not fortify their own city, but should actually join with them in demolishing any city walls still standing outside the Peloponnese. In making this proposal to the Athenians the Spartans concealed the mistrust which was their real motive, arguing instead that if the Persians returned to the attack there would then be no fortified place which they could take as their headquarters, as they had recently done at Thebes: the Peloponnese, they said, could sufficiently provide both a refuge and a base of operations for all of Greece. On the advice of Themistocles, the Athenians managed to get rid of the Spartans and their proposal by replying that they would send delegates to Sparta to discuss the issues raised. Themistocles then recommended that they should send him to Sparta at once, and elect other delegates to join him: these should not leave immediately, but should wait for as long as it took to build the wall up to the minimum defensible height. The whole population in Athens at the time—men, women, and children—should set to work on the wall, sparing no private or public building which would help the construction, but demolishing them all.

So with these instructions given, and intimating that he himself would deal with all other business there, Themistocles set off for Sparta. On his arrival he did not present himself to the authorities, but kept delaying and making excuses. Whenever any official asked him why he was not appearing before the assembly, he said that he was waiting for his fellow delegates: some other business had detained them, but he expected them very shortly and was surprised that they had not yet arrived.

Their friendship for Themistocles led the Spartan authorities to 91 believe what he told them, but as others kept arriving with clear statements that the wall was under construction and already reaching a good height, they could not discount this evidence. Aware of this, Themistocles proposed that rather than allowing the influence of hearsay they should send out some of their own worthies to see for themselves and bring back a reliable report. So this they did, and Themistocles sent a secret message to the Athenians about these envoys, telling them to detain them as unobtrusively as possible and not let them leave until he and his party were back in Athens: by now his fellow delegates, Habronichus the son of Lysicles and Aristeides the son of Lysimachus, had arrived with the news that the wall was in a sufficient state. His fear was that when they learnt the truth the Spartans might then refuse to let them go.

So the Athenians, as instructed, detained the envoys, and Themistocles now finally came before the Spartans and openly declared that Athens was by now sufficiently fortified for the safety of its own inhabitants, and that if the Spartans or their allies wished to make any representations in the future, they should come on the understanding that the Athenians took a clear view both of their own interests and of the common good. Themistocles and his colleagues pointed out that when they had seen fit to abandon their city and take to their ships, this bold decision was taken without reference to the Spartans, and in all subsequent joint deliberation their advice had proved second to none. So now too they saw fit that their city should have a wall, for the greater benefit of their own citizens and the allies at large. An equal and fair contribution to decisions on common policy could only be made from a position of equal strength. So either, said Themistocles, the whole alliance should lose their walls, or the Athenian action should be approved.

On hearing this the Spartans showed no open anger against the 92 Athenians. The ostensible purpose of their original embassy had not been to limit Athens, but to suggest a policy for the common good: and besides they were then on particularly friendly terms in view of the Athenians' determined stand against the Persians. Nevertheless, without showing it, they were vexed at the failure of their plan. The delegates from both sides left for home with no complaints made.

93   So this was how the Athenians walled their city in short time. To
this day the signs of hasty construction can be seen. The foundations
are laid with all sorts of stones, some of them unsquared and placed
just as they came in, and mixed among them are many gravestones
and other pieces of sculpture. The circuit of the city wall was
enlarged in all directions, and in their rush to complete it no building
was spared demolition.

Themistocles also persuaded the Athenians to finish the building
of the Peiraeus, on which a start had been made earlier, in his year of
office as archon. He could see the virtue of the place, with its three
natural harbours, and realized that becoming a seafaring nation was
the key to the acquisition of power. He had been the first to advance
the proposal that the Athenians should take to the sea: and now he
was quick to help lay the foundations of empire.

On his advice they built the wall round the Peiraeus to the thickness
which one can still see. It was wide enough for two wagons bringing up
the stones from opposite directions to pass each other. The interior of
the wall was not rubble or clay, but the whole structure was made of
large blocks of stone cut and squared, with clamps of iron and lead on
the outer faces. The completed height was about half of what
Themistocles intended. His plan was to frustrate any enemy designs by
the size and thickness of the wall, which he thought could be adequately
defended by a small number of those unsuited for other service, while
the rest would man the fleet. His particular concentration on the navy
had its origin, I think, in his perception that the King's forces found it
easier to attack by sea than by land. He considered the Peiraeus more
important than the upper city, and he would often advise the Athenians
that if they were ever hard pressed on land they should go down to the
Peiraeus and take on the world with their ships.

This then was the way in which the Athenians built their walls and
took all other measures immediately after the Persian withdrawal.

94   Pausanias the son of Cleombrotus was now sent out from Sparta
as commander of the Greek forces, with twenty ships from the
Peloponnese: the expedition was joined by the Athenians with thirty
ships, and a good number of the other allies. They first campaigned
against Cyprus, and subdued most of the island. Next they turned to
Byzantium, then in Persian control, and forced its capitulation. This
was still when Pausanias was in command.

95   But Pausanias was already showing an oppressive tendency which
the Greeks resented, especially the Ionians and all others recently

liberated from the King of Persia. These came one after the other to the Athenians, asking them out of kinship to become their leaders and put a stop to any oppression from Pausanias. The Athenians welcomed these approaches, and determined to act on them and generally rearrange matters as they saw best.

Meanwhile the Spartans recalled Pausanias for an inquiry into the reports they had received. Numerous crimes were alleged against him by the Greeks who visited Sparta, and the clear impression was more of a tyranny than a military command. It so happened that his recall came just at the time when their hatred of him caused the allies (except the troops from the Peloponnese) to transfer their allegiance to the Athenians. On his arrival at Sparta he was punished for personal crimes against individuals, but acquitted of the major charges: the main accusation against him was collaboration with the Persians, for which there was thought very clear evidence. The Spartans did not continue his command, but in his place sent out Dorcis and a few colleagues with a small force. The allies would not now accept their leadership. Seeing how things were, Dorcis and his colleagues left for home and the Spartans thereafter sent out no further commanders, fearing that any who did go out would become corrupted, as they had seen in the case of Pausanias. And they wanted to be rid of involvement in the Persian War. They thought the Athenians fully capable of taking the lead, and believed them well disposed towards Sparta at that time.

In this way the Athenians took over the hegemony, with the willing agreement of the allies prompted by their hatred of Pausanias. They then determined which of the cities should provide money and which should provide ships in furtherance of the war against the barbarians: the ostensible purpose was to retaliate for their own losses by ravaging the King's territory. It was now that there was first instituted at Athens the office of 'Treasurers to the Greeks', with responsibility for receiving the tribute (this was the term given to the contributions in money). The original tribute was assessed at four hundred and sixty talents. The treasury was the island of Delos, and the meetings of the allies took place in the temple there.

At first the Athenians were the leaders of autonomous allies who met together to make their policy in common. But in the period intervening between the Persian War and this war there was huge Athenian activity in the prosecution of war and the management of political affairs, activity undertaken against the barbarians, against their own rebellious allies, and against any Peloponnesian state which crossed their path at any time in their various ventures. I have written the following account and made this excursus because all of my predecessors have omitted this period: their histories are either of the Greek world before the Persian invasion or of the Persian War itself. The only one to touch on this subject is Hellanicus in his *History of Athens*, but his treatment is brief and the chronology is imprecise. At the same time this excursus serves to demonstrate how the Athenian empire came into being.

98　　　The Athenians' first action was against Eïon on the river Strymon, then in Persian hands. Under the command of Cimon the son of Miltiades they took the town after a siege, and sold the inhabitants into slavery. They then turned to the Aegean island of Scyros, enslaving the Dolopes who inhabited it and installing their own settlers. They also made war on Carystus, independently of the rest of Euboea, and the Carystians eventually agreed to terms. After this came the revolt of Naxos: the Athenians went to war and blockaded the Naxians into submission. This was the first allied state to lose its freedom—something quite contrary to Greek norms which would subsequently happen to the others one by one.

99　　　There were various reasons for these revolts, but the main causes were failures to pay the tribute or provide the ships, and sometimes desertion from campaigns. The Athenians were exacting managers, and the coercion they applied was oppressive to people who were not used to hardship and had no wish for it. And there were other reasons too why the Athenians were now less popular as leaders. They no longer observed any collective equality in their military campaigns, and it was easy for them to force back any defectors. The allies were in this responsible for their own problems. Most of them, sharing this reluctance to be involved in campaigns which would take them away from home, had the contribution which fell to them assessed in money rather than ships. The result was that the Athenians could spend this income on the development of their navy, and when they revolted the allies found themselves short of resources and inexperienced in war.

100　　Next there took place the land- and sea-battles at the river Eurymedon in Pamphylia, fought against the Persians by the Athenians and their allies. Commanded by Cimon the son of Miltiades the Athenians won both battles on the same day, and captured and destroyed a total of two hundred Phoenician triremes.

Then, after a while, the Athenians faced the revolt of Thasos, occasioned by a dispute over the markets and the mine on the Thracian mainland opposite, which the Thasians controlled. The Athenians sent a fleet to Thasos, won the ensuing sea-battle, and landed on the island. At about the same time they sent out ten thousand settlers, drawn from their own people and their allies, to the Strymon to colonize the place then called Nine Ways and now Amphipolis. They did indeed win possession of Nine Ways, then occupied by Edonians, but when they advanced into the interior of Thrace they were destroyed at Drabescus in Edonia by the combined forces of the Thracians, who saw the founding of the colony as an act of war.

The Thasians, defeated in battle and now under siege, appealed 101 to the Spartans and urged them to help by invading Attica. The Spartans promised to do so (this was kept secret from the Athenians), and would have done so had they not been prevented by the occurrence of the great earthquake, which the Helots and with them the Perioeci of Thuria and Aethaea took as the opportunity to revolt and secede to Ithome. (The Helots were mostly the descendants of the Messenians who had been enslaved long ago: hence the name 'Messenians' given to all the Helots.) The Spartans, then, were engaged in a war with the insurgents in Ithome, and the Thasians, now in the third year of the siege, capitulated to the Athenians. Under the terms of agreement they demolished their walls, surrendered their ships, undertook the payment assessed for immediate indemnity and future tribute, and gave up their rights in the mainland and the mine.

When the Spartans found their war against the Ithome rebels 102 dragging on, they called in their allies, including the Athenians, who came with a substantial force commanded by Cimon. The main reason for inviting the Athenians was that they had a reputation for expertise in siege operations, whereas with their own siege now prolonged the Spartans recognized that they themselves lacked the necessary skills—otherwise they would have taken the place by storm. This campaign led to the first open dispute between the Spartans and the Athenians. When Ithome was still not yielding to assault, the Spartans grew apprehensive of the enterprising and revolutionary spirit of the Athenians, and were conscious as well that they were of different race. Fearing, then, that if they stayed on they might be tempted to collude with the Ithome Helots in a revolution, they dismissed the Athenian force while retaining their other allies. Without revealing their mistrust, they simply said that their services were no longer required. The Athenians realized that some suspicion was afoot, and that their dismissal was not for the innocuous reason given. They took great offence and were indignant that they should be treated like this by the Spartans. As soon as they returned they abandoned the alliance with Sparta first made against the Persians and allied themselves with Argos, the enemy of Sparta, and at the same time both the Athenians and the Argives equally swore an alliance with the Thessalians.

103   After nine years of siege the rebels in Ithome could not hold out any longer, and in the tenth year they agreed terms with the Spartans. Under these terms they had safe conduct to leave the Peloponnese, but should never set foot on it again: any of them caught there would be the slave of his captor. There was also a previous response of the Delphic oracle to the Spartans, telling them to release the suppliant of Zeus of Ithome. So the Helots left the country with their children and women, and in their new hostility to Sparta the Athenians gave them welcome, settling them in Naupactus, a town which they had recently taken from the control of the Ozolian Locrians.

Now the Megarians deserted Sparta and joined in alliance with Athens: the reason was that the Corinthians were gaining the upper hand in a war over disputed boundaries. The Athenians thus acquired both Megara and Pegae, and built for the Megarians the long walls from their city to the port of Nisaea, providing the garrison themselves. This was the first and the main cause of the intense hatred felt by Corinth for Athens.

104   The Libyan Inaros, son of Psammetichus and king of the Libyans who bordered on Egypt, now instigated the revolt of most of Egypt from the Persian King Artaxerxes, starting from Mareia, the inland town opposite Pharos. He installed himself as ruler, and called in the Athenians. They happened to be engaged in an expedition to Cyprus with two hundred of their own and allied ships, but abandoned Cyprus and came to Egypt. Sailing from the sea into the Nile they gained control of the river and of two-thirds of Memphis, then began an attack on the remaining sector, called the White Castle, in which the surviving Persians and Medes had taken refuge together with those Egyptians who had not joined the revolt.

105   An Athenian fleet made a landing at Halieis, and a battle ensued against Corinthian and Epidaurian forces in which the Corinthians were victorious. Later the Athenians fought and won a sea-battle off

Cecryphaleia against a Peloponnesian fleet. After this, war broke out between Athens and Aegina, and a great sea-battle took place off Aegina in which both the Athenians and the Aeginetans were supported by their allies. The Athenians were the victors: they captured seventy of the enemy ships, then landed on Aegina and laid siege to the town. The Athenian general in command was Leocrates the son of Stroebus. Then the Peloponnesians, wanting to help the Aeginetans, sent over to Aegina three hundred hoplites who had previously been supporting the Corinthian and Epidaurian forces: and the Corinthians together with their allies seized the heights of Geraneia and moved down into the Megarid. They reckoned that it would be impossible for the Athenians to send help to the Megarians with such large forces already deployed in Aegina and in Egypt—and, if they did, they would have to move their troops from Aegina. But the Athenians left the army besieging Aegina where it was, and arrived at Megara with a force drawn from the manpower still remaining at home—the oldest and the youngest—with Myronides the general in command. There followed an indecisive battle with the Corinthians: when the two sides parted, each thought they had had the better of the action. After the Corinthians left, the Athenians (who had in fact enjoyed the greater success) set up a trophy. The Corinthian troops, stung by the taunts of cowardice made by the older men back home, made further preparations and about twelve days later returned to set up their own trophy and claim the victory. The Athenians sallied out of Megara, killed the contingent erecting the trophy, then engaged and defeated the rest of their army.

As the Corinthians were retreating after this defeat, quite a large 106 section of them, hard pressed and missing the way back, found themselves in a private estate which was surrounded by a deep ditch with no other exit. Seeing this, the Athenians blocked the entrance with their hoplites, positioned light-armed troops round the perimeter, and stoned to death all those inside. This was a major disaster for the Corinthians. The main body of their army returned home.

At about this time the Athenians also began to build their Long 107 Walls to the sea, one to Phaleron and the other to the Peiraeus. The Phocians now made an expedition into Doris, the mother-country of the Spartans, and took one of the three main towns (these are Boeum, Cytinium, and Erineum). The Spartans came to the aid of the Dorians with fifteen hundred of their own hoplites and ten thousand of their allies: this force was commanded by Nicomedes the son of

Cleombrotus as deputy for the king, Pleistoanax the son of Pausanias, who was still a minor. After forcing the Phocians to capitulate and hand back the town, they were ready to return home. To take the sea route through the Gulf of Crisa exposed them to the Athenians, who had sailed a fleet round and would certainly stop them. They saw equal danger in the land route over Geraneia with the Athenians in possession of Megara and Pegae: besides, the Geraneia passes were difficult and kept under constant guard by the Athenians, so they could see that the Athenians would stop them that way too. They decided, then, to stay in Boeotia while investigating the safest means of passage. A contributory fact was that some Athenians were making secret approaches to them, in the hope that they would put an end to the democracy and the building of the Long Walls.

The Athenians set out to meet them with their full force, including a thousand Argives and contingents from their other allies, a total of fourteen thousand troops. They undertook this expedition because they realized that the Spartans had no means of return, but they also had suspicions of a plot to overthrow the democracy. Their forces were joined by some Thessalian cavalry in accordance with their treaty of alliance, but in the engagement these deserted to the Spartans.

108   The battle took place at Tanagra in Boeotia, and was won by the Spartans and their allies, though there was great slaughter on both sides. The Spartans then proceeded to the Megarid, cut down the plantations, and made their way home over Geraneia and across the Isthmus. But on the sixty-second day after the battle the Athenians marched an army into Boeotia under the command of Myronides, and defeated the Boeotians in a battle at Oenophyta. They took control of the whole of Boeotia and Phocis, demolished the walls of Tanagra, and took as hostages from the Opuntian Locrians one hundred of their wealthiest men. They then completed the building of their own Long Walls. Soon afterwards the Aeginetans too capitulated to the Athenians: the terms were demolition of their walls, surrender of their ships, and assessment to pay tribute in the future. And the Athenians sent a fleet round the Peloponnese, under the command of Tolmides the son of Tolmaeus, which set fire to the Spartans' dockyard, captured the Corinthian-owned town of Chalcis, and, making a landing in the territory of Sicyon, defeated the Sicyonians in battle.

109   The Athenians and their allies still remained in Egypt, where they experienced war in all its aspects. At first they were the masters of Egypt, and the King of Persia sent a Persian named Megabazus to

Sparta with a supply of money, to bribe the Peloponnesians to invade Attica and so draw the Athenians back from Egypt. As he was having no success and the money was being spent without result, Megabazus took himself back to Asia with what remained of the money. The King now sent out another Persian, Megabyxus the son of Zopyrus, with a large army. On his arrival after an overland march Megabyxus defeated the Egyptians and their allies in battle, and drove the Greeks out of Memphis. Eventually he confined them on the island of Prosopitis, and blockaded them there for eighteen months. In the end he drained the canal by diverting the water elsewhere, leaving their ships on dry land and most of the island now joined to the mainland: he then crossed over on foot and took the island.

This, then, after six years of fighting, was the collapse of the Greek 110 enterprise in Egypt. A few from this great number made their way through Libya to Cyrene and survived, but the majority met their death. Egypt became subject again to the King of Persia, except for the marsh people under their king Amyrtaeus. The extent of the marshes made it impossible for the Persians to capture Amyrtaeus, and besides the marsh-dwellers are the fiercest fighters in Egypt. Inaros, the king of Libya who was instrumental in the Egyptian revolt, was betrayed, captured, and crucified. A relief fleet of fifty triremes sent to Egypt by Athens and the rest of the alliance put in to the Mendesian mouth of the Nile without any knowledge of what had happened. They were attacked from land and sea by a Persian army and a Phoenician fleet: most of their ships were destroyed, and the remainder made their escape. Such was the end of the great Athenian and allied expedition to Egypt.

Now Orestes, the son of the Thessalian king Echecratides, was 111 exiled from Thessaly and persuaded the Athenians to restore him. They took with them a force of Boeotians and Phocians, who were now their allies, and marched against Pharsalus in Thessaly. They won control of the immediate area, but could never advance very far from their camp before the Thessalian cavalry stopped them. They failed to take the city, or to achieve any other object of the expedition, and went back with nothing accomplished, bringing Orestes with them. Not long after this a force of a thousand Athenians under the command of Pericles the son of Xanthippus embarked in the ships they had at Pegae (which was now in Athenian control) and sailed along the coast to Sicyon, where they made a landing and defeated those of the Sicyonians who came out to do battle. Immediately thereafter they took Achaean troops on board and sailed across the gulf to attack Oeniadae, a town in Acarnania. They laid siege to the town, but failed to take it and returned home.

112   Three years later the Peloponnesians and the Athenians established a five-year treaty. The Athenians now refrained from any Greek war, but sent an expedition to Cyprus with two hundred of their own and allied ships under the command of Cimon. Sixty of these ships were detached to sail to Egypt, in response to an appeal from Amyrtaeus the king of the marsh people, and the rest of them began a blockade of Citium. But Cimon's death and the onset of famine conditions made them leave Citium. As they sailed off Salamis in Cyprus they met a combined force of Phoenicians, Cypriots, and Cilicians and fought them both at sea and on land, winning both battles. They then set back for home, accompanied by the ships which had now returned from Egypt.

After this the Spartans undertook the so-called Sacred War, in which they won possession of the temple at Delphi and restored it to the Delphians. Then later, when the Spartans had left, the Athenians in turn sent out a force which recaptured the temple and gave it back to the Phocians.

113   Some time later, when the Boeotian exiles had gained possession of Orchomenus and Chaeroneia and a few other places in Boeotia, the Athenians sent out an expedition of a thousand of their own hoplites and various allied contingents to attack these now hostile towns: the general in command was Tolmides the son of Tolmaeus. They took Chaeroneia and enslaved the inhabitants, then started back after installing a garrison. On their return march they were attacked at Coroneia by the Boeotian exiles from Orchomenus, together with some Locrians and Euboean exiles and others of the same persuasion. This force defeated the Athenians, killing some and taking the others alive. The Athenians then withdrew from the whole of Boeotia, making a treaty to that effect conditional on the recovery of their captured men. The exiled party was restored, and all Boeotians regained their independence.

114   Not long after this Euboea revolted from Athens. Pericles had already crossed over to Euboea with an army of Athenians when the news reached him that Megara had revolted, that the Peloponnesians were about to invade Attica, and that the Megarians had slaughtered the Athenian garrison except for a few who made their escape to Nisaea: Megara had brought in troops from Corinth, Sicyon, and

Epidaurus to aid the revolt. Pericles quickly brought his army back from Euboea, and soon afterwards the Peloponnesians invaded Attica under the command of the Spartan king, Pleistoanax the son of Pausanias. They ravaged the land as far as Eleusis and Thria, but returned home without advancing any further. The Athenians crossed back to Euboea with Pericles in command and reduced the whole island. Terms of agreement were settled for all of Euboea except Hestiaea: here the Athenians dispossessed the inhabitants and appropriated their land. Shortly after their return from Euboea 115 the Athenians made a thirty-year treaty with the Spartans and their allies, under which they handed back Nisaea, Pegae, Troezen, and Achaea: these were places which they had taken from the Peloponnesians.

In the sixth year after this war broke out between Samos and Miletus over the possession of Priene. Having the worst of the war, the Milesians came to Athens and made indignant complaint of the Samians. They were supported by some private individuals from Samos itself who wanted a political revolution. So the Athenians sailed to Samos with forty ships and installed a democracy. They took hostages from Samos—fifty boys and fifty men—and deposited them in Lemnos: then they returned home, leaving a garrison on the island. But there were some Samians who would not stay. They made their escape to the mainland and formed a liaison with the leading oligarchs still on the island and with Pissouthnes the son of Hystaspes, then the Persian governor of Sardis. They gathered a force of about seven hundred mercenaries and crossed over to Samos at night. First they led an insurrection against the democrats and captured most of them, then they rescued the Samian hostages from Lemnos and declared their revolt from Athens. They handed over to Pissouthnes the Athenian garrison and the other officials stationed in Samos, and began immediate preparations for an attack on Miletus. And Byzantium joined them in revolt.

When the Athenians became aware of this they sailed for Samos 116 with sixty ships. Sixteen of these were deployed for other purposes, some sent towards Caria to keep a lookout for the Phoenician fleet, others to Chios and Lesbos to summon reinforcements. With the remaining forty-four ships, under the command of Pericles, one of the ten generals, the Athenians met a Samian fleet of seventy ships (including twenty transports) as they were sailing back from Miletus, and engaged them off the island of Tragia: the result was a victory for the Athenians. Later, when reinforcements arrived of forty ships from Athens and twenty-five from Chios and Lesbos, they landed on Samos and, with ground superiority achieved, built walls to invest the city on its three landward sides together with a blockade by sea. Pericles took sixty ships from the blockading fleet for an urgent mission to Caunus and Caria when news came that Phoenician ships were sailing against them (Stesagoras and other Samians had previously left Samos with five ships to call the Phoenician fleet in aid).

117   In this interval the Samians launched their fleet in a surprise attack on the unprotected Athenian naval camp, destroying the guard-ships and winning a sea-battle against the other ships which put out to meet them. So then for about fourteen days they were masters of their own sea and could import and export at will. But when Pericles returned with his fleet the blockade resumed. Later, reinforcements came from Athens—forty ships commanded by Thucydides, Hagnon, and Phormio, and twenty under Tlepolemus and Anticles—together with thirty ships from Chios and Lesbos. The Samians offered some brief resistance at sea, but were unable to hold out long and in the ninth month of the siege were forced to capitulate. The terms of agreement were the demolition of their walls, the giving of hostages, the surrender of their ships, and the payment of full reparations in regular instalments. The Byzantians also agreed terms under which they returned to their previous subject status.

118   Not many years after this there took place the events which I have already described—the affairs of Corcyra and Potidaea, and the various other circumstances which were reasons for this war. All these operations of the Greeks in my account—against each other and against the barbarians—took place in the period of roughly fifty years between the retreat of Xerxes and the beginning of this war. In this period the Athenians consolidated their empire and made great advances in their own independent power. The Spartans could see what was happening, but made only little attempt to prevent it and were inactive for most of the time. They had never been quick to go to war without immediate compulsion, and they were to some extent hampered by wars closer to home: but now the growth of Athenian power was unmistakable, and the Athenians were making inroads on Sparta's allies. At this point, then, the Spartans could tolerate it no longer, and decided that they must go on the attack with all their energies and, if possible, destroy the power of Athens by undertaking this war. They themselves had already determined by vote in their

assembly that the treaty had been broken and the Athenians were guilty of wrongdoing, but they sent to the oracle at Delphi and asked the god whether it would be better for them if they went to war. The god's response, so it is said, was that they would win if they fought in earnest, and that he himself, invited or uninvited, would take their side. And they summoned their allies once more, to put the question 119 of war to their vote. At the congress held when representatives from the alliance had arrived the others spoke their piece, most of them critical of the Athenians and insistent that there should be war. The Corinthians, present also on this occasion, had already gone their private rounds of the other cities individually, soliciting a vote for war: their fear was that otherwise they would be too late to save Potidaea. They were the last to come forward, and they spoke as follows:

'Fellow allies, we cannot now find fault with the Spartans: they 120 have cast their own vote for war, and have gathered us here now to do the same. This is just what leaders of an alliance should do—give equal weight to individual interests, yet with special concern for the common interest: and this responsibility is the counterpart of the special honour they are universally shown on other occasions. Now those of us who have already had dealings with the Athenians need no instruction to be wary of them. But those who live more inland and away from the trade-routes should realize that if they do not protect the coastal cities they will find difficulty in exporting their produce and importing in return the goods which sea gives to land. They should not make a mistaken judgement of what we are now saying as if it did not concern them: they must expect that if they abandon the seaboard the danger will ultimately reach them too, so these present deliberations are about their own interests as much as ours. For this reason they should not be reluctant to choose war in place of peace. Sensible men, for sure, do not disturb themselves if they are not wronged: but brave men wronged go from peace to war, and then make peace again when their fortune in war allows it. Such men are not excited by military success, but neither will they tolerate wrong done to them simply to preserve their enjoyment of peace and quiet. People whose present comfort makes them reluctant to act will quickly find that inaction brings the loss of that agreeable ease which caused their reluctance: and people who make grand presumptions after military success have not realized the fragility of the confidence which excites them. Many badly laid plans have turned successful

when met by greater incompetence on the part of the enemy: and
yet more apparently well-planned strategies have ended in dismal
failure. There is always a gulf between confident plan and execution
in practice: we lay our plans in security, then fail them in the event
through fear.

121   'Now as for us in this present situation, there is wrong being done
to us and we go to war with ample justification: and when we have
beaten off the Athenians, we shall bring the war to a timely conclusion.
There are many reasons why we should win this war. First, because
we are superior in numbers and military experience; second, because
we are all equally disciplined to follow our orders. They are strong at
sea, but we shall fit out a navy for ourselves from the existing resources
which we each have and from the funds at Delphi and Olympia: we
can borrow from there and offer a higher rate of pay to win over their
foreign sailors. Athenian power is based on mercenaries, not their
own people. The same tactic would not work against us, as our power
is men, not money. The likelihood is that one naval defeat will do for
them: but if they hold out, we shall have more time to develop our
skills at sea, and when our expertise matches theirs there is no doubt
that we shall surpass them in courage. This is a quality natural to us
which they cannot be taught, whereas their higher level of skill is
something we can achieve by practice. The money required for this
will come from our contributions. It would be truly disgraceful if,
while the Athenians' allies never fail to pay the tribute which maintains their enslavement, it turns out that we are not prepared to incur
expense on retaliation against our enemies and thereby on our own
safety—indeed on preventing the Athenians from robbing us of this
same hoarded money and using it to our detriment.

122   'And there are other avenues of war open to us. We can foster
revolt among their allies, the surest way of cutting the revenues on
which their strength depends; we can fortify a position in their own
territory; and there will be many other means which cannot now be
foreseen. War is not something that proceeds on set rules—far from
it: for the most part war devises its own solutions to meet any con-
tingency. So the safest course is to handle war in a dispassionate
frame of mind: mistakes multiply when passion is engaged.

       'A further consideration is this. If these disputes were simply
boundary questions among us between rival states of equal power,
we could tolerate that. But as it is the Athenians are a match for all
of us together, and much more powerful than any individual state,

so if we do not combine and fight them with every people and every city united in this one purpose, they will find us divided and have no difficulty in conquering us. This may be a hard message, but you can be sure that our defeat would mean nothing less than downright slavery. That such a possibility should even be mentioned, that there should be any question of so many cities suffering at the hands of one, is a disgrace to the Peloponnese. In that event people would say that we either deserve our fate or are cowards to accept it, and show ourselves a lesser generation than our fathers. Our fathers liberated Greece, but we are not even securing our own freedom: while we make it a principle to depose absolute rulers in any individual city, we are allowing a tyrant city to be established over us all. We do not see how this policy can be innocent of all three of the worst failings—stupidity, cowardice, or indifference. It cannot be that you have avoided these failings only to resort to contempt of the enemy, that notoriously calamitous state of mind which from the number of falls it has caused is better renamed as mindlessness.

'But there is no need to dwell on criticism of the past except in so 123 far as it serves the interest of the present. To secure the future, you must steel yourselves to take in hand the immediate task. You have it from your fathers that success is born from hardship, and you should not change that ethic even if you are now a little in advance of them in wealth and power: what was gained in poverty should not be lost in prosperity. There are indeed many reasons for going into this war with confidence. The god has spoken through his oracle and promised his own support, and all the rest of Greece will be on our side, either through fear or in hope of advantage. And you will not be responsible for breaking the treaty, when the god himself in telling you to go to war considers it already broken: rather you will be avenging its violation. Treaties are not broken by acts of self-defence: they are broken by the initial aggression.

'So with every circumstance in your favour for war, and with this 124 the course we urge on you for our common good, if you believe that community of interest is indeed the surest bond between states as well as individuals, do not now delay in sending help to the Potidaeans (they are Dorians besieged by Ionians, a reversal of what used to happen) or in pursuing the liberation of the others. It is impossible that we should wait any longer, seeing that some of us are already victims, and others will shortly suffer the same fate if it becomes known that we have convened and not found the courage to resist.

No, fellow allies: recognize that we have now reached the crisis point and that the policy we propose is the best way forward, and vote for war. Do not be frightened by the immediate danger, but set your hearts on the more lasting peace which will follow. A peace won through war has a firmer base: to refuse war for the sake of the quiet life runs the greater risk. We should realize that the tyrant city now established in Greece threatens tyranny over all of us alike, with designs on all the states not already in her power. So let us attack and bring her under our control: let us win the future safety of our own homes and the liberation of the Greeks who are now enslaved.'

125   Such was the speech of the Corinthians. The Spartans, now that they had heard all the opinions expressed, asked for the votes of each of their allies there present one by one, both great and small. The majority voted for war. This decision taken, they could not mount an immediate attack in their present state of unpreparedness, and determined that each should set about the appropriate provision with no delay. Even so, nearly a whole year was spent in the necessary preparation before they invaded Attica and openly commenced hostilities.

126   During this time they sent delegations to Athens making various complaints, to ensure that they had the strongest justification for going to war, if the Athenians made no concession. The first Spartan embassy demanded that the Athenians should drive out 'the curse of the goddess', the meaning of which is as follows. In earlier times there was an Athenian called Cylon, an Olympic victor and a powerful man of noble birth who had married the daughter of the Megarian Theagenes, then the tyrant of Megara. In answer to a question put by Cylon to the Delphic oracle the god replied that he should seize the Athenian Acropolis at the time of the greatest festival of Zeus. Cylon borrowed troops from Theagenes and persuaded his friends to join him, and when the time came round for the festival at Olympia in the Peloponnese he seized the Acropolis with the intention of making himself tyrant. He had thought that 'the greatest festival of Zeus' was that at Olympia, and that there was some connection with his own role as an Olympic victor. Whether this 'greatest festival' meant one in Attica or somewhere else was not a question either considered by Cylon or made clear in the oracle. (The Athenians too hold a great festival of Zeus the Kindly which is called the Diasia: this is held outside the city by the whole people, and many make local kinds of offering rather than the usual sacrifices.) But Cylon thought

he had the right interpretation, and so made his attempt. When they saw what had happened the Athenians all rushed back from their fields, surrounded the Acropolis, and laid siege to the men occupying it. After some time the Athenians grew weary of the siege and the majority of them went away, leaving the nine archons in charge of the guard detail and with full authority to deal with the matter as they thought best (in those days the nine archons were chiefly responsible for the administration of public affairs). Cylon and the men under siege with him were beginning to suffer from lack of food and water. Cylon and his brother managed to make their escape: and the others, in severe straits and with some of their number now dying of hunger, sat down as suppliants at the altar on the Acropolis. When the Athenian authorities in charge of the guard saw that they were dying in the temple, they persuaded them to leave their suppliant position with the promise that no harm would come to them, then led them off and put them to death. They even executed a group of them who on their way past sat down in supplication at the altars of the Dread Goddesses. For this crime the murderers and their families after them were held to be accursed and offenders against the goddess. So the Athenians drove out these accursed people, and they were driven out again later by the Spartan Cleomenes supported by the rival faction when there was civil strife at Athens: the living were exiled and the bones of the dead dug up and cast out. Nevertheless they returned afterwards, and their descendants still live in the city.

This then was the curse which the Spartans demanded should be 127 driven out. They pretended that their prime object was to serve the honour of the gods, but in fact they knew that the curse attached to Pericles the son of Xanthippus on his mother's side, and they thought that if he were expelled they would find it easier to deal with the Athenians. Not that they really expected this to happen: their hope was rather to discredit him in the eyes of his fellow citizens and make them think that this family circumstance of his would be a contributory cause of the war. He was the most influential man of his day and the leader of the state. His policy was constant opposition to the Spartans, and he would never let the Athenians make concessions, but was always pressing for the war.

The Athenians made the counter-demand that the Spartans 128 should drive out the curse of Taenarum. This referred to the time when some Helots had taken refuge as suppliants in the temple of Poseidon at Taenarum. The Spartans had recognized their suppliant status and persuaded them to move, then led them off and killed them. They themselves believe that the great earthquake in Sparta happened because of this crime.

The Athenians further demanded that they should drive out the curse of the goddess of the Bronze House, which came about as follows. When the Spartan Pausanias was originally recalled by the Spartiates from his command in the Hellespont, and put on trial by them but acquitted of the charges against him, he was not sent out again in any official capacity, but on his own initiative he took a trireme from Hermione without Spartan authority and sailed to the Hellespont. His pretence was that he had come to help the Greek war-effort, but in fact he was there to continue the intrigue with the King of Persia which he had already started earlier: his aim was to become the ruler of Greece. The favour which first placed the King under an obligation to him and began the whole affair was this. When he was previously in the area after his return from Cyprus, he had captured Byzantium, which was then occupied by Persians, including some relatives and members of the King's own family who were taken prisoner in the town. These he returned to the King without the knowledge of the other allies: his story to them was that the prisoners had managed to escape him. His accomplice in this was Gongylus of Eretria, whom he had put in charge of Byzantium and the men captured there. Gongylus' mission was also to carry a letter to the King, the text of which (as was subsequently discovered) read as follows: 'Pausanias, the leader of Sparta, wishes to do you a service and sends back to you these captives of his spear. I propose, if this meets with your approval, to marry your daughter and bring Sparta and the rest of Greece under your control. I believe that I have the ability to achieve this in collaboration with you. If any of this is pleasing to you, send down to the sea a trusted man to be the intermediary in our further discussions.'

129   Thus far the plain proposal in Pausanias' letter. Xerxes was delighted by the letter, and sent Artabazus the son of Pharnaces down to the sea with orders to take over the satrapy of Dascylium in place of the previous governor Megabates. He gave him a letter of reply which he was to send across to Pausanias in Byzantium without delay, and show him the royal seal: and then he was to carry out with all diligence and loyalty any instructions given him by Pausanias on the King's business. On his arrival Artabazus did all that he was

ordered, and sent across the letter. The text of the King's reply was as follows: 'Thus says Xerxes the King to Pausanias. The service you have done me in saving the men taken at Byzantium across the sea will stand recorded for ever in our house as a benefaction conferred by you. I am also pleased by the words you send me. Let neither night nor day cause you to slacken in the fulfilment of your promises to me, and let there be no impediment for lack of gold and silver to spend or troops to deploy in whatever number wherever they may be required. I have sent you Artabazus, a good man: in conjunction with him be as bold as you will to achieve the best and most successful result for both of us, in my interest and in yours.'

On receipt of this letter Pausanias, who was already held in great 130 esteem by the Greeks for his command at Plataea, took a yet much higher opinion of himself and could not now bear to live in the usual manner. Whenever he left Byzantium he was dressed in Persian fashion, he was accompanied on his tours through Thrace by a body-guard of Persians and Egyptians, and he had Persian food served at his table. He could not contain his ambition, but in small things made it clear what his larger intentions were for the future. He kept himself inaccessible, and treated all alike with such a violent temper that no one could approach him. This was one of the main reasons why the allies changed allegiance to the Athenians.

This was the very behaviour which had caused his original recall 131 when the Spartans heard of it. Now, when he had gone out there again in the ship from Hermione without their authority and was evidently behaving in the same way; when the Athenians had besieged him in Byzantium and forced him out; when he still would not return to Sparta, but established himself at Colonae in the Troad; and when it was reported to them that he was intriguing with the Persians and that there was a sinister purpose to his residence there, then at last the ephors came to the end of their patience. They sent out a messenger with a dispatch-stick and ordered Pausanias to accompany the messenger back to Sparta: otherwise the Spartan citizens would declare war on him. Wishing to attract as little suspicion as possible, and confident that he could bribe his way out of the charges, Pausanias returned to Sparta for the second time. He was at first thrown into prison by the ephors (who have the power to imprison the king), but then later contrived his release and offered to stand trial if any wished to question his actions.

There was no clear evidence available to the Spartan government, 132 either from the personal enemies of Pausanias or from the city as a whole, which would give solid grounds for the punishment of a member of the king's family who had at the time a royal prerogative—he was the cousin and the guardian of the king Pleistarchus, son of Leonidas, who was still a minor. Even so, his flouting of usual custom and espousal of foreign ways gave rise to widespread suspicion that he was not willing to conform to his present position. They reviewed previous examples of his deviation from the established norms of behaviour, especially his treatment of the tripod which the Greeks had dedicated at Delphi as the first-fruits of their victory over the Persians. He had taken it on his own initiative to have it inscribed with this elegiac couplet:

> Leader of Greece in the war which destroyed the forces of Persia,
>   Pausanias dedicates this to Apollo the god.

The Spartans had immediately erased these lines from the tripod and inscribed it instead with the names of all the cities which had taken part in the Persian defeat and the dedication of the monument. Even at the time this offence was regarded as Pausanias' doing, and now that his situation had taken this turn could be seen in a yet clearer light as consistent with his present attitude. They also received reports that Pausanias was involved in some intrigue with the Helots, and this was in fact so: he was promising them emancipation and citizenship if they would join in revolt and help him carry out his whole design. Even so, and even when some of the Helots informed on him, the Spartans would not believe what they were told and refused to make any move against him, following their usual practice in regard to their own people: they were always slow to come to any irrevocable decision concerning a Spartan citizen without incontestable evidence. But then finally, so it is said, the man who was to convey to Artabazus Pausanias' latest letter to the King turned informer. He was a man from Argilus, a former lover and devoted servant of Pausanias. The thought had struck him, to his consternation, that none of his predecessors as messengers had ever yet returned. So he made a counterfeit of Pausanias' seal to avoid discovery if his suspicion proved wrong or if Pausanias asked for the letter back to make some amendment, then opened the letter: as he had rather expected, he found that the contents included the instruction for his own murder.

133   He showed the letter to the ephors, and this at last gave them greater conviction, but they still wanted to hear for themselves some

evidence from Pausanias' own mouth. So a plan was laid. The man went as a suppliant to the temple at Taenarum and built himself there a cabin divided in two by a partition. He concealed some of the ephors in the inner part, and when Pausanias came to him and asked the reason for his supplication, they heard the truth of the whole story. The man protested at what was written in the letter about him and went into all the other details, complaining that he had never once endangered Pausanias in the missions he had run for him to the King, and his reward for that was to meet the same death as most of the other messengers. Pausanias admitted every word of this and asked him not to be angry at the situation: he raised him by the hand to assure him of his safety in leaving the temple, and told him to start his journey at once, so as not to delay the negotiations.

The ephors had heard every detail. For the moment they went 134 away, but with their now certain knowledge they moved to arrest Pausanias in the city. It is said that on the point of his arrest in the street Pausanias could read their purpose in the expression of one of the ephors approaching him, and that another out of friendship gave him a barely perceptible nod of warning. He then ran for immediate refuge to the temple of the goddess of the Bronze House—the precinct was nearby. To avoid exposure to the elements he entered a small room in the temple, and lay low. His pursuers lost him at first, but then took the roof off the building and, once they had found him inside and caught him there, walled up the doors, surrounded the place, and starved him to death. When they saw him on the point of expiry in his condition in that room, they carried him out of the temple still breathing, and he died as soon as he was brought outside. At first they intended to throw his body into the Caeadas ravine, their usual means of disposing of criminals, but then they changed their mind to bury him somewhere close by. Later the god at Delphi gave the Spartans an oracular response telling them to move Pausanias' grave to where he died (and he lies there now in the entrance to the precinct, as shown in the inscriptions on the gravestones). The oracle also declared that they had brought a curse on themselves by what they had done, and told them to give two bodies to the goddess of the Bronze House in requital for the one. So they had two bronze statues made and dedicated those as their requital for Pausanias.

Since the god himself had decreed the curse, the Athenians coun- 135 tered the Spartans with the demand that they should drive it out.

Now the Spartan investigation into Pausanias' intrigue with the Persians produced evidence to implicate Themistocles also, and they sent an embassy to Athens to make this charge and to demand that he should meet the same punishment. The Athenians agreed, but as Themistocles had been ostracized and was living in Argos (and making frequent visits to other parts of the Peloponnese), with the willing collaboration of the Spartans they sent a joint posse of officers to track him down: their orders were to arrest him wherever they found him and bring him back.

136   Themistocles had forewarning, and made his escape from the Peloponnese to Corcyra, where he had the status of a benefactor. But the Corcyraeans said that they could not harbour him for fear of incurring the hostility of Sparta and Athens, and conveyed him to the mainland opposite. Constantly pursued by the posse of officers who were following information about his movements, he was forced in desperation at one point to seek lodging at the house of Admetus, king of the Molossians, who was no friend of his. Admetus was not at home, but Themistocles presented himself as a suppliant to his wife, and she instructed him to take their child in his arms and sit down at the hearth. When Admetus returned shortly afterwards Themistocles revealed who he was, and said that even if he had once opposed a request Admetus had made of the Athenians, this did not justify retaliation now that he was in exile. That would be to victimize him when he was in a much enfeebled state, and the only noble revenge was that fairly taken on equals. He added that his own opposition to Admetus had been on a matter of business and not a question of life or death: whereas if Admetus were to hand him over (he explained by whom and for what he was being pursued) he would be denying him the safety of his life.

137   Admetus listened, then raised Themistocles by the hand together with his own son from where he was sitting with the boy in his arms, the most powerful form of supplication. Not long afterwards the Spartan and Athenian officers arrived. For all their lengthy protestations Admetus refused to hand over Themistocles, but, since he wished to make his way to the King of Persia, sent him across on foot to Pydna on the Aegean coast, a town in the kingdom of Alexander. Here he found a merchant ship setting sail for Ionia, and went on board: but the ship was driven by a storm to the Athenian naval station blockading Naxos. He was unknown to the others on the ship, but, fearful of what might otherwise happen, he explained to the

captain who he was and why he was on the run. He told the captain that if he refused to save his life he would say that he had been bribed to take him on board; his safety depended on no one leaving the ship before the voyage resumed; if he agreed, there would be ample recompense. The captain did as he was asked, and after riding at anchor off the Athenian station for a day and a night eventually put in to Ephesus. Themistocles took care of the captain with a gift of money (after his flight funds had reached him from friends in Athens and from the deposits he had left in safe keeping in Argos). He then travelled inland accompanied by one of the Persians who lived on the coast, and sent a letter to King Artaxerxes, the son of Xerxes, who had recently succeeded to the throne. In this letter he declared: 'I, Themistocles, have come to you. I am the man who has done your house greater harm than any other of the Greeks, for as long as I was forced to defend myself against your father's invasion: but I also did you yet greater benefit when I was in safety and your father in danger during his retreat. A debt of gratitude is owed me' (and here he mentioned the message he had sent from Salamis of an impending Greek withdrawal, and his agency—this was a false pretence—in preventing the destruction of the Hellespont bridges): 'and now I am here with the ability to do you great service, and persecuted by the Greeks for the friendship I feel for you. Give me a year, and then I shall explain to you in person why I have come.'

It is said that the King was impressed by his determination, and 138 told him to do as he proposed. In this intervening year Themistocles learnt all that he could of the Persian language and the way of life in the country. He presented himself after the year was over, and became a man of importance at the King's court and more influential than any Greek had yet been. This was due to his previous reputation, to the hope he held out of enslaving Greece under the King, and most of all to the constant evidence he gave of the quality of his mind.

Themistocles was indeed a man who displayed beyond doubt, and more than any other, natural genius to a quite exceptional and awesome degree. Through the pure application of his own intelligence, and without the aid of any briefing or debriefing, he was a consummate judge of the needs of the moment at very short notice, and supreme in conjecturing the future, more accurate than any in his forecast of events as they would actually happen. He had the gift of explaining clearly all that he himself undertook, and was not lacking in competent judgement on matters outside his experience: and he foresaw better than any the possible advantage and disadvantage in a yet uncertain future. In summary, the intuitive power of his mind and the speed of his preliminary thought gave Themistocles an unrivalled ability to improvise what was needed at any time.

He died of an illness: though some say that he took his own life with poison, realizing that he could not fulfil his promises to the King. However that may be, there is a monument to him in the marketplace of Magnesia in Asia, where he had been governor. The King had given him Magnesia for his bread (which brought him revenue of fifty talents a year), Lampsacus for his wine (considered then the best wine district of all), and Myus for his meat. His family say that at his own request his bones were brought back home and buried secretly in Attica, without the knowledge of the Athenians—burial of a man exiled for treason was illegal.

So ended the stories of Pausanias of Sparta and Themistocles of Athens, the two most eminent Greeks of their time.

139   On their first embassy, then, the Spartans made these demands for the expulsion of the accursed and met with similar counter-demands. Thereafter they sent a series of further embassies to Athens, demanding withdrawal from Potidaea and the restoration of independence to Aegina. Above all, and in the clearest possible terms, they repeated that there would be no war if the Athenians repealed the decree which had denied the Megarians access to the ports in the Athenian empire and to the Athenian market itself. The Athenians rejected the other demands and would not repeal the decree, citing the Megarians' encroachment on both the sacred ground and the neutral strip, and their harbouring of absconded slaves. Finally the last ambassadors arrived from Sparta: they were Rhamphias, Melesippus, and Agesandrus. They made no mention of the previous themes, but simply said this: 'The Spartans wish there to be peace, and there would be peace if you returned their independence to the Greeks.' The Athenians called an assembly and opened the debate, deciding to discuss the whole issue once and for all and give their final answer. Many came forward to speak and opinions were ranged on both sides—for war, and for the repeal of the Megarian decree to remove an impediment to peace. Among the speakers was Pericles the son of Xanthippus, the leading Athenian at that time and a man of the greatest ability both with words and in action. He came forward and gave his advice as follows:

140   'Athenians, my opinion remains that to which I have always held: we must not yield to the Peloponnesians. I recognize, though, that

the spirit which persuades men to war can change when the action is on them, and that resolution varies with fortune. My advice too is very much the same as I have given in the past, and I can see that I must repeat it now: and if some of you are convinced I ask you to maintain your support for the policy which we agree through any reverse we might suffer—or else claim no credit for clear thinking when we meet with success. Events can take as stupid a course as human designs: that is why we blame chance for all that runs counter to our calculation.

'The Spartans' intentions against us have been clear for some time, and yet more so now. The terms of the treaty are that in cases of dispute both sides should go to arbitration, retaining their respective holdings in the interim. They have never yet asked for arbitration nor accepted our offer of it. They want to settle their grievances by war rather than discussion, and they are here now not to pursue complaints but to deliver an ultimatum. They tell us to withdraw from Potidaea, to restore independence to Aegina, and to repeal the Megarian decree: and now these last ambassadors are come here to demand that we return their independence to the other Greeks as well. None of you should think that we would be going to war over a small matter if we refuse to repeal the Megarian decree. They make a great pretence that its repeal would prevent war, but I would not want you to be left with any suspicion that you went to war for a trifling cause. This "small matter" involves the whole confirmation of your resolve, and the test of it. If you give in to them on this, they will assume that fear prompted the concession and immediately impose some greater demand: stand firm on this, and you will make it clear to them that they would do better to treat you as equals. So make up your minds here and now, either to submit before any 141 harm is done, or, if it is to be war (and in my view that is the best course), to make no concessions for reasons either great or small, and to refuse to live in constant fear for our own possessions. Any claim enforced by equals on equals without recourse to arbitration, no matter whether the issue is of the greatest or the least significance, amounts still to enslavement.

'Listen now while I detail the resources for war on either side, from which you can see that we shall be at no disadvantage. The Peloponnesians work their own land, and have no private or public wealth. Then they have no experience of lengthy overseas wars, as their poverty has restricted their warfare to short campaigns against each other. Such people cannot regularly crew ships or send out land armies: this would involve absence from their own properties and the meeting of their own expenses—and in any case they would be denied the freedom of the sea. Wars are sustained by accumulated capital, not by enforced contributions. Men who work their own land are more willing to do war service with their bodies than with their substance: their body is a known quantity which they trust will survive the dangers intact, but they have no guarantee that their money will not be exhausted before the end, especially if, as is likely, they find the war prolonging itself beyond their expectation. In a single pitched battle the Peloponnesians and their allies are capable of resisting the whole of Greece, but they are incapable of maintaining a war against an opposition which differs from them in kind: as long, that is, as they continue without a central deliberative forum, for lack of which they cannot take any immediate decisive action, and as long as all the various tribal groups in a miscellaneous confederacy have equal votes, so each promotes its own concern—a system unlikely to produce any effective results. And as you would expect some are all for vengeance on some enemy of theirs, others are all for minimal damage to their own interests. Their infrequent meetings allow little time for consideration of any common issue, and for the most part they carry on with their own business. Each thinks that their inertia will do no harm, and that it is someone else's responsibility rather than theirs to make some provision for their future: the result is that with all individually sharing this same notion they fail as a body to see their common interest going to ruin.

142   'The most important point is that they will be hampered by lack of money. It will take them time to raise the funds, and that means delay: but the opportunities of war do not wait. And we should not be frightened either of forts built in our territory, or of their navy. It is hard enough for a rival city to establish border-forts even in peacetime, and of course harder still in enemy territory and with our own fortifications no less of a threat to them. If they do build a fort, yes, they could do some harm with raids on part of our land and as a point of reception for deserting slaves, but not sufficient to prevent us sailing to their land and building our own forts there, then defending them with our navy, which is where our strength lies. We have more experience of land operations from our naval base than they have of naval operations from their land base. They will not easily acquire proficiency in seamanship. Even you, who have been

practising since directly after the Persian War, have not yet fully mastered it. So how can men who are farmers, not sailors, achieve anything of any consequence, particularly when they will be denied even their training by the large fleet we shall always have blockading them? A blockade of only a few ships might embolden them to put numbers above inexperience and take their chances: but a full fleet barring them from the sea will keep them inactive, the lack of practice will diminish their skill, and the lack of skill will make them more timid. Seamanship is an art, no different from any other art: it does not admit of casual practice secondary to some other occupation, but demands no other occupation secondary to itself.

'If they do touch the funds at Olympia or Delphi and try to win over our foreign sailors with higher pay, that would be a serious danger if it were not the case that we can still match them with citizens and metics crewing the ships. But this is the case: and, most important of all, we have citizen captains and petty officers in greater numbers and of higher quality than in all the rest of Greece combined. And given the risks they would run, none of our foreign sailors would choose to switch sides for a few days of extra pay, when the price is exile from their own homes and the greater likelihood of defeat. 143

'Such is broadly my view of the Peloponnesian position. Our own position, it seems to me, is both free of the weaknesses I have pointed out in theirs and also has strengths which they cannot equal. If they invade our country by land, we shall sail against theirs: and there will be no equality of effect between the devastation of even a part of the Peloponnese and that of the whole of Attica. They will not be able to acquire more land without fighting for it, whereas we have plenty of other land in the islands and on the mainland—control of the sea is a paramount advantage. Consider: if we were an island, could any be more invulnerable than us? So we should now think ourselves into the closest approximation to islanders, ready to abandon our land and our homes, but keeping close guard on the sea and our city. We must not let anger at our losses draw us into a pitched battle with the Peloponnesians, who far outnumber us. If we win such a battle we shall have to fight them again in no smaller numbers, and if we fail we shall lose our allies too: they are the source of our strength, but they will not acquiesce in our control if we are short of the means to enforce it. Do not mourn the loss of homes and land, but save your mourning for the loss of lives. Property is the product, not the producer of men. If I thought I could persuade you, I would be telling you to go out and destroy your property with your own hands, to show the Peloponnesians that there will be no surrender on this account.

144   'I have many other grounds to encourage the confidence that you will win through, as long as you agree not to extend the empire while the war is on and not to undertake additional risks of your own making—I am more afraid of our own mistakes than of any enemy strategies. But I shall speak again about all this in detail when it is time for action. For now, we should send back the Spartan ambassadors with this answer. We shall admit the Megarians to our market and our ports if the Spartans for their part will conduct no more expulsions of foreigners involving either us or our allies (since nothing in the treaty prohibits either their action or ours); we shall return their independence to the cities in our control if they were independent when we made the treaty, and at such time as the Spartans too restore their own cities to a true independence allowing them individual choice of government rather than conformity to the Spartans' interest; we are willing to go to arbitration under the treaty; we shall not start a war, but if others do we shall defend ourselves. This is a fair answer, and the proper answer for our city to make. You must realize that war is inevitable, and the more willing we are to accept it the less intense will be our enemies' attack. Remember too that for states and individuals alike the greatest dangers give rise to the greatest glory. When our fathers took their stand against the Persians they did not start from resources such as ours, but they abandoned even what little they did possess and then, more by resolve than good fortune, more by courage than strength of armament, they drove back the barbarians and set our city on its path to greatness. We must not fall short of our fathers: we must resist our enemies with every means in our power, and strive to hand on to future generations a city no less great.'

145   Such was the speech of Pericles. The Athenians thought his advice the best, and voted as he urged them. On his motion, the answer they gave to the Spartans followed his proposals in detail and in general: the Athenians would take no orders from Sparta, but were prepared to have the grievances settled by arbitration under the treaty on fair and equal terms. The Spartan ambassadors left for home, and there were no further embassies.

146   These then were the grievances and disputes which arose on either side before the outbreak of war, taking their immediate start

from the affair of Epidamnus and Corcyra. During this time the two sides still maintained communication and travel from one to the other without the formality of heralds—but not without misgivings. What was happening amounted to the collapse of the treaty and a reason for war.

BOOK TWO

1 There follows now the actual outbreak of the war between the Athenians and the Peloponnesians and their respective allies. From this point on there was no communication between the two sides except through heralds, and once started the war was unremitting. My account sets out the events in chronological order, by summers and winters.

2 The Thirty Years Treaty agreed after the conquest of Euboea lasted for fourteen years. In the fifteenth year, when Chrysis was in her forty-eighth year as priestess at Argos, Aenesias was ephor in Sparta, and Pythodorus had two more months of his archonship in Athens, in the sixth month after the battle at Potidaea, and at the beginning of spring, in the first watch of the night an armed force of slightly over three hundred Thebans entered Plataea, a city in Boeotia allied to Athens. They were led by the Boeotarchs Pythangelus the son of Phyleides and Diemporus the son of Onetorides. The Thebans were invited and the gates opened to them by a group of Plataeans, Naucleides and his party, who for motives of personal power wished to eliminate their opponents among the citizens and align the city with Thebes. Their agent in this was one of the most influential men in Thebes, Eurymachus the son of Leontiades.

Plataea had always been hostile to Thebes, so the Thebans, recognizing the imminence of war, wanted to make a pre-emptive strike and seize the place while the peace still held and there was not yet an open state of war. This made it easier for them to enter undetected, as no guard had been set. They grounded their arms in the market-square, but instead of getting straight to work and making for the houses of the opposition, as urged by the collaborators who had invited them, they decided to make reassuring announcements with the preferred aim of bringing the city to a friendly agreement. Their herald proclaimed that any who wished to join them in the ancestral alliance of all Boeotia should pile their arms with theirs: and they thought that the city would readily be won over in this way.

3 When the Plataeans became aware of Thebans within their walls and the sudden occupation of their city, they were terrified and, unable to see them in the darkness, thought the invaders much more numerous than they were. They therefore came to terms and accepted

the proposals without resistance, especially as the Thebans were offering no violence to anyone. However, somehow in the course of the negotiations they came to realize that the number of Thebans was not large, and they reckoned that if they set on them they could easily overpower them: the majority of the Plataeans had no wish to defect from Athens. So they decided to make the attempt. They gathered together by digging through the party walls between their houses, to avoid being seen on the move in the streets; they dragged carts without their draught-animals into the streets to act as a barricade; and they made all other arrangements which seemed suitable in the circumstances. When they were as prepared as they could be, they waited until the last of night just before dawn, then came out of their houses against the Thebans. They wanted to attack in darkness to deny the Thebans the greater confidence and the equality of a fight in daylight: by night the Thebans would be more frightened and disadvantaged by the Plataeans' familiarity with their own city. So they made a sudden attack and quickly engaged at close quarters.

As soon as the Thebans realized that they had fallen into a trap, 4 they closed in on themselves and began to beat off the attacks wherever they came. Two or three times they drove the Plataeans back, but then as the onslaught continued with a huge din, joined by the women and slaves shouting and screaming from the roofs and pelting them with stones and tiles, and with heavy rain falling throughout the night, they panicked and turned to flee. They went running through the city, but the streets were dark and muddy (it was at the end of the month and there was no moon) and most had no idea of the routes to safety, whereas their pursuers knew how to prevent their escape: so the majority met their death. The only gate open was the one through which they had entered, but a Plataean secured it by ramming a spear-butt into the crossbar in place of the pin, so this exit too was now blocked. As they were chased through the city some of them climbed the wall and jumped down outside (most to their deaths), some found an unguarded gate where a woman gave them an axe and, unseen so far, they hacked through the crossbar and just a few of them got out before they were quickly discovered, and others were killed here and there throughout the city. The largest and most concerted group of them blundered into a big building which formed part of the city wall, and the door facing them happened to be open: they had thought this door was a gate giving direct access to the outside. When the Plataeans saw them trapped, they discussed whether they should set fire to the building and incinerate them where they were, or deal with them in some other way. In the end these Thebans and the other survivors still wandering up and down the city came to terms with the Plataeans, agreeing to surrender themselves and their weapons unconditionally. This then was how their enterprise turned out for the Thebans in Plataea.

5 The rest of the Theban army, detailed to arrive in full force while it was still night to support the invading party in case anything went wrong, were already on their way when the news reached them of what had happened, and they hurried to the rescue. Plataea is about eight miles from Thebes, and the rainfall in the night made the going slower for them: the river Asopus was in flood, and not easy to cross. Marching through the downpour and having trouble crossing the river they arrived too late, when their men in Plataea were either dead or captured and held alive. When the Thebans realized the situation they turned their attention to the Plataeans outside the city: there were men and equipment out in the fields, as was bound to be the case when danger struck unexpectedly in peacetime. They wanted to hold any they could capture as hostages for exchange with their own men inside, if indeed any had been taken alive. This was their intention, but while they were still discussing it the Plataeans, suspecting that something like this would happen and fearful for their people outside, sent out a herald to the Thebans denouncing as an impious crime the action they had taken in the attempt to seize their city when there was a treaty in force, and warning them not to harm their people or property outside. Otherwise, they said, they would retaliate by killing the men they had captured alive: but if the Thebans withdrew from their land they would return the prisoners to them. This is the Theban account, and they claim that the Plataeans swore this on oath. The Plataeans disagree: they say that they did not promise to return the prisoners immediately, but only after talks to explore terms, and they deny that they swore an oath. However that may be, the Thebans did withdraw from Plataean territory without doing any harm. The Plataeans quickly brought inside all that was out in the country, then immediately put the prisoners to death. The number of these captives was a hundred and eighty, including Eurymachus, the agent with whom the traitors had dealt.

6 This done, they sent a messenger to Athens, released the bodies to the Thebans under truce, and made arrangements in the city as they thought best in response to the circumstances. News of the situation

at Plataea had quickly reached Athens, and the Athenians immediately arrested all Boeotians in Attica and sent a herald to Plataea with instructions to tell the Plataeans to do nothing drastic in regard to the Theban prisoners until they themselves had come to a decision about them. The Athenians had not yet received the message that the men were dead. The first messenger had set out as soon as the Thebans entered Plataea, and the second shortly after their defeat and capture. The Athenians had no knowledge of the subsequent events, so were dispatching their herald in ignorance: on his arrival he found that the men had already been killed. After this the Athenians marched to Plataea, brought in supplies of food, and left a garrison installed, and evacuated the least fit of the men together with the women and children.

Now that the treaty had overtly been broken by the action at 7 Plataea, the Athenians began making preparations for war, and so did the Spartans and their allies. Both sides had plans to send embassies to the King of Persia and elsewhere in the barbarian world where they hoped they might gain support, and both tried to win the alliance of cities outside their sphere of influence. The Spartans required their adherents in Italy and Sicily to build ships in numbers proportionate to the size of each city, which added to those they already had in Greece would bring the total number of their ships to five hundred. These cities were also required to get ready a specified sum of money: they were to take no further action until all preparations were complete, and in the meantime to allow the Athenians access only in a single ship. For their part the Athenians reviewed their existing alliance, and in particular sent embassies to the places outlying the Peloponnese—Corcyra, Cephallenia, Acarnania, Zacynthus—realizing that the consolidation of support there would enable them to reduce the Peloponnese by encirclement.

There was nothing small-scale in the intentions of either side. 8 Both were eager for war, and with good reason: all men are particularly keen at the start of an enterprise, and at that time there were many young men both in the Peloponnese and in Athens who had no experience of war and welcomed their chance of involvement. All the rest of Greece was agog at this clash of the leading states. Many prophecies were bandied about, and oracle-mongers were full of their verses both in the cities preparing for war and elsewhere. And only a short while before this Delos was shaken by the first earthquake on the island in Greek memory: it was said and believed that this was a sign of things to come. Any other phenomena of a similar kind were sought out and scrutinized.

The general feeling among the Greeks was very much in favour of the Spartans, especially since they had proclaimed that they were liberating Greece. Every individual and every city was keen to take what part they could in supporting the Spartans in both speech and action: and every man thought that things had come to a standstill if he was not personally involved. Such was the anger that most felt for the Athenians, some looking for release from their empire, others fearing their inclusion.

9   These, then, were the preparations made and the attitudes adopted when they started out. The allies with which each side entered the war were as follows. Allied to Sparta were: all Peloponnesians south of the Isthmus except the Argives and the Achaeans (these were neutral: Pellene was the only Achaean city to join the war at the beginning, but later all the rest of Achaea took part also); outside the Peloponnese, Megara, Boeotia, Locris, Phocis, Ambracia, Leucas, and Anactorium. Ships were provided by Corinth, Megara, Sicyon, Pellene, Elis, Ambracia, and Leucas, and cavalry by Boeotia, Phocis, and Locris: the other states provided infantry. Such was the Spartan alliance. The Athenian allies were: Chios, Lesbos, Plataea, the Messenians in Naupactus, most of the Acarnanians, Corcyra, and Zacynthus; and the tribute-paying cities in the various regional groups, coastal Caria, the neighbouring Dorians, Ionia, the Hellespont, the Thraceward district, the islands to the east between the Peloponnese and Crete, and all the Cyclades except Melos and Thera. Of these Chios, Lesbos, and Corcyra provided ships, and the others infantry and money. These were the alliances and resources for war on each side.

10   Immediately after the affair at Plataea the Spartans sent word round the Peloponnese and their allies outside requiring the cities to get ready troops and appropriate provisions for a foreign expedition, with the purpose of invading Attica. When all had made their preparations, each city sent two-thirds of their total forces at the time appointed for their rendezvous at the Isthmus. When the whole armament was gathered there, the Spartan king Archidamus, who was the commander of the expedition, called together the generals and the chief and most influential officials from all of the cities and made this address to them:

11   'Peloponnesians and allies, our fathers undertook many campaigns in the Peloponnese itself and outside, and the older among us are not

without our experience of wars. Even so, we have never yet set out
in greater force than this: this campaign is against a very powerful
city, and our army is at its largest and best. We must not, then, show
ourselves inferior to our fathers or fall short of our own reputation.
All Greece is excited by this enterprise and is watching it intently,
willing us to succeed in our aims—such is the hatred of Athens. So,
though you may think we are invading in massive force with every
confidence that the enemy will not engage us in battle, that is no
reason for taking any less precaution on our march: but in every
contingent officer and soldier alike should constantly expect danger
to his own section. War is unpredictable. Most attacks are sudden,
springing out of anger: and often the smaller force, focused by fear,
has worsted superior numbers caught complacently unprepared.
In enemy country there is constant need for both confidence and
fear—a brave spirit for battle, but also practical precautions inspired
by fear. This way lies the greatest courage in attack and the greatest
security under attack.

'The city we are coming against is far from incapable of defending
itself. It is supremely equipped in every way, so we must have every
expectation that they will engage us in battle. Even if they are not
already deployed pending our arrival, they will surely deploy when
they see us in their territory, ravaging their land and destroying their
property. Anger enters all men when they have in front of their own
eyes the immediate sight of damage they have never seen before: and
when reason retreats passion advances as the determinant of action.
This is more likely to happen with the Athenians than with any
others, since they presume the right to empire and expect to invade
and ravage others' territory rather than see it done to their own.
Remember, then, that we are fighting a great city; and remember that
on the result depends, for good or ill, the ultimate reputation we shall
bring on our ancestors and ourselves. So follow your leaders; make
discipline and security your absolute priorities; and be quick to
respond to orders. Best and safest is when a large army is seen as a
single disciplined body.'

After making this address Archidamus dismissed the meeting. 12
His first act thereafter was to send Melesippus the son of Diacritus,
a Spartiate, to Athens, in case the Athenians might be that much
readier to submit when they saw the Peloponnesians already on their
way. But they refused him entry to the city, let alone access to any
public body: a motion proposed by Pericles had been carried earlier,

that they should not receive any herald or embassy from the Spartans once they had mobilized their army. So they sent Melesippus back without a hearing, and ordered him to be outside their borders that very day: if the Spartans wished to make any representations in future, they should return to their own country before sending their embassies. And they sent escorts with him to prevent any contact with others. When Melesippus reached the frontier and was about to part from them, he said just this before going on his way: 'This day will be the beginning of great disasters for the Greeks.' On Melesippus' return to the camp and the realization that the Athenians would still not give way, Archidamus then finally set out with his army and advanced towards Athenian territory. The Boeotians, who had sent their contingent, including cavalry, to join the main Peloponnesian force, marched with the rest of their army to Plataea and ravaged its land.

13   When the Peloponnesians were still gathering at the Isthmus and had started on their way, without yet invading Attica, Pericles the son of Xanthippus, who was one of the ten Athenian generals, recognizing that the invasion was imminent, suspected that since Archidamus happened to be a guest-friend of his he might possibly spare his own estate from devastation—either as a personal favour or on Spartan instructions to embarrass him, just as they had demanded the expulsion of the accursed on his account. Pericles therefore declared in the assembly that Archidamus was his guest-friend, but that this would have no ill effect on the city; if it turned out that the enemy would not devastate his own estate and properties in the same way as others', he would relinquish them to state ownership, and there should be no suspicion of him in this context.

For the present situation he gave the same advice as he had before. They should prepare for war and bring in their property from the country; they should not go out to battle, but come inside the city and defend it; they should maintain their fleet, which was where their strength lay, equipped and ready; and they should keep a firm hand on their allies. Athenian power, he told them, depended on the revenue received from their allies: and wars were mostly won by sound strategy and financial reserves. They should take confidence, he said, from their finances. Apart from other revenue, the city's annual income in tribute from the allies was by and large six hundred talents; there still remained on the Acropolis a sum of six thousand talents in coined silver (at its highest this capital reserve had stood at nine thousand seven hundred talents, from which had been drawn the expenditure on the Propylaea of the Acropolis and the other buildings, and on Potidaea); in addition there was uncoined gold and silver in the form of private and public dedications, all the sacred vessels for processions and games, the Persian spoils, and other such-like, to the value of at least five hundred talents. He included also the substantial wealth available to them from the other sanctuaries: and if all other means were absolutely exhausted, they could use the gold plates which clothed the goddess herself (he confirmed that the statue was clad in forty talents' weight of refined gold, all of it detachable). These treasures, he said, could be used for the preservation of the city, as long as they were subsequently replaced in equal or greater value.

Such was the encouragement he gave them in matters of finance. As for military resources, he said they had thirteen thousand hoplites, apart from the sixteen thousand in the garrison-posts and deployed along the fortifications. (This was the number on guard duty in the first years of the war, whenever the enemy invaded: they were drawn from the oldest and the youngest age groups, and from the metics who could serve as hoplites. The length of the wall from Phalerum to the circuit-wall of the city was four miles; the garrisoned part of this circuit-wall was a little under five miles long, and there was also an unguarded section between the Long Wall and the Phaleric Wall; the Long Walls to the Peiraeus were four and a half miles in length, and the outer wall was guarded; the total extent of the wall surrounding Peiraeus and Mounychia was six and a half miles, the garrisoned section comprising half of this length.) He also reported that they had twelve hundred cavalry, including mounted archers; sixteen hundred foot-archers; and three hundred seaworthy triremes. These were the resources—those numbers or more in each category—available to the Athenians when they entered the war and the first Peloponnesian invasion was imminent. To this account Pericles added more of his usual arguments to convince them that they would win through in the war.

The Athenians were persuaded by what they heard, and began to 14 bring in from the country their children, their wives, and all their domestic goods, even removing the woodwork from their houses. Their flocks and draught-animals they sent across to Euboea and the islands off the coast. This upheaval was hard for them, as most had always been accustomed to living in the country.

15   This way of life had, from very early times, been more characteristic of the Athenians than of others. In the time of Cecrops and the
first kings down to Theseus, the population of Attica was in separate
cities, each with its own town hall and officials: except when some
danger threatened they did not convene for joint consultations with
the king, but each managed its own affairs and determined its own
policy—and indeed there were occasions when some of them went
to war against the king, for example the Eleusinians with Eumolpus
against Erechtheus. But when Theseus came to be king, with his
combination of power and intelligence he reformed the country. In
particular he dissolved the councils and magistracies in the other cities and centralized all government in what is now the city of Athens,
establishing a single council-chamber and town hall. Each retained
the use of their own land as before, but he obliged them to treat
Athens as their capital, which with all now enrolled grew into the
great city which Theseus handed down to posterity. From him there
started the annual festival of the Union which to the present day the
Athenians still organize at public expense in honour of Athena.

        In earlier times the present Acropolis was the city, together with
an area below it broadly to the south. The evidence for this is as
follows. The oldest temples both of Athena and of other gods are on
the Acropolis itself, and those outside the Acropolis are mostly situated in this part of the city to the south—the temples of Olympian
Zeus, of Pythian Apollo, of Earth, and of Dionysus in the Marshes
(in whose honour the more ancient of the Dionysia are held on the
twelfth day of the month Anthesterion, a festival still observed also
by the Ionians of Athenian descent). There are other ancient temples
too in this area. Then there is the fountain now called Enneacrounos
(the Nine Spouts) after it was given that structure by the tyrants—its
earlier name, when the springs were still in the open, was Callirrhoe
(the Beautiful Fountain). Because of its proximity the Athenians in
the past used this spring on the most important occasions, and from
the old days there survives to the present time the custom of using
its water before marriages and in other religious ceremonies. Because
it was the site of the original settlement the Acropolis is even now
still called by the Athenians *Polis*, the City.

16   For long, then, the Athenians had lived in independent communities throughout the countryside of Attica, and this way of life continued after the political unification, with most Athenians of old and
their descendants down to the time of this war still being born in the

country and living where they were born. So it was not easy for them to uproot and move with their entire households, especially as they had only recently restored their properties after the Persian War. They were distressed and resentful at having to leave their homes and the shrines which had been in continuous use by their families from the old order before unification. They faced a change of life, and to each it was tantamount to exile from his own city.

When they did come into Athens, a few had their own houses or could lodge with friends or relations, but the majority set up home in the empty areas of the city and all the sanctuaries of gods and heroes except the Acropolis and the Eleusinium and any others which were securely locked. The area below the Acropolis known as the 'Pelargic' was under a curse prohibiting occupation, and there was also the tag-end of a Delphic oracle to the same effect, saying 'Best to let the Pelargic rest': but even so it was occupied in the immediate emergency. My view is that the oracle was fulfilled, but in the reverse of the general expectation. It was not the unlawful occupation which caused the disasters to the city, but the war which forced the occupation: without specific reference to the war the oracle was predicting that the area would never be occupied to a good end. Many established themselves even in the towers of the city walls, and anywhere else they could find. The city simply could not accommodate the influx, though eventually they shared out spaces along the Long Walls and in most of the Peiraeus, and people settled there.

Meanwhile they pressed ahead with preparations for the war, gathering allies and fitting out a hundred ships for an expedition against the Peloponnese. Such then was the state of readiness in Athens.

The Peloponnesian army advanced and reached Attica first at Oenoe, the point intended for the launch of their invasion. Here they encamped, and prepared to attack the wall with siege-engines and by other means. Oenoe, lying on the border between Attica and Boeotia, was a fortified place, used by the Athenians as a garrisoned frontier-post in time of war. Preparations for the assault and other delays kept them at Oenoe for some time. This brought severe criticism on Archidamus, who was already thought soft and over-friendly to the Athenians in the build-up to the war for his reluctance to endorse its enthusiastic prosecution: and then when the army was finally gathered, there was held against him the delay at the Isthmus, his slowness on the subsequent march, and particularly this hold-up at Oenoe. During this time the Athenians were bringing their property inside the city, and the Peloponnesians thought that without his procrastination they could have attacked quickly and caught everything still outside. This was the resentment felt by the army towards Archidamus when they were stalled at Oenoe. It is said that he was holding back in the expectation that the Athenians would make some concession while their land was still intact, and would not bear to allow its devastation before their eyes.

19   But when they had tried every means of assault on Oenoe and failed to take it, and there had been no diplomatic communication from Athens, then finally they set out from Oenoe and, about eighty days after the events in Plataea, well on in summer when the corn was ripe, they invaded Attica under the command of Archidamus the son of Zeuxidamus, king of Sparta.

On their first encampment they ravaged the territory of Eleusis and the Thriasian plain, and routed the Athenian cavalry near the lakes called Rheiti. They then advanced through Cropia, keeping Mount Aegaleos on their right, until they reached Acharnae, the largest of the districts of Attica called 'demes'. Here they settled, established their camp, and stayed for a considerable time ravaging the country.

20   It is said that Archidamus had an ulterior purpose in lingering in the Acharnae area with his army in battle order and not on this first invasion descending into the plain of Attica. His hope was that the Athenians, in a city brimming with young men and equipped for war as never before, might perhaps come out to battle rather than tolerate the sight of their land being devastated. So when they did not oppose him at Eleusis or the Thriasian plain, he tried again to tempt them out by this long occupation of Acharnae. He had two concurrent reasons for this policy. He considered the area a suitable position for an established camp, and his expectation was that the Acharnians, who with three thousand hoplites formed a large part of the citizen body, would not stand by to see the destruction of their own property, but would incite the rest of the city to join them in battle. And if the Athenians did not after all come out to oppose this invasion, then that of itself emboldened future invasions to ravage the plain of Attica and advance right up to the city. The thought was that the loss of their own would make the Acharnians less keen to risk their lives for others' land, giving rise to a division of policy. This was Archidamus' plan while he stayed in Acharnae.

As long as the invading army remained in the area of Eleusis and 21
the Thriasian plain, the Athenians did in fact have some hope that
they would not advance any closer. They remembered that fourteen
years earlier the then king of Sparta, Pleistoanax the son of Pausanias,
had invaded Attica with a Peloponnesian army as far as Eleusis and
Thria, but had then turned back without advancing any further (this
was the cause of his exile from Sparta, as he was thought to have been
bribed to retreat). But when they saw the army in Acharnae, less than
seven miles from the city, this was beyond their tolerance. Their land
was being devastated in open view, something which the younger
men had never seen before, and the older men only in the Persian
Wars. Naturally enough, they regarded this with horror, and they
thought, especially the young among them, that they could not
simply stand by but should go out on the attack. Groups gathered in
violent dispute, some demanding an attack, others—the minority—
arguing against. Oracle-mongers chanted all manner of predictions,
eagerly snapped up by each man according to his preference. The
Acharnians were the most insistent on going out to attack: they considered themselves a significant part of the Athenian body, and it was
their land that was being devastated. The city was in every kind of
turmoil, and the people turned their anger on Pericles: forgetting all
his previous advice, they accused him of cowardice in not doing what
a general should and leading them out to battle, and they held him
responsible for all they were going through.

Seeing that their resentment at the present situation was creating 22
a dangerous political mood, yet confident that he was right in his
policy of non-engagement, Pericles would not hold any assembly or
other meeting, for fear that a gathering informed more by passion
than by reason would make the wrong decisions: but he kept the city
under guard, and as calm as he could manage. He did, though, constantly send out cavalry to prevent advance squadrons from the
invading force reaching and damaging the farmland near the city.
There was a skirmish at Phrygii when one section of the Athenian
cavalry and the Thessalians with them fought the Boeotian cavalry
and had the better of it until the hoplites came up in support of the
Bocotians. Then the Thessalians and Athenians were turned back
and suffered a few casualties, but recovered the bodies that same day
without a truce: on the following day the Peloponnesians set up a
trophy. This Thessalian assistance came to the Athenian side under
the terms of their old alliance: contingents arrived from Larisa,

Pharsalus, Peirasia, Crannon, Pyrasus, Gyrton, and Pherae. Their commanders were Polymedes and Aristonous from Larisa (one from each party in the city), and Menon from Pharsalus: and there were commanding officers also from each of the other individual cities.

23   Since the Athenians did not come out to meet them in battle, the Peloponnesians moved on from Acharnae and set about laying waste some of the other demes between Mount Parnes and Mount Brilessus.

While they were still in the country the Athenians sent out round the Peloponnese the hundred ships which they had been fitting out, with a thousand hoplites and four hundred archers on board: the generals in command were Carcinus the son of Xenotimus, Proteas the son of Epicles, and Socrates the son of Antigenes. So this fleet set sail on its expedition, and meanwhile the Peloponnesians, after remaining in Attica for as long as their provisions lasted, went back through Boeotia, taking a different route from that of their invasion. As they passed Oropus they devastated the area known as Graea, inhabited by the Oropians who are subjects of Athens. On their return to the Peloponnese they dispersed to their own cities.

24   When the Peloponnesians had withdrawn the Athenians established garrison-posts to keep guard by land and sea, a guard which they would maintain throughout the war. And they passed a decree reserving one thousand talents from the monies on the Acropolis to be set aside and not spent. The finance for the war was to come from the remaining funds, and they prescribed the death penalty for anyone who suggested or put to the vote a proposal to touch this reserve for any purpose other than the need to repel the enemy if they brought a naval force to attack the city. Together with this fund they set aside their hundred best triremes each year (and appointed trierarchs for them), to be used only in association with that money and in that same emergency, should it arise.

25   The hundred Athenian ships on the expedition round the Peloponnese had been supplemented by fifty ships from Corcyra and a few more from other allies in that region. They did damage at several points on the coast and in particular made a landing at Methone in Laconia and attacked its weak and ungarrisoned wall. There happened to be a Spartiate, Brasidas the son of Tellis, in command of a patrol in this area. When he learnt what was happening he went to the aid of the townspeople with a hundred hoplites. The Athenian forces were dispersed across the countryside or concentrating on the

wall, and Brasidas charged straight through them and burst into Methone: he lost a few of his men in this charge, but he saved the town. For this daring act he was the first in the war to receive public commendation in Sparta.

The Athenians set out to sea and sailed on round the coast. Putting in at Pheia in Elis, they ravaged the land for two days and defeated in battle a picked force of three hundred Eleans who came out to defend it from the Vale of Elis and the dependent territory under immediate attack. When a violent wind sprang up and caught them exposed in a place without anchorage, the majority re-embarked and sailed round the promontory known as Fish Point to the harbour at Pheia, while the Messenians and some others who could not board the ships went on by land and captured Pheia. On their return later the ships picked up these men and put back to sea, abandoning Pheia: by this time the main Elean army had come up in defence. The Athenians sailed on along the coast to other places and ravaged them.

At about the same time the Athenians sent out thirty ships to 26 cruise off Locris and keep a guard on Euboea: the general in command was Cleopompus the son of Cleinias. In a series of landings he ravaged parts of coastal Locris, captured Thronium and took hostages from the population, and at Alope defeated the Locrians who came to do battle for it.

In this same summer the Athenians expelled the Aeginetans and 27 their whole families, children and wives, from Aegina, alleging that they bore major responsibility for bringing the war on Athens. Aegina lies close to the Peloponnese, and it seemed a sensible precaution to occupy the island with their own people sent there as front-line colonists: these settlers were sent to Aegina shortly afterwards. In virtue of their hostility to Athens and the help they had given Sparta at the time of the earthquake and the Helot revolt, the Spartans gave the dispossessed Aeginetans a home and land to cultivate in Thyrea, a territory reaching down to the sea on the borders of Argos and Laconia. Some of the Aeginetans took up home there, and others were dispersed throughout the rest of Greece.

During the same summer, at the beginning of the lunar month 28 (which seems to be the only time at which such a phenomenon can happen), there was an eclipse of the sun in the afternoon: the sun took on a crescent shape before returning full, and some stars could be seen.

29   In this summer too the Athenians appointed Nymphodorus the
son of Pythes, a native of Abdera, as their consular representative
there, and called him to Athens. They had previously regarded him
as an enemy, but his sister was married to the king of Thrace, Sitalces
the son of Teres, and they wanted Sitalces to become their ally:
Nymphodorus had great influence with him.

     This Teres, the father of Sitalces, created the great Odrysian king-
dom and extended it further into the rest of Thrace, though a large
part of Thrace remains independent. There is no connection between
this Teres and the Tereus who took Procne, the daughter of Pandion,
from Athens as his wife. They did not even come from the same
'Thrace'. Tereus lived in Daulia, now part of the region called
Phocis but then inhabited by Thracians, and it was in this country
that the women committed their crime on Itys (and many poets when
speaking of the nightingale have called it 'the Daulian bird'). Further,
it is reasonable to suppose that Pandion would have arranged a
marriage alliance for his daughter at this proximity, with a view to
mutual benefit, rather than with the Odrysians at a distance of many
days' journey. Teres (not even the same name as Tereus) was the
first powerful king of the Odrysians, and it was his son Sitalces
whom the Athenians sought as an ally, looking to him to help them
subdue the towns of the Thraceward region, and Perdiccas.

     So Nymphodorus came to Athens, effected an alliance with
Sitalces and Athenian citizenship for his son Sadocus, and undertook
to bring the war in Thrace to an end: he would persuade Sitalces to
send the Athenians a Thracian force of cavalry and peltasts. He also
reconciled Perdiccas to the Athenians and persuaded them to give
him back Therme. Perdiccas then immediately joined the Athenians
under Phormio in their campaign against the Chalcidians.

     So it was that Sitalces the son of Teres, king of Thrace, and Perdiccas
the son of Alexander, king of Macedonia, became allies of Athens.

30   The Athenians in their hundred ships still off the Peloponnese
captured Sollium, a town belonging to Corinth, and granted to the
people of Palaerus in Acarnania the exclusive rights to occupy the
town and cultivate the land. They also took Astacus by storm, drove
out the tyrant Evarchus who ruled it, and brought the place into their
alliance. They then sailed to the island of Cephallenia and won it
over without a fight: Cephallenia lies opposite Acarnania and Leucas
and consists of four cities, Pale, Cranii, Same, and Pronni. Shortly
after that the ships set back for Athens.

When this summer was turning to autumn the Athenians invaded 31
the territory of Megara with their full force of citizens and metics,
commanded by Pericles the son of Xanthippus. The hundred ships
of the Peloponnesian expedition were now at Aegina on their voyage
home, and when these Athenians heard that the entire army from
Athens was in Megara they sailed there and joined them. This
was the largest combined Athenian armament ever assembled (the
city was still at its height, and the plague had not yet struck). The
Athenians themselves numbered at least ten thousand hoplites
(a further three thousand were in Potidaea): there were also at least
three thousand metic hoplites in the invading force, and in addition
a substantial body of light-armed troops. They laid waste most of the
land and then returned. The Athenians made further invasions of the
Megarid, either with cavalry or with their full force, every year
throughout the war until their capture of Nisaea.

Also at the end of this summer the Athenians fortified Atalante, a 32
previously uninhabited island off the coast of Opuntian Locris, as a
garrison-post to prevent pirates sailing out from Opus and the rest of
Locris to raid Euboea.

Such were the events of this summer after the Peloponnesians had
withdrawn from Attica.

In the following winter Evarchus the Acarnanian, intent on his 33
reinstatement to Astacus, persuaded the Corinthians to sail with
forty ships and fifteen hundred hoplites to restore him, and he himself hired some mercenary help. The leaders of the Corinthian force
were Euphamidas the son of Aristonymus, Timoxenus the son of
Timocrates, and Eumachus the son of Chrysis. The result of this
expedition was that they did reinstate Evarchus: there were other
places along the coast of Acarnania which they wanted to win over,
but when their attempts failed they sailed for home. On their return
voyage round the coast they put in at Cephallenia, and their troops
went ashore in the territory of Cranii. An apparent agreement was
reached which the Cranians then broke with an unexpected attack.
The Corinthians lost some of their men, and had to fight back to
their ships before they could set sail again and return home.

In the same winter, following their traditional institution, the 34
Athenians held a state funeral for those who had been the first to die
in this war. The ceremony is as follows. They erect a tent in which,
two days before the funeral, the bones of the departed are laid out,
and people can bring offerings to their own dead. On the day of the

funeral procession coffins of cypress wood are carried out on wagons, one coffin for each tribe, with each man's bones in his own tribe's coffin. One dressed but empty bier is carried for the missing whose bodies could not be found and recovered. All who wish can join the procession, foreigners as well as citizens, and the women of the bereaved families come to keen at the grave. Their burial is in the public cemetery, situated in the most beautiful suburb of the city, where the war dead are always buried, except those who died at Marathon, whose exceptional valour was judged worthy of a tomb where they fell.

When the earth has covered them, an appropriate eulogy is spoken over them by a man of recognized intellectual ability and outstanding reputation, chosen by the city; after this the people depart. This is how they conduct the funeral: and they followed this custom throughout the war whenever there was occasion.

Over these first dead the man chosen to give the address was Pericles the son of Xanthippus. When the moment arrived he walked forward from the grave and mounted the high platform which had been constructed there so that he could be heard as far among the crowd as possible. He then spoke like this:

35   'Most of those who have spoken here on previous occasions have commended the man who added this oration to the ceremony: it is right and proper, they have said, that there should be this address at the burial of those who died in our wars. To me it would seem enough that men who showed their courage in actions should have their tribute too expressed in actions, as you can see we have done in the arrangements for this state funeral; but the valour of these many should not depend for credence on the chance of one man's speech, who may speak well or badly. It is not easy to find the right measure of words when one cannot quite rely on a common perception of the truth. Those in the audience who are aware of the facts and are friends of the dead may well think that the speaker's account falls short of what they know and wish to hear; and the inexperienced may be jealous, and think there must be exaggeration, if told of anything beyond their own capacity. Eulogies of others are tolerated up to the point where each man still thinks himself capable of doing something of what he has heard praised: beyond that lies jealousy and therefore disbelief. But since this institution was sanctioned and approved by our predecessors, I too must follow the custom and attempt as far as possible to satisfy the individual wishes and expectations of each of you.

'I shall begin with our ancestors first of all. It is right, and also 36 appropriate on such an occasion, that this tribute should be paid to their memory. The same race has always occupied this land, passing it on from generation to generation until the present day, and it is to these brave men that we owe our inheritance of a land that is free. They deserve our praise. Yet more deserving are our own fathers, who added to what they themselves had received and by their pains left to us, the present generation, the further legacy of the great empire which we now possess. We ourselves, those of us still alive and now mainly in the settled age of life, have strengthened this empire yet further in most areas and furnished the city with every possible resource for self-sufficiency in war and peace. I shall not mention our achievements in war, the campaigns which won us each addition to the empire, our own or our fathers' spirited resistance to the attacks of Greek or barbarian enemies—I have no wish to delay you with a long story which you know already. But before I pass on to the praise of the dead, I shall describe first the principles of public life which set us on our way, and the political institutions and national character which took us on to greatness. I think this a suitable subject for the present occasion, and it could be of benefit for this whole gathering, foreigners as well as citizens, to hear this account.

'We have a form of government which does not emulate the practice 37 of our neighbours: we are more an example to others than an imitation of them. Our constitution is called a democracy because we govern in the interests of the majority, not just the few. Our laws give equal rights to all in private disputes, but public preferment depends on individual distinction and is determined largely by merit rather than rotation: and poverty is no barrier to office, if a man despite his humble condition has the ability to do some good to the city. We are open and free in the conduct of our public affairs and in the uncensorious way we observe the habits of each other's daily lives: we are not angry with our neighbour if he indulges his own pleasure, nor do we put on the disapproving look which falls short of punishment but can still hurt. We are tolerant in our private dealings with one another, but in all public matters we abide by the law: it is fear above all which keeps us obedient to the authorities of the day and to the laws, especially those laws established for the protection of the injured and those unwritten laws whose contravention brings acknowledged disgrace.

'Furthermore, as rest from our labours we have provided ourselves 38 with a wealth of recreations for the spirit—games and festivals held throughout the year, and elegantly appointed private houses, giving us a pleasure which dispels the troubles of the day. The size of our city attracts every sort of import from all over the world, so our enjoyment of goods from abroad is as familiar as that of our own produce.

39   'We differ too from our enemies in our approach to military matters. The difference is this. We maintain an open city, and never expel foreigners or prevent anyone from finding out or observing what they will—we do not hide things when sight of them might benefit an enemy: our reliance is not so much on preparation and concealment as on our own innate spirit for courageous action. In education also they follow an arduous regime, training for manliness right from childhood, whereas we have a relaxed lifestyle but are still just as ready as they to go out and face our equivalent dangers. I give you an example. The Spartans do not invade our land on their own, but they have all their allies with them: when we attack others' territory we do it by ourselves, and for the most part have no difficulty in winning the fight in a foreign country against men defending their own property. No enemy has yet met our full force, because we have been simultaneously maintaining our navy and sending out our men on a number of campaigns by land. If they do engage some part of our forces somewhere, a victory over just a few of us has them claiming the defeat of us all, and if they are beaten they pretend that they lost to our full strength. If then we choose to approach dangers in an easy frame of mind, not with constant practice in hardship, and to meet them with the courage which is born of character rather than compulsion, the result is that we do not have to suffer in advance the pain which we shall face later, and when we do face it we show ourselves just as courageous as those who have spent a lifetime of labour. This is one reason for the admiration of our city: and there are others too.

40   'We cultivate beauty without extravagance, and intellect without loss of vigour; wealth is for us the gateway to action, not the subject of boastful talk, and while there is no disgrace in the admission of poverty, the real disgrace lies in the failure to take active measures to escape it; our politicians can combine management of their domestic affairs with state business, and others who have their own work to attend to can nevertheless acquire a good knowledge of politics. We are unique in the way we regard anyone who takes no part in public affairs: we do not call that a quiet life, we call it a useless life. We are all involved in either the proper formulation or at least the proper review of policy, thinking that what cripples action is not talk, but

rather the failure to talk through the policy before proceeding to the required action. This is another difference between us and others, which gives us our exceptional combination of daring and deliberation about the objective—whereas with others their courage relies on ignorance, and for them to deliberate is to hesitate. True strength of spirit would rightly be attributed to those who have the sharpest perception of both terrors and pleasures and through that knowledge do not shrink from danger.

'We are at variance with most others too in our concept of doing good: we make our friends by conferring benefit rather than receiving it. The benefactor is the firmer friend, in that by further kindness he will maintain gratitude in the recipient as a current debt: the debtor is less keen, as he knows that any return of generosity will be something owed, not appreciated as an independent favour. And we are unique in the way we help others—no calculation of self-interest, but an act of frank confidence in our freedom.

'In summary I declare that our city as a whole is an education to 41 Greece; and in each individual among us I see combined the personal self-sufficiency to enjoy the widest range of experience and the ability to adapt with consummate grace and ease. That this is no passing puff but factual reality is proved by the very power of the city: this character of ours built that power. Athens alone among contemporary states surpasses her reputation when brought to the test: Athens alone gives the enemies who meet her no cause for chagrin at being worsted by such opponents, and the subjects of her empire no cause to complain of undeserving rulers. Our power most certainly does not lack for witness: the proof is far and wide, and will make us the wonder of present and future generations. We have no need of a Homer to sing our praises, or of any encomiast whose poetic version may have immediate appeal but then fall foul of the actual truth. The fact is that we have forced every sea and every land to be open to our enterprise, and everywhere we have established permanent memorials of both failure and success.

'This then is the city for which these men fought and died. They were nobly determined that she should not be lost: and all of us who survive should be willing to suffer for her.

'This is why I have dwelt at length on the nature of our city, to 42 demonstrate that in this contest there is more at stake for us than for those who have no comparable enjoyment of such advantages, and also to set out a clear base of evidence to support the praise of the men I am now commemorating. Their highest praise is already implicit: I have sung the glories of the city, but it was the qualities of these men and others like them which made her glorious, and there can be few other Greeks whose achievements, as theirs do, prove equal to their praises. I consider that the way these have now met their end is the index of a man's worth, whether that be first glimpse or final confirmation. Even if some had their faults, it is right that the courage to fight and die for their country should outweigh them: they have erased harm by good, and the collective benefit they have conferred is greater than any damage done as individuals. None of these men set higher value on the continued enjoyment of their wealth and let that turn them cowards; none let the poor man's hope, that some day he will escape poverty and grow rich, postpone that fearful moment. For them victory over the enemy was the greater desire: this they thought the noblest of all risks, and were prepared to take that risk in the pursuit of victory, forsaking all else. The uncertainties of success or failure they entrusted to hope, but in the plain and present sight of what confronted them they determined to rely on themselves, and in the very act of resistance they preferred even death to survival at the cost of surrender. They fled from an ignominious reputation by withstanding the action with their lives. In the briefest moment, at the turning point of their fortune, they took their leave not of fear but of glory.

43 'Such were these men, and they proved worthy of their city. The rest of us may pray for a safer outcome, but should demand of ourselves a determination against the enemy no less courageous than theirs. The benefit of this is not simply an intellectual question. Do not simply listen to people telling you at length of all the virtues inherent in resisting the enemy, when you know them just as well yourselves: but rather look day after day on the manifest power of our city, and become her lovers. And when you realize her greatness, reflect that it was men who made her great, by their daring, by their recognition of what they had to do, and by their pride in doing it. If ever they failed in some attempt, they would not have the city share their loss, but offered her their courage as the finest contribution they could make. Together they gave their lives, and individually they took as their reward the praise which does not grow old and the most glorious of tombs—not where their bodies lie, but where their fame lives on in every occasion for speech and ceremony, an everlasting memory. Famous men have the whole earth as their tomb.

Their record is not only the inscription on gravestones in their own land, but in foreign countries too the unwritten memorial which lives in individual hearts, the remembrance of their spirit rather than their achievement.

'You should now seek to emulate these men. Realize that happiness is freedom, and freedom is courage, and do not be nervous of the dangers of war. The unfortunate, with no hope of improvement, have better reason to husband their lives than those who risk reversal of fortune if they live on and have the most to lose should they fail. To a man with any pride cowardice followed by disaster is more painful than a death which comes in the vigour of courage and the fellowship of hope, and is hardly felt.

'For that reason, to the parents of the dead here present I offer not 44 sympathy so much as consolation. You know that you were born into a world of change and chance, where the true fortune is to meet with honour—the most honourable death for these we commemorate, the most honourable grief for you—and to enjoy a life whose measure of happiness fills both the living and the leaving of it. It is hard, I know, to convince you of this, since you will often have reminders of your sons when you see others blessed with the good fortune which was once your source of pride too: and grief is felt not for the deprivation of joys never experienced, but for the loss of a once familiar joy. Those of you who are still of an age to bear children should hold firm to the hope of further sons. In their own lives some will find that new children help them forget those they have lost, and for the city there will be double benefit—both maintenance of the population and also a safeguard, since those without children at stake do not face the same risks as the others and cannot make a balanced or judicious contribution to debate. Those of you who are past that age should consider it a gain that you have lived the greater part of your life in happiness and that what remains will be short: and you should take comfort in the glory of the dead. Love of honour alone does not age, and in the unproductive time of life the greater pleasure is not the accumulation of gain, as some say, but the enjoyment of honour.

'For those of you here who are sons or brothers of the dead I can see 45 a formidable task. It is common experience that all speak highly of those who are gone, and however you excel in your own qualities you will struggle to be judged even a close second to them, let alone their equals. The living are exposed to the denigration of rivalry, but anything no longer present meets with warm and uncompetitive recognition.

'If I may speak also of the duty of those wives who will now be widows, a brief exhortation will say it all. Your great virtue is to show no more weakness than is inherent in your nature, and to cause least talk among males for either praise or blame.

46   'I have made this speech as custom demands, finding the most suitable words I could. The honour expressed in ceremony has now been paid to those we came to bury: and in further tribute to them the city will maintain their children at public expense from now until they come of age. This is the valuable crown which in contests such as these the city confers on the dead and those they leave behind. The state which offers the greatest prizes for valour also has the bravest men for citizens.

'And now it is time to leave, when each of you has made due lament for your own.'

47   Such was the funeral held in this winter: and with the passing of winter there ended the first year of this war.

At the very beginning of the next summer the Peloponnesians and their allies invaded Attica, with two-thirds of their forces as on the first occasion, under the command of Archidamus the son of Zeuxidamus, king of Sparta. They settled in and began to ravage the land.

They had not been in Attica for more than a few days when the plague first broke out in Athens. It is said that the plague had already struck widely elsewhere, especially in Lemnos and other places, but nowhere else was there recorded such virulence or so great a loss of life. The doctors could offer little help at first: they were attempting to treat the disease without knowing what it was, and in fact there was particularly high mortality among doctors because of their particular exposure. No other human skill could help either, and all supplications at temples and consultations of oracles and the like were of no avail. In the end the people were overcome by the disaster and abandoned all efforts to escape it.

48   The original outbreak, it is said, was in Ethiopia, the far side of Egypt: the plague then spread to Egypt and Libya, and over much of the King's territory. It fell on the city of Athens suddenly. The first affected were the inhabitants of the Peiraeus, who went so far as to allege that the Peloponnesians had poisoned the wells (at that time there were no fountains in the Peiraeus). Afterwards the plague reached the upper city too, and now the number of deaths greatly increased. Others, doctors or laymen, can give their individual opinions of the

likely origin of the plague, and of the factors which they think significant enough to have had the capacity to cause such a profound
change. But I shall simply tell it as it happened, and describe the
features of the disease which will give anyone who studies them some
prior knowledge to enable recognition should it ever strike again.
I myself caught the plague, and witnessed others suffering from it.

It so happened that this year was commonly agreed to have been
particularly free from other forms of illness, though anyone with a
previous condition invariably developed the plague. The other victims were in good health until, for no apparent cause, they were
suddenly afflicted. The first symptoms were a high fever in the head
and reddening and inflammation of the eyes; then internally the
throat and tongue began to bleed and the breath had an unnaturally
foul smell. There followed sneezing and hoarseness of voice, and
shortly the affliction moved down to the chest accompanied by a
violent cough. When it settled in the stomach the turmoil caused
there led to the voiding of bile in every form for which the doctors
have a name, all this with great pain. Most then suffered from an
empty retching which brought violent spasms: in some this followed
as soon as the vomiting had abated, in others much later.

The surface of the body was not particularly hot to the touch or
pallid, but reddish and livid, breaking out in small pustules and
ulcers. But the sensation of burning heat inside the body was so
strong that sufferers could not bear the pressure of even the lightest
clothing or sheets, or anything other than going naked, and their
greatest wish was to plunge into cold water. Many who had no one
to look after them did in fact throw themselves into cisterns, overcome by an insatiable thirst: but as a rule the quantity of water drunk
made no difference. A constant infliction was desperate restlessness
and the inability to sleep. Throughout the height of the disease there
was no wasting of the body, but a surprising physical resilience to all
the suffering, so that there was still some strength in them when the
majority died from the internal fever after six to eight days. If they
survived this period most others died from the consequent weakness
when the disease spread down to the bowels causing heavy ulceration
and the onset of completely liquid diarrhoea.

The disease first settled in the head then progressed throughout
the whole body from the top downwards. If any survived the worst
effects, symptoms appeared when the disease took hold in their
extremities. It attacked genitals, fingers, and toes, and many lived on

49

with these parts lost: some too lost their sight. There were those who on recovery suffered immediate and total loss of memory, not knowing who they were and unable to recognize their friends.

50   Indeed the pathology of the disease defied explanation. Not only did it visit individuals with a violence beyond human endurance, but there was also this particular feature which put it in a different category from all other diseases with which we are familiar: although many bodies lay unburied, the birds and animals which prey on human flesh kept away from them, or, if they did eat, died of it. Evidence of this was the notable disappearance of carrion birds, nowhere to be seen in their usual or any other activity: the dogs, being domestic animals, allowed more immediate observation of this consequence.

51   This then, leaving aside the many variants in the way different individuals were affected, was the general character of the disease. Throughout this time there were no attacks of the usual illnesses: any that did occur ended in the plague.

Some died in neglect and others died despite constant care. Virtually no remedy was established as a single specific relief applicable in all cases: what was good for one was harmful to another. No particular constitution, strong or weak, proved sufficient in itself to resist, but the plague carried off all indiscriminately, and whatever their regime of care. The most dreadful aspects of the whole affliction were the despair into which people fell when they realized they had contracted the disease (they were immediately convinced that they had no hope, and so were much more inclined to surrender themselves without a fight), and the cross-infection of those who cared for others: they died like sheep, and this was the greatest cause of mortality. When people were afraid to visit one another, the victims died in isolation, and many households were wiped out through the lack of anyone to care for them. If they did visit the sick, they died, especially those who could claim some courage: these were people who out of a sense of duty disregarded their own safety and kept visiting their friends, even when ultimately the family members themselves were overwhelmed by the scale of the disaster and abandoned the succession of dirges for the dead. But the greatest pity for the dying and the distressed was shown by those who had had the disease and recovered. They had experience of what it was like and were now confident for themselves, as the plague did not attack the same person twice, or at least not fatally. These survivors were congratulated by all, and in the immediate elation of recovery they entertained the fond hope that from now on they would not die of any other disease.

The suffering was made yet more acute by the influx from the 52 country into the city, and the incomers suffered most of all. With no houses of their own, and forced to live in huts which at that time of year were stifling, they perished in chaotic conditions: the dead and the dying were piled on top of each other, and half-dead creatures staggered about the streets and round every fountain, craving for water. The sanctuaries in which they had encamped were full of corpses—people dying there were not moved: all sacred and secular constraints came to be ignored under the overwhelming impact of the disaster, which left men no recourse. All previously observed funeral customs were confounded, and burial was haphazard, any way that people could manage. Many were driven to shameful means of disposal for lack of friends to help them, so many of their friends already dead: they made use of other people's funeral pyres, either putting their own dead on a pyre constructed by others and quickly setting light to it, or bringing a corpse to a pyre already lit, throwing it on top of the other body in the flames, and then running away.

In other respects too the plague was the beginning of increased 53 lawlessness in the city. People were less inhibited in the indulgence of pleasures previously concealed when they saw the rapid changes of fortune—the prosperous suddenly dead, and the once indigent now possessing their fortune. As a result they decided to look for satisfactions that were quick and pleasurable, reckoning that neither life nor wealth would last long. No one was prepared to persevere in what had once been thought the path of honour, as they could well be dead before that destination was reached. Immediate pleasure, and any means profitable to that end, became the new honour and the new value. No fear of god or human law was any constraint. Pious or impious made no difference in their view, when they could see all dying without distinction. As for offences against the law, no one expected to live long enough to be brought to justice and pay the penalty: they thought that a much heavier sentence had already been passed and was hanging over them, so they might as well have some enjoyment of life before it fell.

Such was the affliction which had come on the Athenians and was 54 pressing them hard—people dying inside the city, and the devastation of their land outside. In this time of trouble, as tends to happen, they recalled a verse which the old men said was being chanted long ago: 'A Dorian war will come, and bring a pestilence with it.' People had disputed whether the original word in the verse was *limos* ('famine') rather than *loimos* ('pestilence'): but not surprisingly in the present situation the prevailing view was that 'pestilence' was the word used. Men accommodate their memories to their current experience. I imagine that if at some time another 'Dorian war' comes after this one, with famine coinciding, the verse will in all likelihood be recited with that meaning.

Those who knew of it also remembered the oracle given to the Spartans, when they enquired whether they should go to war and the god answered that they would win if they fought in earnest, and said that he himself would take their side. The general surmise was that the facts fitted the oracle. The plague had indeed begun immediately after the Peloponnesians had invaded, and it never reached the Peloponnese to any significant extent, but spread particularly in Athens and later in other densely populated areas. So much for the facts of the plague.

55   Meanwhile the Peloponnesians, after ravaging the plain, moved on to the territory called the Coastal Region, penetrating as far as Laureium, the site of the Athenians' silver mines. They laid waste first the part of the territory facing the Peloponnese, then the area lying in the direction of Euboea and Andros.

Pericles was still general, and held to the same view he had taken in the previous invasion, that the Athenians should not go out to
56 offer battle. But while the Peloponnesians were still in the plain and before they had moved on to the coast, he was preparing an expedition of a hundred ships against the Peloponnese, and when all was ready he took them out to sea. He had with him four thousand Athenian hoplites on board the ships, and three hundred cavalry in horse-transports, constructed then for the first time out of old ships: and Chios and Lesbos contributed to the expedition with fifty ships. When this Athenian force set sail, they had left the Peloponnesians in the coastal region of Attica. Arriving at Epidaurus in the Peloponnese they ravaged most of the area, and in an attack on the city they came within hope of capturing it, but did not succeed. They then put out from Epidaurus and devastated the territory of Troezen, Halieis, and Hermione (all these are areas on the coast of the Peloponnese). Moving on from there they came to Prasiae, a coastal town in Laconia: they ravaged some of the land and also took and

sacked the town itself. After this they returned home, to find the Peloponnesians by now withdrawn and no longer in Attica.

For all the time that the Peloponnesians were in Athenian territory, 57 and the Athenians were on their naval expedition, the plague continued to take lives both among the expeditionary force and in the city of Athens—so much so that it was even said that the Peloponnesians cut short their presence in the country for fear of the disease, when they heard from the deserters that there was plague in the city and could see for themselves evidence of the cremations. In fact on this invasion they spent their longest time in the country and ravaged the whole of it: they were in Attica for about forty days.

In the same summer two fellow generals of Pericles, Hagnon the 58 son of Nicias and Cleopompus the son of Cleinias, took over the force which he had just commanded and set off immediately on an expedition against the Thraceward Chalcidians and also Potidaea, which was still under siege. On arrival they brought up siege-engines against Potidaea and tried every possible means of taking the place. But they did not achieve either the capture of the city or any other success consistent with the deployment of such a force, since the plague now broke out there too and took a punishing toll of the Athenian troops, with the original contingent of soldiers, in good health up till then, catching the disease from Hagnon's army. (Phormio and his sixteen hundred escaped, as they were no longer in the Chalcidice area.) So Hagnon returned with his fleet to Athens, having lost to the plague in about forty days one thousand and fifty from his four thousand hoplites: and the original contingent stayed where they were, maintaining the siege of Potidaea.

After the second Peloponnesian invasion, with their land devas- 59 tated for the second time, and under the double burden of plague and war, the Athenians suffered a change of mind. They now began to blame Pericles for persuading them to war and held him responsible for the disasters that had befallen them: and they were ready to make terms with the Spartans—they did in fact send embassies to Sparta, without effect. Reduced to complete desperation, they turned on Pericles. He could see that they were resentful at the present situation and were reacting in all the ways which he had privately predicted: so he called a meeting (he was still general) with the intention of stiffening their resolve and drawing them away from anger to a more benign and confident frame of mind. He came forward and spoke like this:

60   'I was expecting this anger of yours against me (I can understand
its causes), and I have called this assembly in order to refresh your
memory and to suggest that you are wrong to criticize me or to give
in to your present troubles.

'I take the view that the interest of private citizens is better served
when the city as a whole is successful than if there is individual prosperity but collective failure. A man may be personally well off, but
if his country is destroyed he shares in the general ruin: whereas
private misfortune is much more easily survived in a country which
itself enjoys good fortune. Since then the state can bear all individual
troubles, but each individual cannot singly bear the troubles of the
state, it follows—does it not?—that all should rally to the defence of
the state, and not react as you are now: in the shock of the misfortunes in your own homes you are losing sight of our communal
security, and blaming me as the advocate of war—and yourselves for
consenting to it.

'Yet your anger with me is directed at a man who—though I say
it myself—is the equal of any in the intelligence to see what is needed
and the skill to expound it, a man who loves his country and is above
corruption. Intelligence without clear communication is no better
than an empty mind; a man with both these abilities but no loyalty to
his country is less likely to speak for the interests of the community;
let him have loyalty also, but if the man is venal this one fault puts
all his other qualities up for sale. So if you accepted the case for war
in the belief that in these respects I was at least to some extent better
equipped than others, it is not reasonable that I should now bear the
charge of doing wrong.

61   'Certainly if all else is well and people have the choice of war or
peace, it is great folly to go to war. But if, as was the case, the stark
choice is either to submit and endure instant subjection to others or
to face the risks and win through, the greater blame lies in shirking
the danger rather than standing up to it. For my own part, I remain
the same and my position does not shift. It is you who are changing.
What has happened is that your conviction when you were unharmed
has turned to regret now that trouble is on you, and in your weakened state of morale that argument of mine now seems to you mistaken: the pain has already made itself felt by every individual, but
the benefit for all of us is not yet clearly seen. And this major reversal
of fortune, coming out of nowhere, has enfeebled your will to persevere in the policy you approved. Events which happen suddenly,

unforeseen, and quite beyond any reasonable prediction can enslave the spirit: and this is what the plague, coming on top of all else, has done to you. But you are the inhabitants of a great city, you were brought up to a way of life worthy of that city, and you should be prepared to stand firm even in the worst of misfortune and not let your reputation be obliterated. In men's eyes there is as much reason to blame those who lose their established prestige through feebleness as to resent those who brashly aspire to a prestige which they do not deserve. So you must put aside your private sorrows and concentrate on the effort for our communal security.

'As for the likely burden of the war, your suspicion that it will be 62 heavy, and even so no guarantee of our survival, should be sufficiently disproved by the arguments I have already put forward on many other occasions. But I shall make this further point—an inherent advantage in the pure extent of our empire which I think has never yet been fully realized by you nor stressed in my previous speeches. It may seem quite an extravagant claim, and I would not mention it now if I did not see you discouraged without reason. You think of empire solely in terms of rule over our allies, but I can tell you that of the two elements open to man's exploitation, the land and the sea, you are the absolute masters of the whole of one of them, both in the present extent of your control and as far further as you wish to take it: with the naval resources you have at your disposal, no one, neither the King of Persia nor any other nation now on earth, can prevent you from sailing where you will. So this power is clearly of a different order from the utility of houses and land, the loss of which you consider a great deprivation. You should not take this loss so hard. Weigh these things against our naval power and you should come to think of them as no more than a back-garden, a mere accessory of wealth. You should recognize that they will easily be recovered if we keep hold of our freedom and preserve it, whereas submission to others usually brings the permanent loss of all that people had before, however long in their possession.

'You must not let yourselves be seen as doubly inferior to your fathers. They acquired these possessions not by inheritance from others, but through their own exertions, and furthermore kept them safe to hand on to you: and it is a greater disgrace to be robbed of what you possess than to fail in its acquisition. You must tackle the enemy, then, not only with conviction, but with the conviction of superiority. This is not the same as arrogance—even the coward can be arrogant if his stupidity is combined with good luck: but the conviction I speak of derives from a reasoned confidence in superiority over the enemy, and that is what we have. Intelligent use of this confidence makes bold initiatives more secure, given equality of fortune: it does not rely on hope, which is a resort only when there is no other, but on a rational conclusion from the facts, which affords a firmer base for planning strategy.

63 'You all take pride in the prestige the city enjoys from empire, and you should be prepared to fight in defence of it. You cannot shirk the burden without abandoning also your pursuit of the glory. Do not think that the only issue at stake is slavery or freedom: there is also loss of empire, and the danger from the hatred incurred under your rule. You no longer have the option to abdicate from your empire, should anyone out of present fear affect this idea as a noble-sounding means of disengagement. The empire you possess is by now like a tyranny—perhaps wrong to acquire it, but certainly dangerous to let it go. If people of that sort managed to persuade the others they would quickly ruin a city, and even if they set up their own independent state somewhere they would ruin that too. The disengaged can survive only when men of action are ranked beside them. Their policy has no place in an imperial state, but it belongs in a subject city, and what it means is safe servitude.

64 'Do not let yourselves be influenced by that sort among your fellow citizens, and do not be angry with me, when you yourselves joined me in the decision to go to war. The enemy have attacked, as they were always going to do on your refusal to submit; we were prepared for all else, but not for the additional affliction of this plague, the only present circumstance which could not have been foreseen. I know that my increased unpopularity is largely due to the plague: but this is unfair, unless you will also give me the credit for any unexpected success. We should bear blows from the gods with resignation, and blows from the enemy with courage. This has always been the way of this city in the past, and should not now stop with you. You should recognize that Athens has the greatest name among all men because she does not yield to adversity, but has made the greatest sacrifice of lives and labour in war, and has acquired the greatest power of any city in history to the present time. Future generations will retain in perpetuity the memory of this power. Even if we do give a little ground at some point in our time (and it is a law of nature that all things are subject to decline), posterity will

remember that we had the widest empire of Greeks over Greeks, that we held firm in the greatest wars against their combined or separate forces, and that the city we inhabited was the most complete in every facility and the greatest of all.

'All this the disengaged may deplore, but those with their own ambitions will want to emulate us, and those who have failed to gain power will envy us. Hatred and resentment at the time have always been the fate of those who claimed empire over others: but if there must be unpopularity, it is best incurred in the pursuit of the greatest aims. Hatred does not last for long, but present glory and future fame endure for ever in men's memories. You must seek to achieve both, and you will do so if you presuppose a glorious future and a far from inglorious present, and summon all your determination now. You must not negotiate with the Spartans or give them any indication of being oppressed by your present troubles. Among both cities and individuals the strongest are those who in the face of misfortune suffer the least distress of spirit and offer the greatest resistance in action.'

With this sort of argument Pericles tried to dispel the Athenians' 65 anger against himself and to lead their thought away from the terrible conditions of the present. As a political body they accepted his arguments: they stopped sending emissaries to Sparta, and concentrated their energy on the war. Individually, though, they still chafed at their sufferings. The common people were aggrieved to lose even the poor base from which they had started, and the powerful had lost their fine country estates and the grand houses expensively furnished: above all, they now had war in place of peace. The universal anger at Pericles among the Athenians did not subside until they had punished him with a fine. Not long afterwards, as is characteristic of crowd behaviour, they elected him general once more and entrusted all their affairs to his management. By now the individual pain of domestic loss was not so acute, and they considered him better qualified than any to meet the needs of the city as a whole.

Throughout Pericles' leadership of the city in peacetime his moderate policies ensured its preservation in safety, and under his guidance the city reached its greatest height: and when the war came, it is clear that he had provided for the strength of Athens in war too. He survived the outbreak of war by two years and six months. After his death the foresight he had shown in regard to the war could be recognized yet more clearly. He had advised that the Athenians would win through if they kept patient, looked to the maintenance of their navy, and did not try to extend their empire during the war or take any risk that endangered the city. But they did the opposite of all this, and in other ways too which seemed to have no relevance to the war they pursued policies motivated by private ambition and private gain, to the detriment of Athens herself and her allies: any success was more to the honour and benefit of the individual initiator, but failure affected the whole city and harmed the war-effort. The reason for this change was the contrast with Pericles. His power was in his distinguished reputation and his intellect, and he was patently incorruptible. He controlled the mass of the people with a free hand, leading them rather then letting them lead him. He had no need to seek improper means of influence by telling them what they wanted to hear: he already had the influence of his standing, and was even prepared to anger them by speaking against their mood. For example, whenever he saw them dangerously over-confident, he would make a speech which shocked them into a state of apprehension, and likewise he could return them from irrational fear to confidence. What was happening was democracy in name, but in fact the domination of the leading man.

Pericles' successors were more on a level with one another, and because each was striving for first position they were inclined to indulge popular whim even in matters of state policy. The result— inevitable in a great city with an empire to rule—was a series of mistakes, most notably the Sicilian expedition. The error here was not so much a mistaken choice of enemy as the failure of those at home to relate their further decisions to the interests of the force they had sent out. Instead they allowed personal accusations made in the pursuit of political supremacy to blunt the effectiveness of the military, and for the first time there was factional discord in the city. And yet even though the disaster in Sicily lost them the greater part of their fleet as well as the other forces deployed, and there was now civil strife at home, the Athenians still held out for eight years against their original enemies, the Sicilians who joined them, the majority of their allies as they revolted, and the later intervention of Cyrus, the son of the King of Persia, who provided finance for the Peloponnesian navy. They did not give in until they had brought about their own fall by entangling themselves in internal disputes. This demonstrates the more than ample justification Pericles had at the time for his prediction that Athens would very easily win through in a war against the Peloponnesians on their own.

In this same summer the Spartans and their allies mounted an 66 expedition of a hundred ships against the island of Zacynthus, which lies opposite Elis. The people of Zacynthus are colonists from Achaea in the Peloponnese, and they were allied to the Athenians. The expedition had a thousand Spartan hoplites on board, and the commander was the Spartiate admiral Cnemus. They landed and laid waste most of the territory, but when the Zacynthians refused to come to terms with them they sailed back home.

At the end of the same summer a Peloponnesian embassy set out 67 for Asia to meet the King of Persia: the ambassadors were Aristeus of Corinth, the Spartans Aneristus, Nicolaus, and Pratodamus, Timagoras from Tegea, and, acting in a private capacity, Pollis from Argos. Their hope was to persuade the King to provide finance and also to join the war on their side. They first visited Sitalces the son of Teres in Thrace, intending if they could to persuade him to switch from his alliance with Athens and bring his army to the relief of Potidaea, which was under siege by Athenian forces: they also wanted his help to convey them across the Hellespont on their journey to Pharnaces the son of Pharnabazus, who was to send them on to the King. There happened to be with Sitalces two Athenian envoys, Learchus the son of Callimachus and Ameiniades the son of Philemon. They put pressure on Sitalces' son Sadocus, who had been made an Athenian citizen, to hand over the Peloponnesian party to them, to prevent them making their way across to the King and so doing considerable harm to what was now Sadocus' own city. He agreed, and had them arrested on their travel through Thrace before they could embark on the boat that was to take them across the Hellespont: he had sent men to accompany Learchus and Ameiniades, with instructions to hand the Peloponnesian envoys into their custody.

Learchus and Ameiniades took charge of the men and conveyed them to Athens. The Athenians were fearful that if Aristeus escaped he would do them further and greater harm, since he was already known to have been the prime enemy agent at work in Potidaea and the Thraceward area. So on the very day of their arrival, without giving them trial or the opportunity to say what they wanted, they executed every one of them and threw their bodies into a ravine. They claimed in justification the right to safeguard their interests with the same measures already initiated by the Spartans, when they had killed and thrown into ravines any Athenian or allied traders they caught sailing round the Peloponnese in merchant ships. At the beginning of the war it was Spartan practice to treat all those they caught at sea as enemies and kill them, irrespective of whether they were allies of Athens or non-aligned.

68   At about the same time, at the end of the summer, a combined force of Ambraciots and the many barbarians they had incited to join them launched a campaign against Amphilochian Argos and the rest of Amphilochia. The origin of their hostility to this Argos was as follows. Amphilochian Argos and the whole region of Amphilochia were founded on the Ambracian Gulf by Amphilochus the son of Amphiaraus, who on his return after the Trojan War had reason to dislike the situation he found at home in Peloponnesian Argos, and named this new foundation after his native country. The new Argos was the largest city in Amphilochia, populated by the most powerful of the colonists. Many generations later, pressed by misfortunes, these Argives brought in people from Ambracia (which borders Amphilochia) to share their settlement, and it was from these Ambraciot settlers that they first learnt the Greek language which they now speak (the rest of the Amphilochians are barbarians). In time the Ambraciots expelled the Argives and took over the city themselves. When this happened the Amphilochians ceded their country to the protection of the Acarnanians, and together they called in the help of Athens. The Athenians sent them thirty ships with Phormio as general in command. When Phormio had arrived they took Argos by storm and enslaved the Ambraciots, then populated the city with a joint settlement of Amphilochians and Acarnanians. It was after this that the alliance between Athens and Acarnania was first made.

The enslavement of their people was the original cause of the Ambraciots' hostility to the Argives, and the reason why at this later time, during the war, they launched this campaign with their own troops and support from the Chaonians and other neighbouring barbarian tribes. They came up to Argos and gained control of the surrounding territory, but when their attack on the city itself failed to achieve its capture they returned home and each tribe dispersed to their own land.

These were the events of the summer.

69   In the following winter the Athenians sent twenty ships round the Peloponnese with Phormio in command, to make his base in Naupactus and stand guard to prevent any passage in or out of the Gulf of Crisa to or from Corinth. They also sent six ships under the command of the general Melesandrus to Caria and Lycia with the

dual purpose of collecting money there and preventing Peloponnesian freebooters from using that area as a base for attacks on merchant shipping from Phaselis and Phoenicia and the coast of the mainland in between. Melesandrus took a force of allies and of Athenians from the ships inland into Lycia, but was defeated in battle, lost some part of his company, and was himself killed.

In the course of this winter the people of Potidaea came to the 70 end of their ability to hold out against the siege. The Peloponnesian invasions of Attica had done nothing to induce the Athenians to withdraw, and the food had run out: inside Potidaea they had already been forced to eat anything they could find there, including in some cases human flesh. So ultimately they sued for terms with the Athenian generals in charge of the siege, Xenophon the son of Euripides, Hestiodorus the son of Aristocleides, and Phanomachus the son of Callimachus. The generals accepted their proposals, conscious of the suffering of their own troops in a place exposed to the rigours of winter, and of the two thousand talents Athens had already expended on the siege. The terms agreed were that the Potidaean men, children, and women, and the mercenaries also, should evacuate the city, taking with them one cloak each (the women were allowed two) and a set sum of money for their journey. So they left under truce, spreading into Chalcidice or wherever else they could. The Athenians found fault with the generals for agreeing terms without their authority, as they thought they could have achieved the unconditional surrender of the city. Subsequently they sent colonists from their own people to Potidaea and resettled the place.

These were the events of the winter, and so ended the second year of this war chronicled by Thucydides.

In the following summer the Peloponnesians and their allies did 71 not invade Attica, but campaigned instead against Plataea, under the command of Archidamus the son of Zeuxidamus, king of Sparta. As soon as Archidamus had set his army in position and was ready to ravage the land, the Plataeans sent envoys to him with this message:

'Archidamus and Spartans, you do wrong to attack the land of Plataea, and your action is a betrayal both of yourselves and of the fathers from whom you come. We would remind you that when the Spartan Pausanias the son of Cleombrotus had liberated Greece from the Persians with the help of those Greeks who were prepared to share the danger of that battle fought in our territory, he made sacrifice in the market-square of Plataea to Zeus the god of freedom, and with all the allies assembled there he offered a guarantee to the people of Plataea that they would retain possession of their land and city and live there in independence; no one should ever attack them without justification or seek to enslave them; if any attack were made, the allies there present were to defend them in force. Your fathers granted us this privilege in recognition of the courage and loyalty we showed at that time of danger, and you are now doing the opposite, coming here with the Thebans, our greatest enemies, and intent on our subjection. We call to witness the gods by whom those oaths were then sworn, the gods of your fathers, and the gods of our own country, and we tell you not to abuse the land of Plataea or contravene your oaths, but to let us live in the independence which Pausanias awarded as our right.'

72   When the Plataeans had spoken thus Archidamus replied: 'Men of Plataea, what you say is fair, as long as your actions match your words. In the terms of Pausanias' pledge to you, enjoy your own autonomy but also help us to free the others who shared those dangers and joined in that oath to you, and are now subject to the Athenians. We have raised this great force and gone to war for their sake, to liberate them and the others. Your best policy is to join us in this liberation and so maintain your own part in those oaths. If you will not do that, then, as we have urged you before, look after your own affairs and stay neutral: do not join either side; give access to both in friendship, but to neither for purposes of war. That too will satisfy us.'

So spoke Archidamus. The Plataean envoys listened, then went back into the city and reported what had been said to the people. Their reply to Archidamus was that they could not possibly do as he proposed without the approval of the Athenians (their children and women were in Athens), and they were anxious for the whole future of their city: when the Peloponnesians withdrew the Athenians might come and countermand their neutrality, or the Thebans, covered by the agreement to give access to both sides, might make a further attempt to seize the city.

Archidamus sought to meet their concerns with this reassurance: 'Well then, entrust your city and your houses to us Spartans. Specify the boundaries of your land, the number of your trees, and anything else that can be quantified. Move away wherever you wish for the duration of the war, and when the war is over we shall hand back to you all that we take over. Until then we shall hold it in trust, working the land and paying you a return which you will find satisfactory.'

They listened and once again went back into the city. After con- 73
sulting the people, they replied that they wanted first to put the
proposals to the Athenians, and would accept them if the Athenians
agreed; in the meantime the Spartans should make a truce with them
and not ravage their land. Archidamus agreed a truce for the number
of days estimated for the journey there and back, and did not start
the devastation of the land.

The Plataean envoys went to Athens, and after discussions with
the Athenians came back with this message for their fellow citizens:
'Men of Plataea, the Athenians say that at no time in the past, ever
since we first became allies, have they abandoned you to any aggressor, and they will not stand aside now, but will help you as far as they
are able. By the oaths which your fathers swore they adjure you not
to deviate from the alliance.'

Hearing this message relayed by their envoys the Platacans deter- 74
mined not to desert the Athenians, but to bear, if need be, the sight
of their land being ravaged and any other hardship that might follow:
no one should now go outside, but the answer, given from the city
wall, should be that it was impossible for them to accede to the
Spartan proposal.

On this reply, Archidamus proceeded to action. First he called
in witness the local gods and heroes with this invocation: 'All you
gods and heroes who possess the land of Plataea, be our witnesses
now that from the start it was with no wrongful motive, but because
the Plataeans had first broken our communal oath, that we have come
against this land—the land in which our fathers made their prayers
to you before they defeated the Persians, the land which you made a
propitious battleground for the Greeks. Anything we do now will be
no wrong either: we have made many fair proposals without success.
Grant then the punishment of those who first did wrong, and vindi-
cation for those who lawfully seek to impose it.'

After making this appeal to the gods, Archidamus set his army to 75
war. First they surrounded Plataea with a palisade built with the
trees they had cut down, so that no sorties could be made against
them, then they began to construct a ramp against the city wall,
anticipating that with such a large force engaged in the construction
this would be the quickest way of taking the city. They cut timber
from Cithaeron to shore the ramp on either side, building it up in a
criss-cross pattern to act as retaining walls to prevent the lateral
spread of the ramp: for the ramp itself they brought in wood, stone,

earth, and anything else which would serve as filling. They spent seventeen continuous days and nights on this construction, dividing the labour into shifts, so that some were working while others took food and sleep: and the Spartan officers in joint command of each allied contingent kept the men pressed to the work.

Seeing the ramp rising higher, the Plataeans put together a wooden wall and fixed it on top of the city wall opposite the construction of the ramp. They built up the interior with bricks torn from nearby houses, the timber forming a framework to prevent the structure weakening as it grew in height, and they faced it with screens of skins and hides, to keep the workmen and the wood safe from any attack with flaming arrows. This wall rose to a great height, and the ramp kept pace with it no less energetically.

The Plataeans now thought of this next device: they made a hole in the city wall where the mound lay against it and began to carry the 76 earth inside. The Peloponnesians discovered what they were doing and plugged the gaps with clay packed in reed baskets, which could not be worked loose and removed as the earth had been. Frustrated in this way, the Plataeans abandoned this tactic and now dug a tunnel out from the city, calculating its length and depth under the mound, and again began to steal the infill back into the city. For a long time the troops outside had no idea of the undermining which stalled their progress: they kept piling on more earth and the mound kept subsiding into the emptied space.

Fearful that even so they were too few to hold out against such large numbers, the Plataeans devised this further scheme. They ceased work on the superstructure opposite the ramp, and from either end of it, starting from the original low wall, they built a crescent-shaped wall on the inner side projecting into the city, so that if the big wall were taken this secondary wall could hold: the enemy would need to build another ramp against it, and this advance inwards would cost them the same work all over again and also expose them to attack from both sides.

As well as the earthworks the Peloponnesians brought up siege-engines against the city. One was hauled up the ramp and battered down a large part of the superstructure, to the terror of the Plataeans. Other engines were applied at other points of the wall, but the Plataeans dealt with these by lassoing the rams and so deflecting them. They also rigged up huge beams attached at each end by long iron chains to a pair of poles laid across the wall and projecting beyond it. These beams were pulled up to hang at right angles to the rams, and whenever an engine was about to strike they let the chains run free from their hands and the impact of the falling beam would snap off the nose of the ram.

From now on, with their siege-engines ineffective and their ramp 77 met by counter-fortifications, the Peloponnesians concluded that it was impossible to take the city at their present level of assault, and they began to prepare for circumvallation. But first they decided to make an attempt by fire, hoping that with a wind blowing they could set fire to the whole city, given its small extent: they were now thinking of every possible means of securing control without the expense of a siege. They brought up bundles of brushwood and threw them from the ramp into the gap between the wall and the ramp, then when the many hands at work had quickly filled this space they continued to pile the brushwood against the rest of the city wall as far as they could reach from the height of the ramp. They then threw on sulphur and pitch, applied firebrands, and set light to the wood. The result was the greatest man-made sheet of flame ever seen by anyone up to that time (though of course there had been forest fires on the mountains which produced huge flames, the friction of wood on wood caused by the winds giving rise to spontaneous combustion). This was an enormous conflagration, and the Plataeans, who had so far escaped all else, were very nearly destroyed by it. A large part of the city was made inaccessible, and if a wind had arisen to spread the fire, as the enemy hoped, there would have been no further escape. In the event that did not happen, and it is also said that a thunderstorm brought a deluge of water from the sky which extinguished the flames and so put an end to that danger.

After failing in this attempt too, the Peloponnesians sent home the 78 bulk of their forces, but retained a part of the army for the construction of a wall around the city, dividing the circuit between the allied contingents: ditches dug on either side of the wall provided the clay for their bricks. When the whole operation was complete, round about the rising of Arcturus, the Peloponnesians left guards to cover half of the wall (the other half was guarded by Boeotians), then returned home with their troops and dispersed to their own cities. The Plataeans had already evacuated to Athens their children and women, the oldest men and the rest of those who were unfit: there remained under siege four hundred of the Plataeans, eighty Athenians, and a hundred and ten women to cook for them. This was the total number when the siege started, and there was no one else, slave or free, within the city wall. Such then was the setting for the siege of Plataea.

79   In the same summer and at the same time as the attack on Plataea, when the corn was ripening, the Athenians sent an expedition of two thousand of their own hoplites and two hundred cavalry against the Thraceward Chalcidians and the Bottiaeans, under the command of Xenophon the son of Euripides and two other generals. They came up to Spartolus in Bottice and destroyed the corn, and there was also the prospect that agents within the city would bring it over to them. But those of the opposite persuasion sent to Olynthus and secured the arrival of hoplites and a force to garrison the city. When these troops came out of Spartolus to attack, the Athenians joined battle with them right in front of the city. The Chalcidian hoplites and some mercenaries with them were defeated by the Athenians and withdrew into Spartolus: but the Chalcidian cavalry and light troops defeated the cavalry and light troops on the Athenian side (the Athenians had with them a small force of peltasts from the area called Crousis). The battle was hardly over when more peltasts arrived from Olynthus to reinforce the Chalcidians. Seeing this, the light troops in Spartolus took courage from the addition to their forces and from their earlier success, and joined the Chalcidian cavalry and the new reinforcements in a further attack on the Athenians, forcing them to fall back towards the two companies they had left protecting their baggage-train. The Chalcidians gave ground whenever the Athenians came back at them, but when the Athenians were in retreat they pressed their advantage and kept up a barrage of missiles. The Chalcidian cavalry rode up and made attacks at will, causing particular terror among the Athenians and their rout and pursuit for some considerable distance. The Athenians took refuge in Potidaea, and afterwards recovered their dead under truce and returned to Athens with what remained of their army: they had lost four hundred and thirty men and all of their generals. The Chalcidians and Bottiaeans set up a trophy, and after recovering their own dead dispersed to their various cities.

80   Not much later in this same summer the Ambraciots and Chaonians, in an attempt to gain control of the whole of Acarnania and remove it from the Athenian alliance, persuaded the Spartans to fit out an allied fleet and send it with a thousand hoplites against Acarnania. Their argument was that if the Spartans joined them in a

simultaneous attack by sea and on land, so that the coastal Acarnanians could not give support to those in the interior, they should easily annex Acarnania and go on to capture Zacynthus and Cephallenia, thus affecting the Athenians' future ability to sail round the Peloponnese: there was even hope of taking Naupactus. The Spartans agreed. They sent out the hoplites immediately in a few ships with Cnemus, who was still admiral, and gave notice to their allies to prepare the rest of the fleet and sail to Leucas as soon as possible. The Corinthians were particularly keen to support the Ambraciots, who were originally their colonists. While the fleet from Corinth and Sicyon and that area was being fitted out, the contingents from Leucas, Anactorium, and Ambracia had already assembled at Leucas and were waiting there.

Cnemus and his thousand hoplites crossed over the Gulf undetected by Phormio, who was in command of the twenty Athenian ships keeping guard at Naupactus, and immediately began preparations for the land campaign. The Greek troops at his disposal were from Ambracia, Leucas, and Anactorium as well as the thousand Peloponnesians he had brought with him. Of the barbarians joining him, there were a thousand Chaonians (they have no king, but their leaders, Photyus and Nicanor, were the members of the ruling dynasty who held the presidency for that year); combining forces with the Chaonians were Thesprotians, who also have no king; Molossians and Atintanians were led by Sabylinthus, the guardian of the king Tharyps who was still a boy; and Paravaeans were led by their king Oroedus. A thousand Orestians joined the Paravaeans, entrusted by their king Antiochus to the command of Oroedus. Perdiccas too sent a thousand Macedonians, concealing this from the Athenians, but they arrived too late. Without waiting for the ships from Corinth Cnemus set out with this army, and moving through the territory of Argos sacked the unfortified village of Limnaea. They then reached Stratus, the largest city in Acarnania, and thought that if they captured this first the rest of Acarnania would readily come over to them.

When the Acarnanians learnt that a considerable army had 81 invaded by land, and that an enemy fleet was also on its way to attack from the sea, they did not combine in support of Stratus, but each group took measures to protect their own territory, and they sent to Phormio asking for his help: he replied that with a fleet about to sail from Corinth he could not leave Naupactus unguarded.

The Peloponnesians and their allies formed themselves into three divisions and advanced on the city of Stratus. Their intention was to camp nearby and see if they could win the people over by negotiation: if not, they would proceed to action and assault the wall. The order of their advance had the Chaonians and the other barbarians in the centre; on their right the Leucadians and Anactorians and those with them; and on the left Cnemus and the Peloponnesians together with the Ambraciots. The three divisions were quite some distance apart, at times not even within sight of one another. The Greek divisions maintained discipline on the march and kept a lookout, finally pitching their camps in suitable places. The Chaonians, though, had no intention of making camp. Confident in themselves and in their reputation in that part of the mainland as the fiercest of fighters, they thought that if they and the other barbarians advanced at the charge they would take the city without any resistance and gain the credit for themselves.

Seeing the Chaonians still advancing, the men of Stratus reckoned that if they could defeat them while they were thus isolated from the main force, the Greeks would now be less likely to attack. They therefore placed men in ambushes round the city, and when the Chaonians were close fell on them in a coordinated attack from the city and the ambushes. In the resulting panic many of the Chaonians were killed, and seeing their defeat the other barbarians offered no further fight, but turned and fled. Neither of the Greek camps was aware of this battle, since the Chaonians had gone far ahead of them and the presumption was that they had been pressing on to establish their own camp. When the fleeing barbarians descended on them, the Greeks took them in, amalgamated their camps, and stayed there inactive for the rest of the day. The Stratians, lacking as yet the support of the other Acarnanians, did not come to close quarters with them, but kept using their slings from a distance and so reduced the Greeks to frustration, as they could not make any move without armour. The Acarnanians are thought the best at this form of warfare.

82   When night came, Cnemus rapidly retreated with his army to the river Anapus, about nine miles from Stratus. On the following day he took up his dead under truce. The men of Oeniadae now joined him in accordance with their treaty of friendship, and he withdrew into their territory before the Acarnanian reinforcements could arrive. From there all the other contingents returned to their

own homes. The Stratians set up a trophy to commemorate their battle against the barbarians.

The fleet from Corinth and the other allies on the Gulf of Crisa, 83 which was intended to support Cnemus and prevent reinforcement of the inland Acarnanians by those on the coast, never arrived. At about the same time as the battle at Stratus these ships were forced to a sea-battle with Phormio and the twenty Athenian ships guarding Naupactus. Phormio was tracking them as they sailed past and out of the Gulf: he wanted to make his attack in open sea. The Corinthians and their allies were sailing in no expectation of battle. Their ships were fitted out more as transports to carry troops to Acarnania, and they did not think that the Athenians with their twenty ships would dare to make battle against their own forty-seven. But then they noticed that as long as they were sailing along the south coast of the Gulf the Athenians were keeping pace with them along the north coast; and as they crossed from Patrae in Achaea to the mainland opposite on their way to Acarnania, they saw the Athenians bearing down on them from Chalcis and the river Evenus. Their attempt to escape detection by weighing anchor at night had failed, and so it was that they were forced to fight in the middle of the crossing. Each city contributing ships had its own generals: the Corinthian generals were Machaon, Isocrates, and Agatharchidas.

The Peloponnesians deployed their ships in a circle, prows facing outwards and sterns inwards, as large as they could make it without leaving room for an enemy breakthrough: inside the circle they placed the small support craft and their five fastest ships, available to sail out at short range wherever the enemy attacked. The Athenians 84 formed a single line and kept sailing round the Peloponnesians in circles, always grazing close and forcing them into a tighter space, with the constant threat of an immediate attack: but Phormio had briefed the Athenians not to make any attempt until he himself gave the signal. He was hoping that the Peloponnesians would not be able to hold their formation as infantry might on land, but that their ships would foul one another and the smaller craft add to the confusion: and if the usual morning wind blew from the Gulf (it was in expectation of this that he kept circling), they would not be able to stay still for a moment. He reckoned that, with the faster ships, he could choose to attack whenever he wanted, and the best time was with that wind.

When the wind did blow down from the Gulf, the Peloponnesian ships, already in a tight space, were thrown into confusion, the effect of the wind combining with the trouble caused by the smaller craft. Ships kept colliding, and were pushed apart with poles. Amid all the shouting and the fending off with mutual abuse they paid no attention either to the general orders or to their own officers, and in the rough sea they were unable through lack of experience to keep their oars clear of the water, and so made the ships less responsive to the captains' attempts to steer.

That was the moment Phormio chose to give his signal, and the Athenians attacked. First they holed one of the flagships, then began disabling the other ships at every turn. They created such havoc that none of the enemy offered resistance, but all fled to Patrae and Dyme in Achaea. The Athenians pursued them and captured twelve ships, taking on board most of their crews. They then sailed off to Molycrium, set up a trophy at Rhium and dedicated a ship to Poseidon, and returned to Naupactus. With their remaining ships the Peloponnesians immediately sailed round from Dyme and Patrae to Cyllene, the port of Elis. After the battle of Stratus Cnemus also came to Cyllene from Leucas, with the ships of his expedition which had been intended to join this other fleet.

85   The Spartans now sent three commissioners to the fleet to advise Cnemus: they were Timocrates, Brasidas, and Lycophron. The instructions were to prepare for another and more successful battle, and not to allow a small number of ships to deny them the sea. They had been greatly puzzled by the outcome, especially as this was their first attempt at naval warfare. They could not believe that their fleet was so inferior, and suspected that there had been some cowardice: they had failed to appreciate the contrast between the Athenians' long experience and their own brief training. So these commissioners were sent in anger. On their arrival they and Cnemus sent round the cities requesting additional ships and refitted the existing ships for battle.

Phormio likewise sent to Athens, to report the enemy preparations and give news of the battle he had won: he urged the Athenians to send him as many ships as they could without delay, as he was in daily expectation of another battle at any moment. The Athenians sent him twenty ships, but instructed the commander to take them first on an extra mission to Crete. One Nicias, a Cretan from Gortyn who was a consular representative of Athens, had persuaded the Athenians to sail against Cydonia, promising them the annexation of an allegedly hostile city: in fact his motive in bringing in the Athenians was to serve the interests of Cydonia's neighbour, Polichna. So the commander took his ships and left for Crete, where he joined the people of Polichna in ravaging Cydonian territory: and winds and seas too rough for sailing kept him there for some considerable time.

While the Athenians were detained in Crete, the Peloponnesians 86 at Cyllene, now equipped ready for battle, sailed around the coast to Panormus in Achaea, where a land army from the Peloponnese had come to support them. Phormio too sailed round to Molycrian Rhium and anchored outside it with the twenty ships he had deployed in the battle. (This Rhium was friendly to the Athenians. The other Rhium lies opposite, on the Peloponnesian coast: less than a mile of sea separates the two Rhiums, and this gap forms the mouth of the Gulf of Crisa.) So when they saw the Athenians at anchor, the Peloponnesians likewise anchored with seventy-seven ships at the Rhium in Achaea, not far from Panormus and their land army there.

For six or seven days the two fleets lay at anchor opposite each other, training and making preparations for the battle. The Peloponnesians, fearing a repeat of the previous disaster, were determined not to sail west of the Rhiums into the open sea: the Athenians were equally determined not to sail into the narrows, reckoning that the enemy would have the advantage if the battle were in a confined space. Then finally Cnemus and Brasidas and the other Peloponnesian generals, wanting to proceed to an early engagement before any reinforcements could come from Athens, first called together their troops and then, seeing that the majority of them were intimidated by their previous defeat and reluctant to fight, gave this speech of encouragement:

'Peloponnesians, if any of you think that the previous battle is 87 cause to be afraid of the next, this fear is a false deduction. We were ill-equipped then, as you know, and the purpose of our voyage was military transport rather than naval action. It so happened too that luck was largely against us, and it may be that in our first sea-battle inexperience brought some mistakes. The defeat was not the result of any cowardice on our part: and when our spirit has not been crushed, but still has the power of retort, we would be wrong to let it be blunted simply by the outcome of that event. The right view is this. Chance can well cause upsets in human affairs, but true courage lies in constancy of spirit: and no one with that courage would ever justify any cowardly action on grounds of inexperience. In fact your relative lack of experience is outweighed by your superior bravery.

Take the Athenians' expertise, which is what you fear most. True, if expertise is accompanied by courage, in a dire situation it will remember and apply its training, but without strength of spirit no skill is proof against the dangers of battle. Fear drives out memory, and skill without courage is useless. So you should set against their greater experience your own greater daring; and against the anxiety caused by that first defeat set the knowledge that you were then caught unprepared.

'You have the advantage of a superior number of ships and of fighting off friendly territory with a hoplite army in support. In most engagements success goes to those with the greater numbers and the better preparation. So we can find no reason at all for any likelihood of failure: even our previous mistakes now contribute to our advantage, as we shall learn from them. Be confident, then: let us have every man, captain or sailor, doing his duty and staying at his assigned post. We shall manage the attack better than your previous commanders, and give no man an excuse to turn coward. Anyone who does choose cowardice will be suitably punished: the brave will be honoured with the rewards which courage deserves.'

88   Such was the encouragement given to the Peloponnesians by their commanders. Phormio too was concerned for the morale of his men. He could see them gathering in groups to voice their alarm at the sheer number of enemy ships, and called them all to a meeting in order to encourage them and give them his assessment of the present situation. He had always told them before and conditioned them to believe that there could never be a force of ships too large for them to resist its attack, and for long the men themselves had embraced this claim, that as Athenians they would never give way to any rabble of Peloponnesian ships. But on this occasion he was aware that their morale was depressed by the sight in front of their eyes, and he wanted to recall them to confidence. So he convened a meeting of the Athenians and spoke to them like this:

89   'Men, I have called you together because I can see that you have been alarmed by the enemy's numbers, and I would not want you to be afraid when there is nothing to fear. Firstly, they have already been beaten and even they themselves recognize that they are not our equals: that is why they have assembled this disproportionately large number of ships. Secondly, what gives them the confidence to come against us, the belief that courage is their distinctive quality, is based solely on their experience and general success in fighting on land, and

they fancy this will apply to their navy also. But if they enjoy the greater advantage on land, the advantage on this occasion will be ours, and with good reason: they are certainly no more courageous than we are, and each of us is more confident in the element where we have the greater experience. The Spartan leadership is intent on its own reputation and is forcing most of the others into danger against their will: otherwise they would never have attempted another sea-battle after their comprehensive defeat. So do not expect any fearful daring from them. In fact you present a much greater threat to them, and there is more to justify their fear, because you have beaten them before, and they must think that you would not now be offering this paradoxical opposition unless you had a surprise in store for them. When one side has superior numbers, as these have, they usually go into battle reliant on strength rather than intelligence: those who dare to resist them with far inferior numbers, and under no compulsion to fight, only do so in the security of a firm intellectual conviction. They can work this out, and will have been more frightened by our unexpected resistance than if we were opposing them with a reasonable force. Many armies before now have lost to lesser numbers through inexperience, or sometimes lack of courage; and in this situation we have neither fault.

'As far as I can help it, I shall not fight the battle in the Gulf or sail into it. I am aware that a confined space is far from ideal for a few experienced and faster ships fighting against a large number of inexperienced ships. Ramming attacks cannot be properly executed without a clear view of the enemy from a distance, and retreat under pressure, if need be, is equally difficult. There is no room for breakthroughs and turn-backs, the speciality of fast ships, but the sea-battle would inevitably become an infantry-battle, and in that case the larger fleet has the advantage.

'I shall bear all this in mind as best I can. Your responsibility is to stay by your ships in good order and be quick to respond when the command comes, especially as the two stations are so close to each other. Then when we are in action keep discipline and silence paramount, which is essential in most warfare and particularly so in battle at sea—and fight them off as well as you did before. There is much at stake. It is up to you either to annihilate the Peloponnesians' hope in their navy or to bring the Athenians closer to a fear of losing the sea. I remind you again that you have already beaten most of them: and once defeated men do not return to the same dangers with the same resolve.'

90   Such was the encouragement given by Phormio. When the
Athenians would not oblige them by sailing into the narrows of the
Gulf, the Peloponnesians planned to draw them in against their will.
They put out at dawn and sailed along their own coast towards the
interior of the Gulf, maintaining the four columns in which they had
anchored, with what had been the right wing at anchor in the lead.
To this wing they had assigned their twenty fastest ships, so that if
Phormio did think they were making for Naupactus and responded
by sailing along the north coast to defend it, the Athenians could not
escape their attack by sailing ahead of this wing, but these fast ships
would hem them in.
      As they expected, when Phormio saw them putting out to sea, he
was afraid for the unguarded Naupactus, and was forced against his
will to make a hurried embarkation and set sail along the coast, with
Messenian infantry keeping pace in support on land. When the
Peloponnesians saw Phormio's ships coasting in line ahead and now
inside the Gulf and close to the shore, which is exactly what they
wanted, at a single sign of command they suddenly turned their ships
and sailed in line abreast, as fast as each ship could, directly at the
Athenians, hoping to catch all of them. The eleven leading Athenian
ships outran the Peloponnesian wing and its turn into the open
water: but the Peloponnesians caught the other nine, drove them in
flight to the shore and disabled them, and killed all the Athenians
who did not manage to swim away. One ship they captured crew and
all; others they roped and took in tow empty. Some of these empty
ships were rescued even as they were being towed away by the intervention of the Messenians, who plunged into the sea with their
weapons, climbed aboard the ships, and fought from the decks.

91   In this area, then, the Peloponnesians were victorious and had
disabled Athenian ships. Meanwhile their twenty ships from the
right wing were pursuing the eleven Athenian ships which had
escaped their turn into open water. Except for one ship the Athenians
got away and reached Naupactus first, where they took up position
by the temple of Apollo with their prows facing outwards, ready to
fight if the enemy sailed against their territory. The Peloponnesians
arrived after them, singing a paean of victory as they sailed. Far
ahead of the others one ship from Leucas was pursuing the one
Athenian ship left behind. There happened to be a merchant vessel
anchored in the open sea, round which the Athenian ship circled
just in time to ram the pursuing Leucadian amidships and hole it.

This sudden and surprising feat alarmed the Peloponnesians. Moreover, they had allowed success to prevent any disciplined pursuit: some of their ships had lowered their oars and stopped in the water, waiting for the others to catch up (not a wise thing to do with the enemy stationed so close), and others had run aground in the shallows through ignorance of the local conditions.

Seeing all this happening the Athenians took courage, and at a single command sailed out to the attack with a great shout. Their previous mistakes and present disorder limited the Peloponnesian resistance, and after a short while they turned and fled to Panormus, from where they had started. The Athenians gave pursuit, capturing the six nearest ships and recovering those of their own which had earlier been disabled on the shore and taken in tow by the enemy. They killed some of the crew they had captured, and took others alive as prisoners. The Spartan Timocrates had been sailing on the Leucadian ship which was holed near the merchant vessel, and committed suicide when the ship was lost: his body was washed up in the harbour of Naupactus.

On their return the Athenians set up a trophy at the place from which they had sailed out to their victory, and recovered all the bodies and wrecks which were close to their shore: they allowed the enemy to recover their own under truce. The Peloponnesians also set up a trophy to commemorate their success in crippling the Athenian ships on the shore, and they dedicated the ship they had captured alongside this trophy at the Rhium in Achaea. Thereafter, fearful of reinforcements from Athens, all except the Leucadians sailed by night into the Gulf of Crisa and on to Corinth. Not long after the withdrawal of the Peloponnesian fleet, the twenty Athenian ships which should have joined Phormio before the battle arrived at Naupactus from Crete.

So this summer ended.

Before dispersing the fleet which had withdrawn into the Gulf of Crisa and to Corinth, at the beginning of the winter Cnemus and Brasidas and the other Peloponnesian commanders decided to act on a proposal of the Megarians and make an attempt on the Peiraeus, the port of Athens. As was reasonable, given the Athenians' substantial naval superiority, the Peiraeus was open and unguarded. The plan was that each sailor should take his oar, his cushion, and his oar-strap and proceed on foot from Corinth to the sea on the side facing Athens, then make all speed to Megara. Here they were to launch from the Megarians' dockyard at Nisaea the forty ships which happened to be lying there and sail directly to the Peiraeus. There was no fleet on guard there, and no expectation that the enemy would ever make such a sudden attack. The Athenians did not expect them to attempt a more open and premeditated attack either, and they were sure that they would hear of it if such plans were being laid.

Once decided, the Peloponnesians set off immediately. They arrived at Nisaea at night, launched the ships, and set sail—though not now for the Peiraeus, as intended. They were frightened of the risk (and it is alleged that a wind was against them), and sailed instead to the promontory of Salamis which faces Megara. There was a garrison-fort there, and a guard of three ships to prevent any sea-traffic into or out of Megara. The Peloponnesians attacked the fort, towed away the triremes empty, and, catching the rest of Salamis unprepared, set to ravaging the land.

94   Beacons were lit to send the signal of enemy action to Athens, and there ensued a panic as great as any other in the war. People in the upper city thought that the enemy had already invaded the Peiraeus, and the people of the Peiraeus thought that Salamis had been lost and the enemy were just about to sail in to attack them. This could indeed have easily been done, if the Peloponnesians had determined not to lose their nerve: no wind would have stopped them. At dawn the Athenians came running in full force to defend the Peiraeus. They set about launching ships, made a hurried and chaotic embarkation, and sailed this fleet to Salamis, while the army mounted guard on the Peiraeus. When the Peloponnesians became aware of this relief expedition, they quickly set sail for Nisaea: by now they had overrun most of Salamis, and they took with them many prisoners, much booty, and the three ships from the fort at Boudorum. One factor in their withdrawal was their concern for the condition of their own ships, which had long been laid up and were far from watertight. Once back in Megara they returned to Corinth on foot. When the Athenians found that the enemy had already left Salamis, they too sailed back home. From now on they took greater care for the defence of the Peiraeus, among other precautions blocking the entrances to the harbours.

95   At about the same time, at the beginning of this winter, Sitalces the Odrysian, the son of Teres and king of Thrace, mounted a campaign against Perdiccas, the son of Alexander and king of Macedonia, and the Thraceward Chalcidians. Two promises had been made, one

to him and the other by him, and he wanted to enforce the one and fulfil the other. When Perdiccas was under pressure at the beginning of the war he had made Sitalces a promise, if he would reconcile the Athenians to him and refuse to support the restoration and claim to the throne of his brother and enemy Philip: and Perdiccas was not performing his side of the bargain. Sitalces himself, when making alliance with the Athenians, had undertaken to put an end to their war with the Thraceward Chalcidians. So with both these reasons for making his expedition he took with him Philip's son Amyntas, to install him as king of Macedonia, and also the Athenian envoys who happened to be at his court on this business, and Hagnon as military commander, as it was intended that the Athenians would join him against the Chalcidians with a fleet and as large an army as they could send.

Beginning then with the Odrysians Sitalces first made a levy of all 96 the Thracians in his empire between Mounts Haemus and Rhodope and extending to the sea in the direction of the Black Sea and the Hellespont, then of the Getae beyond Mount Haemus and the people living in the other regions south of the Danube and east towards the Black Sea. (The Getae and the others in that area border on the Scythians and share their mode of warfare, all being mounted archers.) He also called into service many of the mountain Thracians, independent people called the Dians who carry daggers and live for the most part round Rhodope: some were hired as mercenaries and others joined as volunteers. He made a levy also of the Agrianians and the Laeaeans and all the other Paeonian tribes within his empire at its furthest reach: this reach extended to the Laeaean Paeonians and the river Strymon, which flows from Mount Scombrus through the territory of the Agrianians and the Laeaeans and formed the boundary between his empire and the Paeonians who from there on were independent. In the direction of the Triballians, also independent, his border tribes were the Treres and the Tilataeans, who live north of Mount Scombrus and extend west to the river Oscius. The Oscius rises in the same mountain as the Nestus and the Hebrus: this is a large uninhabited mountain in the Rhodope range.

The extent of the Odrysian empire as measured by coastline 97 reached from the city of Abdera into the Black Sea as far as the mouth of the Danube. A merchant ship with a constant stern-wind would take at the shortest a full four days and nights to sail round this land. On foot a man travelling light would need at the least eleven days for the journey from Abdera to the Danube. Those are the dimensions of the seaboard. The greatest cross-country distance inland from the sea is from Byzantium to the Laeaeans and the Strymon, and this would take a light traveller thirteen days.

The tribute from all the barbarian tribes and the Greek cities in the Odrysian empire in the time of Seuthes, who succeeded Sitalces as king and raised the tribute to its highest level, was the equivalent of about four hundred talents of silver, paid in gold and silver. Just as much again came in the form of gifts of gold and silver, as well as embroidered or plain fabrics and other goods, made not only to the king himself but also to his fellow Odrysian princes and nobles. Their established custom was the opposite of that in the Persian kingdom—a culture of taking rather than giving, in which to refuse a demand was more shaming than to have a demand refused. This was the custom in the rest of Thrace too, but the power of the Odrysians enabled them to take it yet further, and it was impossible to achieve anything without a gift given. So the kingdom grew to a position of great strength. Of all the nations between the Ionian Gulf and the Black Sea this was the greatest in terms of revenue and general prosperity, though in military strength and size of army a far second to the Scythians. Here there is no comparison. Not only in Europe but even in Asia too no single nation could match the Scythians if they were all of one mind: but the fact is that in this and other ways also they lag behind others in political organization and the technology to develop their resources for a better life. This then was the great territory over which Sitalces was king.

98

He set about preparing his army, and when all was ready he started on the march to Macedonia. His route took him first through his own kingdom, then over the uninhabited Mount Cercina, which forms the boundary between the Sintians and the Paeonians. He traversed it using the road which he himself had cut through the forest on a previous occasion, when he had campaigned against the Paeonians. As they crossed this mountain from Odrysian territory they had the Paeonians on their right and the Sintians and Maedians on their left. Once past the mountain they came to Doberus in Paeonia. On the whole of the march the army suffered no losses except through illness, but did gain additions: many of the independent Thracians joined uninvited in hope of plunder, so that the total force is said to have numbered not less than a hundred and fifty thousand, of which the majority were infantry, but about a third were cavalry. The largest part of the cavalry was supplied by the Odrysians themselves, and after them the Getae. Of the infantry the fiercest fighters were the independent dagger-men who had come down from Rhodope: the rest of the troops were a mixed mass, formidable mostly for their sheer numbers.

So this force gathered at Doberus and prepared for a descent 99 from the heights to invade Lower Macedonia, which was Perdiccas' kingdom. There is also an Upper Macedonia, comprising among other peoples the Lyncestians and the Elimiotians, who are allies and subjects of Lower Macedonia, but retain their own local kingdoms. What is now coastal Macedonia was first acquired by Perdiccas' father Alexander and his forebears, who were originally Temenids from Argos. They won this land and established their kingdom there by forcibly evicting the Pierians from Pieria (they later settled in Phagres and other places across the Strymon below Mount Pangaeum—the coastal area below Pangaeum is still called the Pierian Gulf), and likewise the Bottiaeans (now neighbours of the Chalcidians) from the district called Bottia. They also acquired a narrow strip of Paeonia running down along the river Axius to Pella and the sea; and by driving out the Edonians they took control of the land the other side of the Axius as far as the Strymon, which is called Mygdonia. They displaced the Eordians from what is still known as Eordia (most of them killed, but a small remnant settled near Physca), and the Almopians from Almopia. These new Macedonians conquered other tribes too, and still control them—Anthemus, Grestonia, Bisaltia, and much of the original Macedonia. The whole of this area is now called Macedonia, and Perdiccas the son of Alexander was its king when Sitalces attacked.

The Lower Macedonians were unable to resist the attack of a large 100 army, and gathered in such strongholds and fortified places as they had in the country, which were not many. Those which now exist there were built later by Perdiccas' son Archelaus when he became king: he also cut straight roads and made other military improvements, so that in strength of cavalry and infantry and general resources for war he surpassed all eight of the kings who preceded him.

On leaving Doberus the Thracian army first invaded what had once been Philip's kingdom. They took Eidomene by storm; Gortynia and Atalante and some other places came over by agreement, out of loyalty to Philip's son Amyntas, who was with the Thracians; an unsuccessful attempt was made to capture Europus by siege. The Thracians then advanced into the rest of Macedonia, to the left of Pella and Cyrrhus. They did not go further on to Bottia and Pieria, but set about ravaging the territory of Mygdonia, Grestonia, and Anthemus.

The Macedonians did not even consider any resistance with infantry, but sent for further cavalry from their allies in the interior. Then, though they were few against many, they began making charges into the Thracian army wherever they saw opportunity. They were good horsemen and protected by body-armour, so at any point of attack no one could resist their charge: but it was a dangerous tactic against an enemy many times their number, and each time they found themselves hemmed in by a mass of troops. In the end they desisted, recognizing that they could make no challenge against such numbers.

101   Sitalces now began negotiating with Perdiccas about the issues which lay behind his campaign: and since the Athenian fleet had not arrived (the Athenians, doubting his own arrival, had merely sent him gifts and envoys), he dispatched part of his army against the Chalcidians and Bottiaeans, forcing them inside their walls and ravaging their land. With Sitalcés in occupation of these areas, the peoples living to the south—the Thessalians, the Magnesians, the other subjects of Thessaly, and the Greeks as far as Thermopylae—became afraid that his army might move against them too, and made their preparations. There was similar fear among the northern Thracians inhabiting the plains beyond the Strymon—the Panaeans, the Odomantians, the Droans, and the Dersaeans: all these are independent peoples. Speculation spread even further to the Greek states at war with Athens, where it was rumoured that the Athenians might invoke their pact of alliance and bring in the Thracian army against them too.

In fact Sitalces confined himself to the occupation and devastation of Chalcidice, Bottice, and Macedonia, and when it became clear that he was achieving none of the objects of his invasion, and moreover his army was running out of food and suffering from the winter, he was persuaded to make a rapid withdrawal by Seuthes the son of Sparadocus, who was his nephew and second only to himself in authority. Perdiccas had won over Seuthes with a secret promise to give him his sister in marriage and a dowry with her. Sitalces took Seuthes' advice, and after a total stay of thirty days, eight of them in Chalcidice, returned home quickly with his army. Perdiccas later kept his promise to Seuthes and gave him his sister Stratonice in marriage.

So much, then, for the account of Sitalces' campaign.

In this same winter, after the dispersal of the Peloponnesian fleet, 102
the Athenians at Naupactus under the command of Phormio sailed
round to Astacus and landed there, then marched into the interior of
Acarnania with the four hundred Athenian hoplites from the ships
and four hundred Messenians. They expelled from Stratus and
Coronta and other places the men thought to be unreliable, restored
Cynes the son of Theolytus to Coronta, and returned to their ships.
They decided that, as it was winter, it was not possible to campaign
against Oeniadae, the only place in Acarnania which had always been
hostile to Athens.

The reason for this decision was the river Achelous. This river
flows from Mount Pindus through Dolopia, Agraeis, and Amphilochia,
then through the Acarnanian plain, passing the city of Stratus as it
enters the plain. It flows into the sea by Oeniadae, creating a marsh
round the city which in winter is too full of water to allow any military assault. Most of the Echinades islands lie opposite Oeniadae
close to the mouths of the Achelous: with its strong flow the river
continually forms fresh deposits against them, so that some of the
islands have already been joined to the mainland and the expectation
is that this will happen to them all before long. The current is wide,
deep, and muddy, and the islands close together, forming between
them a frame for the silt which prevents it being washed away: they
lie in staggered rows rather than a single line, so give the water no
straight channels into the open sea. They are small and uninhabited.

The story goes that when Alcmeon the son of Amphiaraus was a
fugitive after the murder of his mother he received an oracle from
Apollo indicating that he should settle in this land: the riddle was
that he would not have release from the terrors until he found and set
up home in a place which at the time when he killed his mother had
not yet been seen by the sun nor yet existed as land, since all the rest
of the earth was polluted by him. He was puzzled, but finally, so they
say, thought of this sedimentation of the Achelous, and reckoned
that over the long period of his wanderings after killing his mother
there would have formed sufficient deposit to support a man's life.
So he settled in the area around Oeniadae, became its ruler, and left
the country its name from his son Acarnan. Such is the traditional
story which has come down to us about Alcmeon.

Phormio and the Athenians left Acarnania and returned to 103
Naupactus. At the beginning of spring they sailed back to Athens,

taking with them the free men among their prisoners of war (who were then released in a man-for-man exchange) and the ships which they had captured.

So ended this winter, and with it the third year of this war chronicled by Thucydides.

BOOK THREE

In the following summer, when the corn was growing ripe, the 1
Peloponnesians and their allies invaded Attica, under the command
of Archidamus the son of Zeuxidamus, king of Sparta. They encamped
and began ravaging the land. As usual, the Athenian cavalry kept up
attacks wherever possible, and prevented the bulk of the light-armed
troops from advancing beyond the hoplites and doing damage to the
areas close to the city. The Peloponnesians remained in Attica for as
long as they had provisions, then withdrew and dispersed to their
various cities.

Immediately after the Peloponnesian invasion, Lesbos (apart from 2
Methymna) revolted from Athens. They had wanted to secede even
before the war, but had received no support from the Spartans, and
they were now obliged to make their revolt earlier than they had
intended. They had been waiting for the completion of works—
the piling of moles to close their harbours, the building of walls,
the construction of ships—and also for the expected arrival from the
Black Sea of archers and corn, and the other goods they were sending
for. But people from Tenedos (no friend of Lesbos) and Methymna,
and some individuals from Mytilene itself who were consular representatives of Athens and in conflict with the others, reported to the
Athenians that Lesbos was being forced into political union with
Mytilene, that all this urgent activity was undertaken in collaboration
with the Peloponnesians and the Boeotians (who were related to the
Lesbians), and that this was preparation for revolt: if no pre-emptive
action was taken immediately, Lesbos would be lost to Athens.

The Athenians were exhausted both by the plague and by the 3
escalation of the war in its early years, and they thought it would be
a major undertaking to open another front against Lesbos, a naval
power with its resources intact. At first, then, they would not accept
the allegations, mainly because they did not want them to be true.
But when they had sent envoys and failed to persuade the Mytilenaeans
to abandon their centralizing policy and put a stop to their preparatory works, they became alarmed and determined on pre-emptive
action. They instantly sent out to Lesbos forty ships which happened
to be ready for an expedition round the Peloponnese: in command
was Cleïppides the son of Deinias, with two other generals. They had

been informed that there was a festival of Apollo Maloeis celebrated outside the city by the whole population of Mytilene, and there was hope of a surprise attack if they hurried. If the attempt succeeded, well and good: if not, Cleïppides was to order the Mytilenaeans to surrender their fleet and demolish their walls; he should tell them that refusal would mean war.

So these ships set off. There happened to be ten triremes from Mytilene on support duty at Athens in accordance with the terms of the alliance: the Athenians detained these and placed their crews under arrest.

The Mytilenaeans were warned by a man who crossed from Athens to Euboea, made his way on foot to Geraestus, found there a merchant ship about to leave, and with a fair wind arrived in Mytilene on the third day after leaving Athens, bringing news of the fleet on its way. Consequently the Mytilenaeans did not leave the city for the festival of Maloeis and took other precautions, fencing the 4 unfinished parts of their walls and harbours and posting guards. The Athenians sailed in shortly afterwards and saw the situation. Their generals delivered the message as instructed. The Mytilenaeans refused to obey, and war was declared.

Unprepared, and obliged to go to war at short notice, the Mytilenaeans did send out their ships to offer battle a little way in front of the harbour, but the Athenian ships chased them back. They then began to negotiate with the Athenian generals, hoping if possible to reach some reasonable agreement which would remove the Athenian ships for the time being. The generals accepted their proposals, as their own fear was that they did not have sufficient forces to wage war against the whole of Lesbos. A truce was made, and the Mytilenaeans sent envoys to Athens (including one of the original informers, who had now changed his mind) in an attempt to persuade the Athenians that they had no revolutionary intent and the fleet could be recalled. At the same time they sent envoys to Sparta in a trireme, undetected by the Athenians who were anchored at Malea to the north of the city—they had no confidence in the success of their embassy to Athens. After a hard journey across open sea the envoys reached Sparta and began negotiations for the sending of some sup- 5 port. When the embassy returned from Athens with nothing achieved, the Mytilenaeans and all the rest of Lesbos apart from Methymna went to war. Methymna had declared in support of the Athenians, and so did Imbros and Lemnos and a few others of the allies.

The Mytilenaeans made a full-scale sortie against the Athenian position, and had the better of the ensuing battle, but lacked the confidence to camp on the field and withdrew. Thereafter they remained inactive, unwilling to take any more risks without further preparation and any help that might be forthcoming from the Peloponnese. They had now been reached by Meleas from Laconia and Hermaeondas from Thebes, who had been dispatched before the revolt but were unable to arrive in advance of the Athenian expedition. After the battle they now sailed in undetected in a trireme, and urged the Mytilenaeans to send back with them another trireme with envoys on board: and so they did.

The Athenians were greatly encouraged by the inactivity of the 6 Mytilenaeans, and called in their allies, who were the quicker to come when they saw no sign of resistance from the Lesbians. They brought some ships round to anchor to the south of the city and fortified two camps either side of the city, establishing a blockade on both harbours. The Athenians thus denied the Mytilenaeans the use of the sea, but all the rest of the land was in the control of the Mytilenaeans and the other Lesbians who had now come to support them, except for the small areas which the Athenians controlled around their camps and at Malea, which was their main station for sea-traffic and their market.

Such was the beginning of the war over Mytilene.

At the same time in this summer the Athenians also sent thirty 7 ships round the Peloponnese, electing Phormio's son Asopius as general in command. This was at the request of the Acarnanians, who had asked to be sent a son or relative of Phormio to lead them. On their voyage these ships ravaged the coastal areas of Laconia. Then Asopius sent the majority of the ships home, while he himself took twelve to Naupactus. Later, he called a full levy of the Acarnanians and campaigned against Oeniadae, his ships sailing up the Achelous and the land army ravaging the territory. When the inhabitants would not submit, he dismissed the land troops and sailed with the Athenians to Leucas, where he made a landing at Nericus. As they were returning to their ships both he and part of his force were killed by the local men who had rallied in defence, assisted by a small garrison. Thereafter the Athenians recovered their dead from the Leucadians under truce and sailed away.

The Mytilenaean envoys who had been dispatched on the first 8 ship were told by the Spartans to present themselves at the Olympic festival, so that the rest of the allies too could hear their case and discuss it. So they came to Olympia. (This was the Olympiad in which Dorieus of Rhodes won his second victory.) At the conference held after the festival they spoke as follows:

9   'Spartans and allies, we are aware of the established way of things among the Greeks: when people secede and desert their previous alliance in time of war, others are glad to welcome them to the extent of their usefulness, but think the less of them for their betrayal of their former friends. And this perception is fair enough in cases where the seceding and the deserted parties have been at one with each other in policy and intent, equally matched in power and resources, and there is no good reason for secession. But this was not so between us and the Athenians, and no one should think the worse of us for leaving them in their hour of danger despite their regard for us in peacetime.

10   'We shall first—especially since we are asking you for an alliance— address ourselves to questions of justice and honesty. We know that no friendship between individuals or association between cities can have any lasting basis unless the partners treat each other with patent honesty and are generally of the same mind: divergence of thinking is the start of differences in action.

'Our alliance with the Athenians began when you withdrew from the Persian War and they stayed on to finish the task. But our purpose in the alliance was not to enslave the Greeks to the Athenians, but to free the Greeks from the Persians. As long as the Athenians led us on an equal basis we were happy to follow: but when we saw them relaxing their hostility to the Persians and advancing the enslavement of their allies, then our fears began. Precluded by the multiplicity of votes from coming together in a common resistance, the allies were enslaved—apart from us and the Chians. With our so-called autonomy and nominal freedom we joined in their campaigns. But on the evidence of previous examples we could no longer trust the Athenians as leaders of the alliance. When they had subjugated our fellow participants in a sworn treaty, it was hardly likely that they would not have done the same to the rest of us, if they had

11   ever become able to do so. If we had all still been autonomous, we could have had greater confidence that the Athenians would take no unilateral action. But with the majority of the allies subjugated and yet the continuing need to deal with us on equal terms, the very fact of this general submission was bound to make it harder for the

Athenians to tolerate our unique claim to equality, the more so as they grew more powerful and we more isolated.

'The only secure basis for an alliance is a balance of fear: then if either partner is inclined to break the terms he is deterred by the knowledge that he would have no superiority in an offensive. The reason why we were left autonomous was solely to the extent that they thought the acquisition of empire was best achieved with plausible rhetoric and the application of moral rather than physical force. They used us as evidence that equal voting partners would not agree to join their campaigns unless those under attack had done some wrong. Similarly, they first conscripted the strongest against the weaker allies, leaving the strongest to the last, when they would be weakened by the removal of the rest. If they had started with us, when all the others still had their own strength and there would have been a focus of resistance, they would not have found the subjugation so easy. Moreover our navies gave them cause for fear: they might at some time unite and present a danger by joining with you or some other power. In fact we survived by cultivating the Athenian state and its leaders of the day: but judging by the examples of their treatment of the others, we did not think that we would have lasted for long if this war had not broken out.

'So what sort of "friendship" or "freedom" was this proving to be? 12 How could we trust it, when relations between us were so insincere? Caution was their motive for cultivating us in time of war, and ours too for cultivating them in peacetime. What is usually secured by mutual good will was in our case a bond of fear, and we were held in the alliance more out of caution than friendship: whichever party was the sooner to find good grounds for confidence would also be the first to make some break. So if any think us wrong to have made the first move while their danger to us is still only a threat in waiting, without waiting ourselves for clear evidence of the reality, this is a mistaken judgement. If we had the equal ability to counter with our own aggressive designs and our own threats held in suspension, why should we ever, in such a position of equality, have come under their power? As it is, when they have the power to attack at any moment, we too should have the right to take our precautions.

'These, then, Spartans and allies, are the reasons and grievances 13 which have led us to secede. They are clear enough to convince any audience of the rationale of our action, and strong enough to frighten us into turning elsewhere for our protection. We had wanted to do so

long ago, when the peace still held and we sent envoys to you to
discuss secession, but that came to nothing when you gave us no
support. But now that the Boeotians have encouraged us to secede,
our response was immediate, and we considered that this would
be a double secession—from the Greek alliance, to join in their liberation rather than the Athenians' oppression of them; and from the
Athenians, to forestall their future attempts to destroy us. Our secession, though, has proceeded faster than we would wish, and left us
unprepared: which is all the more reason for you to take us into your
alliance and send us help as soon as you can, and so demonstrate your
defence of those in need combined with damage to your enemies.

'Your opportunity is greater than ever before. The Athenians have
been crippled by disease and capital expense, and their ships are
either round your coasts or deployed against us, so they are not likely
to have any surplus of ships if you make a second invasion in this
summer, coordinating your attack with ships as well as infantry: they
will either be unable to resist your naval assault or will have to withdraw from both their expeditions against you and us. No one should
think that this will mean running your own danger for a land which
is not your own. Lesbos may seem far away, but the help we can
bring is close to home. The war will not be decided in Attica, as
people might think, but in the territory on which Attica depends for
support. The Athenians derive their income from their allies, and
this will grow yet larger if they put us down: no one else will then
secede, our own resources will be added to theirs, and we would be
in worse state than those already enslaved. But if you give us your
ready support, you will gain a city with a large navy, which is your
greatest need; you will find it easier to defeat the Athenians by drawing away their allies (all the others will now be emboldened to come
over to you); and you will dispel the charge you once incurred of
failure to help those who secede. If you are seen as liberators, your
base for victory will be all the more secure.

14   'Have respect, then, for the hopes which the Greeks repose in you,
have respect for Olympian Zeus, in whose sanctuary we are here as
virtual suppliants, and come to the aid of Mytilene in alliance with
us. Do not abandon us, when the risk we run to our lives is all our
own, but the benefit of success will be shared by all: and all will share
yet more in the harm if you do not accept our cause and we fail.
Prove yourselves men of the quality which Greece expects and our
predicament needs.'

Such was the speech made by the Mytilenaeans. Having heard this 15
appeal, the Spartans and their allies accepted the arguments and took
the Lesbians into alliance. The Spartans instructed the allies there
present to gather at the Isthmus as soon as they could with the usual
two-thirds levy, for the invasion of Attica. They themselves were the
first to arrive, and began preparing slipways at the Isthmus for the
transport of ships overland from Corinth to the sea on the side facing
Athens, so they could make their attack simultaneously with ships
and land forces. The Spartans set about this with energy, but the
other allies were slow to assemble, occupied as they were with the
harvest of crops and sick of campaigning.

The Athenians recognized that these preparations were predicated 16
on a perception of their own weakness. To prove the perception false
and demonstrate their easy ability to meet the attack from the
Peloponnese without moving the fleet at Lesbos, they crewed a hundred ships with metics and their own citizens from all but the two
highest classes, and set sail for the Isthmus in a display of strength,
making landings on the Peloponnese wherever they wished. The
Spartans found this quite astonishing and thought that the Lesbians
must have misled them. When their allies failed to appear and
they also heard news that the thirty Athenian ships sent round the
Peloponnese were ravaging their dependent territory, they considered their expedition a lost cause and returned home. (Later they
made preparations to send a fleet to Lesbos, calling for a total of forty
ships from their allied cities and appointing Alcidas as the admiral to
sail with them.) When the Athenians saw them withdraw, they too
went home with their hundred ships.

[At this time when their ships were at sea the Athenians had the 17
largest number of ships on active service and in fine condition,
though there were similar or even greater numbers at the beginning
of the war. Then there were a hundred guarding Attica, Euboea, and
Salamis, and a further hundred cruising round the Peloponnese,
apart from the ships at Potidaea and in other places: so the total
number of ships in service in the course of one summer was two
hundred and fifty. This and Potidaea were particular drains on their
finances. The men on duty at Potidaea were two-drachma hoplites
(receiving one drachma a day for themselves and one for their servant). There were three thousand of these at first, and this number
was maintained throughout the siege; and then there were the sixteen
hundred with Phormio, who left before the end. All the ships were

paid at this same rate. This then was the initial drain on their finances, and this the largest number of ships which they manned.]

18   At the same time as the Spartans were at the Isthmus the Mytilenaeans made a land campaign with their own troops and supporting forces against Methymna, expecting its betrayal to them. They attacked the city, but when things did not go in the way they had anticipated they went off to Antissa, Pyrrha, and Eresus: they took measures to improve security in these cities and strengthened their walls, then quickly returned home. On their withdrawal the people of Methymna launched their own campaign against Antissa, but a counter-attack from the city left them badly beaten by the Antissans and their supporting forces: many were killed, and the remainder made a hasty retreat. When intelligence reached the Athenians that the Mytilenaeans were in control of the country and their own troops were insufficient to prevent it, at the beginning of autumn they sent out a thousand citizen hoplites with Paches the son of Epicurus as the general in command: they themselves rowed the ships in which they sailed. On arrival they constructed a single wall completely surrounding Mytilene, with garrison-forts built in at strong points. Mytilene was now firmly blockaded both by land and by sea, and winter began.

19   Being short of money for the siege, the Athenians took two measures. For the first time they levied on themselves a property tax to raise two hundred talents; and they sent twelve ships round the allies to collect money, under the command of Lysicles and four other generals. After putting in to various other places and making collections, Lysicles struck up into Caria from Myus and went inland through the plain of the Maeander as far as the Sandian Hill, where he was attacked by the Carians and the Anaeans: both he and a good number of the rest of his force were killed.

20   In this same winter, the Plataeans, still besieged by the Peloponnesians and Boeotians, were beginning to suffer from shortage of food and had no hope of support from Athens or any other prospect of rescue. So they and the Athenians who were with them under siege formed a plan of escape. The original suggestion, put forward by Theaenetus the son of Tolmides, a seer, and Eupompides the son of Daïmachus, one of their generals, was that they should all break out and try to force their way over the enemy walls. Half of them subsequently pulled out, thinking the danger too great, but up to about two hundred and twenty men remained committed to the escape. This is how they set about it.

They constructed ladders of exactly the right length for the enemy wall. They did this by calculating from the courses of bricks in a section of the wall facing them which happened not to have been plastered. The counting of the courses was done by many of them at the same time, so that although some might get it wrong the majority would reach the true figure, especially as they each counted several times and they were not far away, with the wall easily seen for their purpose. So in this way they calculated the length of the ladders, estimating measurements from the thickness of a brick.

The construction of the Peloponnesians' wall was as follows. 21 There were two circuits, one facing Plataea and the other to guard against any external attack from Athens: the two circuits were about sixteen feet apart. In the space between them there were partitioned quarters built for the guards, so the walls were linked throughout and looked like a single thick wall with battlements on both sides. At every tenth battlement there were large towers equal in width to the space between the walls, extending to both the inner and the outer faces, so there was no way past the towers at the side, but only through the middle of them. On nights when there was a rainstorm the guards abandoned the battlements and kept watch from the towers, which were close enough and had roofing. Such then was the wall blockading Plataea.

When the Plataeans had all prepared, they waited for a stormy 22 night of rain and wind, and also no moon, to make their exit. They were led by the same men who had proposed the enterprise. First they crossed the surrounding ditch, then they came up to the enemy wall, undetected by the guards who could not see them in the darkness and could not hear their approach through the bluster of the wind: they had also kept at some distance from one another, to prevent any clatter from the collision of weapons betraying them. They were lightly armed, and had shoes only on their left foot to give them a safer grip in the mud. They now set about scaling the battlements (which they knew to be deserted) in a section of the wall between two towers. First came the men carrying the ladders, and placed them against the wall. Then twelve men lightly armed with dagger and breastplate began to climb up. Their leader was Ammeas the son of Coroebus, and he was the first up: the others followed him and spread out, six going to each of the towers. Then more men came after them, armed only with short spears, while others behind them carried their shields to make it easier for them to climb the wall: they would be given their shields in any encounter with the enemy.

Most of them were up on the wall when the guards in the towers discovered them—one of the Plataeans in grabbing hold of the battlements had dislodged a tile, which fell with a crash. There was an immediate hue and cry, and the whole besieging army rushed up onto the wall. In the darkness and the stormy weather they had no idea what had caused the alarm, and at the same time the Plataeans left behind in the city broke out and attacked the Peloponnesian wall on the opposite side to that which their colleagues were scaling, to distract attention from them as far as possible. The result was that the Peloponnesians were thrown into confusion and stayed where they were, no one taking the initiative to move in support from his own station, and all without a clue of what was going on. Their special force of three hundred detailed to attend any emergency went round outside the wall to the source of the alarm. Beacons were lit to send the signal of enemy action to Thebes, but the Plataeans in the city countered by lighting several beacons on their own walls (they had prepared them in advance for this very purpose) to confuse the beacon-signals received by the enemy, in the hope that they would misinterpret what was happening and not arrive in support until their own escapees had got clear and reached safety.

23   Meanwhile, now that the first of them to reach the top had won control of the two towers by killing the guards in each, the Plataean scaling-party set guards of their own to block the corridors through the towers and prevent any attack by those routes, and got more men up on the towers by ladders placed against them from the top of the wall. So these maintained a fire of missiles from the towers to keep back the troops approaching both below the wall and along it, while the main group now set up a series of ladders against the wall, pushed over the battlements, and climbed across this section of the wall between the towers. As he got over each man stopped at the edge of the external ditch and shot arrows or javelins at anyone coming along the wall to oppose their transit.

When all others had made their way over, the men from the towers came down last and got to the ditch with difficulty. At this point the special detachment of three hundred arrived to intercept them, carrying torches. The Plataeans, standing on the edge of the ditch, could see them the better out of the darkness, and aimed their arrows and javelins at the unprotected parts of the enemies' bodies: they themselves were out of range of the torches, and the less visible for their glare. So even the last of the Plataeans managed to cross the ditch in time, though it was a difficult struggle. Ice had formed there, not firm enough to walk on, but more the watery slush which comes from an east or north wind, and during the night the snow driven by this wind had raised the water level in the ditch so they could hardly keep their heads above it as they crossed. Their escape was in fact largely due to the violence of the storm.

Setting out from the ditch, the Plataeans moved in a body along 24 the road leading to Thebes, with the shrine of the hero Androcrates on their right, reckoning that the Peloponnesians would suppose this the least likely route for them to take, as it led to the enemy—and as they went they could see the Peloponnesians chasing with torches along the road to Cithaeron and Dryoscephalae which leads to Athens. The Plataeans followed the Thebes road for somewhat less than a mile, then turned back and took the mountain road leading to Erythrae and Hysiae, and once in the mountains were able to make their escape to Athens. Two hundred and twelve men made the escape out of an originally larger number: a few had turned back to the city before scaling the wall, and one archer had been captured at the outer ditch. The Peloponnesians gave up the pursuit and returned to their quarters. The Plataeans in the city knew nothing of the outcome, but as those who had turned back reported that there were no survivors, when it was day they sent a herald asking for a truce for the recovery of their dead: they cancelled this approach when they learnt the truth.

This then is how the men from Plataea crossed the enemy wall and reached safety.

At the end of this same winter the Spartan Salaethus was sent out 25 from Sparta to Mytilene in a trireme. He sailed to Pyrrha, then proceeded on foot, making his way undetected into Mytilene along a gully which afforded a path through the encircling wall. He told the presiding officials that there would be an invasion of Attica to coincide with the arrival of the forty ships intended for their aid: he had been sent in advance to inform them of this and to take general charge. The Mytilenaeans took heart and were less inclined now to come to terms with the Athenians.

So ended this winter, and with it the fourth year of this war chronicled by Thucydides.

In the following summer the Peloponnesians dispatched the forty 26 ships to Mytilene with Alcidas (their admiral-in-chief) appointed as

commander, then immediately invaded Attica with their own
and allied forces: their intention was to embarrass the Athenians on
both fronts at once, and so make them less likely to respond to the
fleet sailing for Mytilene. This invasion was under the command
of Cleomenes, the brother of Pleistoanax, acting as regent for
Pleistoanax's son Pausanias, who was king but still a minor. Their
devastation included any new growth in those parts of Attica previously laid waste and extended to the areas left untouched in the
earlier invasions. In fact this invasion caused more distress to the
Athenians than any other, except for the second, as the Peloponnesians
stayed on in constant expectation of hearing news from Lesbos of
action by their ships, which should by then have made the crossing,
and so they pressed ahead with the ravaging of most of Attica. But
when there was still no sign of the expected outcome and their provisions had run out, they withdrew and dispersed to their cities.

27   Meanwhile the Mytilenaeans were forced to come to terms with
the Athenians. The ships from the Peloponnese were taking their
time and still had not reached them, and their food had run out. The
sequence of events was as follows. When even Salaethus had despaired
of the ships, he issued hoplite arms to the ordinary people (who until
now had only been light-armed) with the intention of making an
attack on the Athenians. But once in possession of arms the people
refused to obey the authorities any longer. They gathered in groups
and demanded that the ruling classes should bring out the food in
plain sight and distribute it to all: otherwise they would make their
own agreement with the Athenians and hand the city over to them.

28   The authorities realized that they were powerless to prevent this,
and also recognized their own danger if they were excluded from any
settlement. So both parties together joined in negotiating an agreement with Paches and his army. The terms were that the Athenians
should have the right to make whatever decision they wished about
the people of Mytilene; they themselves would admit the army into
their city, and send an embassy to Athens in their own cause; until
the ambassadors returned Paches would not imprison, enslave, or kill
any Mytilenaean. Such was the agreement, but those Mytilenaeans
who had been most active in dealing with Sparta were terrified at the
entry of the Athenian army and could not bear to wait—for all the
assurances they sat down at the altars as suppliants. Paches persuaded
them to leave their position with a promise to do them no harm,
and lodged them in Tenedos until the Athenians made a decision.

He also sent triremes to Antissa and gained control there too, and generally organized the military side as he saw fit.

The Peloponnesians in the forty ships, who were supposed to 29 reach Mytilene at all speed, had delayed even when sailing round the Peloponnese and took the rest of their voyage at a leisurely pace. Their movement went unreported to the Athenian authorities at home until they put in at Delos: thereafter they touched at Icaros and Myconos, where they first heard that Mytilene had been taken. Wanting to establish the truth, they sailed on to Embatum in the territory of Erythrae, reaching Embatum on about the seventh day after the capture of Mytilene. With the truth now reliably confirmed they debated what to do in the circumstances, and a man from Elis called Teutiaplus spoke as follows:

'My opinion, Alcidas and my fellow Peloponnesian commanders, 30 is that we should sail against Mytilene immediately, just as we are, before our presence is detected. When their troops have only just occupied the city the likelihood is that we shall find much unguarded, and particularly the sea approaches: here they have no reason to expect an enemy attack, and this is where our strength of the moment lies. It is likely too that on the assumption of a victory already won their infantry will have been scattered in billets across the city without any emergency plan. So if we were to attack suddenly and at night, with the help of those inside (if indeed we still have any friends left) I believe we could gain control. And we should not let the danger deter us, but rather regard this as one of those vacant opportunities of war which the successful commander avoids giving himself but exploits when he sees it given by the enemy.'

Alcidas would not accept this argument. Others then, some of the 31 Ionian exiles and the Lesbians who were on board his expedition, urged that if this was too much of a danger for him he should attack and capture one of the cities in Ionia, or Cyme in Aeolis. That would give them a city as a base from which to instigate the revolt of Ionia (as could well be hoped—no one had not welcomed their arrival); they could then deprive the Athenians of a major source of income, and at the same time cause them the expense of any blockade; there was also reason to think that Pissouthnes could be persuaded to join their side.

Alcidas would not hear of this either, but the sum of his determination, after arriving too late to save Mytilene, was to regain the Peloponnese as soon as possible. Putting out from Embatum he 32 began to sail along the coast. He touched at Myonnesus, in the terri-tory of Teos, and there he slaughtered the majority of the prisoners he had taken on his voyage. When he was anchored at Ephesus a deputation arrived from the Samians of Anaea who told him that this was no way to liberate Greece, if he was putting to death men who had not raised their hands against him and were not his enemies, and only allies of Athens under compulsion: if he carried on like this, he would turn few enemies into friends and many more friends into enemies. Alcidas accepted their point, and released those of the Chians whom he still held prisoner, and some of the others. (People had not run away at the sight of his ships, but had greeted them in the belief that they were Athenian, not thinking for a moment that with Athens in control of the sea any Peloponnesian fleet would ever make the crossing to Ionia.)

33   Alcidas set sail from Ephesus as quickly as he could, wanting now to make his escape. He had been spotted earlier, while anchored near Clarus, by the Athenian state triremes the Salaminia and the Paralus, which had arrived in those waters on a mission from Athens. Fearing pursuit, he set out across the open sea with the intention of making no other landfall, if he could help it, before the Peloponnese.

News of Alcidas and his fleet reached Paches and the Athenians from Erythrae, and kept coming in from all directions. The Ionian cities were unfortified, and there was widespread fear that the Peloponnesians would sail round the coast and make plundering attacks on them, even if they did not intend to stay and press this advantage. And the Paralus and the Salaminia had brought direct information of their sighting at Clarus. Paches gave eager chase, main-taining his pursuit as far as the island of Patmos, but returned when there seemed no further chance of catching them. He had hoped to meet them in open sea, but, failing that, he was glad that they had not been cornered somewhere and forced to make camp on land, which would have obliged the Athenians to guard and blockade.

34   On his return voyage along the coast Paches made a particular stop at Notium, the port in the territory of Colophon. Some Colophonians had settled in Notium after the upper city had been captured by Itamenes and the barbarians, brought in by one side in a local power-struggle. The capture of Colophon took place at about the same time as the second Peloponnesian invasion of Attica. There was then fur-ther dissension among those driven out of Colophon who settled in Notium. One party brought in Arcadian and barbarian mercenaries

supplied by Pissouthnes, and occupied a walled-off sector of the town, joined there in common cause by the pro-Persian Colophonians from the upper city. The other party, who had been forced to withdraw and were now in exile, called in Paches. He invited Hippias, the commander of the Arcadians in the walled sector, to a discussion on the understanding that even if he made no satisfactory proposal he would be returned inside the wall safe and sound. Hippias came out to meet him. Paches placed him under arrest (though not in chains), then launched a sudden attack on the wall and took it by surprise. He killed all the Arcadians and barbarians inside, then afterwards brought Hippias back as he had promised: once within the wall he had him seized and shot down. Paches then handed over Notium to the people of Colophon apart from the pro-Persian faction. Later the Athenians made a new colony of Notium with a constitution like their own, sending out founder members and gathering there all the Colophonians scattered in other cities.

On his return to Mytilene Paches forced Pyrrha and Eresus to 35 submission. He captured the Spartan Salaethus, found hiding in the city, and sent him to Athens together with the Mytilenaeans he had lodged in Tenedos and any others he thought responsible for the revolt. He also sent home the bulk of his forces, staying on with the remainder to organize the arrangements for Mytilene and the rest of Lesbos as he saw fit.

When the Mytilenaeans and Salaethus arrived in Athens, the 36 Athenians immediately put Salaethus to death, despite his various proposals which included the offer to secure the Peloponnesian withdrawal from Plataea, still then under siege. They debated what to do with the other men, and in their state of anger they decided to kill not only the Mytilenaeans they had in Athens but also every adult male in Mytilene, and to enslave the children and women. They thought the offence of revolt was aggravated by the fact that, unlike the others, this was not a revolt from subject status, and that a major contribution to the enterprise had been made by the Peloponnesian fleet accepting the risk of the crossing to Ionia in their support: from this they concluded that the revolt had been premeditated for some time. Accordingly they sent a trireme to announce their decision to Paches, with instructions to dispose of the Mytilenaeans as quickly as he could.

On the next day there was an immediate change of heart. On reconsideration the Athenians thought it a savage and excessive decision to destroy a whole city rather than just the guilty. When the Mytilenaean envoys in Athens and the Athenians who supported them sensed this change, they prevailed on the authorities to hold another debate. It was not difficult to persuade them, as they too could see that the majority of the citizens wanted to be given the opportunity for second thoughts. An assembly was immediately called, and various speakers expressed their opinions. Prominent among these was Cleon the son of Cleaenetus, who had carried the previous motion to execute the Mytilenaeans. He was in general the most drastic of the citizens, and at that time by far the most persuasive influence on the people. He now came forward once more and spoke as follows:

37   'I have often thought on previous occasions that democracy is incapable of running an empire, and your present change of mind over Mytilene is a prime example. With no reason for fear or suspicion in the daily conduct of life among yourselves, you apply the same principle to relations with your allies, and do not realize that allowing them to talk you into mistaken policies, or succumbing to pity, is to display a weakness which spells danger for you and brings no gratitude from them. You do not reflect that your empire is a tyranny, exercised over unwilling subjects who will conspire against you. Their obedience is not won by concessions, made to your own detriment, but by a domination based on force rather than popularity.

'Worst of all for us will be if there is no constancy in our decisions, and if we forget that imperfect laws kept valid give greater strength to a city than good laws unenforced. The good sense which comes with intellectual naivety is a more valuable quality than the sophistication which knows no morals, and generally it is the ordinary folk who make the better citizens compared with their cleverer fellows. The clever ones want to appear wiser than the laws and to win in any public debate, as if this was the most important way of displaying their intellect, and the result of such behaviour is usually the ruin of their city. The ordinary folk, on the other hand, with no confidence in their own intelligence, accept the superior wisdom of the laws and do not presume the polished debater's ability to dissect a speech: but as impartial judges rather than competitors they generally reach the right conclusion. That should be the model for us: we should not let the exhilaration of a sophisticated contest of wits lead us to offer you, the Athenian people, advice which belies our true beliefs.

38   'For my part I remain of the same opinion as before. I am surprised at those who have proposed a second debate about Mytilene,

and have thereby introduced an interval of delay, which can only be to the advantage of the guilty party: with the passage of time the victim's anger in pursuit of the offender loses its edge, whereas the punishment which best fits the crime is that exacted closest to the event. I shall be surprised too if anyone will answer me and claim to demonstrate some benefit to us from the Mytilenaeans' offence, or some consequential damage to the allies from our misfortunes. Clearly anyone making the attempt must rely on the power of his oratory to carry the contention that what we completely agreed was not in fact decided at all—or else he must have been induced by personal gain to work up a specious argument designed to mislead you.

'The result of these rhetorical contests is that the prizes go to others while the city bears the risks. And you are to blame for organizing these perverse games. You like to be spectators of speeches and an audience of actions. Good speakers advocating some future course of action are all the evidence you need to judge it possible, and your judgement of past actions relies less on the facts which you have seen with your own eyes than on what you have been told by plausible detractors. You certainly win the prize for gullibility to novel arguments and rejection of the tried and tested. You are slaves to any passing paradox and sneer at anything familiar. Every one of you would like to be an orator himself, but failing that is keen to match his wits against those who do have that skill, and to show himself abreast of the argument. You applaud a sharp point before it is made: you are eager to anticipate what is said but slow to foresee its consequences. You are in effect looking for a different world from that in which we live, and you cannot even think clearly about our present circumstances. Frankly you are in thrall to the pleasure of listening, and you sit here more like spectators at the sophists' displays than men taking decisions for their city.

'I want to move you out of these habits, and so I tell you plainly 39 that Mytilene has done us a greater wrong than any other single city. Now I can feel sympathy with those who have seceded out of intolerance of your imperial rule or under enemy compulsion. But when this action has been taken by people who live on an island, who have walls, who had no reason to fear our enemies except by sea, where they had the defence of their own fleet of triremes, people who retained their autonomy and were held by us in the highest regard—how can this be secession (as if they were the victims of oppressive force), rather than conspiracy and insurrection? They have joined our greatest enemies in an attempt to destroy us, and this is yet worse than direct opposition with their own forces.

'They took no lessons from the fate of their neighbours who had already revolted and been subdued by us, and the prosperity they currently enjoyed was no disincentive to the dangerous course on which they embarked. With reckless confidence in the future, and hopes which exceed their capability but still fall short of their ambition, they have declared war. They have seen fit to promote force over justice, choosing to attack us at what they thought would be the moment of their advantage, not for any wrong done them by us. Unexpected good fortune coming particularly strong and sudden inclines cities to ideas above their station. For the most part men are more secure with a regular rather than an extraordinary measure of success, and one could say that it is easier to avoid disaster than to maintain prosperity. From the first we should never have treated the Mytilenaeans with greater regard than the others, and then we would not have seen this degree of presumption: it is general human nature to despise indulgence and respect an unyielding stand.

'But as things are now they must be punished in a way which fits their crime. And do not attach the blame simply to the oligarchs, while absolving the people. They were all of one mind when it came to the attack on us, though they could have turned to our side and now be reinstated in their city: instead they thought it safer to share the oligarchs' risk, and they joined the revolt. Consider now the effect on our other allies. If they see you applying the same sanctions to secessions forced by the enemy and deliberate revolts, do you not think that all will revolt on the slightest pretext, when the reward for success is liberation and the penalty for failure nothing very drastic? We shall then have to risk money and lives against every city. Success for us will mean taking over a ruined city and losing for ever the future revenue on which our strength depends: failure means adding others to our present enemies and wasting the time we should spend against our established opponents in fighting our own allies.

40　'We should not therefore offer any hope that words can ensure or money can buy a vote of sympathy on the grounds of human error. There was nothing involuntary in the harm they did us, and they knew full well what they were doing when they conspired against us: there can only be sympathy where there is no deliberate intent. That was my contention on the first occasion, and it is my contention now that you should not reverse what you have already decided. I urge you not to fall victim to the three things most prejudicial to empire—pity, addiction to argument, and fairness. Pity is properly reserved as a mutual obligation between people of like mind, not for those who will show no pity themselves and are necessarily in a state of constant hostility. The politicians who delight us with their arguments can still play their games over matters of less importance, but must not be allowed to do so on an issue which will cost the city dear for the cheap pleasure of listening to them, while they themselves take a fancy reward for a fancy speech. And fairness is the way to treat those who will become and remain our friends, not those who will stay as they were, just as much our enemies as before.

'I make this one point in summary. If you follow my advice, justice will be done to Mytilene and your own advantage thereby served: if you decide otherwise, it will be less of a kindness to them than a sentence passed on yourselves. If they were right to revolt, you must be wrong to rule them. But if you lay claim to continued rule irrespective of propriety, then it follows that you should punish them in your own interests too, and forget about equity—or else abandon your empire and make your noble pretences when nobility is no risk. You must demand in self-protection the same penalty as they intended for you. You have survived the plot, but must not be seen more tolerant than those who made it. Consider their likely treatment of you if they had won, especially since they were the aggressors. Those who do harm to another without justification most often press their attack all the way to his destruction, wary of the danger from an enemy left standing: they know that the survivor of a gratuitous attack is the more bitter for his experience than an opponent in open and equal war.

'Do not then be traitors to yourselves. Think back as close as you can to your emotions when the harm was done, how you thought it imperative to subdue Mytilene, and take your vengeance now. Do not weaken on a passing whim or forget the danger which hung over you at the time. Punish them as they deserve, and set a clear example to the rest of the allies that the penalty for revolt will be death. When that is understood, you will be less distracted from the enemy by the need to fight your own allies.'

Such was Cleon's speech. After him Diodotus the son of Eucrates, 41 who in the previous assembly too had spoken most strongly against the execution of the Mytilenaeans, came forward again on this occasion and spoke as follows:

42   'I have no criticism of those who have proposed a review of our
      decision about the Mytilenaeans, and no sympathy with those who
      object to multiple debates on issues of major importance. In my
      opinion the two greatest impediments to good decision-making are
      haste and anger. Anger is the fellow of folly, and haste the sign of
      ignorance and shallow judgement. Anyone who contends that words
      should not be the school of action is either a fool or an interested
      party—a fool, if he thinks there can be any other way of elucidating
      a future which is not self-evident; an interested party, if with a dis-
      creditable case to promote he recognizes the impossibility of a good
      speech in a bad cause and relies on some good slander to bully both
      opposition and audience. Worst of all are those who further tar an
      opponent with the charge of giving a rhetorical performance for
      money. If the accusation were simply of ineptitude, a speaker losing
      the motion might emerge looking dim but not dishonest: but when
      the charge is dishonesty, a speaker carrying the motion is immedi-
      ately suspect, and if he fails he is thought not only dim but dishonest
      too. All this does no good to the city, which loses the advice of those
      too frightened to come forward. Indeed the city would do best if the
      types to which I refer were incompetent speakers, because then there
      would be much less persuasion into error. The good citizen should
      not seek to intimidate the opposition but to prove himself the more
      convincing speaker in fair debate. And the sensible city will not ply
      their best advisers with new honours, but equally will not detract
      from the honour which they already enjoy: and there should be no
      disgrace, let alone punishment, for the man who fails to carry his
      view. Then the successful speaker would not be tempted to insincerity
      or populism by the prospect of yet higher honours, and the unsuc-
      cessful would not adopt the same populist tactic himself in an effort
      to win support from the crowd.

43   'We do the opposite. And what is more, if someone makes the best
      proposal despite a suspicion of personal gain, we allow our resent-
      ment at an unsubstantiated suggestion of profit to deprive the city of
      the manifest benefit of his advice. It has become the norm that good
      advice straightforwardly given is no less suspect than bad. The result
      is that just as the advocate of a completely disastrous policy can only
      win mass support by deception, so the proponent of better policies
      must lie to be believed. Ours is the only city in which an excess of
      criticism makes it impossible to confer benefit transparently and with-
      out subterfuge—anyone openly offering something good is rewarded

with the suspicion that secretly somewhere there is something in it for himself. But even in these circumstances, on the most important issues we speakers should make some claim to a longer perspective than your own short-sighted view, especially as we can be called to account for the advice we give but you are not accountable for the way you take it. If there were equal penalties for proposing and for accepting a policy, you would be more sensible in your decisions. As it is, when something goes wrong you visit your feelings of the moment on the one man who proposed that course and not on the many among you yourselves who concurred in a mistaken policy.

'I am here before you neither as the advocate of the Mytilenaeans 44 nor as their prosecutor. On any sensible view the question at issue for us is not their guilt but the wisdom of our response. I might prove them completely guilty, but I would not for that reason urge their execution if it is not in our interests: I might point to mitigating factors, but would not therefore recommend sparing them unless that is clearly to the good of our city. I believe that the decisions we should be taking are more about the future than the present. And on the very point of Cleon's insistence, that our future interest will be served by imposing the death penalty as a means of preventing further revolts, I too reason from our future security and insist on the opposite conclusion. I beg you not to reject the practicality of my argument for the specious appeal of his. In your present anger at Mytilene you might think his argument has the attraction of justice. But we are not at law with them, so justice is not in point: we are deliberating how to deal with them to our practical advantage.

'In the cities of Greece the death penalty is prescribed for many 45 offences less serious than this and bearing no comparison to it. Even so, hope still induces men to take the risks, and no one has ever embarked on a dangerous scheme in the conviction that he will not survive it. And what rebel city has ever made its move believing that its own forces, with or without allied help, were inadequate for the attempt? Mistakes, individual or collective, are in human nature, and no law will prevent them—witness the whole catalogue of punishments which men have built up with constant additions, all in the hope of reducing the harm done by criminals. It is likely that in earlier ages the punishments prescribed for the greatest crimes were less severe, but as offences continued most of these punishments have over time been raised to the death penalty: yet for all this crime continues.

'So either we must find some still more powerful deterrent, or at least recognize that this deterrent has no effect. Poverty leading through sheer necessity to the courage of desperation; power leading through presumptuous pride to the greed for more; these and the other conditions of life which hold men in the grip of particular passions drive them with an irresistible and overmastering force into dangerous risks. Hope and desire are always ingredients. Where desire leads, hope follows; desire develops the plan, and hope suggests that fortune will be generous; and both are ruinous, as their invisible influence is more powerful than the dangers in plain sight. And fortune does indeed add no less a contribution to the heady mix. Sometimes it presents itself as an unexpected ally, encouraging a man to take risks even from an inferior position, and this is yet more true of cities, inasmuch as there are major issues at stake (freedom, say—or empire), and when the whole community is doing the same each individual takes an irrationally exaggerated view of his own capability. In short, when human nature is set on a determined course of action, it is impossible—and very naive to think otherwise— to impose any restraint through force of law or any other deterrent.

46   'We should not, therefore, allow any belief in the supposed efficacy of the death penalty to distort our judgement, nor should we leave rebels no hope of an opportunity to change their minds and make swift amends for their offence. Consider how things are now: if a city does start a revolt and then recognizes that there is no chance of success, it can come to terms when it is still able to refund our expenses and continue to pay tribute in future. But if we go the other way, do you not think that all will make more thorough preparations than they do at present, and hold out to the very last under siege, if there is one and the same result whether they submit early or late? And how can it not be damaging to us to sit there spending money on a siege without the possibility of terms, and then, if we capture the place, to take over a ruined city, thus losing all subsequent revenue from it? This revenue gives us our strength against the enemy.

'So rather than judging the offenders by the strict letter of the law, to our own detriment, we should seek to ensure by moderation in our punishment that in time to come we still have the financial resource of allied cities capable of their contribution. For our mode of control we should not rely on the rigour of law, but on practical vigilance. Our present way is the opposite. If a free state held forcibly under our rule rebels, as it well might, in pursuit of full autonomy, and we then subdue it, we think we should punish it severely. But the way we should treat free men is not with extreme punishment when they do rebel, but with extreme vigilance before any rebellion and a policy which prevents even the thought of it: and if we do have to put down a revolt we should restrict the blame as narrowly as possible.

'Consider too a further great error you would make if persuaded 47 by Cleon. At present the common people in all the cities are on your side. Either they refuse to join the oligarchs in rebellion, or, if they are forced to do so, they immediately form a potential opposition to the rebels: so when you move to war against an apostate city you have the populace as your allies. If you destroy the common people of Mytilene, who had no part in the revolt and once they were in possession of arms took their own decision to hand the city over to you, you will first of all commit the injustice of killing your benefactors, and secondly you will put the ruling classes in exactly the position they want: when they take their cities into rebellion they will then immediately have the common people on their side, since you will have given advance notice that the same penalty applies indiscriminately to the guilty and the innocent. Even if they were guilty, you should pretend otherwise, to avoid turning into enemies the one class of people who are still our allies. For the maintenance of our empire I consider it much more expedient to tolerate injustice done to us than to justify, as we could, the destruction of people we would do better to spare. And when Cleon speaks of a punishment combining justice and expediency, you will find that in his proposal the two cannot coexist.

'I ask you to recognize that mine is the better case. I do not want 48 you, any more than Cleon does, to be over-influenced by considerations of pity or fairness, but, solely on the basis of the arguments I have put forward, to agree that we should take our time in reaching judgement on the Mytilenaeans sent here by Paches as the guilty parties, and let the others live on in peace. This will be to our future good and the immediate alarm of our enemies, as it shows greater strength to adopt a well-reasoned policy towards one's opponents than to take aggressive action which combines force with folly.'

Such was Diodotus' speech. With the two views expressed so 49 evenly matched the Athenians continued to agonize over the decision and the final show of hands was very close, but Diodotus' motion was carried. At once they sent out another trireme urgently, hoping that it would not arrive after the earlier ship and find the city destroyed: the first trireme had a lead of about a day and a night. The Mytilenaean envoys supplied wine and barley-meal for the ship and promised large rewards if they made it in time. Such was the urgency of the voyage that they continued to row as they ate, barley-meal kneaded with wine and oil, and took it in turns to sleep while others rowed on. By good fortune there was no contrary wind. With the first ship in no hurry on its horrible mission, and this second ship speeding in the way described, the result was that the first ship arrived just enough ahead for Paches to have time to read the decree and prepare to carry out the decision, but then the second ship put in shortly after and prevented the slaughter. This was how close Mytilene came to destruction.

50   On Cleon's motion the Athenians executed the men sent to Athens by Paches as the prime movers of the revolt (these numbered just over a thousand): and they demolished the Mytilenaeans' walls and took over their ships. After that they did not impose tribute on the Lesbians, but instead divided the island (apart from the territory of Methymna) into three thousand allotments, of which they dedicated three hundred to the gods: for the rest they sent out individual land-lords from their own citizens, choosing them by lot. The Lesbians agreed to pay the landlords a yearly rent of two minas for each allotment, and worked the land themselves. The Athenians also took over the towns on the mainland which had been under Mytilenaean control, and these then became subject to Athens.

Such were the events concerning Lesbos.

51   In the same summer, after the recapture of Lesbos, the Athenians sent an expedition, with Nicias the son of Niceratus as general in command, against the island of Minoa, which lies in front of Megara. The Megarians had built a tower on it and used it as a guard-post. Nicias wanted the Athenians to have a base there, closer than Boudorum and Salamis, for their watch on Megara. The objective was to prevent the Peloponnesians launching triremes from the harbour of Megara unobserved, as they had done before, or sending out privateers: and at the same time to stop anything reaching the Megarians by sea. First then Nicias attacked from the sea and took two towers projecting out from Nisaea, using scaling-devices mounted on his ships, thus freeing access to the channel between the island and the mainland: then he walled the side of Minoa facing and close to the mainland, where a bridge across shallow water allows supporting forces to reach the island. His troops completed this work

in a few days, and after that Nicias withdrew with his expeditionary force, leaving a fortification built and a garrison installed on the island.

At about the same time in this summer the Plataeans too ran out 52 of food and, unable to withstand the siege any longer, capitulated to the Peloponnesians. It happened like this. The Peloponnesians launched an assault on the city wall to which the Plataeans could offer no resistance. Realizing how weak they were, the Spartan commander decided not to take the city by storm: this was because he had instructions from Sparta that if there were at some time a truce with Athens and agreement on both sides to return the places they had taken by force of arms, Plataea would be exempt if a voluntary surrender could be claimed. Instead he sent a herald to the Plataeans announcing that, if they were prepared to hand over the city to the Spartans voluntarily and submit to the decision of Spartan judges, there would be punishment for the guilty but nobody would be treated unjustly. That was the herald's message, and the Plataeans, now desperately weak, handed over their city.

The Peloponnesians fed the Plataeans for a few days, until the five men appointed as judges arrived from Sparta. Once there, they presented no charges but simply summoned the Plataeans and asked them this one question: had they done anything to the benefit of the Spartans and their allies in this current war? In reply the Plataeans asked for the opportunity to speak at greater length, and nominated two of their own people to make their case, Astymachus the son of Asopolaus and Lacon the son of Aeimnestus, who was a consular representative for Sparta. These two came forward and spoke as follows:

'We handed over our city, Spartans, because we trusted you. We 53 did not expect to be subjected to this sort of trial, but supposed some more regular legal procedure: and we agreed to appear, as we now do, before no judges other than your own in the belief that this would give us the fairest treatment. Now we are afraid that we were wrong in both assumptions. We have good reason to suspect that at issue for us is the ultimate penalty, and that you will not prove impartial judges. We infer this from the absence of any notified charge against us to which we should respond (on the contrary, we had to seek permission to speak), and from the brevity of your one question, to which a true answer would prejudice us and a false answer invite refutation. Reduced to desperation on all fronts, we can only do what seems to offer our best hope of safety: speak and take our chances. For people in our position the failure to make an argument can incur the charge that, if only it had been made, it could have saved us.

'Our difficulties are compounded by the problem of convincing you. If we had no knowledge of each other, we could with advantage introduce evidence of which you were not aware. But as it is, all that we say will be familiar to you, and our fear is not that you have already judged our moral record inferior to yours and make that your charge against us—far from it—but that we face a predetermined

54   verdict as a favour to others. Nevertheless we shall set out our rights in the quarrel with Thebes and our claims on you and the rest of the Greeks, and try to convince you by reminding you of the services we have rendered.

'In answer to your brief question, whether we have done anything to the benefit of the Spartans and their allies in this war, if this is a question put to us as enemies, we reply that you were hardly wronged if you received no benefit from us; and if you consider us friends, we say that the fault lies rather with those who attacked us. We have shown our integrity both during the peace and against the Persians. It was not we who first broke the recent peace, and at the time of the Persian War we were the only Boeotians to join the fight for the freedom of Greece. Although we are inlanders we fought with the fleet at Artemisium, and in the battle which took place in our own territory we were there in support of you and Pausanias: in all the other dangers which threatened the Greeks in those times we took a part out of proportion to our strength. And, Spartans, a particular service to you was at the time of the greatest panic to grip Sparta, when the Helots revolted after the earthquake and occupied Ithome: we then sent a third of our own men to help you. These things should not be forgotten.

55   'Such was the role we were proud to take for ourselves in those momentous times in the past. Subsequently we and you became enemies, and the fault lies with you. When we asked you for an alliance at a time of Theban pressure on us, you rejected our request and told us to turn to the Athenians, on the grounds that they were close to us and you lived far away. Yet in the war you have not suffered anything exceptional at our hands, nor was there any such likelihood. If we were not prepared to secede from the Athenians at your bidding, that was no wrong done to you. They had helped us against the Thebans when you were reluctant, and after all that time it would

have been dishonourable to desert them, especially as these were people who had done us a good service, had admitted us at our request to their alliance, and had given us a share in their citizenship. It was to be expected, then, that we would welcome and accept their instructions. In the authority which you two powers exercise over your allies, the responsibility for anything done wrong lies with those who lead away from the right course, not those who follow.

'The Thebans have a long history of aggression against us, and 56 you are well aware of the latest example, which is what has brought us to our present state. They attempted to take our city not only in the time of truce but also at a sacrosanct festival season. We were within our rights to take our vengeance on them, in accordance with the universally accepted law that there is no impiety in defending against an enemy who attacks: and it is not fair that we should now suffer on their account. If you take the immediate present as your criterion of justice—your present interest, their present hostility— you will be seen as pandering to expediency rather than making a true judgement of what is right.

'Yet if the Thebans are thought useful to you now, we and the other Greeks were of much greater service to you at the time when you were in greater danger. Now you are attacking and menacing others, but in that time of crisis, when the barbarian was intent on enslaving us all, the Thebans took his side. We can fairly set our solidarity then against our present error, if indeed there has been any error. You will find this a comparison of the great with the small. You will also find that in those critical times when it was rare for any of the Greeks to oppose their courage to the might of Xerxes, those who won the praises did not pursue the interest of their own safety in the face of the invasion, but were prepared to choose the best course and brave the dangers. We were of that number, and were held in the highest regard: but we now fear that those same principles may be our ruin, since we chose an alliance of honour with the Athenians above an alliance of convenience with you. But you should be seen to take a consistent view of the same people: and you should consider that your true interest is served only if what may seem your immediate advantage can be achieved without compromising your firm and constant obligation to the courage of those who fought bravely at your side.

'Think of this too. At present most Greeks regard you as the 57 paradigm of decency. If you pass an unfair verdict on us (and this trial will not go unnoticed—the famous trying the innocent), be careful of the Greeks' reaction. They will find it intolerable that honourable men were victims of a disgraceful decision taken by yet more honourable men, and that spoils from our dead bodies—we who were the benefactors of Greece—are dedicated in the national sanctuaries. It will be seen as a monstrous act if Spartans sack Plataea; if, when your fathers recognized the valour of our city by inscribing its name on the tripod at Delphi, you then obliterate it and its entire population from the whole Greek world, to please the Thebans. This is now the depth of misfortune to which we have come: we were destroyed when the Persians had their victories, and now you, who were once our closest friends, hold us lower than the Thebans and have subjected us to two terrible ordeals, first the threat of starvation if we did not hand over our city, and now the threat of a death sentence in your court. We Plataeans, whose devotion to the Greek cause was out of proportion to our strength, have been rejected by all, alone and unchampioned. Not one of our allies at that time is ready to help us, and we fear that you, Spartans, our last remaining hope, will not prove constant.

58   'And yet we have at least the right to ask you, in the name of the gods who once favoured our alliance and in respect of our own service to the Greeks, to bend now and reconsider anything the Thebans may have persuaded you to do. Demand from them this gift in return, that you should not have to kill when killing dishonours you. Earn for yourselves an honest rather than a corrupt gratitude, and do not trade others' satisfaction for your own infamy. It takes only a brief moment to destroy our lives, but the struggle to remove the disgrace will be long and hard. To punish your enemies would be justified: but we are not enemies—we are supporters who were forced into the war on the other side. So piety demands a judgement which grants us the safety of our lives and recognizes that we gave ourselves up to you freely, with our hands outstretched in supplication (and Greek law prohibits the killing of suppliants), and recognizes too that we have always been your benefactors.

'Look round at the graves of your fathers, killed by the Persians and buried in our land. Each year we gave them public honour with gifts of clothing and all other customary offerings; we brought them the first fruits of all that our earth produces in season; we did this as their supporters in a friendly land, as allies of those who were once our comrades in arms. If you were to take the wrong decision you

would reverse all this. Consider. Pausanias found them burial thinking that he was placing them to rest in a friendly land and among
friendly people. But if you kill us and turn Plataea into Theban territory, what else will you be doing but abandoning your fathers and
kinsmen in an enemy land among their own murderers, and depriving them of the honours which they now enjoy? Moreover, you will
be enslaving the land in which the Greeks won their freedom, you
will desolate the sanctuaries of the gods to whom they prayed before
defeating the Persians, and you will take the sacrifices to your fathers
out of the hands of those who ordained and established them.

   'Spartans, it is not consistent with your reputation to offend 59
against the common code of the Greeks and against your own forebears, or to destroy us, your benefactors, to satisfy the enmity of
others when you yourselves have not been wronged. It would be
consistent to spare us, to let your hearts be moved, to show us
decency and compassion, thinking not only of the horror of our fate,
but of what sort of men we are who would face it: think too on the
instability of fortune, which can inflict disaster on anyone, deserved
or not. And we—as is our right, and as our need compels us—we
invoke the gods who are universally worshipped at altars throughout
all Greece, and pray that our plea will move you. We appeal to the
oaths which your fathers swore not to forget; we are your suppliants at
the graves of your fathers, and we call on the departed not to let us fall
under the Thebans and to prevent the betrayal of their closest friends
to their bitterest enemies. We remind you of that day on which we
achieved the most glorious deeds together with your fathers: and now
on this day we are in danger of meeting the most terrible fate.

   'For men in our position the hardest thing is to bring their speech
to an end, as with that the danger to their life comes close, but end
we must, and we say this now in conclusion. We did not surrender
our city to the Thebans—rather than that we would have chosen the
most abject death by starvation—but we came over to you because
we trusted you: and if we do not convince you, it would be fair to
return us to the state we were in and allow us to make our own choice
of the danger to befall us. We are Plataeans, once the most loyal supporters of the Greek cause and now suppliants dependent on your
good faith. In all this, Spartans, we adjure you not to use your own
hands to deliver us into the hands of the Thebans, who are our
bitterest enemies. You can be our saviours. You are liberating the
other Greeks: do not then destroy us.'

60   Such was the speech of the Plataeans. The Thebans were afraid
that this speech would win some concession from the Spartans, so
they came forward and said that they too wished to speak, since,
mistakenly in their judgement, the Plataeans had been allowed a
longer speech than was needed to answer the question. Permission
was granted, and they spoke as follows:

61   'We should not have asked to make this speech if these men had
given a short answer to the question put to them, and not turned to
accusations against us and irrelevant defence at great length to
charges not even made, with equally irrelevant singing of their own
praises in areas which no one has criticized. So now we must reply to
their accusations and expose their conceit of themselves, so that no
weight is given to either our bad name or their good name, and you
can learn the truth on both counts before making your judgement.

'Our differences began after we had founded Plataea together
with some other places which we had gained by driving out the previous mixed population: this was later than our settlement of the rest
of Boeotia. The Plataeans were not prepared to accept our leadership
as had originally been stipulated, but stood apart from the other
Boeotians and rejected the ancestral traditions. Then when pressure
was put on them, they went over to the Athenians and joined them
in doing us much damage, for which they too have had to suffer in
return.

62   'When the barbarian attacked Greece, they say they were the only
Boeotians not to medize, and they make this a particular point to their
own glorification and our discredit. We say that their only reason for
not medizing was that the Athenians did not medize either: and
on the same principle, when the Athenians later attacked the rest of
Greece, we say in turn that they were the only Boeotians to atticize.
Yet consider the different circumstances in which we and they acted
as we did. At that time the constitution of our city was neither an
oligarchy with equal rights for all nor a democracy, but our affairs
were controlled by a small dominant clique, something as far as could
be from legal process and the ideal of disciplined government, and
very close to tyranny. This clique hoped that a Persian victory would
extend their own power, so they suppressed the common people by
force and invited in the Persians. This act was done without the
whole city having control of its own affairs, and it should not be
blamed for errors committed when there was no rule of law. Anyway,
when the Persians had gone and our city took on a legal constitution,

consider our subsequent record. When the Athenians in their general aggression against Greece were trying to bring our own country under their control and already held most of it because of our internal political struggles, did we not fight them and beat them at Coronea to liberate Boeotia? And are we not now eager participants in the liberation of the rest of Greece, providing cavalry and contributing a greater force than any other of the allies?

'So much for our response to the charge of medism. We shall now 63 set out to show that it is not we but you Plataeans who have done the greater harm to the Greeks and deserve every form of punishment. You claim that it was for vengeance on us that you became allies and citizens of Athens. In that case you should have confined yourselves to inviting their aid against us, and not joined them in their attacks on others. It was open to you to refuse if the Athenians led you in any unwelcome direction, since you already had your alliance with these same Spartans against Persia, of which you yourselves make so much in your defence—that was surely strong enough to keep us away from you and, most important of all, to allow you the security to make your own decisions. But of your own free will, and under no compulsion now, you preferred to choose the Athenian side. You say that it would have been dishonourable to betray your benefactors. Compared with that, affecting the Athenians alone, a far greater dishonour, indeed a crime, was your utter betrayal of the whole community of Greeks with whom you were sworn confederates, when they were intent on the liberation of Greece and the Athenians on its enslavement. Your return favour to the Athenians was in different coin, and you cannot escape the shame of it: you called them in, so you say, because you were being wronged, and then you became their accomplices in wronging others. Yet when favours are traded the true disgrace is the failure to repay like with like, and there is no disgrace in refusing to return a debt justly incurred when its payment leads to injustice.

'You have made two things clear: that when you were the only 64 ones of us not to medize at that time, this was not out of any concern for the Greeks at large but only because the Athenians did not medize either; and that your present policy is to collaborate with the Athenians in opposition to the rest of Greece. And now you claim the benefit of a virtue which you once showed only because others led you to it. This will not do. You chose the Athenians, and must stay in their camp. Do not cite the old confederacy and expect to be saved by it now. You deserted it: you broke your oath and joined in the enslavement of the Aeginetans and others of the confederate allies rather than preventing it. And, in contrast to our medizing, you did this of your own free will, with your constitution stable and unchanged to this day, and under no one's compulsion. When you were given that final offer of peace before the siege began, on condition of your neutrality, you refused. Who then could have done more than you to earn the universal hatred of the Greeks, when the "integrity" which you profess to have shown was to their detriment? You may have acted honourably in the past, as you claim, but your present conduct has shown that to be incidental to your character. What was always your natural inclination has now been revealed in its true light: the Athenians took the path of injustice, and you were their fellow-travellers.

65   'So much then in demonstration that our medism was involuntary whereas your atticism was voluntary. As for the most recent in your list of alleged wrongs, your claim that it was illegal for us to come against your city in the time of truce and at a sacrosanct festival season, even here we do not consider ourselves more at fault than you. If we gratuitously and with hostile intent made an armed attack on your city and ravaged your land, we are at fault. But if some of your own people, those pre-eminent in wealth and birth, invited us in of their free will, wanting to remove you from your external alliance and restore you to the ancestral traditions of the whole Boeotian community—where is our fault? And of course the responsibility for anything illegal lies with those who lead rather than those who follow. But in our judgement neither they nor we were at fault. They were citizens no less than you, and with a greater investment at stake. Their motive in opening their own gates and bringing us into their own city, as friends rather than enemies, was to prevent the worse elements among you growing still worse, and to give the better elements what was due to them. They were the censors of your policy, not wanting to banish anyone physically from the city but to reconnect all to their proper kinship: they would have had you enemies of none, but friends under treaty with all alike.

66   'And here is proof that our actions were not those of enemies. We did no harm to any person, and announced that anyone wanting to be governed under the ancestral constitution of all Boeotia should come over to us. You gladly came over, reached an agreement with us, and initially took no further action. But later you realized that

there were not many of us, and, even if it could perhaps be thought that there was some impropriety in our entering the city without your majority approval, your response was out of all proportion. When you could have followed our example, doing nothing drastic but talking to us and persuading us to leave, you broke the agreement and attacked us. We are not so much aggrieved for those you killed in direct fighting, as there was a certain legality in their fate. But there were others of our men who stretched out their hands in supplication to you: you took them alive into your custody, you promised us that they would not subsequently be killed, and then contrary to all law you put them to death. Was this not an atrocious act? So now you had committed three crimes in a short space of time—the breach of the agreement, the subsequent execution of our men, and your false promise not to kill them if we did no harm to your holdings in the country outside. And yet you claim that we were the criminals and think that you yourselves have nothing to answer for. No, not if these judges here reach the right decision: there will be punishment on all these counts.

'And that is the reason, Spartans, for this detailed exposition, 67 given for your sake but also for ours—so that you can be sure that there will be justice done in the sentence you pass, and we that there is a yet stronger moral base for our retribution. Do not listen to their talk of past virtues, if such there were, and let that soften your resolve. An honourable record can help the cause of an injured party, but should entail double punishment for those guilty of dishonourable conduct, because they are also guilty of betraying their character. And do not let their hand-wringing pleas for pity weigh in their favour, their appeals to your fathers' graves and their own desolation. We can adduce in comparison the much more terrible fate they brought on our slaughtered youth. Some of their fathers fell at Coroneia, fighting to win Boeotia for your side: others are left as old men in desolate homes, and they are much more your rightful suppliants, entreating you to punish the Plataeans. Pity is the proper response to undeserved misfortune: but when men like these suffer their just deserts, that on the contrary is cause for rejoicing.

'Their present desolation is of their own making, since they deliberately rejected the better alliance. They were the criminals, when we had done them no previous harm; they were guided by hatred rather than justice; and even now their punishment will not match their crime, because their sentence will be lawful. They were not, as they claim, holding out their hands in supplication for mercy after a battle, but they submitted themselves under agreed terms to due process of law.

'We therefore ask you, Spartans, to support the law of the Greeks which these men have broken. We have suffered from the breach of that law, and we ask you also to give us just recompense for the loyalty we have shown, and not allow their arguments to displace us from the position we enjoy with you. Make it clear to the Greeks by this example that in your court the issues will not be words but actions. Honourable actions need only a brief report: crimes have elaborate speeches draped over them as a veil. But if all our leaders, as you do now, base their judgement on a single summary point applied to all, people will be less inclined to seek fair words to clothe foul deeds.'

68   Such was the speech of the Thebans. The Spartan judges thought it would still be in order to put the question, whether they had received any benefit from the Plataeans during the war. They reasoned that they had long urged neutrality on the Plataeans (or so they claimed) in accordance with the original treaty made by Pausanias after the Persian War; and subsequently, before beginning the siege, had offered them the opportunity, on that same basis, of refusing commitment to either side. As that offer was rejected, the Spartans considered that their own good intentions had now exempted them from obligation to the treaty, and that the Plataeans had done them wrong. So once more they brought them in one by one and asked them the same question: had they done anything to the benefit of the Spartans and their allies in the war? And as each man said 'No' they took him away and killed him, making no exceptions. Of the Plataeans themselves they slaughtered no fewer than two hundred, and twenty-five of the Athenians who had been under siege with them. The women they sold as slaves.

For about a year they granted occupation of the city to some Megarians who had been exiled as a result of internal strife and to those who survived of their own supporters among the Plataeans. Thereafter they razed the entire city to the ground, foundations and all, and built next to the sanctuary of Hera a hostel two hundred feet square, with two floors of rooms on all sides. They made use of the existing roofing and doors in Plataea, and the beds they made and dedicated to Hera from all the bronze and iron furnishings found within the walls. They also built in her honour a hundred-foot temple in stone.

They made the land public property and leased it out on ten-year lets, taken up by Thebans. Indeed virtually the whole reason for this Spartan aversion to Plataea was to please the Thebans, who they thought would be useful allies in the war just then developing.

Such then, in the ninety-third year of its alliance with Athens, was the end of Plataea.

The forty Peloponnesian ships which had gone to support Lesbos 69 and then fled back across the open sea with the Athenians in pursuit were caught in a storm off Crete, and from there made a straggling return to the Peloponnese. At Cyllene they found thirteen triremes from Leucas and Ambracia, and with them Brasidas the son of Tellis, who had arrived as a commissioner to advise Alcidas. After failing with Lesbos the Spartans planned to enlarge their fleet and sail to Corcyra, where civil war had broken out. The Athenian presence at Naupactus was limited to twelve ships, and they wanted to take action before naval reinforcements could arrive from Athens. Brasidas and Alcidas began their preparations to this end.

The civil war in Corcyra began after the return home of the 70 Corcyraeans captured in the sea-battles over Epidamnus and now released by the Corinthians: the story was that they had been bailed for eighty talents by their consular representatives, but in fact they had agreed to bring Corcyra over to Corinth. And so by approaching their fellow citizens one by one they began working to sever the city's link with Athens. An Athenian ship arrived bringing envoys, and likewise a ship from Corinth. A debate was held, and the Corcyraeans voted to retain their alliance with Athens on the existing terms, but also to renew their former friendship with the Peloponnesians.

The next stage was that a man called Peithias, who was a volunteer consul of Athens and the leader of the people's party, was impeached by these returned Corcyraeans on the charge of enslaving Corcyra to Athens. He was acquitted, and countered with a charge against the five richest men among them, alleging that they had been cutting vine-props from the sanctuaries of Zeus and Alcinous: the fine prescribed for each prop was one stater. They were found guilty, and in view of the enormity of the fine they went and sat as suppliants in the temples, pleading to pay by instalments: but Peithias, who happened also to be a member of the council, persuaded it to enforce the law. Pressed by this legal compulsion, and at the same time informed that Peithias intended while still a council member to persuade the people into a full offensive and defensive alliance with Athens, these men gathered their faction and, armed with daggers, suddenly burst into the council chamber and killed Peithias and some sixty other councillors and private citizens. A few of those who supported Peithias found refuge in the Athenian trireme, which had not yet left.

71 This done, the conspirators called an assembly of the Corcyraeans and proposed that the best policy, and the least likely to lead to enslavement by the Athenians, was to receive neither side in future unless they came in a single ship with peaceful intent, and to regard any larger visitation as an act of war: and they forced the assembly to ratify the motion as proposed. They also sent envoys immediately to Athens, to present the affair in a positive light and to dissuade those who had taken refuge there from doing anything untoward which

72 might provoke an Athenian reaction. But on their arrival the Athenians arrested the envoys as revolutionaries, and deposited them in Aegina together with any of the refugees they had won over.

Meanwhile, after the arrival of a Corinthian trireme with envoys from Sparta, those in control in Corcyra made an attack on the people's party and defeated them in battle. When night came on the people retreated to the acropolis and the higher parts of the city, gathering their forces there and establishing their position: they also held the Hyllaic harbour. The other party took over the agora, where most of them lived, and the adjacent harbour facing the mainland.

73 On the following day there was some minor skirmishing, and both parties sent out into the country, inviting the slaves to join them with promises of freedom. The majority of the slaves came to the support of the people's party, but the other side was reinforced by eight hundred mercenaries from the mainland.

74 A day passed, and then there was another battle, won this time by the people, who had the stronger positions and the greater numbers: they also had the enterprising support of their women, who pelted the enemy with tiles from their houses and faced the fray with a courage beyond their nature. The oligarchs' defeat came late in the afternoon, and their immediate fear was that the people would advance to take the dockyard unopposed and finish them off: they therefore set fire to the houses surrounding the agora and the tenement buildings, to prevent any way through. In this arson they spared neither their own property nor anyone else's, with the result that much merchants' stock was consumed by fire, and the whole city was in danger of destruction, if a wind had arisen to carry the flames in that direction. With the fighting over, each side spent a quiet night

on guard in their own positions. After the victory of the people's party the Corinthian ship stole away, and most of the mercenaries made their way back to the mainland undetected.

On the next day the Athenian general Nicostratus the son of 75 Diitrephes arrived in support from Naupactus with twelve ships and five hundred Messenian hoplites. He attempted to effect a reconciliation, and persuaded the two parties to agree that the ten men most responsible for the discord should be put on trial (but they had already fled), and that the rest should live together in a formal treaty with one another and a defensive and offensive alliance with Athens. This achieved, Nicostratus was ready to sail back. But the leaders of the people's party urged him to leave five of his own ships with them, to reduce the risk of any movement by their opponents, while they would crew an equal number of ships with their own people and send them with him. Nicostratus agreed, and they began drafting their enemies for service in the ships. These men, terrified that they would be sent to Athens, sat down as suppliants in the sanctuary of the Dioscuri. Nicostratus tried to reassure them and persuade them to leave their suppliant position. He failed in this attempt, and the people took this failure as their excuse to go to arms, regarding their opponents' reluctance to sail with Nicostratus as evidence of their disloyal intentions. They seized the weapons from these men's houses, and would have killed those they encountered if Nicostratus had not prevented them. Seeing how matters were developing, the others— to a total of not less than four hundred—took refuge as suppliants in the temple of Hera. The people, anxious to prevent another coup, persuaded them to leave and transported them to the island facing the Heraeum, ensuring that a regular supply of provisions was sent across to them.

This was the stage the civil war had reached when, on the fourth 76 or fifth day after the removal of these men to the island, the Peloponnesian ships arrived from Cyllene, where they had been at anchor after their return from Ionia. There were fifty-three ships in all, and their commander, as before, was Alcidas, with Brasidas joining him on board as adviser.

The ships anchored in the harbour of Sybota on the mainland, then at dawn sailed against Corcyra. This caused chaos among the 77 Corcyraeans, who were already nervous at the internal state of affairs and now had the further alarm of a naval attack. They immediately began getting ready sixty ships, and sent them out successively against the enemy as soon as each was manned, despite the advice of the Athenians that they should let the Athenian ships sail out first and then follow with all their own together. As their ships made this staggered approach to the enemy two of them immediately deserted, in others the men on board started fighting with one another, and the whole action was disorderly. Seeing this confusion the Peloponnesians detailed a squadron of twenty ships to face the Corcyraeans, and formed the rest against the twelve Athenian ships, which included the Salaminia and the Paralus.

78   In their part of the ensuing battle the Corcyraeans, making their ill-organized attacks with only a few ships at a time, got into difficulties. The Athenians, wary of the numbers opposing them and the danger of encirclement, did not engage the whole body of the ships ranged against them or go for the centre, but attacked on the wing and disabled one ship. After that the enemy formed in a circle, and the Athenians kept sailing round it trying to force them into disarray. Seeing this movement and fearing a repetition of what had happened at Naupactus, those detailed to take on the Corcyraeans came to the rescue, and the now combined fleet made a concerted attack on the Athenians. The Athenians now began to back water and retreat in that way. Part of their intention was to give the Corcyraean ships as much time as possible to escape ahead of them, while they themselves retreated slowly, drawing the whole enemy formation after them.

Such was the outcome of this naval engagement, which ended
79   towards sunset. The Corcyraeans were afraid that the enemy would press their victory by sailing against the city, and either rescue the men from the island or take some other decisive action: they therefore brought the men back from the island to the Heraeum, and kept the city under guard. Though they had won the engagement, the Peloponnesians did not chance a direct attack on the city, but with thirteen Corcyraean ships in tow they sailed back to their original base on the mainland. On the following day they still refrained from sailing against the city, though its people were in a turmoil of apprehension and Brasidas, so it is said, was urging Alcidas to sail—but Alcidas outranked him. They did however make a landing on the
80   promontory of Leucimme and began to ravage the fields. Meanwhile, the people's party in Corcyra, terrified of an attack by the Peloponnesian fleet, held talks with the suppliants on the means of securing the city's safety, and persuaded some of them to serve in

their ships: despite all they had managed to crew thirty ships in readiness to meet the attack.

The Peloponnesians ravaged the land until midday, and then sailed back. At nightfall they received beacon-signals indicating the approach of sixty Athenian ships from Leucas. The Athenians had sent these ships, with Eurymedon the son of Thucles as general in command, when they heard of the civil war and the impending dispatch of Alcidas' ships to Corcyra. The Peloponnesians quickly set 81 out for home that very night, sailing close in to land: at Leucas they transported their ships across the isthmus, to avoid being seen if they had sailed round, and so got away.

When the Corcyraeans learnt of the approach of the Athenian and the departure of the enemy ships, they took the Messenian troops inside the city (they had until now been kept outside), and ordered the ships they had manned to sail round to the Hyllaic harbour. While this manoeuvre was being carried out, they seized and killed any of their enemies they could find. When the ships arrived in harbour they took off the men they had persuaded to serve and did away with them. They then went to the Heraeum, persuaded about fifty of the suppliants there to stand trial, and condemned them all to death. When they saw what was happening, the majority of the suppliants, who had not agreed to stand trial, began to kill one another in collective suicide right there in the sanctuary: and there were some who hanged themselves from the trees, others who took their own lives in whatever way they could. Throughout the seven days for which Eurymedon remained there after his arrival with the sixty ships the Corcyraeans continued to murder those of their own people whom they considered enemies. The general charge was of conspiring to subvert the democracy, but some were killed out of private hostility, and others by their debtors who had taken loans and owed them money. Death took every imaginable form; and, as happens at such times, anything went—and then worse still. Fathers killed their sons; men were dragged out of the sanctuaries and killed beside them; some were even walled up in the temple of Dionysus and died there.

That is how savagely the civil war progressed, and it was the more 82 shocking for being the first of the revolutions. Because later virtually the whole of the Greek world suffered this convulsion: everywhere there were internal divisions such that the democratic leaders called in the Athenians and the oligarchs called in the Spartans. In peacetime they would have had neither the excuse nor the will to invite this intervention: but in time of war, when alliances were available to either party to the detriment of their opponents and thereby their own advantage, there were ready opportunities for revolutionaries to call in one side or the other. And indeed civil war did inflict great suffering on the cities of Greece. It happened then and will for ever continue to happen, as long as human nature remains the same, with more or less severity and taking different forms as dictated by each new permutation of circumstances. In peace and prosperous times both states and individuals observe a higher morality, when there is no forced descent into hardship: but war, which removes the comforts of daily life, runs a violent school and in most men brings out passions that reflect their condition.

So then civil war spread among the cities, and those who came to it later took lessons, it seems, from the precedents and progressed to new and far greater extremes in the ingenuity of their machinations and the atrocity of their reprisals. They reversed the usual evaluative force of words to suit their own assessment of actions. Thus reckless daring was considered bravery for the cause; far-sighted caution was simply a plausible face of cowardice; restraint was a cover for lack of courage; an intelligent view of the general whole was inertia in all specifics; and impulsive haste was enlisted among the manly virtues, while full consideration in the light of possible dangers was a specious excuse for backsliding.

People of violent views won automatic credence, and any opposing them were suspect. To lay a plot and succeed was clever: smarter still to detect another's plot. Anyone whose own plot was to remove the need for any plotting was thought to be subverting the party and scared by the opposition. In short, the currency of approval was damage done—either the pre-emptive strike before an opponent could do his own intended damage, or the instigation of those who otherwise had no thought of doing harm.

And indeed family became less close a tie than party, as partisans were more prepared to do the deeds without question. Such associations had no sanction in the established laws, but were formed in defiance of the laws for purposes of self-interest. The partisans' pledges of loyalty to one another were cemented not by divine law but by partnership in some lawless act. Any fair proposals made by the other side were accepted by the stronger party only after precautionary action, and in no generous spirit. Revenge was more important than avoidance of the original injury. If ever there were any sworn reconciliations, the oaths on either side were offered simply to meet some current difficulty and had only temporary force, while one side or the other was without support from elsewhere. But when opportunity presented, the first to take bold advantage of an enemy caught off guard relished this perfidious attack yet more than open reprisal: into his reckoning came both his own safety and the accolade he would also win for intelligence shown in achieving gain through bad faith. Most people would rather be called clever rogues than stupid saints, feeling shame at the latter and taking pride in the former.

The cause of all this was the pursuit of power driven by greed and ambition, leading in turn to the passions of the party rivalries thus established. The dominant men on each side in the various cities employed fine-sounding terms, claiming espousal either of democratic rights for all or of a conservative aristocracy, but the public whose interests they professed to serve were in fact their ultimate prize, and in this out-and-out contest for supremacy they committed the most appalling atrocities and took their acts of vengeance yet further, imposing punishments beyond anything required by justice or civic interest, and limited only by their supporters' appetite at the time: to satisfy immediate party fervour they were equally prepared to suborn convictions in the courts or to use force in their quest for power. So neither side observed any religious constraint, and those who could put a euphemistic gloss on a distasteful action had their reputations enhanced. The citizens who had remained neutral fell victim to both parties: they were destroyed for failing to join the cause, or out of resentment at their survival.

Thus civil wars brought every form of depravity to the Greek world, and simple decency, that major constituent of a noble nature, was laughed out of sight. The division into opposing ideological camps created widespread distrust. No words had the force, and no oath the deterrence, to put a stop to it. All parties with the upper hand reasoned that there was no hope of a secure settlement and, incapable of trusting the other side, looked instead to ensure their own immunity to attack. On the whole the less intelligent had the better prospect of survival. Conscious of their own deficiencies and the intellect of their opponents, and fearful that they would be worsted in argument and outmanoeuvred in pre-emptive tactics by more subtle minds than theirs, they took their chances with immediate action. The others, in their disdainful assumption that they would detect any move in advance and that they had no need to act when they could make their gains by intelligence, were more often caught off guard and so destroyed.

84 [So it was in Corcyra that most of this was perpetrated for the first time: every sort of reprisal taken by their subjects against violent and immoderate rulers who now paid the penalty; men looking for relief from their round of poverty, and driven by their condition to deliver unjust verdicts in the hope of acquiring their neighbours' property; others not motivated by greed, being as wealthy as their victims, but still carried on by passionate bigotry to extremes of savage and implacable attack. With all life thrown into chaos at this time of crisis for the city, human nature triumphed over law: it had always been inclined to criminal breaking of the laws, but now it revelled in showing itself the slave of passion, a stronger force than justice, and the enemy of anything higher. People would not have set revenge above piety or profit above adherence to the law if envy had not worked its corrupting influence on them. And though the commonly accepted laws in such areas underpin everyone's hope of personal rescue if they meet with trouble, men think they have a prior right to set these laws aside when taking vengeance on others—and not leave them intact against a time when they themselves might be in danger and
85 have need of one of them.] Such then were the partisan passions—the first of their kind—with which the Corcyraeans treated one another in their city.

Eurymedon now sailed away with the Athenian fleet. Thereafter the exiled Corcyraean oligarchs (about five hundred had escaped) seized fortified positions on the mainland, gained control of the territory owned there by Corcyra opposite the island, and with that as their base made constant raids on the island Corcyraeans and did considerable harm, leading to a severe shortage of food in the city. They also sent envoys to Sparta and Corinth hoping to negotiate their reinstatement. When these attempts came to nothing, they later equipped themselves with boats and mercenaries and crossed over to the island with a total force of about six hundred. They then burned the boats, to leave themselves no recourse other than conquest of the land, climbed Mount Istone and built a fort there, and began a campaign to destroy the Corcyraeans in the city and gain control of the country.

86 At the end of the same summer the Athenians sent twenty ships to Sicily with Laches the son of Melanopus and Charoeades the son of

Euphiletus as the generals in command. War had broken out between Syracuse and Leontini. Allied to the Syracusans were all the other Dorian cities except Camarina (these cities had also been counted in the Spartan alliance at the beginning of the war, but had not actually taken any part in the fighting), while the Chalcidian cities and Camarina were allied to the Leontinians. From Italy the Locrians were with Syracuse and the Rhegians (on grounds of kinship) with Leontini. The Leontinians and their allies sent to Athens, hoping that an old alliance and the fact that they were Ionians would persuade the Athenians to send them ships, as the Syracusans were isolating them from both land and sea. The Athenians did send ships, ostensibly in response to the call on their kinship, but in reality their motives were to prevent any import of corn from that area to the Peloponnese and to run an experiment to see if it would be possible to bring Sicily under their control. So they established their base at Rhegium in Italy and joined the allies in the prosecution of the war. So this summer ended.

In the following winter the plague struck Athens for the second 87 time: it had never entirely disappeared, but there had been some remission. This second visitation lasted for not less than a year, and the first had lasted for two years. In consequence there was nothing that did more than the plague to demoralize the Athenians and damage their military strength. It killed no fewer than four thousand four hundred of the serving hoplites and three hundred of the cavalry, and the number of deaths among the general populace is beyond computation.

This too was the time of the many earthquakes—in Athens, Euboea, and Boeotia, and especially at Orchomenus in Boeotia.

During the same winter the Athenians in Sicily and the Rhegians 88 made an expedition with thirty ships against the islands called the Islands of Aeolus (impossible to do in summer because of their lack of water). These islands are cultivated by the Liparaeans, who are colonists from Cnidus. They live on one small island in the group called Lipara, and travel from there to farm the other islands, Didyme, Strongyle, and Hiera. The people there think that Hephaestus has his forge on Hiera, as it can be seen emitting copious fire at night and smoke by day. These islands lie opposite the territory of Messana and the Sicels, and they were in alliance with Syracuse. The Athenians ravaged their land, but when the inhabitants would not come to terms they sailed back to Rhegium.

So ended the winter, and with it the fifth year of this war chronicled by Thucydides.

89   In the following summer the Peloponnesians and their allies, under the command of Agis, the son of Archidamus and king of Sparta, went as far as the Isthmus with the intention of invading Attica, but the occurrence of several earthquakes turned them back and no invasion took place. At around this time when the earthquakes were prevalent, the sea at Orobiae in Euboea retreated from what was then the coastline and returned in a tidal wave which hit one part of the town, and as a result of flooding combined with subsidence what was once land is now sea: the tidal wave killed the people who could not escape to higher ground in time. There was a similar inundation at Atalante, the island off Opuntian Locris, which carried away part of the Athenian fort and smashed one of the two ships laid up there. At Peparethus there was also a withdrawal of the sea, but not in this case followed by a surge: and an earthquake demolished part of the wall, the town hall, and a few other buildings. I believe the cause of this phenomenon to be that the sea retires at the point where the seismic shock is strongest, and is then suddenly flung back with all the greater violence, creating the inundation. I do not think that tidal waves could occur without an earthquake.

90   In the same summer there were various campaigns fought in Sicily in various circumstances—both the Sicilian Greeks fighting each other and the Athenians on campaign with their allies. I shall record the most notable actions taken either by the allies in conjunction with the Athenians or by their opponents against the Athenians. Charoeades the Athenian general had already been killed in battle by the Syracusans, leaving Laches in sole command of the fleet. With the allies he made an expedition against Mylae in the territory of Messana. Two tribal regiments of Messanans were on guard at Mylae, and they had also laid an ambush for the troops landing from the ships. The Athenians and their allies routed the men who sprang the ambush and killed many of them, then attacked the fortification and compelled the defenders to an agreement to surrender the acropolis and join them in their march on Messana. Thereafter, on the approach of the Athenians and their allies, the people of Messana also came to terms, giving hostages and providing the other guarantees required of them.

91   In the same summer the Athenians sent thirty ships round the Peloponnese commanded by Demosthenes the son of Alcisthenes

and Procles the son of Theodorus. They also sent sixty ships and two thousand hoplites to Melos: the general in command of this force was Nicias the son of Niceratus. The Melians were islanders who refused to take Athenian orders or join their alliance, and the purpose of this expedition was to bring them over to Athens. When, despite the ravaging of their land, the Melians would still not come to terms, the Athenian fleet left Melos and sailed to Oropus in Graea. They put in there at night, and the hoplites from the ships immediately set out on foot for Tanagra in Boeotia. In response to a signal given, a complete levy of the Athenian army from the city went to meet them at the same place, commanded by Hipponicus the son of Callias and Eurymedon the son of Thucles. They made camp, spent that day ravaging the land around Tanagra, and stayed in camp overnight. On the following day they defeated in battle the Tanagraeans who came out to meet them and a Theban contingent which had arrived in support. They took the weapons from the dead, set up a trophy, and then went back to the city or their ships. Nicias with his sixty ships sailed along the coast of Locris making raids to ravage the land close to the sea, then returned home.

At about this time the Spartans established their colony of 92 Heracleia in Trachis. Their thinking was as follows. The population of Malis is in three divisions: the Paralians, the Irians, and the Trachinians. Of these the Trachinians had been damaged in war by their neighbours the Oetaeans: their original intention had been to attach themselves to the Athenians, but then, not convinced that they could trust them, they sent instead to Sparta with Teisamenus as their chosen envoy. The delegation was joined by men from Doris, the mother-country of Sparta, who had the same request, as they too were suffering damage from the Oetaeans. On hearing their appeal the Spartans decided to send out the colony, partly in a desire to come to the aid of the Trachinians and Dorians, but they could also see that having the city established there would advantage them in the war with Athens. They could equip a fleet there for deployment against Euboea, with only a short crossing, and it would lie usefully on the route to Thrace. All in all they were keen to found the place.

So first they made enquiry of the god at Delphi, and when he gave his approval they sent out the settlers, drawing them from their own people and the Perioeci, and inviting volunteers from the rest of Greece to join them, but excluding Ionians, Achaeans, and some other nationalities. Three Spartans took the lead as founder-colonists: they were Leon, Alcidas, and Damagon. So they established the city and built new walls for it: it is now called Heracleia, and lies about four and a half miles from Thermopylae and just over two miles from the sea. They began to construct dock-yards, and for better protection blocked access on the Thermopylae side right at the pass.

93   As the process of colonizing the city got under way, the Athenians were at first alarmed and thought this new foundation a specific threat to Euboea, as it is a short crossing from there to Cape Cenaeum in Euboea. But in fact there was no subsequent realization of their fears, and Heracleia never gave them trouble. The reason was that the Thessalians, who were dominant in that area, and the peoples whose territory was threatened by this foundation feared the pros-pect of such a powerful neighbour and so kept up a constant war of attrition against the new arrivals, ultimately wearing them down, even though their numbers at first had been very large (all had con-fidently joined a colony established by Sparta, thinking this a guar-antee of security). Moreover a significant contribution to the gradual ruin and depopulation of the colony was made by the very Spartans who came out to govern it: most people were frightened away by their harsh and sometimes unfair administration, which made it increas-ingly easy for their neighbours to gain the upper hand.

94   In the same summer, and at about the same time as the Athenians were occupied at Melos, the Athenians in the thirty ships sailing round the Peloponnese first ambushed and killed a garrison at Ellomenum in Leucadian territory, then later attacked Leucas itself with a larger force: they had been joined by a full levy from Acarnania (except Oeniadae), by troops from Zacynthus and Cephallenia, and by fifteen ships from Corcyra. With their land being devastated on both sides of the isthmus, on the mainland and on the island (where the city of Leucas and the sanctuary of Apollo are situated), the Leucadians were overwhelmed by the scale of the invasion and offered no resist-ance. The Acarnanians begged Demosthenes, the Athenian general, to build a blockading wall, thinking that it would be easy to reduce the city by siege and so get rid of their inveterate enemy.

But just at this point Demosthenes was persuaded by the Messenians that, with such a large force assembled, this would be a good opportunity to attack the Aetolians: they were hostile to Naupactus, and if he conquered them he could easily bring the rest of the mainland thereabouts under Athenian control. Although the

Aetolians were a large and warlike nation, the Messenians pointed out that they lived in unfortified villages widely separate from one another, and used only light arms: it would not be difficult, they said, to overcome them before they could combine. They advised an attack first on the Apodotians, then on the Ophioneans, and finally on the Eurytanians, who form the largest division of the Aetolians, speak the most incomprehensible dialect, and are said to eat raw flesh. With these conquered, it would be easy to bring the rest of the area over to Athens.

Demosthenes agreed this to satisfy the Messenians, but mainly 95 because he reckoned that, without need for reinforcement from Athens, he could use his mainland allies together with the Aetolians to make an overland attack on Boeotia. His route would be through Ozolian Locris to Cytinium in Doris, keeping Mount Parnassus on his right, then down into Phocis. He thought that the Phocians, long-standing friends of Athens, would gladly join his campaign, or, if not, could be coerced: and then Boeotia was just over the border from Phocis. So, despite the protests of the Acarnanians, he set out from Leucas with his entire force and sailed round the coast to Sollium. There he explained his plan to the Acarnanians, but they would not go along with it because of his failure to blockade Leucas. Without them, then, he took the rest of his troops on campaign against Aetolia. These troops were Cephallenians, Messenians, Zacynthians, and the three hundred Athenian marines from his own ships (the fifteen Corcyraean ships had already left). He started from a base established at Oeneon in Locris. These Ozolian Locrians were allies of Athens, and it was arranged that they should bring their full army to join the Athenians in the interior: as they were neighbours of the Aetolians and similarly armed, it was thought that they would be an invaluable addition to the expeditionary force with their experience of the Aetolians' method of fighting and their local knowledge.

Demosthenes camped for the night with his army in the sanctuary 96 of Nemean Zeus (where the poet Hesiod is said to have been killed by the locals, after an oracle had foretold his death 'in Nemea'). At dawn he struck camp and began the march into Aetolia. On the first day he took Potidania, Crocyleium on the second, and Teichium on the third: there he paused and sent back the booty to Eupalium in Locris. His plan was to continue such conquests as far as the Ophioneans, and, if they were not prepared to agree terms, to return to Naupactus and campaign against them later.

The Aetolians had been aware of this venture from the moment it was planned, and as soon as the army had invaded they all rallied in great numbers, including support even from the most distant of the Ophioneans, whose territory extends to the Malian Gulf, the

97 Bomians and the Callians. The Messenians' advice to Demosthenes was along these lines: they repeated their original assurance that the conquest of Aetolia could easily be achieved, and urged him to move against the villages as fast as he could, not giving time for the Aetolians to mass their forces in opposition, but looking to take every village immediately in his path. Confident in his own good fortune, as nothing had resisted his progress, Demosthenes accepted their advice and, without waiting for the Locrians due to reinforce him (his prime lack was of light-armed javelin-men), he advanced to Aegitium, attacked it, and took it by force. The inhabitants had withdrawn to positions in the hills overlooking the town, which was situated on high ground about nine miles from the sea.

By now the Aetolians had rallied to the support of Aegitium, and began attacking the Athenians and their allies. Their method was to charge down the hills on all sides hurling javelins as they ran, withdrawing whenever the Athenian army advanced against them, but pressing back whenever the Athenians gave ground. The battle went on like this for a long time, a sequence of pursuits and retreats, in

98 both of which the Athenians came off worse. As long as their archers had arrows and could use them, the Athenians held out, as the light-armed Aetolians were forced back under fire. But when the archers lost cohesion on the death of their captain, and the main troops had become exhausted by the long and tiring repetition of the same manoeuvres, and the Aetolians kept up the pressure with volley after volley of javelins, then the Athenians finally turned and fled. Unfamiliar with the territory, some found themselves in ravines from which there was no escape, and were killed there—it so happened that their guide to the local paths, a Messenian called Chromon, had been killed. Fast runners and lightly armed, the Aetolians caught many on the run in the immediate rout and shot them down. The majority missed their way and ended up in a wood with no exit: the Aetolians brought fire and burned the wood with them inside. The Athenian army attempted every form of escape and met every form of death, and the survivors made their way with difficulty back to the sea and their original base at Oeneon in Locris. The dead included many of the allies, and of the Athenians themselves about a hundred and

twenty hoplites. Such in number, and all at the same stage of life, this was the finest group of men lost to the city of Athens in the course of this war. Among those killed was the other general, Procles. The Athenians recovered their dead from the Aetolians under truce, withdrew to Naupactus, and then later returned to Athens in their ships. Demosthenes, though, stayed behind in Naupactus and the surrounding area, afraid of the Athenians' reaction to the events.

At about this same time the Athenians in Sicily sailed to the 99 territory of Locri and made a landing there. They defeated the Locrians who came to oppose them, and captured a guard-post by the river Alex.

In the same summer the Aetolians, having earlier dispatched 100 envoys to Corinth and Sparta (these envoys were the Ophionean Tolophus, the Eurytanian Boriades, and the Apodotian Teisandrus), persuaded them to send a force against Naupactus as being responsible for inciting the Athenian invasion. In the autumn the Spartans sent out three thousand allied hoplites, including five hundred from the newly founded city of Heracleia in Trachis. In command of the force was the Spartiate Eurylochus, accompanied by two other Spartiates, Macarius and Menedaïus.

When this army had gathered at Delphi, Eurylochus sent out 101 heralds with a proclamation to the Ozolian Locrians, since his route to Naupactus was through their territory and he also wanted to detach them from the Athenians. The Locrians most eager to cooperate with him were the Amphissans, who were anxious for protection against the hostility of the Phocians. They were the first to volunteer hostages, and they persuaded the other Locrians to do likewise in a general fear of the advancing army: firstly, then, their neighbours in Myonia (where the route into Locris is at its most difficult), and then the people of Ipnea, Messapia, Tritaea, Chaleium, Tolophon, Isus, and Oeanthea. All these peoples also joined the campaign. The Olpaeans gave hostages, but did not join: and the Hyaeans only gave hostages after the capture of one of their villages, called Polis.

With all preparations made and the hostages deposited at Cytinium 102 in Doris, Eurylochus and his army began the march to Naupactus through Locrian territory: on the route he took two of their towns, Oeneon and Eupalium, which had refused to come to terms. Once arrived in the area of Naupactus and joined now by Aetolian support, they began ravaging the land and captured the unfortified suburbs of the city. They then proceeded to Molycrium (a Corinthian colony, but subject to Athens) and captured that too. The Athenian Demosthenes, who was still in the Naupactus area after the outcome of the Aetolian campaign, received advance intelligence of this army and feared for the city: so he went to the Acarnanians and persuaded them to come to the aid of Naupactus (no easy task, in view of his withdrawal from Leucas). They sent a thousand hoplites with him on board his ships, and this force, once inside Naupactus, proved the saving of the place: there had otherwise been the danger that they would not hold out, with an extensive wall to defend and few defenders.

When Eurylochus and those with him learnt of the entry of these troops into Naupactus, and realized that it was impossible for them to take the city by force, they pulled back—but not towards the Peloponnese: instead they withdrew to the region now called Aeolis, to Calydon and Pleuron and the area thereabouts, and to Proschium in Aetolia. This was because the Ambraciots had approached them and urged them to join their own troops in an attack on Amphilochian Argos and the rest of Amphilochia, and on Acarnania too: their argument was that if they gained control of these places the whole of the mainland region would become part of the Spartan alliance. Eurylochus agreed. He dismissed the Aetolians, and kept his army at ease in that area, waiting for the call to support the Ambraciots when they launched their campaign against Argos.

So this summer ended.

103   In the following winter the Athenians in Sicily made an attack on the Sicel town of Inessa, where the acropolis was held by Syracusans. In this they were joined by their Greek allies and by those of the Sicels who had revolted from their enforced subjection to Syracuse and were now fighting on the Athenian side. The attempt to take the place failed, and they turned back. In the course of this withdrawal the Syracusans sallied out from their fortified position and attacked the Athenian allies at the rear of the withdrawing column: this onslaught routed part of the army and killed a good number. After this Laches and the Athenians made several landings from their ships in the territory of Locri. At the river Caïcinus they defeated in battle some three hundred Locrians who came to meet them under Proxenus the son of Capaton, took their arms, and left.

104   In the same winter the Athenians also purified the island of Delos, supposedly in response to an oracle. The tyrant Peisistratus had carried out an earlier purification, but not of the whole island—only

that part of it which could be seen from the sanctuary. On this occasion the whole island was purified, in the following way. All the graves of those who had died on Delos were opened and the contents removed, and the Athenians issued an edict that in future no one should die or give birth in the island: all those close to either condition should be ferried across to Rheneia. The distance between Delos and Rheneia is so short that when Polycrates the tyrant of Samos, who held a naval supremacy for some time and controlled the other islands, captured Rheneia also he dedicated it to Delian Apollo by attaching it to Delos with a chain. After the purification the Athenians then instituted and held for the first time the quadrennial Delian festival.

Long ago there used to be a great gathering at Delos of the Ionians and the neighbouring islanders. The Ionians would come to enjoy the festival with their wives and children, as they now do at the Ephesian festival: athletic and musical contests were held there, and each city brought a chorus. The best evidence of the nature of this festival is Homer, in these verses of the Hymn to Apollo:

And at the time, Phoebus, when Delos is most to your liking,
Here the Ionians gather, long-coated, to meet in your honour,
With them their wives and their children, and all walk the path of your
    precinct;
Here they delight your heart with boxing and dancing and singing.
Every time they hold these games, it is you they remember.

That there was also a musical contest attracting competitors is shown again by Homer in these verses from the same Hymn. He celebrates the Delian chorus of women and concludes his praise with the following lines, in which he also alludes to himself:

Come then now, may Apollo and Artemis also be gracious,
And farewell ladies all. Be mindful of me in the future.
Someone may come here, some other unfortunate mortal, and ask you:
'Girls, please tell me, which of the singers who come to this region
Sings in your view the sweetest song? Who gives you most pleasure?'
You will all answer, naming no names, but prompt to the question,
'He's a blind man, and his home is the rugged island of Chios.'

Such is the testimony of Homer to the antiquity of a great gathering and festival at Delos. In later years the islanders and the Athenians continued to send choruses and offerings, but most elements of the festival, including the games, were abandoned, naturally enough, when Ionia had its troubles. But now the Athenians restored the games and added chariot-races, which had not been held in the past.

105   In the same winter the Ambraciots fulfilled the promise to Eurylochus which had kept his army in the area, and launched a campaign against Amphilochian Argos with three thousand hoplites. They invaded Argive territory and captured Olpae, a strongly forti-fied town set on a hill near the sea: the town had been walled by the Acarnanians, and was used by them and the Amphilochians for their joint assizes. The city of Argos is just under three miles away, on the coast. Some of the Acarnanians went to the support of Argos, while others made camp in the place in Amphilochia called Crenae, keep-ing guard there to prevent the Peloponnesians with Eurylochus from getting past undetected to join the Ambraciots. They sent to Demosthenes, who had commanded the Athenian expedition into Aetolia, asking him to be their leader, and also got word to the twenty Athenian ships which were at that time sailing round the Peloponnese under the command of Aristoteles the son of Timocrates and Hierophon the son of Antimnestus. The Ambraciots at Olpae like-wise sent a messenger to their city calling for a full levy in their sup-port, as they were afraid that Eurylochus and his troops would not be able to get past the Acarnanians, leaving them either a battle on their own or the alternative of a hazardous retreat.

106   When the Peloponnesians under Eurylochus learnt that the Ambraciots had reached Olpae and occupied it, they set out from Proschium to bring support as quickly as they could. Crossing the Achelous, they moved up through Acarnania, which the reinforce-ments sent to Argos had emptied of troops, keeping the city of Stratus and its garrison on their right and the rest of Acarnania on their left. After they had crossed the territory of Stratus, their route took them through Phytia and next along the borders of Medeon, then through Limnaea. And now they passed out of Acarnania into the land of the Agraeans, who were friendly to them. Reaching Mount Thyamus, which is in Agraean territory, they crossed it and came down into Argive land after dark: making their way between the city of Argos and the Acarnanian guard at Crenae, they managed to escape detec-

107   tion and joined the Ambraciots at Olpae. At daybreak the now united forces established themselves at the place called Metropolis and pitched camp there.

Not long afterwards the Athenians arrived in the Ambracian Gulf with their twenty ships to support the Argives; and Demosthenes too arrived with six hundred Messenian hoplites and sixty Athenian archers. The ships moored off Olpae and maintained a blockade of the hill from the sea. The Acarnanians and a few of the Amphilochians (the majority had been forced under Ambraciot occupation) had by now gathered in Argos, and were preparing to fight the enemy: they chose Demosthenes as leader of the whole allied force, in cooperation with their own generals. Demosthenes took them forward and camped near Olpae, where a great ravine separated the two armies. For five days both sides remained inactive, but on the sixth they formed up for battle.

The Peloponnesian army proved larger than his and its line out-flanked him, so Demosthenes, aware of the danger of encirclement, concealed a detachment of hoplites and light-armed troops (to a combined total of four hundred) along a sunken path overgrown with bushes, so that at the moment of engagement they could emerge from the ambush and take the outflanking enemy line from the rear. Preparations were completed on both sides, and they engaged at close quarters. Demosthenes had the right wing with the Messenians and a small number of Athenians: the rest of the line was held by the Acarnanians grouped in their various contingents and the Amphilochian javelin-men who had managed to join the force. On the other side the Peloponnesians and Ambraciots were drawn up in mixed formation, except that the Mantineans stayed in a group towards the left wing, though not at the end of the line: the far left, facing the Messenians and Demosthenes, was taken by Eurylochus and his company.

When the close engagement had begun and the Peloponnesian 108 wing had outflanked their opponents' right wing and were beginning to encircle it, the Acarnanians in the ambush came on them from behind and routed them with the force of their attack. The result was no further resistance from this wing and a contagious panic which turned most of the rest of the army to flight, their terror increased by the sight of Eurylochus' company—the best division they had— being destroyed. The main part in this action was taken by the Messenians who were with Demosthenes on that side of the bat-tlefield. The Ambraciots and the others on the right wing defeated their immediate opposition and pursued them to Argos (the Ambraciots are in fact the most warlike people in that region). When they returned and saw the general defeat of their side, and were then attacked by the rest of the Acarnanians, they made their escape with difficulty to Olpae, losing many of their men in a headlong retreat without order or discipline: out of the whole army only the Mantineans retained formation as they withdrew. The battle ended late in the day.

109   Both Eurylochus and Macarius had been killed, and the command had passed to Menedaïus. The scale of the defeat left him a dilemma. If he stayed where he was, he could not see the means of withstanding a siege, cut off both on land and at sea by the Athenian ships, nor the means of reaching safety if he attempted to withdraw. So next day Menedaïus made overtures to Demosthenes and the Acarnanian generals, asking for a withdrawal under truce, and also the recovery of their dead. They granted the return of the bodies, while they themselves set up a trophy and recovered their own dead, which numbered about three hundred. They refused, though, to proclaim a general truce for the withdrawal of the whole army. Instead, Demosthenes and his Acarnanian colleagues agreed a private truce to allow a quick escape for the Mantineans, Menedaïus and the other Peloponnesian commanders, and any other notables among them. Demosthenes' intention was to strip support from the Ambraciots and their collection of mercenaries, but also, and particularly, to give the Spartans and Peloponnesians a reputation among the Greeks in that area for betraying others to further their own interests. So they took up their dead and gave them hasty burial as best they could, while those given leave to escape made secret plans for their departure.

110   Demosthenes and the Acarnanians now received news that the full force of Ambraciots from the city, responding to the original message from Olpae, was on its way through Amphilochia to join the troops at Olpae, in complete ignorance of what had happened. Demosthenes immediately sent a detachment to ambush the roads and occupy the commanding positions in advance, and prepared to attack in support with the rest of his army.

111   Meanwhile the Mantineans and the others covered by the private truce stole out in small groups, ostensibly on the forage for greens and firewood, and they did begin gathering the supposed objects of their expedition: but when they were at some distance from Olpae they quickened their pace. The Ambraciots and some of the others had also gone out in a body to forage, and when they realized that these men were escaping they too set out at the run to catch up with them. At first the Acarnanians thought this was a mass attempt to

escape when no safe conduct had been granted, and they began to pursue the Peloponnesians. When some of their commanders tried to hold them back and explained that a truce had been made with the Peloponnesians, one of the Acarnanians, seeing this as a betrayal of their own people, threw a javelin at them. After this, however, they let the Mantineans and the Peloponnesians go, but set about killing the Ambraciots—and there was much uncertainty and dispute about who was an Ambraciot and who a Peloponnesian. They killed some two hundred of them: the rest made their escape over the border into Agraeis, where the Agraean king Salynthius, a friend of Ambracia, gave them welcome.

By now the Ambraciots from the city had reached Idomene, a 112 place which consists of two high hills. The advance party sent out from his camp by Demosthenes was quick enough to beat the Ambraciots to the larger of the two hills and take it unobserved as night was falling, and they made camp there: the Ambraciots had been the first to reach and occupy the lesser of the hills. Demosthenes and the rest of his army set out after their supper, as soon as it was dark. He himself led half of the army towards the pass, and the other half took a route through the mountains of Amphilochia. At break of dawn he fell on the Ambraciots when they were still in their beds and had no idea of what had happened. In fact their first thought was that these were their own men, as Demosthenes had deliberately placed the Messenians at the front of his troops and told them to call out in their Dorian dialect to convince the sentries, who in any case would not be able to see them as it was then still dark.

So Demosthenes fell on the Ambraciot army and routed it. Many were killed on the spot, and the rest fled into the mountains. But the paths had been ambushed in advance, and moreover the Amphilochians were familiar with their own territory, in which they had the advantage of light-armed troops against hoplites, while the Ambraciots did not know which way to turn in unfamiliar country: so they blundered into ravines or the ambushes already laid for them, and were killed. They tried every means of escape, and some even turned towards the sea, which was not far away: and when they saw the Athenian ships sailing along the coast just as the action was taking place, they swam out to them, thinking in their immediate terror that, if they had to die, it was better to be killed by the men in the ships than at the hands of the Amphilochians, who were barbarians and their bitterest enemies. Such was the disaster met by the Ambraciots, and few out of many made safe return to their city. The Acarnanians stripped the dead bodies, set up trophies, and went back to Argos.

113   On the following day a herald came to them from the Ambraciots who had escaped from Olpae into Agraeis, to request the recovery of the bodies of those killed, after the first battle, when they had joined the exodus of the Mantineans and the others without the same protection of a truce. When the herald saw the arms and armour of the Ambraciots from the city, he was astonished at their number: he knew nothing of that disaster, and thought these were the arms of the men from his own force. Somebody, mistaken too in thinking the herald was from the Ambraciots at Idomene, asked him why he was surprised, and how many of them had died. He said about two hundred. 'These are obviously not the arms of two hundred,' replied the other, 'but of more than a thousand.' 'So then', said the herald, 'they are not from the men in our fight?' 'Yes they are,' came the reply, 'if you were fighting yesterday at Idomene.' 'But yesterday we did not fight anyone: it was the day before, in the retreat.' 'Well, we did fight yesterday. We fought these here—the Ambraciots coming to your rescue from the city.'

When the herald heard this and realized that the relief force from the city had been destroyed, he gave a cry of horror: appalled by the scale of the calamity now inflicted, he turned straight back without completing his mission or staying to ask for the dead. This was indeed the greatest disaster to befall a single Greek city over so few days in the whole of this war. I have not given the number of those who died, because the reputed loss would seem incredible in proportion to the size of the city. I do know, though, that if the Acarnanians and Amphilochians had been prepared to reduce Ambracia as Demosthenes and the Athenians urged, they would have taken the city without a fight. As it was, they feared that the Athenians in possession of Ambracia would be new neighbours more threatening than the old.

114   Thereafter they assigned a third of the spoils to the Athenians and divided the rest among their cities. The Athenian share was captured at sea, and what are now dedicated in the Athenian temples are the three hundred panoplies reserved for Demosthenes. He brought them with him when he sailed back to Athens (this success had given him greater confidence to return after the disaster in Aetolia). The Athenians in the twenty ships also left for Naupactus.

After the departure of Demosthenes and the Athenians, the Acarnanians and Amphilochians made a truce with the Ambraciots and Peloponnesians who had taken refuge with Salynthius and the Agraeans, granting them safe conduct out of Oeniadae, to which they then transferred from Salynthius' kingdom. For the future the Acarnanians and Amphilochians made a treaty and an alliance with the Ambraciots for a hundred years. The terms were that the Ambraciots should not have to join any Acarnanian campaign against the Peloponnesians, nor the Acarnanians any Ambraciot campaign against the Athenians; otherwise they should come to the defence of each other's country; the Ambraciots should return all Amphilochian territory and hostages which they held; and they should give no support to Anactorium (which was hostile to the Acarnanians). With these terms agreed, they brought their war to an end. Thereafter the Corinthians sent about three hundred of their own hoplites to Ambracia as a garrison, commanded by Xenocleides the son of Euthycles: they had a difficult overland journey to get there.

Such were the events concerning Ambracia.

In the same winter the Athenians in Sicily made a landing from 115 their ships in the territory of Himera, coordinated with a Sicel invasion of the outlying parts of this territory from the interior, and then sailed against the Islands of Aeolus. On their return to Rhegium they found the Athenian general Pythodorus the son of Isolochus arrived to succeed Laches in command of the ships. The allies in Sicily had sailed to Athens and persuaded the Athenians to send more ships in their support: their land was controlled by the Syracusans, but only a few ships denied them the sea, and, intolerant of this, they were gathering a navy in preparation for a challenge. The Athenians began manning forty ships for this expedition: their motives were partly the belief that this would hasten an end to the war in Sicily, and partly also the opportunity to give their navy practice. So they sent out one of their generals, Pythodorus, with a few ships, intending to follow with the dispatch of the main fleet under Sophocles the son of Sostratides and Eurymedon the son of Thucles. At the end of the winter Pythodorus, now holding the command of Laches' ships, sailed against the Locrian fort which Laches had taken previously, but was defeated in battle by the Locrians and withdrew.

At the very beginning of this next spring there was an eruption of 116 liquid fire from Aetna, as had happened before. It destroyed some part of the land of the people of Catana, who live under Mount Aetna, the largest mountain in Sicily. It is said that the last eruption was fifty years earlier, and that there have been three eruptions in all since the Greeks first settled in Sicily.

Such were the events of this winter, and so ended the sixth year of this war chronicled by Thucydides.

BOOK FOUR

In the following summer, about the time when the corn was coming 1
into ear, a fleet of ten Syracusan and the same number of Locrian ships
sailed to Messana in Sicily and captured it: they had been invited
by the Messanans themselves, and Messana now defected from the
Athenians. The main motive on the part of the Syracusans was that
they could see the place was a gateway to Sicily, and they were afraid
that the Athenians would at some time use it as a base from which to
launch an attack on them with larger forces. The Locrian motive was
hatred of the Rhegians, and the wish to reduce them in a campaign
by sea as well as land. They had already made a full-scale invasion of
Rhegian territory to prevent them interfering at Messana, partly
instigated by the Rhegian exiles whom they harboured. Rhegium had
long been in a state of internal dissension, which made resistance to
the Locrians impossible at the present time and thereby intensified
the Locrian attack. After ravaging the land the Locrians withdrew
their infantry, but the ships were kept on guard at Messana, while
others were being manned to join them at the anchorage there and
prosecute the war from that base.

At about the same time in the spring, before the corn was ripe, the 2
Peloponnesians and their allies invaded Attica under the command
of Agis the son of Archidamus, king of Sparta: they established
themselves and began ravaging the land. The Athenians now dispatched to Sicily the forty ships which they had been preparing, and
with them the other two generals, Eurymedon and Sophocles (the
third general, Pythodorus, had already arrived in Sicily). Their instructions were to stop at Corcyra on their route and see to the problems
of the people in the city, who were suffering from the raids of the
exiles on Mount Istone: furthermore, sixty Peloponnesian ships had
already set sail for Corcyra to support the exiles on the mountain,
and the severe shortage of food in the city encouraged their belief
that they could easily gain control. Demosthenes held no command
after his return from Acarnania, but at his own request the Athenians
granted him leave to use these ships at his discretion on their voyage
round the Peloponnese.

When they were sailing off the coast of Laconia they heard that 3
the Peloponnesian ships were already at Corcyra. Eurymedon and

Sophocles wanted to press on to Corcyra, but Demosthenes asked them to put in at Pylos and take some necessary action there before continuing the voyage. They objected, but as it happened a storm arose which forced the ships into Pylos. Demosthenes immediately urged them to fortify the place, saying that this was the whole purpose of his joining their voyage. He pointed out the abundance of timber and stones available, and also the natural strength of the site and the fact that both it and the surrounding area for some distance was unguarded (Pylos is about forty-five miles from Sparta, and lies in what was once Messenian land: the Spartans call it Coryphasium). The generals said that there were plenty of deserted promontories in the Peloponnese which he could occupy if he wanted to waste public money. In Demosthenes' view, though, this site had particular advantages over any other: there was an adjacent harbour; this had been home territory to the Messenians in the past, they spoke the same dialect as the Spartans, and they could do a great deal of damage if they were based there; and also they would give the fort a reliable garrison.

4   He failed to persuade either the generals or the troops (having subsequently shared his plans with their contingent commanders), and was forced to remain inactive while the weather continued unfit for sailing. In the end the troops themselves, with nothing else to do, took it into their heads to gather round and fortify the place. So they set to and began the work. They had no stone-working tools, but chose suitable stones to carry to the site and fitted them together where each went best. If there was need for clay, in the absence of any containers they carried it on their backs, stooped forward so it was more likely to stay in position, and with their hands clasped behind to prevent it slipping off. In every possible way they hurried to finish work on the most vulnerable points before the Spartans could arrive to oppose them. Most of the site had sufficiently strong natural defences to have no need of a wall.

5   In fact the Spartans were holding some festival at the time, and they paid little attention to the news when they heard it. They thought that when they did move against Pylos either the Athenians would not stay to resist, or else they could easily take the place by force: there was also the constraint that their army was still in Attica. The Athenians fortified the mainland aspect of the site and the most vulnerable parts elsewhere in six days. They then left Demosthenes with five ships as its garrison, and pressed ahead with the bulk of the fleet on the voyage to Corcyra and Sicily.

When the Peloponnesians in Attica heard of the occupation of 6 Pylos, they quickly set back for home. The Spartans and their king Agis regarded Pylos as their own affair: but they had also invaded early in the year and, with the corn still green, were running short of food for their numbers, while the onset of unseasonably wintry weather discomforted the troops. For many reasons, then, the result was a withdrawal earlier than intended, and this turned out to be their shortest invasion—they had stayed in Attica for fifteen days.

At about the same time Simonides, an Athenian general, captured 7 Eïon in the Thraceward region, which was a colony of Mende but hostile to Athens. He had gathered a few Athenians from the garrison posts and a larger force from the allies in that area, and the place was betrayed to him. Immediately the Chalcidians and Bottiaeans rallied to the support of Eïon, and Simonides was driven out with the loss of many of his men.

After the Peloponnesian withdrawal from Attica the Spartiates 8 themselves and the Perioeci nearest to Pylos made for the place immediately, while the rest of the Spartans, given that they had only just arrived home from another campaign, followed more slowly. They also sent round the Peloponnese summoning the allies to assist at Pylos as soon as possible, and called back their sixty ships at Corcyra, which were transported across the Leucadian isthmus, escaped detection by the Athenian ships (now at Zacynthus), and arrived at Pylos to join the land army already established there. While the Peloponnesian fleet was still on its way, Demosthenes managed to get two ships out in time to alert Eurymedon and the Athenians in the ships at Zacynthus to the danger at Pylos and tell them to come.

So the Athenian ships sailed at best speed in response to Demosthenes' message. Meanwhile the Spartans were preparing an attack on the fort by land and sea, confident that they would easily take a structure hastily built and thinly manned. In expectation of Athenian reinforcement with the ships from Zacynthus, their intention (if they had not by then already taken the place) was to proceed to block the entrances to the harbour to deny the Athenians any anchorage there. The island called Sphacteria extends down the side of the harbour bay and lies close to it, making the harbour safe and the entrances narrow. The entrance by Pylos and the Athenian fort allows a passage for two ships abreast, and at the other end the gap between island and mainland is less than one mile. The whole island, being uninhabited, was wooded and pathless, and about two and three-quarter miles long.

They planned, then, to block these entrances with ships packed close together and prows facing outwards. Concerned that the island itself could become a base for Athenian action against them, they ferried hoplites across to it and stationed others along the mainland. In this way they thought that both the island and the mainland would be hostile territory to the Athenians; there would be nowhere for them to land elsewhere, as the coast round Pylos, outside the entrance to the bay and facing the open sea, offered no harbour and therefore no base for military support of their people in Pylos; they themselves would avoid the danger of a sea-battle and had every chance of taking the place by siege, since it had been occupied with little preparation and there was no store of food there. With that overall plan they began ferrying the hoplites to the island, choosing them by lot from all of the divisions. Contingents crossed over and returned in rotation, and the last contingent to cross, which was caught there, numbered four hundred and twenty, with attendant Helots in addition: their commander was Epitadas the son of Molobrus.

9   Seeing that the Spartans intended a combined attack with ships and infantry, Demosthenes set about his own preparations. He dragged up on shore under the fort his remaining triremes from the five he had been left, and fenced them with a stockade. He armed their crews with poor-quality shields, most of them made of wicker, as there was no means of acquiring arms in a deserted place, and even these were taken from two Messenian boats, a thirty-oared privateer and a cutter, which had just arrived. The Messenians had about forty hoplites on board, and these were pressed into service with the others. Demosthenes stationed the majority of both the poorly and the fully armed men on the best-fortified and strongest side of the site, facing the mainland, with instructions to repel any attack by the land forces. He himself selected sixty hoplites and a few archers from the whole body of his troops and went outside the wall down to the sea, at the point where he expected the enemy was most likely to attempt a landing. It was a difficult and rocky stretch, fronting the open sea, but he thought they would be keen to force their way ashore here, where the wall was at its weakest (not thinking they would ever be at a naval disadvantage, the Athenians had not built strong fortifications on that side): and if they did force a landing the

place was vulnerable. So he went right to the edge of the sea at that point and stationed his hoplites there, hoping if he could to prevent the enemy coming ashore, and encouraged them with this address:

'Men, you have joined me in facing this danger, and I do not want any of you at a crisis like this trying to show his intelligence by weighing all the odds stacked against us—do not think about it, but just engage the enemy with every hope of winning through on this occasion as you have before. When things have reached the critical point, as they have now, there is no room for calculation and the danger is best met soonest. But actually I can see most factors in our favour, if we are prepared to stand our ground and not let their numbers panic us into throwing away the advantages which we have. This is a hard place for a landing—a potential advantage for us, I think, which will favour our side if we stand firm. But if we give way, even this difficult ground will be open to their advance with no one opposing them, and we shall then have a more formidable enemy because it will not be easy for them to retreat even if we do press back hard. Our best chance of beating them off is while they are still on their ships: once on land they are on equal terms with us.

'And we should not be too fearful of their numbers. They may be a large force, but the difficulty of coming in to land will mean that only a few of them can fight at any one time. This is not the same as an army of superior size meeting us on land in equal combat, but they will be fighting from ships, which for success needs many conditions to combine at the right time on the sea. So I think their difficulties counterbalance our lack of numbers. You are Athenians, and you have experience of naval landings. You know that if an opponent stands his ground and is not intimidated into retreat by the crash of oars and the menace of ships bearing down on him, nothing will then shift him. So I call on you too now to stand firm, to fight them right on the shore, and to save both ourselves and this place here.'

This encouragement from Demosthenes boosted the Athenians' confidence, and they went on down to the sea and deployed along the very edge of the shore.

The Spartans now moved to attack the fort simultaneously with their land army and their ships, which were forty-three in number, and the admiral sailing in command was the Spartiate Thrasymelidas the son of Cratesicles. He made his attack where Demosthenes expected it, and the Athenians defended themselves on both sides, land and sea. The Spartans had divided their fleet into relays of a few ships at a time, as there was no room for more to put in, and they took turns of pause and attack, cheering one another on with every determination to press through somehow and take the fort. Most conspicuous of all in this action was Brasidas. He was commanding one of the triremes and could see that the other commanders and their helmsmen were wary of putting in to this rough coast, even where there seemed a possible opening, and concerned to avoid staving in their ships. He shouted out that it was nonsense to spare the timber and tolerate an enemy fort built in their country; he told the Spartan commanders to force a landing even if that broke their ships, and urged the allies to make a willing sacrifice of their ships, at this present time of need, to repay the Spartans for great benefits conferred; they should run their ships aground and make every effort to get on land and overpower both the men and the fort.

12   What he urged on the others he followed himself, forcing his helmsman to ground the ship. He made for the gangway and tried to get down it, but was forced back by the Athenians and fainted from the multiple wounds he sustained. He fell into the outrigger, and his shield slipped from his arm into the sea. It was washed on land and recovered by the Athenians, who subsequently included it in the trophy they set up to mark this attack. The others tried their best to disembark, but found it impossible in view of the harshness of the terrain and the resolution with which the Athenians held their position. It was quite a reversal of circumstance—Athenians resisting from land (and Laconian land at that) a Spartan attack by sea, and Spartans attempting a naval landing to recover their own territory under Athenian occupation. The Spartans were generally thought at that time to be mostly a land power with unrivalled infantry, and the Athenians a sea power with overall naval supremacy.

13   So throughout this day and part of the next the Spartans continued their attempts to attack, and then desisted. On the third day they sent some of their ships to Asine to fetch wood for the construction of siege-engines, hoping that with these devices they could take the wall facing the bay, which might be high but afforded the best landing underneath it. Meanwhile the Athenian ships arrived from Zacynthus, a total of fifty now, as they had been joined by some of the garrison ships from Naupactus and four Chian ships. When they saw the mainland and the island full of hoplites, and the Spartan ships occupying the harbour and not sailing out to meet them, for lack of any other anchorage they sailed in the first instance to the

uninhabited island of Prote, not far away, and camped there. On the following day they put to sea prepared for a naval battle—in the open sea if the enemy would come out for the fight: otherwise they themselves would sail into the bay.

The Spartans did not put out to meet them, nor had they in fact carried through their intention of blocking the entrances to the bay. Still on land and in no hurry, they began manning their ships and preparing to do battle in the huge harbour with any ships which entered it. Seeing how things stood, the Athenians moved in for the 14 attack through both entrances. Most of the Spartans' ships were by now out from land and facing them. The Athenians fell on these and drove them into flight. They pursued as best they could over the short distance, crippling many of the ships and capturing five, one of them crew and all: the rest escaped to the shore, but the Athenians went in and rammed them. Other ships were still being manned, and these were disabled even before they could put out: some of them, evacuated in terror by their crews, were taken in tow by the Athenians and dragged away empty.

Anguished by the sight of this disaster, which threatened the isolation of their men on the island, the Spartans came running in support, plunged fully armed into the sea, and grabbed hold of their ships to pull them back—in all this flurry every man thought that any effort came to a standstill without the benefit of his personal involvement. There was huge confusion and an inversion of their usual roles in this struggle for the ships: with the energy induced by shock the Spartans were virtually fighting a sea-battle from land, and the Athenians, victors eager to take maximum advantage of their present fortune, were fighting an infantry battle from their ships. They gave each other a hard fight and there were casualties on both sides: when they disengaged the Spartans had saved their empty ships, apart from those captured at the beginning. Each side now returned to their camp. The Athenians set up a trophy, returned the enemy dead, and took possession of the wrecks: and they immediately sent ships on a constant circuit round the island to keep guard on the men who were effectively marooned there. The Peloponnesians on the mainland, joined now by reinforcements from all quarters, kept their position facing Pylos.

When news of the situation at Pylos reached Sparta, it was 15 regarded as a major disaster and the Spartans decided that the authorities should go down to the camp, see for themselves, and take decisions on the spot as they thought best. Once the authorities had seen the impossibility of rescuing their men, they looked to avoid any danger of their coming to grief by starvation or being captured by force of numbers, and so decided to make a truce at Pylos with the Athenian generals (should they agree) while sending envoys to Athens to discuss a settlement and trying to achieve the earliest possible recovery of their men.

16   The generals accepted their proposal, and a truce was worked out on the following terms. The Spartans would bring to Pylos and hand over to the Athenians the ships they had used in the battle and all other warships in Laconia, and they would not take arms against the fort either by land or by sea. The Athenians would allow the Spartans on the mainland to send over to their men on the island a set quantity of prepared food, for each man two Attic quarts of kneaded barley-meal, one pint of wine, and a piece of meat, with half that ration for their attendants: the sending of supplies would be done under Athenian supervision, and no boat should approach the island without their consent. The Athenians would continue to guard the island as before, but would not land on it: and they would not take arms against the Peloponnesian forces either by land or by sea. If either side deviated from these conditions in any way whatever, then the truce would be at an end. The truce would last until the Spartans' envoys returned from Athens: the Athenians would convey them there and back in a trireme. This truce would end on their return, and the Athenians would hand back the ships in the same state in which they had received them.

The truce was agreed on these terms, the ships (about sixty in number) were handed over, and the envoys were dispatched. On their arrival in Athens they spoke as follows:

17   'Athenians, the Spartans have sent us here to negotiate for our men on the island, in the hope that we can persuade you to an arrangement which will both be to your advantage and also allow us the most honourable outcome to the unfortunate situation in which we find ourselves. If we speak at some length, this is not a departure from our usual custom. In our country it is not our habit to use many words where few will suffice, but we do use more when the occasion demands an exposition of the relevant considerations to achieve the desired result. Please do not take what we say as polemic, or as a sermon assuming an unintelligent audience, but think of it as a reminder to the experienced of what you already know about good policy.

'It is open to you to consolidate your present success, retaining what you now control and winning honour and glory besides: and to avoid the common error of men who have no experience of handling a piece of good fortune—one unexpected success makes them over-confident and grasping for more. Those who have met the most reversals of fortune in either direction have good reason to put least reliance on their successes: and experience suggests that this is par-ticularly true both of your city and of us.

'Witness our present misfortunes. We, with the greatest reputa-tion in all Greece, have now had to come to you: and what we are here to ask of you we had previously thought was our own preroga-tive to grant. Yet what has happened to us was not the result of any loss of military strength (nor indeed of any gain in strength causing us to overreach ourselves), but because we made a judgement on the facts at the time, and were wrong: all can make these errors, just as we did. So you should not let the present power of your city and its acquisitions make you think that fortune will always be on your side. Wise men deposit their gains in safe keeping against an uncer-tain future, and are then in a better position to take an intelligent approach to any losses: and wise men recognize that war follows wherever their fortunes lead, and does not confine itself to any area of involvement which they might choose. Such men, by their refusal to let success in war excite their confidence, are least likely to make a false move and most inclined to agree an end to the war when fortune is with them. And this, Athenians, is now your best course with us. You will want to avoid the danger that if you reject our proposal and then fail (as is perfectly possible), even these present successes which you have achieved will subsequently be attributed to luck: whereas it is open to you to leave to posterity an unendangered reputation for both strength and intelligence.

'The Spartans invite you to a treaty ending the war. They offer peace, alliance, and a general state of good friendship and close rela-tions between us. In return they ask for their men on the island, in the belief that it is better for both sides not to prolong the risks they each run, either that the men will find some means of forcing their escape or that they will be blockaded into submission. We think that it is the major enmities which admit of the most lasting settlements—not when one party is resistant and uses his broad advantage over the enemy to enforce restrictive oaths and unequal terms of agreement, but when, despite his ability to do just that, he takes a fair view, makes generosity his victory, and surprises his opponent with a reasonable settlement. The other party now feels no need to resist, as he would if coerced, but rather an obligation to repay generosity in kind, and is all the more ready, from a sense of honour, to abide by the terms to which he has agreed. This is the sort of settlement men reserve for their more serious enemies, not for those with whom they have minor quarrels. And it is in human nature to bow gladly in response to concessions willingly given, but to meet arrogant obduracy with the determination to fight on, taking risks in defiance of judgement.

20   'Now, if ever, is the right time for reconciliation, in both our interests, before we are overtaken by something irremediably divisive, the inevitable result of which will be that you incur our undying enmity, not only collective but individual also, and lose the benefit of what we now invite you to accept. While the war is still undecided, while you stand to gain enhanced reputation and our friendship besides, and we to avoid any dishonour by resolving our predicament on reasonable terms—let us be reconciled. Let the two of us choose peace instead of war, and so bring relief from their pain to the rest of the Greeks. They will give you the main credit for this peace. At the moment they are involved in a war without knowing which side started it: but if the war is ended, as is now largely in your gift, it is you who will receive their gratitude. If you decide for peace, you have the opportunity of friendship with the Spartans, and a firm friendship, when they themselves have invited it and you have granted, not enforced, the alliance. Think too of the likely benefit inherent in this. If we and you are speaking as one, you can be sure that the rest of the Greek world, lacking the power to match ours, will pay us the greatest deference.'

21   Such and no more was the speech made by the Spartans. Their assumption was that the Athenians had earlier wanted a treaty, only to have it denied by their own refusal, and would now gladly accept the offer of peace and return their men. The Athenians took the view that, since they had the men trapped on the island, a peace treaty with the Spartans was now available to them whenever they wanted to make it, and they were inclined to grasp for more. In this they were mainly incited by Cleon the son of Cleaenetus, a demagogue of the time and the most persuasive influence on the masses. He persuaded them to reply that first the men on the island must surrender their arms and themselves and be sent to Athens: once they were

there, the Spartans should give back Nisaea, Pegae, Troezen, and
Achaea (these had not been captured in war, but surrendered under
the previous settlement, to which the Athenians had agreed at a time
of difficulties, when they had more need of a treaty than now); then
the Spartans could recover their men and make a treaty for whatever
length of time was agreed by both sides.

The Spartans made no direct response to this reply, but asked 22
the Athenians to appoint commissioners to meet them in private
session for a full discussion of each point and a settlement on whatever terms were agreed in the debate. Cleon now pressed on in full
force. He said he had always known that the Spartans had no honourable intentions, and this was now clear from their refusal to say
anything in public and their request to confer with a small committee: if they had any sound proposal, they should declare it to all. The
Spartans could see that it was impossible for them to speak in public,
if indeed they were minded to make some concession in view of their
disastrous situation, for fear of compromising themselves with their
allies if they were heard to offer terms which were then rejected.
They could see too that the Athenians were not going to accept their
proposal on any mild conditions. So they left Athens with nothing
achieved.

On their return the truce at Pylos was at an immediate end, and 23
the Spartans asked for the return of their ships according to the
agreement. The Athenians refused to give them back, complaining of
an attack on the wall in breach of the truce and some other apparently
trivial infringements, and insisting on the clause which stated that
any deviation whatever from the terms of the truce would bring it to
an end. The Spartans protested and accused the Athenians of an
injustice over the ships: they then went away and set to war.

Hostilities at Pylos were now in earnest on both sides. The
Athenians kept two ships constantly sailing round the island in opposite directions by day; at night they all anchored in a ring round the
island, except on the side facing the open sea when there was a wind;
and twenty more ships arrived from Athens to help in the blockade,
bringing the total to seventy. The Peloponnesians camped on the
mainland and made attacks on the wall, looking out for any opportunity which might arise to rescue their men.

Meanwhile in Sicily the Syracusans and their allies brought up the 24
further fleet which they had been preparing to join the ships on
guard at Messana, and prosecuted the war from there. In this the

main instigators were the Locrians, enemies of Rhegium, who had made a full-scale invasion of Rhegian territory on their own. They were eager to attempt a naval engagement, as they saw that the Athenians had few ships on the spot, and had learnt that the larger fleet destined for Sicily was occupied in the siege of Sphacteria. They reckoned that if they established control with their fleet they could blockade Rhegium with both ships and land forces, and easily subdue it—and then they would be in a strong position. There is very little distance between the promontory of Rhegium in Italy and Messana in Sicily, and the Athenians would not now be able to lie off Rhegium and command the strait. This strait is the sea between Rhegium and Messana, where Sicily comes closest to the mainland: it is the so-called Charybdis, through which Odysseus is said to have sailed. Its dangerous reputation is understandable given that narrow gap and the currents caused by the influx of water from two great seas, the Tyrrhenian and the Sicilian.

25　　In this intervening space, then, the Syracusans and their allies, with somewhat over thirty ships, were forced to an engagement late in the day to defend a boat which was attempting the crossing, and they put out against sixteen Athenian and eight Rhegian ships. They were defeated by the Athenians and made a hasty retreat as best each could, with the loss of one ship. Night now ended the action.

After this the Locrians left Rhegian land, and the Syracusan and allied ships gathered and anchored at Peloris in the territory of Messana, joined there by their land forces. The Athenians and Rhegians sailed up and attacked when they saw that the ships were uncrewed: but they lost one of their own ships to the throw of a grappling-iron (its crew swam away). Thereafter the Syracusans manned their ships and began towing them on ropes along the shore towards Messana. The Athenians attacked again, but lost another ship when the Syracusans turned nose-on and made the first hit. So the Syracusans, successful in their move along the coast and the ensuing battle, as described, made safe return to the harbour at Messana.

News reached the Athenians that Camarina was being betrayed to the Syracusans by Archias and his party, so they sailed there. Taking this opportunity the Messanans launched a full-scale campaign, both by land and with the allied fleet, against Naxos, the Chalcidian city which was their neighbour. On the first day they forced the Naxians behind their walls and ravaged the countryside: on the next day they sailed the ships round to the river Acesines and ravaged the land there, while their land forces began attacks on the city. At this point the Sicels from the other side of the hills came down in large numbers to help resist the Messanans. The Naxians took heart at this sight and, passing the word that the Leontinians and their other Greek allies were on their way to support them, made a sudden sally out of the city and fell on the Messanans. In the ensuing rout they killed over a thousand, and the remainder struggled to get home, as the barbarians attacked them along the roads and killed most of them. The ships put into Messana and then dispersed to their home ports.

The Leontinians and the other allies, together with the Athenians, now began an immediate campaign against Messana, thinking it crippled. Their plan of attack had the Athenians invading the harbour with their ships while the land forces moved against the city. But a sudden sally was made by the Messanans and a contingent of Locrians under Demoteles, left there as a garrison after the disaster at Naxos: they fell on the Leontinian troops, routed most of them, and killed a good number. Seeing this, the Athenians landed from their ships and came up in support: they caught the Messanans in disarray and chased them back into the city. They then set up a trophy and withdrew to Rhegium. After this the Greeks in Sicily continued to campaign against one another by land without any Athenian involvement.

At Pylos the Athenians continued the blockade of the Spartans on 26 the island, and the Peloponnesians stayed encamped where they were on the mainland. It was a hardship for the Athenians to maintain their guard on the place. They suffered from lack of food and water (there were no springs other than one inadequate source on the acropolis of Pylos, and most had to scrabble in the shingle on the shore to find some sort of drinkable water); conditions were cramped in the small area available for their quarters; with no harbour the ships had to take turns for food on land while the others stayed at anchor in the open sea. The greatest damage to their morale was caused by the unexpected prolongation of the siege, when they had thought that it would only take a few days to reduce a group of men on an uninhabited island with nothing but brackish water.

The reason was that the Spartans had put the word out for volunteers to get food to the island—milled grain, cheese, any other foodstuff suitable for men under siege—with a substantial reward attached and the promise of freedom to any Helot who successfully made the run. And they did get food in. Prominent among those taking this risk were the Helots, who set off from wherever they were in the

Peloponnese and sailed by night to the seaward side of the island, watching particularly for a wind to carry them in. It was easier for them to evade the triremes' guard when the wind was blowing from the sea, as a full blockade was impossible under those conditions, and they themselves would sail in quite recklessly: the boats they ran ashore had an agreed monetary value set on them, and the Spartan hoplites kept guard round the landing-places of the island. Any who took the risk when it was calm were caught. And divers would make their way across from the harbour, swimming underwater and pulling on a cord behind them skins filled with honeyed poppy-seed and crushed linseed: at first they got through undetected, but then a watch was set. The two sides employed every ingenuity, either to send food across or to intercept it.

27   When it was learnt at Athens that their own forces were having trouble and that food was being imported to the men on the island, there was growing concern and a fear that their blockade would be overtaken by winter. The supply of food was a double problem: the place was uninhabited, and they could see that it would be impossible to transport provisions round the Peloponnese, when adequate supplies could not be sent even in summer. They saw too that the blockade could not be maintained indefinitely in an area without harbours, so either they would have to abandon their siege and let the men survive, or the men would wait for stormy weather and sail away in the boats which brought them food. Their greatest fear was of the Spartans themselves: they thought that the lack of any further negotiation meant that the Spartans were in a strong position, and they began to regret their refusal to accept the treaty.

Cleon, aware of the Athenians' resentment of him for preventing the agreement, challenged the truth of the reports from Pylos. Those who had brought the reports proposed that, if they were not believed, inspectors should be sent to see for themselves, and the Athenians chose for this role Cleon himself and Theogenes. Aware now that this would force him either to confirm the reports of those he was impugning, or else be shown a liar if he contradicted them, and seeing that opinion had shifted rather more in favour of military action, Cleon advised the Athenians that they should not be wasting time and opportunity by sending inspectors, but, if they judged the reports true, should be sailing there to deal with the men.

Then, with pointed allusion to Nicias the son of Niceratus, an Athenian general for whom he had a personal enmity, Cleon contested that, if the generals were real men, they could easily fit out a fleet to sail and take the men on the island: if he were in command, he would do exactly that. With the Athenians now beginning to barrack Cleon, 28 asking why he was not already on his way if it seemed so easy to him, and conscious of the personal criticism of himself, Nicias told Cleon that as far as the generals were concerned he could take whatever force he wished and make his attempt. At first Cleon happily accepted the offer, thinking it only a debating point made by Nicias: but when he became aware that Nicias really was prepared to hand over his command, he began to backtrack and said that it was not he but Nicias who was general. He was now alarmed, and had not imagined that Nicias would have the nerve to stand aside. Nicias pressed him again, offered his own resignation from the Pylos command, and called on the Athenians to witness it. As is typical of crowd behaviour, the more Cleon tried to extricate himself from this expedition and withdraw what he had said, the more they cheered on Nicias to hand over the command and shouted at Cleon 'Sail!'

So with no means now of escaping his own claims, Cleon undertook the expedition. He came forward and said that he had no fear of the Spartans; he would sail without requiring a single man from the city for his force, but would take with him the contingents from Lemnos and Imbros which were then in Athens, the peltasts who had come in support from Aenus and elsewhere, and four hundred archers; with this force added to the troops already at Pylos, within twenty days he would either bring back the Spartans on the island alive, or kill them where they were. This brash talk caused a certain amount of laughter among the Athenians, but even so the more sensible elements welcomed it, reckoning that they would thus achieve one or the other of two desired ends—either to be rid of Cleon (which they thought the more likely), or, if they proved wrong in this, to have the Spartans delivered into their hands.

When he had completed all the formalities in the assembly and the 29 Athenians had passed the vote authorizing his expedition, Cleon chose Demosthenes, one of the generals at Pylos, as his colleague, and quickly prepared for departure. He made this choice of colleague because he had heard that Demosthenes himself was already planning the landing on the island: his soldiers were keen to make the attempt, as they were suffering from the hardships of the place and were more besieged than besieging.

Demosthenes' resolve was further strengthened by a fire on the island. The fact that the island, having never been inhabited, was largely wooded and pathless had up till now deterred him, as he thought this gave advantage to the enemy. Even if he landed with a large force the Spartans could do damage with attacks from hidden positions. The tree-cover would deny the Athenians a clear view of the enemy's shortcomings and capabilities, whereas any false move by their own forces would be plain to see, so the enemy could make unpredictable attacks wherever they wished, and the initiative would be theirs. Then again, if he were compelled to close quarters in a wooded area, he thought that the smaller force with a knowledge of the ground would have the advantage over the larger force without that knowledge: and with no sightlines to indicate where support was needed the Athenian army, large though it was, could be destroyed

30 without realizing the extent of the destruction. His experience in Aetolia contributed much to Demosthenes' thoughts at this time: there too a wood had played a part in the disaster.

Lack of space obliged the Athenian soldiers to put in at the extremities of the island to take their midday meal, with guards posted. One of them inadvertently set fire to a small area of wood: a wind got up, and the result was that before they knew it most of the island's tree-cover had been consumed by fire. So Demosthenes, now with a clearer view, could see that there were more men on the island than he had thought (before this he had suspected the Spartans of sending in food for an exaggerated number), which would convince the Athenians of the importance of the enterprise and increase their enthusiasm for it: he could see too that it was now easier to land on the island. He therefore began to prepare for the operation, sending for troops from nearby allies and getting all else ready.

Cleon sent a messenger in advance to tell Demosthenes that he was on his way, and subsequently arrived at Pylos with the force he had requested. When he and Demosthenes were together they first sent a herald to the Spartan camp on the mainland inviting them, should they wish, to tell the men on the island to surrender their arms and themselves to the Athenians without prejudice, on the understanding that they would be kept in reasonable conditions of custody, pending agreement on the larger issue.

31 This proposal was rejected. The Athenians waited for one day, then in that following night embarked all their hoplites in a few ships and set out. Shortly before dawn they made landings on both sides

of the island, from the open sea and on the harbour side, with a total
of about eight hundred hoplites, and advanced at the run to the first
guard-post on the island. The Spartan dispositions were as follows:
in this first garrison there were some thirty hoplites; the majority and
their commander Epitadas occupied the middle and most level part
of the island, round the source of water; and a small detachment
guarded the very end of the island facing Pylos, which was sheer
from the sea and least vulnerable to attack by land. There was in fact
an ancient fort there, built of undressed stones, which they thought
would be of use to them if they were hard-pressed to retreat. Such
was the arrangement of the Spartan forces.

The Athenians rushed the first guards and killed them 32
instantly—they were still in bed or grabbing for their weapons. The
landing had gone unnoticed, as the guards had thought that the ships
were simply moving to their usual nightly anchorage. At dawn the
rest of the army began to land: this consisted of the entire crews of
rather more than seventy ships (except for the lowest-tier oarsmen),
variously equipped; eight hundred archers and no less a number of
peltasts; the Messenians who had come in support; and all the others
stationed at Pylos apart from the guards on the wall. Demosthenes
had organized them into separate groups of more or less two hundred, and these contingents occupied the high points of the ground,
in order to cause the enemy maximum difficulty by surrounding
them on all sides, thus leaving them no single front for any counter-
attack, but exposing them to massed opposition in every direction: if
they moved against those in front of them they would be attacked
from behind, and if against one flank they would be attacked by those
stationed on the other. And wherever they moved, they would always
have at their back their enemy's light-armed troops, the most difficult of all to deal with, as they were effective at long range with
arrows, javelins, stones, and slings. It was impossible even to get near
them: if pursued they could run back and still maintain their threat,
and if it was the enemy retreating they would press them hard. Such
was Demosthenes' strategy when he first planned the landing, and he
now put it into practice.

When the contingent under Epitadas (the main body of the 33
Spartans on the island) saw that their first garrison had been wiped
out and an army was moving against them, they formed for battle and
advanced towards the Athenian hoplites, wanting to come to close
quarters: the hoplites were positioned directly in front of them, with

the light-armed troops on the flanks and behind them. The Spartans could not get at the hoplites or make use of their own expertise, as they were kept back by a barrage of missiles from the light-armed troops on either side, and also the hoplites would not advance to meet them but stayed where they were. They could drive back the light-armed wherever they ran in particularly close to make their attacks, but then these troops would turn again and renew the fight: being lightly equipped they could easily outpace any pursuit in this difficult terrain, left rough by lack of habitation, and the Spartans in their heavy armour could not chase them over such ground.

34   For some little time they continued this long-range skirmishing against each other. But when the Spartans were no longer able to respond with quick sallies wherever they were attacked, the light-armed troops could see that they were now slower to defend themselves, and this sight had greatly increased their own confidence. They could see, too, that they clearly outnumbered the Spartans, and with greater experience of them now did not think them as formidable as they once had: they had made the initial landing in a state of abject terror at the thought of facing Spartans, but had suffered nothing so far to justify their apprehension. Turned now to contempt, they gave a shout and launched themselves in a body against the Spartans, bombarding them with stones, arrows, javelins—whatever each of them had to hand.

    This combination of shouting and onslaught caused panic in an enemy unused to this sort of warfare. Moreover clouds of ash were rising from the newly burned wood, and a man could hardly see in front of his face for the hail of arrows and stones from so many hands, together with the ash. The Spartans were now in real difficulties. Their felt helmets were no protection against the arrows, and the spearheads broke off in their bodies when they were hit; there was nothing they could do to help themselves, with forward vision impaired and their own commands drowned out by the greater volume of the enemy's shouting; danger surrounded them on all sides, and they had no hope of any means of fighting to safety.

35   At length, as the number of wounded grew with their constant wheeling around in the same spot, the Spartans closed ranks and made for the fort at the end of the island (which was not far away) and their garrison there. Seeing them give way, the light-armed troops harried them with fresh confidence and yet louder shouting, and those Spartans caught on the retreat were killed, but the majority

made their escape to the fort and with the guards there took up stations to defend the fort at every point where it was open to attack. The Athenians followed, but the strength of the site made a flanking or encircling movement impossible, so they tried to drive them out with a frontal attack. For a long time, indeed for most of the day, both sides held out through the attrition of battle, thirst, and sun—the Athenians determined to drive the enemy off the high ground, and the Spartans determined not to give way. The Spartan defence was easier now than it had been before, as they did not have to deal with an enemy surrounding them on the flanks.

With no end in sight, the commander of the Messenians came up 36 to Cleon and Demosthenes and told them that they were wasting their efforts: if they were prepared to let him have a section of the archers and the light-armed troops he would go round behind the Spartans by any route he could find, and he thought he could force the approach. He was given the troops he asked for, and set off with them from a point out of sight of the Spartans. He made his way along wherever the precipitous face of the island afforded a footing, on the side of the site where the Spartans had trusted in its natural defences and posted no guards. With difficulty he just managed to get round, unseen, and then suddenly appeared on the height to their rear. The surprise of this caused consternation in the Spartans, but it was what the Athenians were looking for and the sight greatly increased their morale. The Spartans were now under attack from both front and back, and were falling into the same situation (to compare small with great) as at Thermopylae: there the Spartans were destroyed when the Persians went round behind them along the mountain path, and these likewise could no longer resist when exposed now to a double-sided attack. They were few against many, they were physically weakened by lack of food, and they began to withdraw: and the Athenians now controlled the approaches.

Cleon and Demosthenes realized that if the Spartans gave way 37 even a few steps further they would be slaughtered by the Athenian forces, so they stopped the fighting and restrained their own troops. They wanted to bring the Athenians live Spartans, and hoped that on hearing the terms announced the Spartans would be demoralized into handing over their arms and giving in to their desperate situation. They announced that it was open to the Spartans to surrender their arms and themselves to the Athenians, at the Athenians' discretion to decide as they saw fit. On hearing this most of them dropped 38 their shields and waved their hands to indicate acceptance of the terms. The armistice now came into effect and there was a meeting for further discussion between Cleon and Demosthenes and, from the Spartan side, Styphon the son of Pharax. (He was the third of the Spartan commanders. Of the previous two the first, Epitadas, was dead: his nominated successor, Hippagretas, was lying among the corpses, still alive but taken for dead. As the law prescribed, Styphon had been nominated third commander, to take over if anything happened to the other two.) Styphon and his delegation said that they wished to communicate by herald with the Spartans on the mainland and ask for their instructions. The Athenians would not let any of them make the crossing, but sent word themselves for heralds to come over from the mainland. After two or three consultations, the final emissary to sail across from the Spartans on the mainland brought this message: 'The Spartans tell you to make your own decisions about yourselves, but to do nothing dishonourable.' They discussed with their own men, and surrendered their arms and themselves.

For the rest of this day and the following night the Athenians kept them under guard. On the next day they set up a trophy on the island and made general preparations to sail, handing over the prisoners to the custody of the ships' captains: and the Spartans sent a herald and recovered their dead. The numbers killed and taken alive on the island were as follows. A total of four hundred and twenty Spartan hoplites had been ferried to the island. Of these two hundred and ninety-two were brought to Athens alive, and the rest had been killed: the live prisoners included about a hundred and twenty Spartiates. Not many Athenian lives were lost, as the fighting had not been a pitched battle.

39   The whole duration of the blockade of the men on Sphacteria, from the naval battle to the fight on the island, was seventy-two days. For about twenty of these days, when the envoys were away seeking a treaty, the men were supplied with food, but for the rest of the time they depended on smuggled-in provisions. In fact a store of grain and other foodstuffs was found on the island, as the commander Epitadas had not been issuing to his men as full rations as he could afford. So now the Athenians and Peloponnesians withdrew their armies from Pylos, and each side returned home. And, mad though it had seemed, Cleon's promise was fulfilled: he did bring back the men within twenty days, as he had undertaken.

To the Greeks this was the most surprising event of the whole 40
war. They had thought that Spartans would never surrender their
arms, in starvation or any other extremity, but would use them to the
last of their strength and die fighting. They could not believe that
those who surrendered were of the same quality as those who were
killed. Some time later one of the Athenian allies taunted a prisoner
from the island by asking, 'Were the dead, then, your good men and
brave?' The Spartan replied that the 'spindle' (his word for an arrow)
would indeed be a weapon of great value if it could pick out the
brave: by this he meant that the stones and arrows killed whoever
happened to be in their path.

When the men were brought to Athens the Athenians decided to 41
keep them imprisoned and chained until there was some agreement—and to take them out and kill them if the Peloponnesians
invaded their land in the meantime. They established a garrison at
Pylos, manned by the Messenians from Naupactus who sent their
best men for this purpose to what they regarded as their fatherland
(Pylos lies in what was once Messenian territory). These Messenians
kept up plundering raids on Laconia and were able to cause a great
deal of damage as they spoke in the local dialect. With no previous
experience of this sort of predatory warfare, with the Helots beginning to desert and the fear of yet wider revolution affecting the whole
system of their country, the Spartans were seriously worried.
Although not wanting to reveal their concerns to the Athenians, they
continued to send embassies to Athens in the attempt to recover
Pylos and their men. But the Athenians were inclined to reach for yet
greater success: ambassadors came and came again, but every time
the Athenians sent them back empty-handed.

Such, then, were the events concerning Pylos.

Immediately afterwards in the same summer the Athenians 42
campaigned against the territory of Corinth with eighty ships, two
thousand of their own hoplites, and two hundred cavalry in horse-
transports. They were joined by allied troops from Miletus, Andros,
and Carystus, and commanded by Nicias the son of Niceratus with
two other generals.

The fleet sailed and put in at dawn between Chersonesus and
Rheitus, at a beach on this shoreline directly under the hill Solygeius
(this is where in ancient times the Dorians had established position
for their war against the Aeolians inhabiting Corinth: there is now a
village called Solygeia on this hill). From this beach where the ships

put in the distance to the village is just under a mile and a half, to the city of Corinth about seven and a quarter miles, and to the Isthmus two and a half miles. The Corinthians had received from Argos advance notice of the intended expedition, and in good time had gathered a full levy at the Isthmus (except those north of the Isthmus, and the five hundred troops they had on garrison duty in Ambracia and Leucas), and were keeping watch to see where the Athenians would land. In fact the Athenians sailed in undetected before it was light, but when the Corinthians were alerted by signals, they left half of their forces in the area of Cenchreae (in case the Athenians turned against Crommyon) and set off quickly to the defence.

43   One of the two Corinthian generals present in the field, Battus, took a single division to the village of Solygeia to protect it (it was unfortified), while Lycophron began the attack with the rest of the force. The Corinthians fell first on the Athenians' right wing as soon as it had disembarked in front of Chersonesus, and then on the rest of the Athenian army. There was hard fighting, all of it hand-to-hand. The right wing of Athenians and Carystians (these were next to the Athenians on the extreme right) withstood the Corinthian attack and with some difficulty shoved them back. They retreated behind a drystone wall higher up the hill (the whole site sloped steeply upwards), and began pelting the Athenians with stones from the wall. Then they shouted a paean and came back to the attack. Again the Athenians withstood them, and there was more hand-to-hand fighting. Now a division of Corinthians came up in support of their left wing, turned the Athenian right wing, and drove them down to the sea: but the Athenians and Carystians rallied by the ships and fought their way back. There was constant fighting meanwhile between the rest of the two armies, most intense where the right wing of the Corinthians under Lycophron were defending against the left wing of the Athenians, in the expectation that they would otherwise make an attempt on the village of Solygeia.

44   So for some long time they both held out, neither side giving way to the other. But finally, with the Athenian cavalry contributing an advantage over their opponents who had no horses, the Corinthians were turned back and retreated to the summit of the hill, where they grounded their arms and made no further descents, staying there inactive. In this defeat the most casualties were sustained on their right wing, including their general Lycophron. The rest of their army, similarly pressed to retreat, withdrew to the high ground and

took up position there: they were not pursued far, and could make the retreat at their own pace. The Corinthians did not return to the attack, so the Athenians stripped the enemy dead and recovered their own, and immediately set up a trophy.

The other half of the Corinthian forces, who were stationed in Cenchraean territory on guard in case the Athenians sailed against Crommyon, had their view of the battle obscured by Mount Oneium: but when they saw the dust-cloud and realized what was happening, they went straight in support. Support came too from the older men in Corinth when they heard of the situation. At the sight of these combined forces advancing on them the Athenians thought they were facing reinforcements from the neighbouring Peloponnesian states close by, and quickly withdrew to their ships, taking with them the spoils and their own dead (they had to leave two whom they had not been able to find). They embarked and crossed to the outlying islands, from where they sent a herald and recovered under truce the two bodies they had left. In the battle the Corinthians had lost two hundred and twelve men, and the Athenians a little under fifty.

On that same day the Athenians put out from the islands and 45 sailed to Crommyon, which is in Corinthian territory about fourteen and a half miles from the city of Corinth. They anchored there, ravaged the land, and made camp for the night. On the next day they first sailed round the coast to the territory of Epidaurus and made a landing there, then went on to Methana, which lies between Epidaurus and Troezen. They took control of the isthmus of the Methana peninsula and fortified it, establishing a garrison which for some later time carried out raids on the land of Troezen, Halieis, and Epidaurus. When the fortification of the site was finished, the fleet sailed back home.

At the same time as these events, Eurymedon and Sophocles, on 46 their way now with the Athenian ships from Pylos to Sicily, arrived at Corcyra and joined the people in the city in a campaign against the Corcyraean party established on Mount Istone (these had earlier crossed over from the mainland, after the civil war, and were now in control of the countryside and doing great damage). The Athenians attacked their fortified position and took it. The men had fled in a body to a higher point and came to terms, agreeing to hand over the mercenaries and, in their own case, to surrender their arms and submit to the decision of the Athenian people. The generals transported them to the island of Ptychia for custody under truce until they could be sent to Athens: a condition was that if any of them were caught trying to abscond, the truce would be at an end for all of them.

But the leaders of the democratic party in Corcyra, concerned that the Athenians might not execute the captives when they arrived at Athens, devised some sort of pre-emptive measure. They worked on a selected few of those held on the island, suborning their friends to go in with the apparently well-intentioned message that they had best abscond as soon as they could, and they themselves would have a boat ready: the Athenian generals, they said, were about to hand 47 them over to the Corcyraean democrats. The persuasion worked, the boat was provided, and they were caught trying to sail away. The truce was then at an immediate end, and all the men were handed over to the Corcyraeans. A considerable contribution to this outcome, making the story plausible and the perpetrators bold enough to try it on, was the attitude of the Athenian generals, who made it clear that, as they themselves were bound for Sicily, they would not want anyone else to transport the men to Athens and gain the credit for bringing them in.

When the men were delivered to them the Corcyraeans shut them up in a large building. Later they took them out in groups of twenty, shackled together, and made them pass between two parallel files of armed men, who beat and stabbed any personal enemy they saw: men with whips walked alongside, hurrying on those who were slow to 48 approach this gauntlet. A total of sixty were taken out and killed in this way without the men in the building realizing what was happening (they thought they were being moved on to some other place). When they did learn the truth (someone had managed to alert them), they appealed to the Athenians and invited them to kill them themselves, if they wanted them dead. They refused to let any more leave the building, and said they would do their best to prevent anyone entering it.

The Corcyraeans had no intention anyway of forcing their way in through the doors, but climbed up onto the roof of the building, made a hole in the material, and began pelting them with the tiles and shooting down arrows. The men inside protected themselves as best they could, but most were also looking to take their own lives: they used the spent arrows to stab themselves in the throat, or hanged themselves with the cords from some bedsteads which happened to be in the building, or with strips torn from their own clothing. Night fell on this atrocity, but throughout most of the night the killing went on in every form until they were all dead, either by their own hand or shot down from above. In the morning the Corcyraeans threw the bodies criss-cross onto wagons and took them outside the city. The women who had been captured in the fort were enslaved. Such was the annihilation by the democrats of the Corcyraean party based on the mountain, and the civil strife which had grown so violent ended in this—at least for the duration of this war: nothing worth reckoning was left of the other party.

The Athenians sailed off to Sicily, which was their primary destination, and began operations with their allies there.

Towards the end of summer the Athenians at Naupactus joined 49 the Acarnanians in a campaign against Anactorium, a Corinthian city at the mouth of the Ambracian Gulf: it was betrayed to them, and they took it. The Acarnanians sent out settlers of their own to occupy the place, drawing them from all parts of the country. So this summer ended.

In the following winter Aristeides the son of Archippus, one of the 50 generals commanding the Athenian ships sent out to the allies to raise money, arrested at Eïon on the Strymon a Persian, Artaphernes, who was on his way from the King of Persia to Sparta. He was sent to Athens, where the Athenians had his dispatches translated from the Assyrian characters in which they were written, and read them. Amid much other matter the central point in these dispatches was that the King did not understand what the Spartans wanted; many envoys had come, but no two said the same thing; if, then, they wished to make themselves clear, they should send men back to him with the Persian emissary. Some time later the Athenians sent Artaphernes in a trireme to Ephesus, with an embassy of their own. There they were informed of the recent death of King Artaxerxes the son of Xerxes (he had died in this intervening period), and so returned home.

In this same winter the Chians demolished their newly built walls 51 on the orders of the Athenians, who suspected them of revolutionary intent, but not before they had obtained assurances and the best guarantee they could that the Athenians likewise would make no revolution in their policy towards Chios.

So ended this winter, and with it the seventh year of this war chronicled by Thucydides.

The following summer began with a partial eclipse of the sun at the 52 time of the new moon, and an earthquake early in that same month.

The majority of the exiles from Mytilene and the rest of Lesbos had established a base on the mainland, and from here, with mercenaries hired from the Peloponnese and others recruited locally, they set out and captured Rhoeteium—then gave it back unharmed on the payment of two thousand Phocaean staters. Thereafter they went against Antandrus: the city was betrayed to them, and they took it. Their overall strategy was to liberate all the so-called Actaean cities (which had been administered by Mytilene but were now in Athenian control), with Antandrus their prime objective. There was an abundance of timber available there and on the nearby Mount Ida for the building of ships and other apparatus: they could fortify Antandrus and then easily use it as a base from which to make raids on Lesbos (which was not far away) and to gain control of the Aeolian towns on the mainland. They were ready to go ahead with these preparations.

53   In the same summer the Athenians made an expedition against Cythera with sixty ships, two thousand hoplites, and a few cavalry, taking with them troops from Miletus and some other allies: the generals in command were Nicias the son of Niceratus, Nicostratus the son of Diitrephes, and Autocles the son of Tolmaeus. Cythera is an island lying opposite Laconia by Cape Malea. The inhabitants are Spartans in the category of Perioeci. A commissioner for Cythera went over from Sparta to the island every year, and the Spartans kept a permanent hoplite garrison there, regularly replaced. They took good care of the place, as it was a port of call for merchant ships coming in to them from Egypt and Libya, and also served to discourage pirates' raids on Laconia from the sea, the one direction from which it was vulnerable to depredation, as the whole of Laconia lies open to the Sicilian and Cretan seas.

54   The Athenians put in with their expeditionary force. With ten ships and the Milesian hoplites they took the harbour town called Scandeia. With the rest of their forces they landed on the side of the island facing Malea and advanced on the city of Cythera, where they found the whole population already mobilized and camped outside. In the ensuing battle the Cytherans held their ground for a short while, but then turned and fled to their upper city. Thereafter they came to terms with Nicias and his fellow commanders, agreeing surrender to the Athenians at their full discretion short of the death penalty. There had in fact been some earlier communication between Nicias and some of the Cytherans, which speeded the agreement and moderated its immediate and subsequent effect: otherwise the

Athenians would have expelled the Cytherans, on the grounds that they are Spartans and their island lies that close to Laconia. With the terms agreed, the Athenians took over Scandeia, the town by the harbour, and installed a garrison to secure the island. They then sailed to Asine, Helos, and most of the other coastal areas of Laconia, making landings and overnight camps wherever there was opportunity, and ravaged that territory for about seven days.

Seeing the Athenians in possession of Cythera, and expecting 55 similar landings on their own territory, the Spartans did not concentrate their full forces for a pitched battle in any one place, but sent out separate bodies of hoplites to guard the country wherever there was need, and generally maintained a full alert. They feared the possibility of a revolution overtaking their political system, now that they had suffered the massive and unexpected disaster on the island, Pylos and Cythera were in enemy hands, and they were beset on all fronts by a fast-moving war which outpaced their defences. In consequence they took what was for them the unusual step of raising a troop of four hundred cavalry, and a force of archers. And in all military matters they became yet more cautious than ever before, caught as they were in a naval conflict which ran counter to their traditional mode of armament—a naval conflict, moreover, against the Athenians, who always saw a missed opportunity as the loss of an expected success. Fortune too had been against them, and they were shattered by the many blows dealt them in a short time, quite contrary to any reasonable prediction: they now feared some further disaster like that which they had sustained on the island. This made them less confident for battle. Unused to reverses before now, they had lost faith in their judgement and thought that any move they made would end in failure.

In their present ravaging of the coastal areas the Athenians met 56 little resistance for the most part. Wherever they made landings, each local garrison, sharing this general diffidence, thought themselves outnumbered and took no action. One garrison, though, in the neighbourhood of Cotyrta and Aphroditia, did resist and made a charge on the scattered crowd of light-armed troops which sent them flying, but then withdrew again when met by the hoplites. A few of the garrison were killed and their arms taken. The Athenians set up a trophy and sailed back to Cythera.

From there they sailed round to Epidaurus Limera, and after ravaging part of that territory moved on to Thyrea. This is a place in the region called Cynouria, on the borders of Argos and Laconia. It was under Spartan control, and the Spartans had granted it as a home to the dispossessed people of Aegina in virtue of the help they had given Sparta at the time of the earthquake and the Helot revolt, and because, despite being Athenian subjects, they had always inclined to the Spartan cause.

57   While the Athenians were still approaching, the Aeginetans abandoned the fortification which they were in the process of building on the sea-front and retired to the upper city where they lived, just over a mile from the sea. One of the Spartan garrisons in the area had been helping with the construction, but refused the Aeginetans' request to join them behind the walls of the upper city. They could see danger in becoming immured, and withdrew to higher ground, where, reckoning that they would be no match in a battle, they did nothing. At this point the Athenians put in with their fleet, set out immediately in full force, and took Thyrea. They set fire to the city and looted everything in it. Those Aeginetans not killed in the close fighting were taken away and transported to Athens, together with the resident Spartan governor, Tantalus the son of Patrocles, who had been wounded and captured alive. Taken to Athens at the same time were a few men from Cythera, whose removal was thought necessary on grounds of security. The Athenians decided to deposit these men in the islands; to allow the rest of the Cytherans the continued occupation of their own land on payment of a tribute of four talents; to kill all the captured Aeginetans in view of their constant previous hostility; and to imprison Tantalus in the company of his fellow Spartans from the island.

58   In Sicily, in this same summer, the people of Camarina and Gela took the initiative of making a truce just between themselves. And then later all the other Greek Sicilians joined in a conference at Gela, each city sending delegates, to discuss the possibility of a general reconciliation. Many opinions were expressed one way or the other, and there were recriminations and demands as each delegation claimed some disadvantage. Amid all this the most compelling speech was made by Hermocrates the son of Hermon, a Syracusan. He addressed the gathering to this effect:

59   'Fellow Greeks and Sicilians, I come from a city which is not the least powerful in Sicily nor the worst afflicted by the war. What I have to say to you, then, is not local prejudice but a way forward for the general good, my view of the best policy for Sicily as a whole.

'There is no need to give a lengthy description of all the misery inherent in war—you know that already. No one is forced to war unwittingly, and no one is deterred from war if they think they will gain from it. So what happens is that one side sees the advantages as outweighing the dangers, and the other is prepared to face the risks rather than suffer an immediate loss. But if this very conflict is in fact a miscalculation on both sides, there is virtue in counselling reconciliation. And this counsel, if we are prepared to act on it in our present situation, could be of invaluable benefit for us too. It was of course to promote our own individual interests that we went to war in the first place; now we are trying to resolve our differences by discussion; and if we leave this conference without a fair settlement of individual interests, we shall go to war again.

'And yet we should recognize that, if we have any sense, the ques- 60 tion for this meeting will not solely be our local concerns, but whether we can still save the whole of Sicily from what, in my view, is the Athenian design against it. We should regard the Athenians as much more forceful agents of reconciliation than any words of mine. They are the greatest power in Greece; they are here with just a few ships at present to observe our mistakes; they are using the apparent legitimacy of "alliance" to turn our ingrained enmities to their covert advantage. If we start internal wars and call in their support (and these are people who readily launch expeditions even when not invited), if we harm ourselves at our own expense while at the same time clearing the way for their dominance, the likelihood is that they will wait to see us exhausted and then come with a larger force in an attempt to bring all Sicily under their control.

'Yet, if we have any sense, our only purpose in calling in allies 61 and taking on additional risks should be to extend what each of us has by further acquisition—not to harm what we already possess. We should realize that internal dissension, more than anything else, is the ruin of our cities and the ruin of Sicily: all of us who live in this island are threatened by the designs of a common enemy, but we are still divided, city against city. We must recognize this. There must be reconciliation—individual to individual, city to city—and a united effort to save the whole of Sicily. No one should suppose that Athenian hostility is confined to the Dorians among us, while their shared Ionian descent confers immunity on the Chalcidian population. It is not a question of race. This Athenian attack is not motivated by the fact that there are two races here and they hate one of them.

Their motive is to get their hands on the wealth of Sicily—which is our common possession. This is clear enough from their response to the appeal from the Chalcidian community: the Chalcidian cities have never in the past done anything to help Athens under the old alliance, but now the Athenians have found a particular enthusiasm to fulfil their own obligations stipulated in that agreement.

'That the Athenians should be thus acquisitive and calculating is wholly understandable. My complaint is not of those who seek domination, but rather of those who are too ready to submit to it. It has always been in human nature to dominate the subservient—but also to defend against the aggressor. If we recognize this but do not take the proper precautions, or if anyone has come here without the conviction that our most important task is to join together in dealing with the danger which threatens us all—then we are making a mistake. The most immediate way to be rid of this danger is to reach an agreement among ourselves, as the Athenians cannot move against us from home territory, but only from a base provided by those who invited them. In this way our war does not end in further war, but peace brings a trouble-free end to our differences: and our visitors, invited here with a good pretext for doing wrong, will have good reason to leave with nothing done for their trouble.

62   'With regard to the Athenians, this is the great benefit we gain if we take the right decisions. As for ourselves, when peace is universally agreed to be the best state, why should we too not make peace? However our fortunes may differ—prosperity for one, its opposite for another—do you not think peace an advantage in either case, more likely than war to preserve good fortune and put an end to misfortune? Or that peace has its own honours and distinctions, won without danger? And one could continue at length listing the blessings of peace, as long a list as the miseries of war. I ask you to think carefully about this. Do not see anything suspect in what I say, but rather the prospect of salvation for each one of you.

'And if anyone thinks that a just cause or adequate force will ensure some lasting success, he must be prepared for disappointment and not take it too hard when he fails. He should realize that there is a long history of men retaliating against a wrongful attack who, so far from succeeding in their attempted revenge, have not even survived it; and of others who expected that their power would win them some new acquisition, and then, instead of gaining others' possessions, found themselves losing their own. Revenge does not have its just success, simply because it is a response to injustice: and strength acquires no guarantee from the confidence which accompanies it. The greatest determinant of affairs is the incalculable future, which is the most unreliable element of all and yet clearly has the most beneficial effect, as our common fear of the future makes us think twice before setting out to attack one another.

'And now we have double cause for alarm—blind fear of what this 63 hidden future may hold, and the immediate threat of the Athenian presence here and now. We can attribute our failure in what each of us planned and hoped to achieve to the effective constraint of these two factors. So let us send on their way the enemies threatening our land, and for ourselves reach an agreement, if we can, for all time: failing that, let us at least make a truce for as long as possible and defer our private quarrels to some future occasion. In short, let us recognize that if my advice is followed we shall each possess a free city and be our own masters, able to respond honourably, and on equal terms, to anyone doing us good or harm. But if we reject it and submit to the control of others, any action we take, however success-ful, will not be a matter of our own deliberate revenge, but a forced collaboration with our greatest enemies against those who should be our friends.

'Now, as I said at the beginning, I represent a major city, and 64 am more likely to attack others than be attacked. But in view of all these considerations I think it right to back down, and not to do my enemies the damage which redounds to my own harm; not to think, in idiot ambition, that control of my own will implies equal control of fortune, which I do not govern; but to make all reasonable conces-sions. And I ask you all to do the same as I do, imposing this on yourselves rather than having it imposed by the enemy. There is no shame in concessions made within a family—Dorian conceding to Dorian, or Chalcidian to his relatives. The important point is that we are all neighbours, all fellow inhabitants of a single land surrounded by the sea, and all called by one name, Sicilians. We shall fight again, I imagine, when occasion demands, and come to terms again on our own, by negotiation among ourselves. But, if we have any sense, we shall always unite to resist a foreign invader, seeing that harm to any one of us endangers us all: and we shall never in future bring in out-siders as allies or as agents of reconciliation. This policy will ensure that in our present situation we do not deprive Sicily of the double benefit of getting rid of the Athenians and rid of internal war: and that for the future we enjoy on our own a free country less exposed to the designs of others.'

65   Such was Hermocrates' speech, and the Sicilians took his advice. They agreed among themselves a decision to end the war on the terms that each should retain what they already held, except that Morgantina should go to the people of Camarina on payment of a specified sum to the Syracusans. Those allied to the Athenians called in the Athenian command and told them of their intention to agree a treaty which would apply equally to the Athenians. They gave their approval, the agreement was concluded, and after that the Athenian ships sailed away from Sicily.

When the generals returned the Athenians at home imposed the punishment of exile on two of them, Pythodorus and Sophocles, and a monetary fine on the third, Eurymedon, thinking that they had been bribed to withdraw when they could have taken control of Sicily. This was indicative of their attitude in view of their current good fortune: they expected no reverses, but achievement alike of the possible and the near-impossible, irrespective of the forces deployed, whether large or barely adequate. The reason was the success, beyond any rational prediction, of most of their operations, and this had fuelled their hope.

66   In the same summer the people in the city of Megara found themselves hard pressed on two fronts—by the Athenians in the course of the war, with their regular full-scale invasions of Megarian territory twice in every year, and also by their own exiles in Pegae, expelled by the people's party after internal strife and now causing severe trouble with their depredations. The Megarians therefore began discussing among themselves the proposal to take back their exiles and so not expose the city to ruination on both fronts. The friends of the exiles, aware of this agitation, came more into the open than they had before and added their own voice in support of this proposal. The democratic leaders, though, became alarmed, realizing that the people would not be able to stick with them through all this hardship. They therefore entered into discussions with the Athenian generals, Hippocrates the son of Ariphron and Demosthenes the son of Alcisthenes, offering to hand over their city: they saw this as a lesser danger to themselves than the restoration of the exiles whom they had expelled. It was agreed that the Athenians should first seize the long walls (which ran for over a mile from the city to their harbour at Nisaea), in order to preclude any intervention from the

Peloponnesians in Nisaea, where a garrison (of Peloponnesians only) was stationed to ensure security at Megara. Thereafter they would try to deliver the upper city too, and thought that it would come over more readily when that first move had been made.

So when both parties had agreed the plans and made the practical 67 arrangements, the Athenians sailed at nightfall to Minoa, the island facing Megara, with six hundred hoplites under the command of Hippocrates. These took up position in the trench not far from the long walls from which the clay for their bricks was dug, while a second division under the other general, Demosthenes, consisting of light-armed Plataeans and Athenian border-guards, settled in ambush in the sanctuary of Enyalius, closer still to the walls. No one noticed their arrival other than the men briefed about this night's activity. Just before dawn these Megarian conspirators put the following plan into effect. They had a sculling-boat which they had persuaded the commander was for privateering purposes, and with his permission had for some time ensured the opening of the gates at night, when it was their practice to carry the boat on a wagon along the trench to the sea and row out: they would then bring it back before dawn and carry it on the wagon through the gates and inside the walls. Their professed intention was to keep these excursions hidden from the Athenian garrison on Minoa, as no boat would be seen in the harbour at all. On this occasion the wagon was already at the gates, and they were opened as usual to let the boat in: seeing their moment (all this was part of the preconcerted plan) the Athenians charged out from their ambush, running fast to reach the gates before they could be shut again and while the wagon was still between them to prevent their closing. At the same time their Megarian collaborators killed the guards on the gates. The first to run inside (at the point where the trophy now stands) were the Plataeans and border-guards with Demosthenes. The Peloponnesians nearest the scene had now realised what was happening, and as soon as they were inside the gates the Plataeans took on the troops coming up in defence and defeated them, thus securing the gates for the Athenian hoplites now pouring in. As each Athenian got inside he made straight for the wall. 68

A few of the Peloponnesian garrison resisted at first and fought back, and some were killed, but the majority took to flight, terrified by an enemy attack at night and the collaboration in battle against them by the Megarian conspirators, which made them think that the whole of Megara had betrayed them. A contribution was made by the

Athenians' herald, who on his own initiative proclaimed that any Megarian wishing to join the Athenians should ground his arms with theirs. Hearing this, the Peloponnesians stayed no longer: convinced now that they really were faced with a double enemy, they took refuge in Nisaea.

At daybreak, with the walls by now captured and the Megarians in the city in a state of turmoil, those who had done the deal with the Athenians, together with a good number of others who were in the know, urged that they should open the city gates and go out to do battle. Their agreed plan was for the Athenians to rush in when the gates were opened, while they themselves would be identifiable—and so spared in the attack—by a smearing of oil over their bodies. Their own safety in opening the gates was further guaranteed by the arrival, as had also been prearranged, of a force of four thousand Athenian hoplites and six hundred cavalry who had travelled overnight from Eleusis. They had smeared themselves with oil and were already by the gates when one of those in the know revealed the plot to the other party. These gathered and came in a body, insisting that they should not go out to do battle, as they had not ventured this before even when they were in a stronger position, and should not bring the city into obvious danger: if anyone disagreed, there would be fighting there and then inside the city. They gave no indication of knowing what was afoot, but spoke with the apparent conviction of those recommending the best policy: at the same time they stayed on guard close by the gates, with the result that the conspirators could not carry out their intended plan.

69   Realizing that there had been some problem, and that they would not be able to storm the city, the Athenian generals immediately set about the circumvallation of Nisaea, reckoning that if they could take it before any reinforcements arrived, Megara too would capitulate the sooner. They quickly procured from Athens iron and stonemasons and all else they needed. Starting from the walls which they controlled they built a cross-wall facing Megara, and from there drove a ditch and a wall down to the sea on either side of Nisaea, dividing the work among the army in sections. They made use of stones and bricks from the suburb, and cut down trees and brushwood for stockades where they were needed: the suburban houses themselves served as part of the fortification with battlements added.

They spent the whole of that day on the work. By the afternoon of the following day the walls were all but completed, and the people in

Nisaea took fright. They were short of food (they had been taking daily deliveries from the upper city), they did not expect any early support from the Peloponnesians, and they assumed that the Megarians were hostile. They therefore came to terms with the Athenians. These terms were that they should hand over their arms and then each should go free on payment of a set ransom: and that the Athenians should have discretion to do what they wanted with the Spartan commander and any other Spartans in the place. With this agreement made, they came out and left. The Athenians made a breach in the long walls just below the city of Megara, took possession of Nisaea, and saw to all other preparations.

It so happened that the Spartan Brasidas, the son of Tellis, was at 70 this time in the area of Sicyon and Corinth, preparing for an expedition to the Thraceward region. When he heard of the capture of the long walls, fearing for the Peloponnesians in Nisaea and the possible fall of Megara, he sent to the Boeotians asking them to meet him with an army as soon as they could at Tripodiscus (this is the name of a village in the Megarid below Mount Geraneia). He himself went there with two thousand seven hundred Corinthian hoplites, four hundred from Phlius, and six hundred from Sicyon, as well as those of his own troops who had already assembled. He had thought that he could still reach Nisaea before it was taken. But when he learnt of its capture (he had in fact started out for Tripodiscus during that night), he picked a force of three hundred from his army and reached the city of Megara before his presence was known—the Athenians were down by the sea and failed to notice his arrival. He professed the intention and, if possible, the actuality of an attempt on Nisaea: but most of all he wanted to enter the city of Megara and secure it. So he called on the Megarians to admit his force, saying that he had hopes of recovering Nisaea.

Both the factions in Megara were alarmed. The democrats feared 71 that Brasidas would impose the exiles on them and drive out their own party. The concern of the oligarchic party was that this very fear would cause the people to attack them, and that a civil war, with the Athenians lying in wait nearby, would be the end of Megara. So they refused to admit Brasidas, both parties considering it best to keep quiet and see what happened. Both expected a battle between the Athenians and the relieving army, and thought it safer not to declare for whichever side they favoured until that side had won. Having failed to convince them, Brasidas went back to the rest of his army.

72   At dawn the Boeotians arrived. Even before Brasidas sent to them
they had intended to come to the aid of Megara, and had already
gathered in full force at Plataea: they saw that a threat to Megara was
not irrelevant to them. The arrival of Brasidas' messenger made them
much keener still, and they sent forward two thousand two hundred
hoplites and six hundred cavalry, taking the bulk of their forces back
home. The whole army Brasidas now had with him amounted to at
least six thousand hoplites. The Athenian hoplites were formed up
near Nisaea and the sea, with the light-armed troops dispersed across
the plain. The Boeotian cavalry fell on the light-armed and drove
them back to the sea: this was an unexpected attack, as before now
the Megarians had never received any support from any quarter.
The Athenian cavalry rode out in response to engage them, and there
followed a long cavalry battle in which both sides claim to have had
the upper hand. Certainly the Athenians killed the Boeotian cavalry-
commander and a few others who rode right up to Nisaea, and stripped
them of their arms: and as they retained possession of these bodies
and only released them under truce, they set up a trophy. But in the
action as a whole neither side had come out of it with a decisive victory
when they broke off, the Boeotians returning to their own forces and
the Athenians to Nisaea.

73   Brasidas and his army then moved closer to the sea and the city of
Megara. They occupied an advantageous position and formed up for
battle, expecting an Athenian attack and knowing the Megarians
were watching to see which side would win. They thought they were
well placed in two respects: in their position they did not have to
start a battle or deliberately expose themselves to risk; and, since they
had clearly shown themselves ready to stand their ground, they might
well have fair claim to an unopposed victory. At the same time the
situation with the Megarians was working out well. If Brasidas had
not brought his army within sight of Megara, the Megarians would
have had no chance: they would have lost their city as surely as if they
had been defeated in battle. Whereas now there was the possibility
that the Athenians would not offer resistance, and if so Brasidas and
his force would achieve the object of their expedition without a fight.

      And that is indeed what happened. The Athenians did march out
and form up by the long walls, but when no attack was forthcoming
they also took no action. Their own generals reached this same
assessment, reckoning that since they had already succeeded in most
of their objectives there was disproportionate risk in committing to

battle against superior numbers. They might be victorious and capture Megara, but if they failed they would take losses among the finest of their hoplite force: whereas the Peloponnesians had at risk only a small part of the combined forces they could command and of each individual contingent represented there, making it likely that they would want to engage. Both armies stayed waiting for a time, but when there was no movement from either side, first the Athenians went back into Nisaea and then the Peloponnesians returned to their previous position. So now the Megarians friendly to the exiles, assuming Brasidas the victor and the Athenians no longer willing to fight, opened the gates to receive Brasidas himself and the commanders from the other cities, and began discussions with them, ignoring the now shattered pro-Athenian faction.

Later, after the allies had dispersed to their cities, Brasidas also 74 returned to Corinth and resumed preparation for his expedition to Thrace, which had been his original objective. Meanwhile in the city of Megara, once the Athenians too had gone back home, those who had been most involved in dealings with the Athenians quickly left, knowing that they had been discovered: the others made common cause with the friends of the exiles and recalled them from Pegae, first making them swear to solemn assurances that they would forget past quarrels and consider only the best interests of the city. But once in office these men conducted a military review, marshalling the various companies in different places, and picked out from the lines about a hundred of their enemies and of those thought to have been prime collaborators with the Athenians. They forced the people to pass judgement on them with open votes, secured their condemnation, and killed them. They then turned the city into an extreme oligarchy. So revolution was followed by counter-revolution: and there was never a change of government effected by so few which lasted for so long a time.

In the same summer the Mytilenaean exiles were ready to 75 strengthen Antandrus as they had intended. Two of the three generals in command of the Athenian money-raising ships, Demodocus and Aristeides, were in the Hellespont area (the third, Lamachus, had sailed on with ten ships into the Black Sea). When they learnt of the proposed works at Antandrus they feared the place could become as much a danger to Lesbos as Anaea was to Samos: that is where the Samian exiles had established themselves, and they were helping the Peloponnesians with a supply of steersmen for their fleets, keeping the Samians on the island in a state of constant unease, and harbouring emigrants. So the generals raised a force from the allies, sailed to Antandrus, defeated in battle the opposition that came out to meet them, and took the place back again. Not long afterwards, Lamachus, who had sailed into the Black Sea and was anchored at the river Calex in the territory of Heracleia, lost his ships when heavy rainfall in the interior caused a flash flood. He and his troops then made their way on foot through the Bithynian Thracians (who live in Asia, across the water from Thrace), and reached Calchedon, the Megarian colony at the mouth of the Black Sea.

76   In the same summer also, and immediately after the withdrawal from the Megarid, the Athenian general Demosthenes arrived at Naupactus with forty ships. On the matter of Boeotia both he and Hippocrates were in communication with a number of men in the Boeotian cities who wanted to change the existing order and turn it to democracy on the Athenian pattern: and plans had been coordinated, mainly at the instigation of an exile from Thespiae called Ptoeodorus. Some men were going to betray Siphae, a town on the coast of the Gulf of Crisa in Thespian territory. Others from Orchomenus were ready to hand over Chaeroneia (a dependency of the Orchomenus which was once called 'Minyan' but is now known as Boeotian Orchomenus). The Orchomenian exiles took a major part in this plan, and were hiring mercenaries from the Peloponnese: some Phocians were also involved (Chaeroneia lies at the edge of Boeotia, adjoining the territory of Phanoteus in Phocis). The Athenians' task was to take Delium, the sanctuary of Apollo in Tanagraean land facing Euboea. All this was to happen simultaneously on a predetermined day, so that the Boeotians would each be occupied with a disturbance in their own area and would not be able to mobilize any combined force in support of Delium. If the attempt succeeded and Delium was fortified, they were confident that, even if there was not an immediate and complete constitutional revolution in Boeotia, with these places occupied, plundering raids made throughout the country, and a nearby refuge available for any insurgents pressed to retreat, things could not stay as they were: in time Athenian support for the rebels, combined with the fragmentation of the opposing forces, would enable them to turn matters to their advantage.

77   Such was the prearranged plan. When the time came Hippocrates himself was to march against the Boeotians with a force from Athens. Before that he had sent Demosthenes with the forty ships to Naupactus,

to collect an army from the Acarnanians and the other allies in that region and then sail to Siphae in anticipation of its betrayal: they had specified a day on which all these operations should coincide. On his arrival Demosthenes found Oeniadae now forced into the Athenian alliance by the combined pressure of all the Acarnanians. He then raised a full levy of all the allied forces in that area, and first of all led a campaign against Salynthius and the Agraeans which succeeded in winning them over: after that he turned to preparations for keeping his appointment at Siphae, when the time came.

Meanwhile Brasidas, at about this same time in the summer, was 78 making his way to the Thraceward region with seventeen hundred hoplites. When he was at Heracleia in Trachis he sent a messenger ahead to friends in Pharsalus, asking for an escort for himself and his army through Thessaly. Several came to meet him at Meliteia in Achaea Phthiotis—Panaerus, Dorus, Hippolochidas, Torymbas, and Strophacus the consular representative of the Chalcidians—and he was then able to continue his journey. Other Thessalians too joined in escorting him, notably Niconidas from Larisa, who was a friend of Perdiccas.

To pass through Thessaly without an escort was difficult in any circumstances, and yet more so when under arms. All Greeks alike had come to regard as a threat any unauthorized passage by others through their land: and besides the mass of the Thessalians had always been friendly to Athens. So if the Thessalian system had been based on equal rights for all, rather than the traditional dominance of oligarchic cliques, Brasidas could never have gone on. Even as it was, his continued march was met at the river Enipeus by men of the opposite party to that of his escorts, who were ready to stop him, saying that he had no right to make his journey without the consent of the whole Thessalian community. His escorts replied that they would not give him further passage if there were objections; he had appeared without notice, and in providing an escort they were simply fulfilling their obligations as his guest-friends. Brasidas himself added that he came as a friend to Thessaly and its people; he was bearing arms not against them but against the Athenians, with whom he was at war; he knew of no hostility between Thessalians and Spartans which forbade access to each other's territory; he would not of course proceed now if they objected, nor could he, but he did not expect them to prevent him. They listened and left. On the advice of his escorts, Brasidas pressed on at speed with no halts, before a larger

force could gather to stop him. On that day, having started from
Meliteia, he ended at Pharsalus and camped by the river Apidanus:
from there he went to Phacium, and then on to Perrhaebia. At this
point his Thessalian escorts went back, and the Perrhaebians (who
are subjects of Thessaly) brought him to Dium in the kingdom of
Perdiccas: this is a town lying under Mount Olympus in the part of
Macedonia which faces Thessaly.

79   In this way Brasidas managed to hurry through Thessaly before
any opposition could be organized to stop him, and made his way to
Perdiccas and into Chalcidice. Alarmed by the Athenian successes,
both Perdiccas and those in the Thraceward region who were in revolt
from Athens had summoned this force from the Peloponnese. The
Chalcidians thought that they would be the first target of Athenian
aggression (and the neighbouring cities not in revolt were secretly
collaborating in this invitation): Perdiccas was not an open enemy of
Athens, but he too had fears arising from his old quarrels with the
Athenians, and had a particular concern to force the submission of
Arrhabaeus, the king of the Lyncestians.

What made it easier for them to secure the dispatch of an army
from the Peloponnese was the fact that the Spartans were doing badly
80 at the time. With the Athenians putting pressure on the Peloponnese,
and not least on their own territory, the Spartans thought that the
best way of distracting them was to retaliate by sending troops to
their disaffected allies, especially as the allies were inviting Spartan
support with a view to secession and had offered to meet the cost of
the troops' maintenance. At the same time they welcomed an excuse
to send out some of the Helots, to prevent any revolutionary response
to the present situation, now that Pylos was under enemy occupation.

Spartan policy towards the Helots had always been essentially
defensive, and fear of the numbers of vigorous young Helots had
already prompted action. The Spartans invited all Helots who claimed
to have given signal service in war to present themselves for selection, with the promise of freedom for the chosen. This was a ploy:
they reckoned that the first to claim their right to freedom would also
be those most likely to have the spirit for revolt. They selected some
two thousand, who then put on garlands and paraded round the
sanctuaries thinking themselves free: shortly afterwards the Spartans
did away with them, and nobody knew how any of them were killed.

So on this occasion they were glad to send seven hundred
Helots with Brasidas to serve as hoplites. He hired the rest of his

expeditionary force from the Peloponnese. Brasidas himself was 81
very keen to go, and the Chalcidians were eager to have him: so the
Spartans agreed to his expedition. At Sparta he had a reputation for
getting things done, whatever the need, and since being sent abroad
he had proved invaluable to the Spartans. He immediately impressed
the cities with his reasonable and moderate approach, which enabled
him to bring about the secession of most of them, while other places
were betrayed to him and captured. The result was to give the
Spartans the ability to bargain at will (as they subsequently did) in
any mutual return and recovery of places won or lost, and to reduce
the pressure of war on the Peloponnese. And in the later stages of the
war, after the Sicilian affair, the honourable conduct and intelligence
shown by Brasidas at this time—directly experienced by some, heard
of and believed in by others—played a major part in creating enthusiasm for the Spartans among the Athenian allies. He was the first
Spartan sent out to them, he established a reputation for decency in
all his dealings, and left in them a firm expectation that the others too
were of similar character.

For their part, when the Athenians learnt of his arrival in the 82
Thraceward region they declared war on Perdiccas (holding him
responsible for Brasidas' expedition), and took measures to keep a
closer watch on their allies in the area.

Perdiccas immediately took Brasidas and his army along with his 83
own forces on a campaign against Arrhabaeus the son of Bromerus,
king of a neighbouring people, the Lyncestian Macedonians: he had
a quarrel with him, and wanted to subdue him. But when he and the
army together with Brasidas reached the pass into Lyncus, Brasidas
said that before any resort to war he wanted first to go ahead in person and see if he could bring Arrhabaeus into alliance with Sparta by
negotiation. One factor was that Arrhabaeus was sending messages to
the effect that he was willing to refer the matter to Brasidas as intermediary and arbitrator: and the Chalcidian envoys accompanying the
expedition urged Brasidas not to remove the difficulties facing
Perdiccas, otherwise they might find him less eager to assist in their
own affairs. Besides, when Perdiccas' men were in Sparta they had
hinted that he would bring over many of the places in the surrounding
area to the Spartan alliance. In these circumstances, then, Brasidas
asserted an equal and independent interest in addressing the question
of Arrhabaeus. Perdiccas said that he had not brought in Brasidas
to arbitrate in their local quarrels, but rather to take out his own

enemies at his own direction: when he, Perdiccas, was paying half the maintenance of his army, Brasidas had no business to talk with Arrhabaeus. Despite his objections, and now in open dissent, Brasidas did make contact with Arrhabaeus, accepted the assurances he gave, and withdrew his army without any invasion of the country. After this Perdiccas, in pique, reduced his contribution to the upkeep of the army from a half to one-third.

84 Immediately thereafter in the same summer, and shortly before the grape harvest, Brasidas took the Chalcidians with him on a campaign to the Andrian colony of Acanthus. There was dissension in Acanthus whether to admit him or not—on the one side those who had joined the Chalcidians in inviting him, on the other the people at large. Even so, fear for their crop still out in the fields induced the general populace to accept Brasidas' proposal that they should let him in on his own and then make their decision when they had heard what he had to say. Thus admitted, he took his stand before the people (he was not a bad speaker, for a Spartan) and spoke as follows:

85 'Men of Acanthus, my mission here with this army is undertaken at the behest of the Spartans to validate the cause which we proclaimed at the beginning of the war: to fight the Athenians for the liberation of Greece. If we have been rather long in coming, that should be no reproach: we had hoped, mistakenly in the event, that bringing the war to their own country would enable us to crush the Athenians quickly, without involving you in any danger. But we have come now as soon as opportunity allowed, and with your help we shall do our best to defeat them.

'So I am surprised at this exclusion—your gates shut against me, and no apparent welcome of my arrival. We Spartans thought that we would be coming to people who were already our allies in spirit even before our actual appearance, and would be glad to see us here. That is why we have run the substantial risk of many days' journey through foreign territory in our full support of your cause. If you have now changed your minds, if you intend to resist liberation both for yourselves and for the rest of Greece, that could have dire consequences. It is not only a question of your own resistance. Any others I approach are less likely to join me, when they can point to the awkward fact that you, the first I came to, possessed of a notable city and a reputation for intelligence, turned me down. And I shall have no satisfactory explanation to offer: it will be thought either that the freedom I claim to bring is suspect, or that I have come here without the strength or capability to protect you from any Athenian offensive. And yet when I came to the support of Nisaea with this same army which I have with me now, the Athenians were not prepared to engage with us despite their superior numbers: and it is not likely that they could send against you by ship any force of the size they had at Nisaea.

'As for myself, I have not come to do harm. I am here for the 86 liberation of the Greeks. And I have bound the authorities at Sparta by the most solemn oaths to guarantee the autonomy of any people I bring over to alliance with us: and when we speak of alliance, we are not looking to force or inveigle you into fighting on our side—on the contrary, our purpose is to fight on your side to end your enslavement to the Athenians. So I say to you that there is no reason to suspect my motives (I have given you the strongest assurances), nor to think me incapable of protecting you: and every reason for you to come over to me with confidence.

'And if any of you have personal fears which make you wary that I might hand over the city to one group or another, you can trust me absolutely in this. I have not come here to engage in party politics, and I would think it an ambiguous sort of liberty to bring you if I were to ignore our tradition and subject the majority to the few or the minority to the whole. That would be worse than foreign rule, and for us Spartans, so far from gratitude for our efforts and an enhanced reputation, the result would be a blackening of our name. We would be manifestly bringing on ourselves the very same charges which are the basis of our continued war against the Athenians—and all the more resented in us than in those who have never made any pretence to decency. For men of honourable standing it is worse to gain advantage by plausible hypocrisy than by open force: the latter proceeds on the purely contingent justification of superior strength, but the former on deliberate bad faith. You can see from this the degree 87 of circumspection which we apply to the matters which concern us most. We have given you sworn assurances, and you could have no stronger confirmation of sincerity than from men whose actions measured against their words afford cogent evidence that what they say is what they mean, because it coincides with their own interest.

'But if your response to my offer is to say that you are unable to accept, but are sympathetic to our cause and trust that you can refuse without penalty; that liberation does have some obvious dangers for you; that it should of course be conferred on those able to accept it, but not imposed on anyone against their will—if that is your response, I shall first call on the gods and heroes of your country to witness that I have come here for your good and failed to persuade you: I shall then ravage your land and aim to force you. There will be no further scruple in my mind, and I shall consider my action justified by two imperatives—the Spartan interest, and the interest of the Greeks at large. I cannot leave you sympathetic but uncommitted to our side, or the Spartans will be damaged by your continued contribution to the Athenian revenue: and I cannot allow you to frustrate the Greeks' emancipation from slavery. In any other circumstances there would be no reason to act like this, and we Spartans would have no business to liberate the reluctant if it was not in the cause of some common good. Nor are we looking for empire: on the contrary, our purpose is to stop others. We are intent on bringing autonomy to all, and we would prejudice the majority if we were to tolerate your opposition.

'Think carefully, then, and take up the challenge to win first place in starting the liberation of the Greeks, to your everlasting fame. For yourselves the prize is to secure your individual interests from harm, and to crown your whole city with a glorious name.'

88   Such was the extent of Brasidas' speech. The Acanthians debated long, with much said on either side, and then took a secret vote. Influenced both by the seduction of Brasidas' offer and by fear for their crop, they decided by a majority to secede from Athens. They made Brasidas pledge fidelity to the oaths sworn by the Spartan authorities when they sent him out, guaranteeing the autonomy of any people he brought over as allies, and with that pledge given they admitted his army. Not long afterwards Stagirus too, a colony of Andros, joined the revolt.

These were the events of this summer.

89   At the very beginning of the following winter matters were ready for the betrayal of Boeotia to the Athenian generals Hippocrates and Demosthenes, and each had their appointment to keep— Demosthenes at Siphae with his ships, and Hippocrates at Delium. But a mistake was made about the dates for their respective mobilizations, and Demosthenes, with the Acarnanians and many others of the allies in that area on board his fleet, sailed for Siphae too early. His expedition came to nothing, as the enterprise was betrayed by a Phocian from Phanoteus called Nicomachus: he told the Spartans, and they told the Boeotians. As Hippocrates was not yet there to create diversionary trouble in the country, the Boeotians brought a full

levy into action, and both Siphae and Chaeroneia were secured in advance. When the conspirators in the Boeotian cities learnt of this failure, they made no revolutionary move.

Hippocrates had raised a full-scale Athenian army—calling up 90 citizens, metics, and all foreigners then in the city—and arrived at Delium too late, when the Boeotians had already been to Siphae and left. He settled his army there and began to fortify Delium in the following way. They first dug a trench in a circle round the sanctuary and the temple, and piled up the excavated soil to form a wall, which they then secured with wooden stakes driven in on either side: they packed the interior with vine-wood cut from around the sanctuary and stones and bricks stripped from the nearby houses, using every means to raise the height of the fortification. They erected wooden towers at suitable places where no sanctuary building was available for that purpose (there had once been a colonnade there, but it had collapsed). They began construction on the third day after setting out from Athens, and worked throughout that day, the next day, and until lunchtime on the fifth day. Then, when most of the work was complete, the main force retired to a distance of just over a mile from Delium, preparatory to a return home. Most of the light-armed troops continued immediately on the way back, but the hoplites grounded their arms there and waited: Hippocrates had stayed behind to organize the garrison and direct the completion of the remaining parts of the outwork.

During these days the Boeotians were gathering at Tanagra. When 91 the contingents from all the cities had arrived, they could see that the Athenians were moving back home. Since they were no longer in Boeotia (when they grounded their arms the Athenians were just about on the border with the territory of Oropus), all the Boeotarchs, of whom there are eleven, were against giving battle except for one. Pagondas the son of Aeoladas was one of the two Boeotarchs from Thebes (the other was Arianthidas the son of Lysimachidas), and he held the presidency: he wanted to do battle, and thought the risk worth taking. He summoned the troops in successive companies, so that not all should leave their posts at the same time, and tried to persuade the Boeotians to go against the Athenians and take up the challenge. He spoke to them as follows:

'Men of Boeotia, it should never have occurred to some of us com- 92 manders to question the legitimacy of engaging the Athenians in battle if we do not actually catch them still on Boeotian soil. They have crossed the border from their land to ours, they have built a fort here, and they intend the devastation of Boeotia. Of course they are our enemies wherever we find them, including the country from which they set out to inflict hostilities on us. As things stand, if any of you thought non-engagement the safer option, think again. People under attack and defending their own land have no opportunity for careful calculation, unlike those who are secure in their own possessions and deliberately attack others out of greed for more. It is in your tradition to resist any attack by a foreign army, whether in your own country or next door—that has never made any difference. And this imperative applies to the Athenians with by far the greatest force, as beside all else they share a border with us. In relations between neighbouring states mutually assured defence is always the condition of independence. With the Athenians, then, in particular, whose ambition to enslave others extends far beyond their immediate neighbours, how can we not pursue the contest to the utmost? We can see examples of their treatment in the Euboeans across the water from us, and in most of the rest of Greece. We have to realize that, while other sets of adjacent countries generally fight their wars over boundary disputes, defeat for us will mean a single and undisputed boundary fixed which swallows our entire land: if the Athenians invade, they will take forcible possession of all that is ours. That is the price we pay for living next to the Athenians. They are far more dangerous than ordinary neighbours.

'When people attack others—doubtless confident in their strength, as the Athenians now—they find little to fear in a campaign against quietist opponents who will only resist in their own country: less easily controlled are those who go outside their borders to confront them and, given the occasion, start the war themselves. We have experienced this here before with the Athenians. When they had gained control of our land as a result of our internal dissension, we defeated them at Coroneia and established for Boeotia the complete security which has lasted until now. We should remember this. The older among you should seek to emulate their earlier deeds, and the younger—sons of fathers who showed their worth in those days— must strive to keep their family honour untarnished. We can trust to have on our side the god whose sanctuary they have fortified and now occupy against all law; and we can trust the favourable omens of the sacrifices we have made. So let us come to grips with them. Let us show them that they may satisfy their ambitions, if they wish, by attacking those who offer no resistance, but when they come against people whose code of honour is always to fight for the freedom of their own country and never to enslave any other country in defiance of justice, they will not get away unchallenged.'

With this exhortation Pagondas persuaded the Boeotians to 93 confront the Athenians. He quickly mobilized his forces (it was already late in the day) and led them on close to the Athenian army, settling in a position where direct sight of each other was prevented by an intervening hill: here he formed up and prepared for battle. Hippocrates was still at Delium, and when he received a report of the Boeotian advance he sent instructions to his army to take up position. He himself came on shortly afterwards, leaving at Delium about three hundred cavalry to guard the place against any attack and also to watch for an opportunity to charge the Boeotians in the course of the battle. The Boeotians posted a detachment to oppose them: then, when all arrangements were in order, they appeared over the crest of the hill in the formation they had planned. They numbered about seven thousand hoplites, over ten thousand light-armed troops, a thousand cavalry, and five hundred peltasts. The right wing was held by the Thebans and their confederates; in the centre were the men from Haliartus, Coroneia, Copae and the other places round lake Copaïs; the men from Thespiae, Tanagra, and Orchomenus held the left wing; the cavalry and light-armed troops were placed on each wing. The Thebans were formed up to a depth of twenty-five ranks, and the others in whatever formation suited each contingent. This, then, was the scale and disposition of the Boeotian army.

The Athenian hoplites, equal in number to their opponents, were 94 drawn up eight-deep across the whole of their line, with cavalry stationed on either wing. There were no professionally equipped light troops present on this occasion, nor did Athens ever have a regular force of this kind. The full tally of those involved in the invasion was several times greater than that of their opponents, but most of them had come unarmed, given the universal call-up of all foreigners then in Athens as well as the citizens: these had already started for home, and only a few were there to take part in the battle. Formation made and engagement imminent, Hippocrates the general went along the Athenian line with these words of encouragement:

'Men of Athens, this is only a brief exhortation, but for brave men 95 brief is as good as long: and it is more a reminder than an instruction. None of you should think for a moment that there is no cause for us to be facing dangers such as this on foreign soil. At stake in this country now is the future of our own. If we are victorious, the Peloponnesians will lose the use of the Boeotian cavalry and you will never see them invading our land again. In one single battle you can both win this country and promote the freedom of yours. Go to meet them, then, with a spirit worthy of our city—the first city in all Greece, where every one of us is proud to claim his birthright—and worthy of our fathers, who in their time fought and conquered the Boeotians at Oenophyta under Myronides and took possession of their country.'

96   Hippocrates reached halfway along the line with this encouragement, but had no time to go further, as the Boeotians, likewise encouraged by Pagondas with a quick speech there and then, immediately shouted a paean and advanced on them down the hill. The Athenians advanced in turn and met them at a run. The extreme wings of the two armies never engaged, as both were stopped short by gullies in their way. But the rest clashed in a gruelling fight with shields shoving against shields. The Boeotians on the left wing and as far as the centre were losing to the Athenians, who pressed hard on that section and especially on the Thespians. The troops on either side of them had fallen back, so the Thespians were encircled and hemmed in: those who died were cut down defending themselves hand-to-hand. In the confusion of this encirclement some of the Athenians too were killed in mistake by their own side. So this section of the Boeotian line faced defeat, and ran to join that part of their army which was still fighting. Their right wing, where the Thebans were stationed, was getting the better of the Athenians, pushing them back gradually at first then ever more insistently. A further circumstance was that, in response to the difficulties of his left wing, Pagondas launched two squadrons of cavalry round the hill from the blind side, and their sudden appearance over the ridge struck terror into the victorious Athenian wing, who thought that another army was coming to attack them. Pressed now on both sides by the combination of this development and the Theban drive which was breaking their ranks, the entire Athenian army turned to flight.

Some made for Delium and the sea, and some for Oropus: others fled towards Mount Parnes, or in whatever direction they thought could offer some hope of safety. The Boeotians pursued to kill, especially their cavalry and the Locrians who had come in support just as the rout was beginning: but night closed the action, and helped the majority of the fleeing troops to make their escape. On the next day those who had reached Oropus and Delium were transported home by sea, leaving a garrison behind (they were still in possession of Delium). The Boeotians set up a trophy, recovered their own dead and stripped 97 the enemy dead, posted a guard on the field, and returned to Tanagra, where they laid plans for an attack on Delium.

A herald sent by the Athenians to request recovery of the dead was met on his way by a Boeotian herald, who turned him back, saying that he would get no response until he himself had returned from his mission to Athens. He then stood before the Athenians and delivered the message from the Boeotians, to the effect that the Athenians were guilty of breaking the established laws of the Greeks. It was universally accepted that invaders of others' territory kept out of the sanctuaries in that territory: but the Athenians had fortified and taken up occupation of Delium, and all that men do on unconsecrated ground was being done there in the sanctuary, and they had been drawing for their regular supply the holy water which the Boeotians themselves were forbidden to touch except for purification before sacrifice. Therefore on behalf both of the god and of themselves, and calling in witness Apollo and all the deities sharing worship at that altar, the Boeotians gave notice to the Athenians that they could only retrieve their own when they had left the sanctuary.

On receipt of this message the Athenians sent a herald of their own 98 to the Boeotians, to say that they had done no wrong regarding the sanctuary, and would not consciously do it any harm in the future: that had been no part of their original purpose in occupying it, which was to use it as a base for their own defence against those who were in fact doing wrong to them. As for Greek laws, the rule was that those who had control of any territory, large or small, also and always took possession of the sanctuaries, maintaining as far as possible the traditional modes of observance. Indeed the Boeotians themselves, and most others who had driven out the original inhabitants of the land they now occupied, had once invaded sanctuaries belonging to others and now regarded them as their own. The same right of possession would apply to the Athenians too, if they had been able to take over more of Boeotia: as it was, they considered that part which they did occupy to be their own property, and they would not leave it voluntarily. As for sacrilegious use of the water, this was a matter of necessity, not deliberate violation: the Boeotians had attacked their country first, they were acting in self-defence, and had no choice but to use the water. There was every reason to think that actions to

which people were constrained by war or some other emergency
would be pardonable in the god's eyes too. Did not the altars provide
refuge for involuntary offenders? And 'law-breaking' could only be
predicated of malice aforethought: it was not a term applicable to
those driven to some bold act by force of circumstance. As for the
dead bodies, the Boeotians were guilty of much greater impiety in
attempting to barter their return for a sanctuary than the Athenians
in refusing to exchange the sanctuary for the recovery of what was
theirs by right.

They requested, therefore, an unambiguous statement from the
Boeotians that the recovery of their dead was not dependent on their
departure from Boeotian soil (they were not in any case now in the
Boeotians' territory, but on land acquired by force of arms), and
would proceed in the traditional way by formal truce.

99   The Boeotians replied that, if the Athenians were in Boeotia, they
could remove their own only when they left Boeotian territory:
if they were in Athenian territory, they could decide what to do by
themselves. (The Boeotians' thinking was that, although the battle
had taken place on the borders and the dead were in fact lying in the
territory of Oropus, which was a subject possession of Athens, the
Athenians could not recover the bodies without their agreement, and
at the same time they could maintain the pretence of making no truce
in respect of Athenian land. So they thought 'leave our country and
then take what you ask' was a fine response.) The Athenian herald
listened to this answer and left with his mission frustrated.

100   The Boeotians immediately sent for javelin-men and slingers from
the Malian Gulf, and they had been joined after the battle by two
thousand Corinthian hoplites, the Peloponnesian garrison which had
evacuated Nisaea, and the Megarians too. With this force they
marched to Delium and attacked the fortification, employing various
methods including the application of an engine which succeeded in
taking the place. This engine was constructed as follows. They sawed
a great beam in two, hollowed it out completely, then fitted the two
parts precisely together again, like a pipe; at the far end they suspended a cauldron on chains, with an iron nozzle curving down into
it from the beam; most of the rest of the wood was also cased in iron.
From some distance they brought this machine up on wagons against
those parts of the wall which were largely built of vine-wood and
other timber. Wherever they got it close, they applied large bellows
to their end of the beam and made them blow. The pipe was airtight,

so the blast went straight through to the cauldron, which was full of lighted charcoal, sulphur, and pitch. The result was a huge flame which set fire to the wall and made it impossible for anyone to stay manning it: the defenders abandoned the wall and took to flight, and so the fort was captured by this means. Some of the garrison were killed and two hundred taken captive, but most of the others got on board their ships and were transported home.

Delium was captured on the seventeenth day after the battle. Shortly 101 afterwards the Athenian herald, knowing nothing of this event, came once more to ask for the dead: this time the Boeotians agreed their release and did not repeat the previous answer. In the battle there had died a little under five hundred Boeotians, and a little under a thousand Athenians, including their general Hippocrates, with heavy losses too among their light-armed troops and baggage-carriers.

Not long after this battle, Demosthenes, who had sailed at the time only to have the intended betrayal of Siphae come to nothing, took his fleet with the troops from Acarnania and Agraeis on board as well as four hundred Athenian hoplites and made a landing on the coast of Sicyon. Before all his ships were in, the Sicyonians had rallied in defence and they routed those who had already landed and drove them back to the ships, killing some and taking others alive. They set up a trophy and returned the dead under truce.

Within the same days as the events at Delium Sitalces the king of the Odrysians died in the defeat of the army he had led against the Triballians. His nephew Seuthes, the son of Sparadocus, succeeded him as king of the Odrysians and the rest of his dominion in Thrace.

In the same winter Brasidas and his allies in the Thraceward region 102 launched a campaign against Amphipolis, the Athenian colony on the river Strymon. There had been an earlier attempt to colonize the site of the present city by Aristagoras of Miletus when he was in flight from King Dareius, but he was driven out by the Edonians. Then thirty-two years later the Athenians too made an attempt, sending out ten thousand colonists made up of their own people and volunteers from elsewhere: they were wiped out by the Thracians at Drabescus. The Athenians came again in the twenty-ninth year after that, with Hagnon the son of Nicias sent as founder-colonist, expelled the Edonians, and built a colony in this spot, which was previously called Nine Ways. Their base for this operation was Eïon, a trading-post and seaport which they already possessed at the mouth of the river, about three miles distant from the present city. Hagnon named the settlement 'Amphipolis' because, with the Strymon looping round the site on two sides, and a long wall built to define and enclose it from one bend of the river to the other, his foundation had an imposing aspect both seawards and landwards.

103   This then was Brasidas' destination when he set out with his army from Arnae in Chalcidice. Towards evening he reached Aulon and Bormiscus, where lake Bolbe flows into the sea. He made supper there, then marched on through the night. It was wintry weather with snow beginning to fall, which made him press on all the faster, hoping to surprise the people of Amphipolis—except, that is, for the traitors among them. There were settlers from Argilus in the city (Argilus is a colony of Andros) who were the authors of this conspiracy, and others with them, some instigated by Perdiccas, some by the Chalcidians. The town of Argilus is close by, and for long the Athenians had had their particular suspicions of the Argilians and the Argilians their particular designs on Amphipolis. For some time, ever since the arrival of Brasidas provided the opportunity, they had been working with their people who had citizenship in Amphipolis to arrange for the surrender of the city. They now welcomed Brasidas into their own town, defected from the Athenians that very night, and before dawn conducted his army to the bridge over the river. The crossing was at some distance from Amphipolis itself, and there were then no walls running down to it from the city as there are now, but a small garrison had been posted there. Brasidas easily overcame it, helped by two factors—the plot was already in operation, and the weather lent surprise to his attack. He crossed the bridge, and immediately annexed the property of all the Amphipolitans occupying the whole intervening area outside the walls.

104   His crossing of the river came as a sudden shock to the inhabitants of the city. That and the capture of many of their people outside, while others ran for refuge behind the walls, brought the Amphipolitans to a state of utter chaos, made worse by their suspicions of one another. Reports of opinion at the time suggest that Brasidas could well have taken the city if he had decided to proceed directly against it, rather than giving his army leave to plunder. As it was, with everything outside now overrun and no sign of the expected response from those inside, he settled his army and took no further action. The party opposed to the traitors were sufficiently strong in number to prevent the immediate opening of the gates, and with the assistance of the general Eucles (who was there from Athens to protect the place) they

sent for help to the other general in the Thraceward region, Thucydides the son of Olorus, the author of this history. He was at Thasos, an island colonized from Paros, about half a day's sail from Amphipolis. As soon as he received the message he sailed at full speed with the seven ships at his disposal, wanting to reach Amphipolis, if possible, before any move to surrender the city, or, failing that, to secure Eïon.

Brasidas meanwhile was doing his utmost to gain prior control 105 of the city. He was apprehensive of the support from the ships at Thasos, and moreover had learnt that Thucydides owned the rights to work the gold mines in that part of Thrace and consequently had powerful influence with the leading men on the mainland. His fear was that if Thucydides got there first the common people of Amphipolis would look to him to raise an allied force from the seaboard or from Thrace to protect them, and would lose any inclination to come over. He therefore offered moderate terms, issuing this proclamation: any of the Amphipolitans or Athenians in the city who wished to stay could do so in possession of their property and retention of fair and equal rights; any who did not wish to stay could take their effects with them but must leave within five days.

On hearing this proclamation the people in general began to waver, 106 not least because there was only a small proportion of Athenian origin in the largely mixed citizen body, and many of those captured outside had relatives inside. In comparison with what they had feared, they thought the terms of the proclamation fair—the Athenians because they welcomed the chance to leave, reckoning that they were under particular threat and not expecting any rescue soon; and the rest of the people in virtue of their retention of equal political rights and the unexpected release from danger. The supporters of Brasidas now spoke openly in justification of the proposals, as they could see that the people had been converted and were no longer inclined to listen to the Athenian general who was there in person. And so the agreement was made, and they admitted Brasidas on the terms as proclaimed. Such was the surrender of Amphipolis, and late in that same day Thucydides and his ships sailed into Eïon. Brasidas had just gained possession of Amphipolis, and came within one night of taking Eïon: if the ships had not arrived in support that quickly, Eïon would have fallen to Brasidas the following morning.

Thucydides now organized the defence of Eïon, both against 107 any immediate attack by Brasidas and for its future security, and took in those who had chosen under the terms of the truce to leave

Amphipolis and come down to join him at Eïon. Brasidas did make a sudden attempt, sailing down the river in a fleet of boats in the hope of capturing the headland which juts out from the wall and so gaining command of the entrance to the harbour: and he tried an attack by land at the same time. He was beaten back on both fronts, and turned to settling the arrangements at Amphipolis. The Edonian city of Myrcinus went over to him, after Pittacus the king of the Edonians had been assassinated by the sons of Goaxis and his own wife Brauro: and soon afterwards Galepsus and Oesyme (both colonies of Thasos) went over also. Perdiccas arrived immediately after Amphipolis was taken and helped Brasidas to consolidate these new gains.

108   The enemy possession of Amphipolis caused major alarm at Athens, for two reasons in particular. The city was a valuable source both of timber for shipbuilding and of financial revenue: and the Spartans, if granted passage through Thessaly, had always had a route towards the Athenian allies as far as the Strymon, but without control of the bridge could proceed no further, as above Amphipolis the river formed a large lake for some considerable distance, and on the Eïon side there were triremes on watch—but now they had gained easy transit.

And the Athenians were afraid that their allies would defect. Brasidas was giving a general impression of moderation, and wherever he spoke he declared that he had been sent out to liberate Greece. When the cities subject to Athens heard of his taking of Amphipolis, of the offer he had made, and of the mild disposition of the man himself, they were more than ever excited by the prospect of revolt, and began secret negotiations with him, inviting him to come and help them, each of them keen to be the first to defect. They could see no cause for fear, but their underestimation of Athenian power was as great as the subsequent revelation of that power. Their criterion was more vague wish than sound policy: all men tend to wrap their desires in unconsidered hope, while using ruthless logic to banish their aversions. They drew confidence too from the recent blow inflicted on the Athenians by the Boeotians, and from Brasidas' enticing (but untrue) claim that at Nisaea the Athenians had refused to engage his own unsupported army: they believed, then, that no punitive force would be sent against them. Most decisive of all in their willingness to take all risks was the gratifying excitement of the moment and the prospect of their first experience of the Spartans in full cry.

Aware of this, the Athenians dispatched garrisons to the various cities as best they could at short notice and in winter. And Brasidas sent to Sparta calling for reinforcements: in the meantime he made preparations for the building of triremes on the Strymon. The Spartans did not support his request. This was partly the jealousy of their leading men, and also the greater desire to recover their men taken prisoner from the island and to bring the war to an end.

In the same winter the Megarians recaptured their long walls from 109 Athenian control and demolished them to the foundations.

After the taking of Amphipolis Brasidas and his allies campaigned against the peninsula called Acte, which stretches out into the Aegean sea from the canal dug by the Persian King and terminates in the height of Mount Athos. The cities of the peninsula are Sane, an Andrian colony close by the canal and facing the sea towards Euboea, and then Thyssus, Cleonae, Acrothooe, Olophyxus, and Dium. These are inhabited by a mixed population of barbarian peoples, bilingual in Greek and their native languages. There is a small Chalcidian Greek element, but the majority are Pelasgians (descended from the Etruscans who once inhabited Lemnos and Athens), or else Bisaltians, Crestonians, or Edonians. They live in small towns. Most of these came over to Brasidas, but Sane and Dium resisted, and he spent some time ravaging their land with his army.

When this still did not achieve their compliance, he broke off for a 110 campaign against Chalcidian Torone, where the Athenians maintained a garrison. He was invited there by a small group who were prepared to surrender their city. He arrived towards dawn, when it was still dark, and settled with his army around the temple of the Dioscuri, about a third of a mile from the city. His arrival went unnoticed by the general population of Torone and the Athenian guards, but the conspirators knew that he was coming, and a few of them had slipped out ahead to watch for his approach. When they discovered that he was already in place, they smuggled into the city seven of his soldiers lightly armed with daggers (these seven, led by Lysistratus from Olynthus, were the only ones of the twenty originally detailed who had the courage for this entry). They crept in through a gap in the seaward wall and climbed up unseen to the highest guard-post (the city is set on the slope of a hill). They killed the guards there, and then began breaking apart the postern gate which faces Cape Canastraeum.

Brasidas advanced the rest of his army a little way and then 111 halted, sending forward a hundred peltasts to be ready to run in first whenever any gates were opened and the agreed signal given. As time passed and they wondered what was happening the peltasts gradually drew closer to the city. Meanwhile the Toronaeans at work inside with the infiltrated group of soldiers had broken the postern gate and cut through the bar to enable the opening of the gates by the agora. First they led some of the peltasts round the side and let them in through the postern gate, intending to intimidate the general population (who knew nothing of the plot) by the sudden appearance of troops at both rear and front: then they raised the fire-signal which had been specified and now let in the rest of the peltasts through the agora gates.

112   On sight of the agreed signal Brasidas set his army in motion and advanced at the run, the whole army giving a concerted shout which caused widespread panic in the city. Some of his troops pushed straight in through the gates, while others scaled the wall at a place where a collapse was being repaired and there were sawn planks inclined against the wall for the hauling up of stones. Brasidas and the bulk of his army turned immediately upwards to the highest parts of the city, to make sure of its complete capture from top to bottom: the rest of his troops spread out evenly to all other parts.

113   As the capture of their city proceeded the majority of the Toronaeans were distraught, with no idea of what was going on, but the conspirators and those who shared their politics immediately joined the invaders. When the Athenians were alerted (this was a force of about fifty hoplites, sleeping in the agora), a few of them were killed in hand-to-hand fighting but the rest managed to make their escape to safety in the fort of Lecythus, either on foot or by reaching the two ships they had there on guard-duty. Lecythus, previously taken over and occupied by the Athenians, was a headland jutting out to sea and separated from the city by a narrow isthmus. The Toronaeans friendly to the Athenians also took refuge there.

114   When daylight had come and the city was now firmly in his control, Brasidas issued a proclamation to the Toronaeans who had taken refuge with the Athenians, that any who so wished could come out and return to their property with no threat to their civic rights. He also sent a herald to the Athenians requiring them to evacuate Lecythus under truce, taking their belongings with them, on the grounds that it was Chalcidian territory and not theirs. They replied that they would not leave, but asked him for one day's truce for the recovery of their dead. He granted them two days: and in these days he fortified

the buildings near Lecythus while the Athenians likewise strengthened their own position.

Brasidas called a meeting of the Toronaeans and gave them much the same speech as he had delivered at Acanthus. He said that it would not be right to think the worse of the men who had dealt with him to arrange the capture of the city, or to regard them as traitors—they had not been bribed, they were not looking to enslave Torone, but they had acted for the good of the city and its freedom. Nor should the uninvolved fear disadvantage: he had not come to damage the community or any individual. His proclamation to those who had taken refuge with the Athenians was intended to show that he thought none the worse of them for their sympathy in that direction. He expected that once they had experience of the Spartans they would show them similar loyalty—in fact much greater loyalty for the greater justice of their cause: at present they were afraid of the Spartans because they did not know them. He advised them all to make up their minds to be staunch allies, as from that point on they would be held to account for any backsliding. As for past behaviour, the Spartans had no quarrel with them: the iniquity was, on the contrary, that suffered by the Toronaeans themselves under a superior power, and any opposition they had shown to Sparta was pardonable.

Such was the speech with which Brasidas reassured the people of 115 Torone. The truce had now expired, and he launched his assault on Lecythus. The Athenian defences were a wall in poor condition and some houses equipped with battlements, but even so they managed to resist the attack for one day. On the next day, with their opponents preparing to bring up a machine designed to throw fire at the wooden breastwork, and the army already approaching, the Athenians erected a wooden tower on top of a building at a particularly vulnerable point where they thought it most likely that the machine would be applied. They carried up many jars and pitchers of water and large stones, and many men climbed onto the tower. But the overladen building suddenly collapsed with a great crash. To the Athenians close by who witnessed the accident this caused more frustration than alarm, but those further away, and especially those at the greatest distance, thought that the place had already been taken at that spot and set off in flight to the sea and their ships.

When Brasidas saw them deserting the parapets and realized what 116 was happening, he flung his army on and captured the fort immediately, killing any he found inside. Such was the Athenians' exit from

Lecythus, and in their ships and smaller craft they crossed over to Pallene. There was in Lecythus a sanctuary of Athena, and when Brasidas was about to attack he had advertised a reward of thirty minas of silver for the first man to scale the wall: thinking now that there had been more than human agency in the capture, he gave the thirty minas to the goddess and her sanctuary. He then demolished Lecythus, cleared the ground, and dedicated the whole area as a sacred precinct.

He spent the rest of the winter consolidating the places he had gained and planning further acquisitions. And with the passing of this winter there ended the eighth year of the war.

117   At the very beginning of spring in the following summer season, the Spartans and the Athenians made a truce for a year. The Athenian thinking was that this would prevent Brasidas securing any further defections among their allies before they had time for counter-measures: and, if the circumstances were right, they could make a more general agreement. The Spartans had accurately identified the Athenians' fears, and thought that a period of relief from setbacks and pressure would make them more inclined to try for reconciliation and, with the return of the Spartan captives, a longer-lasting peace. Before this run of success by Brasidas, their overriding concern had always been, and still was, the recovery of these men: if he was now allowed to go on to yet greater success and thereby redress the balance, they would lose this chance to recover the men and the rest of their army would have to continue fighting an evenly balanced war with no guarantee of victory.

They therefore made a formal truce for themselves and their allies. These are the texts:

118   Concerning the sanctuary and the oracle of Pythian Apollo we resolve that any who wish should have access according to the established laws, without fraud or fear. This is resolved by the Spartans and their allies here present: and they undertake to use all diplomatic means to persuade the Boeotians and Phocians likewise. Concerning the money belonging to the god, it is resolved that we shall be diligent to discover the guilty parties, properly and justly in accordance with the established laws, both you and we and those others who so wish, all in accordance with the established laws. These are the resolutions of the Spartans and their allies in the matters aforesaid.

A resolution of the Spartans and their allies in the event of the Athenians making a treaty. Both parties to remain within their own territory, retaining possession of what we each now hold: the Athenians at Coryphasium to stay within the bounds of Bouphras and Tomeus; in Cythera to have no communication with the Peloponnesian alliance, neither we with them nor they with us; at Nisaea and Minoa not to go beyond the road leading from the gates at the shrine of Nisus to the temple of Poseidon, and then directly from the temple of Poseidon to the bridge over to Minoa (nor should the Megarians or their allies cross this road); the Athenians to keep the island of Minoa which they have captured, but with no communication in either direction; and at Troezen the Athenians to retain what they now control, as agreed with them by the Troezenians.

In the use of the sea, the Spartans and their allies may sail in their own and allied coastal waters in any oared vessel of a capacity up to five hundred measures, but not in warships.

There shall be safe conduct both by land and by sea for any herald or embassy (with attendants as appropriate) travelling to or from the Peloponnese or Athens in diplomacy to end the war or settle disputes.

During this period there shall be no reception of deserters, either free or slave, either by you or by us.

You shall be legally accountable to us, and we to you, according to established practice, and any matters of contention shall be resolved by arbitration without recourse to war.

These are the resolutions of the Spartans and their allies. If you reach better or fairer resolutions than these, come to Sparta and explain them to us. Neither the Spartans nor their allies will refuse to consider any fair proposals which you make. Those who come should come with full executive authority, as you required of our spokesmen too.

The truce shall be for one year.

A resolution of the council and people. Prytany Acamantis, secretary Phaenippus, president Niciades. Proposer Laches. May it be to the good of the Athenians. Resolved to conclude the truce on the terms agreed by the Spartans and their allies and confirmed by them before the people: the truce to be for one year, and to begin on this day, the fourteenth of the month Elaphebolion. During this period ambassadors and heralds shall travel between the two parties to discuss terms for the ending of the war. The generals and the prytaneis shall first convene an assembly to consider a permanent peace: thereafter, if it is agreed to send and receive embassies concerning an end to the war, the Athenians shall deliberate on any proposals made. The embassies here present now shall immediately ratify the truce before the people, and swear to abide by it for the year.

This was agreed between the Spartans and their allies and the Athenians 119 and their allies on the twelfth day of the Spartan month Gerastius. The agreement was made and ratified by the following: for the Spartans, Taurus the son of Echetimidas, Athenaeus the son of Pericleidas, Philocharidas the son of Eryxilaïdas; for the Corinthians, Aeneas the son of Ocytus, Euphamidas the son of Aristonymus; for the Sicyonians, Damotimus the son of Naucrates, Onasimus the son of Megacles; for the Megarians, Nicastus the son of Cecalus, Menecrates the son of Amphidorus; for the Epidaurians, Amphias the son of Eupaeidas; and for the Athenians the generals Nicostratus the son of Diitrephes, Nicias the son of Niceratus, Autocles the son of Tolmaeus.

So this truce was made, and throughout its duration they continued negotiations for a longer-lasting treaty.

120   Several days were spent in promulgating the truce, and at about this time Scione, a city on Pallene, defected to Brasidas from the Athenians. (The Scionaeans say that they were originally from Pellene in the Peloponnese, but on the return voyage from Troy their ancestors were caught in the storm which hit the Achaean fleet, and driven off course to this place, where they then settled.) On their defection Brasidas crossed over to Scione by night, with a friendly trireme sailing ahead of him while he followed at some distance in a cutter: his thought was that if he encountered a boat bigger than his the trireme would protect him, and if another trireme appeared in opposition it would concentrate on the big ship, not the smaller boat, and in the meantime he could make his escape. This crossing successfully completed, Brasidas called a meeting of the Scionaeans and began by repeating what he had said at Acanthus and Torone. He went on to express the greatest admiration for them, because with Pallene cut off at the isthmus by the Athenian occupation of Potidaea they were virtually islanders, yet of their own accord they had made the move to embrace freedom, and not waited timidly for their own clear good to be forced on them. This indicated that they would face any major test of endurance with equal courage: and, if he managed to arrange things as he intended, he would regard them as truly the most loyal of Sparta's friends, and pay them every honour.

121   The Scionaeans were excited by this speech and with universal enthusiasm (including even those who had originally been against the move) they made up their minds to commit to the war in earnest, and gave Brasidas an honorific welcome—on behalf of the whole community they crowned him with a golden crown as the liberator of Greece, and individuals flocked to festoon him with ribbons as if he were a victor in the games. For the time being he left a small garrison with them while he crossed back again. Shortly afterwards he sent over a larger body of troops, intending, with the Scionaeans now

on his side, to make an attempt on Mende and Potidaea: he expected that the Athenians would react as if Pallene were an island and send out a force to intervene, and he wanted to forestall them. He had also begun some dealings with these cities, with a view to their betrayal.

These, then, were his intentions, but in the meantime a trireme 122 reached him bringing the ambassadors sent out to disseminate notice of the truce, Aristonymus from Athens and Athenaeus from Sparta. His army then returned to Torone, and the ambassadors briefed Brasidas about the agreement. All the Thraceward allies of the Spartans accepted the decision, and Aristonymus was generally satisfied: but by computing the days he realized that the Scionaeans had defected after the truce was ratified, and he declared that they were not covered by it. Brasidas argued at length that they had been in time, and refused to give up the city. Aristonymus reported on the matter to Athens, and the Athenians were all for an immediate campaign against Scione. The Spartans sent envoys to say that this would be a breach of the treaty: they set out their own claim to the city, reliant on Brasidas' testimony, but were prepared to submit the issue to arbitration. The Athenians were in no mood to risk arbitration, but wanted military action as soon as possible. They were furious that even those who could now be classed as islanders were presuming to defect, seduced by Spartan power on land, which would be quite useless in their situation. And in fact the truth of the matter supported the Athenians' claim: the Scionaeans had defected two days after the ratification of the truce. On Cleon's motion and at his persuasion they immediately passed a decree for the destruction of Scione and the execution of its inhabitants. They took no action elsewhere, but began their preparations for this.

Meanwhile Mende defected from them: this is a city on Pallene 123 and an Eretrian colony. Brasidas accepted the defection, seeing no wrong in this, as they had come over to him openly during the truce, and he had his own complaints of Athenian truce-breaking. What had emboldened the Mendaeans too to make this move was the ready determination they saw in Brasidas, as evidenced further by his refusal to give back Scione: and there was also pressure from the conspirators among them—they were only a small minority and would not abandon what they had started, but in fear of the consequences for themselves if they were shown up they had coerced the majority to go against their true inclination. Immediately the Athenians learnt of this revolt they became much more angry still, and began preparations

against both cities. In expectation of an Athenian naval attack
Brasidas evacuated the children and women from Scione and Mende
to Chalcidian Olynthus, and sent across five hundred Peloponnesian
hoplites and three hundred Chalcidian peltasts, with Polydamidas in
overall command. And the two cities coordinated measures for their
own defence against the imminent arrival of the Athenians.

124   Brasidas and Perdiccas meanwhile joined forces and launched a
campaign for the second time against Arrhabaeus in Lyncus. Perdiccas
had with him a full army of the Macedonians under his rule, and also
hoplites from the Greek cities in his kingdom: with Brasidas, in addition to the rest of his Peloponnesians, were Chalcidians, Acanthians,
and contingents from the other cities proportionate to their strength.
The total Greek hoplite force numbered about three thousand, accompanied by nearly a thousand cavalry, Macedonian and Chalcidian combined, and there was a mass of barbarian troops besides. On entering
the territory of Arrhabaeus they found the Lyncestians already
encamped and ready to meet them: so they too took up position for
battle. The two sides had their infantry stationed on two opposing hills,
with a plain between them. First of all the cavalry from both sides
rode down and fought an engagement in the plain. The next move
was made by the Lyncestian hoplites: joined by their cavalry they
advanced down the hill and offered battle. Brasidas and Perdiccas
likewise advanced their troops and engaged. The result was a rout of
the Lyncestians: many were killed, and the remainder escaped to the
high ground and took no further part.

After this they set up a trophy and waited for two or three days,
expecting the intended arrival of the Illyrians hired by Perdiccas.
Then Perdiccas, impatient of sitting idle, was all for pressing on
against the villages in Arrhabaeus' territory. But Brasidas was not
keen and preferred to withdraw, for two reasons: he was concerned
for the fate of Mende, if the Athenian ships got there before he did,
125   and also the Illyrians had not turned up. In the midst of this disagreement news came that the Illyrians had betrayed Perdiccas and
joined Arrhabaeus. The result was that both now decided to withdraw, as the Illyrians were formidable fighters: but because of their
dispute no time had been fixed for the withdrawal to begin. Night
supervened, and the Macedonians and the mass of barbarians took
sudden fright, seized by that unaccountable panic to which large
armies are liable. Convinced that the Illyrians come to fight them
were many times their actual number, and were now virtually on

them, they instantly turned and ran, making for home. At first Perdiccas was unaware of what was happening, but as soon as he realized he was obliged by the action of his troops to leave before he had a chance to see Brasidas (their camps were far apart).

At daybreak Brasidas saw that the Macedonians had already decamped and the Illyrians and Arrhabaeus were about to attack. He now planned his own withdrawal. He formed his hoplites into a compact square, with the mass of light-armed troops placed inside it. He detailed the youngest of his men to be ready to dash out through the ranks at any point where the enemy attacked, while he himself would bring up the rear of the retreat with three hundred picked troops, intending to stand and beat back the first wave of the enemy onslaught. Before the enemy were close on them he found time to give this quick encouragement to his troops:

'Peloponnesians, I imagine that you are terrified by our isolation 126 and the prospect of an attack by barbarians in large numbers: otherwise I should simply be giving you encouragement, and not a lecture as well. But as things are, in view of the desertion of our allies and the size of the force which faces us, I shall try with a few words of reminder and advice to impress on you the essential points. Your quality in battle should have nothing to do with the presence or absence of allies—it is a matter of your own native courage. Nor should you be frightened by mere numbers on the other side. You come from a different system. In regimes such as theirs it is not the many who govern the few, but the other way round, and these few have only won power for their family cliques by supremacy in war.

'Your present fear of these barbarians is due to inexperience. You should realize from your previous encounter with the Macedonians among them—and I can tell you from my own estimate and intelligence received from others—that they will not prove so fearsome. When an apparent strength in an enemy is in fact a weakness, a lesson on the truth of the matter will lend courage to their opponents rather than frighten them: whereas when one side is possessed of a firm inherent advantage, an adversary unaware of it will be over-confident in attack. To the inexperienced these barbarians seem to mean business in a frightening way—the fearful spectacle of their numbers, the unbearable volume of their war-cries, the empty brandishing of their weapons in a show of menace. But when it comes to active engagement with men who are immune to all this, it is a different story. They have no regular formation, and so feel no shame in abandoning a position under pressure. Where honour is concerned, flight or attack makes no difference to their reputation, so even their courage goes untested (and when each man is his own commander it is easy enough to find a good excuse for self-preservation). They obviously think it more effective to intimidate you from a safe distance than to engage hand to hand: if that were not so, their priorities would be reversed.

'Look clearly, then, and you can see that all the terror they create in advance, insistent though it may be on the eyes and ears, in fact amounts to very little. So stand your ground and take what comes, then as opportunity allows continue to retire with discipline and formation maintained, and you will reach safety all the sooner. And for future reference you will discover how rabbles like this behave. If you withstand their first attack, they vaunt their bravery at a distance, all threats and posturing: but if you give way, they are quick to display a safe courage in chasing at your heels.'

127   With these words of advice Brasidas began to withdraw his army. Seeing this, the barbarians charged forward with great yells in a disorderly mass, thinking that Brasidas was on the run and they could catch and destroy him. But the skirmishing parties ran out and met them wherever they attacked, and Brasidas with his picked troops withstood the main charge. So to their surprise the barbarians found their first onslaught resisted: and thereafter the Greeks met and beat back each subsequent wave of attack, and whenever there was a pause continued their retreat. In the end the barbarians pulled the bulk of their army away from Brasidas and the Greeks while they were still in open country, leaving a section to maintain their pursuit and harassment: with the rest they set off at the run after the fleeing Macedonians, killing any they caught up with, and reached the pass in time to secure it (this is the narrow pass into Arrhabaeus' territory which runs between two hills, and they knew that Brasidas had no other route for his retreat). As Brasidas was just about to reach the point of no return they began an encircling movement to cut him off.

128   He realized what was happening and told his three hundred to run as fast as they could, in open order, to the hill which he judged the easier to capture, and try to dislodge the barbarians already stationed on it, before they could be joined there by the larger encircling force. They attacked and defeated the men on the summit, and now the main body of the Greek army made its way up there without much difficulty. The barbarians had in fact taken fright when their men

lost the high ground in this defeat, and gave no further pursuit: they thought that the Greeks had now reached the border and had made good their escape. After gaining control of the high ground, Brasidas could proceed in greater safety, and on that same day he arrived at Arnisa, the first place in Perdiccas' kingdom.

His soldiers were angry on their own account at the premature retreat of the Macedonians, and whenever on the road they came across their ox-carts or any piece of baggage dropped (as naturally happened in a panic-stricken retreat at night), they unyoked the animals and slaughtered them, and appropriated the baggage. From that point on Perdiccas regarded Brasidas as an enemy and developed a lasting hatred for the Peloponnesians—given his experience of Athenian activity this was contrary to his usual inclination, but he ignored the dictates of his best interest and took steps to ensure as soon as possible agreement with the Athenians and dissociation from the Spartans.

On his return to Torone from Macedonia Brasidas found the 129 Athenians already in possession of Mende. Reckoning that it was now impossible for him to cross over to Pallene and intervene, he stayed in Torone inactive, but keeping the place under guard. At about the same time as his campaign in Lyncus the Athenians had put their preparations into effect and sailed against Mende and Scione with fifty ships (including ten from Chios), a thousand of their own hoplites, six hundred archers, a thousand Thracian mercenaries, and peltasts from their allies in the area: the generals in command were Nicias the son of Niceratus and Nicostratus the son of Diitrephes. Setting out in their ships from Potidaea they put in by the temple of Poseidon and marched against the Mendaeans. They had gone out and encamped in a strong position on a hill outside the city, together with three hundred Scionaeans who had come in their support and the Peloponnesian auxiliaries under their commander Polydamidas—a total of seven hundred hoplites. Nicias took with him a hundred and twenty light-armed troops from Methone, sixty picked Athenian hoplites, and all the archers in an attempt to reach them along a path up the hill, but they inflicted casualties on him and he was unable to force his way through. Nicostratus made another approach by a longer route with the rest of their forces, but the hill was hard to climb and the result was complete chaos—indeed the Athenian army came close to defeat. So on that day, with no submission by the Mendaeans and their allies, the Athenians withdrew and

made camp, and when night came the Mendaeans went back into
their city.

130   On the next day the Athenians sailed round to the side facing
Scione, captured the suburb, and spent the whole day ravaging the
land with no one coming out to oppose them (there was in fact some
political discord in the city): and in the course of that night the three
hundred Scionaeans returned home. On the following day Nicias
took half of the army and proceeded to ravage the land as far as the
border with Scione, while with the other half Nicostratus took up a
siege position by the upper gates of the city, where the road leads to
Potidaea. As it happened, this was where the Mendaeans and auxiliaries had their arms piled inside the wall, so Polydamidas formed up
his troops for battle and called on the Mendaeans to go out and fight.
One of the democrats, full of party fervour, shouted back that he was
not going out and had no cause to make war. As soon as the man had
spoken Polydamidas grabbed him by the arm and pulled him about.
At this the democrats immediately took up their weapons and turned
in fury on the Peloponnesians and the opposite party in league with
them. This onslaught routed them completely—it was both the sud-
denness of the attack and also their panic at seeing the gates thrown
open to the Athenians which made them think this was a preconcerted move. Those not killed on the spot fled to the acropolis, their
previous base. By now Nicias was back at the city, and the whole
Athenian army poured into Mende. As the opening of the gates had
not been a formal capitulation, they treated it as a city taken by force
of arms and sacked the entire place: and it was only with difficulty
that the generals prevented the slaughter of the inhabitants too.

After this the Athenians required the Mendaeans to keep their
previous constitution unchanged, and bring to trial in their own
courts any they considered responsible for the revolt. As for the men
on the acropolis, they blockaded them with walls built down to the
sea on either side, and installed a guard.

With the situation at Mende under control, they proceeded against
131   Scione. The Scionaeans and Peloponnesians had come out to face
them and established a strong position on a hill in front of the city,
so placed that it was impossible for their opponents to complete a
surrounding wall without taking the hill. The Athenians attacked in
full force and in the ensuing battle drove off the troops occupying the
hill: they then made camp, set up a trophy, and prepared for the
circumvallation of the city. Shortly afterwards, when this work was

already in progress, the auxiliaries blockaded on the acropolis at Mende forced through the guard by the sea and made their way to Scione during the night: most of them slipped past the Athenian army camped outside and got into the city.

While the wall was being built round Scione, Perdiccas contacted 132 the Athenian generals and came to an agreement with the Athenians (this was because of his hatred for Brasidas arising out of the retreat from Lyncus, and he had begun negotiations immediately after the retreat). It so happened that the Spartan Ischagoras was then on the point of bringing an army overland to reinforce Brasidas. When the agreement was made Nicias asked Perdiccas to give the Athenians some clear evidence of his reliability, and Perdiccas himself did not want any more Peloponnesians arriving in his country, so he exerted influence on his friends in Thessaly (he had always kept on good terms with the leading men there) and ensured that the army was blocked and the whole plan with it—so effectively that the Spartans did not even try for Thessalian cooperation. Nevertheless Ischagoras, Ameinias, and Aristeus did make their own way to Brasidas. The Spartans had sent them to supervise arrangements, and, quite contrary to usual practice, they brought with them from Sparta some of their younger men to be installed as governors of the cities, not wishing these appointments to be left to chance. And Brasidas appointed Clearidas the son of Cleonymus as governor of Amphipolis, and Pasitelidas the son of Hegesandrus in Torone.

In the same summer the Thebans demolished the walls of Thespiae, 133 charging the city with pro-Athenian sympathies. They had long wanted to do this, and now had a ready opportunity after the flower of the Thespian army had been killed in the battle against the Athenians.

Also in the same summer the temple of Hera at Argos burned down. The priestess Chrysis had placed a lighted lamp near the woollen fillets and then fallen asleep, so that the whole place had caught fire and was ablaze before she noticed. In fear of the Argive reaction Chrysis fled that very night to Phlius: and the Argives, following the procedure prescribed by law, appointed another priestess in her place, by name Phacinis. When Chrysis went into exile she had served as priestess over eight years of this war and halfway through the ninth.

Towards the end of the summer Scione had been completely ringed by a wall, and the Athenians withdrew the bulk of their army, leaving a garrison there.

134   In the following winter there was no action between Athenians and Spartans because of the truce. But a battle was fought between the Mantineans and the Tegeans and their respective allies at Laodoceium in the territory of Oresthis, with the victory disputed. Each side had defeated the opposing wing, and both set up trophies and sent spoils to Delphi. But although there were heavy casualties on both sides and the fight was evenly balanced, stopped only by the onset of night, the Tegeans encamped on the field and set up their trophy immediately, whereas the Mantineans withdrew to Boucolion before setting up their own rival trophy later.

135   At the end of this same winter, close on spring, Brasidas made an attempt on Potidaea. He approached by night and got a ladder up against the wall, undetected thus far—a sentry had just passed on the bell, and before he came back to his post the ladder was placed at the point he had vacated. But the guards noticed quickly enough, before Brasidas had the chance to climb up, and he hurriedly withdrew his army without waiting for daybreak.

So ended this winter, and with it the ninth year of this war chronicled by Thucydides.

BOOK FIVE

In the following summer the year's truce was extended until the Pythian games, and during this extension the Athenians evicted the Delians from Delos. They had now decided that some ancient offence meant that the Delians had not been ritually pure at the time of their consecration, and that this was a deficiency in the previous purification which I have described, when they thought they had satisfied the requirements by removing the graves of the dead. Pharnaces offered the Delians a home at Atramyttium in Asia, and any who so wished went and settled there.

When the truce had expired Cleon persuaded the Athenians to grant him a naval expedition to the Thraceward region, and sailed out there in thirty ships with twelve hundred Athenian hoplites and three hundred Athenian cavalry, and larger numbers from the allies. He put in first at Scione, which was still under siege, and took some of the hoplites from the garrison there to add to his forces: he then sailed into the Still Harbour in the territory of Torone not far from the city. Discovering from deserters that Brasidas was not at Torone and that the troops in the place were no match for his, he set out from there with his land army against the city and sent ten ships to sail round into the main harbour. He came first to the additional circuit-wall which Brasidas had built round the city to enclose the suburb also (he had then demolished part of the old wall to join suburb and city into one).

The Spartan governor Pasitelidas and what garrison he had came to defend the wall and attempted to resist the Athenian attack. But when they were weakening under pressure and the ships that had been sent round were now sailing into the harbour, Pasitelidas abandoned the wall and made back for the city at the run: his fear was that otherwise the ships would find the city undefended and take it, and that as the wall fell to the enemy he would be caught between wall and city. In fact he was too late. The Athenians from the ships had already taken Torone, and their infantry followed close on his heels without need for a fight and poured into the city, through the breach in the old wall, just behind him. They killed some of the Peloponnesians and Toronaeans on the spot in hand-to-hand fighting, and took others alive, including the governor Pasitelidas.

Brasidas set out to relieve Torone, but heard of its capture on his way and turned back. He had been within five miles of reaching the city in time. Cleon and the Athenians set up two trophies, one at the harbour and the other by the wall, and then dealt with the Toronaeans: they enslaved the women and children, and sent the men to Athens, together with the Peloponnesians and any other Chalcidians in the place—a total of seven hundred. The Peloponnesian element was subsequently released when the terms of peace were concluded, and the others were recovered by the Olynthians in a man-for-man exchange.

At about this same time the Athenian border-fort at Panactum was betrayed to the Boeotians and captured. Meanwhile Cleon installed a garrison in Torone, then put out and sailed round Athos, making for Amphipolis.

4   At about this time too Phaeax the son of Erasistratus and two fellow envoys sailed for Italy and Sicily on a mission from Athens. When the Athenians had left Sicily after the settlement there, Leontini had enrolled a large number of new citizens and the people were planning a redistribution of land. When they became aware of this the rich and powerful called in the Syracusans and drove out the common people to disperse wherever they could, while they themselves reached an agreement with the Syracusans whereby they deserted their own city, leaving it unpopulated, and took up residence in Syracuse with full citizen rights. Then later some of them regretted their move and left Syracuse, taking over a part of the city of Leontini called Phocaeae, and also the fort of Bricinniae in Leontinian territory. Here they were joined by the majority of the common people previously expelled, and once established they kept up constant war against Syracuse from these two fortified positions. It was on learning of this situation that the Athenians sent out Phaeax, in the hope of persuading their allies there and, if possible, the other Greek Sicilians to unite in a military response to what they saw as Syracusan expansionism, and thus to save the people of Leontini. Once there, Phaeax won over Camarina and Acragas, but failure at Gela made him realize that he would not be able to persuade the others, and he did not continue his approaches. He returned overland to Catana, passing through Sicel country and stopping at Bricinniae to encourage the Leontinians there: he then took ship from Catana.

5   On his voyage both to and from Sicily Phaeax negotiated with some of the Italian cities too about friendship with Athens. He also

came across the Locrian settlers who had been expelled from Messana. (After the agreement made among the Greek Sicilians, there had been internal dissension in Messana, and one of the parties had called in the Locrians: these men had been sent out as settlers, and for a time Messana belonged to Locri.) Phaeax encountered them as they were returning home after their expulsion, but did them no harm, as the Locrians had already made an agreement with him about a settlement with Athens. In the general reconciliation of the Greek Sicilians they alone of the allies had not agreed the treaty with Athens, nor would they have done so now if they did not have a war on their hands against Hipponium and Medma, neighbours and colonies of theirs. Some time later Phaeax arrived back in Athens.

Cleon had now sailed round from Torone against Amphipolis. With 6 Eïon as his base he made an unsuccessful attack on Stagirus, a colony of Andros, but did take by storm the Thasian colony of Galepsus. He sent envoys to Perdiccas, asking him to come with an army according to the terms of the alliance, and others to Polles, the king of the Odomantians in Thrace: these were to bring back with them as many Thracian mercenaries as they could. He then stayed waiting and otherwise inactive in Eïon.

Brasidas heard of these plans and responded by taking up a counter-position on Cerdylium. This is a piece of high ground in Argilian territory the other side of the river, not far from Amphipolis, with a clear prospect all round, so that he could not fail to notice if—as he thought likely—Cleon made a move with his army: he reckoned that Cleon would take a dismissive view of the Spartan numbers and advance inland against Amphipolis with his existing forces. He was meanwhile making his own preparations, calling in fifteen hundred Thracian mercenaries and the entire Edonian force of peltasts and cavalry: he already had a thousand peltasts from Myrcinus and the Chalcidians as well as those in Amphipolis. The total hoplite complement assembled was about two thousand, and three hundred Greek cavalry. Some fifteen hundred of these took up position on Cerdylium with Brasidas, and the rest were marshalled in Amphipolis under Clearidas.

For a while Cleon made no move, but then he was forced to do 7 what Brasidas expected. His soldiers were chafing at the inactivity and comparing the quality of his leadership with that which it would meet on the other side—incompetence and timidity against skill and daring: and into the reckoning they added the reluctance they had

felt to serve under him when the expedition left Athens. Cleon
became aware of their grumbles and saw the need to relieve the bore-
dom of confinement in one place: so he led them out. Success at
Pylos had left him with a conviction of his own shrewdness, and that
was his attitude now. He was confident that no one would come out
and offer battle, and told his troops that this was more of a reconnaissance expedition while he waited for the reinforcements to arrive:
and his purpose in waiting, he said, was not to ensure a safe margin
of superiority if compelled to fight, but to be able to surround the
city completely and take it by storm. So he marched out and established his army on a commanding hill in front of Amphipolis, from
where he could survey for himself the marshy stretch of the Strymon
and the lie of the city on the side towards Thrace. He thought that
he could go back whenever he wanted, without a fight: there was no
sign of anyone on the walls or coming out of the gates—they were all
closed. In fact he regretted not bringing siege-engines with him on
his way up, as he thought the city was undefended and he could have
taken it there and then.

8   As soon as Brasidas had seen the Athenians on the move he had
come down from Cerdylium in response and entered Amphipolis.
He was not going to march out against the Athenians in full line of
battle, as he doubted his own resources and thought his troops
inferior—not in numbers (they were about equal), but in quality, as
the Athenian force sent out on this expedition consisted purely of
citizens, together with the best of the Lemnians and Imbrians. So he
worked out a stratagem for his offensive, reckoning that if he allowed
his opponents a clear view of the actual numbers he had with him
and the basic nature of their equipment he would have less chance of
success than by a surprise attack before they had any advance sight
of his forces—and therefore would have no good reason to assume
superiority. So he made a personal selection of a hundred and fifty
hoplites, assigning the rest to the command of Clearidas, with the
intention of making a sudden attempt on the Athenians before they
had time to leave: he realized that he would not have another similar
chance to catch them on their own, once their reinforcements had
arrived. So he called together all his troops to encourage them and
explain his thinking, and spoke as follows:

9   'Peloponnesians, I need hardly remind you of the obvious: that we
come from a country that has always been free, and the root of this
freedom is courage; and that you are Dorians about to fight Ionians,

with a long history of success against them. I shall, though, explain my plan of attack, as I would not want you to be discouraged by what might appear an inadequate response, when just a few of us take the field rather than all of us together. I imagine that our opponents came up here with an assumption of superiority and confident that no one would go out to offer them battle, and have now abandoned formation and turned to sightseeing in continued disregard of us. Now the successful general is quick to spot such mistakes on the part of the enemy and chooses a strategy which plays to his own strength—not necessarily an open attack in full line of battle, but one which exploits the advantage of the moment. These are the tricks of war and win great acclaim when the enemy is completely fooled to the maximum benefit of one's own side.

'So while they are still unprepared and complacent, and, from what I can see, more inclined to withdraw than to stay in position, before their present vagueness of intent sharpens into some firm purpose I shall take my section and forestall them, if I can, with an attack at the run on the very centre of their army. And then, Clearidas, the next move is up to you. As soon as you see me fall on them, which I hope and expect will cause panic, you must suddenly open the gates and charge out with the Amphipolitans and the other allies under your command, running as fast as you can to engage. This should complete their panic, as the second wave of attack is always more terrifying to the enemy than the force which is already there and fighting them.

'Show your quality, then, Clearidas, as a true Spartiate. And you, my allied friends, follow him bravely. Remember the three essentials of success in war—determination, honour, discipline. Remember too that this day holds your future. Either, if you prove yourselves good men and true, your freedom and a name as allies of the Spartans, or else you must be called slaves of the Athenians. You may at best escape being sold or executed, but your slavery will be yet harsher than before, and you will have set back the cause of liberation for the rest of Greece. You can see how much is at stake, so let me have no faint hearts: and I shall show you that I do not just tell others what to do, but can follow it through in action myself.'

After giving this address Brasidas prepared for his own sortie and positioned the others with Clearidas at the so-called Thracian Gates, ready for their attack as instructed. He had been seen coming down from Cerdylium, and, since the interior of Amphipolis was clearly visible from outside, could be seen now in the city sacrificing at the temple of Athena and making these preparations. At the time Cleon had gone on ahead to reconnoitre, but word was brought to him that the entire enemy army was in full view in the city, and that the feet of many men and horses could be seen under the gates, evidently ready to come out. Hearing this, Cleon came to the spot and saw for himself. Reluctant to fight a decisive battle before the arrival of his reinforcements, and thinking that he could get away in good time, he gave the signal for retreat, and as his troops prepared to leave sent orders that the withdrawal towards Eïon should start off (as was the only possible way) from the left wing. He thought he had plenty of time, so he himself made a quarter-turn with the right wing and began to lead his army away with their unshielded side exposed to the enemy.

At this point Brasidas, seeing the Athenian army on the move, saw his opportunity also. He said to his own section and the rest of the force, 'These men will not stand and face us. I can see it in the jostle of their spears and heads. When troops behave like that, it usually means that they will not withstand an attack. So let me have the gates opened where I said, and let us be out and at them as quick as we can. We can be confident of victory.'

Brasidas then went out by the gate leading to the palisade (this was the first gate in the long wall as it then extended) and ran at speed up the main road, where there now stands a trophy as you reach the steepest part of the hill. He then attacked the Athenian centre. They were already nervous because of their own disorder, and now panic-stricken by the audacity of his attack. He routed them. And now Clearidas, as instructed, came out through the Thracian Gates and bore down on the Athenian army at the same time. The unexpected and sudden double attack threw the Athenians into disarray. Their left wing facing Eïon, which had already gone ahead, immediately broke away and continued to retreat. With that wing now withdrawing from the action Brasidas harried the right wing, and was wounded in the course of this attack. The Athenians did not notice that he had fallen, and his own men near him took him up and carried him out of the battle.

The Athenians on the right wing were more inclined to stand and fight. Cleon himself, who from the start had never intended to stand his ground, fled immediately and was overtaken and killed by a peltast from Myrcinus. But his hoplites rallied on the hill, beat back

Clearidas' attacks two or three times, and would not give in until they were surrounded by the Myrcinian and Chalcidian cavalry and the peltasts, and forced to flee by the volleys of javelins. So now the whole Athenian army had been put to flight. The survivors, those who had not been killed in the immediate close fighting or subsequently by the Chalcidian cavalry and the peltasts, eventually reached Eïon after a difficult and circuitous trek through the mountains.

Brasidas was still alive when he was brought into the city by the men who had come to his rescue and carried him out of the battle. He lived to hear the news that his troops were victorious, and died shortly afterwards. The rest of the army returned from the pursuit with Clearidas, stripped the enemy dead, and set up a trophy.

After this Brasidas was given a state funeral in the city: the whole 11 body of the allies formed a procession in full armour and buried him in front of what is now the agora. The Amphipolitans created a precinct round his tomb, and ever since then they make offerings to him as a hero, and have instituted games and annual sacrifices in his honour. They also adopted him as the founder of their colony, demolishing the buildings erected to honour Hagnon and obliterating any other potentially lasting memorials of his foundation. They regarded Brasidas as their saviour, and a further motive at the time for cultivating their Spartan alliance was fear of the Athenians: now that they were in a state of enmity with Athens they thought that paying founder's honours to Hagnon would be less in their interest, and less to their taste.

They gave back their dead to the Athenians. About six hundred Athenians had been killed, but only seven on the other side: this was because it was never a battle fought in regular formation but more the result, as described, of opportunistic use of circumstance and a panic-making pre-emptive attack. After recovering the dead the Athenians sailed for home, and Clearidas and his colleagues turned to the administration of Amphipolis.

At about this same time, towards the end of summer, a supporting 12 force of nine hundred hoplites was on its way to the Thraceward area under the command of the Spartans Rhamphias, Autocharidas, and Epicydidas. When they reached Heracleia in Trachis they spent some time reforming what they saw as faults in the system there, and were still occupied in Heracleia when the battle took place at Amphipolis. So the summer ended.

At the very beginning of the following winter Rhamphias and his 13 troops proceeded through Thessaly as far as Pierium. But as the

Thessalians were not inclined to let them go further, and as Brasidas, the intended beneficiary of this expedition, was now dead, they turned back for home. They thought there was no longer any purpose they could serve: the Athenians had been defeated and gone away, and they did not feel competent to carry out any of the plans which Brasidas himself had been intending. But their main reason for turning back was that they were aware even when they set out that the Spartans had their minds predominantly on peace.

14   What happened in fact was that immediately after the battle at Amphipolis and Rhamphias' withdrawal from Thessaly neither side took any action to prolong the war, and both turned their thoughts to peace. The Athenians had suffered two blows, at Delium and shortly afterwards again at Amphipolis, and they had lost that confident trust in their own strength which had led them to reject the previous offer of a treaty, when they thought their run of good fortune at the time would bring them ultimate success. They were afraid too that their setbacks would excite further defections among their allies, and they regretted that they had not come to terms after the Pylos affair, when they could have done so with advantage.

The Spartans likewise had their reasons. The war was not going according to plan, as they had expected to break Athenian power within a few years if they ravaged their land; they had met with the disaster on the island, something unprecedented in Spartan history; there were raids on their territory from Pylos and Cythera; the Helots were deserting, and there was always the prospect that those who remained would be supported by their friends abroad in seizing the present opportunity to revolt, as had happened before. A further circumstance was that their thirty-year treaty with the Argives was about to expire, and the Argives would not renew it if the land of Cynouria was not returned to them: the Spartans thought it impossible to fight Argos and Athens at the same time. They also suspected that some of the Peloponnesian cities would defect to the Argives—as in fact they did.

15   Such considerations on both sides decided them that they should come to terms. The Spartans were particularly keen because of their desire to recover the men captured on the island—the Spartiates among these prisoners were men of the first rank, with relatives of equally high status. They had begun negotiations immediately after their capture, but with all going well for them the Athenians were not at the time willing to end the war on reasonable terms. After the

Athenian debacle at Delium the Spartans reckoned that they would now be more receptive, and so were quick to conclude the one-year truce, in the course of which the two sides were to meet for discussion of the longer future.

Then the Athenians had suffered the further defeat at Amphipolis 16 and both Cleon and Brasidas had been killed, the two men on either side who were most opposed to the peace—Brasidas because the war was bringing him success and reputation, and Cleon because he knew that in peacetime his own mischief would be more evident and his denigration of others less credible. In this situation the main contenders for political power in the two cities—Pleistoanax the son of Pausanias, king of Sparta, and Nicias the son of Niceratus, the most successful Athenian general of his day—became yet more enthusiastic for an end to the war. Nicias wanted to preserve his good fortune while he was still undefeated and held in high regard, to enjoy immediate rest from his own labours and give rest to his fellow citizens as well, and to be known in future time as a man who never brought failure on his city. He thought the key to this was lack of risk, and minimal exposure to chance: and lack of risk came with peace.

Pleistoanax's motive was the embarrassment his opponents were causing him over his return from exile, constantly playing on the religious misgivings of the Spartans by bringing up this issue whenever there were setbacks and attributing them to the illegality of his return. (Their allegation was that he and his brother Aristocles had suborned the priestess at Delphi to keep on responding to any Spartan delegates who came to consult the oracle that 'they must bring back the seed of the demigod son of Zeus from a foreign land to their own, or else they would plough with a silver ploughshare'. Eventually the Spartans were persuaded to take action. Pleistoanax had been exiled on suspicion of bribery when he had invaded Attica and then withdrawn: he had taken refuge on Mount Lycaeum, and lived there in a house which at the time was half inside the sanctuary of Zeus—this was because he was afraid of the Spartans. In the nineteenth year they brought him back to the accompaniment of the same dances and sacrifices as when they inaugurated the kings at the original foundation of Sparta.) Pleistoanax, then, was tired of 17 this carping and reckoned that peace, when there would be no setbacks and the Spartans would also have secured the return of the men from the island, should bring him personal immunity from his opponents, whereas in a state of war it was inevitable that the leading men would always be blamed for disasters: so he became anxious for a settlement.

Discussions were held throughout this winter. As time moved on towards spring the Spartans sounded a warning note by sending round instructions to their allied cities to prepare for the building of a fort in enemy territory: this was intended to concentrate Athenian minds. Then after conferences full of claims and counter-claims it was finally agreed between them to make peace on the basis that each side should give back what they had won in war, but that the Athenians should retain Nisaea. (The reason for this was that when the Athenians made their claim for the return of Plataea, the Thebans objected on the grounds that the place had come into their hands through a voluntary surrender, not by force of arms or betrayal: to which the Athenians replied that the same was true of their possession of Nisaea.) The Spartans now called a meeting of their own allies and put it to the vote: except for the Boeotians, the Corinthians, the Eleans, and the Megarians, who were dissatisfied with the terms arranged, all others were in favour of an end to the war. So they made the agreement and formally ratified and swore to a treaty with the Athenians, and the Athenians with the Spartans likewise. This is the text of the treaty:

18 A treaty was made by the Athenians and by the Spartans and their allies on the following terms, to which they swore city by city:

Concerning the common sanctuaries, any who wish shall be free to sacrifice there and travel there and consult the oracles and visit on a delegation, according to established custom, both by land and by sea, without fear. The sanctuary and temple of Apollo at Delphi and the people of Delphi shall be autonomous and shall have full control of their own taxation and their own courts, as regards both themselves and their territory, according to established custom.

The treaty shall be for fifty years between the Athenians and the allies of the Athenians and the Spartans and the allies of the Spartans, and shall be observed both by land and by sea without fraud or violation.

Neither side shall be permitted to bring force of arms with harmful intent against the other by any means or contrivance, neither the Spartans and their allies against the Athenians and their allies nor the Athenians and their allies against the Spartans and their allies. Should any dispute arise between them, they shall have resort to judicial process and affidavits, in whatever way is mutually agreed.

The Spartans and their allies shall restore Amphipolis to the Athenians. In those cities which the Spartans have handed over to the Athenians, people shall be free to leave for wherever they wish and to take their property with them. The following cities shall be autonomous on condition of paying the tribute assessed at the time of Aristeides, and it shall not be permitted for the Athenians or their allies to bring force of arms to their detriment as long as they pay this tribute, now that the treaty has been made: these cities are Argilus, Stagirus, Acanthus, Scolus, Olynthus, Spartolus. These shall be allies of neither side, neither of the Spartans nor of the Athenians: but if the Athenians so persuade the cities, with their consent the Athenians shall be permitted to make them allies.

The people of Mecyberna, Sane, and Singus shall have possession of their own cities in the same way as the people of Olynthus and Acanthus.

The Spartans and their allies shall restore Panactum to the Athenians. The Athenians shall restore to the Spartans Coryphasium, Cythera, Methana, Pteleum, and Atalante; and shall return all Spartans held in the public prison in Athens or in a public prison anywhere else under Athenian rule; and shall release the Peloponnesians besieged in Scione, all other Spartan allies in Scione, and all those sent in by Brasidas; they shall release also any allies of the Spartans in the public prison in Athens or in a public prison anywhere else under Athenian rule. The Spartans and their allies shall likewise return any of the Athenians and their allies whom they hold.

In the case of Scione, Torone, Sermyle, and any other city now held by the Athenians, the Athenians shall decide as they see fit concerning the inhabitants of these and the other cities.

The Athenians shall swear oaths to the Spartans and their allies city by city. Each party shall take the oath which is most binding in their local observance, and seventeen men shall swear from each city. The form of the oath shall be as follows: 'I shall abide by this agreement and this treaty with all justice and honesty.' The oath sworn by the Spartans and their allies to the Athenians shall be identical. Both sides shall renew the oath annually. Pillars of record shall be set up at Olympia, Delphi, and the Isthmus, at Athens on the Acropolis and at Sparta in the Amyclaeum.

If either side has failed to include any point on any issue, it shall be consistent with these oaths on both sides to hold proper consultation and make such amendment to this treaty as is agreed by both sides, the Athenians and the Spartans.

The treaty shall take effect from the following date: in Sparta, in the 19 ephorate of Pleistolas, the fourth day before the end of the month Artemisium; in Athens, in the archonship of Alcaeus, the sixth day before the end of the month Elaphebolion.

The following swore the oaths and poured the libations to ratify the treaty. Of the Spartans: Pleistoanax, Agis, Pleistolas, Damagetus, Chionis, Metagenes, Acanthus, Daïthus, Ischagoras, Philocharidas, Zeuxidas, Antippus, Tellis, Alcinadas, Empedias, Menas, Laphilus. Of the Athenians the following: Lampon, Isthmionicus, Nicias, Laches, Euthydemus, Procles, Pythodorus, Hagnon, Myrtilus, Thrasycles, Theogenes, Aristocrates, Iolcius, Timocrates, Leon, Lamachus, Demosthenes.

20   This treaty was made at the end of winter and the start of spring, immediately after the City Dionysia: exactly ten years had passed, plus a few days, since the beginning of this war. (One should reckon the time by seasons, and not rely on a name-count of the archons or other office-holders in the various cities by whose tenure past events are dated: this method lacks precision, as any given event may have happened at the beginning, in the middle, or at any other point in a term of office. If one counts by summers and winters, as in the narrative here written, with each period being the equivalent of half a year, it will be found that there were ten summers and ten winters in this first war.)

21   It fell by lot to the Spartans to make restitution first. They immediately released the prisoners they held, and sent Ischagoras, Menas, and Philocharidas as envoys to the Thraceward area, to instruct Clearidas to hand over Amphipolis to the Athenians and the others to comply with the terms of the treaty specific to them. But they thought the treaty against their interests and refused: Clearidas too, influenced in favour of the Chalcidians, would not hand over the city, claiming that it was not in his power to do so without their agreement. He himself went directly to Sparta with representatives from the region, to defend himself against any charges of insubordination brought by Ischagoras and his colleagues: he also wanted to know if it was still possible to modify the treaty. He found that the Spartans' hands were tied. They sent him back with instructions to comply fully by handing over the place, or failing that at least to withdraw all the Peloponnesian forces stationed there. He then hurried back on his own.

22   When the allies were convened once more in Sparta, the Spartans urged participation in the treaty on those who had refused to accept it. These gave the same reasons for rejection as before, and said they could only agree a treaty on fairer terms. Having failed to persuade them, the Spartans dismissed their allies and proceeded independently of them to negotiate an alliance with the Athenians. They thought that this would minimize the likelihood of any attack on them by the Argives (who had refused to renew the treaty between them when Ampelidas and Lichas had gone to Argos for that purpose), and that without Athenian aid the Argives on their own would pose no great threat: they saw this also as the best means of ensuring

stability in the rest of the Peloponnese, where there would otherwise be defections to Athens, if that were open. There were envoys from the Athenians in Sparta at the time, and so talks were held and an agreement reached. The record of the oaths taken and the terms of the alliance is as follows:

These are the terms on which the Spartans and the Athenians shall be 23 allies for fifty years.

If any people enter Spartan territory with hostile intent and do harm to the Spartans, the Athenians shall assist the Spartans with all possible force to the best of their ability: and if such people ravage the territory and then depart, their city shall be declared an enemy of the Spartans and the Athenians and shall suffer retribution at the hands of both, and neither city shall cease hostilities before the other. This cooperation shall be fair, prompt, and honest.

And if any people enter Athenian territory with hostile intent and do harm to the Athenians, the Spartans shall assist the Athenians with all possible force to the best of their ability: and if such people ravage the territory and then depart, their city shall be declared an enemy of the Spartans and the Athenians and shall suffer retribution at the hands of both, and neither city shall cease hostilities before the other. This cooperation shall be fair, prompt, and honest.

If the slave population revolts, the Athenians shall aid the Spartans with all their strength to the best of their ability.

Oaths to this effect shall be taken by the same persons on each side who swore to the other treaty also. The oath shall be renewed annually: for this purpose the Spartans shall go to Athens for the Dionysia and the Athenians shall go to Sparta for the Hyacinthia. Each party shall set up a pillar of record, that in Sparta in the temple of Apollo at Amyclae and that in Athens on the Acropolis in the temple of Athena.

If the Spartans and the Athenians decide on any addition to or deletion from this treaty of alliance, it shall be consistent with their oaths to make any such amendment as is agreed by both parties.

The oaths were sworn by the following. Of the Spartans: Pleistoanax, 24 Agis, Pleistolas, Damagetus, Chionis, Metagenes, Acanthus, Daïthus, Ischagoras, Philocharidas, Zeuxidas, Antippus, Alcinadas, Tellis, Empedias, Menas, Laphilus. Of the Athenians: Lampon, Isthmionicus, Laches, Nicias, Euthydemus, Procles, Pythodorus, Hagnon, Myrtilus, Thrasycles, Theogenes, Aristocrates, Iolcius, Timocrates, Leon, Lamachus, Demosthenes.

This alliance was made not long after the peace-treaty; the Athenians gave back to the Spartans the men captured on the island; and the summer of the eleventh year began.

The history of the first war, which lasted continuously for these ten years, has now been written.

25   After the treaty and alliance between the Spartans and the Athenians had been concluded at the end of the ten years' war (this was in the ephorate of Pleistolas in Sparta and the archonship of Alcaeus in Athens), those who had accepted the treaty were at peace, but the Corinthians and some of the Peloponnesian cities kept up agitation against the terms agreed, and quickly enough there was trouble once more in Sparta's relations with her allies. As time went on the Athenians too had cause to mistrust the Spartans for their failure to implement several specific stipulations in the agreement. For six years and ten months the two sides refrained from military operations against the other's territory, but elsewhere the truce had only tenuous effect and they continued to inflict as much damage on each other as they could. In the end they had no choice but to abandon the treaty made after those ten years and resort once more to open war.

26   Thucydides of Athens has written this subsequent history also, setting out the events in chronological order, by summers and winters, up to the destruction of the Athenian empire and the capture of the Long Walls and the Peiraeus by the Spartans and their allies. The total duration of the war to this final point was twenty-seven years. And if anyone claims that the intervening period of agreement cannot be counted as war, the facts will not justify his contention. Let him look at the reality defining this period, and he will find that 'peace' is hardly a reasonable description of a state of affairs in which there had been no full return or recovery of the places specified in the agreement, when moreover there were infringements on both sides in the Mantinean and Epidaurian campaigns among others, the Thraceward allies remained at war with Athens, and the Boeotians would only observe a ten-day truce. So adding together the first ten years' war, the uneasy truce which followed, and the further open warfare after that, if one reckons the duration by seasons one will reach the exact number of years I have given, plus a few days. (One will also find this the only instance in which assertions based on oracles have proved true to the actual outcome: I remember how from the very beginning of the war to its end a popular belief was constantly put about that it must last for 'thrice nine years'.) I lived through the whole of the war, studying it with mature perception and in the intellectual pursuit of an accurate understanding of events.

The fact that I was in exile from my own country for twenty years after my command against Amphipolis gave me the opportunity to observe affairs on both sides (exile adding the Peloponnesian perspective), and to reflect on them in relative calm. So I shall now give an account of the breakdown and collapse of the treaty after those ten years, and then describe the subsequent course of the war.

After the conclusion of the fifty-year treaty, followed by the 27 alliance, the delegations from the Peloponnese summoned for that purpose began to leave Sparta. Most went home, but the Corinthians first turned aside to Argos and held discussions with some members of the Argive government. Their argument was that in making a treaty and an alliance with the Athenians—until then their greatest enemies—the Spartans' motive was not to benefit the Peloponnese but to enslave it. It was therefore incumbent on the Argives to look to the salvation of the Peloponnese. They should pass a decree allowing any independent Greek city prepared to deal on fair and equal terms to enter into a defensive alliance with Argos. Such applications should be heard by a few commissioners specially appointed with full executive powers: they should not be brought before the general assembly, to avoid public knowledge of an application made but rejected by the people. The Corinthians gave their opinion that hatred of the Spartans would bring many into such an alliance. Having recommended this course of action, they returned home.

The Argives privy to this discussion referred the proposal to the 28 authorities and the people. A decree was passed, and the Argives appointed a commission of twelve men through whom any of the Greeks who so wished could enter into alliance, except for the Athenians and the Spartans: terms with either of these could not be made without the consent of the Argive people. The Argives were the more ready to agree this proposal because they could see war coming with the Spartans (their treaty with them was on the point of expiry), and also they had conceived the hope of hegemony in the Peloponnese. At this time Sparta's reputation had sunk very low and her failures excited contempt, whereas the Argives were at the height of their fortune in every way: they had reaped the benefit of non-involvement in the war with Athens and of treaty relations with both sides. So for these reasons the Argives were ready to offer their alliance to those of the Greeks who wished to enter it.

The first to come over to Argos were the Mantineans and their 29 allies, out of fear of the Spartans. During the war against Athens the

Mantineans had forcibly subjected a part of Arcadia, and they thought that the Spartans, especially now that they were free of other concerns, would not tolerate their continued control of this territory: so they gladly turned to Argos, seeing it as a powerful city always at variance with Sparta, and a democracy like their own. The secession of Mantinea caused a stir in the rest of the Peloponnese, with talk of following this example. There was a belief that the Mantineans had made their move on privileged information, and in any case there was general anger against the Spartans, not least for the clause in the treaty with Athens providing that it should be consistent with their oaths to make any addition to or deletion from the treaty as might be agreed between the two cities, Sparta and Athens. This clause was the source of major disquiet in the Peloponnese, and created the suspicion that the Spartans were in league with the Athenians to enslave them: in their view the provision for amendment of the treaty should properly have been drafted to include the whole confederacy. Such fears impelled the majority to follow the lead and make their own alliance with the Argives.

30   The Spartans were aware that this talk was prevalent in the Peloponnese: they knew too that the Corinthians were the ringleaders and intended to make a treaty with Argos themselves. Wanting to forestall events, they sent envoys to Corinth and complained of their instigation of the whole business and their apparent intention to secede from Sparta and become allies of the Argives: this, they said, would be a violation of their oaths, and they were in any case already at fault for not accepting the treaty with Athens, when it was an explicit condition of the League that a majority vote of the allies was binding unless debarred by duty to gods or heroes. The Corinthians had with them the other allies who also rejected the treaty (having summoned them in advance), and replied to the Spartans in their presence. They gave no direct indication of their real grounds for complaint, which were the failure of the Spartans to secure for them from the Athenians the return of either Sollium or Anactorium, and some other ways too in which they thought themselves disadvantaged. Instead they put forward the pretext that they could not betray their friends in the Thraceward area: they pointed out that when these first joined the Potidaeans in revolt Corinth had independently sworn support, and followed that with further oaths later. So they argued that their refusal to enter the treaty with Athens was no violation of their oaths to the League; they had sworn their faith to these

others in the name of the gods, and they would be false to their oaths
if they betrayed them; the wording was 'unless debarred by duty to
gods or heroes', and they considered this a religious debarment. Such
was the case they made of their pre-existing commitments: as for the
alliance with Argos, they said they would consult their friends and do
whatever was right. The Spartan envoys now returned home.

Coincidentally there were in Corinth envoys from Argos also,
urging the Corinthians to enter their alliance without more delay. The
Corinthians told them to attend the next meeting of their assembly.

Very soon afterwards there arrived an embassy from Elis too. 31
They first made an alliance with the Corinthians, then moved on to
Argos and became allies of the Argives by the means prescribed. The
reason for this was a quarrel with the Spartans over Lepreum. War
had broken out in the past between the Lepreans and some of the
Arcadians; the Lepreans had called in the Eleans to fight on their side
with the offer of half of their territory; on the conclusion of this war
the Eleans allowed the Lepreans to retain all of their own land on
payment of a rent to Zeus at Olympia set at one talent. The Lepreans
paid this rent until the war with Athens, then used the war as an
excuse to stop: the Eleans put pressure on them, and the Lepreans
appealed to the Spartans, who agreed to arbitrate. Suspecting that
they would not be fairly treated, the Eleans rejected the arbitration
and proceeded to ravage Leprean territory. The Spartans nevertheless ruled that Lepreum was an independent state, and the Eleans
were at fault: and on the grounds that the Eleans had failed to abide
by the arbitration they sent a hoplite garrison into Lepreum. The
Eleans considered that the Spartans had thus accepted the defection
of one of their cities, and referred to the clause in the agreement
which stated that all parties in the war with Athens should retain at
the end of the war the same territory which they possessed when they
entered it. Thinking themselves unfairly done by, they now seceded
to Argos and joined the alliance in the way prescribed.

Immediately after them the Corinthians also and the Chalcidians
in the Thraceward area became allies of the Argives. The Boeotians,
though, and the Megarians took the same line and stayed aloof, keeping
an eye on the Spartan reaction and recognizing that Argive democracy was less compatible with their own oligarchic governments
than the constitution of Sparta.

At about the same time in this summer the Athenians succeeded 32
in taking Scione by siege: they killed the grown men, enslaved the

children and women, and granted occupation of the land to the Plataeans. They also reinstated the Delians on Delos, cautioned both by their own military failures and by an oracle from the god at Delphi.

At this time too war broke out between the Phocians and the Locrians.

The Corinthians and the Argives, now allies, came to Tegea with the intention of securing its secession from Sparta: they recognized the important part it played, and thought that with Tegea on their side they would control the whole of the Peloponnese. When the Tegeans stated that they would do nothing to oppose Sparta, the Corinthians, all optimism so far, lost some of their campaigning zeal and were struck by the fear that none of the others would now come over to them. Even so, they approached the Boeotians and urged them to ally themselves with Corinth and Argos and join them in all matters of general policy. They also asked the Boeotians to accompany them to Athens and obtain for them too the same ten-day truce which had been effected between the Athenians and the Boeotians shortly after the conclusion of the fifty-year treaty: if the Athenians refused, the Boeotians should renounce their truce and make no further agreement independently of the Corinthians. In response to these requests the Boeotians told the Corinthians that the question of an Argive alliance would have to wait, but they did go with them to Athens, where they failed to obtain the desired ten-day truce: the Athenian answer was that the Corinthians already had a treaty, if indeed they were allies of the Spartans. The Boeotians took no consequent action to renounce their own ten-day truce, despite the demands of the Corinthians and their protestations that this had been agreed. There remained an armistice between Corinth and Athens, but without formal ratification.

33   In this same summer the Spartans, led by their king Pleistoanax the son of Pausanias, launched an expedition in full force to Parrhasia, a part of Arcadia which was subject to the Mantineans. They had been called in by one side in a political struggle, and they also wanted, if possible, to demolish the fort at Cypsela, which the Mantineans had built and garrisoned with their own men: this fort, in Parrhasian territory, was a threat to the Sciritis region of Laconia. The Spartans began to ravage the Parrhasian land, and the Mantineans, leaving their own city under the guard of a force from Argos, went out to defend their allied territory, but returned home when they were unable to save the fort at Cypsela or retain control of the cities in Parrhasia.

The Spartans also went home after restoring independence to the Parrhasians and demolishing the fort.

Also in this same summer, now that the troops which had gone out 34 to the Thraceward area with Brasidas were returned, brought back after the peace-treaty by Clearidas, the Spartans voted to free the Helots who had fought under Brasidas and allow them to live where they wished: shortly afterwards, in view of the quarrel which had developed with the Eleans, they settled them, together with previously liberated cohorts, in Lepreum, on the border between Laconia and Elis. They also dealt with the men who had been captured on the island and surrendered their arms. Their fear was that, if they retained their civic rights, these men might be led to revolutionary measures by the expectation of adverse treatment for what had happened: they therefore disenfranchised them, including some who were in official positions at the time. This involved the removal of all rights to hold office or to buy or sell any property. Some time later these rights were restored to them.

In this same summer too the people of Dium captured Thyssus, a 35 city on Acte, the Mount Athos peninsula. Thyssus was an ally of the Athenians.

Throughout the whole of this summer there continued open communication between Athens and the Peloponnese, but immediately after the peace-treaty the Athenians and the Spartans conceived a mutual mistrust arising from the failure to return to each other the places specified in the treaty. The Spartans had drawn the lot to make restitution first, but they had not given back Amphipolis among other places, nor were they ensuring acceptance of the treaty by their Thraceward allies, the Boeotians, or the Corinthians: they kept on declaring that if this refusal continued they would enforce acceptance jointly with the Athenians, and proposed dates (though without written agreement) by which any not entering the treaty should be declared enemies of both sides. Seeing none of this coming to practical effect, the Athenians began to suspect the Spartans of no honourable intention, and so refused their demand for the return of Pylos (even regretting now the release of the prisoners from the island) and held on to the other places in their control until the Spartans too had performed their part of the agreement. The Spartans claimed that they had done all they could. They had returned the Athenian prisoners they held, they had withdrawn their troops from the Thraceward region, and done all else in their power. In Amphipolis, they said, they did not have sufficient authority to hand over the city: but they would try to bring the Boeotians and Corinthians within the treaty, to get back Panactum, and to secure the recovery of all Athenian prisoners held in Boeotia. They still insisted, though, on the return of Pylos, or at least the withdrawal of the Messenians and the Helots, just as they had withdrawn their troops from Thrace, in which case the Athenians could maintain their own garrison in the place, should they wish. After many lengthy negotiations over this summer they persuaded the Athenians to withdraw the Messenians from Pylos together with all the Helots, including those who had deserted there from Laconia: the Athenians settled the Helots in Cranii on Cephallenia.

So for this summer there was peace and diplomacy between the two sides.

36   But by the following winter there was in office a different set of ephors from that under which the peace-treaty was concluded, and some of these were actually opposed to the treaty. In this winter embassies from the Peloponnesian alliance came to Sparta for a conference attended also by the Athenians, Boeotians, and Corinthians. Much was said between them and nothing agreed. But as the delegates returned home, Cleoboulus and Xenares, who were the ephors most intent on dissolving the treaty, held private talks with the Boeotian and Corinthian envoys, recommending a close coordination of policy in the effort to persuade Boeotia first to ally with Argos and then, with the help of Corinth, to bring Argos into alliance with Sparta. This would remove any pressure on the Boeotians to join the treaty with Athens, as the Spartans would gladly trade the hostility of the Athenians and the dissolution of the treaty for friendship and alliance with Argos. The ephors knew that the Spartans had always desired a satisfactory accommodation with Argos, on the grounds that this would give them greater freedom to conduct a war outside the Peloponnese. Panactum, though, was an issue: the ephors wanted the Boeotians to hand it over to the Spartans, to make a possible exchange for Pylos and so facilitate the resumption of war with Athens.

37   With these instructions from Xenares and Cleoboulus and their supporters in Sparta, the Boeotian and Corinthian envoys set out for home to report, as agreed, to their respective governments. On their way back two Argive officials of the highest rank who had been watching for them on the road met them and discussed with them

their hope that Boeotia would join Corinth, Elis, and Mantinea in alliance with Argos: if that went ahead, their view was that such a coalition would then be free to make war or peace at will with the Spartans or anyone else as need might be. The Boeotian envoys were delighted to hear this, as by happy coincidence the Argives were asking for exactly what their friends in Sparta had charged them to achieve. For their part the Argive officials could see that their proposal was favourably received, and before leaving they promised to send an embassy to the Boeotians. On their return the Boeotian envoys reported to the Boeotarchs what had been said at Sparta and by the Argive officials who had met them. The Boeotarchs welcomed their news and were much encouraged to have this double confirmation, with the request of their friends in Sparta matching the policy promoted by the Argives. Not long afterwards envoys arrived from Argos to formalize the proposals. The Boeotarchs thanked them for their offer, and sent them back with the promise that they would dispatch an embassy of their own to Argos to negotiate the alliance.

In the meantime the Boeotarchs, together with the Corinthians, **38** the Megarians, and the envoys from the Thraceward region, decided that they should first swear oaths of solidarity to one another, pledging to give support in case of need at any time and not to initiate any war or conclude any treaty of peace without common consent: and then with that established the Boeotians and the Megarians (who were with them in this) should make alliance with the Argives. Before the oaths were taken the Boeotarchs referred this plan to the Four Councils of the Boeotians (where the ultimate authority lay), with the recommendation that these oaths of solidarity should be open to all cities prepared to join them in a pledge of mutual assistance. But the members of the Boeotian Councils rejected the proposal, anxious not to offend the Spartans by making a formal agreement with the Corinthians, who had seceded from Sparta. The Boeotarchs had not told them of what had transpired at Sparta, how two of the ephors, Cleoboulus and Xenares, and their supporters were pressing for Boeotia to make an alliance first with Argos and Corinth and then subsequently with Sparta itself—they had thought that even without this information the Council body could not fail to vote through a proposal on which they themselves were already decided. So the plan came to a halt. The Corinthians and the envoys from the Thraceward region went away empty-handed: the Boeotarchs, whose previous intention, if they had pushed this through, was to go on to float an alliance with Argos, now abandoned any referral of the Argive question to the Councils, and did not send the promised embassy to Argos. The whole issue fell into neglect and delay.

39   In this same winter Mecyberna, under Athenian garrison, was attacked and taken by the Olynthians.

There continued constant negotiations between Athens and Sparta over the places still held by the other party, and the Spartans hoped that if the Athenians got Panactum back from the Boeotians they themselves could recover Pylos. They now sent a diplomatic mission to Boeotia with the request that Panactum and the Athenian prisoners should be handed over to Sparta, so that they could recover Pylos in an exchange. The Boeotians refused to countenance this transfer unless the Spartans made an independent alliance with them as they had with the Athenians. The Spartans were conscious that they would be putting themselves in the wrong with the Athenians, as there was a specific agreement that neither side should enter into any alliance or any war without the consent of the other, but in view of their desire to take over Panactum as a means of exchange for the recovery of Pylos, together with the advocacy of the Boeotian cause by those intent on the dissolution of the peace-treaty, they did make the alliance. This was towards the end of the winter and the approach of spring. The demolition of Panactum began immediately.

So ended the eleventh year of the war.

40   At the very beginning of spring in the following summer season the Argives grew concerned. The promised embassy from the Boeotians had not arrived, and they were aware that Panactum was being demolished and that an independent alliance had been concluded between Boeotia and Sparta. Their fear was that they could be isolated and their whole alliance might go over to the Spartans. They believed that the Boeotians had been persuaded by the Spartans to demolish Panactum and join the peace-treaty with Athens, and that this was done with Athenian complicity. The consequence in their view was that it was no longer open to them to make an alliance with Athens either, whereas previously they had imagined that the disputes between Athens and Sparta guaranteed that even if their treaty with the Spartans was not renewed they could at any rate become allies of the Athenians. Faced with this dilemma, and fearful that they could find themselves at war with Sparta, Tegea, Boeotia, and Athens combined, the Argives, who before this had rejected the treaty available with the Spartans and entertained high hopes of

hegemony in the Peloponnese, now hurried to send envoys to Sparta, choosing men for this mission—Eustrophus and Aeson—who they thought would be most congenial to the Spartans. In the present circumstances they considered their best course was to make a treaty of peace with the Spartans, on whatever terms could be agreed, and then to remain inactive.

The Argive envoys arrived and began negotiations with the 41 Spartans about the terms of a possible treaty. At first the Argives demanded that their long-standing dispute over the border-district of Cynouria (containing the cities of Thyrea and Anthene, and occupied by the Spartans) should be referred to the arbitration of some city or individual. The Spartans would not countenance any talk of Cynouria, but said that they were willing, should the Argives wish, to renew the treaty on the previous terms. Even so, the Argive envoys now induced the Spartans to agree to make an immediate fifty-year treaty, with the provision that either side could challenge the other (as long as the challenged city, Sparta or Argos, was free of plague or external war) to fight a one-off battle for the disputed territory, as they had done once before when both sides claimed the victory: but no subsequent pursuit should be allowed over the borders of Argos or Sparta. At first the Spartans regarded this proposal as an absurdity, but later, since in any case they wanted Argos friendly, they agreed to the Argive conditions and had the terms drawn up. But before anything was finalized the Spartans asked the envoys first to return to Argos and present the terms to the people: if there was approval, they should come back to Sparta at the Hyacinthia to take the oaths of ratification. So the envoys then left.

At the same time as the Argives were engaged in this business, the 42 Spartan emissaries—Andromedes, Phaedimus, and Antimenidas— who were charged with taking over Panactum and the prisoners from the Boeotians and handing them back to the Athenians found Panactum already demolished by the Boeotians on their own: the excuse given was that long ago the Athenians and Boeotians had resolved a dispute over the territory by a sworn agreement that neither side should inhabit the place, but both should have joint rights of cultivation. Andromedes and his colleagues did recover the Athenian prisoners, brought them back to Athens, and handed them over: they also reported the demolition of Panactum, thinking this in effect a handover, as no enemy of the Athenians would occupy the place in future. This report infuriated the Athenians, who saw violations by the Spartans both in the demolition of Panactum, which should have been returned intact, and, as they discovered, in the independent alliance they had made with Boeotia, despite their previous assurance of joint pressure on those who rejected the peace-treaty. They reviewed all the other ways in which the Spartans had defaulted on the agreement, and concluded that they had been duped: so they gave a sharp answer to these emissaries and sent them on their way.

43 With relations between Athens and Sparta now come to this state of rupture, those in Athens too who wanted to abandon the peace-treaty were quick to press their case. Prominent among these was Alcibiades the son of Cleinias, still of an age which would be thought young in any other city, but respected for the distinction of his family. He did actually believe that greater advantage lay in an accommodation with Argos, but there was also an element of piqued pride in his opposition to the Spartan treaty, in that the Spartans had negotiated the peace through Nicias and Laches, ignoring his own claim because of his youth and showing no regard for what had been a long family tradition of service as consular representatives for Sparta: his grandfather had renounced this office, but he himself had taken particular care of the Spartan prisoners from the island with a view to its reinstatement. With a comprehensive sense of grievance, then, he had spoken against the peace-treaty from the beginning, claiming that the Spartans were not to be trusted and that their only reason for making peace with Athens was to use this treaty to marginalize the Argives and then renew their campaign against the Athenians when they had no allies: and now too, once relations with Sparta had been ruptured, he immediately sent a private message to Argos, asking them to come as soon as they could, bringing representatives also from Mantinea and Elis, to invite Athens into their alliance. This was now their opportunity, he said, and he himself would be fully active in promoting their cause.

44 On receipt of this message, and the realization that the Spartan alliance with Boeotia had been made without reference to the Athenians, and that there was now a major rupture between Athens and Sparta, the Argives diverted their attention from the envoys they still had at work negotiating a treaty in Sparta and concentrated on Athens. They reflected that this was a city in long-standing friendly relations with them, which was a democracy like their own, and which would be a powerful ally on the sea, if they found themselves at war. So they immediately dispatched an embassy to negotiate an

alliance with the Athenians, joined in this by envoys from Elis and Mantinea.

Soon there arrived an embassy from Sparta also, consisting of three men who were thought acceptable to the Athenians, Philocharidas, Leon, and Endius. This embassy was sent in haste because the Spartans feared that otherwise the Athenians would be angry enough to make an alliance with Argos: the envoys were also to request the return of Pylos in exchange for Panactum, and to explain that the Spartan alliance with Boeotia was not made with any intent prejudicial to the Athenians. Their presentation on these issues to the council, 45 and their statement that they had come with full authority to reach agreement on all matters of dispute, alarmed Alcibiades: he feared that if the same account was given to the assembly, the people could actually be won over and the Argive alliance rejected. He therefore followed this stratagem with the Spartan envoys: he persuaded them, adding his personal guarantee, that if they disavowed the possession of full authority when they appeared before the assembly, he would secure them the return of Pylos (using his own influence with the Athenians as strongly in their support as it had so far been in opposition) and ensure reconciliation in all other matters. His real purpose in these dealings was to distance the Spartan envoys from Nicias and to give himself the opportunity to denounce the Spartans in the assembly as insincere in their professed intentions and never consistent from one statement to the next—and so to achieve alliance with Argos, Elis, and Mantinea. The plan worked. When the envoys appeared before the people and were asked if they had full authority, they replied that they did not, a statement quite contrary to what they had said in the council. At this the Athenians lost patience, and with Alcibiades inveighing against the Spartans yet more strongly than ever they followed his lead and were ready to bring in the Argive envoys and their colleagues and make an alliance there and then. But there was an earth tremor before any business could be concluded, and the assembly was adjourned.

The assembly was reconvened on the following day. Despite hav- 46 ing been caught himself by the trick which had induced the Spartan envoys to disclaim full authority, Nicias still argued the greater merit of retaining friendship with Sparta. He proposed that they should postpone the Argive question until they had sent a further delegation to the Spartans and discovered their intentions, insisting that the continued avoidance of war was as advantageous to Athens as it was discreditable to Sparta: Athens was well set, and their best plan was to preserve this good fortune for as long as they could, whereas in Sparta's poor state any opportunity to go straight back to the lottery of war would be a godsend. Nicias persuaded the Athenians to send an embassy, including himself, to demand of the Spartans that, if they had honourable intentions, they should rebuild Panactum and hand it back together with Amphipolis, and renounce their alliance with the Boeotians unless they joined the peace-treaty, in conformity with the specific agreement that neither side should make terms with any third party without the consent of the other. The Athenians instructed their envoys to add that if they themselves were prepared to deal dishonourably they would by now have made an alliance with the Argives, who were presently in Athens for that very purpose. So they dispatched Nicias and his colleagues on their embassy with a comprehensive brief, including these and all other points of contention.

On their arrival at Sparta the envoys delivered their message and concluded with the threat that, if the Spartans would not renounce their alliance with the Boeotians if they failed to join the peace-treaty, the Athenians would for their part make an alliance with the Argives and their confederates. Prevailed upon by the associates and political supporters of the ephor Xenares, the Spartans refused to renounce the Boeotian alliance, but at the request of Nicias they did renew on oath their previous undertakings. Nicias feared that otherwise he would leave with a completely empty hand and face criticism at home—as indeed he did—as the one held responsible for the treaty with Sparta in the first place. When on his return the Athenians heard that nothing had been won from Sparta they took immediate offence and considered this a betrayal by the Spartans. At an assembly attended by the Argives and their allies (Alcibiades had ensured their presence) the Athenians made a treaty and alliance with them, of which this is the text:

47 A treaty was made for a hundred years between the Athenians and the Argives, the Mantineans, and the Eleans, binding on both themselves and all subject allies on either side, to be observed without fraud or violation both by land and by sea.

Neither side shall be permitted to bring force of arms with harmful intent against the other by any means or contrivance, neither the Argives, Eleans, or Mantineans and their allies against the Athenians and the subject allies of the Athenians nor the Athenians and the subject allies of the Athenians against the Argives, Eleans, or Mantineans and their allies.

The Athenians and the Argives, the Mantineans, and the Eleans shall be allies for a hundred years on the following terms:

If enemies invade the territory of the Athenians, the Argives and Mantineans and Eleans shall bring such aid to Athens as may be requested by the Athenians, with all possible force to the best of their ability: and if the enemies ravage the territory and then depart, their city shall be declared an enemy of the Argives and Mantineans and Eleans as well as the Athenians and shall suffer retribution at the hands of all these cities, and no one of these cities shall be permitted to cease hostilities against that city without the agreement of all.

If enemies invade the territory of the Argives, the Mantineans, or the Eleans, the Athenians shall likewise bring such aid to Argos, Mantinea, or Elis as may be requested by these cities, with all possible force to the best of their ability: and if the enemies ravage the invaded territory and then depart, their city shall be declared an enemy of the Athenians as well as the Argives, the Mantineans, and the Eleans and shall suffer retribution at the hands of all these cities, and no one of these cities shall be permitted to cease hostilities against that city without the agreement of all.

The signatory cities of Athens, Argos, Mantinea, and Elis shall not allow the passage of any armed force for purposes of war through their own land or water, or that of their respective subject allies, unless such passage is granted by formal vote of all the signatory cities.

A city sending troops to the aid of another shall provision those troops for up to thirty days from their arrival in the city which requested aid, and likewise provide for their return. If the summoning city wishes to make use of the troops for a longer period, it shall pay a rations allowance of three Aeginetan obols a day for each hoplite, light-armed trooper, and archer, and one Aeginetan drachma a day for each cavalryman.

The summoning city shall have command of the troops when the war is within its own territory. If all the cities agree on a joint external campaign, the command shall be equally shared between all the cities.

The Athenians shall swear to the treaty on behalf of themselves and their allies: the Argives and the Mantineans and the Eleans and their allies shall swear city by city. The oaths shall be sworn over full-grown victims, and in each case shall be the oath which is most binding in local observance. The form of the oath shall be as follows: 'I shall abide by the alliance on the terms agreed with all justice, fidelity, and honesty, and I shall not violate it by any means or contrivance.'

The oaths shall be taken at Athens by the council and the city magistrates, and shall be administered by the prytaneis; at Argos by the council and the Eighty and the Artynae, administered by the Eighty; at Mantinea by the Demiurgi and the council and the other magistrates, administered by the Theori and the Polemarchs; at Elis by the Demiurgi and the ministers of state and the Six Hundred, administered by the Demiurgi and the Thesmophylaces.

The oaths shall be renewed as follows: the Athenians shall go for that purpose to Elis and Mantinea and Argos thirty days before the Olympic festival; the Argives and Eleans and Mantineans shall go to Athens ten days before the Great Panathenaea.

The articles of agreement concerning the treaty and the oaths and the alliance shall be recorded on stone pillars, to be inscribed and set up by the Athenians on the Acropolis, by the Argives in the sanctuary of Apollo in the agora, and by the Mantineans in the sanctuary of Zeus in the agora: and all parties shall jointly deposit a bronze plaque at Olympia at the coming Olympic festival.

If the signatory cities consider it desirable to make any addition to these terms, any such addition as may be jointly agreed by all the cities in consultation shall be binding.

48   Such was the treaty and the alliance now made, and the existing treaty between Athens and Sparta was not on that account renounced by either party. The Corinthians, although allies of Argos, abstained from this new alliance: they had already refused to join the earlier offensive and defensive alliance agreed between Elis, Argos, and Mantinea, and now said that they were content with the original defensive alliance, which provided for mutual assistance but did not require a commitment to any joint offensive. In this way the Corinthians distanced themselves from the allies and began to turn their thoughts back to Sparta.

49   This summer there was a celebration of the Olympic festival (it was the Olympiad in which Androsthenes of Arcadia won his first victory in the pancratium). The Spartans had a ban imposed on them by the Eleans, which excluded them from the precinct and therefore from making sacrifice or competing in the games. This was for their failure to pay the fine resulting from a judgement which the Eleans secured against them under Olympic law: the charge was that the Spartans had violated their territory during the Olympic truce by bringing armed force against the fort at Phyrcus and sending hoplites into their town of Lepreum. The fine was two thousand minas—two minas for each hoplite, as the law prescribes. The Spartans sent envoys to protest that the sentence was unjustified, claiming that the hoplites had been sent to Lepreum before the announcement of the truce at Sparta. The Eleans replied that the truce (which they proclaim first to themselves) was already in force throughout Elis, and

the Spartans had sprung this violation on them when they were observing peace under the truce and expected others to do likewise. The Spartan rejoinder was that in that case the Eleans should not have bothered to proclaim the truce in Sparta at all, if they thought it had already been violated; this could not have been their view when they did in fact make the proclamation; and from that point on the Spartans had made no armed incursion into their territory. The Eleans maintained their position, refusing to credit any protestation of innocence: but if the Spartans would return Lepreum to them, they offered to remit their own share of the fine and pay on the Spartans' behalf the percentage which falls due to the god.

When that offer was rejected, they made another: the Spartans need 50 not return Lepreum if they did not want to, but in view of their desire to be granted access to the precinct they should take a public stand at the altar of Olympian Zeus and swear before all the Greeks that they would without fail pay the fine after the festival. The Spartans would not accept this either: so they were barred from the precinct and made their sacrifices at home, while the rest of the Greeks, except the people of Lepreum, sent their formal delegations to the festival. Even so the Eleans took precautions against the possibility that the Spartans might force their way in to sacrifice. They set an armed guard of their younger men, and were joined in this by troops from Argos and Mantinea, each sending a thousand, and by some Athenian cavalry who were in Harpine waiting for the festival to begin. The whole gathering at the festival was terrified that the Spartans might arrive under arms, yet more so when Lichas the son of Arcesilas, a Spartan, received a public beating in the racecourse from the festival police. He had won the race with his chariot and pair, which in view of the Spartan debarment from the games was registered to the national stable of Boeotia, and the victory was so announced: but he had walked onto the racecourse and put a garland round the head of his charioteer, to demonstrate that the chariot was his own. This greatly intensified the general anxiety, and it was thought that there would be a crisis. The Spartans, though, fell quiet and let the festival pass without incident.

After the Olympics the Argives and their allies came to Corinth to ask the Corinthians to join them. There happened to be a Spartan embassy there too. Many discussions were held with no final outcome, as an earthquake intervened on which the various delegates dispersed for home.

So the summer ended.

51 In the following winter there was a battle between the people of Heracleia in Trachis and the Aenianes, the Dolopes, the Malians, and some of the Thessalians. These were neighbouring tribes hostile to Heracleia, as the place had been built and fortified in specific threat to their territory. From its very foundation they had kept up attrition against the city as far as they could, and now they defeated the Heracleians in this battle: among the Heracleian dead was their Spartan governor, Xenares the son of Cnidis.

So ended this winter, and with it the twelfth year of the war.

52 At the very beginning of the following summer the Boeotians took control of Heracleia, which was in poor state after the battle and subject to depredations, and dismissed the Spartan Agesippidas for misgovernment. Their motive in taking over the place was the fear that, with the Spartans embroiled in difficulties in the Peloponnese, it might otherwise fall to the Athenians. Even so, the Spartans were angry at this move.

In the same summer Alcibiades the son of Cleinias, one of the Athenian generals, undertook a joint venture with the Argives and their allies. He took a small force of Athenian hoplites and archers to the Peloponnese, augmented it with troops supplied by the allies there, and led this army on a tour of the Peloponnese in general consolidation of the alliance, in the course of which he persuaded the people of Patrae to build walls down to the sea, and made plans himself to create another fortified position on the Rhium promontory in Achaea: this project was stopped by the intervention of the Corinthians, the Sicyonians, and others whose interests would be harmed if a fort were built there.

53 In the same summer war broke out between Epidaurus and Argos. The occasion and pretext was the failure of the Epidaurians to fulfil their obligation to send a sacrificial victim, in payment for their pasture-rights, to the temple of Apollo Pythaeus, over which the Argives had the main control. Even without this excuse Alcibiades and the Argives had determined, if they could, to bring Epidaurus into their alliance, in order to keep Corinth quiet and allow the Athenians a shorter support route from Aegina, avoiding the need to sail round Scyllaeum. So the Argives prepared for the invasion of Epidaurus as if this was their own campaign to enforce the sacrifice due.

54 At about this time too the Spartans, led by their king Agis the son of Archidamus, marched out in full force as far as Leuctra on their border facing Mount Lycaeum, with the ultimate destination

unknown even to the cities which had supplied their contingents. But the sacrifices made before crossing the frontier proved unpropitious, so the Spartans returned home and sent word to their allies to prepare for an expedition when the coming month was over (this was Carneius, a sacred month for the Dorians). With the Spartans gone back, the Argives set out on the fourth day before the end of the month preceding Carneius, and held the calendar at that date throughout their invasion and ravaging of Epidauria. The Epidaurians called on their allies, but some pleaded in excuse the sanctity of the month, and others advanced to the border of Epidauria but then took no further action.

While the Argives were in Epidauria embassies from the various 55 cities met for a conference at Mantinea on the invitation of the Athenians. As discussion proceeded the Corinthian Euphamidas pointed out the present discrepancy between theory and practice: they were sitting there talking about peace, while there was a state of armed conflict between the Epidaurians and their allies and the Argives. They should first of all go to both camps and stop the war, and then they could resume talk of peace. On his persuasion they went out and secured the Argive withdrawal from Epidauria. The conference was subsequently reconvened, but they could still reach no agreement, and the Argives reinvaded Epidauria and continued to ravage the territory. The Spartans marched out in response, as far as Caryae: but here too the sacrifices at the frontier were unfavourable, and they turned back. The Argives devastated about a third of Epidauria before returning home. On learning that the Spartans were on the march, the Athenians had sent a thousand hoplites to support Argos under the command of Alcibiades, but this force went back when it became clear that it was no longer needed.

So this summer passed.

In the following winter, undetected by the Athenians, the Spartans 56 sent by sea to Epidaurus a garrison of three hundred men under the command of Agesippidas. The Argives came to Athens and complained that, when the treaty specified that no participant should allow enemy passage through their territory, the Athenians had failed to prevent this coastal voyage to Epidaurus: and if they did not retaliate by bringing the Messenians and the Helots back to Pylos to harass the Spartans, Argos would have cause for grievance. On Alcibiades' persuasion the Athenians inscribed at the foot of the pillar recording the Spartan treaty a statement to the effect that the Spartans had not kept to their oaths, and they brought back the Helots from Cranii to Pylos to resume raiding Spartan territory: beyond that they took no other action. Throughout this winter war continued between Argos and Epidaurus—there was no pitched battle, but a series of ambushes and raids in which there would be casualties on one side or the other. Towards the end of winter and the approach of spring the Argives came up to Epidaurus with scaling-ladders, thinking that the war would have left the city short of defenders and open to storm: but the attempt failed, and they turned back.

So ended the winter, and with it the thirteenth year of the war.

57   In the middle of the following summer the Spartans launched an expedition against Argos with a full levy of their own troops and the Helots, commanded by their king, Agis the son of Archidamus. Seeing their allies in Epidaurus under pressure, with the rest of the Peloponnese either seceded from them or disaffected, they thought the situation would deteriorate further if they did not act quickly to contain it. They were joined in this expedition by the Tegeans and the other Arcadians who were allies of Sparta. The rest of their allies, from within and without the Peloponnese, gathered at Phlius. The Boeotians sent a contingent of five thousand hoplites and the same number of light-armed troops, together with five hundred cavalry, each with an attendant foot-soldier; the Corinthians sent two thousand hoplites; the others contributed in proportion to their relative strength, though the Phliasians provided their entire force, as the army was mustering in their territory.

58   The Argives had prior intelligence both of the initial Spartan preparations and of their departure on the march to join the others in Phlius. They now deployed their own army, reinforced by the Mantineans (together with their allies) and three thousand hoplites from Elis. They advanced and met the Spartans at Methydrium in Arcadia. Both sides established position on high ground, and the Argives prepared for action, as they now had the Spartans on their own: but in the night Agis managed to move his army without detection and made his way to the allies in Phlius. The Argives became aware of this at first light, and marched first to Argos then onto the Nemea road, by which they expected that the Spartans and their allies would make their descent into the plain. Agis did not take this expected route, but, detailing the Spartans, Arcadians, and Epidaurians to go with him, followed another, difficult path down into the Argive plain; the Corinthians, Pellenians, and Phliasians set

out before dawn on a different route; and the instruction for the Boeotians, Megarians, and Sicyonians was to come down by the Nemea road, where the Argives were waiting, so that if the Argives turned back into the plain to meet his own division they could use their cavalry in pursuit. These dispositions made, Agis invaded the plain and began to ravage Saminthus and the surrounding area.

It was now daylight, and the Argives had learnt of Agis' move- 59 ment. They therefore started back from Nemea to defend their city, and on the way they encountered the forces from Phlius and Corinth: they killed a few of the Phliasians, and a slightly greater number of their own men fell to the Corinthians. The Boeotians, Megarians, and Sicyonians made for Nemea as instructed, but found the Argives already gone—they were now down in the plain, and when they saw their property being devastated they began forming up for battle. The Spartans likewise prepared to meet them. The Argives were now trapped and cut off on all sides: in the plain the Spartans and their division blocked access to the city; the Corinthians, Phliasians, and Pellenians were on high ground behind them; and the pass to Nemea was occupied by the Boeotians, Sicyonians, and Megarians. And they had no cavalry, as the Athenians, alone among their allies, had not yet come in support.

The main body of the Argives and their allies did not see this danger in their present position: in fact they thought they were well placed for battle, with the Spartans isolated in Argive territory that close to the city itself. But two leading Argives, Thrasylus (one of the five generals) and Alciphron (the consular representative for Sparta), approached Agis when the two armies were on the point of engagement and discussed with him the case for not committing to battle: the Argives were willing, they said, to offer and accept fair and equal terms of arbitration if the Spartans had any complaint against Argos, and to make a treaty for the maintenance of peace in the future.

The two Argives making this offer did so of their own accord with- 60 out authority from the people. Agis likewise accepted their offer on his own authority, and with no wider consultation beyond informing one of the officials attached to the expedition he agreed a treaty for four months, within which the Argives must fulfil their undertakings. He then immediately withdrew his army, without a word of explanation to any of the allies. The Spartans and their allies followed his orders as the law required, but they were deeply critical of Agis among themselves, thinking that with the Argives cut off on all sides

by horse and foot they had had the perfect opportunity to engage, and
were now leaving with nothing to show for the scale of this deployment.
This was the finest Greek army ever raised so far, as was most clearly
seen when the entire force was gathered at Nemea before disbanding.
It consisted of the Spartans in full strength and contingents—picked
troops in every case—from Arcadia, Boeotia, Corinth, Sicyon, Pellene,
Phlius, and Megara: and it looked a match not only for the Argive alliance but for any additions also which might augment it.

So the army made the withdrawal in this spirit of dissatisfaction
with Agis, and then the various contingents dispersed home. For
their part the Argives were yet more critical of those who had negotiated the treaty without consulting the people. They too thought that
they could never have had a better opportunity, and now the Spartans
had escaped, when they could have brought them to battle close to
their own city and with a strong array of allies on their side. So on
their return to Argos they began to stone Thrasylus in the bed of the
Charadrus watercourse (this is where they hold courts martial before
entering the city). He saved his life by taking refuge at the altar: but
even so they confiscated his property.

61   After this there arrived a supporting force of a thousand Athenian
hoplites and three hundred cavalry, under the command of Laches
and Nicostratus. Despite this reinforcement the Argives were unwilling to break the truce with Sparta, and told the Athenians to go back:
and they would not agree their request to present a case to the assembly until pressure from the Mantineans and Eleans (who had not yet
left Argos) eventually forced them to comply. The Athenians, with
Alcibiades there with them as ambassador, argued in front of the
Argives and their allies that it was wrong to make the truce in the first
place without the agreement of the other members of the alliance,
and that now was the time, with the opportune arrival of the Athenians,
to take the war in hand. These arguments convinced the allies, and
they set out on an immediate expedition against Orchomenus in
Arcadia—all of them except the Argives: they were no less convinced,
but hung back at first and then came to join the others later. The combined forces invested Orchomenus and began a siege with repeated
assaults. A particular factor in their desire to win over Orchomenus
was the presence there of some hostages from Arcadia deposited in
the place by the Spartans. Fearing the weakness of their wall and the
numbers of the opposing force, and the likelihood that they would be
killed before anyone came to their help, the Orchomenians agreed

terms: the conditions were that they would join the alliance, give hostages of their own to the Mantineans, and hand over the hostages deposited by the Spartans.

In possession now of Orchomenus, the allies went on to debate 62 which should be the next of their remaining targets. The Eleans pressed for Lepreum, and the Mantineans for Tegea: the Argives and the Athenians sided with the Mantineans. Furious that they had not voted for an attack on Lepreum, the Eleans went home. The other allies began preparations at Mantinea for an expedition against Tegea: and some of the Tegeans were collaborating inside the city for its surrender.

When their army returned home from Argos after the four-month 63 treaty had been concluded, the Spartans severely criticized Agis for not presenting them with the conquest of Argos, when in their opinion there had never before been a better opportunity: gathering allied forces of that number and quality was no easy matter. When news followed of the capture of Orchomenus, their resentment grew yet deeper still and in an uncharacteristically precipitate fury they proposed to raze Agis' house to the ground and fine him one hundred thousand drachmas. He begged them to do none of this, and promised to redeem the charges against him with a military success under his command: if he failed, they could then do with him as they pleased. They deferred the fine and the demolition of his house, but for the time being introduced a regulation which was unprecedented in their history: they appointed a commission of ten Spartiates to advise the king, without whose agreement he had no authority to withdraw an army from enemy land.

Meanwhile a message reached them from their friends in Tegea 64 indicating that, if they did not come at once, Tegea would secede from Sparta to join Argos and its allies, and was already on the brink of secession. The Spartans reacted with unprecedented speed, sending out a full levy of citizens and Helots. This army marched to Orestheium in Maenalia. Here they sent instructions to their allies in Arcadia to muster and follow close on their heels to Tegea: and, though their own entire force had come out as far as Orestheium, they now sent back one-sixth of their citizen troops, including the older and the younger cohorts, to keep guard at home. With the rest of their army they came on to Tegea, and shortly afterwards their Arcadian allies joined them. They sent also to Corinth, Boeotia, Phocis, and Locris, asking for supporting troops to meet them at

Mantinea as soon as possible. These allies had short notice, and it was not easy for them to cross the intervening enemy territory which blocked their way without waiting for each other and combining their forces for this march: even so, they set about it with all speed. The Spartans meanwhile took with them the complement of their Arcadian allies and invaded the territory of Mantinea. They made camp near the temple of Heracles and began ravaging the land.

65   When the Argives and their allies saw the enemy in action they took up a strong and virtually unassailable position and deployed for battle. The Spartans immediately launched an assault, and had come within range of stone or javelin before one of the Spartan veterans, seeing the strength of the position they were attacking, called out to Agis that he seemed intent on curing one mistake with another, by which he meant that Agis was trying to redeem the discredit of his withdrawal from Argos by this intemperate determination to attack. Whether influenced by this interjection or because he himself had suddenly changed his mind for this or another reason, Agis quickly withdrew his army before it came to engagement. Returning to Tegean territory he then began diverting the flow of river water into Mantinean land: this was a constant source of conflict between the Mantineans and the Tegeans, as widespread damage was caused in whichever direction the flow was turned. Agis' plan was to bring the Argives and their allies down from their high ground in response to this diversion of the water, once they heard of it, and to fight them on the level. So he spent the rest of this day down there engaged in the waterworks. The Argives and their allies were at first astonished at the sudden Spartan withdrawal from so close, and did not know what to make of it. But then when the Spartans had withdrawn out of sight, and they themselves were left idle with no orders to pursue, they turned again to criticism of their generals. Added to their previous complaint that they had let the Spartans go when they were nicely caught close to Argos, they now held it against the generals that the Spartans were running away with no one pursuing them, and this inactivity meant salvation of the Spartan cause and betrayal of their own. The generals were disconcerted at first, but subsequently led their army down from the high ground and advanced into the plain, where they camped with the intention of proceeding against the enemy.

66   On the following day the Argives and their allies formed up in the battle-order they planned to use should they encounter the enemy.

The Spartans were returning from the waterworks to their original base by the temple of Heracles when they suddenly saw the opposing army close by, advanced now from the high ground and already in full battle-order. This moment was the greatest military shock in Spartan memory, and gave them little time to organize their response. They reacted at speed. Every man went immediately to his own position, and detailed orders were given by their king Agis, as their law required. (When the king is in the field he is in complete command. He personally determines the requisite orders and gives them to the polemarchs; they pass them on to the divisional commanders, and then in sequence the orders are transmitted from divisional commander to company commander to unit commander to unit. Any subsequent instructions needed follow the same route and arrive quickly. Virtually the whole of the Spartan army is a system of command within command, and responsibility for action is widely shared.)

On this occasion the Sciritae were drawn up on the left wing, 67 a position to which they have always had an exclusive right unique in the Spartan army. Next in line were the veterans of Brasidas' campaigns in the Thraceward region and with them the previously liberated Helots; then came the main range of the Spartans' own divisions, with the troops from Heraea in Arcadia beside them; next the Maenalians, and on the right wing the Tegeans, with a few Spartans holding the extreme right of the line; the cavalry were positioned on both wings. Such was the Spartan formation. Facing them on the other side were the Mantineans on the right wing (posted there because the action was taking place in their territory); alongside them their allies from Arcadia; then the select Argive regiment of a thousand which the city had long maintained in military training at public expense; next to them the rest of the Argives, then their allies from Cleonae and Orneae; and finally the Athenians holding the left wing, supported by their own cavalry.

This, then, was the make-up and disposition of the forces on either 68 side. The Spartan army appeared the larger, but I could not have given an accurate account of the numbers in each contingent or the total numbers on either side. The secrecy of their system prevented knowledge of the Spartan strength, and estimates on the other side were suspect, given the natural tendency of men to exaggerate the numbers contributed by their own city. The following calculation, though, affords a view of the Spartan numbers on this occasion. They had seven divisions in the field, apart from the Sciritae who numbered six hundred. There were four companies to each division, and four units to each company. Four from each unit fought in the front rank. The depth of the line varied, as each divisional commander was allowed his own discretion, but on average the line was eight ranks deep. Along the whole line, then, and excluding the Sciritae, the front rank consisted of four hundred and forty-eight men.

69   The two armies were now ready to engage, and in the brief interval the various contingents were addressed by their own commanders along the following lines. The Mantineans were urged to remember that they would be fighting not only for their own country but also for sovereignty or subjection; they had tasted both; their task was to retain the one and prevent return to the other. The Argives were reminded of their ancient hegemony and the historical division of power in the Peloponnese; they must not allow the permanent loss of their power; and at the same time they must take final revenge for all the wrong done them by the enemy on their border. The address to the Athenians appealed to their national pride: they were fighting alongside many brave allies, and it was their duty to outdo them all; moreover, defeating the Spartans in the Peloponnese would secure and extend their own empire, and no one would ever invade their land again. Such were the exhortations addressed to the Argives and their allies. On the Spartan side there was encouragement given individually to the separate contingents, but the Spartans themselves followed their military code and confined exhortation to the reminder of what they all knew well, their duty to be brave: they were well aware that long practical training was a more effective ingredient in success than any fine speech giving encouragement at the last minute.

70   They now proceeded to the engagement, the Argives and their allies advancing with grim determination and in high feeling, the Spartans more slowly and to the tune of the many pipers included in their ranks—this was no religious observance, but a means of keeping a rhythmical step to the advance and preventing any break in the

71   line, as often happens when large armies move to the attack. While they were still closing king Agis took a tactical decision. As they engage, all armies tend to the right, pushing out their right wing with the result that both sides then outflank their opponents' left wing with their right. This is because each individual hoplite is anxious to bring his own undefended side as close as possible to the shield of his colleague on the right, and reckons that tight locking is the best protection. This fault is started by the line-leader of the right wing, who

wants to keep his own undefended side clear of the enemy at all times, and then the others follow with the same motivation. In this engagement the Mantineans on the right wing were far outflanking the Sciritae, and the Spartan and Tegean overlap of the Athenians on the left was yet more extensive, in proportion to the greater size of the Spartan army. Agis feared encirclement of his left wing and decided that the Mantineans outflanked them dangerously. He therefore sent orders to the Sciritae and the Brasidean veterans to move across from the main line and cover the Mantineans, and instructed the polemarchs Hipponoïdas and Aristocles to bring up two divisions from the right of the Spartan forces and insert them to fill the resulting gap: his thought was that he would still have plenty of troops on the right, while there would be a stronger line facing the Mantineans.

What actually happened was that Aristocles and Hipponoïdas 72 refused to carry out the manoeuvre on the grounds that the advance was already under way and they had not been given sufficient notice (they were subsequently convicted on a charge of cowardice and banished from Sparta): and by now the enemy were on him. With no divisions coming across to take the place of the Sciritae, Agis ordered the Sciritae themselves to close up again, but they too were not able now to fill the gap. Despite this complete failure of professional skill the Spartans then gave a remarkable demonstration of their ability to win the day by courage alone. As the engagement began, the Mantineans on the right wing routed the Sciritae and the Brasidean veterans, then together with their allies and the thousand select Argives pushed through the still open gap in the opposing line and caused havoc in that section of the Spartans, surrounding them completely then driving them back in defeat all the way to their wagons, where they killed some of the older men posted to guard them. In this part of the field, then, the Spartans had the worst of it. But the rest of their army, and especially the centre, where Agis was positioned with his bodyguard of the three hundred so-called Knights, fell on the main body of the Argives (the older troops known as the Five Companies), the Cleonaeans, the Orneans, and those of the Athenians who were posted beside them. This assault routed them completely: most offered no resistance, but gave way immediately under the Spartan attack, and some were even trampled underfoot in the rush to avoid capture.

With the centre giving way, the Argive and allied line was now 73 broken in two places. Moreover the outflanking right wing of Spartans and Tegeans was threatening to encircle the Athenians, who were now in double jeopardy, facing encirclement on the left wing and already defeated in the centre: and without the good work of their supporting cavalry the Athenians would have taken more punishment than any other part of the allied army. It also happened that Agis, seeing his own left wing in trouble against the Mantineans and the thousand select Argives, ordered his whole force to go to the aid of the losing section. This move, as the opposing army wheeled away from them and passed them by, gave the Athenians the opportunity to get clear unmolested, together with the defeated element of the Argives. But the Mantineans and their allies and the Argive special forces abandoned any thoughts of pressing the enemy further when they saw their own side defeated and the Spartans bearing down on them: they turned and fled. Most of the Argive special forces survived, but the Mantinean losses were more serious. In fact the whole retreat in flight was neither hard-pressed nor protracted. The Spartans fight their battles long and resolute to the turning point, but once they have turned the enemy they do not pursue for any great time or distance.

74   This, or something very close to it, is how this battle evolved. It was the largest battle that had been joined between major Greek cities for a very considerable time. The Spartans displayed the weapons taken from the enemy dead and immediately went on to set up a trophy and strip the bodies: they took up their own dead and carried them to Tegea, where they were buried, and released the enemy dead under truce. The numbers killed were seven hundred Argives, Orneans, and Cleonaeans; two hundred Mantineans; and of the Athenians, together with their settlers from Aegina, two hundred, including both generals. On the Spartan side there had not been sufficient pressure on the allies to cause any significant loss: for the Spartans themselves it was difficult to establish an exact figure, but some three hundred were said to have died.

75   When the battle was imminent the other Spartan king, Pleistoanax, set out in reinforcement with the older and the younger troops and reached as far as Tegea, but returned home on learning of the victory. The Spartans sent word to Corinth and their allies beyond the Isthmus to countermand the request for troops, then they too returned home, dismissed their allies, and, as this was the month for it, celebrated the festival of Carneia. By this one military action the Spartans redeemed their reputation in Greek eyes. The prevalent criticism at the time had been of cowardice in the debacle on the island and general

irresolution and torpor: it was now thought that fortune might have brought them low, but there was still the same spirit in them.

On the very day before this battle the Epidaurians invaded the Argolid in full force, knowing it was short of defenders, and killed a large number of the garrison the Argives had left behind when their main army went out on campaign. There now arrived in support of the Mantineans, but too late for the battle, a force of three thousand Elean hoplites and a further thousand Athenians in addition to the original contingent. The total complement of these allies marched immediately on Epidaurus, while the Spartans were celebrating the Carneia, and began to wall off the city, allocating sections of the circuit among themselves. The others soon gave up the work, but the Athenians pressed on to complete their own designated task, the fortification of the Heraeum promontory. They all contributed to the garrison left in this fort, and then went back to their own cities.

So the summer ended.

At the very beginning of the following winter, the Carneia now 76 celebrated, the Spartans took their army out again, and when they had reached Tegea sent forward peace proposals to Argos. They had always had friends in Argos who wanted to end the democracy, and after the outcome of the battle these men were in a much better position to persuade the majority to an agreement: their plan was first to make a peace-treaty with the Spartans and to follow that with an alliance, thus opening the way for an attack on the democrats. And now there arrived in Argos their consular representative at Sparta, Lichas the son of Arcesilas, bringing two proposals from the Spartans: they could have war if they wished, or alternatively they could be at peace. There was much argument (Alcibiades happened to be there too), but the men in league with the Spartans, now emboldened to come out in the open, persuaded the Argives to accept the peace proposal. This is the text:

It is determined by the assembly of the Spartans to make agreement with 77 the Argives on the following terms:

They shall return to the Orchomenians the children taken hostage, and the men to the Maenalians. They shall also return to the Spartans the men now held in Mantinea.

They shall depart from Epidaurus and demolish the walls they built. If the Athenians will not withdraw from Epidaurus, they shall be enemies of the Argives and the Spartans and of the allies of the Spartans and the allies of the Argives.

If the Spartans hold any children as hostages, they shall return them to each city from which they come.

Concerning the sacrifice due to the god, the Argives at their discretion shall either require an oath of the Epidaurians or else take an oath themselves.

The cities in the Peloponnese, both small and large, shall all be independent according to established custom.

If anyone from outside the Peloponnese enters Peloponnesian territory with harmful intent, the two parties shall in consultation with each other organize the defence in whatever way they decide most equitable to the Peloponnesians.

The allies of the Spartans outside the Peloponnese shall have the same standing as the Spartans, and the allies of the Argives outside the Peloponnese shall have the same standing as the Argives, and they shall retain their present territory.

The Spartans shall publish these terms to their allies and conclude the agreement if they too are content: if the allies have any comments, they should relay these comments to Sparta.

78   The Argives accepted this proposal from the start, and the Spartan army returned home from Tegea. Thereafter, with communication now established between the two parties, it was not long before the same group of men had taken matters further and engineered that the Argives should renounce their alliance with Mantinea, Athens, and Elis and make a treaty and alliance with Sparta. The text of this treaty was as follows:

79 It has been determined by the Spartans and the Argives that there should be a treaty and alliance between them for fifty years on the following terms:

Both parties shall deal on fair and equal terms according to established custom.

The other cities in the Peloponnese shall be participants in this treaty and alliance as independent cities each in its own right and retaining its own territory, dealing on fair and equal terms according to established custom.

The allies of the Spartans outside the Peloponnese shall have the same standing as the Spartans, and the allies of the Argives shall have the same standing as the Argives, and they shall retain their present territory.

If there is need for any combined military expedition the Spartans and the Argives shall decide the most equitable contribution for the allies and consult together on the conduct of the war.

If any of the cities within or without the Peloponnese has a dispute, whether about boundaries or any other matter, it shall be resolved in this way: a quarrel between any two allied cities shall be referred to a third city deemed fair and acceptable by both cities. Private citizens shall pursue their legal rights according to established custom.

Such was the treaty and alliance agreed, and the two parties settled 80 the question of gains made from each other in the war and any other issues. Now pursuing a common policy, they voted not to receive any herald or embassy from the Athenians unless they evacuated their forts and left the Peloponnese, and not to enter into any agreement or any war other than jointly. Among other energetic initiatives, both sent embassies to the Thraceward area and to Perdiccas, and managed to persuade Perdiccas to join them. He did not immediately defect from the Athenians, but was minded to do so now that he had the example of the Argive defection (his own family originally came from Argos). With the Chalcidians they renewed their previous oaths of alliance and swore new ones. The Argives also sent envoys to the Athenians requiring them to evacuate the fort at Epidaurus. In view of the fact that they formed only a small part of the composite garrison, the Athenians sent Demosthenes to bring out their contingent. On his arrival Demosthenes proposed an athletics match outside the fort. This was a ploy. When the rest of the garrison had come out for the match he shut the gates on them. Later the Athenians took the unilateral decision to renew their treaty with the Epidaurians and handed over the fort to them.

After the Argive defection from the original alliance the Mantineans 81 held out at first, but then, powerless without the Argives, they too agreed a truce with Sparta and abandoned any claim to control cities in Arcadia. The Spartans and Argives now undertook a joint campaign with a thousand troops each. The Spartans went on alone to impose a narrower oligarchy on Sicyon, and then the two forces combined to put an end to the democracy in Argos, and established an oligarchy there favourable to the Spartan interest. This was as winter was just giving way to spring, and so ended the fourteenth year of the war.

In the following summer the people of Dium on the Athos penin- 82 sula seceded from the Athenians to the Chalcidians, and the Spartans restructured the political situation in Achaea to conform better than before to their own interests.

In Argos the democrats gradually regrouped and gained enough confidence to attack the oligarchs, waiting for the exact time when the Spartans were celebrating the festival of the Gymnopaediae.

In the ensuing battle within the city the democrats were victorious, and the oligarchs were either killed or expelled. For some time the Spartans refused to come in answer to the summons from their friends in Argos, but eventually they did postpone the Gymnopaediae and set out in support. At Tegea they heard that the oligarchs had been defeated, and would not advance any further despite the appeals of the surviving oligarchs: instead they went back home and continued the celebration of the Gymnopaediae. Later, embassies arrived at Sparta both from the party now in power at Argos and from the exiles. After hearing lengthy arguments on both sides delivered in the presence of their allies, the Spartans decided that those now in the city were the guilty party, and resolved to march on Argos—but this was followed by delays and procrastination. In the meantime the democrats at Argos, fearful of the Spartans and now once again courting an Athenian alliance as their best recourse, began building long walls down to the sea, so that, if they were blockaded by land, they could still have the benefit of importing essentials by sea, with Athenian help. Some of the other Peloponnesian cities were complicit in this building work, which involved the entire adult population of Argos—men, women, and slaves—and was supported by carpenters and stonemasons from Athens.

So the summer ended.

83   In the following winter, aware of the progress of these fortifications, the Spartans and their allies (with the exception of the Corinthians) sent an army against Argos: there was also an element in Argos itself working for their cause. The expedition was led by Agis the son of Archidamus, king of the Spartans. The anticipated base of support in the city came to nothing. The army did, though, capture and destroy the walls under construction, then took Hysiae in the Argolid and killed all the free men who came into their hands. This done, they withdrew and disbanded to their various cities. After this the Argives in their turn marched into Phliasian territory and returned when they had ravaged it: this was because Phlius had harboured the Argive exiles, most of whom had taken up residence there.

During this winter also the Athenians blockaded Macedonia as a result of their grievances against Perdiccas. They complained of the agreement he had made to join the Argives and Spartans: and also that when they had prepared an army to go out against the Thraceward Chalcidians and Amphipolis, under the command of Nicias the son of Niceratus, he had reneged on their alliance and his withdrawal was the main reason why the expedition was aborted. He was therefore an enemy.

So ended this winter, and with it the fifteenth year of the war.

In the following summer Alcibiades took a fleet of twenty ships 84 to Argos and arrested those Argives who were still thought suspect and sympathetic to Sparta—three hundred men, whom the Athenians then deposited in neighbouring islands under their control. And the Athenians sent a force against the island of Melos, consisting of thirty of their own ships together with six from Chios and two from Lesbos, twelve hundred of their own hoplites, with three hundred archers and twenty mounted archers, and about fifteen hundred hoplites from their allies in the islands. The Melians are Spartan colonists who, unlike the other islanders, would not submit to Athenian domination: at first they remained neutral and took no part in the war, but later were forced into an openly hostile stance when the Athenians tried to coerce them by ravaging their land.

The commanding generals, Cleomedes the son of Lycomedes and Teisias the son of Teisimachus, established their force on the island, but before doing any harm to the country sent forward spokesmen to negotiate with the Melians. The Melians did not give them access to the people at large, but required them to state their business before the authorities and the privileged few. The Athenian envoys began as follows:

'Since we are not to address the people at large, presumably so that 85 we do not have the chance to bamboozle the masses with a single uninterrupted presentation of seductive and unchallenged arguments (we are well aware that this is the purpose of our invitation to this gathering of the few), you gentlemen here might wish to make assurance doubly sure. We suggest that neither of us make set speeches, but we invite you at any point to criticize and answer any proposition with which you are not happy. First of all, then, are you content with this proposal?'

The Melian councillors replied: 'We have no objection to the rea- 86 sonable principle of a calm exchange of views, but your military presence—a fact, not just a threat—seems at odds with it. In our view you have come with your own preconceived judgement of this discussion. The result is likely to be that if we win the moral argument and so do not submit, we face war; and if we grant your argument, we face servitude.'

87   *Athenians*. Well of course if all you can think of is your own forecast of the future, and if you have met us here without the explicit
purpose of considering how to save your city in the present circumstances which are plain to your eyes, we might as well stop now. But
if that is your purpose, we can continue.

88   *Melians*. It is natural and understandable that people in our position should cast about for words and thoughts. But yes, this meeting
is indeed about our survival, and we agree that the discussion should
proceed in the way you propose.

89   *Ath*. Well, we shall not bulk out our argument with lofty language,
claiming that our defeat of the Persians gives us the right to rule or that
we are now seeking retribution for some wrong done to us. That would
not convince you. Similarly we do not expect you to think there is any
persuasive power in protestations that though you are a Spartan colony
you have never joined their campaigns, or that you have not done us
any harm. So keep this discussion practical, within the limits of what
we both really think. You know as well as we do that when we are talking on the human plane questions of justice only arise when there is
equal power to compel: in terms of practicality the dominant exact
what they can and the weak concede what they must.

90   *Mel*. To our way of thinking, at any rate, there is advantage (and
we must speak of advantage, since you have put justice to one side
and made expediency the basis of discussion)—there is advantage in
your preserving the principle of the common good: that is, that anyone who finds himself in danger should receive fair and equitable
treatment, and be able to improve his position if he can make a strong
case for something less than the full rigour of what could happen to
him. This principle is proportionately in your interest much more
than ours, given the massive retaliation you would face as an example
to others should you fall from power.

91   *Ath*. Even if our empire is brought to an end, we are not anxious
about the consequences. It is not ruling powers like the Spartans who
are vindictive to their defeated enemies (and in any case we are not
dealing with the Spartans now): the greater cause for fear is if their
own subjects turn on their previous rulers and gain control. But that
is a danger you can leave to us. Right now we want to make clear to
you that we are here in the interests of our own empire, yes, but what
we shall say is designed to save your own city. Our desire is to take
you under our rule without trouble: it is in both our interests that
you should survive.

Mel. And how could it be in our interest to be your slaves? How 92 does that compare with your interest in being our masters?

Ath. Because submission offers you the alternative to a much more 93 terrible fate: and because we gain by not destroying you.

Mel. So can we not be friends rather than enemies? Would you not 94 accept our inactive neutrality?

Ath. Your friendship is more dangerous to us than your hostility. 95 To our subjects friendship indicates a weakness on our part, but hatred is a sign of our strength.

Mel. And do your subjects see the logic of this? Do they then make 96 no distinction between those who have no dependent connection and the rest who are mostly your own colonies, and in some cases have revolted and been put down?

Ath. Well, they certainly think that neither category is short of a 97 case in justice, but they see it as a matter of power—if the independents survive, it is because we are too frightened to attack them. So quite apart from the resulting extension of our empire your subjection will give us greater security. It is particularly important that we, as a naval power, should not let islanders get away from us, especially you in your relatively weak position.

Mel. Do you not think that our alternative offers you security? 98 Since you have diverted us from talk of justice and want us to follow your doctrine of expediency, we must try again by another route and state our own interest, which might convince you if it happens to coincide with yours. At present there are several neutrals: do you want to make enemies of them all? When they see what you are doing here they will expect an attack on themselves before long. And this would simply serve to strengthen your existing enemies and bring you others who, left to themselves, would have had no such intention.

Ath. We do not see much danger from those mainland states 99 whose freedom will make them very reluctant to initiate defensive measures against us. The greater threat is the islanders—both the few not yet in our control, like you, and those already chafing under the compulsion of empire. These are the people most likely to take an irrational risk and bring themselves and us into entirely foreseeable danger.

Mel. Surely, then, if such desperate measures are taken by you to 100 preserve your empire, and by your subject slaves to escape it, it would be complete dishonour and cowardice if we who are still free do not go to any lengths rather than submit to slavery.

101   *Ath.* No, not if you take a sensible view. You are not in an equal contest, so questions of honour maintained or shame avoided have no relevance. You should be thinking more of your survival, and that means not resisting a force much stronger than you.

102   *Mel.* But we know that wars sometimes take on a more impartial fortune which belies any discrepancy in numbers. If we yield now, all hope is gone: but with action taken there is still hope that we can stand upright.

103   *Ath.* Hope counsels risk. When men with other resources besides hope employ her, she can harm but not destroy. But those who stake their all (and hope is spendthrift) only recognize her for what she is when they are ruined and she has left them no further chance to act on their realization. You are weak and one throw from destruction. Do not let yourselves fall into this trap. Do not do what so many others do under pressure: human means can still save them, but when visible hopes recede they turn to the invisible—divination, oracles, and other such sources of disastrous optimism.

104   *Mel.* We can assure you that we do not underestimate the difficulty of facing your power and a possibly unequal fortune. Yet, as for fortune, we trust that our righteous stand against injustice will not disadvantage us in divine favour; and that Spartan help will make up for our deficiency in strength—if for no other reason, they will be bound to fight for us out of kinship and a sense of honour. So our confidence is not as completely illogical as you suggest.

105   *Ath.* Well, we do not think that we shall be short of divine favour either. There is nothing in our claim or our conduct which goes beyond established human practice as shown in men's beliefs about the divine or their policy among themselves. We believe it of the gods, and we know it for sure of men, that under some permanent compulsion of nature wherever they can rule, they will. We did not make this law; it was already laid down, and we are not the first to follow it; we inherited it as a fact, and we shall pass it on as a fact to remain true for ever; and we follow it in the knowledge that you and anyone else given the same power as us would do the same. So as for divine favour, we can see no reason to fear disadvantage. As for your trusting fantasy about the Spartans, that a sense of honour, of all things, will bring them to your aid, we can only admire your innocence and pity your folly. Among themselves and under their own regulations at home the Spartans are as virtuous as can be. But their treatment of others is a different story, and a long one, best

summarized by saying that of all the people we know the Spartans make the most blatant equation of comfort with honour, and expediency with justice. Such principles are hardly conducive to your rescue, which does now look an illogical proposition.

Mel. But that is the very point in which we can now place our 106 greatest trust—the Spartans' perception of their own interest. They will want to avoid the consequence of abandoning Melos—their own colony. Among the Greeks at large this would brand them faithless in the eyes of their friends and provide ammunition for their enemies.

Ath. You seem to forget that interest goes hand-in-hand with safety, 107 while the pursuit of justice and honour involves danger, something which the Spartans are generally loath to face.

Mel. On the other hand, we think that, even though there may be 108 dangers, the Spartans will be more inclined to undertake them on our behalf, and to consider them a better investment than they would in other cases, given that for practical purposes we lie close to the Peloponnese and our kinship offers them a surer guarantee of loyalty.

Ath. Yes, but what reassures potential parties to a conflict is obvi- 109 ously not mere sympathy with those who have invited them but some clear superiority in practical strength. The Spartans have a particular eye for this—at any rate they have so little confidence in their own resources that they only attack others in the company of numerous allies: so it is hardly likely that they will make their own crossing to an island when we control the sea.

Mel. But they can send others. The Cretan sea is a vast area, in 110 which ships can hide and escape more easily than a superior naval power can catch them. And if that fails they can turn to invade your land and go after the remaining allies you have—those not visited by Brasidas. Then the focus of your efforts will not be some unconnected piece of territory, but your very own land and that of your allies.

Ath. Some such diversion is quite possible—it has happened before: 111 you know our record as well as we do, and you will be aware that the Athenians have never abandoned a single siege under external threat. But what strikes us is that, though you agreed that this would be a negotiation for your survival, at no point in this long discussion have you said anything which people might take as grounds for thinking that you will survive. Your strongest arguments are all in the future and no more than hopes: and your present resources are too slim to have any chance against the opposition already in place. Please ask us to withdraw and then, while you still can, come to a more sensible conclusion—so far there has been no logic in your attitude. You cannot, surely, be intending to embrace that false sense of shame to which men turn when danger looms obvious and honour is threatened: the results are almost always catastrophic. Often enough men with their eyes still open to what they are in for are lured on by the seductive power of what they call 'honour': victims of a mere word, they deliberately bring on themselves a real and irretrievable disaster, and through their own foolhardiness incur a more shameful loss of honour than pure misfortune would have inflicted. If you are sensible you will avoid this, and take the view that there is no disgrace in yielding to a great city which offers you moderate terms—alliance and retention of your own land on payment of tribute. Given the choice between war and security, you will not want to choose the worse out of obstinate pride. The general rule of success is to stand up to equals, respect superiors, and treat inferiors with moderation. Please then consider afresh when we have withdrawn, and keep constantly in your minds the thought that you are deliberating for your country: you have only the one country and only the one decision on which it stands or falls.

112   The Athenians now withdrew from the conference. Left to themselves, the Melians confirmed the general grounds of their refusal, and gave this answer: 'Athenians, our original decision has not changed, and we shall not consent in this short time to lose the freedom of a city which has been inhabited for seven hundred years. We shall put our trust in the good fortune from the gods which has until now preserved our city, and for human help we shall look especially to the Spartans, and we shall thus try to save ourselves. But we too have terms to offer: we ask you to accept us as friends and neutrals, and to leave our land with a treaty made between us as best serves both our interests.'

113   Such was the Melians' response. The Athenians' final word as they left the conference was this: 'Well then, to judge by these deliberations of yours you must be the only men, it seems to us, who think the future is more certain than the evidence of your own eyes, and regard speculation as present fact, as if mere wishing will make it so. Spartans, fortune, and hope—the more you stake your trust in this trio, the greater will be your downfall.'

114   The Athenian spokesmen returned to the army. As the Melians showed no sign of submission, the Athenian generals immediately

began hostilities and built a wall completely encircling the city of Melos, dividing the work among their various contingents. Later they left a garrison of their own and allied troops to keep guard on the place both by land and by sea, and went back with the bulk of their forces. The remainder stayed behind and kept up the siege.

At this same time the Argives invaded Phliasia and lost about eighty 115 men in an ambush mounted by the Phliasians and their own exiles. And the Athenians in Pylos carried out a major plundering raid on Spartan territory. Even so, the Spartans did not on that account renounce the treaty and go to war, but they made it known that anyone who wished to launch reprisal raids on the Athenians from their territory was welcome to do so. The Corinthians did clash with the Athenians over some grievances specific to them, but the rest of the Peloponnesians remained inactive. In a night assault the Melians captured the section of the Athenian wall opposite their agora, killed a few men, and brought in as much corn and other commodities as they could. They then went back and took no further action: and the Athenians saw to improved security for the future.

So the summer ended.

In the following winter the Spartans planned an expedition against 116 the Argolid, but turned back home when their frontier sacrifices proved unfavourable. This intended invasion made the Argives suspect certain of their own citizens: they arrested some of them, but others managed to escape.

At about this time the Melians once more took another part of the Athenian wall which was scantily guarded. In response a further force was sent out from Athens, commanded by Philocrates the son of Demeas. Now under tight siege, and also betrayed by some internal treachery, the Melians volunteered surrender to the Athenians at their absolute discretion. Of the Melian population the Athenians executed all the grown men who came into their hands and enslaved the children and women. Later they colonized the place themselves, sending out five hundred settlers of their own.

BOOK SIX

1 In the same winter the Athenians conceived a renewed ambition to subjugate Sicily, hoping to achieve this with a naval expedition on a greater scale than those under Laches and Eurymedon. Most Athenians were ignorant of the extent of the island and the size of its population, both Greek and barbarian, and had no idea that they were undertaking a war almost as formidable as their war against the Peloponnesians. To circumnavigate Sicily would take a merchant ship nearly eight days, and yet this large island is separated from the mainland by only two miles of sea.

2 Here follows an account of the original settlement of Sicily, and a complete list of the various peoples who occupied the island. The most ancient were the Cyclopes and the Laestrygonians, who are said to have inhabited some part of the country, but I can give no information about who they were, where they came from, or where they subsequently went: we can only go by what the poets tell us, and individuals are free to form their own opinion about them. It is clear that after these the Sicanians were the first to settle the island, though they themselves claim to have been the original natives: enquiry reveals the truth that they were in fact Iberians, displaced by Ligurians from their homeland by the river Sicanus in Iberia. At that time the island took from them the name Sicania, having previously been called Trinacria. To this day the Sicanians still live in the western parts of Sicily. During the capture of Troy some of the Trojans managed to escape the Achaeans and made their way by ship to Sicily, where they settled land adjoining the Sicanians: their generic name was the Elymians, and their cities were called Eryx and Egesta. Their settlement was joined by a number of Phocians who had fought at Troy and then been driven by a storm first to Libya and from there to Sicily. The Sicels, whose original homeland was in Italy, crossed over from Italy to Sicily under pressure from the Opicans. According to a probable story they made this crossing on rafts, waiting for a wind to rise which favoured their passage, but they could well have had other means of sailing across. There are still Sicels in Italy even now, and the country takes its name from a Sicel king called Italus. Entering Sicily with a large army they defeated the Sicanians in battle and pushed them back to the southern and western parts of the country.

They changed the island's name from Sicania to Sicily, and lived there, occupying the most fertile land, for about three hundred years after their arrival until Greeks came to Sicily. They still inhabit the central and northern areas of the island. The Phoenicians also at one time occupied enclaves on coastal promontories all round Sicily and settled in the outlying small islands, for the purpose of trade with the Sicels. When the Greeks began to arrive in large numbers by sea, the Phoenicians abandoned most of their settlements and concentrated their population in Motya, Soloeis, and Panormus close to the Elymians, both for the security afforded by their alliance with the Elymians and also because this is the area giving the shortest sea passage from Sicily to Carthage.

This, then, is the list of the barbarians who inhabited Sicily and the regions where they settled.

The first Greeks to colonize Sicily sailed from Chalcis in Euboea, 3 with Thucles as their leader, and founded Naxos. They set up an altar to Apollo Archegetes which still stands outside the city (and delegates to festivals make sacrifice at this altar before they sail from Sicily). In the following year Archias of Corinth, one of the Heracleidae, founded Syracuse, first driving out the Sicels from the island of Ortygia. This, no longer now completely surrounded by water, is the site of the inner city: some time later the outer city was included within the walls and its population grew large. In the fifth year after the foundation of Syracuse Thucles and the Chalcidians set out from Naxos, evicted the Sicels by force of arms, and founded first Leontini, then Catana: the Catanaeans chose their own founder-colonist, one Evarchus.

At about this same time Lamis arrived in Sicily bringing colon- 4 ists from Megara. He settled a place called Trotilum on the river Pantacyas, but later moved from there to join the Chalcidian community in Leontini for a short while, until they expelled him. He then went on to found Thapsus, where he died. His colonists uprooted themselves from Thapsus and founded the city known as Megara Hyblaea when Hyblon, a Sicel king, in betrayal of his own people made them a gift of the land and escorted them to it. There they lived for two hundred and forty-five years until they were removed from their city and land by Gelo the tyrant of Syracuse. Before this removal, and a hundred years after their own foundation, they sent out Pammilus to found Selinus: he had come from their mother-city of Megara to help them establish this new colony. The foundation of Gela, in the forty-fifth year after Syracuse was founded, was a joint enterprise by Antiphemus from Rhodes and Entimus from Crete, each bringing their own colonists. The city took its name from the river Gelas, but the area which is now the acropolis and was the first to be fortified is called Lindii. The colony was established with Dorian institutions. Almost exactly a hundred and eighty years after the foundation of their own city, the Geloans founded Acragas, naming it after the river Acragas: they appointed Aristonous and Pystilus as founder-colonists, and gave it the same institutions as Gela.

Zancle was originally settled by raiders who came there from Cumae, the Chalcidian city in Opicia. Later they were joined by a substantial number of colonists from Chalcis and the rest of Euboea who shared in the distribution of land: the founder-colonists were Perieres from Cumae, and from Chalcis Crataemenes. Zancle was the original name given by the Sicels, as the place is shaped like a reaping-hook, for which the Sicel word is *zanklon*. Later these first inhabitants of Zancle were displaced by Samians and other Ionians who put in to Sicily when they had to sail away to escape the Persians. Not long afterwards the Samians were expelled by Anaxilas the tyrant of Rhegium: he refounded the city with a mixed population, and renamed it Messana after his own ancestral homeland.

5 Himera was colonized from Zancle by Eucleides, Simus, and Sacon. The majority of the immigrant colonists were Chalcidians, but the foundation included some exiles from Syracuse, the so-called Myletidae, who had been defeated in a civil war. The language of the colony was a mixture of Chalcidian and Doric, but the predominant institutions were Chalcidian. Acrae and Casmenae were founded by the Syracusans, Acrae seventy years after Syracuse itself, and Casmenae some twenty years after Acrae. Camarina was first founded by the Syracusans, almost exactly a hundred and thirty-five years after the foundation of Syracuse: the founder-colonists were Dascon and Menecolus. A revolt by the people of Camarina brought war with Syracuse and had them driven out of their home. Some time later Hippocrates the tyrant of Gela took the land of Camarina as ransom in exchange for some Syracusan prisoners and repopulated the place as his own foundation. Then again the people were displaced by Gelo, and Camarina was founded for the third time by the Geloans.

6 These were the many nationalities, Greek and barbarian, who made up the population of Sicily, and such was the size of the island on which the Athenians had become eager to make war. Their real reason was the ambition to dominate the whole of Sicily, but they also had

the decent pretext of a desire to help their own kinsmen and the allies they had already acquired. A particular incentive was provided by the presence of an embassy from Egesta making increasingly urgent appeals for aid. The Egestans had gone to war with their neighbours in Selinus over some questions of intermarriage and a disputed piece of territory: the Selinuntians had brought in the Syracusans on their side, and the war was strangling Egesta both on land and by sea. So the Egestan envoys reminded the Athenians of the alliance made in the time of Laches and the previous war over Leontini, and urged them to send ships in their defence. Their main argument among much else was that if the Syracusans were not punished for the expulsion of the Leontinians but went on to destroy the remaining allies of the Athenians, and so took complete control of Sicily, there was the danger that at some point they would bring a major force to support the Peloponnesians—Dorians helping their Dorian kin, colonists helping their founders—and help to bring about the overthrow of Athens itself. It would be a sensible precaution, then, for the Athenians to join their remaining allies in opposition to the Syracusans, especially as the Egestans would provide sufficient funds for the war. The Athenians heard these arguments constantly repeated by the Egestans and their supporters in assembly after assembly, and finally voted to send a preliminary board of inquiry to Egesta to establish whether they did have the funds they claimed in their treasury and their temples, and also to ascertain the state of the war with Selinus.

So the Athenian envoys had been dispatched to Sicily. In the same 7 winter the Spartans and their allies (except the Corinthians) launched an expedition into the Argolid. They ravaged a small area of the land and carried off a quantity of corn in the wagons they had brought; they settled the Argive exiles in Orneae and left them a small detachment of troops for their protection; they then brokered a temporary truce between Orneae and Argos to prevent any depredations of each other's land, and went back home with the rest of their army. Not long afterwards the Athenians arrived with thirty ships and six hundred hoplites. The full Argive army joined them in an advance on Orneae and began the first day of a siege: but at night the men in Orneae managed to get away, as the besieging army was camped at some distance from the town. When the Argives discovered this on the next day, they razed Orneae to the ground and then returned home, followed shortly by the Athenian fleet.

The Athenians also transported to Methone on the border of Macedonia a force of their own cavalry together with the Macedonian exiles resident in Athens, and began doing damage to the territory of Perdiccas. The Spartans sent a request to the Thraceward Chalcidians to fight in support of Perdiccas: they had a truce with the Athenians terminable at ten days' notice, but they refused.

So the winter ended, and with it the sixteenth year of this war chronicled by Thucydides.

8   At the beginning of spring in the following summer season the Athenian envoys returned from Sicily. With them were Egestan representatives bringing sixty talents of silver bullion, as a month's pay for the sixty ships which they would ask Athens to send. The Athenians called an assembly at which they heard from the Egestan and their own envoys a number of attractive falsehoods, in particular the claim that ample funds were available in the Egestan temples and treasury. They voted to send sixty ships to Sicily and appointed as commanding generals, with absolute discretionary power, Alcibiades the son of Cleinias, Nicias the son of Niceratus, and Lamachus the son of Xenophanes. They were to help Egesta against Selinus; if campaigning conditions allowed, they should also assist in the re-establishment of Leontini; and in general they should take all such measures in Sicily as they judged in the best interests of the Athenians. Four days after this another assembly was held to decide what provision should be made for the rapid fit-out of the ships and to vote anything further the generals might need for the expedition. Nicias had not wanted election to this command. He thought the city had made a wrong decision, and was using a superficial and specious excuse for designs on the whole of Sicily, which would be a huge undertaking. In an attempt to change their minds he came forward and gave his advice to the Athenians along these lines:

9   'This assembly is convened to discuss our provision for the naval expedition to Sicily. But in my opinion we should examine further the very question whether such an expedition is advisable: we should not decide matters of major importance on such superficial consideration and allow foreigners to sway us into entering a war which is none of our concern. For myself I have nothing against war. It has made my reputation, and I have less fear than most for my own life, although I believe that the man who does take some thought for his life and property is no less a good citizen, as such men have the greatest personal interest in the success of their city. But I have never before

let reputation dictate a view which I did not hold, and now too I shall tell you only what I think best. I realize that my words would have little force against your characteristic temperament if I were simply to advise you to preserve what you have and not risk present advantage for an uncertain future: but I shall argue that your enthusiasm is misplaced and your aims will be hard to achieve.

'I warn you that sailing to Sicily takes you away from the many 10 enemies you have here in Greece and seems designed to invite yet others to come over and join them. Perhaps you think that the peace-treaty you have concluded offers some security. Even if you make no move it will still be a peace in name only—that is the way some people from here and in Sparta have seen to it—but if you meet some serious opposition and fail, our enemies will be quick to make their attack. They only agreed the treaty in the first place under pressure of circumstances and in a situation where their credit was less than ours: and then the treaty itself is still rife with disputes between us. Some cities persist in rejecting this agreement, such as it is, and they are far from the weakest. Some of these are in open war with us, and others are only abiding by their ten-day truce because the Spartans have not yet taken action. In all likelihood they would eagerly join the Greek Sicilians in offensives against us if they found our forces split in two, as would be the result of our present intention—before now they would have given much to have these Sicilians on their side. We need to consider these factors. The city is in a delicate position, and we should not endanger it further by chasing after a new empire before we have secured the old: the Thraceward Chalcidians rebelled years ago and have still not been reduced, and there are others on the mainlands whose allegiance is dubious. And here we are apparently intent on rushing aid to Egesta as an injured ally, while we have done nothing so far to redress our own long-standing injuries from these defections.

'Yet if we subdue the rebels we can subsequently keep them under 11 control, whereas even if we are successful in Sicily we would find it difficult to maintain our hold on such a distant and populous island. And it is senseless to choose to attack the sort of people over whom victory will bring no lasting control, while failure will leave you worse off than you were before making the attempt. In my view, to judge from their present situation, the Sicilian Greeks would be even less of a threat to us if they came under Syracusan rule (this is of course the scenario with which the Egestans are trying to alarm us most).

As things are, individual states might possibly send support to Sparta
as a favour, but that way, as part of a Syracusan empire, they are
unlikely to make war on another empire: just as they could combine
with the Peloponnesians to destroy our empire, they would run the
comparable risk of losing their own to a similar combination on our
part. The Greeks in Sicily will be most in awe of us if we do not come
at all, or failing that if we make a display of our strength and then
quickly leave: but if we suffer any reverse that awe will turn to contempt and they will not hesitate to join the campaign of our enemies
at home. We all know that respect increases with distance and when
reputations are not put to the test. You Athenians can vouch for that
from your own experience of the Spartans and their allies. You
dreaded them at first, but now that to your surprise you have had the
better of them and your initial fears were not realized, you have dismissed them from the reckoning and extended your ambition to
Sicily. But one should not be over-excited by enemy setbacks: true
confidence depends on superior strategy. And you should make no
mistake that Spartan embarrassment will have them looking even
now for any possible means of dealing us a blow which will restore
their good name—the more so since they have invested so much for
so long in cultivating a reputation for courage. So if we take a sensible view, the real issue for us is not sending aid to some barbarians
at Egesta in Sicily, but maintaining a defensive alert at home against
the designs of an oligarchic state.

12   'We should also remember that we have only recently made some
partial recovery from the effects of a major plague and a major war,
with funds building up and the population growing back. These
resources should rightly be used for our own benefit here at home,
and not wasted in the cause of this bunch of exiles who beg our help
with whatever set of plausible lies suits their purpose. They are
happy to let others take the risks while their own contribution is
confined to words: a successful outcome brings no grateful return
from them to justify the support given, and failure could well be
equally disastrous for their supporters.

    'It may be that someone who is delighted to receive this command
presses a case for the expedition. He is only concerned with his own
interest, not least because he is still rather young for office. He wants
to maintain the glamour of his racing-stable and hopes that this
appointment will help with his expenses. Do not allow this man his
personal preening at the city's risk. Bear in mind that such people

embezzle public funds for their private extravagance; and that this proposed enterprise is a serious business, not one for impetuous handling under a young man's control.

'I see now that the young man of whom I speak has packed this 13 assembly with other young men to support him, and this gives me some concern. For my part, then, I call for support among the older of you. If you find yourself sitting next to one of these young claqueurs, do not be embarrassed into thinking that a vote against war brands you a coward, and do not fall victim—as they may well do—to the disastrous allure of distant promise. You know that for the most part greed fails and foresight succeeds. So if you care for your country, now dicing with the greatest danger it has ever risked, vote them down. Your vote should be in favour of leaving the Greek Sicilians to live in their own land and settle their own affairs, as long as they continue to respect the present boundaries between them and us, which have proved effective barriers—the Ionian Gulf for the coastal route and the Sicilian Sea for an open crossing. And our specific reply to the Egestans should be that since they started their war with Selinus without reference to Athens they must also see to its conclusion by themselves. In future we must abandon our habit of making these one-sided alliances, which lead us to give help when others are in trouble with no prospect of reciprocal support when we need it ourselves.

'So, Chairman, if you see it as your responsibility to protect the 14 interests of the city, and want to show yourself a patriot, I ask you to put this to the vote and invite the Athenians to give their opinions once more. If you are nervous of calling for a second vote, you should consider that in front of so many witnesses you cannot be accused of a breach of procedure, and that you have it in your power to restore the city to health when it has taken a wrong decision. This is the honourable exercise of office—to benefit one's country as best one can, or at least be no conscious party to its harm.'

Such was Nicias' speech. Most of the Athenians who subsequently 15 came forward spoke in favour of the expedition and against any annulment of the previous vote, but there were some who took the other side. The most insistent advocate of the expedition was Alcibiades the son of Cleinias. His motives were opposition to Nicias (they had always had political differences, and now Nicias had made insulting reference to him), and above all a strong desire to have the command: he hoped that this would give him the conquest of Sicily and Carthage, and that success would also restore his own fortunes, bringing cash as well as glory. He had a position to maintain in the eyes of his fellow citizens, and his devotion to racehorses and other expensive pursuits went beyond his existing means. This extravagance of his was later a significant factor in the ultimate defeat of Athens. The general public became wary of the excesses of his unconventional and hedonistic lifestyle and of the huge ambition apparent at every turn in all areas of his involvement: they thought he was aiming at tyranny, and turned against him. So, even though in the public sphere his command of strategy was unrivalled, on a personal and individual level the people took exception to his behaviour, and replaced him with others: by so doing they caused the city's downfall not long afterwards.

Alcibiades now came forward and addressed the Athenians as follows:

16   'Athenians, not only do I have a better claim to command than any other (I have to start with this point, since Nicias has impugned my credentials), but I also think I deserve it. Those pursuits for which I am criticized bring me personal fame, as they did my family before me, but they also bring benefit to my country. My outstanding performance at the Olympic festival made the Greeks revise and even exaggerate their estimate of the power of Athens, when they had expected the city to be exhausted by war. I entered seven chariots—more than any private citizen had ever done before. I won the victory, and second and fourth place too: and my whole display at the games was of a piece with my victory. Quite apart from the regular honour which such successes bestow, the plain fact of their achievement also hints at reserves of power. And then again my sponsorship of productions and any other public duty on which I may "preen" myself, though naturally exciting envy at home, does make its own contribution to the impression outsiders form of our strength. So there is use in this sort of "folly", when a man expends his own resources for national as well as personal benefit. And there is nothing wrong if someone with good cause for pride does not treat others as equals, just as those in poor state do not expect others to share their misfortune. If we are in trouble, people shun us: by the same token no one should complain if the successful look down on him—or else he should give others equal treatment before claiming parity of esteem for himself. I know that these proud and successful men, and all who have achieved some pre-eminent distinction, meet with resentment in their own lifetime (especially from their peers, but also in any

company they keep). Yet when they are gone, individuals in future generations make spurious claims to be their descendants, and their native country, far from disowning them as aberrant citizens, takes proud credit for the achievements of its own sons. I aspire to this kind of fame, and that is why my conduct as a private citizen is criticized. But I ask you to consider whether I have any rival in the management of public affairs. Without any significant danger or expense to you I put together a consortium of the most powerful states in the Peloponnese and forced the Spartans to stake everything on the outcome of a single day's fighting at Mantinea. The result is that, even though they had the better of the battle, they have never yet recovered any solid confidence.

'This is what my supposed "immaturity" and "egregious folly" 17 achieved—successful diplomacy with the Peloponnesian powers which convinced them with its passionate sincerity. So now too there is no need to be cautious of my relative youth: while I still enjoy that vigour, and Nicias retains his reputation for good luck, take advantage of what we both can offer. You have already voted for the expedition to Sicily and should not change your minds in the belief that it will come up against some great power. Sicily may have large cities, but they are full of mixed rabbles and prone to the transfer or influx of populations. As a result no one feels that he has a stake in a city of his own, so they have taken no trouble to equip themselves with arms for their personal safety or to maintain proper farming establishments in the country. Instead, individuals hoard whatever money they can extract from public funds by persuasive speaking or factional politics, in the knowledge that, if all fails, they can go and live elsewhere. A crowd like that are hardly likely to respond unanimously to any proposal or to organize themselves for joint action: more probable is that individual elements will go with any offer that attracts them, especially if they are in a state of internal dissension (and that is what we hear). Moreover, their hoplite numbers are nothing like what they claim, just as we have seen in the other Greek states too, whose own estimates of their numbers proved a gross exaggeration, when in fact they could barely muster an adequate force for this war.

'So, on the information I have received, that is the situation we shall find in Sicily—easy enough: and it will be made easier still when our offensive is joined by the many barbarians there who hate the Syracusans. Here at home, if you think it through, there is nothing to prevent us. Our forefathers had these same enemies as we are

told we would leave behind us if we sail, and the Persians to face as
well: yet they built our empire, and that was solely on the strength of
naval superiority. And now too the Peloponnesians have never had
so little hope against us. Even at the height of their powers, they can
only invade us by land, and they can do this whether or not we sail
to Sicily. By sea they can do us no harm, and we shall still have a fleet
left to match theirs.

18   'What plausible argument, then, can we give ourselves for hanging
back, or what excuse to our allies over there for not helping them?
We have sworn an alliance with them, after all, and should go to their
aid without objecting that they have not aided us. That is not why we
took them on as allies. We did not expect them to reciprocate by
coming over here to help us, but we wanted them to give trouble to
our enemies there and so prevent them from attacking us here. This
is how we and all other imperial powers have built up an empire, by
readily responding to any request, Greek or barbarian, for our intervention. If we were all to sit tight or let racial discrimination dictate
where we give support, we should add little to our empire and in fact
run the risk of losing it altogether. Faced with a dominant power,
people do not just defend themselves when attacked, but they take
pre-emptive action to forestall the attack. And we cannot ration ourselves to some voluntary limit of empire. Given the position we have
reached, we have no choice but to keep hold of our present subjects
and lay designs on more, because there is the danger that, if we do
not rule others, others will rule us. Inactivity is not an option for you.
It may be for others, but you cannot contemplate it without a corresponding change in your whole culture and practice.

'So the logic is that a campaign there will increase our power here,
and we should sail. This will flatten any Peloponnesian pretensions
when they see us scornful enough of the present lull to sail against
Sicily: and if the people there come over to our side we shall have a
good chance of mastering the whole of Greece. At the very least we
shall damage the Syracusans, which will benefit both us and our
allies. Our ships will be our security, enabling us to stay if we succeed
or to come back—we shall be superior at sea to the whole of Sicily
combined. Do not let Nicias deflect your purpose with his quietist
talk and his attempt to create a division between young and old. When
our fathers were young men they brought this city to its present
greatness under the tried and tested system which allowed them to
share decision-making with their seniors, and now too you should

look to advance the city yet further by the same means. Bear in mind that youth and age only show their virtues in combination, and that the most effective policies are a blend of every sort of opinion—shallow, middle-of-the-road, or highly specialized. Remember too that if the city is at rest its mechanism will seize like anything else out of use, and everyone's skill will atrophy, whereas constant campaigning will add to our experience and train us to fight our cause with action rather than rhetoric. My conclusion is this: to my mind a city which has never believed in quiet will very quickly go under if it makes the change to quiescence, and the greatest security in national life is when people deviate least from their traditional character and practice, whatever its faults.'

Such was Alcibiades' speech. After hearing him, and also the 19 Egestans and Leontinian exiles, who came forward to make their case and beg for assistance with reminders of the sworn agreement, the Athenians were yet more than ever enthusiastic for the expedition. Nicias realized that he now had no hope of deterring them with his original argument, but thought that he might well change their minds by insisting that the resources required would be massive. He came forward again and spoke as follows:

'Athenians, I can see that you are completely set on going to war, and 20 I pray that all will be well and as we wish: but I shall share with you my thoughts on how we stand. From what I have been told, the cities we are proposing to attack are powerful, independent of one another, and in no need of the change of regime which would be welcomed by people looking to move from forcible subjection to a more comfortable state: so they will hardly want to exchange their freedom for our rule. And for a single island Sicily contains a large number of Greek states. Apart from Naxos and Catana (which I expect will side with us out of kinship with the Leontinians) there are seven other cities fully equipped with broadly the same sort of forces as our own, and not least among them the main objects of our expedition, Selinus and Syracuse. They have considerable numbers of hoplites, archers, and javelin-men, and also large fleets of triremes and the population to crew them. In addition to their private wealth, there is treasure in the temples of Selinus and the Syracusans have income from the tithes paid by some of the barbarians. Their particular advantages over us are the possession of a substantial cavalry and the availability of locally grown rather than imported corn.

'Against such a power we need more than the bare complement of 21 marines. A large force of infantry must sail too, if we want to do justice to our ambition and not find the country closed to us by a mass of cavalry—especially if the cities combine in fear of us and we acquire no more allies beyond the Egestans who could provide us with cavalry to take on theirs. It would shame us to be driven out of the island, or to send for reinforcements because we had not thought through our original plans. We must take with us from home adequate supplies and equipment for the whole enterprise, bearing in mind that we are planning a naval expedition far from our own country, under campaigning conditions very different from your experience when meeting some enemy in this part of the world, with the help of your subject states. Here further supplies can be easily obtained from friendly territory, but there you will have cut yourselves off in a wholly alien country, with communication home taking more than four months in the winter.

22   'These then are what I consider the requirements: a considerable force of hoplites from Athens itself and our allies, both our own subjects and any we can persuade or pay to join us from the Peloponnese; a large number of archers and slingers to deal with the enemy cavalry; sufficient ships for overwhelming naval superiority, so there is no extra problem in bringing in supplies; merchant ships to transport the grain, wheat and roasted barley, we shall also need from home; master-bakers conscripted under hire in fair proportion from our mills, so that our forces will still have food if we are detained by adverse sailing conditions, as few cities will be able to cater for such a large army. Generally we must equip ourselves as completely as possible, and not leave anything dependent on others. In particular we need to have with us from here a very substantial sum of money: you should assume that the funds from Egesta said to be available to you there are most probably a fiction.

23   'Even if we equip and send out from Athens a force of our own which is not merely the proposed "match" for the enemy (no match, though, for their fighting strength in hoplites), but, more than that, a force superior to them in all departments, we shall still not find it easy to achieve both conquest and a safe return. You should think of this as like an expedition to establish a colony in an alien and enemy country, when the prime need is to win control of the territory on the very day of landing, in the knowledge that failure will mean a hostile environment at every turn. This is what I fear, and I can see that we shall need much good planning and yet more good luck, which is something hard for humans to ensure. For these reasons I would

want to minimize my exposure to fortune in this expedition, and only sail with the assurance of an armament as far as we can tell fit for the task. This I consider the best security for the city at large and for those of us on the expeditionary force. If anyone thinks otherwise, I gladly resign my command to him.'

This speech of Nicias was calculated to achieve one or other of two 24 outcomes: either he would deter the Athenians by his insistence on the magnitude of the enterprise, or, if the campaign was forced on him, he would ensure that he sailed with the best chance of safety. In fact, so far from losing their enthusiasm for the expedition in view of the logistic burden it would impose, the Athenians were yet more determined, and his speech achieved the opposite effect: they thought that Nicias had given good advice, and there would now be an ample margin of safety. All alike were smitten with a passionate desire to sail. The older men looked forward to conquest at their destination, or at least no reversal for such a large armament; the young men of military age longed for foreign travel and the sights abroad, quite confident of a safe return; and the general mass of troops saw immediate pay and the prospect of further resources to fund a lifetime of public benefits. This huge enthusiasm of the majority meant that anyone who did in fact disagree kept quiet, fearing that a contrary vote would brand him unpatriotic.

Finally one of the Athenians came forward, called on Nicias, and 25 said that there must be no more excuses or delays: he should now declare in front of them all what forces he wanted the Athenians to vote him. Nicias was reluctant to reply, saying that he would prefer to have time to discuss the matter with his fellow commanders: but as far as he could see at present, they would need to sail with at least a hundred triremes from Athens itself (of which an agreed number would be troop-transports), and send for others from their allies; the hoplite force embarked, Athenian and allied, should be a total of at least five thousand, and more if possible; the generals would see to proportionate enlistment of the other units they would take with them—archers from home and from Crete, and slingers—and any other provision they thought appropriate.

On hearing this the Athenians immediately voted the generals 26 absolute discretionary power to take whatever decisions on the size of the force and the whole management of the expedition they judged in the best interests of the Athenians. Preparations now began. Requests were sent to the allies, and recruitment lists compiled at Athens.

In recent years recovery from the plague and from a continuous war had built up the city with a new generation of young men and funds accumulated during the armistice, with the result that all was now in greater supply.

27   While these preparations were still in train, most of the stone Herms in the city of Athens had their faces mutilated in one night (these Herms, square-shaped in the local fashion, are common outside the doors of both private houses and temples). Nobody knew the perpetrators, but large rewards were publicly offered for information leading to their detection, and a decree was also passed giving immunity to any citizen, foreigner, or slave who volunteered knowledge of any other desecration. The Athenians took the matter more seriously still, thinking that it had ominous import for the expedition and was the prelude to a conspiracy for revolution and the overthrow of democracy.

28   Information came from some metics and their servants, not about the Herms, but concerning some earlier mutilations of statues by young men in a drunken frolic: and they also alleged that the Mysteries were being parodied in private houses, naming Alcibiades among the offenders they accused. This was seized on by those who had particular reason to resent Alcibiades for blocking their own path to any clear political supremacy, and thought that if they could get rid of him they would take over the leadership of the people. So they were concerned to blow up the whole affair and make strident claims that the profanation of the Mysteries and the mutilation of the Herms were part of a plot to subvert the democracy, and that Alcibiades was behind it all: as contributory evidence they cited the undemocratic excesses of his general lifestyle.

29   Alcibiades took immediate steps to defend himself against the information laid and was ready to stand trial to establish his guilt or innocence before the expedition sailed (all preparations were now in place): if he was guilty of any of this, he said, he would pay the penalty, but if acquitted he should retain his command. He insisted that the Athenians should not credit attacks made on him in his absence, but if he really was a criminal they should proceed to execute him there and then: it was not sensible to send him out in command of such a major armament with such a serious charge against him unresolved. His enemies feared that the army would support him if there was an immediate trial, and that the people would take an indulgent view in recognition of his role in persuading the Argives and some of the

Mantineans to join the expedition. They therefore played for delay and toned down the excitement, putting up other speakers to propose that for the present Alcibiades should sail with the expedition and not hold back its launch, but should return and face trial within a set period of days. Their intention was that he should be recalled under summons for trial when they had a stronger case against him, which would be easier to manufacture in his absence. So it was decided that Alcibiades should sail.

As a result the launch of the expedition to Sicily began shortly 30 afterwards, in the middle of summer. Prior notice had been given for most of the allies, the merchantmen carrying corn, the smaller boats, and all the other attendant vessels to muster at Corcyra, from where the whole fleet would cross the Ionian Gulf to the promontory of Iapygia. The Athenians themselves and any allies already with them went down to the Peiraeus early in the morning of the appointed day and began to man the ships for departure. Virtually the whole of the rest of the population of Athens, citizens and foreigners alike, joined them at the Peiraeus. The native Athenians came to bid individual farewells to their own people—friends, relatives, sons—with mixed emotions, hope for a successful conquest combining with tearful anxiety whether they would ever see them again, when they thought of how far over the sea their mission was taking them from home. At 31 this last minute, when imminent parting reminded of dangers ahead, they were invaded by all the fears which had never occurred to them when they voted for the expedition: but their spirits revived at the immediate spectacle of power in front of them, the pure quantity of every form of equipment they could see with their own eyes. The foreigners and the rest of the crowd came there to witness for themselves a remarkable enterprise which would otherwise have seemed incredible.

This first expeditionary force was indeed at that time the costliest and most magnificent Greek armada ever to sail from a single city. In numbers of ships and hoplites the force taken by Pericles to Epidaurus and subsequently by Hagnon to Potidaea was just as large, comprising as it did four thousand hoplites, three hundred cavalry, and a hundred triremes from Athens itself, together with fifty triremes from Lesbos and Chios and a good number of allied troops too on board. But those were short journeys requiring little logistic provision, whereas this expedition was planned for a long absence and equipped for both naval and land warfare as need might be.

Every care and huge expense was lavished on the fleet by the trierarchs and the state. Public funds provided wages of one drachma a
day for each sailor, and had supplied sixty warships to be crewed and
forty troop-transports, with first-class officers assigned to them. The
trierarchs supplemented the state pay for the upper bench of rowers
and the petty officers, and spared no expense on the figureheads
and other fittings: every one of them went to extreme lengths to
prove his own ship the best in both splendour and speed. The infantry were selected from up-to-date service-lists, and there was intense
rivalry among them over the quality of their arms and personal
equipment.

So while the Athenians were thus competing with one another in
their various spheres of operation, to the rest of the Greeks it seemed
more like a display of power and capability than a preparation for
war. Anyone computing the combined public and private expenditure on this expedition would have found that in total a vast sum of
money was leaving the city. Public costs were not only the expense
already committed but also the funds sent with the generals. Private
money had been spent by individuals on their own equipment and by
the trierarchs on their ships, with more costs to come: add to that the
pocket money for a long campaign which everyone would have taken
over and above their state pay, and all that servicemen or merchants
had with them on board for trading purposes. And what made this
armament the talk of Greece was the astonishing daring of it and the
pure magnificence of the spectacle, let alone the overwhelming scale
of military force brought against its objective: and it was recognized
that this was the longest expeditionary voyage ever undertaken from
a home state, and an enterprise of unprecedented ambition in the
relation of intended gain to present holding.

32   When the ships were manned and all supplies now stowed on
board ready for the launch, a trumpet sounded the call for silence,
and the customary prayers before departure were recited, not ship by
ship but with one herald speaking for them all: and throughout the
force bowls of wine were mixed and servicemen and officers together
made libations from cups of gold and silver. The prayers were joined
by the crowd of citizens and other well-wishers on land. When they
had sung the paean and completed the libations the fleet set out.
They sailed in column at first, then raced each other as far as Aegina.
From there they made all speed to reach Corcyra, where the allies
were gathering with the rest of their force.

Meanwhile reports of the armada began to reach Syracuse from several quarters. For some time they were given no credence, but eventually an assembly was called at which speeches were made on both sides of the question, some crediting the reports of the Athenian expedition and others rejecting them. Among the speakers was Hermocrates the son of Hermon, who came forward in the belief that he was reliably informed in the matter and advised the Syracusans as follows:

'You may well disbelieve me, as you have others, when I tell you 33 the truth about this armada, and I realize that those who either originate or pass on apparently incredible reports not only fail to convince others but find themselves regarded as fools. But no such fear will stop me speaking, when the city is in danger and I persuade myself that I have more reliable information than anyone else. I tell you, whatever your incredulity, that the Athenians have launched a major expedition against you, with both naval and land forces. Their pretext is support of their allies in Egesta and the re-establishment of Leontini, but in truth they want Sicily, and especially our city: they reckon that if they can win Syracuse it will be easy to win the rest of the country. Realize, then, that they will be here soon, and consider how best to defend yourselves with your present resources. I warn you not to underestimate the enemy and be caught off guard, still less to disbelieve the impending attack and take no precautions at all.

'Those who do believe what I say should not be panicked by this daring expression of Athenian power. They can do us no more harm than we can do to them, and the very scale of their armament can work to our advantage. It places us in a much better position with the other Greek Sicilians, who will be more ready to join us in the fight if they are alarmed for their own safety: and if we do manage to defeat the Athenians or at least send them home with their object frustrated (I really have no fear that they will achieve what they expect), this will be a particularly glorious triumph for us—and I have every hope of it. Rarely has any large expedition, Greek or barbarian, sent out far from home met with success. The invaders never outnumber the local inhabitants and their neighbours, who all combine under the threat, and if the attempt fails for lack of supplies in a foreign land, even though the failures are largely self-inflicted, the intended victims still reap the glory. An example is these very Athenians: after the unexpected and manifold failure of the Persian invasion, they rose to power on the supposition that the invaders had

Athens as their objective. I am hopeful that the same will prove true
in our case.

34   'So let us set to with a will. There are preparations to be made here
at home; we should send out to the Sicels to consolidate alliances and
try to make new friends and allies; we should send envoys to the rest
of Sicily emphasizing that this is a danger common to us all, and also
to the Italian cities, in the hope that they will join our cause or at least
refuse to allow the Athenians access. And I think we would do well
to send to Carthage too. They will not be surprised at a threat from
Athens—in fact they live in constant fear that at some point the
Athenians will attack their city. So they may well take the view that
to ignore our predicament could bring on their own, and be prepared
to give us covert help—or it might be open help: at any rate help in
one form or another. Of all the present possibilities they can give the
most powerful support, if that is what they decide: they have huge
resources of gold and silver, which work for success in war as in all
else. And we should send to Sparta and Corinth, asking them to
come to our assistance here as soon as they can, and to reopen the war
there in Greece.

'I tell you what I think is our best opportunity. In your usual preference for inaction you are hardly likely to embrace it, but I shall tell
you nevertheless. If all Sicilian Greeks together, or at least as many
as will join us, were prepared to launch our entire existing fleet, with
two months' rations on board, and take up position at Taras and the
promontory of Iapygia to oppose the Athenians, thereby making it
clear to them that before any fight for Sicily they must contest their
crossing of the Ionian Gulf, that would be the best way to confound
them. We would force them to take into account that our advance
guard has a base in friendly territory (Taras is sympathetic to us),
that they have a great stretch of open water to traverse with their
entire complement of ships, that it will be difficult to retain formation over such a long voyage, and that their slow and sporadic
approaches will make them easy prey for us. They may on the other
hand leave behind their heavier vessels and attack with a concentration of their fast warships: in that case, if they have had to use oars,
we can fall on them when they are exhausted, or if we decide otherwise we can always retire to Taras. They will have crossed over with
only the supplies needed for a naval engagement, and will then find
themselves in a dilemma on these desolate shores: if they wait here
they will be blockaded, and if they try to sail on past us they will be

cut off from their support ships with no assurance of a sympathetic welcome in any of the coastal cities—a discouraging prospect.

'So I believe that these considerations will inhibit them from leaving Corcyra at all. Either the time they spend in discussing strategy and sending out spying missions to establish our numbers and position will push them into the winter season, or frustration at this unexpected obstacle will cause them to disband the expedition— especially as I hear that the most experienced of their generals was reluctant to take the command and would welcome the excuse offered by any sign of serious opposition from us. I am quite sure that the reports would exaggerate our strength, and of course men set the level of their resolve by what they hear: they are daunted when the enemy takes the initiative, or at least makes it clear that any attack will be resisted, as that brings the realization that the danger is not one-sided. This will be the Athenian experience now. They have set out against us in the belief that we shall not resist, a reasonable conclusion in view of the fact that we did not join the Spartans to their detriment, but if they see us taking a bold step which confounds their belief, it is the unexpected opposition which will deter them rather than any accurate estimate of our power.

'So I ask you to follow my advice, ideally by taking the bold step I have suggested. Failing that, I urge you to make all other preparations for war without delay. Every one of you should take it into his head that contempt for an approaching enemy is best shown through courage on the actual field of battle, whereas the most useful immediate reaction is to assume danger and recognize that security depends on realistic precautions under threat. They are coming for sure: and I have no doubt that they are already at sea and virtually on us.'

Such was Hermocrates' speech. It provoked vehement argument 35 in the Syracusan assembly: some asserted that there was no way that the Athenians could be coming, and Hermocrates was talking nonsense; others argued that, even if they did come, they would sustain more damage than they could inflict; and some outright cynics tried to ridicule the whole question. Only a small element believed what Hermocrates was saying and shared his fear of imminent danger. Now Athenagoras came forward to speak. He was the leader of the democratic party and at the time the most persuasive influence on the general public. He addressed the assembly as follows:

'The Athenians mad enough to come over here and walk straight 36 into our hands? Only a coward or a traitor would not welcome that prospect! But what surprises me in the people who are spreading these reports to alarm you is not the extremes to which they are prepared to go, but their stupidity in thinking that their motives are not transparent. They have their own reasons for being afraid, and want to put the whole city in a state of emergency so that their particular fears are concealed in a general panic. And this is what lies behind these present rumours; they do not come out of nowhere, but they have been deliberately made up by people who are always involved in this sort of agitation. You would be well advised to discount the reports put about by these men and instead base your view of the probabilities on what a shrewd and highly experienced enemy would do—and I certainly rate the Athenians as such. They are hardly likely to turn their backs on the Peloponnesians and a war in Greece which is far from settled, and deliberately set out on another war of comparable scale. Indeed, considering the number and strength of our cities, I imagine they are glad that we are not attacking them.

37   'Even if they were to come, as alleged, I think that Sicily is better placed than the Peloponnese to finish them off, given our superior all-round capabilities. Our own city by itself is far more than a match for the armament said to be coming against us, even if that were twice as large. This much is certain: they will not be bringing horses with them, and will procure no cavalry here other than a handful from Egesta; as they have to come by sea they will not have hoplite numbers to match ours (it is challenge enough to make this long voyage with ships alone, never mind heavy loading); and a campaign against a city as powerful as ours requires general provision of supplies and equipment on a massive scale. So in my considered opinion—and I will go this far—I doubt that they would escape total destruction even if they brought with them a city as large as Syracuse, established it on our borders, and fought us from there: yet more so when the whole of Sicily is enemy territory (it will unite against them), when they must make a camp as soon as they are out of their ships, and then have no resources beyond basic supplies and a collection of tents—our cavalry will see to it that they cannot advance far. In fact I do not think they will win any ground at all, such is the superiority I believe our forces will have over theirs.

38   'But, as I say, the Athenians are well aware of all this and I am sure have no intention of jeopardizing their own interests. It is people here who are fabricating stories which are neither true nor ever likely to be true. This is not the first time, and I have always known what

they are up to: they want to do or say all that they can, including this sort of rumour and others yet more mischievous, to intimidate you ordinary people of Syracuse into accepting their control of the city. And I do fear that constant attempts may ultimately bring them success. We are very bad at taking precautions before trouble is on us, at spotting danger and following up with action. That is why our city has so seldom been at rest—a history of disputes and struggles undertaken more among ourselves than against any external enemy, and we have had tyrannies too and oppressive cliques in power. If you will come with me in this, I shall try to ensure with all vigilance that nothing of this sort happens in our day. This means persuading you, the general public, to take punitive action against those who have such designs, not just when their guilt is blatant (it is hard to catch them at it), but for what they would do if they could: one should retaliate in advance against an enemy's intention, not simply after the event, as the first to drop his guard will be the first to suffer. It means also exposing the oligarchic party, keeping them under close surveillance, and educating them too, which I think the best way of stopping their mischief.

'And indeed—a question I have often asked myself—what is it that you young men actually want? Is it immediate elevation to office? Well, that is forbidden by law. If you were qualified there would be no legal bar: it is simply that the law disqualifies those of your age. Are you then reluctant to share equal rights with a mass of others? But they are people just like you, so how could it be right to deny them like entitlement? I shall be told that there is no sense or equity 39 in democracy, and that the moneyed classes are best equipped to govern best. To that I reply first of all that "demos" denotes the whole people, and "oligarchy", government by the few, denotes only a part; secondly, that the rich are the best financial stewards, policy is best developed by people of sense, and decisions on the arguments advanced are best taken by the general public; and that these three categories, both separately and including all participants, have equal value in a democracy. An oligarchy, though, gives the people their full share of danger, while hogging the benefits and depriving others to establish its own monopoly of advantage. This is what your grandees and your young men are working to achieve, but it is a lost cause in a great city.

'To these people I make a direct last-minute appeal. At present you are utterly devoid of sense: if you do not understand the error of

your ways, you must be the most stupid of all the Greeks known to me, or else the most immoral, if you know perfectly well what you
40 are doing and persist in it. But I urge you even now to learn or reform and work for the general good of the whole city. You should realize that this way you stand to win your fair share—and the good patriots among you a greater share—of the privileges open to the entire community: whereas if you pursue a different path you risk losing all. And let us have no more of these reports you put about—we know their purpose and will not let you get away with it. Even if the Athenians do come, this city of ours will prove its worth and repel them: we have generals who will see to that. And if, as I believe, there is not a shred of truth in all this, the city is not going to be panicked by these reports of yours into electing you to power and so subjecting itself to self-inflicted slavery. The city will form its own view. It will judge that in your case words are tantamount to action, and will never let you talk it out of the freedom it enjoys: it will seek to preserve that freedom by taking active measures to stop you.'

41 Such was Athenagoras' speech. One of the generals now stood up, proposed that no more speakers should be allowed, and gave his own summary of the situation. 'There can be no measured debate', he said, 'when speakers simply trade insults and the audience is happy to sit back and let them carry on. The proper course is to focus on the reports we are receiving and to explore the measures which each individual and the city at large can take for our successful defence against invasion. And even if in the end there proves no emergency, it will do our civic pride no harm to parade the full splendour of our cavalry and hoplites and all the other ornaments of war (we generals shall see to the arrangements and hold a review): no harm either in sending those envoys to the other cities to take soundings and for any other purpose thought appropriate. We have already taken care of some matters, and we shall bring any resulting information before you.' After these words from the general the Syracusans broke up their assembly.

42 By now the Athenians and all allied forces had gathered at Corcyra. The generals first of all held a final review of the fleet and organized their anchorage and campsites. They divided the fleet into three squadrons, each assigned by lot to one of the three generals: this was to avoid any difficulties which a mass sailing might cause in finding water, harbourage, and provisions for all when they made their landfalls, and it was also thought that having a general attached to each

squadron would make for better discipline and easier command. Their next step was to send out an advance group of three ships to Italy and Sicily, to establish which of the cities would give them access. Their instructions were to meet the main fleet in mid-voyage, so that this information would be available before they put in.

And now the Athenians set sail from Corcyra with their entire 43 armament and began the crossing on their way to Sicily. The extent of this armament was as follows. There were a hundred and thirty-four triremes in all, and two Rhodian penteconters: of these a hundred were Athenian (sixty being warships and the rest troop-transports), and the remainder of the fleet was provided by Chios and the other allies. The total number of hoplites was five thousand one hundred. Athenian citizens in this number were fifteen hundred from the service-list of the qualified classes and seven hundred of the thetic class serving as marines: the rest were allied troops, mainly from the subject states, but including five hundred from Argos and two hundred and fifty Mantinean and other mercenaries. There was a total of four hundred and eighty archers (the eighty from Crete); seven hundred Rhodian slingers; a hundred and twenty Megarian exiles, light-armed; and one horse-transport carrying thirty cavalry and their mounts.

Such was the scale of the battle force sailing in this first expedi- 44 tion. The fleet included thirty cargo-ships to carry their grain supplies, the bakers, masons, and carpenters, and all the tools needed for siege operations: also a hundred smaller vessels, requisitioned to sail with the cargo-ships. A good number of other small ships and merchantmen chose to attach themselves to the military expedition for trading purposes. So this whole miscellany of ships now set out from Corcyra to cross the Ionian Gulf. The entire fleet reached land at the promontory of Iapygia, or at Taras, or wherever their course took them, and then sailed along the coast of Italy. The Italian cities would not grant them access to markets or entry within their walls, but did allow them water and anchorage (Taras and Locri refused even this). At length they reached Rhegium at the toe of Italy, where the fleet was reunited. Denied entry to the city, they made camp outside in the sanctuary of Artemis (where the Rhegians set up a market for them), dragged the ships on shore, and rested. They held talks with the Rhegians, pressing them as Chalcidians to support their fellow Chalcidians of Leontini: the Rhegians said that they were not going to take sides, but would abide by any decision reached in consultation with the other Greeks in Italy. The Athenians now gave thought to the best means of conducting the campaign in Sicily: and they were also waiting for the advance ships to return from Egesta, as they needed to know whether the funds of which the Egestan envoys had spoken at Athens were actually there.

45   Meanwhile unambiguous reports of the Athenian fleet at Rhegium were reaching the Syracusans from many sources, including their own agents. In the light of this they set about preparations in earnest, and there were no more doubts. They sent round to the Sicel towns, dispatching troops or envoys as appropriate, and installed garrisons in the local forts. In the city itself they held an inspection to check the condition of equipment and horses, and generally prepared themselves for the rapid and virtually immediate onset of war.

46   The three advance ships now returned from Egesta to join the Athenians at Rhegium. They reported that of all the funds promised they could find evidence of no more than thirty talents. The immediate effect on the generals was to dent their confidence. They had suffered two early setbacks, this news from Egesta and also the refusal of the Rhegians to join their side, when they were the first state the Athenians had attempted to win over, and the most promising, given their kinship with the Leontinians and their long-standing friendly relations with Athens. Nicias had expected the Egestan debacle, but his two colleagues found it utterly baffling. What had happened was that the Egestans had played a trick when the original board of inquiry had arrived from Athens to examine their finances. They took the Athenians to the sanctuary of Aphrodite at Eryx and showed them the range of dedications there—bowls, flagons, censers, and much else besides—which were all of silver and gave a much exaggerated impression of what was in fact a slender financial reserve. They also held private dinner parties for the crews of the triremes: at each of these entertainments the hosts brought out, as if they were their own, gold and silver goblets collected from all over Egesta itself and bor- rowed from the neighbouring cities, Phoenician and Greek alike. All were using virtually the same props, but this apparently universal display of plenty hugely impressed the Athenians from the triremes, and when they arrived back in Athens they put it about that they had seen a great quantity of riches. When word now spread that the money was not there in Egesta, the troops were loud in their recrim- inations against their men who had fallen for a trick and taken every- body with them at the time.

The generals now held a conference in the light of the present situation. Nicias' opinion was that they should sail with their full 47 force against Selinus, which was the main purpose of their expedition. If the Egestans provided funds for the entire campaign, they would make their plans accordingly: but if not, they would demand maintenance for the sixty ships which the Egestans had requested and stay there until the Selinuntians were brought to terms with Egesta by force or negotiation. That achieved, they should sail along the coast to display the power of Athens to the other cities and demonstrate their active support of friends and allies. They should then turn back home, unless they were presented with an early and unexpected opportunity to help the Leontinians or win over one of the other cities: but they should not endanger Athens by squandering their own resources.

Alcibiades declared that, when they had sailed out with such a 48 large force, they could not possibly make an ignominious return with nothing achieved. They should send out proclamations to all the cities except Selinus and Syracuse, and work on the Sicels too, trying to induce revolt in those subject to the Syracusans and to make allies of the others, which would bring them food supplies and further troops. The first focus of persuasion should be Messana, as it lay right on the strait, the gateway to Sicily, and its harbour would provide the best strategic position for the Athenian fleet to wait and watch. Then finally, when they had won over the cities and knew who would fight on which side, they should attack Syracuse and Selinus—unless of course Selinus settled with Egesta and Syracuse allowed the re-establishment of Leontini.

Lamachus gave his opinion that they should sail directly to Syracuse 49 and do battle right up against the city as soon as possible, while the inhabitants were still unprepared and in a state of maximum confusion. Every army, he said, inspires the greatest terror at the very beginning: but if its appearance is long delayed, people recover their courage and are far from impressed at the eventual sight of it. But if the Athenians made a sudden attack, while the enemy were still in fearful suspense, they would have the best chance of victory: all would combine to spread panic—the sight of them (they would never seem so numerous as on that first view), the dread of the consequences, and above all the immediate danger of battle. It was likely too that their refusal to believe in the Athenian approach would leave a good number stranded out in the countryside, and the attempted movement of

people and property into the city would provide rich pickings for the
Athenian army if it was then camped in front of Syracuse and con-
trolling the area. Such a strategy would incline the other Sicilian
Greeks to abandon any alliance with Syracuse and come over to the
Athenians, without waiting to see which side would win. Lamachus
also proposed that they should move their fleet to anchorage at
Megara, and make that their naval station: the place was deserted,
and a short distance from Syracuse by sea or land.

50   After expressing this view Lamachus nevertheless gave his
support to Alcibiades' proposal. Alcibiades then sailed across to
Messana in his own ship and tried to negotiate an alliance, but failed
to persuade them: the Messanans replied that they would not admit
the Athenians to their city, but offered to set up a market for them
outside. So Alcibiades sailed back to Rhegium. The generals immediately crewed and provisioned sixty ships from across the squadrons
and sailed down the coast to Naxos, leaving the rest of the force and
one of their own number at Rhegium. The Naxians did admit them
to their city, and they sailed on to Catana. Receiving no welcome
from the Catanaeans (there was a pro-Syracusan element in the city),
they moved on to the river Terias and camped there. On the next day
they sailed this fleet in column towards Syracuse, except for ten ships
which they sent ahead on reconnaissance to sail into the Great
Harbour and see whether there was any fleet launched. These ships
were to sail in close and make proclamation from their decks that the
Athenians had come in virtue of their alliance and kinship to restore
the Leontinians to their own land: any Leontinians in Syracuse
should therefore feel free to come over to the Athenians as their
friends and benefactors. This proclamation given, and a good survey
made of the city, the harbours, and the terrain which would have to
be the base of their operations in war, the Athenian fleet sailed back
to Catana.

51   The Catanaeans now held an assembly, and, although they would
still not allow the army into the city, they invited the generals to come
in and address them as they wished. While Alcibiades was speaking,
and all local attention was focused on the assembly, the Athenian soldiers managed to take apart a badly built postern gate without anyone
noticing, and crowded in to shop in the marketplace. When they saw
the troops inside the city the relatively few pro-Syracusans took immediate fright and slipped away, but the main body of the Catanaeans
voted for an alliance with the Athenians and invited them to bring the

rest of their forces from Rhegium. On this the Athenians sailed back to Rhegium and now set out for Catana with their entire armament. As soon as they arrived they started establishing their camp.

They began to receive reports from Camarina that if they went 52 there the people would come over to them: reports too of the manning of a Syracusan fleet. So they sailed with their entire force down the coast to Syracuse first of all. Finding no evidence of a fleet being manned, they carried on round towards Camarina, where they put in to the open beach and sent a herald to the city. The Camarinaeans refused to admit them, saying that their sworn agreement was to receive any Athenian visitation in a single ship, but greater numbers only at their own invitation. Thus frustrated, the Athenians sailed · away. They did land on a part of Syracusan territory and do some plundering, but when the Syracusan cavalry came to the defence and killed some of the light-armed troops dispersed over the area, they took themselves back to Catana.

There they found that the state ship Salaminia had arrived from 53 Athens to order Alcibiades home to answer the public charges against him. Also required were some other members of the force who were among those informed against together with Alcibiades for profanation of the Mysteries or named in connection with the Herms. After the expedition sailed the Athenians had continued vigorous inquiry into both affairs, the Mysteries and the Herms. They made no assessment of the informers, but accepted any accusation whatever as grounds for suspicion, and arrested and imprisoned utterly respectable citizens on the evidence of some worthless types. In their view the paramount need was thorough investigation leading to detection, and they were not going to let questions of an informer's worth prevent the examination of anyone accused, however respectable he might seem. The people were aware, by oral tradition, that the tyranny of Peisistratus and his sons had grown oppressive towards the end, and also that its overthrow was not brought about by their own efforts or by Harmodius, but was the result of Spartan intervention. This knowledge kept them in a state of constant anxiety and universal suspicion.

It was in fact the mere circumstance of a love affair which drove 54 Aristogeiton and Harmodius to their desperate act. By a detailed narrative of this affair I shall demonstrate the complete inaccuracy of all other versions, including the story which the Athenians themselves tell of their own tyrants and the event in question. When Peisistratus died in his old age, still in power as tyrant, it was not Hipparchus, as most people think, but Hippias, the eldest son, who succeeded to the tyranny. Harmodius was a celebrated beauty in the flower of his youth, and the lover who claimed him was a middle-ranking commoner called Aristogeiton. Hipparchus the son of Peisistratus tried to seduce Harmodius, but he refused his advances and told Aristogeiton. In all the passionate jealousy of a lover, and terrified that Hipparchus would use his power to take Harmodius from him by force, Aristogeiton immediately began to plot the overthrow of the tyranny, as best he could in his social station. Meanwhile Hipparchus made a second attempt to seduce Harmodius, with no greater success: his reaction was not to contemplate any use of force, but to look for some covert means of humiliating Harmodius without his motive becoming clear.

And indeed violence would have been foreign to the overall character of the tyrants' regime, which was far from oppressive to the general public. They established their rule without creating any bitterness, and of all tyrants these evinced the strongest traits of decency and intelligence. Although they taxed the Athenians at only five per cent of their produce, they still beautified the city, supported wars through to the end, and maintained sacrificial offerings in the temples. In most respects the city was left free to enjoy its previous constitution, except to the extent that the tyrants always ensured high office for one of their own people. Among others of the family to hold the annual archonship was Peisistratus the son of the tyrant Hippias, named after his grandfather. In his term of office he dedicated the altar of the Twelve Gods in the Agora and the altar of Apollo in the sanctuary of Apollo Pythius. The inscription on the altar in the Agora was obscured from view when the people of Athens subsequently built an extension to the altar. But one can still see now the faint lettering of the inscription in the Pythium, which reads:

> Here Peisistratus, Hippias' son, in the close of Apollo
> Pythius, placed this gift marking the office he held.

55   That Hippias succeeded to the tyranny as the eldest son I can definitely confirm from my own knowledge based on particularly reliable oral sources. It can also be deduced from these plain facts. Of the legitimate sons of Peisistratus it is clear that only Hippias had children. That is indicated not only by the inscription on the altar but also by the column set up on the Acropolis at Athens concerning the criminality of the tyrants. On this column there is no mention of

any child of Thessalus or Hipparchus, but five children of Hippias are listed, born to him by Myrrhine the daughter of Callias son of Hyperochides: and it is a fair presumption that the first son to marry was the eldest. On this same column Hippias' name is inscribed immediately after his father's: again the presumption must be that Hippias was first in line and became tyrant after his father. And in any case I cannot think that Hippias could easily have taken over the tyranny straight away, if Hipparchus had been tyrant at the time of his murder and Hippias had tried to establish his own rule there and then. As it was, his by now characteristic hold of fear over the citizens and strict discipline in his bodyguards enabled him to maintain control with a wide margin of security. He certainly did not show the diffidence of a younger brother unfamiliar with the continuous exercise of power. What happened with Hipparchus was that the notoriety of his incidental murder fuelled the subsequent belief that he was tyrant.

So, to resume, when Harmodius rejected his advances, Hipparchus 56 carried out his intention of humiliating him. Harmodius had a young sister who was a virgin. Hipparchus and his people invited her to present herself as one of the basket-bearers in a religious procession, but then sent her away, claiming that she had never been invited in the first place because she did not meet the qualification. Harmodius was furious at this, and Aristogeiton yet more incensed on his behalf. They already had everything arranged with their fellow conspirators, and were just waiting for the Great Panathenaea, the one day when a body of citizens under arms, as participants in the procession, would excite no suspicion. The plan was that they themselves would strike the first blow, and their colleagues in the procession would then immediately move to deal with the guards. For security's sake only a small number were privy to the conspiracy: but their hope was that, however few the protagonists, those unaware of the plot but with arms at hand would instantly join in the opportunity for their own liberation.

When the day of the festival came, Hippias went outside the walls 57 to the place called the Cerameicus, where he and his guards were busy arranging the various elements of the procession into their sequence. Harmodius and Aritogeiton, ready armed with their daggers, moved forward to do the deed. But when they saw one of the conspirators in friendly conversation with Hippias (who made himself approachable to everyone), they stopped in alarm, thinking that they had been betrayed and were on the point of arrest. Before that could happen they determined to take their vengeance first, if possible, on the man who had wounded them both and driven them to risk all. They dashed inside the gates just as they were and found Hipparchus by the shrine called Leocoreium. Blind to all else they went straight for him in the height of passion, a lover's jealousy in one, in the other the fury of a man insulted. They stabbed him repeatedly and killed him. A crowd gathered, and Aristogeiton managed to escape the guards in the first instance: but he was later caught and received no gentle treatment. Harmodius was killed there and then.

58　When the news was brought to Hippias in the Cerameicus, his immediate reaction was not to go to the scene of the crime, but to walk over to the contingent of armed men waiting to take part in the procession, before they could learn what had happened (they were at some distance from the scene). Giving no hint in his expression of anything untoward he asked them to leave their arms and move across to another area to which he pointed them. They moved as directed, thinking that he had some instruction to give them. He then told his guards to remove the arms, and proceeded immediately to pick out those he suspected of complicity and anyone found carrying a dagger (shield and spear only being the regular arms for these processions).

59　That is how the conspiracy of Harmodius and Aristogeiton turned out for them: it began with a lover's resentment, and the final desperate act was the result of a last-minute failure of nerve. The consequence for the people of Athens was that the tyranny now entered a more oppressive stage, as Hippias was increasingly fearful for his security. He executed a good number of citizens, and also began to look abroad in the search for some ready asylum should there be a revolution. That was at any rate the reason for subsequently marrying his daughter Archedice to Aeantides the son of Hippoclus the tyrant of Lampsacus—a surprising alliance of Athenian and Lampsacene, but Hippias was aware that Hippoclus and his family had great influence with the Persian King Dareius. Her tomb is at Lampsacus, and bears this inscription:

Under this earth lies the daughter of Hippias, who was the greatest
　Man of his time in Greece. Her name is Archedice.
Though her father, her husband, her brothers, her sons were all tyrants,
　Her own mind stayed firm, free of presumptuous pride.

Hippias remained as tyrant of Athens for three more years. In the fourth year he was deposed by the Spartans and Alcmeonidae among the Athenian exiles. Given safe conduct to Sigeium and on to Aeantides at Lampsacus, he then made his way to King Dareius. Twenty years later, and by then an old man, he came back from there to Marathon with the Persian expedition.

With this history in mind, and recollecting all the other traditional 60 information they had about the tyrants, the Athenian people were now fiercely suspicious of the alleged profaners of the Mysteries and thought that it was all part of some oligarchic or tyrannical conspiracy. Inflamed by such suspicions they had already put in gaol many men of high standing, and there was no end in sight—every day there was greater ferocity and yet further arrests. At this point one of the prisoners who was a prime suspect was persuaded by a fellow prisoner to give information, whether true or not (there are conjectures both ways, and nobody either then or subsequently has been able to establish the truth about the perpetrators). What convinced the prisoner was his companion's argument that, even if he had not actually committed the crime, he should claim immunity for turning state's evidence, which would both save his own life and put an end to the prevailing climate of suspicion in the city: a confession of guilt with the promise of immunity gave him a better chance of survival than to deny it and face trial. So this prisoner laid information against himself and against others in the matter of the Herms. The people of Athens were greatly relieved to gain what they supposed clear evidence of the truth, having previously seethed at the possibility that they might never discover who was plotting against their democracy, and they immediately released the informer and all his fellow prisoners not named in his deposition. Those accused they brought to trial. They executed all they could arrest, and pronounced sentence of death on those who had fled, advertising a monetary reward for anyone who killed them. In all this it was unclear whether the victims were justly punished, but there was no doubt of the beneficial effect on the city at large.

In the case of Alcibiades, with the enemies who had attacked him 61 before he sailed with the expedition keeping up their agitation, the Athenians took a severe view. Now that they thought they had the truth about the Herms, they were yet more convinced that he was responsible, as charged, for the profanation of the Mysteries, with the same purpose and as part of the anti-democratic conspiracy. And it so happened that at the time of this ferment in Athens a small Spartan force came as far as the Isthmus, having some business with the Boeotians.

It was believed at Athens that the arrival of this force had nothing to do with the Boeotians but was a prearranged move plotted by Alcibiades, and that if they had not been quick enough to act on the information received and make the arrests, the city would have been betrayed: indeed there was one night when the people took their arms and slept out in the sanctuary of Theseus (the Theseium in the city, that is). At about the same time too Alcibiades' friends in Argos were suspected of planning an attack on the Argive democracy, and this prompted the Athenians to hand over the Argive hostages held in the islands to the people of Argos, to deal with as they pleased.

Suspicion had concentrated on Alcibiades from all directions, so that the Athenians were determined to bring him to trial and execute him: hence the dispatch of the state ship Salaminia to Sicily, to fetch Alcibiades and others against whom information had been laid. The Salaminia's orders were to give notice that he must follow the ship home to answer the charges, but not to arrest him: they were anxious to cause no stir in Sicily which might affect either their own troops or the enemy, and they were particularly concerned not to lose the Mantineans and the Argives, believing that it was Alcibiades' influence which had persuaded them to join the expedition. So Alcibiades and his fellow accused set out from Sicily in his own ship and sailed on the way to Athens in company with the Salaminia. When they reached Thurii, they followed no further. Fearful of sailing home to a prejudiced trial, they left their ship and disappeared. The crew of the Salaminia spent some time searching for Alcibiades and his fellows, but called off the search when there was no sign of them, and left for home. Alcibiades, now an exile, found passage shortly afterwards in a vessel sailing from Thurian territory to the Peloponnese. The Athenians condemned him and his colleagues to death in their absence.

62   After this the remaining two Athenian generals in Sicily split their force into two parts, dividing the command between them by lot, then sailed with the entire force towards Selinus and Egesta: they wanted to know whether the Egestans would produce the money, and also to reconnoitre the situation at Selinus and discover the state of the quarrel with Egesta. Sailing round with the coast on their left, along the side of Sicily which faces the Tyrrhenian Gulf, they put in to Himera, which is the only Greek city in that part of the island. They were not made welcome, and sailed on. As they continued their voyage they took the coastal town of Hyccara, which despite its

Sicanian population was hostile to Egesta. They enslaved the inhabitants and handed over the town to the Egestans, whose cavalry had
joined them. Their own infantry now set out back on foot through
Sicel country all the way to Catana, while the transports took the sea
route there with the enslaved people on board. Nicias sailed round
direct from Hyccara to Egesta, where his business included the collection of those thirty talents: that achieved, he rejoined the main
force. The sale of the slaves realized another hundred and twenty
talents. They sent round to their allies among the Sicels asking for
consignments of troops: and with half of their own force they
marched against the enemy town of Hybla Geleatis, but failed to take
it. So the summer ended.

At the very start of the following winter the Athenians began 63
preparations for the attack on Syracuse. The Syracusans too for their
part prepared to go on the offensive against the Athenians. Their
initial fear and expectation of an immediate Athenian attack had not
been realized, and with each passing day they had grown in confidence. Now that they saw the Athenian fleet occupied far away
from them at the other end of Sicily, and the march on Hybla resulting in the failure of the attempted assault, they took a yet more dismissive view of the Athenians, and—as the common people tend to
do when their spirits are up—they insisted that their generals should
lead them out to Catana, since the Athenians were not coming against
them. Syracusan cavalry were always riding up to keep a watch on
the Athenian camp and taunting them: a favourite sneer was to ask
whether their real purpose in coming was more to find themselves a
new home abroad alongside the Syracusans than to resettle the
Leontinians in their old home.

The Athenian generals were well aware of the situation. Their 64
plan was to draw the entire Syracusan army as far as possible away
from the city and then use this opportunity to sail their ships round
under cover of night and establish a suitable base without interference: they reckoned that this would give them a better chance than an
opposed landing from the sea or an observed march by land, which,
in the absence of cavalry of their own, would expose their light troops
and the whole crowd of unarmed attendants to severe damage from
the numerous cavalry on the Syracusan side. This way, though, they
could gain a base without any significant cavalry attrition on the way:
and the Syracusan exiles accompanying them advised of the position
close by the sanctuary of Olympian Zeus (a position which they did

in fact go on to occupy). So to further their plan the generals employed
the following stratagem. They sent into Syracuse a man of firm loyalty
to their own side who was believed by the Syracusan generals to be
in sympathy with them. This man was a Catanaean, and he professed
to come from the men in Catana whose names the generals recognized as the remaining group of their partisans in the city. His story
was that the Athenians spent their nights in Catana itself, leaving
their arms in their day-camp, and if the Syracusans were prepared to
bring out their entire army to make a dawn raid on the camp on a day
to be agreed, their party in Catana would block the Athenians in the
city and set fire to their ships, giving the Syracusans an easy chance
to attack the stockade and take the camp. There were, he said, many
Catanaeans ready to take part in an action which was already planned,
and he was their emissary.

65   Given their overall confidence and their intention, even without
this proposal, to have preparations in train for a march on Catana,
the Syracusan generals were far more inclined to believe the fellow
uncritically, and immediately agreed a day on which they would arrive.
They then sent him back and, since by now they had an allied presence in the city (Selinuntians and some others), they put the whole
of their own Syracusan army on alert for an expedition. When their
preparations were complete and the agreed days of departure and
arrival were on them, they marched out towards Catana and camped
for the night by the river Symaethus in Leontinian territory. When
the Athenians had confirmation of their approach, they decamped,
took on board their warships and other vessels all their own forces
and all the Sicels and any others who had joined them, and sailed off
at nightfall for Syracuse. At dawn on the following day the Athenians
began disembarking at the site opposite the sanctuary of Olympian
Zeus to establish their base there. At the same time the Syracusan
cavalry who had ridden on ahead to Catana found that the whole
Athenian army had taken ship, and returned with this news to the
infantry. The entire force now turned back to defend the city.

66   They had a long march to Syracuse, and in the meantime the
Athenians used the lull to establish themselves in an advantageous
position, which would allow them to start battle whenever they wished
and minimized the trouble the Syracusan cavalry could cause them
either during an engagement or before it. On one side they were protected by walls, houses, trees, and a marsh, and along the other side
by precipitous ground. They felled the trees nearby and carried the

trunks down to the seashore, where they drove them in to form a palisade opposite their line of ships: they also threw up a hasty barricade
of rough stones and logs at Dascon, the easiest point of access for the
enemy, and broke down the bridge over the river Anapus. No one
came out from the city to hinder this work. The first to appear in
opposition were the Syracusan cavalry, and then later the whole body
of infantry gathered to join them. Their first move was to advance
close to the Athenian base, but when the Athenians would not come
out to meet them they retired and made camp on the other side of the
Helorum road.

On the following day the Athenians and their allies prepared for 67
battle. Their order had the Argives and Mantineans occupying the
right wing, the Athenians the centre, and the rest of the allies the left.
Half of the army constituted the van, ranged eight ranks deep. The
other half was formed up close to the sleeping-quarters in a hollow
square, also eight ranks deep, with instructions to be on the alert to
move up in support of any part of the line under particular pressure:
and they placed the porters inside this square of reserve troops. The
Syracusans drew up their entire hoplite force sixteen deep, consisting of a full levy of their own citizens and such allies as had come to
join them (mainly Selinuntians: but they also had a total of two hundred cavalry from Gela, and about twenty cavalry and fifty archers
from Camarina). They placed their cavalry, numbering no fewer
than twelve hundred, on the right wing, with the javelin-men next to
them.

The Athenians wanted to make the first attacking move, and at the
point of readiness Nicias went up and down the line with these words
of encouragement for each individual national contingent and for the
army as a whole:

'Men, all of us here face the same challenge, so there is no need for 68
a long address. And I think the very strength of our force should
build your confidence more than any fine speech could do for a
weaker army. When we are Argives and Mantineans, Athenians and
the best of the islanders, we can all have high hopes of victory in the
company of so many allies of such quality— especially as our opponents are not picked troops like ourselves but a city militia called out
in defence. And what is more they are Sicilians. They may look down
on us, but they will not stand up to us: their skill does not match their
ambition. I would have you all bear in mind too that we are far from
home and the only friendly land nearby is what you can win by your

own exertion in battle. So my message to you is the opposite of the exhortation which I am sure the enemy commanders are giving to their own troops. They will be speaking of a battle for their country: but I must remind you that this is not your country, and you must conquer it or else face a difficult retreat, harried by cavalry in great numbers. So remember your own worth, and move confidently to the attack: you have less to fear from the enemy than from the pressure and difficulty of our present situation.'

69   With this address Nicias led his army straight into battle. The Syracusans were not expecting to have to fight that soon, and some of them had actually gone off into the city, which was not far away. They came running back in hurried support and, though late, joined the main body wherever they could find a station. In this and all other battles the Syracusans lacked nothing in spirit or daring, but their otherwise exemplary courage could extend only as far as their skill allowed, and when this failed they were forced to lose the object of their resolve. Despite their expectation that the Athenians would not initiate an attack, and their consequent need for a hasty defence, they took up their arms and advanced straight for the enemy. The action began with skirmishes between the stone-throwers, slingers, and archers on either side, with drives one way or the other as is usual in these light-armed engagements. Then the soothsayers presented the customary sacrificial victims, and the trumpeters called the hoplites to join battle. The two armies advanced. At issue for the Syracusans was a fight for their own country, and for each man among them immediate survival and future liberty. On the other side the Athenians were fighting to add a foreign country to their own and to save their own from a damaging defeat; the Argives and the independent allies were eager to share the Athenians' achievement of their aim, and then with the battle won to have sight of their own land once more; and the main spur for the subject allies was the consciousness that their only hope of surviving the immediate moment lay in victory (a subsidiary hope was that if they had helped the Athenians to a further conquest their own conditions of subjection might be eased).

70   When the armies were engaged hand-to-hand, for a long time there was no advantage on either side, and in the course of the battle thunder and lightning came on with a deluge of rain. This contributed yet further to the terror of the first-time soldiers who were least familiar with war, but the more experienced of the Athenians put the

storm down to the season of the year and were much more surprised by the continued resistance of the opposition. But then first the Argives drove back the left wing of the Syracusans, followed by similar Athenian success against the section facing them, and now the rest of the Syracusan line began to break up and the whole army was put to flight. The Athenians did not pursue to any distance, as the numerous Syracusan cavalry, uninvolved in the defeat, kept them pinned down, charging and turning back any Athenian hoplites they saw breaking out in pursuit. So the Athenians followed in a body as far as it was safe to do so, then withdrew and set up a trophy. The Syracusans gathered on the Helorum road and re-formed as best they could in the circumstances, but still sent a detachment of their own troops to guard the Olympieium, fearful that the Athenians would lay hands on the treasures there. The rest of their army returned to the city.

The Athenians did not in fact go near the temple, but took up their 71 own dead and placed them on a pyre, then spent the night where they were. On the following day they gave back the Syracusan dead under truce and collected the bones of their own from the pyre: about two hundred and sixty of the Syracusans and their allies had been killed, and some fifty of the Athenians and their allies. They then took the enemy spoils with them and sailed back to Catana. It was now winter, and they thought they could not prosecute the war in Sicily any further without acquiring cavalry to prevent complete domination by the Syracusan horse—so this meant sending for cavalry from Athens and recruiting from their local allies. They also needed more funds collected from Sicily itself and sent from Athens, and wanted to win over some of the cities (which they hoped would be more amenable after the result of the battle). All that, and they had to see to the provision of food and all other supplies needed for an attack on Syracuse in the spring. So with this programme in mind 72 they sailed off to Naxos and Catana, intending to winter there.

The Syracusans buried their dead and then held an assembly, at which Hermocrates the son of Hermon came forward to speak. He was a man of unsurpassed intelligence with a proven record also of experience and exemplary courage in war. He now sought to boost their morale and prevent them resigning themselves to what had happened. Their resolution, he said, had not been defeated: the problem had been lack of system. Yet the margin of deficiency had been less than might have been expected, given that they were up against the most experienced soldiers in Greece and were little more than laymen against professionals. The major problems were the number of generals (there were fifteen of them) and the multiplicity of command, together with the lack of systematic response to command among the troops. If they confined authority to just a few generals of experience, and spent this winter organizing the hoplite force—maximizing numbers by providing arms for those without their own, and introducing compulsory training as well—they would have a good chance, he said, of overcoming their opponents. They already had the courage, and discipline in action would follow. Both qualities would develop together, discipline honed in the school of danger, and courage taking bolder form with the confidence of greater expertise. The generals elected should be few in number and have absolute discretionary power, confirmed by a sworn guarantee that the people would allow them to command as they knew best: this way confidential matters would be better protected, and all other arrangements placed on an orderly and accountable basis.

73   The Syracusans paid attention to him and voted in all his recommendations. They elected just three generals—Hermocrates himself, Heracleides the son of Lysimachus, and Sicanus the son of Execestus. They also sent envoys to Corinth and Sparta, asking for their aid as allies and urging the Spartans to intensify an open war against the Athenians on their behalf, which would either pull the Athenians back from Sicily or leave them less able to send reinforcements to the army already there.

74   The Athenian fleet back in Catana now sailed straight for Messana in the expectation that the city would be betrayed to them. But the intrigues they had engaged in came to nothing. On his recall and dismissal from command Alcibiades, aware that he must go into exile, had divulged to the Syracusan party in Messana what he knew was planned. They had already killed the conspirators, and those who shared their own politics now formed an armed faction which prevailed on the city not to admit the Athenians. The Athenians stayed there for about thirteen days, but with wintry weather, shortage of provisions, and no success they went back to Naxos, where they fenced their camp with stockades and prepared to spend the winter there. They also sent a trireme to Athens for funds and cavalry, looking for both to arrive at the beginning of spring.

75   During the winter the Syracusans built a wall adjoining the city, which took in the Temenites sanctuary and extended along the whole

of the region which faces Epipolae: this was to exclude the possibility of being walled off at closer quarters in the event of a defeat. They also built garrison-forts at Megara and in the Olympieium, and drove stakes into the sea at all the landing-places. Knowing that the Athenians were wintering in Naxos, they took a full levy of their army to Catana and returned home after ravaging some of the territory and burning the Athenian camp and its huts. They heard that the Athenians were sending an embassy to Camarina in an attempt to win the people over on the strength of their former alliance, made under Laches: so they sent a counter-embassy of their own. They had their suspicions that the Camarinaeans had not been particularly enthusiastic in sending what help they did for the first battle, and might be unwilling to give any more support in the future, now that they saw the Athenians successful in that battle: they could be persuaded to renew the old friendship and join the Athenian side. So the two groups arrived at Camarina, Hermocrates and some colleagues from Syracuse, and an Athenian delegation including Euphemus. The Camarinaeans held an assembly, at which Hermocrates, looking to prejudice them against the Athenians, spoke as follows:

'Men of Camarina, our reason for this mission is not the fact of the 76 Athenian military presence (we have no fear that this will intimidate you), but rather the possibility of a diplomatic approach which could sway you if you do not hear what we have to say first. You know the pretext for their coming to Sicily, but we can all suppose their real intention. In my view they are not here to repossess the Leontinians but to dispossess us. They cannot plausibly claim any consistency. They displace populations in Greece, yet want to replace populations in Sicily; they profess concern on grounds of kinship for the Chalcidians of Leontini, but have enslaved and keep subject the Chalcidians in Euboea, from where Leontini was colonized. That programme of control in Greece and their attempts now in Sicily are one of a kind. They accepted the leadership freely offered them by the Ionians and their own allied colonies for a campaign of reprisal against the Persians, but then forced them into subjection on a variety of pretexts—failure to provide troops, misuse of troops against one another, any specious charge they could bring in any particular case. This front against the Persians was not, then, the Athenians fighting for Greek freedom, nor the Greeks fighting for their own: the Athenians were looking to replace Persian enslavement with theirs, and the Greeks to make a change of slave-master—to one just as clever, but clever for the worse.

77 'But enough of this. We are not here now to parade the injuries done by the Athenians—the charges are easily made, and you know them already. Our purpose is much more to accuse ourselves. We have had the examples of the Aegean Greeks enslaved because they did not support one another, we now have the same tricks being played on us here—all this talk of "resettling our kinsmen of Leontini" and "helping our allies in Egesta"—and yet we are reluctant to band together and show them that what they have here are not Ionians, not Hellespontines, not islanders used to a constant succession of slave-masters, Persian or whoever, but Dorians, free inhabitants of Sicily and sons of an independent Peloponnese. Or are we waiting until we are picked off one by one and city by city, when we know this is the only way in which we can be conquered? When we can see them resorting to the stratagem of persuading some of us to split away, encouraging others to inter-city wars by the offer of alliance, and spreading mischief wherever they can with cosy private proposals? And do any of us think that when his fellow in some other part of the country is being destroyed the same fate will not later reach him—that the first to suffer will be alone in his misfortune?

78 'I can imagine someone here reckoning that the hostility is between Syracusan and Athenian, and does not involve him, so taking amiss any suggestion that he should risk himself for what is after all my city. Well, he should reflect that he will not simply be fighting for my city: this will be a fight, in my territory, for his own city just as much as for mine, and he will be the more securely placed to carry on that struggle if I have not been disposed of first, so he can have me to fight with him in his cause and not be left on his own. He should reflect too that the Athenian purpose is not so much to punish Syracusan hostility, but to use me as a lever to ensure his compliance. And if anyone is motivated by envy, or it could be fear (greatness attracts both), to want Syracuse damaged enough to teach us a lesson, but with enough life left in her to protect his own interests, he is asking for something beyond human power to achieve: a man cannot regulate fortune to match his own inventory of desires. And if he miscalculates, while they are mourning his own ruin he may well wish that he still had my prosperity to envy. But that will be impossible if he has abandoned us and refused to take his share in these dangers which are more real than they may sound. On the face of it he would be preserving our power: in reality he would be ensuring his own salvation. And you of all people, men of Camarina, should have foreseen

this and not be so lukewarm in your support as you are now: you are neighbours of ours, and next in the line of danger. You should have come to us, not we to you. You would have been begging for our help if the Athenians had landed first on your territory, and in the situation as it is you should have presented yourselves at Syracuse with the same call of "no surrender". But so far neither you nor any of the others have shown this initiative.

'Cowardice may have you professing the need to be fair as between 79 us and the invaders, and pleading your alliance with the Athenians. But that alliance was made against the possibility of an enemy attack on you, and was not meant to have application to your friends: and you were to help the Athenians when harm was done to them, not, as now, when they themselves are doing harm to others. Look—even the Rhegians, despite being Chalcidians themselves, are not prepared to join the Athenians in resettling their fellow Chalcidians of Leontini. Strange, then, if the Rhegians suspect the reality behind the specious justification and choose principle over logic, while you are happy with any plausible excuse for helping your natural enemies and joining them—the worst enemies we have—in the destruction of your yet more natural kinsmen. This will not do. You must fight back, and not be intimidated by the scale of their forces. This is nothing to fear if we all stand together—only if the opposite happens and we lose our cohesion, which is what they are trying to achieve. Even when they met us on our own and had the better of the battle, they did not succeed in their objective and made a hasty retreat.

'So there is no reason for despair if we can all combine and make 80 a more wholehearted contribution to the alliance, especially as we expect help from the Peloponnesians, who completely outclass the Athenians in military expertise. And no one should think it fair to us or safe for you to adopt the cautious policy of denying help to either side on the grounds that you are allies of both. Fair in theory is not the same as fair in practice. If the result of your refusal to join us is that the victim falls and the aggressor wins, it follows that by this very abstention you have failed to protect the survival of the victims and also failed to prevent a crime by the aggressors. The nobler course, surely, is to align with the injured parties who are also your kinsmen, and so to preserve the common interests of Sicily and save these Athenian friends of yours from their error.

'To sum up the Syracusan case. We see no point in giving you or the others a detailed lecture on what you yourselves can see as well as we can. But we do appeal to you, and in so doing make this statement in front of you all. If we fail to persuade you, the truth of the matter will be this: we Dorians are under attack by Ionians, our inveterate enemies, and we are betrayed by fellow Dorians—you! If the Athenians destroy us, your decision will have given them the means, but the credit will be all in their name: and what will be the prize of their victory?—the very people who enabled that victory. If on the other hand we win through, you again will pay the penalty for putting us in that danger. Think, then, and make your choice: either immediate safety in immediate servitude, or the chance of winning through with us, and so avoiding both the shame of submission to Athenian slave-masters and a bitter feud with us, which would not be short-lived.'

81   Such was Hermocrates' speech. After him the Athenian envoy Euphemus spoke as follows:

82   'We came here for the renewal of our former alliance, but the criticisms launched by my Syracusan counterpart oblige me to add some words in justification of our empire. Now in fact he made the most important point himself when he said that the Ionians are inveterate enemies of the Dorians. Such indeed is the case. As Ionians living next door to a greater number of Dorians in the Peloponnese we had to consider the best means of avoiding subservience to them. We acquired a navy, and after the Persian Wars broke free from the Spartan command and leadership, as there was no more reason for them to dictate to us than the other way round, except to the extent of their greater power at the time. Our own city then took on its role as leader of the King's previous subjects. Our thinking was that this way, with the power now to defend ourselves, there would be the least danger of falling under the Peloponnesians: and even on the strictest view there was no injustice in our subjection of the Ionians and the islanders, which the Syracusans describe as "enslavement of our kinsmen". We were their mother-city, and they joined the Persian invasion against us; they did not have the courage to revolt and lose their homes, as we did when we abandoned our city; they chose slavery for themselves and wanted to impose the same state on us.

83   'This gives one reason for our empire—we have earned it. We supplied the largest navy and unhesitating determination in the service of Greece, while those who are now our subjects were equally energetic in the Persian cause to our intended detriment. A second reason was our desire to build up strength against the Peloponnesians.

We make no fancy claims to justify our empire on the grounds that we were the sole agents in overthrowing the barbarians, or that we put ourselves at risk for the freedom of our allies, rather than for a general freedom including our own. No one can be blamed for taking the appropriate steps to ensure his own safety. It is concern for our security which brings us here now, and we can see that you and we have the same interests. The evidence we offer for this lies in the very accusations made against us by the Syracusans which serve to intensify your own suspicious fears (and we know that when people are in an agony of suspicion over some issue they take comfort for the time being in arguments which appeal to their mood, but when it comes to practical application they go on to follow their own interests).

'We have told you that fear is the reason for maintaining our empire at home: and it is fear too which brings us here to put matters on a secure footing in conjunction with our friends. We have not come to enslave you, but to prevent you being enslaved. And let me hear 84 no objections that your welfare is none of our concern. The truth is that with you intact and strong enough to resist the Syracusans there is less likelihood of their sending support to the Peloponnesians and so damaging us. This alone makes you a prime concern for us. For the same reason there is good cause for us to restore the Leontinians, not to subject status like their kinsmen in Euboea, but to the most powerful position possible, so that they can carry out harassment on our behalf from their own land on the borders of Syracuse. In Greece we can match our enemies on our own, so when Hermocrates claims that there is no consistency in liberating the Chalcidians here while keeping them subject at home, the fact is that it suits our purpose to have the Chalcidians of Euboea as monetary contributors only, without military capability, whereas here it suits our purpose that the Leontinians and our other friends should be completely independent.

'For a tyrant or an imperial city nothing advantageous is inconsist- 85 ent, and the only bond is reliability: in every case the circumstances determine enemy or friend. And our advantage here requires that we do not weaken our friends but use their strength to render our enemies powerless. You should trust us in this. At home too we manage our allies in a variety of ways according to their particular utility. The Chians and Methymnaeans, for example, are independent as long as they provide us with ships; the majority are under rather greater compulsion to pay tribute; and there are others left in completely free alliance with us (though they are islanders, and we could easily take them over), because they lie in strategic positions around the Peloponnese. So it is logical that our policy in Sicily too should reflect our interests, and, as we have said, our fear of the Syracusans. Their aim is to dominate you. They plan to unite you in suspicion of us, and then by force or default (if we have failed and left) to take Sicily under their own control. This is inevitable if you others join them. Such a combined force will tax our capability, and with us gone the Syracusans will have the strength to deal with you.

86   'If anyone thinks otherwise, the very facts refute him. When you called us in aid on that first occasion, the threat you held before us was of the danger to ourselves if we allowed you to fall under the Syracusans. It can hardly be fair now to reject the argument with which you sought to persuade us in the first place, or to be suspicious of the larger force which we have now brought to meet their strength. Your suspicions should much more be directed against them. We cannot remain here without your help, and even if we were to turn to the bad and make conquests, we could not retain control with communication so long by sea and the impossibility of garrisoning major cities which have resources comparable to those of mainland centres. Whereas these people are established right on your border, and theirs is no temporary camp but a city much larger than the complement of our forces here. They are always scheming against you, and they never miss an opportunity (as already demonstrated, for example, by their treatment of Leontini): and now they have the gall to invite you to take sides against the very people who are blocking their schemes and have so far saved Sicily from falling under their domination. Do they think you that naive? The security to which we invite you is altogether more real. It is already inherent in our relations with each other, and we urge you not to turn your backs on it. Consider. With or without allies the Syracusans outnumber you and will always have an open road against you, but you will not often be given the chance of beating them with the support of an army as powerful as ours. If your suspicion of our motives means that this army leaves Sicily with its purpose unfulfilled—or even in defeat—the time will come when you will long to see even a fraction of it back again, but by then you will be beyond help.

87   'So, men of Camarina, we ask you and the others to pay no attention to these Syracusan travesties. We have told you the whole truth about the suspicions held against us, and we shall now summarize the arguments which we think you will find convincing. Our position

is this. We dominate people at home so that others should not control us, and we liberate people in Sicily to prevent them being used to our harm; we are obliged to busy ourselves, because we have many interests to protect; our intervention here is not gratuitous, but both now and previously it is the response of allies to requests for help from those of you here suffering oppression. Do not appoint yourselves judges or regulators of our behaviour and try to change it (hard to do that now in any case), but take and use whatever aspect of our restless character serves your purpose as well as ours. You should not think of this character of ours as a universal curse—it has actually benefited far more Greeks than it has harmed. Whoever the people and wherever the place (even where we have no presence), any potential victim and any intending aggressor can expect a ready response from us, and the prospect in the one case of our decisive assistance and in the other of fearful consequences if we intervene: the result is that the aggressor is forced to think again, and the potential victim has his position rescued without the need for action on his part. This is the security we offer you now, equally available to you and to anyone else who asks for it. Do not reject it. Follow the others' example and join with us: then you can change your stance towards Syracuse from constant wariness to an equality of threat at any time.'

Such was Euphemus' speech. The Camarinaeans found themselves **88** in a difficult situation. They were well disposed to the Athenians (except to the extent that they thought them aiming at the domination of Sicily), and always at odds with the Syracusans because they shared a border. But a contributory fear was that the Syracusans, uncomfortably close neighbours, could win through even without support from Camarina, and for that reason they had originally sent that small squadron of cavalry and now decided that for the future they would favour the Syracusans with their practical help, keeping it as modest as possible, while for the time being, to maintain a show of even-handedness to the Athenians (who had after all proved superior in the recent battle), they would give the same answer to both. So after consideration along these lines they replied that, since they were formally allied to both parties now at war with each other, they thought the only policy consistent with their oaths was to give help to neither. Both sets of envoys now left.

While the Syracusans continued their own preparations for the war, the Athenians encamped at Naxos made overtures to the Sicels in an effort to win over as many as they could. The Sicels concentrated in the plains were Syracusan subjects and not many had revolted, but the settlements in the interior were and always had been independent, and with few exceptions these Sicels immediately joined the Athenians and began supplying the army with food: some contributed money also. The Athenians took offensive action against those who refused to come over, and forced some of them into submission: elsewhere they were frustrated when the Syracusans sent garrison troops to assist the defence. They transferred their naval station from Naxos to Catana, rebuilt the camp which had been burned down by the Syracusans, and settled there to see the winter through. They dispatched a trireme to Carthage proposing friendship, in the hope of obtaining some assistance from that quarter, and also sent to Etruria, where some of the cities were volunteering military aid. They sent round the Sicels and to Egesta requesting as many cavalry as they could supply, and busied themselves preparing stocks of all the materials needed for siege operations—brick-making frames, iron, and so forth—ready for vigorous prosecution of the war as soon as spring came.

The envoys sent by the Syracusans to Corinth and Sparta tried on their way to persuade the Italian Greeks that they were under similar threat, and should concern themselves with the Athenian activity. Once in Corinth, they presented the case for Corinthian aid on grounds of kinship. The Corinthians immediately took the initiative and voted for a full commitment to the support of Syracuse. They detailed envoys of their own to accompany the Syracusan party to Sparta, so they could join them in the attempt to involve the Spartans too with an appeal to resume more open war in Greece and to send some assistance to Sicily.

The Corinthian envoys' arrival at Sparta coincided with that of Alcibiades and his fellow exiles. From Thurian territory his immediate move at the time had been to cross over in a cargo-vessel to Cyllene in Elis first of all, and then later to make his way to Sparta: the Spartans themselves had invited him, but he would only come with a guarantee of safe conduct, as he was wary of their reaction to his part in the Mantinean affair. So, as it happened, the Spartan assembly heard not only the Corinthian and Syracusan envoys but Alcibiades too urging the same request on them. The ephors and the relevant authorities already had it in mind to send delegates to Syracuse to forestall any accommodation with the Athenians, but they were not keen to offer military help. Alcibiades now came forward and made a speech designed to sharpen the Spartan resolve and spur them to action. This is what he said:

'I must first deal with the prejudice against me, so that when I speak 89 of common interest you do not allow suspicion to deny me a fair hearing. My ancestors renounced the consular representation of Sparta because of some complaint, but I took it up again and did you good service particularly in the aftermath of your misfortune at Pylos. I remained always energetic on your behalf, but when you were making peace with the Athenians you chose to conduct your negotiations through my enemies, so investing them with influence and slighting me. When I then turned to my dealings with the Mantineans and the Argives, and any other means of getting back at you, the harm done served you right for your treatment of me. Some of you may have been angry with me at the time—unfairly—and should now reconsider in the light of the true facts. And anyone who thought the worse of me also for inclining to the people should realize that this too is no good ground for offence. My family has always been hostile to tyranny, and for that reason (since any element opposed to arbitrary power is labelled "the popular party") the leadership of the ordinary people fell to us and has stayed with us ever since. And also, living as we did in a democratic state, we had no choice but to conform for the most part to the prevailing conditions. We did, though, try to temper the inherent irresponsibility of democracy by practising a more moderate form of politics. But there were others, in the past and now, influencing the masses for the bad: and it was these people who drove me out. Whereas we championed the whole nation, and thought it right that all should help maintain the form of government they had inherited, under which the city did in fact enjoy its greatest power and independence. Yes, those of us of any intelligence recognized democracy for what it is, and, given that I have become its prime victim, I am in a better position than any to criticize it. But there is nothing new to be said about an acknowledged folly—and we thought it unsafe to make the change from democracy when we had you as enemies on our doorstep.

'These, then, are the circumstances which have caused the preju- 90 dices against me. But there is an issue now on which you must make a decision and I can guide you with whatever privileged information I possess. Let me explain. We sailed to Sicily intending first of all to subdue the Sicilian Greeks, if that could be done; then to move on to a like subjugation of the Greeks in Italy; and finally to make an attempt on the Carthaginian empire and Carthage itself. If all or most of this succeeded, our plan was then to attack the Peloponnese. We would bring with us this entire additional force of overseas Greeks, as well as hiring a large number of barbarians, including Iberians and others who are at the present time acknowledged to be the best fighters among the barbarians in that part of the world; we would use the plentiful timber in Italy to build many further triremes; with our fleet thus augmented we could effectively encircle the Peloponnese and impose a blockade; and at the same time army operations on land would be taking cities either by direct attack or by walling them under siege. Our hope was that these means would enable us to reduce you easily, and we could then go on to dominate the entire Greek world. Further supplies of money and food would be amply provided by these foreign acquisitions, quite apart from the revenue we receive in Greece.

91   'You have heard, from one who knows them in every detail, the substance of our intentions in dispatching this present expedition: and the remaining generals will, if they can, put the same strategy into effect. Let me explain now how Sicily will be lost if you do not intervene. Despite their lack of experience the Sicilian Greeks could even now win through if they offered a united resistance. The Syracusans on their own—with their full army already defeated in battle and enemy ships blockading them—will not be able to hold out against the Athenian forces now in their country. And if this city is taken, the rest of Sicily falls, and Italy too in quick succession: and then the danger from that quarter of which I have just warned will shortly be on you. So no one should think that this is an issue simply about Sicily. It will be about the Peloponnese also, if you do not take immediate action. You should send on ship to Sicily a force of men who will take the oars themselves and serve as hoplites as soon as they arrive, and—yet more valuable in my view than this army—a Spartiate commander to organize the present muster of troops there and press the shirkers into service. This will encourage the friends you already have there and make the uncommitted less afraid to join you.

'Here in Greece at the same time you should instigate more open war, to convince the Syracusans of your involvement and so stiffen their resistance, and to reduce the Athenians' ability to send reinforcements to their army in Sicily. And you should build a fort at Deceleia in Attica. The Athenians have always been particularly afraid of this, and reckon it the only stratagem of war not tried against them. The most effective way of damaging your enemy is to hit them with what you realize is their greatest fear, once that is made clear to you (and you can take it that all participants in war are authorities on what frightens their own side most). I could make a long list of what you stand to gain, and the enemy to lose, by the fortification of Deceleia, but will confine myself to the main points. Most of the structure of the land economy will fall into your hands—you can seize everything standing, and the slaves will come over of their own accord; the Athenians will immediately be deprived of the revenue from the silver mines at Laureium and the private income they now enjoy from the land and the law courts; above all, they will see a fall-off in the flow of tribute, as their allies will pay them less attention when they conclude that you are at last fighting the war in earnest. How far any of this is realized—and with speed 92 and energy—lies, Spartans, in your power. That all of it is possible, I have no doubt: and I do not think I shall be proved wrong.

'I hope that none of you will think the worse of me for joining its greatest enemies in a vigorous attack on my own land, when once I was known for my patriotism, or will suspect me of the usual exile's zeal in what I tell you. I am indeed an exile: but what I have forfeited is the malignity of my persecutors, not my ability to do you service, if you will listen to me. The greater enemies of my country are not those like you who have damaged it in open hostility, but the people who have forced its friends to become its enemies. The patriotism I retain is for the city which guaranteed my citizen rights, not for the city which has done me wrong. I do not think of myself as attacking my own country—what is there now is no longer mine—so much as reclaiming my country as it once was. The true patriot unjustly robbed of his country does not hesitate to attack it, but his very love for it makes him seek any means of recovering it. So, Spartans, I would ask you to make use of me. I am ready for any danger or privation, and you need have no qualms when you see that the common saying "the worst enemy makes the best friend" applies to me too, in that I know the Athenians' plans and could guess at yours. As for you, I would ask you to realize the major importance of this present issue, and not to hold back from sending these expeditions to Sicily and into Attica. A small fraction of your army assisting in Sicily would preserve large interests, and you could crush the Athenians' power once and for all. And then you could live your own lives in safety and

enjoy the hegemony over the whole of Greece, based not on force but
on grateful good will.'

93   Such was Alcibiades' speech. The Spartans had in fact already
been contemplating an expedition against Athens, but they were still
dithering and keeping a cautious eye on events. They were much
more inclined to action when they heard Alcibiades spelling out the
detail with what they considered to be expert knowledge. The result
was that they now began to turn their thoughts to the fortification of
Deceleia and, as an immediate measure, determined to send some
assistance to their friends in Sicily. They appointed Gylippus the son
of Cleandridas to the command in Syracuse, and told him to arrange,
in consultation with the Syracusan and Corinthian envoys, the best
and quickest means of getting help to Sicily with present resources.
He began by asking the Corinthians to send two ships immediately
to meet him at Asine, and to fit out as many more as they were minded
to send and have them ready to sail as soon as it was the season. With
these arrangements agreed the envoys left Sparta.

And there arrived at Athens the trireme from Sicily which the
generals had dispatched to request money and cavalry. The Athenians
heard the case and voted to send the army both the money for supplies and also the cavalry.

So the winter ended, and with it the seventeenth year of this war
chronicled by Thucydides.

94   At the very beginning of spring in the following summer season
the Athenians in Sicily put out from Catana and sailed down the
coast to Sicilian Megara (as I have mentioned before, the Syracusans
had removed the inhabitants in the time of the tyrant Gelo, and were
still in possession of the place). They landed, ravaged the fields, and
attacked a fortified Syracusan outpost. Failing to take it, they moved
on by land and sea to the river Terias: here they went inland, ravaged
the plain, and burned the corn. They encountered a few Syracusans
and killed some of them, then set up a trophy and returned to their
ships. They sailed back to Catana, took on provisions, and marched
with their full army against the Sicel town of Centoripa, inducing it
to capitulate: on their way back they burned the corn of the Inessians
and the Hyblaeans. On their return to Catana they found that the
cavalry they had requested from Athens had arrived—two hundred
and fifty men with all their equipment except horses, which were to
be supplied locally—together with thirty mounted archers and three
hundred talents of silver.

During this same spring the Spartans launched an expedition 95
against Argos, and had proceeded as far as Cleonae when an earthquake
occurred and they turned back. Thereafter the Argives invaded the
neighbouring territory of Thyrea and took a great deal of booty from
the Spartans, which was sold for no less than twenty-five talents. And
shortly afterwards, in the summer of this same year, the popular party
in Thespiae made an attack on the party in government, but their
attempt failed when the Thebans intervened. Some of the insurgents
were arrested, and others fled to exile in Athens.

In this summer the Syracusans learnt that the Athenian cavalry 96
had arrived and an attack on Syracuse was imminent. They reckoned
that if the Athenians failed to gain control of Epipolae (a steep area
lying directly above the city), it would not be easy for them to wall
off Syracuse, even if they proved superior in battle. So they determined to guard the approaches to Epipolae and prevent the enemy
making their way up through them unobserved. They could have no
other means of access, as the rest of the area has steep edges and
slopes right down to the city, and all of it is visible from inside the
city: the Syracusans call it Epipolae ('the Heights') because it forms
a plateau above the surrounding terrain. Hermocrates and his colleagues had just recently taken up their appointment as generals, and
the whole army was paraded at dawn for a military review in the
meadowland beside the river Anapus, at which first six hundred of
the hoplites were picked as a special force to guard Epipolae and to
be available for rapid deployment in any other emergency. They
were under the command of Diomilus, an exile from Andros.

During the night before this day of the Syracusan review the 97
Athenians had managed, without detection, to bring their entire
armament from Catana and put in at the place called Leon, about
three-quarters of a mile from Epipolae. The infantry disembarked
here, and the ships anchored at Thapsus (a peninsula projecting into
the sea with a narrow waist, not far from Syracuse by sea or land).
The Athenian naval section blocked the isthmus with a palisade and
stayed where they were in Thapsus. The infantry went straight for
Epipolae at the run, and reached the plateau by the Euryelus route
before the Syracusans were aware or could get there from the
meadowland where the review was taking place. All hurried to meet
the threat, as fast as each could run, including Diomilus and his six
hundred: but they had to cover almost three miles from the meadow
before engaging the Athenians, and as a result their attack was made

in some disorder. The Syracusans were defeated in the battle on Epipolae and withdrew into the city. Diomilus and about three hundred others were killed. After this the Athenians set up a trophy and returned their dead to the Syracusans under truce, then on the following day came down against the city itself. The Syracusans did not come out to meet them, so they went back and constructed a fort at Labdalum, on the edge of the Epipolae cliffs facing Megara, to serve as a repository for their stores and money when they moved forward either to do battle or to build walls.

98   Not long afterwards three hundred cavalry joined the Athenians from Egesta, and about a hundred more sent by the Sicels, the Naxians, and some others. They already had two hundred and fifty of their own (with horses now either provided by the Egestans and the Catanaeans or purchased elsewhere), so their total complement of cavalry amounted to six hundred and fifty. Leaving a garrison installed at Labdalum the Athenians advanced to Syce, where they established position and quickly built their 'circle'. The Syracusans were amazed at the speed of construction, and came out intending to do battle—they could not stand by and watch it happen. With both armies now forming up for engagement the Syracusan generals saw that their own troops were disordered and having difficulty achieving formation, and took them back into the city, except for a detachment of the cavalry who stayed behind and threatened to put an effective stop to any stone-gathering by the Athenians outside a short range. But a counter-attack by one tribal regiment of the Athenian hoplites together with their whole cavalry force sent the Syracusan cavalry back in flight, and killed some of them. The Athenians set up a trophy to mark this victory in a cavalry battle.

99   On the following day the Athenians began building their wall to the north of the circle, with the rest of their troops bringing stones and timber to line the whole of the intended route to the place called Trogilus, which offered them the shortest stretch of fortification from the Great Harbour to the sea on the other side. On the advice of their generals, and of Hermocrates in particular, the Syracusans decided to risk no more full-scale engagements with the Athenians. They thought their better option was to build counter-walls across the intended line of the Athenian wall. If they were quick enough with their building, they would block the Athenians each time: and as part of this process, if the Athenians did try to intervene they would respond by sending out a section of their army to erect stockades

and so take control of the approach routes before the Athenians could stop them. The Athenians would then have to suspend their construction work to bring all their forces to bear on the Syracusans in their way. So they came out and began building a cross-wall at right angles below the Athenian circle, starting from their own city wall: they cut down the olives in the Temenites sanctuary and erected wooden towers at intervals. The Athenian ships had not yet sailed round from Thapsus into the Great Harbour, but the Syracusans still controlled sea-traffic and the Athenians were bringing in their supplies from Thapsus by land.

When the Syracusans were satisfied with their stockading and the 100 extent of cross-wall built (with no interference from the Athenians, who feared that a division of their forces would make them vulnerable, and in any case were busy on their own wall-building), they left one tribal regiment to guard these structures and withdrew into the city. The Athenians now destroyed the pipes laid underground to bring drinking water into the city. Then, seeing their chance when most of the Syracusan guards were in their tents at midday (some had even gone back into the city), and there was lax security at the stockade, they detailed three hundred men picked from their own hoplites together with a select number of light troops armed for the purpose to go at the run in a sudden attack on the cross-wall. Half of the rest of the army went with one of the generals towards the city, in case the Syracusans came out to intervene, and the other half under the other general went against the stretch of stockade by the pyramid. The three hundred attacked their part of the stockade and captured it. The defenders abandoned it and ran for refuge in the fortification surrounding Temenites. Their pursuers pressed in after them, but once inside they were forced out again by the Syracusans, and some of the Argives and a few Athenians fell there in the action. The whole army now converged, destroyed the cross-wall, tore out the stockades, carried off the stakes to their own base, and set up a trophy.

The Athenians spent the following day building walls from the 101 circle to the edge of the cliff which on this side of Epipolae looks out over the marsh to the Great Harbour: this—down the cliff and straight across the level of the marsh—gave them the shortest line of wall to the harbour. The Syracusans too used this time to come out and lay another stockade extending from the city across the middle of the marsh, with a ditch dug alongside it, to prevent the Athenians continuing a wall to the sea. With their work completed as far as the cliff, the Athenians attacked the new Syracusan stockade and ditch. They sent orders to their ships to sail round from Thapsus into the Great Harbour of Syracuse, and before dawn brought their land forces down from Epipolae to the level area below and crossed the marsh by laying down doors and duckboards where the ground was firmest, if muddy. At dawn they took almost all of the stockade and ditch, and captured the remnant shortly afterwards. A pitched battle ensued in which the Athenians were victorious. The Syracusans on the right wing fled back to the city, and those on the left fled towards the river. To prevent their crossing, the three hundred picked Athenian troops ran at full speed for the bridge. This alarmed the Syracusans, and since they had most of their cavalry there with them, they made a concerted attack on these three hundred, sent them flying, and charged into the Athenian right wing: this onslaught spread the panic to the whole of the front division of the wing. Lamachus saw what had happened, and came across in support from his left wing, bringing the Argives with him and a few archers. He had just followed others over a ditch when he and the few who crossed with him found themselves cut off from the rest, and he was killed together with five or six of his companions. The Syracusans immediately snatched up the bodies and rushed them across the river out of enemy reach. Then they too retreated as the rest of the Athenian army now bore down on them.

102   Meanwhile, when the Syracusans who had initially fled into the city saw what was going on, they recovered their morale and came out again in battle order to face the immediate Athenian opposition, at the same time sending a detachment against the circle on Epipolae, thinking it would be undefended and open to capture. They did capture and ransack the two-acre outwork, but the circle itself was saved by Nicias, who happened to have been left there because of illness. He ordered the camp-servants to set fire to the various tackle and other timber piled in front of the wall, realizing that this was their only possible hope in the absence of defenders. And so it turned out: the fire kept the Syracusans back, and they retreated. Help too was coming up to the circle from the Athenians below, who had chased off the opposition there, and also the Athenian ships from Thapsus were now sailing, as ordered, into the Great Harbour. Seeing all this, the Syracusans up on the plateau made a hasty retreat, and the whole Syracusan army withdrew to the city, convinced now that with their present forces they were incapable of preventing a wall to the sea.

After this the Athenians erected a trophy and gave back their 103
dead to the Syracusans under truce, likewise recovering the bodies of
Lamachus and his companions. With their entire armament, naval
and military, now at hand, they set about walling off the Syracusans.
Starting from the cliff-edge of Epipolae they began building two
lines of wall to run from there to the sea. Supplies for the army came
in from all over Italy. Many of the Sicels who had previously been
waiting on events now allied themselves with the Athenians, and
three penteconters arrived from Etruria. All else too was proceeding
as they hoped. The Syracusans thought they had no prospect now
of saving the city by force of arms, as no help had reached them,
not even from the Peloponnese, and they could only talk in terms
of an accommodation, both among themselves and in their overtures
to Nicias (who was now the sole commander after the death of
Lamachus). No settlement came of it, although, as one would expect
of men in despair and closer than ever to a complete siege, many
proposals were made to Nicias and yet more canvassed within the
city. There was some internal suspicion also arising from their predicament, and they deposed the generals under whom they had
arrived at this state, crediting them with a malign influence, either
jinx or treachery. In their place they elected Heracleides, Eucles, and
Tellias.

Meanwhile the Spartan Gylippus and the ships from Corinth were 104
already at Leucas, intending to bring rapid help to Sicily. Here they
received a stream of alarming reports (all of them equally false) to
the effect that Syracuse was by now completely walled off. Gylippus
now had no further hope of Sicily, but would try to secure Italy. To
that end he and the Corinthian Pythen set off in two Spartan and
two Corinthian ships to cross the Ionian Gulf as fast as they could
to Taras, and the Corinthians were to follow after crewing two
Leucadian and three Ambraciot ships in addition to their own ten.
From Taras Gylippus first sent envoys to Thurii, and renewed the
Thurian citizenship conferred on his father, but failed to win the
people over. He then put out to sea and sailed on down the coast of
Italy, but in the Gulf of Terina he was caught by the prevailing
offshore wind which blows strongly from the north in this region,
and was driven out into the open sea, where he suffered a storm of
extreme violence. He made it back to Taras, and there dragged on
shore and repaired the ships most badly damaged in the storm.
Nicias had heard of his approach, but, just as the Thurians had done,

took a dismissive view of the number of his ships: he thought this expedition had no more than a piratical purpose, and for the time being posted no watch.

105 At about the same time in this summer the Spartans and their allies invaded the Argolid and ravaged most of the country. The Athenians came to the assistance of the Argives with thirty ships. This was a blatant violation of their treaty with the Spartans. Before now they had sent raiding-parties out of Pylos, made landings elsewhere in the Peloponnese (but not in Laconia), and fought as allies of the Argives and Mantineans: but they had always refused the frequent Argive requests to join them in even a token armed landing on Laconian soil, with minimum damage done to the land and a quick departure. But now, under the command of Pythodorus, Laespodias, and Demaratus, they landed and ravaged the country at Epidaurus Limera, Prasiae, and all the other targets of their attack, so finally giving the Spartans an unanswerable case for retaliation against Athens.

When both the Athenian fleet and the Spartans had left Argos, the Argives invaded Phliasia, devastated some of the land and killed a number of the men, then went back home.

BOOK SEVEN

After repairing their ships Gylippus and Pythen sailed down the 1 coast from Taras to Epizephyrian Locri. They now learnt the true situation, that Syracuse was not yet completely walled off, and it was still possible for an army to reach the city by coming over Epipolae. So their debate was now how to approach Sicily: should they take the risk of the east coast route and a direct entry to the harbour of Syracuse, or first sail along the north coast to Himera, collect troops from Himera itself and any others they could persuade, and make the approach by land? They decided to sail for Himera, not least because the strait was unguarded: on learning that they were in Locri, Nicias, despite his earlier view, had sent four Athenian ships to Rhegium, but these ships did not arrive in time to intercept. So Gylippus and Pythen could pass through the strait unchecked, and reached Himera after putting in first at Rhegium and Messana. Once there they persuaded the Himeraeans to fight on their side, and not only to join the expedition themselves but also to provide hoplite arms for those of their sailors who were unarmed (they were leaving the ships beached at Himera): and they sent to the Selinuntians asking them to bring an army and meet them at a designated place. They were also promised a modest contribution of troops by the Geloans and some of the Sicels, who were much readier now to come over after the recent death of Archonides (a local Sicel king and a powerful figure sympathetic to the Athenians), and the arrival of Gylippus from Sparta with evidently serious intent. Gylippus now gathered his forces: about seven hundred of his own sailors and marines armed as hoplites; from Himera a thousand hoplites and light-armed combined, and a hundred cavalry; some light troops and cavalry from Selinus, and a few from Gela; and about a thousand in all from the Sicels. With this army Gylippus marched for Syracuse.

Meanwhile the Corinthians were making their best speed in 2 support with the rest of the ships from Leucas. One of their commanders, Gongylus, was the last to set off and the first to arrive in his single ship at Syracuse, shortly before Gylippus. He found the Syracusans about to hold an assembly to discuss ending the war, and was able to pre-empt that discussion and talk them round with the encouraging news that more ships were on their way, and so was

Gylippus the son of Cleandridas, sent by the Spartans as commander. The Syracusans took heart, and when they heard that Gylippus was now close at hand they went out immediately with their whole army to meet him. He had just captured a Sicel fort at Ietae on his way, and was now approaching Epipolae in full battle order. He went up by Euryelus (the same route initially taken by the Athenians) and joined with the Syracusans in an advance on the Athenian fortifications. He had arrived just at the time when the Athenians had completed nearly a mile of their two lines of wall to the Great Harbour, with only a short stretch left to the sea on which they were still working, and their other wall to the north and the sea by Trogilus already had stones laid along most of its route, and part was completed, part left half-finished. This was how close Syracuse came to destruction.

3   The sudden approach of Gylippus and the Syracusans caused consternation among the Athenians at first, but they formed in battle order to meet them. Gylippus halted his troops at close range and sent forward a herald to tell the Athenians that he was prepared to make a truce if they would take their belongings and leave Sicily within five days. They ignored this proposal and sent his herald back without an answer. The two sides now began forming for battle. Seeing the Syracusans in confusion and having difficulty achieving formation, Gylippus took his army back to more open ground. Nicias did not follow with the Athenians, but kept them where they were by their own wall. When Gylippus saw that the Athenians were not coming out to meet him, he led his troops away to the spur called Temenitis and camped there for the night. On the following day he led out his army and stationed the bulk of it opposite the Athenians' walls, to prevent them intervening anywhere else, while leading a detachment against the fort at Labdalum, which was out of sight of the Athenians: he took the place and killed all found inside it. On the same day the Syracusans captured an Athenian trireme on guard duty at the Little Harbour.

4   The Syracusans and their allies next began to build a single line of wall starting from their own upper city wall and running across Epipolae at right angles to the direction of the enemy's northern wall, such that if the Athenians failed to stop it they could no longer achieve their circumvallation. The Athenians had now completed their wall to the sea and come back up to the higher ground. One part of the Athenian wall was weak, and Gylippus took his army on a night assault against it. The Athenians had pickets camped outside the

wall, and marched out to meet him as soon as the alarm was raised: seeing the situation, Gylippus quickly took his troops back. The Athenians reinforced that part of the wall to a greater height, and undertook guard duty there themselves, giving their allies designated sections to guard along the rest of the fortification.

Nicias now decided to fortify Plemmyrium (as it is called). This is a headland opposite the city which projects into the Great Harbour and narrows its entrance. If this were fortified, Nicias thought the import of supplies would be made easier: they would be able to keep watch on the Little Harbour of Syracuse from a lesser distance, and not be obliged, as now, to make their interceptions from deep within the Great Harbour whenever there were naval movements by the Syracusans. And he was already beginning to concentrate more on the naval dimension of the war, as he could see that the arrival of Gylippus had now made the Athenians' prospects by land less encouraging. So he transferred the fleet and some troops to this spot and built three forts there, in which the bulk of their stores was lodged: and this was where the large transports and the warships now anchored. The result was the beginning, and the major cause, of the deterioration of the ships' crews. Water was scarce, and no supply close at hand. And when the sailors went out for firewood too they suffered casualties from the Syracusan cavalry who dominated the area: to prevent damage done by any forays from the force at Plemmyrium the Syracusans had stationed a third of their cavalry in the fortified village at the Olympieium. Nicias was receiving reports now of the imminent arrival of the rest of the Corinthian ships, and sent twenty ships to intercept them, with instructions to lie in wait for them around Locri and Rhegium and the general approach to Sicily.

Gylippus continued the building of the wall across Epipolae, 5 making use of the stones which the Athenians had already laid out for their own wall, and all the while he repeatedly led out the Syracusans and their allies and drew them up in battle order in front of the wall: and on each occasion the Athenians would take formation opposite them. When he thought the moment right Gylippus offered battle. The close-quarter fighting took place in the area enclosed by the two lines of fortification, where the Syracusan cavalry could not be put to any use, and the Syracusans and their allies were defeated. They recovered their dead under truce, and the Athenians set up a trophy. Gylippus assembled his troops and told them that the fault was his, not theirs; by making formation too close between the walls he had deprived them of the benefit of their cavalry and javelin-men; so he would now lead them out again. And he urged them to remember that in military strength they could hold their own, and in terms of morale it was unthinkable that as Peloponnesians and Dorians they should not be determined to crush these Ionians and islanders and their ragbag of allies, and drive them out of the country.

6   At the next opportunity Gylippus did lead them out again. Nicias and the Athenians had taken the view that even if the enemy were not prepared to offer battle, it was vital to prevent them carrying on the line of their counter-wall: their construction was already close to crossing the end of the Athenian wall, and if it went further the result for the Athenians was the same whether they fought and won all their battles or never fought at all. So they went out against the Syracusans. For the engagement Gylippus took his hoplites further away from the wall than before, and placed his cavalry and javelin-men on the Athenian flank in the open space left where the work on both walls had ceased. In the ensuing battle the cavalry charged into the left wing of the Athenians opposite them and put them to flight: this led to a general defeat and the whole Athenian army was broken by the Syracusans and driven back within their lines. In the following night the Syracusans continued building their wall and managed to carry it across and past the Athenian line of construction. There could now be no further Athenian interference, and the Athenians had completely lost all prospect of walling off the city, irrespective of any victories in the field.

7   After this the rest of the Corinthian ships sailed in, together with the ships from Ambracia and Leucas, a total of twelve, commanded by the Corinthian Erasinides. They had got through undetected by the Athenian guardships, and once there they helped the Syracusans to build the rest of their cross-wall. Gylippus meanwhile had gone elsewhere in Sicily to raise troops, looking for both naval and land forces, and also to win over any cities which were sluggish in the cause or had so far kept completely out of the war. More envoys, Syracusan and Corinthian, were sent to Sparta and Corinth to request a further consignment of troops in freighters, smaller vessels, or whatever form of shipping was available to convey them, given that the Athenians too were sending for reinforcements. In generally high morale the Syracusans also manned a fleet and began practising for future attempts at this form of warfare.

8   Aware of this, and seeing the day-by-day increase in the enemy strength and the Athenians' own predicament, Nicias likewise

communicated with Athens. It had been his practice to send regular dispatches with a detailed account of events, but this time he went into particular detail, as he thought the situation was critical, and all would be lost if the Athenians did not take immediate action either to recall the expedition or to send out considerable reinforcements. Concerned that his message might be distorted by his emissaries, through incompetence at public speaking, failure of memory, or adjustments to suit the mood of the masses, he put his dispatch in writing, thinking this the best way to guarantee that the Athenians heard his personal opinion undiluted in the transmission, and could make their decision on the true facts of the case. So his emissaries set off, armed with his letter and full instructions on the line they should take. He now saw to it that the army kept on the defensive and took no avoidable risks.

Towards the end of this same summer Euetion, an Athenian general, joined with Perdiccas in an attack on Amphipolis, with a large force of Thracians assisting them. He failed to take the city, but brought triremes round into the Strymon and began a siege from the river, with his base in Himeraeum.

So this summer ended.

In the following winter the men sent by Nicias arrived at Athens, 10 delivered orally all they had been told to say, answered any questions put to them, and presented Nicias' letter. The city clerk came forward and read this letter to the Athenians. Its content was as follows:

'Athenians, you know the earlier course of events from my many 11 previous dispatches, but there is now yet greater need for you to hear of our present situation and make your decision in that knowledge. You sent us against the Syracusans, and we had won most of our battles with them and built the lines of fortification where we are now stationed: but then the Spartan Gylippus arrived with an army from the Peloponnese and further troops acquired from some of the cities in Sicily. He was defeated by us in the first engagement, but on the next day we were forced back to our lines by their numerous cavalry and javelin-men. So now, in the face of enemy numbers, we have had to stop our work on circumvallation and are reduced to inaction (it is not as if we could bring our full army to bear, as the defence of our walls takes up a good part of our hoplite force). Meanwhile the enemy have built a single line of wall, which crosses ours, so that there is now no possibility of walling them off, unless a large army is brought up to attack and take this cross-wall. The result is that we, who are supposed to be the besiegers, are rather the besieged ourselves, at least by land: we cannot venture any distance into the country either, because of their cavalry.

12　　'They have also sent envoys to the Peloponnese for reinforcements, and Gylippus has gone out to the cities in Sicily, to persuade the uncommitted to join his cause and, if possible, to secure further land and naval forces from the others. My understanding is that they plan to combine an infantry attack on our walls with a naval operation at sea. And this "at sea" ought not to shock you. The situation with our own fleet is well understood by the enemy too. At first the fleet was in prime order, the ships good and dry and the crews in fine condition: but now the ships are waterlogged after so much time in the sea, and the crews have been ruined. We cannot beach our ships and air them out, as the enemy ships match or even exceed our numbers and present us with the constant expectation of an attack. They are exercising in plain view; they can choose their own time to commence operations; and they have greater freedom to dry their ships, as they are not, like us, actively involved in a blockade.

13　　'We could hardly enjoy this last advantage even if we had a substantially superior number of ships and were not obliged, as we are now, to use our whole fleet on guard duty: if we remove even a small part of our coverage, we shall lose our supplies, which have to come in past the enemy's city and even now have a difficult passage. What has been, and still is, the ruin of our crews is that some of our sailors, who have to go far for firewood, forage, and water, are picked off by the cavalry; the slaves are deserting, now that the enemy can match our forces; the foreigners pressed into service in the ships are taking the first opportunity to return to their cities in Sicily; and those initially attracted by high pay and what they thought was the prospect of making money rather than war are now surprised to find the enemy resistance so strong and extending to naval opposition also— some are disappearing on the excuse of pursuing deserted slaves, or simply vanishing where they can (and Sicily is a large country): there are others who have persuaded the trierarchs to replace them with slaves from Hyccara while they continue their trading. All this has reduced the quality of the fleet.

14　　'This letter is addressed to people who are as well aware as I am that a crew is only at its peak for a short while, and that the key sailors are the few who know how to start a ship and keep the rowing together. The most desperate aspect of the present situation is that despite my command I can do nothing to stop this attrition (your Athenian ways are hard to control), and we have no source of replacement crew to fill the ships, in contrast to the enemy's abundant supply. What we have at our disposal is simply what we brought with us, so our losses inevitably reduce that number: our remaining allies here, Naxos and Catana, are unable to help. If only one more factor shifts to the enemy's advantage—if, that is, the regions of Italy which provision us change sides when they see the state we are in and no help coming from you—we shall be besieged into surrender and they will have won the war without a further blow struck.

'I could have sent you a different and more agreeable report, but that would not have served you better: you need to make your decisions with a clear view of the situation here. And I know the way you are. You like to have matters presented in the most agreeable light, and then find fault later if the outcome fails to match the report. So I thought it safer to reveal the truth.

'As things are, you can be assured that neither your troops nor 15 your commanders have failed you in the original purpose of our mission. But when all Sicily is uniting against us, and they are expecting a further army from the Peloponnese, you must make a decision now on the understanding that our forces here in Sicily cannot hold out even against the present opposition. You must either recall these forces or send another army and fleet of equal size to reinforce them, together with a considerable sum of money. And you should send someone to replace me. I am suffering from a kidney disease, and I cannot stay on here. I claim your indulgence in this, as when I was in good health I did you much good service in my commands. But do what you intend to do at the very beginning of spring, with no delays. The enemy will acquire new resources in Sicily in short time: the reinforcements from the Peloponnese will take longer, but even so, if you are not careful, they will either get past you (as they did earlier) or simply move before you do.'

Such was the content of Nicias' letter. When they had heard it 16 read, the Athenians did not relieve Nicias of his command, but, pending the election and arrival of other generals to join him, they assigned two of the officers already there on the spot, Menandrus and Euthydemus, to act as co-commanders so that Nicias should not have to bear the whole burden alone and unwell. And they voted to send another fleet and another army recruited from Athenians on the hoplite service-list and from the allies. As fellow generals for Nicias they elected Demosthenes the son of Alcisthenes and Eurymedon the son of Thucles. They sent Eurymedon to Sicily as soon as possible (round about the winter solstice) with ten ships and a hundred and twenty talents of silver: he was also to assure the Athenian forces in Sicily that help was on its way and their concerns would be met.

17 Demosthenes stayed behind to prepare for the launch of the main expedition in early spring—sending out to the allies to requisition troops, and getting ready money, ships, and hoplites at Athens. The Athenians also sent twenty ships round the Peloponnese, to guard against any attempted crossings to Sicily from Corinth or the rest of the Peloponnese.

The envoys from Sicily had now arrived at Corinth and reported the improved situation there. The Corinthians, convinced that their first dispatch of ships had been crucial, now grew more confident still. They prepared to send hoplites of their own to Sicily in freighters (the Spartans would do the same from the rest of the Peloponnese), and crewed twenty-five warships to offer battle with the Athenian squadron on watch at Naupactus: they hoped that the need to concentrate on this opposing force of triremes would reduce the chances that the Naupactus squadron could block the sailing of their freighters.

18 The Spartans also began preparing for their invasion of Attica, as had long been their intention and was now being urged on them by the Syracusans and Corinthians, who had heard of the Athenian reinforcements planned for Sicily, and imagined that an invasion would stop them: and Alcibiades maintained his insistence on the case for fortifying Deceleia and keeping the war at full stretch.

Above all, the Spartans had developed some confidence. They thought the Athenians would be easier prey now that they had a double war on their hands, against Sparta and in Sicily, and considered that this time the Athenians had been the first to break the treaty. They recognized that in the earlier period of war the initial transgression had been more on their side, in that Thebans had entered Plataea in time of peace, and they themselves had refused the Athenians' challenge to arbitration when the previous treaty expressly prohibited recourse to arms if there was an offer of arbitration. They interpreted their misfortunes as just punishment for this, and took very much to heart the disasters inflicted on them at Pylos and elsewhere. But now that the Athenians had based those thirty ships in Argos and used them to devastate parts of Epidaurus and Prasiae and other places, while keeping up constant raids out of Pylos and always refusing Spartan proposals of arbitration whenever there was disagreement about some disputed clause in the treaty, the Spartans came to the conclusion that the guilt of transgression, formerly attached to them, had finally shifted to the Athenians—and this made them eager for war. So in this winter they sent round their allies for supplies of iron and got ready the other tools needed for the construction of a fort. They also began preparing on their part, and requiring the rest of the Peloponnese to do likewise, the support to be sent in the freighters to their friends in Sicily.

So the winter ended, and with it the eighteenth year of this war chronicled by Thucydides.

At the very beginning of the following spring, and earlier than on any previous occasion, the Spartans and their allies invaded Attica under the command of Agis the son of Archidamus, king of Sparta. They first ravaged the land in the area of the plain, then began to fortify Deceleia, dividing the work among the various contingents. Deceleia is about eleven miles from Athens, and roughly the same distance or a little more from Boeotia. The fort was built with a view to the devastation of the plain and the best tracts of land, and could be clearly seen from the city of Athens. 19

While the Peloponnesians and their allies were engaged on this work in Attica, in the Peloponnese itself the dispatch of the hoplites in the freighters was being organized at about the same time. The Spartans sent a force chosen from the best of the Helots and the previously liberated cohorts, a combined total of six hundred hoplites with the Spartiate Eccritus as their commander, and the Boeotians sent three hundred hoplites under the command of two Thebans, Xenon and Nicon, and Hegesandrus from Thespiae. These were the first to set off, putting out to the open sea from Taenarum in Laconia. Not long after them the Corinthians dispatched five hundred hoplites, some from Corinth itself and others bought-in mercenaries from Arcadia, with the Corinthian Alexarchus appointed their commander: and the Sicyonians sent two hundred hoplites along with the Corinthians, under the command of Sargeus from Sicyon. The twenty-five Corinthian ships which had been crewed over the winter maintained a blocking station opposite the twenty Athenian ships at Naupactus until these hoplites had got safely away from the Peloponnese in the freighters. This was of course the original purpose of crewing these ships, to distract the Athenians' attention from the freighters to the triremes.

20   While this was going on and Deceleia was being fortified, the
Athenians also took action early in the spring. They sent thirty ships
round the Peloponnese under the command of Charicles the son of
Apollodorus, with instructions to put in at Argos and take on board
Argive hoplites requisitioned under the terms of their alliance, and
they sent Demosthenes on his way to Sicily with the expedition as
planned. He had with him sixty Athenian and five Chian ships,
twelve hundred Athenian hoplites from the service-list and as many
others as could be obtained from all over the islands, together with
any useful military help available elsewhere among the subject allies.
Demosthenes was instructed first of all to join Charicles' fleet in
operations on the coast of Laconia. So he sailed to Aegina and waited
there for any remnants of his force to catch up and for Charicles to
return from Argos with the hoplites on board.

21   Meanwhile in Sicily, at about this same time in the spring,
Gylippus arrived back at Syracuse bringing with him as many troops
as he could obtain from all over the various cities which he had persuaded to contribute. He assembled the Syracusans and told them
that they should man the largest fleet they could and make trial of a
battle at sea: he hoped that this would have a significant effect on the
war and so justify the risk. Hermocrates strongly supported this
recommendation, and urged them not to despair of taking on the
Athenians in a naval attack. There was nothing traditional or permanent about the Athenians' expertise at sea, but they had previously
been landsmen yet more than the Syracusans, and it was only the
Persian invasion which forced them to turn sailors. To daring men
like the Athenians, those who met them with daring of their own
would present the greatest threat: the very technique they used
against others—intimidation by the pure boldness of their attack,
often without military superiority—could equally well be employed
as a weapon against them by the Syracusans. He was quite sure, he
said, that if the Syracusans were bold enough to offer an unexpected
challenge to the Athenian fleet, the advantage achieved by this element of surprise would outweigh any damage Athenian expertise could
inflict on Syracusan inexperience. So he told them not to be timid,
but to go ahead and try out their navy.

With Gylippus, Hermocrates, and some other speakers all urging
this course of action, the Syracusans were fired with enthusiasm for
22   battle at sea, and began manning the ships. When the fleet was ready,
Gylippus brought round his entire infantry force under cover of

night in preparation for a land attack on the forts at Plemmyrium, while at a preconcerted signal the Syracusan triremes set out. Thirty-five sailed directly from the Great Harbour, and forty-five sailed round from the Little Harbour (where they had their dockyard), intending to link up with the ships in the Great Harbour and make a combined attack on Plemmyrium, so that the Athenians would face trouble from both directions, land and sea. But the Athenians quickly manned sixty ships in response, sending twenty-five to do battle with the thirty-five Syracusan ships in the Great Harbour, and with the rest going to meet the enemy squadron sailing round from the dockyard. There followed a sustained struggle outside the mouth of the harbour, the Syracusans trying to force entry and the Athenians trying to keep them out.

The Athenians in Plemmyrium had gone down to the waterside to 23 watch the sea-battle, and Gylippus took this opportunity to make a sudden attack on the forts at first light. He took the largest fort first, then later the two smaller forts, whose garrisons did not stay to resist when they saw the ease with which the large fort was taken. Some of the troops from the first fort to be captured ran to board their boats and a nearby freighter, and only just managed to make it to the main Athenian base with one fast trireme in pursuit (at the time the Syracusan ships in the Great Harbour were having the better of the engagement). But when the two smaller forts were taken the Syracusans were now losing the sea-battle, and the Athenian troops escaping from these forts had an easier transit to their base. What had happened was that the Syracusan ships fighting outside the mouth of the harbour had forced through the Athenian defence and then sailed inside in total disorder, falling foul of each other and so handing victory to the Athenians, who routed both this fleet and the ships which had at first had the better of them in the harbour. The Athenians disabled eleven Syracusan ships and killed most of the crews, except for the crews of three ships who were taken prisoner. They themselves lost three ships. They salvaged the Syracusan wrecks and set up a trophy on the islet in front of Plemmyrium, then returned to their own base.

So although the Syracusans had come off badly in the naval 24 engagement, they did now hold the forts on Plemmyrium, and they set up three trophies, one for each fort. They demolished one of the two forts taken in their later attack, but repaired and garrisoned the other two. Many men were killed or taken prisoner in the capture of the forts, and a substantial quantity of goods was lost from all three. The Athenians had used them as a warehouse, and they contained a good deal of merchants' stock as well as corn, and also much belonging to the trierarchs—the mainsails and other equipment of forty triremes were stored there and taken by the enemy, as were three triremes which had been drawn up on the beach. The capture of Plemmyrium was one of the first and greatest of the debilitating blows suffered by the Athenian forces. There was now no safe approach for the import of provisions, as the Syracusans had ships deployed in the seaways to intercept, and all subsequent convoys had to fight their way through: and the capture spread general dismay and low morale throughout the army.

25 After this the Syracusans sent out a squadron of twelve ships with Agatharchus of Syracuse on board as their commander. One of these ships sailed off to the Peloponnese carrying envoys who were to report good hopes on their part in Sicily and to urge yet stronger prosecution of the war in Greece. The remaining eleven sailed to Italy on the intelligence that ships laden with supplies for the Athenians were approaching. They intercepted these ships and destroyed most of them, and also burned a supply of shipbuilding timber which was lying ready for the Athenians in the territory of Caulonia. They then moved on to Locri, and while they were anchored there one of the freighters from the Peloponnese sailed in carrying hoplites from Thespiae. The Syracusans took these hoplites on board their own ships and set off round the coast for home. The Athenians had twenty ships on the watch for them off Megara, and captured one of the ships and its crew, but could not prevent the others making their escape back to Syracuse.

There was some skirmishing in the harbour over the wooden piles which the Syracusans had driven into the seabed in front of the old docks, to give their ships safe anchorage behind the piles, where the Athenians could not sail in and ram them. The Athenians brought up opposite the docks a 250-ton freighter equipped with wooden towers and screens, and then, working from small boats, attached ropes to the piles and winched them up or broke them off, or else dived down and sawed through them. The Syracusans kept up a barrage of missiles from the docks, and the men on the freighter responded. Eventually the Athenians managed to remove the majority of the piles, but the most troublesome part of this palisade was the hidden stakes: some had been driven in so that they did not show above the surface of the water, which presented the same danger of damage to an approaching ship as a sunken reef not seen in time. These too were dealt with by hired divers who went down and sawed them off. Even so, the Syracusans drove in another palisade. And so it went on, all the devices and tricks one would expect when two opposing forces were based so close to each other, constant skirmishing, every sort of stratagem.

The Syracusans also sent out Corinthian, Ambraciot, and Spartan envoys to the other cities with the news of the capture of Plemmyrium and an explanation of the defeat at sea in terms of their own disorder rather than any superior strength on the part of the enemy. The envoys were to present a general picture of optimism and to ask for both naval and military assistance against the enemy: reinforcements were expected for the Athenians, and if they could destroy the present armament before these came, the war would be over and won.

Such was the activity on both sides in Sicily.

When Demosthenes had gathered the full body of the reinforce- 26 ments he was to take to Sicily, he put out from Aegina and sailed to the Peloponnese where he linked up with Charicles and the thirty Athenian ships under his command. With the Argive hoplites taken on board they sailed on to Laconia. Here they first ravaged some of the country round Epidaurus Limera, then landed in the part of Laconia opposite Cythera, where the temple of Apollo stands. They ravaged some of the land and fortified a peninsular site there to provide a safe-haven for deserting Spartan Helots and a base, like Pylos, from which raiding-parties could do their plunder. As soon as he had helped capture this place Demosthenes sailed on round to Corcyra, to take on allied troops there and then make all speed for Sicily. Charicles stayed behind to complete the fortification, then installed a garrison in the place and took his thirty ships home, the Argives with them.

In this same summer thirteen hundred Thracian peltasts arrived 27 at Athens from the dagger-carrying tribe known as the Dians. They had been due to sail with Demosthenes to Sicily, but had come too late, and the Athenians decided to send them back to where they came from in Thrace. They thought it too expensive to retain them (each earned a drachma a day) in view of the hostilities from Deceleia.

The initial construction of the fort at Deceleia had been undertaken during this summer by the whole Peloponnesian army, and thereafter it was kept occupied, as a constant threat to Athenian land, by a regular succession of garrisons sent out from the allied cities. It did immense harm to the Athenians, and the consequent destruction of property and loss of life was a crucial element in the city's decline. The earlier invasions had been relatively brief, and had not prevented benefit from the land in the rest of the year. But now the occupation was continuous; sometimes additional troops were drafted in, but even the regular garrisons would overrun the countryside and despoil it for their own needs; and the Spartan king Agis was there in person, well aware of the importance of prosecuting this aspect of the war. All this caused serious damage to the Athenians. They were denied all their land; more than twenty thousand slaves had deserted, and many of these were skilled workers; all their flocks and draught animals had been killed; and their horses, now that the cavalry had to ride out every day to harass Deceleia or protect the countryside, were going lame with the constant punishment on compacted ground, or else sustaining actual wounds.

28   The transport of provisions from Euboea, which had previously taken the quicker route from Oropus overland through Deceleia, now had to follow the sea passage round Sounium, at great expense. Athens was obliged to import all else as well, and came to resemble a military outpost rather than a city. By day the Athenians took turns of guard duty at the battlements, and at night the entire citizen body except for the cavalry was kept on alert, some on the walls and others under arms elsewhere: summer and winter, this wore them out. But the greatest pressure on them was that they had to carry on two wars at the same time, and in this they were gripped by a passionate tenacity of purpose which would have seemed incredible to anyone who did not subsequently witness it. The measure of this is the fact that, under siege from a Peloponnesian fort in their own country, they still did not give up Sicily, but maintained there a comparable siege of Syracuse, a city which on its own could rank with Athens; and that their strength and determination went so far beyond the reasonable expectations of the Greeks (who at the beginning of the war variously gave them one, two, or at the most three years of survival if the Peloponnesians invaded their country) that in the seventeenth year after that first invasion, and by now completely exhausted by the war, they went to Sicily and took on a new war just as onerous as their long-standing conflict with the Peloponnese. All this, combined now with the huge damage being inflicted by Deceleia and other costs hitting hard, had crippled them financially. It was at this time

that they imposed on their subject allies, in place of tribute, a five-per-cent tax on all seaborne traffic, reckoning that this would bring them greater income. Their expenses had not remained at the earlier level, but had grown considerably as the war had grown, and their revenues were failing.

So, anxious not to incur further expenditure in their present 29 financial difficulties, the Athenians took immediate steps to send back the Thracians who had arrived too late for Demosthenes. They appointed Diitrephes to ship them home, with instructions to make what use of them he could to do harm to the enemy as he sailed along the coast (their route would take them through the Euripus channel). He landed them first in the territory of Tanagra for a quick raid, then at nightfall he sailed across the Euripus from Chalcis in Euboea to land in Boeotia and lead them against Mycalessus. He camped for the night, undetected, by the temple of Hermes, less than two miles from Mycalessus, and at daybreak assaulted and captured this small city. The assault took the inhabitants off guard, as they had never expected that people would come up so far inland to attack them. Their walls were weak, dilapidated in parts and elsewhere built low, and in any case they had felt secure enough to leave their gates open. The Thracians poured into the city and began sacking the houses and temples and slaughtering the people. They spared neither old nor young, but automatically killed every person they found, children and women also, and even the very beasts of burden and any other living creature they could see. These Thracians, when they have nothing to fear, are as bloodthirsty as any other barbarian race, even the worst, and here in Mycalessus they brought total panic and destruction in every form, including the invasion of the largest school in the place, when the pupils had just come in for their lessons: they butchered the entire school. This was the greatest disaster affecting the whole city which they had ever suffered, more sudden and terrible than any other.

As soon as they heard of it the Thebans came to the rescue. They 30 caught the Thracians before they had gone far, relieved them of their booty, and chased them back in flight to the sea at the Euripus, where their convoy of ships was anchored. Of those who died the majority were killed in the attempt to embark, as they did not know how to swim and the ships' crews, seeing what was happening on land, had pulled back to moor out of bowshot. In the retreat itself the Thracians put up a surprisingly sensible defence against the Theban cavalry which led the attack, using their local tactic of quick charges followed by closed ranks, and only a few of them were killed at this stage. Some others had been caught still looting in the city, and died there. The total number of Thracians killed was two hundred and fifty, out of thirteen hundred. The relieving force of Thebans and others lost about twenty cavalry and hoplites combined, including one of the Theban Boeotarchs, Scirphondas. Of the Mycalessians, a whole swathe of the population was wiped out. Such was the fate of Mycalessus, visited by a calamity which, relative to the size of the city, was more pitiable than any other in this war.

31   Demosthenes had sailed on towards Corcyra after the fort on the Laconian coast was established. On his way he found a freighter anchored at Pheia in Elis ready to transport the Corinthian hoplites to Sicily. He destroyed the ship, but the men escaped and later took passage in another vessel. He went on to Zacynthus and Cephallenia, where he collected some hoplites and sent for more from the Messenians at Naupactus, then crossed to Alyzia and Anactorium in Acarnania on the mainland opposite, both being places under Athenian control. While he was thus engaged he was met by Eurymedon on his way back from Sicily, where he had been sent in the previous winter to bring funds to the Athenian forces: Eurymedon's main report was that after he had set sail news had reached him of the capture of Plemmyrium by the Syracusans. They were joined also by Conon, the commander at Naupactus, who reported that the twenty-five Corinthian ships stationed opposite them showed no sign of abandoning hostilities and clearly intended to fight. He asked them to send reinforcements, as his eighteen ships were not enough to enter battle with the enemy's twenty-five. So Demosthenes and Eurymedon sent ten of the fastest ships in their own fleet to go with Conon and join the squadron at Naupactus, while they themselves continued the final recruitment for the expedition. Eurymedon sailed to Corcyra, where he ordered the manning of fifteen ships and raised a levy of hoplites (he had now cut short his journey home and assumed the joint command with Demosthenes to which he had been elected). Demosthenes meanwhile was collecting a force of slingers and javelin-men from the environs of Acarnania.

32   The envoys from Syracuse who had gone out to the other Sicilian cities after the capture of Plemmyrium succeeded in their mission and were now ready to bring back the troops they had gathered. Nicias had prior intelligence of this, and sent word to the Sicel allies

of Athens who controlled the territory through which they would
have to pass (these were the people of Centoripa and Alicyae, and
some others). He told the Sicels not to let the enemy through, but to
combine forces and stop them, as there was no chance that they
would even try an alternative route (this was because the Acragantines
would not allow them passage through their territory). So when
these Greek Sicilian troops had started on their way the Sicels com-
plied with the Athenians' request and set an ambush for them
deployed in three divisions. This sudden attack caught them off
guard, and the Sicels killed some eight hundred of them, including
all the envoys except one of the Corinthians. This man brought the
survivors to Syracuse: they numbered about fifteen hundred. In 33
these same days also the Syracusans received reinforcements from
Camarina, consisting of five hundred hoplites, three hundred javelin-
men, and three hundred archers. The Geloans too sent a squadron of
five ships, together with four hundred javelin-men and two hundred
cavalry. By this time, apart from the neutral Acragas, virtually the
whole of Sicily, including the cities which before now had been waiting on events, was united in support of the Syracusans against the
Athenians.

After this disaster in Sicel country the Syracusans deferred any
immediate attack on the Athenians. Meanwhile Demosthenes and
Eurymedon, their recruitment from Corcyra and the mainland now
complete, took their whole armament across the Ionian Gulf to the
promontory of Iapygia. Setting out again from there they touched at
the Iapygian islands called the Choerades and took on board their
ships a hundred and fifty Iapygian javelin-men of the Messapian race
offered by a local dynast, Artas, with whom they renewed an old
friendship. They then reached Metapontium in Italy, where they
persuaded the Metapontians under the terms of their existing alliance to let them have three hundred javelin-men and two triremes to
join their expedition. With these additions they sailed on down the
coast to the territory of Thurii. Here they found that the anti-
Athenian party had recently been expelled in a coup. They intended
in any case to muster the whole armament here and hold a review to
see if any element was missing. At the same time they wanted to
prevail on the Thurians not only to give the expedition their most
active support, but also, in view of this turn of political fortune, to
make a full offensive and defensive alliance with Athens. These two
purposes kept them in Thuria for a while.

34   At about this same time the Peloponnesians in the twenty-five ships
stationed opposite the Naupactus squadron to protect the freighters
sailing for Sicily now prepared for battle. They manned some further
ships to bring their fleet close to the Athenian complement, and
moved their anchorage to Erineus, in the territory of Rhype in Achaea.
The place where they anchored was a crescent-shaped bay. Supporting
infantry from Corinth and their local allies was deployed on the
projecting headlands either side, and the ships formed a solid line
between them. The naval commander was the Corinthian Polyanthes.
The Athenians sailed out of Naupactus against them with thirty-three
ships under the command of Diphilus. For a while the Corinthians
made no movement, but then, when it seemed the right moment, the
signal was raised and they sailed out to engage the Athenians. There
followed a protracted battle with neither side yielding to the other.
Three Corinthian ships were destroyed. No Athenian ship was completely wrecked, but some seven were put out of commission when
Corinthian ships with their catheads strengthened for this specific
purpose rammed them head on and sheared off their outriggers. The
engagement was ambiguous enough for both sides to claim victory,
but the Athenians gained possession of the wrecks when the wind
blew them out into the open sea and the Corinthians made no further
move to attack. The two fleets separated with no pursuit, and no
prisoners taken on either side—the Corinthians and Peloponnesians
were fighting close to land, so their crews could easily escape capture,
and on the Athenian side no ship had been wrecked. As soon as the
Athenians had sailed back to Naupactus the Corinthians set up a
trophy, regarding themselves as the victors because they had put
the greater number of ships out of commission. Their definition of
no defeat mirrored their opponents' definition of no victory. The
Corinthians thought that anything less than a complete loss was a
win, whereas the Athenians took anything less than a complete victory as a defeat. Even so, when the Peloponnesians had sailed away
and the infantry dispersed, the Athenians marked their own claim to
victory with a trophy set up in Achaea, a little over two miles from
what had been the Corinthian base at Erineus. Such was the outcome
of the naval engagement.

35   Demosthenes and Eurymedon, their expedition now joined by
seven hundred hoplites and three hundred javelin-men provided by
the Thurians, ordered their ships to sail round to the territory of
Croton while they themselves first held a review of all their land

forces at the river Sybaris and then led them on down through Thuria. When they had reached the river Hylias the Crotonians sent them word that they would not allow the army passage through their land: so they turned down to the sea and camped for the night at the mouth of the Hylias, and their ships met them there. On the following day they embarked the army and sailed on along the coast, touching at the cities they passed with the exception of Locri, until they reached the promontory of Petra in the territory of Rhegium.

Meanwhile the Syracusans, aware of their approach, were keen to make another trial of their own fleet and also to deploy the land army which they had been gathering for the express purpose of a pre-emptive attack before these reinforcements arrived. Learning from their experience in the previous sea-battle, they had made some modifications to their ships which they saw could give them an advantage. In particular they had shortened and strengthened the prows, giving them thicker catheads braced by struts extending nine feet to, and a further nine feet through, the sides of the prow (this was how the Corinthians too had adapted their ships for the head-on tactics they used against the Naupactus squadron). The Syracusans thought that they could thus gain an advantage over the Athenian ships, which were not similarly built to withstand this sort of attack, but had slender prows designed for their preferred technique of encircling and ramming amidships rather than head on. They also reckoned that a battle in the Great Harbour, involving many ships in a confined space, would work in their favour. They could use their massive thick rams to smash the Athenians' thin and hollow prows in head-on collisions, and without adequate room the Athenians would not be able to employ against them the technical manoeuvres on which they most relied—encirclement and penetration through gaps in the line: the Syracusans would do their best to offer no opportunity for penetration, and the lack of space would preclude encirclement. Head-on ramming, which had previously been put down to the captains' inexperience of naval warfare, would now be their favoured mode of attack, and they expected to gain great advantage from it. Athenian ships forced to back water out of the battle could only retire towards land, and that land was close by and closely confined to the area of their own base. The Syracusans would control the rest of the harbour, so if the Athenians came under pressure they would all have to crowd into the same small area with consequent fouling and confusion (and indeed in all their sea-battles nothing did greater harm to the

36

Athenians than their inability to back water into any part of the harbour, as the Syracusans could). Nor would the Athenians be able to sail round them into wider water, as the Syracusans could turn and re-enter from the open sea at will, and back water whenever they wished: moreover, Plemmyrium would be enemy territory to the Athenians, and the mouth of the harbour was not wide.

37 Such were the tactical refinements devised by the Syracusans to suit their own degree of skill and naval strength. They were also more confident now after the earlier sea-battle, and they launched a coordinated attack by land and sea. Shortly before the fleet went into action Gylippus led out the infantry based in the city and took them against the section of the Athenian wall which faced Syracuse, while the troops stationed in the Olympieium (such hoplites as were there, the cavalry, and the Syracusan light infantry) attacked the wall from the other direction. Immediately after this the Syracusan and allied ships sailed out. At first the Athenians thought that the enemy attempt would be an infantry operation only, but they were then disconcerted to see the ships also suddenly bearing down on them. Some took position on the wall or in front of it to meet the attacking force, while others went out to oppose the numerous cavalry and javelin-men fast approaching from the Olympieium and the outskirts of Syracuse, and the other section manned the ships or went down to fight from the beach. When the ships were crewed they put out seventy-five

38 against the Syracusan fleet of about eighty. For most of the day there was attack and retreat and constant skirmishing with neither side able to achieve anything of note, other than one or two Athenian ships disabled by the Syracusans. They eventually parted, and at the same time the Syracusan infantry withdrew from the attack on the Athenian wall.

On the following day the Syracusans kept quiet, giving no indication of what they intended to do next. In view of the drawn result of the previous day's fighting Nicias expected another attack, and required the trierarchs to repair any damage to their ships. He also moored freighters in front of the palisade which the Athenians too had fixed in the seabed as a protective dock for their ships: he placed the freighters two hundred feet apart, so that any ship under pressure could make a safe retreat and sail out again unmolested. These preparations occupied the Athenians for the whole day until nightfall.

39 On the next day the Syracusans employed the same offensive as before, though at an earlier hour, and engaged the Athenians by land

and sea. The two fleets faced each other in the same way, and again spent much of the day skirmishing. Eventually Ariston the son of Pyrrhichus, a Corinthian and the best ship's captain on the Syracusan side, persuaded the Syracusan naval commanders to send a request to the city authorities to arrange for the immediate transfer of the general market down to the seashore, making it compulsory for all those with stocks of food to bring them for sale there by the sea. The idea was to disembark the sailors and have them buy their lunch from these traders right by their ships: with only a short interval they could then surprise the Athenians with a second attack on the same day.

The commanders agreed and sent the message, and the market 40 was set up. The Syracusans suddenly backed water and rowed for home, then quickly disembarked and had their meal on the shore. The Athenians took their withdrawal to the city as an acknowledgement of defeat, disembarked at leisure, and busied themselves with various tasks including the preparation of lunch, in the belief that they would do no more fighting on that day at least. But suddenly the Syracusans were re-embarked and bearing down on them again. The Athenians, most of them unfed, took to their ships in chaotic disorder and had a difficult time of it getting under way to face them. For a while the two fleets maintained a wary stand-off, but soon the Athenians decided that any further delay could lose them the battle through the sheer exhaustion of their men, and they should attack at once. So, raising a cheer throughout the fleet, they struck forward and began the fight. The Syracusans withstood the attack and used the head-on tactics they had planned: their modified rams sheared off the Athenians' outriggers along much of a ship's length, and their javelin-men on the decks inflicted considerable damage on the Athenians. Still greater damage was done by the Syracusans who weaved among the enemy ships in light boats, ducking under the banks of their oars or rowing up to their sides and hurling javelins at the sailors.

Relentless use of these battle tactics eventually brought the 41 Syracusans victory, and the Athenians turned tail and made for the refuge of their own base through the channels between the freighters. The Syracusan ships pursued them as far as the freighters, but were prevented from going further by the heavy metal 'dolphins' swung out on cranes from the freighters and suspended over the channels. Two Syracusan ships in the heat of victory came too close to the freighters and were destroyed: one of them was captured crew and all. When the Syracusans withdrew they had disabled seven Athenian ships and badly damaged many others: the crews they mostly took alive, but some they killed. They set up trophies to mark both sea-battles. They were now firmly confident of substantial superiority at sea, and they expected to have the better of the land campaign as well.

42   While the Syracusans were preparing for another attack on both elements, Demosthenes and Eurymedon arrived with the reinforcements from Athens. They had with them, I calculate, seventy-three Athenian and allied ships, together with about five thousand hoplites from Athens itself and their allies, a good number of javelin-men both barbarian and Greek, slingers, archers, and full provision of all else required. The immediate effect on the Syracusans and their allies was deep dismay at the thought that they now had no prospect of a final release from danger, when they saw that, despite the fortification of Deceleia, the Athenians had sent against them a second expedition just about as large as the first, and that Athenian power seemed unlimited in every direction. The effect on the original Athenian force was the development of some confidence after difficult times.

Demosthenes saw how matters stood, and realized that he could not afford to waste time or repeat the experience of Nicias. Nicias had inspired fear on first arrival, but this turned to contempt when he did not apply immediate pressure on Syracuse but spent the winter at Catana, and so Gylippus had time to bring an army from the Peloponnese and steal a march on him. The Syracusans would never even have sent for this army if Nicias had attacked at once. Confident of their own ability to deal with the Athenians unaided, they would have learnt their mistake only when they were completely walled off by a superior enemy, so that any reinforcements called for then could not have helped them to the same extent. Reviewing all this, and recognizing that for him too his maximum and most frightening impact was right now, on this very first day, he wanted to take immediate advantage of the panic caused at this moment by the arrival of his force. Seeing that the Syracusan cross-wall which had prevented the Athenian circumvallation was only a single wall, and was easily captured if the approach up to Epipolae were secured and the force stationed there taken out (nobody would then resist them), he lost no time in taking forward this attempt. He thought it was his quickest way of finishing the campaign. Either he would succeed and take

Syracuse, or else he would bring the expedition home and save pointless attrition both of the Athenian troops there with him and of the overall resources of the city.

First of all, then, the Athenians went out and ravaged the Syracusans' land round the river Anapus, regaining for the moment their original military control on both land and sea, as the Syracusans offered no opposition on either element other than the cavalry and javelin-men from the Olympieium. Thereafter Demosthenes decided 43 first to try using siege-engines against the cross-wall. But when the engines he had brought up were set on fire by the enemy defence on the wall, and all the other attacks made by the Athenian forces at various points were repulsed, he thought he should delay no longer, and with the agreement of Nicias and his fellow commanders he proceeded to the attempt on Epipolae as planned.

An unobserved approach and ascent during the daytime seemed impossible. So, after ordering provisions for five days and gathering all the masons and carpenters, together with a supply of arrows and all the tools needed for siege-works, should they be successful, at about the first watch of the night Demosthenes led out the entire army and marched towards Epipolae. He was accompanied by Eurymedon and Menandrus, but Nicias was left behind in the Athenian lines. They reached the foot of Epipolae at Euryelus, where the first Athenian force also had made its original ascent. The Syracusans had guards posted, but the Athenians were able to advance undetected on the Syracusan fort built there and take it, killing some of the garrison. The majority of the guards made their escape to bring the immediate news of this attack to the three separate camps (for Syracusans, other Sicilian Greeks, and allies) in fortified forward positions on Epipolae, and also to alert the Syracusan six hundred, who were the advance guard on this part of Epipolae. The six hundred rushed to the defence, but Demosthenes and the Athenians met them and, for all their vigorous resistance, sent them back in retreat. The force with Demosthenes pressed on immediately, to exploit their present momentum and lose no speed in the achievement of their objective: others proceeded straight away to take possession of the Syracusan cross-wall (the guards did not wait to face them) and began pulling down the battlements. The Syracusans and their allies, together with Gylippus and his troops, were now coming out in defence from their encampments, but when they clashed with the Athenians they were still dazed by the unexpected boldness of this night attack and they were initially forced into retreat. The Athenians now continued their advance in increasing disorder, thinking they had won and wanting to drive their way as quickly as they could through all the enemy contingents which had not yet engaged, to prevent any rally by the enemy if they slackened the pace of their attack. The Boeotians were the first to make a stand: they counter-attacked, routed the Athenians, and put them to flight.

44   The Athenians were now thrown into such helpless confusion that it has not been easy to establish from either side a detailed account of what exactly happened. Events are clearer in daytime operations, but even then the participants have no overall picture, but only a vague knowledge of what was going on in their own particular area. In a night battle—and this was the only one fought between large armies in the whole of the war—how could anyone be certain of anything? There was a bright moon, and as happens in moonlight they could see each other as human shapes from some distance, but without any confident recognition of friend or foe. Large numbers of hoplites from both sides were milling about in a confined space. Some of the Athenians were already beaten, while others, so far undefeated, continued the original attack. A large part of their army either had just come up or was still making the ascent, and they did not know which way to turn. The rout of their forward troops had now created complete confusion, and the general noise made it difficult to distinguish one side from the other. The Syracusans and their allies, aware that they were gaining the upper hand, cheered one another on with loud shouts (no other form of communication was possible in the darkness) and withstood all attacks. The Athenians were trying to locate their own troops, and took as hostile anything coming from the opposite direction, even if it was their own side now running back in defeat. Having no other means of recognition they were constantly asking for the password, and so not only caused chaos among themselves, all asking at the same time, but also revealed the password to the enemy. They did not have the same opportunity to learn the enemy password, as the Syracusans, getting the better of the battle and keeping their forces concentrated, had less difficulty in recognizing their own side. The result was that if a superior force of Athenians encountered a group of enemy, the enemy could get away by knowing the Athenian password, whereas the other way round, if the Athenians could not respond when challenged for the password, they were killed. But nothing did greater harm than the confusion caused

by the singing of the paean, which had a virtually identical sound on both sides. Whenever the Argives, Corcyraeans, or other Dorian contingents on the Athenian side raised their paean, the effect was to frighten the Athenians just as much as the enemy's paeans. So in the end, once the panic had started, all over the army friends were colliding with friends and nationals with their fellows, not only terrifying one another but actually proceeding to combat, which was stopped just in time. Now under full pursuit, and with only a narrow path back down from Epipolae, many jumped to their death over the steep sides.

When the survivors got down to level ground, the majority, and especially the members of the first expedition who best knew the local geography, made their escape back to their camp. Some of the later arrivals lost their way and wandered about the countryside, until day came and Syracusan cavalry sweepers destroyed them.

On the following day the Syracusans set up two trophies, at the 45 top of the way up to Epipolae and at the spot where the Boeotians had made the first stand, and the Athenians recovered the bodies of their dead under truce. A good number of Athenians and their allies had died, but more sets of weapons were captured than there were bodies: this was because those forced to jump over the sides, whether to die or survive, had first abandoned their arms.

This unexpected success had buoyed up the Syracusans' con- 46 fidence once more to its previous level, and they now sent Sicanus with fifteen ships to Acragas: the city was in a state of revolution, and he was to win it over if he could. And Gylippus had gone off by land on another mission to raise further troops from the rest of Sicily. After the result on Epipolae his hope was now to take the Athenian walls by storm.

Meanwhile the Athenian generals held a council of war in the light 47 of the disaster they had suffered and the comprehensive malaise now prevalent in the army. They saw their initiatives failed and the troops chafing at the length of their stay. The men were oppressed by sickness (both because this was the time of year when diseases are most common, and because they were camped in a marshy and unhealthy place) and also by the general hopelessness of the situation as they saw it. Demosthenes was against staying any longer. He maintained the view he had taken when risking the attack on Epipolae. That had failed, so he voted for a departure without delay, while it was still possible to cross the open sea and in military terms they at least had naval superiority with the arrival of the second fleet. The interests of

Athens, he said, were better served by a war directed against the
enemy building forts in the Athenians' own country, rather than
against the Syracusans, with little hope now of an easy conquest: and
it made no sense to waste huge sums of money on a pointless siege.

48   Such was the argument of Demosthenes. Nicias privately shared
the view that they were in poor state, but did not want to voice any
admission of their weakness or to have many involved in what would
then be an open vote for withdrawal, sure to be reported back to the
enemy: this would greatly lessen their chances of making a quiet
retreat at a time of their own choosing. There were other considerations too. His knowledge of the enemy's situation (and he was better
informed about this than his colleagues) still gave him hope that the
Syracusans would find themselves in worse state than the Athenians
if the siege was maintained—they would be worn down by financial
exhaustion, especially now that the Athenians with their present fleet
had greater control of the sea. And there was an element in Syracuse
working for surrender to the Athenians, which kept in constant
touch with him and urged him not to withdraw. With the information which he had Nicias was in fact still in two minds and reviewing
the options, but his overt statement at the time was a refusal to bring
back the expedition. He was well aware, he said, that the Athenians
would not forgive them for leaving Sicily without their own express
vote of recall. Judgement on them would be passed by men who had
not shared their own first-hand experience of the situation, but would
make up their minds on what they heard at second hand in the criticisms of others—any misrepresentation by a clever speaker would
convince them. And many or most of the troops with them, who
were now complaining of dire straits, once back in Athens would
broadcast the opposite complaint that their generals had betrayed
them and been bribed to go home. Knowing the Athenian character
as he did, for his part he would prefer to take his own risk of dying,
if die he must, at the hands of the enemy rather than face execution
by the Athenians on a dishonourable charge without any justice. And
despite all, he said, the Syracusans' situation was yet worse than
theirs. With the need to support mercenary troops, the expenditure
on keeping the forts garrisoned, and the maintenance of a large navy
for a full year now, they were already in financial difficulty which
would soon be desperation. They had spent two thousand talents so
far and had large debts besides, and if they lost any part of their present
force through inability to pay the wages, their military position would

be ruined, as it depended on mercenaries who, unlike their own troops, had no obligation to serve. So, he concluded, they should maintain the siege to wear the enemy down, and not allow finance (in which their own resources were far superior) to dictate their departure.

Nicias was insistent on this line of argument because he saw 49 exactly how things were in Syracuse, including the financial problems and the existence there of a significant pro-Athenian element, whose communications with him urged no withdrawal: and at the same time he had greater confidence than before in at least naval superiority. But Demosthenes would not agree to prolong the siege on any grounds whatsoever. If, he said, they could not take the expedition back without a vote of the Athenian assembly, but must continue to wear the enemy down, they should do this after first moving their base to Thapsus or Catana, from where their land forces could overrun much of the countryside, so maintaining themselves at the enemy's expense and doing them harm with their depredations, and their ships could fight their battles in the open sea. The present confined space worked to the enemy's advantage, but with ample room for manoeuvre they could exploit their expertise and make their retreats and attacks without the need to keep putting out from or in to a narrow and restricted base. In short, he said, he could not in any way approve staying any longer in the same place: they should move elsewhere now, as soon as possible, and without delay. Eurymedon expressed the same view. Nicias still objected, and this caused hesitation and delay, giving rise also to a suspicion that his insistence might be based on some superior information. And so it was that the delay continued, and the Athenians stayed where they were.

Meanwhile Gylippus and Sicanus arrived back at Syracuse. 50 Sicanus had had no success with Acragas, as while he was still at Gela on his way there the faction friendly to the Syracusans had been expelled. Gylippus brought with him a substantial further army from Sicily and also the hoplites sent out in the freighters from the Peloponnese in the spring, who had reached Selinus from Libya. They had first been driven off course to Libya, where the Cyrenaeans had given them two triremes and pilots for their voyage. Proceeding along the coast they joined forces with the people of Euesperides, who were under siege from the Libyans. After defeating the Libyans they sailed on round to the Carthaginian trading-post of Nea Polis, which is the closest point to Sicily (the voyage takes two days and a night), and made the crossing from here to Selinus.

On their arrival the Syracusans immediately began preparations for another double attack on the Athenians by sea and land. The Athenian generals now saw the enemy reinforced by a fresh army, while their own situation showed no improvement but rather a daily deterioration in every respect, not least the increasing pressure of sickness among the men. The generals regretted not moving their base earlier, and since even Nicias was now less opposed to the idea (only stipulating that there should be no open vote), with as much secrecy as they could they gave everyone notice of an evacuation of the camp, and told them to be ready to move when they received the order. All was prepared and they were on the point of sailing away when there was an eclipse of the moon, just then at the full. At this most of the Athenians felt misgivings and called on the generals to postpone the operation: and Nicias (who was rather too much inclined to divination and the like) refused even to discuss any earlier move until they had waited for the thrice nine days prescribed by the soothsayers. So, with this the reason for their sudden delay, the Athenians had stayed on.

51   The Syracusans had their own intelligence of this, and were much more determined now to give the Athenians no quarter. They took the evacuation plan as Athenian acknowledgement of their loss of both naval and military superiority: and to prevent them settling down somewhere else in Sicily where they would be harder to fight, they wanted to force them as soon as possible to a sea-battle where they were, and where the conditions favoured Syracuse. So they manned their ships and spent what they considered a sufficient number of days on exercises. When the time came, on the first day they attacked the Athenian walls. A small detachment of hoplites and cavalry came out against them through one of the gates, but they cut off some of the hoplites, routed the rest of the detachment, and chased after them. As there was only a narrow way back through the gate, the Athenians lost seventy horses and a few of the hoplites.

52   This time the Syracusans withdrew their army. But on the next day they sailed out with a fleet of seventy-six ships and at the same time brought their land forces against the walls. The Athenians put out to meet them with eighty-six ships, engaged, and began the battle. Eurymedon, in command of the Athenian right wing, was trying to encircle the enemy ships, and in this attempt he had extended his line too far round towards land: after defeating the Athenian centre the Syracusans and their allies then cut him off in a bay deep inside

the harbour. There Eurymedon was killed, and the ships he had with him in his squadron were destroyed. The Syracusans now began pursuing and driving ashore the entire remainder of the Athenian fleet.

When Gylippus saw the enemy ships being defeated and driven 53 back to shore beyond their palisade and the confines of their base, he took part of his army along the spit to intervene, with the intention of killing the sailors as they landed and making it easier for the Syracusans to tow away the ships from a shore now under friendly control. This part of the Athenian perimeter was guarded by the Etruscans. They could see a disorderly approach by Gylippus' troops and came out to confront them: they fell on the leading column, routed them, and drove the whole force into the marsh called Lysimeleia. But afterwards the Syracusans and their allies brought up a larger force, and now the Athenians, in fear for their ships, came to support the Etruscans and joined battle with the enemy. They defeated and pursued the Syracusans, killing a few hoplites, and rescued most of their ships and brought them back to their base: but eighteen ships were captured by the Syracusans and their allies, and all the crews were executed. In an attempt to set fire to the remainder of the Athenian fleet the Syracusans filled an old merchant ship with brushwood and pine logs and, with the wind in the right direction, set light to it and let it drift towards the Athenians. Put in fear again for their ships the Athenians devised counter-measures to extinguish the flames and keep the fireship at a distance, and so averted the danger.

After this the Syracusans set up trophies to mark their victory in 54 the sea-battle and also their success in cutting off the hoplites and capturing the horses in the engagement at the upper Athenian wall. The Athenians likewise marked with trophies the Etruscans' drive of the enemy infantry into the marsh and their own defeat of the second force.

With the Syracusans now the decisive victors at sea also (despite 55 their original fear of the additional fleet brought by Demosthenes), the Athenians were in complete despair. The reversal was a great shock to them: yet greater still was their regret that they had ever launched the expedition. These were the only cities they had come up against which were actually comparable in character to their own—under democratic government like them, and strong in ships, cavalry, and size of population. They could not therefore bring any distinct advantage against them to secure their compliance, neither the promise of a change of regime nor the threat of much superior military strength. They were failing in most respects, and now this unimaginable defeat at sea took an already low morale to much greater depths.

56   The Syracusans now had the immediate freedom of movement round the harbour, and planned to block its mouth, so that, even supposing it were their intention, the Athenians would lose any chance of slipping away by sea. The focus of their attention was not now simply their own escape from danger, but also how to deny escape to the Athenians. They thought, as was indeed the case, that present circumstances made their own position far the stronger, and that, if they could defeat the Athenians and their allies both by land and by sea, the rest of the Greeks would see this as a heroic prize to have won. Throughout Greece the immediate effect would be either freedom from subjection or removal of the threat, since, they believed, the remaining Athenian forces would not be capable of sustaining the next phase of the war: and they, the Syracusans, would be credited as the authors of this deliverance, to the great admiration of the rest of the world and future generations. And this was a prestigious contest in other ways too: they were proving their superiority not only over the Athenians but over a whole host of Athenian allies as well; again, it was not only them fighting for themselves, but others had come to support their stand, and they had taken their place as leaders alongside Corinth and Sparta; they had offered their own city to bear the brunt of the danger which threatened them all; and they had developed their navy to substantial strength.

There was now gathered in contention for Syracuse what was certainly the largest number of nations ever to converge on a single city, a number exceeded only by the full tally of those involved in this war for or against the cities of Athens and Sparta.

57   Here follows a list of the various nationalities who were there on either side to attack or defend Sicily and took part in the war over Syracuse. They had come to share either in the conquest of the country or in its rescue, but their particular alignment was not determined by any justifying cause or kindred loyalty so much as by purely contingent factors of self-interest or compulsion.

The Athenians themselves, as Ionians, came over against Dorian Syracuse of their own free will. They were joined in the expedition by the Lemnians, the Imbrians, the Aeginetans occupying Aegina at the time, and also the Hestiaeans settled at Hestiaea in Euboea: all these were Athenian colonists, speaking the same dialect as the Athenians and retaining the same institutions.

Of the others who joined the expedition some were subjects, others were independent allies, and there were also some mercenaries. The tribute-paying subjects were the Eretrians, Chalcidians, Styrians, and Carystians from Euboea; the Ceans, Andrians, and Tenians from the islands; and the Milesians, Samians, and Chians from Ionia (of these last the Chians did not pay tribute, but were independent as long as they provided ships instead, and took part in the expedition on that basis). Almost all of these were Ionians and of Athenian descent (the only exception being the Carystians, who are of the Dryopian race), and although they were subjects and therefore obliged to participate, at least they did so as Ionians against Dorians. Then there were the Aeolians—the Methymnaeans (contributing ships rather than subject to tribute), and the Tenedians and Aenians, both of these tribute-paying. These Aeolians found themselves compelled to fight against their own race, as the Boeotians on the Syracusan side were also Aeolians and the founders of the colonies from which they came: the only outright Boeotians fighting their own were the Plataeans, not surprisingly in view of their mutual hostility. The Rhodians and the Cytherans too, both Dorian peoples, had to fight against their kin. The Cytherans were Spartan colonists, but served in the Athenian army against the Spartans under Gylippus; the Rhodians (who are of Argive descent) were required to make war not only on the Dorian Syracusans but also on their own colonists the Geloans, who were fighting on the Syracusan side. Among the islands lying off the Peloponnese the Cephallenians and Zacynthians were independent, but as islanders they were under some pressure to take part because the Athenians controlled the sea. The Corcyraeans, who were not only Dorians but unquestionably Corinthians too, served with the Athenians against Corinthians and Syracusans, despite being colonists of the former and kinsmen of the latter: they could make a specious claim of compulsion, but in fact they were motivated just as much by their hatred of the Corinthians. The Messenians too were brought into the war—this now being the term for the inhabitants of Naupactus and the garrison at Pylos, which at the time was still in Athenian hands. And there were a few Megarian exiles whose circumstances had them fighting against the Selinuntians, who were Megarians too.

The others participating in the campaign did so on a more voluntary basis. The Argives went with the Ionian Athenians to fight as

Dorians against Dorians not so much in virtue of their alliance with
Athens as out of hatred of the Spartans and, at the individual level,
the opportunistic hope of personal advantage. The Mantineans and
other Arcadians came as mercenaries. They had always been ready to
join any war offered to them, and now they were equally happy, as
long as there was gain in it, to regard the Arcadians serving with the
Corinthians as their enemies. So too the Cretans and Aetolians, also
attracted as mercenaries. The Cretans had founded Gela jointly with
the Rhodians, but it turned out that, so far from coming to assist
their own colonists, they were prepared to attack them for pay. And
some of the Acarnanians gave their support as allies, partly for
motives of gain, but mainly out of loyalty to Demosthenes and good
will towards the Athenians.

All these were from countries east of the Ionian Gulf. Of the
Greeks in Italy, the Thurians and the Metapontians joined the
Athenian side as a necessary consequence of the state then prevailing
in their internal conflicts; and among the Sicilian Greeks the Naxians
and the Catanaeans sided with the Athenians. Barbarian support
came from the Egestans, who had invited the Athenians in the first
place, and from most of the Sicels; from outside Sicily there were
some Etruscans, who had a quarrel with the Syracusans, and Iapygian
mercenaries.

That is the list of all the nationalities under arms on the Athenian
side.

58   On the opposite side the Syracusans were supported by the
Camarinaeans, their immediate neighbours, and the Geloans, whose
territory came next after Camarina; and then by the Selinuntians,
who lived the far side of the still neutral Acragas. All these inhabited
the part of Sicily which faces south towards Libya: in the region
fronting the Tyrrhenian Sea to the north the Himeraeans were the
only Greek inhabitants, and also the only people from that area to
support Syracuse. These were the Greek states, all Dorians and all
independent, who fought on the Syracusan side. The only barbarians
with them were the Sicels who had not defected to the Athenians.

From the Greeks outside Sicily aid was sent to Syracuse by the
Spartans, who provided a Spartiate commander and a force consisting of Helots and men from the newly liberated cohorts; by the
Corinthians, the only allies to bring both a fleet and a land force; by
the Leucadians and the Ambraciots, in virtue of their ties of kinship;
there were mercenaries from Arcadia (sent by the Corinthians), and

an obligatory force from Sicyon; and, from outside the Peloponnese, a contingent sent by the Boeotians. Yet as a proportion of the total resources this external aid was smaller in every category than the contribution made by the Sicilian Greeks themselves: theirs were big cities, which together had mustered a large number of hoplites, ships, and horses, and a wealth of other troops besides. And within this the proportion supplied by the Syracusans on their own was greater than virtually all the rest combined, reflecting both the size of their city and the fact that they were in the greatest danger.

Such then were the allies mustered on either side. Both sides now 59 had their full complement in place, and neither would receive any further help in any form.

The Syracusans and their allies naturally thought that there was a heroic prize to be won if they could follow their victory achieved at sea with the capture of the entire Athenian expeditionary force, huge as it was, by preventing any possible means of escape either by sea or on foot. So they immediately began to block the mouth of the Great Harbour (which was about three-quarters of a mile wide) with triremes and other boats large and small anchored broadside, and to make other preparations in case the Athenians still persisted in offering battle at sea. There was nothing small-scale in any of their plans now.

Seeing the blockade of the harbour, and inferring the enemy's 60 overall intention, the Athenians realized that they needed to make some decisions, and held a meeting of the generals and contingent commanders to review the situation in the light of their present difficulties. Chief among these was the question of food. They did not have enough left for their immediate needs (having sent word to Catana to cancel the supply when they thought they were about to leave), and would have none in the future unless they gained control of the sea. They decided therefore to abandon their upper walls and build a cross-wall to create an enclave right by the ships no larger than was absolutely necessary for the accommodation of their stores and their sick. They would leave a garrison here, take on board every single other infantryman to fill every available ship, seaworthy or not, and fight it out at sea. If successful, they would move to Catana. If not, they would burn their ships and make a retreat on foot in full battle order to the nearest friendly territory they could reach, whether barbarian or Greek. Once made, they put this decision into action. They quietly withdrew from the upper walls and manned the

entire fleet, compelling everyone of remotely serviceable age to go on
board. The total number of ships manned was about a hundred and
ten. They filled the decks with large numbers of archers and javelin-
men from Acarnania and other foreign parts, and took all other
measures they could, given the constraint of their situation and the
plan they had formed.

When all was nearly ready, Nicias saw that the men were despondent
at the unfamiliar experience of a heavy naval defeat but also impatient to risk battle as soon as possible, as they were short of rations.
He therefore first called them all together and addressed them with
encouragement along these lines:

61   'Soldiers of Athens, allied soldiers, the coming contest will have
the same importance for every one of us. We shall all be fighting for
our lives and for our country, just as much as the enemy. If we win
now with our ships, everyone can see his own home-city once more,
wherever that may be. We should not be downhearted. We should
not behave like utter novices who are thrown by early defeats and for
ever afterwards let those first disasters shape their expectations of a
fearful outcome. No. All you Athenians here have long experience of
many wars, and all you allies have constantly fought with us on our
campaigns. Remember, then, how wars take unexpected turns: and
prepare yourselves for this battle in the hope that fortune will stand
on our side, and determined to renew the fight in a manner worthy of
this vast army which you see before you, and of which you are part.

62   'We have consulted the ships' captains and put in place, as far as
our circumstances allow, all the measures which, given the narrow
confines of the harbour, we thought could help us deal with the
inevitable crowding of ships and the enemy's use of troops deployed
on deck, factors which have done us harm in previous engagements.
We shall have on board a large number of archers and javelin-men as
well as a mass of other troops, which would not be our tactic if we
were fighting a true sea-battle in open water, as the increased weight
of the ships would interfere with our manoeuvring skills, but here,
in what will necessarily be more of a land-battle fought from ships,
they will serve us well. And we have worked out the corresponding
changes needed in the structure of our ships, including the installation of iron grapnels to counteract the effect of the enemy's strengthened catheads, which did us so much harm. Any ship ramming us
will be caught by the throw of these grapnels and prevented from
backing off again, if the marines follow up and do their job. As I say,

we have been reduced to fighting a land-battle on board ship, and it is clearly in our interest to avoid backing water ourselves and to deny that opportunity to the enemy, especially as the whole shore, apart from the section occupied by our land-forces, is in enemy hands.

'With this in mind you must fight it out to your utmost, and not 63 allow yourselves to be driven ashore. When ship clashes with ship, refuse to separate until you have swept the hoplites from the enemy deck. These instructions are as much for the hoplites as for the sailors, since this task falls mostly to the men on deck, and even now we still retain overall superiority with our infantry. As for the sailors, I urge you, and not only urge but beg you not to take your previous reverses too much to heart: you have better resources on deck now, and a greater number of ships. Some of you are not citizens, but so far have been regarded as honorary Athenians and admired for that throughout the Greek world, because you speak our language and have assimilated our culture. Remember what a joy that privilege is, too precious to lose. You have shared with us the benefits of our empire, and your share extends yet further to the fear inspired in our subjects and your own security under the law. You alone have had the freedom to be our partners in this empire, and owe it now the duty not to let it down. So show your contempt for these Corinthians—you have beaten them many times before—and for these Sicilian Greeks, none of whom was prepared even to attempt resistance when our fleet was at its prime. See them off, and make it clear that even when weakened by setbacks you have the expertise to overcome any combination of strength and good fortune in the opposition.

'Now another word to the Athenians among you. I would remind 64 you that back home there are no more ships like these in the dockyards and no more men of an age for hoplite service. If you meet with anything other than victory, your enemies here will immediately sail over there, and our people left at home will be unable to withstand their present enemies in Greece and these new invaders combined. Then you here will immediately be in the hands of the Syracusans (and you know what your intentions were against them), and your people at home will be in the hands of the Spartans. So in this one contest now before you you will be fighting both for yourselves and for them. Now, if ever, is the time to be strong. Reflect, one and all, that you who will soon be on these ships are the Athenian army and navy, you are the whole of your city, you are the great name of Athens. For Athens' sake any man with skill or courage out of the ordinary should display it now: he will never have a better opportunity to help himself and save his country.'

65 After this address Nicias immediately gave orders to man the ships. It was easy enough for Gylippus and the Syracusans to realize that the Athenians were going to fight, as they could see the actual preparations. But they had also been told in advance about the installation of the grapnels, and they had included counter-measures in the general fitting out of their ships for all the various contingencies: they stretched hides over the prow and much of the upper structure of each ship, so that any grapnel thrown would slip off and find no purchase. When all was ready, the generals and Gylippus addressed their men with encouragement along these lines:

66 'Syracusans and allies, we have made a glorious beginning, and the challenge before us now is to secure a glorious conclusion. Most of you evidently know this, or you would not be so strongly committed to the task: but in case anyone is not fully aware, we shall spell it out. The Athenians, already possessing the greatest imperial power ever held by Greeks past or present, came to this country to enslave Sicily first, and then, if successful, to proceed to the enslavement of the Peloponnese and the rest of Greece. You were the first of all men to withstand that once all-conquering navy: you have defeated it in previous battles, and there is every reason to expect that you will defeat it now. When men find their assumed strength cut short, what remains of their self-esteem is left weaker than if they had not thought themselves superior in the first place, and the unexpected blow to their pride has them caving in when in fact they still retain some power to resist. In all probability this will be the state of the 67 Athenians now. Whereas in our case that first instinct which led us to take our chances despite our inexperience at the time is now more firmly based: add to that the realization that we are the champions if we have beaten the champions, and every man's hope is redoubled. And generally in any enterprise high hopes inspire high commitment.

'As for their mimicry of our fighting arrangements, we are familiar enough with our own style to adapt to any aspect of it used against us. But when they experiment with crowds of hoplites on their decks, and crowds of javelin-men, Acarnanians and others, who are simply landlubbers put on a ship and will have no idea how to throw a javelin from the sitting position, is it not inevitable that they will unbalance the ships and create chaos among themselves as they all attempt a style of deployment which is foreign to them? And they will derive no benefit either from the size of their fleet, in case any of you is worried that he will have to fight superior numbers. A large fleet in a confined space will be slower to carry out intended man-oeuvres, and much more easily damaged by the means we have ready for them. The truth of the matter is this, and we are confident in the accuracy of our sources. The Athenians are overwhelmed by their difficulties. The hopeless situation in which they find themselves has forced them to the desperate resort of trusting to luck rather than strategy and risking all in the only way they can—either a break-out to sea or, failing that, a retreat by land. They know that whatever happens they could not be worse off than they are at present.

'So, with the opposition in this disarray, with the fortune of our 68 greatest enemies now playing into our hands, let us take them on with real passion. We should remember that the right to satisfy feelings of anger in the punishment of an aggressor is universally accepted, and that revenge on one's enemies, soon to be in our power, is indeed, as the saying goes, the sweetest of all things. It will be clear to all of you that the Athenians are not only enemies but the worst of enemies. They came against our country to enslave it. If they had succeeded in this, they would have brought the ultimate suffering on our men, the worst indignities on our children and women, and on the whole city the most shameful name there can be. So there must be no relent-ing. Do not think that all is achieved if they simply leave with no more danger to us: they will do that anyway, even if they defeat us. But if the outcome is as we wish, and as it promises to be, it will be a glorious challenge for us to have won, to see the Athenians pun-ished and to restore to the whole of Sicily that freedom, now more deeply rooted, whose fruits she used to enjoy. As for dangers, they rarely come with less penalty for failure or greater benefit in success.'

After giving this encouragement to their own troops, the Syracusan 69 generals and Gylippus began to man their ships as soon as they saw the Athenians doing the same. Nicias, aghast at the situation and aware both of the extent of the danger and now of its immediacy (the ships were on the point of rowing out), went through all the agony of thought which generals experience on the brink of major battles—too little done, not enough said. He appealed again to each of the trier-archs, calling them by their father's name, by their own name, by the name of their tribe; he urged those who had claim to distinction on their own account not to betray that claim, and those with famous ancestors to maintain their family honours untarnished; he reminded

them of their fatherland, the freest country there was, where every
man could live his life in unregimented liberty; and he continued in
the vein familiar at such moments of crisis, when men do not try to
avoid the impression of conventional language (such as the standard
references on all occasions to 'our wives and children and the gods of
our fathers'), but invoke what they think could be helpful at a time
of distress.

   When he had said all that he thought time allowed (though still
not enough for his satisfaction), Nicias turned back and led the land
forces down to the sea, extending the line over as wide an area as he
could, so that they could be as effective as possible in cheering on
their fellows on board the ships. The Athenian generals embarking
with the fleet were Demosthenes, Menandrus, and Euthydemus.
They now set out from their base and made straight for the gap left in
the barrier across the harbour mouth, hoping to force their way out.

70   The Syracusans and their allies had already put out and deployed
with about the same number of ships as before, using some of them
to guard the exit and ring the rest of the harbour, so that they could
make a simultaneous attack on the Athenians from all sides: at the
same time they had their land forces ready to give support wherever
their ships might have to put in to shore. The Syracusan fleet was
commanded by Sicanus and Agatharchus, each taking a wing of the
whole fleet, with Pythen and the Corinthians in the centre. When
the first Athenian squadron reached the barrier the initial force of
their attack gave them the better of the enemy ships stationed there,
and they began trying to break the links. But soon afterwards the
Syracusans and their allies came bearing down on them from all
sides, and the fighting was not now confined to the barrier but spread
throughout the harbour. The ensuing battle was more fiercely fought
and on a greater scale than any of the previous engagements. There
was intense urgency among the rowers on either side to respond to
every order to attack, and an intense contest of wits between the
opposing captains; when ship clashed with ship the marines too were
keen to prove their performance on deck no less professional; each
and all strove to excel in the duties assigned to them.

   With many ships meeting in a small space (and this was a battle
in a very small space between a very large number of ships—the
combined total came to nearly two hundred), there was little direct
ramming because of the lack of room to pull back for a charge
through the line: more often there were accidental collisions, ship

crashing into ship when attempting to escape or in pursuit of another. When one ship was bearing down on another, the men on the decks kept up a constant barrage of javelins, arrows, and stones: and when the two closed, the marines fought hand to hand in an effort to board the other. In many areas of the battle there was so little room that a ship which had rammed an enemy in one direction would find itself rammed from another, with the consequence that one ship would have two or sometimes even more ships entangled round it, and the captains were faced with the need to defend or attack against the enemy not just one at a time, but in multiples from all sides. And all the while the great din of so many ships crashing into one another both terrified the crews and made it impossible for them to hear the orders shouted by the coxswains—and indeed on both sides they were shouting loud, not only technical directions but also encouragement of the immediate struggle for victory. On the Athenian side they were urging their men to force their way out and now or never make one more supreme effort to win a safe return to their own country: on the other side the coxswains shouted reminders to the Syracusans and their allies of the glory there was in preventing the escape of the enemy, and the prestige every man would bring to his home-city if he had played his part in victory. And on both sides the generals would add their voice if they happened to see a ship backing without clear cause. They would call to the trierarch by name and ask him what he and his men thought they were doing. Had they now decided (this was the Athenian question) that enemy-infested land was a more congenial prospect than the sea which Athens, with no small labour, had made her element? Was that why they were going backwards? The Syracusans were asked whether, when they knew perfectly well that the Athenians were desperate for any means of escape, they themselves were now in flight from the fugitives.

While the sea-battle hung in the balance the two land armies on 71 the shore were gripped in an agony of conflicting emotions, with the local troops rooting for yet further triumph and the invaders terrified of ending up in a situation even worse than the present. For the Athenians everything depended on their ships, and their anxiety for the outcome was intense beyond words. Localized action varied throughout the theatre of battle, and so inevitably the men lining the shore had varying perspectives: the action was quite close in front of their eyes, and they were not all looking at the same arena. So if some saw their own side winning in their particular part of the battle, they would take instant encouragement and begin calling on the gods not to deprive them of this hope of salvation; others who had witnessed an area of defeat turned to loud cries of lament, and from the mere sight of what was happening were in more abject terror than the actual combatants. Yet others, focused on a part of the battle which was evenly balanced, went through all the agonies of suspense: as the conflict lasted on and on without decisive result, their acute anxiety had them actually replicating with the movement of their bodies the rise and fall of their hopes—at any moment throughout they were either on the point of escape or on the point of destruction. And as long as the battle at sea remained in the balance you could hear across the Athenian ranks a mixture of every sort of response—groans, cheers, 'we're winning', 'we're losing', and all the various involuntary cries let out by a great army in great danger. The suspense was just as agonizing for the men on board, until finally, after a long-protracted battle, the Syracusans and their allies routed the Athenians, pressed after them in clear triumph with whoops and cheers, and chased them back to land. Then all in the naval force who had not been captured out on the water made shore wherever they could and cascaded out of their ships to run for the camp. The land troops could hardly believe what was happening, and—no possible variety of response now—in one universal surge of emotion gave vent to cries and tears of anguish. Some ran to defend the ships, some to guard the remaining stretch of wall: but others—the majority—began looking out for themselves and the means of their own safety. The panic at this moment was the greatest ever experienced by an Athenian army. They had now suffered a similar fate to that which they inflicted at Pylos. There the destruction of the Spartans' ships had meant the further loss of their men who had crossed over to the island: and now too the Athenians could not hope for a safe escape by land, unless events took an unexpected turn.

72   So, after a hard-fought battle in which both sides lost many ships and many men, the Syracusans and their allies, with victory now assured, recovered their wrecks and their dead and sailed back to the city, where they set up a trophy. The scale of the Athenians' immediate calamity was such that they did not even think of asking to retrieve their dead or their wrecks: they planned to leave that very night. But Demosthenes came up to Nicias and proposed that they should man their remaining ships once more and attempt to force their way out at dawn. He argued that they still had more serviceable ships left

than the enemy: the Athenians had a residual fleet of about sixty ships, and their opponents less than fifty. Nicias concurred, and the generals were ready to man the ships: but the sailors, shattered by their defeat and convinced that they could no longer win, refused to embark.

So the Athenians were all now agreed on a retreat by land. The 73 Syracusan Hermocrates suspected their intention, and realized the danger if such a large army could get away by land and settle somewhere else in Sicily with a mind to renew the war against Syracuse. He therefore went to the authorities and spoke as he thought, arguing that they should not stand by and let the Athenians get away during the night, but the entire Syracusan and allied army should go out now, barricade the roads, and occupy any narrow passes with a guard set there in advance. The authorities very much shared his view, and thought this the right plan, but they doubted whether the men would readily accept such an order. They had only just now been able to enjoy some relaxation after a great sea-battle, and at festival-time too (this happened to be the day of a sacrifice to Heracles): in celebration of their victory most had indulged in holiday drinking, and the very last command they could be expected to obey at this time was an order to take up arms and march out. The authorities saw this as an insuperable difficulty, and Hermocrates could not change their minds. So, still afraid that the Athenians could start off in the night and manage to cover the most difficult terrain unopposed, he proceeded with a plan of his own devising. When it was growing dark, he sent some of his associates with a cavalry escort to the Athenian camp. They rode up within earshot and called to some of the soldiers. They presented themselves as friends of the Athenians (and Nicias did have some informants within the city), and told the men to take the message to Nicias that he should not withdraw his army in the night, as the Syracusans were guarding the roads: he should take his time to prepare and leave during the day. This message delivered, they went back, and the recipients reported it to the Athenian generals. They considered the message to 74 be genuine, and so made no move overnight. When, despite their intention, they did not manage to get away promptly in the morning, they decided to wait for the following day, so that the soldiers had time to pack up as best they could the items they were most likely to need, and then to set out with everything else left behind, taking with them only such supplies as they still had for bodily sustenance.

Meanwhile the Syracusans and Gylippus had already gone out
with their land forces to block the local roads likely to be taken by the
Athenians, set guards at the places where streams and rivers could
be crossed, and deploy for battle in what they decided was the best
position to intercept the Athenian army and stop it. At the same time
their navy rowed up to the beached Athenian ships and began towing
them away. The Athenians themselves, as they intended, had set fire
to a few of them: but the Syracusans could now, without any interference or opposition, attach their tow-ropes to all the others, wherever they had run aground, and bring them back to the city.

75   Thereafter, when Nicias and Demosthenes thought their preparations complete, the army at last began its departure on the third day
from the sea-battle. The pity of it was not only the fact that they were
retreating after the loss of their entire fleet, and with those high
hopes now turned to imminent danger both for themselves and for
the city of Athens, but in the very act of leaving the camp every man
had to endure painful and heart-rending sights. The dead bodies
were unburied, and to see a friend lying there brought distress and
fear at the same time in equal measure. The living who were being
left behind—the wounded and the sick—were much more distress-
ing even than the dead to their living comrades, and in more pitiful
state than those who had been killed. The cries of entreaty they
started up ('take us with you') reduced the others to despair. They
would call out for help to every friend or relative they could see; they
clung to their tent-mates even as they moved off, and followed as far
as they could; when strength and body failed they fell back with
anguished groans and a stream of curses. So the whole army was in
tears, and this despairing pity made it hard for them to move out,
even though it was a move from enemy country when they had
suffered disasters too great for tears already, and were in fear of
suffering more in an uncertain future. And there was also a sense of
shame and a strong element of self-reproach. They looked like nothing so much as a column of refugees from a city taken by siege, and
a large city at that: the total mass of men on the move numbered not
less than forty thousand. Every one of them was carrying with him
anything he had been able to take of potential use, and even the hoplites and the cavalry, in contrast to their usual practice when under
arms, carried their own food. They had either lost their attendant
slaves, or distrusted them (the slaves had long been deserting, and
the greatest number did so now). But what they had with them was

not enough, as the food in the camp had run out. This sharing of
hardship in their general degradation had at least the consoling aspect
of 'safety in numbers', but even so was not easy to accept at the time,
especially when they thought of what initial brilliance and pride had
come to such a humiliating end. This was indeed the greatest reverse
experienced by any Greek army. They had come with the intention
of enslaving others, and now found themselves leaving in fear of
enslavement themselves; they had set out to the accompaniment of
paeans and prayers for success, and were now retreating with quite
different imprecations in their ears; they were on foot, not on ship,
and reliant now on infantry rather than navy. And yet the pure scale
of the danger still hanging over them made all this seem bearable.

In view of the army's low morale and the huge change in their 76
situation, Nicias went along the ranks giving encouragement and
consolation as best he could in the circumstances. He increasingly
raised his voice as he moved from section to section, warming to the
task and hoping to do some good by broadcasting his message as far
as it could reach:

'Even in our present state, Athenians and allies, we must have 77
hope. Before now men have reached safety from yet worse situations
than this, and I would not have you being too hard on yourselves
because of the defeats you have suffered or of the present hardships
which belie your worth. Look at my own case. I am no stronger than
any of you (you can see how my disease has affected me), but I was
once thought second to none in the good fortune of my private and
wider life, and I am now at the same cusp of danger as the meanest
among you. And yet my life has been spent in constant observance of
the gods and constant justice and fairness in my dealings with men.
This gives me, despite all, some confident hope for our future, and
our misfortunes do not alarm me as in any way a reflection of our
worth. They could well abate. The enemy have had their full share
of success, and if we incurred any god's resentment when we launched
our expedition, we have now been punished enough. Others before
now have gone to war against other countries, doing what human
nature will do, with consequences which human nature can bear. We
too have cause to hope now for a gentler divine dispensation (merit-
ing now the gods' pity rather than their resentment), and if you look
over your own concerted ranks—the number and quality of hoplites
on the march—you should not be too much dismayed. You should
have in mind that wherever you settle you form an immediate city,

and no other city in Sicily will easily resist your attack or dislodge
you, once established. Take your own responsibility for maintaining
security and discipline on the march, and every one of you should
remember that in any place where he may have to fight victory will
give him his new homeland and his fortress. We shall press on night
and day alike, as we are short of food for the journey. If we can reach
some friendly Sicel territory (and fear of the Syracusans keeps them
firm in our support), you can then consider yourselves secure. We have
sent ahead to them, telling them to meet us and bring more food.

'Finally, soldiers, and in short, you must realize that the only
option is to be brave—there is no nearby refuge for the faint-hearted.
Remember too that if you can escape the enemy now, all the others
among you will reach the homes you must long to see, and the
Athenians here will raise up once more to greatness the fallen power
of their city. It is men who make a city—not walls, not ships without
the men to fill them.'

78   Nicias went all through the army with such words of encouragement, at the same time restoring proper formation wherever he saw
gaps in the ranks or other irregularities. Demosthenes likewise traversed the troops under his command with the same or similar
exhortations. The army marched in hollow-rectangle formation,
Nicias' division in front and Demosthenes' following, with the porters and most of the other troops inside the frame of hoplites. When
they reached the ford across the river Anapus they found a force of
Syracusans and allies drawn up there ready to meet them. They
routed this force and gained control of the crossing, then proceeded
on their march, but the Syracusans kept up constant harassment,
with their cavalry riding alongside and their light troops hurling
javelins.

On this day the Athenians covered about four and a half miles,
before making camp for the night on high ground. On the next day
they started early in the morning and proceeded for just over two
miles, then came down to a level stretch of land and camped there.
It was an inhabited area, and they wanted to get any foodstuff
they could from the houses, and also draw water from there to carry
with them—there was no ready supply of water for several miles
along their intended route. Meanwhile the Syracusans had gone on
ahead and were building a wall to block the next pass. This was a
steep hill with precipitous ravines on either side, known as the
Acraean Rock.

On the following day the Athenians moved forward, and this time they were harassed on both sides by large numbers of Syracusan and allied cavalry and javelin-men, throwing volleys of missiles and riding up close. The Athenians fought on for a long time, but eventually turned back to their previous camp, where they now did not have the same access to provisions, as the cavalry made it impossible to move outside the camp.

In the morning they started early, resumed the march, and forced 79 their way to the hill where the pass had been walled off. Here they found themselves faced by enemy infantry drawn up in defence of the wall many ranks deep (as the place afforded little width). The Athenians attacked and began an assault on the wall, but under a bombardment of missiles from large numbers of the enemy on the steep hill above (with height lending range to their casts) they failed to carry the assault, and drew back again to rest. It so happened that the battle was accompanied by a storm of thunder and rain, as is not unusual at this time of year, with autumn coming on: but this demoralized the Athenians yet further, and they thought that here too everything was conspiring to destroy them. While they were resting Gylippus and the Syracusans sent a detachment of their army to wall them off from the rear and so prevent retreat by the way they had come: but the Athenians managed to counter this move with a detachment of their own troops. Thereafter the Athenians withdrew their whole army more into the plain and camped for the night.

On the next day they began to march on. The Syracusans now surrounded them and attacked from all sides, wounding many. They would retreat if the Athenians advanced against them, but pressed in hard whenever the Athenians fell back, concentrating their attack on the troops at the rear, in the hope that they could gradually turn small-scale routs into universal panic. The Athenians struggled on like this for a long time, and after advancing two-thirds of a mile or so they halted in the plain to rest. The Syracusans too broke off and went back to their own camp.

During the night Nicias and Demosthenes agreed on a change of 80 plan, in view of the poor state of their army (a complete lack of provisions now, and a large number of casualties from the constant enemy attacks). They decided to light as many campfires as possible and lead the army away, not on their originally intended route, but in the opposite direction to that in which the Syracusans were watching for them, towards the sea. The overall course of their march was not now

aimed at Catana, but to the other side of Sicily, towards Camarina
and Gela and the other cities, Greek or barbarian, in that region. So
they lit plenty of fires and set off in the night. As can happen in any
army, especially a very large one, panic-fears broke out—not least
because they were marching at night, through enemy territory, and
with the enemy not far away—and they fell into confusion. Nicias'
division, reflecting his generalship, stayed together and got far ahead,
but the larger half of the army with Demosthenes lost contact and
proceeded in worse order. By dawn, though, they had all reached the
sea, and took the so-called Helorum road, intending to go as far as
the river Cacyparis and then follow the river up into the interior,
where they expected to be met by the Sicels they had sent for. When
they reached the river they found a guard of Syracusans already there
and busy blocking the passage with a wall and a palisade. They
forced their way through, crossed the river, and continued in the
same direction towards another river called the Erineus, as this was
the route advised by their guides.

81   The reaction of most of the Syracusans and their allies, when day
came and they realized that the Athenians had left, was to blame
Gylippus for deliberately letting them go. They set off in fast pursuit,
easily discovering the route the Athenians had taken, and caught up
with them at about the time of the midday meal. They came first on
the troops with Demosthenes, who were behind the others and progressing more slowly, still in disorder from the panic of the previous
night. The Syracusans immediately attacked and fought them, and
their isolation from the rest of the Athenian army made it easier for
the enemy cavalry to encircle them and keep them confined in one
spot. Nicias' army was now a good five miles ahead. He was leading
them on at a faster pace, taking the view that their best chance of
survival in the circumstances was not to stand and fight, if they could
avoid it, but to retreat as quickly as they could, only fighting when
they had no option. On the other hand Demosthenes had for the
most part to suffer more intense harassment as he was at the rear of
the retreat and so the first target for enemy attacks, and now that he
saw the Syracusans in pursuit he chose to draw up his army for battle rather than continue the march. This delay cost him encirclement
by the enemy, and both he and the Athenians with him were now in
serious trouble. They were forced to crowd into a plot of land with a
wall surrounding it and a road on either side: it was quite thickly
planted with olive trees. Here they were subjected to a barrage of

missiles from all round the perimeter. The Syracusans had good reason to prefer this mode of attack to close fighting. To take the risk of engaging desperate men would have now transferred the advantage from them to the Athenians, and there was a general reluctance to sacrifice their lives unnecessarily when success was already assured: in any case they thought that this method of fighting would overpower the Athenians and lead to their capture.

`And so it was. All day they kept shooting at the Athenians and 82 their allies from all sides, and when they saw them finally reduced to utter exhaustion by their wounds and all other effects of the constant attrition Gylippus and the Syracusans and their allies made a proclamation, first of all inviting any of the islanders who so wished to come over to their side with a guarantee of freedom (some of the island cities did go over, but not many). Thereafter an agreement was offered to the whole of the rest of the force with Demosthenes: they should surrender their arms, but no one would suffer death by violence, in imprisonment, or through deprivation of the basic needs of life. The whole six thousand surrendered themselves, and handed in all the money they had with them, throwing it into upturned shields: four shields were filled. The captives were immediately taken back into the city. On this same day Nicias and his division reached the river Erineus. He crossed it and camped his army in an area of high ground.

On the next day the Syracusans caught up with Nicias and told 83 him that Demosthenes' division had surrendered: they invited him to do the same. He did not believe them, and arranged a truce for a horseman to go and see. When the horseman had gone and come back with confirmation of the surrender, Nicias sent a message to Gylippus saying that he was prepared to agree on behalf of the Athenians to reimburse the Syracusans for their full expenses in the war, on condition that they let his army free to go: until the money was paid he would give Athenian citizens as hostages, a man for each talent. The Syracusans and Gylippus would not accept these proposals, but instead attacked and surrounded this division as they had the other, keeping up a barrage of missiles from all sides until late in the day. Nicias' men too were in a terrible condition through lack of food and other necessities, but even so they intended to wait for the dead of night and then continue their march. They were just taking up their arms when the Syracusans detected what was happening and raised the paean. It was plain now that they could not steal away, so

the Athenians put down their arms again—all except for about three
hundred men, who broke through the enemy guard and set off wherever they could in the darkness.

84   When day came Nicias led his army on, and the Syracusans and
their allies kept up their harassment as before, bombarding them
from all sides and shooting them down with javelins. The Athenians
were making for the river Assinarus as fast as they could. They
thought that if they could only cross this river they would have some
relief from the constant pressure of attacks on all sides by the large
number of enemy cavalry and the mass of light troops: and also they
were exhausted and urgent to drink. When they reached the river
they flung themselves in, all discipline now gone, and with every man
trying to get across first and the enemy hard on them they had a
difficult time of it. Forced to crowd together as they attempted to
cross, they stumbled over one another and some were trampled underfoot: they fell foul of their own spears and other gear, some dying
there and then from the spears, and others carried downstream
entangled in the baggage. The Syracusans had men ranged on the far
bank of the river (which was steep), and from that height they rained
down missiles on the Athenians below, most of them in a chaotic
crush slaking their thirst in the shallow water of the river. The
Peloponnesians came down the bank to the attack, and began slaughtering the Athenians, particularly those still in the river. The water
quickly turned foul, blood mingling with mud, but the Athenians
drank on, and most fought among themselves to reach it.

85   In the end, when the bodies were lying heaped on one another in
the river, and the army had been utterly destroyed, most of them
there along the river and any who had escaped being accounted for
by the cavalry, Nicias surrendered himself to Gylippus. He trusted
Gylippus more than the Syracusans, and asked him to do whatever
he and the Spartans wanted with his own person, but to stop the
slaughter of his men. In response to this Gylippus gave the order to
start taking prisoners. So the survivors—excluding a good number
appropriated by the Syracusan soldiers—were brought in alive, and
the three hundred who had broken through the guard during the
night were rounded up by a detachment sent in pursuit. The total
number of state prisoners taken from the Athenian army was not
great, in contrast to the large number kidnapped and dispersed, such
that the whole of Sicily became full of them: this was because their
capture was not the result of a formal capitulation, as it had been with

Demosthenes' army. A substantial proportion of the army died. The slaughter at the river was the main loss of life in the retreat, and as great a slaughter as any in the whole of this war. A good number also had died in the frequent attacks on the army as it marched. But even so many escaped, either immediately at the time or by running away later after they had been enslaved. For all these the point of refuge was Catana.

The Syracusans and their allies now gathered their troops together 86 and returned to the city with the spoil they had won and as many of the prisoners as they could take with them. All the other captured Athenians and allies they sent down into the quarries, reckoning this the most secure place to keep them under guard: as for Nicias and Demosthenes, despite the objections of Gylippus, they cut their throats. Gylippus had thought that it would be a fine prize and a crowning achievement to bring the opposing generals back to Sparta. It so happened that of these two Demosthenes was regarded by the Spartans as their greatest enemy, and Nicias as their greatest friend, the reason in both cases being the affair at Pylos and the island: by persuading the Athenians to make a peace-treaty, Nicias had ensured the release of the Spartan men captured on the island. This had disposed the Spartans in his favour, which was Nicias' main ground of reliance in surrendering himself to Gylippus. But (so it was said) there were some Syracusans afraid that if put to torture on the question he might reveal their communications with him and cause them trouble amid the general success, and others, especially the Corinthians, who feared that, given his personal wealth, bribes in certain quarters might enable him to escape and do them further mischief in the future. These won the consent of their allies and had him executed. For such reasons, or something very like them, Nicias met his death. Of all the Greeks in my time he was the least deserving of this depth of misfortune, since he conducted his whole life as a man of principle.

The prisoners in the quarries were harshly treated by the 87 Syracusans in the early days of their captivity. Large numbers were confined in a deep and narrow space. Direct sun and suffocating heat, with no shelter, oppressed them first by day, and then the autumnal nights that followed brought cold and a contrasting extreme of temperature which ruined their health. In such a cramped space they had to do everything just where they were: and with the dead bodies piling up too (men dying of their wounds, through the changes of temperature, and other such causes), the stench was unbearable. They were also afflicted by hunger and thirst (over eight months the daily ration for each man was half a pint of water and a pint of cereal), and suffered every other misery imaginable when men are thrown into a place like that. This was the condition of all the captives together for some seventy days: thereafter the Syracusans sold the others as slaves, but kept in that confinement the Athenians and any Sicilian or Italian Greeks who had fought on their side. The total number of state prisoners taken is hard to establish exactly, but was not less than seven thousand.

This proved the most significant occurrence in the whole of this war, and, it seems to me, in the whole of recorded Greek history—unparalleled triumph for the victors, and unparalleled disaster for the vanquished. This was, as they say, 'total annihilation'. Beaten in every way on every front, extreme miseries suffered on an extreme scale, and army, fleet, and everything else destroyed, few out of all those many made their return home.

Such were the events in Sicily.

BOOK EIGHT

When the news reached Athens, for a long time they could not 1
believe that their forces had been so utterly destroyed, and would not
credit even the unambiguous reports brought back by soldiers who
had actually witnessed the events and made their escape. Then when
they had to accept the truth they turned on the politicians who had
taken part in advocating the expedition (as if they themselves had not
voted for it), and were furious too with the oracle-mongers, the seers,
and all others whose professed revelations of the divine will had at
the time encouraged their hope of conquering Sicily. On every side
there was nothing for them but pain, and they were plunged into fear
and the utmost consternation at what had happened. The burden of
loss lay heavy on individual families and on the city at large—so
many hoplites gone, so many cavalrymen, such a swathe of youth
and no replacement to be seen. And when at the same time they could
not see an adequate number of ships in the docks, adequate funds in
the treasury, or an adequate supply of officers for the ships, they
despaired of surviving the situation as it was. They thought that their
enemies in Sicily, particularly after such a crushing victory, would
immediately send a fleet against the Peiraeus, that their enemies in
Greece itself, with all their resources now doubled in this way, would
bring every force to bear on them both by land and by sea, and that
their own allies would revolt and join the enemy.

Nevertheless they decided that, as far as lay in their power, they
should not give in. Specific decisions were to build up a fleet (procur-
ing timber from wherever they could) and a financial resource; to take
steps to secure their allies, most particularly Euboea; to make sensible economies in state expenditure at home; and to elect a board of
older men to oversee the agenda for debate at any given time as occasion demanded. As tends to happen in a democracy, the people were
ready to embrace any form of discipline in the panic of the moment,
and they proceeded to implement the decisions they had taken.

So the summer ended.

In the following winter there was an immediate surge of excite- 2
ment throughout the rest of Greece at the massive Athenian failure
in Sicily. States which had so far been neutral thought that they should
stay out of the war no longer, but volunteer to join the campaign

against Athens even if not invited. They each reckoned that they would have been targets of Athenian aggression if the Sicilian venture had succeeded, and that the final stages of the war would be short: it would be a glorious thing to have taken part. The allies of the Spartans shared a new determination, stronger than ever before, to bring their long suffering to a speedy end. But most insistently of all the Athenian subjects were now eager to revolt from Athens, whether or not they had the power to do so: they interpreted the situation in the light of their own emotions, and did not give the Athenians any chance of surviving the next summer. All this was encouraging to the Spartan state, and yet more so the likely prospect of their allies in Sicily coming to join them at the beginning of spring in full force, now that they had necessarily developed a strong navy. Confident on all fronts, they determined to prosecute the war with unhesitating vigour. They reckoned that with the war brought to a glorious conclusion they would be permanently free of dangers of the sort which the Athenians would have presented if they had added the Sicilian dimension to their power; and that once they had crushed the Athenians they themselves would be guaranteed the leadership of all Greece.

3   So right at the beginning of this winter their king Agis set out with an armed force from Deceleia and collected money from the allies to help pay for the fleet. He then turned to the Malian Gulf, where the Oetaeans were long-standing enemies: he confiscated the bulk of their cattle and exacted payment from them. Here also he put pressure on the Achaeans of Phthiotis and the other Thessalian subjects in this region. Despite the indignant protests of the Thessalians he forced them to give hostages and money, sent the hostages for safe keeping to Corinth, and tried to compel them into the alliance. The shipbuilding requisition which the Spartans imposed on the allied states was for a total of a hundred new ships. The numbers stipulated were twenty-five each from Sparta itself and Boeotia, fifteen from Phocis and Locris, fifteen from Corinth, ten from Arcadia, Pellene, and Sicyon, and ten from Megara, Troezen, Epidaurus, and Hermione. All other preparations were made for an immediate resumption of war at the approach of spring.

4   The Athenians too used this winter to carry out their own preparations as intended. They procured timber and built ships; they fortified Sounium to protect the corn-ships on their route round to Athens; they abandoned the fort they had built in Laconia when

sailing round the Peloponnese on their way to Sicily, and made other economies wherever there seemed unnecessary expenditure; and most of all they kept a close watch on their allies to prevent revolt.

During the same winter, while both sides were engaged in this activity and busy equipping themselves to all intents as though they were only just beginning the war, the Euboeans became the first of the Athenian subjects to send envoys to Agis to discuss revolt from Athens. He accepted their proposals and sent to Sparta for Alcamenes, the son of Sthenelaïdas, and Melanthus to come as the intended commanders in Euboea. They arrived with a force of about three hundred newly liberated Helots, and Agis began arranging their transport across. But just then envoys arrived from the Lesbians also, who were equally keen to revolt. As their case was actively supported by the Boeotians, Agis was persuaded to defer intervention in Euboea and turned to promoting the Lesbian revolt. He appointed Alcamenes (who had been about to sail to Euboea) as their governing commander, and promised them ten ships, with the Boeotians promising another ten. This was done without reference to the Spartan state: as long as Agis was at Deceleia with his own army there, he had full authority to send a force wherever he wished, to levy troops, and to raise money. Indeed it could be said that at this particular time he had much greater control over the allies than the Spartan government at home, as he had an army at his own disposal and was an immediately formidable presence wherever he chose to go.

While he was negotiating with the Lesbians, the Chians and Erythraeans, also eager to revolt, turned for help not to Agis but to Sparta. They were accompanied by a representative of Tissaphernes, who had been appointed military governor of the west by King Dareius the son of Artaxerxes. Tissaphernes was equally interested in securing the involvement of the Peloponnesians, and offered to provide their maintenance. He had recently received a demand from the King for the tribute due from his province, and he was in arrears as far as the Greek cities were concerned because the Athenians made collection impossible. He thought that if he could damage the Athenians he would be better able to get his tribute: and at the same time he hoped to present the King with a Spartan alliance, and thereby to carry out a further instruction from the King, which was to take alive or kill Amorges, the bastard son of Pissouthnes, who was in revolt in the Carian region.

6   The Chians and Tissaphernes thus shared the same objective and
presented a combined case. At about the same time there arrived in
Sparta Calligeitus the son of Laophon, a Megarian, and Timagoras
the son of Athenagoras, a Cyzicene, both exiles from their own country and resident at the court of Pharnabazus the son of Pharnaces.
They had been commissioned by Pharnabazus to secure the dispatch
of a fleet to the Hellespont for his own purposes. Like Tissaphernes,
he was keen, if possible, to induce the cities in his province to revolt
from the Athenians, for the same reason of tribute, and he wanted to
be the one to present the King with a Spartan alliance.

       The two parties representing Pharnabazus and Tissaphernes were
acting independently of each other, and when both were at Sparta
there developed a fierce competition between them to win the prior-
ity of Spartan support: one party wanted ships and troops sent to Ionia
and Chios first, the other to the Hellespont. The Spartans themselves were much more inclined to accept the proposals of the Chians
and Tissaphernes, as their cause was also promoted by Alcibiades,
who had a strong link of ancestral guest-friendship with Endius, one
of the ephors at the time. (This friendship was the source of the
Laconian name Alcibiades in his family: Endius' father was called
Alcibiades.) Nevertheless the Spartans first sent an inspector to
Chios—one of the Perioeci called Phrynis—to establish whether the
Chians did have the number of ships they claimed and the general
capability of the city accorded with the account given. When he
reported that what they had been told was true, the Spartans immediately made an alliance with the Chians and Erythraeans, and voted
to send them forty ships, on the assumption that, from what the
Chians said, there was already a fleet there of at least sixty ships.
Their original intention was to send ten of their own ships in this
number, commanded by Melanchridas, their current admiral-in-
chief. But an earthquake occurred, and after that they transferred the
command from Melanchridas to Chalcideus, and reduced the
number of ships under fit-out in Laconia from ten to five.

       So the winter ended, and with it the nineteenth year of this war
chronicled by Thucydides.

7   At the very beginning of spring in the following summer season the
Chians pressed for the dispatch of the ships, as they were afraid that
the Athenians would get wind of their intrigue (like all the others,
they had tried to keep their overtures secret). So the Spartans sent
three Spartiates to Corinth with instructions to arrange the immediate

transport of the ships across the Isthmus from the Corinthian Gulf to the sea facing Athens, and then give the whole fleet sailing orders to Chios, including the ships which Agis was fitting out for Lesbos. The total number of allied ships at the Isthmus was thirty-nine. Pharnabazus' agents Calligeitus and Timagoras took no part in the 8 expedition to Chios. They had brought money with them, twenty-five talents, but made no offer to contribute to the costs of this expedition, preferring to wait and finance a separate expedition later. When Agis saw that the Spartans were set on going to Chios first, he himself had no objection, but the allies convened a conference at Corinth to take their own view. They decided to sail first to Chios under the command of Chalcideus, who was fitting out the five ships in Laconia; to go on from there to Lesbos under Alcamenes, Agis' choice for that command; and then finally to reach the Hellespont, with Clearchus the son of Rhamphias appointed to this last command. They decided also to transport only half of the ships across the Isthmus at first, and send these immediately on their way: the idea was to split the Athenians' attention between the ships setting out and the ships still to follow across the Isthmus. They were prepared to make the voyage in this quite open manner, as they had come to regard the Athenians as impotent, with no significant naval power yet in evidence. They followed their decision immediately with the transport of twenty-one ships over the Isthmus.

The others were in a hurry to sail, but the Corinthians were reluctant to join them until they had celebrated the Isthmian festival, which fell at that time. Agis was willing to let them observe the Isthmian truce, and to take on the expedition by himself. The Corinthians objected, and there ensued a delay, during which the Athenians began to get some inkling of the Chian business. They sent one of the generals, Aristocrates, to confront the Chians. When they denied any plot, the Athenians required them, as a guarantee of good faith, to send back with Aristocrates a contribution of ships to the allied war-effort: and they sent seven. The reason for this compliance in sending the ships was that the Chian people at large knew nothing of the negotiations with Sparta, and the oligarchs who were in the plot did not want to provoke a breach with the people before securing their own ground—and they had lost hope of any Peloponnesian intervention because of the delays.

Meanwhile the Isthmian festival was being celebrated. The Athenians 10 had been included in the proclamation of the festival truce, and had

sent a delegation to attend. While they were there they acquired more
precise information about the Chian business, and on their return
they took immediate steps to ensure that the ships at Cenchreae
could not get away without their knowledge. After the festival the
Peloponnesians set sail for Chios with twenty-one ships under the
command of Alcamenes. The Athenians intercepted them with an
equal number of ships and tried at first to draw them out into the
open sea. The Peloponnesians did not venture very far after them,
but turned back. At this the Athenians also withdrew, as they had
the seven Chian ships in their number and thought them unreliable.
But later they crewed further ships to bring the total to thirty-
seven, and when the Peloponnesians resumed their voyage along the
coast they chased them into Speiraeum, an uninhabited harbour in
Corinthian territory just short of the border with Epidauria. The
Peloponnesians lost one ship out at sea, but gathered the rest into this
harbour and anchored there. The Athenians attacked both by sea
with their ships and from the land with troops they had put ashore.
There followed a disorderly scrimmage of a battle in which the
Athenians damaged most of the Peloponnesian ships on the shore
and killed their commander Alcamenes: some of their own men
fell too.

11   When they broke off the Athenians set a guard of enough ships to
blockade the enemy, and anchored the rest of their fleet at the nearby
islet, where they made camp. They also sent to Athens for reinforcements, as on the following day Corinthian troops arrived in support
of the Peloponnesian ships, and shortly after them the other people
of the area. The Peloponnesians could see the difficulty of maintaining a guard on such a desolate place, and were uncertain what action
to take, even considering setting fire to the ships: in the end they
decided to drag the ships on shore and sit it out with their land
forces on guard until some suitable opportunity of escape presented
itself. When Agis heard of their situation he sent them Thermon, a
Spartiate, to take charge. The first news to reach the Spartans at
home was that the ships had put out from the Isthmus (Alcamenes
had been instructed by the ephors to send a horseman when the
departure was under way), and they were immediately ready to send
out their own five ships with Chalcideus in command and Alcibiades
with him. They were on the point of leaving when the second
message came with news of the fleet's confinement in Speiraeum.
Disheartened that their first move in the Ionian war had met with

failure, they were minded to cancel any dispatch of ships from their home waters and even to recall some which had already sailed.

When Alcibiades heard of this he went back to Endius and the 12 other ephors and urged them not to abandon the expedition. His arguments were that they would have sailed and arrived before the Chians heard what had happened to the other fleet; that once he reached Ionia he would have no difficulty in persuading the cities to revolt; he would describe the Athenian weakness and the Spartan commitment, and his would be taken as a uniquely authoritative voice. He took Endius aside and emphasized the honour to be won if he were the agent of revolt in Ionia and a Spartan alliance with the King: he should not let this prize fall to Agis (there was no love lost between Alcibiades and Agis). He convinced the other ephors as well as Endius, and set sail with the five ships in company with the Spartan Chalcideus. They made all speed on the voyage.

At about this same time the sixteen Peloponnesian ships which 13 had served with Gylippus throughout the Sicilian war were on their way back. Off Leucas they were intercepted and mauled by the twenty-seven Athenian ships stationed there under Hippocles the son of Menippus to watch for ships coming from Sicily: but all except one got past the Athenians and sailed into Corinth.

Chalcideus and Alcibiades arrested all they met in the course of 14 their voyage, to prevent any reports of their coming. They put in first at Corycus on the mainland, where they released their prisoners and had a preliminary meeting with some of the Chians in the plot, who advised them to sail straight into the city unannounced. So they suddenly arrived at Chios to the surprise and alarm of the general public. The oligarchs had so arranged it that the council was sitting at the time, and Chalcideus and Alcibiades were given the floor. They announced that many more ships were on their way (keeping quiet about the blockade at Speiraeum), and the Chians formally declared secession from Athens, followed shortly by the Erythraeans. They then took three ships to Clazomenae and induced revolt there too. The Clazomenians immediately crossed to the mainland and began fortifying Polichna, in case they needed to retreat there from the small island on which their city stands. All the revolted cities were now engaged in building fortifications and preparing for war.

The news from Chios quickly reached Athens. The Athenians 15 recognized that they now had a clearly major crisis on their hands: with the most important allied state gone over to the enemy, the rest of their allies would hardly stay quiet. In the alarm of the moment they immediately abrogated the penalties set for anyone suggesting or putting to the vote a proposal to touch the reserve of a thousand talents which they had jealously guarded throughout the war. They now voted to broach this reserve and use it to man a large number of ships. From the blockading fleet at Speiraeum they voted to send directly to Chios the eight ships under the command of Strombichides the son of Diotimus which had broken off guard duty to pursue Chalcideus and his squadron, but returned when they failed to catch him: another twelve would be sent in support shortly afterwards under Thrasycles, these too taken from the blockade. They removed the seven Chian ships participating in the blockade at Speiraeum, freed the slaves serving in them, and imprisoned the free men in the crews. They quickly manned another ten ships and sent them in partial replacement of the total number withdrawn from the blockade of the Peloponnesians, and planned to fit out and crew thirty more. There was urgency all round, and nothing was spared in the operation for the recovery of Chios.

16   Meanwhile Strombichides with his eight ships arrived at Samos. He took on an additional Samian ship and sailed to Teos, where he warned the inhabitants to stay loyal. But Chalcideus too was now bearing down on Teos from Chios with twenty-three ships, supported by the Clazomenian and Erythraean land forces keeping pace along the coast. Strombichides was informed in time and put back to sea. When he was well out in the open water he could see the size of the fleet coming from Chios, and turned to run for Samos, pursued by the enemy fleet. The Teians at first refused entry to the land forces, but then admitted them after the Athenians had fled. These troops waited for a while, expecting the return of Chalcideus from the pursuit. When time passed and he still did not come, they began on their own initiative to demolish the wall which the Athenians had built to protect the city of Teos on the landward side, and they were joined in this by a few barbarians who arrived under the command of Stages, one of Tissaphernes' deputies.

17   After chasing Strombichides back to Samos, Chalcideus and Alcibiades armed the sailors from the ships they had brought from the Peloponnese and left them in Chios, then manned those ships and a further twenty with Chians and sailed for Miletus, intending to bring about its revolt. Alcibiades was friendly with the leading men in Miletus, and wanted to win over the Milesians before any more

ships arrived from the Peloponnese. This would crown the achievement of widespread revolt among the Ionian cities solely with the help of the Chians and Chalcideus, and so win that prize for the Chians, for himself and Chalcideus, and, as he had promised, for Endius as the originator of the expedition. They made most of the voyage unobserved, and reached Miletus not far ahead of Strombichides and Thrasycles, who had just arrived from Athens with twelve ships and joined in the chase. They succeeded in bringing Miletus to revolt, and when the Athenians sailed in hard on their heels with nineteen ships, the Milesians refused to admit them. The Athenians then took up a blockading position at Lade, the island facing the city.

And now, immediately after the revolt of Miletus, the first Spartan alliance with the King was negotiated by Tissaphernes and Chalcideus, as follows:

The Spartans and their allies made an alliance with the King and 18 Tissaphernes on these terms:

All the territory and all the cities which are in the King's possession, or were in the possession of the King's forefathers, shall belong to the King: and whatever revenues or other goods once accrued to the Athenians from these cities, the King and the Spartans and their allies shall jointly ensure that the Athenians receive neither monies nor any other goods.

The King and the Spartans and their allies shall jointly pursue the war against the Athenians: and termination of the war shall only be allowed if agreed by both parties, by the King and by the Spartans and their allies.

If any revolt from the King, they shall also be the enemies of the Spartans and their allies: and if any revolt from the Spartans and their allies, they shall be the King's enemies likewise.

So the alliance was agreed on these terms. 19

Immediately after this the Chians manned a further ten ships and sailed to Anaea, wanting to find out how things stood at Miletus and also to bring the cities in that region into the revolt. A message came from Chalcideus telling them to go back, as Amorges was approaching overland at the head of an army. They sailed back to Dios Hieron, where they caught sight of sixteen ships which Diomedon was bringing from Athens to follow the earlier squadron under Thrasycles. As soon as they saw them, they scattered—one ship to Ephesus, the rest making for Teos. The Athenians captured four ships abandoned by their crews after reaching land in time, but the other five found refuge in the city of Teos. The Athenians then sailed away to Samos. The Chians put out to sea again with their remaining ships and, together with the land forces, secured the revolt of Lebedus and then Aerae. After that both army and ships returned to their various home cities.

20   At about this same time the twenty Peloponnesian ships at Speiraeum (which had been driven there earlier and then blockaded by an equal number of Athenian ships) made a sudden break-out, defeated the Athenians in battle at sea, and captured four of their ships. They then sailed back to Cenchreae and prepared once more for the expedition to Chios and Ionia. And Astyochus, who was just now succeeding as overall admiral-in-chief, arrived from Sparta to command them.

After the land forces had withdrawn from Teos Tissaphernes came in person with an army and completed the demolition of what remained of the fortification at Teos: he too then withdrew. Shortly after his departure Diomedon arrived with ten Athenian ships and established formal agreement with the Teians to allow the Athenians admission to their city on the same basis as the Peloponnesians. He sailed on round to Aerae, but left when his attack on the city failed to take it.

21   This was also the time of the revolution in Samos, when the people rose up against the men in power, helped by the Athenians from the three ships which they had there at the time. The Samian people killed in all up to two hundred of the most powerful men, condemned another four hundred to exile, and distributed their land and houses among themselves. The Athenians subsequently voted them independence on the grounds that their loyalty was now assured, and they continued their political reforms. Among other measures they withdrew all civic rights from the former landowners and prohibited any future marriage alliances, bride or groom, between them and the people or the people and them.

22   The Chians lost none of their original enthusiasm for promoting revolt elsewhere, even before the Peloponnesians arrived in force, and a contributory motive was to involve as many cities as they could in sharing the risk of defection. Their next move in the summer was to send an expedition of thirteen of their own ships against Lesbos, following the Spartans' declared plan of progressing from Chios to Lesbos, and thence to the Hellespont. At the same time the infantry available from the Peloponnesians already there and their allies in the region marched round towards Clazomenae and Cyme. The Spartiate Eualas commanded the land force, and the ships were commanded

by Deiniadas, one of the Perioeci. The fleet sailed first to Methymna, and secured its revolt. Four ships were left there, and the rest went on to secure the revolt of Mytilene.

Meanwhile Astyochus, the Spartan admiral-in-chief, set out from 23 Cenchreae with four ships, as planned, and reached Chios. On the third day after his arrival the Athenian fleet, numbering twenty-five, sailed to Lesbos under the command of Leon and Diomedon (Leon had brought a subsequent reinforcement of ten ships from Athens). On the same day, towards evening, Astyochus also put out to sea with the addition of one Chian ship and sailed for Lesbos, to offer what assistance he could. He arrived at Pyrrha, then on the next day at Eresus, where he learnt that Mytilene had been taken by the Athenians in one quick attack. They had sailed straight into the harbour without any warning, captured the Chian ships there, then put troops ashore and defeated the force which met them: so they were now in possession of the city. Astyochus heard this from the Eresians and from the Chian ships which had been left earlier at Methymna with Euboulus, but were now running for home after the capture of Mytilene and happened to meet him at Eresus (there were three of them now—one had been caught by the Athenians). So instead of pressing on to Mytilene Astyochus first secured the revolt of Eresus, then armed the men from his own ships and sent them round by land to Antissa and Methymna, putting Eteonicus in command, while he took the sea route with his and the three Chian ships. His hope was that the appearance of his force would encourage the Methymnaeans and keep them firm in their revolt. But when it turned out that everything was going against him in Lesbos, he took his land party back on board and sailed away to Chios. The allied land forces originally destined for the Hellespont were also dispersed back to their home cities. Shortly afterwards six more of the allied Peloponnesian ships from Cenchreae arrived to join Astyochus in Chios.

After restoring conditions in Lesbos the Athenians sailed on from there to capture from the Clazomenians the place they were fortifying on the mainland, Polichna. They brought them all back to their city on the island, except for the main instigators of the revolt, who absconded to Daphnus. So Clazomenae rejoined the Athenian alliance.

In this same summer the Athenians blockading Miletus with their 24 twenty ships at Lade made a landing at Panormus in Milesian territory, where the Spartan commander Chalcideus was killed when he brought up a few troops in opposition. On the third day after that the Athenians sailed across again and set up a trophy, which the Milesians pulled down, considering it erected without any complete conquest of the territory. Leon and Diomedon now used the Athenian fleet from Lesbos to prosecute war against the Chians from their ships, launching their attacks from the Oenoussae islands opposite Chios, from Sidoussa and Pteleum, fortified positions they held on the Erythraean peninsula, and from Lesbos itself: their marines were hoplites taken from the service-list and pressed into this role. Landings were made at Cardamyle and Boliscus, where the Chian forces coming to resist them were defeated with many casualties and the general area devastated: they were defeated again in another battle at Phanae, and in a third battle at Leuconium.

After this the Chians no longer came out to fight, and the Athenians comprehensively ravaged their richly cultivated land which had remained inviolate from the Persian Wars until then. Except for the Spartans, the Chians are the only people I know of who have combined prosperity with prudence, and matched the growth of their city with a corresponding stability of well-ordered government. Their very revolt (which may seem on the face of it a lack of caution) was not undertaken until they had a good number of firm allies to share the risk, and could see that after the Sicilian disaster Athens was in a dire state undeniable even by the Athenians themselves. And if they were undone by one of those miscalculations to which human affairs are prone, their mistake was shared by many others who, like them, thought that Athenian power would soon be completely destroyed. As it was, denied the sea and despoiled by land, some of them were prepared to bring their country back to the Athenians. The authorities became aware of this, but took no direct action themselves. Instead they brought the Spartan admiral Astyochus over from Erythrae with the four ships he had there, and discussed with him how best to put down the conspiracy by moderate means, either taking hostages or in some other way. This, then, was the state of affairs in Chios.

25   Towards the end of this summer Athens sent out an expedition of a thousand Athenian hoplites, fifteen hundred Argives (the Athenians providing hoplite armour for the five hundred of the Argives who had come light-armed), and a thousand from the allies. This force embarked in forty-eight ships (including some troop-transports) under the command of the generals Phrynichus, Onomacles, and Scironides, and sailed to Samos, then crossed over to Miletus and

took up position there. The Milesians came out to meet them with eight hundred hoplites of their own, together with the Peloponnesian troops who had come with Chalcideus and a body of mercenaries hired by Tissaphernes, who was there in person with his cavalry. These now engaged the Athenians and their allies in battle. The Argives on their wing charged ahead in some disorder, contemptuous of the opposition and convinced that no Ionians would withstand their attack. They were defeated by the Milesians and nearly three hundred of their men were killed. The Athenians first defeated the Peloponnesians, then drove back the barbarians and the rest of the miscellaneous opposition, but did not engage with the Milesians, as after the rout of the Argives they had retreated inside their city when they saw the other forces losing. The Athenians, now masters of the field, took up a position right in front of the city of Miletus. (A particular circumstance of this battle was that the Ionians on both sides had the better of the Dorians: the Athenians were victorious over the Peloponnesians facing them, and the Milesians over the Argives.) The Athenians set up a trophy and began preparations to wall off the city (it stands on a narrow-necked peninsula), reckoning that if they could reduce Miletus to compliance the other cities also would easily be won back.

But meanwhile, late in the afternoon, they heard reports of the 26 fleet of fifty-five ships from the Peloponnese and Sicily which was now nearly on them. At the instigation of the Syracusan Hermocrates, who had been foremost in urging the Sicilian Greeks to take their part in the final overthrow of Athens, twenty ships had come from Syracuse and two from Selinus; and the Peloponnesian ships under preparation were now ready. The Spartan Therimenes had been put in charge of conveying both squadrons to the admiral-in-chief Astyochus. They first sailed to Leros, an island some way short of Miletus. Here they learnt that the Athenians were at Miletus, and so sailed on into the Iasian Gulf to find out more about the Milesian situation. Alcibiades came on horseback to Teichioussa, a place in Milesian territory which was the point in the Gulf where the fleet had sailed in and made their camp. He told them about the battle (he had been there in person and fought on the side of the Milesians and Tissaphernes), and advised them, if they did not want to see the ruin of their campaign in Ionia and indeed of their whole cause, to go as quickly as they could to the relief of Miletus and not allow the city to be walled off.

27   They were ready to go at daybreak. But when the Athenian general Phrynichus received clear information about this fleet from Leros, although his fellow commanders wanted to stay where they were and fight it out at sea, he said no: he would not undertake such a fight himself, nor would he allow them or anyone else to do so if he could help it. When it was open to them to postpone battle until they had precise knowledge of the number of enemy ships they faced and the relative number they could muster themselves with time spent on proper preparation, he would never take such an unconsidered risk simply to avoid an accusation of dishonour. There was nothing dishonourable in Athenians making a strategic retreat from an enemy navy. The real harm would be defeat, whatever the circumstances, which would not just bring dishonour on the city but also plunge it into extreme danger. After the disasters it had suffered the city could barely afford to take offensive initiatives even with secure preparation and at a time and place it could choose, except in an emergency: still less should it court risks of its own making if there was no compulsion to run them. Phrynichus proposed that as soon as they could they should take on board the wounded, the whole infantry, and the gear they had brought with them (but leaving behind, to lighten the ships, any spoil obtained from enemy country), and sail back to Samos, where they could gather all their ships and continue attacks from there as opportunity offered. His view prevailed, and he took the action proposed. This decision was seen, not only at the time but also in hindsight, as confirming Phrynichus' reputation for intelligence, as shown both here and in all other matters within his control. So just before nightfall the Athenians pulled out from Miletus in this way, their victory incomplete. Once at Samos the Argives quickly sailed home in disgust at their own defeat.

28   At dawn the Peloponnesians put to sea from Teichioussa and arrived at Miletus after the Athenians had left. They stayed for one day, then on the next day took with them the Chian ships which, under Chalcideus at the time, had been pursued into the harbour, and sailed back to Teichioussa intending to fetch the tackle which they had unloaded there. When they arrived they were approached by Tissaphernes with his land army: he persuaded them to sail against Iasus, where his enemy Amorges had stationed himself. They made a sudden attack on Iasus and took it, aided by the inhabitants' assumption that the ships could only be Athenian. In this action the Syracusans won particular plaudits. Amorges (who was the bastard

son of Pissouthnes, and in revolt from the King) was captured alive by the Peloponnesians and handed over to Tissaphernes to take back to the King if he so wished (those were his instructions from the King). They then plundered Iasus and the army appropriated a very great quantity of treasure, as the place had long been wealthy. They did no harm to the mercenaries with Amorges, but took them over and conscripted them into their own ranks, since most of them came from the Peloponnese. The town itself they handed over to Tissaphernes together with all their captives, slave or free, for whom they had agreed with him a price of one Daric stater each. They then returned to Miletus. Pedaritus the son of Leon had been sent out from Sparta to be governor in Chios, and they had him escorted as far as Erythrae by Amorges' mercenary troops. In Miletus itself they installed Philippus as governor.

So the summer ended.

In the following winter, when Tissaphernes had made arrange- 29 ments for Iasus to be garrisoned, he came on to Miletus and distributed a month's pay, as he had promised at Sparta, to all the ships at the rate of one Attic drachma a day for each man. Thereafter he proposed to pay at a half-drachma rate, until he could consult the King: if the King gave permission, he would pay the full drachma. This matter of pay was not pressed by Therimenes (who was not the admiral, but had simply been in charge of delivering the ships to Astyochus), but the Syracusan general Hermocrates did raise objections, as a result of which an increase of five ships' worth was agreed in the total pay, giving each man a little more than half a drachma a day. Tissaphernes was now offering thirty talents a month for fifty-five ships, and extra payment in the same proportion for any ships beyond that number.

During the same winter the Athenians at Samos received from 30 home a further reinforcement of thirty-five ships with the generals Charminus, Strombichides, and Euctemon. They now assembled their whole fleet, including the ships engaged at Chios, for the purpose of allotting forces to the two main operations, which were a naval blockade at Miletus and the dispatch of a fleet and infantry to Chios. It fell to Strombichides, Onomacles, and Euctemon to take thirty ships to Chios together with troop-transports carrying a portion of the thousand hoplites who had gone to Miletus: the other generals were based in Samos with seventy-four ships to dominate the sea and keep up attacks on Miletus.

31   Astyochus happened to be in Chios at the time, selecting hostages
to hold against the possible betrayal of the island to Athens, but when
he heard of the arrival of the fleet with Therimenes and the improvement of the allies' prospects, he abandoned this task and put to sea
with his ten Peloponnesian ships and ten Chian, first attacking
Pteleum without success, then sailing on to Clazomenae. Here he
demanded that the pro-Athenian party should remove to Daphnus,
and Clazomenae come over to the Peloponnesians: he was joined in
this demand by Tamos, a Persian deputy governor of Ionia. When
the Clazomenians refused, he launched an attack on the city (which
was unwalled) but failed to take it. He then sailed away in a strong
wind which carried his ship to Phocaea and Cyme, while the rest of his
fleet put in to the islands lying off Clazomenae—Marathoussa, Pele,
and Drymoussa. Detained there by the winds for eight days, they
plundered or consumed the property deposited by the Clazomenians
for safe keeping in the islands, and took what remained on board their
ships when they sailed to Phocaea and Cyme to rejoin Astyochus.

32   While he was still in that area Astyochus was approached by
envoys from Lesbos with proposals for a second revolt. He was ready
to accept, but the Corinthians and the other allies were unenthusias-
tic in view of the previous failure. So he put out and set sail for
Chios, where his ships finally arrived from various directions after
being scattered by a storm. After this Pedaritus, who had earlier been
making his way by land from Miletus, now reached Erythrae and
made the crossing to Chios with his attendant troops. He also had at
his disposal the five hundred or so armed crewmen left in Chios by
Chalcideus from his five ships. When some of the Lesbians came and
repeated their offer to revolt, Astyochus presented to Pedaritus and
the Chians the argument for intervening with their fleet to secure the
defection of Lesbos: by this action they would either bring more
allies to their side, or, even if not wholly successful, do some damage
to the Athenians. But they would not hear of it, and Pedaritus
refused to let him have the Chian ships.

33   Astyochus then took the five Corinthian ships, a sixth from
Megara, one more from Hermione, and the ships he had brought
with him from Laconia, and sailed with these for Miletus to take up
his full command of the navy as admiral-in-chief. As he left he made
it repeatedly clear to the Chians that they could expect no help from
him whatever when they themselves might be in need. He made land
at Corycus in Erythraean territory and camped there for the night.

The Athenian naval and infantry force sailing from Samos to Chios also put in there and anchored on the other side of the hill which was all that separated the two fleets and kept them unaware of each other's presence. But in the night a letter came from Pedaritus with the information that some Erythraean prisoners had been released from Samos on the promise that they would betray their city to the Athenians, and had now arrived in Erythrae for that purpose. So Astyochus immediately set sail back to Erythrae. (That was how close he came to falling into the hands of the Athenians.) Pedaritus sailed across to meet him, and together they investigated the story of this supposed treachery. When they found that the whole thing was a ruse to get the fellows safe out of Samos, they dropped the charges and sailed back, Pedaritus to Chios and Astyochus to his original destination of Miletus.

Meanwhile the Athenian force had also left Corycus, and as their 34 ships were rounding the Arginum promontory they chanced on three Chian warships and gave chase as soon as they sighted them. A violent storm blew up and the Chian ships just managed to reach the safety of their harbour, but the three Athenian ships foremost in the pursuit were wrecked and blown ashore close to the city of Chios, their crews either captured on land or lost at sea. The rest of the Athenian fleet found refuge from the storm in the harbour under Mount Mimas called Phoenicus. From there they sailed on later to put in at Lesbos, and began preparing for the fortification they intended to build in Chios.

During this same winter the Spartan Hippocrates set out from 35 the Peloponnese with ten Thurian ships (commanded by Dorieus the son of Diagoras, and two colleagues), one Laconian ship, and one Syracusan. They sailed across and put in at Cnidus, which had now revolted from Athens under the influence of Tissaphernes. When they learnt of this arrival the Peloponnesian authorities at Miletus ordered them to use half of their ships to keep guard on Cnidus and to station the other half around Triopium to seize the merchant ships putting in there from Egypt (Triopium is a promontory at the end of the Cnidian peninsula, with a sanctuary of Apollo). The Athenians heard of this and sent a fleet from Samos which captured the six ships on guard duty at Triopium (though the crews escaped). They then sailed on to Cnidus and launched an attack on the unwalled city which nearly succeeded in taking it. They attacked again on the following day, but in the night the inhabitants had improved their defences and had been joined by the crews escaped from the ships at Triopium. Unable now to do as much damage as before, the Athenians left and sailed back to Samos after ravaging the Cnidians' land.

36　　At about the same time Astyochus arrived at Miletus to take command of the fleet. At this stage the Peloponnesians based there were still comfortably placed in all essentials: the pay was adequate, the troops had the added security of the huge spoils taken from Iasus, and the Milesians were committed in support of the war. They did, though, think that the first agreement with Tissaphernes made between him and Chalcideus was deficient and tended to their disadvantage. So before Therimenes left they made another agreement, as follows:

37　An agreement between the Spartans and their allies and King Dareius and the King's sons and Tissaphernes. There shall be a treaty and friendship between the parties on these terms:

Whatever territory and cities belong to King Dareius, or belonged to his father or forefathers, neither the Spartans nor the allies of the Spartans shall go against these for the purpose of war or any other detriment, and neither the Spartans nor the allies of the Spartans shall exact tribute from these cities: nor shall King Dareius or the subjects of the King go against the Spartans or their allies for the purpose of war or any other detriment.

If the Spartans or their allies make any request of the King, or the King of the Spartans or their allies, whatever action they take by mutual agreement shall be valid.

Both parties shall jointly pursue the war against the Athenians and their allies: and if they terminate the war, both parties shall do so jointly.

Whatever troops are in the King's territory, at the summons of the King, shall be maintained at the King's expense.

If any of the cities which are party to this agreement with the King go against the King's territory, the others shall intervene and assist the King to the full extent of their power: and if any in the King's territory, or in any territory over which the King has dominion, go against the territory of the Spartans or their allies, the King shall intervene and give assistance to the full extent of his power.

38　　After the conclusion of this agreement Therimenes handed over the fleet to Astyochus, then sailed away in a cutter and was never seen again. The Athenians had now transferred their forces from Lesbos to Chios and, with superiority on both land and sea, began fortifying Delphinium, a place not far from the city of Chios which was in any case strong on the landward side and also offered harbours.

The Chians took no action. They had already been badly beaten in many battles, and anyway their internal relations were in a poor state: now that Tydeus the son of Ion and his followers had been executed by Pedaritus as pro-Athenian agents, and the rest of the population forced under tight control, no one could trust anyone else, and for that reason it was thought that they themselves would not be a match for the Athenians, nor would the mercenaries brought by Pedaritus. They did, though, send to Miletus and ask for the help of Astyochus. When he refused, Pedaritus sent a letter to Sparta accusing him of misconduct. This, then, was the situation the Athenians found in Chios. Their fleet at Samos made several attempts to attack the enemy ships at Miletus, but as these would never come out to fight, the Athenians withdrew to Samos and took no further action.

In this same winter, round about the solstice, the twenty-seven ships 39 which the Spartans had been persuaded to fit out for Pharnabazus (through the agency of Calligeitus the Megarian and Timagoras the Cyzicene) set out from the Peloponnese and sailed for Ionia: the commander on board was the Spartiate Antisthenes. With these ships the Spartans also sent out eleven Spartiate men as commissioners to advise Astyochus, one of whom was Lichas the son of Arcesilas. Their instructions, on arrival at Miletus, were to assist Astyochus in the general management of affairs for the best outcome, and, at their discretion, to send on this fleet as it was, or a larger or smaller number of ships, to Pharnabazus at the Hellespont, putting Clearchus the son of Rhamphias in command (he was sailing with the expedition). The eleven commissioners also had authority, again at their discretion, to depose Astyochus from his command and appoint Antisthenes in his place: in view of Pedaritus' letter the Spartans had their doubts about Astyochus. These ships, then, set out from Malea across the open sea and were putting in to Melos when they chanced on a squadron of ten Athenian ships, three of which they captured empty of their crews and then burned. Fearing now that the ships which had got away from Melos would report their approach to the Athenians at Samos (as indeed they did), they took the precaution of sailing a longer way round via Crete to put in at Caunus in Caria. They thought they were now safe, and from there they sent a message to the fleet at Miletus requesting an escort along the coast.

At the same time the Chians and Pedaritus kept sending messages 40 to Astyochus, despite his continued reluctance, urging him to bring his whole fleet to their assistance: they were being blockaded, and he should not stand by while the greatest of the allied cities in Ionia was cut off by sea and devastated by raids on land. A relevant factor was that the Chians had large numbers of slaves (a denser slave population than any state other than Sparta), and their punishments for any misdeeds were all the harsher because of their numbers. So when the Athenian forces seemed firmly installed in Chios with a fortified base, the majority of the slaves immediately deserted to them, and their knowledge of the country was instrumental in doing it the greatest damage. The Chians insisted on the need for help, while there was still some hope and the possibility of prevention, with the fortification of Delphinium in progress but not yet completed, and the Athenians beginning a longer circuit wall to protect both camp and ships. Although disinclined in view of his earlier threat, when Astyochus saw the allies enthusiastic in this cause he too determined to support the Chians.

41   But in the meantime he received the message from Caunus announcing the arrival of the twenty-seven ships and the Spartan commissioners. He thought there was nothing more important than to provide a convoy for such a large reinforcement of ships which would extend their control of the sea, and to ensure the safe passage of the Spartans who had come to report on his conduct. So he immediately abandoned the Chios plan and sailed for Caunus. In the course of his voyage down the coast he made a landing at Cos Meropis, an unwalled city left in ruins after being hit by the largest earthquake in living memory. The inhabitants had fled to the mountains, and Astyochus sacked the town and in a series of raids plundered everything he could take from the countryside (except for the free men rounded up—these he let go). From Cos he reached Cnidus at night, but could only follow the Cnidians' urgent recommendation not to disembark his men, but to sail on directly, without any pause, against the twenty Athenian ships which Charminus (one of the generals from Samos) had out on patrol looking for the twenty-seven ships expected from the Peloponnese—the very ships which Astyochus had come to escort. The Athenians in Samos had heard from Melos of their approach, and Charminus was patrolling the area round Syme, Chalce, and Rhodes, and off the coast of Lycia: he now had the further information that the ships were at Caunus.

42   So without any pause, and before his movements could be detected, Astyochus sailed on towards Syme, hoping to catch the Athenian ships somewhere in the open sea. Heavy rain and cloudy conditions

disoriented his ships in the darkness and created confusion. The fleet became split up, and when day broke the left wing could now be seen by the Athenians, while the rest of the ships were still straggling the other way round the island. Charminus and the Athenians hastily put out to sea against them with fewer than their total of twenty ships, thinking the ships they could see were the fleet from Caunus for which they had been watching. They attacked immediately, disabled three and damaged others, and were having the better of the action until the unexpected appearance of the larger part of Astyochus' fleet had them blocked on all sides. They then turned to run, losing six ships as they did so, but escaping with the rest to the island of Teutloussa, and from there to Halicarnassus. After this the Peloponnesians put in to Cnidus, where they were joined by the twenty-seven ships from Caunus: the entire combined fleet then sailed across to erect a trophy on Syme, and went back to anchor at Cnidus.

When the Athenians at Samos heard of this sea-battle and its result, 43 they took their whole fleet and sailed to Syme. They made no attack on the fleet at Cnidus, nor did the Peloponnesians come out to attack them. They simply collected the ships' equipment they had left at Syme, and after touching at Loryma on the mainland sailed back to Samos.

All the Peloponnesian ships were now together at Cnidus, and necessary repairs were being carried out. At the same time, since Tissaphernes had arrived, the eleven Spartan commissioners discussed with him any aspects of the previous agreements which they found unsatisfactory, as well as the future conduct of the war as would best serve the interests of both parties. Lichas was the keenest critic of the situation as it was. He said that both treaties, those negotiated with Chalcideus and then with Therimenes, were badly drawn. It was monstrous for the King now to claim possession of all the territory over which he or his forefathers had once held dominion in the past. That would mean renewed slavery for all the islands, for Thessaly, for Locris, and for all Greece as far as Boeotia, and instead of bringing them freedom the Spartans would be imposing Persian rule on the Greeks. He therefore demanded a different treaty on better terms. Certainly, he said, Sparta was not going to observe the present agreements, and did not want maintenance at all if those were the terms for it. Tissaphernes took offence at this and left the meeting in a rage without settling anything.

The Spartans meanwhile made the decision to sail to Rhodes. 44 They had been receiving communications from some of the most powerful men in Rhodes, and hoped to bring over an island which was strong in numbers of sailors and infantry alike, thinking also that with their alliance as it would then stand they would be able to maintain their fleet by themselves, without asking Tissaphernes for money. So in this same winter they sailed as soon as they could from Cnidus, and their first landing in Rhodian territory was at Cameirus, with ninety-four ships. Their arrival terrified the people at large, who knew nothing of the negotiations and began to run away, not least because their city had no walls. The Spartans then called a meeting of the Cameirans, inviting also people from the other two cities on the island, Lindus and Ialysus, and persuaded the Rhodians to secede from Athens. So Rhodes came over to the Peloponnesian alliance. The Athenians became aware of the Spartan intentions at the time, and sailed with their fleet from Samos in an attempt to forestall them. They appeared in the offing, but were just too late and sailed away for the time being to Chalce, then back to Samos. Later they carried on hostilities against Rhodes with naval attacks launched from Chalce and Cos. The Peloponnesians meanwhile collected some thirty-two talents from the Rhodians, dragged their ships up on shore, and took no other action for eighty days.

45   But in the meantime and even earlier, before the Peloponnesian move to Rhodes, another sequence of events was developing. After the death of Chalcideus and the battle at Miletus the Peloponnesians began to have their suspicions of Alcibiades, and the result was a letter reaching Astyochus from Sparta with orders to have Alcibiades killed (he was a personal enemy of Agis, and thought untrustworthy in other ways too). In his initial alarm Alcibiades took refuge with Tissaphernes, and then began working on him to do as much damage as he could to the Peloponnesian cause, and became his constant mentor. He had Tissaphernes cut down the sailors' pay from one Attic drachma a day to half a drachma, and that at irregular intervals. He instructed Tissaphernes to tell the Peloponnesians that the Athenians, with their longer experience of naval management, paid their sailors only half a drachma, not from any shortage of funds but to prevent their men feeling flush enough to compromise their fitness by spending money on unhealthy pursuits, or deserting their ships if they were not held hostage by pay still owing. He also told him to bribe the trierarchs and the allied generals into agreement. (Only the Syracusans refused: their general Hermocrates was the sole voice protesting on behalf of the whole alliance.) When cities came asking

for money Alcibiades saw them off in person and acted as Tissaphernes' mouthpiece. He told the Chians that they must have lost all shame: they were the wealthiest people in Greece, and despite the protection of a mercenary army they were now expecting others to risk both lives and money in defence of their freedom. To the other cities he replied that, when they had been paying large sums to the Athenians before their revolts, it was scandalous if they were not now prepared to make equal or greater contributions in their own cause. He explained that at present finance was understandably tight, as Tissaphernes was supporting the war at his own expense, but that if at some point funds for maintenance came through from the King, Tissaphernes would restore full pay and give appropriate subsidy to the cities.

Alcibiades also advised Tissaphernes not to be in too much of a 46 hurry to conclude the war, and not to plan on giving one and the same side superiority on both land and sea by bringing up the Phoenician fleet he had under preparation or paying for more Greek sailors. He should allow the division of power to continue, and then it would always be open to the King to set the others on whichever side proved troublesome to him. But if a combination of land and sea power produced a victor, the King would have no obvious ally to help him crush the victorious side, unless he was prepared, at great expense and risk, to enter the lists himself sooner or later and take the contest through to its conclusion. The more economical course, at a fraction of the expense and no danger to the King himself, was to let the Greeks wear themselves out against each other. The Athenians, he said, would be more suitable partners in the King's empire. They were not so ambitious to expand their power on land, and both the principle and the practice of their conduct of the war matched the King's interests very well. The Athenians would cooperate in a policy of enslavement, with the Aegean area subjugated to them and all the Greeks living in the King's territory subjugated to the King: whereas the Spartans were coming on the contrary as liberators, and it was not likely that when they were liberating Greeks from Greeks they would stop short of liberating Greeks from barbarians, unless the Persians managed somehow to get them out of the way soon. So he advised him first to wear both sides out, then, when he had clipped Athenian power as much as he could, to get the Peloponnesians out of his country.

To judge by his actions, Tissaphernes was largely inclined to follow this course. He evidently thought well of Alcibiades' advice in these matters and placed his full confidence in him. As a result he kept the Peloponnesians on poor rates of pay, and would not let them fight any sea-battle, always saying that the Phoenician fleet would arrive soon and then they could fight from a position of superiority. In this way he gradually weakened their cause and reduced the efficiency of their navy, which at its peak had been in formidable condition. And generally he made it clear beyond any possibility of concealment that he had little enthusiasm for supporting them in the war.

47   In giving this advice to Tissaphernes and the King, Alcibiades, now under their patronage, was telling them what he genuinely thought was in their best interests. But at the same time he was working for his own return to his country. He knew that the day would come (if he did not destroy his country before then) when he could persuade the Athenians to recall him: and he thought his best means of persuasion was to be seen as the intimate of Tissaphernes. So it transpired. The Athenian army at Samos became aware of his strong influence with Tissaphernes. This was partly because Alcibiades himself included the promise of making Tissaphernes their friend in his messages to the most powerful men in the army, asking them to put it about to the better class of people that he was willing to come back and join them in an oligarchy, but not in the malign sort of democracy which had driven him out. But yet more important was the fact that the trierarchs and leading Athenians at Samos had made up their own minds to overthrow the democracy.

48   This movement began in the base at Samos and later spread from there to the city of Athens. At first some individuals from Samos crossed over to the mainland and held discussions with Alcibiades. He offered the prospect of winning them the friendship first of Tissaphernes and then of the King himself, if the democracy was abandoned (this would overcome the King's reservations). The wealthiest Athenians, who were the most imposed on, now began to conceive great hopes of getting the government into their own hands and also of defeating the enemy. On their return to Samos they brought suitable colleagues into a conspiratorial group, while publicly announcing to the troops at large that the King would be their friend and would provide money if Alcibiades were recalled and democracy abandoned. The common soldiers may have felt some immediate distaste at the deal, but the straightforward hope of pay from the King kept them quiet. After making this announcement to the whole army, the group planning the oligarchy gave further

consideration to Alcibiades' proposal both among themselves and within a wider circle of their fraternity members.

The others thought it straightforward enough and sound, but Phrynichus (who was still general) would have none of it. In his view—and he was right—Alcibiades cared no more for oligarchy than he did for democracy, and his sole motivation was somehow to change the existing political order so that his friends could have him called back. Their own overriding concern, he said, must be to avoid civil strife. And it was not a straightforward matter for the King to take the Athenian side: that would set him at odds with the Peloponnesians, who were now just as much in evidence on the sea and controlled some of the most important cities in his dominions; he did not trust the Athenians, and he had the ready alternative of making allies of the Peloponnesians, who had so far done him no harm. As for the allied states, Phrynichus said he was certain that no difference would be made by the conspirators' evident promise to install oligarchies, simply on the grounds that Athens itself would not be a democracy. The seceded states would not come back, and those still in the alliance would not be any more loyal. Oligarchy or democracy was all one to them if they were still enslaved: what they wanted was their freedom, irrespective of their ultimate form of government. In any case, Phrynichus continued, they thought the so-called 'great and good' would oppress them as much as the democracy: it was they who were the authors and facilitators of crimes done by the people, and they who benefited most from them. If it was up to the oligarchs there would be a violent regime and executions without trial, whereas the people offered the allies a legal refuge and a restraint on oligarchic excesses. The cities had learnt this from actual experience, and he had no doubt of their view. So Phrynichus declared that as far as he was concerned there was no merit in Alcibiades' proposal or its present development.

But the conspirators at this gathering stuck to their original deci- 49 sion. They approved the present proposals and planned to send Peisander and other envoys to Athens, to negotiate about the recall of Alcibiades and the overthrow of democracy in the city, and to ratify friendship between Tissaphernes and the Athenians.

Knowing that there would be a proposal for the restoration of 50 Alcibiades (and that the Athenians would accept it), Phrynichus was now concerned, in view of his own express opposition, that if Alcibiades did return he would do him some harm for attempting to

stand in his way. He therefore had recourse to the following stratagem. He secretly sent word by letter to Astyochus the Spartan admiral
(who at the time was still at Miletus) to the effect that Alcibiades was
undermining the Spartan cause by promoting friendship between
Tissaphernes and the Athenians. He included full detail in his letter,
and added the hope that Astyochus would understand his motive in
doing down a personal enemy even at some disadvantage to his own
country. Astyochus had no intention of punishing Alcibiades (with
whom in any case he now had less frequent dealings), but went up to
see him in Magnesia and to see Tissaphernes too, and, turning
informer himself, he told them both the content of the letter from
Samos. (It was said that Astyochus had sold himself to Tissaphernes,
and was taking private payments for this and other information: that
was also why he had not pressed harder in the matter of the reduced
wages.) Alcibiades immediately sent a letter to the authorities in
Samos denouncing Phrynichus for what he had done, and demanding his execution. This disconcerted Phrynichus, and the revelation
did indeed leave him in a very dangerous position. So he sent another
letter to Astyochus, protesting at the earlier breach of confidence,
and saying now that he was prepared to give the Spartans the opportunity to destroy the whole Athenian army in Samos. He gave detailed
indications of how this could be done (Samos being unwalled), and
said that, when the Athenians were now threatening his life, he could
not be blamed for taking this or any other action to avoid destruction by his most virulent enemies. Astyochus revealed this too to
Alcibiades.

51   Phrynichus had planned on Astyochus' continued betrayal of
confidence, and then an immediate further letter from Alcibiades
on this issue. He now anticipated this by informing the army that he
had clear intelligence of enemy intentions to attack their base while
Samos was still unfortified and not all their ships were in harbour.
They must therefore fortify Samos as quickly as they could, and
maintain all else on defensive alert. As general he was within his
powers to command this action on his own authority. So they set
to the work, and in consequence the fortification of Samos (which
was intended in any case) was completed all the sooner. Not long
afterwards the letter came from Alcibiades, warning that the army
had been betrayed by Phrynichus and the enemy were about to
attack. It was thought that Alcibiades could not be trusted, that he
was privy to the enemy's plans and was imputing complicity to

Phrynichus out of personal hatred. So this letter did Phrynichus no harm, but actually served to confirm the information given in his own statement.

After this Alcibiades continued to work on Tissaphernes, trying to 52 bring him round to friendship with the Athenians. Tissaphernes was wary of the Peloponnesians, as they had more ships in the area than the Athenians, but even so he was inclined, if at all possible, to go along with Alcibiades, especially when he reflected on the quarrel with the Peloponnesians at Cnidus over the treaty of Therimenes (this had taken place before the move to their present station in Rhodes). On that occasion Alcibiades' previous argument, that Spartan policy was to liberate all the cities, had been borne out by Lichas when he declared it an intolerable clause in the agreement that the King should have possession of the cities which at some time in the past had been under either his or his forefathers' rule. Alcibiades was playing for high stakes, and applied himself assiduously to his courtship of Tissaphernes.

Meanwhile Peisander and the other envoys sent by the Athenians 53 in Samos arrived at Athens and spoke at length to the assembled people, summarizing as the essential point that with the recall of Alcibiades and a modification of their democracy they could secure the King as their ally and defeat the Peloponnesians. There was much general opposition to the proposal about the democracy, Alcibiades' enemies were loud in protesting that it would be monstrous to allow the return of a law-breaker, and the Eumolpidae and Ceryces cited the Mysteries as the reason for his banishment and invoked the gods against his recall. Amid all this opposition and outrage Peisander came forward again and called out each objector, asking them in turn whether they could see any hope of survival for the city unless someone persuaded the King to change to their side—when, as he pointed out, the Peloponnesians had a fleet at least as large as their own out at sea and ready for action, they had more cities in their alliance, and they were being financed by the King and Tissaphernes, whereas Athens had no money left. When in answer to his question they all acknowledged that they could see no other hope, Peisander went on to present them with the stark conclusion. 'Well,' he said, 'this is not going to happen unless we win the King's trust by adopting a more prudent form of government and restricting eligibility for office to a select few; unless we concentrate now on survival rather than the constitution (we can always change things later, if there is anything

we do not like); and unless we bring back Alcibiades, who is the only
man alive who can make this happen.'

54   The people at first reacted angrily to this talk of oligarchy, but as
Peisander continued his clear explanation of why there was no alternative means of survival, fear, combined with the hope of future
reversal, brought them to accept. So they voted that Peisander should
sail with ten others to negotiate with Tissaphernes and Alcibiades for
what they judged the best outcome. Peisander had also denounced
Phrynichus, and the people relieved him and his colleague Scironides
of their commands and sent Diomedon and Leon to the fleet to
replace them as generals. (This denunciation was the claim that
Phrynichus had betrayed Iasus and Amorges: and Peisander made it
because he feared that Phrynichus would not be in favour of negotiation with Alcibiades.) Peisander also canvassed all the cabals which
were already established in the city for mutual support in lawsuits
and elections to office, and urged them to unite and work in common
for the overthrow of the democracy. After making other arrangements to speed the matter in hand, Peisander and his ten colleagues
proceeded on their voyage to Tissaphernes.

55   Leon and Diomedon had by now joined the Athenian fleet, and
in the same winter they sailed against Rhodes. They found the
Peloponnesian ships pulled up on shore, but made a landing and
defeated the Rhodian force which came out to oppose them. They
then retired to Chalce, and made that rather than Cos the base of
their operations: it was easier from there to track any movements of
the Peloponnesian fleet.

A Laconian called Xenophantidas now arrived in Rhodes, sent
from Chios by Pedaritus to report that the Athenian fortification was
now complete, and that Chios would be lost if the entire fleet did not
come to its aid. The Peloponnesians at Rhodes were minded to give
assistance. But meanwhile Pedaritus himself, with his own mercenary
force and the whole Chian army, made an attack on the Athenian wall
protecting their ships. He took part of the wall and a few ships drawn
up on land, but the Athenians came out against them, routed the
Chians first, and then defeated the force with Pedaritus. Pedaritus
himself and a large number of Chians were killed, and a great quantity
56   of arms captured. After this the Chians were yet more tightly blockaded by both land and sea, and the famine there was now severe.

Meanwhile Peisander and his fellow Athenian envoys reached
Tissaphernes and began discussions about an agreement. Alcibiades

could not rely on Tissaphernes' response (he was more afraid of the Peloponnesians than of the Athenians, and was still inclined, as Alcibiades himself had advised, to wear down both sides), so he resorted to the ploy of setting Tissaphernes' demands of the Athenians so high that there could be no agreement. It seems to me that Tissaphernes also wanted the negotiations to fail. He was motivated by his fears, while Alcibiades, seeing that Tissaphernes was unlikely to agree on any terms, did not want the Athenians to conclude that he was incapable of influencing Tissaphernes: rather that Tissaphernes was primed and ready to reach agreement, but the Athenians themselves were not offering sufficient inducement. With Tissaphernes there in person, Alcibiades acted as his spokesman and made such exorbitant demands that, even though they went a long way to accommodate them, the Athenians bore the blame for the breakdown of the talks. He demanded first that the whole of Ionia should be ceded to the King, then subsequently added the off-lying islands and some other places. The Athenians made no objection thus far, so finally at their third meeting (fearful now that his complete lack of influence would be shown up) he demanded that the King should be allowed to build ships and sail off his own coast wherever and with whatever number of ships he wanted. At that point the Athenians had enough: they could see no way forward, and thought they had been duped by Alcibiades. So they left in a rage and took themselves to Samos.

Immediately after this, and in the same winter, Tissaphernes went 57 down to Caunus. He wanted to bring the Peloponnesians back to Miletus, and to avoid a complete breach of relations by offering them continued maintenance on whatever terms he could obtain in a further agreement. He was afraid that if they were otherwise short of the means of maintaining that number of ships, either they would be obliged to fight the Athenians and lose, or their crews would desert: in either case the Athenians would achieve what they wanted without any help from him. His main fear, though, was that they would plunder the mainland in search of food. Looking ahead, then, with all this taken into consideration, and wishing as he did to keep the two Greek powers evenly matched, Tissaphernes invited the Peloponnesians to meet him at Caunus, made his offer of maintenance, and concluded a third treaty with them, as follows:

In the thirteenth year of the reign of King Dareius, and in the ephorate of 58 Alexippidas at Sparta, an agreement was made in the plain of the Maeander between, on the one hand, the Spartans and their allies, and, on the other, Tissaphernes and Hieramenes and the sons of Pharnaces, concerning the respective interests of the King and of the Spartans and their allies.

All the King's territory which lies in Asia shall remain the King's: and the King shall determine as he pleases in respect of his own territory.

The Spartans and their allies shall not go against the King's territory for any detriment, neither shall the King go against the territory of the Spartans or their allies for any detriment. If any of the Spartans and their allies go against the King's territory for detriment, the Spartans and their allies shall intervene to prevent it: and if any of those in the King's dominion go against the Spartans or their allies for detriment, the King shall intervene to prevent it.

Maintenance for the ships now present shall be provided by Tissaphernes according to the agreement, until such time as the King's ships arrive. When the King's ships have come, the Spartans and the allies may, if they choose, take responsibility on themselves for the maintenance of their own ships: if they wish to continue to receive maintenance from Tissaphernes, Tissaphernes shall provide it, but at the end of the war the Spartans and their allies shall pay back to Tissaphernes whatever money they have received.

When the King's ships have come, the ships of the Spartans and their allies and the King's ships shall jointly pursue the war in whatever way is decided by Tissaphernes and the Spartans and their allies. And if they wish to agree a settlement with the Athenians to end the war, the terms of that settlement shall be the same for both parties.

59 So the treaty was agreed on these terms. Tissaphernes now began preparations to bring up the Phoenician ships (as specified in the treaty) and to fulfil his other undertakings. He was anxious to be seen making a start, at any rate.

60 Towards the end of winter the Boeotians took Oropus, despite an Athenian garrison there. The place was betrayed to them in a joint operation involving men from Eretria as well as Oropus itself. Their ulterior motive was the revolt of Euboea: Oropus lies opposite Eretria, and in Athenian hands would inevitably present a considerable danger to Eretria and the whole of Euboea. So with Oropus now secured the Eretrians came to Rhodes and invited the Peloponnesians to intervene in Euboea. They, though, were more concerned to relieve the distress of Chios, and set sail from Rhodes with their entire fleet. When they reached Triopium they caught sight of the Athenian fleet out at sea on their way from Chalce. Neither side attacked the other, and the Athenians went on to arrive at Samos and the

Peloponnesians at Miletus, now recognizing that they could not bring help to Chios without engaging the Athenians at sea.

So this winter ended, and with it the twentieth year of this war chronicled by Thucydides.

At the very beginning of spring in the following summer season, 61 Dercylidas, a Spartiate, was dispatched overland by the coastal route to the Hellespont with a small army to secure the revolt of Abydos (which is a Milesian colony). And the Chians, with Astyochus still doubting his ability to help, were forced by the stranglehold of the blockade to fight it out at sea. A fortunate circumstance was that while Astyochus was still at Rhodes they had received from Miletus a new governor after the death of Pedaritus, a Spartiate called Leon, who had come out as lieutenant to Antisthenes, and he brought with him twelve ships which had been guarding Miletus: these were five Thurian ships, four Syracusan, one from Anaea, one Milesian, and Leon's own ship. The entire Chian land forces broke out and seized a strong position, while their thirty-six ships were launched against the Athenians' thirty-two, and came to battle. It was a hard fight, and when they turned back to the city as evening came on the Chians and their allies had not been worsted in the action.

Very soon after this Dercylidas reached the Hellespont overland 62 from Miletus, and Abydos seceded to him and to Pharnabazus, followed two days later by Lampsacus. Strombichides in Chios heard of this and hurried to intervene with twenty-four Athenian ships, which included some troop-transports carrying hoplites. He defeated the Lampsacenes who came out to meet him, and took Lampsacus (which was unwalled) in one quick attack. He carried off the movable goods and the slaves, but returned the free inhabitants to their homes. He then went on to Abydos, but the people would not concede and repeated attacks failed to take the place. So he sailed over to Sestos, a city on the Chersonese opposite Abydos which had once been in Persian hands, and turned it into a fortress to keep guard on the whole of the Hellespont.

Meanwhile the Chians gained greater control of the sea. That, and 63 the news of the sea-battle and the departure of Strombichides and his ships, emboldened Astyochus and the Peloponnesians at Miletus. Astyochus took two ships through to Chios and brought back the allied ships which had gone there: then with his entire fleet united he sailed out against Samos. The Athenians were now in a state of mutual suspicion, and did not come out to meet him: so he sailed back to Miletus.

The reason was that about this time or somewhat earlier the democracy at Athens had been overthrown. When Peisander and his fellow envoys came to Samos after their meeting with Tissaphernes, they took steps to establish yet firmer control within their own army, and in Samos itself encouraged the most powerful men to join them in the attempt to set up an oligarchy, despite the fact that the Samians had been through a revolution to avoid coming under oligarchic government. At the same time the Athenian revolutionaries in Samos conferred among themselves and took the view that they should leave Alcibiades out of it, as he was evidently unwilling to join them and in any case was hardly suitable for participation in an oligarchy: given that they were already compromised, they should take it on themselves to ensure that the movement did not stall. They also determined to maintain the war-effort, and make ready contributions of money or any other requisite from their own resources, as this would now be an imposition not at the behest of others but for their own benefit.

64   With this general confirmation among themselves they proceeded immediately to dispatch Peisander and half of the envoys to Athens to take matters forward at home, instructing them to set up oligarchies in all the subject cities at which they put in on their voyage: the other half of the envoys were sent variously to other subject places. They also sent Diitrephes, who was then at Chios, to take up the command in the Thraceward region to which he had already been appointed. When he arrived at Thasos he put down the democracy there. But within two months of his departure the Thasians began fortifying their city: they had no more need for an aristocracy backed by Athens when they were daily expecting their liberation by the Spartans. There was a group of Thasian exiles driven out by the Athenians and now based in the Peloponnese. In conjunction with their friends at home they were working hard to obtain ships and bring about the revolt of Thasos. So now what had happened was exactly what they wanted—a redirection of government without any danger to themselves, and the overthrow of the democracy which would have opposed them. So in the case of Thasos the result was the opposite of that intended by the Athenians involved in introducing the oligarchy, and I imagine the same was true of many other subject states also. Once they had acquired a 'sensible' government with no restraints on their actions, the cities went straight for outright freedom, and had little time for the specious 'law and order' offered by the Athenians.

In the course of their voyage to Athens Peisander and his col- 65
leagues, as agreed, put down the democracies in the various cities
along their route, and from some of the places they took on board
hoplites who would support them. When they reached Athens they
found most of the work already done by the members of the cabals.
A group of younger men had conspired to have one Androcles
quietly murdered: he was a leading champion of the people and had
been instrumental in the banishment of Alcibiades. They had two
reasons for killing him, the second stronger than the first: the fact
that he was a demagogue, and, looking forward to the return of
Alcibiades and the friendship he would secure with Tissaphernes,
the belief that this would place them in his good books. There were
some other inconvenient people also quietly disposed of in the same
way. The conspirators had prepared the ground with a public manifesto, to the effect that there should be no state pay for anyone not on
active military service, and that participation in government should
be restricted to a maximum of five thousand, those to be the citizens
most capable of serving the state with both property and person.

This was only a pretence intended to play well with the general 66
public, as the authors of the revolution were certainly going to keep
the government of the city in their own hands. There were still even
so meetings of the assembly and of the council (that is, the council of
five hundred chosen by lot): but the agenda was controlled by the
clique of conspirators, all speakers came from their number, and their
speeches were vetted in advance. No one else now would express any
contrary view, as there was general fear at what they saw as the extent
of the conspiracy. If anyone did speak up, he quickly met his death
in some convenient way. There was no attempt to search for the
perpetrators, and none of the suspects was ever brought to trial. The
people were terrorized into silence, and thought themselves lucky to
escape violence, even if they never said a word. They imagined the
conspiracy to be much more widespread than it actually was, and this
kept them demoralized: they had no means of discovering the truth,
as the pure size of the city made it impossible for everyone to know
everyone else. For this same reason it was impossible to identify
sympathizers with whom to share grievances and plan any counter-
action: the choice of confidant could only be either a stranger or an
intimate who could not be trusted. All the democrats now approached
one another with suspicion, on the possibility that any one of them
could be involved in what was going on. There were indeed some

participants whom no one would ever have expected to turn oligarch. It was these examples which intensified mutual suspicion among the people at large, and by giving solid cause for the democrats to mistrust one another greatly contributed to the security of the oligarchs' position.

67   This, then, was the situation Peisander and his colleagues found on their arrival at Athens, and they immediately applied themselves to the next stages. First they convened an assembly of the people and proposed the election of ten commissioners with authority to draw up recommendations for the best management of the city and lay their proposals before the people on a fixed day. Then, when this day came, they held the assembly in the confined space of the sanctuary of Poseidon at Colonus, about a mile outside the city. The only proposal brought forward by the commissioners was simply that any Athenian should have impunity to introduce any resolution he wished: but they also specified severe penalties for anyone indicting the proposer for illegality, or using other means to do him harm. And now the real scheme was proposed without further concealment. The motion was that all existing offices in the present order of government should be abolished, and there should be no state pay for office; that a presiding board of five should be elected, that these five should elect another hundred, and each of these hundred co-opt three more; that these Four Hundred should meet in the council-chamber with absolute authority to govern the city in whatever way they might consider best; and that they should summon meetings of the Five Thousand as and when they might so decide.

68   The proposer of this motion, and to all appearances the most committed agent in the overthrow of the democracy, was Peisander. But in fact the man who had developed the whole scheme to this point and worked longest for its achievement was Antiphon. He was a man of quality, equal to any of his contemporaries in Athens, and exceptionally gifted in his powers of thought and expression. He was reluctant to come forward in the assembly or on any other public stage. This, and a reputation for cleverness, meant that the people at large were suspicious of him: but for individuals consulting him about a case they had to argue in the law courts or the assembly he was the one man who could give them outstanding service. And when later the regime of the Four Hundred had fallen and the people were intent on reprisals, and he was brought to trial for his part in setting up this regime, the speech he gave in his own defence was

without doubt the finest ever made, up to my time, by any man on a capital charge. Phrynichus also showed himself exceptionally committed to the oligarchy. He had his own reasons to be afraid of Alcibiades (knowing that Alcibiades was aware of his dealings with Astyochus when he was at Samos), and thought it unlikely that he would ever be recalled under an oligarchy. Once Phrynichus had subscribed to the cause, he was seen as particularly dependable when there were dangers to face. Another leading figure among the revolutionaries was Theramenes the son of Hagnon, a man of considerable eloquence and intellectual power.

So it was not surprising that in the hands of so many able men the enterprise succeeded, despite its inherent difficulty: it was not an easy task to terminate the liberty of the Athenian people almost exactly a hundred years after the deposition of the tyrants, when they had been not only free of subjection to anyone else but also, for over half of that period, accustomed to imperial power over others.

No opposition was expressed in the assembly, but all these propos- 69 als were ratified and the assembly then dismissed. After that the next move was to have the Four Hundred occupy the council-chamber, and this was achieved in the following way. All Athenians did daily duty either on the walls or on parade, with arms ready to hand because of the enemy at Deceleia. On this particular day those not involved in the plot were allowed to leave the parade-ground as usual, and the conspirators had been told to loiter not exactly right by their arms, but not too far away: if anyone tried to oppose what was going on, they were to take up their arms and intervene. There were also on hand some Andrians and Tenians, three hundred Carystians, and some of the Athenian settlers who had been sent out to occupy Aegina: these had been brought in with their own arms for this very purpose, and were given the same instructions. With this deployment in place the Four Hundred arrived, each carrying a concealed dagger, accompanied by the hundred and twenty young men they used as their enforcers. They broke in on the regularly appointed councillors meeting in the council-chamber and told them to take their pay and leave. They had themselves brought with them money to pay for the unexpired period of the councillors' term of office, and handed it to each of them as they left the building.

With the council retiring in this way without objection, and the rest 70 of the citizen body keeping quiet and causing no trouble, the Four Hundred installed themselves in the council-chamber. For the present they chose their own presiding officers by lot, and observed the traditional prayers and sacrifices to the gods on assuming their administration. Soon, however, they made wholesale changes in the democratic system. They stopped short of recalling the exiles (because Alcibiades was one of them), but otherwise took resolute control of the city. They put some (not many) to death—those whom they thought it convenient to get out of the way—and imprisoned or exiled some others. They also communicated with Agis, the Spartan king, who was at Deceleia, saying that they were willing to make peace and expected him to be readier to agree terms with them than with the fickle democracy they had supplanted.

71   Agis took the view that Athens could not be in a settled state, and that the people would not so quickly surrender their long-standing freedom. He thought that the sight of a large enemy army would keep them unsettled (and in any case he was not at all convinced that the ferment in Athens was now over), so he gave no conciliatory answer to the emissaries of the Four Hundred and in fact sent for substantial reinforcements from the Peloponnese. Not much later he took his own garrison force from Deceleia together with the newly arrived troops and came down to the very walls of Athens. His hope was that ferment among the Athenians would make them more likely to capitulate on Spartan terms, or even allow him immediate capture amid the chaos caused by the combination of internal and external threats: if that meant that the Long Walls would be unguarded he could hardly fail to take them. But as he came up closer the Athenians gave no sign whatever of any internal disturbance. They sent out their cavalry and a detachment of hoplites, light-armed troops, and archers, shot down some of his men who had advanced too far, and took possession of a number of arms and dead bodies. Agis now realized how things stood in the city, and took his army back. He and his own troops stayed on in their station at Deceleia: he kept the reinforcements in Attica for a few days, then sent them home. Thereafter the Four Hundred resumed their diplomatic approaches to Agis, and he was now more receptive. At his suggestion they also sent envoys to Sparta to discuss terms for the peace they wanted to conclude.

72   They also sent ten men to Samos to reassure the forces there and explain that the oligarchy presented no detriment to the city or its citizens, but had been established to preserve the national interest, and that there were five thousand (not just four hundred) involved in the administration—and this despite the fact that because of military

campaigns and official business abroad the Athenians had never yet held an assembly on a matter important enough to achieve an attendance of five thousand. These emissaries were sent out with instructions to make these and other appropriate arguments as soon as the Four Hundred were formally installed. Their fear, realized in the event, was that the general body of Athenian sailors would not be prepared to stay with an oligarchic regime, and that trouble would start at Samos and end in their overthrow.

A reaction against the oligarchic movement had already set in at 73 Samos, and the following events took place at about the same time as the Four Hundred were being organized in Athens. Some of the Samians who had earlier led the revolution against the men in power, and had counted as 'the people' at the time, were now changing sides under the influence of Peisander (after his arrival in the island) and the Athenians in his coterie at Samos. They formed themselves into a group of some three hundred conspirators and planned to attack the others who were now 'the people'. There was an Athenian called Hyperbolus, a worthless fellow who had been ostracized, not out of fear of his power or position, but because he was a pest and a disgrace to the city. In collusion with Charminus, one of the generals, and a number of other Athenians in Samos, and as a guarantee of their complicity, these men had Hyperbolus murdered. They colluded with them in other acts of violence also, and were ready and willing to launch an attack on the majority party. The people learnt of their intentions and gave this information to the generals Leon and Diomedon (who had been appointed to office by the democracy and were not happy with the move to oligarchy), and also to Thrasyboulus and Thrasyllus (the former a trierarch, the latter a serving hoplite) and the others who were seen to be most constant in their opposition to the oligarchic conspiracy. They begged them not to stand by inactive while they were destroyed and Samos alienated from Athens, when Samos was the one remaining bastion of the Athenian empire. This appeal had its effect. The men they had approached went round the troops individually to ensure their resistance, with particular attention to the Parali, the crew of the ship Paralus who were all freeborn Athenians and ready to attack oligarchy anywhere, real or imaginary: and whenever Leon and Diomedon had to sail elsewhere they always left some ships behind for the protection of the Samians. So when the three hundred made their attack, all the crews, and especially the Parali, rallied to the defence, and the majority party emerged victorious. They killed some thirty of the three hundred, and punished the three main instigators with exile. They offered the others an amnesty, and incorporated them into the subsequent democracy.

74 The Samians and the army in Samos now sent the Paralus at full speed to Athens to report the developments, not knowing that the Four Hundred were now in power. On board was an Athenian who had been a fervent supporter of the counter-revolution, Chaereas the son of Archestratus. When they sailed in the Four Hundred immediately arrested two or three of the Parali, confiscated their ship, and transferred the rest of the crew to a troop-ship detailed for guard duty round Euboea. When Chaereas saw the situation he managed somehow to make a quick escape and got back to Samos. There he gave the troops a greatly exaggerated account of horrors at Athens—free men flogged like slaves, no opposition to the government tolerated, wives and children sexually abused, plans to arrest and imprison the relatives of all military personnel at Samos who were not of their party, and to execute these hostages if they did not conform. And he added a good number of other falsities.

75 On hearing this the first reaction of the troops was to turn on the main authors of the oligarchy and any others who had supported them, and they were on the point of shooting them down. But they desisted when the moderates restrained them and warned that they could ruin everything, with the enemy fleet on watch close by and prepared for action. After this, Thrasyboulus the son of Lycus and Thrasyllus (the two main leaders of the counter-revolution) were ready to declare their hand and re-establish democracy among the Athenians at Samos. They had all the soldiers, especially those of the oligarchic party, swear the most binding oaths that they would without fail support the democracy and maintain unity, commit themselves to continued prosecution of the war against the Peloponnesians, and regard the Four Hundred as enemies beyond any negotiation. The same oath was sworn by all Samians of adult age, and the Athenian army recognized a solidarity with the Samian people in all that they did and all that might result from the risks they shared: they could see that neither the Samians nor they themselves had any other place of safety, and that if they lost either to the Four Hundred or to the enemy at Miletus that would be the end of them.

76 So for a while there was a power-struggle, one side trying to impose democracy on the city, and the other trying to impose oligarchy on the armed forces. The soldiers proceeded directly to call an

assembly, at which they deposed their former generals and any of the trierarchs they suspected, and elected other trierarchs and generals in their place: Thrasyboulus and Thrasyllus were among the new generals chosen. Individuals stood up in the assembly and offered a variety of points for their own encouragement. It was no cause for worry, they said, that the city had revolted from them: this was the revolt of a minority against a majority, and the majority were better able to provide for themselves in every way. They controlled the entire fleet, and could force the other subject cities to provide funds just as much as any navy based in the Peiraeus. Samos was a strong state to have on their side—in the Samian war it had come very close to wresting control of the sea from the Athenians—and their base of operations against the enemy would be the same as before. Their possession of the fleet made them better able to bring in supplies than the Athenians at home. In fact it was only their own position in forward defence at Samos which had so far enabled the Athenians to keep the Peiraeus open: and now, if it came to it, if the Athenians refused to give them back their constitution, the fleet at Samos would be better able to close the sea to the city Athenians than vice versa. In any case, in terms of winning the war, the home state was of little or no use to them and was no great loss, considering that the Athenians at home could no longer give them any money (the troops were paying for themselves) or any sensible political decision—which was the reason why states controlled armies. In this respect the people at home had made a serious error in subverting the ancestral constitution. They in Samos were maintaining it, and would do their best to reimpose it at home: so there was at least as much good political advice available in Samos as in Athens. And then there was Alcibiades: if they recalled him with an immunity, he would gratefully bring them the King's alliance. Above all, and if all else failed, with such an extensive fleet at their command they had many possibilities of finding refuge—cities and land—elsewhere.

After holding this assembly and building their morale with speeches 77 along these lines, they turned with equal energy to preparations for continuing the war. The ten envoys dispatched to Samos by the Four Hundred heard how things stood when they reached Delos, and stayed there without proceeding further.

At about this same time there was also unrest among the 78 Peloponnesian troops in the fleet at Miletus, who bandied about vociferous complaints that Astyochus and Tissaphernes between them were ruining their cause. Astyochus, they said, had refused to fight earlier when they were in better condition and the Athenian fleet was small, and was refusing to fight now, when there was said to be civil strife among the Athenians and their ships were still dispersed. They could well be worn out with waiting for Tissaphernes to produce his Phoenician ships, which seemed mere talk and no substance. As for Tissaphernes, he was not only failing to bring up these ships, but his irregular and incomplete payment of wages was weakening the fleet. They said there should be no more delay, and it was time for a decisive battle. The Syracusans were particularly insistent.

79   The allies and Astyochus became aware of this agitation. They held a conference at which they agreed to go for a decisive battle at sea, a resolution confirmed as news came in of the trouble at Samos. So they put to sea with their entire fleet of a hundred and twelve ships, making for Mycale, where they had told the Milesians to go round to meet them on foot. At the time the Athenians had their eighty-two ships from Samos lying at Glauce on the promontory of Mycale (at this point the distance from Samos to the mainland at Mycale is very short). When they saw the Peloponnesian ships approaching, they retreated back to Samos, thinking that they did not have sufficient numbers to stake all on one battle now. Besides, they had received advance information from Miletus that the enemy were looking to fight, and they were expecting Strombichides to return from the Hellespont to reinforce them with the ships which had gone from Chios to Abydos—a courier had been sent to summon him. So for these reasons the Athenians retreated to Samos, while the Peloponnesians sailed in to Mycale and made camp there, together with the land troops from Miletus and other local areas. On the next day they were ready to sail against Samos, but news came that Strombichides had arrived with the ships from the Hellespont, and they immediately sailed off back to Miletus. With their fleet now augmented the Athenians went on the attack themselves, sailing against Miletus with a hundred and eight ships. They now wanted the decisive battle, but as no one would come out to meet them they sailed back to Samos.

80   The Peloponnesians refused to fight because they doubted their ability to match the full Athenian fleet, but they were also concerned to find the money to support their own large number of ships, especially as Tissaphernes was such a poor paymaster. So in this same

summer, and immediately after this refusal to come out against the Athenians, they sent Clearchus the son of Rhamphias with a squadron of forty ships to Pharnabazus, as was his original commission when he left the Peloponnese. Pharnabazus had been inviting them to come, and was ready to pay for their maintenance: at the same time Byzantium was communicating with them about revolt from Athens. So this Peloponnesian squadron put out into the open sea (to avoid being seen on its voyage by the Athenians), but was caught in a storm. Clearchus and the majority of the ships made Delos, and then returned to Miletus (Clearchus himself subsequently took his way to the Hellespont by land to assume his command): but the ten ships under the Megarian general Helixus weathered the storm and reached the Hellespont, then secured the revolt of Byzantium. Thereafter the Athenians at Samos, informed of these developments, sent a naval force to keep guard on the Hellespont, and there was a minor sea-battle off Byzantium, eight ships against eight.

Ever since he had restored the democracy at Samos, Thrasyboulus 81 remained insistently of the view that Alcibiades should be recalled, and his fellow leaders agreed with him. He finally persuaded the mass of troops at an assembly, and they voted through both the recall and an immunity. Thrasyboulus then sailed to Tissaphernes and brought Alcibiades back with him to Samos, convinced as he was that their only hope of survival was if Alcibiades could win Tissaphernes over to their side from the Peloponnesians. An assembly was called, at which Alcibiades first spoke of his own circumstances, complaining about the exile imposed on him and blaming it for his actions. He then talked at length about the political situation, giving them strong hopes for the future and greatly exaggerating his own influence with Tissaphernes. In this he had several purposes. He wanted to frighten the oligarchy at home and ensure the dissolution of the cabals; to increase his prestige among the Athenians at Samos and encourage their own confidence; and to dash the enemies' present hopes by alienating them as far as he could from Tissaphernes. So Alcibiades boasted on with huge promises: Tissaphernes had assured him that if he could trust the Athenians they would not lack for maintenance as long as he had money of his own to give, even if in the end he had to sell his own bed; that he would bring up the Phoenician ships, already now at Aspendus, on the Athenian rather than the Peloponnesian side; but that he would only trust the Athenians if Alcibiades was restored unharmed to be their guarantee.

82   On hearing all this, and a great deal more, the Athenians promptly
elected Alcibiades general alongside their existing generals, and
allowed him full control of their affairs. Every man among them held
more precious than anything else this new hope of personal safety
combined with retribution on the Four Hundred. From what they
were told they conceived an immediate disdain for the enemy close
at hand, and were ready to sail straight for the Peiraeus. Despite
popular pressure for this course, Alcibiades flatly refused to let them
sail against the Peiraeus and turn their backs on the nearer enemy.
He said that since he had been elected general he must first sail to
Tissaphernes and discuss with him the conduct of the war. He left
immediately after this assembly, to give the impression of complete
cooperation between the two of them. He also wanted to increase his
prestige in Tissaphernes' eyes and make it clear to him that he had
now been appointed general and was in a position to do him good—or
harm. In effect, Alcibiades was using Tissaphernes to put pressure on
the Athenians, and the Athenians to put pressure on Tissaphernes.

83   When the Peloponnesians at Miletus heard of Alcibiades' recall,
their already existing mistrust of Tissaphernes deepened into a yet
greater alienation. What had happened was that by the time of the
Athenians' attempted attack on Miletus, when they had not been
prepared to come out and fight, Tissaphernes had become much more
remiss in his payments, and this question of Alcibiades now had
intensified a longer-standing resentment against Tissaphernes. As
before—and not this time just the common soldiery, but some of the
officers also—they gathered in groups to take stock of their grievances: they had never yet received their full pay; what came was too
little and too infrequent; if no one would take the fleet out to fight or
move it to a reliable source of maintenance, the men would start
deserting; all this was the fault of Astyochus, who was toadying to
Tissaphernes for his own profit.

84   While they were still taking stock there was an actual fracas involving Astyochus. The Syracusan and Thurian sailors were for the most
part free men (more so than in other contingents), and so were particularly forthright in besieging Astyochus with demands for pay. He
gave them a somewhat dismissive answer accompanied by threats,
and even raised his stick against Dorieus when he supported the
claims of his own men. At this the crowd of troops saw red, as sailors
will, and surged forward to strike Astyochus down. He saw it coming
and ran for refuge at a nearby altar. In the end he was not hurt, and

the confrontation was dissipated. Another incident was a surprise assault made by the Milesians on the fort which Tissaphernes had built in Miletus: they captured it and expelled the guards he had posted there. This action met with the approval of the other allies, especially the Syracusans. Lichas, though, was not pleased. He said that the Milesians and the others living in the King's territory should pay all reasonable deference to Tissaphernes and keep on good terms with him until they brought the war to a successful conclusion. This and other similar pronouncements caused much resentment among the Milesians, and when Lichas subsequently died of disease they refused to allow the Spartans present at the time to bury him where they wanted.

Relations with Astyochus and Tissaphernes were in this state of 85 discord when Mindarus arrived from Sparta to succeed Astyochus as admiral-in-chief. Astyochus handed over the command and sailed for home. Tissaphernes sent with him to Sparta a spokesman from his own court circle, a bilingual Carian called Gaulites, who was to complain of the Milesian action in the matter of his fort and at the same time defend him against their counter-charges. He knew that the Milesians were travelling to Sparta specifically to denounce him, and that with them was Hermocrates, who was likely to expose Tissaphernes as a double-dealer, in league with Alcibiades to damage the Peloponnesian cause. Tissaphernes had had a grudge against Hermocrates ever since the question of the delivery of pay for the fleet: and in the latest stage, after Hermocrates had been exiled from Syracuse and other generals had arrived to command the Syracusan ships at Miletus (these were Potamis, Myscon, and Demarchus), Tissaphernes had made much more vehement attacks on him now that he was an exile, alleging among other things that the reason for Hermocrates' display of hostility was that he had once asked Tissaphernes for money and been refused. So then Astyochus, the Milesians, and Hermocrates all sailed off to Sparta. By now Alcibiades had left Tissaphernes and crossed back to Samos.

The envoys sent out earlier by the Four Hundred to give reassur- 86 ing explanations to the Athenians in Samos now arrived from Delos, after Alcibiades had returned. An assembly was held at which they attempted to make themselves heard. At first the soldiers would not listen, and kept up a clamour for 'death to the destroyers of demo- cracy'. Quiet was restored with some difficulty, and the envoys then had their hearing. They gave out that the change of government was made for the salvation of the city, not for its destruction, and there was no intention of betraying it to the enemy (if there were, this could have been effected in the recent enemy invasion when the new government was already in place); that all members of the Five Thousand would have their turn in the administration; and that the men's families back home were not being abused—as scandalously alleged by Chaereas—or suffering any other detriment, but staying perfectly secure in their own property.

As they went on and on they increasingly lost their audience. The soldiers turned angry and voiced a range of opinions, most calling for an attack on the Peiraeus. It was then that Alcibiades can be said for the first time to have done an outstanding service to his country. With the Athenians at Samos ready to sail against their own people at home—in which case, without any doubt, the enemy would immediately have taken possession of Ionia and the Hellespont—Alcibiades stopped them. At that particular moment no other man would have been capable of restraining the crowd, but he had them drop the idea of a naval attack and spoke forcefully to shame them out of any inclination to vent their anger on the individual envoys. He took it upon himself to answer the envoys and send them back. His answer was that he had no objection to the government of the Five Thousand, but they must get rid of the Four Hundred and restore the council of five hundred as in the old constitution. If they had made economies to provide better keep for their troops on service, that he could wholly applaud. Generally, they must stand firm and make no concessions to the enemy. If the city was kept safe, there was every hope of a reconciliation among themselves: but once there was any failure either at Samos or at home, there would be no one left to be reconciled with.

There were also present some envoys from Argos, bringing offers of help addressed to 'the Athenian people in Samos'. Alcibiades thanked them, and sent them back with the message that help would be welcome when it was called for. These Argives had come with the crew of the Paralus, who as related earlier had been assigned to the troop-ship on patrol round Euboea. They were then given the task of conveying to Sparta some Athenian envoys sent by the Four Hundred (these were Laespodias, Aristophon, and Melesias). When they were off Argos in the course of their voyage they arrested the envoys and handed them over to the Argives, on the grounds that they were among those chiefly responsible for the overthrow of the democracy.

The Parali did not return to Athens, but took their trireme from Argos to Samos, bringing with them the Argive envoys.

In this same summer there came a time when Peloponnesian vex- 87 ation with Tissaphernes reached its height, for all the other reasons as well as the return of Alcibiades, and they thought he was now clearly siding with Athens. So at this time, and evidently in an attempt to dispel their suspicions, Tissaphernes prepared to travel to Aspendus and fetch the Phoenician ships, and he invited Lichas to accompany him. He announced that he would second his deputy governor Tamos to the army, to take personal charge of the payment of maintenance during his own absence. Accounts vary, and it is not easy to discover what Tissaphernes had in mind when he went to Aspendus, or why having gone there he did not bring back the ships. That a Phoenician fleet of a hundred and forty-seven ships had come as far as Aspendus is certain: but as to why they never came further there are many conjectures. Some think that in removing himself to Aspendus Tissaphernes was continuing his policy of wearing down Peloponnesian morale (and certainly the provision of maintenance was no better when delegated to Tamos, in fact rather worse). Others think that he had brought the Phoenicians up to Aspendus in order to make money by selling the crews their discharge (and so had no intention of putting them to active service). Yet others see his motive in the context of his denunciation at Sparta: he wanted, that is, to have it reported of him that there was no dishonesty, that he was known to have gone to fetch the ships, and that they were indeed manned and ready. But it seems to me quite clear that in not bringing up the fleet his motive was the attrition and containment of the Greek powers— damage done by his long absence on the way to Aspendus and the time he would spend there, and stalemate preserved by not strengthening either side with the support he could give. If he had wanted, he could indeed without doubt have brought the war to a decisive conclusion by taking a plain part. If he had brought up the ships he would in all probability have handed victory to the Spartans, who were now facing the Athenian fleet with equal numbers and no sense of inferiority. What really exposes Tissaphernes is the excuse he gave out for not bringing up the ships, which was that the number mustered was less than the King had specified: but in that case he could doubtless have won yet greater favour by saving the King money and achieving the same result at less expense. Whatever his motive, Tissaphernes now came to Aspendus and met the Phoenicians: and at his suggestion the Peloponnesians sent Philippus, a Spartan, with two triremes for the supposed purpose of fetching the ships.

88   When Alcibiades learnt that Tissaphernes was on his way to Aspendus, he took thirteen ships and sailed for Aspendus himself, promising the army at Samos a major benefit which he could guarantee: he would either bring back with him the Phoenician ships on the Athenian side, or at least prevent them going to the Peloponnesians. He had probably known all along that Tissaphernes had no intention of bringing up the ships, and wanted to compromise him as much as he could in the eyes of the Peloponnesians as his own friend and a friend of the Athenians, and thereby to increase the pressure on him to join the Athenian side. So Alcibiades set out on his voyage eastwards, making directly for Phaselis and Caunus.

89   The envoys sent by the Four Hundred to Samos now arrived back at Athens and reported what Alcibiades had said—the need to stand firm and make no concessions to the enemy, his high hopes of reconciling army and city and winning through against the Peloponnesians. This was a great encouragement to the rank and file of the oligarchic movement who had felt uneasy for some time and would gladly have abandoned the whole business if there was any safe way out. They were already beginning to group together and share their criticisms of the state of affairs, and they were led in this by some of those who were actually generals or held other office in the oligarchy, such as Theramenes the son of Hagnon and Aristocrates the son of Scelias, and some others. These men had taken a leading part in the revolution, but now (or so they said) they were seriously afraid of the army at Samos and of Alcibiades, afraid too that their colleagues who were sending delegations to Sparta might go their own way without wider consultation and do damage to the city. So they thought they should move away from an extreme oligarchy, and instead make the Five Thousand a reality rather than a pretence, and establish a constitution of greater equality. This was the phrase they used as a political smokescreen, but in fact most of them harboured private ambitions and fell into the syndrome which is characteristically fatal to an oligarchy succeeding a democracy. From the very first day members of an oligarchy have no truck with mere equality, and they all think they deserve unquestioned first place: whereas in a democracy the result of an election is easier to bear when the loser can console himself with the thought that he was not competing with his equals. What most clearly influenced them was the strong position of Alcibiades at

Samos and their own belief that the oligarchy could not last: so each
of them was manoeuvring to establish his own claims as the foremost
champion of the people.

Those among the Four Hundred most prominently opposed to 90
this sort of compromise were Phrynichus (who at the time when he
was general in Samos had spoken out against Alcibiades), Aristarchus
(a particularly vehement and long-standing opponent of democracy),
Peisander, Antiphon, and a number of other influential figures. They
had already been sending their own delegations to Sparta to press for
the peace agreement they wanted—they had done this as soon as
their position was established, and again when Samos declared
against them for democracy—and they had started their fortification
at the place called Eëtioneia. They intensified both activities when
their own envoys returned from Samos and they saw a shift in the
attitude both of the general public and of those in their movement
previously thought secure. Alarmed by developments both at home
and in Samos they hurriedly dispatched Antiphon and Phrynichus
and ten others to Sparta, with authorization to make peace with the
Spartans on any remotely tolerable terms, and they speeded yet more
energetically the construction work on the fortification at Eëtioneia.
According to Theramenes and his party, the purpose of this fortification was not to bar the Peiraeus to any attack by the fleet at Samos,
but rather to allow the enemy access at will with both naval and land
forces.

Eëtioneia is a claw of land closing the entrance to the Peiraeus.
The wall now being built joined the existing wall, which faced the
land on the west, to form an enclave where a small number of men
stationed there could command the approach from the sea. The old
wall facing the land and the new wall being built on the inner side
facing the sea both terminated at one of the two towers guarding the
narrow mouth of the harbour. They also walled off the largest storehouse in the Peiraeus, which was closest to the new fortification and
directly connected to it. They took control of the storehouse themselves, and compelled all corn-merchants to transfer their existing
stock and unload all further imports into it: the sale of corn was only
allowed from this depot.

For some time Theramenes had been airing his views, and when 91
the envoys returned from Sparta with nothing achieved by way of an
agreement for the people as a whole, he declared that this fortification could well be the ruin of Athens. It so happened that at this same

time, in response to the Euboeans' invitation, a Peloponnesian fleet
of forty-two ships (including some Italian ships from Taras and Locri,
and a few from Sicily) was now lying at Las in Laconia getting ready
to sail to Euboea under the command of the Spartiate Agesandridas,
the son of Agesandrus. Theramenes claimed that these ships were
destined not for Euboea but for the support of the party fortifying
Eëtioneia, and warned that without immediate precautions they
could all be lost before they knew it. This charge was not simply a
canard, and came close enough to the thinking of the men against
whom it was laid. For them the ideal was oligarchy at home and the
continuation of empire over the subject allies; failing that, the retention of their ships and walls, and their independence; and if this too
was denied them, they had no intention of becoming the prime victims
of a restored democracy, but would bring in the enemy and agree the
loss of walls and ships, and any fate whatever for the city, as long as
they themselves could save their own skins.

92   This was why they were so keen to press ahead with the building
of this fortification and incorporate into it posterns and entrances
and other means of introducing the enemy: they wanted to have it
finished when the time came. Now as yet this sort of talk had been
confined to a few and largely kept secret. But then after his return
from the embassy to Sparta Phrynichus was stabbed in the crowded
marketplace by one of the border-guards in a planned assassination.
He had just left the council-chamber and not gone far: he died on the
spot. The assassin made his escape, but his accomplice, a fellow from
Argos, was caught and put to torture by the Four Hundred. He did
not give the name of anyone who had commissioned the murder, and
said nothing more than that he knew there had been large gatherings
at the house of the border-guard commander and in other houses
elsewhere. The fact that no untoward action followed this affair
encouraged a bolder approach from Theramenes and Aristocrates
and all others (whether members of the Four Hundred or not) who
shared their view. At the same time the ships from Las had now sailed
round, taken station at Epidaurus, and raided Aegina. Theramenes
declared that if they were really on their way to Euboea it made no
sense for them to have sailed up the gulf to Aegina and then returned
to anchorage at Epidaurus: they must have been called in for the
purpose which he had always maintained, and so doing nothing was
now no longer an option. After much more inflammatory talk and airing of suspicions the people finally took positive action. The hoplites

in the Peiraeus engaged in the construction of the wall at Eëtioneia (among whom was Aristocrates as company commander of the contingent from his own tribe) seized Alexicles, who was a general in the oligarchic party and particularly implicated with the cabals, and took him off to imprisonment in a private house. Others involved in this kidnap included one Hermon, the commander of the border-guards stationed at Mounichia: and, most importantly of all, the rank and file of the hoplites were in support.

When this was reported to the Four Hundred, who happened to be in session in the council-chamber, they were immediately ready to take to arms (though some did not agree) and turned on Theramenes and his associates with threats. Theramenes defended himself and said that he was prepared to go right now and assist in the rescue of Alexicles. He took with him one of the generals who shared his view and went down to the Peiraeus. Aristarchus also went to the scene with some of the younger cavalrymen. There ensued widespread confusion and alarm. Those in the city thought that the Peiraeus was already in the hands of the counter-revolutionaries and the prisoner had been killed, and those in the Peiraeus thought that they were in imminent danger of an attack from the city. In the city the older men struggled to restrain the party members who were running through the streets to fetch their arms, and Thucydides, the consular representative for Athens in Pharsalus, who happened to be in Athens at the time, worked tirelessly to confront every man he met and plead with him not to destroy his country when the enemy was lying ready so close by. These efforts eventually brought calm and the two sides kept their hands off each other.

When Theramenes (who was himself a general) reached the Peiraeus he put on a show of remonstration with the hoplites, whereas Aristarchus and the opposition expressed genuine fury. Most of the hoplites stayed of the same mind and were ready to resist in earnest. They began by asking Theramenes if he thought the wall was being built to any good purpose, and whether it would not be better demolished. He replied that if they decided to demolish it, that was his decision also. At this the hoplites and a crowd of men from the Peiraeus immediately got up on the fortification and began to pull it down. The call had gone out to the people that anyone who wanted government by the Five Thousand instead of the Four Hundred should come and join the work. They still covered themselves by speaking of the Five Thousand, rather than calling outright for those who wanted a democracy, as they feared that the Five Thousand might actually exist, and careless talk from one man to the next could cause trouble. This was exactly why the Four Hundred did not want the Five Thousand either to exist or to be known not to exist. Their view was that to have that number of participants in government would be tantamount to democracy, whereas keeping the whole question obscure would promote a general and mutual fear of everyone else.

93   On the next day the Four Hundred, shaken as they were by the events, still held a meeting in the council-chamber. And the hoplites in the Peiraeus released Alexicles from his arrest, completed the demolition of the wall, and proceeded to the theatre of Dionysus near Mounichia, where they grounded their arms and held an assembly. On the decision taken there they marched straight to the city and again grounded their arms, this time in the Anaceium. Selected members of the Four Hundred came to meet them there and talked with them individually, looking to persuade any they saw as reasonable men to show an example of calm and restrain the others. They promised that they would publish the names of the Five Thousand, and that all these would have their turn on the Four Hundred with the method of rotation to be determined by the Five Thousand themselves. In the meantime they begged them to take no action which could ruin the city and drive it into the hands of the enemy. There were many such individual discussions, which left the whole hoplite body in milder mood than it had been, and much more concerned now for the wider national interest. They agreed that an assembly should be held on a specified day in the precinct of Dionysus to discuss the means of restoring harmony.

94   When the day came for this assembly and the people were on the point of gathering in the precinct of Dionysus, news came that the forty-two ships with Agesandridas were sailing from Megara along the coast of Salamis. All in the popular party thought that this was exactly what Theramenes and his associates had long been saying, that this fleet was destined for the fortification at Eëtioneia, and it was just as well that the wall had been demolished. It could be that some prearranged agreement had kept Agesandridas hovering around Epidaurus and that area, but it is likely that he lingered there on his own initiative in view of the prevailing agitation at Athens, with the hope of intervening at the critical moment. The Athenians' reaction to this news was to rush straight down to the Peiraeus with

every available man, thinking that an enemy threat more serious than any from their own internal conflict was now not far off them and heading right for their harbour. Some went on board the ships which were lying ready, others began to launch more ships, and yet others went to the defence of the walls and the mouth of the harbour.

In fact the Peloponnesian ships sailed on past, rounded Sounium, 95 and came to anchor between Thoricus and Prasiae: they then went on to Oropus. The Athenians had to put out a fleet in haste and were obliged to use crews who had not trained together—a consequence both of the civil disturbances at home and of the need to take immediate action to protect their most vital interest (now that Attica was closed to them they depended completely on Euboea). With Thymochares as general in command they sent a number of ships to Eretria, which made a combined total of thirty-six when they arrived and were added to the ships already at Euboea. They had to fight as soon as they got there. Agesandridas gave his men their lunch and then took his ships out from Oropus, which is about six and a half miles across the sea from the city of Eretria. As he bore down on them, the Athenians too gave orders for the immediate manning of their fleet, thinking that they had the crews close by their ships. But in fact they were not shopping for their lunch in the marketplace, as the Eretrians had deliberately arranged that the only food for sale was at the houses on the far edge of town: this was in order to slow the manning of the Athenian ships so that the enemy could attack before they were ready and force the Athenians to come out against them whatever their state of preparedness. Indeed a signal had been raised at Eretria telling the fleet at Oropus when it was time to sail to the attack. Disorganized to this extent, the Athenians did put out their ships and engage in battle off the harbour of Eretria: for a short while they managed to hold their own, but were then turned to flight and chased back to land. Those who took refuge in the city of Eretria, assuming it to be friendly, fared worst of all: the inhabitants butchered them. Others who made the Athenian-held fort in Eretria survived, as did the ships which reached Chalcis. The Peloponnesians captured twenty-two of the Athenian ships, variously killed or made prisoners of the crews, and set up a trophy. Not long afterwards they secured the revolt of the whole of Euboea apart from Oreus (which was still under Athenian control), and saw to general arrangements for the island.

When news reached the Athenians of the events in Euboea, the 96 panic which set in was greater than any before. Not even the disaster in Sicily, which had seemed so comprehensive at the time, nor anything else so far had frightened the Athenians as much as this. With the army at Samos in revolt, no ships in reserve or crews to man them, dissent at home which could break into civil war at any moment, and now to crown it all this immense blow which had lost them their ships and, most crucially, lost them Euboea, a more important lifeline than Attica itself—how could they not be reduced to despair, and with good reason? But what caused them the greatest and most immediate alarm was the fear that the enemy might be bold enough to exploit their victory and sail straight for them, against a Peiraeus empty of ships: and they imagined the enemy all but there already. And indeed, if the Peloponnesians had been bolder, they could easily have done this. Then they could either have exacerbated the divisions in the city by simply lying off the Peiraeus, or, if they had to stay longer and start a blockade, they would have forced the fleet in Ionia, despite its opposition to the oligarchy, to come to the help of their kinsmen and the city as a whole: and in that case the Hellespont, Ionia, the islands, and everything as far as Euboea—virtually the whole Athenian empire—would have fallen into their hands. Not for the first time (there had been many other examples) the Spartans showed themselves, of all possible enemies, the ideal opponents in a war fought by the Athenians. The marked difference in national character (the Athenians quick and enterprising, the Spartans slow and unadventurous) gave a particular advantage to the Athenians as a naval power. The Syracusans proved the point: they were the most closely comparable in character to the Athenians, and so the most successful in fighting them.

97   At any rate the Athenians' reaction to the news was to man twenty ships despite all, and to call an immediate assembly, the first to meet again in the traditional place for assemblies known as the Pnyx. At this assembly they deposed the Four Hundred and voted to transfer government to the Five Thousand (to be constituted of all those who could provide their own hoplite armour), and to abolish all pay for any public office, with the sanction of a curse on anyone infringing this rule. There followed a series of subsequent assemblies as a result of which they appointed legal commissioners and voted in the other elements of a new constitution. And now for the first time, at least in my lifetime, the Athenians enjoyed a political system of substantial and obvious merit, which blended the interests of the few and the many without extremes, and began to restore the city from the wretched

situation into which it had fallen. They also voted for the recall of Alcibiades and other exiles with him, and sent messages both to him and to the army at Samos urging them to take an active part.

On this counter-revolution Peisander and Alexicles and their asso- 98 ciates and the other leading figures in the oligarchy slipped out of the city to Deceleia, all except Aristarchus, who, as one of the generals at the time, hastily took with him some of the most barbarous of the archers and made for Oenoe. This was an Athenian fort on the border with Boeotia, which was at present under siege in a unilateral action by the Corinthians (though they had also called in the Boeotians) in response to a defeat inflicted by the garrison at Oenoe which killed some of their troops returning home from Deceleia. In collusion with the besiegers Aristarchus tricked the garrison by telling them that the Athenian authorities had made a general peace agreement with the Spartans, and one of the conditions was that they must hand over Oenoe to the Boeotians. Trusting the word of a general, and cut off by the siege from all other information, the garrison came out under truce. In this way Oenoe was captured and occupied by the Boeotians: and the oligarchic revolution at Athens came to an end.

At about the same time in this summer there were developments 99 also among the Peloponnesians at Miletus. No provision at all was now forthcoming from any of those to whom Tissaphernes had delegated their maintenance when he went to Aspendus; neither the Phoenician ships nor Tissaphernes himself had so far made any appearance; Philippus, who had been detailed to accompany Tissaphernes, and also Hippocrates, a Spartiate in Phaselis at the time, had both sent letters to Mindarus, the admiral-in-chief, saying that the ships would never come and Tissaphernes had been playing them false throughout; and Pharnabazus was still inviting them, eager to secure their fleet for his own purpose of inducing the rest of the cities in his province to revolt from the Athenians (just like Tissaphernes, and like him he expected to profit from the revolts). So for all these reasons Mindarus finally moved his fleet from Miletus. With strict discipline enforced and at very short notice, so as not to alert the Athenians at Samos, he put out to sea with seventy-three ships and sailed for the Hellespont (sixteen ships had already gone there earlier in this same summer, and overrun part of the Chersonese). He was caught in a storm and forced by the wind to put in at Icaros, where bad weather kept him for five or six days before he went on to arrive at Chios.

100 When Thrasyllus heard that Mindarus had sailed out of Miletus, he too immediately put to sea from Samos with fifty-five ships, anxious that Mindarus should not reach the Hellespont before he did. On learning that Mindarus was at Chios, and thinking that he would spend some time there, Thrasyllus posted lookouts at Lesbos and on the mainland opposite, to detect and report any movement by the Peloponnesian ships, while he himself sailed along the coast to Methymna and ordered a supply of barley and other provisions so that, if there was a prolonged delay, he could use Lesbos as a base for attacks on Chios. At the same time he wanted to sail against the Lesbian town of Eresus, which had revolted from Athens, and take it if he could. What had happened was that some of the most powerful citizens of Methymna, now in exile, had brought over from Cyme some fifty hoplites of their own political persuasion together with mercenary troops hired on the mainland, a total of about three hundred in all, led by a Theban, Anaxandrus, in virtue of the kinship connection. These first of all attacked Methymna, but their attempt was cut short by the arrival of some of the Athenian garrison from Mytilene: beaten back again in a battle outside the walls, they made their way over the mountain and secured the revolt of Eresus. So Thrasyllus sailed to Eresus with all his ships, intending to launch an assault. Thrasyboulus had already got there before him, having set out from Samos with five ships as soon as news came of the exiles' landing: but he had arrived too late to prevent the revolt and was now lying at anchor off Eresus. Thrasyllus and Thrasyboulus were joined also by two ships returning home from the Hellespont and by the Methymnaeans' ships, bringing the total of the fleet gathered there to sixty-seven. Using the troops from these ships they began preparations for an attack on Eresus with siege-engines and all other means in the hope of taking the place by storm.

101 Meanwhile Mindarus and the Peloponnesian fleet at Chios spent two days provisioning and had their wages paid by the Chians (three Chian 'fortieths' for each man). On the third day they put out from Chios and sailed fast, not across the open sea (to avoid meeting the ships at Eresus), but keeping Lesbos on their left and making for the mainland. They touched at the harbour of Carteria in Phocaean territory, and took their lunch there, then sailed on past Cyme and had their dinner at Arginousae on the mainland opposite Mytilene. Leaving there well before dawn they sailed along the coast to reach Harmatus, which is on the mainland directly facing Methymna.

They lunched there and hurried on, sailing round the promontory of Lectum and past Larisa, Hamaxitus, and the other towns in that area, and finally reached Rhoeteium on the Hellespont before midnight. Some of their ships also put in at Sigeium and other neighbouring places.

The Athenians who were at Sestos with eighteen ships realized 102 from the beacon-signals lit by their own lookouts and from the sudden appearance of multiple watch-fires on the enemy shore opposite that a Peloponnesian fleet was approaching the strait. In that very night they sailed as fast as they could towards Elaeus, hugging the shore of the Chersonese and hoping to get out into the open sea away from the enemy ships. They did go undetected by the sixteen ships at Abydos, which had received previous notice of the approach of a friendly fleet and been told to keep a close watch on the Athenians in case they tried to sail out of the strait. But at dawn they caught sight of Mindarus' ships, which immediately gave chase. Not all of the Athenian ships managed to outrun them. Most made their escape towards Imbros and Lemnos, but the four hindmost were caught off Elaeus: one of these ran aground near the sanctuary of Protesilaus and was captured crew and all; two others were captured without their crews; and one more, abandoned by its crew, was burned off the shore of Imbros. After this the entire Peloponnesian fleet, joined now 103 by the ships from Abydos to make a total of eighty-six, blockaded Elaeus for the rest of that day: but the town would not capitulate, and the fleet sailed off to Abydos.

The Athenians, failed by their lookouts and not thinking it possible that an enemy fleet could pass them by undetected, were happily settling to the assault on the walls of Eresus. When they learnt the reality, they immediately abandoned Eresus and sailed with all speed to the defence of the Hellespont. On their way they chanced on and captured two Peloponnesian ships which had pressed the pursuit rather too boldly into the open sea. On the following day they arrived at Elaeus and anchored there. They were joined by the ships which had escaped to Imbros, and spent five days in preparation for the impending battle.

The engagement then began, and proceeded as follows. The 104 Athenians started sailing in column close in to the shore towards Sestos, and seeing this movement the Peloponnesians likewise put out from Abydos to face them. With battle now a certainty, the Athenians— seventy-six ships—extended their line along the Chersonese from

Idacus to Arrhiani, and the Peloponnesians—eighty-six ships— extended theirs from Abydos to Dardanus. The Peloponnesian right wing was held by the Syracusans, and Mindarus himself was on the other wing with the fastest ships in the fleet. The Athenian left wing was commanded by Thrasyllus, and the right by Thrasyboulus: the other generals took various positions in between. The Peloponnesians were keen to make the first moves to engage. They wanted, if possible, to outflank the Athenian right wing with their left to debar their exit from the strait, and to drive the Athenian centre back to land (which at that point was at no great distance). The Athenians realized what they were trying to do, and countered by extending their own line on the flank where the enemy was hoping to block them. They were getting the better of this manoeuvre, but by now their left wing had gone beyond the headland called Cynossema. The result of these moves to right and left was that the centre of the line became weak and over-extended, not least because the Athenians had a smaller complement of ships and the sharp angle described by the coast round Cynossema prevented sight of what was happening on the other side of it.

105   So the Peloponnesians fell on the centre and drove the Athenian ships off the water, then disembarked themselves to follow up on land their decisive superiority in the action. No help could be brought to the centre either by the right wing with Thrasyboulus or by the left wing with Thrasyllus. Thrasyboulus was being pressed hard by the pure number of ships against him, and the left wing not only had their view obstructed by the headland of Cynossema but were also tied down by the Syracusans and others who were opposing them with equal forces. But then, over-confident after their victory, the Peloponnesians began chasing individual ships at random and part of their line fell into disarray. Seeing their opportunity, Thrasyboulus and his wing stopped extending their line and suddenly turned to attack the ships ranged against them. They routed these and next took on the scattered ships of the victorious Peloponnesian centre, giving them such a mauling that most of them turned to flight without any resistance. And by now the Syracusans too had given way to Thrasyllus' wing, and were the more urgent to make their own escape when they saw the others in flight.

106   After this rout the Peloponnesians fled for the most part to the river Meidius at first, and then later to Abydos. The Athenians captured relatively few ships (as the narrow confines of the Hellespont

allowed the enemy to reach places of refuge close by), but this victory at sea could not have come at a better time for them. Up till this point they had been wary of the Peloponnesian navy because of a series of small defeats as well as the disaster in Sicily, but now they could shake off their habit of self-depreciation and abandon any further respect for the enemy's ability at sea. From the enemy forces they did even so capture eight Chian ships, five Corinthian, two Ambraciot, two Boeotian, and one each from Leucas, Sparta, Syracuse, and Pellene: their own losses amounted to fifteen ships. They set up a trophy on the headland of Cynossema, brought in the wrecks, and returned the enemy dead under truce. They then sent a trireme to announce the victory at Athens. The arrival of this ship with news of an unhoped-for success, following soon on the blows they had suffered with Euboea and the revolution at home, greatly increased Athenian morale: they now thought that with full commitment to their own cause they could still win through.

The Athenians at Sestos quickly repaired their ships, and on the 107 fourth day after the sea-battle sailed for Cyzicus, which had revolted. On their way they sighted the eight ships from Byzantium anchored at Harpagium and Priapus: they sailed in to the attack, defeated the opposition on land, and captured the ships. When they arrived at Cyzicus (which was unwalled) they took back the city and exacted a payment from it. Meanwhile the Peloponnesians sailed from Abydos to Elaeus and recovered those of their captured ships which were still seaworthy (the rest had been burned by the Elaeusians), and sent Hippocrates and Epicles to Euboea to bring up the ships which were there.

At about this same time Alcibiades sailed back with his thirteen 108 ships from Caunus and Phaselis to Samos, to announce that he had prevented the Phoenician ships from going to the Peloponnesians and had made Tissaphernes a greater friend of the Athenians than ever before. He then crewed an additional nine ships and went off to exact a large sum of money from the Halicarnassians and to fortify Cos. With that done and a governor installed in Cos he sailed back to Samos towards the beginning of autumn.

When Tissaphernes learnt that the Peloponnesian fleet had sailed from Miletus to the Hellespont, he decamped from Aspendus and set out for Ionia. Now the people of Antandrus (who are Aeolians) had taken advantage of the Peloponnesian presence in the Hellespont to bring some hoplites from Abydos overland across Mount Ida and install them in their city. They were suffering oppression by the Persian Arsaces, who was Tissaphernes' deputy. This Arsaces had committed an atrocity on the Delians who had settled in Atramyttium when the Athenians removed them from Delos to purify the island. Arsaces pretended an unspecified cause of hostilities and invited the best of the Delians to serve in his army. He led them out in apparent friendship and alliance, but waited for them to take their midday meal and then surrounded them with his own troops and shot them down. This example made the Antandrians fear similar violence on themselves, and since in any case Arsaces was imposing intolerable burdens on them they drove out his garrison from their acropolis.

109   Tissaphernes saw this as the work of the Peloponnesians, added to the similar expulsions of his garrisons at Miletus and Cnidus. He realized that his stock was very low with them, and feared that they could do him further harm. At the same time he was vexed to find that Pharnabazus had secured their services in less time and at less expense, and was more likely than himself to achieve success against the Athenians. He therefore determined to go and meet them at the Hellespont, to complain of the business at Antandrus and to present the most plausible defence he could to the various charges made against him including the question of the Phoenician ships. His first stop was at Ephesus, where he offered sacrifice to Artemis.

APPENDIX

Weights, Measures, and Distances; Money; Calendar

Weights, Measures, and Distances

The different Greek states used their own systems, and the same words can denote different absolute weights (for instance) in the systems of different states. Particularly in connection with things other than precious metals, degrees of precision were probably not high.

For weights, the Athenian scale (with the values of the late fifth and fourth centuries, about 18 per cent greater than the values of the sixth century) was:

1 obol	= 0.77 g	= ¼₀ oz
6 obols = 1 drachma	= 4.6 g	= ⅙ oz
100 drachmae = 1 mina	= 460 g	= 1 lb
60 minas = 1 talent	= 27.6 kg	= 61 lb

For measures of capacity the principal Athenian units were:

1 *kotyle* (wet or dry)	= 0.273 l	= ½ imp. pint	= ⅔ US pint
12 *kotylai* = 1 *chous* (wet)	= 3.28 l	= 5¾ imp. pints	= 7 US pints
12 *choes* = 1 *metretes* (wet)	= 39.31 l	= 8⅔ imp. gallons	= 10½ US gallons
4 *kotylai* = 1 *choinix* (dry)	= 1.09 l	= 2 imp. pints	= 2⅓ US pints
48 *choinikes* = 1 *medimnos* (dry)	= 52.42 l	= 11½ imp. gallons	= 14 US gallons

The principal unit for measuring longer distances was the stade, comprising 600 feet. The Athenian stade was about 176 metres = 193 yards. Distances were commonly estimated rather than exactly measured, and Thucydides' informants may not always have been thinking in terms of the same stade as he did, but it has been shown that most of Thucydides' distances imply a stade of between 150 and 200 metres = between 165 and 220 yards.[1] In our translation the equivalent distances in terms of miles are given.

---

[1] See R. A. Bauslaugh, 'The Text of Thucydides 4.8.6 and the South Channel at Pylos', *JHS* 99 (1979), 1–6.

Money

Coins were named after the weight of precious metal (commonly silver) which they contained; but by the late fifth century Athenian coins were slightly lighter than their nominal weight: thus the standard 4-drachma coin at Athens weighed about 17.2 g = 0.6 oz. It is impossible to give meaningful equivalences in terms of present-day monetary values. In the late fifth century an unskilled worker at Athens could earn half a drachma a day, and a skilled 1 drachma; a juryman received half a drachma (increased from the mid-century rate of 2 obols); soldiers and sailors normally received half a drachma but might be paid more for particular campaigns. A man was considered rich enough to be liable for the trierarchy and other liturgies if his property was worth about 4 talents; one of the largest fifth-century estates is said to have been worth 200 talents, but there cannot have been many worth more than 20 talents. For the tribute from the Delian League, see 1.96, 2.13 with notes; for Athens' revenues at the beginning of the Peloponnesian War see 2.13 with notes.

Calendar

Years were identified by an annual official (in Athens the archon), or by the years of reign or office of a ruler or official who served for an extended period: 2.2 dates the outbreak of the Peloponnesian War by the systems used in Argos, Sparta, and Athens. A year commonly began at the new moon after a solstice or equinox. Each normal year consisted of twelve lunar months of 29 or 30 days, *c*.354 days in all; but to keep the calendar in step with the seasons some years had a thirteenth, 'intercalary' month added to bring the total to *c*.384 days (documents quoted in 4.118–19 and 5.19 give equivalences in the Spartan and Athenian calendars in spring 423 and spring 421, and show that the two did not keep in step with each other between those points). In Athens, the year began at the new moon after the summer solstice, and the months with approximate equivalents in our calendar were as follows (the intercalary month, when added, was usually a second Posideon, placed after the first):

1. Hecatombaeon	July	7. Gamelion	January
2. Metageitnion	August	8. Anthesterion	February
3. Boedromion	September	9. Elaphebolion	March
4. Pyanopsion	October	10. Munychion	April
5. Maemacterion	November	11. Thargelion	May
6. Posideon	December	12. Scirophorion	June

EXPLANATORY NOTES

These notes seek to help a range of readers, including readers without a great deal of background knowledge, to understand both Thucydides' subject matter and his treatment of it. I give references to other ancient texts for material not provided by Thucydides; and sometimes to books (but in these notes not to periodical articles) in English which provide a helpful discussion of matters which cannot be discussed at length in these notes. I list here some books which are not cited regularly in the individual notes but will regularly be helpful to those who wish to pursue matters further. Full bibliographical details are given in the Select Bibliography.

On Greek history in general there are chapters by experts, with source references and modern bibliography, in the latest edition of the *Cambridge Ancient History*: in particular, for readers of Thucydides, vol. v², on the period 478–404; also vols. ii. 1/2³ on the bronze age, iii. 1² on the tenth to eighth centuries, iii. 3² on the eighth to sixth centuries, iv² on the late sixth and early fifth centuries including the Persian Wars. Shorter histories of Greece include, in the Routledge History of the Ancient World, R. Osborne, *Greece in the Making, 1200–479 BC*, and S. Hornblower, *The Greek World, 479–323 BC*; in the Blackwell History of the Ancient World, J. Hall, *A History of the Archaic Greek World, ca. 1200–479 BCE*, and P. J. Rhodes, *A History of the Classical Greek World, 478–323 BC*.

A four-volume series by D. Kagan gives a detailed history of the Peloponnesian War and what went before it, with discussion of the views of many scholars over the past century: *The Outbreak of the Peloponnesian War, The Archidamian War, The Peace of Nicias and the Sicilian Expedition, The Fall of the Athenian Empire*—and he has also written the single-volume *The Peloponnesian War*. G. E. M. de Ste. Croix, *The Origins of the Peloponnesian War*, ranges more widely than its title suggests. Other recent books on the Peloponnesian War include G. L. Cawkwell, *Thucydides and the Peloponnesian War*; J. F. Lazenby, *The Peloponnesian War: A Military Study*; V. D. Hanson, *A War Like No Other: How the Athenians and Spartans Fought the Peloponnesian War* (vivid and stimulating, but not always reliable on details). On naval matters, J. S. Morrison, J. F. Coates, and N. B. Rankov, *The Athenian Trireme*, is of fundamental importance.

Out of many books on Thucydides, J. H. Finley, jun., *Thucydides*, and S. Hornblower, *Thucydides*, are the best overall treatments; a good and up-to-date introduction for non-specialists is P. Zagorin, *Thucydides: An Introduction for the Common Reader*. K. J. Dover, *Thucydides*, in the series Greece & Rome: New Surveys in the Classics, reviewed the themes perceived as most important in the 1970s. A recent collection of studies by different authors is A. Rengakos and A. Tsakmakis (eds.), *Brill's Companion to Thucydides*. There are two major commentaries in English: A. W. Gomme, A. Andrewes, and K. J. Dover, *A Historical Commentary on Thucydides*; S. Hornblower, *A Commentary on Thucydides*.

There are editions with translation and commentary by P. J. Rhodes of Books 2, 3, and 4.1–5.24 (and Book 1 envisaged); there are editions with commentary of Book 2 by J. S. Rusten (with a linguistic emphasis: and Book 1 envisaged), and of Books 6 and 7 by K. J. Dover. There is a single-volume commentary based on the Penguin translation, D. Cartwright, *A Historical Commentary on Thucydides*. References by name alone are to the comments of these on the passage under discussion; our debts to Gomme, Andrewes, and Dover and to Hornblower go far beyond the points at which they are explicitly cited.

The largest-scale and most authoritative atlas, of an austere kind simply showing topography and locating sites, is R. J. A. Talbert (ed.), *Barrington Atlas of the Greek and Roman World*; smaller and cheaper, and including some thematic maps and plans of battle sites, is N. G. L. Hammond (ed.), *Atlas of the Greek and Roman World in Antiquity*.

BOOK ONE

The narrative of the Peloponnesian War proper begins in Book 2, and from there onwards Thucydides uses a framework of seasonal years, divided into summers and winters, and very rarely steps outside it (see first note on Book 2). The structure of Book 1 is complex but coherent (see analysis on p. lviii)—and there is no need to suppose, as some scholars have done, that what we now have has been revised from an earlier version with a different emphasis.

Thucydides begins (1–23.3) by claiming that the Peloponnesian War was greater than any previous war, and in what is often called his 'archaeology' (2–19) he gives an outline of the growth of power in Greece to justify that claim. He was a writer proud of the trouble he took to get the facts right, and digresses to make that point (20), before repeating his claim that previous wars were not as great as the Peloponnesian War (21). Criticism of other writers leads to a digression on his method and aim in writing his history (22), which is followed by a final statement of the greatness of the Peloponnesian War (23.1–3).

The remainder of Book 1 is devoted to the causes of the war and to the events leading up to it. In the second half of 23 Thucydides distinguishes between 'the real reason, true but unacknowledged' and 'the openly proclaimed grievances on either side'. He then sets out to give a definitive account of the grievances, 'so that nobody in future will need to look for the immediate cause', and gives a detailed narrative of two episodes, concerning Corcyra in 435–433 (24–55) and Potidaea in 433–432 (56–66), in each of which Athens came to fight against Sparta's ally Corinth. Corinth and other states then decided to put pressure on Sparta as leader of the Peloponnesian League to take action against Athens, and Thucydides reports a meeting in Sparta in 432, in which two other grievances, concerning Aegina and Megara, emerge (67–88): there are speeches by Corinthians and by Athenians 'come there on other business', and by the Spartan king Archidamus and ephor Sthenelaïdas. The upshot was a decision by Sparta that Athens was in the wrong and a war against Athens was necessary, and the summoning of a formal congress of the Peloponnesian League to ratify that decision.

Thucydides ends that section by repeating his belief that his 'real reason', Spartan fear of Athenian power, counted for more than the particular grievances which he has been reporting; and he then sets out to justify his belief by giving an account of the growth of Athenian power from the foundation of the Delian League to continue the war against Persia after the defeat of the Persian invasion of Greece in 480–479 (89–118, with another statement of the belief in 118). He resumes his main narrative with the congress of the Peloponnesian League in 432 (119–25). The Peloponnesians were not ready to start fighting immediately, so the winter of 432/1 was devoted to preparations and diplomatic exchanges (126–46). This leads Thucydides into another digression on earlier history (126–38): on Cylon's attempt to become tyrant in seventh-century Athens, which had resulted in a curse which Sparta tried to exploit against Athens; on the downfall of Pausanias in Sparta after the Persian Wars, leading to a curse which Athens in turn tried to exploit; and on the downfall of Themistocles of Athens at the same time. Book 1 ends with Athens' response to the pressure from Sparta (139–46), featuring a speech by Pericles in Athens which claims that the grievances were merely pretexts, appeasement would achieve nothing, and if war had to come Athens was well placed to win it.

The one point at which Thucydides seems to lose sight of his overall purpose is 126–38, where the stories of Cylon and Pausanias arise from their use in the propaganda of 432/1 but Thucydides then proceeds from Pausanias to Themistocles: he sees these two as 'the two most eminent of the Greeks of their time' (138), and he sees Themistocles as a precursor of his hero Pericles.

1.1–23.3 Introduction

1.1 *Preface.* Thucydides introduces himself and his subject as Herodotus had introduced himself and his subject; whereas Herodotus 'presented the results of [his] enquiry [*historie*]', Thucydides 'wrote this history of the war', or, more literally, 'put together in writing [*xynegrapse*] the war'. Herodotus wrote about the Persian Wars and (generously interpreted) their background, 'to preserve the fame of . . . remarkable achievements'; Thucydides wrote about the Peloponnesian War (much more strictly interpreted), 'reckoning that this would be a major war and more momentous than any previous conflict'. So we see from the beginning that, although much of his writing is matter-of-fact, Thucydides' history also has a superlative side to it. Although he never names Herodotus, there are various points where he clearly has Herodotus in mind.

'He began his work right at the outbreak'; he lived beyond the end of the war (see e.g. 5.26); and there has been much discussion of how much of his history was written at different times and how far what was written early was revised later, on which see Introduction, pp. xxv–xxviii.

He begins by justifying his claim that the Peloponnesian War was greater than any previous war, and insists from the outset on his credentials as a historian: 'accurate research' into the distant past was impossible, but he 'enquired as far into the past' as he could, looking for 'evidence which [he could] trust'. The last sentence of the chapter opens a ring (cf. Introduction, p. xlii), which will be closed at the beginning of 1.20.

1.2–19 *'Archaeology'*. Here Thucydides outlines the development of Greece
from the earliest times to the period after the Persian Wars: he is not
aware of the 'dark age' between the break-up of the bronze-age civiliza-
tions after *c*.1200 and the emergence of archaic Greece *c*.800, but thinks of
an uninterrupted progress from the more primitive to the more advanced.
He accepts the main lines of the traditional stories, and does not as
Herodotus did (Hdt. 1.1–5 contr. following chapters) distinguish between
a legendary distant past and a knowable more recent past, but he omits any
religious dimension and approaches the stories in a rationalist spirit (see
especially 1.9–11, on the Trojan War). In this section he gives reasons for
his statements, as he does not when writing the history of his own time:
he argues from Homer (1.3, 5, 9, 10), from the names given to the Greek
people (1.3), from current practice among more primitive people (1.5–6),
from burial practices (1.8), from how later generations might interpret
the physical remains of Athens and of Sparta (1.10); he frequently cites
tekmeria (pieces of evidence), *semeia* (indications), and *martyria* (testimony); where he cannot be certain he estimates likelihood (*eikos*). (For a
passage on facts and evidence by a contemporary of Thucydides see
Antiph. 5. *Chorus-Member* 31.) Modern historians do not always think he
has arrived at the right answers, but he has certainly looked in the right
kinds of way for evidence to support his account. The theme of his summary is the increase of power, on land and particularly at sea, and the
growth of population and wealth which made that increase possible.

1.2–3 In Thucydides' earliest phase the Greeks were so disunited that there
was no single name applicable to them all, and they were not settled but
underwent frequent population movements. However, his contrast may
be between planting crops for the year and planting olives and vines for
the long term (Gomme) rather than between hunting-and-gathering and
agriculture (Hornblower). Attica was not the most fertile part of Greece,
but it was not in fact the most infertile. The classical Athenians claimed
that they were autochthonous, were directly descended from the original
population of Attica: it is at least true that the city of Athens is one of the
few sites in Greece which were occupied continuously from the bronze
age to the archaic period. Modern historians distinguish between a
migration from Greece to the Aegean islands and western Asia Minor in
the dark age, when life was insecure, in the tenth and ninth centuries, and
the sending-out of colonies in the archaic period, to facilitate trade and
to export people for whom there was insufficient food at home, from the
eighth century onwards. Athens was generally regarded as the mother-
city of the Ionians in a strict sense, those Greeks who settled in the
middle stretch of the islands and the Asiatic coast, with Aeolians to the
north and Dorians to the south (the word 'Ionians' could be used more
loosely to refer to all the eastern Greeks: cf. note to 1.94–5), but we cannot now determine how large a part Athens played in this process. When
the Greeks worked out a chronological framework for the stories of their
past, they placed the Trojan War at what by our reckoning is the beginning of the twelfth century and Homer in the eighth century.

1.4 Minos was a legendary ruler of Crete, dated earlier than the Trojan War: the truth behind the legends is that what archaeologists have called the 'Minoan' civilization of Crete (not Greek in its language) was the first advanced civilization in the Greek world, and in the sixteenth and fifteenth centuries was able at any rate to influence the Greek mainland, the Aegean islands (the Cyclades are the islands of the southern Aegean, which encircle Delos), and western Asia Minor. The Carians (cf. 1.8) in the classical period occupied the south-western corner of Asia Minor: they were not Greek, but their history was bound up with that of the Asiatic Greeks; it is not now believed that they occupied the islands.

1.5 Before the existence of agreements to guarantee peaceful intercourse, visits to neighbouring territory were likely to be for plunder, and would be led by powerful men able to afford a ship and recruit a crew. The question is found in Homer, but piracy does seem to be a matter for reproach: *Od.* 3.71–4 = 9.252–5. Thucydides envisages the early Greeks as living in separate villages (cf. 1.10, on Sparta), which over time by the process known as *synoikismos* ('coming to live together') joined to form more substantial cities; and he cites people in the more primitive part of Greece in his time (listed from east to west along the north coast of the Gulf of Corinth) as evidence for what the more advanced part had been like in the past.

1.6 Carrying arms on a day-to-day basis is seen as characteristic of primitive and insecure peoples (cf. the 'frontier mentality' in the USA). Athens, although not abandoned in the dark age, lagged behind Peloponnesian cities in the archaic period, and is not likely to have been the first city to adopt a more luxurious and relaxed lifestyle. However, in Thucydides' own time Athens was the most prosperous Greek city while its rival Sparta was self-consciously old-fashioned and austere, and what is said here is probably an inference from that. The 'Ionian' tunic (*chiton*, undergarment) was made of linen and was elaborate, while the 'Dorian' was made of wool and simple. The hairstyle mentioned here is referred to as an old men's fashion by Aristophanes (*Eq.* 331, *Nub.* 984); but in Thucydides' time long hair was affected by upper-class young Athenians and also by Spartans: elaborate clothing and long hair are inappropriate for physical hard labour (and the Spartans had Helots, for whom see note to 1.101–3, to farm their land)—but of course fashion and convenience often do not coincide. The elaborate fashion is more likely to have originated in Ionia and to have passed to Athens; for the late fifth century the 'Old Oligarch' remarks that in Athens citizens dress no better than metics (foreign residents) and slaves. ([Xen.] *Ath. Pol.* 1.10)—and we may compare the development of jeans from working men's trousers to universal fashion.

Nudity for athletics goes back further than Thucydides seems to have thought: vase painting and sculpture show that the practice was well established in the sixth century. As in 1.5 he argued from current practice in the more primitive part of Greece, here he argues from current practice among the barbarians; Hdt. 1.10 remarks that among the barbarians it is thought disgraceful even for men to be seen naked.

1.7-8 Thucydides envisages development from unfortified to fortified and from inland to coastal cities; and in fact long-established cities such as Athens, Corinth, and (particularly) Sparta were inland and developed separate harbour towns. His thinking is that when life became more settled the accumulation of wealth became easier and more desirable, so that access to the sea became more worthwhile, but when there was more to defend there was greater need to fortify cities. For the Carians, cf. 1.4 (it is thought that Thucydides assumed too readily that the burials on Delos were in a manner not merely used by the Carians but distinctive of the Carians); the Phoenicians never settled in the Aegean on a significant scale, but there is archaeological evidence that they visited it and perhaps colonized on a small scale in the dark age and archaic period. For the 'purification' of Delos in 426/5, cf. 3.104: even innocent death gave rise to pollution, so it had to be kept away from sanctuaries as far as possible.

1.9-11 More than Herodotus (who did not believe that Helen was in Troy: 2.112-20), Thucydides accepts the traditional account of a Greek war against Troy, in the north-western corner of Asia Minor, to recover Helen, the wife of king Menelaus of Sparta, from her abductor Paris; but he approaches it in a rationalist spirit. How much truth, if any, there is behind the legend continues to be disputed by scholars. Thucydides does not deny the story of an oath sworn by Helen's suitors to support her and her husband (cf. Paus. 3.20), but he thinks it more important that Menelaus' brother Agamemnon was the most powerful ruler in Greece. In the Catalogue of Ships (Hom., *Il.* 2.484-760) Agamemnon had 100 ships of his own and provided a further 60 for the Arcadians (lines 569-80, 603-13); the account of his sceptre is given in *Il.* 2.100-9.

In Thucydides' time the 'cyclopean' walls of Mycenae were visible but other signs of its wealth were not; and it is certainly true that of the two most powerful cities of his own world Athens was particularly well equipped with fine public buildings and Sparta was not (it consisted of four adjoining villages, and Amyclae a short distance away).

The ships are assumed to resemble the more old-fashioned ships which Thucydides knew, and the *Iliad*'s two figures for crews are taken to represent the maximum and the minimum. Thucydides exaggerates by rounding up the *Iliad*'s 1,186 ships to 1,200: 1,200 × 85 = 102,000 men; 1,186 × 85 = 100,810 men; which would compare well with 378 × 200 = 75,600 men in the Greek ships used against Persia in 480 (Hdt. 8.48, cf. 82), or perhaps 40,000 men altogether in Athens' Sicilian expedition of 415-413 (Hornblower, iii, appendix 2). Even in Thucydides' time forces going away from home took provisions only for a limited period and expected to live off what could be obtained locally after their arrival.

1.12 After the Trojan War Thucydides continues to use the corpus of Greek legend: Odysseus' ten-year journey back to Ithaca was a well-known delayed return; the murder of Agamemnon on his return, by his wife Clytemnestra and her lover Aegisthus, was a well-known instance of internal strife; and among the settlements founded elsewhere was the alleged foundation of Rome by fugitives from Troy (a story already current in Thucydides' time: Hellanicus *FGrH* 4 F 84). On Boeotia Thucydides is trying to reconcile the tradition of a migration from Thessaly with the mention of Boeotians in the *Iliad* (2.494–510). The truth behind the widespread tradition of an invasion of the Peloponnese by the strand of the Greek people known as Dorians is hard to establish, but it does at least seem to be true that those Peloponnesians who were called Dorians and who spoke the Dorian dialect of Greek were more recent arrivals there than the other inhabitants. For Athens and the Ionians, cf. 1.2; colonies in the rest of the Mediterranean world were founded, in many but by no means in all cases, by Peloponnesians, from the eighth century onwards (cf. note to 1.2–3, and for colonies in Sicily see 6.3–5).

1.13–19 In the rest of the 'archaeology' the main theme is the development of naval power. The Greeks were fond of lists in which, for instance, *A* was the greatest philosopher for *x* years, then *B* for *y* years, and so on; and behind Thucydides' account there seems to lie the notion of a succession of 'thalassocracies', of control of the sea by successive states for specified periods. Such a list, constructed from well-known instances of success and failure at sea, will have had some connection with reality but will of course have been greatly over-simplified. For a list of this kind, preserved by Eusebius, see Diod. Sic. 7.11.

Another theme is the rule of 'tyrants'. Aristocracies, ruling collectively through annually appointed officials, had in most places supplanted the earlier kingships (whose powers had been limited, as in Homer, by tacit understanding rather than by formal rules). In many but not all cities, particularly in the seventh and sixth centuries, these were challenged by men, often themselves on the fringes of the aristocracy, who traded on local grievances to seize power for themselves. Tyrant was not a formal position to which a man was appointed: some ruled autocratically but others worked through existing institutions; some were popular, at any rate at first when they promised to redress grievances, but in the end their own power became a new source of grievance, and no tyranny lasted longer than a century. Thucydides connects the rise of tyrants with the growth of wealth; more specifically, we may say that in self-sufficient agricultural communities there was little opportunity for social mobility, but the more varied opportunities for gaining and losing wealth in the archaic period produced men as rich as the aristocrats who owned the largest quantities of good land, who began to want political and social recognition.

1.13 The first development in shipbuilding was the distinction between 'long' ships for fighting and 'round' ships for carrying cargo. The trireme improved on the earlier fifty-oared 'penteconter' (1.14) by having three banks of oars and oarsmen, thus gaining additional power without additional length. It is disputed whether the trireme was invented by the Greeks or by the Phoenicians, and how early, but no state seems to have had large numbers of triremes before the fifth century.

Ameinocles of Corinth is not otherwise attested. Corcyra (cf. 1.24–55) was colonized by Corinth *c*.733, and if Thucydides' dates (whether reckoned from 421 or from 404) are right nothing can be said about these episodes; but it is possible that they result from generation counts using over-long generations, and should be scaled down to refer to the late seventh century, when Corinthian pottery was reaching Samos (J. B. Salmon, *Wealthy Corinth: A History of the City to 338 BC* (Oxford University Press, 1984), 108) and a war between Corinth and Corcyra is attested (Hdt. 3.49–53).

Corinth is 'wealthy' in Hom., *Il.* 2.570. It probably gained more from exploiting trade across the Isthmus of Corinth between the Saronic and Corinthian Gulfs (to avoid sailing round the Peloponnese) than overland trade along the Isthmus between central Greece and the Peloponnese; *c*.600 a causeway, the *diolkos*, was constructed to enable ships to be transported across the Isthmus (cf. Salmon, *Wealthy Corinth*, 136–9; Thucydides mentions the transporting of ships but not the *diolkos* in 3.15, 8.7–8).

Cyrus II was King of Persia *c*.560–530, controlling western Asia Minor from *c*.546, and Cambyses was King 530–522; Polycrates was tyrant of Samos, very close to the Asiatic mainland, *c*.532–522. Cyrus and Cambyses did not have a fleet in the Aegean; but Polycrates is credited with various achievements, including an empire on the mainland as well as in the islands (Hdt. 3.39; cf. 3.122), which cannot easily be assigned to the period of his reign, and it may be that as a famous figure he has attracted achievements which in fact belong earlier in the sixth century. However, the dedication of Rheneia is probably his (see 3.104).

Phocaea, an Aeolian city in Asia Minor, colonized Massalia in southern Gaul *c*.600, and may have come into conflict with Carthage then. Phocaeans who fled from Asia Minor to Corsica *c*.540 after the Persian conquest had 60 ships with which they won an expensive victory over the Carthaginians and Etruscans at Alalia (Hdt. 1.166).

1.14 Dareius I was King of Persia 522–486; the Persians invaded Greece in 490 and (under his successor Xerxes, 486–465) in 480–479; Herodotus credits Gelo of Syracuse in Sicily with 200 triremes and Corcyra with 60 warships in 480 (7.158, 168). An intermittent war between Athens and Aegina began *c*.505; in the late 490s Athens had 50 ships available and obtained a further 20 from Corinth (Hdt. 6.89). In 483/2 Themistocles persuaded the Athenians that a surplus from the silver mines should not be distributed among the citizens but be spent on new ships (Hdt. 7.144; *Ath. Pol.* 22.7, giving the date), as a result of which Athens had a fleet of 200 triremes when the Persians invaded in 480 (Hdt. 8.1 with 14, 8.44 with 46). The war against Aegina was Themistocles' ostensible reason; preparations for the Persian invasion had in fact begun, but the need to resist the invaders at sea may not yet have been clear, and the importance of Athens' ships at Artemisium and at Salamis in 480 may be good luck for his reputation rather than confirmation of his foresight.

1.15 Pheidon of Argos is said to have given his city a brief period of power, probably in the first half of the seventh century (Strabo 358/8.3.33, cf.

Hdt. 6.127). Sparta conquered neighbouring Messenia in the late eighth and seventh centuries, but in the mid-sixth century gave up the attempt to make further conquests and started building up the network of alliances which developed into what scholars call the Peloponnesian League (cf. note to 1.19 below). The war between Chalcis and Eretria is the so-called Lelantine War, fought for the control of a plain in Euboea between the two cities (Strabo 448/10.1.12), probably in the late eighth century; it did not spread to the rest of Greece as a unified war, but several local wars fought about that time fit into a pattern with friends of Chalcis on one side and friends of Eretria on the other.

1.16 For the strength of the Ionians, cf. what is said of Polycrates in 1.13. Croesus was king of Lydia, in western Asia Minor and bounded by the river Halys on the east, from *c*.560; after Cyrus' defeat of the Medes in 550/49 Croesus tried to expand into the gap, but he was defeated by Cyrus *c*.546. The islands close to the Asiatic mainland made token submission to Cyrus but did not seriously become his subjects; it is these islands which Dareius subjected in the early years of his reign.

1.17 Tyrants tended not to distinguish between what was their own and what was their state's, so in strengthening their family and its image they strengthened their state and its image too, and some states were strong when ruled by tyrants. In Sicily, Thucydides is thinking particularly of Gelo (ruling in Gela from 491/0 and in Syracuse 485/4–478/7) and his brother Hiero (ruling in Syracuse 478/7–467/6)—after the battle of Marathon, despite what is said in 1.18.

1.18 Spartan intervention led to the expulsion of Hippias from Athens in 511/0 (cf. 1.20, 6.53, 59), and that was probably the origin of the claim that Sparta had always been opposed to tyrants and had deposed tyrants throughout Greece (see e.g. the list, in which some items are more credible than others, in Plut., *Malice of Herodotus* 859 C–D). The best-attested instances earlier than 511/0 are in Sicyon in the 550s and in Naxos in the 520s or 510s. In fact, after expelling Hippias from Athens, *c*.504 the Spartans considered reinstating him but were dissuaded by Corinth (Hdt. 5.90–4). Probably in the sixth century they were not opposed to tyranny on principle but on some occasions their successes in foreign policy happened to result in the overthrow of a tyrant. On Sparta's internal affairs, Thucydides is alluding to a regime described as 'good order' (*eunomia*) and attributed to Lycurgus, which ancient writers assigned to the early eighth century or earlier still (we do not know what information or reasoning lies behind Thucydides' 'four hundred years') but most scholars now date to the early seventh century, after the first phase of the conquest of Messenia. This was a deal by which the aristocrats gave the Spartan citizens a defined position in the state (thus avoiding the risk of tyranny) in return for their support against the conquered peoples of Laconia and Messenia. The political and military organization of the citizens, and a first distribution of conquered land and Helots to work it, can be assigned to that occasion; there was an ongoing development after that, but by the fifth century the Spartans were proud of being different from other Greeks and in particular from the Athenians, and were attributing all their distinctive institutions to Lycurgus.

After Athens and Eretria had supported the Ionian Revolt against Persia in the 490s (Hdt. 5.28–6.42), the Persians invaded mainland Greece in 490, with Eretria and Athens as their main targets. Eretria was captured, but at Marathon the Persians were defeated by Athens (with help from Plataea; promised help from Sparta did not arrive until after the battle: Hdt. 6.94–124). The Persians returned in 480, with a force which Herodotus implausibly reckoned at over five million. Sparta as the strongest state in Greece was accepted as leader of the resistance; after an attempt to halt the Persians in central Greece, at Thermopylae and Artemisium, had failed, there was no hope of saving Athens, and the Athenians were persuaded by Themistocles to abandon their city and rely on their navy (cf. note to 1.14); the Persians were then defeated at sea at Salamis in 480 and on land at Plataea (and at Mycale in Asia Minor) in 479 (Hdt. 7–9). For developments after that, see 1.89–118.

1.19 After Athens had become self-consciously democratic, by the reforms of Ephialtes in 462/1, it took to imposing democracies on some states in its alliance, the Delian League, when they rebelled, and it came to be seen throughout the Greek world as a champion of democracy. Sparta, with a measure of equality among its unusually restricted citizen body, was not a typical oligarchy, but in reaction against Athens it came to be seen as a champion of oligarchy and encouraged oligarchy among its allies in the Peloponnesian League; but it did not often interfere in the members' internal affairs before the fourth century.

For Athens' gradual change from requiring ships to demanding the payment of tribute by its allies cf. 1.96, 99. After Athens' defeat of Samos in 440–439 (1.115–17) Chios and the cities of Lesbos were the only remaining ship-providing members of the Delian League; the cities of Lesbos, apart from Methymna, lost that status when they revolted against Athens in 428–427 (cf. 3.2–50). Between the Persian War and the Peloponnesian War Athens increased in citizen numbers, wealth, and power; in Sparta the earthquake of c.465/4 (cf. 1.101–3) in fact began a decline in citizen numbers which was never to be reversed. Nevertheless it is probable that the last sentence of this chapter refers to each side, not only to the Athenian side.

1.20 *Difficulty of getting history right.* Having completed his survey of the growth of power in Greece, Thucydides digresses to insist that he has investigated thoroughly and critically while other Greeks do not. What is said here of Harmodius and Aristogeiton is compatible with the longer account given in 6.53–9 (see notes there), and indeed what is said here is not wholly intelligible without information given only there (which suggests that what is said here was written at the same time as or later than what is said there). The opinion which he rejects as mistaken was not held by Herodotus, who believed as Thucydides does that Hippias was the eldest son of Peisistratus and was the reigning tyrant, and that the tyranny did not end until Hippias was expelled in 511/0 (5.55–65); but Hippias' expulsion was due to the Alcmaeonid family and to Sparta, and by the time of Thucydides many Athenians did not want to be grateful to the Alcmaeonidae or to Sparta and therefore put more emphasis on the killing of Hipparchus in 514.

The 'false beliefs' at the end of the chapter were held by Herodotus. Hdt. 6.57 says that if the kings (Sparta had not one king but two) are absent from the *gerousia* (the council of elders, comprising the two kings and twenty-eight men aged over sixty) the members most closely related to them 'take on their privileges and cast two votes for the kings they are representing and then one for themselves'—which does seem to be the view attacked here, though some scholars deny it; we have no other evidence on the matter. There is no doubt that Hdt. 9.53 refers to a 'Pitana division' at the battle of Plataea in 479. Pitana was one of the villages of Sparta (cf. note to 1.9–11), and the articulation of the citizen body after the Lycurgan reform was based in part on five 'obes' which seem to have corresponded to the five villages. It is usually thought either that there was a division in the Spartan army based on Pitana but that was not its official name, or that there was a Pitana division in 479 but not in Thucydides' time and Thucydides did not know that the army organization had been changed. The Roman emperor Caracalla, in an archaizing spirit, created a 'Pitana division' in his army: Hdn. 4.8.3.

1.21 *Previous wars not as great as Peloponnesian War.* 'Stories written more to please the ear' and 'the unreliable realms of romance' are to be contrasted with Thucydides' history (1.22). At this time texts were commonly made public by being read aloud, and it is stated that the Athenians made an award to Herodotus for reading out part of his history (Diyllus *FGrH* 73 F 3, from Plut., *Malice of Herodotus* 862 B; Eusebius under 446/5 in the Armenian version, under 445/4 according to Jerome).

1.22 *How Thucydides has written his history.* In a second digression, arising out of his criticism of other writers, Thucydides gives an account of his history. For discussion, see Introduction, pp. xxx–xxxvi; he proudly reiterates that he has taken the trouble to get the facts right, as others do not (on disagreements between witnesses, cf. 7.44, 71), and maintains that his history has been written not to give immediate pleasure but to be useful. Under the influence of the late-fifth-century intellectuals known as sophists (see also note to 1.76), he was very fond of contrasts such as that between word or surface appearance (*logos*) and deed or underlying reality (*ergon*) (cf. Introduction, p. xxxiv), and his starting this chapter with speeches (*logos*) and continuing with events (*erga*) is a particular application of that contrast.

1.23.1–3 *Greatness of Peloponnesian War.* In the first half of this chapter Thucydides ends this introduction by stating again that the Peloponnesian War was greater than any previous war, even the Persian War (his 'four battles' are Artemisium and Salamis in 480 at sea, Thermopylae in 480 and Plataea in 479 on land, with Mycale in 479 omitted as being in Asia Minor). His superlatives begin, reasonably enough, with captured cities, refugees, and slaughter. But he then writes of natural phenomena—earthquakes, eclipses, and droughts—as if it was because of the war that they were particularly frequent, whereas in his usual more sober moods he would have said that their frequency during the war was purely coincidental (cf. Introduction, p. xlv; in fact his history does not mention any droughts). On the plague which afflicted Athens between 430 and 426, see 2.47-54, 3.87.

1.23.4-146 Causes of the Peloponnesian War

1.23.4-6 *Grievances and disputes, real reason.* In the second half of this chapter Thucydides embarks on what will be the theme of the remainder of Book 1, the causes of the Peloponnesian War and the events leading up to the war. For the Thirty Years Treaty of 446/5, see 1.115. Thucydides distinguishes between grievances (*aitiai*) and disputes (*diaphorai*), which were openly proclaimed, and a real reason (*prophasis*), which was true (*alethestate*, the superlative 'truest') but unacknowledged. The difference lies not so much in the words chosen (in 1.118 *prophasis* is used of the grievances) as in the facts that the grievances were openly proclaimed while the alternative explanation was unacknowledged (except by Thucydides), and that he considered his alternative explanation to be the truest. The alternative is by no means absent from Book 1—from the Corcyraeans' warning to Athens that 'fear of your power is fuelling Spartan desire for war' (1.33) to the Spartans' final demand to Athens that 'there would be peace if [Athens] returned their independence to the Greeks' and Pericles' insistence that the grievances were merely pretexts (1.139-40). Presumably, as Aristophanes seems to reflect complaints in Athens that the war had been brought about by Pericles' intransigence over Megara (Ar., *Ach.* 514-38, *Pax* 605-18), other people in general tended to blame the war on one or another of the particular grievances, and Thucydides was insistent that he knew better. Although he refers to 'grievances on either side causing the breach of the treaty', his main grievances are the grievances of the Peloponnesians against Athens, and his real reason is the fear of Athens which compelled Sparta to go to war: technically, it was the Peloponnesians who started the war, and it suited Thucydides the Athenian to explain why the Peloponnesians went to war against Athens.

Although he considers the grievances less important, Thucydides' insistence that he knows better has led him to give his account of the grievances, in the (vain) hope that 'nobody in future will need to look for the immediate cause'. However, it is a problematic account, in which the episodes of Corcyra (1.24-55) and Potidaea (1.56-66) are reported in detail but the grievances of Aegina and Megara are mentioned only briefly (e.g. 1.67) in the remainder of the narrative. See Introduction, p. xiii-xv.

1.24-55 *Corcyra (435-433).* Corcyra was a colony of Corinth (cf. note to 1.13), which was topographically on the edge of the Greek world, and had kept outside the main stream of that world's history with its friendships and enmities and was not on good terms with Corinth. A quarrel between the two over their joint colony Epidamnus led to war; Corcyra was victorious at Leucimme in 435; but, when Corinth called on its allies for support in a further attack, in 433 Corcyra appealed to Athens for support. Hoping to avoid an open breach of the Thirty Years Treaty (since Corinth was a member of the Peloponnesian League), Athens granted Corcyra a purely defensive alliance, but at Sybota did have to intervene in defence of Corcyra. Thus Athens and Corinth fought against each other for the first time since the treaty.

1.24 Corcyra is the modern Kerkyra/Corfu, off the north-west coast of mainland Greece; Epidamnus is Durrës in Albania, *c.*125 miles (200 km) to the north. The Ionian Gulf, between north-western Greece and southeastern Italy, was named after the legendary wanderings of Io, driven mad by Hera after her seduction by Zeus, and has no connection with the Ionians. Though not consistent, Thucydides tends to supply geographical information on places at the edge of the Greek world but not on places at the heart of it.

Corcyra was founded *c.*733, and Epidamnus *c.*625 (so Corinth and Corcyra were not yet on bad terms then). Foundation narratives regularly involve a 'founder-colonist' (*oikistes*) as leader of the venture, and, although the foundation of a colony may often have been a less organized process than the narratives suggest, the involvement of such a leader need not be doubted. The details about Phalius are not necessary for the narrative: it has been observed that Thucydides often gives such details in the case of Corinth, and may have spent some time there during his exile (cf. Introduction, p. xxv).

'People' (*demos*) in Greek can be used either of the whole citizen body or, as here, of the lower class, or democratic party, as opposed to the upper class, or aristocratic or oligarchic party. The Epidamnian 'representatives' were envoys (*presbeis*), men sent to negotiate; these, when their attempt to negotiate failed, then became suppliants (*hiketai*), asking for divine protection and throwing themselves on the mercy of the Corcyraeans. Corcyra was itself fairly democratic at this time but contained a significant number of men with oligarchic sympathies (cf. the details in 3.69–85), and presumably the exiled oligarchs of Epidamnus had stronger links with Corcyra (cf. 1.26), or links with more influential Corcyraeans, than the democrats controlling the city.

1.25 In 'enquired of the god' Thucydides is uncritically using conventional language; this is not good evidence that he was after all a believer (see Introduction, p. xliv). It is more remarkable, perhaps an authentic reflection of what was said in Corinth, that he stresses a religious aspect of Corinth's hostility to Corcyra. Nothing in the *Odyssey* (books 6–8) suggests a location for fairy-tale Phaeacia, but the identification with Corcyra had become standard, and there was a sanctuary of Homer's king Alcinous there (3.70).

1.26 Ambracia and Leucas are between the Gulf of Corinth and Corcyra; Apollonia is between Corcyra and Epidamnus (the overland journey was difficult, and not attempted by the larger force of 1.27).

1.27 The 3,000 hoplites here become 2,000 in 1.29: probably the text is corrupt in one place or the other.

1.28 The Corcyraeans have in fact no 'present alliances' (cf. 1.31), but in this context it suits them to suggest that as colonists of Corinth they are friends of the Peloponnesians and enemies of Athens, whereas in Athens they will suggest that Corinth is an enemy of both Athens and Corcyra (e.g. 1.35). Arbitration provided an opportunity for point-scoring: a state could appear virtuous if it was willing to go to arbitration when its opponent was not, but it could minimize the risks if it objected to any suggested arbitrators likely to rule against it, and here each state wanted to dictate the position from which arbitration would be entered into.

1.29 Heralds (*kerykes*), in contrast to envoys (1.24), are men sent not to negotiate but to make a formal proclamation. In 'bracing' their old ships the Corcyraeans were fitting *hypozomata*, internal cables tying the bow to the stern: Morrison, Coates, and Rankov, *The Athenian Trireme*², 169–71, 196–8, 220–1. Epidamnus after its defeat by Corcyra drops out of the story.

1.30 A trophy (*tropaion*), literally a commemoration of the enemy's turning to flee, was a monument displaying spoils taken from a defeated enemy. Leucimme was one of the headlands at the south end of Corcyra; despite the apparent implication of 1.29, the battle was presumably fought there, not at Actium (50 miles, 80 km, to the south). For Cheimerium, see note to 1.46–7.

1.31–45 For the debate in Athens Thucydides gives a Corcyraean speech 1.32–6, a Corinthian speech 1.37–43, the Athenian decision 1.44–5.

1.32–6 The Corcyraeans begin with right (*dikaion*, 'just'), but since they have no existing relations with Athens they have to concentrate on benefit (*xymphora*), a prominent theme when Thucydidean speakers emphasize the realities of power. Their prediction of war between Athens and the Peloponnesians (1.33) is answered only weakly by the Corinthians (1.42) and is reaffirmed in Thucydides' narrative (1.44): Athens' decision to wind up the Acropolis building programme and devote surplus revenue to the dockyards and walls, probably in 434/3 (ML 58, translated Fornara 119), and its renewal of alliances with Rhegium and Leontini in the west, in 433/2 (ML 63–4, translated Fornara 124–5), confirm that this does not reflect Thucydidean hindsight but the Athenians did this early expect a war to which the west (1.36) would be relevant.

1.37–43 The Corinthians, using a common feature of second speeches, claim that, if the first speech had kept to the point, the second would do so too, but, since the first did not, the second is compelled (1.37) to answer the first. The Corinthians claim that right is on their side, but find it harder to argue that support for them will benefit Athens. Several of their points are far from cogent, and to this reader Corcyra seems to have the better of the argument. Corinth did maintain unusually close links with its colonies (though it was the general Greek understanding that a colony was an independent state), but note that at the end of this episode it had to capture Anactorium (1.55).

1.40 What is said about Samos is not repeated in the narrative of that episode (1.115–17), perhaps simply because Thucydides remembered that he had said it earlier. The cases were not in fact parallel: Samos was recognized in the Thirty Years Treaty as a member of the Athenian bloc, but Corcyra was not a member of either the Peloponnesian or the Athenian bloc and Corinth had no formal rights over it. If Sparta was indeed willing to support Samos in 440–439, that would have been a breach of the treaty, and Sparta (or some Spartans) will have been more actively hostile to Athens than the narrative of 433–432 suggests.

1.41 'The accepted Greek norms' are not formal agreements (though Thucydides uses *nomoi*, which in other contexts means 'laws') but the unformulated yet generally accepted principles on which the Greek states dealt with one another. For the twenty ships supplied to Athens, see note to 1.14.

1.42 The reference to Athens' treatment of Megara is probably an allusion not to the grievance which will first be mentioned in 1.67 but to Athens' taking Megara out of the Peloponnesian League between *c.*460 and 446 (1.103–15).

1.44 It seems to have been Athens' practice to spread major decisions over two days, with discussion on the first and the vote on the second. Here Thucydides is frustratingly reticent: we should like to know who favoured Corinth and who Corcyra, how many changed their minds and why; and very probably he had been present, and knew and could have told us. Probably, as claimed by Plutarch (*Per.* 29), Pericles was in favour of supporting Corcyra, and obtained what he wanted but not easily (cf. the note on Lacedaemonius in 1.45). In limiting themselves to a defensive alliance (Thucydides' verbal distinction between *xymmachia* = full alliance and *epimachia* = defensive alliance is not generally observed in Greek) the Athenians were adopting an interpretation of the Thirty Years Treaty by which they would not be in breach of the treaty if they fought only to defend the territory of Corcyra. Even this was not the decision of a state anxious to stay at peace: it would have suited Athens perfectly well if Corcyra and Corinth had weakened each other while Athens remained uninvolved (cf. the Corinthians in 1.40): see Introduction, p. xiv.

1.45 An inscription (ML 61, translated Fornara 126) records money taken by the generals named here from the treasury of Athena for this campaign at the beginning of 433/2. Lacedaemonius was a son of Pericles' opponent Cimon, with a name advertising the family's Spartan connections. Plutarch thinks Pericles had him appointed to this campaign to humiliate him (*Per.* 29); more probably, either Lacedaemonius (like Thucydides) had broken away from Cimon's political position or (more likely) he had not and his appointment is a sign that those opposed to the alliance were strong enough to get their man chosen as one of the commanders. Commanders did not necessarily approve of the campaigns on which they were sent: cf. Nicias and the Sicilian expedition of 415–413 (Books 6–7, with note to 6.17).

1.46–55 Thucydides proceeds to the Sybota campaign of 433.

1.46–7 The geographical detail is not all necessary for the narrative, and it is not clearly expressed. The harbour near Ephyre is the *Glykys Limen* ('sweet harbour') at the mouth of the Acheron; the Thyamis reaches the sea opposite central Corcyra; Cheimerium is the region between those two rivers in general, and the promontory near which the Corinthians camped is Varlam, at a latitude between the south of Corcyra and the island of Paxos. The Sybota islands are just off the mainland, opposite the southern end of Corcyra: this battle was fought in the same area as the battle of Leucimme in 435 (1.29–30).

1.48 Three days' provisions were taken because the Corinthians were not sure that they would return to their camp the same day: if victorious, they hoped to land on Corcyra.

1.49–50 The older style of naval warfare involved grappling and boarding, after which the soldiers would fight on the decks. The Athenians in the fifth century had developed manoeuvres to turn naval battles into sailors' battles at sea, such as breaking through the enemy lines and then turning sharply (*diekplous*: cf. note to 7.36–41), and Thucydides the Athenian regards the older style as unsophisticated. The Corcyraean left was successful against the Corinthian right, and sailed to the camp at Cheimerium (about 10 miles, 15 km, away), but on the Corcyraean right the Athenians eventually had to join in the fighting. The battle left the Corinthians in command of the water, and they collected wrecks and bodies at mainland Sybota, directly opposite the islands (triremes were often disabled in battle but could not easily be sunk: Morrison, Coates, and Rankov, *The Athenian Trireme*[2], 127–8).

1.50–1 There must have been a second debate in Athens, not reported by Thucydides, which resulted in the decision to send a further twenty ships (Hornblower). This time Thucydides names two generals, the inscription (ML 61, translated Fornara 126), with a date about three weeks later than the previous occasion, names three, and only one name appears in both texts. There have been ingenious attempts to save Thucydides' reputation, but the easiest explanation is that he has slipped here; Dracontides, named in the inscription, is known as an opponent of Pericles from the democratic end of the spectrum.

1.52–3 The Corinthians were afraid that the Athenians would consider the Thirty Years Treaty to be at an end and themselves now to be openly at war with Corinth, but the Athenians continued to insist on their interpretation, that they had committed themselves only to defending Corcyra and the treaty still held.

1.55 In 1.46 there was one ship from Anactorium (inside the Gulf of Ambracia) on the Corinthian side, perhaps sent by a pro-Corinthian minority. For Corinth's use of the prisoners from Corcyra, see 3.70 and note.

1.56–66 *Potidaea (433–432).* Potidaea was a colony of Corinth but a tribute-paying member of the Delian League. In this episode Athens put pressure on Potidaea, Potidaea obtained help from Corinth (which in its attempt not to break the Thirty Years Treaty sent not an official Corinthian force but volunteers and mercenaries), and in 432 there was a battle in which again Athenians fought against Corinthians. The Athenians then settled down to besiege Potidaea.

1.56 Potidaea was on the isthmus of Pallene, the western prong of Chalcidice in the north-west Aegean. Thucydides starts by suggesting that Athens acted against Potidaea because of its Corinthian connection after the episode of Corcyra, but he goes on to indicate that king Perdiccas of Macedonia was another cause of concern, and the record of tribute collected suggests that Athens had been putting pressure on Potidaea for some years. It is in fact surprising that until now Athens continued to allow Potidaea to receive officials from Corinth. The 'Thraceward' region is the term used by the Athenians to refer to the Greek states settled on and near the north coast of the Aegean.

1.57 Perdiccas II was king of Macedonia from the mid-fifth century to 413: during his reign he changed sides many times between Athens and Sparta (though he may have seen them as changing sides with regard to him); his father Alexander I was king in the early fifth century and played a part in the Persian Wars. Derdas was probably ruler of Elimeia, a part of Upper Macedonia south-west of the plain of Lower Macedonia. The Chalcidians here (Thucydides' use of the term is perhaps anticipatory) are not the inhabitants of Chalcidice as a whole but primarily those on the coast near Olynthus, north of the three prongs; and the Bottiaeans lived in that northern part of Chalcidice too, perhaps to the west of Olynthus (cf. 2.99).

For 'two' other generals the manuscripts have 'ten', but there were only ten Athenian generals altogether, and some were occupied elsewhere; and (as with the two expeditions to Corcyra (1.45, 51, with notes)) Athens often gave the command of an expedition to three generals. Archestratus was the commander who, for whatever reason, was most prominent in Thucydides' mind, but he was not, and Thucydides' expression does not imply that he was, officially superior to his colleagues.

1.58 There had been earlier occasions when attacks on Attica were made or contemplated to distract Athens from another campaign (1.101, 109, 114; cf. 1.105): on this occasion Sparta's promise was not fulfilled until the beginning of the Peloponnesian War in 431 (2.14–23). The negotiations took place in the winter of 433/2, and the campaigning belongs to 432. Olynthus, not previously a large or important city, was about 7 miles (11 km) north of Potidaea (cf. 1.63), and the Chalcidians who took part in this synoecism (cf. note to 1.5: Thucydides here uses *anoikizein*, particularly appropriate for moving inland) were from cities in the vicinity of Olynthus, including the northern part of Sithone, the middle prong; lake Bolbe, where they were given farmland, is some distance further north. The enlarged city tends to be referred to as Olynthus in literary texts but as the Chalcidians in its own documents.

1.60 In the case of Corcyra, the Athenians limited themselves to a defensive alliance so that they could claim they were not breaking the Thirty Years Treaty (see 1.45); here under the treaty Athens was entitled to coerce Potidaea, and to keep their hands clean the Corinthians sent volunteers and mercenaries, not an official force of the Corinthian state. Aristeus is not the Aristeus sent to Corcyra in 1.29.

1.61 Callias, the general uppermost in Thucydides' mind (cf. Archestratus in 1.57), may be identified with the proposer of the financial decrees of 434/3 (or at any rate the first of them) and the renewed alliances with Rhegium and Leontini of 433/2 (cf. note to 1.32–6). The Athenians' route is problematic. Therme is at the north-east corner of the Thermaic Gulf (Thessalonica), and Pydna is on the west side. Beroea is inland, to the west of Pydna, but to go there would not be to leave Macedonia, and to go via there to Strepsa (the result of an emendation: probably south-east of Therme though some place it north-west) would be strange (Gomme; contr. Hornblower). Gigonus was on the coast north-west of Potidaea. Some have thought that there was another Beroea, or that Beroea is a copyist's error for Brea, an unlocated place to which Athens had sent settlers in the 440s or 430s (ML 49, translated Fornara 100); the problem remains unsolved. Pausanias was perhaps a brother of Derdas (1.57).

1.62 If the mention of Iolaus is to make sense, it must mean that he commanded at Potidaea as deputy for Perdiccas (Hornblower; contr. Gomme). The battle is the one in which Socrates saved the life of Alcibiades: Pl., *Chrm.* 153 A–C, *Symp.* 219 E–220 E; Alcibiades was to return the compliment at Delium (see note to 4.96).

1.63 Thucydides gives the distance from Olynthus to Potidaea as 60 stades, implying a stade of 202 yards (185 m), comfortably within his normal range (see Appendix). Gomme points out that, although Potidaea was visible from Olynthus, the road taken by the Athenians from Gigonus to Potidaea was not. The signals will have been raised to indicate that the battle was beginning and the reserve should come from Olynthus to support Aristeus (1.62).

1.64 The Athenians built a wall in order to blockade Potidaea. This is what a 'siege' normally amounted to in the fifth century; in their siege of Plataea, 429–427, the Spartans combined a blockade with the latest in military technology (2.71–8; cf. 3.20–4). Potidaea had its own wall on the south side of the city, and had refused Athenian demands to demolish it (1.56).

1.66 That Corinth had been acting *idiai* could mean either that it had been 'acting alone', independently of the Peloponnesian League as a whole (Hornblower) or that it had been 'acting privately', using simply volunteers and mercenaries, not officially (Gomme); but the second is the better explanation of why this 'was not yet the outbreak of the war, and they were still in a state of truce' (contrast the Theban attack on Plataea in 431, which Thucydides does treat as the beginning of the war: 2.2–6).

1.67–88 *First meeting in Sparta (432).* In an elaborate piece of scene-setting Thucydides gives us a Corinthian speech (1.68–71); a response by Athenians 'come there on other business' (1.73–8); and then, with foreigners removed from the assembly, a speech by king Archidamus advising caution (1.80–5) and a speech by the ephor Sthenelaïdas demanding immediate action (1.86). The vote is in favour of immediate action, and the Spartans then summon a formal congress of the Peloponnesian League.

1.67 Corinth takes the lead, both as the strongest and most independent-minded of Sparta's allies and as the one which, over Corcyra and Potidaea, has come into direct conflict with Athens. Aegina had been a member of the Delian League since it was subdued by Athens *c.*457 (1.108): Thucydides gives no more information than this about its complaint, and does not make it clear whether autonomy was allegedly promised in the Thirty Years Treaty or in a bilateral treaty; cf. Introduction, p. xiv. Megara had been an ally of Athens between *c.*460 and 446 (1.103, 114–15): Thucydides does not give much further information about its complaint (1.139 adds a little), but clearly much was made of it at the time (cf. 1.139, 140).

1.68–71 The Corinthian speech introduces the contrast between Spartan slowness and conservatism and Athenian energy and innovation which is to pervade Thucydides' history, and the description of Athens in 1.70 fits well with the speeches of Pericles. If the Spartans had indeed wanted to support Samos in 440 (cf. 1.40), they, or some of them, were not as reluctant to confront Athens as the Corinthians here allege. On Athens' fortification, see 1.89–93 (Sparta wanted to prevent it but was outwitted), and on the Long Walls, see 1.107. Against the Persians Sparta sent only a small force to Thermopylae in 480, but probably in a genuine belief that that would suffice until reinforcements could follow (Hdt. 7.198–239); to say that Xerxes' failure was due to his own mistakes is distinctly one-sided. For the promise to Potidaea, see 1.58. The threat to look for alternative allies must, as noted by an ancient commentator, envisage Argos, which was neutral to 421 and allied with Corinth for a while after that (cf. 5.14, 27–32).

1.72–8 We do not know what the Athenians' 'other business' was. Thucydides gives them a speech in which, as he states, they do not defend themselves against accusations but justify and indeed flaunt their power: deterrent in the sense that they warn Sparta against attacking Athens. The contrast between older and younger is a frequent motif. On Athens' contribution to the Persian Wars, see 1.18; according to Herodotus, Athens provided 200 out of 378 ships in 480 (8.1, with 8.14, 48; cf. 8.82); on Themistocles, cf. Hdt. 8.40–96 (evacuation of Athens and Salamis), 8.123–5 (in Sparta).

1.75–7 This gives us the first account in a speech of Athens' empire; here as elsewhere speakers unashamedly use the language of political realism (despite 'later', the sequence 'fear–prestige–our own interests' may be logical rather than chronological). For Athens' becoming leader after 479, see 1.94–5; for Athens' unpopularity, see 1.98–9; for the ending of the good relationship between Athens and Sparta, see 1.101–2. On Sparta and the Peloponnesians, see 1.19; after the Peloponnesian War Sparta did in fact become more interfering and unpopular, but it is not impossible that what is said in 1.76–7 could have been written by Thucydides, and indeed said by Athenian speakers, long before then.

1.76 For 'the natural instinct' Thucydides uses the word *physis*, a favourite word of the sophists (see note to 1.22), who in various ways contrasted *physis*, 'nature', which cannot be other than it is, with *nomos*, in the sense of 'convention', what has been decided by some human beings in their own interests and could have been decided otherwise by others. Pausanias in and after 478 provides an example of the misbehaviour of Spartans abroad (1.94–5, 128–34).

Another theme of 1.76–7 is the Athenians' use of their law courts. They do seem to have been exceptionally given to litigation; like other Greek states they made treaties regulating the trial of lawsuits between citizens of their state and of other states, and one way in which they exercised their power in the Delian League was by transferring major lawsuits from local courts to Athenian courts, which would be more likely to favour Athenians against allies and to favour supporters of Athens among the allies. The point at the beginning of 1.77 seems to be not that because they were at a disadvantage when treaty cases were tried in allied courts they have transferred such cases to Athens (Gomme, Hornblower) but (*a*) that in treaty cases the Athenians submit to the disadvantage of trials in the other state where that is what the treaty requires, rather than having all such cases tried in their own courts, (*b*) that some local cases have been transferred to Athenian courts (which for the purposes of this speech are deemed to be impartial); and that by indulging in both of these practices rather than simply imposing their own will they have gained a reputation for addiction to litigation (thus R. Meiggs, *The Athenian Empire* (Oxford University Press, 1972), 228–33).

1.78 'The incalculable element' and 'chance' are important for Thucydides (cf. Introduction, pp. xliii–xliv): his history unlike Herodotus' involves no divine plan, but there are occurrences, such as the plague at Athens (cf. 2.61), which cannot be predicted and provided for.

1.79–85 The first Spartan speech is by Archidamus. His father had died young, and he had himself been king (see 1.20) since perhaps *c*.469. On Athens' resources, see 2.13. The Spartans do indeed invade Attica in the early years of the war (e.g. 2.18–23, in 431), and the Athenians do indeed avoid a major battle with the invaders and rely on their sea power for survival (cf. Pericles in 1.143, 2.13: we may wonder how far Archidamus could have foreseen that); the Spartans' earliest attempt to support a revolt against Athens in the Aegean was a failure (Mytilene in 428–427, 3.2–50); Pericles in his first speech comments on their financial weakness (1.142–3).

1.82 The mention here of 'further allies, Greek or barbarian' is the first pointer to the involvement of the Persians, for the past half-century the national enemy, in the war (see 2.7): for Sparta, Persia offered the best hope of redressing the financial imbalance, and did in and after 412 provide support (see Book 8); Athens needed at least to prevent Persia from helping Sparta, did make a treaty of some kind c.423 (see note to 4.50), and from 411 to 407 hoped in vain that Persian help might be diverted from Sparta to Athens (see notes to 8.47, 76).

1.84 This chapter gives a Spartan view of the contrast between Sparta and Athens: Sparta is brave, disciplined, and not too clever for its own good.

1.86 Sthenelaïdas' speech has a truly laconic flavour, and one would like to think that this reflects the speech actually made by him (though no non-Spartan will have heard it: 1.79). The ephors, first reliably attested in the mid-sixth century, were five annually elected officials to whom, while they did not abolish the kings, the Spartans had transferred many of the civilian powers of the kings: in particular, they sat with the *gerousia* (see note to 1.20) and presided in the *gerousia* and the assembly. Deciding by acclamation (regarded as childish by Arist., *Pol.* 2. 1270 B–1271 A; for a description of the procedure see Plut., *Lyc.* 26) was probably a survival from an era before the Greeks had taken to counting votes. In constructing a 'constitution' of the Peloponnesian League, de Ste. Croix (*Origins of the Peloponnesian War*, 105–23; cf. 339–30) was probably more systematic than the Spartans themselves; but at the end of the sixth century (Hdt. 5.90–3; contr. 5.74–5) it became an accepted principle that if the Spartans required military support from their allies their own decision had to be endorsed by a congress of the allies.

1.87 The 'fourteenth year' is 433/2, the treaty having been made in 446/5; the war proper will begin in the fifteenth year, 432/1 (2.2). Here Thucydides is probably reckoning not by the seasonal years which he uses for his narrative of the war (2.2) but by Athenian official years.

1.88 Thucydides ends this section by repeating his 'real reason' from 1.23.

1.89–118 *'Pentecontaetia': growth of Athenian power, to justify Thucydides' real reason.* Thucydides writes of 'roughly fifty years' in 1.118, and the term *pentecontaetia* for this period of not quite fifty years is used by an ancient commentator on 1.97. This excursus is intended to show how the Athenians became so powerful as to make Sparta afraid. It is not a history of the Delian League, and we may assume that the League engaged in a good deal of activity against the Persians which Thucydides has not mentioned; but even on its own terms it is unsatisfactory, in that Thucydides does not mention the abandonment of regular warfare against Persia but continuation of the League, c.450 (see note to 1.111–12), and after the Thirty Years Treaty of 446/5 (1.115) he mentions only (but at

length) the war of 440-439 against Samos (1.115-17), and does not
explain here (though he mentions elsewhere some items which help us
to explain) why it was that by 432 Sparta was no longer happy with the
balance which that treaty tried to establish.

Our other main sources for this period are Diod. Sic. 11.39-12.28
(with the events of 435-432, which he misdates, in 12.30-4, 38-41) and
Plutarch's Lives, particularly *Cimon* and *Pericles*: for the most part they
give differing and additional details for episodes which Thucydides mentions, rather than episodes which he does not mention. From the 450s the
Athenians took to inscribing decrees of the assembly and other public
documents on stone in exceptionally large quantities, and these give us
information particularly on the Delian League of a kind which we do not
find in the literary texts.

1.89 The siege of Sestos is included by Herodotus as the last episode in the
war of 480-479 (9.114-21), and it is included here by Thucydides
because it is the first Greek campaign undertaken under Athenian rather
than Spartan leadership. In 479 Leotychidas had commanded at sea and
at the battle of Mycale while Pausanias had commanded on the Greek
mainland and at the battle of Plataea. Leotychidas will not be mentioned
again by Thucydides, but probably in 478 when Pausanias commanded
in the Aegean he campaigned against those in northern Greece who had
supported Persia, and is said to have been flagrantly guilty of taking
bribes in Thessaly (Hdt. 6.72).

1.89-93 The story of Themistocles, Sparta, and the rebuilding of Athens'
walls became notorious, and is repeated in Plut., *Them.* 19, and other
texts. It is one of a number of stories in which, though honoured in
Sparta in 480/79 like no other foreigner (1.74), after the Persian Wars
Themistocles turned against Sparta while his opponent Cimon was
strongly pro-Spartan (see note to 1.101-3). One of Themistocles' fellow
envoys to Sparta in this story (1.91), and a confidant of his in other
stories, is Aristeides, the original organizer of the Delian League (see
notes to 1.96-7, 5.18): the main tradition represents the two as rivals (e.g.
Ath. Pol. 28.2), but after 479 they are better seen as on the same side,
against Cimon (*Ath. Pol.* 23.3-4 tries to reconcile the two views).
Habronichus had been with the Greek army at Thermopylae in 480 and
reported what happened there to the navy at Artemisium (Hdt. 8.21).

As in his 'archaeology' (1.8, 10), in 1.93 Thucydides cites archaeological evidence to confirm that the rebuilding was done in haste; but,
while there are indeed pieces of sculpture built into the wall, Thucydides
may give an exaggerated impression: see Hornblower and the works
which he cites.

1.93 On the Peiraeus, see again Plut., *Them.* 19. Some scholars, over-impressed
by Hdt. 7.143 on Themistocles' recent prominence, have doubted either
that the office mentioned is his archonship or that his archonship was in
493/2 (Dion. Hal., *Ant. Rom.* 6.34.1), but mistakenly. Athens could not
rely on the Peiraeus until it was securely in possession of Salamis (late

sixth century: ML 14, translated Fornara 44. B), but the intermittent war against Aegina which began c.505 (Hdt. 5.79–89) will have shown the need for a more secure harbour than the bay of Phalerum: cf. Hornblower. In his emphasis on sea rather than land power Themistocles is represented as foreshadowing Pericles: see note to 1.143. Most of what survives is of the wall as rebuilt in the 390s, and that at least does not support Thucydides' claim that the wall was of solid stone throughout (Gomme).

1.94–5 Pausanias had commanded at Plataea in 479: he was regent for his cousin Pleistarchus (see 1.132). The story of his downfall will be told in 1.128–34. Here as there Thucydides is convinced of Pausanias' guilt where it can never have been proved: presumably the information came from sources in Sparta which he considered reliable. Cyprus had been in contact with Greece in the bronze age; in the classical period some of its inhabitants were Greek or at any rate thought of themselves as Greek, and when the Greeks were aggressive against Persia they tried to claim Cyprus for the Greek world. Byzantium was on the European side of the Bosporus, and would be important to the Persians if they tried to return to Europe.

It is important to Thucydides that, although it developed into an Athenian empire, the Delian League began innocently, and so for him it was the allies who invited Athens to take the lead and who refused to accept Dorcis. Herodotus (8.3) and *Ath. Pol.* 23.4 point to an Athenian initiative; at any rate the Athenians could not have become leaders without willingness on both sides. Also, for Thucydides, the Spartans 'wanted to be rid of . . . the Persian war'; but for *Ath. Pol.* 23.2 they were reluctant to give up the lead and Diod. Sic. 11.50 suspiciously has a debate which unexpectedly led to a decision not to challenge Athens. Sparta had other worries at this time, and although there were no doubt some who thought otherwise Thucydides probably reports the majority view correctly. For the narrow and broad senses of 'Ionian' see note to 1.2–3. Not all the members of the Delian League, even at its foundation, were Ionian in the narrow sense, but considerations of kinship were often invoked in interstate affairs, and it suited Ionian Athens to represent the league which it led as an Ionian league.

1.96–7 Thucydides' account of what, because of its original headquarters, scholars call the Delian League is full of problems. The organization was in fact done by Aristeides (5.18, *Ath. Pol.* 23.3–5), though he is not mentioned in connection with the League subsequently. The 'ostensible purpose' is puzzlingly limited: many members (especially Aegean islanders) had not suffered from the Persians, elsewhere Thucydides refers to the liberation of Greeks still under Persian rule (3.10), it must have seemed likely that the Persians would return and desirable to guard against that, and *Ath. Pol.* 23.5 has a full and permanent offensive and defensive alliance. In view of the emphasis on innocent beginnings, 'ostensible purpose' is presumably contrasted with what became of the League later rather than with concealed sinister intentions at the time.

It need not be doubted that the Treasurers to the Greeks were Athenian from the start: providing them, like providing military commanders, was part of Athens' function as leader. The levying of regular contributions was something new in a Greek alliance: 460 talents is a surprisingly large figure for the tribute at the start, even if it includes a cash equivalent for ships: I have suggested that it comes from an optimistic assessment list for those who joined or were expected to join (Rhodes, *The Athenian Empire*, Greece & Rome: New Surveys in the Classics, 17 (Oxford University Press, 1985; reissued with addenda, 1993), 7–8; cf. note to 2.13). The treasury 'was' Delos, a major Ionian sanctuary, and was moved to Athens in 454/3 (the first of the 'Athenian tribute lists', *IG* i³ 259, is the list for spring 453); meetings (in which Athens probably had one vote like each of the allies: cf. note to 3.10–11) 'took place' there, and were probably discontinued when the treasury was moved (later we find decisions taken only by Athens). That the allies were 'autonomous' (a word perhaps coined to refer to that degree of independence which they hoped to retain in a league under a leader) was probably taken for granted rather than spelled out: there had not yet been a Greek alliance whose members were not autonomous.

1.97 This is the only place where Thucydides names another historian: Hellanicus of Lesbos, an older contemporary, whose *Atthis (History of Athens)* was the first of a series of such works. From that we have only fragments quoted by other writers, but it is sadly just as true of Thucydides' own account of this period that 'his treatment is brief and the chronology is imprecise' (Thucydides is not necessarily claiming that Hellanicus' chronology was 'inaccurate', i.e. wrong: cf. 5.20, where he uses the same term).

1.98–100 Eïon on the Thracian coast was important as a surviving outpost of Persian power in Europe (we learn from Plut., *Cim.* 7 that it was taken over and settled by the Athenians); its capture was perhaps in 476. Scyros, in the northern Aegean, was irrelevant to an anti-Persian league, but it lies on the vital route from the Hellespont to Athens (and we learn from Plut., *Thes.* 36 and *Cim.* 8, that Cimon brought back to Athens what was said to be the skeleton of the legendary hero Theseus); its capture was perhaps in 475. Carystus had been sacked by the Persians in 490, and therefore supported them in 480 (Hdt. 6.99, 8.66, 112, 121; 9.105 mentions this episode): coercing it could be justified as punishing a Persian sympathizer, but it too lies near the route from the Hellespont to Athens. We are not told why Naxos revolted or in what ways it lost its freedom, but what happened to Thasos (1.101) indicates the likely nature of the settlement: this is mentioned as the first use of force against an existing member.

1.99 Naxos leads to Thucydides' comment on revolts and their suppression. The Athenians were taking a permanent alliance to mean permanent warfare, which the allies had probably not envisaged when they joined the League and which imposed a heavy burden on their manpower if they contributed their own ships and crews: paying tribute in cash was less troublesome but made the allies less able to dissent from Athenian policy or to resist Athenian action against them.

1.100 The Eurymedon enters the sea by the south coast of Asia Minor, not far to the west of Cyprus. It is possible that the Persians were assembling forces there with a view to trying to return to Greece; the Athenians must have felt secure in the Aegean to risk going so far from it. This battle is perhaps to be dated 469, in which case the episodes of Carystus and Naxos will fall in the second half of the 470s.

1.100–1 The revolt of Thasos can be dated fairly securely 465/4–463/2, and this time we are given a reason: Athenian covetousness; this is the clearest instance yet of the Athenians' using the League in pursuance of their own interests. Other island states had possessions on the adjacent mainland, and we may wonder how the Athenians justified their position to the allies. Nine Ways, a short distance inland from Eïon, they had attempted to occupy after taking Eïon; they colonized it as Amphipolis in 437/6 (4.102).

An unfulfilled Spartan promise to distract Athens by invading Attica, when the Athenians were still led by the pro-Spartan Cimon and Sparta was to ask for Athenian help shortly afterwards (1.103), is suspicious: more probably this was invented when Athens and Sparta had become enemies and some Spartans asked why the rise of Athens had not been halted before it was too late.

1.101–3 The earthquake killed a large number of Spartan citizens, and began a decline which was never reversed. In addition to the full citizens, the population of Laconia and Messenia included Perioeci ('dwellers around', men free to run the affairs of their own communities but subject to Sparta in foreign policy) and Helots (a word which probably means 'captives', serfs who farmed the land for its citizen owners). Thuria was certainly and Aethaea presumably in Messenia: this was essentially a revolt of the Messenians against Sparta (and was reckoned as Sparta's Third Messenian War). We learn from Plut., *Cim.* 16 that the Athenians were divided, with the pro-Spartan Cimon (who had given the name Lacedaemonius to one of his sons: 1.45) wanting to help Sparta and Ephialtes not. Cimon took 4,000 hoplites (Ar., *Lys.* 1137–44). It was probably while they were in Messenia that in 462/1 Ephialtes got the upper hand in Athens and carried out his democratic reform (*Ath. Pol.* 25.1–2), and it was probably in reaction to this that the Spartans distrusted the Athenian soldiers, fearing that they might be ordered to change sides, and dismissed them. On returning to Athens Cimon tried to reverse the reform but, by the procedure which enabled the Athenians to send a man into honourable exile for ten years, was ostracized (Plut., *Cim.* 17). The alliance by virtue of which the Athenians had been appealed to and which they then renounced was that made in 481 by the Greeks intending to resist the Persian invasion, still considered to be in force despite the foundation of the Delian League. Argos was the one Peloponnesian state which never acknowledged Spartan superiority; Thessaly was hostile to Sparta as a result of Leotychidas' punitive expedition after the Persian Wars (see note to 1.89).

This episode has given rise to chronological difficulties. If in this excursus Thucydides mentioned each single event in correct chronological sequence, there is not room for a ten-year war between what he mentions before and what he mentions after, so it used to be fashionable to emend the 'tenth' year in 1.103 to a lower figure. But Thucydides need not have mentioned each event in correct sequence. Diod. Sic. (11.63-4) narrates the whole war under 469/8 and in 11.84 briefly mentions its end under 456/5, while giving a duration of ten years; Philochorus (*FGrH* 328 F 117, translated Fornara 67. A) put the earthquake and the war under 468/7, but Pausanias (4.24.5, translated Fornara 67. C) put them under 464/3. Most probably Thucydides has mentioned the earthquake and the beginning of the war in the chronologically correct place, and for tidiness' sake has told the whole story as one unit: this will yield a war from 465/4 to 456/5, with a suitable ending date for Athens to be able to settle the refugees in Naupactus, after Tolmides' campaign in 1.108 (cf. Introduction, p. xxvii).

1.103, 105-8 Thucydides now interweaves two narratives spanning *c.*460-455. Athens' breach with Sparta led to the beginning of the First Peloponnesian War, in which the Athenians began to extend their power on the Greek mainland. It started when Megara, on the Isthmus of Corinth, defected from the Peloponnesian League to Athens; and (while Sparta was still engaged in the Messenian War) Megara's enemy Corinth led the opposition to Athens. Aegina, in the middle of the Saronic Gulf, had been at war with Athens between *c.*505 and 483/2 (see note to 1.14), and Athens as a naval power was not going to tolerate a hostile island so near.

Long walls, built first for Megara (1.103) and afterwards (but probably planned if not actually started earlier) for Athens, joined an inland city to its harbour town in a single fortified area, which was safe against an enemy's blockade as long as it remained in control of access by sea. In the 440s the Athenians built for themselves a third Long Wall, parallel to and a short distance south-east of the original Peiraeus wall (Andoc. 3. *Peace* 7, Aeschin. 2. *Embassy* 174, cf. Pl., *Grg.* 455 E, Plut., *Per.* 13).

The Phocians' attack on neighbouring Doris (1.107), which the Dorians of the Peloponnese believed to be their original homeland (the Spartans perhaps shared with Doris one of the two Dorian votes in the Delphic Amphictyony), did elicit action by Sparta. Pleistarchus (see note to 1.94-5) had died without leaving a son; his successor was Pleistoanax, and the regent Nicomedes was Pausanias' brother. By possessing Megara, and its harbour on the Gulf of Corinth, Pegae, the Athenians were able to threaten the Spartans' return both by land and by sea (Thucydides regularly calls the inner part of the Gulf, east of Rhium and Antirrhium, the Gulf of Crisa). It is hard to be sure how serious the internal threat to Athens was, but Ephialtes was murdered after his reform (*Ath. Pol.* 25.4); Plutarch (*Cim.* 17, *Per.* 10) has a story that the ostracized Cimon tried to

rejoin the Athenians at Tanagra; he was rejected, but his friends, to disprove accusations of Spartan sympathies, fought exceptionally boldly and
were killed. Opuntian Locris (1.108) is northern Locris, east of Thermopylae.
Tolmides' campaign attacked the Spartans' harbour town of Gytheium;
Chalcis was just outside the narrowest part of the Gulf of Corinth, on the
north side; it was probably in this campaign that the Athenians captured
Naupactus, just inside, on the north side (cf. 1.103).

Thucydides' only chronological indications are that Oenophyta was
fought on the sixty-second day after Tanagra (1.108) and that the Egyptian
war fought at the same time as this lasted six years (1.110). An inscribed
Athenian casualty list commemorates men who died in Cyprus, Egypt,
Phoenicia, Halieis, Aegina, and Megara in the same year (ML 33, extracts
translated Fornara 78). The year is perhaps a campaigning year, rather
than an official year beginning in mid-summer; it is apparently the first
year of both wars, and is likely to be 460 or 459. Tanagra and Oenophyta
are perhaps to be dated 457, and Tolmides' campaign 456.

1.104, 109–10 While in the 450s the Athenians set about increasing their
power in mainland Greece, they did not abandon the war against the
Persians. For Cyprus, cf. 1.94. Egypt was a part of the Greek world in
the sense that there had been Greek mercenaries and traders there since
the seventh century; from now until the end of the Persian empire it
would frequently be in revolt against Persia, and it was seen as another
place in which the Greeks could stand up to the Persians. The casualty
list mentioned above reveals, as Thucydides does not, that at least at the
beginning of this war the Athenians were also active on the coast of
Phoenicia.

Persia did not keep large forces in the provinces, but in time could
move large forces to where they were needed, and so like other revolts
this one began promisingly but ended in failure. The attempt to pay the
Spartans to attack Athens is the first attested instance of what was to be
a favourite Persian way of interfering in Greek affairs (but Hdt. 9.2, 41,
mentions it as a possibility in the context of 479). Memphis was a short
distance upstream from the apex of the Nile delta, Prosopitis (1.109) was
in the south-west part of the delta.

The end will have come in 455 or 454. Thucydides gives the impression that all 200 ships of the original force (1.104) and some of the ships
in the relief expedition (1.110) were lost, with a corresponding number
of men (not all Athenian). Those who find it hard to believe in so large a
disaster so briefly mentioned have used the 40 ships of Ctesias (FGrH
688 F 14 §36 [32], translated Fornara 72) to support the argument that the
Greek force was much smaller, either throughout the war or after the
beginning; but it is not clear that Thucydides is wrong. Amyrtaeus appealed
to Athens again in 451 (1.112); and a gift of corn by Psammetichus in
445/4 (Philoch. FGrH 328 F 119, Plut., Per. 37) was perhaps an unsuccessful attempt to gain Athenian support for a further rising. The moving
of the Delian League's treasury to Athens in 454/3 (see note to 1.96–7)
was perhaps prompted by fear of a Persian resurgence in the Aegean.

1.111-12 In campaigns of 454 Athens' expansion loses its momentum: the one success, against Sicyon, like Tolmides' earlier success there (1.108) seems to have had no consequence. This is the earliest mention of Pericles, both chronologically and in the sequence of Thucydides' history: it is low-key, in the same style as the other mentions of commanders between 478 and 446.

The five-year treaty (1.112) probably belongs to early 451 (so it will have expired when the fighting of 446 took place: 1.114); at the same time a thirty-year treaty was made between Argos and Sparta (5.14). If Cimon was ostracized in 461, and stories of his early recall (Plut., *Cim.* 17-18, *Per.* 10) are untrue, he will have returned to Athens in 451, and the treaty with the Peloponnesians, as well as the campaign in Cyprus in which he was killed, will reflect his influence.

The 'Athenian tribute lists' and other Athenian inscriptions show us that in the late 450s and early 440s Athens had trouble with some members of the Delian League, who in at least one case seem to have had the support of Persia (Erythrae, on the mainland of Asia Minor opposite Chios: ML 40, translated Fornara 71). Thucydides does not mention that; more seriously, he does not mention that the regular fighting against Persia for which the League was founded came to an end after Cimon's death. A majority of scholars believe that it was formally ended by a treaty, the Peace of Callias, known to everybody from the fourth century onwards but not mentioned in any fifth-century text (unless Hdt. 7.151 is an oblique allusion to it). I am among those who think that the treaty was invented in the fourth century to make more vivid the contrast between the shameful King's Peace of 387/6, by which the Asiatic Greeks were returned to Persia, and the glorious past—but it still seems to be true that the war ended. Yet the Delian League was kept in being, for Athens' own purposes, and this transformation ought to have been mentioned in an account of the growth of Athens' power.

Three bodies had a particular interest in Delphi and its sanctuary of Apollo: the city of Delphi; the Phocians, in whose territory it lay; and the Amphictyony (league of neighbours), a body of mostly central-Greek peoples dominated by the Thessalians, which had gained control of the sanctuary through the First Sacred War at the beginning of the sixth century. Athens seems to have given control of the sanctuary to the Phocians after Oenophyta, while making some kind of agreement with the Amphictyony (*IG* i³ 9, translated Fornara 82). In this Second Sacred War Sparta gave the sanctuary to the city of Delphi and Athens gave it back to the Phocians; since they did not fight directly against each other, they could claim that their five-year treaty was not broken. Plutarch (*Per.* 21) says that Pericles commanded the Athenians; Philoch. *FGrH* 328 F 34. b puts the Athenian response 'in the third year', which could be right.

1.113-15 The revolt of Boeotia was in late 447 or early 446, that of Euboea and Megara in 446. Pleistoanax (cf. 1.107), invading after the expiry of the five-year treaty (1.112), turned back after ravaging the part of Attica nearest to the Megarid, presumably because he had been given assurances that the Athenians would come to terms. But it was believed that Pericles had bribed him, both by Spartans who thought he should have gone on to attack Athens, and by Athenians who saw no cause for shame in bribery which was in Athens' interests (Ar., *Nub.* 859 with schol., translated Fornara 104; Plut., *Per.* 23), and Pleistoanax was exiled (cf. 2.21, 5.16). In Euboea (1.114) the Hestiaeans, in the north, were singled out for harsh treatment because they had killed the crew of an Athenian ship (Plut., *Per.* 23).

The Thirty Years Treaty was made in 446/5: Athens gave up its mainland acquisitions, so that superficially Sparta seemed in the end to have put a stop to the growth of Athens' power; but in return the division of the Greek world into a Spartan bloc based on the mainland and an Athenian bloc based on the Aegean was recognized (cf. 1.31), and the following years were to show that the Athenians' desire to expand had not been curbed (cf. Introduction, p. xiii).

1.115–17 Miletus was on the coast of Asia Minor, a little to the south of the adjacent island of Samos, Priene was to the north of Miletus, and Miletus and Samos had clashed over Priene before. Nothing is known of the involvement of distant Byzantium in this episode beyond what Thucydides says. The war began in 441/o and continued into 440/39. Samos was still a ship-providing member of the Delian League (see notes to 1.19, 99), and Athens had continued to tolerate an oligarchy there (probably Athens insisted on a democracy not only at the point mentioned by Thucydides but also after the war). If there was a Peace of Callias between Athens and Persia, the Persians were breaking it by supporting Samos; and, if the Spartans had persuaded the Peloponnesian League to support Samos (see note to 1.40), they would have broken the Thirty Years Treaty. It is perhaps because of Persia's involvement, to show that they would still take action when necessary, as well as because the Samians challenged Athens very effectively (cf. 8.76), that the Athenians intervened here on such a large scale. The Thucydides of 1.117 was neither the historian nor his (probable) grandfather Thucydides the son of Melesias, who had been ostracized. Hagnon and Phormio were both major figures, and Hagnon's son Theramenes will play a major role in Book 8. After the war, it is not clear what the Samians' obligations were once their reparations had been paid, but they were not assessed for tribute in the regular manner.

Important as the episode may be, it is striking that Thucydides narrates it in more detail than the other episodes in the excursus, and that he does not include in this excursus any other episodes after the Thirty Years Treaty (see Introduction, p. xiii).

1.118 Thucydides ends the excursus by referring back to Corcyra and Potidaea and the other grievances, here using the word *prophasis* (used of his 'real reason' in 1.23) of them. He has not said as much as he might about how the Athenians 'consolidated their empire' (see note to 1.111–12);

he tries to combine the view of Sparta as slow to act, expressed by the Corinthians in 1.68–71, with his view of the real reason for the war, that when Athens did become too powerful Sparta did find it intolerable. The sanctuary at Delphi, which gave its strong support to the Spartans, had presumably come under the control of the pro-Spartan city of Delphi again after the Thirty Years Treaty (cf. 1.112).

1.119–25 *Congress of Peloponnesian League in Sparta (432).* After the excursus justifying his emphasis on his 'real reason' (1.89–118), Thucydides resumes the narrative from 1.88: the Spartan assembly has already decided on war, but to commit the Peloponnesian League it needs a majority vote from the League's members.

1.120–4 Thucydides begins with another Corinthian speech. The motif that Athens' naval power is a threat to inland as well as to coastal cities is new.

1.121 The suggestion that the Peloponnesians can provide money of their own and borrow from Delphi and Olympia, and can build a navy to defeat the Athenian navy, answers the caution of Archidamus in 1.80: probably Corinth was the only member of the League with significant wealth in cash, and there is no clear evidence that money was obtained from Delphi and Olympia; and the Peloponnesians seem not to have understood how far Athens' navy surpassed others in skill (cf. 2.83–92). Payment of oarsmen was standard, but many of Athens' oarsmen were non-Athenians (cf. 1.143).

1.122 Revolt among Athens' allies was also mentioned cautiously by Archidamus (1.81). *Epiteichismos*, the building of a hostile fort inside the enemy's territory, makes its first appearance here: the Athenians built such forts in the Archidamian War (first at Atalante in 431: 2.32; most notably at Pylos in 425 and Cythera in 424: 4.2–41, 53–7), but the Peloponnesians did not build a fort in Attica until they occupied Deceleia in 413 (7.19, 27–8). The description of Athens as a 'tyrant city' (1.122, 124) will be used unashamedly by the Athenians Pericles (2.63), Cleon (3.37), and Euphemus (6.85); cf. Ar., *Eq.* 1110–20.

1.124 The idea of solidarity among Dorians and among Ionians, and of the military superiority of the Dorians, occurs on various occasions (more often on the Peloponnesian side: Hornblower), but ethnic solidarity could always be overridden when other considerations seemed more important; cf. note to 1.94–5 on the Delian League as an Ionian league. No Corinthians will have heard Archidamus' speech (cf. 1.79), but the Corinthians then in Sparta will have been able to discover what he said. It is a greater obstacle to belief in Thucydides' speeches as authentic reports that Pericles' speech in Athens (1.140–4) responds to points made in this speech. See Introduction, p. xxxv.

1.125 The Peloponnesians were not sufficiently prepared to begin the war in 432, but the campaigning season was not yet at an end. 'Nearly a whole year' is probably the right interpretation of Thucydides' 'not a year ... but less': this congress perhaps met in August (Gomme), and the first

Peloponnesian invasion of Attica—Thucydides wavers between that and the Theban attack on Plataea (2.2–6) as the starting point of the war—probably began in late May 431 (2.19; cf. note to 2.2–6).

1.126–38 *Digression on past episodes raised in propaganda: Cylon, Pausanias, Themistocles.*

1.126–7 The exchange of propaganda included attempts to weaken the opposing side by exploiting curses. The Athenian curse affected Pericles because his mother was from the cursed family, the Alcmeonids (not named by Thucydides, whose great-uncle Cimon had an Alcmeonid wife too). Cylon was an Olympic victor in 640, and tried to become tyrant in 636, 632, 628, or 624. The story is told also by Hdt. 5.71, Plut., *Sol.* 12 and schol. Ar., *Eq.* 445 (three versions); *Ath. Pol.* 1 has the end of an account on the same lines as Plutarch's. Trying to become tyrant and killing suppliants could both be represented as wicked, and different slants on the story were possible. Thucydides may be reacting against a version in which Cylon did make his attempt at the time of the Diasia; he is certainly reacting against Herodotus' claim that control of the state was in the hands of the mysterious 'chiefs of the *naukraroi*', while only Plutarch states explicitly that the man responsible was the archon, Megacles of the Alcmeonid family. The Dread Goddesses are the Erinyes/Eumenides (Furies), and their altars were on the Areopagus, to the west of the Acropolis. For the invocation of the curse by Cleomenes, in 508/7 against Cleisthenes, see Hdt. 5.70–2, *Ath. Pol.* 20.2.

Pericles has been mentioned in a matter-of-fact way in the Pentecontaetia (see note to 1.111–12), but in 1.127 he is presented for the first time as a major figure; the comment on his refusal to make concessions anticipates 1.139–46.

1.128–34 The curse of Taenarum (the southern tip of the Mani, on the west side of the Laconian Gulf) is disposed of quickly: for the earthquake of *c*.465/4 see 1.101; the episode mentioned need not have been immediately before that. For Pausanias, see 1.94–5, to which this narrative provides a sequel. 'To help the Greek war-effort' is probably the right interpretation of Thucydides' 'for the Greek war'. That Gongylus of Eretria was used as a go-between is supported by the fact that he was given land by the Persians (cf. Xen., *Hell.* 3.1.6, *An.* 7.8.8); but, apart from the improbability that the letters quoted (1.128–9) would have survived, Pausanias' offer to marry the King's daughter looks like an elaboration of the rumour reported by Herodotus (5.32) that he married Megabates' daughter. There were two Persian satrapies in western Asia Minor: Hellespontine Phrygia in the north, with its capital at Dascylium near the Propontis, and Ionia, with its capital at Sardis (cf. 8.5–6).

1.130 Pausanias' embracing of Persian luxury at Byzantium may be contrasted with his earlier reaction, in 479 after the battle of Plataea (Hdt. 9.80–2).

1.131 The dispatch-stick (*skytale*), or rather a strip of cloth which for decipherment had to be wrapped round the stick which he possessed, conveying the order to return to Sparta, has been thought to conflict with the statement that he went to Hermione 'without . . . authority', but he was still regent.

1.132 The bronze 'serpent column' which supported a gold tripod survives in the Hippodrome in Istanbul, and the list of cities is on that (ML 27, translated Fornara 59): we do not know where on the whole monument Pausanias' couplet was inscribed; according to [Dem.] 59. *Neaera* 96–8 the Plataeans prosecuted Sparta before the Delphic Amphictyony and demanded the erasure.

1.134 Pausanias was removed from the temple so that he should not pollute it by dying inside. Here as before Thucydides is confident of Pausanias' guilt in matters which were never proved: it is likely that when Pausanias returned to the Hellespont region and did not cooperate with the Athenians he did seek to cooperate with the Persians; it is perhaps less likely that he planned to free the Helots, but when they did revolt not long after his death (1.101) he was a convenient scapegoat. Thucydides gives us no indication of chronology, but probably Pausanias was expelled from Byzantium by the Athenians *c*.470 (cf. Just., *Epit.* 9.1.3) and the rest of the story belongs to the first half of the 460s.

1.135–8 Even with Pausanias Thucydides seems not merely to be providing the information needed to explain the curse cited by Athens against Sparta but in a Herodotean manner to be telling an exciting story for its own sake. The downfall of Themistocles is another exciting story, and it is of no relevance to the exchange of propaganda in 432/1: rather, Pausanias and Themistocles were 'the two most eminent Greeks of their time' (1.138), and in his intellectual qualities (1.138) Themistocles is presented as a forerunner of Pericles. Cf. Introduction, p. xxviii. For Themistocles after the Persian Wars, see note to 1.89–93.

1.135 Themistocles' ostracism marked a decision by the Athenians against him and for Cimon; as a result of the charges mentioned here he was condemned in his absence for medism, treasonable collaboration with the Persians; ironically, though he then became a dependant of the Persians, we have no good reason to think he was guilty of medism before his condemnation. Argos and other states in the northern Peloponnese fought against Sparta in the 470s–460s; Themistocles' departure from Argos may be due in part to the return to power of the old aristocracy which had lost its supremacy *c*.494 (Hdt. 6.83).

1.136 That Themistocles first fled westwards is consistent with the very slight indications that he was interested in the west (de Ste. Croix, *Origins of the Peloponnesian War*, 176, 378–9). Plutarch (*Them.* 24) states that he had favoured Corcyra when arbitrating between Corcyra and Corinth; we do not know when or how he had opposed Admetus. In his version of the story (*Them.* 22–9), Plutarch takes Themistocles across the Aegean past Thasos (probably) to Cyme: if we knew which route was correct that would help us to date the episode, but probably these are rival embroideries on the simpler fact that in crossing the Aegean he had to keep out of the hands of the Athenians. Plutarch says that later writers had Themistocles meet not Artaxerxes (who became King in 465) but Xerxes, the King he had fought against in 480, but that is so much more effective dramatically that the less exciting Artaxerxes version must be true: Themistocles was ostracized perhaps *c*.470, but did not reach Asia before 465.

1.137 The 'message . . . from Salamis' presupposes an alternative version of the (probably invented) story in Hdt. 8.108–10 that after Salamis the Greeks pursued the Persian fleet only to Andros, Themistocles wanted to continue to the Hellespont but was outvoted, and he then sent a message claiming the credit for the abandonment of that plan.

1.138 For the praise of Themistocles, cf. especially the praise of Pericles in 1.139, 2.60 (by himself), 65. The granting of territory was a regular Persian means of rewarding favourites: Magnesia and Myus were on the Maeander, inland from Miletus, and Lampsacus on the Hellespont; there are coins of Magnesia with Themistocles' name and others with his son's name, and in the hellenistic period there was a festival in his honour at Lampsacus. According to Paus. 1.1.2 Themistocles was given honourable burial—perhaps later.

1.139–46 *Athenian response to Spartan pressure (432).* After demanding the expulsion of the Alcmeonids, the Spartans next raised three of Thucydides' four 'grievances' (the episode of Corcyra was at an end, so no demand could be made in that connection), and for Megara Thucydides gives a little more information than he gave in 1.67. The final demand echoes Thucydides' 'real reason'. Pericles, having been given one formal introduction in 1.127, here occupies centre stage for the first time and is given another introduction and his first speech (1.140–4).

1.140 For Pericles' insistence on not yielding, cf. 1.127; he will again claim to be unchanging in 2.61, as will Cleon in 3.38. For the extent to which Sparta had for some time been willing to fight, see note to 1.37–43; if the 'grievances' are indeed mere excuses, Thucydides' 'real reason' for the war is confirmed.

1.141–3 For the Peloponnesians as farmers lacking accumulated wealth, cf. Archidamus in 1.80 and the Corinthian response in 1.121 (the Spartans themselves did not farm their land but had Helots to do it for them); for the nature of the impending war, cf. Archidamus; for Peloponnesian disunity, cf. the Corinthians in 1.122; for hostile forts within Attica and the Peloponnesians' naval hopes (1.142), cf. the Corinthians in 1.122 and 121; for the possibility of the Peloponnesians' borrowing from Olympia and Delphi (1.143), cf. the Corinthians in 1.121. The word which we translate as 'captain', *kybernetes*, denotes the helmsman who, under the trierarch (the rich citizen assigned to a ship to command it and pay its running expenses), was its professional commander. 1.143 anticipates Pericles' strategy of not resisting invasions of Attica but relying on Athens' control of the sea and of the Delian League (cf. 2.13); the notion that Athens would be even stronger if it were an island can be found in [Xen.] *Ath. Pol.* 2.15, probably written in the mid-420s.

1.144 The advice not to be over-ambitious by trying to extend the empire during the war is praised by Thucydides in 2.65—and is advice which was not followed after Pericles' death.

1.146 Renewed mention of 'grievances and disputes', and of Epidamnus and Corcyra, closes the ring which was opened in 1.23; but the period during which communication was maintained and the two sides were not yet formally at war is 432/1, after the Peloponnesians' decision to go to war.

BOOK TWO

2.1 Formal beginning of the war

The Peloponnesian War began in the spring of 431. Thucydides signals one formal beginning with the attack on Plataea, but that was 'while the peace still held' (2.2), and he signals a second formal beginning with the invasion of Attica (2.10, 19). Since each state had its own calendar (cf. 2.2), and many started their year in the middle of the campaigning season (cf. 5.20), Thucydides uses his own seasonal calendar, beginning the year in spring (usually early March, but see note to 8.44) and dividing it into summers of about eight months and winters of about four, and in 2.2 anchoring his system to the year-reckoning of three major states. He rarely digresses outside this framework (most notably in 4.50; the backtracking in 8.45 need not go outside the current winter). Probably (though some disagree) precise astronomical dates are intended only when explicitly mentioned (as at 2.78; contr. 2.19).

2.2–32 First summer (431)

2.2–6 *Thebes' attempt to seize Plataea.* The Thirty Years Treaty was made in 446/5 (1.115); the war began in the first half of 431. With the OCT we retain the manuscripts' 'two more months' and 'sixth month' in 2.2, which would imply October 432 for the battle at Potidaea, early April 431 for the attack on Plataea, early June for the Athenian new year and late June in 431/0 for the invasion of Attica (cf. Hornblower); but there is a strong case for emending to 'four more months' and 'tenth month', and dating Potidaea June 432, Plataea early March 431, the invasion of Attica late May and the Athenian new year early July (cf. Gomme).

Since 519 Plataea, on the north slope of the mountain range separating Attica from Boeotia, and near to the roads between Boeotia and the Peloponnese, had resisted incorporation in the Boeotian federation which Thebes dominated and had been allied to Athens (Hdt. 5.39–42; date, Thuc. 3.68); the Boeotarchs were the principal officials of the federation. As often happened in Greece, Plataea had a minority party which hoped with outside support to get control of the city (NB 5.4, where the upper-class men of Leontini even choose to merge their city with Syracuse). Thucydides indicates in 3.56, 65, that the attack was made at a time of sacred truce. Here and in the later sections on Plataea (2.71–8, 3.20–4, 52–68) he gives a vivid and detailed account: the capture of Plataea did not seriously affect the course of the war; but Plataea was near to Athens so he could easily obtain information and details of ingenious devices he seems to have found interesting in their own right, and the story of this small town, caught up in the war between the great powers and not saved by its ally Athens, helped him to make important points about the war. The story is repeated in [Dem.] 59. *Neaera* 98–106.

2.5   Here we have a rare instance of Thucydides' mentioning alternative accounts and not deciding between them (cf. Introduction, p. xxxi). Hornblower stresses that the Thebans' charge that the Plataeans were breaking an oath is a reply to the Plataeans' charge that the Thebans were breaking their oath to the Thirty Years Treaty (in A. H. Sommerstein and J. Fletcher (eds.), *Horkos: The Oath in Greek Society* (Bristol Phoenix Press, 2007), 138–47 at 144–5).

2.6   It is striking that before the war had formally begun the Athenians were able to find and arrest all the Boeotians in Attica.

2.7–17   *Final preparations and resources.* The Persians had by Greek standards unlimited resources: help from them offered the Peloponnesians the best chance of matching the wealth of Athens, and in 412–404 finally enabled them to win the war; Athens needed at least to prevent them from helping the Peloponnesians. However, although Athens more than once sent forces to the west (first in 427: 3.86), the western Greeks did not send forces to support the Peloponnesians at all until after the defeat of Athens' expedition of 415–413, and not on a large scale even then (see 8.26).

2.8   This repeats the theme of the greatness of the war from 1.1–23. Except in 447–446 there had not been much fighting in mainland Greece since 454 (see 1.112–17). For the suggestion, uncharacteristic of Thucydides, that oracles and natural phenomena might be meaningful, cf. 1.23 and see Introduction, pp. xliv–xlv; he has overlooked an earlier earthquake on Delos mentioned by Hdt. 6.98. The enthusiasm for Sparta's intention to liberate Greece suggests that in 431 Thucydides' 'real reason' for the war was not 'unacknowledged' (cf. 1.23): the narrative as a whole does not confirm that Athens was so widely hated, but the claim fits such passages as the Athenian speech in 1.75–8 and Sparta's ultimatum in 1.139.

2.11   Archidamus' speech will not have been heard by Thucydides and probably was not particularly memorable: what Thucydides supplies is consistent with his own view of Athens' unpopularity, and with the caution of Archidamus' speech in 1.79–85 and of Archidamus' actual advance.

2.12   The original model for Melesippus' solemn announcement is Hom., *Od.* 8.81.

2.13   It is not clear how easily the Peloponnesians could have identified Pericles' lands and avoided damaging them. Because Thucydides was an

Athenian, and because Athens believed in open government as Sparta did not (see 5.68), it is credible that Pericles made a speech of the kind summarized here and that Thucydides could then or later obtain the detailed figures. Pericles' strategy, of allowing Attica to be overrun and using the cavalry but not risking a major hoplite battle, is that already indicated in 1.143. As in 1.96, Thucydides gives a surprisingly high figure for the tribute: the 'tribute lists' point to *c*.400 talents; perhaps his higher figure comes from an optimistic assessment list. Probably the 6,000 talents 'on the Acropolis' were in the treasury of Athena (an ancient commentator on Aristophanes quotes a version of this passage pointing to a regular balance of *c*.6,000 talents rather than a maximum of 9,700, which might be historically correct: cf. textual note); much of the wealth 'from the other sanctuaries' was now in a consolidated treasury of the Other Gods, kept with that of Athena. The siege of Potidaea cost 2,000 talents (2.70), but it is now thought that another 2,000 talents would have paid not simply for the Propylaea, the entrance building at the west end, but for the whole of the Periclean work on the Acropolis. Athens did indeed borrow from the sacred treasuries (see note to 3.19), and in the last years of the war melted down some other dedications, but the gold on Pheidias' statue of Athena was left untouched until 296/5 (*FGrH* 257a F 4, Paus. 1.25.7): at this date 40 talents of gold were worth 560 talents of silver. As for soldiers, the 'youngest' were those aged 18–19 and the 'oldest' perhaps those aged 40–59; the total number of adult male citizens may have approached 60,000; there were at least 3,000 metics, foreign residents, able to fight as hoplites (cf. 2.31).

2.14–16 It is not clear how thorough the evacuation of Attica was, or how many of those who left their rural homes stayed away after the invaders had left. Classical Attica was divided into 139 demes, local political units; but it now appears that the countryside was largely deserted during the dark age of which Thucydides was unaware (see note to 1.2–19), and resettled during the archaic period. The legendary early kings, from Cecrops to Theseus, were traditionally dated before the Trojan War, and by the late fifth century Theseus had come to be regarded as a harbinger of democracy (e.g. Eur., *Supp.*): as in 1.1–23 Thucydides accepts the legends but interprets them in a rationalist spirit; and as there he cites evidence to support his beliefs about the past. The temples which he mentions were to the south-east of the Acropolis; there was also early occupation north and north-west of the Acropolis (including the area of the classical Agora). There is a fountain in Thucydides' south-eastern area, but the only fountain dated archaeologically to the Peisistratid period is the 'south-east fountain-house' in the Agora. Inscriptions confirm that in the fifth century the Athenians regularly did call the Acropolis *polis*.

2.17 The Eleusinium was between the Acropolis and the Agora. The 'Pelargic' was probably at the north-west corner of the Acropolis—and here Thucydides has a rationalizing interpretation of an oracle, which eliminates the need for foreknowledge (cf. Introduction, p. xliv).

2.18–23 *The Peloponnesian invasion of Attica.* Oenoe is in the far north-west of Attica and not on the direct route from the Peloponnese: it is not clear (and seems not to have been clear to Archidamus' soldiers) what, apart from giving the Athenians a further chance to negotiate, was the point of this diversion. 'In the build-up to the war', more literally 'in setting the war in motion', echoes the Homeric 'set Ares in motion' (e.g. *Il.* 2.381).

2.19 The date and the formal mention of Archidamus mark the last point at which the war could be said formally to have begun. Eleusis and the Thriasian plain are in the west of Attica, the part nearest to the Isthmus of Corinth; from there the invaders did not head for Athens but went to Acharnae, in the north of the central plain. That was indeed the largest of the Athenian demes (Thucydides remembers here that he is not writing for Athenian readers only: cf. Introduction, pp. xxxix–xl).

2.20 We retain the manuscripts' 'three thousand hoplites', but it is generally agreed that, large as Acharnae was, it was not that large: see the textual note for two suggested corrections, but we cannot be sure of the right solution.

2.21 For the invasion of Pleistoanax in 446, cf. 1.114, and for his return from exile see 5.16. For the warlike reputation of the Acharnians, cf. Aristophanes' *Acharnians*, of 425.

2.22 In 431 Pericles was accused of not fighting energetically enough; in 430 he was blamed for the war (2.59). This is one of a few texts which indicate that during the Peloponnesian War the generals had some involvement with the *prytaneis* (the standing committee of the council of five hundred) in deciding when to convene meetings of the assembly (cf. 2.59, 4.118). Phrygii (not a deme) was in the north-east of the central plain. For the alliance with the Thessalians, cf. 1.102: they did not fight for Athens again, but according to 4.78 most of the people remained pro-Athenian.

2.23 The invaders moved to the north-east of Attica and returned home via Boeotia: Oropus was lost to the Boeotians in 412/1 (8.60), so what is said of it here was written earlier and not corrected (cf. Introduction, p. xxvii).

2.24–32 *Athenian counter-measures.* The final reserve fund of 1,000 talents was used in 412—when the conditions specified here were not fulfilled, so the assembly had first to vote to override those conditions (8.15). The keeping in reserve of the 100 best triremes is more problematic: there was no immediate prospect of a naval attack on Athens, and to keep the best ships out of use seems perverse, but it is possible that this was indeed decided in 431 but not adhered to for long. Another problem concerns the naval campaigns of 431 and 430: they involved large numbers of ships and men and cost large sums of money, but Thucydides writes of them in a disjointed (for 431: 2.17, 23, 25, 30) and low-key manner as if they were unimportant. Various explanations have been suggested: it may be that Thucydides reflects Pericles' cautious public pronouncements but privately Pericles hoped that demonstrations of invulnerability would lead the Peloponnesians to acknowledge that Athens could not be defeated.

2.25 For Corcyra's link with Athens, cf. 1.24–55; in this chapter we have the first appearance of Brasidas, the most energetic Spartan commander in the Archidamian War.

2.26 Locris without further specification is northern, 'Opuntian' Locris, east of Thermopylae and facing the northern part of Euboea.

2.27 For Aegina's hostility to Athens, cf. the brief mentions in 1.67, 139, 140; for the Helot Revolt, cf. 1.101–3 and for Athens' conquest of Aegina, cf. 1.105, 108. Pericles is said to have called Aegina the eyesore of the Peiraeus (Arist., *Rh.* 3. 1411A). Thyrea was on the east coast of the Peloponnese: the Athenians attacked and destroyed the settlement in 424 (4.56–7).

2.28 A lunar eclipse is reported as a natural phenomenon without ulterior significance (cf. Introduction, p. xlv): the natural explanation was accepted by Pericles (Plut., *Per.* 35) and was attributed to his friend Anaxagoras of Miletus (Plut., *Nic.* 23).

2.29 Thrace was an area in which Thucydides had a personal interest (see Introduction, p. xxiv). A 'consular representative' is a *proxenos*, a man who lives in his own state but acts as a collective guest-friend (*xenos*: see G. Herman, *Ritualised Friendship and the Greek City* (Cambridge University Press, 1987)) of another state and looks after the interests of that state and of visitors from it (notice the role of the Athenian *proxenoi* in Mytilene in 428: 3.2). For an episode in Thrace in 430, see 2.67; and on the Odrysian kingdom and a campaign in 429/8 which Athens failed to support, see 2.95–101. The digression on the legendary Tereus (who was married to Procne, daughter of the Athenian king Pandion, but raped her sister Philomela, and in revenge Procne killed her own son Itys; in the end Tereus and the two women were turned into birds, Procne into a nightingale) is uncharacteristic of Thucydides (cf. Introduction, p. xxxiii). Possibly a dramatist had connected Teres with Tereus and Thucydides could not resist the temptation to correct the error. No instance of 'Daulian bird' survives in Greek literature, but there are several in Latin, e.g. Catull. 65.14. Peltasts are light infantry, particularly from Thrace, named after their shield, the *pelte*.

2.30 Here, as at other points, Thucydides seems to think notes on the islands off the west coast of Greece more necessary than notes on mainland cities.

2.31 The attack on Megara, in response to the dispute mentioned in 1.67, 139, 140, 144, is the first of a series of biannual attacks which the Athenians made until in 424 a plot to betray the city to them left them in possession of the harbour town of Nisaea but not of the city (4.66–74).

2.33–46 First winter (431/0)

2.33 *A Corinthian campaign in the north-west.* This is a reaction to Athens' naval campaign of summer 431 (see in particular 2.30).

2.34–46 *The public funeral in Athens.* The earliest surviving Athenian casualty list is of men killed at Drabescus c.464 (*IG* i³ 1144; cf. 1.100), and according to Paus. 1.29.4 that was the first public funeral, but many think Thucydides' 'traditional' should point to an earlier date. Diod. Sic. 11.33.3 dates the institution of the funeral games (not mentioned by Thucydides) and the speech to 479. If the institution was an old one, Marathon in 490 was not the only exception (Plataea in 479 was another: Hdt. 9.85.2). Casualty lists are commonly arranged by the ten tribes instituted by Cleisthenes. Public tombs were located in the outer Cerameicus, to the north-west of the walled inner city, between the Sacred Gate and the Academy.

According to Dem. 20. *Lept.* 141 the speech was an institution peculiar to Athens. We possess part or all of four other speeches, and Plato's *Menexenus* contains a parody of this speech, purporting to be by Pericles' mistress Aspasia. For studies of Athenian funeral speeches, see J. E. Ziolkowski, *Thucydides and the Tradition of Funeral Speeches at Athens* (New York: Arno, 1981); N. Loraux trans. A. Sheridan, *The Invention of Athens: The Funeral Oration in the Classical City* (Harvard University Press, 1986): there tends to be a standard pattern, but this speech is unusual in concentrating on the way of life of contemporary Athens rather than on the glorious achievements of previous generations.

Pericles had made the speech at least once before, for the dead of the Samian war of 440–439 (Plut., *Per.* 8, 28, cf. 1.115–17); his remark that the spring had been taken out of the year (Arist., *Rh.*, 1.1365 A, 3.1411 A) is perhaps from that speech. It should not be doubted that Pericles made the speech on this occasion; Thucydides probably heard the speech, and it is entirely possible that he reports its main lines correctly. In fact the Athenians who died in this first year of the war will not have been very numerous and will not have died very gloriously, but Pericles/Thucydides uses this speech to expound an Athenian ideal (and there is no balancing speech to expound a Spartan ideal).

2.36 That 'the same race has always occupied' Attica was regularly claimed: cf. 1.2, 2.14–16. Pericles was born in the 490s; the Delian League was founded in the 470s by men of his father's generation, and he was a leading figure in Athens from the 450s onwards. Mention of a topic which one says one will pass over is a common rhetorical device.

2.37 The discussion of democracy is the first of a number of explicit or implicit contrasts between Athens and Sparta. By the reforms of Ephialtes in 462/1 Athens became self-consciously democratic (the word *demokratia* may have been coined in that context), and within ten years it could respond to provocation by imposing democracy on a member state of the Delian League (Erythrae, late 450s: ML 40, translated Fornara 71). In fact in fifth-century Athens most civilian appointments were made by allotment, i.e. by 'rotation', and while there were stipends for offices members of the lowest property class were not eligible for appointment. Rusten notes the contradiction between the 'open and free' Athenians and the 'obedient' Athenians. The Spartans' way of life encouraged supervision of one another and uniformity; but Sparta and all Greek states would claim to live under the rule of law, which they saw as a guarantee of freedom rather than an obstacle to it (cf. 1.84, Hdt. 7.104). Athens probably had more personal freedom than many states, certainly than Sparta, but the ostentatious lifestyle of Alcibiades was to give offence (cf. 6.28).

2.38 For Athens' large number of festivals—represented here as occasions for relaxation rather than worship of the gods—and (thanks to its control of the sea) ability to import foreign goods, cf. [Xen.] *Ath. Pol.* 2.9, 3.2; 2.7, 11–12, Isoc. 4. *Paneg.* 42.

2.39 Expulsion of foreigners was a Spartan practice (cf. 1.144), and the training system for young Spartans was notorious; there must have been training opportunities for Athenian soldiers, but we have little evidence before the introduction of a programme for 18- and 19-year-olds in the 330s (cf. *Ath. Pol.* 42).

2.40 'Beauty without extravagance, and intellect without loss of vigour' perhaps contrasts Athens both with austere Sparta and with luxurious Persia (L. Kallet, in K. A. Morgan (ed.), *Popular Tyranny* (University of Texas Press, 2003), 131–4). Athens' political machinery required, and clearly obtained, large-scale participation in public affairs by the citizens, but there were some 'quiet Athenians' (L. B. Carter, *The Quiet Athenian* (Oxford University Press, 1986)). For public discussion of policy, see 2.60, 3.37–8, 42–3. The rejection of self-interest seems to be undermined even here, and other Thucydidean speeches including that of Pericles in 2.60–4 suggest that the Athenians pursued their interests realistically and unashamedly.

2.41 The theme of Athens as an education to Greece was taken up in the fourth century by Isocrates (4. *Paneg.* 47–50). For Thucydides' attitude to Homer, cf. 1.10, 21; in 1.10 he says that Athens' buildings would suggest even greater power than it actually had.

2.43 Here the speech turns from praise for the dead and their city to exhortation to the survivors. It is a common theme in Greek literature that happiness and prosperity are not lasting, and the best life ends at a high point before they are lost (cf. the lesson attributed to Solon in Hdt., 1.29–33).

2.44–5 The message to the bereaved seems bleak to modern readers, and since Pericles was regarded as aloof (cf. Plut., *Per.* 5, 7) ancient readers may have reacted similarly. A good citizen was expected to have a stake in the city by owning land in its territory and producing children to ensure its continuing existence; many bereaved parents may have had other sons still living, but it is unlikely that many could have expected to have further children. Athenian women were excluded from public, except religious, life, which may have seemed normal rather than oppressive; respectable women were commonly referred to as a man's daughter or wife rather than by their own name.

2.46 State maintenance for war orphans is attributed to Solon by Diog. Laert. 1.55, but according to Arist., *Pol.* 2.1268 B Hippodamus claimed to be creating something novel when he instituted this in Miletus in the fifth century.

2.47–68 Second summer (430)

2.47–54 *The plague in Athens.* Thucydides' account of Athenian ideals in Pericles' funeral speech is followed by his account of the suffering and demoralization of the plague. His account is detailed and overtly matter-of-fact, but that is not inconsistent with his using it to make a point. Apart from that contrast, as in the whole of his history (cf. 1.22) Thucydides seeks to be useful; and perhaps here as elsewhere he wants to show that he can give a better account than others. He uses medical terms, though not the most obscure and technical terms, and without the existence of contemporary medical works it would probably not have occurred to him to give so detailed an account of a disease. (There was a plague in the story of the Trojan War, but that receives only a brief mention in the *Iliad*: 1.43–61.)

2.48 The overcrowding of Athens during the Peloponnesian invasions will have hastened the spread of the disease (Diod. Sic. 12.45.2) and have worsened the suffering of those who caught it (cf. 2.52). Importation from abroad recalls Athens' boasted ability to import goods of all kinds (2.38). Diod. Sic. 12.58.3–5 blames stagnant water and inferior crops after a wet winter, and the failure in 430 of the 'etesian' winds which normally blow from the north-west in the summer: we cannot tell whether this is authentic memory omitted by Thucydides or later speculation. Many attempts have been and continue to be made to identify the disease; but there are good grounds for thinking that after nearly 2,500 years it is likely to be either extinct or so changed that it cannot be equated with any present-day disease on the basis of the symptoms reported here (A. J. Holladay, ed. A. J. Podlecki, *Athens in the Fifth Century and Other Studies in Greek History* (Chicago: Ares, 2002), 123–65; these chapters by Holladay and J. F. C. Poole).

Pious and impious perished alike (2.47, 53), but there was a feeling that the gods needed to be appeased: it may be in response to the plague that a sanctuary of Heracles *Alexikakos* (averter of evil) was established in the city, Delos was 'purified' in 426/5 (3.104), and in 420/19 (after the Peace of Nicias) the cult of the healing god Asclepius was brought to Athens from Epidaurus.

2.53 Thucydides believed in morality if not in religion, and here he blames the plague for a decline in standards in Athens (but it is clear from 2.51 that some Athenians behaved unselfishly); the late fifth century was also a time when the sophists were challenging all the traditional beliefs, including the existence of gods and of absolute standards of conduct (cf. Introduction, p. xliii).

2.54 Thucydides gives a rationalizing account of a traditional verse: *loimos* and *limos* are first found together in Hes., *Op.* 243; in modern Greek they would be pronounced alike, but they were not in antiquity. For the oracle, cf. 1.118.

We learn from 3.87 that the plague originally lasted for two years and returned in 427/6, and that it killed about a third of the field army (and presumably at least that proportion of the total population): cf. 2.58, where 1,050 out of 4,000 men taken to Potidaea succumbed. There is an account by the Roman poet Lucretius, 6.1090–1286, which is based on Thucydides but has both omissions and additions.

2.55–8 *The summer's campaigns (i)*. This year's Peloponnesian invasion of Attica (2.55, 57) was the longest-lasting (the shortest was in 425: 4.6) and (cf. 3.26) the most damaging. We cannot tell how thorough it was, but probably it did considerable short-term but little long-term damage to Athenian agriculture (cf. V. D. Hanson, *Warfare and Agriculture in Classical Greece* (University of California Press, ²1998)); although Laureium (in the south-east of Attica) and the mines are mentioned, the working of the silver mines does not seem to have been brought to a halt in the 420s (contrast the more serious effects of the Spartans' year-round occupation of Deceleia, from 413: 7.27–8).

2.56 The Athenian naval expedition was as large as but is dealt with as perfunctorily as that of 431 (cf. on 2.24–32): all the places mentioned, apart from Prasiae, were in the Argolid, and Pericles may have hoped to put pressure on Argos to abandon its neutrality (see note to 1.68–71) and join Athens. For Potidaea (2.58), cf. 1.56–66, 2.67, 70; For Hagnon, see note to 1.115–17; Phormio's force (cf. 1.65) is mentioned here to make it clear that it was not among the men exposed to the plague.

2.59–65 *Pericles under attack*. Whereas in 431 Pericles was considered insufficiently belligerent (2.21–2), in 430 he was blamed for the war and the Athenians tried to make peace with Sparta. Sparta may have hoped to continue the war until Athens surrendered unconditionally, but 2.65 suggests that the Athenians withdrew from the negotiations after Pericles had persuaded them to fight on. For Pericles and meetings of the assembly, see note to 2.22.

2.60–4 In this, his last speech in Thucydides, Pericles emphasizes the people's responsibility for decisions taken in the assembly (2.60, 61, 64; cf. Thucydides' comment in 8.1).

2.60 Pericles' account of his own merits is in familiar terms but shocks modern readers when attributed to himself, yet it may reflect what he actually said: for his intellectual qualities, cf. 2.65, and 1.138 (Themistocles), 8.68 (Antiphon), also 2.15, 34; on his patriotism, cf. Alcibiades on his own defection to Sparta (6.92); with his incorruptibility contrast what is said of his successors in 2.65 and of Alcibiades in 6.12, 15.

2.61 For the claim that Pericles is unchanging, cf. 1.86 (the Spartans according to Sthenelaïdas), 1.140 (Pericles), 3.38 (Cleon).

2.62 For the benefits of Athens' sea power, cf. the 'Old Oligarch', [Xen.] *Ath. Pol.* 2.5, 11–12; for the empire as the creation of Pericles' father's generation, cf. 2.36.

2.63 The contrast between freedom to rule over others and the 'slavery' of subjection to others is widespread: in Thucydides, 1.76, 3.45, 5.69, 6.18, 87, 7.75, 8.64. Athens enjoyed that highest kind of freedom for most of the time between 478 and 338. On the empire as a tyranny, cf. 1.122, 124 (Corinthians), 3.37 (Cleon); that the Athenians were wrong to acquire the empire is not suggested by Athenian speakers elsewhere and was probably not meant to be taken seriously here. On the 'disengaged', cf. 2.40, 6.18.

2.64 'Blows from the gods' is a conventional expression, not a serious suggestion that misfortunes such as the plague ('which could not have been foreseen') were sent by the gods. For the hatred incurred by Athens as a ruling power, cf. 1.76.

2.65 On the sufferings of the poor and rich, contrast [Xen.] *Ath. Pol.* 2.14, claiming that only the rich suffered; but Thucydides is more likely to be right. For his view of the volatility of crowds, cf. 4.28, 6.63. Probably Pericles was deposed from office (Diod. Sic. 12.45.4, Plut., *Per.* 35), put on trial and fined, but re-elected either for the end of 430/29 or normally for 429/8. (This should be distinguished from the trial of Plut., *Per.* 32, which occurred c.437.) He died c. September 429—weakened by the plague but not immediately killed by it (Plut., *Per.* 38). For his strategy, cf. 2.13: departures from it after his death included the major hoplite battles at Delium in 424/3 (unplanned: 4.89–101) and at Mantinea in 418 (5.65–75); the episode at Pylos and the rejection of a Spartan peace offer in 425 (4.2–41); and especially the campaigns in Sicily in 427–424 (passages between 3.86 and 4.65), 422 (5.4–5), and 415–413 (6–7). However, it can be maintained that Pericles' was a strategy for avoiding defeat rather than achieving victory, and things were done later which were or could have been beneficial, such as the occupation of Pylos in 425 and of Cythera in 424 (4.53–7); the campaigns (not in fact successful) against Megara in 424 (4.66–74) and Boeotia in 424/3; the alliance with Argos and other Peloponnesians in 420 (5.40–8).

'The domination of the leading man' represents wishful thinking by Thucydides: Athens' institutions did not allow any one man to achieve overwhelming power (cf. Rhodes, in P. Flensted-Jensen *et al.* (eds.), *Polis and Politics . . . M. H. Hansen* (Copenhagen: Museum Tusculanum Press, 2000), 465–77), and Pericles was not without opponents either before or after the outbreak of the war. Fourth-century writers could see Pericles either as the last of the good old politicians or as the first of the inferior new; in fact, leaders after Pericles were still rich but mostly no longer from the old aristocracy, and, whereas men such as Cimon and Pericles were both political and military leaders, a divide opened afterwards between political leaders such as Cleon and military leaders such as Demosthenes.

What is said here of the Sicilian expedition of 415–413 is hard to reconcile with the account in Books 6–7 and cannot have been thought at the same time; the end of 2.65 in its present form cannot have been written until after the end of the war (see Introduction, pp. xxvii–xxviii). In Books 6–7 failure seems to be due to 'mistaken choice of enemy' compounded by errors made on the spot; the 'personal accusations' mentioned here are presumably those which led to the exile of Alcibiades (6.27–9, 53, 60–1). 'Civil strife at home' began with the revolutions of 411 (8.63–98). 'Eight' years is Shilleto's suggestion for the manuscripts' 'three', and should denote the Thucydidean years 412/1–405/4, followed by surrender in the ninth year, 404/3. The Sicilians did not send much help to Sparta; on the whole, Athens regained the Aegean islands and the Hellespont region but was less successful on the Aegean coast of Asia Minor; Persia began supporting Sparta in 412 (8.5), and did so more effectively after Cyrus was sent to the Aegean in 407 (Xen., *Hell.* 1.3.8–14, 4.1–7). The final 'internal disputes' perhaps refers particularly to Athens' ongoing problems with Alcibiades; also, after Athens' defeat at Aegospotami in 405 the demagogue Cleophon wanted to continue fighting but the oligarch Theramenes eventually negotiated peace with Sparta.

With this premature obituary notice Pericles disappears from Thucydides' history, apart from one cross reference in 6.31.

2.66–8 *The summer's campaigns (ii)*. The force which attacked Zacynthus was the largest Peloponnesian naval force attested during the Archidamian War. The Spartan admiral (*nauarchos*) was probably at this time appointed for an expedition rather than for a set term, but *c*.409 Sparta changed to an annual office beginning in the spring.

2.67 The embassy to Persia is the first mentioned after Thucydides recorded in 2.7 that both sides intended to make approaches to Persia: the Corinthian Aristeus was the supporter of Potidaea in 432 (1.60–5); Hdt. 7.133–7 reports this episode in connection with the fathers of the first two of the Spartans; Pollis of Argos, presumably a friend of Sparta, went in a private capacity because Argos was at this time neutral. Pharnaces was satrap of Hellespontine Phrygia, in north-western Asia Minor.

2.68 This chapter deals with places around the Gulf of Ambracia, in north-western Greece: Ambracia, a Corinthian colony, was to the north of the Gulf and Argos to the east. As on other matters of early history Thucydides accepts the legendary account, yet supposes that Argos, colonized by Greeks, had to learn Greek from Ambracia: more probably, in fact, Argos was barbarian by origin but the names of Argos and Amphilochia had led to a false link with the story of Amphilochus. Phormio's expedition was presumably a few years before the Peloponnesian War, and was the cause of the close ties between him and the Acarnanians (cf. 3.7). The participants in the Peloponnesian War were not involved in the episode in this chapter, but they were to be involved in later episodes (see 2.80–2 for the next).

2.69–70 Second winter (430/29)

Athenian campaigns and the capitulation of Potidaea. For Naupactus, where Athens had settled Messenian refugees in the 450s after the Third Messenian War, see 1.103. Caria is at the south-western corner of Asia Minor and Lycia to the east of it: some cities here were members of the Delian League but seem not to have paid tribute regularly, and here as in

3.19 and 4.50 Thucydides is probably referring to special levies rather than the regular collection of tribute.

2.70 The story of Potidaea is continued from 2.58: for the cost of the siege, cf. 2.13 (without a figure); the possessions which the inhabitants could not take became booty for the Athenians. Although the Athenians 'found fault with the generals', they seem not to have deposed or punished them (cf. 2.79).

2.71–92 Third summer (429)

2.71–8 *The siege of Plataea (i)*. For what preceded this siege, see 2.2–6. Two possible motives for the Peloponnesians' attacking Plataea rather than Athens are to avoid the plague in Athens and to please the Boeotians. For undertakings entered into in 479, cf. 3.58; the festival and games of the hellenistic period (Diod. Sic. 11.29, Plut., *Arist.* 21) are not attested in the classical.

2.73 The Athenian promise of support was inconsistent with Pericles' strategy (cf. 2.13), and apart from the garrison of 2.6 no help was sent.

2.74 For Archidamus' calling on the local gods and heroes, cf. Brasidas at Acanthus (4.87).

2.75 'Seventeen' days is one possible correction of the manuscripts' 'seventy', which is certainly wrong.

2.76–7 The 'siege-engines' (2.76) were battering-rams, the most advanced kind of siege machinery available in the fifth century, and circumvallation (2.77) was at this time the normal form taken by a siege.

2.78 The 'rising of Arcturus' before the sun was *c*.20 September. The story is continued in 3.20–4, 52–68.

2.79 *An Athenian campaign in the north-east*. Potidaea had surrendered (2.70), but the Chalcidians based on Olynthus remained hostile to Athens. Xenophon's colleagues were presumably those named in 2.70. Thucydides uses the campaigns of this summer to make particular points: this chapter shows the Athenian hoplites defeated by cavalry and light infantry.

2.80–2 *A Spartan campaign in the north-west*. This is a sequel to 2.66, 68, and shows the Peloponnesians let down by the indiscipline of their barbarian allies. Of those listed in 2.80, the Thesprotians and Molossians were in fact Greek-speaking. Perdiccas of Macedonia, 'concealing [his involvement] from the Athenians', had gone over to the Athenian side in 431 (2.29).

2.83–92 *Naval battles in the Gulf of Corinth*. This episode demonstrates the overwhelming superiority of the Athenians at sea. Naupactus, and Rhium and Antirrhium (as the Molycrian Rhium of 2.86 is often called), were on a long narrow stretch of water, and Phormio with a smaller but more expert fleet wanted to attack in the open water of the Gulf of Patrae to the west of that; the part to the east is called the Gulf of Crisa (cf. 1.107). See the remarks on tactics attributed to Phormio in 2.89.

2.84 For the Peloponnesians' tactics, cf. the less skilled Greeks against the more skilled Persians at Artemisium in 480 (Hdt. 8.10-11, 16): their best ships were wasted inside the circle, and the Athenians forced them to contract their circle and fall into confusion. (It appears that Magellanic penguins use similar tactics to catch fish: *The Times*, 26 October 2006, 35.)

2.85 The Spartans were given to appointing advisers to commanders who failed to come up to scratch. To present-day readers it is amazing that the Athenian reinforcements urgently needed by Phormio were sent via Crete, not involved in the Peloponnesian War and indeed not greatly involved in the main stream of Greek history in the classical period: it has been suggested that the Athenians hoped to interfere with ships travelling between north Africa and the Peloponnese; it is hard to decide whether Thucydides' low-key remarks here and in 2.92 are intended to imply disapproval.

2.87, 89 Thucydides is unlikely to have known what the commanders actually said, and these speeches will represent what he judged appropriate (cf. Introduction, p. xxxv-xxxvi). For Phormio to risk the second battle, against a fleet nearly four times the size of his, was very daring: it was a risk which he need not have taken, and although he was in the end victorious he could easily not have been.

2.90 The Messenians must have marched out from Naupactus to support Phormio's fleet as the Peloponnesian fleet had an army to support it (cf. 2.86). The open water of this chapter is the middle of the narrow channel, not the much more open water to the west and east.

2.91 The 'sudden and surprising feat' by which the Athenians turned defeat into victory exemplifies the characteristics attributed to them by the Corinthians in 1.70.

2.93-103 Third winter (429/8)

2.93-4 *The Peloponnesian fleet.* The proposal to attack the Peiraeus is attributed to the Megarians, but will have appealed to the energetic Brasidas. The Athenians were not expecting an attack, had taken no precautions, and had 'no fleet on guard there' (but must have had many ships in the harbour); since the Peloponnesians had to walk to Nisaea, Megara's harbour on the Saronic Gulf, there were presumably no ships available at Cenchreae, Corinth's harbour. This is one of the texts which prove that a trireme had as many oars as oarsmen.

2.94 The promontory named as Boudorum was probably the more northerly of the two embracing the mainland promontory south-east of Megara. Thucydides is scornful of the Peloponnesians' excuse for abandoning their original plan. Normally it was being kept in the water for a long time that was bad for ships (cf. 7.12; also Hdt. 7.59, Xen., *Hell.* 1.5.10); but when they had dried out they needed to be recoated with pitch (cf. Morrison, Coates, and Rankov, *The Athenian Trireme*², 277-8), and since the Peloponnesian ships were launched at short notice that had presumably not been done.

2.95–101 *A campaign by Sitalces, the Odrysian.* For Sitalces, cf. 2.29, 67; we are not told what promise Perdiccas had made to him. Athens had supported Philip against Perdiccas *c.*433/2 (1.57). The peoples enlisted by Sitalces lived in an area bounded by the Black Sea in the east, the Aegean in the south, the longitude of Chalcidice in the west, and the Danube in the north; for the account of the kingdom in terms of journey times, see Hdt. 4.86, 101. Four hundred talents of silver is comparable to the amount of tribute which Athens collected from the Delian League before the war (see note to 2.13). Gifts were of course both given and taken both in Thrace and in Persia, but the Persian Kings received so much more revenue than they needed that they were accustomed to reward their favourites with lavish gifts (e.g. Xen., *Cyr.* 8.2.7–10). According to Hdt. 5.3, the Thracians were the largest nation after the Indians, and would be the strongest if united; the Persian empire, outside Thucydides' geographical limits, was stronger than Thrace but was a collection of many nations.

2.98 Sitalces' route began well to the north, after which he entered Macedonia by travelling southwards through the Axius valley to the Thermaic Gulf.

2.99 Lower Macedonia was the land around the Thermaic Gulf, and Upper Macedonia the hill country surrounding it to the south, west, and north. For the legendary account of the royal family's origin, see Hdt. 8.137–9, cf. 9.45: classical Greeks accepted the Argeads' claim to derive from the Temenid branch of the descendants of Heracles, in Peloponnesian Argos (cf. 5.80); it may in fact be true, as stated by App., *Syr.* 333, that they were from the Argos in Orestis, west of the Thermaic Gulf near the modern Kastoria. Alexander I was king in the early fifth century, nominally subject to Persia and used as a go-between in the Persian Wars.

2.100 Archelaus succeeded Perdiccas as king, and attracted a circle of artists and writers, including the tragedian Euripides.

2.101 The failure of the Athenians to support Sitalces is surprising: since becoming an Athenian ally in 431 (2.29) he had done nothing for them except allow them to capture the Peloponnesian envoys bound for Persia (2.67), but the Athenians can hardly have failed to hear of the movement of his large army. The great campaign achieved little, and is barely relevant to the Peloponnesian War, but it gave Thucydides the opportunity to give an account, in the Herodotean manner, of a region with which he had a particular connection (cf. Introduction, pp. xxiv, xxxix).

2.102–3 *Phormio in Acarnania.* Astacus must have expelled the tyrant Evarchus, expelled by Athens earlier but reinstated by Corinth (2.30, 33). Athens' 'hoplites from the ships' were the *epibatai*, of whom normally each trireme carried ten. Pericles had failed to take Oeniadae in the 450s (1.111). The geographical phenomenon will not have been directly familiar to readers in most parts of the Greek world, but it is mentioned also by Hdt. 2.10—and even today not all of the islands have been joined to the mainland. Thucydides then switches from physical geography to legend, which he accepts in his usual manner. Amphiaraus was one of the Seven Against Thebes, attacking one of Oedipus' sons on behalf of another, and he ordered his children to avenge his death on his wife Eriphyle, who had forced him to take part in the campaign; Amphilochus (2.68) was Alcmeon's brother.

2.103 Phormio after returning to Athens plays no further part in the narrative, and in 3.7 his son is sent to succeed him. Stories of his being fined but having the fine paid for him (Androt. *FGrH* 324 F 8, cf. Paus. 1.23.10) seem to belong to an earlier occasion; probably he simply died, and Thucydides omitted to mention that either here or in 3.7.

BOOK THREE

3.1–18 Fourth summer (428)

3.1 *Peloponnesian invasion of Attica.* The corn was 'growing ripe' about late May. For the Athenians' response with cavalry, cf. 2.19, 22. The Peloponnesians' staying 'for as long as they had provisions' indicates a shorter period than the forty days of 430 (2.57).

3.2–6 *Revolt of Mytilene (i).* By the device of ring composition the account of the revolt's origin is begun and ended with similar words, 'obliged to make their revolt earlier than they had intended' (3.2), 'obliged to go to war at short notice' (3.4). The Lesbians, like the Boeotians, belonged to the Aeolian strand of the Greek people. The other cities of Lesbos, apart from Methymna, were Pyrrha, Eresus, and Antissa (cf. 3.18); and the Lesbians were among the few members of the Delian League still not paying tribute but providing ships (see note to 1.19). For consular representatives (*proxenoi*), see note to 2.29; for political union (*synoikismos*) see note to 1.5.

3.3 The forty ships were presumably intended as replacements for those brought back by Phormio (2.103; cf. 3.7). Cleïppides was the father of Cleophon, a prominent demagogue in the last years of the Peloponnesian War. The great panhellenic festivals were protected by sacred truces, but local festivals were often seen by attackers as opportunities rather than impediments (cf. 3.56). It is not clear how Mytilene's obligation to Athens was formulated (Chios and Lesbos together supplied fifty ships for the naval campaign of 430: 2.56), nor whether the crews were kept under arrest merely long enough to hold back the news of Cleïppides' expedition or until the end of the revolt.

3.4 Malea is the peninsula at the south-east corner of Lesbos, but Thucydides clearly wrote and meant 'north', and has probably misapplied the name.

3.5 Imbros and Lemnos are islands in the north Aegean which were acquired and settled by the Athenians early in the fifth century. 'From Laconia' is used by Thucydides only here and in 8.55: perhaps Meleas was not an ordinary Spartan citizen but had some special status.

3.7   *Asopius in the north-west*. For Oeniadae and for the disappearance of Asopius' father Phormio from Thucydides' history, see note to 2.103.

3.8-18   *Revolt of Mytilene (ii)*. The Olympic festival was held at the second full moon after the summer solstice, in 428 on 14 August. Olympia was in the Spartan orbit, and the festival provided an appropriate occasion to publicize Mytilene's need for help, but Mytilene's envoys should have reached Sparta, and Sparta should have been able to summon a meeting of the Peloponnesian League, well before that. Dorieus of Rhodes came from a family of athletes (Pindar, *Olympian* 7 was written for his father), and was victor in the pancratium (all-in wrestling) in 432, 428, and 424 (there is an inscription recording his victories, *SIG*³ 82). Thucydides' primary purpose in mentioning him is to identify the festival (cf. 5.49); but later, perhaps under the influence of Hippias of Elis, it became normal to use the winner of the stadium (foot-race). The single *polis* of Rhodes was not founded until 408/7, and in the official list of victors Dorieus will have been attributed to Ialysus.

3.9-14   The Mytilenaeans' speech concentrates on their justification for revolt, and that moral argument is weakened by the prudential argument in 3.13 that the present is a good occasion.

3.10-11   The parallel between the individual and the state is widespread in Greek, and reaches its culmination in the discussion of justice in Plato's *Republic*. For Sparta's withdrawing from the Persian War and Athens' staying on, see 1.89, 94-5; the purpose of freeing the Greeks from the Persians is conspicuously absent from 1.96. For the Athenians' originally leading 'on an equal basis', cf. 1.97, 99; for their later 'relaxing their hostility to the Persians', with or without a formal treaty, see note to 1.111-12, and for their 'advancing the enslavement of their allies', cf. 1.99. 'Multiplicity of votes' (3.10) and 'equal voting partners' (3.11) probably point to a structure in which each member including Athens had one vote in the council—but after the moving of the treasury to Athens in 454/3 meetings of the council seem to have been discontinued (see note to 1.96-7). It is not true that the weaker allies were attacked first: Naxos (1.98) and Thasos (1.100-1) were among the strongest, and Naxos presumably and Thasos certainly had until they revolted provided ships.

3.13   In 'reasons and grievances' Thucydides uses the words *prophasis* and *aitia*, used separately of different kinds of explanation in 1.23, together for the same explanation. Athens has made the Greeks their own enemies, so that, paradoxically, Mytilene has to secede from the Greeks in order not to harm them but to free them (C. W. Macleod, *Collected Essays* (Oxford University Press, 1983), 91). For the plague in Athens, see 2.47-54; if the only Athenian naval squadrons currently active were those of Cleïppides (3.3) and Asopius (3.7), the Athenians were far from being stretched. For Athens' dependence on the Delian League, cf. Archidamus in 1.81, 83, Pericles in 2.13; for the argument that Mytilene's navy could end up in the possession of Athens or at the disposal of Sparta, cf. the Corcyraeans' argument in 1.36. Mytilene will indeed find itself 'in worse state than those already enslaved' (in contrast to, for example, Potidaea, 2.70). For suppliants see note to 1.24.

3.15 This was the one occasion when Sparta attempted an invasion of Attica at a time other than the spring, and it collapsed because, while the Spartans did not have to do their own farming, their allies did (cf. note to 1.141–3), and they were busy harvesting their grapes and olives (the grain harvest was earlier). For the *diolkos* across the Isthmus, see note to 1.13.

3.16 The Athenians' manning a fleet 'with metics and their own citizens from all but the two highest classes' is mentioned because normally an unknown proportion of their oarsmen were volunteers from the allied states and slaves (for slaves, see note to 7.13), and the citizens of the third out of the four property classes fought as hoplites: it must have been assumed that men who were not practised oarsmen could still do the job adequately. 'Thirty ships' is probably a piece of carelessness: the reference is to Asopius' squadron, but this raiding must have been done by the eighteen ships which he sent back to Athens (3.7). Alcidas was the Spartans' admiral (*nauarchos*: see note to 2.66–8); all that we know of him is what Thucydides reports in Book 3, but he seems to have been a disastrous commander.

3.17 This chapter is problematic. Most of the details seem to refer not to 428 but to the beginning of the war, hence the 'then' inserted at the beginning of the second sentence of the translation; the hundred ships 'guarding Attica, Euboea, and Salamis' are not compatible with what Thucydides states elsewhere, and the drain on the Athenians' finances is relevant to 3.19 but is not appropriate in this context. Some scholars have thought that the chapter belongs after 2.56; more probably it is correctly placed here but is the work of an interpolator.

3.18 Paches is alleged in late texts to have raped two Mytilenaean women after killing their husbands (*Anth. Pal.* 7.614), and to have committed suicide in the law court when convicted in his *euthynai*, his examination on retirement from office (Plut., *Arist.* 26, *Nic.* 6). It is again considered noteworthy (cf. 3.16) that his hoplites rowed their own ships.

3.19–25 Fourth winter (428/7)

3.19 *Athenian financial difficulties.* Here as at Potidaea (2.13, 70) a siege was expensive, because the soldiers had to be paid for a long period. A record of borrowing by the Athenian state from its sacred treasuries (ML 72; extracts translated Fornara 134) shows that in each of the years 432/1–430/29 well over 1,000 talents were borrowed, but in 429/8 c.600 talents and after that no more than 300 talents in a year: the Athenians realized that they were using up their reserves too rapidly, cut down on expensive naval expeditions like those of 431 and 430, and took measures to increase their income. It is unclear whether Thucydides means that the property tax (*eisphora*) was now levied for the first time ever or the first time during the war or the first time to raise as much as 200 talents: the possibility of an *eisphora* is mentioned in a decree probably of 434/3 (ML 58, translated Fornara 119, B. 15–19), but it may be that none had occurred before this winter. There may have been a reassessment of the tribute in 428, but, as in 2.69 and 4.50, the ships to the allies mentioned here were sent probably for a special levy rather than as part of the regular collection of tribute. Lysicles is probably the man who was a politician and who lived with Aspasia after Pericles' death (Ar., *Eq.* 132 with schol., Plut., *Per.* 24). The Anaeans were men exiled from Samos and settled on the mainland opposite after the war of 440–439 (3.32, cf. 1.115–17).

3.20–4 *The siege of Plataea (ii): escape of Plataeans.* The story of the siege of Plataea is continued from 2.71–8. After two summers Athens had sent no help, and was not now likely to do so. In [Dem.] 59. *Neaera* 103 the men drew lots to decide which should escape.

3.21 The besiegers' walls and ditches seem to have been unparalleled in their elaboration.

3.22 Thucydides claims that the escapers had their right foot bare to get a better grip—but having both feet bare would have been better still, and he has suppressed a religious explanation, that baring one foot was part of a rite for the gods of the underworld, who were presumably being invoked to help the enterprise (P. Lévêque and P. Vidal-Naquet, in Vidal-Naquet, *The Black Hunter* (Johns Hopkins University Press, 1986), 61–88, at 64). To fool the besiegers the escapers set out northwards, towards Thebes, but then turned to the east and made their way southwards to one of the passes leading through Mount Cithaeron to Attica.

3.25 *Revolt of Mytilene (iii).* Nothing is known of Salaethus except what Thucydides tells us. His entry into Mytilene to take charge of the defence preparations prefigures Gylippus' entry into Syracuse in 414 (6.93, 7.1–2), but there is no indication that this account was written or revised after 414 with Gylippus in mind. His enterprise contrasts with the lack of enterprise of Alcidas (3.26).

3.26–86 Fifth summer (427)

3.26 *Peloponnesian invasion of Attica.* With Krüger we print 'forty ships' in agreement with the other passages mentioning this squadron: the OCT retains the manuscripts' 'forty-two'. Unlike the aborted invasion of late summer 428 (3.13, 15), this was the usual invasion by land only: it was this invasion and Alcidas' expedition (foreshadowed in 3.16) which were 'to embarrass the Athenians on both fronts at once'. The previous invasions had been commanded by Archidamus, and the next was to be commanded by his son and successor Agis (3.89): the use of the other royal house this year suggests that Archidamus was ill but not yet dead. For the exile of Pleistoanax, see 1.114, and for his return, see 5.16.

3.27–50 *Revolt of Mytilene (iv).* Unless the attackers gave up or there was an act of treachery, a siege by blockade would end with the city's being starved into surrender (cf. Plataea, 3.52). The events of 3.27 make it clear that Mytilene was ruled by an oligarchy. Scholars investigating the popularity of the Athenian empire with its subjects have argued over whether the lower classes had supported the revolt (cf. Cleon in 3.39), and refused to fight now because they were starving, or had been opposed to the revolt from the beginning (cf. Diodotus in 3.47): Thucydides' narrative seems to support the first view.

3.28 The generals who accepted the surrender of Potidaea in 430/29 were criticized for agreeing to terms which the assembly considered too lenient (2.70), so Paches referred this decision to Athens.

3.29 The Peloponnesians 'sailing round the Peloponnese' were to return to Cyllene, in Elis (3.69), and had probably set out from there.

3.30 Teutiaplus, himself from Elis, uses for 'strength' the word *alke*, a pun on the inappropriate name of the feeble Alcidas, who was the first Spartan commander to venture into the Aegean but was clearly not willing to risk an encounter with the Athenians.

3.31 Ionian exiles have not previously been mentioned; the Lesbians were presumably the crews of the two ships mentioned in 3.4-5. Pissouthnes was the Persian satrap at Sardis who had supported the Samians against Athens in 440-439 (1.115).

3.32 Ephesus and Chian exiles friendly to Sparta are among those named in an inscription listing contributors to a Spartan war fund, which belongs to the time of the Peloponnesian War though its exact dating is disputed (ML 67, translated Fornara 132, plus a new fragment: text and translation most easily consulted in W. T. Loomis, *The Spartan War Fund*, Historia Einzelschriften, 74 (1992)).

3.33 Clarus, the seat of an oracle, was a short distance inland from Notium, harbour town to the further-inland Colophon (3.34). The Salaminia and the Paralus were two triremes which the Athenians used for formal state business, though they could be used as ordinary warships too (cf. 3.77).

3.34 This is one of the few places where Thucydides steps outside his chronological framework, to mention at a single point an episode which had begun in 430 but reached its climax now (cf. Introduction, p. xxvii).

3.35 When Paches sent prisoners from Tenedos to Athens, he was breaking the agreement of 3.28, unless (which is possible) he had received orders from Athens.

3.36 If the Athenians did turn down a serious possibility of saving Plataea, they were remarkably callous; but it is unlikely that the Spartans would have abandoned the siege simply to save Salaethus. Since Mytilene had surrendered unconditionally, the Athenians were entitled to treat it as severely as they wished: they are not known to have acted so severely before the Peloponnesian War, but this treatment was to become common during the war (on the Spartan side, cf. 5.83, and Alcidas in 3.32). Thucydides describes the decision as taken in a 'state of anger', and says that the next day the Athenians thought it 'a savage and excessive decision', cf. 'horrible mission' in 3.49; in the debate Cleon will reject appeals to pity (3.37, 38, 40), while Diodotus will object to decisions taken in anger (3.42, 44). 'The authorities' who were persuaded to hold a second debate were the *prytaneis* (see note to 2.22): despite 6.14 there was probably no general rule against that.

Cleon was one of the leading figures in Athenian politics, from or before Pericles' death in 429 until his own death in 422 (5.6–12). He was one of the first politicians of a new kind, not from the old aristocracy (his father was a rich tanner), and not regularly holding office (though he was in the end to be a general), but basing his position on his ability to make persuasive speeches in the assembly and law courts. Cf. the characterization of him at 4.21 and in *Ath. Pol.* 28.3, and the picture of him given by Aristophanes (esp. *Knights*): he was ostentatiously populist, with a wild style and wild policies; he was disliked by Thucydides (for whose exile he may have been responsible: see note to 4.122) and by Aristophanes; the word 'demagogue' (*demagogos*, 'people-leader') may have been coined to refer to him and to men like him. The statement that he 'was . . . at that time . . .' must have been written or rewritten after his death (cf. Introduction, p. xxvii).

3.37–40 In his speech Cleon does not pander to the people (contr. 2.65) but stands out against them: the great demagogue criticizes democracy, and in a clever speech he criticizes clever speakers. Echoes of the Mytilenaean speech at Olympia (3.9–14) are presumably due to Thucydides' sense of what was appropriate, but Cleon in real life may have echoed Pericles in real life as Cleon in Thucydides echoes Pericles in Thucydides.

3.37 When Cleon says, 'your empire is a tyranny', after Pericles had said it was 'like a tyranny' (2.63), it is not clear whether Thucydides intends Cleon to seem more extreme than Pericles. Thucydides comments on the assembly's lack of 'constancy' in 2.65 and elsewhere. For complaints of excessive cleverness, cf. the Spartan Archidamus in 1.84; for 'the ordinary folk', cf. the Syracusan Athenagoras in 6.39.

3.38 'I remain of the same opinion' echoes Pericles in 1.140, 2.61. The Greeks had no concept of a loyal opposition, and men often accused opponents of deliberately espousing wrong policies as a result of bribery. For the sophists, see note to 1.22: many of them claimed to teach skills needed in public life, including that of persuasive speaking, and Aristophanes' *Clouds* caricatures the philosopher Socrates as a sophist who taught how to make the worse argument prevail.

3.39 For the 'revenue on which our strength depends', cf. Pericles in 2.13.

3.41 Diodotus is otherwise unknown, but there is no need to doubt that he did exist and did oppose Cleon in the debates on Mytilene.

3.42–8 In his speech Diodotus defends the principle of debate while reusing the attack on inappropriate cleverness, and he argues that even if it were deserved savage retribution would not be in Athens' best interests.

3.43 Despite the claim that speakers could be called to account, it was a problem which Athens in the late fifth century had to address that the accounting procedures to which office-holders were subject did not apply to speakers who held no office: the *graphe paranomon*, by which speakers and their decrees could be attacked in a law court (cf. 8.67), may have been introduced about this time in an attempt to deal with the problem. For the people's responsibility for decisions, cf. Pericles in 2.60.

3.45–6 This is a remarkable passage, arguing against the death penalty on the grounds that those who are bound to be put to death have no incentive for restraint in their wrongdoing: cf. Thucydides' own comment in 2.53 on the conduct of those who expected to die from the plague. The contrast between 'human nature' (*physis*) and 'law' (*nomos*, seen as arbitrary human convention) was a favourite of the sophists: see note to 1.76. For argument from what was 'likely' (*eikos*) in the past, cf. Thucydides' reasoning in his 'archaeology' (1.2–19 with notes).

3.46 A refund of Athens' expenses had been demanded from Samos in 439 (1.117).

3.49 The Athenian assembly regularly voted by show of hands—probably without a precise count, but on this occasion, although the majority was small, the decision was presumably not challenged. It has been calculated that the voyage of about 187 nautical miles (345 km) might have taken about forty hours for the first ship and about twenty for the second.

3.50 To kill over a thousand men was still severe; it has been estimated that the adult male population of the whole of Lesbos, including non-rebellious Methymna, may have been *c.*22,500. For 'landlords' Thucydides uses *klerouchoi*, which as a technical term denotes men given land in a settlement outside Athens but retaining Athenian citizenship. An inscription (*IG* i³ 66) and a speech (Antiph. 5. *Murder of Herodes* 77) suggest that the Mytilenaeans not put to death retained ownership of their property: either Thucydides is wrong or there was a revision of the original terms not long afterwards.

3.51 *Minoa.* This low-key chapter separates two major episodes, and contains Thucydides' first mention of Nicias, who was to be prominent until his death in Sicily in 413. He came from a family whose wealth was based on the silver mines; like Cleon he was the first member of his family to have a public career, but unlike Cleon he emulated the style of the aristocratic politicians. As a military commander he had his successes, but he seems to have been more eager to avoid failure than to achieve success. For the Athenians' blockade of Megara, cf. 1.67; since autumn 431 they had been attacking Megara twice a year (2.31); in 429 the Peloponnesians had set out from Megara intending to attack the Peiraeus and had raided Salamis (2.93–4). No island now exists which fits Thucydides' description: probably his Minoa was the present-day promontory Teicho, which projects between two promontories of Salamis, and the harbour of Nisaea was to the west of it.

3.52–68 *The siege of Plataea (iii): fall of Plataea.* Plataea like Mytilene was led to surrender by shortage of food. Places taken by force were to be returned under the Peace of Nicias in 421 (5.17), and it may be that this passage was written after 421 and Thucydides has guessed at an intention in the light of that (Hornblower). The offer made by the uncharacteristically anonymous Spartan commander will have encouraged the Plataeans to hope for more generous treatment than they eventually received. The five Spartan judges were probably one from each of the five obes (local units). Plataea's Spartan consul has the suitable name Lacon, and his father may be the Aeimnestus of Hdt. 9.72.

3.53–9 The Plataeans' speech cannot deny that Plataea is a staunch ally of Sparta's enemy Athens, so concentrates on Plataea's services in the past and the hostility of Thebes; as always in Thucydides, the appeal to the gods is in vain.

3.54 It was indeed the Thebans who broke the Thirty Years Treaty by attacking Plataea in 431 (cf. 2.2–6). It would have been tactless to mention Plataea's support for Athens at Marathon in 490, when the Spartans did not arrive until after the battle (Hdt. 6.108, 120); at Thermopylae in 480 not only Plataea but also Thespiae and (allegedly unwillingly, but cf. below on the Thebans' speech) Thebes were represented (Hdt. 7.202, 222); at Artemisium but not at Salamis some Plataeans rowed in Athenian ships (Hdt. 8.1, 44); the last battle against the Persians in Greece, in 479, was fought in Plataea's territory and Plataeans took part (Hdt. 9.12–89). For the revolt of the Helots, 465/4–456/5, see 1.101–3: this is the only text to mention a Plataean contingent.

3.55 Sparta's rejection of Plataea occurred in 519 (cf. 3.68): Plataea, resisting Thebes' attempt to incorporate it in a Boeotian federation, appealed to king Cleomenes of Sparta, but he replied that Sparta was too far away and advised an appeal to Athens (Hdt. 6.108). Fourth-century orators report that after the fall of Plataea the surviving Plataeans were given Athenian citizenship (e.g. [Dem.] 59. *Neaera* 104–6); but Thucydides seems to be reporting an earlier grant of what came to be called *isopoliteia*, the right to exercise the privileges of citizenship when in Athens.

3.56 That the Theban attack in 431 was in a festival season is not denied by the Thebans in 3.65 but was not mentioned in 2.2–6. The Plataeans refer here to a 'universally accepted law', in 3.58 to 'Greek law' and in 3.59 to the 'common code of the Greeks', in 3.66 the Thebans refer to the 'legality' of killing in war but describe the killing of men who had surrendered as 'contrary to all law', and the interpolated 3.84 refers to 'commonly accepted laws'. The Greek word *nomos* covers a range from written laws via 'unwritten laws' (Pericles in 2.37) to accepted conventions. There was no formal international law in the Greek world, but there were general assumptions (e.g. about the inviolability of heralds: see note to 3.72; also note to 1.41); each city had its own laws, but there was enough similarity between them for it to be possible to talk of Greek law.

3.57 For the tripod at Delphi, cf. 1.132; for the destruction of Plataea after Thermopylae, cf. Hdt. 8.50.

3.58 The alliance is that made by the Greek states which combined in 481 to resist the Persian invasion (Hdt. 7.145, cf. 7.132). For suppliants, see note to 1.24; it was widely acknowledged that the rights of those making a just supplication should be respected, but the rights of enemies who surrendered were secure only if guaranteed by the terms of surrender—if then: the Plataeans had probably broken an undertaking to the Thebans who surrendered to them in 431 (2.5, cf. the Thebans in 3.66). For the tombs of those killed in the battle of Plataea, cf. Hdt. 9.85.

3.61–7 The Thebans' speech represents the Plataeans as hostile to their fellow Boeotians and as accomplices of Athens rather than true friends of the Greeks; Thebes' support for Persia in 480 (in fact not certain before the Greeks' defeat at Thermopylae, and inevitable after that) is blamed on an unrepresentative clique ruling the city.

3.61 The tradition was that the Boeotians had arrived in their territory from Thessaly, in which case Plataea in the south may well have been one of the later sites to be occupied; Plataea is included in Boeotia in the Catalogue of Ships (Hom., *Il.* 2.494–510); we have no evidence on the relations between Plataea and the other Boeotians before 519.

3.62 Attitudes to a distant state were often conditioned by attitudes to a neighbour: according to Herodotus, Phocis did not medize because Thessaly did, Argos did not join the Greek alliance because it would not accept the leadership of Sparta (Hdt. 8.30, 7.148–52). 'Medize' is used frequently by Herodotus and others of collaboration with the Medes, i.e. the Persians, and the analogous 'atticize' will have been coined in the time of the Delian League. Probably 'democracy' was coined in Athens in the second quarter of the fifth century, and 'oligarchy' was coined to denote its opposite (though opponents of democracy tended to prefer 'aristocracy'). *Isonomia* ('equal rights for all') and other compounds of *iso-* seem to have been in vogue *c.*500 to denote constitutional government as opposed to tyranny (for which see note to 1.13–19), and Thucydides here and in 4.78 uses *dynasteia* ('small dominant clique') to contrast the quasi-tyranny of a small body with a more moderate oligarchy. How a particular regime should be categorized will not always have been self-evident; it may well be that early-fifth-century Thebes had a typical aristocratic regime, from which Thucydides' Thebans are trying to distance themselves. On Athens and Boeotia in the mid-fifth century, cf. 1.107–8, 113: it has been suggested that Tanagra was disputing Thebes' claim to the leadership of Boeotia.

3.63 The anti-Persian alliance of 481 did not include 'the whole community of Greeks': cf. above.

3.64 There is no evidence that the Plataeans joined with the Athenians against Aegina (on which cf. 1.105, 108) or any other states, but it is not unlikely. For the Spartans' final offer, cf. 2.72. There was a tendency (though not always followed) in the ancient world to believe that people's fundamental goodness or badness does not change, and that good actions by the bad are hypocritical while bad actions by the good are doubly bad because out of character.

3.65 It was all too common for members of a minority party in a state to prefer having the upper hand with outside support to not having it: cf. 2.2–6. Here it appears that the supporters of Thebes were rich and oligarchically inclined, and they wanted the Plataeans to be not 'enemies of none' but friends of Thebes and Sparta rather than of Athens. However, Plataea had been separate from the 'traditions of the whole Boeotian community' for at least ninety-three years.

3.66 Thebes' allegation of 'three crimes' trumps Plataea's allegation of 'two terrible ordeals' in 3.57.

3.67 At Coroneia in 447/6 the Thebans were fighting for liberation from Athens, not necessarily for attachment to Sparta (cf. 1.113).

3.68 If the figures here and in 2.74 and 3.24 are all accurate, there are forty-two Plataeans unaccounted for: some at least will have died during the siege, but Hornblower wonders whether some now claimed to have benefited the Spartans and were spared; the women (cf. 2.78), or some of them, may already have been slaves. For Megarian exiles, cf. 4.66; the Plataean supporters of Sparta had presumably gone into exile after the episode in 431. The sanctuary of Hera was outside the city (cf. Hdt. 9.52). Some have doubted the correctness of the 'ninety-third' year, but without good reason.

3.69–85 *Civil war in Corcyra (i).* The story of the Peloponnesian ships is resumed from 3.33; they perhaps took a southerly route, 'off Crete', to avoid the islands of the Athenian empire. Brasidas had shown himself to be an energetic commander in episodes reported in 2.29, 2.85–94. For the twelve ships at Naupactus, see 3.7 (but the twelve now include the Salaminia and Paralus, in the Aegean in 3.33).

3.70 To explain the civil war Thucydides steps outside his chronological framework (cf. Introduction, p. xxvii). Most of the Corcyraean prisoners will have been taken in the battle of Sybota in 433 (1.55); they were probably sent back to Corcyra not long before summer 427. For the ransom, we correct the manuscripts' incredibly large 'eight hundred' talents to eighty. Athens' original alliance with Corcyra was purely defensive (1.44), but in 431 Corcyra had joined the Athenians in raiding western Greece (2.25). It cannot be confirmed that there had been a 'former friendship with the Peloponnesians' (contr. 1.31, 32, 37); but this decision for neutrality represents a victory for the anti-Athenian party. It is not clear what was distinctive about Peithias as a 'volunteer' consul. If rich men considered a fine of 1 stater (3 Corinthian drachmas) enormous, they must have taken many thousands of props over an extended period: taking them from a sanctuary was not necessarily sacrilege, but could be viewed as such by their opponents. Alcinous was king of the *Odyssey*'s Phaeacians (see note to 1.25).

3.71 The declaration of neutrality here is stronger than that in 3.70. Those who had fled to Athens on the trireme of 3.70 secured the sending of the sixty ships to be mentioned in 3.80.

3.72 Envoys, unlike heralds, were not regarded as inviolable. Archaeologists on the basis of meagre remains have located the ancient city to the south of the modern town, with the harbours on either side of the Kanoni peninsula; but there is no island nearby, and Gomme argued that probably the Hyllaic harbour was where the modern, north-facing harbour is; the acropolis the headland south-east of that; the other harbour south of the headland; and the agora near that.

3.73 It is not clear why the slaves supported the democrats: Greek democrats were not opposed to slavery, and Hornblower suggests that the slaves simply expected the democrats to win.

3.74 For the involvement of the women, cf. Plataea in 431 (2.4), and for fires, cf. Plataea again (2.4, 77).

3.75 Nicostratus will appear as general several times until 418/7, and is probably the Nicostratus of Ar., *Vesp.* 81–4. Thucydides often refers to 'leaders of the people's party', reflecting the fact that these were usually not themselves ordinary, poor men. The island is probably Vido, north of the modern harbour.

3.76 For mainland Sybota, cf. 1.50.

3.78 For the naval tactics, cf. Phormio near Naupactus in 429 (2.83–4): it is likely enough that both sides were conscious of what had happened there. Alcidas is again feeble, as when he was sent to support Mytilene (cf. 3.29–33). For Leucimme, cf. 1.30.

3.80 This is the first appearance of Eurymedon, who held several commands (mostly in the west: we do not know whether he had connections there) until he died at Syracuse in 413. Unlike Nicostratus in 3.75, he made no attempt to restrain the democrats.

3.81 The total width of the isthmus was 4 miles (6 km): the Corinthians are said to have dug a canal in the seventh century (Strabo 451/10.2.8), and there was a navigable channel at some later times; we do not know exactly what the situation was now. Not all democrats will have been poor, lower-class men; and Greeks who incurred large debts were usually not poor. 'Every imaginable form' of death is a favourite Thucydidean expression in such contexts: cf. 3.83, 98. Those who died in the temple of Dionysus had been left to starve—and not removed before they expired, as Pausanias was in 1.134.

3.82–3 Here Thucydides digresses from this particular episode to discuss in general terms the growing evil of civil war and the collapse of moral standards during the Peloponnesian War: cf. his comments on the Athenian plague (2.53). For his view of human nature, cf. 1.22. The word translated as 'party' is *hetaireia*, used of associations particularly of upper-class young men, which might be purely social or might have a lawful or unlawful political dimension (cf. 6.27, 8.65). The point about divine law is that invocation of the gods was a common means of reinforcing pledges. These chapters are ambiguous over cleverness: revolutionaries reached extremes of ingenuity and sought a reputation for cleverness, and simple decency was mocked (as usual in Thucydides, laughter is unkind), but those who were less intelligent and made up their minds quickly had the better chances of survival; intellectuals do not make the most effective revolutionaries.

3.84 This chapter was rejected in antiquity and is rejected by most modern scholars as an interpolation: it is not blatantly un-Thucydidean, but the verdict of antiquity should be accepted.

3.85 The episode at the end of this chapter may have occurred later than the summer of 427 (cf. Introduction, p. xxvii). Mount Istone is probably Pantokrator, north of the city and the highest mountain in the island. Corcyra was to send fifteen ships to support Athens in 426 (3.95), and Thucydides will continue the Corcyraean narrative in 4.2, 46-8.

3.86 *Athens and the west (i)*. This is the first of a series of disjointed sections on Athenian involvement in the west which will continue to 424 (4.58-65); Thucydides' treatment is avowedly selective (3.90). In these sections he regularly refers to 'Sicily', though the activity which he reports was not limited to Sicily. For the interest in the west of both sides, cf. 1.36, 44 (Athens), 2.7 (Sparta). This is the first appearance of Laches, who was involved in the truce with Sparta in 423 (4.118) and the Peace of Nicias in 421 (5.19), and commanded and was killed at Mantinea in 418 (5.61, 74); Plato's dialogue *Laches* investigates the nature of courage. On the Sicilian cities named here, see 6.2-5; we cannot say how long before this point the war between Syracuse and Leontini had begun. The Leontinian deputation to Athens included the celebrated orator Gorgias (Pl., *Hp. Mai.* 282 B, Diod. Sic. 12.53-4): the 'old alliance' is probably that renewed in 433/2 (see note to 1.32-6). If the Peloponnesians did import corn from the west it would reduce their need to farm their land and give them more freedom to fight, but we do not know to what extent they did. In 424 the Athenian commanders, who by then had a larger force, were punished for accepting the treaty of Gela and not conquering Sicily (4.65): some scholars have wondered whether the Athenians already entertained that ambition in 427.

3.87-8 Fifth winter (427/6)

3.87 *Plague in Athens; earthquakes.* In 413 Sparta's occupation of Deceleia 'did immense harm to the Athenians, and . . . was a crucial element in the city's decline' (7.27): probably this comment on the demoralization caused by the plague was written before then, but Thucydides could use such superlatives without a specific time reference, so that is not certain. Comparison with the figures in 2.13 indicates that the plague killed about a third of Athens' population. The bare report of 'the many earthquakes' is neither related to the war nor used to display Thucydides' rationalism. The article suggests that this was remembered as a year of unusually frequent earthquakes; for Thucydides' temptation to believe that they might after all have some deeper significance, cf. 1.23 and Introduction, p. xlv.

3.88 *Athens and the west (ii).* The Aeolian Islands (as they are still called) lie to the north of the eastern part of Sicily; Aeolus was the legendary ruler of the winds (e.g. Hom., *Od.* 10.1–27). Nowadays Strongyle is the most fiery island. Similar material, attributed to Antiochus of Syracuse, is found in Paus. 10.11, and Antiochus may be Thucydides' source too (cf. Introduction, p. xxix). For the Sicels, cf. 6.2. Thucydides regularly uses the Athenian/Ionian form Messene, but we follow the normal English practice of using the Dorian form Messana for this city to distinguish it from Messene/Messenia in the Peloponnese.

3.89–102 Sixth summer (426)

3.89 *Peloponnesian invasion of Attica; earthquakes.* Archidamus had died between the previous spring and now (see note to 3.26). The Spartans might have called off their invasion either through fear of physical danger or because they saw a religious significance in the earthquakes: Diod. Sic. 12.59.1 prefers the religious explanation; Thucydides uses these occurrences to link tidal waves (of the kind now known by the Japanese term *tsunami*) with earthquakes. Orobiae, a dependency of Hestiaea, was towards the north-west end of Euboea opposite Opuntian Locris (for which cf. 1.108); Peparethus is one of the islands north-east of that end of Euboea.

3.90 *Athens and the west (iii).* This is the one point at which Thucydides states that he limits himself to recording 'the most notable actions'. That must be true of the whole of his history; but his brief and disjointed account of Athens' activities in the west between 427 and 424 makes us particularly aware that he cannot have recorded every incident, and here we have an independent account supplying details which he omits: a papyrus fragment from Antiochus of Syracuse or a writer following him mentions activities of Charoeades and Laches at the beginning of this summer (*PSI* xii 1283 = *FGrH* 577 F 2, col. i).

3.91 *Melos and Boeotia.* The force sent round the Peloponnese (cf. 3.94–8) introduces us to Demosthenes, Athens' most adventurous commander in the earlier part of the war. He was sometimes unsuccessful (e.g. 3.95–8), but he learnt from his mistakes (cf. 3.107–14), and he was responsible for Athens' spectacular success at Pylos in 425 (4.3–23, 26–41). He took reinforcements to Sicily in 413, and was captured and put to death then.

For Melos, cf. 2.9. It is said to have been founded from Sparta (5.84, cf. Hdt. 8.48), and it was now the only Aegean island outside the Athenian orbit; inclusion in the optimistic tribute assessment list of 425 (ML 69, translated Fornara 136, i. 65) does not prove that it paid. It appears among contributors to a Spartan war fund in an inscribed list whose dating is uncertain (ML 67, translated Fornara 132: see note to 3.32). For its eventual conquest by Athens in 416, see 5.84–116.

The attack on Boeotia is the first recorded use of the full Athenian army during the war except in the attacks on Megara (2.31): in the event it achieved little, but it showed that the Athenians could defeat the

Boeotians if they attacked suddenly and the Boeotians could not obtain Peloponnesian support (but contrast the Delium campaign of 424/3: 4.89–101). This is Thucydides' only mention of Hipponicus, a man from a rich and distinguished family and a later husband of Pericles' wife. Some scholars have thought that the two-pronged attack on Boeotia, and with it Demosthenes' move towards Boeotia from Naupactus (see 3.94–8, at 95), had been planned coherently in advance. However, Nicias' attack on Melos was surely intended seriously, and how long it would take could not have been predicted; Demosthenes' campaign is said to have been prompted by the Messenians at Naupactus, and it was even less certain whether and if so how quickly he could reach Boeotia. Unless Thucydides' account is seriously misleading, a fully coordinated plan does not seem credible; the most we can assume is that Demosthenes knew an attack on Boeotia was intended and thought he might arrive there in the same year.

3.92–3 *Spartan colony at Heracleia in Trachis.* The Greek text here is 'in Trachinia', but in the translation we have used the form which Thucydides uses elsewhere. The site was a short distance to the west of Thermopylae (and the head of the gulf has silted up considerably since Thucydides' time); the Malians lived to the west and north of the gulf, and the Oetaeans to the south-west of them. Doris was to the south of the Oetaeans: whatever the truth behind the legendary 'Dorian invasion', the Dorian Greeks of the Peloponnese regarded Doris as their homeland (cf. 1.12, 107). This is the first of a number of passages in which people outside the heartland of central and southern Greece are said to be afraid of Athenian ambitions (cf. 3.113–14, 4.60–1, 63, 92, 6.76–7; and an Athenian reply, 6.82–7); Spartan hankering for power in northern Greece surfaces from time to time (cf. Leotychidas, in note to 1.89).

Consultation of Delphi before the foundation of a colony was commonplace: it is remarkable that Thucydides sees fit to mention it, and in the language used here, but the language need not imply that Thucydides himself believed in the god (cf. Introduction, p. xliv). The founders are all men with significant names, perhaps chosen partly for that reason, but Thucydides does not remark on this: Leon the lion (associated with Heracles), Alcidas (a name borne by Heracles) and Damagon ('leader of the people'). They presumably did not stay long: other rulers are named in 5.51–2.

3.93 In Euboea the Athenians had no trouble until 411 (cf. 8.95–6), and the colony was not a success, as Thucydides steps outside his chronological framework to indicate, but it was used as a staging-post by Brasidas on his way to the Thraceward region (the text here suggests that the Spartans were thinking of such a journey when they founded Heracleia, but Thucydides may be indulging in hindsight: 4.78; cf. 5.12). For its vicissitudes, see 5.51–2, 8.3; in 395 it was captured by the Boeotians and given to the Thessalians (Diod. Sic. 14.38.4–5, 82.6–7).

3.94–8 *Campaigns in north-western Greece (i).* Ellomenum is not otherwise attested: W. M. Murray in the *Barrington Atlas* places it on the east coast of the island, but it could have been on the mainland opposite. Leucas was attacked by Athens in 428 (3.7); Zacynthus was an ally of Athens from the beginning of the war (2.9, cf. 2.7), and Cephallenia was won over in 431 (2.7, 30). The Messenians were those at Naupactus; the Aetolians (on whose primitive nature cf. 1.5) lived inland to the north of Naupactus. It is not clear, and Thucydides perhaps did not ask himself, what is meant by 'the rest of the mainland thereabouts'. The light arms of the Aetolians (cf. Eur., *Phoen.* 133-40) were to prove effective in mountainous country against Demosthenes' hoplites. The note on the primitive nature of the Aetolians, qualified by 'are said', is reminiscent of Herodotus.

3.95 For Demosthenes' intention of reaching Boeotia, see note to 3.91, above: by going inland through Aetolia he was not taking the easier route through Ozolian Locris, along the coast, from which he could continue past Amphissa to Cytinium. Phocis had been friendly to Athens in the middle of the century (1.107-8, 111-12), but was reckoned among Sparta's allies at the beginning of the war (2.9). The Corcyraeans would presumably, like the Acarnanians, have preferred to campaign against Leucas.

3.96 The digression on Hesiod shows Thucydides in atypically relaxed mood: for the confusion over Nemea in the Peloponnese and this sanctuary of Nemean Zeus, cf. 'the greatest festival of Zeus' in the story of Cylon, 1.126. The sanctuary was perhaps at Oeneum, on the coast; the towns captured by Demosthenes were inland from there, south of the river Daphnus (now Mornos).

3.97 Aegitium was to the east of Teichium, again south of the river.

3.98 The Athenians' archers would have run out of ammunition before the Aetolians' javelin-men. For the use of fire, cf. Sphacteria in 425 (4.29-30). The Athenian hoplites here are apparently the marines of 3.95 (for this service the Athenians sometimes used hoplites, sometimes *thetes*: 6.43, 8.24). One hundred and twenty dead was a high proportion of a body of 300, and these were the worst Athenian losses which Thucydides has reported since the beginning of the war (at Delium in 424/3 the Athenians were to lose nearly 1,000, but from a total of *c.*7,000: 4.101, with 4.90, 93-4); 'in the course of this war' probably refers to the Archidamian War, not to the Peloponnesian War as a whole. Probably Demosthenes was deposed after this defeat; but (whether or not he knew that he had been deposed) since no successor had arrived he later acted as general to save Naupactus (3.102), and the Acarnanians invited him and he agreed to command their forces (3.105-14).

3.99 *Athens and the west (iv)*. This is the shortest of Thucydides' sections on the west. Although, as usual, he begins with a reference to Sicily, this episode took place on the 'toe' of Italy.

3.100-2 *Campaigns in north-western Greece (ii)*. The envoys will have been sent about the time of Demosthenes' invasion of Aetolia, and this is possibly the occasion of an inscribed treaty between Sparta and Aetolia (ML 67 *bis*, in the 1988 reissue). The Spartan commanders are an early instance of Sparta's using not a king but a citizen (often with other citizens as advisers) to command land forces which did not include Spartan citizens: the technical term 'harmost', frequent in Xenophon, is used by Thucydides only at 8.5.

3.101 Delphi was sympathetic to the Spartans (cf. 1.118). Literary writers do not always use the forms of names attested in inscriptions, and we have retained the manuscripts' versions of the city names, but according to inscriptions 'Ipnea' should be 'Hypnia': the places are probably mentioned in order from east to west.

3.102 Molycrium was west of Naupactus, at or near Antirrhium, where the gulf is at its narrowest. On failing to take Naupactus Eurylochus moved further west, to an area which was perhaps already controlled by the Achaeans of the northern Peloponnese, as it was in the early fourth century: like Demosthenes in Aetolia, he was persuaded to abandon one set of allies in order to support another, with disastrous results.

3.103–16 Sixth winter (426/5)

3.103 *Athens and the west (v).* Inessa was an inland site south-west of Mount Aetna: for a time in the middle of the century it had been the second home of the city of Aetna founded originally at Catana by Hiero of Syracuse (Diod. Sic. 11.49, 76, 91).

3.104 *Athens' purification of Delos.* Cf. 1.8, where this figures in an argument to support Thucydides' view of early Greece. Birth and death were regarded as polluting, and to be kept away from sanctuaries (cf. Pausanias' death, 1.134). Thucydides is perhaps disparaging Athens' willingness to act in response to oracles; for the earlier purification by Peisistratus, likewise in response to oracles, cf. Hdt. 1.64. Olympia and Delphi were in the Spartan orbit, so in attending to Delos Athens was perhaps attempting to redress the divine balance; Diod. Sic. 12.58.6–7 explains the purification as an appeasement of Apollo after the plague, but by disturbing the dead the Athenians were committing sacrilege in the name of religion. On all this, see Hornblower, who wonders whether Thucydides himself had some connection with the purification—but probably he could not have taken part both in that and in the naval side of the campaign of 3.105–14, of which he shows detailed knowledge. Rheneia is about 750 yards (700 m) from Delos: for the episode involving Polycrates, perhaps towards the end of his reign, cf. 1.13. For Athens' later attempt to go beyond this purification, see 5.1, 32. The first celebration of the new festival will have been *c.* February 425; probably in 417, Nicias led the Athenian delegation with a great show of magnificence (Plut., *Nic.* 3–4: cf. note to 6.16), but there is no good evidence linking him with the purification. Hornblower argues that the Ephesian festival is not that of Artemis but the Panionia, the Festival of All the Ionians, and suggests that that was originally held at the Panionium on Cape Mycale and moved back there in 373.

The Hymn to Apollo is one of the poems transmitted to us as the *Homeric Hymns*: a hymn to Delian Apollo (from which Thucydides quotes lines 146–50, 165–72) followed by a hymn to Pythian (i.e. Delphic) Apollo. Some ancient writers attributed the hymn to Cynaethus of Chios, perhaps of the late sixth century (Hippostratus *FGrH* 568 F 5 = schol. Pind. *Nem.* 2.1c); the Delian part of the hymn is perhaps to be dated to the early sixth century (G. S. Kirk, in *Cambridge History of Classical Literature*, i (Cambridge University Press, 1985), 110–15); Thucydides in attributing the hymn to Homer is echoing current opinion. Thucydides' text differs at many points from that transmitted in the manuscripts of the hymn, but probably he was correctly quoting the version known to him. The last line quoted reflects the tradition that Homer was blind and was from Chios. By Ionia's 'troubles' Thucydides probably refers to the conquest of mainland Ionia first by the Lydians and then particularly by the Persians, and the Ionian Revolt against the Persians, in the sixth and the early fifth century.

3.105–14 *Campaigns in north-western Greece (iii).* Not all the sites mentioned in these chapters have been securely identified. Map 4 shows the identifications of W. K. Pritchett, *Studies in Ancient Greek Topography*, viii (Amsterdam: Gieben, 1992), 1–78; and also, in brackets, two alternative identifications by N. G. L. Hammond, *Studies in Greek History* (Oxford University Press, 1973), 471–85, with 473 fig. 21, which some scholars think more likely to be right (Hammond's Argos is a more substantial site than Pritchett's, but is *c*.3 miles, 4.5 km, inland). The manuscripts sometimes use the singular Olpe and sometimes the plural Olpae: we follow Pritchett in believing that the same place is meant, and in the translation we consistently use Olpae. They sometimes use the singular Idomene and sometimes the plural Idomenae, this time for an easily intelligible reason (see note to 3.112, below), and we consistently use Idomene.

Joint assizes of the Acarnanians and Amphilochians were probably instituted after the episode in which Phormio was involved, not long before the Peloponnesian War, mentioned in 2.68. For Demosthenes' status, see note to 3.98, above. The twenty Athenian ships had perhaps been sent to replace those which he had had, which by now will have returned to Athens without him: that Demosthenes was not now an Athenian general did not prevent this force from cooperating with him.

3.106 The Peloponnesians' route will have taken them to the west of the two lakes on the eastern border of Acarnania, to Limnaea, at the south-eastern corner of the Gulf of Ambracia.

3.107 The ravine was that of the river which reaches the coast between Olpae and Metropolis. Demosthenes' ambush shows that he had learnt from his defeat at Aegitium (cf. 3.97): the sunken path will have been in the ravine. The Peloponnesians' mixed formation was probably adopted so that the better troops from the Peloponnese could stiffen the others; since the army did not include Spartan citizens (cf. 3.100), it is not clear who will have formed Eurylochus' company.

3.108 The incautious pursuit by the Ambraciots shows that they had not learnt the lesson of 429 (cf. 2.80–2); it must be not just they but the whole army who 'made their escape . . . to Olpae'.

3.109 Macarius and Menedaïus were Eurylochus' citizen advisers (cf. 3.100), who took over the command after he had been killed. Mercenaries have not been mentioned before: they may be identical, or overlap, with the allies of 3.100.

3.111 The Greek text of the second sentence has no second element with *de* to answer a first element with *men*: the translation gives what we take to be the intended meaning, but we are not sure precisely what Thucydides' text was.

3.112 The Greek text varies between the singular Idomene (here) and the plural Idomenae: in view of the two hills the variation is easy to understand; the larger hill is the more southerly. The 'pass' will have been to the west of the two hills, and the mountain route to the east. For men caught still in bed, cf. the Spartans on Sphacteria, 4.32. There was not a single Dorian dialect, but there was a family resemblance between the Dorian dialects, and Demosthenes presumably thought that the Ambraciots would take any Dorian-speakers to be Peloponnesian and friendly; in 4.3, 41, Demosthenes was to make more specific use of the dialect of the Messenians from Naupactus. For light-armed troops against hoplites, cf. the Aetolians opposing Demosthenes (3.97–8); but despite Thucydides' 'unfamiliar country' the Ambraciots were less than 10 miles (16 km) from their own city. The Amphilochians probably were barbarian in the sense of non-Greek (see note to 2.68); but here 'barbarian' implies uncivilized. For 'few out of many', cf. 1.100, 7.86.

3.113 This vivid informal dialogue is unique in Thucydides: it provides an impressive climax to an impressive narrative, and is reminiscent of tragedy. For the superlative ('the greatest disaster'), cf. 3.98 on Aegitium; probably here as there 'this war' is the Archidamian War; cf. 7.30 on the disaster at Mycalessus in 413. On casualty figures Thucydides uniquely, and to great effect, withholds what he claims to know because it would not be believed: cf. the Behistun Inscription of the Persian King Dareius I (Brosius 44, §58). For his confidence in an unfulfilled conditional statement, cf. 2.94, on the Peloponnesians' aborted attack on the Peiraeus in 429/8.

3.114 Dedications were made about this time by 'the Messenians and Naupactus' at Olympia (*SIG*³ 80 = ML 74, translated Fornara 135) and Delphi (*SIG*³ 81 = *F. Delphes* III. iv 1 + *SEG* xix 392); for the statue at Olympia, see e.g. C. M. Robertson, *A Shorter History of Greek Art* (Cambridge University Press, 1981), 126, with pl. 171. It is interesting that not even the Athenians could be sure of getting their booty home by sea; in fact not all was lost (*IG* ii² 403, 7–12 refers to repairs in the fourth century to a statue of Athena Nike dedicated after this success). The treaty reflects distrust of a powerful Athens, and amounts to an agreement by the Acarnanians and Ambraciots to resist further intervention in their region by both Athenians and Peloponnesians: although the Athenians had had the better of the fighting, they derived no benefit from it. The Corinthian colony of Anactorium had supported the Peloponnesians (2.9, 20–2), but in 425 Athens helped the Acarnanians to capture it (4.49). The Acarnanians will support the Athenians in Boeotia in 424/3 (4.77).

3.115–16 *Athens and the west (vi)*. Himera was originally Chalcidian, i.e. Ionian (cf. 6.5), but had been resettled from Dorian Acragas (Diod. Sic. 11.49.3, cf. Hdt. 7.165). Thucydides does not explain why Laches was superseded: he appears to have been deposed and recalled to Athens (schol. Ar., *Vesp.* 240), but his ongoing career suggests that he was not put on trial or at any rate not convicted. Pythodorus was an associate of the philosophers Parmenides and Zeno, of Elea in Italy (Pl., *Prm.* 126 B, 127 A–D, etc.). The forty ships now prepared (cf. 4.2), added to the original twenty and those of Pythodorus, would make over sixty, i.e. more than the Athenians originally intended to send in 415 (6.8). Sophocles may be the man of that name who was to be one of the Thirty oligarchs ruling Athens in 404/3 (Xen., *Hell.* 2.3.2). The Locrians must have recaptured their fort after Laches had left (cf. 3.99).

3.116 For Thucydides' interest in volcanic activity, cf. 3.88. There is a vivid account of the previous eruption by Pind., *Pyth.* 1.21–8: it is dated 479/8 by the Parian Marble, *FGrH* 239 A 52. Thucydides' third eruption must have been earlier than that; his silence on the eruption of 396/5 (Diod. Sic. 14.59.3) does not prove that he had died or stopped working by then, though it is likely that he had done so (cf. Introduction, p. xxv).

BOOK FOUR

4.1–49 Seventh summer (425)

4.1 *Athens and the west (vii)*. The corn came 'into ear' about late April, after Thucydides' spring had begun in early March (see note to 2.1), and it was ripe about late May (see note to 3.1). Internal dissension in Rhegium has not been mentioned before.

4.2–6 *Pylos (i)*. This is an episode which Thucydides singles out for detailed and vivid treatment. It was an exciting episode; it was important for its effect on the course of the war, and would have been even more important if the Athenians had succeeded in following it up by provoking a Messenian revolt (cf. 4.41). At various points he stresses the element of chance, and we may suspect that he has over-emphasized that and played down elements of planning—because the success was due in part to Cleon, of whom he disapproved (cf. esp. 4.27–8), and because he thought the Athenians in refusing to settle with the Spartans were in an un-Periclean way 'grasping for more' (4.21, 41, cf. 4.17).

Civil strife in Corcyra had been continuing since 427 (3.69-85). For Demosthenes in 426, see 3.94-8, 100-2, 105-14; now he was probably a general elect for 425/4. He must have given some indication of his plans, to influential supporters (perhaps including Cleon: see note to 4.28) if not to the assembly, to have obtained the permission mentioned here.

4.3 Laconia for Thucydides includes Messenia. The storm must have arisen by chance, but Pylos seems to have been a site which Demosthenes had in mind (though he had not been able to bring tools for fortification). He occupied the headland to the north of the island of Sphacteria (cf. Map 5); the present-day lagoon did not exist, or at any rate was too shallow for warships; the Spartans' name Coryphasium will be used in treaties (4.118, 5.18).

4.4 'The troops' should perhaps be deleted from the first sentence (it is unlikely that Demosthenes would have communicated with them through the commanders of the tribal contingents); presumably both soldiers (probably more than the usual ten per ship) and sailors took part in the fortification.

4.5 The Spartan festival was presumably not a major one, since it had not prevented the dispatch of the army to invade Attica. As Hornblower remarks, in Thucydides men who think something can easily be done are usually mistaken.

4.6 It is not clear why the Spartans invaded Attica too early; their longest invasion, in 430, had lasted about forty days (2.57).

4.7 *An episode in the north-east.* Thucydides interrupts the account of Pylos to chronicle a campaign elsewhere of little importance. This Eïon is not the city at the mouth of the Strymon (1.98, 4.50, 102, etc.) but was somewhere to the north of the three prongs of Chalcidice. The 'Chalcidians' here are those who in 433 were incorporated in the *polis* of Olynthus and given land near lake Bolbe (1.58), and the Bottiaeans also lived north of the three prongs (cf. 2.99).

4.8-23 *Pylos (ii).* For Spartan use of the isthmus of Leucas, cf. 3.81; the Spartan camp was probably to the north-east of the great bay, near the modern Gialova. Thucydides reveals casually that the Athenian fleet had not 'pressed ahead' (4.5) to Corcyra, but was waiting at Zacynthus, about 70 miles (115 km) from Pylos. Having sent two of his ships to summon the rest, Demosthenes now had three ships, and about 600 men.

In general, Thucydides seems well informed on the topography of this campaign, but two figures in the manuscripts' text of 4.8 are factually wrong: the passage to the north of Sphacteria is about 110 yards (100 m) wide, but the passage to the south is twelve times as wide, and the length of Sphacteria is about 4,800 yards (4,400 m). We believe (though not all do) that the errors are more probably due to a copyist than to Thucydides himself, and have accepted two emendations: 'eight or nine <stades>', i.e. 'less than one mile', rather than 'eight or nine (*sc.* ships)' for the southern passage (implying a stade at the short end of Thucydides' range: see Appendix), and 'twenty-five' rather than 'fifteen' stades for the length of the island ('two and three-quarter miles': implying a stade in the middle of his range: this second emendation is widely accepted); cf. textual note.

The Spartans did not in fact block the entrances (cf. 4.13): we do not know the basis for Thucydides' statement that they intended to do so. The 'divisions' from which the men to go to Sphacteria were picked were the *lochoi*: according to 5.68 there were six regular *lochoi* and one of liberated Helots in 418, but it is possible that there were in fact six *morai* each of two *lochoi* (see note to 5.68), and that the 420 men represent one *enomotia* of 35 men from each of the twelve *lochoi* (A. J. Toynbee, *Some Problems of Greek History* (Oxford University Press, 1969), 376-7). Helots generally accompanied the hoplites on campaign as attendants (cf. Hdt. 7.229, 9.10).

4.9 Demosthenes' ships will have been in the small bay to the south-east of the headland. The Messenians probably arrived (from Naupactus) not by chance but because Demosthenes had been in touch with them. Most of the men will have been stationed on the east side of the fort, and Demosthenes with his squadron to the south-west; he had not expected to be outnumbered at sea, because he had not thought the Spartan ships from Corcyra would arrive before the Athenian ships.

4.10 In his speech Demosthenes is made to predict the Spartans' actions correctly. He rejects the Thucydidean and Athenian virtues of intelligence and calculation—but then (as noted by Gomme) goes on to perform the calculation.

4.11 The Spartans originally had 60 ships (4.2, 8): the other seventeen were perhaps watching for the Athenian fleet. We are not told how large their land force was (scarcely as large as the 12,000 of Diod. Sic. 12.61.2) or who commanded it. Brasidas had been an adviser to Alcidas at Corcyra in 427 (3.69), and presumably had gone to Corcyra again with this fleet: Hornblower follows up the suggestion of J. G. Howie that in Book 4 and the beginning of Book 5 Thucydides has constructed a distorted picture in order to present the *aristeia* (heroic career) of Brasidas, like the *aristeia* of a Homeric hero.

4.12 For the gangway (for disembarking) and outrigger (through which the highest-level oars were threaded) of a trireme see Morrison, Coates, and Rankov, *The Athenian Trireme*², 236 ('gangplank'), 161-7, 198 fig. 56 (outrigger). On the reversal of circumstances for the land power Sparta and the sea power Athens, cf. 4.14; and there are other passages in the Pylos narrative which focus on reversal or paradox.

4.13 Asine was on the coast of the Messenian Gulf; Prote was about 9 miles (15 km) north-west of Pylos.

4.14 If the Spartan ships were in the north of the bay, using the southern as well as the narrow northern entrance will have increased the distance travelled by many of the Athenians' ships but will have enabled the whole fleet to get into the bay more quickly. For every man's thinking that his personal involvement was essential, cf. 2.8, and contrast Pericles' depiction of the Peloponnesians in 1.141.

4.15 The Spartans had not been overwhelmingly defeated, as suggested here and (even more) in 7.71, but the defeat may have been seized on by men who were already interested in ending the war. The 'authorities' are probably the five ephors and the *gerousia* of twenty-eight elders plus the two kings.

4.16 For the truce Thucydides may be quoting, or be close to, the actual words: he does not use official formulas, but we should not expect that of an agreement made not by the regular bodies but by the men in command on the spot. That the Spartans should have agreed to hand over all the warships in Laconia is a surprising concession (noted by Hornblower). The food allowance was generous: nearly 4 imp. pints (2.2 litres) of meal, and a quarter of that volume of wine (cf. Hdt. 6.57 on the allowance for Spartan kings dining at home, using the somewhat larger Spartan measure; contr. 7.87 on the much less generous allowance for the Athenians captured by Syracuse in 413). Kneaded barley-cakes were moistened and eaten uncooked; the 'attendants' were Helots (cf. 4.8).

4.17–20 The Spartans in Athens are in a weak position, and can only invite the Athenians to make peace while their position is strong because they cannot count on its remaining strong indefinitely—but, as all too often when the side in a weak position offered to make peace, the side in a strong position did hope its position would remain strong indefinitely. For speaking 'at some length', contrast Sthenelaïdas in 1.86, and Brasidas' 'brief demonstration' in 5.9.

4.18 'Wise men' are men of prudence (*sophrosyne*), commonly considered a Spartan virtue. It was a major theme of Herodotus' history that good fortune cannot be relied on to continue (e.g. Hdt. 1.30–3, on Solon's visit to Croesus). The argument at the end of 4.18 is that, if the Athenians make peace while they are winning, they will seem both strong and intelligent, but, if they continue fighting and eventually lose, their earlier successes will seem due not to strength but to luck.

4.19 In offering peace and alliance the Spartans are offering to abandon their current allies and the cause of Greek freedom, as they will do in 421 (5.14–24). On making friends by placing others under an obligation, cf. Pericles in 2.40; 'taking risks in defiance of judgement' is said to be characteristic of the Athenians by the Corinthians in 1.70.

4.20 'Something irremediably divisive' would be the death of the Spartans on Sphacteria (cf. 4.15, where 'coming to grief' renders another euphemism); after the truce has failed the Spartans will in 4.38 tell the men to do 'nothing dishonourable'. Formally it was clear that the Peloponnesians had begun the war in 431, through the Theban attack on Plataea (2.2) and the invasion of Attica preceded by the sending of a herald (2.12); but in 432/1 each side accused the other of breaking the Thirty Years Treaty. When Athens and Sparta made peace and alliance in 421, the rest of the Greek world did not 'pay [them] the greatest deference'.

4.21 The Athenians had wanted a treaty in 430 (2.59, 65); Aristophanes in his *Acharnians* of early 425 perhaps indicates that some continued to want peace. By not giving Cleon a full speech in reply, Thucydides perhaps emphasizes the Spartans' reasonableness and Cleon's unreasonableness; for the description of him, cf. 3.36 with note. According to Plut., *Nic.* 7, Nicias (cf. 4.27) was in favour of peace; Philoch. *FGrH* 328 F 128 seems to have said that the vote had to be taken three times (but surely in the assembly, not in the council). The 'previous settlement' is the Thirty Years Treaty of 446/5 (1.115).

4.22 For doubts cast on the honourable intentions of a Spartan embassy, cf. Alcibiades in 420 (5.44–5): we do not know what further concessions the Spartans might have been willing to make, but Cleon's demands included the return of places which it was not in Sparta's power to give.

4.23 It is not clear whether the 'apparently trivial infringements' of the truce were trivial only in the eyes of Sparta or this view is being endorsed by Thucydides; similarly the Athenians' 'injustice over the ships' may be the view simply of Sparta or also of Thucydides himself. Athens' 'two ships constantly sailing round' were not enough for an effective blockade, and we should expect others to have been stationed near the likely escape routes (cf. J. B. Wilson, *Pylos 425 BC* (Warminster; Aris & Phillips, 1979), 98–9). The twenty additional ships were presumably sent after the failure of the negotiations.

4.24–5 *Athens and the west (viii)*. The enmity between Locri and Rhegium is repeated from 4.1; but the invasion mentioned here is not that of 4.1, which had ended with the Locrians' withdrawal, but another. Twenty Athenian ships had gone in 427 (3.86), and Pythodorus had taken 'a few' (3.115); we do not know if more than one had returned to Athens with Laches. Even in this passage, whose main focus is elsewhere, Sphacteria is in Thucydides' Greek simply 'the island'. At its narrowest point the strait between Italy and Sicily is *c*.1¾ miles (2.8 km) across, but Messana and (more so) Rhegium were further south. For Scylla and Charybdis, see Hom. *Od.* 12.234–59: the identification was regularly accepted by later Greeks, but this is the earliest surviving text to mention it; the Tyrrhenian Sea is north of the gap, and the Sicilian south (6.13 distinguishes between the Ionian Gulf, close to Italy, and the Sicilian, the open water further south); the waters are not in fact very dangerous.

4.25 'Night now ended the action' is a common ending to battle narratives, but of course it may have been a common ending to battles in real life. Peloris is the headland at the extreme north-east of Sicily. The grappling-iron will have been thrown from the land (but they will be mounted on ships is 7.62, 68), and the Syracusan ships were then towed to keep them so close to the land that the enemy ships could not attack. It is not clear what the successful Syracusan manoeuvre was: 'nose-on' is possibly but not certainly correct. The Sicels were the native inhabitants of eastern and central Sicily (cf. 6.2): they are 'the barbarians' below (but by now they were hellenized). It is not made clear whether the Leontinians and others were on their way to Naxos or this was just a convenient rumour. The Athenians when they joined in the attack must have returned from Camarina: we are not told the outcome of that episode.

4.26–41 *Pylos (iii)*. This section begins surprisingly, with the Athenians in difficulties, after the previous section ended with them in an apparently strong position. They had about 14,000 men: there was no local supply of food; there is no spring on the acropolis now. The 'open sea' includes the great bay, but its northern shore was in the hands of the Spartans. There were seventy-two days (cf. 4.39) between the battle of 4.14 and the fighting on Sphacteria. For Helots running the blockade the 'monetary value' was the sum to buy a replacement promised to any who lost a boat.

4.27 The Athenians' fear of the onset of winter is mentioned, but that was still some way ahead: the meeting of the assembly mentioned here will have been about the end of July. Thucydides attributes to Cleon disreputable motives which he must simply have inferred from his perception of Cleon's character. Reports insisting on the need for prompt action may have been sent by Demosthenes. Theogenes is one of the men who will swear to the treaties of 421 in 5.19, 24; we do not know whether he was chosen as an associate or as an opponent of Cleon. Probably Nicias, elected as a general for 425/4, had already been appointed to command at Pylos but was in no hurry to go there.

4.28 Cleon had not, as far as we know, held any military office, and he seems to have been taken aback when Nicias offered to hand over the command to him: this element in the campaign was not planned. For Thucydides' view of crowds, cf. 2.65, 6.63. Probably Cleon became an extraordinary eleventh general for 425/4. He had probably been in touch with Demosthenes, and Demosthenes had probably told him privately and/or the assembly in a report what kind of troops he needed: the contingents from Lemnos and Imbros (islands in the north-east Aegean settled by Athenians), peltasts (Thracian light infantry), and archers had perhaps been summoned by the assembly which had given the command to Nicias. The twenty-day promise was irresponsible, but it was to be fulfilled (cf. 4.39); it is striking that Thucydides suggests that failure accompanied by the death or discrediting of Cleon would have been a worthwhile outcome.

4.29 Demosthenes was by now an ordinary general for 425/4 (see note to 4.2–6), and the assembly made him and Cleon joint commanders of the campaign. For 'large force . . . damage' we should perhaps follow Gomme in emending to 'force . . . much damage': the issue at this point is visibility, not the relative size of the forces.

4.30 In 426 Demosthenes had suffered in Aetolia when the enemy deliberately set fire to a wood (see 3.98), and some scholars suspect that the fire here, described by Thucydides as unintended, was in fact intended. Afterwards Demosthenes will have been able to see not only how many the Spartans were but also where they were positioned. The force which Cleon brought had probably been requested by himself (Gomme) rather than by Demosthenes (Hornblower). The Athenians' landing-places were probably where the island narrows about a third of the way from south to north, with the Spartans' first guard-post south from there; the source of water 'Grundy's Well'; and the ancient fort on Mount Elias (see Map 5).

4.32 The main Athenian force will have landed near the centre of the island, on each side. We do not know how many ships Cleon had brought; the lowest-tier oarsmen will have had to stay on the ships to control them. Probably more Messenians had come from Naupactus, in addition to those mentioned in 4.9; stone-throwers and slingers have not been mentioned before.

4.33-5 Much of this is narrated from the viewpoint of the Spartans: Thucydides may have questioned the Spartan prisoners in Athens.

4.34 The Athenians' 'abject terror at the thought of facing Spartans' is irrational, since the commanders were confident that they had the right forces for the job, and Thucydides may have exaggerated it to highlight the successful outcome.

4.36 The Messenians had been at Naupactus for thirty years, and it is unlikely that anybody among them already knew of a route; they probably climbed to the summit from the east coast (this kind of mountaineering exploit was to be repeated more spectacularly by Alexander the Great's forces at the Sogdian Rock in 327: Arr., *Anab.* 4.18-19). At Thermopylae in 480 the Persians had sent a contingent by a route through the hills (revealed by a man with local knowledge) to descend in the rear of the Greeks holding the pass (Thucydides uses the same Greek word for path, *atrapos*, as Hdt. 7.175); there the Spartans did not surrender (Hdt. 7.210-19). The Spartans here lacked food not because there was none left (cf. 4.39) but because they had not been able to eat that day.

4.38 No Spartans were allowed to go to the mainland because the Athenians did not want to lose any of their captives. Paus. 1.15.4 mentions shields taken from the Spartans: for one with the dedicatory inscription 'The Athenians from the Spartans from Pylos', see J. M. Camp, *The Athenian Agora* (London: Thames & Hudson, 1986), 71-2 with figs. 45-6.

4.39 The Athenians did not all return home: a garrison was left at Pylos (cf. 4.41), and Eurymedon and Sophocles with the original fleet continued to Corcyra and Sicily. It is not clear whether Cleon's twenty days are to be counted from the assembly of 4.27-8 or (as in Plut., *Nic.* 7) from his leaving Athens, but the fighting on Sphacteria and his return to Athens will have occurred during August.

Aristophanes' *Knights* of 424 shows that Cleon took the lion's share of the credit and was rewarded with the right to dine in the *prytaneion* (town hall) and a front seat in the theatre; whether the suggestion that Demosthenes resented this is historically correct or is Aristophanic invention we do not know.

4.40 Probably 'the whole war' of which this was the most surprising event is simply the Archidamian War (cf. Introduction, p. xxvi); for the surprise of Athens' failure in Sicily in 415–413, see 7.87. Expectation of the Spartans' conduct will have been based on Thermopylae (see above). 'Good men and brave' are *kaloi k' agathoi*, a term used with various emphases to refer to upper-class men and the virtues (including military) associated with them: Thucydides uses it only here and in 8.48. 'Spindle' as a metaphor for arrow is used in tragedy, and here it may recall the notion of the three Fates as spinners (Hom., *Od.* 7.197).

4.41 By keeping their Spartan prisoners the Athenians were able not only to prevent further invasions of Attica but to maintain continuous pressure on the Spartans. Spartan citizen numbers were declining (see notes to 1.19, 5.68), which will have added to the seriousness of the loss of these men. Thucydides makes much of raids from Pylos and, later, Cythera (cf. 4.55, 5.14; also 5.35): certainly the morale of the Spartans was damaged, but the Athenians seem not to have achieved the large-scale destabilization which they hoped for and the Spartans feared.

4.42–5 *An Athenian campaign in the Corinthiad.* Thucydides gives a detailed account (he perhaps took part in the campaign: Gomme), but the campaign was not important except that it resulted in the establishment of another Athenian raiding-post in the Peloponnese. The horse-transports were perhaps modified triremes with oarsmen on the highest level only (Morrison, Coates, and Rankov, *The Athenian Trireme*[2], 156, 227–30). For the so-called Dorian invasion of the Peloponnese, see 1.12 with note: Corinth seems to have been a younger city than Sparta or Argos, and stories of its foundation were fitted awkwardly into the story of the Dorian invasion (see Salmon, *Wealthy Corinth*, 38–54). Argos, neutral in the Archidamian War (cf. 5.14), evidently had enough contact with both sides for Athenian plans to pass through Argos to Corinth. The signals were presumably torch signals.

4.43 By attacking the Athenian right wing with their left the Corinthians were reversing normal hoplite tactics (cf. 5.71): this reversal was most notoriously used in Thebes' defeat of Sparta at Leuctra in 371. The Corinthians' withdrawal was to the south-east slopes of Mount Oneium. A paean is a prayer for victory (or, as in 2.91, a thanksgiving after victory).

4.44 The contribution of the Athenian cavalry is celebrated in Ar., *Eq.* 595–610. The older men were a category within a hoplite army normally used for garrison duty: for Athens, cf. 1.105, 2.13. It is striking that Nicias behaved like a defeated commander to recover his last two dead (cf. Plut., *Nic.* 6).

4.45 'Methana' with 'peninsula' should perhaps be deleted, as in the OCT. In the next few years Troezen reached an agreement with Athens (cf. 4.118) and Halieis became an ally (*IG* i[3] 75), but Epidaurus remained anti-Athenian. The purpose of the landing near Solygeia is unclear, but this activity was presumably intended to put pressure on Argos and to ease communication if Argos could be tempted out of its neutrality.

4.46-48.5 *Civil war in Corcyra (ii)*. Ptychia is probably modern Vido, the island mentioned without name in 3.75.

4.47 It will have been public knowledge that the Athenians were bound for Sicily, and Eurymedon had acquiesced in an earlier massacre (cf. 3.81). Hornblower compares the manner of the slaughter with what the Nazis did at Auschwitz and elsewhere.

4.48 For those who killed themselves before their enemies could kill them, compare the earlier episode (3.81). The women whose fate was slavery have not been mentioned before. 'This war' is probably the Archidamian War (cf. Introduction, p. xxvi); the passage was probably written before the episode of (probably) 411 mentioned by Diod. Sic. 13.48. Victory for Athens' friends was of no immediate help to Athens: Thucydides does not mention Corcyra again until its involvement in the Sicilian expedition of 415-413 (e.g. 6.30, 7.26, 33).

4.48.6 *Athens and the west (ix)*. The Athenians had withdrawn from the fighting in 4.25. Thucydides gives no details of further fighting before the end of this war (4.58-65).

4.49 *A campaign in north-western Greece*. For Anactorium, cf. 2.9, 80-2; the treaty of 426/5 had bound Ambracia not to support Anactorium (3.114). In 421 Corinth would object that Anactorium was not to be returned under the Peace of Nicias (5.30).

4.50-1 Seventh winter (425/4)

4.50 *Negotiations with Persia*. For Aristeides' colleagues, see 4.75; for money-raising expeditions, cf. 2.69, 3.19. There was certainly a new assessment of the allies' tribute in 425, involving significant increases (*IG* i³ 71; extracts ML 69, translated Fornara 136), but this expedition was probably not sent to collect regular tribute.

For negotiations with Persia, cf. 2.7 with note to 2.7-17. By 'Assyrian characters' Thucydides probably means Aramaic, the normal language of secretaries in the Persian empire and earlier in the Assyrian empire. Sparta's problem presumably was that it had embarked on the war ostensibly to liberate the Greeks (cf. 2.8) but the price for Persian support, as in 412-411, would be the return of the Asiatic Greeks to Persia (cf. 8.18 with note). We can probably infer from Ar., *Ach.* 61-127 that there had been at least one Athenian approach to Persia. Thucydides now strays outside his chronological framework (cf. Introduction, p. xxvii): Artaxerxes died at the end of 424 or the beginning of 423. Thucydides does not tell us, but it appears from Andoc. 3. *Peace* 29 and an Athenian decree (ML 70, translated Fornara 138, with an important new fragment ML addenda (1988), p. 313) that once Dareius II was established on the throne Athens did make a treaty with him: Athens will certainly not have been willing to abandon the Asiatic Greeks, but a non-aggression pact could have satisfied both sides. This is one of Thucydides' most culpable omissions: apart from one sentence in 5.1, the Persians are not mentioned again until 413/2 (8.5-6).

4.51 *Athenian suspicion of Chios.* After the revolt of Mytilene in 428, Chios and the Lesbian city of Methymna were the only members of the Delian League still providing ships. The revolt of Mytilene had been preceded by wall-building (3.2). Chios obeyed Athens, but this was not abject submission. An inscription listing contributors to a Spartan war fund (see note to 3.32) includes 'exiles of the Chians who are friends of the Spartans': it is not certain whether these were exiled now and paid shortly afterwards or are the men exiled *c.*411 (Diod. Sic. 12.65).

4.52–88 Eighth summer (424)

4.52 *Eclipse and earthquake; activity of Mytilenaean exiles.* The eclipse (on 21 March) and earthquake are mentioned simply as interesting occurrences; for Thucydides' awareness of the connection between solar eclipses and the new moon, cf. 2.28. Thucydides has not explained when and how the Mytilenaeans had been exiled, or where their base was (cf. Introduction, p. xli); for exiles harassing their island state from the mainland, cf. Corcyra, 3.85. Two thousand Phocaean staters were equivalent to 8 Athenian talents: this ransoming of a whole city is an unusual occurrence. The Actaean cities were those from Antandrus to the Hellespont (cf. 3.50, where the term is not used), and probably 'the Aeolian towns on the mainland' are the same (Gomme). For the timber, cf. Xen., *Hell.* 2.1.10.

4.53–7 *An Athenian campaign against Cythera and Laconia.* An inscription records payments to Nicias and his colleagues *c.*10 May (ML 72. 20–2). The same three generals will swear to the truce of 423 (4.119). Cythera is explained in a manner normally used by Thucydides for more remote places; we do not know whether Spartan commissioners and garrisons were sent to other Perioecic communities, but Cythera was in a particularly sensitive position (cf. Hdt. 7.235, quoting the wish of the sixth-century Chilon that Cythera were at the bottom of the sea; Xen., *Hell.* 4.8.7–8). 'Laconia' here includes Messenia.

4.54 The manuscripts have 2,000 Milesian hoplites, certainly too many (though accepted by Hornblower) and perhaps repeated in error from 4.53. Scandeia was on the east side of the island, and Cythera in the centre. The Athenians already possessed Scandeia, but after the agreement 'took [it] over' formally. Asine is the city of that name on the west side of the Laconian Gulf, not the better-known Asine in Messenia (cf. 4.13); Helos was at the head of the Gulf (many Greeks thought, probably wrongly, that it was the origin of the term Helot: contrast note to 1.101–3).

4.55 Sparta had a body of *hippeis*, 'horsemen', in fact hoplites who acted as a royal bodyguard; the cavalry and archers recruited now were probably not Spartan citizens. For Spartan pessimism and lethargy, cf. 1.69–71, 118, and what Hermocrates says of the Greek Sicilians in 4.63; for events 'contrary to any reasonable prediction', cf. 2.61, 4.65. In fact the run of Spartan reverses and Athenian successes will not continue beyond this point.

4.56 Cotyrta and Aphroditia were on the east side of the Laconian Gulf, Epidaurus Limera and Thyrea on the east coast of the Peloponnese. The note on the Aeginetans is repeated from 2.27 (cf. Introduction, p. xxvii); they are not mentioned in the account of the Helot revolt in 1.101–3, and their support for Sparta is not mentioned in 2.27.

4.57 'The islands' are the Cyclades; the word 'tribute' indicates that Cythera was to be treated as a member of the Delian League, a humiliation for Sparta. The Aeginetans are not known to have done anything hostile to Athens since the beginning of the war and their expulsion from Aegina.

4.58–65 *Athens and the west (x)*. Gela, on the south coast of Sicily, colonized from Rhodes and Crete (cf. 6.4), has not been mentioned before. This is the first appearance of Hermocrates, who will be always important in opposition to Athens but not always in power in Syracuse. It is surprising that the perfunctory and disjointed narrative of this war should end with a major speech (4.59–64): perhaps the speech was written after 415–413, when Sicily and Hermocrates seemed more important than they did in the 420s.

4.59 The point of Hermocrates' opening remark is that Syracuse is less in need of the peace for which he will argue than the other cities. The reasons why men accept the risks of warfare are well put.

4.60 'If we have any sense' will recur in 4.61 and 4.64. For the Athenians' alliance with Leontini and their alleged ulterior motive, cf. 3.86. 'Clearing the way' for dominance is a metaphor from tree-felling. The Athenians were to come with a larger force in 415–413 (cf. Books 6–7), but not because the Greek Sicilians were exhausted and not with a successful outcome.

4.61 The Chalcidians belonged to the Ionian strand of the Greek people: in 6.77 Hermocrates will express Dorian contempt for the Ionians (on which cf. 1.124 with note). For the view that domination is natural, cf. the Athenians in 1.76, 5.89, 105. Since Sicily is a long way from Athens, the Athenians could campaign there only because they had been invited by allies who could provide a base.

4.62 On the praise of peace Hornblower compares Milton, Sonnet 16, lines 10–11: 'Peace hath her victories | No less renowned than war'. 'Instead of gaining . . . found themselves losing' is the strongest form of the device of 'presentation by negation' (Hornblower).

4.63 Treaties in the fifth century were made sometimes for all time (e.g. Athens' alliances with Rhegium and Leontini: ML 63–4, translated Fornara 124–5), sometimes for a fixed period (e.g. the Thirty Years Treaty of 446/5: 1.115).

4.64 Hermocrates suggests that it is more important that the Athenians are foreign invaders, from outside Sicily, than that they have ties of kinship with the Chalcidians within Sicily; he is careful not to say that Syracuse, already powerful in Sicily, will be able to dominate the island if its opponents are denied Athenian support.

4.65 Morgantina, in the interior, was not at all near either to Camarina or to Syracuse. Thucydides says nothing else about Morgantina, and not enough about Camarina (cf. 4.25) to make sense of his narrative. There must have been a lapse of time between the making of the treaty at Gela and the punishment of the generals at Athens: probably this section has been placed at the point appropriate to the latter (G. S. Shrimpton, *History and Memory in Ancient Greece* (McGill–Queen's University Press, 1997), 277–8). It is not clear why Eurymedon was treated more leniently than his colleagues: perhaps he was tried last, and popular anger was beginning to be assuaged. Eurymedon was sent to Sicily again in 414/3 (cf. 7.16); Sophocles was perhaps to be one of the Thirty oligarchs who ruled Athens in 404–403 (Xen., *Hell.* 2.3.2); nothing further is known of Pythodorus. For the Greeks' tendency to blame bribery when a success was not achieved, cf. note to 3.38. Thucydides' narrative has told us nothing of what happened after the arrival of the Athenian reinforcements (cf. 4.48.6), and has not suggested that the Athenians were in a position to take control of Sicily before that; for their western ambitions in 424, cf. Ar., *Eq.* 174, 1304–4 (mentioning not Sicily but Carthage). In relying on their current good fortune they were ignoring the warning of the Spartans in 4.17–18; cf. Hermocrates on the incalculability of the future in 4.62–3.

4.66–74 *Athens and Megara (i).* In 2.31 Thucydides mentioned that the Athenians invaded the Megarid each year, but not that they did so twice each year: probably that extra detail was not deliberately withheld (contr. Hornblower), but it was a deliberate choice not to mention each invasion in its place as each Spartan invasion of Attica was mentioned in its place. For Megara's two harbours and the long walls joining Nisaea to the city, cf. 1.103; Sparta had allowed the exiles to occupy Plataea from 427 to 426 (cf. 3.68). Hippocrates' father Ariphron was the elder brother of Pericles. Hippocrates here makes his first appearance in Thucydides, but an inscription shows that he had already served as general in 426/5 (ML 72, translated Fornara 134, 3). Here we have a classic instance of party leaders' preferring to be on the winning side in their city even at the cost of submission to an outside power: cf. 3.65.

4.67 'Had agreed the plans and made the practical arrangements' is literally 'had made all their arrangements in deeds and words', a very artificial use of one of Thucydides' favourite contrasts. Minoa had been captured by Athens in 427 and no longer belonged to Megara (cf. 3.51). The Plataeans will have been men who escaped from the city in 428/7 (cf. 3.20–4). Enyalius was an epithet for (e.g. Hom., *Il.* 17.210–11) or an alternative name for or embodiment of (e.g. Ar., *Pax* 457) Ares. The gates will have been in the long walls, on the side towards Athens; the commander will have been the Spartan commander of the garrison in Nisaea.

4.68 The gates in this chapter are those from the city to the area between the long walls; the threatened fighting inside the city would be between pro-Athenian and anti-Athenian Megarians.

4.69 Men and materials had to be obtained from Athens because investing Nisaea was not part of the original plan.

4.70 Facts about Brasidas' north-eastern campaign emerge gradually, probably not through deliberate narrative dislocation to heighten the dramatic effect but because, not yet far from the manner of oral composition, Thucydides mentions details only as they become relevant. He shows detailed knowledge of Brasidas' campaigns, and often attributes thoughts to him: he will have had little opportunity to meet Brasidas after he was exiled, and his most likely source is Clearidas (cf. 4.132: suggested by H. D. Westlake, *Studies in Thucydides and Greek History* (Bristol Classical Press, 1989), 78-83). Tripodiscus was about 7 miles (11 km.) west of Megara; the cities from which Brasidas obtained soldiers were all fairly near.

4.72 The Boeotians were concerned for Megara both because its territory adjoined theirs and because they claimed to be the founders of Megara (e.g. Hellanicus *FGrH* 4 F 78; for a rival Athenian claim, cf. note to 4.118).

4.73 It is surprising to read that the Athenian generals thought 'they had already succeeded in most of their objectives': they seem to have given up too easily; they had given Brasidas the victory by default, and had made it certain that they would not get control of Megara. We have not been told how the Athenian force had been selected, and whether it did indeed comprise their best hoplites.

4.74 The Athenians presumably left a garrison in Nisaea. For the Megarians' use of a military review, cf. Xen., *Hell.* 2.4.8-10: the point of open voting was that it could be seen who, if anybody, dared to vote for acquittal (contrast the secret vote at Acanthus, 4.88). We do not know how long Megara remained oligarchic: Thucydides' language perhaps implies that it was not so when he wrote the last sentence of this chapter.

4.75 *The Athenians in the north-east.* For the Mytilenaean exiles and Antandrus, cf. 4.52. For the money-raising ships, cf. 4.50, where Aristeides is the only general named. Demodocus is probably the Demodocus of [Pl.] *Theages* (see esp. 127 E). Lamachus had probably first served as a general in the 430s (cf. Plut., *Per.* 20); he is mocked for his belligerence in Aristophanes' *Acharnians* (566-625, etc.), and was to die in Sicily in 414. For Anaea, cf. 3.19, 32. Heracleia Pontica, about 125 miles (200 km) from the Bosporus on the south coast of the Black Sea, was a colony of the Megarians and Boeotians (cf. Ps.-Scymn. 972-5): we do not know whether it was now on good terms with Megara; its inclusion in the tribute assessment of 425 (*IG* i³ 71, iv. 126-7) does not guarantee that it was on good terms with Athens; and it may be mere coincidence that Lamachus went there when Athens was trying to get control of Megara. Editors have commonly emended Calex to Cales, from Arr., *Bithyniaca* 20, but we cannot be sure that Arrian in the second century AD used the same form as Thucydides (Hornblower, following D. M. Lewis).

4.76-7 *Athens and Boeotia (i).* Demosthenes had been based at Naupactus in 426 and had been interested in advancing on Boeotia from there (cf. 3.95

with note to 3.91). Thucydides implies that the first approach was made to Demosthenes and Hippocrates while they were in the Megarid, but they returned to Athens and set out with fresh forces: since the plan depended on secrecy, we may wonder how much was divulged to the assembly. The cities were organized in a federation led by Thebes, and both the federation and the individual cities were oligarchic (cf. 5.38, *Hell. Oxy.* 19 Chambers). A Thespian is more likely than a Theban (most manuscripts) to have been opposed to the federation. Ptoeodorus is a characteristically Boeotian name, derived from Apollo Ptoeus, whose sanctuary was north of Thebes. The three places chosen for intervention were in the south-west, the north-west, and the south-east of Boeotia: how good the Athenians' chances of success were depends on how much actual or potential support there was for them to exploit. Chaeroneia here is a dependency of Orchomenus, but in the federation as organized in the 390s it was grouped with two cities east of Orchomenus (*Hell. Oxy.* 19.3 Chambers). Orchomenus was the city most likely to challenge Thebes for dominance: Thucydides distinguishes it from the Orchomenus in Arcadia (mentioned in 5.61); for its being 'Minyan', cf. Hom., *Il.* 2.511. Delium was a sanctuary of Delian Apollo.

4.77 We should probably not infer from 'he had sent' that (contrary to normal practice) Hippocrates was technically superior to Demosthenes. The Acarnanians were not breaking the treaty of 426/5 (cf. 3.114), since on this campaign they would not be fighting against any other participants in that treaty; after this they will not be mentioned again until 413 (7.57). For Oeniadae, cf. 2.102, 3.7; it will not appear in Thucydides again.

4.78–88 *Brasidas in the north-east (i).* For Sparta's colony of Heracleia, cf. 3.92–3: unless that section was written with hindsight, it suggests that a campaign like this was already being contemplated in 426. Pharsalus, the principal city in south-western Thessaly, was on the Athenian side in 431 (cf. 2.22) but was to be aligned with Sparta in the 370s (Xen., *Hell.* 6.1.2–17). Thucydides reports the names of several men (good Thessalian names, Hornblower; Torymbas is probably the Thessalian name behind the manuscripts' Torylaus), though they do not make a significant contribution to the narrative. Larisa was the principal city in north-eastern Thessaly: in 431 it had supported Athens with commanders 'from each party in the city' (cf. 2.22). It was common to pass under arms through the territory of states with which one was not at war, but such states might well feel threatened, and it may be that the frequency of the practice and of the perceived threat increased during the Peloponnesian War (cf. the treaty quoted in 5.47). Thucydides envisages a situation in which the majority of the Thessalians, and perhaps the formal decision-making bodies, were pro-Athenian but oligarchic cliques had a degree of influence not reflected in the formal structures; for his view of narrow oligarchies, cf. 3.62. For guest-friendship, see note to 2.29 and Herman, *Ritualised Friendship*, discussing this instance on p. 119. 'Knew of no hostility' seems to be formal diplomatic language: cf. RO 42. 8, probably

of 362. While the Spartans in general were slow, Brasidas is often
reported as acting quickly (cf. W. R. Connor, *Thucydides* (Princeton
University Press, 1984), 128 n. 45).

4.79 Thucydides explains the origin of Brasidas' expedition here, when he
enters the region. The appeal had been sent before the episode at
Megara, when Athens' run of successes ended. The Chalcidians who
appealed openly will have been those incorporated in Olynthus (cf. 1.58).
Perdiccas was last mentioned, as allied to Athens but secretly supporting
Sparta, in 429 (2.80).

4.80 Although since Athens' success at Pylos the Spartans had been afraid of
a major Helot uprising, none occurred (cf. note to 4.41). The 'elimination' of 2,000 active Helots had happened at some unspecified time in
the past (and the Spartans will have been afraid of 'young' rather than of
'stupid' Helots, the alternative reading): Thucydides evidently believed
the story, but we cannot tell how, or how reliably, he learned of it; Diod.
Sic. 12.67.4 has the men killed at home.

4.81 Thucydides suggests here that the Spartans were glad to send the expedition, but a different impression will be given in 4.108. This chapter
bestows high praise on Brasidas; but, although he will claim that he has
come as a genuine liberator (4.85–7), he will threaten to use force against
those who do not cooperate with him voluntarily (4.87). Bargaining for
'mutual return and recovery of places' was to take place in the Peace of
Nicias in 421 (5.17). The 'Sicilian affair' is the episode of 415–413: this
passage was written or revised after that (cf. Introduction, p. xxvii).

4.82 Probably Athens' 'closer watch' on the allies was simply a matter of
greater alertness: there had been no secret about Brasidas' plans, and
probably Thucydides and Eucles (cf. 4.104) had already been sent to the
region.

4.83 The Lyncestians lived to the west of the Macedonian plain, well away
from the area in which the Athenians were interested. If Perdiccas were
to defeat Arrhabaeus, he might cease to need Brasidas, and cease to join
Brasidas in supporting the Chalcidians. When he was paying half of
Brasidas' maintenance, presumably the Chalcidians were paying the
other half; by reducing but not ceasing his contribution he retained a
hold over Brasidas (Hornblower); and there was to be another joint campaign against Arrhabaeus later (cf. 4.124–8).

4.84 The grape harvest would be in September: its mention is not simply an
indication of date, but helps to explain why Acanthus went over to
Brasidas (cf. Xen., *Hell.* 7.5.14, Aen. Tact. 7.1). The last mention of
'people' in this chapter refers not to 'the people at large' but to a citizen
assembly. Brasidas' persuasive speech can be contrasted with the laconic
speech of Sthenelaïdas in 1.86: although Thucydides cannot have heard
the original, to an unusual extent its authenticity is supported by references to it in the narrative (cf. Introduction, p. xxxvi). Hornblower notes
that it is the basis of a 'periodically adjusted manifesto', with similar

speeches made in other cities later. For the question of Athens' popularity with the member states of the Delian League, cf. note to 3.27–50: each side in the debate can find some support in this episode.

4.85 For the liberation of Greece, cf. 2.8; for Sparta's expectation that invasions of Attica would bring victory, cf. 5.14. Brasidas argues, as speakers today still argue, that those who exert themselves on behalf of others (without consulting them) deserve their gratitude and support. A first rejection would have shown only that he was unpersuasive, not that he was untrustworthy. At Nisaea he had had a larger force, which in hoplites outnumbered the Athenians: Thucydides will remark in 4.108 that his claim here was untrue.

4.86 The implication of the 'oaths' is that the Spartans at home were, or Brasidas thought they were, less committed to the freedom of the cities than he was. If 'autonomy' (cf. note to 1.96–7) was incompatible with the presence of a Spartan governor, the promise was soon to be broken, apparently by Brasidas himself (cf. 4.132). It was not yet Spartan practice to impose oligarchies on its allies, as Athens sometimes imposed democracies on its allies (cf. 1.19 and note); for the desire of the allies to choose for themselves rather than have even a congenial constitution imposed on them, cf. 8.48, 64.

4.87 For calling on the local gods and heroes, cf. Archidamus at Plataea (2.74); Brasidas assumes that if Acanthus does not openly join Sparta it will continue to pay tribute to Athens. When the Peloponnesian War ended Sparta would not resist the temptation to take over the Athenian empire.

4.88 This is one of the earliest references to a secret vote in Greece: contrast the open vote at Megara (4.74). Brasidas' speech was attractive, but Thucydides commonly uses that word of what is deceptive, and 4.108 will describe his words as 'enticing (but untrue)'. Stagirus (or Stagira) is best known as the birthplace of the philosopher Aristotle.

4.89–116 Eighth winter (424/3)

4.89–101.4 *Athens and Boeotia (ii)*. It appears that the principal reason for the Athenians' failure was the leaking of the plot; but it may be that the plot was leaked when it was because of Demosthenes' approach, and certainly the fact that Hippocrates had not yet gone to Delium made it easier for the Boeotians to act firmly in the west.

4.90 Probably Hippocrates went at what he thought was the agreed time, when news from Siphae had not yet reached Athens. It was unusual, though not unprecedented, for metics to be used on a campaign outside Attica; the 'foreigners' were presumably from the member states of the Delian League. Around 7,000 hoplites (cf. 4.93–4) is a surprisingly low number, set against the 13,000 of 2.13 and the 4,400 killed by the plague of 3.87: perhaps this quick mobilization fell short of the available total. Given the threats elsewhere, the Boeotians probably did not send all their manpower to Tanagra. As elsewhere (cf. especially the siege of Plataea, 2.75–8, 3.20–4), Thucydides is interested in the details of sieges and fortifications; but, despite his detailed knowledge of these works and of the topography, as a general in the north (cf. 4.104–5) he cannot have been present.

4.91 The eleven Boeotarchs (cf. 2.2) came from the eleven electoral units of Boeotia (cf. *Hell. Oxy.* 19.3 Chambers): two were from Thebes in its own right, and since the destruction of Plataea (before which there may have been only nine) Thebes had claimed a further two on account of Plataea and its dependencies. Pagondas was identical with, or else from the same family as, the Pagondas of Pindar, fr. 94b Maehler; Arianthidas is probably identical with the [—]thius included in the 'navarchs monument' at Delphi with which the Spartan Lysander commemorated his victory over Athens in 405 (ML 95, *d*), and Hornblower wonders whether he supported Pagondas (Thucydides' Greek does not state, and it need not be true, that 'all . . . except for one' were against fighting). Oropus, on the coast south-east of Delium, with an important sanctuary of Amphiaraus, was claimed both by Athens and by Boeotia: it was currently in Athenian hands, not incorporated in Attica but ruled as subject territory, and hence its status could be variously referred to by Boeotians and Athenians.

4.92 For the Euboeans, in 447/6, see 1.113–14; Philoch. *FGrH* 328 F 130 mentions an Athenian campaign in 424/3, about which Thucydides says nothing. Pagondas' point about boundaries is that other Greek states fight neighbours to settle where the boundary between them should be drawn, but Athens wants to conquer Boeotia. For a precedent from the middle of the century Pagondas selects the Boeotian victory at Coroneia, in 447/6 (cf. 1.113); Hippocrates in 4.95 will select the Athenian victory at Oenophyta, *c*.457 (cf. 1.108).

4.93 Probably the Thebans took the right wing on account of their leading position in Boeotia. The Athenians' eight-deep formation (see 4.94) was typical, but the Boeotians seem to have been fond of a deeper formation which added weight to the attack. For the different depths of different contingents, cf. the Spartan army at Mantinea in 418 (5.68).

4.94 Most of the Athenian force had gone to build the fort, not to fight (cf. 4.90); it is hard to believe that their number was 'several times greater' than that of the Boeotians.

4.96 This and the battle of Mantinea in 418 (5.70–4) were the two most substantial hoplite battles of the Peloponnesian War. The Athenians were at a disadvantage in advancing uphill, but it was still better to advance than to stand and await the enemy's charge. The 'gruelling fight with shields shoving against shields' is typical of hoplite battles as traditionally viewed: that view has been challenged, but is probably correct for most hoplite battles if not for all. The Thespians' grave has been found (see Pritchett, *GSW*, iv.132–3, and part of their casualty list, *IG* vii 1888; the casualty list from Tanagra, *IG* vii 585, may belong to this campaign too): altogether there may have been *c*.300 Thespian dead. Since the men who 'had fallen back' and the men who 'were encircled' were not the same, the manuscripts' text at that point cannot stand. Among the Athenians who fled was the philosopher Socrates, found and supported by Alcibiades (Pl., *Symp.* 221 A–B, *Lach.* 181 B). The Locrians who supported the Boeotians were the north-eastern, Opuntian, Locrians.

4.97 The exchange of messages which begins here, Thucydides' longest passage in indirect speech, recalls the dialogue between an Ambracian herald and the Acarnanians in 3.113. This episode may be reflected in Euripides' *Suppliants*, in which the Thebans refuse to let the Argive women recover their dead. The 'established laws of the Greeks' are general understandings, not formal written laws.

4.98 Apart from their support for Brasidas at Megara (cf. 4.70, 72), the Boeotians are not recorded as having acted against Athens recently. The Athenians argue disingenuously: they did not control the sanctuary by virtue of controlling the surrounding territory, but had conquered it in order to use it for military purposes (probably knowing that it had a water supply). For the Boeotians' alleged origin in Thessaly, cf. 1.12. Greeks did do in war things which they might have felt inhibited from doing otherwise, but it would not normally have been thought that the mere fact of war automatically legitimized any breach of normal restrictions. It was, however, normal for victors to return the dead to enemies who acknowledged their defeat.

4.99 It appears that the battlefield was in the territory of Oropus; but, if the Athenians claimed possession of Delium because they currently occupied that, by the same criterion the battlefield now belonged to the Boeotians.

4.100 The Boeotians seem to have expected the recapture of Delium to be more difficult than it proved to be; for uses of fire, cf. 2.77, 4.115.

4.101 The ships taking the Athenians home will not have hurried, and their voyage will have taken days rather than hours. The casualties of 7.1 per cent on the winning side were a little above average for a hoplite battle; 14.3 per cent on the losing side about average (and the losing commander was often killed).

4.101.5 *The death of Sitalces.* For Sitalces, cf. 2.95–101; also 2.29. The Odrysians and their kings have not been mentioned since 429/8 and will not be mentioned again: this is an unusually disconnected insertion in Thucydides' narrative.

4.102–8 *Brasidas in the north-east (ii).* For Amphipolis, Eïon, and Argilus, see Map 6. The fact that Amphipolis was an Athenian colony made its going over to Brasidas particularly shocking. The earliest attempts at settlement were on the hill with a summit at 133 m., slightly to the north. (The settlements are dated by schol. Aeschin. 2 *Embassy* 31 (67 Dilts), translated Fornara 62.) For Aristagoras of Miletus, who went to Myrcinus, further north, in 496/5, see Hdt. 5.124–6 (Thucydides agrees with

Herodotus that he was 'in flight' as the Ionian Revolt faced defeat, but gives information not given by Herodotus). The Athenians killed at Drabescus were the men sent in 465/4 at the time of the war with Thasos (cf. 1.100; the scholiast gives the wrong archon beginning Lysi-). Hagnon's foundation was in 437/6: he seems to have been venerated as a hero while still alive (cf. 5.11). For Eïon, cf. 1.98. At Amphipolis a large circuit wall has been found, but not a wall cutting off the whole loop of the river.

4.103 Argilus' 'people who had citizenship in Amphipolis' were presumably Argilians who had joined in Hagnon's colony; whether they could still or again be regarded as citizens of Argilus would be for Argilus to decide. The bridge at Amphipolis was about two-thirds of a mile (1 km) from the north-west corner of the city wall. Settlement patterns varied, and we cannot be sure how many of the Amphipolitans had their permanent homes outside the city walls.

4.104 Nothing is known about Eucles and the forces with him except what is said here and in 4.106 (for the chronology, see note to 4.82). Thucydides here plays a part in his own history, but writes of himself austerely and as he might have written of any other general; we are not told why or by whose decision he had gone to Thasos, or whether his not being at Eïon was blameworthy. He did at least succeed in securing Eïon, but he was exiled (cf. 5.26).

4.105 For Thucydides' family, see Introduction, pp. xxiv–xxv: his mining rights and personal connections were inherited from Miltiades' wife, the elder Hegesipyle, and his wealth would if necessary have enabled him to hire troops at his own expense. The principal mining area was around Mount Pangaeum, between the Strymon and Thasos. The 'Athenians in the city' are presumably not the Amphipolitans of Athenian origin (mentioned in 4.106) but Eucles' garrison troops.

4.106 The colonists of 437/6 can hardly have been fewer than the 10,000 of 465/4 (cf. 1.102), and Athens would have been able to supply only a small proportion of them. Probably there was an emergency assembly, addressed by Brasidas and by Eucles, which voted to accept Brasidas' terms. We do not know what became of Eucles: it is possible but not certain that he let Amphipolis go too easily, but after this decision there was no point in his staying. Thucydides discreetly makes the point that he himself did the best he could in the circumstances.

4.107 The active Brasidas still made an attempt on Eïon. Perdiccas was last mentioned in 4.83, reducing but not entirely stopping his support for Brasidas.

4.108 Fir was the preferred wood for shipbuilding, and Macedonia and Thrace were the best sources of it. Amphipolis as a colony did not pay tribute to Athens: it may have supplied money as a charge on the mines (L. Kallet-Marx, *Money, Expense and Naval Power in Thucydides' History, 1–5.24* (University of California Press, 1993), 175–6). The lake, lake Cercinitis, was drained in the 1930s. The 'subsequent revelation' of Athenian power, successful except in the battle in which Cleon was killed, was in 422–421. This chapter fits uncomfortably with 4.81, which gives a wholly favourable picture of Brasidas and does not suggest that there were any disadvantages in going over to him (cf. Introduction, p. xxviii).

4.109.1 *Athens and Megara (ii).* This short interruption notes, presumably in its chronological place, another setback for the Athenians.

4.109.1–116 *Brasidas in the north-east (iii).* Acte is the eastern prong of Chalcidice. For Mount Athos, the shipwreck of a Persian fleet in 492, and the canal dug before Xerxes' invasion of Greece in 480, see Hdt. 6.44–5, 7.22–3. Thucydides probably mentions the cities in correct anti-clockwise order (Herodotus' order is different). The name Pelasgian was given by the Greeks to various non-Greek peoples: for the belief that Pelasgians settled in Athens for a time but were expelled and moved to the north-Aegean island of Lemnos, cf. Hdt. 6.136–40.

4.110 Torone was on the west side of Sithone, the middle prong. Thucydides' point in calling it (and Olynthus in 4.123) Chalcidian is not clear: Torone may not have been a colony of Chalcis in Euboea, and Olynthus certainly was not (see Hdt. 8.127); and Torone can hardly have been part of the Chalcidian state centred on Olynthus (see note to 1.58, and 4.114 below). Possibly all the cities of Chalcidice were thought, wrongly, to have originated from Chalcis (cf. Hornblower). The temple of the Dioscuri was north-east of the city; Canastraeum was the east-facing tip of Pallene, the western prong.

4.112 Aen. Tact. 8.3, 21.1, in the fourth century, warns against leaving in the countryside materials which could be used by an attacker.

4.114 In Amphipolis (cf. 4.105), Brasidas' proclamation was to men considering whether to go over to him; here it was to men who had fled from a city he had captured (and the only Athenians were the garrison troops). Here 'Chalcidian' refers to the state centred on Olynthus (note the Olynthian who was the first to enter the city, 4.110); but Brasidas ought to have offered Torone freedom in alliance with him, not incorporation in the Olynthian state. His 'meeting' was an ad hoc assembly of the citizens who had not fled to Lecythus; but a lawful assembly could be convened only by the authorities of Torone. 'From that point on they would be held to account': Brasidas again combines sticks with carrots, and will not tolerate further oppositon after he has made his offer.

4.115 We are not told whether the Toronaeans in Lecythus joined the Athenians in flight or returned to the city.

4.116 Thirty minas of silver—3,000 Athenian drachmas or 2,100 heavier, Aeginetan drachmas—was an enormous sum for a soldier whose pay would be not more than 1 drachma a day: the text may be corrupt. Thucydides does not record his own view, but Brasidas regarded the collapse of the defenders' building as due to divine intervention, and Thucydides regarded Brasidas' view and his resulting action as significant (cf. Introduction, p. xliv).

4.117–33 Ninth summer (423)

4.117–19 *The year's truce.* Thucydides' readers know that there were Spartans interested in peace (cf. 4.41, 108), but this is his first indication that there were Athenians interested in peace (it is uncertain how much desire to end the war lies behind Aristophanes' *Acharnians*, of early 425, before the success at Pylos). He writes as if both sides were unanimous, which is unlikely to be true; presumably there were preliminary talks before the formal agreement was made. The text in the middle of the chapter is difficult, and some words may be missing (cf. textual notes): the argument seems to be that currently the Athenians were under pressure and had not put their Spartan prisoners to death; but, if Brasidas tried to go on from strength to strength, either (*a*) he might succeed but the Athenians might react by killing the prisoners, or (*b*) he might fail in which case the Athenians might no longer be interested in peace.

4.118 Thucydides here begins a practice, continued in Books 5 and 8, of directly quoting treaties. This is more probably an experiment in narrative technique than a sign of incompleteness intended to be converted to paraphrase in the final polishing (cf. Introduction, p. xxxii). Of the four documents here, the first two appear to be messages from the Peloponnesians to Athens, based on decrees of the Peloponnesians; the third is a decree of Athens, formulated in the normal style of Athenian decrees; the last is a record, from the Spartan side, of the ratification of the treaty: Thucydides probably obtained these from an Athenian source.

Athens had not been formally excluded from Delphi during the war, but Delphi sympathized with the Peloponnesians (cf. 1.118), and the route to it from Athens lay through Boeotia and Phocis; there must have been some financial matter about which Athens had complained. Coryphasium was the Spartan name for Pylos (cf. 4.3); for possible identifications of Bouphras and Tomeus, see Map 5. See for Cythera 4.54, 57; for Nisaea 4.69, 73; for Minoa 3.51, 4.67. For Troezen, see 2.56, 4.45; but Thucydides has not previously mentioned the agreement. For oared vessels the manuscript text refers awkwardly to talents and to 'measures': probably 'talents' is to be deleted and the 'measures' are amphorae; the effect will have been to allow boats of up to thirty oars. Heralds would normally have safe conduct without special provision, but embassies would not (cf. note to 3.72). Greek states had a tendency to give men full authority on particular occasions without specifying precisely how full: the intention here seems to have been that the men sent were authorized to swear to the treaty unless the other party proposed modifications.

In the Athenian decree the manuscripts omit 'council and'; but in inscribed decrees of the second half of the fifth century the council is invariably mentioned, and the omission is more likely to be due to a copyist than to Thucydides. The date 14 Elaphebolion was perhaps *c*.25 March 423, which fits a Thucydidean year beginning early March (cf. note to 2.1). For the involvement of the generals in convening the assembly, cf. 2.22, 59. Towards the end of the chapter there are clearly words missing from the manuscripts' text: 'if it is agreed to send and receive embassies' gives the sense required.

4.119 Presumably the whole Spartan alliance was bound by the treaty, though not all members are mentioned as swearing to it; Athens apparently committed its allies without consulting them. Since each city had its own calendar with its own irregularities, it is not surprising that 12 Gerastius in Sparta = 14 Elaphebolion in Athens here but a different equation applies in 421 (5.19). The Spartan Athenaeus son of Pericleidas has names advertising a family with Athenian connections (cf. the Athenian Cimon's son Lacedaemonius, 1.45); Pericleidas had asked Athens for help against the Messenians in the 460s (Ar., *Lys.* 1138-44). Philocharidas will reappear in the diplomacy of 421-420 (5.19, 24, 44). The Corinthian Aeneas may be a nephew of the Aristeus of 1.60, so not from a pro-Athenian family; for Euphamidas, cf. 2.33, 5.55. The three Athenians commanded against Cythera as generals for 425/4 (4.53), and had evidently been re-elected for 424/3.

4.120-32 *Brasidas in the north-east (iv).* For Thucydides' mention of an alleged Trojan War foundation, cf. the Elymians in Sicily (6.2). Brasidas praises Scione because, unlike other cities, it volunteered to join him; but despite his promises, he withdrew most of his forces to fight Arrhabaeus, and the Athenians arrived in his absence (4.124-9), and in the Peace of Nicias Sparta abandoned Scione to Athens (5.18).

4.121 The honours for Brasidas resemble those for victorious athletes (Pericles was thus honoured when he delivered the funeral oration after the Samian war of 440-439: Plut., *Per.* 28), but are not quasi-religious.

4.122 The ambassadors in their journey must have counted the days from the ratification of the truce: on the defection of Scione, Thucydides, uncharacteristically, gives alternative versions and chooses between them (cf. Introduction, p. xxxi). Cleon, making his first appearance since the Pylos episode, takes a hard line on Scione: it is possible that he was responsible for Thucydides' exile, and that this contributed to Thucydides' dislike of him. The Athenians felt free to act here, because they believed the truce to have been broken, but they did not take military action elsewhere.

4.123 By accepting the defection of Mende, Brasidas was surely breaking the rule that each side should possess what it possessed when the truce was ratified (cf. Connor, *Thucydides*, 137): the narrative makes it likely that the minority favourable to Brasidas were inclined to oligarchy (cf. 4.130). For 'Chalcidian Olynthus', cf. note to 'Chalcidian Torone', 4.110.

4.124 We are not told how hard it was to resist Perdiccas' pressure, but Brasidas' abandonment of his new allies at this point looks irresponsible. The Chalcidians of this campaign are those of the state centred on Olynthus. Thucydides here distinguishes the (Lower) Macedonians both from Greeks and from outright barbarians. The pass of 4.128 is the Kirli Dirven pass, west of lake Petres, and the battle will have been fought north-west of that, but perhaps not beyond Monastir as suggested by

N. G. L. Hammond (*A History of Macedonia*, i (Oxford University Press, 1972), 104–8 with maps 7 and 8).

4.125 For the panic of large armies, cf. what is said in 2.65, 4.28, 6.63, 8.1, on the moods of a crowd within a city; for Brasidas' formation for the withdrawal, cf. the Athenian retreat from Syracuse in 413 (7.78).

4.126 Probably Brasidas was speaking to his whole army, but chose (or Thucydides chose on his behalf) to address all the men as Peloponnesians; the allies who have deserted are not any part of his force but Perdiccas' force. The word translated 'family clique' is *dynasteia*, for which cf. 3.62; whereas even in Sparta and under the regimes which it favoured among its allies the hoplites had a measure of political power. Brasidas' military point is that knowing that the enemy's reality will not live up to the appearance justifies courage, while failure to know about a real strength may lead opponents to take unjustifiable risks.

4.127 His prediction of the enemy's empty show is borne out: this kind of characterization was to become a regular way of describing a barbarian horde (cf. 2.81)—not simply as a literary motif but because by comparison with the Greeks and Romans the armies of less sophisticated peoples were like that.

4.128 There is a ridge on each side of Brasidas' road, the later Via Egnatia, and the one to his right (west) would offer the better opportunity. His men's angry treatment of the Macedonians was spontaneous, but he allowed it to happen. Perdiccas' eventual agreement with the Athenians will be mentioned in 4.132.

4.129 Thucydides backtracks to mention what had happened in Chalcidice while Brasidas was in Lyncus (cf. Introduction, p. xxvii). The obedience of Chios after the episode of 4.51 is mentioned in a fragment of Eupolis' comedy *Poleis* (fr. 246 Kassel and Austin). The temple of Poseidon was outside Mende, to the west. The manuscripts' seven hundred hoplites in Polydamidas' force are too few (cf. 4.123), and we should expect a mention of light-armed troops too. Methone, on the west side of the Thermaic Gulf, was a city within the Delian League whose loyalty Athens worked hard to retain (cf. ML 65, translated Fornara 128). Thucydides is frustratingly vague about how the Athenians 'came close to defeat'.

4.130 The Athenians' sack of Mende was an unfair reaction, when they had been opposed by a minority and had been let into the city by democrats who refused to fight against them: the previous constitution was presumably democratic, and any ill will from punishing the pro-Spartan faction would be incurred not by the Athenians but by the pro-Athenian democrats.

4.132 An Athenian treaty with Perdiccas and Arrhabaeus (*IG* i³ 89) has sometimes, but not in *IG* i³, been assigned to this context. The Spartan Ischagoras will reappear in the diplomacy of 421 (5.19, 21, 24). There was a Spartan law forbidding men of military age to leave Sparta without permission (Isoc. 11. *Bus.* 18): Ischagoras and his colleagues could surely have obtained permission, and perhaps did, but perhaps Thucydides' informant complained of a breach of the law. Spartan city governors of the kind mentioned here were later given the title harmost (*harmostes*: cf. 8.5 with note): the Greek text does not make it clear who had not wished the appointments to be left to chance, but it is fairly certain that Brasidas appointed the governors, and to that extent at least he broke his earlier promises (cf. 4.85–8). Clearidas will refuse to hand back Amphipolis to Athens after the Peace of Nicias (cf. 5.21, 34).

4.133.1–3 *Boeotia; Argos.* Because of the one-year truce, Thucydides has little other material for the summer of 423. There were to be further bouts of Athenian sympathy in Thespiae, in southern Boeotia, in 414 (6.95) and in the fourth century; the battle against the Athenians was that at Delium (cf. 4.96). It is surprising that Thucydides sees fit to mention the fire which destroyed the temple of Hera, *c.*5 miles (8 km) north-east of Argos (where the building of a new temple had already been begun): his most likely reason is that the priestess was used as a basis for chronology (cf. 2.2).

4.133.4 *Brasidas in the north-east (v).* For the siege of Scione, cf. Ar., *Vesp.* 209–10, of early 422.

4.134–5 Ninth winter (423/2)

4.134 *Mantinea and Tegea.* The two cities, *c.*10 miles (16 km) apart in south-eastern Arcadia (cf. 5.64), were old rivals, and both had interests in western Arcadia. It is striking that this quarrel between members of the Peloponnesian League could break out when the Peloponnesian War was suspended but not ended. Presumably the right wing of each army was successful (cf. 5.71); Pausanias saw the Mantinean dedication at Delphi (10.13.6).

4.135 *Brasidas in the north-east (vi).* It appears that, to ensure that sentries stayed awake at night, a bell had to be passed from one to the next (cf. Ar., *Av.* 1160); when one man went to pass on the bell, his own section of wall was for a short time unguarded.

BOOK FIVE

5.1–12 Tenth summer (422)

5.1 *Delos.* The translation, with Canfora's emendation, reproduces what Thucydides must have meant, but the manuscripts' text would mean 'came to an end until the Pythian games'. The games were held about August in the third year of each Olympiad: the truce must have been extended for about five months, and (although Thucydides stresses Cleon's eagerness to attack Scione) the Athenian assembly must have agreed to that extension.

The purification was reported in 3.104; the offence was perhaps the massacre of Aeolian pilgrims (Hyp. fr. A.1.4 in the Loeb *Minor Attic*

Orators, ii). Atramyttium was at the head of the gulf north-east of Lesbos, and there is no evidence that it ever belonged to the Delian League. Pharnaces was the satrap of Hellespontine Phrygia (cf. note to 1.128–34).

5.2–3 *Brasidas in the north-east (vii).* Thucydides' presentation suggests to an uncharacteristic extent that Cleon obtained the assembly's permission to do what he wanted. He will have been one of the regular generals for 422/1, and in this short campaign (about August–September) he was successful: his capture of Torone by direct assault was a rare achievement. The Still Harbour was to the south of the city. Torone seems to have become Brasidas' headquarters; there can have been no secret about Cleon's expedition, and on the facts presented by Thucydides Brasidas' absence appears culpable.

5.3 Panactum was probably at Kavasala, north of Eleusis and east of Plataea. The narrative is unnecessarily disjointed: this sentence could as well have been placed after the sentence about Cleon which follows.

5.4–5 *Athens and the west (xi).* Thucydides backtracks to continue the western narrative from 4.65. Phaeax first appears in comedy in Ar., *Eq.* 1377–80; he was one of the men who attracted votes in the ostracism of (probably) 415, for which see note to 6.6. Leontini had moved towards democracy, and the upper-class citizens chose to merge their city with Syracuse rather than have their land taken from them. Whatever the western Greeks thought, the Athenians will not have thought that their western alliances were ended by the treaty of 424. Acragas, not previously mentioned by Thucydides, was on the south coast of Sicily west of its mother-city Gela, and after Syracuse was the richest and strongest city on the island.

5.5 Locri had not joined in the treaty of 424; it was now contemplating a treaty; but we hear no more of that, and in 415 it was anti-Athenian again (cf. 6.44).

5.6–12 *Brasidas in the north-east (viii).* For the topographical details, see Map 6. In these chapters Thucydides frequently attributes thoughts to Cleon and Brasidas. Neither lived long to report his thoughts to others; information on Brasidas may be derived from Clearidas (cf. note to 4.70). The Odomantians (cf. 2.101) lived east of the Strymon, inland from Amphipolis. Cerdylium was perhaps the hill at 339 m., directly west of Amphipolis.

5.7 The comments on Cleon's leadership seem unfair: he had been successful at Torone; his forces were a fair match for Brasidas' forces, but it was reasonable to wait for his reinforcements and to attack Amphipolis after they arrived. The statement that his troops had been reluctant to serve under him is remarkable, and we may wonder whether it has been projected back from their discontent at this stage. It is hard to see the point of reconnaissance in force: perhaps Cleon hoped to tempt Brasidas to fight in circumstances in which the Athenians could win. Marshall's emendation, which we accept, makes 'his purpose in waiting . . .' part of what he said to his troops. The hill in front of Amphipolis is perhaps that at 133 m. to the north-east of the city.

5.8 Brasidas took his whole force back to the city: he needed his men with him, not on the far side of the river. Although his hoplites were not Spartan citizens, it is surprising that he should have considered his army inferior in quality to Cleon's. The Athenian hoplites were presumably citizens (literally 'undiluted'), and possibly a selected body of the better hoplites; Cleon had taken Lemnians and Imbrians (Athenian cleruchs) to Pylos in 425 (cf. 4.28).

5.9 Different parts of Brasidas' speech are addressed to different parts of his force; in view of the content of the earlier part, the opening 'Peloponnesians' is not unreasonable.

5.10 The Thracian Gates were at the north-east corner of the city. Cleon appears to have continued further north, so could not himself see what was happening in Amphipolis; feet of men and horses could not have been seen under the gates from his hill, so if this is a true report and not just vivid writing some Athenians must have risked going very close to the city. Cleon seems not to have given detailed instructions in advance for the withdrawal to be carried out when signalled. Apparently the Athenian force had been facing west or south-west, with its left wing nearest to Eïon, and the whole phalanx now made a quarter turn to the left, to face south or south-east, with the unshielded right flank exposed to the enemy. The palisade, joining the north-west corner of the city wall to the bridge, seems to have been built after Brasidas had occupied Amphipolis: Brasidas will have taken the road skirting the northern stretch of the wall. Cleon as commander will have been on the right wing in the original formation, which became the rear in the withdrawal. His death is made to seem as disgraceful as possible: his men were inclined to fight back but he was not, and he was killed by a barbarian peltast. Brasidas fought bravely, and learnt of his victory before dying.

5.11 Religion plays a significant part in Thucydides' treatment of Brasidas (Hornblower), and after his death Brasidas was venerated as a hero. More remarkably, the buildings in honour of Hagnon show that he, though still alive, had been venerated as a hero (I. Malkin, *Religion and Colonization in Ancient Greece* (Leiden: Brill, 1987), 228–32); this is one of the first secure instances in Greece of religious honours for a living man. Fear of the Athenians is not surprising: what had been defeated was a small army, and Athens might well have sent a larger force to avenge the defeat and recover Amphipolis. The disparity between casualties on the winning and losing side was greater in such circumstances than in a regular hoplite battle (cf. note to 4.101).

5.12 Heracleia continued to have a chequered history: see next 5.51–2.

5.13–24 Tenth winter (422/1)

5.13 *Brasidas in the north-east (postscript)*. Rhamphias and his men, though 'aware . . . that the Spartans had their minds predominantly on peace', must have been sent at the prompting of Spartans who were not thinking of peace. But Brasidas' death removed the Spartan most eager to continue the war, and Athens' defeat increased the likelihood that Athens would agree to terms acceptable to Sparta.

5.14-24 *The Peace of Nicias.* The previous offer which Athens had rejected was made in 425 (4.17-22, cf. 4.41). For the Spartans' original expectations, cf. 4.85, 7.28, but note the warning of Archidamus in 1.81. The Helots were not rebelling on the scale which Athens hoped and Sparta feared (cf. note to 4.41); for the earlier revolt, cf. 1.101-3. Thucydides has not previously mentioned the treaty between Sparta and its Peloponnesian rival Argos: the fact that after its expiry Argos would be free to fight against Sparta would be a major consideration in the next few years.

5.15 Thucydides' point seems to be that the captives included important men, with important relatives who were not captured but still in Sparta. In his account of the one-year truce (4.117-19) the motive which he stressed was Athens' desire to break Brasidas' run of successes in the north-east.

5.16 On the deaths of Cleon and Brasidas, cf. Ar., *Pax* 261-86: even in Brasidas' case Thucydides suggests a personal rather than a patriotic motive. Nicias, however, though his reluctance to take risks is emphasized, is allowed to think of the citizens' as well as of his own advantage. Pleistoanax' return from exile (cf. 1.114, 2.21) has not been mentioned before: his exile lasted perhaps from 445/4 to 427/6; apart from his working for peace we know nothing of his activities since his return. What follows has a strongly Herodotean flavour (Hornblower). Pleistoanax' grandfather Cleomenes was said to have corrupted the Delphic oracle in the 490s (Hdt. 5.62-5). The 'demigod son of Zeus' was Heracles, the supposed ancestor of the Spartan kings; ploughing with a silver ploughshare seems to be an allusion to famine. Mount Lycaeum was in southwestern Arcadia. Pleistoanax' father Pausanias had died when trapped in a sanctuary (cf. 1.134). The dances and sacrifices will belong to a later reconstruction of Sparta's origins—perhaps made for this occasion.

5.17 The possibility of the Peloponnesians' building a hostile fort was mentioned in 1.122 (the Corinthians), 1.142 (Pericles). The conferences apparently involved ten Spartans and ten Athenians, and no allies of either (cf. Diod. Sic. 12.75.4). The return of conquered territory did not apply to Potidaea and Aegina (already in the Athenian bloc at the beginning of the war) or to north-western Greece (covered by the treaty of 3.114). Sparta's meeting was of all the Peloponnesian League, including Boeotia, but probably not Sparta's new allies in the north-east. The objectors' reasons will emerge below (esp. 5.29-31); in addition, all the allies might object that Sparta had embarked on the war to liberate the Greeks from Athens (2.8, cf. 4.85-7) but now was accepting a return to the position of 431 in order to recover its prisoners from Pylos. The Boeotians (5.26 with note) and Chalcidians (6.10) made 'ten-day' truces with Athens; later the Corinthians asked for one but Athens refused (5.32). The fact that several of Sparta's allies refused to join the peace, and that Sparta was not punctilious in enforcing the peace (cf. 5.21, on

Amphipolis), was a serious flaw: superficially the terms indicated that Sparta had failed to break the power of Athens, but Athens was unwise to agree to this incomplete peace.

5.18 None of Athens' allies, inside or outside the Delian League, were consulted or invited to swear; for Sparta's allies, cf. above; but the intention was that all the allies of each should be bound by the treaty. For Delphi, cf. the one-year truce (4.118). Amphipolis was never recovered by Athens, and was finally taken by Philip of Macedon in 357. Aristeides was responsible for the original assessment of the Delian League's tribute (e.g. *Ath. Pol.* 23.5), presumably at a lower level than Athens was demanding after 425 (cf. note to 4.50). Sane is not the Sane on Athos (4.109) but the Sane on Pallene (Hdt. 7.123). For Coryphasium as the Spartans' name for Pylos, cf. 4.3: because of Sparta's incomplete implementation, Athens refused to return Pylos and other places occupied, but it eventually withdrew the Messenians from Pylos (5.35); Cythera fought for the Athenians in 413 (7.57). Olympia and the Isthmus were within the territory of states which refused to join the peace, Elis and Corinth, but the pillars may still have been set up there; the Amyclaeum was the sanctuary of Apollo and Hyacinthus at Amyclae, about 3 miles (5 km) south of Sparta proper. Sparta's allies noticed with anger that they were not to be consulted about amendments (cf. 5.29).

5.19 The Greek dating formulas state 'on the *x*th day of the waning month': Athens counted the days backwards in the last decade of the month, and our translation assumes that Sparta did likewise. Sparta's seventeen men are the two kings, the five ephors, and ten others; Athens' seventeen include ten in tribal order from Procles to Leon; and the two sets of ten will have been those involved in the conferences of 5.17. The Athenian Lampon was a man active in religious matters from the 440s onwards.

5.20 We are still just in Thucydides' year 422/1; his next year begins in 5.24. Thus according to his own scheme the war lasted slightly less than ten years—yet most scholars accept that the Greek text means 'plus a few days': that is presumably based on some kind of calculation in terms of solar years (Andrewes). In any chronological scheme precise dating requires not simply the year but the point within the year; because of the differences between states' calendars the same point could belong to different years (as we reckon them) in different states; and what Thucydides particularly needed to say here was that the length of the Archidamian War might be nine, ten, or eleven years according to the calendar being used. Cf. his objection to Hellanicus' chronology, in 1.97.

5.21 The allotment (cf. 5.35) was not mentioned in the treaty as quoted by Thucydides; it is not clear why the two sides should not have been required to implement the treaty simultaneously. The Chalcidians of Olynthus had refused the treaty, so were not bound to implement it; but they were some distance from Amphipolis, and could hardly have prevented Clearidas from handing over Amphipolis if he had been determined to do so.

5.22 Lloyd-Jones's emendation assumes that the allies left Sparta and returned—about two weeks later. For what the Spartans thought about Argos we accept the explanation and emendation of Gomme. Lichas is to make a number of later appearances: most relevantly here, he was Argos' consular representative in Sparta (cf. 5.76). Mantinea and Elis did join Argos and Athens (5.47), but there was no likelihood that Corinth or Megara would join Athens.

5.23 The terms are largely symmetrical; but Athens was to support Sparta against a rising of the Helots, whereas there was no danger of a rising of the chattel slaves at Athens. The Dionysia at Athens was slightly before the anniversary of the treaty (cf. 5.20); the Hyacinthia at Sparta was perhaps about the same time (cf. 5.41).

5.24 The oath-takers are the same as in 5.19, but there are differences in the order of the names: it is possible that in that respect the manuscripts correctly report what Thucydides wrote and that he correctly reproduced the documents which he saw. Athens did restore Sparta's prisoners although Sparta failed to restore Amphipolis. The end of the chapter as it now stands reflects Thucydides' later realization that the Peace of Nicias had not ended the war; but he may originally have written something like '. . . the men captured on the island. The war between the Athenians and the Peloponnesians, which lasted continuously for these ten years, has now been written.'

5.25-35 Eleventh summer (421)

5.25-6 *Thucydides' second preface.* Thucydides came to realize that the Peace of Nicias had not ended the war, and so wrote this second preface to introduce his narrative of the war's continuation: in 5.25 he looks ahead over the period of increasingly insecure peace to the renewed outbreak of open war. The ephor and archon are those named in 5.19. The six years and ten months seem precise but are problematic: if we count from the making of the Peace, which seems to be implied, we reach midwinter 415/4, where there is not a crucial change; the points at which Athens and Sparta ceased sparing each other's territory were Athens' raid on Laconia, in summer 414 (6.105), and Sparta's occupation of Deceleia, in spring 413 (7.19).

5.26 Here Thucydides echoes 1.1, and, for 'chronological order, by summers and winters', 2.1. This chapter must have been written after the end of the war, but Thucydides' surviving narrative ends in the autumn of 411 (cf. Introduction, pp. xxv–xxviii). By 'the Mantinean and Epidaurian campaigns' Thucydides means those which begin in 5.53, including the battle of Mantinea in 418, which is recounted in 5.64–75. A 'ten-day' truce is probably one which could be ended at ten days' notice (e.g. Andrewes), though some scholars believe it had to be renewed every ten days (e.g. Hornblower). 'Plus a few days' uses the same Greek verb as was used in 5.20: Plut., *Lys.* 15 allows us to date Lysander's entry into Athens, after Athens had accepted Sparta's peace terms, in late April 404, and it is reasonably certain that that acceptance was slightly over twenty-seven years after the attack on Plataea in 2.2–6; for Thucydides' uncharacteristic acknowledgement that the oracle was right, cf. Introduction, p. xliv. The restoration of exiles was prescribed in the peace treaty of 404 (Xen., *Hell.* 2.2.20); behind a reference to Thucydides' being recalled 'after the defeat in Sicily' (Marcellin., *Vit. Thuc.* 32, cf. Paus. 1.23.9) perhaps lies an offer which he did not accept. For a suggestion that he spent part of his exile in Corinth, cf. Introduction, p. xxv.

5.27–32 *Formation of Argive alliance.* For fear of joint domination by Sparta and Athens, cf. the end of 5.29, and earlier, 4.20; also Ar., *Pax* 1080–2. Argos had never acknowledged Sparta's supremacy, and defections from Sparta's alliance would give it the opportunity to challenge Sparta's leading position. The suggestion that open application to the assembly should be avoided is the first sign of the lack of trust which was to bedevil the negotiations of the next few years (cf. esp. 5.38).

5.28 The details in 5.40 may indicate that by the beginning of Thucydides' summer 420 the treaty had expired. For the advantage to Argos of non-involvement in the Archidamian War, cf. Ar., *Pax* 475–7.

5.29 For Mantinea's pursuit of its local interests during the Archidamian War, cf. 4.134. This is the first of a number of passages in which Thucydides notes the affinity of states with similar constitutions (cf. 5.31, 44; also 5.76, 81–2); Hornblower stresses the ongoing connection between Mantinea and Argos. On the provision for amendment Thucydides here uses the words of the alliance between Sparta and Athens (5.23), but the substance appears in the Peace of Nicias though in different words (5.18).

5.30 For the rules of the Peloponnesian League, cf. de Ste. Croix, *Origins of the Peloponnesian War*, 105–23, 339–40—though probably the reality was less clear and coherent than his presentation of it. For Sollium, cf. 2.30, for Anactorium, 4.49: these had been taken by the Acarnanians, allies of Athens but not members of the Delian League and perhaps not committed to the Peace of Nicias—but by 413 Anactorium was in Athenian hands (7.31).

5.31 For Lepreum, between Olympia and Messenia in territory claimed by Elis, see T. H. Nielsen, in Hansen and Nielsen, *Inventory*, 543–4. We cannot date the war with Arcadia, but it was probably after 479, when Lepreum was independent of Elis (Hdt. 9.28, with 9.77). Lepreum was reconquered by Elis before the end of the fifth century (Xen., *Hell.* 3.2.23–5); with its region of Triphylia it was made independent by Sparta at the beginning of the fourth century, and was later incorporated into Arcadia. The clause cited by the Eleans does not appear in the Peace of Nicias as quoted in 5.18: Andrewes suggests that they were trying to apply within the Peloponnesian alliance the principle stated in 5.17, 'that each side should give back what they had won in the war'; Hornblower prefers to think of a pre-war agreement between the Peloponnesians. The Chalcidians will be those centred on Olynthus.

5.32 For the fate of Scione, cf. 4.122, 5.18; but according to 4.123 the children and women had been evacuated to Olynthus. For the Plataeans, cf. note to 3.55: Gomme pointed out that they could preserve their identity better in Scione than by being absorbed into Athens. For the Delians, cf. 5.1. Thucydides says no more about the war between the Phocians and Locrians, but 5.64 considers both as potential allies of Sparta in 418. Mantinea had joined the Argive alliance (cf. 5.29), and Mantinea and its neighbour Tegea are often found on opposite sides (cf. 4.134). It is not clear why Athens treated Boeotia and Corinth differently: Hornblower notes that Corinth was estranged from Sparta but Boeotia was not.

5.33-35.1 *Summer campaigns.* Parrhasia was the far south-west of Arcadia; Sciritis proper was northern Laconia to the east of the Eurotas, but land further west may at this time have been considered part of Sciritis.

5.34 Here we encounter for the first time 'previously liberated cohorts' (*neodamodeis*): Thucydides never explains, but they seem to have been Helots who, unlike those serving under Brasidas (cf. 4.80), were liberated when recruited into the army; presumably the citizens of Lepreum agreed to receive them, as a larger citizen body would strengthen them in their independence. After its anxiety to recover the prisoners from Pylos, it is remarkable how Sparta distrusted them after their return.

5.35 Dium had remained loyal to Athens in 424/3 (4.109), but was to defect to Sparta in 417 (5.82).

5.35.2-8 *Non-fulfilment of treaty.* After the Peace there were various incidents which one side could have regarded as a breach of it by the other (notice particularly 5.56), but it did not suit either side to regard the Peace as at an end until 413 (cf. Introduction, p. xix). The immediate 'mutual mistrust' here differs from, and cannot belong to, the same spell of thinking and writing as 'As time went on' in 5.25: cf. Introduction, p. xxviii. For the allotment and Sparta's failure to return Amphipolis to Athens, cf. 5.21. As with the ex-Helots settled by Sparta in Lepreum, presumably the citizens of Cranii agreed to take these Helots: we are given no indication of how numerous they were.

5.36-9 Eleventh winter (421/0)

Spartan intrigues with Boeotia. The first sentence of 5.36 is the best indication that Sparta's official year began in the autumn—probably at the new moon after the equinox. The manuscripts' text in the middle of 5.36 is very clumsy: 'persuade Boeotia first itself to ally with Argos and then with Boeotia to bring Argos into alliance with Sparta', and then after a long parenthesis it is Cleoboulus and Xenares who want 'greater freedom to conduct a war outside the Peloponnese': we have therefore adopted a series of emendations favoured by Gomme and Andrewes. For Panactum, cf. 5.3. Cleoboulus and Xenares expected Boeotia to cooperate in Sparta's plans, although it had not joined in the Peace of Nicias; they also assumed that Boeotia would be able to align the Argive alliance with Sparta, though 5.37 shows the Argives thinking otherwise.

5.37 A later reference, 5.47, suggests that the highest officials in Argos at this time were the Artynae, though other texts point to a board of Demiurgi.

5.38 The Boeotarchs (cf. 2.2, 4.91) began not by responding to Argos but by swearing solidarity with other states outside both the Argive alliance and the Peace of Nicias. *Hell. Oxy.* 19. 2–4 Chambers states that in the individual cities of Boeotia the full citizens possessed of a property qualification were divided into four councils which in turn prepared business for the other three, and that each of the eleven units of the federation supplied one Boeotarch and sixty members of the federal council; it appears from this passage that the federal council was divided into quarters in the same way as the citizen bodies of the individual cities. Here by expecting tame acquiescence and not divulging their ulterior purpose the Boeotarchs failed to obtain the agreement which they would have obtained if they had divulged it; but Andrewes points out that that purpose might then have become known to the Argives, who did not share it.

5.39 It is a sign of the unfinished nature of this part of his history (cf. Introduction, p. xviii) that Thucydides twice repeats in this chapter what he has already said in 5.36 about the Spartans' hopes for Panactum and Pylos. The Boeotians, who presumably remained members of the Peloponnesian League, and who in 5.38 wanted to remain on good terms with Sparta, now wanted a direct alliance like that which Sparta had made with Athens. That alliance, as quoted in 5.23, does not include the clause mentioned here, but it may have been assumed, or else added under the provision for amendment. We have to wait until 5.40 to be told that it is the Boeotians who demolished Panactum, and until 5.42 to be told their pretext.

5.40–50 Twelfth summer (420)

5.40–8 *Various intrigues.* Thucydides perhaps places Argos' knowledge of the demolition of Panactum too soon (though Hornblower is unworried): the Spartans discover that it has happened in 5.42. It was a hindrance to Sparta's dealings with Athens that Panactum was demolished, and either the Argives were or Thucydides was irrational about this (to save Thucydides from that, Gomme wanted to emend 'demolish' to 'hand over'). What Argos aimed at, peace with Sparta and neutrality, was in effect a renewal of the thirty-year treaty which seems by now to have expired.

5.41 According to Paus. 2.38.5, there was eventually an arbitration in favour of Argos. For Cynouria, cf. 4.56 (and 2.27, which does not use the name). Thucydides does not mention Anthene elsewhere; we should expect him to mention the surviving Aeginetans as occupants of Thyrea. For the battle 'once before', in the mid-sixth century, fought originally by three hundred champions on each side, see Hdt. 1.82.

5.42 Thucydides' language suggests that he does not accept the Boeotian claim: the Peace of Nicias had stated that Panactum was to be returned to Athens (5.18), but the Boeotians had not sworn to the Peace.

5.43 For a comment on Alcibiades' flamboyant and selfish character we have to wait until 6.15: though more relevant there, it is not irrelevant here. He was born in 451/0 (Davies, *APF*, 18, cf. Plut., *Alc.* 15), and after his father's death at Coroneia in 447/6 (cf. 1.113) he was brought up by Pericles, who was a cousin on his mother's side. He was first mentioned in comedy in 427 (Ar. fr. 198. 6 Kock/Edmonds = 205. 6 Kassel and Austin, from *Banqueters*); that he was involved in the reassessment of the Delian League's tribute in 425 (cf. note to 4.50), as alleged by [Andoc.] 4. *Alc.* 11, is unlikely, but we can accept what Thucydides says of his looking after the Spartans captured at Pylos in that year; he is now attested as the proposer of a decree in 422/1 (*SEG* 1 45). For once Thucydides does not say that 'in word' he considered alliance with Argos a better policy but 'in deed' he was motivated by pique (cf. Introduction, p. xxxiv), but accepts both considerations as genuine. The likeliest occasion for the renunciation of the consular position by his grandfather, another Alcibiades, is the breach between Athens and Sparta in 462/1 (cf. 1.102); it seems not to have saved him from being ostracized (Lys. 14. *Alc.* 1. 39, [Andoc.] 4. *Alc.* 34). We learn, but not until 8.6, that 'Alcibiades' was a Spartan name, which had entered this family because of its Spartan connection.

5.44 For links between Argos and Athens in the legendary past (if that is what is meant) see e.g. Aesch., *Eum.* 762–74. In the fifth century Argos had been an ally of Athens from *c.*462/1 (cf. 1.102) until the making of its thirty-year treaty with Sparta. For the absence of the Corinthians from this alliance (contr. 5.27, 31), cf. 5.48. Of the Spartan envoys, Philocharidas was one of the Spartans involved in making the one-year truce of 423 and the Peace of Nicias (4.119, 5.19); Leon could be the founder of Sparta's colony at Heracleia (cf. 3.92), but the name is not rare; Endius belonged to the family with which Alcibiades' family was connected (8.6).

5.45 It is hard to accept the story of deceit exactly as Thucydides tells it. Greek states had a tendency to give men full authority (make them *autokratores*) on particular occasions without specifying how and how far their powers were enhanced, but it is unlikely that Sparta was willing to make major concessions to Athens, or undertook to accept whatever terms its envoys could be persuaded to agree to in Athens. Presumably Alcibiades did deceive the Spartans somehow, but we cannot reconstruct exactly what happened. Thucydides sees no ulterior significance in the earthquake (cf. Introduction, p. xlv), which in fact merely delayed the outcome.

5.46 Gomme noted that Nicias was trying to play the strong man, but could hardly expect the Spartans to rebuild Panactum. The oath sworn to him by the Spartans was presumably additional to the annual renewal prescribed in 5.23.

5.47 The copy of the treaty published in Athens has survived (Tod 72 = *IG* i³ 83). There are a number of verbal disagreements (though fewer than used to be supposed: see Hornblower), as there are between inscriptions when multiple copies of a text survive: the Greeks do not seem to have thought word-for-word identity mattered. It is possible, but cannot be verified, that Thucydides has reproduced verbatim the text which he saw (Gomme suggested the copy set up at Olympia). Argos, Mantinea, and Elis were already allies, so this treaty takes the form of an alliance between Athens and all of them, whether individually or collectively. The alliance begins with defensive provisions, but the reference later to 'a joint external campaign' shows that it is a full offensive and defensive alliance. For the issue of passage through the allies' territory, cf. 4.78 with note to 4.78–88. 3 Aeginetan obols = 4.3 Athenian obols, and 1 drachma is double that in each system (see Appendix). Athens swore for all its allies, as in the Peace of Nicias (see note to 5.18). We should expect the treaty to specify which city magistrates were to swear for Athens, as for the other participants: the generals are the most likely, but practice varied from one occasion to another, and on some occasions a large number of men swore. The Olympic festival was held about August; the Panathenaea at the end of the first month of the Athenian year, about July (see Appendix); the Olympics and the Great Panathenaea were each quadrennial, the Olympics falling in 420 (cf. 5.49–50) and the next Great Panathenaea in 418. The intention seems to have been that renewal should be about the same time in alternate years (Hornblower). Documents of Elis were regularly published at Olympia, so the copy there will have served both for Elis and for the alliance as a whole (Andrewes).

5.48 For the original alliance as a defensive alliance, cf. 5.27; the subsequent upgrading of that to a full alliance has not been mentioned before. Andrewes notes that Corinth's objection to Sparta was only to its making peace with Athens, and as the likelihood of renewed war increased Corinth returned to its normal allegiance.

5.49–50 *Sparta banned from Olympic games.* As in 3.8, Thucydides identifies the festival by the winner of the pancratium. Phyrcus has not been identified; for Lepreum (which the Spartans did not regard as belonging to Elis), see note to 5.31. Festival truces covered those travelling to attend the festival and the territory of the state holding the festival (Hornblower).

5.50 Harpine was upstream from Olympia. When Sparta went to war against Elis *c.*402–400, that was to take revenge for its exclusion now (there is no reason to believe, as some have done, that Sparta was excluded on subsequent occasions too: see Hornblower). Gomme, characteristically, suggested that the earthquake merely served as an excuse for ending discussions which were clearly going to achieve nothing.

5.51 Twelfth winter (420/19)

Heracleia in Trachis. Xenares is probably the man first mentioned as ephor in 5.36 (Andrewes, Hornblower: Gomme was agnostic).

5.52–5 Thirteenth summer (419)

Mostly Argos. On Spartan misrule in Heracleia, cf. 3.93, where the same Greek expression is used. Alcibiades will have been general for 420/19. Isoc. 14. *Team of Horses* 15 perhaps refers to this episode; for Patrae, cf. note to 2.83–92. Gomme regarded the flamboyant campaign as typical of Alcibiades.

5.53 Hornblower notes that it was in 420/19 that the cult of Asclepius was introduced into Athens from Epidaurus (see note to 2.48). The war between Argos and Epidaurus will continue until 418/7, when Argos makes peace with Sparta after the battle of Mantinea (5.77, 80). Thucydides expects his readers to know about the temple of Apollo, strictly Pythaeeus, which was perhaps at Asine, south-east of Argos; Epidaurus perhaps had a lesser share in its administration; we have retained the otherwise unattested *botamion* and translate it 'pasture-rights', on which see Hornblower (who takes the Botamia to be a festival), but some manuscripts have *parapotamion*, 'the area across the river' (see textual note). Corinth and Epidaurus were old friends (cf. 1.27), but it is not clear how Epidaurus' defection would 'keep Corinth quiet'.

5.54 Leuctra (or Leuctrum) was in the north-west of Laconia: going there would suggest that Sparta's objective was Elis, but would not exclude a turn towards Mantinea. The cities referred to are apparently those of Sparta's Perioeci (Hornblower, contr. Gomme and Andrewes). For Sparta's mustering an army without stating the objective, cf. Hdt. 5.74 (but this decision was probably not taken by Agis on his own, as that by Cleomenes was: cf. the kings' right to make war claimed in Hdt. 6.56). On *diabateria*, sacrifices before crossing the frontier, which are attested particularly for Sparta, see Pritchett, *GSW*, iii. 68–71. For Sparta's avoidance of campaigning at the time of the Carneia (the month corresponded approximately to our August), cf. Hdt. 6.106, 7.206; Argos was to manipulate its calendar again in the 380s (Xen., *Hell.* 4.7.2–3, cf. 5.1.29). The Carneia did not prevent or delay the battle of Mantinea in 418 (cf. 5.75); see also on 5.82.

5.55 Thucydides is perfunctory in his treatment of a conference which achieved nothing: Andrewes points out that it could have been instigated either by Athenians wanting to preserve the Peace or by Athenians wanting to score points against Sparta. Euphamidas may be the man of that name mentioned in 2.33, 4.119. Caryae was in the north-east of Laconia, on the route to Argos via Arcadia.

5.56 Thirteenth winter (419/18)

Argos. Sparta's winter naval expedition was unexpectedly daring. Andrewes suggests that Argos was regarding not the whole of the sea but the Saronic Gulf as Athenian 'territory'; the Athenian reaction was to declare the Spartans to be in breach of the Peace of Nicias, but not yet to declare the Peace to be at an end.

5.57–75 Fourteenth summer (418)

5.57–60 *Spartan attack on Argos.* See Map 7. 'Middle' indicates that this episode was later than the normal beginning of the campaigning season, in Thucydides' spring: he does not explain why Sparta acted now rather than earlier. For the use of attendant infantry with cavalry, cf. Xen., *Hell.* 7.5.23–4, *Hipparch.* 5.13, and Caes. *BG* 1.48.5.

5.58 Methydrium was to the west of Mantinea, which the Spartans were avoiding. The Corinthian contingent set out 'before dawn' (the meaning of the manuscripts' text) on its route to the Argive plain, but Agis must have started earlier and travelled by night.

5.59 The Argive army was between the Boeotian contingent and Agis' contingent; Agis' contingent was between the Argive army and the city of Argos. Thucydides apparently judges Agis' position to be more favourable (but see Hornblower); whether that is correct depends on how near the Boeotian contingent was; the commanders on each side were willing to make a truce, but the soldiers on each side thought their commanders had thrown away an opportunity of victory. It is possible that the non-arrival of the Athenians was due to a reduced enthusiasm for conflict at this stage (cf. next note but one), but Andrewes thought it might be due only to logistical problems.

5.60 'The officials' with Agis will have included the polemarchs, the officers ranking next below himself (cf. 5.66), and two of the ephors (Xen., *Lac.* 13.1, 5). That this was 'the finest Greek army ever raised so far' is surprising in the light of such passages as 2.9, 11; some commentators have inferred from 'seen' that the exiled Thucydides himself saw this army. The Charadrus, dry at most times in the year, ran round the north and east of the city of Argos: Hornblower notes the contrast between the (more disciplined) Spartan and the Argive reactions.

5.61–3 *Argive attack on Orchomenus and Tegea.* Gomme was excessively sceptical of such political explanations, but it is possible that Alcibiades had not been elected general for 418/7 and that that reflects a change of mood in Athens.

5.62 Elis' interest in Lepreum is clear, but the loss of Tegea would have done much more to weaken Sparta.

5.63 If the truce had led to a treaty between Sparta and Argos (cf. 5.59), Agis could have claimed that it was justified; but Argos' joining in the attack on Orchomenus showed that it would not, and so weakened his position. He was perhaps tried by the *gerousia* (including the other king) and the ephors (D. M. MacDowell, *Spartan Law* (Edinburgh: Scottish Academic Press, 1996), 133–4; Hornblower). For demolition of the house, cf. the treatment of Leotychidas after his campaign of probably 478 in Thessaly (Hdt. 6.72); Agis probably could not have paid so large a fine (equivalent to more than 23 Athenian talents), though Andrewes suggests that the kings were exempt from the ban on owning silver. Advisers had previously been imposed on unsuccessful admirals (e.g. 2.85). The manuscripts' text would mean 'withdraw . . . from the city', but Haase's 'from enemy land' fits what Agis had done and makes better sense of the Greek verb. Agis' command at Mantinea was unfettered (see. 5.66), and we hear no more of threats to him after his victory at Mantinea.

5.64–75.3 *Battle of Mantinea.* See Map 8. Sparta's route up the Eurotas valley via Orestheium was not the most direct but was the easiest (cf. its use in 479: Hdt. 9.11). The temple of Heracles has been located in the northern part of the hourglass-shaped plain, south-east of Mantinea (W. K. Pritchett, accepted by Andrewes in his addenda (vol. v, p. 457) and by Hornblower).

5.65 The Argive position was probably on the lower slopes of Mount Alesium, east of Mantinea. 'Curing one mistake with another' was a proverbial phrase, found in Hdt. 3.53 and in tragedy; and 'for this or another reason' is Herodotean too (e.g. Hdt. 4.147): this is a surprising way for Thucydides to write of Agis' change of tactics. By 'returning to Tegean territory' Agis moved into the southern part of the plain: the water-courses were probably not the same then as now, but he seems to have interfered shortly to the south of the gap (Andrewes, vol. v, pp. 457–8; Hornblower). The facts that he went 'out of sight' of the Argives, and that when returning northwards (5.66) he was caught unprepared by the Argives, are easier to explain if we can assume that the Pelagos wood, first mentioned in the second century AD by Paus. 8.11.1, 5, already existed and blocked the view through the gap where the plain narrows (accepted by Andrewes, doubted by Hornblower).

5.66 The Spartans had been in frightening situations before, notably at Thermopylae in 480 and at Pylos in 425 (4.2–41); the point here is that they had never before been so seriously surprised. As Gomme remarks, Sparta was not unique in having subsidiary units and commanders in its army, but the Spartan system was exceptionally elaborate and efficient.

5.67 For the Sciritae, see note to 5.33–35.1; Hornblower argues that Brasidas' veterans include his mercenaries as well as his Helots. Because of the dynamics of a hoplite phalanx, to be explained in 5.71, the right wing was the most honourable position, and the left wing ranked next (cf. Hdt. 9.26–8). On the Argive side, Hornblower follows T. H. Nielsen in suggesting that the 'allies from Arcadia' were Maenalians, opposed to those fighting for Sparta. This is the first mention of Argos' select force, with which we may compare the Sacred Band of 300 Thebans (e.g. Plut., *Pel.* 18–19), and the *eparitoi* of the Arcadian federation (e.g. Xen., *Hell.* 7.4.33), in the fourth century.

5.68 After complaining of Spartan secrecy and claiming that accurate numbers could not be given for either side (Hornblower compares Hdt. 4.81, 7.170), Thucydides gives an account of the Spartan army which would permit a calculation: 3,584 + 600 Sciritae ?+ 300 Knights = 4,184 or 4,484 Spartans (it is not clear whether the Knights of 5.72 are included in this structure). However, there is a slightly different account of the Spartan army in Xen., *Lac.* 11.4; and, while it is possible that each is correct for the time to which it refers, there is a good case (accepted by Andrewes and Hornblower) for believing that each is a slightly inaccurate account of the same structure. If so, Thucydides should perhaps have said, 'They had seven regiments [*morai*: six regular regiments and one of liberated Helots]. . . . There were two divisions [*lochoi*] to each regiment, four companies [*pentekostyes*] to each division, and four units [*enomotiai*] to each company.' The result would then be 6,144 regular army + 1,024 Brasidean veterans + 600 Sciritae ?+ 300 Knights = 7,768 or 8,068 Spartans (including Perioeci, perhaps 60 per cent of the total), from a five-sixths levy (cf. 5.64). Spartan citizen numbers were declining (cf. notes to 1.19, 101–3); but this correction would put more of the decline after 418 and less before (see e.g. de Ste. Croix, *Origins of the Peloponnesian War*, 331–2). Variation in depth of line between contingents of a mixed army was common, but it is surprising to find it even within the Spartan contingent.

5.69 For the alternatives of sovereignty (sc. over others) and subjection, with nothing between, see note to 2.63; for Argos' claim to supremacy in the Peloponnese, see note to 1.101–3; if Sparta were defeated in a major land-battle in the Peloponnese, the threat to Athens would indeed be at an end.

5.70 The advance to music was surely standard, and not only for Sparta (but the Spartan version was perhaps particularly intimidating: cf. Polyaenus, *Strat.* 1.10, Plut., *Lyc.* 22); it is surprising even that Thucydides insists on its secular purpose, but it is presumably mentioned here because this was the great hoplite battle of the Peloponnesian War.

5.71 All Greeks will have known of hoplites' tendency to shift to the right, and of the reason for it, but the fact is needed to explain what happened on this occasion.

5.72 What is striking is that, when Agis decided on corrective action, two of the polemarchs disobeyed. Thus the Spartans began the battle with a gap in their line, and they ought now if ever to have been defeated—but their general good order (not just 'courage alone') was still enough to secure victory over allies not sufficiently practised in fighting together. The 'so-called Knights' were in fact hoplites (cf. Hdt. 8.124).

5.73 This chapter ends with a comment which is slightly surprising: the Spartans may have been exceptionally resolute in persisting to the 'turning point' (the point where the opposing phalanx gave way), but it was characteristic of Greek armies in general not to engage in long pursuits.

5.74 This was not only the largest-scale hoplite battle in the Peloponnesian War (the last battle on a comparable scale had been that at Tanagra *c*.457: 1.107–8). It was also of major significance, since victory restored Sparta's standing in the Peloponnese (cf. 5.75), whereas defeat would have undermined it fatally (cf. 5.69). For the 'settlers from Aegina', cf. 2.27.

5.75.1–3 Pleistoanax set out with the reinforcements presumably because it was known that reinforcements were on their way to the other army (cf. 5.75.4–6); if Hdt. 5.75 is correct, the rule stated there about one of the kings must have been relaxed (Hornblower). For the Corinthians and others, cf. 5.64.

5.75.4–6 *Epidaurian attack on Argos.* Uncharacteristically, at this point Gomme suggested that Athens' sending its forces in instalments was the result of political disagreement, and it was Andrewes who responded that the initial sending of too small a force, on this occasion and on others, was due to overconfidence. We may wonder how the battle would have turned out if these men and the Eleans had arrived in time.

5.76–81 Fourteenth winter (418/17)

Peace in the Peloponnese. Thucydides' winter began some months after Carneius (cf. on 5.54), and it is perhaps better to delete 'the Carneia now celebrated' as an interpolation. For the link between democracy and alignment with Athens, cf. in general note to 1.19, and for Argos, 5.29, 31, 44. What Thucydides proceeds to give us—for a settlement which lasted only a short time—is a preliminary agreement on the conditions for peace and the basis for an alliance (Spartan decree in 5.77), followed by a 'treaty and alliance', which is in fact a treaty of alliance, not dealing with the other issues (5.78–80, with text quoted 5.79). Sparta had sent Lichas to Argos before (5.22).

5.77 This document (both this and the next are quoted in Doric Greek) begins with current issues which must be resolved if there is to be peace: for the Orchomenians, cf. 5.61 (not referring to children), for the men in Mantinea, cf. 5.61; Maenalian hostages have not previously been mentioned. Argos cannot compel Athens to withdraw from Epidaurus, but is to join Sparta in opposition if Athens will not withdraw. No children held by Sparta have been mentioned. The sacrifice is to Apollo Pythaeus (cf. 5.53); what exactly the solution was is hard to fathom (cf. Hornblower). The remainder of the document prepares for the alliance, covering the Peloponnese as a whole, and the allies of Sparta and of Argos (in Crete?) outside the Peloponnese. With Argos allied to Sparta, opposition is now to be expected only from outside the Peloponnese, and in particular from Athens, and it seems to be envisaged that Sparta and Argos are to be joint leaders of an enlarged Peloponnesian alliance. That would be a major development, in which Sparta's existing allies might not tamely acquiesce (cf. the fears expressed about the alliance of 421 between Sparta and Athens (5.27, 29)).

5.78 It is not clear whether the allies had time to respond between the agreement of 5.77 and the alliance of 5.79.

5.79 The alliance first repeats points from the agreement; Hornblower follows M. Ostwald in thinking that all rule over Peloponnesian cities by other Peloponnesian cities is forbidden. Then it is stated more clearly that joint campaigns are to be the joint responsibility of Sparta and Argos. Provision for the resolution of disputes is added, on standard lines.

5.80 We do not know of any territory which either might have returned to the other, but there may have been prisoners of war to be returned. Perdiccas has not been mentioned since 5.2, where he was pro-Athenian: 5.83 indicates that he did become an ally of Sparta and Argos. For the alleged Argive origin of his family, cf. 2.99. Demosthenes' trick enabled Athens on its own to hand over the fort, not in conjunction with the other garrison forces: Andrewes notes that if the Athenians had realized that Argos' new alignment would not last long they might have delayed over this. The treaty which they renewed with Epidaurus will have been the Peace of Nicias.

5.81 Mantinea's truce was for thirty years (Xen., *Hell.* 5.2.2), and Mantinea rejoined the Peloponnesian League. Nothing is said about Elis, but it was in control of Lepreum once more by *c*.402 (Xen., *Hell.* 3.2.25). It is possible but not certain that the thousand Argives mentioned here were the special force of 5.67; probably there was some joint action before the Spartans went without the Argives to Sicyon (where presumably there was already some form of oligarchy). It is probably this counter-revolution in Argos to which Aen. Tact. 17.2–4 refers.

5.82 Fifteenth summer (417)

Mostly Argos. Of the Achaean cities, only Pellene had supported the Spartans in 418 (5.58–9). Achaea had closer connections with central Greece than with the rest of the Peloponnese, and its loyalty to Sparta seems to have been weak (cf. 2.9, where again Pellene is singled out; 3.92). The Gymnopaediae at Sparta was held in midsummer (cf. Pl., *Lg.* 1.633 C): the Spartans may have intercalated days to postpone the date of the festival (cf. Argos in 5.54), but Hornblower doubts that; for a story connected with this episode, see Paus. 2.20.1–2. Argos did not formally renew its alliance with Athens until spring 416 (*IG* i³ 86 with ML 77, this part translated Fornara 144, 29–30). Plut., *Alc.* 15 attributes the long walls to Alcibiades. Some Mantineans continued to sympathize with Athens (cf. 6.29), and they may have been among the other Peloponnesians who assisted.

5.83 Fifteenth winter (417/16)

Argos; the north-east. Corinth supported Sparta in 418 (5.57, 64, 75). Its abstention from this attack on Argos is not explained: it attacked Athens in 416 (5.115), but abstained from another Spartan campaign in 416/5 (6.7). The one sentence devoted to Hysiae contrasts strongly with the extended treatment of Athens' dealing with Melos which is to follow (cf. Introduction, p. xxxviii).

ML 77 (cf. above: a financial record for 418/7–415/4) shows that there was Athenian activity in the north-east which Thucydides does not mention: Nicias' aborted campaign seems to be that referred to in lines 20–1 of this inscription and dated about May 418/7, i.e. before the Argive counter-revolution of 5.82.

5.84–115 Sixteenth summer (416)

Mostly Athenian attack on Melos. Hornblower notes that much of Book 5 'has been about the greater and stronger imposing their will on the smaller and weaker'. Alcibiades was presumably a general for 417/6 (stated by Diod. Sic. 12.81.2). Thucydides does not mention him in connection with Melos, and neither does Diod. Sic. However, [Andoc.] 4. *Alcibiades* 22–3 alleges that he recommended the enslavement of the Melians, and bought and had a son by a Melian woman—an allegation which on chronological grounds is not impossible but which could not have been made until after spring 415, the latest possible date for that text if it were an authentic text written for the occasion to which it ostensibly belongs (the ostracism which resulted in the banishment of Hyperbolus, for which see note to 6.6). That allegation reappears in Plut., *Alc.* 16. For Melos, see 2.9, 3.91 and note to 3.91; its alleged Spartan origin will be invoked in the dialogue which follows; we know nothing about its conduct after the Peace of Nicias to explain this Athenian attack; its being the only Aegean island outside the Delian League was an ongoing provocation to Athens, but Andrewes concludes from the substantial use of allied forces that the attack was not blatantly unjustified. The two generals are not mentioned elsewhere by Thucydides.

Here uniquely Thucydides gives us not opposing speeches but a formal dialogue (5.85–113). It is credible that in an oligarchic state the Athenians were asked to present their case not to the assembly but to 'the authorities and the privileged few' (cf. the dialogue proposed by Sparta for negotiations with Athens in 4.22). Thucydides will not have found out easily what was said, since he was in exile from Athens (F. E. Adcock, *Thucydides and his History* (Cambridge University Press, 1963), 33, assumed that the Melians who betrayed the city to Athens (5.116) were spared); but his dialogue can reasonably be judged by the same criteria as his speeches, and accepted as his honest reconstruction, on the basis of such information as he did obtain, of the kinds of argument that he would expect to be used. That is not incompatible with his emphasizing, to an extent which may not fairly represent what was actually said, the Athenians' ruthless insistence on the realities of power. (Cf. Introduction, pp. xxxvi, xlv–xlvi.) Hornblower cites as a precursor Hesiod's parable of the hawk and the nightingale (*Op.* 203–11).

5.85 At 4.88 Thucydides describes Brasidas' speech at Acanthus as a 'seduction'. Melian oligarchs may have kept the Athenians from the assembly as a matter of course, rather than for the reason which Thucydides makes the Athenians allege.

5.86 At 4.88 Thucydides notes that Acanthus was influenced not only by Brasidas' speech but also by his threat of force.

5.89 For renunciation of the argument from the Persian Wars, cf. Euphemus in 6.83; also 1.73. The Athenians claim not that might is right (as some sophists would have done, and cf. Dem. 15. *Liberty of Rhodians* 29) but that when one party is overwhelmingly superior in might the question of right does not arise.

5.90 The Melians reply that it is advantageous that those superior in might should not do all they are capable of (cf. the Athenians in 1.76, Diodotus in 3.44–7). For prediction of the overthrow of the Athenian empire, cf. Pericles in 2.63–4: when Athens was finally defeated, in 404, it was treated more leniently by Sparta than some of Sparta's allies wished (Xen., *Hell.* 2.2.19–20).

5.94–5 For rejection of a counter-suggestion of friendship and neutrality, cf. Brasidas at Acanthus (4.97).

5.96 In describing Athens' subjects as its colonies the Melians are accepting the representation of the Delian League as an Ionian league (cf. notes to 1.2–3, 94–5).

5.97 On the importance of islanders to Athens, cf. 4.120–2.

5.104 Andrewes regarded the absence of a reply to the Melians' claim of a 'righteous [in a religious sense] stand against injustice' as 'more damaging to Athens than anything else in the Dialogue'. Neither the gods (or what Thucydides might call 'chance': cf. Introduction, p. xliii) nor the Spartans did in fact help Melos, but Hornblower stresses that it was not unreasonable for the Melians to hope for Spartan help.

5.105 For a belief in nature (*physis*) which was characteristic of the sophists cf. Introduction, pp. xlv–xlvi; the ascription to the gods as well as to men of the principle that 'wherever they can rule, they will' (cf. especially 1.76) is striking. If the dialogue had not been kept on a level of generality, Sparta's willingness to betray the freedom of the Greeks when it was in Sparta's interests to do so, which no doubt did 'brand them faithless in the eyes of their friends' (5.106: cf. notes to 4.50, 5.17, 8.18), could have been cited in support of the disparaging comment on Sparta.

5.107 Pericles in a very different spirit had spoken of the burdens accompanying the pursuit of honour (2.63–4).

5.108 Melos is not particularly near to the Peloponnese (*c*.75 miles, 120 km), but is nearer to Laconia than any other substantial island among the Cyclades.

5.110 The 'Cretan sea' is the southern Aegean.

5.111 The Athenians had not abandoned an attack on others because of a threat to Attica: at the beginning of the 450s a Peloponnesian attack did not make them give up their siege of Aegina (1.105); in 446 Pericles returned from Euboea to face the Peloponnesian invasion but went back to Euboea afterwards (1.114)—and in 413 the Peloponnesian occupation of Decelea (7.19) would not make the Athenians give up their siege of Syracuse (which Andrewes thought Thucydides had in mind when he wrote this passage). For the use of shame here, cf. Phrynichus in 8.27. Only here are we told that what Athens offered to Melos was ordinary tribute-paying membership of the Delian League.

5.112 Hornblower notes that only here, in the Melians' last utterance, is a form of address used. We do not know the basis for the seven hundred years of Melos' freedom: it is possible that Melos was actually settled from Sparta in the ninth or eighth century (P. A. Cartledge, *Sparta and Lakonia* (Routledge, ²2002), 94), but the fifth-century belief was more important than the reality (I. Malkin, *Myth and Territory in the Spartan Mediterranean* (Cambridge University Press, 1994), 74–8).

5.115 For the resumption of raids (by former Helots or their descendants) from Pylos, see 5.56. Just as Athens did not declare the Peace of Nicias to be at an end in 5.56, Sparta now did not declare the Peace to be at an end and resume fighting to distract the Athenians from Melos. Corinth had neither sworn to the Peace of Nicias nor obtained a separate treaty with Athens subsequently.

5.116 Sixteenth winter (416/15) (beginning)

Argos; Melos. Philocrates will have been a general for 416/5; probably Cleomedes and Teisias were re-elected for this year and remained on Melos. Melos was fertile, and it is possible that its population was as much as 5,000 in all, 1,250 adult males. Hornblower notes the irony of the Spartan colony's becoming an Athenian colony. Thucydides' elaborate presentation of this episode, in which the Athenian sledgehammer crushed the last nut in the Aegean, immediately before his elaborate presentation of the Sicilian campaign of 415–413, in which the Athenians disastrously overreached themselves, is surely intentional (cf. Introduction, pp. xxi, xxxvii). Ar. *Av.*, 186, of 414, does not suggest any sensitivity about Melos; but, no doubt partly because of Thucydides' presentation of it, Athens' treatment of the Melians became one of the most notorious acts of Athenian imperialism (e.g. Xen., *Hell.* 2.2.3, Isoc. 12. *Panath.* 62–6).

BOOK SIX

6.1–7 Sixteenth winter (416/15) (conclusion)

6.1 *Athens' Sicilian expedition (i): planning.* In Thucydides' text as our manuscripts transmit it, almost the whole of Books 6–7 is devoted to the Athenians' Sicilian expedition of 415–413; but the beginnings and ends of those books do not coincide with new summers or winters in the narrative, and the division into books is not due to Thucydides himself (cf. Introduction, p. xxvi). The impression given by these books is that the Athenian project was over-ambitious (suggested in this chapter), but that even so it might have succeeded in the short term if Nicias had been less dilatory in 414 (cf. 6.103, 7.2; also 7.48–9, 73). This is at odds with the suggestion in 2.65 that the failure was due not to misjudgement but to political dissension in Athens and consequent failure to support the project properly. That passage and this narrative were certainly thought, and almost certainly written, at different times: probably the narrative not long after the events (but see note to 6.15), and the comment in 2.65 after the end of the war, by which time there had been a good deal of political dissension in Athens (cf. Introduction, p. xxviii).

The force sent in 427–424 had by 424 comprised sixty ships or slightly more (cf. 3.115): originally sixty were intended in 415 (cf. 6.8), but probably more soldiers with them, and more ships were eventually sent (cf. 6.25, 31, 43). In view of the campaigns of 427–424 and 422, and earlier contacts, the claim that 'most Athenians were ignorant' of Sicily, which suits his suggestion of misjudgement here, is perhaps the most unfair claim in Thucydides' history; Plut., *Nic.* 12 writes, we do not know on what basis, of excited conversations and sketch maps. The circumference of Sicily is *c.*575 miles (930 km); Ephorus *FGrH* 70 F 135 suggests a voyage of five days and nights; Thucydides was presumably thinking of daytime only. The width of the strait at its narrowest point is *c.*1¾ miles (2.8 km), implying 20 stades of 153 yards (140 m) (shorter than his usual stade, but surely just estimated: see Appendix).

6.2–5 *Early history of Sicily.* See Map 2; and on all the cities of Sicily and Italy, see T. Fischer-Hansen *et al.*, in Hansen and Nielsen, *Inventory*, 172–248, 249–320. What Thucydides' argument needs here is an account of Sicily in 415: what he actually gives is an account of its early history and in particular of the foundation of Greek colonies there. Presumably he had discovered information which he wished to publicize; and Hornblower follows H. C. Avery in stressing the passages which compare the Athenian expedition with a colonizing expedition (esp. 6.23). Thucydides' main source seems to have been Antiochus of Syracuse (*FGrH* 555), who wrote a history of Sicily down to 424. His intervals of time can be translated into absolute dates from the destruction of Megara Hyblaea (6.4) *c.*483/2, and it has been argued that Antiochus counted back in 35-year generations from that and other points in the early fifth century. In some cases other texts give divergent dates, which are likely to have been arrived at equally artificially. Thucydides' dates are accepted by A. J. Graham in *CAH* iii. 3², 103–9, and archaeological evidence suggests that they are at any rate approximately correct. Earlier traces of Greek presence are not necessarily evidence of a Greek *polis*; in many cases (as Thucydides sometimes notes) the *polis* took over an already occupied site. In Thucydides' order, the dates are within a year or two of: Sicel migration 1034/3, Naxos 734/3, Syracuse 733/2, Leontini and Catana 729/8, Megara Hyblaea 728/7, Selinus 628/7, Gela 689/8, Acragas 581/0, Acrae 663/2, Casmenae 643/2, Camarina 598/7.

6.2 By the time of Thucydides it was generally believed that the Cyclopes and Laestrygonians of Hom., *Od.* 9–10 lived in Sicily; Euripides located his *Cyclops* near Mount Aetna (cf. the location of the Phaeacians in Corcyra: 1.25, 3.70). For Thucydides' qualified acceptance of the epic account, cf. 1.10. That the Sicanians were the original inhabitants of the island and were pushed to the west by the Sicels migrating from Italy was generally believed; archaeologically the two peoples are not distinguishable, and by the classical period they had become substantially hellenized. The Sicanians are not mentioned again apart from a Sicanian town in 6.62. (The term for Greek Sicilians is Siceliots.) Trinacria seems to be a version of Thrinakie in Hom., *Od.* 11.107. Thucydides is the earliest surviving author to write of Trojan fugitives in Sicily; the actual origin of the Elymians is unknown (they had a third city, Entella). No other text takes Phocians to Sicily (except Paus. 5.25.6, perhaps derived from Thucydides): some have thought of the Phocaeans from Asia Minor (who colonized elsewhere in the western Mediterranean, and cf. Sicilian Phocaeae in 5.4), but here Thucydides is writing of barbarians, and a better emendation would be to Phrygians (later assimilated to the Trojans: cf. Paus.); but Hornblower after discussion tentatively retains Phocians. Thucydides' Opicans were the Oscans, of southern Italy. Archaeological evidence suggests that the Phoenicians did not precede the Greeks in Sicily, but arrived in the west about the same time as the Greeks arrived in the east, and they did not attempt to expand eastwards before the fifth century; the Phoenician colony of Carthage is *c*.150 miles (240 km) from Motya.

6.3   Naxos is the first landing-point for ships sailing to Sicily via southern Italy; the Chalcidians had already founded colonies in the bay of Naples (cf. 6.4); the name Naxos suggests the involvement of Aegean Naxos (as claimed by Hellanicus, *FGrH* 4 F 82). The aristocracies of various Dorian cities claimed descent from Heracles (for Corinth cf. 1.24); for the 'island' of Ortygia, see Map 9.

6.4   'Betrayal' is defended by Hornblower, who notes that 'it offers an unexpected native perspective'. For the destruction of Megara Hyblaea, see Hdt. 7.156; Hornblower remarks that this is the first of many Herodotean echoes in Book 6. Archaeologists have been torn between Thucydides' date of *c*.628/7 for Selinus and 651/0 (Diod. Sic. 13.59.4). The name of a Megarian co-founder of Selinus seems to have dropped out, and can be supplied from *SEG* xliii 630 as Myscus or Euthydemus (cf. Hornblower). The name Lindii recalls Lindos on Rhodes; Hdt. 7.153 mentions one settler from the island of Telos but omits Crete. Thucydides mentions Dorian institutions in Gela perhaps because Rhodes was unambiguously Dorian but the status of Crete was less clear. Cumae was founded on the mainland of the bay of Naples, *c*.650, from the earlier colony on the island of Pithecusae and from Cyme in Asia Minor: for secure contact with Greece the settlers there needed to control the strait between Sicily and Italy (for the identification with the Homeric Scylla and Charybdis, cf. 4.24); Zancle was founded *c*.730, and Rhegium on the Italian side soon afterwards. For the Samians and others, fleeing from the Persians *c*.494 at the end of the Ionian Revolt, see Hdt. 6.22–4; the refoundation of Zancle as Messana is attributed to Cadmus from Cos by Hdt. 7.164, while confused late texts associate the change with Anaxilas and with Messenians fleeing from the Peloponnese (Strabo 268/6.2.3, Paus. 4.23.6–10).

6.5   A scholiast on Pind., *Ol.* 5 dates the revolt of Camarina Ol. 57 = 552–548, but the archaeological record shows no break in the mid-sixth century.

Hdt. 7.154–6 has the city awarded to Hippocrates by arbitrators $c.493/2$; Gelo ruled in Syracuse $485/4$–$478/7$; Diod. Sic. 11.76.5 reports the refounding by the Geloans under $461/0$.

6.6 *Athens' Sicilian expedition (ii): planning.* In saying that the Athenians 'had become eager' to make war, Thucydides uses a word commonly applied to irrational impulses (Hornblower). For 'real reason' he uses the same words as in 1.23, *alethestate prophasis*; for the ambition and for Chalcidian Leontini as an Ionian city, cf. 3.86 (where kinship is the *prophasis* = ostensible motive, contrasted with the ambition which is the real motive), 7.76–7; and for the current state of the Leontinians, cf. 5.4. A much-discussed Athenian inscription, from a year when the archon's name ended *-on*, is concerned with the exchange of oaths between Athens and Egesta (ML 37, translated Fornara 81): examination seems finally to have established that the year was not in the 450s but was $418/7$ (Antiphon); for Thucydides not to have mentioned the alliance under that year, or as something recent here, would be shocking but not an omission of which he was incapable, but the problems are less if we can believe that what happened in $418/7$ was the renewal of an alliance made $c.427$, 'in the time of Laches', and that *pace* Dover and Hornblower the Greek here can mean 'the previous war over Leontini'. It is interesting, if true, that the Athenians were cautious about Egesta's ability to pay—but yet were to be deceived (cf. 6.46).

Another event mentioned not here but only in 8.73 is the ostracism, to be dated to spring 416 or more probably spring 415, proposed by Hyperbolus, which was expected to result in the removal of either Nicias or Alcibiades, but in fact resulted in the removal of Hyperbolus himself. Thucydides perhaps omitted it in its place because it failed to resolve the conflict between the two men and their policies.

Diod. Sic. 13.2.6, cf. 30.3, has a secret meeting of the council and generals which discussed what to do with Sicily when it was conquered; in 8.1 Thucydides will refer to oracles and soothsayers, but here he says nothing about the consultation of the Delphic or any other oracle (cf. Hornblower).

6.7 *Various campaigns.* Cf. the Corinthians' abstention from a Spartan campaign in $417/6$ (5.83); but in 416 they made their own attacks on Athens (5.115). Orneae had been on the Argive side in 418 (5.67). For Methone, cf. 4.129. The Chalcidians will again be those centred on Olynthus (contr. Dover): in 421 they had not accepted the Peace of Nicias but had joined the Argive and Corinthian alliance (cf. 5.36, 31), but we have not previously been told that they, like the Boeotians (5.26), had a ten-day truce with Athens.

6.8–62 Seventeenth summer (415)

6.8–26 *Athens' Sicilian expedition (iii): preparations.* The crew of a trireme numbered $c.200$, so what is said here implies pay of 1 drachma per man per day (cf. 6.31). 'Attractive' is the word used to describe Brasidas'

speech at Acanthus (4.88, cf. 4.108, where it is 'enticing (but untrue)')
and what the Athenians could have said to a Melian assembly (5.85,
where we translate 'seduction'). It will be revealed in 6.46 that the
Egestans' promises are indeed false. A fragmentary inscription, if correctly assigned to 415, indicates that this first assembly not only decided
on an expedition of sixty ships, but in deciding on three generals considered and rejected the alternative of just one (presumably Alcibiades); and
a later assembly may have set aside a sum of 3,000 talents (ML 78, major
fragments translated Fornara 146). For the appointment of generals 'with
absolute discretionary power', cf. note to 5.45. We are not told how far
Nicias made his opinions clear at the first assembly.

6.9   At the second assembly we are given two speeches by Nicias, with one by
Alcibiades between them: Nicias' predictions are borne out by subsequent events, while Alcibiades' are not. Nicias in his first speech stresses
the insecurity of Athens' position in Greece, argues against the plan to
conquer Sicily and attacks Alcibiades' motives for championing the plan.
The Egestans were Elymians (cf. 6.2). Nicias was undefeated, but his
reputation will have been for competence combined with caution; and he
had been behind the truce of 423 and the peace of 421. 'To preserve what
you have and not risk present advantage for an uncertain future' matches
the policy attributed to Pericles in 1.144, 2.65, cf. 2.13, 63; also 4.62
(Hermocrates), 5.87 (Melian dialogue).

6.10 Despite Sparta's hopes (2.7), the Sicilian Greeks had not yet intervened
in the Peloponnesian War, and even after the failure of this Athenian
campaign they did so only on a small scale (cf. 8.26); but Hornblower
stresses that large-scale intervention could still have been predicted at the
time. Corinth was the state most clearly 'in open war' with Athens (cf.
5.115).

6.11 Because Sicily is a long way from Athens, and is a large island which had
many cities, it would indeed have been difficult for Athens to retain control if the attempt at conquest succeeded: Euphemus will make the same
point in 6.86. However, the argument that an empire would not attack
another empire is not plausible. The transposition of 'but if we suffer . . .
enemies at home' to after 'We all know . . . put to the test', accepted in
the OCT, spoiled the logic and ought never to have been made. The last
words of the chapter are difficult, but seem to suggest that Sparta is more
of an enemy because it is oligarchic and thus opposed to the Athenian
democracy.

6.12 The plague had ended in 427/6 (3.87), and the Peace of Nicias had been
made in 421: since 421 Athens will have had comparatively little expenditure and few casualties; there seems to have been a decision to repay with
interest the sums borrowed from the sacred treasuries, but despite
Andoc. 3. *Peace* 8 we do not know how much actually was repaid, and an
inscription covering 418–414 shows that borrowing had not totally
ceased (ML 77, translated Fornara 144). After stressing that the Egestans
are barbarians, in 6.11, Nicias here denigrates the Leontinians as a

'bunch of exiles'. Alcibiades was born in 451/0, and is first attested as general in 420/19 (cf. note to 5.43); Nicias was born before 469 (Davies, *APF*, 404). Horse-breeding was regularly associated with wealth (e.g. Ar., *Nub.* 12–18). We are left to guess how a general might improperly enrich himself, but helping himself to booty would be one possibility. Hornblower notes that Nicias' considerable wealth (cf. Davies, *APF*, 403–4) is mentioned only in 7.86.

6.13 Seating in the Athenian assembly was not regulated (e.g. M. H. Hansen, *The Athenian Democracy in the Age of Demosthenes* (Oxford: Blackwell, 1991), 137–8); members voted as individuals (normally openly, by raising their hands). There were no parties with a party discipline, but leading politicians would tend to have groups of supporters, attached to them for different reasons and with different degrees of loyalty, and these could be called on to attend and vote on crucial occasions. Opposition between older and younger members is not mentioned on other occasions in Athens (though the categories are often contrasted, e.g. for Athens in 6.24), but it suits Nicias' argument to suggest that the young Alcibiades' supporters are hot-headed young men, lacking the experience and wisdom of age. For the Ionian Gulf, cf. 1.24; the Sicilian Sea is here distinguished from it as the open water further south, but contr. 4.24. Pericles in his funeral speech suggested that Athens did help others with 'no calculation of self-interest, but an act of frank confidence in our freedom' but that that did then place the others under an obligation to help Athens (2.40); Alcibiades will reply in 6.18; Euphemus will repeat that it is in Athens' interests to keep the enemies of Syracuse strong and independent (6.83–7). For the Greek tendency to approve of intervention to help those who (are perceived to) have been wronged, cf. P. A. Low, *Interstate Relations in Classical Greece: Morality and Power* (Cambridge University Press, 2007), ch. v, esp. p. 201.

6.14 The Greek vocative is *prytani*: the fifty members of the council from one tribe acted as the *prytaneis*, standing committee and presiding committee, for a tenth of the year, and each day one of them was chairman. There seems to have been no formal ban on reconsidering a decision, unless that decision was accompanied by an 'entrenchment clause' forbidding reconsideration (and note the reconsideration of the decision about Mytilene, 3.36–50), so breaking the *nomoi* here cannot mean more than breach of custom.

6.15 Opposition between Nicias and Alcibiades has been shown most clearly in Nicias' attempting to preserve the peace of 421 while Alcibiades worked for alliance with Argos and confrontation with Sparta on land in the Peloponnese (5.44–8); they were also men of very different temperaments and social standing (see notes to 3.51 for Nicias, 5.43 for Alcibiades). For the third general, Lamachus, cf. 4.75, 5.19, 24. In 6.90 Alcibiades will speak in Sparta of ambitions to conquer Carthage; here Thucydides himself takes those ambitions seriously (it is hard to be sure whether the references to Carthage in Ar., *Eq.* 173–4, 1303–4, are comic exaggeration or reflect suggestions actually made in the mid-420s). Thucydides here expresses faith (perhaps excessive) in Alcibiades' strategic ability, but acknowledges that his lifestyle led the Athenians to distrust him; for fear of tyranny, cf. note to 6.53.3-59. Even if most of Books 6-7 was written shortly after the events (see note to 6.1), the allusions here to Athens' downfall must be later.

6.16 Alcibiades defends first his personal position and then the Sicilian project. His extravagant participation in the Olympic games was in 416 (some texts say he came first, second, and third: Eur. *ap*. Plut. *Alc*. 11, Isoc. 16. *Team of Horses* 34); it was probably in 417 that Nicias, less self-centredly, had acted lavishly as leader of the Athenian delegation to the festival of Apollo on Delos (Plut., *Nic*. 3-4). 'Sponsorship of productions' was organized through the system of liturgies, by which the richest citizens were called on to accept personal and financial responsibility for a ship in the navy (as 'trierarchs': cf. 6.31) or a group of performers in a festival. In the light of 6.15, readers are presumably expected to find the passage on justified pride arrogant, though it probably seemed less offensive in classical Greece than it would in our world. Given the unsuccessful outcome, what is said of the Argive alliance and the battle of Mantinea is a forced attempt to make the best of a bad job.

6.17 Scholars have tended to think that the Athenians collectively did the counterpart of 'tak[ing] advantage of what . . . both can offer', i.e. appointed both so that each would counteract the excesses of the other; but more probably both had been appointed because each had a sufficient body of supporters in the assembly (cf. note to 1.45, a comparable instance). Sicily had suffered many population movements from the early fifth-century tyrants and from the reaction which followed their downfall; cf. more recently the fate of Leontini in 5.4. The conflict between Hermocrates and Athenagoras (6.32-41) and the fact that there were men willing to betray Syracuse to Nicias (cf. 6.103, 7.48-9, 73), will show that there was indeed internal dissension in Syracuse. 'This war' represents Alcibiades as sharing Thucydides' view that all of what we now call the Peloponnesian War was one war (cf. 5.25-6). Some but not all of the Sicels did support Athens: see 6.88, 98, 103, 7.1, 32, 57-8, 77, 80. In the early stages of building their empire the Athenians had not faced opposition in Greece: see 1.96-102.

6.18 Alcibiades here responds to Nicias' remarks on Athens' western allies: what he says of the need to persist with imperial policies echoes Pericles in 2.42, 63. For the attribution of Athens' success to 'our fathers', cf. Pericles in 1.144, 2.36, 62; for the argument against quietism, cf. Pericles in 2.63-4. The argument (originally medical) for a blend of different elements will be used by Athenagoras in 6.39.

6.19 Nicias' second speech (6.20-3) concentrates on the theme announced here; we may wonder if Thucydidean hindsight has contributed to it (cf. Introduction, p. xxxv).

6.20 Syracuse was comparatively democratic, though Athenagoras will suggest that oligarchic sympathizers were looking forward to an opportunity to seize power (6.38–9), and after the failure of the Athenian expedition there was a move further in the direction of democracy (Arist., *Pol.* 5.1304 A 27–9, Diod. Sic. 13.33–5). The seven cities are presumably Syracuse, Selinus, Gela, Acragas, Messana, Himera, and Camarina (identified by a scholiast: cf. 6.3–5; Megara Hyblaea and Leontini did not currently exist, Acrae and Casmenae were not major cities). Shortage of cavalry was to prove a problem for the Athenians (cf. esp. 6.70–1).

6.21 On arrival the Athenians found it harder to gain allies than they had hoped (cf. 6.44, 50–2). The Greeks disliked winter voyages, but contact was not impossible: see 6.74, 88, 7.16.

6.22 Having declared a belief in the temple treasures of Selinus (6.20), Nicias disbelieves in those of Egesta—justifiably (cf. 6.46). Pericles had remarked on intelligent planning (1.144, 2.40, 60), and on the plague as a blow beyond reasonable expectation (2.61). In contrast to 425 (4.28), Nicias' offer to resign his command was not this time accepted.

6.24 Nicias achieved his second objective, a larger force, but it was sent with greater confidence; it might have been easier for the original force to withdraw unscathed at the end of 415, or if it stayed and failed the failure would not have been so costly in men and resources (Dover). Thucydides' word for 'passionate desire' is *eros*, used only here and in Diodotus' speech ('desire', 3.45); Nicias in 6.13 used a compound, which we render 'disastrous allure'.

6.25 Plut., *Nic.* 12, *Alc.* 18, calls the unnamed Athenian Demostratus, perhaps by over-hasty inference from Ar., *Lys.* 387–97, but Hornblower is not sure he is wrong (on Demostratus' identity, see the inconclusive discussion of Davies, *APF*, 105–6). The Cretan archers came as mercenaries (cf. 7.57).

6.26 For the compilation of recruitment lists, see note to 6.31.

6.27–9 *Religious scandals in Athens (i)*. The Herms (representations of the god Hermes) first made in Athens were square in section, with an erect phallus and a head on top (cf. Hdt. 2.151); probably, in addition to damage to the face (perhaps seen as more impious than damage to the phallus), the phallus was broken where that was still intact (cf. Ar., *Lys.* 1093–4). Presumably both the scale and the timing of the act (shortly but not immediately before the departure: cf. note to 6.30–52) led the Athenians to take this more seriously than previous mutilations. A plot against the democracy is unlikely (though it is significant that one was suspected); a last-ditch attempt to create unfavourable omens by attacking the patron god of travellers and prevent the Sicilian expedition (not by the pious Nicias, but by other opponents of the expedition) is more likely; Andocides (cf. 6.60) claims that the act was planned as a pledge, a wrongful act to bind the members of a *hetaireia* (cf. note to 8.48) to which he belonged, but that he both objected and was injured and unable to take part (Andoc. 1. *Mysteries* 60–8).

6.28 It is clear that after the mutilation there were men ready with accusations against Alcibiades and associates of his. The Mysteries (without further specification, the Eleusinian Mysteries) involved secrets disclosed only to the initiated: it was impious to disclose these improperly, and probably also to hold mock celebrations even if only initiates were present.

6.29 Most able-bodied citizens fought as soldiers or rowed in the navy at some time, and there was not normally a sense of opposition between fighting men and civilians (though from 412, when Samos became the main base of the Athenian navy, there was opposition between the Athenians at Samos and those at home: 8.72–3, etc.). No doubt men who had been persuaded by Alcibiades to vote for the expedition and were about to serve on it would not want to lose him as commander.

6.30–52 *Athens' Sicilian expedition (iv): voyage to Sicily, Syracusan reaction.* The mutilation of the Herms was perhaps in late May, and the departure of the expedition in early June. No doubt this was an exceptionally well-attended and dramatic occasion, but it also suits Thucydides' purpose to give an elaborate account of it, to be contrasted with the total failure of 413. On Corcyra as a staging-post, cf. 1.36; Iapygia is the southernmost point of the 'heel' of Italy.

6.31 For the force of 430, cf. 2.56, 58 (where allied soldiers are not mentioned). For trierarchs, cf. note to 6.16 (the system was one which encouraged competition). Probably 1 drachma a day was an exceptional payment, because of the long absence from Athens, and 3 obols (8.45) was normal: see Pritchett, *GSW*, i. 14–24 (who accepts 3.17 as authentic, as we do not). 'Petty officers' is the best interpretation of *hyperesiai* (cf. Dover). 'Good' service-lists might simply be lists which include those who should be included and omit those who should not (Dover, whence our translation 'up-to-date'), but there are some indications that in the fifth century there was scope for preferential enlistment of men who were willing and experienced.

6.32 Hornblower remarks that by providing a Syracusan debate after the Athenian debate Thucydides 'suggests a larger parallel between the two cities'. Hermocrates correctly believes in the Athenian expedition (and even knows about Nicias' reluctance: 6.34), Athenagoras wrongly does not and suggests that rumours have been put about by oligarchic plotters (nothing we know about Hermocrates supports that, but see note to 6.72–88.6), and a general gives qualified support to Hermocrates. None of the speakers mentions Athens' interventions in the 420s.

6.33 On the failure of the Persians, cf. the Corinthians in 1.69; the Delian League was founded ostensibly in the interests of all the Greeks, and according to Thucydides on the initiative of the allies (cf. 1.94–7).

6.34 Thucydides has already accepted Alcibiades' ambitions concerning Carthage (6.15); but it is hard to believe that the Carthaginians feared an attack by Athens. Corinth is mentioned not only as the strongest member of the Peloponnesian League after Sparta but as the mother-city of Syracuse (cf. 6.3). We agree with Dover (though not all have done) that the Syracusan navy was probably much less skilled than the Athenian (cf. 7.36), and that if it had gone to Taras to fight against the Athenians it would probably have been heavily defeated; whether Thucydides thought that, we cannot tell.

6.35 For the description of Athenagoras, cf. the descriptions of Cleon in 3.36, 4.21; and he resembles Cleon in denouncing his opponents as conspirators (e.g. Ar., *Eq.* 235–9). We know nothing about him, but he need not be an invented character. His judgement of the situation is wrong, but that does not mean that every statement attributed to him was considered by Thucydides to be wrong.

6.36 For another claim that the war in Greece is 'far from settled', cf. Nicias in 6.10, and Thucydides himself in 6.1.

6.37 On cavalry, cf. Nicias in 6.20; the Athenians in fact took just thirty horses (6.43). Nicias in 6.23 had said that the Athenians would be virtually founding a city in Sicily; and cf. 7.75.

6.38 Syracuse was ruled by the Deinomenid tyrants from 485 to 466, and was unstable for some time after that, but there is no evidence of trouble after *c*.450: Dover and Hornblower have wondered whether this was written with hindsight after the seizure of power by Dionysius I in 406–405. Hermocrates, already prominent in 424 (4.58–65), was presumably somewhat older than Alcibiades, i.e. over 35.

6.39 Surprisingly, we are here given the view held by some classical Greeks that democracy displays 'no sense' (cf. Alcibiades in 6.89) 'or equity', but the rich should have the political power (because by owning the most property they have the greatest stake in the state), and in reply a defence of moderate democracy: the rich are the best financial stewards, if only because they are thought least likely to succumb to bribery and other temptations (Arist., *Pol.* 4. 1293 B 38–9: cf. Athens' limiting the treasurers of Athena to the highest property class: *Ath. Pol.* 8.1, 47.1); the 'people of sense' or intelligence (*xynetoi*) are the best at developing policy; and 'the general public', literally 'the many', are best at listening and deciding (which is not quite the same as the argument accepted hesitantly by Aristotle, that the many are better collectively than their individual members: *Pol.* 3. 1281 A 40–1282 A 41). The 'Old Oligarch' claimed that in democratic Athens the common people leave the dangerous offices to the rich but are eager to hold the profitable ones ([Xen.] *Ath. Pol.* 1.3).

6.40 Successful democracies, such as the Athenian, succeeded in persuading rich men not to regard the regime as hostile to them but to cooperate with it and pursue honour through it (cf. the note on trierarchs, 6.16).

6.41 It is not clear whether the generals had a constitutional position which entitled them to end the debate, but Thucydides' language does not imply that they did. The upshot is that preparations are to be made on the assumption that the Athenians are coming, but Hermocrates' expedition to Taras is rejected.

6.42 The three generals were constitutionally equal, so the assignment of squadrons by lot was appropriate; for other allotments cf. 6.62, 8.30. *Pace*

Hornblower, the fact that these generals had 'absolute discretionary power' (6.26) is irrelevant.

6.43 Hornblower compares this list with the Catalogue of Ships in Hom., *Il.* 2.484–760; it is placed here because it was at Corcyra that the whole expeditionary force was assembled; a complete catalogue of the forces eventually involved on each side will be given in 7.57–8. Dover argued that troop-transports were modified triremes, rowed at least in part by the soldiers, but could be reconverted to serve as fighting ships; Morrison, Coates, and Rankov suggest that these had broader hulls than normal triremes (*The Athenian Trireme²*, 151–6), but that horse-transports were converted triremes with oarsmen only on the highest level (pp. 156, 227–30). Marines were often *thetes*, members of the lowest census class (but contr. 3.98, 8.24, with note to 3.98). The thirty cavalry are not heard of again.

6.44 A siege of Syracuse seems already to have been contemplated. Hornblower, comparing 7.33 on Metapontium, wonders if Thucydides has exaggerated the hostility of the Italian Greeks. Locri had been made an Athenian ally in 422 (cf. 5.5), but clearly was one no longer. Considerations of kinship were often invoked but often overridden (cf. e.g. 1.95, 7.57, with notes to 1.94–5 and 7.57); Rhegium had an alliance with Athens which had been renewed in 433/2 (cf. note to 1.32–6).

6.45 Thucydides here closes a ring (cf. Introduction, p. xlii) by reusing words used in 6.32 of the initial Syracusan reaction.

6.46 Hornblower notes Thucydides' failure here to mention that now or later Athens did receive substantial sums of money from Rhegium and other states (*IG* i³ 291). No doubt there had been wishful thinking by the original Athenian investigators, but it is hard to believe the story exactly as Thucydides tells it (cf. the trick in 5.45; as Dover remarked, Egesta was remote and had no near neighbours). Eryx was on a hill by the coast, *c.*16 miles (25 km) west of Egesta: the wealth of the sanctuary did not prove that Egesta was wealthy (Dover), and silver was much less valuable than gold (Hornblower).

6.47–50 Nicias, disapproving of the expedition and unsurprised at the Athenians' cool reception and the lack of funds from Egesta, wanted to do the bare minimum and withdraw while it could be claimed that the expedition had been sent under a misapprehension; Alcibiades, with his taste for intrigue, wanted to make friends and influence people (but when he departed into exile he undermined the Athenians' attempt to win over Messana: 6.74); Lamachus wanted to make an immediate attack and catch Syracuse unprepared. Commentators mostly think that Lamachus' plan was the best and was judged the best by Thucydides (cf. 7.42). Whether it was the best depends on how unprepared Syracuse was: 6.32–41, 45, does not make that clear, but Thucydides could have exaggerated to enhance the unexpectedness of the outcome. For what is said about the position of Messana in 6.48, cf. 4.1; for the impact of a force immediately on arrival, in 6.49, cf. 5.9, 7.42; for catching men outside their city, cf. 2.5, 4.103. Unsurprisingly, the two generals in favour of the expedition made common cause, agreeing on the plan of the persuasive Alcibiades.

6.50 Alcibiades' ship will have been literally his own: cf. his ancestor Cleinias' ship in 480 (Hdt. 8.17). At Messana, Alcibiades' charm failed to work, and Hornblower notes that Thucydides does not give him a speech (comparable to Brasidas' speech at Acanthus: 4.84–7). Naxos gave the Athenians money (*IG* i³ 291, 1–2). Here and later Thucydides expects his readers to have a general knowledge of Syracusan topography; it is remarkable if the Athenians were able not only to make their proclamation but also to reconnoitre afterwards without interference.

6.51 Catana also gave the Athenians money (*IG* i³ 291, 15–16).

6.52 Camarina was presumably divided (Hornblower): the agreement mentioned will have been made with Athens in 427 (cf. 6.75), and without renouncing that Camarina will have made an alliance with Syracuse in 424 (cf. 6.67, 88).

6.53.1–2 *Religious scandals in Athens (ii): recall of Alcibiades.* For the Salaminia, cf. 3.33 with note. Thucydides' aristocratic bias shows in his comment on the respectability of the accused and the worthlessness of the accusers.

6.53.3–59 *Harmodius and Aristogeiton.* Thucydides lets the religious scandals prompt a detailed account of the killing of Hipparchus by Harmodius and Aristogeiton, on which he expostulates briefly in 1.20. It seems that fears about Alcibiades (6.61, cf. 6.28) led him to think of the Peisistratid tyranny; fears of Spartan intervention (6.61) led him to think of the Spartan intervention which ended the tyranny; that episode had been dealt with adequately by Herodotus, but he was carried away by his confidence that the normal (though not Herodotean) view of Hipparchus' killing was erroneous to correct the error. In fact he protested too much: even in his account of the episode attentive readers will find remarks which presuppose that Hipparchus was not killed only because of a personal grudge. Hornblower notes that Thucydides tells the story in Herodotus' manner, but emphasizes the homosexual dimension which Herodotus omitted (Hdt. 5.55–62). With this narrative, cf. *Ath. Pol.* 17.3–18, in general agreement with Thucydides but with some divergences.

6.54 Tyrant was not an office to which a man was appointed: although Thucydides was right to make Hippias the eldest son, it may be better to think of joint rule by Hippias and Hipparchus (cf. *Ath. Pol.* 18.1). As well as playing down the assassination, Thucydides plays down Aristogeiton (but not Harmodius, whereas for Herodotus the two men were from the same immigrant family); *Ath. Pol.* 18.1–2 by an inept combination of sources seems about to make Hipparchus the Peisistratid in love with Harmodius but then gives that role to his brother Thessalus. Writers who made the killing of Hipparchus the ending of the tyranny made the tyranny degenerate after Peisistratus' death (e.g. Diod. Sic. 10.17.1); Thucydides makes it degenerate only after Hipparchus' death; *Ath. Pol.*

16.7, 19.1, makes it degenerate at both points. *Ath. Pol.* 16.4 attributes to Peisistratus a 10 per cent tax: perhaps that is generic (as the English 'tithe' can be) and Thucydides is correct (Dover). A fragment of the inscribed archon list survives for the 520s: it includes members of leading families evidently induced to collaborate with the regime, together with Hippias in 526/5 and (probably) the younger Peisistratus in 522/1 (ML 6, translated Fornara 23, fr. *c*). For the altar of the Twelve Gods (by the Panathenaic Way, south-east of the Stoa of the Basileus), see *The Athenian Agora: A Guide to the Excavation and Museum*⁴ (Athens: A.S.C.S.A., 1990), 96–7 no. 31. The inscription on the altar of Apollo survives (ML 11, translated Fornara 37): its lettering is not particularly faint, but probably it was enhanced with paint which had worn away by Thucydides' time.

6.55 Thucydides gives reasons for his beliefs about earlier history as he does not with contemporary history (cf. Introduction, pp. xxxii–xxxiii). He cites another inscription to show that Hippias was Peisistratus' eldest son: that he was named first is more cogent than that he was the only one with children (Hdt. 5.65 is perhaps just careless); the pillar seems (despite Hornblower's agnosticism) to have recorded a condemnation of the Peisistratids. By 'legitimate' sons Thucydides means (anachronistically) those born to Peisistratus by his Athenian wife; *Ath. Pol.* 17.3–4 reduces the three to two by supposing Thessalus to be an alternative name for one of his two sons by his later, Argive wife.

6.56 *Ath. Pol.* 18.2 (probably through carelessness) makes the festival for which the girl was rejected the Panathenaea; the assassination occurred at the Great Panathenaea of 514/3. *Ath. Pol.* 18.4 (cf. 15.4–5) explicitly denies that the men in the procession carried arms and after the killing were disarmed by Hippias: we do not know on what grounds, or which author is right (Dover; Hornblower thinks Thucydides is right).

6.57 *Ath. Pol.* 18.3 has Hippias on the Acropolis to receive the procession; probably all that was genuinely remembered was that Hipparchus was at the Leocoreium (unidentified: against the suggestion that it was the 'crossroads enclosure' between the Stoa of the Basileus and the altar of the Twelve Gods (*The Athenian Agora: A Guide*⁴, 86–7 no. 27) is the fact that that site has produced no evidence of cult activity earlier than the second half of the fifth century (J. M. Camp, *The Athenian Agora* (London: Thames & Hudson, 1986), 47–8, 78–9)). The Cerameicus extended inside and outside the Sacred Gate and the Dipylon Gate to the north-west of the Agora. *Ath. Pol.* 18.4–6 has a story of Aristogeiton's being tortured and—truthfully or not—naming accomplices.

6.59 Hippoclus of Lampsacus was one of the Greek rulers taken by Dareius on his Scythian expedition of *c*.514 (Hdt. 4.138): what was surprising about this marriage alliance is that Lampsacus had been an enemy of the Athenian-ruled settlement in the Chersonese (Hdt. 6.37–8). The epigram is attributed to Simonides by Arist., *Rhet.* 1.1367 B 20–1. For the story of Hippias' expulsion in 511/0, see Hdt. 5.62–5, *Ath. Pol.* 19; for Hippias at Marathon, see Hdt. 6.102, 107–8, cf. 6.121.

6.60–1 *Religious scandals in Athens (iii): verdicts in Athens, flight of Alcibiades.* The reference in 6.27 is only to 'overthrow of democracy', but 6.15 mentioned tyranny in connection with Alcibiades, and after the excursus tyranny is naturally mentioned along with oligarchy. The unnamed informant was Andocides, as we learn from his defence speech in 400 (Andoc. 1. *Mysteries* 49–69, claiming that he was involved with the mutilators but did not mutilate any Herms himself). Thucydides thought him not worth naming (Hornblower, following C. B. R. Pelling; Plut., *Alc.* 20.6 remarks that Thucydides does not name any of the informants); he may have obtained information from Andocides (Hornblower notes that both were in exile in the last years of the Peloponnesian War and both had north-Aegean connections); this is one of the rare passages in which he admits to uncertainty (cf. Introduction, p. xxxi). We have substantial fragments of the 'Attic *stelai*', recording the sale of property confiscated from the men condemned (*IG* i³ 421–30: extracts ML 79, translated Fornara 147. D): if the aim of the mutilators was to prevent the Sicilian expedition (cf. note to 6.27–9), it is ironic that in the end they helped to pay for it.

6.61 The purpose of profaning the Mysteries, in private, was presumably to give a guilty thrill to those involved; the inscriptions show that some men were condemned on both charges. For Boeotian hopes of exploiting Athens' troubles, and the mobilization (not all men to the same place), cf. Andoc. 1. *Mysteries* 45. The Theseium in the city was not the popularly called Theseium, in fact the Hephaesteium, on the west side of the Agora, but in an area not yet excavated, east of the Panathenaic Way between the Agora and the Acropolis (J. Travlos, *Pictorial Dictionary of Ancient Athens* (London: Thames & Hudson, 1971), 578–9). For the Argive hostages, cf. 5.84; for Alcibiades' role in persuading Mantineans and Argives to join the Sicilian expedition, cf. 6.29.

6.62 *Athens' Sicilian expedition (v).* Thucydides' treatment of this episode is perfunctory. As Hornblower notes, after Alcibiades' departure Nicias and Lamachus must have discussed what to do; in effect, they decided to continue with his plan. Some other writers made Hyccara (which was slightly nearer to Egesta than to Himera) a Sicel town (e.g. Diod. Sic. 13.6.1): Thucydides seems to suggest that it would have been expected to support Egesta; 120 talents was perhaps the price of 7,200 captives. With Dover we prefer 'sent' to 'sailed round to their allies', since most of the Sicels lived inland; Hybla was inland from Catana.

6.63–93 Seventeenth winter (415/14)

6.63–71 *Athens' Sicilian expedition (vi): the Athenians' first attempt on Syracuse.* For Thucydides' view of the volatility of the common people, cf. 2.65, 4.28, and for eagerness to go out and fight, cf. 2.21–2.

6.64 The Athenians' lack of cavalry is important in this episode. For the topography of Syracuse, see Map 9. Thucydides assumes a considerable amount of topographical knowledge in his readers; it is not clear whether he had been to Syracuse or simply had detailed information. The sanctuary of Olympian Zeus (two columns remain standing) was somewhat under 1 mile (over 1 km) inland, west of the Great Harbour and south of the river Anapus.

6.66 Dover argued that Dascon was the southern half of the western shore of the Great Harbour; in the *Barrington Atlas*, R. J. A. Wilson's text makes it the headland, Punta Caderini, at the north end of that stretch, but it is wrongly marked on map 47. The road to Helorum passed the sanctuary and continued to the south.

6.67 We might have expected the Athenians to take the attacking position on the right wing; for their eight-deep formation, cf. note to 4.93; Hornblower remarks on this early instance of a division between attacking force and reserve force. Camarina's contribution will be represented as half-hearted in 6.75, cf. 88.

6.68 The Athenians were successfully carrying out a bold plan, and Nicias' speech is surprisingly pessimistic (his use of the same motif in 7.75 is far more appropriate), but it fits a commander whose heart was not in the enterprise.

6.69 The battle seems to have been fought north of the Anapus, and Thucydides uses it to mention features characteristic of hoplite battles. The divinatory sacrifice, mentioned only here, occurs before the hoplite engagement but after the skirmishing has begun. For independent and subject allies of Athens, cf. Euphemus in 6.85.

6.70 It is not credible (though many have believed it) that Thucydides is contrasting inexperienced Syracusans with experienced Athenians. He could be contrasting the inexperienced with the experienced on both sides, but we have accepted Hornblower's argument that he is writing wholly about the Athenian force. For 'drove back' Thucydides uses *othein*, the verb commonly applied to that pushing against the enemy which was characteristic of hoplite phalanxes. Victorious Greek armies did not normally pursue over a long distance (cf. note to 5.73), but after this battle the Athenians would probably have chased the Syracusans back to the city if not prevented by the cavalry.

6.71 According to Diod. Sic. 13.6.4, the Athenians did take possession of the temple (but before the battle: perhaps this is just careless writing); according to Plut., *Nic.* 16 they set out to raid the temple but were prevented by Nicias. The upshot was that the Athenians had carried out an enterprising plan and won a victory, but derived no benefit from it.

6.72–88.6 *Athens' Sicilian expedition (vii): winter preparations.* The Athenians in fact went first to Catana, then to Naxos (6.74), but later in the winter back to Catana (6.88). The introduction of Hermocrates is surprisingly full for a man who has been mentioned several times before (esp. 4.58, 6.32, but neither with the praise bestowed here); the Spartan Brasidas was credited with both intelligence and courage in 4.81, and as an expounder of wise policies Hermocrates recalls the Athenian Pericles. Complaints about multiplicity of command go back to Hom., *Il.* 2.204-5.

Despite the generals' 'absolute discretionary power' (cf. note to 5.45), when things went badly they were to be deposed (6.103). This passage is echoed by Xen., *Anab.* 6.1.18.

6.74 Alcibiades' undermining of the Athenian intrigues at Messana is mentioned only here, when the Athenians discover it.

6.75 The new Syracusan wall, after a loop to the west round Temenites, probably ran to the north: the effect was to increase considerably the length of wall which the Athenians would have to blockade. For Camarina's diplomatic position, cf. note to 6.52. Hornblower notes that the battle between Athenian and Syracusan forces (6.66–70) is now followed by a battle of words. The Athenian Euphemus cannot be identified (the name is not rare): unlike Cleon's opponent in the Mytilene debate, Diodotus (cf. 3.41), he is not given even a patronymic; but he could be, or be related to, the Euphemus who proposed an amendment to Athens' decree for Egesta (ML 37, translated Fornara 81, 15).

6.76 Hermocrates' speech is a good instance of ring composition (Hornblower), beginning and ending with Athenian imperialism, enclosing the theme of Ionians and Dorians, with Camarina's fear of Syracuse (justified by what was reported in 6.5, although Camarina was originally founded by Syracuse) at the centre. For 'displace populations' Thucydides uses the adjective *anastatos*, which he uses elsewhere only of Syracuse's treatment of Camarina (6.5). For the revolt of Euboea and its suppression in 446, cf. 1.114. Hermocrates accepts the innocent beginning of the Delian League (cf. 1.94–5) which Euphemus in 6.82–3 will reject; the reference to Ionians and colonies (which does not cover all the early members of the Delian League—and Thucydides probably did not ask himself which states he meant by 'colonies') enables Hermocrates to concentrate on the Athenians' treatment of their own kin. For the change in the nature of the League, cf. 1.99, and 1.115 on the origin of the Samian war.

6.77 In 'you know them already' and 'examples' Thucydides 'daringly . . . allows Hermokrates to parody the Periclean funeral oration' (Hornblower, comparing 2.36–7). Here we have a variant on the stereotype of Dorians as more valiant than Ionians (cf. 1.124). For the notion that those not in danger yet will be in danger later, cf. the Corinthians in 1.120.

6.78 The Athenians had tried in 422 to arouse fears of Syracusan domination (5.4). For the metaphor of 'regulating', cf. Alcibiades in 6.18, where the cognate verb is translated 'ration ourselves'.

6.79 For the claim that an alliance should be made only for virtuous purposes, cf. the Corinthians on Corcyra in 1.39–40. In the recent battle Syracuse had not been on its own, and indeed Camarina had been among its allies (cf. 6.65, 67).

6.82 Euphemus' speech is often compared with the Athenian speech at Sparta in 1.73–8, but Euphemus, while claiming that it is not in Athens' interests to have designs on the Sicilians, is more aggressive—and indeed, in contrast to Hermocrates in 6.76 and Thucydides himself in 1.94–5, he suggests that from the foundation of the Delian League the Athenians did set out to be stronger than the Peloponnesians, and that they justly subjected Ionians and islanders who had joined the Persians in attacking them (in fact by no means all of the islanders had). The Athenians in 480 abandoned their city but refused to defect to the Persians (Hdt. 8.40–1, 136–44, 9.4–5).

6.83 For refusal to give a more unselfish justification of the empire, cf. 5.89, in the Melian dialogue.

6.84 Euphemus implies that the Athenians want to weaken Syracuse but not destroy it (Dover). He speaks of 'liberating' the Chalcidians of Leontini, a verb normally used of themselves by Athens' enemies and not used by Hermocrates in 6.76.

6.85 For Athens' empire as a tyranny, cf. 1.122 (Corinthians), 2.63 (Pericles), 3.37 (Cleon). After the suppression in 427 of the revolt of Mytilene (cf. 3.50), Lesbian Methymna and Chios were the only members of the Delian League still providing ships, but that was a status which they had managed to retain, not one which was guaranteed to them (cf. note to 1.19); the 'completely free' islanders are from the states around the Peloponnese, whose contingents had joined Athens' expedition at Corcyra (6.30, 32, 42; cf. the catalogue in 7.57).

6.86 Hornblower wonders whether 'larger' is deliberately ambiguous between 'than is needed' (C. F. Smith, the Loeb editor) and 'than in the 420s' (Dover). Although it suits Euphemus' argument, it is surprising to find here an echo of Nicias' point (6.11) that Athens could not retain control of Sicily against opposition, and a suggestion that the Athenian expedition might fail.

6.88 The Camarinaeans, afraid of the ambitions of both but more directly threatened by Syracuse, remain theoretically perched on the fence but prepared to continue with grudging help to Syracuse. Money from the Sicels is mentioned in *IG* i³ 291 (cf. note to 6.46). This approach to Carthage stands in contrast to Athens' alleged hopes of conquering it (6.15, 90): contact continued, and in 406 Athens praised Carthage and may actually have made it an ally (ML 92, translated Fornara 165).

6.88.7–93 *Alcibiades in Sparta.* For the threat to the Italian Greeks, cf. 6.90, 104. The enthusiasm of the Corinthians is contrasted with the caution of the Spartans: cf. what the Corinthians say to the Spartans in 1.71. According to Isoc. 16 *Chariot Team* 9, Plut., *Alc.* 23, Alcibiades went first to Argos, and to Sparta only after hearing of his condemnation in Athens: if that is correct, Thucydides' account is misleading. The 'relevant authorities' mentioned with the ephors are presumably the kings and *gerousia*.

6.89 Alcibiades' speech begins and ends with a defence of his current stance. For the renunciation of the consular position and Alcibiades' services in the 420s, cf. 5.43. Those who would criticize his inclination to the people would be upper-class men who had not behaved similarly. Hornblower suggests that Thucydides is repeating the Alcmeonidae's opposition to tyranny from Hdt. 6.121, 123, rather than reporting what Alcibiades actually said—which is possibly but not necessarily correct. The line between upper class and 'people' could be drawn in different places according to circumstances and the needs of an argument (cf. 8.92). Thucydides regularly writes of 'leaders of the people' who are not themselves ordinary men (cf. 3.75). Until the failure of the Sicilian expedition, upper-class Athenians did acquiesce in the democracy, and men of all classes benefited from the empire (cf. overseas possessions listed in the 'Attic *stelai*', cited in note to 6.60–1). What Alcibiades says is appropriate for his Spartan audience, but it is hard to fit 'a more moderate form of politics' to what we know of him: while flaunting his superiority he had tried to beat the populist demagogues at their own game. Here, like Athenagoras in 6.39, he takes 'people' to mean the whole populace, not just the lower-class majority; Hornblower notes that conservatives have quoted the argument for maintaining a successful regime as if it were Thucydides' own opinion, and as if democracy were not immediately afterwards condemned as 'acknowledged folly'.

6.90 For the aims of the expedition, cf. 6.1, 6, 15: this is the most extravagant version. On the timber of southern Italy, cf. 7.25 and R. Meiggs, *Trees and Timber in the Ancient Mediterranean World* (Oxford University Press, 1982), 462–6.

6.91 If Syracuse had fallen to Athens, the other western Greeks might well have followed at the time: Athens' problem would have been retaining control (cf. 6.11, 86). For men who row their transport ships but then fight as hoplites, cf. 3.18: 7.1 shows that this proposal was adopted. Deceleia will be occupied by the Spartans, and with the effects which Alcibiades predicts, but not until 413 (cf. 7.19, 27–8). The reference to the law courts is puzzling: Dover suggests that with many of the citizens under arms sessions of the courts might be suspended for lack of jurors.

6.92 Alcibiades tries to rebut the objection that as an exile disloyal to his own city he may not become loyal to and trustworthy by Sparta (cf. the Mytilenaeans in 3.9). In 8.76 Athenian democrats on Samos will claim that (they are the true Athens and) the oligarchic city has revolted from them. For enemies and friends, cf. Soph., *Aj.* 679–82; for the good will attracted by Sparta, cf. 2.8 (but Hornblower notes that after Euphemus' Athenian claim to liberation, in 6.87, Alcibiades does not use that language). Rule by force was often contrasted with rule by law (e.g. Arr., *Anab.* 4.11.6, *SIG*³ 274. VI. 1–2; cf. Pind. fr. 169 Snell and Maehler).

6.93 It is not clear how much effect Alcibiades had, or was believed by Thucydides to have had: Spartan help was sent to Syracuse, but on a small scale (in addition to Gylippus, the two ships of 6.104); Deceleia was not fortified until 413. It may be that the Spartans had been thinking in general terms and Alcibiades proposed Deceleia as the site; but Deceleia was known to the Spartans and spared in their invasions in the Archidamian War (cf. Hdt. 9.73). Asine will be the city of that name on the coast of the Messenian Gulf (cf. 4.13).

6.94–105 Eighteenth summer (414) (beginning)

6.94 *Athens' Sicilian expedition (viii): Athenian campaigns.* For Syracuse's taking over of Megara, cf. 6.4. The river Terias was between Megara and Catana; Centoripa was inland from Catana (it is mentioned as an Athenian ally in 7.32), and Inessa (not in the *Barrington Atlas*) and Hybla between them. Corn burned at this time of year will have been stored corn, not growing corn (Dover). ML 77. 73–6 records payments from the treasury of Athena of the 300 talents and a further 4 talents, 2,000 drachmas about mid-March and early April.

6.95 *Mainland Greece.* Cleonae had been an ally of Argos at the battle of Mantinea (5.67); for the Spartans' turning back in response to an earthquake, cf. 3.89. For Thyrea, disputed between Sparta and Argos, cf. 5.41. The sale of booty regularly occurred but is not regularly mentioned: 25 talents was presumably an exceptionally large outcome. For Athenian sympathizers in Thespiae, in southern Boeotia, cf. 4.133.

6.96–103 *Athens' Sicilian expedition (ix): siege of Syracuse begun.* See Map 9; Thucydides gives some comments on locations, but not consistently or fully. Epipolae was mentioned in 6.75 but is described only now; the steep edges (not quite as steep as the reader of Thucydides might imagine) were everywhere except at 'the approaches'; the whole plateau was visible from inside the Syracusans' new wall of 6.75, but not from inside the old city wall. Hornblower notes that in Thucydides' presentation, as Syracuse corresponds to Athens, Epipolae corresponds to Deceleia. The Syracusan generals had been elected at the beginning of winter (6.73), but apparently their year of office began in the spring; the meadowland will have been west of the Great Harbour, north of the Olympieium.

6.97 Thapsus was between Megara and Syracuse; Euryelus (where there are remains of a fourth-century and hellenistic fort) was at the 'waist' of Epipolae, about 4½ miles (7 km) west of the north–south stretch of coast; Leon will have been on the coast north or north-east of Euryelus (and at least double Thucydides' 6–7 stades/¾ mile (1–1.3 km) from it); Labdalum towards the east end of the northern ridge of Epipolae. Despite the confidence of Hermocrates (6.72–3), the Syracusan defence starts badly, with amazement and defeats in 6.97–8, and again, leading to talk of capitulation, in 6.102–3.

6.98 The 650 Athenian cavalry were still no match for the Syracusan (1,200 in 6.67). Syce, 'fig tree', will have been towards the southern edge of Epipolae; despite the word, the Athenian fort was not necessarily circular. The Athenian army was regularly organized in tribal regiments, and 'Athenian' hoplites here is presumably to be taken literally, but Athenians made up less than a third of the hoplites attacking Syracuse.

6.99 The Athenian plan was to build walls northwards and southwards from the 'circle', so that Syracuse would be completely cut off by land, and the Syracusans needed to prevent that. Trogilus, the northern destination, was probably the inlet of S. Panagia. The stockades would be temporary defences to protect the Syracusans while they were building their counter-wall: Dover suggests that they were at the edge of the plateau, and this first wall on the slope below that and above the marsh. Use of olive wood from the sanctuary will have been an act of impiety, presumably thought to be justified by the emergency.

6.100 Syracuse had probably just three tribes (cf. the three generals, 6.73), and Dover suspects that only a certain age-range within one tribe was left to guard the wall. Attacking at lunch-time was an often-used stratagem (e.g. Hdt. 1.63, 6.78). Thucydides could surely have discovered which Athenian general took which position: after this anonymity, the death of Lamachus in 6.101 and the illness of Nicias in 6.102 are all the more striking. The 'pyramid' presumably made sense to those who knew Syracuse at the time: in most manuscripts it is corrupted to 'gate'.

6.101 Here we have the second Syracusan counter-wall. For a combination of ditch and stockade, cf. Xen., *Hell.* 5.4.38; for another use of doors along with other timber, see Hdt. 8.51. The river will be the Anapus. According to Plut., *Nic.* 18 Lamachus and a Syracusan cavalryman killed each other in single combat.

6.102 The 'two-acre outwork' (10 *plethra*/c.2¼ acres, c.9,000 m²) Dover places east of the 'circle' (AA on Map 9). In 7.15 we shall be told that Nicias suffered from a kidney disease: that was possibly but not certainly his illness now. For his use of fire to keep the enemy away cf. Xen., *Hell.* 7.2.8, Aen. Tact. 32. 12.

6.103 The double wall to the sea is the southern wall, to the Great Harbour. Hornblower wonders whether the depth of the Syracusans' despair has been exaggerated for greater contrast with Gylippus' arrival and their eventual victory; but we must surely accept as authentic the approaches to Nicias and the deposition of the generals—despite the 'absolute discretionary power' and the 'sworn guarantee' of 6.72. In the Greek world unsuccessful commanders were frequently suspected of having been bribed by the enemy (cf. 4.65). The Heracleides elected cannot be the same as the Heracleides deposed (cf. 6.73): Xen., *Hell.* 1.2.8 has Syracusans called Heracleides and Eucles commanding in the Aegean in 409, but Hornblower warns that Heracleides was a common name in Syracuse (Eucles was not, but here one manuscript has Eurycles).

6.104 *Athens' Sicilian expedition (x): Gylippus in Italy.* Leucas (1.30) and Ambracia (2.80) were both colonies of Corinth. On Gylippus' father Cleandridas (cf. 6.93) we have with the OCT and Hornblower accepted the reading of one manuscript and Valla; Dover supposed what that states to be impossible as an occurrence and with most manuscripts read 'relying on the fact that his father had once held Thurian citizenship'. Cleandridas was exiled from Sparta with Pleistoanax in 446/5 (cf. 1.114, 3.21, with Diod. Sic. 13.106.10, Plut., *Per.* 22). 'Gulf of Terina' is an error on Thucydides' part: that was on the west side of the 'toe' of Italy, but he means the sea on the east side.

6.105 *Mainland Greece.* The Spartan raid on the Argolid is a resumption of the raid of 6.95, abandoned because of an earthquake, and the Argives' raid on the east coast of Laconia is a sequel to their raid then. Athens' blatant violation of the Peace of Nicias is explained in what follows: since the Peace the Athenians had not attacked Spartan territory and the Spartans had not attacked Athenian territory, but now the Athenians did attack Spartan territory. Consequently the Spartans considered that the Peace had finally been ended by the Athenians, and so in 413 they did invade Attica and occupy Deceleia (cf. 7.18–19). Pythodorus is probably the man of that name in 5.19, 24; Laespodias will reappear in 8.86.

BOOK SEVEN

7.1–9 Eighteenth summer (414) (conclusion)

7.1–8 *Athens' Sicilian expedition (xi): Gylippus' arrival in Syracuse.* For Nicias' earlier view, see 6.104. Alcibiades had advised the sending of men who would first row and then fight as hoplites (6.91). Archonides of Herbita had cooperated with Ducetius in founding Cale Acte on the north coast (Diod. Sic. 12.8.2, 446/5), and the Archonides mentioned here will be that man or his son; a later Archonides founded Halaesa (Diod. Sic. 14.16.1–4, 403/2); an Athenian decree for (probably) Thucydides' Archonides was reinscribed in 385/4 (*IG* i³ 228).

7.2 Gongylus was to be killed in the battle of 7.5 (Plut., *Nic.* 19). For the Peloponnesians' arriving just in time to prevent Syracuse's capitulation, cf. 6.103; Thucydides writes similarly of the arrival of Athens' second decision about Mytilene just in time to prevent the implementation of the first (3.49). Alcibiades' proposal was that a Spartan should be sent to take overall command (6.91); Dover notes that as the campaign progresses Gylippus becomes less prominent; Hornblower, perhaps too subtly, thinks what is said here is deliberately ambiguous.

7.3 Plut., *Nic.* 19 has a more detailed account of this episode. At the end of this chapter, the Greek text does not specify the 'Little' Harbour, and in 7.4 it does not specify 'Little' and 'Great', but that passage makes the meaning clear.

7.4 The building of this counter-wall (SC3 on Map 9) was crucial in preventing the Athenians from completing their blockade, as is stressed at the end of 7.6, and Nicias seems to have been culpable in not completing the Athenian wall to Trogilus before Gylippus arrived. We are given reasons for the fortification of Plemmyrium, but it was to prove disastrous: cf. 7.23–4.

7.5 Gylippus' acceptance that the first defeat was his fault is remarkable.

7.6 The 'next opportunity' was on the next day, according to Plut., *Nic.* 19.

7.7 For the Corinthian commander we follow most manuscripts and the OCT in reading Erasinides: Hornblower prefers one manuscript's Thrasonides, as being the commoner name.

7.8 Thucydides' version of the letter will be given in 7.11–15, in the context of its receipt in Athens; Dover notes that other letters from commanders are attested.

7.9 *Amphipolis*. An Athenian inscription has been restored with a payment to Euetion and colleagues at the beginning of 414/3, but *IG* i³ 371, 3–4, leaves the name unrestored. Perdiccas when last mentioned (6.7) was opposed to Athens: this is Thucydides' last mention of him, and also of Amphipolis—which was never recovered by Athens and was taken by Philip II of Macedonia in 357.

7.10–18 Eighteenth winter (414/13)

7.10–17.2 *Athens' Sicilian expedition (xii): Nicias' letter to Athens*. Hornblower notes that the messengers must have had their oral session with the council; and that the Thucydidean letter (whose relationship to the original must be comparable to that of the speeches: cf. Introduction, pp. xxxiv–xxxvi) functions like a speech, but is more technical and introduces factual material not in the narrative. The 'city clerk' was not the principal secretary of the state but a skilled man elected to read documents to the council and assembly (cf. *Ath. Pol.* 54.5).

7.11 Formally, the force had been sent to support Egesta against Selinus, to re-establish a Leontini independent of Syracuse and to achieve what more it could (6.8). The arrival of Gylippus is mentioned, but the departure of Alcibiades (6.53, 60–1) and the death of Lamachus (6.101) are not. For the transformation of besiegers into besieged, cf. the Athenians at Pylos (4.29).

7.12 For the need to dry out triremes, cf. note to 2.94.

7.13 Editors used to emend the text to distinguish between sailors and slaves, but it now seems to be established that Athens did use slave oarsmen and that 'our' sailors, the slaves, and the foreigners are three categories of sailors (cf. Hornblower). For the prospect of making money, cf. 6.24; for slaves from Hyccara, cf. 6.62.

7.14 The first comment on the Athenian character refers to the men in the Athenian force, and the second to the Athenians at home, two aspects of democratic volatility; the thought will be attributed to Nicias again in 7.48.

7.15 That the Athenians in Sicily should be either recalled or reinforced repeats what is attributed to Nicias in 7.8. For Nicias' illness, cf. 6.102 (but Hornblower thinks his kidney disease may have been new). It was not only the Athenians at home who failed to prevent the Peloponnesians from reaching Sicily (silence of 6.93, 104) but also Nicias (6.104, 7.1, 7).

7.16 As Hornblower stresses, Thucydides reports the decisions taken, with no hint of the debate which must have preceded them. Menandrus and Euthydemus were presumably elected as additional generals for 414/3 (cf. Cleon in 425/4: note to 4.28). Menandrus is probably the general of 405/4 (Xen., *Hell.* 2.1.16), Euthydemus probably the oath-taker of 5.19, 24.

Demosthenes was last heard of in 418/7 (5.80); Eurymedon in 424, when he was campaigning in Sicily and was fined for acquiescing in the treaty of Gela (4.65). The reinforcements were given one of Athens' most enterprising generals and one with Sicilian experience: whether they were already generals for 414/3 (and likely to be re-elected for 413/2) or elected early for 413/2 (and authorized to act immediately) is not stated, but the first is more likely (Develin, *AO*, 152–3, contr. Dover; no comment in Hornblower). The figure of 120 talents is found in one manuscript and Valla's translation, and ought not to have been bracketed as an editorial insertion in the OCT.

7.17.3–18 *Preparations of Peloponnesians.* Naupactus has not been mentioned since 4.66–7, but the fact that Athens did not interfere with the first Peloponnesian reinforcements, and the sending of twenty Athenian ships in 7.17.2, do not prove that there had been no Athenian ships there since 421 (Hornblower, contr. Dover).

7.18 Athens' sending of reinforcements to Sicily would reduce the manpower left in Athens and improve the prospects for the fortification of Deceleia (Dover thought the lack of ships to inflict reprisals on the Peloponnese particularly important). For the attack on Plataea, cf. 2.2–6, 3.56. For the Spartans' refusal to go to arbitration, cf. 1.140; the embassies of 1.126 were not sent in the spirit of Archidamus' proposal of 1.82, 85. For Athens' raid on Laconia, cf. 6.105; for raids from Pylos, cf. 5.56, 115; Thucydides has not mentioned recent Spartan offers of arbitration.

7.19–87 Nineteenth summer (413) (beginning)

7.19–20 *Mainland Greece, including Deceleia.* According to Diod. Sic. 13.9.2 Alcibiades went with Agis: if he returned when the fort had been built (cf. 7.27), Plut., *Alc.* 23 need not conflict with that, *pace* Dover. Deceleia, on the southern slopes of Mount Parnes, north-north-east of Athens, was in fact nearer to the Boeotian plain than to the city of Athens. For Sparta's 'previously liberated cohorts', cf. 5.34. For the strengthening of pro-Spartan elements in Thespiae and Sicyon, cf. 6.95, 5.81, respectively.

7.20 Charicles is probably the man of that name who was apparently democratic and zealous in his search for religious offenders in 415 (Andoc. 1. *Mysteries* 36) but was one of the Thirty in 404/3 (Xen., *Hell.* 2.3.2). We seem to have too many generals for 414/3, and it is possible that Charicles, and Conon in 7.31, were not generals but admirals (*nauarchoi*) (cf. Hornblower on 7.31). Cawkwell has suggested that most of the island states in the Delian League were not obliged to supply soldiers (*Thucydides and the Peloponnesian War*, 115–20, noting the small number of islands mentioned in 7.57); the other 'subject allies' must be those on the mainlands of Greece, Thrace and Asia Minor (those mentioned by Cawkwell were not subject allies). For cooperation between Demosthenes and Charicles, cf. the arrangement of 4.2.

7.21–5 *Athens' Sicilian expedition (xiii): Plemmyrium, Great Harbour.* Although Hermocrates was again influential, nothing stated by Thucydides suggests that he had been reinstated as general and 7.73 suggests that he had not (cf. 6.103). Already in the 490s Athens had fifty ships and acquired another twenty from Corinth (Hdt. 6.89). For the hope that an inexperienced fleet could defeat an experienced Athenian fleet, cf. the Spartans in 429 (2.83–92).

7.22 The Athenians were in a good state of alertness if they manned sixty ships in response to the Syracusans' before daybreak.

7.23 The motif of men on land concentrating on the sea-battle will be repeated in 7.71. For the Syracusans' initial success which turned to failure, cf. again the Spartans in 429 (2.90–2).

7.24 Triremes used their sails for voyaging, not for fighting, so the sails would be stored on land when fighting was expected. Before the Athenians fortified Plemmyrium (7.4), it had apparently been unoccupied: now the stores there had been lost, and it was garrisoned by the Syracusans.

7.25 The Syracusans' morale was now good, and they intercepted ships coming to the Athenians as the Athenians had failed to intercept ships coming to the Syracusans. For Thespiae, cf. 7.19. With the skirmishing in the harbour we see Thucydides' interest in ingenious military devices, cf. e.g. the siege of Plataea (2.71–8, 3.20–4). The translation's '250-ton' renders 'of 10,000', which we take to be 10,000 talents. For the emphasis on the Syracusans' disorder, cf. the Spartans' belief that their first defeat in the Gulf of Corinth could not have been due to lack of skill (2.85).

7.26 *Demosthenes' voyage to Sicily (i)*. Cythera should have been returned to Sparta after the Peace of Nicias (5.18), but 7.56 confirms that it was not. The notion of a refuge to encourage and receive deserting Helots goes beyond what Thucydides has said before.

7.27–30 *Mainland Greece: Deceleia, Mycalessus*. For the Dians, cf. 2.96. What is said of the effects of Sparta's occupation of Deceleia is written from a standpoint later than summer 413—how much later, we cannot tell, but Athens' ability to rely on Euboea (cf. 2.14) ended in autumn 411 (8.95–6). The longest of the earlier invasions, lasting forty days, was in 430 (2.57). 'Even the regular garrisons would overrun the countryside' attempts to make sense of the transmitted text: that is probably corrupt, but no convincing emendation has been proposed. We do not know the basis for the number of deserting slaves: the manuscripts are divided between 'many . . . skilled workers' (which we accept) and an expression for 'most' which Thucydides does not use elsewhere; they presumably include but are not limited to slaves working in the silver mines (a recent study suggests that these numbered not more than 11,000).

7.28 Normally, but evidently not always, sea transport was preferred to land transport for heavy and bulky goods. For Oropus, cf. 2.23. The cost of importing food and other goods would fall directly on the individual consumers, but this would render them less able to support the state's war-effort. For expectations of the Athenians' willingness and ability to persevere in the war, cf. 5.14, 8.2, 24. Evidence for the Delian League's tribute after 421 is scanty and not reliably datable, but the annual amount collected was probably nearer to 1,000 than to 500 talents. Whether the Athenians later (perhaps in 410) reverted to the tribute from this tax is uncertain also.

7.29 Diitrephes is probably a relative of Nicostratus son of Diitrephes (3.75). It is not clear how far he controlled or could have controlled what happened, but the episode did not prevent him from serving as general again in 411 (8.64). Mycalessus was c.4 miles (6.5 km) from the coast immediately south of the narrows: it was not one of the constituent cities of the Boeotian federation (it seems to have been a dependency of Tanagra), but it was not very small. The horror of this episode is summed up twice, at the end of 7.29 and of 7.30: it was a barbarian atrocity inflicted on innocent and unexpecting victims; for the indiscipline and savagery of barbarians and near-barbarians, cf. 2.81, 3.94, 4.124-8.

7.31 *Demosthenes' voyage to Sicily (ii).* Pheia was on the headland north-east of the mouth of the Alpheius, Alyzia opposite Leucas (so north of Zacynthus and Cephallenia); Anactorium had been given to the Acarnanians in 425 (cf. 4.49, 5.30). For Eurymedon's mission, cf. 7.16. Conon was to be important in the last years of the Peloponnesian War and in the 390s: here he was perhaps not a general but an admiral (cf. note to 7.20); with his reluctance to engage twenty-five enemy ships with his eighteen, contrast Phormio in 2.83-92. There is no allusion here to Eurymedon's role in Corcyra in 3.80-1, 4.46-8.

7.32-3 *Athens' Sicilian expedition (xiv).* For Centoripa, cf. 6.94; (H)alicyae was an Elymian city between Egesta and Selinus: its alliance with Athens was inscribed on the same stone as the decree for Egesta, for which see on 6.6. For Syracuse's rival Acragas, cf. 5.4, where it responded favourably to the Athenian Phaeax: as Hornblower remarks, it is surprising that it did not positively support the Athenians now.

7.33 With Camarina 'news of the capture of Plemmyrion achieved what rhetoric could not' (Dover, contrasting 6.75-88). Messana, not mentioned after 6.74, was another state which remained neutral. For Iapygia, cf. 6.30: the Messapians lived on the 'heel' of Italy. Hornblower suggests that Metapontium was an exception to the Athenians' hostile reception in Italy mentioned in 6.44; 7.35, 57 indicate that Thurii was won over.

7.34 *Battle in Gulf of Corinth.* Cf. Morrison, Coates, and Rankov, *The Athenian Trireme*[2], 163-7. Erineus, on the coast, and Rhype, inland, were slightly further east than Naupactus. Diphilus had presumably succeeded Conon. The 'catheads' (*The Athenian Trireme*[2], 211) were ear timbers projecting to each side of the bow, in front of and protecting the outriggers (for which cf. note to 4.12) and supporting platforms for the anchors: the Corinthian ships attacked the prows of the Athenian and then continued along one side. For varying assessments of victory and defeat, cf. 1.70.

7.35 *Demosthenes' voyage to Sicily (iii).* Identifications are not certain, but possibly the river Hylias was slightly nearer to Croton than to Thurii (*Barrington Atlas*), and Petra was Leucopetra, south of Rhegium.

7.36–41 *Athens' Sicilian expedition (xv): battle in Great Harbour.* The 'previous sea-battle' was that of 7.25; and presumably the Syracusans had heard of the Corinthians' modification of their ships for the battle of 7.34. The Athenian manoeuvres were *periplous*, sailing round the enemy's line (cf. Morrison, Coates, and Rankov, *The Athenian Trireme*[2], 293), and *diekplous*, by which (probably) individual ships sailed through gaps in the enemy's line, perhaps first shearing away an enemy ship's oars and then turning abruptly to ram (contr. *The Athenian Trireme*[2], 43, 60). As with the hoplite battle in 6.69–70, Thucydides makes points here which apply to other sea-battles too.

7.39 Plut., *Nic.* 25 attributes to Ariston the naval tactics of 7.36 (as does Diod. Sic. 13.10.2), and reports that he died in the final sea-battle. Attacking when the enemy were eating was a favourite device: cf. e.g. Hdt. 1.63 (Peisistratus), Thuc. 8.95, Xen., *Hell.* 2.1.27–8 (one version of the battle of Aegospotami): Plut., *Nic.* 20 attributes that also to Ariston, and claims that Nicias did not want to fight a sea-battle before the reinforcements arrived but was forced into it by Menandrus and Euthydemus (who presumably were re-elected as regular generals for 413/2).

7.41 The 'dolphins' were downward-facing semicircles (Hornblower), suspended until they could be dropped on an enemy ship: this was another favourite device (cf. Ar., *Eq.* 762, Pherecrates fr. 12 Kassel and Austin; also Thuc. 2.76, the Plataean response to battering-rams, and Diod. Sic. 13.78.4, blocks of stone).

7.42–6 *Athens' Sicilian expedition (xvi): arrival of Demosthenes, night battle.* Dover calculates that 'seventy-three' ships is exactly right, if Eurymedon had left nine ships in Sicily and joined Demosthenes with one, and suggests that *malista* denotes not approximation but a calculation by Thucydides. Until the final outcome of the campaign Thucydides maintains the tension by highlighting moments of expected Athenian victory and moments of expected Syracusan victory—and for the genuine uncertainty, cf. 7.49. Here the strategy proposed by Lamachus in 6.49 is endorsed, but it is not made clear whether the endorsement is Demosthenes' or Thucydides' or both.

7.43 The siege-engines will be battering-rams, as used at Plataea (cf. 2.76). In Map 9 we adopt Dover's view that the Syracusans' three camps were attached to the south side of their counter-wall, but Hornblower prefers to think of camps to the north of that wall and not far from the south–north wall of 6.75. For the six hundred, cf. 6.96–7.

7.44 For the difficulty of finding out what happened, cf. in general 1.22, 50, and on the final battle in the Great Harbour, 7.71; also Eur., *Supp.* 846–56. Dover (p. 478) points out that the space was not particularly confined: Thucydides was either misinformed or carried away. On the hazards of

using passwords, cf. Aen. Tact. 24–5; paeans (see note to 4.43) are not
in Thucydides used by Athenians or Ionians. The cliffs of Epipolae
(see note to 6.96–103) will have been dangerous enough at night for
frightened men who did not know the terrain.

7.45 There were 2,500 deaths on the Athenian side, according to Diod. Sic.
13.11.5, 2,000 according to Plut., *Nic.* 21.

7.46 Sicanus was one of Hermocrates' colleagues in 6.73, deposed in 6.103,
but apparently reinstated later (cf. 7.70).

7.47–50 *Athens' Sicilian expedition (xvii): Athenian withdrawal delayed.* The
debate is represented as one between Demosthenes and Nicias:
Eurymedon is mentioned only as agreeing with Demosthenes, and
Menandrus and Euthydemus not at all (Hornblower). This is probably a
fact about Thucydides' narrative rather than a fact about the actual debate,
but it may well be a fact about what actually happened that the views of the
ordinary soldiers and sailors now become increasingly prominent.
Hornblower wonders if malnutrition was contributing to the Athenians'
sickness; the marshes outside Syracuse caused trouble for attackers on
other occasions too (cf. Diod. Sic. 13.114.1–2, in 405; 14.70.4–71, in 392;
perhaps also the plague of 15.24.2–3/73.1, before 368).

7.48 The reference to an 'open vote' implies at least a much larger meeting of
officers, and probably a meeting of the whole force or at least all the
Athenians in it. Nicias' opinion that there were still men in Syracuse
wanting to surrender to Athens (cf. 6.103) seems to be endorsed by
Thucydides in 7.49, cf. 7.73. Dover considers Nicias' argument 'as disgraceful a proposition as [of] any general in history: rather than risk
execution, he will throw away the fleet and many thousands of other
people's lives, and put his country in mortal peril'—but at least the risk
was genuine and Demosthenes and Eurymedon will have been conscious
of it (cf. Kagan, *The Peace of Nicias and the Sicilian Expedition*, 319, citing
Demosthenes' refusal to return to Athens after his defeat in Aetolia, 3.98,
and Eurymedon's fine for accepting the treaty of Gela, 4.65).

7.50 The Peloponnesians' detour via Libya was not intentional like the detour
via Crete of the Athenian force mentioned in 2.85, 92, but like the
Athenians the Peloponnesians delayed to take part in a campaign unconnected with the Peloponnesian War. Euesperides was the later Berenice,
modern Benghazi; Cyrene was a colony of Thera, itself allegedly a colony
of Sparta, Euesperides was a colony of Cyrene, and there is an inscription
of *c.*350–320 in which it appoints two Syracusan consular representatives
(*SEG* xviii 772). The Peloponnesians continued along the north African
coast to obtain a short sea crossing to Sicily. The eclipse was on 27 August:
it is not clear whether Thucydides means that lunar eclipses can occur
only at the full moon, as he states in 2.28 that solar eclipses can occur
only at the new moon. The eclipse alarmed 'most of the Athenians',
and the soothsayers prescribed a delay of 'thrice nine days' (cf. 'thrice
nine years' in 5.26). Thucydides himself would not have regarded the
eclipse as ominous, and perhaps thought that the educated Nicias should

not have done (cf. Introduction, pp. xliii–xliv); Pl., *Lach.* 198 E 2–199 A 1 maintains that a general should be not the servant but the master of the seer.

7.51–72 *Athens' Sicilian expedition (xviii): last battles in Great Harbour.* Thucydides has said that there were Syracusans giving information to Nicias; he does not say how information about the Athenians reached the Syracusans. The Athenians will have abandoned their horses in order to escape into the fortifications.

7.52 The Athenian line perhaps originally ran north-west to south-east, facing north-east, with Eurymedon trapped in the northern part of the Great Harbour (Dover); Diod. Sic. 13.13.2–3 gives the positions of other commanders, on both sides, and has Eurymedon trapped at Dascon, for which see note to 6.66.

7.53 For the Etruscans, cf. 6.88, 103. Lysimeleia is probably the marsh of 6.66.

7.55 Despite the plural 'cities', which anticipates 7.56, Thucydides' main point in this chapter is the similarity of Athens and Syracuse, which is implied throughout his narrative and stated most explicitly here (cf. 8.96). That Syracuse afterwards 'changed from *politeia* to democracy' (Arist., *Pol.* 5.1304 A 27–9, cf. Diod. Sic. 13.33–5) is not incompatible with Thucydides' regarding as democracy the current regime, even as modified to allow for three powerful generals (cf. the implications of Athenagoras' speech, 6.36–40; generals, 6.72–3, 103).

7.56 Here Thucydides moves from Athens and Syracuse to the large number of allies on each side, thus preparing the way for the catalogue which follows.

7.57 Compare the more concise catalogue of allies on each side in 431 (2.9); also the Homeric Catalogue of Ships (Hom., *Il.* 2.484–760), and Herodotean catalogues, including the list of nations in Xerxes' army (7.61–96) and the list with ethnic origins of the contingents in the Greek fleet (8.43–8). Dover's analysis shows how Thucydides mingles criteria of status, geography, and race in organizing these lists; attention is particularly focused on contingents fighting on the other side than the criteria would lead one to expect. For 'the Aeginetans [in fact Athenians] occupying Aegina at the time', cf. 2.27. For the status of Chios and Methymna, providing ships, and independent on sufferance but not under guarantee, cf. 6.85 with note. The Plataeans will be those settled in Scione in 421 (cf. 5.32); for the Messenians comprising 'the inhabitants of Naupactus and the garrison at Pylos', cf. 1.103 and 4.41, 5.35, 56; for the Megarian exiles, cf. 6.43. The Aetolians last appeared, as enemies of Athens, in 426 (3.94–102); the Acarnanians were still grateful to Demosthenes for his support in 426/5 (3.105–14).

7.58 One would expect the 'Spartiate commander' to be Gylippus, and that is probably what Thucydides means, but another Spartiate commanded the force of Helots and men from the newly liberated cohorts, Eccritus

(7.19: not mentioned elsewhere). The Sicyonians, brought as members of the Peloponnesian League, are contrasted with the Arcadian mercenaries.

7.59   The width of the harbour mouth at its narrowest is *c*.1,100 yards (1 km), so Thucydides' 8 stades imply an unusually short stade (see Appendix); but distances across water were particularly hard to estimate.

7.60   For meetings attended by more than the generals, cf. 7.48 with note. The 'contingent commanders' were the taxiarchs, commanders of the tribal regiments (cf. *Ath. Pol.* 61.3); probably in this force, distant from Athens, each tribe had a taxiarch, irrespective of normal appointments (Dover); we do not know how the allied contingents were organized, or whether their commanders were admitted to councils such as this. Dover points out that here only the slaves are likely to have included men too old or too young for active service. The cross-wall is AD on Map 9. Hornblower notes that the process of manning the ships is not completed until 7.65. Evidence for the date of the battle at the Assinarus (7.84) suggests that the Athenians had waited for the 'thrice nine days' of 7.50 (contr. Dover, note to 7.72.4).

7.61   After a long period without speeches (none so far in Book 7), we are given a set of speeches before the crucial battle and one more after, all the Athenian speeches being by Nicias. For the Athenians this was the last chance of avoiding disaster, and the pessimistic notes sounded by Nicias are at any rate appropriate to his character.

7.62   The Athenians' response to the Syracusans' modification of their ships (7.36) is reported through this speech: fighting a land-battle from ships was the older style of naval warfare, which Athenian fifth-century developments had seemed to render obsolete (cf. 1.49).

7.63   The sailors who are not Athenians but 'honorary Athenians' were metics who had settled in Athens (cf. note to 2.13: thus Hornblower, following a scholiast; contr. Dover): if this reports what Nicias actually said, it was a tactless remark when the sailors also included men from the subject states.

7.64   Everything from the beginning of 7.62 has been addressed to the sailors, and the Athenians of this chapter are the Athenian sailors (Hornblower; contr. Dover). The fear that the victorious Syracusans would immediately sail against Athens will be repeated in 8.1, but will not be fulfilled (as Nicias predicted in 6.11). The idea that the men are the city will recur more emphatically in Nicias' speech after the battle (7.77), and cf. Thucydides' use of it in 7.75.

7.65   For information reaching the Syracusans from the Athenians, cf. 7.51. Other Thucydidean speeches have been attributed to a plurality of speakers (e.g. the Corcyraeans and the Corinthians, 1.31–44): this attribution to the Syracusans and Gylippus is particularly awkward, but 'our country' in 7.68 implies a Syracusan speaker and Syracusan hearers.

7.66   The remark on Athens' imperial power echoes Pericles' last speech (2.64), and the Athenian intentions echo those reported by Alcibiades in

Sparta (6.90). 'Enslave' here is probably metaphorical of those subjected to an imperial ruler, but contrast 7.68, with note, below.

7.67 For javelin-men in the Syracusan navy, cf. 7.40. The Athenians' options, 'a break-out to sea or . . . a retreat by land', have been presented to Thucydides' readers in the narrative (7.60).

7.68 In 6.72 it was the Syracusans who suffered from disarray ('lack of system'), but the Athenians had already suffered from it in the night battle on Epipolae (7.43: 'disorder'). The suffering and indignities suggested here are those all too often inflicted on the conquered, as at Melos (5.116), and go beyond subjection. Hornblower stresses the appropriateness to the fertile Sicily of the agricultural metaphor at the end of the chapter.

7.69 As Hornblower suggests, the 'conventional language' of Nicias' supplementary appeal was surely commoner in real life than in the pages of Thucydides. For the 'unregimented liberty' of Athens, cf. Pericles in 2.37; for the appeal to ancestors and 'the gods of our fathers', cf. the Plataeans in 2.71, 3.59. The 'barrier across the harbour mouth' is that of 7.59.

7.70 The Athenians had about 110 ships (7.60) and the Syracusans about 76 (7.70, with 7.52), so the total was indeed 'nearly two hundred'. Thucydides' account of this great sea-battle, abounding in superlatives, is 'more of an atmospheric evocation and a report of emotions and morale . . . than a piece of conventional military history' (Hornblower); there are echoes of it in Polyb. 1.44.4–5 and elsewhere, and in Sall., *Iug.* 60. Sicanus was a fellow general of Hermocrates, deposed with him but evidently reinstated (cf. 6.73, 103, 7.46); for Agatharchus, cf. 7.25; Pythen had come with the Peloponnesian ships (6.104). For collisions when there were many ships in a confined space, cf. the battle of Salamis in 480 (Hdt. 8.84–90).

7.71 For the difficulty of seeing what was happening, cf. the night battle on Epipolae (7.44, with note).

7.72 Cf. the Ambraciot herald's reaction to shocking defeat in 3.113. With the refusal of the Athenian sailors to embark again we have one moment of mutiny.

7.73–4 *Athens' Sicilian expedition (xix): Athenian withdrawal delayed.* We may doubt whether the continuing danger from the Athenians after their ignominious withdrawal from Syracuse would be as great as is suggested. The 'authorities' must at least include the generals; Hermocrates had not been reinstated (see note to 7.21–5). The Syracusans do not risk giving an order which might lead to mutiny on their side—but Hornblower wonders whether the authorities were as strongly in favour of Hermocrates' plan as Thucydides suggests. Later instances of Syracusan drunkenness are recorded, for instance in 355 (Diod. Sic. 16.18.5–19.1). For Syracusans in touch with Nicias, cf. 6.103, 7.48–9. The trick practised now recalls the trick practised by the Athenians in 415 (6.64–5).

7.75–87 *Athens' Sicilian expedition (xx): Athenian withdrawal and defeat.* In 7.75 Thucydides contrasts the humiliation of this withdrawal with the confidence of the dispatch of the expedition in 6.30–2. The day of withdrawal is the third day from the battle by inclusive counting. This is the beginning of a diary in which, if the naval battle was on day 1 and the withdrawal on day 3, the arrival at the river Assinarus (7.84) was on day 10: if Plut., *Nic.* 28 gives the date of the battle, and the Athenians did wait a month after the eclipse of 27 August in 7.50, this will be equivalent to 29 September–8 October. For disasters too great for tears, cf. Bacchyl. fr. 2 Snell and Maehler, Hdt. 3.14. For the departing men as a city in flight, cf. note to 7.64 (normally the population of a captured city was not allowed to leave, but contr. Potidaea, 2.70, Amphipolis, 4.105–6): Hornblower sees an allusion to the fall of Troy. The figure of 40,000 (with 240 triremes lost) recurs in Isoc. 8. *Peace* 86, but it cannot be right unless a large number of slaves is included, and what is said of desertions makes that unlikely (cf. Hornblower, vol. iii, appendix 2). The end of ch. 75 reads is if it were intended to end a stretch of narrative: cf. note to 7.87.

7.76 Now that the disaster which he both feared and helped to bring about has arrived, Nicias appears in a more positive light.

7.77 Hornblower finds it hard to derive much encouragement from Nicias' introduction; but remarks by the Melians in 5.85–113 and Thucydides' final comment on Nicias (7.86) suggest that Greeks could even when it was unrealistic cling to a hope that they would not suffer more than they deserved. The conclusion echoes Ajax in Hom., *Il.* 15.734–8. Macleod, *Collected Essays*, 143–4, noted an echo of 1.143, in Pericles' first speech, which 'sharply reminds us that the whole expedition flouts the defensive policy of Pericles'.

7.78 For the hollow-rectangle formation, cf. 4.125 (another retreat), 6.67. The army originally headed inland, hoping to be able to turn north towards Catana (cf. 7.80 and Diod. Sic. 13.18.6). Probably, as suggested by P. Green, *Armada from Athens* (Garden City, NY: Doubleday, 1970), 321–4, its route was west as far as the modern Capocorso bridge and then north-west, the Acraean Rock was the south face of Monte Climiti, and the ravine was Cava Castelluccio: cf. Kagan, *The Peace of Nicias and the Sicilian Expedition*, 340–9, with 341 map 12, accepting all Green's identifications.

7.79 While Thucydides notes that the thunderstorm was not unusual at that time of year, he suggests that the men saw it as a sign of divine displeasure (cf. Introduction, p. xlv).

7.80 For the lighting of fires to conceal departure, cf. the Greeks at Artemisium in 480 (Hdt. 8.19). The 'other side of Sicily' is the south-west coast as opposed to the east coast: a message about this change of plan must have been sent to the Sicels; the army will have reached the Helorum road (cf. 6.66) and the southern part of the east coast near the modern Cassibile. The Cacyparis will be the modern river Cassibile; Green makes the Erineus the Asinaro = Fiume di Noto (pp. 330) and the Assinarus the Tellaro (*Armada from Athens*, 334–5), and that is more likely than the view of Dover and Hornblower that the Assinarus is the Asinaro and the Erineus therefore a river between that and the Cassibile.

7.81 Blaming Gylippus anticipates the disagreement between (some) Syracusans and him after the capture of the surviving fugitives (7.86, with note).

7.82 In the event, Demosthenes was executed and the prisoners were not adequately supplied with the basic needs of life (7.86-7). That only 6,000 men in his contingent lived to surrender casts further doubt on the 40,000 of 7.75. It is not clear whether we are to think of money filling four shields as a surprisingly large or a surprisingly small amount: see Hornblower.

7.83 Nicias attempted not total surrender but a deal: as Dover notes, the Athenians could raise money more easily than they could replace lost men.

7.84 The account of this last episode is 'one of the most appallingly memorable chapters' in Thucydides (Hornblower). It seems to be suggested that the Peloponnesians in the Syracusan force were particularly vindictive.

7.85 Together, 7.82 and 7.87 suggest that only 1,000 men in Nicias' contingent were taken alive. One man who made it to Catana was the speaker of Lys. 20. *Polystratus* 24-7, who was back in Athens by 410; another was the Callistratus of Paus. 7.16.4-6, killed in subsequent action against the Syracusans.

7.86 The quarries were below the southern escarpment of Epipolae, east of the Athenians' wall from the 'circle' to the Great Harbour; the difficulty of escaping from them is remarked on by Cic., *2 Verr.* 5.68. Thucydides reports only what actually happened; but Diod. Sic. 13.19.4-33.1 and Plut., *Nic.* 28 have stories behind which seems to lie a debate in which the demagogue Diocles (who was to head a democratic revolution in 412) argued for what was eventually done, while both Hermocrates and Gylippus urged milder treatment. Nicias' wealth, not mentioned when it could be set beside that of Alcibiades, in 6.8-26, was derived from the silver mines (cf. Xen., *Vect.* 4.14, Plut., *Nic.* 3-4). Thucydides' obituary verdict on him is surprising, both because there is no comparable verdict on Demosthenes (since the council of war following the nocturnal defeat on Epipolae, 7.47, the Athenian chapters have focused principally on Nicias) and because it is not the verdict we should expect, given that Thucydides has represented Nicias as damagingly over-cautious and that he himself does not elsewhere express admiration for the kind of virtue attributed to Nicias. The Greek text specifies the *arete* with which Nicias conducted his whole life, and that must refer not to manly courage but to what Nicias is made to claim in his last speech, 'constant observance of the gods and constant justice and fairness in [his] dealings with men' (7.77). Thucydides does seem to have thought that, despite his faults, Nicias was a good man who did not deserve such a shameful end; cf. what he says of 'simple decency' in 3.83.

7.87 For the prisoners' rations, contr. the more generous allowance of the truce at Pylos (4.16). Presumably those kept for the full eight months were ransomed or sold as slaves after that. For 'total annihilation',

cf. Hdt. 2.120 (on Troy). The ending of Book 7 at this point is not due
to Thucydides himself (cf. Introduction, p. xxvi); we have already had
one apparent ending, in 7.75, and 8.1 (the last chapter devoted to summer 413) will show the Athenians shocked but resolving to continue the
struggle.

BOOK EIGHT

8.1 Nineteenth summer (413) (conclusion)

Athens' reaction to defeat in Sicily. With the initial disbelief Hornblower
compares the Syracusans' disbelief in 415 (6.32, 45). For the responsibility of citizens for decisions in the assembly, cf. Pericles in 2.60, 64, Cleon
in 3.43. The religious support for the expedition has not been mentioned
before, but it suits the sceptical Thucydides to note that the support
proved unfounded (cf. Introduction, p. xliv). Despite the Athenians'
fears (cf. 7.64), the Sicilian Greeks would not send much help to the
Peloponnesians (cf. 8.26, 35). A main source of timber for shipbuilding
was Macedonia (cf. Andoc. 2. *Return* 11; ML 91, translated Fornara 161);
another was the Troad (cf. 4.52). For the importance of Euboea, cf. 2.14,
7.28. It is not made clear how the *probouloi* appointed to oversee the
agenda (Thucydides uses the cognate verb) interacted with the council
and (cf. note to 2.22) the generals: in Ar., *Lys.* 387 ff. a *proboulos* is a
target for mockery (cf. perhaps *Thesm.* 808–9); the two *probouloi* known
are Hagnon (cf. 1.117 with note to 115–17) and the tragedian Sophocles;
they perhaps had to be over 40 (cf. *Ath. Pol.* 29.2). For what 'tends to
happen in a democracy', cf. 2.65, 4.28, 6.63.

8.2–6 Nineteenth winter (413/12)

Preparations for war in Greece. For the excitement, cf. 2.8, at the beginning of the war, but it is hard to imagine who the neutrals mentioned
here might be: as Andrewes notes, Thucydides is carried away in piling
up the odds against the nevertheless resilient Athens. What is now foreshadowed is not liberation of the Greeks from Athenian domination, as
in 2.8, but domination of the Greeks by Sparta.

8.3   For the Oetaeans, cf. 3.92; Heracleia, last mentioned as in Boeotian
hands, may by now have been recovered by Sparta (it was Spartan in 409:
Xen., *Hell.* 1.2.18). We do not know whether the hundred ships were all
built: what is most surprising is that only fifteen were required from the
naval power Corinth (cf. 1.36).

8.4   The fortification of Sounium shows that the Athenians were not totally
excluded from the countryside by the Spartan occupation of Deceleia;
the fort in Laconia is that of 7.26.

8.5   Applicants from the more northerly part of the Aegean and Asia Minor
were rivalled by applicants from the more southerly part, each with a

Persian satrap behind them, and Sparta had to choose between two strategies: immediately the southern strategy was adopted, owing to Chios' ships (8.6) and Alcibiades' links with Miletus (8.17), but it was the northern strategy, with the possibility of cutting off Athens' corn supplies, which was eventually to win the war for Sparta. Alcamenes' father was probably the Sthenelaïdas of 1.86. The word for 'governing commander' is *harmostes*, used only here by Thucydides but frequently by Xenophon (e.g. *Hell.* 1.3.15) of Spartans commanding garrisons or non-citizen armies. At a distance from Sparta, Agis had to make decisions on his own, but it is not clear whether he had been given enhanced powers (and notice 8.7); there is no sign now of the advisers with whom he was saddled in 5.63. Apart from the last sentence of 5.1, this is Thucydides' first mention of the Persians since 4.50 (and, in view of their importance from now to the end of the war, he might have given them more prominence earlier if he had lived to produce the final version of his history). Probably Tissaphernes had defeated Pissouthnes and replaced him as satrap at Sardis at the end of the 420s (cf. Ctesias *FGrH* 688 F 15.53 [52]), and had more recently been appointed 'military governor of the west'—a position whose implications are unclear, but Pharnabazus was not obviously subordinate to him. Amorges may have been in revolt, and supported by the Athenians, for a few years (perhaps since *c*.414): according to Andoc. 3 *Peace* 29 it was that support which finally induced the Persians to support Sparta, and it may also be that which induced Dareius to demand 'arrears' of tribute from cities in the Athenian orbit.

8.6 Pharnabazus was satrap at Dascylium: we learn from 8.8 that he sent money. For Alcibiades and Endius, cf. 5.44–5: if Alcibiades had indeed made a fool of Endius in 420, this further cooperation is remarkable. Foreign connections were often reflected in naming practices: see Herman, *Ritualised Friendship*, 19–22. Changes of plan as the result of an earthquake were not uncommon (cf. 3.89, 6.95, and Introduction, p. xlv), but, if it was the earthquake which here led to a change of commander and the scaling-down of the expedition, that is striking.

8.7–28 Twentieth summer (412)

Chios leads revolt of Ionia. In the case of Chios, the approach to Sparta was concealed not only from Athens but also from the Chian citizens (cf. 8.9). For hauling ships across the Isthmus, cf. 3.15. Agis' powers were not such as to prevent the Spartans from commandeering the ships being prepared for his plan (cf. 8.5).

8.8 Rhamphias is probably the man of that name in 1.139, 5.12; his son Clearchus was to be the original commander of Cyrus' 10,000 Greek mercenaries, and was killed in the battle of Cunaxa, in 401.

8.9 Hornblower suggests that the earthquake of 8.6 may have reinforced the Corinthians' scruples. In 8.7 we were at the beginning of spring: the Isthmia seems to have been celebrated about the time of the solstice, but the truce will have begun earlier. Aristocrates is probably the man of that name in 8.89. For the guarantee of good faith, cf. that demanded of Chios by Athens in 4.51. Probably Chios was ruled by a moderate oligarchy (cf. 8.24), and probably not all the men with political rights were involved in this plot.

8.10 For the location of Speiraeum, see Map 3, and Salmon, *Wealthy Corinth*, 6, with 21 fig. 5.

8.11 The 'other people of the area' must be Epidaurians. The Peloponnesians' contempt for the Athenians (8.8) had proved unfounded, and the confidence of 8.2 quickly evaporated.

8.12 According to Plut., *Alc.* 23, *Ages.* 3, Alcibiades had had an affair with Agis' wife: that may be true even if it is not true that he was the father of Agis' putative son Leotychidas (Xen., *Hell.* 3.3.1–4, not naming the father; Plut.)—which would mean that Agis lived to be nearly 60 without fathering a son who survived.

8.13 The Peloponnesian ships of 6.104, 7.2, and 7.7 total 17, but Gongylus' ship may have been lost when he was killed (Plut., *Nic.* 19). Hippocles had perhaps succeeded Diphilus at Naupactus and, like his predecessors there, may not have been a general (cf. 7.31, 34); some ostraca were cast against him, presumably when Hyperbolus was ostracized (see note to 6.6).

8.14 Principal places in the eastern Aegean mentioned in Book 8 are shown on Map 1. Corycus was the southern extension of the Erythrae peninsula; Clazomenae was on the gulf of Smyrna, east of Erythrae (the people had moved from the mainland to their island, apparently in the mid-sixth century: Str. 645/14.1.36, Paus. 7.3.9); the location of Polichna is uncertain.

8.15 In 431 the Athenians had decreed that their last 1,000 talents were to be used only if Athens was attacked by sea (2.24). For Strombichides' father Diotimus, cf. 1.45: the family was consistently democratic and anti-Spartan (cf. Davies, *APF*, 161–5), and Strombichides was put to death by the Thirty in 404 (Lys. 30. *Nicomachus* 14, cf. 13. *Agoratus* 13). Thrasycles was one of the men who swore to the treaties of 421 (5.19, 24). Slaves listed in a Chian inscription of about this date may be men enlisted as sailors and then freed (L. Robert, *Études épigraphiques et philologiques* (Paris: Champion, 1938), 118–26).

8.16 Samos was deprived of its navy in 439 (1.117), but as Andrewes suggests may have been allowed to keep one or two ships. Teos was due south of Clazomenae; the Athenians' wall was probably a recent one, built to protect the city against Tissaphernes.

8.17 For the long-standing rivalry of Samos and Miletus, cf. 1.115 with note to 1.115–17. In antiquity Miletus was on the coast and Lade (on which the Ionians based themselves for the deciding battle of the Ionian Revolt, in 495: Hdt. 6.7–8) was an offshore island: now Miletus is inland and Lade is a hill near the coast.

8.18 This treaty is the first of three between the Spartans and the Persians in 412–411 (the others are quoted in 8.37, 58). While the third has a more elaborate preamble which may reflect a higher status, the first two took immediate effect and were not merely preliminary drafts. Whatever territory the Persians seriously intended to claim, they were here alarmingly extensive about what they could claim (cf. Lichas in 8.43), and even abandoning the Asiatic Greeks to Persia (as in 8.58) would conflict directly with Sparta's original aim of liberating the Greeks from Athens (cf. note to 4.50); Amorges was currently in revolt from the Persians (cf. 8.5), while there were no rebels from Sparta against whom Persia might be invoked; there were not yet sufficient Spartan forces in the east for the maintenance of them to be an issue. Apart from a general commitment to a joint war against Athens, the advantages here were all with the Persians.

8.19 For Anaea, south of Ephesus, cf. 3.19 with note—and Ephesus must by now have joined the revolt. North of Ephesus, Dios Hieron was west of Notium (cf. note to 3.33), and Lebedus west of that; Aerae was west of Teos. Diomedon was to be strongly democratic in 411 (8.73), and was one of the generals involved in and executed after the battle of Arginusae in 406 (Xen., *Hell.* 1.7.29). In 8.16 the Athenians had fled from a larger enemy fleet; here the Chians fled from a larger Athenian fleet.

8.20 Thucydides presents Astyochus as tactless and incompetent. Probably at this stage the Spartan admiral-in-chief was still appointed for a particular campaign (cf. note to 2.66–8) rather than (as from *c*.409) for a year. Teos seems not to have had active enthusiasm for either side, but to have tried to stay out of trouble (and is not mentioned again until it was raided by the Spartans in 406: Diod. Sic. 13.76.4).

8.21 Probably the Athenians had installed a democracy in Samos in 439 (cf. note to 1.115–17): in that case, probably, they tolerated a return to (at any rate, comparative) oligarchy later, and what happened now was the overthrow of that regime (which itself was pro-Athenian in 8.16) (Andrewes, contr. Hornblower). The fragmentary *IG* i³ 96 seems to reflect Athens' settlement with the new regime.

8.22 The chapter begins with a Chian initiative, but it turns out that both land and sea forces were commanded by Laconians, the sea force by one of the Perioeci. Methymna was the one city on Lesbos which had not joined in the revolt of 428–427, and (like Chios) continued to contribute ships to the Delian League (cf. 3.2, 5, 50; 6.85, 7.57).

8.23 The Athenians seem to have given up the blockade of Cenchreae, to concentrate on the Aegean (Hornblower). Leon is probably not the Leon of 5.19, 24; like Diomedon, he was democratic in 411 (8.73), and he is probably the Leon of Salamis put to death by the Thirty in 404/3 (Xen., *Hell.* 2.3.39). Hornblower remarks that Astyochus ought to have made straight for Mytilene. In summer 411 Mytilene and Methymna were to be on the Athenian side but Eresus on the Spartan (8.100). Daphnus, unlocated, was on the Athenian side in 407 (ML 88, translated Fornara 163).

8.24 The Oenoussae islands were at the north end of the strait between Chios and the mainland; the Athenians proceeded anticlockwise from

Cardamyle, in the north-east of the island. For the Athenians' marines, see notes to 3.98, 6.43, and for their service-lists, see note to 6.31. Chios had been largely untroubled since the Persian reprisals in 493 at the end of the Ionian Revolt (Hdt. 6.31–2); for its prosperity, cf. Alcibiades in 8.45. 'Prudence' (*sophrosyne*) and 'well-ordered government' (*kosmos*: here the verb is used) often though not always have oligarchic overtones; in this comparison with Sparta Thucydides is praising primarily stability, but his comments on democracy (e.g. 2.65, 4.28, 6.63, 8.1) suggest that he did not consider that conducive to stability. For expectations of Athenian collapse, cf. 8.1–2; in general the Athenians proved more successful at recovering control in the islands than on the mainland, even though it was the mainland which Sparta was willing to hand over to Persia.

8.25 Phrynichus, an important man in Book 8, was by now in his sixties (Andrewes), but there is little evidence for his earlier career. Onomacles was an extreme oligarch in 411 (decree *ap.* [Plut.] *X Orat.* 833 F), who escaped after the overthrow of the Four Hundred and was one of the Thirty in 404/3. Scironides (if that is the right form of the name: see Andrewes and Hornblower) was to be deposed in 8.54; no more is known of his career. For perceptions of Ionians and Dorians, cf. notes to 1.124, 4.61, 6.77.

8.26 Hermocrates had not had his way over the treatment of the captives in 413 (cf. note to 7.86); he still had some influence, and we learn in 8.29 that he came with the Syracusan contingent, but the Sicilian contribution to the war in the east was not large. Leros (only one manuscript does not garble the name) is in fact *c.*34 miles (55 km) south-west of Miletus; Teichioussa was on the mainland, *c.*16 miles (26 km) south-east of Miletus; the evidence of the tribute lists shows that both were in some sense Milesian (cf. M. H. Hansen, in Hansen and Nielsen, *Inventory*, 114). Alcibiades presumably came from Miletus.

8.27 For an Athenian strategic retreat, cf. 8.16. Phrynichus did not have superior authority (cf. note to 1.57): he had to, and managed to, persuade his fellow commanders, allied as well as Athenian. For 'risks of its own making', cf. Pericles in 1.144; for the reputation for intelligence, cf. 2.34 on the man chosen to deliver Athens' funeral oration. It appears that Thucydides' verdict was, as it still is, controversial. The Athenians had 68 ships to the Peloponnesians' 80: Andrewes (supported by Lazenby, *The Peloponnesian War*, 178, and by 8.30) thought Phrynichus' caution mistaken, and Hornblower at least judges Thucydides' praise surprising; Thucydides may here have misapplied the Periclean caution of which he approved (cf. 1.143, 2.13). Samos was to be the Athenians' main base in the eastern Aegean for the rest of the war. The Argives were probably both humiliated by their defeat of 8.25 and annoyed at the decision not to fight now.

8.28 Iasus (claiming to have been founded first from Argos and afterwards from Miletus: Polyb. 16.12) seems not to have been as rich as Thucydides thought. For the assumption that a fleet in the Aegean would be

Athenian, cf. 3.32 (when that assumption had greater justification). A Daric stater was equivalent to 20 Athenian drachmas (Xen., *Anab.* 1.7.18), well below the market value of slaves.

8.29–60 Twentieth winter (412/11)

8.29–44 *Campaigns in the Aegean.* At 8.5 Tissaphernes' rate of pay was not specified; when the King was eventually consulted, he approved only the half-drachma rate (Xen., *Hell.* 1.5.5). For Astyochus as admiral, cf. 8.20, 33. This is the first of a number of passages in which Greeks from the west are not easily cowed; the upshot here was that Tissaphernes paid 30 talents for 55 ships, whereas at the half-drachma rate he would have paid 30 talents for 60 (how much was actually paid to the individual sailors we do not know).

8.30 Strombichides must have returned to Athens since his last appearance, in 8.17. For allotment, cf. 6.42: Hornblower is perhaps too surprised that the matter was not decided in Athens.

8.31 A plan for Chios must have been decided since 8.24. Tamos was an Egyptian, who in 401 commanded a fleet for Cyrus against Tissaphernes, and then fled to Egypt and was killed there (Xen., *Anab.* 1.2.21, 4.2; Diod. Sic. 14.19.2–6, 35.3–5). The narrative of this winter shows that naval operations could continue in the winter but ran serious risks from the weather. Phocaea and Cyme were north of Clazomenae.

8.32 For the failure of Lesbos' first attempted revolt, see 8.22–3. We are going to encounter internal disagreements on both the Spartan and the Athenian side: uncharacteristically, on this occasion Astyochus was more enterprising than his opponents.

8.33 By taking over the main fleet at Miletus Astyochus entered fully into the command to which he had been appointed. A message about the prisoners must have reached Pedaritus from Erythrae; despite the disagreement of 8.32 he and Astyochus could cooperate when necessary. Hornblower wonders if the prisoners had indeed intended to work for the Athenians, but finally accepts that it was the Athenians who were deceived.

8.34 Arginum was the point nearest to Chios on the Erythrae peninsula; Mimas was the northern extension of the peninsula, and Phoenicus on its west side. The fortification alluded to at the end of the chapter must be that on Chios to be mentioned in 8.38, but Thucydides' text does not make that clear here.

8.35 Hippocrates is probably the man who was second-in-command to Mindarus at Cyzicus in 410 and was killed at Calchedon in 408 (Xen., *Hell.* 1.1.23, 3.5–6). For Dorieus, originally from Rhodes, see 3.8 with note to 3.8–18. In Thurii the supporters of Athens got the upper hand in 413 (7.33, 57), but will have lost it after Athens' defeat in Sicily. Hornblower rejects recent arguments and accepts that classical Cnidus was not at the tip of the long peninsula, near the Triopium (a sanctuary of Apollo which was a major sanctuary of the Dorians), but some way to the east. The merchant ships from Egypt may have been carrying corn to Athens.

8.37 In the first treaty (8.18) the emphasis was on Dareius' owning territory; here it is on his and the Spartans' not attacking each other's territory, but the potential extent of his claim was not reduced. This time the Spartans undertook not to exact tribute from cities in Dareius' sphere; in return Persia undertook to pay for Spartan forces—but only if invited by the Persians, and with nothing said about the rate of pay. 'Party to this agreement' (Dover *ap*. Andrewes) is the best interpretation of a phrase which troubled some editors: the final clause strengthens the non-aggression provision of the first clause.

8.38 Therimenes' cutter was presumably overwhelmed by a storm. Delphinium was to the north of Chios town. Tydeus' father was perhaps the tragic poet Ion. The 'tight control' seems to denote a narrower oligarchy than the regime of 8.9, 24. Plut., *Lacaen. Apophth.* 241 D-E has a story that some Chians went to Sparta to complain about Pedaritus.

8.39 The solstice was on 24 December. For the ships requested by Pharnabazus and for Clearchus, cf. 8.6-8. For the advisers, cf. 2.85, 3.69, 5.63: Lichas (for whom cf. 5.22 with note) seems to have been not one of eleven equals but the leader; in the event, Astyochus was not deposed, and Antisthenes is not heard of again (except in 8.61) in the Peloponnesian War. Now that Melos was in Athenian hands (5.116), it was risky of the Spartans to put in there. Caunus was north-east of Rhodes.

8.40 Material on the slaves at Chios is collected at Ath. 6.265 B-266 F: here as in 8.24 Thucydides compares Chios with Sparta (assimilating Sparta's Helots to chattel slaves); presumably Chios' slave population was 'denser' in proportion to the free than Athens', but not in total numbers.

8.41 Meropis was at the north-east end of the island of Cos (and is marked as Cos on Map 1); until 366/5 there was another city, Astypalaea, at the south-west end. Syme and Chalce were, respectively, north and west of Rhodes.

8.42 For attempts to work out which ships were where, see Andrewes and Hornblower: the problems are reduced if the Athenians used a harbour on the south side of Syme. Charminus' defeat is mocked in Ar., *Thesm.* 804. Teutloussa was a small island immediately south of Syme; Halicarnassus was north-east of Cos.

8.43 The Athenians did not 'attack' but simply 'touched at' Loryma (Hornblower), on the promontory east of Syme: they took a roundabout route to avoid sailing past Cnidus. With the emendation *eneinai*, which we accept, the spelling-out of what territory Persia might claim is a part of the indirect speech attributed to Lichas (and not an authorial explanation by Thucydides). Lichas' stance was to change (cf. 8.84); but later Callicratidas was to object to receiving Persian support at too high a price (Xen., *Hell.* 1.6.6-11).

8.44 We learn from 8.61 that some ships remained at Miletus. At this time Rhodes had three principal cities: they jointly went over to the Spartans;

and by synoecism (cf. note to 1.58) in 408/7 a new city of Rhodes was founded at the north-east tip of the island, where the modern Rhodes town is (Diod. Sic. 13.75.1). Inscriptions of Lindus point to a constitutional structure resembling that of Athens (*IK Rhodischen Peraia* 251, *SIG*³ 110 n. 4), whereas a decree attributed to the Rhodians collectively just before the synoecism was enacted by a council without an assembly (*SIG*³ 110): Hornblower warns about making the same assumption for all three cities, but it seems that as at Chios (cf. 8.9 with note, 8.24) the men favouring Sparta were oligarchically inclined. Dorieus, mentioned in 8.35, is not mentioned here: Hornblower wonders whether he was under judicial sentence; and he notes that Athens had allowed the Rhodians to retain some ships (cf. Samos, 8.16). We retain the manuscripts' 'eighty days', which Andrewes calculates cannot have ended earlier than 5 April (and which with 8.60 proves that Thucydides did not have a fixed date for the end of winter).

8.45–56 *Intrigues of Alcibiades.* 'In the meantime and even earlier' marks the beginning of the most extensive chronological dislocation in Books 2–8 (cf. Introduction, p. xxvii), and there are points, to which Thucydides might have attended in his final revision, where it is imperfectly dovetailed with the rest of the narrative. As Hornblower stresses, the Peloponnesians' suspicion of Alcibiades was an accelerating process, not a datable event. The death of Chalcideus and the battle of Miletus were reported in 8.24–5; but Alcibiades was still cooperating with the Spartans in 8.26, and this chapter need not take us back earlier than the beginning of Thucydides' winter 412/1. For Alcibiades and Agis, see 8.12 with note. Earlier, 8.36 suggested that what is said here about pay is not a repetition of what was stated in 8.29 but a later reduction, not from one drachma but from the rate fixed in 8.29; for Athenian rates of pay, cf. note to 6.31. Alcibiades acted as spokesman for Tissaphernes in his dealings with both sides: how much influence he had with Tissaphernes, and how correctly he represented Tissaphernes' own position, is not certain (cf. 8.56 with note below).

8.46 This is the first mention of the Phoenician fleet: as Andrewes points out, Phoenicia was outside Tissaphernes' satrapy, and the fleet was the King's rather than his. In the 390s the Spartans, when fighting for the Asiatic Greeks against Persia, did prove more willing than the Athenians had been to penetrate the interior of Asia Minor (whether Thucydides lived long enough to discover that is uncertain: cf. Introduction, p. xxv); but the Athenians remained unhappy with conceding Persia's claim to the Aegean coast of Asia Minor, and did so only when forced to accept the King's Peace of 387/6.

8.47 For Alcibiades' view of democracy, cf. 6.89, and Phrynichus' comment in 8.48. Both the 'most powerful' Athenians at Samos and the wider 'better class of people' are presumably upper-class men who could be expected to favour oligarchy.

8.48 If the pamphlet of the 'Old Oligarch' ([Xen.] *Ath. Pol.*) is correctly dated to the mid-420s (e.g. the edition of J. L. Marr and P. J. Rhodes

(Oxford: Aris & Phillips, 2008)), there were already in the time of Cleon men who disliked the democracy; in 415 there was a probably unjustified fear that the religious scandals were a sign of a plot against the democracy (cf. 6.27 with note to 6.27–9); since 413 the democracy was no longer justified by success, and the bribe offered to the poorer Athenians, who would lose politically from a change to oligarchy, was financial support from Persia to win the war. For 'fraternities' (*hetairika* = *hetaireiai*), cf. 6.27 and 8.54 with notes. Thucydides thought highly of Phrynichus (cf. 8.27): Phrynichus' cynical view of Alcibiades is endorsed, his suggestion that the Persians would not support the Athenians was to be borne out, and so was his view that a change to oligarchy would not make Athens more popular with the allies (cf. 8.64). For the 'great and good', *kaloi k' agathoi*, cf. 4.40 with note (where the different context justifies a different translation): Phrynichus himself seems not to have been from an upper-class background (cf. Lys. 20. *Polystratus* 11–12). The 'Attic *stelai*' listing property confiscated from the men condemned after the scandals of 415 (cf. note to 6.60–1) show that rich Athenians had been able to acquire land in allied territory on a large scale. What is said of the nature of an oligarchic regime may have been retrojected by Thucydides from what actually happened in 411 (Hornblower after N. G. L. Hammond).

8.49 Peisander, mocked in comedy as a glutton and a coward, had been an enthusiastic investigator of the scandals of 415, and with Charicles (see 7.20 with note) is remarked on as a man who afterwards changed sides (Andoc. 1. *Mysteries* 36).

8.50 As Hornblower remarks, Thucydides was interested in clever tricks, and perhaps also told this story 'partly . . . to entertain, relief before the horrors of the revolution'. Phrynichus' 'plan A' was an attempt to discredit Alcibiades with Astyochus, which failed; his 'plan B' involved a letter which this time he expected to be shown to Alcibiades, and this succeeded because he prepared the Athenians for the letter which Alcibiades sent in reaction to it. We are now about the time of the solstice (8.39): Magnesia was south-east of Ephesus, on the Maeander.

8.52 The Peloponnesians' move to Rhodes was in 8.44. Thucydides here confirms statements attributed to Alcibiades in 8.46 and to Lichas in 8.43 (cf. Introduction, p. xxxvi).

8.53 Andrewes had Peisander and colleagues leave Samos immediately after 8.49 and delay for some time in Athens; better, Hornblower follows more recent studies in having them leave Samos about mid-February. It is generally accepted that Aristophanes' *Lysistrata* was produced at the Lenaea of 411, in February, and his *Thesmophoriazusae* at the Great Dionysia of 411, in April. *Lysistrata*, in which a *proboulos* is mocked (cf. note to 8.1) but there is no sign of anything sinister afoot, was perhaps performed just before Peisander's arrival; in *Thesmophoriazusae* Aristophanes allowed himself discreet hints (esp. 361–2, 1143–6) but no more. 'If the democracy was abandoned' (8.48) became in Peisander's propaganda 'a modification of their democracy', 'a more prudent form of government', and an emergency measure which could be reversed later. The Eumolpidae and Ceryces ('heralds') were the hereditary groups (known as *gene*) which provided the principal functionaries of the Eleusinian cult: see R. Parker, *Athenian Religion: A History* (Oxford University Press, 1996), 293–7, 300–2. For initial objections, cf. the reaction at Samos (8.48); Andrewes notes that it is hard to visualize Peisander's dealing with objectors exactly as reported here.

8.54 The ten sent back with Peisander were probably one from each tribe. For Iasus and Amorges, cf. 8.27–8, where Athens' support for Amorges is not made so clear. The 'cabals' (*xynomosiai*) are best seen as groups at the sinister end of the range of the fraternities mentioned in 8.48.

8.55 Here the dispatch of Leon and Diomedon (8.54) feeds into the period of Peloponnesian inactivity at Rhodes (end of 8.44), and Thucydides resumes the single thread of the narrative. The Chian strand is continued from 8.40. For the designation 'Laconian', cf. 3.5.

8.56 We are not told where the meeting with Tissaphernes took place. What Alcibiades said was presumably public knowledge. On his influence with Tissaphernes, cf. note to 8.45–56; Thucydides believed that, even if the strategy was Alcibiades', Tissaphernes while willing to put pressure on the Spartans by talking to the Athenians was not willing to switch his support to the Athenians (which he would have found hard to justify to the King). If even these oligarchic Athenians were willing to abandon mainland Asia Minor and also the offshore islands, that is remarkable (cf. note to 8.46). If there was a Peace of Callias between Athens and Persia in the middle of the century (cf. note to 1.111–12), that might have forbidden the Persians to bring ships into the Aegean; even without that, it is credible that the Persian challenge to Athens' naval power in the Aegean was more than even these Athenians could concede.

8.57–9 *Third Spartan–Persian treaty.*

8.58 For the higher status of this treaty, see note to 8.18; it no longer seems that the regnal year dates this to the end of March or later (Hornblower, contr. Andrewes), but if the text of 8.44 is sound (see note) it could be as late as early April while still falling within Thucydides' winter. The move from Caunus (8.57) to the plain of the Maeander for ratification is not explained. Hieramenes may have been a representative of the King (D. M. Lewis, *Sparta and Persia* (Leiden: Brill, 1977), 104); 'the sons of Pharnaces' in effect denoted Pharnabazus. This time Persia's territorial claim was restricted (immediately but still not definitively) to mainland Asia Minor, but there it was absolute. Maintenance was now limited to the Peloponnesians' ships already present—possibly though not certainly at the half-drachma rate of 8.45—and anything provided after the arrival of the King's ships (which never did arrive: cf. 8.87) would be only a loan.

8.60 *Oropus captured from Athens by Boeotians.* For Oropus as Athenian territory, cf. 2.23; for Euboean hostility to Athens, cf. 8.5.

8.61–109 Twenty-first summer (411) (unfinished)

8.61–63.2 *Campaigns in the Aegean.* Dercylidas was harmost in Abydos later in the war (Xen., *Hell.* 3.1.9), and was to be prominent in the 390s: he was ingenious, and fond of being away from Sparta (Xen., *Hell.* 3.1.8, 4.32). Pedaritus' death was reported in 8.55, and Astyochus and the Peloponnesians left Rhodes in 8.60, so Leon will have arrived during Thucydides' winter 412/1. The word which we translate as 'lieutenant' is *epibates*, which normally denotes a marine; its precise significance here is unknown. For the Samian exiles at Anaea, cf. 3.19, 8.19. For the ending of fighting at nightfall, cf. 1.51.

8.62 For the capture of Sestos from the Persians by the Athenians and others in 479/8, cf. 1.89.

8.63.3–71 *Revolution of the Four Hundred in Athens.* For the revolution among the Samians, cf. 8.21: the leaders of those who opposed 'the most powerful men' then have in turn become the most powerful men. That Alcibiades was 'unwilling' to join the Athenian oligarchs reflects a judgement on his performance in 8.56 (Andrewes); that he was 'hardly suitable' perhaps reflects Phrynichus' judgement in 8.48, reinforced by the episode of 8.50–1.

8.64 Diitrephes is probably the man of 7.29; his command in the Thraceward region has not been mentioned before. In ML 83, translated Fornara 153, we have two Thasian laws offering rewards to men who give information on plots, best attributed to the oligarchic regime which was installed now. Thasos was recovered by Athens and made democratic again in 407 (Xen., *Hell.* 1.4.9, cf. *SEG* xxxviii 851, A. 4, 19, B. 2–3, 20). '"Sensible" government' (*sophrosyne*), an expression often associated with Sparta and with oligarchy (cf. note to 4.18), seems from what follows to be ironic, as 'the specious "law and order"' (*eunomia*), also associated with Sparta (cf. 1.18 with note), openly is.

8.65 Some of the 'various cities' visited are to be mentioned in 8.69. For the 'fraternities' or 'cabals', cf. 8.48, 54. Androcles' role in 415 is mentioned by Andoc. 1. *Mysteries* 27; he is the only man other than Cleon of whom Thucydides uses the term 'demagogue'. It appears that Alcibiades' failure to gain Tissaphernes' support for Athens was not yet known in the city. Civilian stipends would not be needed if political power was restricted to the richer citizens, and their abolition could be represented as a desirable economy in Athens' straitened circumstances (cf. 8.86); 'the citizens most capable of serving the state with both property and person' was a formula used at this time to denote those of hoplite status and above: cf. *Ath. Pol.* 29.5; 8.97 and *Ath. Pol.* 33.1 on the intermediate regime of 411/o; Xen., *Hell.* 2.3.15, 48 for Theramenes in 404. For the number, cf. 8.72: it is unlikely that there were by now as few as 5,000 citizens of hoplite status and above; it suits the different contexts that 5,000 is a maximum here but a minimum in *Ath. Pol.* 29.5.

8.66 We have two accounts of what happened now: by Thucydides, who was a contemporary but outside Athens, and who emphasizes the violence and intimidation (and, as Andrewes notes, writes as if all the oligarchs were extremists); and in *Ath. Pol.* 29–32, which was written nearly a century later, and is based partly on Thucydides and partly on a source using documents to show how the revolutionaries tried to make their revolution seem respectable by democratic criteria of respectability. There is tendentiousness in both accounts, but on details which serve no partisan purpose *Ath. Pol.* is likely to be right. Identifying the council as of five hundred and appointed by lot stresses that this was the normal democratic council; appointment by lot, to select from men considered equally eligible, was not restricted to but was often considered characteristic of democracy. Athens was much larger, and much further from being a 'face-to-face' community, than most Greek cities. Lys. 25. *Overthrowing Democracy* 9 mentions Phrynichus and Peisander as two men who changed from democracy to oligarchy; Andoc. 1. *Mysteries* 36 mentions Peisander and Charicles (the latter, for whom see 7.20 with note, is not mentioned in 411–410 but was one of the Thirty in 404/3).

8.67 *Ath. Pol.* 29.2–3 has thirty commissioners, the ten *probouloi* (cf. 8.1) and twenty others (cf. Androtion *FGrH* 324 F 43, Philoch. *FGrH* 328 F 136), and quotes the decree giving them their instructions. *Ath. Pol.* does not mention that the assembly was held at Colonus: that may particularly have deterred poorer, and more poorly armed, citizens from attending, but there must have been some respectable pretext. *Ath. Pol.* 29.4 gives more detail than Thucydides on the suspension of the normal safeguards; 29.5 begins with more detail on the abolition of civilian stipends, and continues with the entrusting of the state to 'not less than five thousand' (cf. 8.65 with note) for the duration of the war, and the appointment of a hundred men to register the Five Thousand. Then *Ath. Pol.* 30 gives a constitution 'for the future' and 31 a constitution 'for the immediate crisis' which begins with a method of appointing the Four Hundred totally different from that of Thucydides, these constitutions said to be the work of another board of a hundred. Probably the Four Hundred (recalling Solon's council, which preceded Cleisthenes' five hundred: *Ath. Pol.* 8.4, 31.1) were appointed as stated by Thucydides, and the two constitutional documents, reflecting disagreement among the oligarchs once they got down to details, were published when the Four Hundred formally inaugurated their rule (for which see 8.70). The process of registering the Five Thousand was at least begun (cf. Lys. 20. *Polystratus* 13–14), but under this regime the list was never published and no meetings of a body purporting to be the Five Thousand were held (cf. 8.92–4).

8.68 *Ath. Pol.* attributes the positive proposals as well as the suspension of safeguards to the commissioners: it may be that Peisander was one of the commissioners and claimed to be speaking on their behalf. With the leading men of different kinds Hornblower compares the three speakers in the Persian constitutional debate in Hdt. 3.80–3. There was an orator Antiphon in whose name are preserved three individual law-court speeches and three 'tetralogies', each comprising two prosecuting and two defending speeches in hypothetical homicide cases. Thucydides' Antiphon will be the author of the three individual speeches; the author of the tetralogies may be another man; and 'Antiphon the sophist' (*Vorsokr.* 87), from whom we have fragments critical of conventional beliefs, may be yet another. The life of Antiphon (the orator) in [Plut.] *X Orat.* 832 B–834 B ends with two documents on the trial of Antiphon and other oligarchs. *Ath. Pol.* 32.2 has a list of the leaders apparently derived from Thucydides but omitting Phrynichus—an omission due perhaps not to the author but to a subsequent copyist. Theramenes was the son of Hagnon, one of the *probouloi* (see note to 8.1): he was to fall out with the extremists in 411 (8.89–97), remained active under the democracy, and in 404 he played a major part in bringing the regime of the Thirty into existence, but again fell out with the extremists and on that occasion was put to death by them. *Ath. Pol.* 28.5 remarks that opinions on him were divided. Thucydides, though he clearly disapproved of the regime of the Four Hundred, writes approvingly of these men. The tyranny was ended by the expulsion of Hippias in 511/0 (6.59), so this was exactly the hundredth year after by inclusive counting, and the Delian League was founded in 478/7 (1.94–7): despite the statement that ending the Athenians' freedom was 'not an easy task', 8.69–70 shows that the democrats failed to resist.

8.69 Pay for jurors, probably in the 450s, was Athens' first civilian payment (*Ath. Pol.* 27.3–4); the others were probably introduced between then and the outbreak of the Peloponnesian War. *Ath. Pol.* 32.1 gives dates: the democratic council's year (at this time distinct from the calendar year) was due to end on 14 Scirophorion = 9 July; it was in fact paid off on 14 Thargelion = 9 June, and the Four Hundred's formal inauguration (Thucydides does not clearly distinguish the two occasions) was on 22 Thargelion = 17 June. We need to allow time between the Colonus assembly and 9 June, and between the commissioners' appointment and the Colonus assembly, so Peisander will have arrived in Athens towards the end of May.

8.70 Thucydides here uses the normal *prytaneis* for the presiding officers, whereas in 8.67 he uses *proedroi* ('presiding board', the title of a new board created in the fourth century, after his death) for the five men who formed the core of the Four Hundred: neither is a reliable guide to the terminology actually used. Inscriptions show that some democratic officials remained in office to the end of 412/1. Though disliking the regime, Thucydides notes that there was not a wild reign of terror (contr. Chaereas in 8.74). At 8.63, despite failing to get Persian support, the oligarchs had still been 'determined to maintain the war-effort'; but once in power they tried to negotiate an end to the war.

8.71 However, they did not simply capitulate, and they trusted the cavalry and others they sent out to resist Agis. The delegation to Sparta mentioned here should be distinct from that of 8.86.

8.72–7 *Return to democracy by Athenians at Samos*. Certain kinds of business in the assembly required a quorum of 6,000, and even if we limit the claim to the period after 431 it can hardly be true that attendance had never reached 5,000 (though it may have been true recently with the navy based at Samos).

8.73 What is said of the Samians begins with a summary of 8.21, 63, and then adds the 300 conspirators. Hyperbolus was a demagogue in the mould of Cleon, who was a serious politician but for some reason was considered particularly contemptible by Thucydides and others (cf. Ar., *Pax* 679–87, Plato Com. fr. 203 Kassel and Austin *ap.* Plut., *Nic.* 11, *Alc.* 13): for his ostracism, see note to 6.6. Thrasyboulus (of the deme Steiria: there was another prominent Thrasyboulus, of Collytus) was to be prominent in the remainder of the war, as a supporter of Alcibiades (cf. 8.81), in 403 took the lead in fighting back against the Thirty, and remained active until he died on campaign *c*.389. Thrasyllus seems to have been more strongly democratic, and was one of the generals executed after the battle of Arginusae in 406. For the Paralus, see note to 3.33; for slaves as well as foreigners in the other crews, see note to 7.13.

8.74 Chaereas was to serve as a general in the Hellespont in 411/0 (Diod. Sic. 13.49–51); his account of the 'horrors' is to be contrasted with 8.70. 'Free men flogged like slaves' (a more literal translation would be 'flogging as a punishment for everybody') reflects the fact that free men were not normally subject to corporal punishment. Sexual abuse was commonly alleged against tyrants: e.g. Hdt. 3.80.

8.75 At the end of the war the Athenians showed their gratitude to the loyal Samians: ML 94, trans. Fornara 66, and RO 2 (parts of the same inscription).

8.76 Having declared enmity against Athens under the Four Hundred, the Athenians at Samos held assemblies and appointed officials as if they were a separate *polis*. The Samian war was that of 440–439 (1.115–17). The oligarchs had claimed to be reverting to older and better Athenian practice (cf. *Ath. Pol.* 29.3, 31.1; and note on the Four Hundred at 8.67): democrats in reply claimed that for Athens the traditional constitution was democracy. The Athenians continued to hope—in vain, and it is not clear with how much encouragement—that Persian support might be diverted to them, until the cooperation between the King's son Cyrus and the Spartan Lysander began in 407. For the idea of a large force as a city on the move, cf. the Athenians at the beginning and end of the great Sicilian expedition (6.63, 7.75).

8.78–80 *Peloponnesian fleet to Hellespont*. The Peloponnesians' dissatisfaction was cumulative, but notice especially the long period of inactivity at Rhodes (8.44).

8.79 Mycale is the promontory directly opposite Samos, on the south side of which the Greeks defeated the Persians in 479 (1.89, Hdt. 9.96–107): at its narrowest point the strait between the north side and Samos is about 2 miles (3 km) wide. For Strombichides' squadron, cf. 8.62.

8.80 For Clearchus and Pharnabazus, cf. 8.8, 39. Byzantium was a colony of Megara: Helixus and Clearchus were still there in 408 (Xen., *Hell.* 1.3.14–22). As Hornblower remarks, Byzantium was important, and this note of its revolt is surprisingly low-key.

8.81–2 *Alcibiades joins Athenian fleet at Samos.* Until his return to Athens in 407 Alcibiades was a commander of the fleet, appointed by the fleet, but as far as the *polis* was concerned remained under the sentence passed on him in 415. For the Phoenician fleet, cf. 8.46, 58–9, 78: we have not previously been told that it was at Aspendus, in the gulf of Pamphylia north-west of Cyprus.

8.83–5 *Mindarus succeeds Astyochus as Spartan admiral.*

8.84 For Dorieus, cf. 3.8 with note to 3.8–18, 8.35. Hornblower remarks on the tendency of Spartan officers to use violence against other Greeks, as they might against Helots. Lichas had himself earlier been unhappy with Persia's terms (8.43, 52): for the suggestion that they must be accepted for the duration of the war cf. the Athenian oligarchs' suggestion that oligarchy must be accepted for the duration of the war (8.53; *Ath. Pol.* 29.5). We do not know when he died (cf. note to 8.87–8, and for one alternative suggestion see Introduction, p. xxv).

8.85 Mindarus was to be defeated and killed in the battle of Cyzicus in 410. For the Carian Gaulites, cf. Mys (Hdt. 8.133–5) and perhaps Pigres (Xen., *Anab.* 1.2.17): they will in fact have been trilingual, in Carian, Greek, and Aramaic. Xen., *Hell.* 1.1.27–31 seems to date Hermocrates' exile to 410, and some scholars have believed that, but more probably Thucydides is not anticipating here but correctly dates the exile to 411. It seems that the various deputations convinced the Spartans of Tissaphernes' unreliability (Lewis, *Sparta and Persia*, 110–13).

8.86 *Alcibiades restrains Athenian democrats at Samos.* On the oligarchs' propaganda, note the willingness to negotiate with Sparta but also the resistance to Agis in 8.70–1, and the envoys' instructions in 8.72. Alcibiades' restraining the democrats in 8.82 was probably an earlier intervention, not an anticipation of this. It is striking that Alcibiades earned his strongest praise from Thucydides when, like Pericles (2.65), he restrained the crowd (Hornblower compares also Solon fr. 37. 6–7 West *ap. Ath. Pol.* 12.5)—but we with hindsight might say that, since Athens was defeated in the end, it would have been less damaging if the defeat had come now. Alcibiades accepted the restricted body of full citizens, and by implication the abolition of civilian stipends, but not the despotic council of the Four Hundred. The story of the Parali is continued from 8.74. Laespodias is probably the man of 6.105; Melesias may be a son of Pericles' opponent Thucydides son of Melesias and an uncle of the historian (cf. Introduction, p. xxiv).

8.87–8 *Tissaphernes goes to Aspendus.* For Tamos, cf. 8.31. Here, uncharacteristically, Thucydides briefly admits to uncertainty (cf. Introduction, p. xxxi), but by the end of the chapter he has decided on the correct explanation: a suggestion of D. M. Lewis that the ships may have been needed against a revolt in Egypt (cf. *Sparta and Persia*, 133), was accepted by Andrewes but is rejected by Hornblower. Philippus is probably the man of 8.28: the fact that he went instead of Lichas may, but does not necessarily, mean that Lichas was dead or dying (cf. note to 8.84).

8.88 For Caunus, cf. 8.39; Phaselis was beyond it, on the gulf of Pamphylia south-west of Aspendus.

8.89–98 *Four Hundred replaced by Five Thousand in Athens.* This is the first mention of uneasiness among 'the rank and file of the oligarchic movement'. For Theramenes, see note to 8.68. Aristocrates, probably the Aristocrates of 5.19, 24, and 8.9, was to be a general under the restored democracy in 407/6 and 406/5; a choregic dedication of his survives (*IG* i³ 964). Thucydides does not allow for any genuine dislike of the current regime, but regards that as a mere smokescreen covering selfish ambition (cf. Introduction, p. xxxiv).

8.90 Aristarchus is a common name, and we cannot identify this holder of it; Xen., *Hell.* 2.3.2 adds Aristoteles (one of the Thirty in 404/3) and Melanthius (unknown). This is the first mention of the fortification at Eëtioneia, for which see Map 10. Hornblower defends the usual interpretation against the alternative suggested by Andrewes: Eëtioneia itself was to be a fortress, walled on both sides; the other tower was at Acte, on the south side of the harbour entrance. It is possible that Thucydides has been careless and that ten men including Antiphon and Phrynichus were sent to Sparta (Develin, *AO*, 162).

8.91 Las was north of Laconian Asine. Hornblower cites ML 82, translated Fornara 152, in which Eretria honours Hegelochus of Taras, and he suggests that Hegelochus was a son of the seer Teisamenus of Elis (Hdt. 9.33), that he acted as seer for the battle of 8.95, and that his son was the Hegias who acted as seer for the battle of Aegospotami in 405 (Paus. 3.11.5). Agesandridas' father may be the Agesandrus of 1.139. According to *Ath. Pol.* 32.3 the Spartans were demanding the dissolution of Athens' naval empire; according to Thucydides (but what he gives us may be no more than his own conjecture) retention of the empire was the oligarchs' preferred option but they would not insist on it; it will in fact have been an obstacle to a settlement that the oligarchs in Athens were in no position to commit the navy at Samos. At the end of the war Athens did have to accept demolition of the Peiraeus and Long Walls and the loss of all but twelve warships (e.g. Andoc. 3. *Peace* 11–12; cf. 5.26).

8.92 According to Lys. 13. *Agoratus* 70–1, Lycurg., *Leocrates* 112, the plotters were Thrasyboulus of Calydon and Apollodorus of Megara; an inscription of 409 (ML 85, translated Fornara 155) records honours for Thrasyboulus and lesser honours for several others, and orders an investigation into charges of bribery in connection with honours for Apollodorus. For Aegina as an Athenian settlement since 431, see 2.27. Alexicles is not otherwise known. Hermon was sent to Pylos in 410/09 (ML 84, translated Fornara 154, 10). If the manuscripts' text is right, some of the Four

Hundred did not agree with the hostile response to Theramenes; but perhaps we should with Andrewes and Hornblower accept the deletion of *plen*, to make the text mean that those who did not approve (of the kidnapping of Alexicles) made a hostile response to Theramenes. The ambiguous Theramenes in the presence of the Four Hundred concealed his support for the mutineers. According to Lycurg., *Leocrates* 115 the restored democracy put Alexicles and Aristarchus to death. Thucydides of Pharsalus was probably related to the Menon of 2.22. That the mutineers really wanted democracy will again be a Thucydidean inference: Andrewes stressed that the next day they were willing to compromise (8.93).

8.93 Mounichia was on the east side of Peiraeus, and the theatre of Dionysus was between that and the harbour of 8.90. The Anaceium (temple of the *Anakes*, i.e. Castor and Pollux) was on the north slope of the Acropolis (Paus. 1.18.1–2): for a possible location, see S. G. Miller, in M. H. Hansen (ed.), *Sources for the Ancient Greek City State* (Copenhagen: Royal Danish Academy, 1995), 210–11, with 242 and fig. 1. The precinct of Dionysus, south of the east end of the Acropolis, contained the theatre and to the south of it a small temple (Travlos, *Pictorial Dictionary of Ancient Athens*, 537–52, with 540 fig. 677).

8.94 Thucydides offers two possible explanations of Agesandridas' movements but firmly accepts the second (cf. Introduction, p. xxxi).

8.95 Thoricus and Prasiae were on the east coast of Attica, a short distance north of Sounium, where the east coast meets the south-west-facing coast. For the importance of Euboea, cf. 2.14, 7.28, 8.1. Thymochares was perhaps defeated by Agesandridas again later this year, in the Hellespont (Xen., *Hell.* 1.1.1; but the beginning of *Hell.* is problematic): he may belong to a family which produced several leading men between the mid-fourth century and the mid-third. In Xenophon's version of the battle of Aegospotami in 405 the Spartans succeeded with a similar trick (Xen., *Hell.* 2.1.27–8; but contr. Diod. Sic. 13.106.1–5). Oreus, at the north end of Euboea, is elsewhere referred to by its earlier name, Hestiaea (1.114, 7.57).

8.96 Hornblower notes the piling up of disasters for Athens: the defeat in Sicily (8.1), the revolt of Chios (8.15), and now the loss of Euboea. For the Spartans' lack of boldness, cf. especially their aborted attack on the Peiraeus in 429 (2.93–4): even if Thucydides is exaggerating, an attack on the Peiraeus now would have had very serious consequences. For the contrast between the Spartans and the Athenians, cf. the Corinthians in 1.70–1. Hornblower notes that the Syracusans followed the Athenians in willingness to innovate—by copying a Corinthian innovation (7.36 with 7.34); 7.55 compared Athens and Syracuse in a different way.

8.97 The Pnyx was to the west of the Acropolis: the democracy had been set aside by an assembly held not there but at Colonus (8.67). Probably the decision taken now was to retain the oligarchic principles of no civilian stipends and a limited citizen body (cf. 8.65) but to return to the democratic principle that the assembly (thus limited) rather than the council (which was perhaps of 500 but elected) should be the powerful body (cf. Alcibiades in 8.86, the mutineers in 8.89, 92), and this is what Thucydides means by a blend. *Ath. Pol.* 33 paraphrases Thucydides' narrative and judgement, adding only the date: this change occurred about the beginning of the third month of 411/0. The function of the commissioners will have been to draft laws for the new constitution: we know nothing more about them or their laws, but in 410 the restored democracy embarked on a recodification of Athens' laws (Lys. 30. *Nicomachus* 2–3). For the status of Alcibiades, cf. note to 8.81–2: he acted as a commander of the fleet in the time of this regime and of the restored democracy, but did not return to Athens until 407.

8.98 A farm belonging to Peisander was given to Apollodorus of Megara (cf. note to 8.92: Lys. 7. *Olive Stump* 4); for Aristarchus, cf. Xen., *Hell.* 1.7.28. The archers were the Scythian force maintained to keep order (Andoc. 3. *Peace* 5, schol. Ar. *Ach.* 54).

8.99–109 *Campaigns in the Aegean and Hellespont.* The Aegean narrative is continued from 8.87; for Hippocrates, cf. 8.35, and for Pharnabazus' invitation, cf. 8.80. Icaros was west of Samos.

8.100 For Thrasyllus, cf. 8.73. Eresus had revolted before but the Athenians had recovered it (8.23). For Cyme, south-east of Lesbos, cf. 8.22, 31. The kinship connection is between the Boeotians and the Aeolians of Lesbos: cf. 7.57.

8.101 We do not know how large a sum Chian 'fortieths' represent. Phocaea was south-west of Cyme, just outside the gulf; from Cyme the Peloponnesians crossed to the north side and the strait between Lesbos and the mainland (Hornblower sees the mention of Arginousae as an anticipation of the battle in 406 which Thucydides did not live to write about); Eresus was on the south-west-facing coast of Lesbos, and the Athenians there would not know about ships sailing through the strait. Hamaxitus will have been reached before Larisa; Sigeium was just outside the Hellespont, and Rhoeteium inside it on the Asiatic side. Hornblower notes Thucydides' stress on the speed of the voyage: 189 nautical miles (349 km) in two days, two-thirds on the second day (for the single ships sailing from Athens to Mytilene in 427, see note to 3.49).

8.102 Sestos (cf. 8.62) was on the European shore of the Hellespont, opposite Abydos (for which cf. 8.61); Elaeus was just inside the Hellespont, and the islands of Imbros and Lemnos (cf. note to 4.28) outside. Protesilaus was said to have been the first Greek killed in the Trojan War (cf. Hdt. 9.116, 120); it is of course accidental that his sanctuary occurs both at the end of Herodotus' history and at the end of what survives of Thucydides' unfinished history.

8.104 The Peloponnesians' line extended from Abydos in the direction of the Aegean as far as Dardanus (north-east of Rhoeteium); the Athenians' line was opposite; the headland of Cynossema on the European side made each end of these lines invisible to the other. For the Peloponnesians' over-confidence which turned victory into defeat, cf. the second battle in the Gulf of Corinth in 429 (2.90–2). Hornblower notes the irony of the Syracusans' defeat after their victory over the Athenians in Sicily in 413.

8.106 The river Meidius was probably that flowing into the Hellespont opposite Cynossema (Rhodius in Strabo 595/13.1.28 and in *Barrington Atlas*, map 51).

8.107 Cyzicus was in the Propontis, on the isthmus of the major peninsula projecting into it; Harpagium was to the west of that, and Priapus further west. For the eight ships from Byzantium, cf. 8.80.

8.108 The movements of Alcibiades are continued from 8.88: the earlier narrative suggests that he greatly exaggerated his influence. In Xen., *Hell*. 1.4.8 he collected 100 talents from the region of Halicarnassus. For Antandrus, cf. 4.52, 75: Hdt. 7.42 called it Pelasgian (i.e. non-Greek); for the Delians at Atramyttium, cf. 5.1, 32.

8.109 For Miletus and the Persians, cf. 8.84; nothing has been said before of a garrison at Cnidus. On Persian interest in Artemis at Ephesus, see Lewis, *Sparta and Persia*, 108, with n. 1. In all major manuscripts except one the last sentence translated here is followed by one more, based on but not matching Thucydides' own markers of summer and winter, and certainly a later interpolation: 'When the winter after this summer ends, the twenty-first year is completed'. On the abrupt ending of Thucydides' history, see Introduction, p. xxv.

NOTES ON THE GREEK TEXT

No scribe at any date is likely to have copied a substantial portion of the text in front of him without making errors of his own, and perhaps also emending (whether correctly or incorrectly) what he took to be errors in the text in front of him, so no manuscript copy of Thucydides' text is likely to be identical either with any other copy or with the text which Thucydides himself wrote. It is not always easy for modern scholars to identify and correct their predecessors' errors, and neither we in deciding what text to translate nor any other modern editors are likely to have succeeded at every point in recovering what Thucydides himself wrote (though every editor aims to do that).

Thucydides' text is known to have existed in the ancient world in a number of different versions: our medieval manuscripts transmit a version which divides the text into eight books, but there is no indication of a division made by Thucydides himself, and we know that other versions existed which divided the text into a larger number of books.

Modern texts are based primarily on eight medieval manuscripts, written between the tenth and the fourteenth centuries (each of the other surviving manuscripts is a descendant of one or another of those). In addition we have a number of papyrus fragments, written between the third century BC and the sixth century AD, which contain parts of the text. We also have indirect evidence for the text of Thucydides. There are places where ancient authors and commentators (themselves transmitted to us by generations of copyists) quote or expound Thucydides, and sometimes their text is different from that of our surviving copies. Lorenzo Valla, who completed a Latin translation of Thucydides in 1452, had access to manuscripts independent of those which now survive; and some independent manuscripts also lie behind the sixteenth-century printed editions of Henri Estienne (Stephanus) and Aemilius Portus.

We have taken as our starting-point the Oxford Classical Text of H. Stuart Jones, equipped with an improved apparatus criticus in 1942 by J. E. Powell (and with an improved index in 1963 by an unidentified scholar); and below we supply textual notes for all points where the text which we translate is different from the OCT, and for some points where we follow the OCT but some current scholars do not. Not all of these divergences have a significant effect on the sense or the detail, but where they do the textual issues are discussed in the Explanatory Notes.

The edition which most authoritatively reports the readings of the manuscripts is that of 1972–2000 by J. B. Alberti (the 'J' resulting from the

Latinization of 'Giovanni'). A recent discussion of the manuscripts and attempt at a stemma are given by K. Maurer, *Interpolation in Thucydides*, Mnemosyne Suppl. 150 (1995).

1.2.6 Reading μετοικεσίας τὰ ἄλλα (variant in one MS, cf. μετοικήσεις τὰ ἄλλα Ullrich), not μετοικίας ἐς τὰ ἄλλα.

1.27.2, 29.1 Retaining with OCT τρισχίλιοι (27), δισχιλίοις (29): probably one is corrupt but we do not know which.

1.30.1 Reading (with most MSS) Κερκύρας, not Κερκυραίας.

1.57.6 Reading δυοῖν (Busolt) for δέκα, which OCT marks as corrupt.

1.61.3 Retaining with OCT Βέροιαν (MSS: Βρέαν Bergk) . . . Στρέψαν (Pluygers).

1.67.3 Reading εἴ τίς τι ἄλλος (Reiske), not εἴ τίς τι ἄλλο.

1.90.3 Retaining καὶ αὐτοὺς καὶ γυναῖκας καὶ παῖδας, which OCT deletes.

1.103.1 Retaining with OCT δεκάτῳ (τετάρτῳ Krüger, ἕκτῳ Gomme, πέμπτῳ at one time Lewis).

1.109.3 Reading Μεγάβυξον (Gomme), not Μεγάβυζον.

1.126.6 Reading (with the MSS) θύουσι πολλοὶ οὐχ ἱερεῖα, ἀλλὰ θύματα ἐπιχώρια, not πολλὰ (Hermann) . . . ἀλλ' <ἀγνὰ> θύματα (Hemsterhuis).

1.128.1 Retaining ἀπὸ Ταινάρου, which OCT deletes.

1.134.4 Retaining ἐς τὸν Καιάδαν, οὗπερ τοὺς κακούργους εἰώθασιν ἐσβάλλειν (OCT deletes οὗπερ τοὺς κακούργους εἰώθασιν).

1.136.4 Reading ἀσθενέστερος (with some MSS), not ἀσθενεστέρου.

1.141.4 Reading ναῦς πληροῦν (Herwerden), not ναῦς πληροῦντες.

2.2.1 Retaining with OCT δύο μῆνας (τέσσαρας Krüger) . . . μηνὶ ἕκτῳ (δεκάτῳ Gomme).

2.4.2 Reading προσβαλλόντων (with some MSS), not προσβαλόντων.

2.4.5 Reading αἱ πλησίον θύραι (with some MSS), not αἱ θύραι.

2.13.3 Retaining with OCT the MSS text: see Explanatory Note.

2.15.4 Reading τὰ γὰρ ἱερὰ <τὰ ἀρχαιότατα> (Gomme after Stahl) ἐν αὐτῇ τῇ ἀκροπόλει τῆς τε Ἀθηνᾶς (correction in some MSS) καὶ ἄλλων θεῶν: OCT marks as corrupt.
Retaining τῇ δωδεκάτῃ, which OCT deletes.

2.16.1 Deleting μετεῖχον (Driessen).

2.20.4 Retaining with OCT τρισχίλιοι γὰρ ὁπλῖται (πολῖται Polle, χίλιοι καὶ διακόσιοι, i.e. ΧΗΗ for ΧΧΧ, Whitehead after Gomme).

2.22.3 Reading Πειράσιοι (with a papyrus), not Παράσιοι (MSS), which OCT deletes.

2.40.2 Retaining with OCT ἑτέροις (ἑτέροις <ἕτερα> Richards).
Reading αὐτοὶ ἤτοι κρίνομέν (with some MSS), not οἱ αὐτοί.

2.42.4 Reading ἀφίεσθαι (Poppo), not ἐφίεσθαι.

2.44.1 Reading ἐπίστασθε (Herwerden), not ἐπίστανται.

2.52.2 Reading <καὶ> ἀποθνῄσκοντες (Gomme).

2.65.12 Reading ὀκτὼ (Shilleto) μὲν ἔτη for τρία, which OCT marks as corrupt.

2.65.13 Deleting αὐτὸς (Gomme), which OCT retains.

2.73.2 Retaining Πλαταιῆς, which OCT deletes.

2.75.3 Reading ἑπτακαίδεκα (Steup) for ἑβδομήκοντα, which OCT marks as corrupt.

2.77.6 Retaining ἐξ οὐρανοῦ (omitted by some MSS), which OCT deletes.

2.80.5 Reading (with the MSS) Φώτυος, not Φώτιος.

2.89.5 Reading τοῦ παραλόγου (Steup), not τοῦ παρὰ πολύ.

2.89.9 Reading (with most MSS) τῶν πολεμικῶν, not τῶν πολεμίων.

2.90.1 Reading (with some MSS) παρὰ τὴν ἑαυτῶν γῆν, not ἐπί.

2.90.2 Reading πλέοντες (Dobree), not πλέοντα (which Croiset deleted).

2.96.1 Retaining ἐς τὸν Εὔξεινόν τε πόντον καὶ τὸν Ἑλλήσποντον, which OCT deletes.

2.97.3 Reading ὅσωνπερ ἦρξαν (Dobree), not ὅσον προσῆξαν.

2.100.4 Reading Βοττίαν (Rhodes), not Βοττιαίαν.

2.102.4 Reading τοῦ μὴ σκεδάννυσθαι (Poppo), not τῷ μὴ σκεδάννυσθαι, which OCT deletes.

3.9.2 Reading ἐπινοίᾳ (Hude), not εὐνοίᾳ.

3.10.4 Reading ἐπειγομένους (Ross), not ἐπαγομένους.

3.10.5 Reading ἀμύνεσθαι (with some MSS), not ἀμύνασθαι.

3.12.1 Deleting πίστιν (Classen), which OCT retains.

3.17 Bracketing this chapter as an interpolation (with OCT).

3.23.5 Retaining ἢ βορέου, which OCT deletes.

3.26.1 Deleting δύο καὶ (Krüger), which OCT retains.

3.30.4 Retaining with OCT τὸ κενὸν (τὸν καιρὸν Schulz).

3.38.1 Deleting ὂν after ἀντίπαλον (Haase), which OCT retains.

3.39.6 Reading ἡμῖν (with one MS), not ὑμῖν.

3.44.2 Reading <οὐδ'> (Gomme) ἐᾶν (Lindau) for εἶεν, which OCT marks as corrupt.

3.45.4 Reading ἑκάστῃ (Duker), not ἑκάστη.

3.52.2 Reading κολάσειν (Krüger), not κολάζειν.

3.53.1 Retaining ἢ ὑμῖν, which OCT deletes.

3.56.7 Reading ἔχουσι (Heilmann), not ἔχωσι.

3.58.5 Reading ἐρημώσετε (Herwerden), not ἐρημοῦτε.

3.61.1 Reading οὗτοι (Hude), not αὐτοί.

3.62.5 Reading ἵππον (Cobet), not ἵππους.

3.64.3 Reading ὑμῶν (with some MSS), not ἡμῶν.

3.65.3 Reading φιλίους, οὐ πολεμίους (Steup), not φιλίως, οὐ πολεμίως.

3.67.5 Reading <ἂν> ἀνταποδόντες (Dobree).

3.68.1 Deleting ἃ after ὕστερον (Heilmann), which OCT retains.

3.70.1 Reading ὀγδοήκοντα (Rhodes), not ὀκτακοσίων.

3.82.5 Reading τυχών τε (Dion. Hal.), not τυχών.

3.84 Bracketing this chapter as an interpolation (with OCT).

3.92.1 Retaining ἐν Τραχινίᾳ (with MSS and OCT), but for consistency with other passages we translate 'in Trachis'.

3.94.2 Reading ῥᾳδίως τ' ἂν ἐκπολιορκῆσαι πόλεώς τε (with some MSS), not ῥᾳδίως γ' ἂν ἐκπολιορκῆσαι καὶ πόλεως.

3.94.3 Reading ἠπειρωτικὸν (e.g. Classen and Steup), not Ἠπειρωτικὸν.

3.102.5 Deleting τὴν after Αἰολίδα (Steup) and ἐς before τὰ ταύτῃ (Herwerden), which OCT retains.

3.104.3 Punctuating with comma after Ἐφέσια (Fraser), where OCT has no punctuation.

3.107–13 For Olpe/Olpae see Explanatory Note to 3.105–14.

3.111.2 OCT marks part of the text as corrupt, but the general sense is clear.

3.112–3 For Idomene/Idomenae, see Explanatory Note to 3.112.

3.113.4 Punctuating with question mark after μαχομένων ἐστίν, not full point.

4.2.3 Reading προεπεπλεύκεσαν (Classen), not παρεπεπλεύκεσαν.

4.4.1 Retaining with OCT τοὺς στρατιώτας (deleted Köstlin).

4.8.6 Reading ὀκτὼ ἢ ἐννέα <σταδίων> (Bauslaugh).

Reading πέντε καὶ εἴκοσι σταδίους (Burrows), not πέντε καὶ δέκα σταδίους.

4.9.1 Reading προεσταύρωσε (Bloomfield), not προσεσταύρωσε.

4.13.2 Reading πεντήκοντα (with some MSS), not τεσσαράκοντα.

4.19.2 Reading πολεμίου (Stahl), not πολέμου.

4.25.2 Deleting ἐς τὰ οἰκεῖα στρατόπεδα, τό τε ἐν τῇ Μεσσήνῃ καὶ ἐν τῷ Ῥηγίῳ (Steup), which OCT retains.

4.25.8 Reading προσέβαλλον (Poppo), not ἐσέβαλλον.

4.25.9 Reading οἱ Σικελοὶ <οἱ> (Krüger).

4.27.3 Reading Θεογένους (with most MSS), not Θεαγένους (cf. 5.19.2, 24.1).

4.28.4 Reading <καὶ> τοξότας (Portus).

4.29.3 Reading <καὶ> πολλοὶ γὰρ (Wilamowitz) (πολλὰ γὰρ without <καὶ> Gomme), not πολλῷ γὰρ without <καὶ>.

4.30.3 Reading αὐτοὺς (Bauer), not αὐτοῦ.

Reading ὥστε (Gomme), not τότε, and placing ὥστε . . . ποιεῖσθαι after ἐσπέμπειν (with the MSS), not after οὖσαν (OCT after Krüger).

4.32.3 Reading τὰ μετέωρα καταλαβόντες (Spratt), not τὰ μετεωρότατα λαβόντες.

Reading ἔχουσι (with most MSS), not ἔχωσι.

4.40.2 Reading ἀπιστούντων (Gomme), not ἀπιστοῦντές.

4.41.3 Reading ἀπαθεῖς (Stephanus), not ἀμαθεῖς.

4.42.4 Reading αὐτῶν (Poppo), not αὑτῶν.

4.43.1 Reading ξυνέβαλλεν (with most MSS), not ξυνέβαλεν.

4.44.2 Reading τοιούτῳ τρόπῳ (de Romilly), not τούτῳ τῷ τρόπῳ.

4.44.4 Reading καὶ ὡς ἔγνωσαν, where OCT (with some MSS) deletes ὡς.

4.45.2 Retaining ἐν ᾧ ἡ Μεθώνη ἐστί, which OCT after Stahl deletes.

4.46.1 Reading <ταῖς> ναῦσιν (Hammond after Gomme).

4.46.4 Reading αὐτοὺς ἐλθόντας (Poppo), not τοὺς ἐλθόντας.

4.47.3 Reading προσιόντας (with most MSS), not προϊόντας (one MS, cf. Duker).

4.50.2 Reading τοὺς Λακεδαιμονίους (Cobet), not πρὸς Λακεδαιμονίους.

4.52.3 Reading τὴν ἄλλην παρασκευὴν (Poppo), not τῇ ἄλλη σκευῇ.

4.54.1 OCT (with the MSS) reads δισχιλίοις Μιλησίων ὁπλίταις, but the numeral is almost certainly corrupt, and we have omitted it.

4.56.1 Reading <γενόμενοι> ἐν τῷ τοιούτῳ (Dobree), which yields sense; but more words may have dropped out (Gomme).

4.59.4 Reading βουλόμενοι (with some MSS), not βουλευόμενοι.

4.62.2 Reading οὐχ ἡσυχία μᾶλλον ἢ πόλεμος (with the MSS), not ἡσυχίαν . . . πόλεμον (Herwerden), τὸ μὲν παύσειεν . . . τὸ δὲ ξυνδιασώσειε (Steup), not παῦσαι . . . ξυνδιασῶσαι.

4.62.3 Reading δυνάμει τι (Krüger), not δυνάμει τινί.

4.63.1 Reading τοὺς ἤδη (Reiske), not τὸ ἤδη, which OCT marks as corrupt. Reading ἕκαστός τις (with one MS), not ἕκαστός τι.

4.67.3 Reading ἐκδρομή (Gomme), not φυλακή.

4.69.2 Reading διελομένη <ἤγεν> (Madvig).

4.72.4 Reading τελευτήσαντες <ἐπεκράτησαν>, ἀλλ' ἀπεκρίθησαν οἱ μὲν (Bernadakis), not τελευτήσαντες ἀπεκρίθησαν, ἀλλ' οἱ μὲν, which does not give a satisfactory sense.

4.73.2 Reading ἐπειδή τε . . . [καὶ] αὐτοῖς (Gomme), not ἐπειδή γε . . . καὶ αὐτοῖς.

4.73.4 OCT (with the MSS) reads τοῖς δὲ ξυμπάσης τῆς δυνάμεως . . . ἐθέλειν τολμᾶν, which is difficult, and possibly corrupt, but the general sense is clear.

4.75.2 Reading Κάληκα (with the MSS), not Κάλητα.

4.76.2 Reading ἐκ Θεσπιῶν (a variant in some MSS), not ἐκ Θηβῶν.

4.77.2 Reading Οἰνιάδας τε ὑπὸ 'Ακαρνάνων (one MS, cf. Poppo), not Οἰνιάδας δὲ ὑπό τε 'Ακαρνάνων.

4.78.1 Reading Τορύμβας (Masson), not Τορύλαος.

4.80.3 Reading νεότητα (with most MSS), not σκαιότητα.

4.85.7 Reading νηΐτην (Hude), not νηΐτῃ.

4.93.2 Reading Ἱπποκράτει <ἔτι> ὄντι (Rutherford).

4.94.1 Reading ἄοπλοί τε <οἱ> πολλοὶ (Krüger).

4.96.3 Reading κυκλωθέντων <αὐτῶν> (Gomme).

4.98.2 Reading πρὸ τοῦ (Stahl), not πρὸς τοῖς.

4.102.4 Retaining διὰ τὸ περιέχειν αὐτήν, which OCT after Dobree deletes.

4.108.1 Deleting with OCT (after Kistemaker) ἐνόμιζεν.

4.108.4 Reading ἐψευσμένοι (with one MS), not ἐψευσμένοις.

4.113.1 Reading ταὐτά (Classen), not ταῦτα.

4.117.2 Reading ἕως ὅτε (schol. on Ar., *Pax* 479), not ὡς ἔτι; but the text and the sense are difficult, and there may be wider corruption (possibly some words have dropped out: Steup).

4.118.5 Deleting τάλαντα (Wallinga), which OCT retains.

4.118.10 Reading ἐκελεύετε (Kirchhoff), not κελεύετε.

4.118.11 Reading ἔδοξεν <τῇ βουλῇ καὶ> τῷ δήμῳ (Gomme).

4.118.14 We follow Kirchhoff in supposing that some words have dropped out between εἰρήνης and βουλεύσασθαι. The translation supplies what is likely to have been the sense of the missing words.
Reading εἴπῃ (Gomme), not ἐσίη.

4.119.1 Deleting with OCT (after Kirchhoff) καὶ ὤμοσαν.

4.120.1 The MSS reading ἐπήρχοντο, retained by OCT, is probably corrupt (Gomme), but the required sense is clear.

4.123.2 Deleting καὶ before καταβιασαμένων (Classen), which OCT retains.

4.124.1 Reading αὑτοῦ (Poppo), not αὐτοῦ.

4.129.3 ξύμπαντες [δὲ] (deletion by OCT after Krüger) ἑπτακόσιοι ὁπλῖται is probably corrupt: the numeral is suspect (too few), and there may be a lacuna in which a number was given for light-armed troops also.

5.1 Reading διεγένοντο (Canfora), not διελέλυντο.

5.5.2 Deleting τοῖς before κομιζομένοις (Dobree), which OCT retains.

5.7.3 Reading περιμένειν (Marshall), not περιέμενεν.

5.15.1 OCT marks ὁμοίως as corrupt, but the general sense is clear.

5.15.2 Reading οὔπω (with some MSS), not οὔπως.

5.16.1 Reading οἱ ἐν ἑκατέρᾳ (with some MSS), not ἑκατέρᾳ.

5.18.5 With Steup reading τάσ<δε> δὲ πόλεις, not τὰς δὲ πόλεις, and punctuating with a full point after ἔχοντας and a colon after εἶναι, not a colon after ἔχοντας and a full point after εἶναι.

5.19.2 Reading (with the MSS) Θεογένης, not Θεαγένης (cf. 4.27.3); also in 5.24.1 (where the MSS have Θεαγένης).

5.20.1 Deleting ἡ ἐσβολὴ ἡ ἐς τὴν Ἀττικὴν καὶ (Müller), which OCT retains.

5.22.1 Reading αὖθις (Lloyd-Jones), not αὐτοί.

5.22.2 Reading Ἀργείους <ἐπιέναι> . . . <καὶ> [νομίσαντες] (Gomme), where OCT retains the MSS text.

5.23.6 Reading ὅτι ἂν δοκῇ ἀμφοτέροις, εὔορκον εἶναι (Herwerden), not ὅτι ἂν δοκῇ, εὔορκον ἀμφοτέροις εἶναι.

5.31.2 Reading καταλυσάντων (Krüger), not καὶ λυσάντων.

5.31.6 Reading <τὰ> ἀπὸ τῶν Λακεδαιμονίων (Haase), not ὑπὸ τῶν Λακεδαιμονίων (which seems, wrongly, to take περιορώμενοι as passive).

5.35.1 Reading ἐν τῇ Ἀθωΐδι Ἀκτῇ Διῆς (Meineke), not ἐν τῇ Ἄθω Ἀκτῇ Διῆς (OCT after Didot) or ἐν τῇ Ἄθῳ Δικτηδιῆς or variations (MSS).

5.36.1 Reading παραινοῦντες ὅτι μάλιστα ταῦτά (Reiske) τε γιγνώσκειν καὶ πειρᾶσθαι Βοιωτοὺς <πείθειν> (Hude) . . . αὖθις μετὰ Κορινθίων (Ullrich) . . . no parentheses . . . ἡγουμένους (some MSS), not ταῦτα . . . μετὰ Βοιωτῶν . . . , then οὕτω . . . γενέσθαι in parentheses, then ἡγούμενοι (OCT with most MSS).

5.38.3 Reading μετ᾽ αὐτῶν Λακεδαιμονίων (Stahl), not μετὰ τῶν Λακεδαιμονίων.

5.40.2 Retaining with OCT καθελεῖν, not παραδοῦναι (Gomme).

5.42.1 Reading Ἀνδρομέδης (with most MSS) and Ἀνδρομέδην (with some MSS), not Ἀνδρομένης . . . Ἀνδρομένη.

5.46.5 Ending the parenthesis at Ἀλκιβιάδου (Steup), not at ξύμμαχοι.

5.47.7 Reading αὐτῆς (Duker), not αὐτῆς (OCT) or αὐτῇ (MSS).

5.49.3 Reading παρ᾽ αὐτοῖς (printed without comment by many editors), not παρ᾽ αὑτοῖς.

5.53 Retaining with OCT βοταμίων (παραποταμίων some MSS): see Explanatory Note.

5.55.1 Reading ἐφ᾽ ἑκατέρων (correction in one MS), not ἀφ᾽ ἑκατέρων.

5.55.4 Reading στρατηγός, πυθόμενοι (with one MS) [δὲ] (Portus) . . . ἀπῆλθον (most MSS), not στρατηγός· πυθόμενος (most MSS) δὲ . . . ἀπῆλθεν (some MSS).

5.58.4 Reading ὄρθριον (with most MSS), not ὄρθιον.

5.62.2 Reading αὐτῶν Τεγεατῶν (with the MSS), not αὐτῶν τῶν (OCT after Stahl).

5.63.4 Reading ἐκ τῆς πολεμίας (Haase), not ἐκ τῆς πόλεως: see Explanatory Note.

5.65.4 Retaining τοὺς Ἀργείους καὶ τοὺς ξυμμάχους, which OCT after Haacke deletes.

5.66.2 Punctuating with a colon after ἐξεπλάγησαν and a full point after ἐγίγνετο (Andrewes), not a full point after ἐξεπλάγησαν and a comma after ἐγίγνετο.

5.76.1 Retaining with OCT ἐπειδὴ τὰ Κάρνεια ἤγαγον (deleted Krüger, perhaps correctly: see Explanatory Note).

5.77, 79 The text of the treaties in these two chapters is given in the Laconian dialect. Dialect being particularly liable to corruption, there are several uncertainties of text and meaning: we have followed OCT except at 5.79.4, where we read διακριθῆμεν <ἇδε>· αἰ [δέ] τις . . . (Dover ap. Andrewes), not διακριθῆμεν. αἰ δέ τις . . .

5.83.4 OCT marks ἀπάραντος as corrupt: the sense required is clear, and among the suggested emendations Andrewes cites ἀποστάντος (Poppo).

5.110.2 Deleting καὶ before γῆς (Duker), which OCT retains.

6.2.3 Retaining with OCT Φωκέων (Φρυγῶν Ridgeway, perhaps correctly; Φωκαιῶν Pais, cf. 5.4.4): see Explanatory Note.

6.4.1 Retaining with OCT προδόντος (παραδόντος Classen, and perhaps a sign of disturbance in one MS).

6.4.2 Reading Πάμμιλον (with some MSS: cf. Hdn. 1.162), not Πάμιλλον, retained by OCT, *LGPN* iii.A and Hornblower (who remarks that Πάμμιλον may be the correct form of the name but the text here should not be emended). Myscus or Euthydemus should be inserted as the subject of ξυγκατῴκισεν (Hornblower, cf. *SEG* xliii 630): see Explanatory Note.

6.6.1 Reading προγεγενημένοις (with some MSS), not προσγεγενημένοις.

6.9.2 Reading νῦν ἄλλα ἢ ἂν (Stahl after Valla), not νῦν, ἀλλὰ ἢ ἂν.

6.11.4 Retaining the MSS order (OCT after Rauchenstein places εἰ δὲ σφαλείημέν . . . ἐνθάδε ἐπιθοῖντο after . . . τῆς δόξης δόντα): see Explanatory Note.

6.12.1 Omitting εἶναι after ἐνθάδε (with one MS), which OCT retains.

6.15.4 Reading διαθέντος (correction in one MS, cf. Herwerden), not διαθέντι (OCT with correction in one MS) or διαθέντα (MSS).

6.25.2 Reading αὐτῶν Ἀθηναίων (ὧν ἔσεσθαι . . . δοκῶσι), καὶ ἄλλας . . . εἶναι (correction in one MS), not (αὐτῶν δ᾽ Ἀθηναίων ἔσεσθαι . . . εἶναι).

6.26.1 Retaining Ἀθηναίοις, which OCT deletes.

6.31.1 Punctuating with comma after τῇ ὄψει (Dover), not after ἑώρων. Reading αὕτη <ἡ> πρώτη (Dobree).

6.38.4 Reading πειθὼν τοὺς [δὲ] τὰ τοιαῦτα μηχανομένους κολάζειν (Weil), not πειθών, τοὺς δὲ . . . κολάζων.

6.39.2 Reading εἰ <γὰρ> μὴ μανθάνετε (Gomme).

6.40.1 Reading ὧνπερ (Dover after a scholiast) τὸ τῆς πόλεως πλῆθος, not ἥπερ τὸ τῆς πόλεως πλῆθος, which OCT after Krüger deletes.

6.49.4 Reading ἐφορμισθέντας (Schaefer) or ἐφόρμησιν τὰ (Böhme), not ἐφορμηθέντας.

6.54.5 Reading ἐπαχθεῖς ἦσαν . . . κατεστήσαντο (Hude), not ἐπαχθὴς ἦν . . . κατεστήσατο.

6.62.5 Reading περιέπεμψαν (correction in one MS), not περιέπλευσαν.

6.69.3 Reading ξυγκαταστρεψάμενοι . . . ὑπακούσονται (correction in one MS), not ξυγκαταστρεψανένοις . . . ὑπακούσεται.

6.82.2 Reading [καὶ] παροικοῦντες (Classen), not καὶ παροικοῦσιν.

6.87.4 Reading ἀδεὲς (Reiske), not ἀδεεῖ (OCT after Krüger) or ἀδεεῖς (MSS).

6.88.4 Reading οὐ πολλοὶ (Canter), not οἱ πολλοί.

6.88.6 Reading πλινθεῖα (Dover after a scholiast), not πλινθία.

6.89.6 Reading ὅσῳ καὶ μέγιστα ἠδίκημαι, λοιδορήσαιμι (Stephanus after a scholiast and Valla), not ὅσῳ καὶ λοιδορήσαιμι.

6.97.1 Reading νυκτὸς <ᾗ> (Madvig) τῇ ἐπιγιγνομένῃ ἡμέρᾳ ἐξητάζοντο ἐκεῖνοι (Classen), not νυκτὸς τῇ . . . ἐξητάζοντο καί.

6.100.1 Reading πυραμίδα (with two MSS), not πυλίδα.

6.101.1 Reading <πρὸς> τὸν κρημνὸν (Stahl).

6.104.2 Retaining with OCT καὶ τὴν τοῦ πατρὸς ἀνανεωσάμενος πολιτείαν (one MS and Valla), not κατὰ τὴν τοῦ πατρός ποτε πολιτείαν (most MSS).

7.1.3 Reading στρατιᾷ (with most MSS), not πανστρατιᾷ.

7.2.4 Deleting τοῦ κύκλου (Dover), which OCT retains.

7.7.1 Deleting μέχρι (Dover), which OCT retains.

7.7.3 Reading ὁπωσοῦν (Hude), not ὅπως ἂν.

7.13.2 Retaining τῶν ναυτῶν τῶν μὲν, where OCT after Poppo deletes the second τῶν.

7.21.3 Retaining αὐτοῖς before φαίνεσθαι, which OCT after Badham deletes.

7.22.1 Reading παρεσκεύαστο (with some MSS), not παρεσκευάσατο.

7.27.4 Retaining with OCT ἐξ ἀνάγκης τῆς ἴσης φρουρᾶς καταθεούσης τὴν χώραν, but it is probably corrupt: see Explanatory Note.

7.27.5 Reading τούτων πολὺ μέρος (with most MSS), not τούτων τὸ πολὺ μέρος.

7.28.2 Reading που (with one MS), not ποιούμενοι, which OCT marks as corrupt.

7.32.2 Reading ἑνός του Κορινθίου (Herwerden), not ἑνὸς τοῦ Κορινθίου.

7.48.6 Reading ᾧ (correction in one MS), not ὦν.

7.49.2 Reading τρίβειν αὐτούς (with the MSS), not τρίβειν αὐτοῦ (OCT after Krüger).

7.57.5 Reading καὶ ἄντικρυς (Böhme), not καταντικρὺ.

7.70.7 Punctuating with comma after ποτε, not after αὖθις.

7.75.4 Reading πολλῶν ἐπιθειασμῶν (Poppo, cf. Valla), not ὀλίγων ἐπιθειασμῶν.

7.76 Reading ἀεί τι μᾶλλον (Weidgen), not ἔτι μᾶλλον.

8.10.1 Reading ἐπηγγέλθησαν γὰρ αἱ σπονδαί (with one MS and a papyrus, cf. Valla), not just ἐπηγγέλθησαν γάρ.

8.18.3 Reading ἔστωσαν twice (with the MSS), not ὄντων (OCT after Tucker).

8.19.2 Deleting καὶ before ὅτι Ἀμόργης (Poppo after Valla).

8.19.4, 20.2 Reading Αἱρᾶς, Αἱρᾶς (Rubinstein), not Αἱρᾶς, Αἱρᾶς (OCT after Hude); the MSS have ερας vel sim.

8.22.1 Reading πλήθει παρόντων (Wilamowitz), not πλήθει παρόντες.

8.23.4 Reading ἀποστήσας, καὶ τοὺς . . . νεῶν ὁπλίσας (Powell, cf. a papyrus), not ἀποστήσας καὶ ὁπλίσας, καὶ τοὺς . . . νεῶν ὁπλίτας.

8.27.2 Retaining ἔξεστιν, which OCT after Dobree deletes.

8.38.3 Reading ἐς ὀλίγον (with the MSS), not ἐς ὀλίγους (OCT after Dobree).

8.39.3 Reading προσέβαλλον (with one MS), not προσέβαλον.
Reading τῆς Καρίας (Wilamowitz, cf. Valla), not τῆς Ἀσίας.

8.43.3 Reading ἐνεῖναι (OCT after Bekker), not ἐνῆν (MSS): see Explanatory Notes.

8.44.4 Retaining with OCT ὀγδοήκοντα, not πεντήκοντα (Wilamowitz at one time) or τεσσαράκοντα (Pritchett): see Explanatory Note.

8.45.3 Reading στρατηγὸς ὢν (with one MS) after Ἑρμοκράτης.

8.46.3 Retaining with most MSS (cf. Valla) τῶν βαρβάρων, which OCT deletes.
Reading πη before ἐξέλωσι (Goodhart and Tucker), not μὴ.

8.53.1 Retaining with the MSS καὶ before ἀφικόμενοι, which OCT deletes.

8.56.4 (OCT, but most edd. begin a new §5 here) Reading with one MS ἐνταῦθα δὴ οὐκέτι, ἀλλ' ἄπορα, where after οὐκέτι most MSS add τι and OCT marks a lacuna.

8.68.2 Omitting with some MSS μετέστη . . . κατέστη, which OCT retains but marks as corrupt, suspecting that alternative versions of the text have been conflated.

8.73.4 and subsequently Reading the correct Θράσυλλος / -ον / -ῳ (Stahl, with one MS in every instance except this first), not Θράσυλος / -ον / -ῳ.

8.77 Retaining οἱ δέκα πρεσβευταί, which OCT after Herwerden deletes (cf. 8.86.1).

8.82.1 Deleting τε before παρόντας (Goodhart).

8.86.1 Retaining πρεσβευταί, which OCT after Herwerden deletes (cf. 8.77).

8.86.9 Retaining with one MS πεμπτοὺς, not πέμπουσι, which OCT after Bekker reads and deletes.

8.89.2 Reading στρατηγούντων (Bergk), not στρατηγῶν τῶν, of which OCT after Classen deletes στρατηγῶν, and Reeve ap. Andrewes further deletes τῶν.
Deleting with OCT and some MSS ἔπεμπον after πρεσβευομένους.
Reading ᾤοντο (Delebecque) ἀπαλλαξείειν (Abresch), not οὐ τὸ ἀπαλλάξειν (MSS): OCT prints οὐ τὸ †ἀπαλλαξείειν, but the obelus ought rather to have been attached to οὐ τὸ (cf. Andrewes).

8.92.6 Retaining with OCT πλὴν before ὅσοις, which Haase deleted and a papyrus omits: see Explanatory Note.

8.94.1 Retaining ἐν Διονύσου, which OCT after Goodhart deletes.
Reading with Arnold and one MS πᾶς τις τῶν πολλῶν, where other MSS add ὁπλιτῶν after πολλῶν, and OCT after Stahl deletes τῶν πολλῶν ὁπλιτῶν.

8.99.1 Retaining ὅτε ἐπὶ τὴν Ἄσπενδον παρῄει, which OCT after Hude deletes.

8.100.5 Reading with one MS καὶ αἱ Μηθυμναῖαι, where OCT reads καὶ Μηθυμναῖαι (most MSS) <πέντε> (Dobree).

8.109.2 Bracketing as an interpolation with OCT ὅταν ὁ μετὰ τοῦτο . . . ἔτος πληροῦται (which one MS omits): see Explanatory Note.

INDEX

References are to Book and chapter (e.g. 2.68 refers to Book 2, chapter 68): the chapters are indicated in the text by marginal numbers.

Where relevant, the entry for a place or a country should be understood to include the inhabitants of that place or country. Actions taken by 'the Peloponnesians' are indexed under 'Sparta/Spartans' when the Spartans are also involved.

The headings of the more important entries are given in bold capitals, and references of particular relevance or importance are printed in bold. Where a date is given in bold, it has continued application until the next indication of date in that entry or paragraph. All dates are BC. (Dates from 431 on given in the form, e.g., '428/7' denote the winter season, late 428 to early 427: '428' denotes the summer season of 428.) The headings of a number of general topics are given in italics.

For the most part, this index does not include the names of fathers, or of those recorded as swearing to treaties or alliances, unless they recur in another context.

Abdera, city in Thrace 2.29, 2.97

Abydos, city on Hellespont: Milesian colony 8.61; (411) revolts from Athens 8.61-2, (8.79); Peloponnesian ships at Abydos 8.102 (cf. 8.99), joined by entire fleet, 8.103; 8.104, 8.106, 8.108

Acamantis, Athenian tribe 4.118

Acanthus, city in Chalcidice: Andrian colony 4.84; (424) won over by Brasidas and secedes from Athens 4.84-8; 4.114, 4.120; (423) in Brasidas' army 4.124; (422/1) provision in Peace of Nicias 5.18

Acarnan, son of Alcmeon, legendary eponym of Acarnania 2.102

ACARNANIA 2.68, 2.80-3, 3.7, 3.106; story of Alcmeon and his son Acarnan 2.102; maintain the old ways 1.5; expert slingers 2.81 (cf. 7.31); mostly allies of Athens 2.9, 7.57; Oeniadae only city constantly hostile to Athens 1.111, 2.102, 3.7 (cf. 3.94) —(454) Athenian attack on Oeniadae 1.111; (?early 430s) with Amphilochians and Phormio defeat Ambraciots in Argos, make alliance with Athens 2.68; (431) envoys from Athens at start of war 2.7; (431) Athenians capture Sollium and Astacus, driving out tyrant Evarchus 2.30; (431/0) Corinthian expedition restores Evarchus 2.33;

(429) Ambraciot and Spartan campaign against Acarnania 2.80-3; (429/8) Phormio in Acarnania 2.102-3; (428) campaign with Asopius (2) against Oeniadae 3.7; (426) attack Leucas with Athenians under Demosthenes 3.94-5; send help to Naupactus 3.102; (426/5) invite Demosthenes to lead them against Ambraciots and Peloponnesians 3.105-14; fear Athenians as neighbours more than Ambraciots 3.113; defensive alliance with Ambracia 3.114; (425) Anactorium betrayed, and settled by Acarnanians 4.49; (424) compel Oeniadae into Athenian alliance 4.77; Demosthenes raises forces from Acarnania for Boeotian expedition 4.77, 4.89, 4.101; (413) forces raised by Demosthenes for war in Sicily 7.31, 7.57 (their loyalty to him), 7.60, 7.67 —and Ambracia 2.80-2, 3.102, 3.105-14 and Phormio 2.68, 2.81, 2.102-3, 3.7 and Demosthenes 3.94-5, 3.102, 3.105, 7.57

Acesines, river in Sicily 4.25

Achaea 1.111, 1.115, 2.83, 2.84, 4.21, 5.82, 7.34; colonized Zacynthus 2.66; neutral at start of war 2.9; excluded from Spartan colony at Heracleia 3.92

Achaeans, Homeric name for
Greeks 1.3, 4.120, 6.2
Achaea Phthiotis, dependency of
Thessaly 4.78; (413/2) forced
by Agis to give money and
hostages 8.3
Acharnae, largest of Attic demes 2.19–23
Achelous, river in W. Greece 2.102,
3.7, 3.106
Acheron, river in Thesprotia 1.46
Acherousian lake, in Thesprotia 1.46
Achilles 1.3
Acrae, city in Sicily: founded by
Syracusans 6.5
Acraean Rock, near Syracuse 7.78
Acragas (1), city in Sicily: founded
from Gela 6.4; (422) won over by
Phaeax 5.4; neutral in Sicilian
war 7.32–3, 7.58; (413) Syracusan
mission to win it over 7.46, 7.50
(pro-Syracusan faction expelled)
Acragas (2), river in Sicily 6.4
ACROPOLIS of Athens: site of
original settlement, still called
Polis 2.15; seized by Cylon 1.126;
Athenian treasury 2.13, 2.24; expen-
diture on Propylaea and other
buildings of, 2.13; gold-clad statue of
Athena 2.13; temple of Athena 2.15,
5.23; kept free of occupation in influx
of population from the country 2.17;
pillars of record set up on, 5.18, 5.23,
5.47, 5.56, 6.55
Acrothooe, city on Acte peninsula 4.109
Actaean cities, on mainland of Asia from
Antandrus to Hellespont 4.52
Acte, peninsula of Chalcidice 4.109,
5.35; canal dug by Xerxes 4.109
Actium, city at mouth of Ambracian
Gulf 1.29, 1.30
Admetus, king of the Molossians: and
Themistocles 1.136–7
Aeantides, son of Hippoclus,
married to Hippias' daughter 6.59
Aegaleos, mountain in Attica 2.19
Aegean Sea 1.98, 4.109
AEGINA, island in Saronic Gulf:
early fleet of penteconters 1.14;
(c.505–483/2) war with Athens 1.14,
1.41; helped Sparta in Helot
revolt 2.27, 4.56; (460–459) defeated
by Athenians in sea-battle and
besieged 1.105; capitulate and tribute
imposed (c.457) 1.108, 3.64; (432)
instigate war, complaining of lost
autonomy 1.67, 1.139, 1.140,
2.27; (431) expelled by
Athenians, Aegina occupied by
Athenian settlers 2.27; offered home
in Thyrea by Spartans 2.27, 4.56–7;
(424) Thyrea captured by Athenians
and Aeginetans executed 4.57;
(411) raided by Peloponnesian
fleet 8.92; Aeginetan coinage
5.47; 2.31, 3.72, 5.53, 6.32, 7.20, 7.26
—Athenian settlers: 2.27; in battle of
Mantinea (418) 5.74; at Syracuse
7.57; supporting Four Hundred
(411) 8.69
Aegitium, town in Aetolia 3.97
Aenesias, Spartan ephor 2.2
Aenianes, tribe neighbouring Heracleia
(1) 5.51
Aenus, city in Thrace: Boeotian
colony 7.57; (425) sends peltasts in
support of Athens 4.28; subject ally of
Athens, with Athenians at
Syracuse 7.57
Aeolians, racial subdivision of
Greeks: original inhabitants of
Corinth 4.42
—Aeolian countries and
cities: 'Actaean cities' from Antandrus
to Hellespont 4.52; Aenus 7.57;
Antandrus 8.108; Boeotia, Lesbos
7.57 (cf. 3.2, 8.5); Cyme 3.31;
Tenedos 7.57
Aeolis (1), region of Asia Minor 3.31
Aeolis (2), region of Greece to W. of
Ozolian Locris 3.102
Aeolus, islands of: colonized from
Cnidus 3.88; (427/6) allied with
Syracuse, attacked by Athenians and
Rhegians 3.88; (426/5) attacked
again by Athenians 3.115
Aerae, city in Ionia: (412) revolts
from Athens 8.19, 8.20
Aesimides, Corcyraean commander 1.47
Aeson, Argive envoy to
Sparta (420) 5.40
Aethaea, district of Messenia 1.101
Aetna, volcano in Sicily 3.116
Aetolia 3.94–8; maintain the old
ways 1.5; Aetolian arms and
tactics 3.94, 3.95, 3.97–8; hostile to
Naupactus 3.94, 3.100; (426) defeat

Athenian expedition under Demosthenes 3.94–8, 4.30; persuade Sparta and Corinth to attack Naupactus 3.100, and give support 3.102; (413) Aetolian mercenaries with Athenians in Sicily 7.57

Agamemnon 1.9–10

Agatharchidas, Corinthian general 2.83

Agatharchus, Syracusan commander 7.25, 7.70

Agesandridas, Spartan commander 8.91, 8.94–5

Agesandrus: father of Agesandridas 8.91; Spartan ambassador (432) 1.139

Agesippidas, Spartan governor of Heracleia (1), dismissed by Boeotians (419) 5.52; in command of garrison for Epidaurus 5.56

AGIS, son of Archidamus, king of Sparta: (426) leads aborted (earthquake) invasion of Attica 3.89; leads invasion of 425: 4.2, 4.5–6; (422/1) signatory of Peace of Nicias and alliance 5.19, 5.24; (419) leads aborted (unfavourable sacrifices) expedition 5.54; (418) leads expedition against Argos 5.57–60; criticized by allies and Spartans for accepting treaty with Argives and withdrawing 5.60, 5.63, 5.65; punishment proposed and deferred, commission of Spartiate advisers appointed 5.63; in command at battle of Mantinea 5.65–6, 5.71–3; (417/6) leads Peloponnesian expedition against Argos 5.83; (413) leads invasion of Attica and fortification of Deceleia 7.19; (413 on) presence at Deceleia 7.27, 8.3, 8.5; his powers and authority there 8.5, cf. 8.7–9; (413/2) collects money for fleet from allies 8.3; approached by Euboea and Lesbos for help in revolting from Athens 8.5, cf. 8.7; (412) sends Thermon to Peloponnesian fleet blockaded in Speiraeum 8.11; (411) approached by Four Hundred, and takes troops to the walls of Athens 8.70–1
— hostility between Agis and Alcibiades 8.12, 8.45

Agraeis, region of Aetolia 2.102, 3.106 (friendly to Peloponnesians, 426/5), 3.111, 3.113–4, 4.77 (won over by Demosthenes, 424), 4.101

Agrianians, Paeonian tribe 2.96

Alcaeus, Athenian archon at time of Peace of Nicias (422/1) 5.19, 5.25

Alcamenes, son of Sthenelaïdas (8.5), Spartan commander 8.5, 8.8, 8.10, 8.11; (412) killed in battle at Speiraeum 8.10

ALCIBIADES (1), son of Cleinias (5.43 etc.): Laconian name 8.6; Olympic victor 6.16; his family consular representatives for Sparta 5.43, 6.89; guest-friendship with Spartan ephor Endius 8.6, cf. 8.12, 8.17
— ambition 6.15–16; independent/private action 5.43, 5.45; character 5.43, 6.12 (Nicias), **6.15**, 8.48 (Phrynichus), 8.86; diplomacy 5.43–8, 6.16–17, 6.29, 6.61, cf. 6.88–9; suspected of plot to subvert democracy 6.28, 6.60–1; indirect responsibility for defeat of Athens 6.15; on empire 6.17–18; on democracy 6.89, 8.47
— speeches: (415) in assembly debating Sicilian expedition 6.16–18; (415/4) at Sparta 6.89–92; (411) at assembly in Samos (reported) 8.81
— hostility of and to Nicias 5.43, 5.45, 6.12–13, 6.15–16; Agis 8.12, 8.45; Phrynichus 8.48, 8.51, 8.54, 8.68, 8.90; enemies of Alcibiades at Athens 6.28–9, 6.61, 8.53
— in Athens: took care of Spartan prisoners from Sphacteria 5.43, 6.89; (422/1) opposition to Peace of Nicias, and motives 5.43, 6.89; (420) engineers Athenian alliance with Argos 5.43–8, cf. 6.88–9; (420/19) Athenian general, expedition to Peloponnese with Argives and allies 5.52; with Argives, intent on bringing Epidaurus into the alliance 5.53, 5.55; (419/8) persuades Athenians to add rider to record of treaty with Sparta 5.56; (418) ambassador with Athenian force sent to support Argos, argues for prosecution of war 5.61; (418/7) in Argos when peace with Sparta debated 5.76; (416) arrests Spartan sympathizers in Argos 5.84; **(415)** appointed to Sicilian command 6.8; speech in assembly advocating

Sicilian expedition, 6.16–18; alleged
profanation of Mysteries 6.28–9, 8.53
—in Sicily: **(415)** at conference of
generals at Rhegium 6.48, 6.50; fails to
win over Messana 6.48, 6.50; in
assembly at Catana 6.51; summoned
home from Sicily to answer charges
(6.29), 6.53, 6.61; leaves escort of
Salaminia at Thurii, and finds passage
to Peloponnese 6.61, 6.88; had
divulged Athenian plans to pro-
Syracusans in Messana 6.74;
condemned to death in his absence 6.61
—in Sparta: (415/4) speech in
Spartan assembly 6.89–92; on
Athenian intentions in Sicilian
expedition and ultimate ambitions
6.90; advises building of fort
at Deceleia 6.91, 7.18; apologia for
turning against Athens, and offers
his services to Sparta 6.92; **(413/2)**
supports request for help from Chios
and Tissaphernes 8.6, 8.12; **(412)**
with Chalcideus in Spartan naval
expedition to Chios and Ionia 8.11–12,
8.14, 8.17; confident of his ability
to persuade revolt in Ionia 8.12;
with Chalcideus secures revolts
of Chios 8.14, Erythrae 8.14,
Clazomenae 8.14, Teos 8.16,
Miletus 8.17 (friendly with leading
men there); fought at battle of
Miletus, meets Peloponnesian
reinforcing fleet and urges relief of
Miletus 8.26; **(412/1)** Spartan
suspicion, letter to Astyochus
ordering his death 8.45
—in Asia: **(412/1)** takes refuge
with Tissaphernes and advises on
measures against Peloponnesian
interest 8.45–6; working for return
to Athens 8.47, 8.48; discussion
with oligarchic plotters from
Samos 8.48; outwitted by
Phrynichus 8.50–1; ensures
failure of Athenian negotiations with
Tissaphernes 8.56; **(411)** excluded
from oligarchic plot 8.63
—in Samos: **(411)** recalled, with
immunity, to Samos 8.81; presentation
at assembly in Samos, and his
motives 8.81–2; elected general by
Athenians in Samos 8.82; forbids
immediate sailing for Peiraeus

8.82; at assembly restrains inclination
to attack Peiraeus, and answers
emissaries of Four Hundred and envoys
from Argos 8.86, 8.89, cf. 8.90; sets
out for Aspendus, promising to deal
with the Phoenician ships 8.88;
returns 8.108; exacts money from
Halicarnassus and fortifies Cos,
installing governor 8.108; **(411)**
Athenian assembly votes to recall
Alcibiades and other exiles, 8.97
—and Tissaphernes 8.6, 8.26,
8.45–7, 8.52, 8.56, 8.65, 8.81, 8.82,
8.85, 8.88, 8.108
—alleged influence with Tissaphernes
8.47, 8.48, 8.56, 8.65, 8.81, 8.82, 8.108
—question of his recall 8.47–50,
8.53–4, 8.65, 8.70, 8.76, 8.81, 8.97
Alcibiades (2), father of Endius 8.6
ALCIDAS, Spartan admiral-in-
chief: **(427)** appointed 3.16, 3.26;
dilatory in expedition to Mytilene, and
returns to Peloponnese 3.27, 3.29–33;
rejects advice of Teutiaplus and
others 3.30–1; slaughters prisoners
3.32; chased by Paches 3.33, 3.69;
joined by Brasidas as 'commissioner' at
Cyllene 3.69; commander of expedition
to Corcyra 3.76–81; pulls rank on
Brasidas 3.79; retreats on news of
Athenian reinforcements 3.81; **(426)**
founder-colonist of Heracleia (1) 3.92
Alcinous, sanctuary in Corcyra 3.70
Alciphron, consular representative for
Sparta in Argos 5.59
Alcisthenes, father of
Demosthenes: 3.91 etc.
Alcmeon, son of Amphiaraus, father
of Acarnan, legendary founder
of Acarnania 2.102
Alcmeonidae, Athenian clan,
instrumental in deposition of
tyrant Hippias 6.59
Alex, river in territory of Locri 3.99
Alexander, king of Macedonia, father
of Perdiccas 1.57, 1.137, 2.29;
establishment of kingdom by
Alexander and his forebears 2.99
Alexarchus, Corinthian commander of
troops sent to Sicily (413) 7.19
Alexicles, general in oligarchy at
Athens: **(411)** kidnapped by hoplites
in Peiraeus, and released 8.92–3;
escapes to Deceleia 8.98

Alexippidas, Spartan ephor 8.58

Alicyae, Sicel town 7.32

Almopia, district of Macedonia 2.99

Alope, in Opuntian Locris 2.26

Alyzia, in Acarnania 7.31

AMBRACIA 2.68, 2.80–2; Corinthian colony 2.80, 7.58; ship-providing ally of Sparta 2.9, 2.80, 3.69, 8.106; (435–433) support Corinth at Epidamnus and Corcyra 1.26, 1.27, 1.46, 1.48; (430) campaign against Amphilochian Argos, and reason for hostility 2.68; (429) campaign against Acarnania, with Chaonians and Spartan force 2.80–2; (426) persuade Spartans to join campaign against Amphilochia and Acarnania 3.102, 3.105–14; scale of the disaster at Idomene 3.113; (426/5) defensive alliance with Acarnania and Amphilochia, 3.114; Corinthian garrison installed 3.114; (414) three Ambraciot ships to accompany Corinthians to Italy/Sicily 6.104, 7.7, 7.58; (411) lose two ships at Cynossema 8.106
— Ambracian Gulf 1.29, 1.55, 2.68, 3.107, 4.49

Ameiniades, Athenian envoy to Sitalces (430) 2.67

Ameinias, Spartan commander 4.132

Ameinocles, Corinthian shipbuilder 1.13

Ammeas, Plataean, leader of scaling party 3.22

Amorges, bastard son of Pissouthnes, in revolt from King of Persia 8.5, 8.19, 8.28; (412) captured in sack of Iasus 8.28, 8.54

Ampelidas, Spartan envoy to Argos (422/1) 5.22

Amphiaraus: father of Amphilochus 2.68; father of Alcmeon 2.102

AMPHILOCHIA 2.68; legendary foundation by Amphilochus, 2.68; Amphilochians, other than those in Argos, barbarians 2.68, 3.112; history of Ambraciot hostility 2.68; (430) Ambraciot campaign against Amphilochian Argos 2.68; (426/5) Ambraciot and Spartan campaign against Amphilochia and Argos 3.102, 3.105–14; fear Athenians as neighbours more than

Ambraciots 3.113; defensive alliance with Ambracia 3.114

Amphilochus, son of Amphiaraus, legendary founder of Amphilochian Argos 2.68

AMPHIPOLIS, city in Thrace on river Strymon 4.102–9, 5.6–11; site originally called Nine Ways 1.100, 4.102; history of its colonization 4.102; renamed Amphipolis by Hagnon 4.102; value to Athens 4.108; (424/3) surrenders to Brasidas, and Thucydides fails to save it 4.103–8, cf. 5.26; (423) Clearidas appointed Spartan governor 4.132; (422) battle for Amphipolis between Athenians under Cleon and Brasidas' army 5.6–11; funeral and honours for Brasidas (adopted as founder of the city), buildings and memorials in honour of Hagnon demolished 5.11; (422/1) restoration to Athens specified in Peace of Nicias 5.18, refused by Clearidas 5.21, 5.35, 5.46; (417) Athenian expedition against Amphipolis under Nicias aborted 5.83; (414) with Perdiccas and Thracians, Athenians attack Amphipolis and attempt siege 7.9
— Thracian gates 5.10; temple of Athena 5.10

Amphissa, in Ozolian Locris: (426) cooperate with Spartan expedition to Naupactus 3.101

Amyclae, in Laconia: temple of Apollo (Amyclaeum) 5.18, 5.23

Amyntas, son of Philip: (429/8) Sitalces' attempt to install him as king of Macedonia 2.95, 2.100

Amyrtaeus, king of the marsh people in Egypt 1.110, 1.112

Anaceium, temple of Castor and Pollux in Athens 8.93

Anactorium, city at mouth of Ambracian Gulf, joint Corcyraean and Corinthian foundation (1.55): 1.29, 1.46, 1.55, 5.30, 7.31; ally of Sparta 2.9; (429) provides ships and troops for campaign against Acarnania 2.80–1; hostile to Acarnania 3.114; (425) betrayed to Athenians and Acarnanians, and settled by Acarnanians 4.49

Anaea, on mainland opposite Samos, base of Samian exiles 3.19, 3.32, **4.75**, 8.19, 8.61

Anapus (1), river in Acarnania 2.82

Anapus (2), river near Syracuse 6.66, 6.96, 7.42, 7.78

Anaxandrus, Theban leader of Methymnaean exiles (411) 8.100

Anaxilas, tyrant of Rhegium 6.4

Andocides, Athenian commander 1.51

Androcles, Athenian demagogue, instrumental in banishment of Alcibiades, murdered (411) 8.65

Androcrates, hero with shrine by Plataea-Thebes road 3.24

Andromedes, Spartan envoy (420) 5.42

Andros, Aegean island 2.55, 4.42, 6.96; colonized Acanthus 4.84, Argilus 4.103, Sane 4.109, Stagirus 4.88, 5.6; subject ally of Athens, with Athenians at Syracuse 7.57; some Andrians support Four Hundred (411) 8.69 (cf. 8.65)

Androsthenes, Arcadian Olympic victor 5.49

Aneristus, Spartan ambassador to Persia, executed by Athenians (430) 2.67

Antandrus, Aeolian city on mainland NE of Lesbos 4.52, 4.75; (411) bring hoplites from Abydos and expel Persian garrison 8.108-9

Anthemus, in Macedonia 2.99, 2.100

Anthene, city in Cynouria 5.41

Anthesterion, Attic month 2.15

Anticles, Athenian general 1.117

Antimenidas, Spartan envoy (420) 5.42

Antiochus, king of Orestians 2.80

Antiphemus, Rhodian co-founder of Gela 6.4

Antiphon, architect of oligarchy at Athens (411): his character and quality **8.68**; leading member of extremists among Four Hundred, sent to negotiate peace with Sparta 8.90; his speech in self-defence after fall of Four Hundred 8.68

Antissa, city in Lesbos 3.18, 3.28, 8.23

Antisthenes, Spartan commander 8.39, 8.61

Aphrodite, goddess: sanctuary at Eryx 6.46

Aphroditia, in Laconia 4.56

Aphytis, on Pallene peninsula (Chalcidice) 1.64

Apidanus, river in Thessaly 4.78

Apodotians, division of population of Aetolia 3.94, 3.100

APOLLO, god: Phoebus 3.104; Apollo Archegetes 6.3; Delian Apollo 1.13, 3.104, 4.76, 4.97; Apollo Maloeis 3.3; Pythian Apollo 2.15, 4.118, 6.54; Apollo Pythaeus 5.53 —at Delphi 1.132, 4.118, 5.18; festival at Delos 3.104; festival of Apollo Maloeis at Mytilene 3.3; oracle to Alcmeon 2.102; Homeric Hymn to Apollo quoted 3.104 —temples/sanctuaries: Actium 1.29; Amyclae 5.18, 5.23; Argos 5.47; Apollo Pythaeus at Asine (2)(?) 5.53; Pythian Apollo at Athens 2.15, 6.54; Delium 4.76, 4.97-8; Delphi 4.118, 5.18; Laconia, opposite Cythera 7.26; Leucas 3.94; Naupactus 2.91; altar of Apollo Archegetes at Naxos (2) 6.3; Triopium (Cnidus) 8.35

Apollonia, in Illyria, colony of Corinth 1.26

arbitration 1.28, 1.34, 1.37, 1.39, 1.78, 1.85, 1.140-1, 1.144, 1.145, 4.122, 5.31, 5.41, 5.59, 5.79, 7.18

ARCADIA: stable population 1.2; provided with a fleet by Agamemnon 1.9; Arcadian Olympic victor Androsthenes 5.49; Arcadian mercenaries 3.34, 7.19, 7.57-8 (on both Athenian and Syracusan sides) —war between some Arcadians and the Lepreans 5.31; partly subjected by Mantineans during Archidamian War 5.29, but independence restored to Parrhasia by Spartans (421), 5.33, and all other Mantinean control abandoned in 417/6, 5.81; (418) in Peloponnesian expedition against Argos 5.57-60; Argive alliance attacks and wins Orchomenus 5.61; Arcadian allies of Sparta (5.64, 5.67) and Argos/Athens (5.67) at battle of Mantinea; (413/2) required to build ships for Peloponnesian League 8.3

Arcesilas, father of Lichas: 5.50 etc.

Archedice, daughter of Hippias 6.59

Archegetes: altar of Apollo Archegetes at Naxos in Sicily 6.3

Archelaus, son of Perdiccas, king of Macedonia 2.100

Archestratus, Athenian general 1.57
Archetimus, Corinthian
  commander 1.29
Archias (1), leader of pro-Syracusan
  party in Camarina 4.25
Archias (2), Corinthian founder of
  Syracuse 6.3
ARCHIDAMUS, son of Zeuxidamus
  (2.19 etc.), king of Sparta, father of
  Agis (3.89); guest-friend of Pericles
  2.13; (432) speech at first conference in
  Sparta 1.79–85; his view of Spartan
  character and practice 1.84; (431)
  speech at Isthmus before invasion of
  Attica 2.11; leads 1st Peloponnesian
  invasion of Attica 2.10–13, 2.18–23;
  criticized for delays 2.18; (430) leads
  2nd invasion of Attica 2.47; (429) leads
  campaign against Plataea 2.71–8; (428)
  leads 3rd invasion of Attica 3.1
Archonides, Sicel king 7.1
Arcturus, star 2.78
Argilus, city in Thrace near
  Amphipolis: Andrian colony 4.103;
  1.132; (424/3) welcomes Brasidas,
  defects from Athens, plots surrender of
  Amphipolis 4.103; 5.6; (422/1)
  provision in Peace of Nicias 5.18
Arginoussae, on mainland
  opposite Mytilene 8.101
Arginum, promontory on
  Erythraean peninsula 8.34
Argives, Homeric name for Greeks 1.3
Argos, Agamemnon's kingdom 1.9,
  2.68; the Argives' 'ancient
  hegemony' 5.69
ARGOS: Council, Eighty, Artynae
  5.47; priestesses 2.2, 4.133; select
  regiment of 1,000: 5.67, 5.72–3; Five
  Companies 5.72; temple of Hera,
  burned down 4.133; sanctuary of
  Apollo, 5.47; Charadrus watercourse,
  site of courts martial 5.60; Temenids
  from Argos ancestors of Macedonian
  kings 2.99; Perdiccas' family originally
  from Argos 5.80; Themistocles in
  Argos after ostracism 1.135, 1.137
  —(462/1) alliance with Athens, and
  both with Thessalians 1.102; (?457)
  contingent at battle of Tanagra 1.137; neutral at start of
  Peloponnesian War 2.9, 5.28; (425)
  give Corinth advance notice of

Athenian expedition 4.42; 30–year
  treaty with Sparta, about to expire in
  422/1, and associated Spartan
  fears 5.14, 5.28, 5.40–1 (not
  renewed 5.22)
  —(421) set up defensive alliance
  against Sparta 5.27–32: hoping for
  hegemony in Peloponnese 5.28, 5.32,
  5.40; joined by Mantinea 5.29,
  Elis 5.31, Corinth and Chalcidians
  5.31; Boeotians and Megarians
  wary 5.31–2; Tegea refuses 5.32,
  5.40; (421/0) attempts to involve
  Boeotia 5.36–8; (420) Megarians
  subsequently enthusiastic 5.38; (420)
  alarm at failure to achieve alliance with
  Boeotia, and seek treaty with
  Sparta 5.40–1, 5.44
  —(420) treaty and alliance with
  Athens, Mantinea, and Elis 5.43–8
  (text, 5.47); provide troops to support
  Elean guard at Olympia 5.50; (419)
  expedition of Argive alliance to
  Peloponnese under Alcibiades
  5.52; (419–418) war with Epidaurus 5.26, 5.53–6, 5.57, 5.75, 5.77
  (pretext and motive, 5.53);
  manipulate calendar 5.54; demand
  Athenian retaliation for Spartan
  garrison in Epidaurus 5.56; (418)
  Peloponnesian expedition against
  Argos 5.57–60; withdrawn and
  4–month treaty agreed, Argive resentment at unauthorized treaty 5.59–60,
  5.65; allies persuade Argos to continue
  war: attack on Orchomenus (2) and
  preparations against Tegea 5.61–2;
  battle of Mantinea 5.65–75 (Argive
  losses, 5.74); (418/7) treaty renounced
  by Argives 5.78
  —(418/7) treaty and alliance with
  Sparta 5.76–80 (texts, 5.77,
  5.79): jointly persuade Perdiccas to
  join them, and renew alliance with
  Chalcidians 5.80; (418–417)
  suppression and restoration of
  democracy 5.81–2
  —(417) building of long walls, with
  Athenian help 5.82; (417/6) their
  destruction by the Spartans 5.83;
  invade and ravage Phliasia 5.83; (416)
  invade Phliasia, ambushed 5.115;
  (416/5) destroy Orneae 6.7; (415–413)

Argives in Athenian Sicilian expedition 6.29, 6.43, 6.61, 6.67, 6.68–70,
6.100, 6.101, 7.57 (motives); (414)
abortive Spartan expedition against
Argos: Argos invades Thyrea 6.95;
Spartan invasion of Argolid: Athenians
send ships to assist Argives 6.105, 7.18;
Argives invade and ravage Phliasia 6.105;
(413) Argive hoplites requisitioned by
Athens under terms of alliance 7.20,
7.26; (412) Argive hoplites in Athenian
expedition to Miletus, defeated by
Milesians 8.25; return home in disgust
at their defeat 8.27
—democracy at Argos 5.31, 5.41,
5.44, 5.60, 5.76; enemies of democracy 5.76, 5.78, 5.82–3, 6.61; (418/7)
oligarchy imposed after Argive/Spartan
alliance 5.81; (417) defeat of oligarchs,
and restoration of democracy 5.82;
(416) 300 Spartan sympathizers arrested
by Athenians 5.84 (further arrests
5.116); (415) these hostages handed to
the people of Argos 6.61; (411) Argos
sends envoys offering help to 'the
Athenian people in Samos' 8.86;
envoys sent by Four Hundred to Sparta
handed over to Argives 8.86
Argos, Amphilochian: in legend founded
by Amphilochus, of Peloponnesian
Argos 2.68; (430) Ambraciot
campaign against Argos 2.68;
2.80; (426/5) Ambraciot and Spartan
campaign against Argos and
Amphilochia 3.102, 3.105–14
Arianthidas, Boeotarch from
Thebes 4.91
Aristagoras, of Miletus, attempted
to colonize Nine Ways/Amphipolis
(496/5) 4.102
Aristarchus, one of the extreme oligarchs
in the Four Hundred 8.90, 8.92; (411)
betrays Oenoe to Boeotians 8.98
Aristeides (1), son of Lysimachus
(1.91): (479/8) Athenian delegate to
Sparta with Themistocles 1.91;
(478/7) fixed original level of tribute
for members of Delian League 5.18
Aristeides (2), son of Archippus (4.50),
Athenian general 4.50, 4.75
Aristeus (1), son of Adeimantus,
Corinthian commander 1.60–3,
1.65; (430) Peloponnesian

ambassador to King of Persia,
arrested, executed in Athens 2.67
Aristeus (2), son of Pellichus,
Corinthian commander 1.29
Aristeus (3), Spartan commander 4.132
Aristocles (1), brother of
Pleistoanax 5.16
Aristocles (2), Spartan polemarch
disgraced after battle of Mantinea
(418) 5.71–2
Aristocrates: (422/1) Athenian signatory
of Peace of Nicias and alliance 5.19,
5.24; (412) Athenian general, sent to
Chios 8.9; (411) a leader of the
moderate oligarchs at Athens 8.89, 8.92
Aristogeiton, with Harmodius assassin
of Hipparchus (514) 1.20, 6.53–9
Ariston, Corinthian ship's captain 7.39
Aristonous (1), Thessalian
commander 2.22
Aristonous (2), Geloan
founder-colonist of Acragas 6.4
Aristonymus, Athenian
ambassador 4.122
Aristophon, envoy of Four
Hundred to Sparta (411) 8.86
Aristoteles, Athenian general 3.105
Arnae, in Chalcidice 4.103
Arne, in Thessaly: Boeotians
expelled from Arne 1.12
Arnisa, in Macedonia 4.128
Arrhabaeus, king of Lyncus: hostility
of Perdiccas 4.79, 4.83; (423)
campaign of Perdiccas and
Brasidas against him 4.124–8
Arrhiani, in Chersonese 8.104
Arsaces, Persian, deputy of Tissaphernes:
(411) committed atrocity on Delians in
Atramyttium 8.108
Artabazus, Persian liaising between
Xerxes and Pausanias (1) 1.129, 1.132
Artaphernes, Persian envoy from King to
Sparta, arrested at Eïon (1) and sent to
Athens (425/4) 4.50
Artas, Iapygian dynast, provides
javelin-men for Athenian force in
Sicily (413) 7.33
Artaxerxes, son of Xerxes, father of
Dareius (2) (8.5), King of Persia
(465–424) 1.104; and
Themistocles 1.137–8; death 4.50
Artemis, goddess 3.104; 6.44 (sanctuary
at Rhegium); 8.109 (at Ephesus)

Artemisium (1), promontory of
Euboea: battle of (480) 3.54
Artemisium (2), Spartan month 5.19
Artynae, magistrates at Argos 5.47
Asia 1.6 (wearing of loincloths), 1.9
(Pelops brought wealth from Asia),
1.138, 2.67, 2.97, 4.75, 5.1, 8.58
Asine (1), in Messenia 4.13, 6.93
Asine (2), in Laconia 4.54
Asopius (1), father of Phormio 1.64
Asopius (2), son of Phormio, Athenian
general, led campaign against
Oeniadae, killed in Leucas (428) 3.7
Asopus, river in Boeotia 2.5
Aspendus, city on coast of
Pamphylia 8.81, 8.87–8, 8.99, 8.108
Assinarus, river in Sicily: (413) scene of
slaughter of Nicias' division 7.84
Astacus, in Acarnania: (431) captured by
Athenians and tyrant Evarchus driven
out 2.30; (431/0) Evarchus reinstated
by Corinthians 2.33; 2.102
Astymachus, Plataean spokesman
(427) 3.52
ASTYOCHUS, Spartan admiral-
in-chief: (412) takes command of
expedition to Chios and Ionia 8.20,
8.23; (in Lesbos) secures revolt of
Eresus, but withdraws to Chios
8.23; (in Erythrae) consulted by
Chians on pro-Athenian conspiracy
8.24, 8.31; receives reinforcing fleet
from Peloponnese and Sicily
8.26; (412/1) failed attack on Pteleum
(2) and Clazomenae 8.31; ready to
accept Lesbian proposals for a second
revolt, but opposed by allies,
Pedaritus, and Chians 8.32; warns
Chians not to expect any help
themselves 8.33, cf. 8.38, 8.40; sails to
Miletus to take up his command as
admiral-in-chief 8.33, 8.36, 8.38;
narrowly escapes encounter with
Athenians at Corycus 8.33; with
Pedaritus, investigates alleged plot to
betray Erythrae to Athenians 8.33;
refuses Chian request for help, and
accused by Pedaritus of misconduct 8.38; relents 8.40, but abandons
planned relief 8.41; Spartans send
commissioners to 'advise' Astyochus
8.39, 8.41–3; at Cnidus and Syme
(sea-battle with Athenians)

8.41–3; receives letter from Sparta
ordering death of Alcibiades 8.45;
betrays Phrynichus' confidence to
Alcibiades and Tissaphernes, 8.50–1,
8.68; said to have sold himself to
Tissaphernes 8.50, cf. 8.83; sets out
to relieve Chios, but kept back by sight
of Athenian fleet 8.60–1; (411) sails
against Samos, but battle refused by
Athenians 8.63; agitation against
him among Peloponnesians at
Miletus 8.78–9, 8.83–5; succeeded
as admiral-in-chief by Mindarus, and
returns to Sparta 8.85
Atalante (1), island off coast of Opuntian
Locris: (431) fortified by Athenians
2.32; (426) hit by tsunami 3.89;
(422/1) provision in Peace of
Nicias 5.18
Atalante (2), in Macedonia 2.100
Athena, goddess: 'curse of the
goddess' 1.126–7; 'curse of the
goddess of the Bronze
House' 1.128, 1.134–5
— statue (2.13) and temple (2.15, 5.23)
on Acropolis; temple in Amphipolis
5.10; sanctuary at Lecythus 4.116
Athenaeus, Spartan: (423) signatory of
one-year truce 4.119; ambassador for
the truce 4.122
Athenagoras, leader of democratic party
at Syracuse: (415) speech in Syracusan
assembly 6.35–40
ATHENIAN EMPIRE: genesis 1.75–7
(Athenians at Sparta, 432), 1.95–7,
3.10–11, 6.76, 6.82; consolidation
1.118, 2.36, 3.10–11; defence of
realpolitik 1.75–7, **5.85–113** (Melian
dialogue); unpopularity 1.75–6, 1.99,
2.8, 2.11 (cf. Pericles 2.41), 2.63–4
(Pericles), 3.37 (Cleon), 5.99
(Athenians at Melos); empire as
enslavement 1.69, 1.98, 1.122, 1.124,
3.10–11, 3.63–4, 3.70–1, 4.87, 4.92,
5.9, 5.86, 5.92, 5.100, 6.76–7, 6.80,
7.66, 8.48; 'tyrant city' 1.122, 1.124,
2.63 (Pericles), 3.37 (Cleon), 6.85
(Euphemus); Athenians dangerous as
neighbours 3.113, 4.92; attitude of
subject allies to oligarchy/demo-
cracy 8.48 (Phrynichus), 8.64;
vulnerability after Athenian defeat
at Eretria (411) 8.96

—treasury 1.96; tribute 1.19, 1.56
(Potidaea), 1.80, **1.96** (original
assessment), 1.99, 1.101, 1.108, 1.121,
2.13, 6.85, 6.91, **7.28** (replaced by 5%
tax, 413), 7.57; ships, not tribute 1.19
(Chios and Lesbos), 6.85, 7.57 (Chios
and Methymna); tribute-paying
regions 2.9; tribute-paying subjects/
independent allies 6.85, 7.57
— Pericles on empire 1.143, 1.144,
2.13, 2.36, 2.63–4; Cleon on
empire 3.37, 3.40; Diodotus on
empire 3.46–7; Alcibiades on
empire 6.17–18; Hermocrates on
Athenian empire 6.76–7; Euphemus
on Athenian empire 6.82–5, 6.87
— settlers sent to: Scyros 1.98,
Nine Ways/Amphipolis 1.100,
Aegina 2.27, 7.57, Hestiaea 1.114,
7.57, Potidaea 2.70, Notium 3.34,
Lesbos 3.50, Melos 5.116
— revolts/defections/losses:
(general) 1.75, 1.99, 1.122, 1.143, 2.65,
3.39, 3.46–7, 4.80, 4.81, 4.108, 4.117,
5.14, 5.91, 5.110–11; fear of revolts
after Sicilian disaster 8.1–2, 8.4,
8.15; Persians looking to
foster revolts 8.5–6
—(470s) Naxos 1.98, 1.137;
(465/4–463/2) Thasos 1.100–1;
(446) Euboea 1.23, 1.114 (cf. 4.92);
(446) Megara 1.114; **(440–439)**
Samos 1.40, 1.41, 1.115–7; Byzantium 1.115, 1.117; (432) Potidaea 1.58,
1.62–5; (432 on) Thraceward
Chalcidians 1.58–9, 2.29, 2.58, 2.79,
4.79–81, 4.84–8, 4.103–16, 6.10;
(428–427) Lesbos 3.2–6, 3.8–18,
3.25, 3.27–50; (424) Acanthus and
Stagirus 4.88; **(424/3)** Argilus 4.103,
Amphipolis 4.103–7, Myrcinus,
Galepsus, Oesyme 4.107, most of Acte
peninsula 4.109, Torone 4.110–16
(recaptured, 422: 5.2–3); **(423)**
Scione 4.120–3, 4.129–33, 5.2, 5.18,
5.32 (recaptured); Mende 4.123–4,
4.129–30 (recaptured); (417) Dium
secedes to Chalcidians 5.82
— revolts in Ionia, led by Chios:
(412) Erythrae 8.5–6, 8.14,
8.16; Clazomenae 8.14, 8.16
(recovered 8.23); Chios 8.5–10, 8.12,
8.14–15, 8.24; Teos 8.16, 8.20;

Miletus 8.17; Lebedus, Aerae 8.19;
Methymna 8.22–3; Mytilene 8.22
(recaptured 8.23); Eresus 8.23
(again in 411); **(412/1)** Cnidus
8.35; Rhodes 8.44; **(411)**
Abydos 8.61–2; Lampsacus 8.62
(recaptured 8.62); Byzantium
8.80; Euboea 8.5, 8.60, 8.91–5;
Eresus 8.100, 8.103; Cyzicus 8.107
(recaptured 8.107)
ATHENS (physical, social, and
political): once inhabited by
Etruscans 4.109; early political
history and topology of Athens 1.2,
2.15–16; kings 2.15; tyrants 1.18,
1.20, 1.126 (Cylon's attempt), 2.15,
6.53–60; tyrants deposed by Spartans
1.18, 6.53, 6.59, 8.68; more
impressive appearance than Sparta
1.10; rebuilding and fortification
after Persian War 1.69, 1.89–93;
Long Walls 1.69, 1.107, 1.108, 2.13,
2.17, 5.26 (capture), 8.71
— Acropolis, *q.v.*; temples 2.15,
3.114; Anaceium 8.93; temple of
Athena 2.15, 5.23; sanctuary of Apollo
Pythius 2.15, 6.54; precinct of
Dionysus 8.93–4; altars of Dread
Goddesses 1.126; Eleusinium 2.17;
Leocoreium 1.20, 6.57; Theseium
6.61; altar of Twelve Gods in agora
6.54; public cemetery 2.34; Cerameicus 6.57–8; fountain Enneacrounos, previously known as Callirrhoe
2.15; 'Pelargic' area 2.17; Pnyx
8.97; Phalerum/Phaleric wall 1.107,
2.13; Peiraeus, *q.v.*
— autochthonous 1.2, 2.36;
unification of Attica under
Theseus 2.15–16; population 1.80,
2.38, 2.44, 6.12, 6.26, 8.66; overcrowding 2.17, 2.52; accustomed
to living in the country 2.14–16;
tribes 2.34, 4.118; tribal regiments 6.98; thetic class 6.43;
metics 1.143, 2.13, 2.31, 3.16, 4.90,
6.28, 7.63 ('honorary Athenians')
— festivals: Diasia 1.126; City
Dionysia 5.20, 5.23; Dionysia
(Anthesteria) 2.15; Panathenaea
1.20, 5.47, 6.56–7; Union 2.15
— political and social system 2.37, 2.40
(Pericles), 3.37 (Cleon); archons 1.126,

2.2, 5.19, 6.54; assemblies 1.31–44,
1.139–45, 2.13, (2.22), 2.59–65, 3.36–49,
4.16–22, 4.27–9, 4.118, 5.45–6, 6.8–26,
7.10–16, 8.53–4, 8.66, 8.67–9, 8.93–4,
8.97 (second debates: 3.36, 3.38, 3.42,
6.14); city clerk 7.10; council 5.45,
5.47, 8.66, 8.69, 8.86; overseeing board
of older men (established 413) 8.1;
prytany/prytaneis 4.118, 5.47, 6.14
(chairman of assembly); 'Treasurers to
the Greeks' 1.96; fraternities/cabals
8.48, **8.54**, 8.65, 8.81, 8.92; ostracism
1.135 (Themistocles), 8.73
(Hyperbolus); public duties
('liturgies'), 6.16 (Alcibiades),
(8.48, 8.63); *see also* trierarchs
—state pay 6.24, 8.65, 8.67, 8.69,
8.97; state funeral for war
dead 2.34; state maintenance for
war orphans 2.46; state triremes
(Paralus and Salaminia) 3.33, 3.77,
6.53, 6.61, 8.73–4, 8.86
ATHENS/ATHENIANS: relaxed
life-style 1.6, 2.39, 3.37;
character 1.70 (Corinthians),
1.102 (Spartans), 2.40 (Pericles),
3.37–8 (Cleon), 3.42–3 (Diodotus),
4.55, 4.65, 6.9 (Nicias), 6.18
(Alcibiades), 6.87 (Euphemus), 7.14
(Nicias), 7.21 (Hermocrates), 7.34,
7.48 (Nicias); Athenians and
Spartans compared/contrast-
ed 1.6, 1.18–19, 1.69–71, 1.73–4
(contributions in Persian War), 2.39
(Pericles), 8.96; ambition/grasping
for more 4.21 (cf. 4.17), 4.41 (contra
Pericles, 1.144), 4.65, 6.1, 6.6 (Sicily),
6.10–11, 6.13 (Nicias), 6.24, 6.31;
resilient/resourceful beyond others'
expectations 1.105, 2.65, 2.83, 2.89,
3.16, 4.5, 4.8, 7.28, 7.42, 8.24; 'an
education to Greece' 2.41 (Pericles)
—colonized: Ionia and islands 1.2,
1.12, 2.15; Nine Ways/Amphipolis
1.100, 4.102; Imbros 7.57;
Lemnos 7.57
—war with Aegina (*c*.505-483/2)
1.14, 1.41; abandoned city in Persian
War 1.18, 1.74, 1.91, 1.144 (returned
1.89, 2.16); Athenian contribution to
Persian War 1.73–5; (479–478) with
Ionian and Hellespontine allies capture
Sestos 1.89; (478) with Greek alliance

subdue Cyprus and capture Byzantium
1.94; (478/7) formation of Delian
League 1.97; (?476) capture of Eïon
1.98; (?475) capture of Scyros 1.98;
(470s) force capitulation of Carystus
1.98; revolt of Naxos, blockaded into
submission 1.98, 1.137; (?469)
Athenians and allies defeat Persians in
battles of Eurymedon 1.100;
(465/4–463/2) revolt of Thasos,
besieged into submission 1.100–1;
(465/4) Athenian colonizing force
destroyed by Thracians at Drabescus
1.100, 4.102; (?462) Cimon's expedition
to help Spartans with Helot revolt leads
to first open dispute between Spartans
and Athenians 1.102; (462–461)
Athenian alliance with Argos and
Thessaly 1.102, 1.107
—first Peloponnesian War
(*c*.461–446) 1.103, 1.105–8, 1.114–15:
(461/0) Megara defects from Sparta to
Athens, Athenians build long walls to
Nisaea 1.103, 1.107; (460–459) lose
battle of Halieis, win sea-battle off
Cecryphaleia, defeat Aegina in
sea-battle and start siege, defeat
Corinthians invading Megarid
1.105–6; (457) lose battle of Tanagra,
win battle of Oenophyta and gain
control of Boeotia and Phocis, Aegina
capitulates 1.108; (456) fleet sent
round Peloponnese under Tolmides
1.108; (454) fruitless expedition to
Thessaly, Pericles in Corinthian
Gulf 1.111; (451) five-year treaty
1.112; (446) revolt of Megara and
Peloponnesian invasion of Attica
1.114; Thirty Years Treaty, return
of places won from the
Peloponnesians 1.115 (cf. 4.21)
—Athenians in Cyprus 1.104 (460),
1.112 (451, death of Cimon); (460–454)
disastrous campaign in Egypt, 1.104–5,
1.109–10, 1.112; (*c*.458–457) building of
Long Walls 1.107–8; (449) recapture
temple at Delphi 1.112; (447/6) lose
Boeotia at battle of Coroneia 1.113 (cf.
3.62, 3.67, 4.92); (446) put down revolt
of Euboea 1.114; (440–439) revolt of
Samos, siege and surrender 1.115–17
(cf. 1.40, 1.41), revolt and capitulation of
Byzantium 1.115, 1.117; (433)

defensive alliance with Corcyra 1.44–5, and naval support of Corcyra against Corinth 1.45, 1.47–9, 1.51–5; (433–432) Athenians take precautions in Potidaea, and send expedition against Perdiccas 1.56–61; **(432)** revolt of Potidaea 1.58, 1.62–5; Athenian reinforcing expeditions 1.61, 1.64; defeat of Potidaeans and Corinthians, and Potidaea besieged 1.62–5; summary of grievances between Athenians and Peloponnesians 1.66, 1.146; speech of Athenians at first Peloponnesian conference 1.72–8; pre-war propaganda on both sides 1.126–38; Spartan final demands and Athenian final answer 1.139–45 —**resources for the war** 1.1, 1.19, 1.80, 1.143 (Pericles), 2.9 (allies), 2.11, **2.13** (Pericles), 2.20, 2.24, 2.31, 2.62 (Pericles), 3.13 (dependent on allies for income); *see also* finance —**(431)** Athenian reaction to events in Plataea, and garrison installed 2.6 (cf. 2.78, 3.20, 3.68); preparations for war 2.7, 2.17, 2.24 (reserve fund); **allies on Athenian side** 2.9; general Greek feeling against Athens at start of war 2.8, 2.11; Spartan ambassador rejected unheard 2.12; evacuation of Attica into Athens 2.14, 2.16–18, 2.52, 2.62; 1st Peloponnesian invasion of Attica 2.18–23; reaction to invasion, and resentment of Pericles 2.21–2; send naval expeditions round Peloponnese 2.17, 2.23, 2.25, 2.30, and to coast of Locris 2.26; expel Aeginetans, and send settlers to Aegina 2.27; alliances with Sitalces (cf. 2.95) and Perdiccas 2.29; invade Megarid 2.31; (431/0) **state funeral for the war dead** 2.34–46; (430) 2nd invasion of Attica 2.47, 2.55–7 —**plague in Athens (**430–429, 427/6), 1.23, 2.31, 2.47–54, 2.57–8, 2.64, 3.3, 3.13, 3.87; origin and spread 2.47–8, 2.54, 2.58; moral collapse 2.52–3, 2.61; death toll 2.58, 3.87; debilitating effect 3.3, 3.13, 3.87; second visitation (427/6) 3.87; recovery 6.12, 6.26 —**(430)** naval expedition against Epidaurus and Peloponnesian coast

under Pericles 2.56, 6.31; same force taken on by Hagnon against Potidaea 2.58; turn against Pericles after 2nd invasion and plague, and ready to make terms with Sparta 2.59, 2.65; fine Pericles, but re-elect him general 2.65; execute Peloponnesian ambassadors arrested in Thrace on way to Persia 2.67; **(430/29)** squadron based in Naupactus under Phormio 2.69; capitulation of Potidaea 2.70; **(429)** Plataeans consult Athenians before responding to Spartan demands 2.72–4; defeat at Spartolus 2.79; naval successes (Phormio) in the Corinthian Gulf 2.83–92; reinforcements for Phormio sent first to Crete 2.85–6, 2.92; **(429/8)** Peloponnesian attack on Peiraeus (aborted) and Salamis 2.93–4; panic at Athens 2.94; fail to support Sitalces against Chalcidians 2.95, 2.101; Phormio campaigns in Acarnania 2.102–3; **(428)** 3rd invasion of Attica 3.1; expedition round Peloponnese under Asopius, attacking Oeniadae and Leucas 3.7 (cf. 3.16); display of naval strength, to the surprise of Spartans 3.16; **(428/7)** measures to raise finance 3.19 —**revolt of Mytilene (**428–427) 3.2–6, 3.8–18, 3.25, 3.27–50; Athenian expedition in response 3.3–6; reinforcements sent under Paches, and Mytilene besieged 3.18; **(427)** Mytilene capitulates 3.27–8; Paches captures Notium, and forces submission of Pyrrha and Eresus 3.34–5; 'Mytilenaean debate' in assembly at Athens 3.36–49; 2nd trireme sent to countermand order to kill Mytilenaeans 3.49; settlement imposed on Lesbos 3.50 —**(427)** 4th invasion of Attica 3.26; Nicias captures and fortifies island of Minoa 3.51; Athenian involvement in civil war in Corcyra 3.70–2. 3.75–81, 3.85 (naval engagement against Peloponnesians 3.75–8) —**first expedition to Sicily (**427–424) 3.86, 3.88, 3.90, 3.99, 3.103, 3.115, 4.2, 4.24–5, 4.48, 4.58–65; war between Syracuse and Leontini, allies

on either side, Athenians called in by
Leontinians, Athenian motives 3.86;
(426) Messana capitulates to
Athenians 3.90 (defects 4.1); (426/5)
Pythodorus succeeds Laches 3.115;
(425) reinforcement of 40 ships
dispatched 3.115, 4.2, 4.48; first naval
engagements 4.24–5; (424) Conference
of Gela ends internal war, and Athenians
leave 4.58–65; Athenian generals
punished for leaving Sicily 4.65
—(426) expeditions round
Peloponnese, against Melos, and full
levy at Tanagra, defeating Tanagraeans
and Thebans 3.91; fear (unrealized)
of threat to Euboea from Spartan
foundation of Heracleia (1) 3.92–3;
disastrous expedition to Aetolia under
Demosthenes 3.94–8 (Athenian
losses, 3.98); Demosthenes and
Acarnanians save Naupactus from
Peloponnesian attack by land 3.100–2;
(426/5) Demosthenes' successes in
Amphilochia against Peloponnesians
and Ambraciots 3.105–14; (425) 5th
invasion of Attica 4.2, 4.5–6
—(425) the Pylos campaign 4.3–6,
4.8–23, 4.26–41; fleet bound for
Corcyra and Sicily puts in to Pylos and
fortifies the place 4.3–4; Spartans send
army and fleet, land hoplites on
Sphacteria 4.8; Demosthenes beats
back attempted Spartan landings
4.9–13; truce agreed, ended on failure
of Spartan embassy to Athens
4.15–23; hardship for the Athenians at
Pylos 4.26–7, 4.29; Cleon incites
rejection of Spartan offer of peace
4.21–2, and forced to take command
at Pylos himself 4.27–30; Athenian
landing on Sphacteria and surrender
of Spartan hoplites 4.31–9; prisoners
sent to Athens, Messenian garrison
installed at Pylos 4.41
—(425) capture and loss of Eïon
(2) 4.7; campaign in Corinthiad,
fortification of Methana isthmus
4.22–5; Eurymedon and Sophocles
in Corcyra, defeat Corcyraean
oligarchs 4.46–8; with Acarnanians,
capture Anactorium 4.49; (425/4)
arrest of Persian emissary to Sparta,
sent back with Athenian embassy 4.50;

suspect Chians and require demolition
of walls 4.51; (424) 'Actaean cities'
in Athenian control (cf. 3.50)
threatened by Mytilenaean exiles, and
Antandrus taken 4.52 (recaptured by
Athenians 4.75); campaign against
Cythera (surrenders 4.54) and coastal
areas of Laconia 4.53–7; capture and
loot Thyrea, surviving Aeginetans
taken to Athens and killed 4.57;
campaign at Megara, capture long
walls and Nisaea, but refuse to fight
relieving force with Brasidas 4.66–74;
Boeotian campaign 4.76–7,
4.89–101: plan coordinated with
Boeotian democrats 4.76–7;
(424/3) failure of coordination and
betrayal frustrate Demosthenes'
expedition 4.89; Hippocrates fortifies
sanctuary of Delium 4.90; Pagondas
persuades Boeotians to attack
4.91–3; battle of Delium 4.93–7
(Athenian and Boeotian losses, 4.101);
diplomatic quibbling over recovery of
dead 4.97–9; sanctuary captured by
Boeotians 4.100; (424/3) loss of
Amphipolis to Brasidas 4.102–6, 4.108
(alarm at Athens); Thucydides saves
Eïon (1) 4.107; loss of Torone and fort
at Lecythus 4.110–16; (423) one-year
truce, and motives 4.117, 5.15
(texts, 4.118; extended, 5.1); defection
of Scione to Brasidas 4.120–1,
Athenian reaction 4.122 (besieged by
Athenians 423–421: 4.131, 4.133, 5.2,
5.18; captured 5.32); defection of
Mende 4.123 (recaptured 4.129–30);
(422) evict Delians from Delos 5.1
(reinstated, 421: 5.32); recapture of
Torone under Cleon 5.2–3; fort at
Panactum betrayed to Boeotians 5.3;
mission of Phaeax to Italy and
Sicily 5.4–5; battle at Amphipolis,
Athenians defeated by Brasidas and
Cleon killed 5.6–11; Athenian loss of
confidence after Delium and
Amphipolis 5.14
—(422/1) desire for peace on both
sides, motives national and personal
(Nicias, Pleistoanax) 5.13–17; Peace
of Nicias ratified 5.17 (text, 5.18–19);
subsequent alliance between Sparta
and Athens 5.22–4; Athenians return

Spartan prisoners 5.24 (regretted, 5.35); (421–420) growing mutual distrust at non-fulfilment of treaty 5.25, 5.35 (Athenians refuse to return Pylos), 5.39, 5.42–6; opposition to the peace-treaty in Sparta (new ephors, 5.36) and Athens (Alcibiades, 5.43–5); the issue of Panactum 5.39–40, 5.42, 5.46; (420) fruitless embassy to Sparta under Nicias 5.46; Athenians enter treaty and alliance with Argos, Mantinea, and Elis, engineered by Alcibiades 5.43–8 (text, 5.47)
— (419) Alcidiades in Peloponnese consolidating Argive alliance 5.52; Athenians summon conference at Mantinea 5.55; send army to support Argos against Epidaurus 5.55; (418) arrive late in support of Argos against Pelopon-nesian expedition 5.59, 5.61, and argue for prosecution of war; in **battle of Mantinea** 5.67, 5.69, 5.71–4 (Athenian losses, 5.74); send further troops, too late for the battle, and join allied attack on Epidaurus, fortifying Heraeum 5.75, 5.77; (418/7) renew treaty with Epidaurus, and hand over Heraeum fort 5.80; (417) help Argive democrats build long walls to sea 5.82; (417/6) blockade Macedonia; (416) expedition against Melos 5.84–116 (**Melian dialogue** 5.85–113; fate of Melian population 5.116); (416/5) renewed interest in Sicily, confirmed by Egestan embassy appealing for aid against Selinus 6.1, 6.6; board of inquiry sent to Egesta 6.6, 6.8, 6.46; operations in Orneae and Macedonia 6.7
— **second expedition to Sicily** (415–413), *see* **SICILIAN EXPEDITION**
— (415) reaction to mutilation of Herms and alleged profanation of Mysteries 6.27–9, 6.53, 6.60–1, cf. 8.53; spectacle of armada for Sicilian expedition at Peiraeus 6.30–2; recall of Alcibiades from Sicily 6.53, 6.61; Alcibiades condemned to death in his absence 6.61; (414) assist Argos

against Sparta and ravage parts of Laconia, justifying Spartan retalia-tion 6.105, 7.18; attack Amphipolis and attempt siege 7.9; (413) 6th invasion of Attica and fortification of Deceleia 7.19, 7.27 (damage caused by Deceleia, 7.27–8); Demosthenes sent with reinforcements to Sicily 7.20 (raids Laconia, fort established opposite Cythera 7.26; recruitment in W. Greece 7.31, 7.33; in Italy 7.33, 7.35); financial straits, replacement of tribute by 5% tax 7.28; returning Thracian peltasts commit atrocities in attack on Mycalessus 7.27, 7.29–30; sea-battle with Corinthians in Gulf 7.34, 7.36
— (413) reactions in Athens to defeat in Sicily 8.1; (413/2) reactions in Greece, among Athenian subjects, in Sparta 8.2; Athenian preparations for resumption of war in Greece 8.1, 8.4–5 (rebuilding of navy 8.1, 8.4); (412) get wind of oligarchic plot at Chios, demand ships as guarantee, intercept and blockade Peloponnesian expedition to Chios 8.9–11, 8.14–15, 8.20; intercept but fail to stop Peloponnesian ships returning from Sicily 8.13; revolt of Chios and reaction at Athens 8.14–15; Athenian ships in E. Aegean 8.15–17, 8.19, 8.23; revolt of Miletus, Athenian blockade 8.17, 8.24; democratic revolution in Samos, now granted independence by Athenians 8.21; revolt of Methymna and Mytilene 8.22–3; Athenians recapture Mytilene 8.23; defeat Chians and ravage the island 8.24; send expedition against Miletus, victorious, but withdraw to Samos on approach of Peloponnesian fleet 8.25–7; (412/1) whole Athenian fleet assembled at Samos and based there 8.30, 8.35, 8.38, 8.39, 8.41, 8.44, 8.47–8, 8.60, 8.63; revolt of Cnidus, Athenians capture guard-ships and attack the city 8.35; fortify Delphinium and blockade Chios 8.34, 8.38, 8.40, 8.55–6, 8.61; naval patrol worsted by Astyochus' fleet at Syme 8.41–2; too late to prevent secession of Rhodes, but attack from Chalce and Cos 8.44,

8.55; Oropus betrayed to Boeotians
8.60; (411) Chians break out and fight
Athenians at sea 8.61, 8.63; revolt of
Abydos and Lampsacus, Strombichides
recovers Lampsacus and fortifies
Sestos 8.62, recalled from Hellespont to
reinforce fleet at Samos 8.79
— oligarchic plot and revolution
(412/1–411): leading figures 8.68,
8.89, 8.90, 8.98 (individual motives, 8.89); belief that oligarchy
could not last 8.72, 8.89; (412/1)
originated among trierarchs and
leading Athenians at Samos 8.47–51,
8.53, 8.56, 8.63, 8.73; discussions with
Alcibiades, who promises Persian
support if democracy abandoned 8.48;
reaction of troops at Samos 8.48;
Phrynichus opposed to plans 8.48;
Peisander sent to Athens to promote
oligarchic movement, and Athenian
reaction 8.49, 8.53–4;
Athenians vote to send Peisander
and others to negotiate with
Tissaphernes and Alcibiades 8.54
(negotiations fail 8.56, 8.63); (411)
attempt to set up oligarchy in
Samos 8.63, 8.73; reaction, oligarchic
coup defeated, democracy restored, led
by Thrasyboulus and Thrasyllus
8.72–7, 8.86; Peisander sent again to
Athens, setting up oligarchies on his
route 8.64–5; Diitrephes puts down
democracy in Thasos 8.64; convenient
murders, and oligarchic manifesto at
Athens 8.65; suspicion and fear at
Athens 8.66; assemblies vote through
measures resulting in establishment of
the **Four Hundred** 8.67, 8.69
— Athenians in Samos as rival
state (411) 8.75–7, 8.81–2, 8.86,
8.88–90, 8.96, 8.97, 8.108; hold
assemblies 8.76, 8.81, 8.86, appoint
generals and trierarchs 8.76, 8.82, and
receive envoys 8.86; oath to support
democracy, prosecute the war, and
hold Four Hundred as enemies 8.75,
8.90; reasons advanced for confidence
8.76; recall Alcibiades with an
immunity, and elect him general
8.81–2; Alcibiades refuses to let them
sail against the Peiraeus 8.82; give

rough hearing to emissaries of Four
Hundred, and call for attack on Peiraeus,
restrained by Alcibiades 8.86; envoys
from Argos offer help to 'the Athenian
people in Samos' 8.86; fear of Athenians
in Samos and of Alcibiades among
oligarchs at Athens 8.72, 8.81, 8.89–90
— regime of Four Hundred
(411): quality of the leading
figures 8.68; government established
by oligarchic conspirators at
Athens 8.67–75; ratified by
assembly 8.67, 8.69; occupy
council-chamber 8.69–70; wholesale
reforms 8.70; communication with
Agis, and his practical response
8.70–1; emissaries sent to Samos 8.72,
8.77, 8.86, 8.89; emissaries sent back
with reply from Alcibiades 8.86, 8.90;
envoys sent to Sparta 8.86, 8.89,
8.90–1 (authorized to make peace on
any tolerable terms); opposition
between moderates (Theramenes,
etc., 8.89), uneasy at developments,
and extremists (Phrynichus,
etc., 8.90) 8.89–92, 8.94; extremists
seek peace with Sparta and hasten
fortification of Eëtioneia 8.90–1, 8.94;
priorities of extremists 8.91–2;
murder of Phrynichus 8.92; kidnap
and subsequent release of Alexicles
8.92–3; hoplites support moderate
party and demolish Eëtioneia
fortification 8.92–3; near civil
war 8.92, 8.94, 8.95, 8.96; hoplites
placated by promise of more liberal
regime 8.93; Four Hundred
deposed and government tranferred
to the **Five Thousand** 8.97;
leading oligarchs escape to Deceleia,
Aristarchus betrays Oenoe to
Boeotians 8.98; reprisals 8.68
— the **Five Thousand** (411):
supposed government in oligarchic
manifesto at Athens 8.65, 8.67, 8.72,
8.86, 8.89; of uncertain existence
8.92, but Four Hundred promise to
publish the names 8.93; assembly
after loss of Euboea deposes Four
Hundred and transfers government
to the Five Thousand (constituted
of all who could provide their

own hoplite armour) 8.97;
merits of the new political system 8.97
—(411) Agis brings troops to the
walls of Athens 8.71; Peloponnesian
fleet defeats Athenians off Eretria, and
Euboea revolts 8.94–5; reaction at
Athens 8.96–7; assembly votes to
recall Alcibiades and other exiles 8.97;
Athenian fleet from Samos follows
Peloponnesian fleet to Hellespont
8.100–3; Athenian victory at battle of
Cynossema 8.104–6; effect on morale at
Athens 8.106; recapture Cyzicus 8.107
—final defeat of Athens (404) 5.26,
6.15 (indirect responsibility of
Alcibiades), 7.27 (contribution of
Deceleia)
—panics at Athens 2.94 (Peloponnesian attack on Salamis, 429/8)), 4.108
(capture of Amphipolis, 424/3), 7.71
(in Athenian army, 413), 8.1 (after defeat
in Sicily, 413), 8.94 (expecting attack on
Peiraeus, 411) 8.96 (after loss of
Euboea, 411)
—Athens and Argos 1.102, 5.44,
5.43–8, 5.56, 5.59, 5.61, 5.65–75
(battle of Mantinea), 5.78, 5.80, 5.82,
5.84, 6.61, 6.105, 7.57, 8.25, 8.86
—Athens and Perdiccas 1.57, 1.61,
1.62, 2.29, 2.80, 4.79, 4.82, 4.128,
4.132, 5.6, 5.80, 5.83, 6.7, 7.9
—Athens and Tissaphernes
(hopes of alliance) 8.47–8, 8.53–4,
8.56, 8.65, 8.76, 8.81
—campaigns: (c.505–483/2) Aegina
1.14, 1.41; (470s) Sestos, Cyprus,
Byzantium, Eïon (1), Scyros, Carystus,
Naxos 1.89, 1.94, 1.98, 1.137;
(465/4-463/2) Thasos 1.101; (460–459)
Halieis, Cecryphaleia, Megarid 1.105–6;
(460–454) Egypt 1.104, 1.105, 1.109-10,
1.112; (c.460–457) Aegina 1.105, 1.108,
3.64; (457) Tanagra, Oenophyta
1.107–8; (456) expedition round
Peloponnese under Tolmides 1.108;
(454) Thessaly, Sicyon, Oeniadae
1.111; (451) Cyprus 1.112; (447/6)
Coroneia 1.113; (446) Megara,
Euboea 1.114; (440–439) Samos
1.115-17; (433) Corcyra 1.31-55; (432
on) Potidaea and Chalcidians 1.56-66,
2.13, 2.29, 2.58, [3.17]; (431) naval
expeditions round Peloponnese 2.17,

2.23, 2.25, 2.30; Megara 2.31; (430)
expedition under Pericles to Peloponnesian coast 2.56; (429) expedition
against Chalcidians 2.79; (428–427)
Lesbos 3.3–6, 3.18, 3.25, 3.27–8,
3.35; (428) naval expeditions round
Peloponnese 3.7, 3.16, [3.17]; (427)
Corcyra, against Peloponnesians 3.75–8,
3.80, 3.85; (427–424) first expedition
to Sicily, *see above*; (426) naval
expeditions round Peloponnese 3.91,
3.94; Melos, Tanagra, Locris 3.91,
3.94; Leucas (with Acarnanians) 3.94;
Aetolia 3.94–8, 4.30; (426/5)
Amphilochia 3.105-14; (425)
Pylos 4.8–16, 4.23, 4.26–41;
Corinthiad 4.42–5; Corcyra, against
oligarchs 4.46–8; (424) Cythera and
Laconia 4.53–7; Megara, Nisaea
4.66-74, 4.85; (424/3) Boeotia, Delium
4.76-7, 4.89–90, 4.93–7, 4.100-1, 4.108,
5.14-15; (423) Scione and Mende
4.122-3, 4.129-33; (422) Torone
5.2–3, and Amphipolis 5.6-12; (418)
Mantinea 5.65-75; (417/6) campaign
against Chalcidians and Amphipolis
aborted 5.83; (416) Melos 5.84-116;
(416/5) Macedonia 6.7; (415–413)
second expedition to Sicily, *see*
SICILIAN EXPEDITION; (412) naval
operations in E. Aegean and Ionia
8.15-17, 8.19-20, 8.23-4; Miletus
8.25-7, cf. 8.30, 8.38; (412/1) Chios
8.30, 8.33, 8.34, 8.38, 8.40, 8.55-6,
8.61; (411) offer battle at Miletus 8.79,
8.83; Eretria 8.95-6; Cynossema 8.103-6
—Athenian navy 1.142–3 (Pericles),
2.13 (Pericles), 2.62, 2.85, 2.88, 3.115
(practice), 6.82, 7.21 (Hermocrates); development 1.14, 1.90, 1.93, 1.99, 6.82,
7.21; numbers in Persian War, 1.74;
numbers at start of Peloponnesian War
[3.17]; spectacle of navy in Peiraeus before
Sicilian expedition 6.30-2; deterioration in Sicily 7.4, 7.12-13; disadvantaged by Syracusan modification of
ships and tactics 7.36, 7.40-1;
rebuilding after defeat in Sicily 8.1, 8.4
—Athenian naval superiority 1.93
(Themistocles), 1.142 (Pericles), 2.62
(Pericles), 2.85, 2.93, 3.32, 3.78,
3.80-1, 4.12, 5.109, 6.17-18, 6.22,
7.21, 7.47-9, 7.55 (lost in Sicily),

8.57, 8.60, 8.80, 8.106
—Athenian cavalry 2.13, 2.19,
2.22, 2.31, 2.56 (cf. 6.31), 2.79, 3.1,
3.87 (death toll in plague), 4.42, 4.44,
4.53, 4.72, 4.93, 5.2, 5.50, 5.61, 5.67,
5.73, 6.7, 6.94, 6.98 (total of 650 at
Syracuse), 7.27, 7.28, 7.51, 8.71
Athos, mountain at end of Acte peninsula
(Chalcidice) 4.109, 5.3, 5.35, 5.82
Atintanians, barbarian tribe in
Epirus 2.80
Atramyttium, in Mysia: (422) offered
by Pharnaces as home for evicted
Delians 5.1; (411) Delians in
Atramyttium massacred by
Arsaces 8.108
Atreus, son of Pelops 1.9
ATTICA: thin soil 1.2; autochthonous
population 1.2, 2.36; early history
1.2; colonization of Ionia 1.2, 1.12,
2.15; early political history, unification
under Theseus 2.15–16; demes 2.19,
2.23; 'coastal region' 2.55–6; evacuation of Attica before Peloponnesian
invasion 2.14, 2.16–18, 2.52,
2.62; Deceleia denies Athenians the
use of Attica 7.27–8, 8.95–6
—Peloponnesian invasions of
Attica: (446) under Pleistoanax
1.114, 2.21, 5.16; 1st invasion of
Peloponnesian War (431) 2.10–13,
2.18–23; 2nd invasion (430) 2.47,
2.55–7; 3rd invasion (428) 3.1; 4th
invasion (427) 3.26; invasion of 426
aborted (earthquake) 3.89; 5th
invasion (425) 4.2, 4.5–6; 6th
invasion, and fortification of
Deceleia (413) 7.19
Aulon, in Chalcidice 4.103
Autocharidas, Spartan commander 5.12
Autocles, Athenian general 4.53; (423)
signatory of one-year truce 4.119
Axius, river in Macedonia 2.99

BARBARIANS: no generic term in
Homer 1.3; barbarian ways of
life 1.6; bloodthirsty 7.29;
Eurytanians said to eat raw flesh
3.94; lack of discipline 2.81, 4.126–7;
Brasidas' denigration of barbarians
(Illyrians) as fighters 4.126; barbarian
mercenaries 2.96, 3.34, 3.73–4, 3.85,
3.109, 4.46, 4.124–5, 4.129, 5.6, 6.90,

7.27, 7.29–30, 8.25; bilingual
barbarians 4.109, 8.85
—Amphilochians mostly barbarians 2.68, cf. 3.112; Illyrians 1.24,
1.26, 4.124–8; Scythians 2.96, 2.97
(Scythian archers as police in
Athens 8.98); barbarian inhabitants of
Sicily 6.2, 6.17, Egestans as 'barbarians'
(Nicias) 6.11 (cf. Alcibiades 6.18);
Thracian tribes 1.100, 2.96, 2.98,
2.101, 4.102 (destroy Athenian
colonizing force at Drabescus, 465/4),
7.27, 7.29–30 (Dians commit atrocities
at Mycalessus, 423)
—Epidamnus attacked by barbarians
1.24; (433) barbarians in Thesprotia
support Corinthians against
Corcyra 1.47; both sides seeking
barbarian support at beginning of
war 1.82 (Sparta), 2.7; Chaonians,
etc. support Ambraciots against
Amphilochia (430) 2.68, and against
Acarnania (429) 2.80–1; barbarians in
Brasidas' army (423) 4.124–5
Battus, Corinthian general 4.43
Beroea, in Macedonia 1.61
Bisaltia, in Macedonia 2.99, 4.109
Bithynian Thracians 4.75
Black Sea 2.96, 2.97, 3.2, 4.75
Boeotarchs, *see* BOEOTIA
BOEOTIA: Boeotians driven out of
Arne by Thessalians 1.12, settle
Boeotia 3.61, cf. 4.98; previously
called Cadmeïs 1.12; fertile, 1.2; of
Aeolian race 7.57 (cf. 3.2, 8.5);
Boeotian ships in expedition to
Troy 1.10; colonized Tenedos,
Aenus, Methymna 7.57; ally of
Sparta, providing cavalry 2.9;
national chariot-racing stable
5.50; Boeotarchs 2.2, 4.91,
5.37–8, 7.30; Four Councils of
Boeotians 5.38; pan-Boeotian
alliance 2.2, 3.61, 3.65–6
—Plataeans 'only Boeotians to
oppose Persians' 3.54; civil strife
after Persian War 3.62, 4.92; (457)
defeated by Athenians at Oenophyta,
and Athenians take control of
Boeotia 1.108, 3.62; (454) join
Athenians in Thessalian campaign
1.111; (447/6) defeat Athenians at
Coroneia and regain independence

1.113, 3.62, 3.67, 4.92; **(431)** all
Boeotians in Attica arrested 2.6; ravage
Plataean land 2.12; Peloponnesians
return from 1st invasion via
Boeotia 2.23; **(429)** at siege of
Plataea 2.78, 3.20; **(428)** encourage
revolt of Lesbos 3.2 (cf. 3.5,
3.13); **(427/6)** earthquake 3.87; **(426)**
Demosthenes plans overland attack on
Boeotia 3.95; **(424)** Boeotians with
Brasidas at Megara 4.70, 4.72–3;
(424/3) Boeotian pro-democracy parties
coordinate plans with Athenians 4.76–7
(abandoned 4.89); pre-empt Athenian
attack, defeat Athenians at Delium
4.89–101 (their forces at Delium
4.93); **(423)** in one-year truce Boeotians
to be persuaded to allow universal
access to Delphi 4.118; **(422)** capture
Athenian fort of Panactum 5.3 (5.36,
5.39–40, 5.42); **(422/1)** dissent from
treaty and alliance with Athens 5.17,
5.22, 5.26, 5.35, 5.36, 5.40; **(421)** wary
of alliance with Argos 5.31; **(421/0)**
Spartan-inspired proposals for alliance
of Boeotia with Corinth and Argos
come to nothing 5.36–8, 5.40; alliance
with Sparta, as condition for transfer of
Panactum 5.39–40, 5.42, 5.44, 5.46;
(419) take over Heracleia (1)
5.52; **(418)** in Peloponnesian
expedition against Argos 5.57–60;
summoned to assist Spartans at
Mantinea 5.64 (request countermanded,
5.75); **(415)** meet small force of
Spartans at Isthmus 6.61; **(413)** send
300 hoplites to Sicily 7.19, 7.58; first
to rout the Athenians on Epipolae 7.43,
7.45; **(413/2)** required to build ships
for Peloponnesian League 8.3; support
Lesbian request for help in revolting
from Athens 8.5; **(412/1)** capture
Oropus 8.60; **(411)** with Corinthians
besiege Oenoe, which is betrayed to
them 8.98; lose two ships at
Cynossema 8.106
— Boeotian cavalry 2.9, 2.12, 2.22,
3.62, 4.72, 4.93, 4.95–6, 5.57–8;
Theban cavalry 7.30
Boeum, town in Doris 1.107
Bolbe, lake in Macedonia 1.58, 4.103
Boliscus, in Chios 8.24
Bomians, Aetolian tribe 3.96

border-guards, Athenian
(*peripoloi*) 4.67, 8.92
Boriades, Aetolian envoy 3.100
Bormiscus, in Chalcidice 4.103
Bottia, district of Macedonia 2.99, 2.100
Bottiaeans (1), inhabitants of Bottia,
evicted by Macedonians 2.99
Bottiaeans (2), inhabitants of
Bottice 1.57–8, 2.79, 2.101, 4.7
Bottice, region of Chalcidice 1.65,
2.79, 2.101
Boucolion, in Arcadia 4.134
Boudorum, Athenian fort on
promontory of Salamis 2.93–4, 3.51
Bouphras, near Pylos 4.118
BRASIDAS, son of Tellis (2.25 etc.),
Spartan commander: the Spartan
most opposed to peace 5.16; 'not a
bad speaker, for a Spartan'
4.84; public commendation
2.25; jealousy of Spartans 4.108,
cf. 4.117; character and effectiveness
4.81, 4.108, 4.121, 4.123; religious
observance 4.87, 4.116, 5.10; sent as
adviser to Cnemus (429) 2.85, to
Alcidas (427) 3.69, 3.76, 3.79; as
arbitrator 4.83; and Perdiccas 4.83,
4.107, 4.124–8, 4.132
—(431) at Methone 2.25; (429)
speech at Rhium 2.87; (429/8)
proposed attack on Peiraeus 2.93;
(425) at Pylos 4.11–12 (wounded, 4.12,
and loses shield); (424) at Megara/
Nisaea 4.70–4, 4.85, 4.108; (424–423)
expedition to Thraceward region
(through Thessaly, 4.78), 4.70, 4.74,
4.78–88, 4.102–16, 4.120–9, 4.132,
4.135; (424) speech at Acanthus 4.85–7,
cf. 4.120; (424/3) achieves surrender of
Amphipolis and makes attempt on Eïon
(1) 4.103–7; propaganda about
Athenian refusal to fight at Nisaea 4.85,
4.108; calls for reinforcements from
Sparta, refused 4.108; at Torone/
Lecythus 4.110–16; speech to
Toronaeans 4.114, cf. 4.120; (423) at
Scione 4.120–2, 5.18; speech to
Scionaeans 4.120; fêted as liberator of
Greece 4.121; at Mende 4.123–4;
campaign with Perdiccas against
Lyncus 4.124–8; speech to his troops
at Lyncus 4.126; appoints governors of
Amphipolis and Torone 4.132; (423/2)

attempt on Potidaea 4.135; (422) fails
to relieve Torone 5.2–3; at Amphipolis 5.6–11; killed 5.10; funeral and
honours in Amphipolis (adopted as
founder) 5.11; (421) Helots who
fought under Brasidas freed by
Spartans 5.34; (418) Brasidas' veterans
at battle of Mantinea 5.67, 5.71–2
Brauro, wife of Pittacus, helped to
assassinate him 4.107
Bricinniae, fort in Leontinian
territory 5.4
Brilessus, mountain in Attica 2.23
Bronze House, goddess of 1.128, 1.143
(precinct)
Byzantium, city on Bosporus: 2.97; (478)
won from Persian control 1.94,
1.128; Pausanias (1) forced out of
Byzantium by Athenians 1.131;
(440–439) revolts from Athens 1.115,
1.117 (returned to subject status);
(411) revolts from Athens, and minor
sea-battle 8.80 (the 8 Byzantine ships
captured by Athenians 8.107)

cabals/fraternities at Athens 8.48,
8.54, 8.65, 8.81, 8.92
Cacyparis, river in Sicily 7.80
Cadmeïs, previous name of Boeotia 1.12
Caeadas, ravine used for disposal of
criminals in Sparta 1.134
Caïcinus, river in territory of Locri 3.103
Calchedon, Megarian colony at mouth of
Black Sea 4.75
Calex, river in territory of
Heracleia (2) 4.75
Callians, Aetolian tribe 3.96
Callias (1), Athenian general 1.61–3;
killed at Potidaea 1.63
Callias (2), father of Callicrates 1.29
Callias (3), father of Hipponicus 3.91
Callias (4), father-in-law of Hippias 6.55
Callicrates, Corinthian commander 1.29
Calligeitus, Megarian exile,
agent of Pharnabazus 8.6, 8.8, 8.39
Callirrhoe, previous name of fountain
Enneacrounos 2.15
Calydon, city in Aeolis (2) 3.102
Camarina, Dorian city in Sicily: founded
by Syracusans, and subsequent
refoundations 6.5; allied to Leontini in
427: 3.86; pro-Syracusan party 4.25;
(424) truce with Gela, leading to

conference of Gela 4.58; 4.65; (422)
won over by Phaeax 5.4; (415) refuse to
admit Athenians 6.52; (415/4) support
Syracuse with small force 6.67;
Athenians and Syracusans bid for
their support in assembly 6.75–88;
(413) send reinforcements to
Syracuse 7.58; 7.80
Cambyses, son of Cyrus, King of Persia
(530–522) 1.13, 1.14
Cameirus, city in Rhodes 8.44
Canastraeum, cape at tip of Pallene
peninsula (Chalcidice) 4.110
Carcinus, Athenian general 2.23
Cardamyle, in Chios 8.24
Caria 1.4, 1.8 (pirates, colonized Delos),
1.116, 2.9 (coastal Caria tribute-paying
region of Athenian empire), 2.69, 3.19
(Athenian money-collecting force
destroyed, 428/7), 8.5, 8.39
Carneia, Spartan festival 5.75–6
Carneius, sacred month in Dorian
calendar 5.54
Carteria, harbour in territory of
Phocaea 8.101
Carthage: sea-battle with Phocaeans
1.13; Alcibiades' ambition to
conquer Carthage 6.15; Athenian
ambitions against Carthage
(Alcibiades) 6.90; possible source
of help for Sicily 6.33; for Athenians
6.88; short sea passage to Sicily
6.2; trading-post Nea Polis 7.50
Caryae, in Laconia 5.55
Carystus, city in Euboea: of Dryopian
race 7.57; (470s) forced to capitulate
by Athenians 1.98; (425) with
Athenians in Corinthiad 4.42–3;
subject allies, with Athenians in
Syracuse 7.57; (411) some
Carystians support Four
Hundred 8.69 (cf. 8.65)
Casmenae, city in Sicily: founded by
Syracusans 6.5
CATANA: city in Sicily, under Mt Aetna
(partial destruction in eruption of
426/5: 3.116): founded by Thucles and
Chalcidians 6.3; pro-Syracusan
party 6.50–1, 6.64; (415) expected to
side with Athens on kinship
grounds 6.20; first refuse, then accept
Athenians and form alliance 6.50–1;
Catanaean assembly 6.51; (415–414)

Catana as Athenian base 6.51–2, 6.62,
6.63–5, 6.71–2, 6.74–5, 6.88, 6.94, 6.97,
7.42; (415/4) Syracusans ravage
territory and burn Athenian camp 6.75;
(414) provide horses for Athenian
cavalry 6.98; one of the Athenians'
'remaining allies' (Nicias) 7.14, 7.57;
(413) Demosthenes advocates move from
Syracuse to Thapsus or Catana 7.49,
7.60; Catana providing food to
Athenians at Syracuse 7.60; first aim of
Athenian retreat 7.80; refuge for
escaped or kidnapped Athenians 7.85
Caulonia, in Italy 7.25
Caunus, in Caria 1.116, 8.39, 8.41–2,
8.57, 8.88, 8.108
cavalry: Peloponnesian cavalry provided
by Boeotia, Phocis, Locris 2.9;
cavalry pay 5.47; cavalrymen's
attendants 7.25; cavalry battles 2.22,
4.72, 4.124, 6.98
Cecrops, legendary king of Attica 2.15
Cecryphaleia, small island off
Aegina 1.105
Cenaeum, cape in Euboea 3.93
Cenchreae, port in Corinthiad 4.42,
4.44, 8.10, 8.20, 8.23
Centoripa, Sicel town: (414) capitulates
to Athenians 6.94; 7.32
Ceos, Aegean island: subject ally of
Athens, with Athenians at
Syracuse 7.57
Cephallenia, W. Greek island: 1.27, 2.7
(envoys from Athens at start of war),
2.30 (won over by Athenians), 2.33
(failed Corinthian attempt, 431/0),
2.80; (426) join Athenians and
Acarnanians against Leucas 3.94, and
Athenians against Aetolia 3.95; 5.35
(Helots from Pylos settled there), 7.31,
7.57 (with Athenians in Sicily as
independent ally)
Cerameicus, district of Athens 6.57–8
Cercina, mountain in Macedonia 2.98
Cerdyllum, high ground opposite
Amphipolis 5.6, 5.8, 5.10
Ceryces, Athenian clan with oversight of
Eleusinian Mysteries 8.53
Cestrine, in Epirus 1.46
Chaereas, fervent Athenian
democrat: (411) brings to Samos
exaggerated account of regime of
Four Hundred 8.74, 8.86

Chaeroneia, in Boeotia 1.113, 4.76, 4.89
Chalce, E. Aegean island 8.41, 8.44,
8.55, 8.60
Chalcideus, Spartan commander:
(413/2) replaces Melanchridas as
admiral 8.6; (412) commands
expedition to Chios and Ionia 8.8,
8.11–12, 8.14–17, 8.32; with
Alcibiades secures revolts of Chios
(8.14), Erythrae (8.14), Clazomenae
(8.14), Teos (8.16), Miletus (8.17,
8.25, 8.28); with Tissaphernes
negotiates 1st treaty between Sparta
and Persia 8.17–18, 8.36, 8.43; killed
at Panormus (3) 8.24, 8.45
CHALCIDIANS in Thraceward
region: (432) persuaded by Perdiccas
to uproot to Olynthus 1.58
—(432 on) in revolt from and at war
with Athens 1.56–9, 1.61–5, 2.29, 2.58,
2.79 (defeat Athenians at Spartolus,
429); (425) drive Athenians out of Eïon
(2) 4.7; (424) invitation and arrival of
Brasidas 4.79–82; at Acanthus 4.84–8;
(424/3) Argilus 4.103, Amphipolis
4.103–8, Torone 4.110–14; (422)
Cleon's expedition 5.2–3, 5.6–11; 5.26,
5.30, 5.83 (Athenian expedition under
Nicias aborted, 417), 6.10 (still in revolt,
415); supported by Corinth 1.56,
1.60–6, 5.30; in Brasidas' army
4.123–4 (423), 5.6 (422)
—(429/8) Sitalces' campaign against
Chalcidians 2.95, 2.101; (422/1)
provision in Peace of Nicias 5.18; (421)
refuse compliance with Peace of
Nicias 5.21, 5.26, 5.35; join Argive
alliance 5.31; (421/0) frustrated in
attempt to bring Boeotia into the
alliance 5.38; (418/7) alliance confirmed
with Argos and Sparta 5.80; (417)
Dium secedes to Chalcidians 5.82;
(416/5) refuse Spartan request to
support Perdiccas against Athenians 6.7;
10–day truce with Athenians 6.7
—Chalcidian cavalry 2.79,
4.124, 5.10
Chalcidice 1.65, 2.58, 2.70, 2.101, 4.79,
4.103, (4.110, 4.123)
Chalcis (1), city in Euboea: first Greeks
to colonize Sicily 6.3; founded Naxos
(2), Leontini, Catana (6.3), Zancle
(6.4), Himera (6.5); founded Cumae in

Opicia (Italy) 6.4; Chalcidian (i.e.
Ionian) cities in Sicily 3.86, 4.25, 4.61,
4.64, 6.3–5, 6.76, 6.79, 6.84,
7.57; early war with Eretria
1.15; 7.29, 8.95; subject ally of
Athens, with Athenians in Sicily 7.57
Chalcis (2), Corinthian dependency in
Aetolia: (456) captured by Athenians,
1.108; 2.83
Chaleium, in Ozolian Locris 3.101
chance/the incalculable 1.78, 1.84,
1.122, 1.138, 1.140, 1.142, 2.11, 2.44,
2.61, 2.64, 2.87, 3.59, 4.18, 4.55,
4.62–4, 4.65, 5.16, 5.46, 5.75, 5.102,
6.23, 6.78, 7.61, 7.71, 8.24
Chaonians, barbarian tribe in Epirus:
political structure 2.80; (430) join
Ambraciots against Amphilochia 2.68;
(429) against Acarnania 2.80–2
Charadrus, watercourse outside Argos,
site of courts martial 5.60
Charicles, Athenian general 7.20, 7.26
Charminus, Athenian general 8.30,
8.41; (411) colluded with oligarchic
conspirators in Samos 8.73
Charoeades, Athenian general: (427)
commanded in 1st Athenian
expedition to Sicily 3.86; (426)
killed in battle with Syracusans 3.90
Charybdis, strait between Sicily
and Italy 4.24
Cheimerium, in Thesprotia 1.30, 1.46,
1.48
Chersonese 1.11, 8.62, 8.99, 8.102, 8.104
Chersonesus, in Corinthiad 4.42–3
CHIOS, E. Aegean island: supposed
birthplace of Homer 3.104; rich land,
unravaged from Persian War to
412: 8.24, 8.45; combined prosperity
with stability 8.24; dense slave
population 8.40; ships, not tribute
1.19, 6.85, 7.57; ship-providing allies of
Athens 1.116–17, 2.9, 2.56 (cf. 6.31),
4.13, 4.129, 5.84, 6.43, 7.20, cf. 8.9; with
Athenians in Sicily 7.57; 'autonomy' in
Athenian empire 3.10; (427) prisoners
held by Alcidas released 3.32; (425/4)
Athenian suspicions, walls
demolished 4.51
—revolt from and war with Athens
(413/2–411): (413/2) apply to Sparta,
alliance made 8.5–8, without
knowledge of common people 8.9,

8.14; (412) Athenians get wind 8.9–10,
8.15; revolt, and reaction in Athens
8.14–15; with Spartans, promote revolt
elsewhere 8.16–17, 8.19, 8.22–3
(Lesbos), 8.28; defeated by Athenians
at Mytilene 8.22–3; Athenians wage
war from Lesbos, Chians defeated and
country ravaged 8.24, 8.38; pro-
Athenian elements 8.24, 8.31, 8.38;
Pedaritus sent as Spartan governor
8.28, 8.32; (412/1) Athenian
expedition against Chios 8.30, 8.33–4,
8.38, 8.40, 8.55–6, 8.61; offend
Astyochus 8.32–3; Athenians fortify
Delphinium 8.34, 8.38, 8.40; Chians
appeal to Astyochus 8.38, 8.40, 8.60,
Tissaphernes (rejected) 8.45,
Peloponnesians at Rhodes 8.55; defeated by Athenians, Pedaritus killed,
blockade tightened, famine in Chios
8.55–6, 8.61; (411) Leon comes as new
governor, with ships 8.61; Chians
break out, and sea-battle with
Athenians 8.61, 8.63; Peloponnesian
fleet at Chios, paid by Chians 8.99–101;
lose eight ships at Cynossema 8.106
Choerades, Iapygian islands off
Taras 7.33
Chromon, Messenian, guide to Athenians
in Aetolia (426) 3.98
Chrysippus, murdered by Atreus 1.9
Chrysis, priestess at Argos 2.2; (423)
accidentally burns down temple of
Hera 4.133
Cilicia 1.112
Cimon (1), son of Miltiades (1.98 etc.),
Athenian general: (470s) captures
Eïon (1) 1.98; (?469) defeats
Persians in battles of Eurymedon
1.100; (?462) brings Athenian force to
help Spartans in Helot revolt 1.102;
(451) leads expedition to Cyprus,
dies there 1.112
Cimon (2), father of Lacedaemonius 1.45
Cithaeron, mountain in
Boeotia 2.75, 3.24
Citium, city in Cyprus 1.112
civil strife (stasis): 1.2, 1.12, 1.23, 1.24,
1.115, 1.126, 2.65 (Athens); 3.2, 3.27
(Mytilene); 3.34; 3.62, 4.92
(Boeotia); 3.68, 4.66 (Megara); 4.1,
4.130, 5.4, 5.5, 7.33, 7.46, 7.50, 8.21,
8.92–6 (Athens); in Corcyra (427–5),

3.70–81, [3.84], 4.2, 4.46–8; in the Greek world, 3.82–3, [3.84]

Clarus, in Ionia 3.33

Clazomenae, in Ionia: (412) revolts from Athens and fortifies Polichna 8.14; 8.16, 8.22; Polichna captured by Athenians, Clazomenians rejoin Athenian alliance 8.23; (412/1) failed attack by Astyochus 8.31; property in off-lying islands looted by Astyochus' fleet 8.31

Cleaenetus, father of Cleon: 3.36 etc.

Cleandridas, father of Gylippus 6.93; Thurian citizenship conferred on him 6.104

Clearchus, son of Rhamphias (8.8 etc.), Spartan commander 8.8, 8.39, 8.80

Clearidas, Spartan appointed governor of Amphipolis (423) 4.132; (422) in battle for Amphipolis 5.6, 5.8–10; (421) refuses to hand back Amphipolis after Peace of Nicias 5.21; brings back troops from Thraceward region after peace 5.34

Cleinias (1), father of Alcibiades: 5.43 etc.

Cleinias (2), father of Cleopompus: 2.26 etc.

Cleïppides, Athenian general 3.3

Cleoboulus, Spartan ephor, opposed to peace treaty 5.36–8

Cleombrotus, father of Pausanias (1) 1.94 etc., and of Nicomedes 1.107

Cleomedes, Athenian general at Melos (416) 5.84

Cleomenes (1), Spartan king 1.126

Cleomenes (2), brother of Pleistoanax, regent for his nephew Pausanias (2): (427) leads 4th Peloponnesian invasion of Attica 3.26

CLEON, son of Cleainetus (3.36 etc.), Athenian demagogue (3.36) and general: the Athenian most opposed to peace 5.16; 'more sensible elements' want to be rid of him 4.28; character 3.36, 4.21, 5.7, 5.10, 5.16; enmity for Nicias 4.27–8; Cleon on democracy 3.37; on empire 3.37, 3.40 —(427) carries 1st motion to execute Mytilenaeans 3.36; speech in 'Mytileneaean debate' 3.37–40; carries motion to execute Mytilenaeans

sent to Athens 3.50; (425) persuades Athenians to reject Spartan offer of peace 4.21–2; forced into accepting Pylos command 4.27–8; at Pylos 4.30–9, cf. 5.7; (423) carries motion for destruction of Scione 4.122; (422) recaptures Torone 5.2–3, and Galepsus, but fails at Stagirus 5.6; at Amphipolis 5.6–10; disaffection of his troops 5.7; killed 5.10

Cleonae (1), in Argolid: (418) in battle of Mantinea 5.67, 5.72, 5.74; 6.95

Cleonae (2), city on Acte peninsula (Chalcidice) 4.109

Cleopompus, Athenian general 2.26, 2.58 (at Potidaea)

Cnemus, Spartan admiral: (430) campaign against Zacynthus 2.66; (429) campaign against Acarnania 2.80–2; 2.84; Spartan commissioners sent to advise him 2.85; speech at Rhium 2.87; (429/8) proposed attack on Peiraeus 2.93

Cnidus, E. Aegean peninsula: colonized Aeolus islands 3.88; sanctuary of Apollo at Triopium 8.35; (412/1) revolts from Athens 8.35; attacked and ravaged by Athenians from Samos 8.35; 8.41; whole Peloponnesian fleet gathered at Cnidus 8.42–4, 8.52; (411) expulsion of Persian garrison 8.109

Colonae, in Troad 1.131

colonies, colonization 1.12, 1.24–7, 1.34, 1.38, 1.56; colonization of Cyclades by Minos 1.4; of islands by Carians and Phoenicians 1.8; of Ionia 1.2, 1.12, 2.15; of Italy and Sicily by Peloponnesians 1.12; of Sicily 6.3–5; consultation of Delphi 3.92; invitation of volunteers 1.27, 3.92, 4.102; relations of colonies and mother-cities: 1.25, 7.57 (Corcyra/Corinth); 1.56; 5.104, 5.106 (Melos/Sparta); 6.6 (Syracuse/Corinth)

Colonus, outside Athens: sanctuary of Poseidon, site of assembly in 411: 8.67

Colophon, in Ionia: (430) captured by Persians 3.34; (427) Notium restored to Colophonians by Paches 3.34

Conon, Athenian commander at
Naupactus (413) 7.31
consular representatives (proxenoi)
2.29, 2.85, 3.2, 3.52, 3.70, 4.78, 5.43,
5.59, 5.76, 6.89, 8.92
Copae, in Boeotia 4.93
Copaïs, lake in Boeotia 4.93
CORCYRA, W. Greek island: on route
to Italy and Sicily, 1.36, 1.44; colonized
Epidamnus 1.24; early sea-battle
with Corinthians 1.13; early use of
triremes 1.14; Themistocles a
benefactor 1.136; previous
isolationist policy 1.31, 1.32,
1.37; wealth 1.25; naval power 1.25,
1.33, 1.35, 1.36, 1.44, 1.68, 3.77,
3.82; ship-providing allies of
Athens 2.9, 2.25, 3.94, 7.31, 7.57;
relations with Corinth 1.25, 7.57;
assemblies 3.70–1; council 3.70
—sanctuaries of Zeus and Alcinous
3.70; temple of Hera (Heraeum) 1.24,
3.75, 3.79, 3.81; sanctuary of
Dioscuri 3.75; temple of Dionysus
3.81; Hyllaic harbour 3.72, 3.81;
island facing Heraeum 3.75, 3.79;
promontory of Leucimme 1.30, 1.47,
1.51, 3.79
—(435) besiege Epidamnus,
defeat Corinthians in sea-battle of
Leucimme 1.26–30; (433) apply to
join Athenian alliance 1.31–6 (speech
at Athens 1.32–6); defensive alliance
with Athens 1.44–5, 3.70; with
Athenian help, worst Corinthians
in sea-battle of Sybota 1.47–55;
Corcyraean prisoners and their
return 1.55, 3.70; (431) envoys
from Athens at start of war 2.7;
(415) muster-station for Sicilian
expedition 6.30, 6.32, 6.34, 6.42–4,
7.26; (413) hoplites and ships raised to
support Athenians in Sicily 7.31, 7.57
—civil war (427–425) 3.70–81, [3.84],
4.2, 4.46–8: (427) envoys from
Athens, Corinth, and Sparta at start of
civil war 3.70, 3.72; oligarchic envoys
to Athens arrested 3.72; democratic
refugees in Athens 3.70–2; oligarchic
coup kills Peithias and others 3.70;
oligarchic, then democratic victory 3.72–4; arrival of Athenian ships
from Naupactus 3.75; naval

engagement with Peloponnesians
3.77–8, and arrival of further Athenian
fleet 3.80–1; murder and suicide of
oligarchs 3.81; (425) oligarchs cross
from mainland and harass city from
Mt Istone (3.85), 4.2; Peloponnesian
fleet to support them recalled to
Pylos 4.2–3; famine in city 3.85,
4.2; oligarchs defeated by Athenians
and democrats, and wiped out (murder
and suicide) 4.46–8
CORINTH: situation, and
wealth 1.13; original inhabitants
Aeolians 4.42; Isthmian festival
8.9–10; colonized Ambracia (2.80),
Apollonia (1.26), Corcyra (1.24–5,
7.57), Leucas (1.30), Potidaea (1.56),
Sollium (2.30), Syracuse (6.3,
cf. 6.88); builders of first triremes
1.13; early sea-battle with Corcyraeans
1.13; relations with Corcyra 1.25,
7.57; loaned ships to Athenians against
Aegina 1.41; defeat Athenians at
Halieis, defeated by Athenians in
Megarid (460–459), 1.105–6;
Corinthian Chalcis captured by
Athenians (456) 1.108; aid revolt of
Megara (446) 1.114; opposed
Peloponnesian intervention in revolt of
Samos (440–439) 1.10–11; ship-
providing allies of Sparta 2.9, 7.58, 8.3
—(435) support Epidamnus, defeated
by Corcyraeans in sea-battle of
Leucimme 1.25–31; (435–433) build up
navy thereafter 1.31, (1.36); (433)
speech at Athens 1.37–43; worsted by
Athenians and Corcyraeans in
sea-battle of Sybota 1.46–55; take
Anactorium 1.55; anger against
Athens 1.55–7, 1.103; approaches by
Perdiccas 1.57; Corinthian force at
Potidaea 1.60–6; (432) summon allies
to Sparta 1.67; speeches at Sparta
1.68–71, 1.120–4; (431) Sollium
captured by Athenians 2.30; (431/0)
expedition to Acarnania and Cephallenia 2.33; (430/29) Phormio at
Naupactus to prevent traffic to/from
Corinth, 2.69; (429) defeated by
Phormio in Gulf 2.80, 2.83–4,
2.90–2; (429/8) starting point for
attack on Peiraeus/Salamis 2.93–4;
(427) send envoys to Corcyra at start of

civil war 3.70, 3.72; (426/5) install
garrison in Ambracia 3.114, 4.42;
(garrison in Leucas 4.42, cf. 3.7,
3.94); **(425)** battle with Athenians
attacking Corinthiad 4.42–4; lose
Anactorium to Athenians and
Acarnanians 4.49; (424) hoplites in
Brasidas' army at Megara 4.70;
(424/3) hoplites supporting Boeotians
at Delium 4.100; (423) signatories of
one-year truce 4.119
—(422/1) dissent from treaty and
alliance with Athens 5.17, 5.22, 5.25,
5.35; **(421)** urge Argives to set up
defensive alliance 5.27, 5.32, and
join it 5.31; Spartan complaints
5.30; seek truce with Athens
5.32; **(421/0)** Spartan-inspired
proposals for alliance of Boeotia with
Corinth and Argos come to nothing
5.36–8; secede from Sparta 5.38
(cf. 5.30); **(420)** abstain from Athens/
Argos alliance and incline to Sparta
5.48; Argives and allies ask Corinthians
to join them 5.50; (419) prevent
Alcibiades fortifying Rhium 5.52; **(418)**
in Peloponnesian expedition against
Argos 5.57–60; summoned to assist
Spartans at Mantinea 5.64; request
countermanded 5.75; (417/6) do not
join Peloponnesians against Argos 5.83
(nor in 416/5: 6.7); (416) unspecified
clash with Athenians 5.115; (415/4)
vote to support Syracuse, and send
envoys to Sparta 6.88, 6.93; **(414)**
send two ships to Italy/Sicily 6.93,
6.104; to follow with more ships 6.104,
7.2, 7.4, 7.7 (escape interception),
7.58; troops requested for Sicily 7.7, cf.
7.12 (Nicias), 7.17, 7.18; (414–413) fleet
opposing Athenians at Naupactus 7.17,
7.19, 7.31, 7.34 (sea-battle); **(413)** send
hoplites to Sicily 7.17, 7.19, 7.31,
7.58; in final sea-battle in Great
Harbour 7.70; only allies to send
both fleet and land force to Sicily 7.58;
return of ships (412) 8.13; (413/2)
required to build ships for Peloponnesian
League 8.3; **(412)** League conference
at Corinth 8.8, Corinthians hold up
agreed action for Isthmian festival
8.9–10; support the ships blockaded at
Speiraeum 8.11; (412/1) oppose

Lesbian proposals for second
revolt 8.32; **(411)** besiege
Oenoe 8.98; lose five ships at
Cynossema 8.106
Coroneia, in Boeotia: site of Athenian
defeat by Boeotians (447/6) 1.113,
3.62, 3.67, 4.92; 4.93 (at battle of
Delium, 424/3)
Coronta, in Acarnania 2.102
Corycus, on mainland opposite Chios, in
Erythraean territory 8.14, 8.33–4
Coryphasium, Spartan name for
Pylos 4.3, 4.118, 5.18
Cos, E. Aegean island: 8.44, 8.55, 8.108
Cos Meropis, city in Cos: ruined by
earthquake 8.41; (412/1) sacked by
Astyochus 8.41
Cotyrta, in Laconia 4.56
Cranii, city in Cephallenia 2.30,
2.33; (421) Helots from Pylos
settled there 5.35, 5.56
Crannon, in Thessaly 2.22
Crataemenes, from Chalcis,
co-founder of Zancle 6.4
Crenae, in Amphilochia 3.105–6
Crestonia, *see* Grestonia
Cretan Sea 4.53, 5.110
Crete 2.9, 2.85–6, 2.92, 3.69; 6.4, 7.57
(co-founders of Gela); 8.39; (415)
Cretan archers in Sicilian expedition
6.25 (mercenaries, 7.57)
Crisa, Gulf of (Corinthian Gulf)
1.107, 2.69, 2.80, 2.83–4, 2.86,
2.89–93, 4.76, 8.7
Crocyleium, town in Aetolia 3.96
Croesus, king of Lydia (from *c*.560):
(*c*.546) defeated by Cyrus 1.16
Crommyon, in Corinthiad 4.42, 4.44–5
Cropia, in Attica 2.19
Croton, city in Italy 7.35
Crousis, district of Chalcidice 2.79
crowd behaviour 2.65, 4.28, 6.63, 8.1,
8.86
Cumae, city in Italy (Opicia):
co-founder of Zancle 6.4
Cyclades, Aegean islands 1.4, 2.9
(tribute-paying region of Athenian
empire)
Cyclopes, supposed original
inhabitants of Sicily 6.2
Cydonia, city in Crete 2.85
Cyllene, port/dockyard of Elis 1.30,
2.84, 2.86, 3.69, 3.76, 6.88

Cylon, Olympic victor, attempted
tyranny in Athens 1.126
Cyme, city in Aeolis (1) 3.31, 8.22,
8.31, 8.100, 8.101
Cynes, Acarnanian restored by
Athenians to Coronta 2.102
Cynossema, headland in Chersonese:
(411) scene of sea-battle between
Athenians and Peloponnesians 8.104–6
Cynouria, region on borders of
Argos and Laconia 4.56, 5.14, 5.41
Cyprus 1.94, 1.104, 1.112, 1.128
Cypsela, Mantinean fort in Parrhasian
territory 5.33
Cyrene, city in N. Africa 1.110, 7.50
Cyrrhus, in Macedonia 2.100
Cyrus (1), King of Persia
(*c*.560–530) 1.13, 1.16
Cyrus (2), son of Dareius (2) 2.65
Cythera, island S. of Laconia: Spartan
colony 7.57; (424) capitulates to
Athenian expedition 4.53–7; 4.118;
5.14 (raids on Spartan territory);
(422/1) provision for return to Sparta
in Peace of Nicias 5.18; (413)
Athenian fort in Laconia opposite
Cythera 7.26
Cytinium, town in Doris 1.107, 3.95,
3.102
Cyzicus, city on S. shore of Propontis
8.6, 8.39; (411) revolts from Athens
and recaptured 8.107

Damagon, Spartan founder-colonist of
Heracleia (1) 3.92
Danaans, Homeric name for Greeks 1.3
Danube, river 2.96, 2.97
Daphnus, unidentified place near
Clazomenae 8.23, 8.31
Dardanus, on Asian shore of
Hellespont 8.104
Dareius (1), King of Persia
(522–486) 1.14, 1.16, 4.102, 6.59
Dareius (2), son of Artaxerxes,
King of Persia (424–404) 8.5–6, 8.28,
8.37, 8.58
Dascon (1), Syracusan founder-colonist
of Camarina 6.5
Dascon (2), area on SW shore of
Syracusan Great Harbour 6.66
Dascylium, capital of a Persian
satrapy 1.129
Daulia, in Phocis 2.29; 'Daulian bird'
(nightingale) 2.29

DECELEIA, in Attica: (425/4)
Alcibiades advises Spartans to build
fort there 6.91, (6.93), 7.18; (413)
Spartans begin fortification 7.19,
7.20, 7.27; damage caused to Athens
by Deceleia 7.27–8, 8.69, 8.95;
7.42, 8.70–1, 8.98; (411) leading
members of Four Hundred
escape to Deceleia 8.98
Deiniadas, Spartan commander
(one of the Perioeci) 8.22
Delium, sanctuary of Apollo in territory
of Tanagra: (424/3) seized and
fortified by Athenians, battle of
Delium against Boeotians 4.76,
4.89–101, 5.14–15
DELOS, Aegean island: treasury of
Delian League 1.96; earthquake
2.8; purification by Peisistratus
3.104; (426/5) by Athenians 1.8,
3.104, 8.108; (422) further
purification by Athenians, and
eviction of Delians 5.1 (reinstated,
5.32); earlier Delian festival, and
revival by Athenians (426/5)
3.104; (422) evicted Delians
offered home in Atramyttium by
Pharnaces 5.1; (411) Delians in
Atramyttium massacred by Arsaces
8.108; 3.29, 8.77, 8.80, 8.86
DELPHI: funds at Delphi 1.121,
1.143; Greek dedication at Delphi after
Persian War 1.132, 3.57; spoils of war
sent to Delphi 4.134; provision in
treaties for universal access 4.118
(one-year truce, 423), 5.18 (Peace of
Nicias, 422/1); under Peace of Nicias
Delphi to be autonomous, and pillar
recording the Peace set up 5.18;
Sacred War (449) 1.112; 3.101
— the oracle: as arbitrator
1.28; consultations 1.25 (Epidamnians), 1.118 (Spartans), 1.126
(Cylon), 3.92 (Spartans re Heracleia),
5.16 (Spartans); responses 1.103
(to Spartans), 1.118, 1.123, 2.54
(to Spartans), 1.126 (to Cylon), 1.134
(to Spartans); oracles 2.17
('Pelargic' area of Athens), 5.32
(reinstatement of Delians); alleged
suborning of oracle by Pleistoanax
and his brother 5.16
Delphinium, near city of Chios: (412/11)
fortified by Athenians 8.34, 8.38, 8.40

demagogues 4.21 (Cleon), 8.65
(Androcles)
Demaratus, Athenian general 6.105
Demarchus, Syracusan commander:
(411) sent to fleet at Miletus 8.85
demes, districts of Attica 2.19, 2.23
Demiurgi, magistrates at Mantinea
and Elis 5.47
democracy: views of: Alcibiades 6.89,
8.47; Athenagoras 6.38–40; Cleon,
3.37; Diodotus 3.42–3; Pericles
2.37; nature of Athenian, under
Pericles 2.65; Athenian support for
democratic parties 3.82, 4.76,
5.82; democracy in Argos, 5.81–2;
in Samos, 1.115, 8.73, 8.75; attitude
of subject allies to democracy/
oligarchy 8.48, 8.64; democracies put
down by Peisander, etc. (411)
8.64–5; *see also* crowd behaviour
Demodocus, Athenian general 4.75
DEMOSTHENES, son of Alcisthenes
(3.91 etc.), Athenian general: (426)
commands naval expedition round
Peloponnese 3.91; against Leucas, with
Acarnanians 3.94; against Aetolia
3.94–8, 4.30; plans overland attack on
Boeotia 3.95; defeated in Aetolia,
does not return to Athens 3.98 (cf.
3.114); persuades Acarnanians to come to
aid of Naupactus 3.102; (426/5) invited
to lead against Ambraciot invasion of
Amphilochia 3.105–14; private truce to
sully Spartan reputation in NW
Greece 3.109, 3.111; urges reduction of
Ambracia 3.113; 300 panoplies reserved
for Demosthenes 3.114; (425) at
Pylos 4.3–5, 4.8–16, 4.23, 4.26,
4.29–39; speech to troops at Pylos
4.10; chosen by Cleon as his
co-commander 4.29; (424) at
Megara 4.66–73; at Naupactus,
gathering troops for Boeotian expedition 4.76–7; (424/3) expedition to
Siphae compromised by betrayal to
Boeotians 4.89, 4.101; unsuccessful
landing on coast of Sicyon 4.101;
(422/1) signatory of Peace of Nicias and
alliance 5.19, 5.24; (418/7) in charge of
handing over fort at Heraeum 5.80;
(414/3) elected general to join Nicias in
Sicily 7.16–17, 7.26–7; (413) joins
Charicles' fleet in operations on coast of
Laconia 7.20, 7.26; recruitment in

W. Greece 7.31, 7.33, cf. 7.57
(Acarnanian loyalty); in S. Italy 7.33
—in Sicily (413): arrival and
assessment of situation 7.42; assault on
Epipolae fails 7.43–5; advocates
departure from Sicily 7.47, or at least
moving from Syracuse 7.49; commands
in final sea-battle 7.69; proposes
another attempt to break out 7.72;
exhortations to troops at start of
retreat 7.78; change of plan in
retreat 7.80; his division
surrenders 7.80–2; executed by
Syracusans 7.86
Demoteles, commander of Locrian
garrison at Messana 4.25
Dercylidas, Spartan commander:
(411) sent overland to Hellespont,
secures revolt of Abydos 8.61–2
Derdas, Macedonian opposed to
Perdiccas 1.57, 1.59
Dersaeans, northern Thracian
tribe 2.101
Deucalion, father of Hellen 1.3
Dians, dagger-carrying Thracian
tribe 2.96, 2.98, 7.27; (413)
commit atrocities in attack on
Mycalessus 7.29–30
Diasia, festival of Zeus the Kindly
at Athens 1.126
Didyme, one of the Lipara islands 3.88
Diemporus, Boeotarch: (431) led
Theban entry into Plataea 2.2
Diitrephes (1), father of
Nicostratus: 3.75 etc.
Diitrephes (2), Athenian
general: 7.29; (411) puts down
democracy in Thasos 8.64
Diodotus, son of Eucrates (3.41),
Athenian politician: (427) speech in
'Mytilenaean debate' 3.42–8
Diomedon, Athenian general: (412)
commands a fleet in E. Aegean
8.19–20, 8.23 (recaptures
Mytilene), 8.24; (412/1) sent as
replacement general to Samos
8.54–5; (411) supports Samian
democrats 8.73
Diomilus, Andrian exile, in command of
Syracusan rapid-deployment force,
killed on Epipolae (414) 6.96–7
Dionysia: (= Anthesteria) Athenian and
Ionian festival 2.15; City Dionysia
at Athens 5.20, 5.23

Dionysus, god: temple of Dionysus in the Marshes at Athens, 2.15; temple at Corcyra 3.81; theatre of Dionysus near Mounichia 8.93; precinct of Dionysus in Athens 8.93–4

Dioscuri, gods: sanctuary in Corcyra 3.75; temple at Torone 4.110; Anaceium in Athens 8.93

Dios Hieron, in Ionia 8.19

Diotimus, Athenian general 1.45; father of Strombichides 8.15

Diphilus, Athenian general 7.34

Dium (1), in Macedonia 4.78

Dium (2), city on Acte peninsula (Chalcidice): (424/3) resists Brasidas 4.109; (421) captures Thyssus 5.35; (417) secedes from Athens to Chalcidians 5.82

Doberus, in Paeonia 2.98–100

Dolopes, *see* Dolopia

Dolopia, region of central Greece 2.102; Dolopes original inhabitants of Scyros 1.98; (420/19) Dolopes in battle against Heracleia (1) 5.51

Dorcis, Spartan commander sent to replace Pausanias (1) 1.95

DORIANS: generic racial term 1.124, 2.9; occupation of Peloponnese 1.12, 1.18, 1.24, 4.42; Dorian dialect 3.112, 4.3, 4.41, 6.5; sacred month Carneius 5.54; Dorian/Ionian antipathy 1.102, 1.124, 3.86, 3.92, 4.61, 5.9, 6.77, 6.80, 6.82, 7.57, 7.63, 8.25; 'Dorian war' prophecy 2.54; Dorian cities in Sicily 3.86, 4.61, 4.64, 6.77, 7.57–8; Dorian paeans in night-battle on Epipolae (413) 7.44

Dorieus, from Rhodes: Olympic victor 3.8; (412–411) commands 10 Thurian ships in Spartan fleet 8.35; (411) threatened violence by Astyochus 8.84

Doris, region of central Greece: mother-country of Sparta 1.107 (supported by Sparta against Phocis), 3.92 (appeal to Sparta against Oetaeans); 3.95, 3.102

Dorus, Thessalian friend of Brasidas 4.78

Drabescus, in Edonia (Thrace): (465/4) scene of destruction of Athenian colonizing force by Thracians 1.100, 4.102

Dread Goddesses, their altars in Athens 1.126

Droans, northern Thracian tribe 2.101

Drymoussa, island off Clazomenae 8.31

Dryopians, race inhabiting Carystus in Euboea 7.57

Dryoscephalae, in Boeotia 3.24

Dyme, in Achaea 2.84

Earth (Ge): temple of, in Athens 2.15

earthquakes 1.23, 2.8, 3.87, 3.89, 4.52, 5.45, 5.50, 6.95, 8.6, 8.41; great Spartan earthquake (*c.*465/4) 1.101, 1.128, 2.27, 3.54, 4.56

Eccritus, Spartan commander of troops sent to Sicily (413) 7.19

Echecratides, Thessalian king, father of Orestes 1.111

Echinades, islands opposite Oeniadae 2.102

eclipses, of sun 1.23, 2.28, 4.52; of moon 7.50

Edonia, region of Thrace 1.100, 2.99, 4.102, 4.107, 4.109, 5.6 (Edonians in Brasidas' army, 422)

Eëtioneia, claw of land narrowing entrance to Peiraeus: (411) fortified by Four Hundred 8.90–2; the wall demolished by hoplites and men of Peiraeus 8.92, 8.94

EGESTA, city in Sicily: of Trojan origin 6.2; barbarians 6.11 (Nicias), 7.57; (416–415) at war with Selinus, and appeal to Athens for help 6.6, 6.8, 6.13, 6.47–8, 6.62; offer funds 6.6, 6.8; funds doubted by Nicias 6.22, 6.46, and found to amount to only 30 talents 6.46–7, collected by Nicias 6.62; Hyccara captured and handed to Egestans 6.62; (414) provide horses for Athenian cavalrymen 6.98; Athenian allies 7.57; Egestan cavalry 6.37, 6.62, 6.88, 6.98

Egypt: revolt from and recovery by Persia 1.104, 1.109–10, 1.112; (460–454) disastrous Athenian expedition to Egypt 1.104, 1.105, 1.109–10, 1.112; plague spread from Ethiopia to Egypt 2.48; marsh people 1.110, 1.112; trade 4.53, 8.35; Egyptian bodyguard of Pausanias (1) 1.130

Eidomene, in Macedonia 2.100

Eïon (1), in Thrace, at mouth of
Strymon: (?476) captured from
Persians 1.98; 4.50; 4.102; (424/3)
defended against Brasidas by
Thucydides 4.104, **4.106–7**,
4.108; (422) Cleon's base for campaign
against Amphipolis 5.6, 5.10

Eïon (2), in Thraceward region: colony
of Mende, captured and lost by
Athenians (425) 4.7

Elaean district of Thesprotia 1.46

Elaeus, city at SW extremity of
Chersonese 8.102–3, 8.107; sanctuary
of Protesilaus 8.102

Elaphebolion, month in Athenian
calendar 4.118, 5.19

Eleusinium, temple in Athens 2.17

Eleusis, in Attica 1.114, 2.15
(legendary war against
Erechtheus), 2.19–21, 4.68

Elimiotians, people of Upper
Macedonia 2.99

ELIS: Six Hundred, Demiurgi,
Thesmophylaces 5.47; Elean control
of Olympia 5.31, 5.49–50; Vale of
Elis 2.25; dockyard at Cyllene 1.30
(burned by Corcyraeans, 435),
2.84; help Corinth against
Corcyra 1.27 (435), 1.46 (433); ship-
providing ally of Sparta 2.9
—(431) Pheia attacked and Eleans
defeated by Athenians 2.25; (427)
Teutiaplus' advice to Alcidas
rejected 3.29; (422/1) dissent from
Peace of Nicias and alliance 5.17,
5.22; (421) alliance with Corinth, and
then Argos 5.31, 5.37; quarrel with
Sparta over Lepreum 5.31, 5.34,
5.49–50; (420) Elis, Mantinea, and
Argos make treaty of alliance with
Athens 5.43–8; ban Sparta from
Olympic festival 5.49–50; (418)
support Argives against Spartans 5.58,
5.61, and insist on prosecution of war
5.61–2; return home when allies vote
against attack on Lepreum 5.62; send
hoplites too late for battle of Mantinea,
and join allied attack on Epidaurus 5.75;
(418/7) Argives renounce alliance with
Elis, etc. 5.78

Ellomenum, in Leucadian
territory 3.94

Elymians, Trojan settlers in Sicily 6.2

Embatum, in the territory of Erythrae
(1) 3.29

Endius, son of Alcibiades (2) (8.6),
Spartan ephor 8.6, 8.12; guest-friend
of Alcibiades (1) 8.6; (420) envoy to
Athens 5.44–6; (412) persuaded by
Alcibiades to send support for Ionian
revolt 8.12, 8.17

Enipeus, river in Thessaly 4.78

Enneacrounos, fountain in Athens 2.15

Entimus, Cretan co-founder of Gela 6.4

Enyalius, god (= Ares): sanctuary near
Megara 4.67

Eordia, district of Macedonia 2.99

Ephesus, in Ionia 1.137, 3.32–3, 4.50,
8.19, 8.109; Ephesian festival 3.104

Ephyre, in Thesprotia 1.46

Epicles, Spartan commander 8.107

Epicydidas, Spartan commander 5.12

Epidamnus, on Illyrian coast of
Adriatic: 1.24–9; jointly colonized by
Corcyra and Corinth 1.24–5; (435)
handed over to Corinth 1.25;
besieged, and surrenders to
Corcyraeans 1.26–9; the Epidamnus
affair the first of the causes of the
war 1.146; 1.34, 1.38, 1.39, 3.70

EPIDAURUS: (460–459) with
Corinthians defeat Athenians at
Halieis 1.105; (446) aid revolt of
Megara, 1.114; (435) help Corinth
against Corcyra 1.27; (430) attacked
by Athenians under Pericles 2.56,
6.31; (425) attacked by Athenians
under Nicias 4.45; (419/8) war
with Argos 5.26, 5.33–6, 5.57, 5.75,
5.77; Spartans send garrison to
Epidaurus 5.56; (418) in
Peloponnesian expedition against
Argos 5.58; Argive allies prepare for
siege of Epidaurus, and build fort at
Heraeum 5.75; (418/7) in treaty with
Sparta Argives agree withdrawal from
Epidaurus 5.77; Athenians renew
treaty with Epidaurians and hand over
Heraeum fort 5.80; (413/2) required
to build ships for Peloponnesian
League 8.3; (411) Peloponnesian fleet
stationed at Epidaurus 8.92, 8.94

Epidaurus Limera, in Laconia 4.56,
6.105, 7.18, 7.26

EPIPOLAE, heights above
Syracuse 6.75, **6.96**, 6.101–3, 7.1–5,
7.42–6; spur Temenitis 7.3; (414)

seized by Athenians, and Syracusans
defeated 6.97; Gylippus on
Epipolae 7.2–3, 7.43; 3rd Syracusan
counter-wall running across
Epipolae 7.4, 7.5, 7.42; battles on
Epipolae: (414) first 6.97; second 7.5;
third 7.6; (413) fourth 7.43–6;
see also Euryelus, Labdalum, Syce

Epitadas, Spartan commander on
Sphacteria (425) 4.8, 4.31, 4.33,
4.38 (killed), 4.39

Erasinides, Corinthian commander 7.7

Erechtheus, legendary king of Attica 2.15

Eresus, city of Lesbos: 3.18, 3.35; (412)
revolts from Athens 8.23; (411)
revolts again 8.100; Athenians begin
but abandon siege 8.100, 8.103

Eretria, city of Euboea: colonized
Mende 4.123; early war with
Chalcis 1.15; subject ally of Athens,
with Athenians at Syracuse 7.57;
Athenian fort in Eretria 8.95; (412/1)
betray Oropus to Boeotians, invite
Peloponnesians to assist revolt of
Euboea 8.60; (411) aid Peloponnesians
to defeat Athenian fleet 8.95; butcher
defeated Athenian crews 8.95

Erineum, town in Doris 1.107

Erineus (1), bay on coast of Achaea 7.34

Erineus (2), river in Sicily 7.80, 7.82

Erythrae (1), in Ionia: 3.29, 3.33, 8.24,
8.28, 8.32; Athenian forts on
Erythraean peninsula 8.24,
8.31; (413/2) apply to Sparta for
help in revolting from Athens, and
alliance made 8.5–6; (412) revolt 8.14,
and support Chalcideus against
Teos 8.16; (412/1) trick of
Erythraean prisoners in Samos 8.33

Erythrae (2), in Boeotia 3.24

Eryx, city in Sicily 6.2, 6.46
(sanctuary of Aphrodite)

Eteonicus, Spartan commander 8.23

Ethiopia: original outbreak of plague 2.48

Etruria: (415/4) some cities volunteer
aid to Athenians in Sicily 6.88; (414)
send three penteconters to Athenians
6.103; (413) with Athenians at
Syracuse (7.57), repel attack by
Gylippus 7.53–4

Etruscans: once inhabited Lemnos
and Athens 4.109

Eualas, Spartan commander 8.22

EUBOEA: colonization of Sicily from
Chalcis in Euboea 6.3–5, 6.76; (470s)
Carystus capitulates to Athenians
1.98; (447/6) Euboean exiles at
battle of Coroneia 1.113; (446)
revolt from Athens, put down by
Pericles 1.114 (cf. 1.23, 4.92, 6.76,
6.84); (431) livestock from Attica
sent across to Euboea 2.14; (427/6)
earthquake; (426) tsunami at
Orobiae 3.89; Heracleia (1)
potential threat to Euboea 3.92–3
—tribute-paying subjects, with
Athenians in Sicily 7.57; importance
for Athenian food supplies 2.14,
7.28, 8.1, 8.95–6, 8.106; Athenian
guard on Euboea (431) 2.26,
2.32, [3.17], (413) 8.1, (411) 8.74,
8.86, 8.95
—second revolt: (413/2) first
approaches to Agis 8.5; (412/1)
betrayal of Oropus, and approach to
Peloponnesians in Rhodes 8.60; (411)
fleet sent from Laconia, defeat of
Athenians at Eretria, revolt of all
Euboea except Oreus 8.91–5;
resulting panic at Athens 8.96;
Peloponnesian fleet at Euboea
brought up to Hellespont 8.107

Euboulus, Chian commander 8.23

Eucleides, founder-colonist of Himera 6.5

Eucles (1), Athenian general in
Amphipolis (424/3) 4.104, 4.106

Eucles (2), Syracusan general: elected
(414) 6.103

Eucrates, father of Diodotus 3.41

Euctemon, Athenian general 8.30

Euesperides, city in N. Africa 7.50

Euetion, Athenian general 7.9

Eumachus, Corinthian commander 2.33

Eumolpidae, Athenian clan with
oversight of Eleusinian Mysteries 8.53

Eumolpus, legendary leader of
Eleusinians against Erechtheus 2.15

Eupalium, in Ozolian Locris 3.96, 3.102
(captured by Spartans, 426)

Euphamidas, Corinthian commander:
2.33; (423) signatory of one-year
truce 4.119; (419) at conference
of Mantinea 5.55

Euphemus, Athenian delegate to
Camarina (415/4) 6.75; his
speech in the assembly 6.82–7

Eupompides, Plataean general:
(428/7) leader of escape 3.20
Euripus, channel between
Euboea and mainland 7.29–30
Europe 1.89, 2.97
Europus, in Macedonia 2.100
Eurybatus, Corcyraean commander 1.47
Euryelus, western approach to
Epipolae 6.97, 7.2, 7.43
Eurylochus, Spartan commander against
Naupactus (426) and then
Amphilochia (426/5) 3.100–2,
3.105–9 (killed)
Eurymachus, Theban in league with
pro-Theban party in Plataea 2.2;
(431) captured and killed 2.5
EURYMEDON (1), son of Thucles (1)
(3.80 etc.), Athenian general: (427)
leads reinforcing fleet at Corcyra
3.80–1, 3.85; (426) leads full levy of
Athenians against Tanagra 3.91;
(426/5–424) joint commander of
reinforcements to Sicily 3.115, 4.2–3,
4.8, 6.1; (425) at Corcyra 4.46–
8; (424) fined on return from
Sicily 4.65; (414/3) elected general to
join Nicias in Sicily 7.16, 7.31; (413)
recruitment in Corcyra 7.31, 7.33, in
S. Italy 7.33; in assault on Epipolae
7.43; supports Demosthenes in
conference of generals 7.49; killed in
final battle in Great Harbour 7.52
Eurymedon (2), river in Pamphylia:
(?469) scene of double victory
over Persians 1.100
Eurystheus 1.9
Eurytanians, division of population of
Aetolia 3.94, 3.100
Eustrophus, Argive envoy to
Sparta (420) 5.40
Euthydemus: (422/1) Athenian
signatory of Peace of Nicias and
alliance 5.19, 5.24; (414/3)
appointed co-commander with Nicias
in Sicily 7.16; (413) commands in
final battle in Great Harbour 7.69
Evarchus (1), tyrant of Astacus in
Acarnania 2.30 (expelled by
Athenians, 431), 2.33 (reinstated
by Corinthians)
Evarchus (2), colony-leader of
Catana 6.3
Evenus, river in Aetolia 2.83

famine 1.23; 1.112 (Cyprus), 2.70
(Potidaea), 3.52 (Plataea), 3.85, 4.2
(Corcyra), 8.56 (Chios)
finance: war a matter of finance 1.11,
1.83 (Archidamus, *contra* 1.121), 2.13
(Pericles)
—Athenian 2.13, 2.24 (reserve fund,
cf. 8.15), 3.13, [3.17], 3.19, 7.27–9,
8.76; Athenian power dependent on
revenue from allies 2.13, 3.13, 3.31,
3.39, 3.46, cf. 6.90, 6.91, 7.28;
money-collecting ships 2.69, 3.19, 4.50,
4.75; expense of Potidaea siege 2.13,
2.70, [3.17]; expense of Sicilian
expedition 6.31, 7.16–17, 7.47; funds
built up during armistice 6.12,
6.26; sale of slaves 6.62; financially
crippled by 413: 7.28, 8.1, 8.53;
economies 8.1, 8.4, 8.86
—Spartan 1.80, 1.83, 1.121,
1.141–2, 2.65, 8.3, 8.53, 8.80;
Syracusan 7.48
Fish Point, promontory in Elis 2.25
Five Thousand, *see* ATHENS
food supplies: for Athens 1.81, 7.28,
8.4, 8.76, 8.90; importance of
Euboea 2.14, 7.28, 8.1, 8.95–6; for
Athenians in Pylos 4.27; for Athenians
in Sicily 6.22, 6.44, 6.71, 6.74, 6.88,
6.103, 7.4, 7.13, 7.14, 7.24, 7.60;
Sicily has advantage of locally grown
corn, 6.20; corn from Sicily to
Peloponnese 3.86, from Black Sea to
Mytilene 3.2; for Peloponnesian
fleet (412/1) 8.57
Four Hundred, *see* ATHENS

Galepsus, in Thrace: colony of
Thasos 4.107, 5.6; (424/3) defects
to Brasidas 4.107; (422) retaken
by Cleon 5.6
Gaulites, Carian sent by Tissaphernes
to represent him at Sparta (411) 8.85
Gela, Dorian city in Sicily: founded from
Rhodes and Crete 6.4, 7.57; Geloans
founded Acragas 6.4, and Camarina
6.5; Hippocrates tyrant of Gela
6.5; the acropolis called Lindii
6.4; (424) truce with Camarina, leading
to Conference of Gela 4.58;
(422) reject approach by Phaeax 5.4;
(415/4) support Syracuse with
cavalry 6.67; (414) give support to

Gylippus 7.1; (413) send reinforcements to Syracuse 7.33; 7.58; 7.80

Gelas, river in Sicily 6.4

Gelo, tyrant of Syracuse 6.4, 6.5, 6.94

Geraestus, in Euboea 3.3

Geraneia, mountain in Megarid 1.105, 1.107, 1.108, 4.70

Gerastius, month in Spartan calendar 4.119

Getae, tribe bordering Scythia 2.96, 2.98

Gigonus, in Chalcidice 1.61

Glauce, on promontory of Mycale 8.79

Glaucon, Athenian commander 1.51

Goaxis, an Edonian 4.107

Gongylus (1), an Eretrian, accomplice of Pausanias (1) 1.128

Gongylus (2), Corinthian commander: (414) arrives in Syracuse in time to pre-empt discussion to end war 7.2

Gortyn, city in Crete 2.85

Gortynia, in Macedonia 2.100

Graea, area inhabited by Oropians 2.23, 3.91

GREECE/GREEKS: name Hellas/Hellenes 1.3; early history to Trojan War 1.2–11, from Trojan War to Persian War 1.12–18; old settlements 'a collection of villages' 1.10; early shifts of population, 1.2, 1.12; maintenance of old ways, and bearing arms 1.5–6; development of Greek navies 1.4, 1.13–15; split by early war between Chalcis and Eretria 1.15; split between Athens and Sparta 1.18, cf. 3.82; Greek confederacy against Persia 1.18, 1.94–5, 1.102, 3.63–4; Greek dedication at Delphi after Persian War 1.132, 3.57

— attitude of Greeks at beginning of Peloponnesian War 1.123, 2.8, 2.11, 2.12, 3.13 (cf. 3.57–8), 4.20, 7.28; Greek view of Spartans 3.57–8, 3.93, 4.18, **4.40**, 4.108, **5.75**; surprise at Spartan surrender on Sphacteria 4.40; astonishment at scale of Athenian expedition to Sicily 6.31, cf. 7.28; Syracusans hope for Greek recognition of their success 7.56; Greek reaction to Athenian defeat in Sicily 8.2, 8.24; attitude to others' passage through their land 4.78; Greek conventions/norms 1.41,

1.77, 1.98, 1.132, 3.9, 3.56, 3.58, 3.59, [3.84], 4.97–8, 4.118 (one-year truce), 5.18 (Peace of Nicias), 7.68

— (428/9) general fear of Thracian army 2.101; (427 on) civil war throughout Greece, 3.82–3, [3.84], rival factions calling in either Athenians or Spartans (3.82); (426) volunteers invited for Spartan colony of Heracleia (1) 3.92

— racial sub-divisions: *see* Aeolians, Dorians, Ionians

Grestonia, district of Macedonia 2.99, 2.100, 4.109 ('Crestonia')

guest-friendship 2.13 (Pericles/ Archidamus), 4.78 (Brasidas/ Thessalians), 8.6 (Alcibiades/Endius)

GYLIPPUS, son of Cleandridas (6.93, cf. 6.104), Spartan commander in Sicily: (415/4) appointed, and first arrangements made 6.93; **(414)** takes four ships to Italy 6.104, then to Sicily 7.1; gathers army in Sicily and marches on Syracuse 7.1; joins Syracusans on Epipolae, captures Labdalum 7.2–3; failed night assault on Athenian wall 7.4; first defeated by, then defeats Athenians on Epipolae, and 3rd counter-wall completed 7.5–6, cf. 7.11 (Nicias); (414–413) raises troops in Sicily 7.7, cf. 7.12 (Nicias), 7.21, 7.46, 7.50; **(413)** with Hermocrates, advises adoption of naval warfare 7.21; captures Athenian forts at Plemmyrium 7.22–4; leads attack on Athenian wall, coordinated with naval offensive 7.37–8; in night-battle on Epipolae 7.43; brings Peloponnesian reinforcements from Selinus 7.50; defeated on shore 7.53; address before final battle in Great Harbour 7.66–8; measures to block Athenian retreat 7.74; blamed for letting Athenians go 7.81; gains surrender of Demosthenes' division 7.82; Nicias surrenders to him 7.85, 7.86; objects, without success, to execution of Nicias and Demosthenes 7.86; (412) ships serving with him in Sicily return, escaping interception 8.13

Gymnopaediae, festival at Sparta 5.82
Gyrton, in Thessaly 2.22

Habronichus, Athenian delegate to
  Sparta with Themistocles 1.91
Haemus, mountain in Thrace 2.96
Hagnon, son of Nicias (2) (2.58 etc.),
  father of Theramenes (8.68),
  Athenian general: (439) against
  Samos 1.117; (430) against
  Potidaea 2.58, 6.31; (429/8) with
  Sitalces 2.95; (437/6) founder-colonist
  of Amphipolis 4.102; (422) stripped
  of founder's honours 5.11; (422/1)
  signatory of Peace of Nicias and
  alliance 5.19, 5.24
Haliartus, in Boeotia: (424/3) at battle
  of Delium 4.93
Halicarnassus, city in Caria 8.42, 8.108
  (money extracted by Alcibiades, 411)
Halieis, in SE Argolid 1.105, 2.56, 4.45
Halys, river in Asia 1.16
Hamaxitus, town in Troad 8.101
Harmatus, town in Troad 8.101
Harmodius, with Aristogeiton assassin
  of Hipparchus (514) 1.20, 6.53–9
Harpagium, on S. shore of
  Propontis 8.107
Harpine, near Olympia 5.50
Hebrus, river in Thrace 2.96
Hegesandrus (1), father of
  Pasitelidas 4.132
Hegesandrus (2), Thespian commander
  of Boeotians sent to Sicily (413) 7.19
Helen 1.9
Helixus, Megarian general: (411)
  secures revolt of Byzantium 8.80
Hellanicus, historian: his
  History of Athens 1.97
Hellas/Hellenes: origin of the
  names for Greece/Greeks 1.3
Hellen, son of Deucalion: gave
  name to Hellas 1.3
Hellenic Sea 1.4
HELLESPONT: Persian bridges over
  Hellespont 1.137; (479/8) Hellespon-
  tines and Ionians revolted from Persia
  capture Sestos with Athenians 1.89;
  Pausanias returns to Hellespont 1.128;
  tribute-paying region of Athenian
  empire 2.9, cf. 6.77; 2.67, 2.96, 4.75
  —(413/2–411) Pharnabazus wants
  Spartans to send fleet to Hellespont

8.6, 8.8, 8.39, 8.62, 8.80, 8.99; (412)
  Peloponnesians plan to progress from
  Aegean to Hellespont 8.7, 8.22, 8.23
  (land force withdrawn); (411)
  Dercylidas sent overland to Hellespont
  8.61–2; Sestos fortified by Athenians
  as guard on Hellespont 8.62;
  Strombichides recalled from
  Hellespont to join Athenian fleet at
  Samos 8.79; Clearchus sent to
  Hellespont with fleet for Pharnabazus
  8.80; Byzantium revolts and
  Athenians send naval force to guard
  Hellespont 8.80; would be lost if
  Athenians at Samos sailed against
  Athens 8.86, or to help Athens
  8.96; Mindarus moves Peloponnesian
  fleet from Miletus to Hellespont
  8.99–103, 8.108; battle of
  Cynossema, 8.104–6
Helorum, town S. of Syracuse:
  Helorum road 6.66, 6.70, 7.80
Helos, town in Laconia 4.54
HELOTS: descendants of enslaved
  Messenians 1.101; Spartan fear of
  Helots 4.80, cf. 5.23; elimination of
  potentially troublesome young
  Helots 4.80; (465/4–456/5) Helot
  revolt 1.101–3 (settled by Athenians
  in Naupactus, 1.103), 1.128, 2.27, 3.54,
  4.56; intrigue with Pausanias (1) 1.132;
  Helots deserting 4.41, 5.14, 5.35,
  7.26; liberated cohorts (*neodamodeis*)
  5.34, 5.67, 7.19, 7.58, 8.5
  —(425) at Pylos/Sphacteria 4.8,
  4.26; (424) in Brasidas'
  army 4.80; (421) Helots who fought
  under Brasidas freed and settled in
  Lepreum 5.34; Athenians withdraw
  Helots from Pylos 5.35; (419/8)
  brought back to Pylos at insistence of
  Argives 5.56; (418) in Spartan
  expedition against Argos 5.57; in
  Spartan expedition to Mantinea
  5.64; (413) constitute Spartan
  force sent to Sicily 7.19, 7.58
Hephaestus, god: thought to have his
  forge on Hiera 3.88
Hera, goddess: temple at Argos,
  burned down (423), 4.133; temple at
  Corcyra 1.24, 3.75, 3.79, 3.81;
  Heraeum at Epidaurus 5.75;
  sanctuary at Plataea, and temple

built by Spartans after razing
Plataea 3.68
Heracleia (1), Spartan colony in
Trachis: on route to Thrace 3.92, cf.
4.78, 5.12; (426) established 3.92–3;
threat to Euboea never materializes
3.93; join Spartan expedition against
Naupactus 3.100; (422) some Spartan
reforming of the system 5.12;
(420/19) defeated in battle by
neighbouring tribes 5.51; (419)
taken over by Boeotians 5.52
Heracleia (2) (Pontica), on the
Black Sea 4.75
Heracleides (1), Syracusan general:
(415/4) elected 6.73; (414)
deposed 6.103
Heracleides (2), Syracusan
general: (414) elected 6.103
Heracles, sons of (Heracleidae) 1.9, 1.12,
1.24, 6.3
Heracles: temple at Mantinea 5.64,
5.66; festival of Heracles at
Syracuse 7.73
Heraea, in Arcadia: on Spartan
side at battle of Mantinea (418) 5.67
Heraeum, promontory at Epi-
daurus 5.75, 5.80
heralds 1.29, 1.146, 2.1, 2.2, 2.5,
2.6, 2.12, 3.24, 3.52, 3.101, 3.113,
4.30, 4.38, 4.44, 4.68, 4.97–9, 4.101,
4.114, 4.118, 6.32, 6.52, 7.3
Hermaeondas, Theban envoy to
Mytilene (428) 3.5
Hermes, god: temple outside
Mycalessus 7.29
Hermione, in SE Argolid: 1.128,
1.131; (435) helps Corinth against
Corcyra 1.27; (430) land ravaged by
Athenians 2.56; (413/2) required to
build ships for Peloponnesian
League 8.3; (412/1) a ship in
Spartan fleet 8.33
HERMOCRATES, son of Hermon
(4.58 etc.), leading Syracusan 6.72;
(424) at Conference of Gela, 4.58–65;
(415) speech urging action in view of
Athenian expedition 6.32–4; (415/4)
speech recommending structural
reforms 6.72–3; elected one of three
generals 6.73, 6.96 (deposed 6.103);
speech in assembly at Camarina 6.76–80;
(414) advises counter-walls 6.99;

(413) speech advising adoption of naval
warfare 7.21; tricks Athenians into
delaying retreat 7.73–4; (412)
instigates participation of Sicilian ships
in Peloponnesian war effort 8.26;
(412/1) protests at Tissaphernes' cut in
pay for Peloponnesian fleet 8.29, 8.85;
protests at bribery to agree pay-cut 8.45;
(411) hostility of Tissaphernes, goes to
Sparta to expose him 8.85; exiled from
Syracuse and replaced as commander of
Syracusan ships at Miletus 8.85
Hermon (1), father of
Hermocrates: 4.58 etc.
Hermon (2), commander of
border-guards at Mounichia 8.92
Herms: (415) mutilation of
Herms in Athens, and
reaction 6.27–9, 6.53, 6.60–1
Hesiod, poet 3.96
Hestiaea, city in Euboea: (446)
dispossessed by Athenians after
Euboean revolt 1.114, and Athenians
settled there (in Athenian army at
Syracuse 7.57); subsequently called
Oreus (8.95, only city in Athenian
control after revolt of Euboea, 411)
Hestiodorus, Athenian general 2.70
Hiera, one of the Lipara islands,
supposed forge of Hephaestus 3.88
Hieramenes, Persian, party to 3rd treaty
with Sparta (412/1) 8.58
Hierophon, Athenian general 3.105
Himera, city in Sicily: colonized from
Zancle 6.5; only Greek city on
N. side of Sicily 6.62, 7.58; (426/5)
attacked by Athenians and Sicels
3.115; (415) refuse to welcome
Athenians 6.62; (414) provide arms
and troops for Gylippus 7.1;
support Syracuse 7.58
Himeraeum, in Thrace, near
Amphipolis 7.9
Hippagretas, 2nd Spartan
commander at Sphacteria 4.38
Hipparchus, son of Peisistratus (1),
assassinated by Harmodius and
Aristogeiton (514) 1.20, 6.54–7
Hippias (1), son of Peisistratus (1), tyrant
of Athens 1.20, 6.54–9; (511/0)
deposed, given refuge in Lampsacus
and then with Dareius (1) 6.59; (490)
with Persians at Marathon 6.59

Hippias (2), commander of Arcadian mercenaries at Notium (427) 3.34
Hippocles, Athenian commander 8.13
Hippoclus, tyrant of Lampsacus 6.59
Hippocrates (1), Athenian general: (424) at Megara 4.66–73; with Demosthenes, plans expedition against Boeotia 4.76–7; (424/3) commands in Delium campaign 4.89–97; killed in battle of Delium 4.101
Hippocrates (2), tyrant of Gela 6.5
Hippocrates (3), Spartan commander 8.35, 8.107; (411) in Phaselis, warns Mindarus of Tissaphernes' duplicity 8.99
Hippolochidas, Thessalian friend of Brasidas 4.78
Hipponicus, son of Callias (3), Athenian general: (426) leads full levy against Tanagra 3.91
Hipponium, in Italy: Locrian colony, at war with Locri (422) 5.5
Hipponoïdas, Spartan polemarch, disgraced after battle of Mantinea (418) 5.71–2
Homer, epic poet 1.3 (his date, and his names for the Greeks), (1.5), 1.9, 1.10 (Catalogue of Ships), (1.13), 2.41; 'Hymn to Apollo' quoted 3.104
hope 2.42, 2.51, 2.62, 3.39, 3.45, 4.65, 4.108, 5.103, 5.113, 6.13, 7.77
hoplites: Spartan supremacy 1.141, 1.143, 4.12 (cf. 4.34, 6.11); Athenian numbers at start of war 2.13, 2.31; hoplite pay [3.17], 5.47; attendant slaves 7.75; Athenian recruitment lists 6.26, 6.31, 6.43, 7.16, 7.20, 8.24; hoplites v. light-armed troops 3.97–8, 4.32–5; tendency to push to the right 5.71; as rowers 3.18 (cf. 3.16), 6.91, 7.1; as marines 8.24
human nature 1.22, 1.76, 3.39, 3.45, 3.82, [3.84], 4.19, 4.61, 4.108, 5.105, 7.77, 8.24
Hyacinthia, Spartan festival 5.23, 5.41
Hyaeans, people in Ozolian Locris 3.101
Hybla Geleatis, town in Sicily 6.62–3, 6.94
Hyblon, Sicel king 6.4
Hyccara, town in Sicily: (415) captured by Athenians, and Sicanian inhabitants enslaved 6.62, 7.13
Hylias, river in Italy 7.35

Hyllaic harbour in Corcyra 3.72, 3.81
Hyperbolus, Athenian demagogue, ostracized: (411) murdered by oligarchic conspirators in Samos 8.73
Hysiae (1), in Boeotia 3.24
Hysiae (2), in Argolid: (417/6) captured by Peloponnesians and men executed 5.83

Ialysus, city in Rhodes 8.44
Iapygia, promontory at heel of Italy 6.30, 6.34, 6.44, 7.33; Iapygian islands (Choerades) 7.33; (413) dynast Artas provides javelin-men for Athenians 7.33
Iasian Gulf: 8.26
Iasus, in Caria: (412) sacked by Peloponnesians and handed over to Tissaphernes 8.28–9, 8.36, 8.54
Iberia: original home of Sicanians 6.2; potential mercenaries 6.90
Icaros, Aegean island 3.29, 8.99
Ida, mountain in Troad 4.52, 8.108
Idacus, on Chersonese 8.104
Idomene, in Amphilochia: (426/5) battle, Ambraciots defeated by Demosthenes 3.112–13
Ietae, Sicel fort captured by Gylippus (414) 7.2
Illyrians 1.24, 1.26, 4.124–8 (in Lyncus campaign, 423)
Imbros, N. Aegean island: Athenian colony 7.57; (428) support Athens in Lesbian revolt 3.5; (425) in Cleon's army at Pylos 4.28; (422) in Athenian army at Amphipolis 5.8; with Athenians in Sicily 7.57; 8.102, 8.103
Inaros, king of Libyans 1.104, 1.110
Inessa, Sicel town 3.103
Iolaus, Perdiccas' deputy at Potidaea (432) 1.62
IONIA: colonized from Athens/Attica 1.2, 1.12, 1.95, (2.15), 6.82; Ionian fashion 1.6; Ionians at earlier Delian festival, and Ephesian festival 3.104; early naval power 1.13; subjugated by Cyrus 1.16; in Sicily (Zancle) after Ionian revolt 6.4; lead request for Athenian hegemony after liberation from Persia 1.75, 1.95, 6.76; tribute-paying region of Athenian empire 2.9; Ionian cities

unwalled 3.33, cf. 8.14, 8.16; Persian deputy governor of Ionia 8.31
— (427) Ionian exiles with Spartan expedition to Mytilene 3.31; (426) excluded from Spartan colony of Heracleia (1) 3.92; (413/2) Spartan expedition to Ionia agreed, 8.6–7; (412) Chians lead revolt of Ionia, 8.7–28; (412/1) whole of Ionia as price for Persian support of Athenians 8.56; (411) would be lost if Athenians at Samos sailed against Athens 8.86, or to help Athens 8.96
Ionian Gulf 1.24, 2.97, 6.13, 6.30, 6.34, 6.44, 6.104, 7.33, 7.57
Ionians: generic racial term 1.124, 2.15, 3.104, 6.77; Ionian/Dorian antipathy 1.102, 1.124, 3.86, 3.92, 4.61, 5.9, 6.77, 6.82, 7.57, 7.63, 8.25
Ipnea, in Ozolian Locris 3.101
Irians, division of population of Malis 3.92
Isarchidas, Corinthian commander 1.29
Ischagoras, Spartan commander: 4.132; (422/1) signatory of Peace of Nicias and alliance 5.19, 5.24; envoy to Thraceward region after Peace of Nicias 5.21
Isocrates, Corinthian general 2.83
Isthmian festival at Corinth 8.9–10
Isthmus, Corinthian 1.13, 1.108, 2.9, 3.15, 3.16, 3.18, 3.89, 4.42, 6.61; (431) Peloponnesian forces gathered at Isthmus before invasion of Attica 2.10, 2.13, 2.18; record of Peace of Nicias to be set up at Isthmus 5.18; slipways for transport of ships across Isthmus, 3.15, 8.7–8
— Leucadian isthmus, Peloponnesian ships transported across 3.81, 4.8; 3.94; Methana isthmus 4.45; Potidaea isthmus 1.62, 1.64, 4.120; Thapsus isthmus 6.97
Istone, mountain in Corcyra occupied by oligarchs (427–425) 3.85, 4.2, 4.46
Isus, in Ozolian Locris 3.101
Italus, Sicel king giving name to Italy 6.2
ITALY: named from Sicel king Italus 6.2; colonies founded by Peloponnesians 1.12; Corcyra on route to Italy and Sicily 1.36, 1.44; Athenian ambition to subjugate Greeks in Italy (Alcibiades) 6.90–1; (431) Spartan adherents required

to build ships and provide money 2.7; (422) mission of Phaeax 5.4–5; (415–413) Athenians' reception in Italy 6.34, 6.42, 6.44, 6.88, 7.33, 7.35, 7.57; supplies for Athenians from Italy 6.103, 7.14; Italian allies of Athenians at Syracuse 7.57 (imprisoned with Athenians 7.87); (415/4) Syracusan approaches to Italian Greeks 6.34, 6.88; (414) Gylippus in Italy 6.104, 7.1; (411) Italian ships with Spartan fleet 8.91
— cities: see Croton, Cumae, Locri, Metapontium, Rhegium, Taras
Itamenes, Persian, captured Colophon (430) 3.34
Ithome, mountain in Messenia: occupied by the Helots in revolt (465 on) 1.101–3, 3.54
Itys 2.29

kinship: 7.57; Ionian 1.95, 3.86, 6.6, 6.20, 6.44, 6.46, 6.50, 6.76, 6.79, 7.57; Dorian 1.26, 1.107, 5.104, 5.108, 6.6, 6.79–80, 6.88, 7.57–8; Aeolian/Boeotian 3.2, 3.65, 7.57, 8.5, 8.100

Labdalum, Athenian fort on Epipolae 6.97–8, 7.3
Lacedaemonius, Athenian general 1.45
Laches, Athenian general: (427) leads 1st Athenian expedition to Sicily 3.86, 3.88, 6.1, 6.6, 6.75; in sole command after death of Charoeades 3.90, 3.103; (426/5) superseded in Sicily 3.115; (423) formal proposer of one-year truce 4.118; (422/1) negotiator (5.43, with Nicias) and signatory of Peace of Nicias and alliance 5.19, 5.24; (418) leads Athenian force in support of Argos 5.61; killed in battle of Mantinea 5.74
Lacon, Plataean spokesman (427) 3.52
Laconia 2.25, 2.27, 2.56, 3.7, 4.3, 4.12, 4.16, 4.53–7, 5.35, 6.105, 7.19, 7.20, 8.6, 8.91; Sciritis region 5.33; (413) Athenian fort established opposite Cythera 7.26, 7.31, 8.4 (abandoned, 413/2)
Lade, island facing Miletus: (412) Athenian blockade of Miletus from Lade 8.17, 8.24
Laeaeans, Paeonian tribe 2.96, 2.97

Laespodias, Athenian general
6.105; (411) envoy of Four Hundred
to Sparta 8.86

Laestrygonians, supposed original
inhabitants of Sicily 6.2

Lamachus, Athenian general: (424)
loses ships at river Calex 4.75;
(422/1) signatory of Peace of Nicias
and alliance 5.19, 5.24; **(415)**
appointed to Sicilian command 6.8; at
conference of generals 6.49–50; (414)
killed in battle outside Syracuse 6.101,
6.103

Lamis, Megarian founder of colonies in
Sicily 6.4

Lampsacus, city on Hellespont:
Hippoclus tyrant of Lampsacus 6.59;
refuge of Hippias 6.59; given to
Themistocles 1.138; (411) revolts
from Athens, and recaptured 8.62

Laodoceium, in Arcadia: battle between
Mantinea and Tegea (423/2) 4.134

Larisa (1), in Thessaly 2.22, 4.78

Larisa (2), town in Troad 8.101

Las, port in Laconia 8.91, 8.92

Laureium, Athenians' silver
mines 2.55, 6.91

Learchus, Athenian envoy to
Sitalces (430) 2.67

Lebedus, in Ionia: (412) revolts
from Athens 8.19

Lectum, SW promontory of Troad 8.101

Lecythus, headland off Torone: (424/3)
Athenian fort there captured by
Brasidas 4.113–16; sanctuary of
Athena 4.116

Lemnos, N. Aegean island: once
inhabited by Etruscans
4.109; Athenian colony 7.57;
hit by plague 2.47; (428) support
Athens in Lesbian revolt 3.5;
(425) in Cleon's army at Pylos 4.28;
(422) in Athenian army at
Amphipolis 5.8; with Athenians
in Sicily 7.57; 8.102

Leocoreium, shrine in Athens 1.20, 6.57

Leocrates, Athenian general 1.105

Leon (1): (426) Spartan founder-colonist
of Heracleia (1) 3.92; (420) envoy to
Athens 5.44–6

Leon (2), Athenian signatory of Peace of
Nicias and alliance (422/1) 5.19, 5.24

Leon (3), Athenian general: (412)
commands a fleet in E. Aegean 8.23

(recaptures Mytilene), 8.24; (412/1)
sent as replacement general to
Samos 8.54–5; (411) supports
Samian democrats 8.73

Leon (4), father of Pedaritus 8.28

Leon (5), Spartan replacing Pedaritus
as governor of Chios (411) 8.61

Leon (6), place on coast near
Epipolae 6.97

LEONTINI, city in Sicily: founded from
Chalcis in Euboea 6.3–4, 6.76; of
Ionian descent 3.86, cf. 6.6; part of city
called Phocaeae 5.4; fort of Bricinniae
5.4; (427) war with Syracuse, allies on
either side, help sent by Athenians
3.86, cf. 6.6; (425) campaign against
Messana with Athenians 4.25; (422 on)
the people driven out of Leontini, and
war with Syracuse 5.4, 6.6, 6.8, 6.19,
6.86; (415) Leontinian exiles press
case for support at Athenian
assembly 6.19
—restoration of Leontinians a
reason/pretext for Athenian
expeditions to Sicily 3.86, 6.6,
6.8, 6.12, 6.19, 6.33, 6.44, 6.46–8,
6.50, 6.63, 6.76–7, 6.84

Leotychidas, Spartan king at battle of
Mycale (479) 1.89

Lepreum, in Elis: (421) cause of
quarrel between Elis and Sparta 5.31,
5.34, 5.49–50; freed Helots settled
there 5.34; (418) Eleans fail to
persuade Argive alliance to
attack Lepreum 5.62

Leros, E. Aegean island 8.26–7

LESBOS, E. Aegean island: related to
Boeotians 3.2 (cf. 3.5, 3.13), 7.57;
'autonomy' in Athenian empire
3.10–11, 3.39; ships, not tribute 1.19,
3.3, 6.85; ship-providing allies of
Athens 1.116–17, 2.9, 2.56
(cf. 6.31), 5.84
—revolt from Athens (428–427)
3.2–6, 3.8–18, 3.25, 3.27–50: except
Methymna 3.2, 3.5, 3.50; forcing of
political union with Mytilene 3.2;
Mytilenaeans present case to
Peloponnesian League 3.8–15, and
form alliance 3.15; siege of Mytilene
3.18, 3.25, 3.27–8; settlement
imposed 3.50
—(428) internal wars 3.18; (424)
Lesbian exiles seize Antandrus as

base for raids on Lesbos 4.52, 4.75 (defeated by Athenian force); **second revolt**: (413/2) approach Agis, and help promised 8.5, 8.7, 8.8; **(412)** Peloponnesians plan to proceed from Chios to Lesbos to Hellespont 8.7, 8.22, with Chians secure revolt of Methymna and Mytilene 8.22; Athenians recapture Mytilene 8.23; Eresus revolts 8.23; Lesbos Athenian base for war against Chios 8.24; (412/1) proposals for another revolt welcomed by Astyochus but rejected by allies and Chians 8.32; (411) Athenian fleet begins siege of Eresus 8.100 (abandoned, 8.103)

LEUCAS, W. Greek island: colony of Corinth 1.30; Corinthian garrison 4.42 (cf. 3.7, 3.94); ship-providing ally of Sparta 2.9, 2.80–1, 2.91, 3.69; (435, 433) support Corinth against Corcyra 1.26, 1.27, 1.46; (435) ravaged by Corcyraeans 1.30; (429) base for Peloponnesian attack on Acarnania 2.80, 2.84; in Peloponnesian fleet defeated by Phormio 2.91–2; (428) repel Athenian attack under Asopius (2) 3.7; (426) attacked and ravaged by Athenians and Acarnanians, but not besieged 3.94, 3.95 (cf. 3.102); (414–3) provide ships in support of Syracuse 6.104, 7.7, 7.58; (411) lose a ship at Cynossema 8.106; 8.13 — temple of Apollo 3.94; Leucadian isthmus 3.81, 3.94, 4.8

Leucimme, promontory of Corcyra 1.30, 1.47, 1.51, 3.79; (435) battle of Leucimme 1.26–30

Leuconium, in Chios 8.24

Leuctra, in Laconia 5.54

Libya 1.104, 1.110, 6.2; plague spread from Ethiopia to Libya 2.48; trade 4.43; (413) Peloponnesians in Libya, driven off course 7.50

Lichas, son of Arcesilas (5.50 etc.): consular representative of Argos in Sparta 5.76; (422/1) Spartan envoy to Argos 5.22; (420) given public beating at Olympic games 5.50; (412/1) one of commissioners sent to advise Astyochus 8.39, 8.43

(critical of previous treaties with Persia, cf. 8.52); (411) resented by Milesians for advising acceptance of Persians 8.84; (411) invited to accompany Tissaphernes to Aspendus, 8.87; dies in Miletus, refused burial where the Spartans wanted 8.84

light-armed troops: effectiveness against hoplites 3.97–8, 3.112, 4.32–6; no regular force at Athens 4.94; over 10,000 on Boeotian side at Delium (424/3) 4.93

Ligurians: drove Sicanians out of Iberia 6.2

Limnaea, village in Acarnania 2.80, 3.106

Lindii, name of the acropolis at Gela 6.4

Lindus, city in Rhodes 8.44

Lipara, group of the Aeolus islands 3.88, 3.115

Liparaeans, colonists from Cnidus, inhabitants of Aeolus islands 3.88

Locri (Epizephyrian, 7.1), city in Italy: (427) allies of Syracuse 3.86; **(426/5)** Athenian landings and defeats of Locrians 3.99, 3.103; Locrian defeat of Athenians 3.115; **(425)** with Syracuse, capture Messana 4.1; hostility to Rhegium 4.1, 4.24–5; refused treaty with Athens (424) but make agreement with Phaeax (422) 5.5; **(422)** Locrian settlers take over Messana, then expelled 5.5; war with Hipponium and Medma 5.5; (415) refuse Athenian expedition any access 6.44; (411) provide ships for Peloponnesian fleet 8.91; 7.4, 7.25, 7.35

Locris, Opuntian: (457) hostages taken by Athenians after battle of Oenophyta 1.108; (447/6) with Boeotians at battle of Coroneia 1.113; (431) allies of Sparta 2.9; Athenian guard on Locris 2.26, 2.32; (426) tsunami at Atalante, 3.89; coast ravaged by Athenians 3.91; (424/3) support Boeotians at Delium 4.96; (413/2) required to build ships for Peloponnesian League 8.3

Locris, Ozolian: maintain the old ways 1.5; sanctuary of Nemean Zeus 3.96; (456/5) Athenians capture Naupactus from Locris 1.103; (426)

allies of Athens, support campaign against Aetolia 3.95, 3.97; cooperate with Spartan expedition against Naupactus 3.101; (421) war with Phocis 5.32; (418) summoned to assist Spartans at Mantinea 5.64, request countermanded 5.75

Loryma, on mainland promontory E. of Syme 8.43

Lycaeum, mountain in Arcadia 5.16, 5.54

Lycia 2.69, 8.41

Lycophron (1), Spartan commissioner sent to advise Cnemus (429) 2.85

Lycophron (2), Corinthian general 4.43–4

Lyncus, kingdom in Macedonia: 2.99, 4.79, 4.83; (423) campaign of Perdiccas and Brasidas against Arrhabaeus, Lyncestian king 4.124–8, 4.132

Lysicles, Athenian general: (428/7) in command of money-collecting ships, killed in Caria 3.19

Lysimeleia, marsh outside Syracuse 7.53 (cf. 6.66)

Lysistratus, Olynthian leader of entry into Torone (424/3) 4.110

Macarius, Spartan commander against Naupactus (426) and then Amphilochia (426/5) 3.100, 3.109 (killed)

MACEDONIA: 2.99–100; Lower/ Upper Macedonia, development of kingdom 2.99–100; Macedonian kings originally Temenids from Argos 2.99; Perdiccas, king of Macedonia, *q.v.*; (432) Athenian expedition to Macedonia 1.57–61; (429/8) Sitalces' campaign against Macedonia 2.95, 2.98–101; (424–423) Brasidas in Macedonia 4.78, 4.83, 4.124–8 (Lyncus campaign); (417/6) blockaded by Athenians 5.83; (416/5) ravaged by Athenians from Methone (2) 6.7 —Macedonian exiles in Athens 6.7; Macedonian cavalry 1.61–3, 2.100, 4.124

Machaon, Corinthian commander 2.83

Maeander, river in Caria 3.19, 8.58

Maedians, Thracian tribe 2.98

Maenalia, region of Arcadia 5.64; (418) on Spartan side at battle of Mantinea 5.67, 5.77

Magnesia, in Ionia: Themistocles governor of Magnesia, his memorial there 1.138; (412/1) Astyochus meets Alcibiades there 8.50

Magnesians, subjects of Thessaly: fear of Thracian army (429/8) 2.101

Malea (1), cape in Laconia 4.53–4, 8.39

Malea (2), promontory on Lesbos 3.4, 3.6

Malis, region of NE Greece: three divisions of population 3.92; (420/19) in battle against Heracleia (1) 5.51 —Malian Gulf 3.96, 4.100, 8.3

Maloeis Apollo, festival at Mytilene 3.3

MANTINEA, city in Arcadia: subjected part of Arcadia 5.29, 5.33, 5.81; disputes with Tegea 4.134, 5.65; (426/5) in Peloponnesian force in Amphilochia 3.107–9, 3.11; (421) join Argive alliance 5.29, 5.37; fort at Cypsela demolished by Spartans 5.33; (420) with Elis and Argos make alliance with Athens 5.43–8; support Elean guard at Olympia 5.50; (419) conference at Mantinea summoned by Athenians 5.55; (418) support Argives against Spartans 5.58, 5.61, and insist on prosecution of war 5.61–2; battle of Mantinea (5.26), 5.64–75, (6.16); Mantinean losses 5.73–4; (418/7) alliance renounced by Argives 5.78; agree truce with Sparta, and abandon control of cities in Arcadia 5.81; (415) Mantineans (mercenaries) in Athenian expedition to Sicily 6.29, 6.43, 6.61, 6.67, 6.68, 7.57 —Council, Demiurgi, Theori, Polemarchs 5.47; sanctuary of Zeus 5.47; temple of Heracles 5.64, 5.66

Marathon, battle of (490) 1.18, 1.73, 2.34 (burials); Hippias with Persians at Marathon 6.59

Marathoussa, island off Clazomenae 8.31

Mareia, town in Egypt 1.104

marines on board triremes 3.95, 6.21, 6.43, 7.1, 7.62, 7.70, 8.24

Massalia, in S. Gaul: colonized by Phocaeans 1.13

Mecyberna, in Chalcidice: (422/1) provision in Peace of Nicias 5.18; (421/0) captured by Olynthians 5.39

Medeon, in Acarnania 3.106

Medes 1.104

medism: 1.74; 1.95, 1.128–35
(Pausanias); 1.90, 3.56, 3.62,
3.64–5 (Thebans)

Medma, in Italy: Locrian colony,
at war with Locri (422) 5.5

Megabates, Persian, replaced as
satrap of Dascylium 1.129

Megabazus, Persian sent to bribe
Peloponnesians to invade Attica
(?457) 1.109

Megabyxus, Persian commander in
Egypt 1.109

MEGARA: 4.66–74; colonized
Calchedon (4.75), Thapsus, Megara
Hyblaea, Selinus (6.4, 7.57); Theagenes
tyrant of Megara 1.126; ship-providing
ally of Sparta, 2.9; (?460) defect from
Sparta and ally with Athens, (1.42),
1.103, 1.105; Athenians build long walls
to Nisaea 1.103; (446) revolt from
Athens 1.114; (?early 430s on) barred
from Athenian market 1.67, 1.139,
1.140, 1.144; (435, 433) support Corinth
against Corcyra 1.27, 1.46, 1.48; (431)
invaded by Athenians, and twice every
year to 424: 2.31, 4.66; Athenian ships
at Boudorum prevent traffic in or
out 2.93, 3.51; (429/8) propose attack
on Peiraeus 2.93–4; (427) Athenians
capture and fortify island of Minoa
3.51; exiled oligarchs granted
occupation of Plataea 3.68; (424)
depredations from Pegae by oligarchs 4.66; democrats plot to hand over
city to Athenians 4.66–8, 4.71, 4.73–4
(failure); Athenians capture long walls
and Nisaea 4.68–9; Megara saved by
Brasidas 4.70–3; oligarchs recalled, and
establish extreme oligarchy 4.74;
(424/3) support for Boeotians at battle
of Delium 4.100; long walls recaptured
from Athenians and demolished 4.109;
(423) agree one-year truce, 4.118–19;
(422/1) dissent from treaty and alliance
with Athens 5.17, 5.22; (421) wary of
alliance with Argos 5.31, but
subsequently (421/0) enthusiastic 5.38;
(418) in Peloponnesian expedition
against Argos 5.58–60; (415) Megarian
exiles with Athenians in Sicily 6.43,
7.57; (413/2) required to build ships for
Peloponnesian League 8.3; (412/1)

Megarian ship in Spartan
fleet 8.33; 8.94
— long walls 1.103, 4.66–70, 4.73,
4.109; sanctuary of Enyalius 4.67
— Megarid 1.105, 1.108, 2.31, 4.70,
4.76

Megara Hyblaea, in Sicily: founded by
Megarian colonists from Thapsus,
later removed by Gelo 6.4, 6.94;
(415) deserted, and proposed by
Lamachus as station for Athenian
fleet 6.49; (415/4) fort built there by
Syracusans 6.75, 6.94 (attacked by
Athenians); 6.97; 7.25

Meidius, river near Abydos 8.106

Melanchridas, Spartan admiral 8.6

Melanthus, Spartan commander 8.5

Meleas, Spartan envoy to Mytilene
(428) 3.5

Melesandrus, Athenian general:
(430/29) killed in Lycia 2.69

Melesias, envoy of Four Hundred to
Sparta (411) 8.86

Melesippus, Spartan envoy to
Athens 1.139 (432), 2.12 (431)

Meliteia, in Achaea Phthiotis 4.78

Melos, Aegean island: Spartan
colony 5.84, 5.89, 5.104, 5.106;
neutral at start of war 2.9, 5.84; (426)
Athenian expedition fails to subdue
Melos 3.91, 3.94, cf. 5.84; (416)
Athenian expedition against Melos,
and siege 5.84, 5.114–16; **Melian
dialogue** 5.85–113; (416/5) fate of
Melian population 5.116; (412/1)
Spartan fleet at Melos on way to
Miletus 8.39, 8.41

Memphis, city in Egypt 1.104, 1.109

Menandrus, Athenian commander:
(414/3) appointed co-commander
with Nicias in Sicily 7.16; (413) in
assault on Epipolae 7.43; commands
in final sea-battle 7.69

Menas, Spartan: (422/1) signatory of
Peace of Nicias and alliance 5.19,
5.24; envoy to Thraceward region
after Peace of Nicias 5.21

Mende, city on Pallene peninsula
(Chalcidice): Eretrian colony
4.123; founded Eïon (2) 4.7;
temple of Poseidon 4.129; civil
strife 4.130; (423) Brasidas' designs

4.121; defects from Athens 4.123–4; recaptured 4.129–31

Mendesian mouth of Nile 1.110

Menecolus, Syracusan founder-colonist of Camarina 6.5

Menedaïus, Spartan commander against Naupactus (426) and then Amphilochia (426/5) 3.100, 3.109

Menon, Thessalian commander 2.22

mercenaries: Aetolian 7.57; Arcadian 3.34, 7.19, 7.57–8; barbarian 2.96, 3.34, 3.73–4, 3.85, 3.109, 4.46, 4.124–5, 4.129, 5.6, 6.90, 7.27, 7.29–30, 8.25; Cretan 7.57; Iapygian 7.57; Iberian 6.90; Illyrian 4.124–5; Mantinean 6.43, 7.57; Peloponnesian 1.31, 1.60, 4.52, 4.76, 4.80, 6.22, 8.28; Thracian 2.96, 4.129, 5.6, 7.27; sailors in Athenian navy 1.121, 1.143, 7.13; mercenary pay 7.27; 1.115, 2.33, 2.70, 2.79, 7.48, 8.28, 8.38, 8.55, 8.100

Messana, city in Sicily: originally called Zancle 6.4; (426) forced to submit by Athenians 3.90; (425) captured by Syracusans and Locrians, defects from Athens 4.1; base for Syracusan fleet, naval and land engagements with Athenians 4.24–5; attack Naxos (2), defeated 4.25; (424–422) internal strife, taken over by settlers from Locri, subsequently expelled 5.5; (415) Alcibiades fails to win over Messana 6.48, 6.50; pro-Syracusan party there, 6.74; (415/4) Athenian attempt on Messana frustrated, plans betrayed by Alcibiades 6.74; 3.88; 7.1

Messapia, in Ozolian Locris 3.101

Messapians, tribe in heel of Italy 7.33

MESSENIANS: original inhabitants of Messenia in Peloponnese enslaved, and name 'Messenians' given to all Helots 1.101, cf. 4.3, 4.41; (456/5) after Helot revolt, settled by Athenians in Naupactus 1.103

—'Messenians in Naupactus': allies of Athens 2.9, 2.25, 2.90, 2.102, 3.75, 3.81, 4.3, 4.9, 4.32, 4.36, 4.41, 7.31, 7.57; usefulness of their Doric dialect 3.112, 4.3, 4.41; (426) persuade Demosthenes to attack

Aetolia 3.94–5, 3.97; (426/5) with Demosthenes in Amphilochia against the Ambraciots 3.107–12; (425) at Pylos/Sphacteria (4.3), 4.9, 4.32, 4.36; form garrison at Pylos, and raid Laconia 4.41, cf. 7.57; (421) withdrawn from Pylos 5.35; Argives demand their return 5.56; (413) with the Athenians at Syracuse 7.31, 7.57

Metapontium, city in Italy: (413) supplies troops and ships to Athenians 7.33, 7.57

Methana, peninsula between Epidaurus and Troezen: (425) isthmus fortified by Athenians 4.45; (422/1) to be restored to Sparta under Peace of Nicias 5.18

Methone (1), in Laconia 2.25

Methone (2), on Thermaic Gulf 4.129, 6.7

Methydrium, in Arcadia 5.58

Methymna, city in Lesbos: Aeolian city, colonized from Boeotia 7.57; Athenian ally contributing ships 6.85, 7.57, cf. 8.100; with Athenians in Sicily 7.57; did not join revolt of Lesbos (428–427) 3.2, 3.5, 3.50; (428) attacked by Mytilenaeans, attack Antissans and defeated 3.18; (412) revolt from Athens 8.22–3; (411) Methymnaean exiles fail in attack on Methymna, secure revolt of Eresus 8.100

metics, resident aliens in Athens 1.143, 2.13, 2.31, 3.16, 4.90, 6.28, 7.63 ('honorary Athenians')

Metropolis, in Acarnania 3.107

Miciades, Corcyraean commander 1.47

MILETUS, city in Ionia: colonized Abydos 8.61; Aristagoras attempted to colonize Nine Ways (496/5) 4.102; ally of Athens 4.42, 4.53–4, 7.57 (at Syracuse); (440–439) war with Samos 1.115–16; (412) revolt from Athens 8.17; Athenian blockade from Lade 8.17, 8.24; defeated by Athenian expedition 8.25; Athenians prepare to wall off city 8.25–6, but withdraw on arrival of Peloponnesian fleet 8.27; Spartan Philippus installed as governor 8.28; (412/1) Athenian naval attacks on Miletus 8.30, 8.38; (412–411) Peloponnesian fleet based

in Miletus 8.29, 8.33, 8.36, 8.38, 8.39;
(returned) 8.60–3, 8.78–9, 8.83–5,
8.99; (411) Milesian infantry support
Peloponnesian fleet at Mycale 8.79;
capture Tissaphernes' fort in
Miletus 8.84, 8.85, 8.109; send
envoys to Sparta to denounce
Tissaphernes 8.85; Peloponnesian
fleet moved from Miletus to
Hellespont 8.99, 8.108
Miltiades, father of Cimon (1): 1.98 etc.
Mimas, mountain to N. of Erythraean
peninsula 8.34
Mindarus, Spartan commander: (411)
succeeds Astyochus as admiral-in-
chief 8.85; moves Peloponnesian fleet
from Miletus to Hellespont, via Chios
8.99–103; speed of voyage 8.101;
chases Athenian ships at Sestos
8.102–3; at battle of Cynossema 8.104
mines: in Thrace (gold) 1.100–1,
4.105; Athenian silver mines at
Laureium 2.55, 6.91
Minoa, island in front of Megara 3.51,
4.67, 4.118
Minos 1.4, 1.8
'Minyan', older name for Boeotian
Orchomenus 4.76
Molossians, people in Epirus 1.136, 2.80
Molycrium, on N. side of mouth of
Corinthian Gulf: Corinthian colony,
subject to Athens 3.102; (426)
captured by Spartans 3.102; 2.84;
Molycrian Rhium 2.86
Morgantina, city in Sicily 4.65
Motya, Phoenician settlement in Sicily 6.2
Mounichia, harbour in Athens 2.13,
8.92, 8.93 (theatre of Dionysus)
Mycale, mainland promontory opposite
Samos: battle of, in Persian War (479)
1.89; (411) Peloponnesian fleet at, 8.79
Mycalessus, city in Boeotia: (413) attack
and massacre by Thracian mercenaries
7.29–30; temple of Hermes 7.29
Mycenae 1.9, 1.10
Myconos, Aegean island 3.29
Mygdonia, region of Macedonia 1.58,
2.99, 2.100
Mylae, in territory of Messana: (426)
forced to submit by Athenians 3.90
Myletidae, Syracusan clan, exiled and
joined foundation of Himera 6.5
Myonessus, in territory of Teos in
Ionia 3.32

Myonia, district of Ozolian Locris 3.101
Myrcinus, city in Edonia (Thrace):
(424/3) goes over to Brasidas
4.107; (422) in Brasidas' army at
Amphipolis 5.6, 5.10
Myronides, Athenian general 1.105;
1.108, 4.95 (wins battle of
Oenophyta, 457)
Myrrhine, wife of Hippias 6.55
Myscon, Syracusan commander: (411)
sent to fleet at Miletus 8.85
Mysteries: (415) allegations of
profanation 6.28, 8.53;
reaction and inquiry at Athens 6.53,
6.60–1
MYTILENE, main city of Lesbos: (428)
attempting to force political union of
Lesbos 3.2; civil strife 3.2,
3.27; triremes impounded at
Athens 3.3; attack on Methymna
3.18; (428–427) revolt from and
war with Athens 3.3–6, 3.18, 3.25,
3.27–8, 3.35–6, 3.50; send envoys to
Athens and Sparta 3.4–5; presentation of case to Peloponnesian League
at Olympia 3.8–15; alliance with
Sparta 3.15; besieged by Athenians
3.18, 3.25, 3.27–8 (capitulation);
Spartans send Salaethus, 3.25, then
40 ships 3.26 (delayed and ineffective,
3.29–33); Mytilenaean debate in
Athens (Cleon and Diodotus) 3.36–49;
second trireme countermands death
penalty 3.49; execution of
Mytilenaeans sent to Athens by
Paches, and settlement imposed
3.50; (424) Mytilenaean exiles plan
offensive from mainland and take
Antandrus 4.52, recaptured by
Athenians 4.75; (412) revolt again
8.22, and Mytilene recaptured by
Athenians 8.23; (411) Athenian
garrison in Mytilene defeats
Methymnaean exiles attacking
Methymna 8.100
Myus, in Caria 3.19; given to
Themistocles 1.138

Naucleides, leader of pro-Theban party
in Plataea 2.2
NAUPACTUS, in Ozolian Locris: temple of Apollo 2.91; (456/5) captured by
Athenians, and Helots from Messenia
settled there 1.103; 'the Messenians in

Naupactus' allies of Athens, 2.9 etc. (*see* MESSENIANS); (430/29) Phormio based there with 20 ships 2.69, 2.80, 2.81, 2.83, 2.84, 2.90–2, 2.102–3; (427) 12 ships there under Nicostratus 3.69, intervene in Corcyra 3.75; (426) Aetolians hostile to Naupactus 3.94, 3.100; Demosthenes stays in Naupactus area after failure in Aetolia (3.96), 3.98; Spartan expedition against Naupactus 3.100–2; saved by Acarnanian support at request of Demosthenes 3.102; (425) some of garrison ships go to Pylos 4.13; Athenians at Naupactus capture Anactorium 4.49; (424) Demosthenes at Naupactus raising troops for Boeotian expedition 4.76–7; (414–413) Corinthian fleet in opposition to Athenian squadron at Naupactus 7.17, 7.19, 7.31, 7.34 (sea-battle); (413) Demosthenes recruits Messenians at Naupactus for Sicily 7.31

Naxos (1), Aegean island: (470s) revolt from Athens and subjugation 1.98; 1.137

Naxos (2), city in Sicily: first Greek colony, from Chalcis, in Sicily 6.3; altar of Apollo Archegetes 6.3; (425) defeat Messanans, with aid of Sicels 4.25; (415) expected to side with Athens on kinship grounds 6.20; admit Athenian expeditionary force, 6.50; (415/4) Athenians camp there for the winter 6.72, 6.74–5; (414) send cavalry to Athenians 6.98; one of the Athenians' 'remaining allies' (Nicias) 7.14, 7.57

Nea Polis, Carthaginian trading-post 7.50

Nemea (1), in Ozolian Locris: sanctuary of Zeus 3.96

Nemea (2), in Argolid 5.58–60

Nericus, in Leucas 3.7

Nestus, river in Thrace 2.96

Nicanor, leader of Chaonians 2.80

Niceratus, father of Nicias (1): 3.51 etc.

Niciades, chairman of prytaneis for Athenian assembly resolving one-year truce (423) 4.118

NICIAS (1), son of Niceratus (3.51 etc.), Athenian general: wealth 7.86; good fortune 5.16, 6.17, 7.77; aversion to risk 6.23–4, 5.16; dilatory 7.42; religious 7.77; superstitious 7.50; illness 6.102, 7.15 (kidney disease), 7.16, 7.77; hostility of Cleon 4.27–8; hostility of and to Alcibiades 5.43, 5.45–6, 6.12–13, 6.15–16; Spartan good will 7.86; Nicias on Athenian character 6.9, 7.48; communication with/from enemy 4.54 (Cythera), 7.48–9, 7.73, 7.86 (Syracuse); agony of command 7.16, 7.69; Thucydides' assessment 7.86

—in Athens: (427) leads expedition to Minoa 3.51; (426) leads expedition to Melos, Tanagra, Locris 3.91; (425) resigns Pylos command to Cleon 4.27–8; leads expedition to Corinthiad 4.42–5; (424) leads expedition to Cythera and Laconia 4.53–7; (423) signatory of one-year truce 4.119; in command against Scione/Mende 4.129–33; asks Perdiccas for evidence of reliability 4.132; (422/1) main Athenian proponent of peace 5.16, 5.46; with Laches negotiates peace of Nicias 5.43, 5.46, 7.86 (on its fragility 6.10); signatory of Peace and alliance 5.19, 5.24; (420) fruitless embassy to Sparta 5.46; (417) in command of aborted expedition to Thraceward region 5.83; (415) appointed, against his will (cf. 6.23–4, 6.34), to Sicilian command 6.8; speeches in assembly about Sicilian expedition 6.9–14, 6.20–3; pressed to specify forces required 6.25; generals given absolute discretion 6.26; doubts reality of supposed Egestan funds 6.22, 6.46

—in Sicily: (415) in conference of generals at Rhegium 6.47; (415/4) address before battle outside Syracuse 6.68; (414) saves Athenian 'circle' on Epipolae 6.102; approached for an accommodation by Syracusans 6.103; ignores news of Gylippus' approach 6.104, then sends ships too late to intercept 7.1; fortifies Plemmyrium and moves fleet there 7.4; fails to intercept Corinthian ships 7.4, 7.7; sends letter to Athenians 7.8, 7.10–15

(urges either recall or reinforcement, 7.8, 7.15, asks to be relieved of
command, 7.15); (414/3) not relieved
of command, but generals elected to
join him 7.16–17; (413) has Sicel
allies ambush reinforcements on way to
Syracuse 7.32; organizes defences for
Athenian naval station 7.38; agrees
assault on Epipolae, but left behind
7.43; advocates continuation of
siege 7.48–9; agrees move of base
from Syracuse, delayed by
eclipse 7.50; address before final
sea-battle 7.61–4; appeal to
trierarchs 7.69; agrees another
attempt to break out, but sailors
refuse 7.72; tricked by Hermocrates
into delaying retreat 7.73–4; address
at beginning of retreat 7.76–7; change
of plan in retreat 7.80; offers to
reimburse Syracusan expenses
7.83; his division slaughtered at river
Assinarus 7.84–5; surrenders
to Gylippus 7.85, 7.86; executed by
Syracusans 7.86
Nicias (2), father of Hagnon: 2.58 etc.
Nicias (3), Cretan from Gortyn, consular
representative of Athens 2.85
Nicolaus, Spartan ambassador to Persia,
executed by Athenians (430) 2.67
Nicomachus, Phocian, revealed plans
for betrayal of Boeotia (424/3) 4.89
Nicomedes, Spartan commander 1.107
Nicon, Theban commander of Boeotians
sent to Sicily (413) 7.19
Niconidas, Thessalian friend of Brasidas
and Perdiccas 4.78
Nicostratus, son of Diitrephes (1) (3.75),
Athenian general: (427) takes fleet from
Naupactus in support of Corcyra
3.75–8; attempts reconciliation 3.75;
naval engagement with Peloponnesians
3.76–8; (424) leads expedition to
Cythera and Laconia 4.53–7; (423)
signatory of one-year truce 4.119; in
command against Scione/
Mende 4.129–33; (418) leads Athenian
force in support of Argos 5.61; killed
in battle of Mantinea 5.74
Nile, river 1.104, 1.110
Nine Ways, in Thrace 1.100; colonized
by Athenians (437/6), renamed
Amphipolis 4.102

Nisaea, port of Megara 1.103, 1.114,
1.115, 2.31, 2.93–4, 3.51, 4.21, 4.66,
4.68–70, 4.72–3, 4.85, 4.108; (424)
Peloponnesian garrison 4.66–70,
4.100; Athenian circumvallation and
capture of Nisaea 4.69, 4.118; (422/1)
Athenians to retain Nisaea under
Peace of Nicias 5.17
— long walls from Megara to
Nisaea 1.103, 4.66–70, 4.73;
shrine of Nisus 4.118; temple of
Poseidon 4.118
Nisus, shrine at Nisaea 4.118
Notium, port of Colophon: captured
by Paches (427), later colonized by
Athenians 3.34
Nymphodorus, of Abdera, appointed
consular representative for Athens
(431) 2.29

Odomantians, N. Thracian
tribe 2.101, 5.6
Odrysians, Thracian people: their king
Sitalces becomes ally of Athens
(431) 2.29; 2.95–8, 4.101;
Odrysian empire, extent and
wealth 2.97; Odrysian cavalry 2.98
Odysseus 4.24
Oeanthea, in Ozolian Locris 3.101
Oeneon, in Ozolian Locris 3.95, 3.98,
3.102 (captured by Spartans, 426)
Oeniadae, in Acarnania: 2.102; only
Acarnanian city constantly hostile to
Athens, 1.111, 2.102, 3.7 (cf. 3.94);
2.82, 3.114, 4.77 (forced by Acarnanians
into Athenian alliance, 424)
Oenoe, Athenian fort on border with
Boeotia: (431) attacked without
success by Peloponnesians in 1st
invasion of Attica 2.18–19; (411)
besieged by Corinthians and
Boeotians, betrayed to Boeotians 8.98
Oenophyta, in Boeotia: (457)
battle of, 1.108, 4.95
Oenoussae islands, opposite Chios 8.24
Oesyme, in Thrace: Thasian
colony, defects to Brasidas (424/3)
4.107
Oetaeans, people in Thessaly 3.92, 8.3
oligarchy: Spartan encouragement of, 1.19,
3.82, 5.81–2; in Megara 4.74, Thessaly
4.78, Sicyon 5.81, Argos 5.81, Samos
8.63, 8.73–4; Athenagoras on, 6.38–40;

attitude of subject allies to oligarchy/ democracy 8.48, 8.64; oligarchies installed by Peisander, etc. (411) 8.64–5; inherent weakness of, 8.89

Olophyxus, city on Acte peninsula (Chalcidice) 4.109

Olorus, father of Thucydides (1) 4.104

Olpae, town in Amphilochia 3.105–8, 3.110–11, 3.113; (426/5) captured by Ambraciots 3.105; battle of, defeat of Ambraciots and Peloponnesians 3.107–8

Olpaeans, in Ozolian Locris 3.101

Olympia: sanctuary of Zeus 3.14, 5.31, 5.50; funds at Olympia 1.121, 1.143; records of treaties set up at Olympia 5.18, 5.47; Elean control of Olympia, 5.31, 5.49–50; (428) conference of Peloponnesian League at Olympia 3.8–15

Olympic festival/games 1.6, 1.126, 3.8, 5.47, 5.49–50 (Spartans banned, 420), 6.16; Olympic law and truce 5.49; festival police 5.50; pancratium 5.49; chariot-race 5.50, 6.16; Olympic victors: 1.126 (Cylon of Athens), 3.8 (Dorieus of Rhodes), 5.49 (Androsthenes of Arcadia), 5.50 (Lichas of Sparta, under false colours), 6.16 (Alcibiades of Athens)

Olympieium, sanctuary of Olympian Zeus near Syracuse 6.64–5, 6.70, 6.75, 7.37, 7.42; fortified village there 7.4

Olympus, mountain in Thessaly 4.78

Olynthus, city in Chalcidice: (432) Chalcidians persuaded by Perdiccas to uproot to Olynthus 1.58; 1.62–3, 2.79, 4.110, 4.123, 5.3; (422/1) provision in Peace of Nicias 5.18; (421/0) Olynthians capture Mecyberna 5.39

Oneium, mountain in Corinthiad 4.44

Onomacles, Athenian general: (412) in command of expedition to Miletus 8.25, (8.27); and against Chios (412/1) 8.30

Ophioneans, division of population of Aetolia 3.94, 3.96, 3.100

Opicia, region of S. Italy 6.4; Opicans drove out Sicels 6.2

Opus, in Opuntian Locris 2.32

oracles 1.25, 1.103, 1.118, 1.126, 1.134, 2.17, 2.54, 2.102, 3.96, 3.104, 5.16, 5.32; consultations of oracles in time of trouble 2.47 (plague), 5.103; oracle

proved true 5.26; oracle-mongers 2.8, 2.21, 8.1; soothsayers 6.69, 7.50, 8.1; *see also* DELPHI

Orchomenus (1), in Boeotia 1.113, 3.87 (earthquake), 4.76 (once called 'Minyan' Orchomenus); (424/3) at battle of Delium 4.93

Orchomenus (2), in Arcadia: (418) besieged by and comes to terms with Argive alliance 5.61–3; hostages taken 5.61, 5.77

Orestes, exiled son of Thessalian king: (454) attempted restoration by Athenians 1.111

Oresthenium, in Arcadia 5.64

Oresthis, region of Arcadia 4.134

Orestians, barbarian tribe in Epirus 2.80

Oreus, city in Euboea, previously called Hestiaea: only city still in Athenian control after revolt of Euboea in 411: 8.95

Orneae, in Argolid: (418) in battle of Mantinea 5.67, 5.72, 5.74; (416/5) Argive exiles settled there by Spartans, Orneae destroyed by Argives 6.7

Orobiae, in Euboea: (426) hit by tsunami 3.89

Oroedus, king of Paravaeans 2.80

Oropus, territory on border of Boeotia and Attica: subject possession of Athens 2.23, 4.99; 2.23, 3.91, 4.91, 4.96, 4.99, 7.28; (412/1) betrayed to Boeotians 8.60; (411) Peloponnesian fleet for Euboea based at Oropus 8.95

Ortygia, the inner city of Syracuse, once an island 6.3

Oscius, river in Thrace 2.96

ostracism 1.135 (Themistocles); 8.73 (Hyperbolus)

Paches, Athenian general: (428) leads expedition to Mytilene and begins siege 3.18; (427) accepts capitulation of Mytilene 3.28; chases Alcidas' fleet 3.33; captures Notium 3.34; reduces Pyrrha and Eresus, sends suspect Mytilenaeans to Athens 3.35 (executed, 3.50); trireme sent ordering Paches to execute all men in Mytilene 3.36; second trireme countermands order 3.49

Paeonia, region of Thrace 2.96, 2.98, 2.99

Pagondas, Boeotarch from Thebes:
(424/3) persuades Boeotians to
engage Athenians at Delium 4.91–3,
4.96

Palaerus, in Acarnania 2.30

Pale, city in Cephallenia 2.30; (435)
supports Corinth against Corcyra 1.27

Pallene, peninsula of Chalcidice 1.56,
1.64, 4.116, 4.120–1, 4.123, 4.129

Pammilus, Megarian founder of
Selinus 6.4

Pamphylia 1.100

Panactum, Athenian fort on Attica/
Boeotia border: (422) betrayed to
Boeotians 5.3; to be restored to
Athenians under Peace of Nicias
(422/1) 5.18, 5.35; (421–420)
bargaining-counter for return of
Pylos 5.36, 5.39, 5.42, 5.44,
5.46; (420) demolition 5.39–40, 5.42

Panaeans, northern Thracian tribe 2.101

Panaerus, Thessalian friend of
Brasidas 4.78

Panathenaea, festival at Athens 1.20,
5.47, 6.56–7

Pandion, father of Procne 2.29

Pangaeum, mountain in Thrace 2.99

panic in armies 3.108, 4.125, 4.128,
7.44, 7.71, 7.80–1

Panormus (1), in Achaea 2.86, 2.92

Panormus (2), Phoenician settlement
in Sicily 6.2

Panormus (3), in Milesian
territory 8.24

Pantacyas, river in Sicily 6.4

Parali, crew of Athenian state trireme
Paralus, committed democrats (8.73):
(411) help defeat oligarchic coup in
Samos 8.73; some arrested, others
assigned to a troop-ship by
Four Hundred 8.74, 8.86; hand over
to Argives envoys from Four Hundred
to Sparta, and take Argive envoys to
Samos 8.86

Paralians, division of population of
Malis 3.92

Paralus, Athenian state trireme 3.33,
3.77, 8.73–4, 8.86

Paravaeans, barbarian tribe in
Epirus 2.80

Parnassus, mountain in Phocis 3.95

Parnes, mountain in Attica 2.23, 4.96

Paros, Aegean island: colonized
Thasos 4.104

Parrhasia, district of Arcadia 5.33

Pasitelidas, Spartan: (423) appointed
governor of Torone 4.132; (422)
killed in Athenian recapture of
Torone 5.3

Patmos, Aegean island 3.33

Patrae, in Achaea 2.83, 2.84; (419)
persuaded by Alcibiades to build walls
to sea 5.52

PAUSANIAS (1), son of Cleombrotus
(1.94), father of Pleistoanax (1.107
etc.): 1.94–6, 1.128–35, 1.138;
guardian of king Pleistarchus 1.132;
in command at battle of Plataea (479)
1.130, 2.71, 3.54, 3.58; guarantee
of independence for Plataea
2.71–2, 3.68; capture of Byzantium
(478) 1.94, 1.128–9; commander of
Greek forces after Persian War,
resented, recalled 1.94–6; put
on trial 1.95, 1.128; recalled
again 1.131; affectation of Persian
ways 1.130; intrigue with Xerxes
1.95, 1.128–9, 1.131; intrigue
with Helots 1.132; starved to
death 1.134

Pausanias (2), son of Pleistoanax, king
of Sparta as minor, with his uncle
Cleomenes (2) as regent 3.26

Pausanias (3), Macedonian, (?)brother
of Derdas 1.61

Pedaritus, Spartan: (412) appointed
governor of Chios 8.28, 8.32; (412/1)
refuses to help revolt of Lesbos 8.32; investigates alleged plot to
betray Erythrae 8.33; executes
pro-Athenians in Chios 8.38;
complains to Sparta of Astyochus'
refusal to help Chios 8.38–9; appeals
again to Astyochus 8.40; appeals for
help to Peloponnesians in Rhodes,
defeated and killed in attack on
Athenian wall 8.55, 8.61

Pegae, Megarian port on Corinthian
Gulf 1.103, 1.107, 1.111, 1.115, 4.21,
4.66, 4.74

PEIRAEUS, port of Athens: fortified on
advice of Themistocles 1.93; Long
Wall to Peiraeus 1.107; Peiraeus/
Mounichia walls 2.13; towers guarding
mouth of harbour 8.90; corn
warehouse 8.90; no fountains in 430:
2.48; (431) accommodates some of
influx from country 2.17; (430) plague

hits in Peiraeus first 2.48; (429/8)
Peloponnesian attack proposed but
aborted, defences improved 2.93–4;
(415) spectacle of fleet for
Sicily 6.30–2; (413) fear of Sicilian
naval attack 8.1; (411) Athenians in
Samos dissuaded from attacking
Peiraeus 8.82, 8.86, cf. 8.90; Eëtioneia
fortified by Four Hundred, wall
demolished by hoplites 8.90–2, 8.94;
hoplites in Peiraeus support
Theramenes and moderates 8.92–3;
alarm at near civil war between Peiraeus
and city 8.92, 8.94; Athenians rush to
Peiraeus in fear of imminent attack
8.94; fear of Peloponnesian attack after
defeat at Eretria 8.96; (404) captured
at end of war 5.26

Peirasia, in Thessaly 2.22

PEISANDER, Athenian politician:
(412/1) sent from Samos to Athens to
promote oligarchic movement 8.49,
8.53–4; sent from Athens to
negotiate with Tissaphernes and
Alcibiades 8.54; negotiations
fail 8.56, 8.63; denounces
Phrynichus 8.54; (411) sent again to
Athens, and installs oligarchies en
route 8.64–5, 8.67–8; leading
extremist among Four Hundred 8.90;
escapes to Deceleia 8.98

Peisistratus (1), tyrant of Athens 1.20,
3.104, 6.53–5

Peisistratus (2), son of the tyrant
Hippias 6.54

Peithias, 'volunteer consul' of Athens at
Corcyra, leader of people's party,
killed in oligarchic coup (427) 3.70

Pelargic area, below Acropolis in
Athens 2.17

Pelasgians, branch of non-Greek
peoples 1.3, 4.109

Pele, island off Clazomenae 8.31

Pella, in Macedonia 2.99, 2.100

Pellene, in Achaea: original home of
Scionaeans 4.120; only Achaean city
on Peloponnesian side at start of
war 2.9; (418) in Peloponnesian
expedition against Argos 5.58–60;
(413/2) required to build ships for
Peloponnesian League 8.3; (411) lose
a ship at Cynossema 8.106

PELOPONNESE: takes name from
Pelops 1.9; fertile, subject to changes
of population 1.2; Dorian occupation 1.12, 1.18; two-fifths occupied by
Spartans 1.10; founded most colonies
in Italy and Sicily 1.12, cf. 6.77;
Pericles on Peloponnesian strengths
and weaknesses 1.141–3; all
Peloponnese except Argos and
Achaea allied to Sparta 2.9; plague
did not reach Peloponnese 2.54
— Athenian expeditions to/round
Peloponnese: (456/5) 1.108; (431)
2.17, 2.23, 2.25, 2.30; (430) 2.56;
(428) 3.7, 3.16, [3.17]; (426) 3.91,
3.94; (426/5) 3.105, 3.107; (419)
5.52; (414/3) 7.17; (413) 7.20, 7.26
— Peloponnesian mercenaries 1.31,
1.60, 3.34, 4.52, 4.76, 4.80, 6.22, 6.43,
7.19, 7.57–8, 8.28

PELOPONNESIAN LEAGUE 1.19,
1.40, 1.43, 1.76, 1.83, 1.141, 2.9, 3.8,
3.15–16, 4.22, 4.118, 5.30, 5.54, 5.57,
5.60, 5.77, 5.99; (432) 1st conference
at Sparta 1.67–88; 2nd conference at
Sparta 1.119–25; (428) conference at
Olympia 3.8–15; (422/1) conferences
to ratify Peace of Nicias 5.17, 5.22;
(421/0) conference at
Sparta 5.36; (412) conference at
Corinth 8.8
— (431) full levy for invasion of
Attica 2.10; (429) allied naval force
defeated in Corinthian Gulf
2.83–92; (428) fail to support second
invasion of Attica 3.15–16; (425)
summoned to support at Pylos 4.8 (cf.
4.22); (422/1) Spartans fear defections
to Argos 5.14; (422/1–421) dissent
from treaty/alliance with Athens, and
defections to Argive alliance 5.17,
5.22–4, 5.25, 5.27–32, 5.35; (419–418)
widespread disaffection 5.52, 5.57;
(418) expedition to Argos
(5.57–60) 'finest Greek army ever
raised so far' 5.60; resentment of Agis
for withdrawing 5.59–60; (414/3)
required to prepare for fort at Deceleia
and support for Sicily 7.18; (413)
forces sent to Sicily in freighters 7.7,
7.17, 7.18, 7.19, 7.25, 7.31, 7.34,
7.50; (413 on) supply succession
of garrisons for Deceleia, 7.27,
8.98; (413) reaction to Athenian
defeat in Sicily 8.2; (413/2)
money collected, and ship-building

required 8.3; (412) plan to progress
from Chios to Lesbos to Hellespont
8.7, 8.22, 8.23; (412/1) oppose
Lesbian proposals for 2nd
revolt 8.32, but support relief of
Chios 8.40; (411) ship losses at
Cynossema 8.106
PELOPONNESIAN WAR: importance
and scale 1.1, 1.21, 1.23, 2.8, 2.12;
inevitability 1.36, 1.44 (*contra* 1.42),
1.118, 1.144; 'Dorian war' prophecy
2.54; 'thrice nine years' 5.26;
pre-war propaganda 1.126–38,
2.13; last Spartan demands and
Athenian reply 1.139, 144–5; actual
outbreak, 2.1ff.; preparations, and
allies on either side 2.7–9; general
Greek attitude at start of war 1.123,
2.8, 2.11, 2.12, 3.13 (cf. 3.57–8),
4.20, 7.28; Spartan motives
(Brasidas) 4.85–7; 'first war' 10 years
to Peace of Nicias 5.24–6;
preparations for resumption of war
(413/2) 8.2–5; end of the war 5.26,
6.15, 7.27, 8.87
—causes, 1.23–146: growth of
Athenian power 1.89–118; (435–433)
Epidamnus/Corcyra 1.24–55, 1.146;
(433–432) Potidaea 1.56–66, 1.139;
Megara 1.67, 1.139, 1.140;
Aegina 1.67, 1.139; 'real reason'
1.23, 1.33, 1.88, 1.118
—land power v. sea power 1.18,
1.81, 1.83, 1.121, 1.141–3, 2.62,
2.89, 4.12, 4.122
—'First Peloponnesian War' 1.103,
1.105–8
—peace moves/desire to end war:
Athenian: (430) after 2nd invasion
and plague, rejected by Sparta 2.59,
2.65, 4.21; (422/1) after battle of
Amphipolis 5.14, 5.16; (411) envoys
sent by Four Hundred 8.86, 8.89,
8.90–1; **Spartan**: (425) after
Pylos disaster, rejected by
Athens 4.15–22, 4.41, 5.15; (424/3)
4.108; (422/1) 5.14–17; **both**: (423)
one-year truce 4.117–19, extended
5.1 (motives on both sides, 4.117);
(422/1) Peace of Nicias 5.14–19
(motives on both sides, 5.13–17)
Pelops, gave his name to
Peloponnese 1.9
Peloris, in territory of Messana 4.25

Peparethus, Aegean island 3.89
PERDICCAS, son of Alexander
(1.57 etc.), father of Archelaus (2.100),
king of Macedonia (Lower Macedonia
2.99) 1.56–9, 1.61–2, 2.29, 2.80,
4.78–9, 4.82–3, 4.124–5; his family
originally from Argos, 5.80; influence
in Thessaly 4.132; (429/8) Sitalces'
campaign against Perdiccas and
Macedonia 2.95, 2.98–101; and
Seuthes 2.101; (424–423) against
Arrhabaeus/Lyncestians 4.79, 4.83,
4.124–5; and Brasidas 4.79, 4.83,
4.107, 4.124–5, 4.128, 4.132; (424/3)
involved in conspiracy to betray
Amphipolis 4.103, 4.107; (418/7)
joins Spartan/Argive alliance 5.80,
5.83; (417/6) Athenians blockade
Macedonia and declare Perdiccas an
enemy 5.83; (416/5) his territory
ravaged by Athenians 6.7; (414)
attacks Amphipolis with Athenians 7.9
—relations/alliances with Athens
1.57, 1.61, 1.62, 2.29, 2.80, 4.79, 4.82,
4.128, 4.132, 5.6, 5.80, 5.83, 6.7, 7.9
PERICLES, son of Xanthippus
(1.111 etc.), Athenian general:
under 'the curse of the goddess' 1.127,
2.13; guest-friend of Archidamus 2.13;
influence and policy 1.127;
constant in his view 1.127, 1.140, 2.13,
2.61, 2.65; unpopularity
2.21–2, 2.59, 2.65; contrast with his
successors 2.65; on empire 1.143,
1.144, 2.13, 2.36, 2.63–4; on
democracy 2.37; on women 2.45
—(454) leads expeditions to Sicyon
and Oeniadae 1.111; (446) crushes
revolt of Euboea 1.114; (440–439)
crushes revolt of Samos 1.116–17;
(431) carries motion refusing
access to Spartan embassies 2.12;
Athenian resentment in 1st
invasion 2.21–2; leads campaign
against Megara 2.31; (430)
leads expedition to E. coast of
Peloponnese 2.56, 6.31; Athenians
turn against him after 2nd
invasion and plague 2.59, 2.65
(fined, then re-elected general);
(429) dies 2.65
—speeches: (432) advocating
war 1.140–4; (431) encouragement
before invasion 2.13; (431/0)

funeral oration 2.35–46; (430)
response to disaffection 2.60–4
—Thucydides' assessment 1.127,
1.139, 2.65; Pericles' assessment
of himself 2.60
Perieres, from Cumae, co-founder
of Zancle 6.4
Perioeci, category of inhabitants of
Laconia: some joined the Helot
revolt 1.101; 3.92, 4.8, 4.53
(Cythera), 8.6, 8.22
Perrhaebia, region N. of Thessaly 4.78
Perseus 1.9
PERSIA: Persian tribute 8.5–6;
culture of giving 2.97; subjugate
Ionia under Cyrus and Dareius (1)
1.16; (460–454) revolt and recovery
of Egypt 1.104, 1.109–10;
(479–478) lose Sestos 1.89; (478)
lose Byzantium 1.94; (?457) attempt
to bribe Peloponnesians to invade
Attica 1.109; affected by
plague 2.48; (430) capture
Colophon 3.34
—intrigues with Greeks: Pausanias (1),
1.95, 1.128–9, 1.131; Themistocles
1.135, 1.137–8; (440) Samian
oligarchs 1.115; *see also*
ALCIBIADES
—Greek negotiations with Persia:
(431) both sides seeking Persian
support at beginning of war 2.7; again
in 425/4: 4.50; (430) Peloponnesian
embassy to Persia arrested 2.67;
(413/2) Persians seeking alliance with
Sparta 8.5–6, 8.12; (412) 1st treaty
with Sparta 8.17–18, 8.36, 8.43;
(412/1) 2nd treaty with Sparta 8.36–7,
8.43, 8.52; 3rd treaty with
Sparta 8.58
see also **TISSAPHERNES**
PERSIAN WAR: 1.18, 1.23, 1.69, 1.73–4,
1.89, 1.90, 1.97, 2.21, 3.10, 3.54, 3.56–8,
5.89, 6.17, 6.33, 6.82; Greek dedication
at Delphi 1.132, 3.57; Persian spoils on
Acropolis at Athens 2.13; Greek
alliance for retaliation 1.75, 1.94–7,
1.102, 3.10, 6.76, 6.82
—battles: (490) Marathon 1.18, 1.73,
2.34, 6.59; (480) Salamis 1.14,
1.73–4, 1.137; Artemisium 3.54;
Thermopylae 4.36; (479) Mycale 1.89; Plataea 1.130, 2.71, 2.74,
3.54, 3.58; (?469) Eurymedon 1.100

Petra, promontory in territory of
Rhegium 7.35
Phacium, in Thessaly 4.78
Phaeacians, supposed original inhabitants
of Corcyra 1.25 (cf. sanctuary of
Alcinous, 3.70)
Phaeax, Athenian envoy sent on mission
to Italy and Sicily (422) 5.4–5
Phaedimus, Spartan envoy (420) 5.42
Phaeinis, priestess at Argos 4.133
Phaenippus, secretary for Athenian
assembly resolving one-year truce
(423) 4.118
Phagres, in Thrace 2.99
Phaleron, a harbour of Athens 1.107;
the Phaleric wall 2.13
Phalius, Corinthian founder-colonist of
Epidamnus 1.24
Phanae, in Chios 8.24
Phanomachus, Athenian general 2.70
Phanoteus, in Phocis 4.76, 4.89
Pharnabazus (1), father of
Pharnaces (2) 2.67
Pharnabazus (2), son of Pharnaces (2),
Persian satrap: (413/2–411) seeks
Spartan alliance and fleet for
Hellespont 8.6, 8.8, 8.62, 8.80, 8.99,
8.109; rivalry with Tissaphernes 8.6,
8.8, 8.99, 8.109
Pharnaces (1), father of Artabazus 1.129
Pharnaces (2), son of Pharnabazus (1),
father of Pharnabazus (2) (8.6, 8.58)
2.67; (422) settles dispossessed
Delians in Atramyttium 5.1
Pharos, in Egypt 1.104
Pharsalus, city in Thessaly 1.111, 2.22,
4.78, 8.92
Phaselis, city on coast of Pamphylia 2.69,
8.88, 8.99, 8.108
Pheia, in Elis 2.25, 7.31
Pherae, in Thessaly 2.22
Philip, brother of Perdiccas 1.57, 1.59,
1.61; father of Amyntas 2.95, 2.100
Philippus, Spartan: (412) installed as
governor of Miletus 8.28; (411) sent
to Aspendus 8.87, warns Mindarus of
Tissaphernes' duplicity 8.99
Philocharidas, Spartan diplomat
4.119, 5.19, 5.21, 5.24; (420)
envoy to Athens 5.44–6
Philocrates, Athenian general 5.116
Philoctetes 1.10
Phlius/Phliasia, in NE Peloponnese:
(435) help Corinth against

Corcyra 1.27; (424) in Brasidas' army at Megara 4.70; 4.133; (418) Peloponnesian expedition against Argos gathers at Phlius 5.57–8 (Phliasians in that expedition 5.57–60); (417/6, 416, 414) invaded three times by Argives 5.83, 5.115, 6.105

Phocaea, in Ionia: colonized Massalia, defeated Carthaginians in sea-battle 1.13; 8.31, 8.101; Phocaean staters 4.52

Phocaeae, part of the city of Leontini 5.4

Phocis, region of central Greece: after Trojan War some Phocians joined Elymian settlement in Sicily 6.2; once inhabited by Thracians 2.29; allies of Sparta 2.9, but 'long-standing friends of Athens' 3.95; (?458) attack on Doris countered by Spartans 1.107; (457) Athenians take control of Phocis after battle of Oenophyta 1.108; (454) allies of Athens in Thessalian campaign 1.111; (449) Athenians restore temple at Delphi to Phocians 1.112; (426) hostility to Amphissans 3.101; (424) some Phocians involved in Boeotian pro-democracy movement 4.76; (423) in one-year truce Phocians to be persuaded to allow universal access to Delphi 4.118; (421) war with Locris 5.32; (418) summoned to assist Spartans at Mantinea 5.64, request countermanded 5.75; (413/2) required to build ships for Peloponnesian League 8.3

Phoebus, name of Apollo 3.104

Phoenicians: pirates 1.8; traders 2.69, 6.2; Phoenicians in Sicily 6.2, 6.46; Phoenician fleets 1.16, 1.100 (destroyed at Eurymedon, ?469), 1.110 (with Persians in Egypt), 1.112, 1.116; Phoenician fleet promised by Tissaphernes 8.46, ('the King's ships' in 8.58), 8.59, 8.78, 8.81, 8.87, 8.88, 8.99, 8.108, 8.109

Phoenicus, harbour under Mt Mimas 8.34

PHORMIO, son of Asopius (1) 1.64, father of Asopius (2) 3.7, Athenian general: (440/39) at Samos 1.117; (?430s) expedition to Amphilochian Argos 2.68; (433–432, 431) at Potidaea/Chalcidice 1.64–5, 2.29,

2.58, [3.17]; (430/29) based in Naupactus with 20 ships 2.69, 2.80, 2.81, 2.83, 2.84, 2.90–2, 2.102–3; (429) naval successes in the Gulf 2.83–92; speech to Athenians at Molycrian Rhium 2.89; (429/8) expedition to Acarnania 2.102–3 —and Acarnanians 2.68, 2.81, 2.102–3, 3.7

Photyus, leader of Chaonians 2.80

Phrygii, in Attica 2.22

Phrynichus, Athenian general: reputation for intelligence 8.27; (412) in command of expedition to Miletus 8.25, 8.27; refuses to engage Peloponnesian fleet and withdraws to Samos 8.27; (412/1) opposed to oligarchic plan 8.48; outwits Alcibiades 8.50–1; denounced by Peisander and relieved of command 8.54; (411) committed oligarch 8.68; leading extremist among Four Hundred, sent to negotiate peace with Sparta 8.90; murdered 8.92 —hostility to Alcibiades 8.48, 8.51, 8.54, 8.68, 8.90

Phrynis, one of the Perioeci, sent as inspector to Chios (413/2) 8.6

Phthiotis, region of Thessaly 1.3, 4.78 (Achaea), 8.3

Phyrcus, Elean fort 5.49

Physca, in Macedonia 2.99

Phytia, in Acarnania 3.106

Pieria, district of Macedonia 2.99, 2.100

Plerium, in Thessaly 5.13

Pindus, mountain in Thessaly 2.102

piracy 1.4–5, 1.7–8, 1.13, 2.32, 2.69, 3.51, (3.114), 4.53, 4.67

Pissouthnes, Persian governor of Sardis 1.115, 3.31, 3.34; father of bastard son Amorges (*q.v.*) 8.5, 8.28

Pitana division at Sparta: never existed 1.20

Pittacus, king of Edonians: assassinated (424/3) 4.107

PLATAEA, city in Boeotia 2.2–6, 2.71–8, 3.20–4, 3.52–68; founded from Thebes 3.61; hostility to Thebes 2.2, 3.54, 3.55, 3.56, 3.59, 7.57; rejected inclusion in pan-Boeotian alliance 2.2, 3.55, 3.61, 3.64–6; allies of Athens 2.9, 2.72–4, 3.55–6, 3.61, 3.63–4, 3.68, 4.67,

7.57; (519) help refused by Sparta, given by Athens against Thebes 3.55, 3.61; (479) battle of Plataea in Persian War 1.130, 2.71, 2.74, 3.54, 3.58; Plataeans in Persian War 3.54, 3.56–8; Pausanias' guarantee of Plataean independence 2.71–2, 3.68; (within 464–455) help Spartans in Helot revolt 3.54
—(431) entry of Thebans into Plataea and their defeat 2.2–6, 2.19, 3.56, 7.18; pro-Theban party 2.2, 3.65, 3.68; land ravaged by Boeotians 2.12; (429) Spartan campaign against Plataea, 2.71–8; exchanges with Archidamus 2.71–4; consultation of Athenians 2.72–3; (429–427) siege: 2.75–8, 3.20–4 (escape of 212 Plataeans, 428/7), 3.52 (capitulation), 3.53–9 (speech before Spartan judges), 3.68 (verdict, execution, and end of Plataea); (427) occupied by Megarians, then razed to the ground 3.68; (424) Plataean troops with Athenians at Megara 4.67; (422/1) not handed back under Peace of Nicias 5.17, cf. 3.52; (421) Plataeans granted occupation of Scione 5.32; (415–413) with Athenians in Sicily 7.57

Pleistarchus, king of Sparta as minor, ward of Pausanias (1) 1.132

Pleistoanax, son of Pausanias (1), father of Pausanias (2) (3.26), king of Sparta (as minor, 1.107) 5.16–17; (446) led invasion of Attica 1.114, 2.21, 5.16; (?445/4) exiled from Sparta on suspicion that he was bribed to withdraw from Attica 2.21, 5.16; his return after 18 years, and criticism by his opponents (said to have suborned Delphic oracle) 5.16–17; (422/1) leading Spartan proponent of peace 5.16–17; signatory of Peace of Nicias and alliance 5.19, 5.24; (418) commands (unneeded) reinforcements for Agis at Mantinea 5.75

Pleistolas, Spartan ephor at time of Peace of Nicias (422/1) 5.19, 5.24, 5.25

Plemmyrium, headland opposite Ortygia (Syracuse): (414) fortified by Athenians, and fleet moved there 7.4; (413) forts captured by

Gylippus 7.22–4, 7.31; significance of this loss 7.24, 7.36

Pleuron, city in Aeolis (2) 3.102

Pnyx, hill in Athens, regular place of assemblies 8.97

Polemarchs: military officials at Mantinea 5.47; officers in Spartan army 5.66, 5.71

Polichna (1), city in Crete 2.85

Polichna (2), town on mainland opposite Clazomenae: (412) fortified by Clazomenians 8.14; captured by Athenians 8.23

Polis, village in Ozolian Locris 3.101

Polles, king of Odomantians in Thrace 5.6

Pollis, Argive ambassador to Persia, executed by Athenians (430) 2.67

Polyanthes, Corinthian commander 7.34

Polycrates, tyrant of Samos (c.532–522) 1.13, 3.104

Polydamidas, Spartan commander at Mende (423) 4.123, 4.129, 4.130

Polymedes, Thessalian commander 2.22

Poseidon, god: temples at Taenarum 1.128, Mende 4.129, near Nisaea 4.118; sanctuary at Colonus 8.67; ship dedicated to Poseidon by Athenians (429) 2.84

Potamis, Syracusan commander sent to fleet at Miletus (411) 8.85

POTIDAEA, city on Pallene peninsula (Chalcidice) 1.56–66, 2.70; Corinthian colony, tribute-paying ally of Athens 1.56; the key to the Thraceward region 1.68 (cf. 2.67); (432) Athenian precautionary demands 1.56–7; Potidaeans send envoys to Athens and Sparta 1.58; revolt from Athens 1.58; supported in revolt by Corinth 1.60–3, 1.65, 5.30; (432–430/29) besieged by Athenians 1.64–5, 1.67–8, 1.119, 2.13, 2.58 (reinforcements under Hagnon, cf. 6.31, affected by plague), 2.67; (430/29) reduced to starvation, and capitulate 2.70; colonized later by Athenian settlers 2.70; (423) base for Athenian attack on Mende 4.129; (423/2) Brasidas' unsuccessful attempt on Potidaea (4.121), 4.135; 2.79, 4.120, 6.31
—one of the causes of the war 1.56, 1.66, 1.68, 1.118, 1.139, 1.140;

expense of the Athenian
campaign 2.13, 2.70, [3.17]
Potidania, town in Aetolia 3.96
Prasiae (1), in Laconia: (430) taken and
sacked by Athenians 2.56; 6.105, 7.18
Prasiae (2), on E. coast of Attica 8.95
Pratodamus, Spartan ambassador to
Persia, executed by Athenians
(430) 2.67
Priapus, on S. shore of Propontis 8.107
Priene, in Ionia 1.115
Procles (1), Athenian general 3.91, 3.98
Procles (2), Athenian signatory of Peace of
Nicias and alliance (422/1) 5.19, 5.24
Procne, daughter of Pandion 2.29
Pronni, city in Cephallenia 2.30
Propylaea, on Athenian Acropolis 2.13
Proschium, in Aetolia 3.102, 3.106
Prosopitis, island below Memphis 1.109
Prote, island off Messenia 4.13
Proteas, Athenian general 1.45, 2.23
Protesilaus, sanctuary near Elaeus 8.102
Proxenus, Locrian (Italian)
commander 3.103
prytaneis/prytany, presiding
section of Athenian council 4.118,
5.47, 6.14, 8.70
Pteleum (1), unknown location: provi-
sion in Peace of Nicias (422/1) 5.18
Pteleum (2), Athenian fort on Erythraean
peninsula 8.24, 8.31
Ptoeodorus, Thespian exile promoting
democratic movement in Boeotia 4.76
Ptychia, island off Corcyra 4.46 (cf. 3.75)
Pydna, in Macedonia: (432) besieged by
Athenians 1.61; 1.137
PYLOS, in Messenia (cf. 4.41): 4.3–6,
4.8–16, 4.23, 4.26–41, 4.55; Spartan
name Coryphasium 4.3, 4.118,
5.18; (425) advantages of the
place 4.3; fort built by Athenians
4.4–5; attempted Spartan landing
repulsed 4.9–13; sea-battle in
harbour 4.13–14, cf. 7.71; Spartans
marooned on Sphacteria 4.14–16, 4.23,
4.26–7; hardships for Athenians
4.26–7, 4.29; Cleon forced to take up
Pylos command 4.27–9, 4.39; battle
on Sphacteria and surrender of
Spartans 4.31–9; garrison established,
raids on Laconia 4.41, cf. 5.56, 5.115,
6.105, 7.18, 7.26, 7.57; (422/1) to be
restored to Sparta under Peace of

Nicias 5.18; captured Spartans
returned 5.24, 7.86 (regretted, 5.35);
(421) restoration refused, but
Messenians and Helots withdrawn
5.35 (Helots brought back, 419/8: .
5.56); (421–420) Spartan hopes to
exchange Panactum for Pylos 5.36,
5.39, 5.42, 5.44–5; (413) Pylos affair
determines Spartan view of
Demosthenes and Nicias 7.86
—effect of Pylos disaster on
Spartans 4.41, 4.55, 4.80, 4.108,
4.117, 5.14–15, 5.17, 7.18, 7.71
Pyrasus, in Thessaly 2.22
Pyrrha, city in Lesbos 3.18, 3.25,
3.35, 8.23
Pystilus, Geloan founder-colonist
of Acragas 6.4
Pythangelus, Boeotarch, leads
entry into Plataea (431) 2.2
Pythen, Corinthian commander: (414)
takes ships to Italy/Sicily, 6.104,
7.1; (413) in final battle in Great
Harbour 7.70
Pythian games 5.1
Pythodorus (1), Athenian archon 2.2
Pythodorus (2), Athenian general:
(426/5) replaces Laches in
Sicily 3.115, 4.2; (424) exiled
on return from Sicily 4.65
Pythodorus (3), Athenian general
6.105; signatory of Peace of Nicias
and alliance (422/1) 5.19, 5.24

Rhamphias, Spartan commander 5.12–14;
ambassador to Athens (432) 1.139
Rhegium, city in Italy: (427 on) allies of
Leontini, and Athenian base for 1st
Sicilian expedition 3.86, 3.88, 3.115,
4.25; naval cooperation with
Athenians 3.88, 4.25; hostility of
Locri 4.1, 4.24–5; (415) refuse to join
Athenians against Sicily 6.44–6,
6.79; 6.50–1, 7.1, 7.4, 7.35
—Anaxilas tyrant of Rhegium 6.4;
sanctuary of Artemis 6.44;
promontory of Petra 7.35
Rheiti, lakes in Attica 2.19
Rheitus, in Corinthiad 4.42
Rheneia, island next to Delos 1.13, 3.104
Rhium (1), Molycrian 2.84, 2.86
Rhium (2), in Achaea, opposite
Molycrian Rhium 2.86, 2.92, 5.52

Rhodes, E. Aegean island: Dorians, of
Argive descent 7.57; co-founders of
Gela 6.4, 7.57; (415–413) with
Athenians in Sicily 6.43, 7.57;
(412/1) revolt from Athens 8.44;
Athenian attacks 8.44, 8.55;
Peloponnesian fleet moves to
Rhodes 8.44 (exacts money), 8.52,
8.55, 8.61, then from Rhodes to
Miletus 8.60; 3.8, 8.41
Rhodope, mountain in Thrace 2.96, 2.98
Rhoeteium, on Hellespont 4.52, 8.101
Rhype, in Achaea 7.34

Sabylinthus, leader of Molossians and
Atintanians 2.80
Sacon, founder-colonist of Himera 6.5
Sacred War (449) 1.112
Sadocus, son of Sitalces: (431) given
Athenian citizenship 2.29; (430)
hands over Peloponnesian embassy to
Athenians 2.67
Salaethus, Spartan sent to aid of Mytilene
(428/7) 3.25, 3.27, 3.35–6
Salaminia, Athenian state
trireme 3.33, 3.77, 6.53, 6.61
Salamis (1), island in Saronic Gulf:
battle of Salamis (480) 1.14, 1.73–4,
1.137; fort at Boudorum 2.93–4, 3.51;
(429/8) Salamis attacked by Peloponnesian fleet, 2.93–4; [3.17], 8.94
Salamis (2), city in Cyprus 1.112
Salynthius, king of Agraeis 3.111, 3.114;
(424) won over by Demosthenes 4.77
Same, city in Cephallenia 2.30
Saminthus, in Argolid 5.58
SAMOS, E. Aegean island: early navy
and naval strength 1.13; Polycrates
tyrant of Samos (c. 532–522) 1.13,
3.104; unwalled 8.50–1 (cf. 1.117);
in Sicily (Zancle) after Ionian revolt
6.4; subject ally of Athens, with
Athenians in Sicily 7.57; Samian
exiles in Anaea (3.19), 3.32,
4.75; (440) war with Miletus,
Athenians intervene and impose
democracy 1.115; (440–439) revolt
from Athens, 1.40, 1.41, 1.115–17,
8.76; besieged, revolt crushed, walls
demolished and navy forfeited 1.117
—(412) Athenian fleets at
Samos 8.16–17, 8.19, 8.21, 8.25;
revolution of people against olig-

archs 8.21, cf. 8.63, 8.73; Athenians
grant independence to Samos 8.21;
Athenians withdraw from Miletus to
Samos 8.27; (412–411) entire
Athenian fleet assembled and based in
Samos 8.30, 8.33, 8.35, 8.38, 8.39,
8.41, 8.44, 8.47–8, 8.60, 8.63,
8.79; Athenian oligarchic plot
originated in base at Samos 8.47–51,
8.53, 8.56, 8.63; (412/1) Samos
fortified 8.51; (411) attempt to set
up oligarchy in Samos 8.63, 8.73;
reaction, oligarchic coup defeated
(8.73), democracy restored 8.72–7,
8.86; 'one remaining bastion of
Athenian empire' 8.73; Alcibiades
recalled to Samos 8.81; Alcibiades
at Samos, 8.81–2, 8.86, 8.108;
emissaries from Four Hundred sent
to Samos 8.72, 8.77, 8.86, 8.89
—(411) Athenians in Samos as rival
state 8.75–7, 8.81–2, 8.86, 8.88–90,
8.96, 8.97, 8.108 (see further under
ATHENS/ATHENIANS)
Sandian Hill, in Caria 3.19
Sane (1), city on Acte peninsula
(Chalcidice): colony of Andros,
(424/3) resists Brasidas 4.109
Sane (2), city on Pallene peninsula
(Chalcidice): provision in Peace of
Nicias (422/1) 5.18
Sardis, city in Lydia 1.115
Sargeus, Sicyonian commander 7.19
Scandeia, harbour town in Cythera 4.54
Scione, city on Pallene peninsula
(Chalcidice): (423) defects to
Brasidas 4.120–1; Athenian campaign
in response 4.129–33; (423–421)
under siege 4.131–3, 5.2, 5.18
(provision in Peace of Nicias), 5.32
(captured)
Sciritis, region of Laconia 5.33;
Sciritae in Spartan army 5.67; (418)
in battle of Mantinea 5.67–8, 5.71–2
Scironides, Athenian general: (412)
joint commander of expedition to
Miletus 8.25, (8.27); (412/1)
relieved of command, with
Phrynichus 8.54
Scirphondas, Theban Boeotarch,
killed at Mycalessus (413) 7.30
Scolus, in Chalcidice: provision in
Peace of Nicias (422/1) 5.18

Scombrus, mountain in Thrace 2.96

Scyllaeum, promontory in territory of Hermione 5.53

Scyros, Aegean island: (?475) captured by Athenians 1.98

Scythians 2.96, 2.97

Selinus, Dorian city in Sicily: founded by Megara 6.4, 7.57; (416/5) war with Egesta, and supported by Syracuse 6.6, 6.8, 6.13, 6.47–8, 6.62; resources for war (Nicias) 6.20; (415–413) Selinuntian troops supporting Syracuse 6.65, 6.67, 7.58; supporting Gylippus 7.1; (413) Peloponnesian reinforcements land at Selinus 7.50; (412) two ships in Peloponnesian expedition to Miletus 8.26

Sermyle, in Chalcidice 1.65, 5.18

Sestos, city on Chersonese: (479–478) besieged and captured from Persians by Athenians and allies 1.89, 8.62; (411) fortified by Athenians as guard on Hellespont 8.62, 8.102; Athenian ships at Sestos chased by Mindarus' fleet 8.102; 8.104, 8.107

Seuthes, nephew of Sitalces (2.101): king of Odrysia after Sitalces 2.97, 4.101; and Perdiccas 2.101

ships and shipbuilding: ships in Trojan expedition 1.10; early shipbuilding in Corinth 1.13; Athenian ships in battle of Salamis 1.14; condition and care of ships 2.94, 7.12; repair of ships 1.52, 6.104, 7.1, 7.38, 8.43, 8.107
— penteconters 1.14, 6.43, 6.103; 30-oared privateer 4.9; cutters 1.53, 4.9, 4.120, 8.38; sculling-boat 4.67; fireship 7.53; troop-transports 1.116, 2.83, 6.25, 6.31, 6.43, 6.62, 7.4, 8.25, 8.30, 8.62, 8.74; horse-transports 2.56, 4.42, (6.7), 6.43; merchant ships 2.91, 2.97, 4.53, 6.1, 6.22, 6.30, 6.44, 6.88, 7.23, 7.25; freighters transporting Peloponnesian troops to Sicily (413) 7.7, 7.17–19, 7.25, 7.31, 7.34, 7.50; freighters used as protection 7.25, 7.38, 7.41
— timber for shipbuilding 4.52 (Mt Ida), 4.108 (Amphipolis), 6.90 (Italy), 7.25 (Caulonia), 8.1, 8.4; shipbuilding on both sides in 413/2: 8.3–4
see also triremes

Sicania, early name of Sicily 6.2

Sicanians, early settlers of Sicily, from Iberia 6.2; Sicanian population of Hyccara 6.62

Sicanus (1), river in Iberia 6.2

Sicanus (2), Syracusan general: elected (415/4) 6.73, deposed (414) 6.103; (413) on mission to Acragas 7.46, 7.50; commands in final sea-battle 7.70

SICELS, native inhabitants of Sicily: 3.88, 3.103, 5.4, 6.2, 6.34, 6.45, 6.48, 6.62, 6.88, 7.1; crossed over from Italy, defeated Sicanians 6.2; dispossessed by Greek colonists 6.3; Sicel kings 6.2, 6.4, 7.1; (426/5) revolt from Syracusan control and fight on Athenian side 3.103, 3.115, cf. 6.17, 6.88; (425) support Naxos against Messanans, 4.25; (415–413) support for and sought by Syracusans 6.34, 6.88, 7.1 (support for Gylippus), 7.58; support for and sought by Athenians 6.17, 6.48, 6.62, 6.65, 6.88, 6.103, 7.32, 7.57, 7.77, 7.80; (413) ambush troops coming to aid of Syracuse 7.32
— Sicel towns: Alicyae 7.32; Centoripa 6.94, 7.32; fort at Ietae 7.2; Inessa 3.103, 6.94; Sicel cavalry 6.88, 6.98

SICILIAN EXPEDITION (415–413): Athenian ambitions/motives in Sicily 3.86, 4.60–1, 4.65, 5.4, 6.1, 6.6, 6.8, 6.24, 6.33, 6.69, 6.76, 6.83–7, 6.90, 7.66; pretext and real reason 6.6, 6.8, 6.33, 6.76; general ignorance of scale of undertaking 6.1 (cf. 6.36); allies on Athenian side 7.57; costliest Greek armada 6.31; later regret 7.55; reason for failure 2.65; lack of cavalry 6.22, 6.37 (cf. 6.43), 6.64, 6.88; failure to intercept hostile ships 6.104, 7.1, 7.4, 7.7, 7.25; sickness among troops 7.47, 7.50; deterioration of ships and crews, 7.4, 7.12–13; shortage of food 7.60, 7.75, 7.77–8, 7.80, 7.83; almost all Sicily united against Athens 7.15, 7.33; length of communication with Athens 6.21, 6.86; similarity of Syracusans and Athenians 7.55, 8.96; Thucydides' assessment of the disaster 7.87

—(416/5) renewed ambition 6.1,
6.6, stirred by envoys from Egesta 6.6,
6.8, 6.11; (415) enthusiasm 6.19, 6.24,
6.31; appointment of generals and their
brief 6.8 (resources voted 6.26);
arguments of Nicias and Alcibiades in
assembly 6.8–26; spectacle of
expeditionary force at Peiraeus 6.30–2;
reactions in Syracuse 6.32–41, 6.45;
numbers of forces gathered at
Corcyra 6.43–4; initial setbacks
(Rhegium and Egesta) 6.44–6, cf. 6.79;
conference of generals at Rhegium 6.46–50; reception in Italy 6.34,
6.42, 6.44, 7.33, 7.35, and Sicily
6.50–2, 6.62; reconnaissance of Great
Harbour 6.50, 6.52; base moved from
Rhegium to Catana 6.51; recall of
Alcibiades 6.53, 6.61; capture of
Hyccara 6.62; (415/4) Athenians move
to base opposite Olympieium 6.64–6;
victory in battle outside Syracuse 6.67–
71, 6.79, 6.88, 6.91; need for cavalry and
funds 6.71, 6.74, 6.93 (arrive from
Athens 6.94, from Sicily 6.98); winter
in Naxos 6.72, 6.74–5, 6.88, then
Catana 6.88, 7.42; preparations for
spring offensive 6.88; embassy to
Camarina 6.75, Euphemus'
speech 6.82–7
—(414) Athenians move from Catana,
seize Epipolae, defeat Syracusans 6.97; capture and destroy
Syracusan counter-walls 6.100, 6.101,
and win pitched battle 6.101; begin full
circumvallation 6.103 (near
completion, 7.2); fortify Plemmyrium
and move fleet there 7.4 (effect of this
on condition of ships' crews 7.4, 7.13);
first defeat, then defeated by Gylippus
and Syracusans on Epipolae, all prospect
of circumvallation lost 7.5–6, cf. 7.11
(Nicias), 7.42; Nicias' letter to
Athenians 7.8, 7.10–15; (414/3)
Athenians vote further resources and
elect generals 7.16–17; (413)
1st sea-battle, forts at Plemmyrium
captured 7.22–4; supply-ships
intercepted 7.25; attack on Athenian
wall coordinated with naval offensive,
2nd sea-battle 7.37–8; 3rd sea-battle,
won by Syracusans 7.40–1
—(413) reinforcements arrive with
Demosthenes and Eurymedon
7.42; Athenian defeat in

night-battle on Epipolae 7.43–5;
conference of generals 7.47–9; planned
move from Syracuse delayed by eclipse
of moon 7.50; attack on Athenian
wall 7.50–1; 4th sea-battle, lost by
Athenians and resulting despair 7.52–5,
7.60; Eurymedon killed 7.52; Syracusans defeated on shore 7.53–4;
conference of generals, decision to fight
out or retreat 7.60, cf. 7.67; Athenians
lose 5th and final sea-battle 7.69–72;
sailors refuse further attempt to break
out 7.72; **retreat from Syracuse,**
7.75–85; Demosthenes' division
caught and surrenders 7.80–2;
slaughter of Nicias' division and
surrender 7.84–5; prisoners kept in
quarries 7.86–7; Nicias and Demosthenes executed 7.86
—walls/forts built by Athenians:
fort at Labdalum 6.97–8, 7.3; 'circle'
at Syce 6.98, 6.102; north wall
towards Trogilus 6.99, 7.2, 7.4, 7.6,
7.60 (abandoned); south walls to Great
Harbour 6.101, 6.103, 7.2, 7.4;
cross-wall to create enclave 7.60

Sicilian Sea 4.24, 4.53, 6.13

SICILY: name of island 6.2; size of
island 6.1, 7.13; history of barbarian
(6.2) and Greek settlement 6.2–5;
colonies founded by Peloponnesians
1.12, 6.77; nature and size of
population 6.1–6, 6.17, 6.20, 6.36–7,
7.55, 7.58; Sicilian tyrants 1.17–18,
6.4–5; Dorian and Chalcidian/Ionian
cities 3.86, 4.25, 4.61, 4.64, 6.3–5,
7.57–8; Phoenicians in Sicily 6.2,
6.46; strait between Messana and
Rhegium ('Charybdis') 4.24; Corcyra
on route to Italy and Sicily 1.36, 1.44
—Athenian expeditions: (427–424)
1st expedition 3.86, 3.88, 3.90, 3.99,
3.103, 3.115, 4.2, 4.24–5, 4.65; (422)
mission of Phaeax 5.4; (415–413) 2nd
expedition, *see* SICILIAN
EXPEDITION
—internal campaigns: 3.86 (war
between Syracuse and Leontini, 427),
3.90, 4.25; (424) conference of Gela
4.58–65, agreement to a treaty 4.65,
5.4–5; (422) Leontinians driven out,
war with Syracuse 5.4 (cf. 6.6, 6.8,
6.19, 6.86); (416/5) war between
Selinus and Egesta 6.6, 6.8, 6.13,
6.47–8, 6.62

—appeals for Sicilian unity 4.58–65 (Hermocrates), 6.77–80 (Hermocrates), 6.91 (Alcibiades); 'all Sicily uniting against us' (Nicias) 7.15, 7.33; fear of Syracusan domination 6.78, 6.85–7 (*contra* Nicias in 6.11); (414–413) troops requested/raised in support of Syracuse 7.7, 7.12, 7.21, 7.25, 7.32, 7.46, 7.50; expectation of Sicilian involvement in Greece after Athenian defeat 7.64, 8.1, 8.2; Sicilian ships in Peloponnesian fleets 8.26, 8.35, 8.91

—cities: *see* Acragas, Camarina, **CATANA, EGESTA,** Eryx, Gela, Himera, Hybla Geleatis, Hyccara, **LEONTINI,** Megara Hyblaea, Messana, Morgantina, Naxos (2), Selinus, **SYRACUSE,** Thapsus

Sicyon, city W. of Corinth: ship-providing ally of Sparta 2.9, 2.80; (456, 454) Athenian landings, Sicyonians defeated 1.108, 1.111; (446) aid revolt of Megara 1.114; (435) diplomatic support for Corcyra 1.28; (424) in Brasidas' army at Megara 4.70; (424/3) repel Athenian landing 4.101; (423) signatories of one-year truce 4.119; (419) prevent Alcibiades fortifying Rhium 5.52; (418) in Peloponnesian expedition against Argos 5.58–60; (418/7) narrower oligarchy imposed by Spartans 5.81; (413) send troops to Sicily 7.19, 7.58; (413/2) required to build ships for Peloponnesian League 8.3

Sidoussa, Athenian fort on Erythraean peninsula 8.24

sieges: Athenian expertise 1.102; cost of, 2.13, 2.70, 2.77, [3.17], 3.19, 3.31, 3.33, 3.46, 7.47; materials for siege operations 4.69, 6.88, 7.43; siege-engines 2.18, 2.58, 2.76–7, 4.13, 4.100, 4.115, 5.7, 7.43, 8.100

Sigeium, city on Hellespont 6.59, 8.101

Simonides, Athenian general: (425) captures and loses Eïon (2) 4.7

Simus, founder-colonist of Himera 6.5

Singus, in Chalcidice: provision in Peace of Nicias (422/1) 5.18

Sintians, tribe on borders of Macedonia 2.98

Siphae, town in Thespian territory: (424) to be betrayed to Athenians 4.76–7; (424/3) failure of plan 4.89–90, 4.101

Sitalces, son of Teres, father of Sadocus (2.29), king of Thrace: his Odrysian empire 2.97; ally of Athens 2.29, 2.67, 2.95; (429/8) campaign against Macedonia/Perdiccas and Chalcidians 2.95–101 (size of his force 2.98); (424/3) killed in campaign against Triballians 4.101

slaves and slavery: densest slave populations in Sparta and Chios 8.40; inhabitants of captured cities sold into slavery 1.98, 1.113, 2.68, 3.36, 3.68, 4.48, 5.3, 5.32, 5.116, 6.62, cf. 7.87; sale of slaves 6.62, 8.28; recruitment of slaves 3.73; slaves in Athenian navy 7.13; attendant on Athenian hoplites and cavalrymen 7.75; deserting slaves 1.139, 1.142, 2.57, 4.41, 4.118, 5.14, 5.35, 6.91, 7.13, 7.27, 7.75, 8.40; Helot revolts 1.101–3, 1.128, 2.27, 3.54, 4.56, 5.23

Socrates, Athenian general 2.23

Sollium, in Acarnania: Corinthian colony, captured by Athenians (431) 2.30; 3.95, 5.30

Soloeis, Phoenician settlement in Sicily 6.2

Solygeia, village on hill Solygeius in Corinthiad 4.42–3

Solygeius, hill in Corinthiad 4.42

Sophocles, Athenian general: (425) in joint command of reinforcements to Sicily 3.115, 4.2–3; at Corcyra 4.46–8; (424) exiled on return from Sicily 4.65

Sounium, southern promontory of Attica 7.28, 8.4, 8.95

SPARTA (physical, social, and political): unimpressive as a city 1.10; political system unchanged for over 400 years 1.18, combined prosperity with stability 8.24; Peloponnesian hegemony 1.19, 1.76, 1.144 (*see also* **PELOPONNESIAN LEAGUE**); encouragement of oligarchy 1.19, 3.83, 5.81–2, 8.9, 8.14; Spartan kings 1.20, 1.131, 5.16, 5.63, 5.66; ephors 1.87, 1.131, 1.133–4, 2.2, 5.19, 5.36, 6.88, 8.12, 8.58; assemblies 1.67–87 (procedure, 1.87), 5.77, 6.88–93; Spartiates, 1.128, 2.12, 2.25, 2.66, 3.100, 4.8, 4.11, 4.38, 5.9, 5.15, 5.63, 7.19, 8.7, 8.11, 8.22,

8.39, 8.61; Perioeci 1.101, 3.92, 4.8,
4.53, 8.6, 8.22; Helots, *q.v.*; dense
population of slaves 8.40;
commissioners to advise failing
commanders 2.85 (Cnemus), 3.69,
3.76, 3.79 (Alcidas), 8.39 (Astyochus),
5.63 (to advise king); commissioner
for Cythera 4.53; appointment of
governors abroad 4.132, 5.51–2, 8.28,
8.61; public commendation 2.25
(Brasidas)
— army organization: polemarchs
5.66, 5.71–2; two reserve commanders
3.100, 3.109, 4.38; chain of command
5.66; units 5.68; pipers 5.70; 300
Knights (king's bodyguard) 5.72;
Sciritae 5.67–8, 5.71–2; 'Pitana
division' 1.20
— Amyclaeum 5.18, 5.23; Caeadas
ravine 1.134 (cf. 2.67); dockyard at
Gytheium 1.108; festivals 4.5,
(Hyacinthia) 5.23, 5.41, (Carneia)
5.75–6, (Gymnopaediae) 5.82
SPARTA/SPARTANS: simple
fashions 1.6; **character** 1.68–71
(Corinthians), 1.77, 1.84
(Archidamus), 1.118, 1.132, 5.105
(Athenians); slow to act 1.68–71,
1.84, 1.118, 1.132, 3.13, 4.85, 5.64
('unprecedented speed'), 5.82, 6.88,
6.93, 8.96; secrecy 5.68, 5.74;
expulsions of foreigners 1.144 (cf.
2.39); 'laconic' 4.17 (cf. Sthenelaïdas,
1.86), 4.84 (Brasidas 'not a bad
speaker, for a Spartan'), 5.69;
behaviour abroad 1.77, 1.95, 3.93,
4.81 (Brasidas), 4.108, 4.130, 5.52,
8.84; diffidence/pessimism 1.69–71,
1.118, 4.15, 4.17–20, 4.41, 4.55–6,
4.80–1, 5.14, 5.28, 5.46, 5.57, 5.109,
8.11 (development of confidence,
414/3: 7.18); failure of nerve 2.94,
8.95; over-confidence in apparent
victory 2.91–2, 8.105; religious
scruples 1.118, 1.128, 2.74, 3.89,
4.116, 5.16, 5.54, 5.55, 5.116, 6.95,
7.18, 8.6 (earthquakes, 3.89, 6.95,
8.6); education/training 1.84, 2.39,
5.69; discipline, 1.84, 1.121, 2.11,
2.39, 2.81, 4.40, 5.66 (lack of
discipline, 2.91, 5.72); **Spartans and
Athenians compared/contrasted**
1.6, 1.18–19, 1.69–71, 1.73–4

(contributions in Persian War), 2.39
(Pericles), 8.96
— Greek view of Spartans 3.57–8,
3.93, 4.18, 4.40, 4.108, 5.75;
'liberators' 1.69, 1.122, 1.124–5, 2.8,
2.72, 3.13, 3.32, 3.59, 4.85–7, 4.108,
4.121, 5.9, 8.43, 8.46, 8.52; unpopularity 1.95 (Pausanias); 3.93, 5.52
(Heracleia); 5.27, 5.29, 5.57 (among
Peloponnesian League); jealousy of
Brasidas 4.108, cf. 4.117; hoplite
supremacy 1.141, 1.143, 4.12; fear of
Spartan hoplites 4.34, cf. 6.11; naval
inferiority 1.74, 1.80, 1.121, 1.142,
2.85, 2.87, 2.91–2, 3.32 (intended
Spartan navy, 2.7)
— colonized: Melos 5.84, 5.89,
5.104, 5.106; Cythera 7.57;
Heracleia (1) 3.92–3
— deposed Athenian tyrants 1.18,
6.53, 6.59; led Greek alliance in Persian
War 1.18, 1.75, 1.77, 1.94–5
(abandoned, 1.95), 6.82; attempt to
prevent refortification of Athens
1.90–2; (465/4) earthquake and Helot
revolt 1.101–3, 1.128, 2.27; (?462) first
open dispute with Athens 1.102;
(461/0) Megara defects from Sparta to
Athens 1.103, 1.107; (460–459)
defeated by Athenians in sea-battle at
Cecryphaleia 1.105; (?458/7) intervene
to protect Doris against Phocis 1.107;
(457) defeat Athenians at Tanagra
1.107–8; (451) five-year treaty 1.112;
(449) 'Sacred War', Spartans give
control of Delphic sanctuary to
Delphians 1.112; (446) invasion of
Attica 1.114, 2.21, 5.16; (446) **Thirty
Years Treaty** 1.115; (432) 1st
conference of Peloponnesian League at
Sparta, 1.67–88; 2nd conference
1.119–25; vote for war, 1.87, 1.118,
1.125; pre-war propaganda on
both sides 1.126–38; Spartan
final demands, and Athenian
final answer 1.139–45
— **resources for the war**: 1.1,
1.80–2 (Archidamus), 1.121,
1.141–2 (Pericles), 2.11, 2.65
(Persian finance); allies on Spartan
side 2.9; allied providers of
ships 2.9, 8.3; rest of Greece in
support of Sparta 1.123, 2.8, 2.11

—(431) preparations for war 2.7–8; 1st invasion of Attica 2.10, 2.18–23; offer Thyrea to expelled Aegine-tans 2.27; (430) 2nd invasion 2.47, 2.55–7; failed expedition to Zacyn-thus 2.66; execute all caught at sea 2.67; (429) campaign against Plataea 2.71–8; against Acarnania 2.80–2; (429/8) naval attack on Peiraeus (aborted) and Salamis 2.93–4; (428) 3rd invasion 3.1; having refused earlier, accept request to help Lesbos/Mytilene secede 3.2, 3.13, 3.15; allies fail to support planned further invasion of Attica 3.13, 3.15; (428/7) continued siege of Plataea, escape of Plataeans 3.20–4; (427) 4th invasion 3.26; send Salaethus, then 40 ships, to aid of Mytilene 3.16, 3.25–6; slow progress and return of this expedition 3.27, 3.29–33, 3.69; enforce surrender of Plataea 3.52; court to try Plataeans 3.52–68; naval intervention in civil war at Corcyra 3.69, 3.72, 3.76–81; (426) invasion of Attica aborted (earthquake) 3.89; establish colony of Heracleia in Trachis 3.92–3; persuaded by Aetolians to campaign against Naupactus 3.100–2; coopera-tion of Ozolian Locrians 3.101; persuaded by Ambraciots, join campaign against Amphilochia and Acarnania 3.102, 3.105–14; defeat at Olpae 3.107–8; preferential truce to sully Spartan reputation in NW Greece 3.109, 3.111; (425) 5th invasion 4.2, 4.5–6; support sent for Corcyraean oligarchs 4.2–3 (recalled to Pylos, 4.8); Pylos affair 4.6, 4.8–23, 4.26–41; naval battle 4.13–14; reaction to disaster, embassy to Athens offering peace 4.15–22, 4.41, cf. 4.108, 5.15; capture of Spartans on Sphacteria 4.29–39; Greek surprise at Spartan surrender 4.40; (425/4) negotiations with Persia, intercepted 4.50; (424) demoralized after Athenian capture of Cythera 4.55–6; Brasidas saves Megara 4.70–3; respond to request for help from Perdiccas and Chalcidians in revolt 4.78–81, 4.83; Brasidas secures secession of

Acanthus 4.84–8; (424/3) Brasidas captures Amphipolis 4.102–6, and Torone 4.110–16; Spartans refuse Brasidas' request for reinforcements 4.108; (423) one-year truce 4.117–19; Brasidas in Lyncus 4.124–8; reinforc-ing army blocked by Thessalians 4.132; (422) lose Torone to Athenians 5.2–3; win battle for Amphipolis 5.6–12; (422/1) desire for peace terms 5.13–17; fears on impending expiry of treaty with Argos 5.14, 5.22 (cf. 5.43); Peace of Nicias 5.17–19, and alliance with Athens 5.22–4; alliance made independently of dissenting allies 5.22, subsequent trouble with Peloponnesian League 5.25; captives from Sphacteria returned 5.24 (their treatment in Sparta, 5.34) —(421) defections from Peloponnesian League to Argive alliance 5.27–32, 5.52; quarrel with Elis over Lepreum 5.31; expedition to Parrhasia 5.33; mutual mistrust after treaty with Athenians 5.35; (421/0) attempt to engineer Boeotian alliance with Corinth and Argos 5.36–8; ephors opposed to Peace of Nicias 5.36–9; alliance with Boeotia, in hope of acquiring Panactum as bargaining-counter for Pylos 5.39–40, 5.42, 5.44, 5.46; (420) agree 50-year treaty with Argos 5.41; banned by Eleans from Olympic festival 5.49–50; (419/8) send garrison to Epidaurus 5.56; (418) expedition against Argos 5.57–60; resentment of Agis for withdrawing 5.60, 5.63, 5.65; appoint commissioners to advise him 5.63; battle of Mantinea against Argive alliance 5.64–75 (Spartan losses, 5.74; reputation redeemed in Greek eyes, 5.75); (418/7) alliance with Argos 5.76–80, truce with Mantineans 5.81; establish oligarchy in Argos 5.81–2; expedition against Argos, destroy long walls and capture Hysiae 5.83; (416/5) invade Argolid 6.7; (415/4) support for Sicily urged by Syracusans, Corinthians, and Alcibiades 6.88–92; urged to reopen war in Greece (6.34), 6.73, 6.91, 7.25 (413); decide help for Sicily and appoint Gylippus 6.93;

(414) expedition against Argos aborted (earthquake), Argives invade Thyrea 6.95; invade Argolid, Athenian response taken as clear breach of treaty 6.105, 7.18; (414/3) preparations for Deceleia and help for Sicily 7.18 (cf. 7.7); (413) 6th invasion of Attica, fortification of Deceleia 7.19, 7.27–8; troops sent to Sicily, 7.19, 7.58; (for Spartans in Sicily, 414–413, *see* GYLIPPUS): (413/2) Spartan ambitions after Athenian defeat in Sicily, 8.2; preparations and ship-building requisition, 8.3
— in Ionia and E. Aegean (413/2–411): (413/2) approached by both Pharnabazus and Tissaphernes, decide help for Chios and Ionia 8.5–6; (412) plan to progress from Chios to Lesbos to Hellespont 8.7, 8.22; ships blockaded at Speiraeum 8.10–11, 8.14–15, 8.20; secure revolt of Chios, Erythrae, and Clazomenae 8.14; of Miletus 8.17; 1st treaty with Persia 8.17–18; Astyochus ineffective in Lesbos 8.23; defeated in battle of Miletus 8.25; reinforcing fleet secures Miletus 8.26–8; sack Iasus 8.28, 8.36; (412/1) based in Miletus 8.29, 8.33, 8.36, 8.38–9; 2nd treaty with Persia 8.36–7; fleet for Pharnabazus dispatched to Ionia 8.39 (thence to Hellespont, 411: 8.80); send commissioners to advise Astyochus 8.39, 8.41–3; suspicion of Alcibiades, his death ordered 8.45; appeals from Chios 8.38, 8.40, 8.55, 8.60; sail to Rhodes, secure its secession from Athens 8.44; based in Rhodes 8.44, 8.52, 8.55, 8.60; 3rd treaty with Persia 8.57–8; sail to relieve Chios, return to Miletus on sight of Athenian fleet 8.60; (411) unrest in fleet at Miletus 8.78, 8.83–5; set out for decisive sea-battle, retreat when Athenian fleet reinforced, refuse battle at Miletus 8.79, 8.83; deputations to Sparta denouncing Tissaphernes 8.85, 8.87; reaction to recall of Alcibiades 8.83, 8.87; Mindarus moves fleet from Miletus to Hellespont 8.99–103, 8.108; defeated in battle of Cynossema 8.104–6
—(411) envoys sent by Four Hundred 8.86, 8.89, 8.90–1; send

fleet to aid revolt of Euboea 8.91–2 (raid Aegina, 8.92), 8.94–5; defeat Athenian fleet at Eretria and secure revolt of Euboea 8.95; fail to exploit vulnerability of Athens/Peiraeus 8.96
— invasions of Attica: (their ineffectiveness 1.81, 2.70, 4.85, 5.14, 7.27–8); (465/4) promised to Thasians 1.101; (?457) Persian attempt to bribe Peloponnesians to invade 1.109; (446) invasion under Pleistoanax 1.114, 2.21, 5.16; (432) promised to Potidaeans 1.58, 1.71; (431) 1st invasion of Peloponnesian War 2.10–13, 2.18–23; (430) 2nd invasion 2.47, 2.55–7; (428) 3rd invasion 3.1; allies fail to support planned further invasion 3.13, 3.15; (427) 4th invasion 3.26; invasion of 426 aborted (earthquake) 3.89; (425) 5th invasion 4.2, 4.5–6; (413) 6th invasion, and fortification of Deceleia 7.19
—campaigns: (460–459) Cecryphaleia 1.105; (457) Tanagra 1.107–8; (430) Zacynthus 2.66; (429–427) Plataea, 2.71–8, 3.20–4, 3.52–68; (429) Acarnania 2.80–2; (429/8) Peiraeus (aborted) and Salamis 2.93–4; (427) Mytilene 3.16, 3.26, 3.27, 3.29–33, 3.69; Corcyra 3.69, 3.76–81; (426/5) Naupactus 3.100–2; Amphilochia 3.105–14; (425) Corcyra 4.2–3; Pylos 4.8–16, 4.23, 4.26, 4.29–41; (424) Megara 4.70–4; (424–423) Thraceward region 4.70, 4.74, 4.78–88, 4.102–16, 4.120–9, 4.132, 4.135; (423) Lyncus 4.124–8; (422) Amphipolis 5.6–12; (421) Parrhasia 5.33; (418) Argos, 5.57–60; Mantinea 5.64–75; (417/6) Argos/Hysiae 5.83; (416/5) Argolid 6.7; (414) Argolid 6.105; (413) troops sent to Sicily 7.19, 7.58; (412–411) Chios, Ionia, E. Aegean 8.5–7, 8.10–29, 8.31–3, 8.35–6, 8.38–9, 8.44, 8.60, 8.78–9, 8.83–5; Iasus (412) 8.28, 8.36; (411) Euboea 8.91–2, 8.94–5; Hellespont 8.80, 8.99–103; Cynossema 8.104–6
— Sparta and Argos 5.14, 5.22, 5.27–31, 5.36, 5.41, 5.43, 5.52, 5.57–61, 5.63, 5.65–75, 5.76–81, 5.82–3, 5.116, 6.95
— Sparta and Tissaphernes, and pay for the Peloponnesian fleet (412–411), *see* TISSAPHERNES

Spartolus, in Bottice: (429) Athenian defeat there 2.79; (422/1) provision in Peace of Nicias 5.18

Speiraeum, harbour on E. coast of Peloponnese: (412) Peloponnesian fleet blockaded there by Athenians 8.10–11, 8.14–15, 8.20 (break-out)

Sphacteria, island enclosing harbour at Pylos (*q.v.*) 4.8, 4.14–17, 4.23, 4.26–7, 4.28, 4.29–39, 4.55; (425) Spartan hoplites marooned there 4.14–16, 4.23, 4.26–7; fire on the island 4.30; battle and surrender of Spartans 4.31–9; (422/1) captured Spartans returned under Peace of Nicias 5.24; their treatment at Sparta after return 5.34

Stages, a deputy of Tissaphernes 8.16

Stagirus, in Chalcidice: colony of Andros 4.88, 5.6; (424) secedes from Athens 4.88; (422) unsuccessful attack by Cleon 5.6; (422/1) provision in Peace of Nicias 5.18

Stesagoras, Samian oligarch 1.116

Sthenelaïdas, Spartan ephor, father of Alcamenes (8.5): (432) speech and management of vote at 1st conference at Sparta 1.85–7

Stratonice, sister of Perdiccas, married to Seuthes 2.101

Stratus, largest city in Acarnania: (429) defeats attack by Ambraciots, Peloponnesians, and Chaonians 2.80–2, 2.83, 2.84; 2.102, 3.106

Strepsa, city in Thrace 1.61

Strombichides, son of Diotimus (8.15), Athenian general: (412) commands a fleet in E. Aegean 8.15–17; too late to prevent revolt of Miletus, starts blockade from Lade 8.17; (412/1) in joint command of fleet sent to Samos, detailed against Chios 8.30; (411) recaptures Lampsacus, fails at Abydos, fortifies Sestos 8.62–3; returns from Hellespont to Samos 8.79

Strongyle, one of the Lipara islands 3.88

Strophacus, Thessalian friend of Brasidas 4.78

Strymon, river in Thrace 1.98, 1.100, 2.96, 2.97, 2.99, 2.101, 4.50, 4.102, 4.107, 4.108, 5.7, 7.9

Styphon, third Spartan commander on Sphacteria 4.38

Styra, in Euboea: subject ally, with Athenians in Sicily 7.57

supplication 1.24, 1.103, 1.126, 1.128, 1.133, 1.136–7, 3.28, 3.58–9, 3.66, 3.67, 3.70, 3.75, 3.80–1, 4.98, 5.60, 8.84; Greek law prohibiting killing of suppliants 3.58, 3.66, 3.67

Sybaris, river in Italy 7.35

Sybota (1), islands off Thesprotia 1.47, 1.54; (433) battle of Sybota 1.48–55

Sybota (2), harbour in Thesprotia 1.50, 1.52, 1.54, 3.76

Syce, site of Athenian 'circle' on Epipolae 6.98

Symaethus, river in Sicily 6.65

Syme, E. Aegean island 8.41–3

SYRACUSE: founded by Archias of Corinth 6.3, cf. 6.88; founded Acrae, Casmenae, Camarina 6.5; population 6.3, 6.20, 6.37, 7.28, 7.55, 7.58; tyrants 6.38 (Gelo, 6.4, 6.5, 6.94); Myletidae clan exiled 6.5; democracy 7.55; assemblies 6.32–41, 6.72–3, 7.2, 7.21; party divisions 6.36–40; pro-Athenian elements 7.48–9, 7.73; resources/ finance 6.20, 7.48 (Nicias); special force of 600: 6.96–7, 7.43; festival of Heracles 7.7

—(island of) Ortygia 6.3; Temenites sanctuary 6.75, 6.99; Olympieium 6.64–5, 6.70, 6.75, 7.4, 7.37, 7.42; Little Harbour 7.3, 7.4, 7.22 (dockyard); Great Harbour 6.50, 6.99, 6.101–2, 7.2, 7.4, 7.22–3, 7.36, 7.59; Plemmyrium 7.4, 7.22–4, 7.36, 7.31; Dascon 6.66; Lysimeleia 7.53; Helorum road 6.66, 6.70, 7.80; Epipolae, *q.v.*

—Syracusan character 6.34, 6.38; closest in character to Athenians 8.96; spirit/courage 6.69, 6.72; pride in achievement against Athenians 7.56, 7.66–8; fear of Syracusan domination 6.78, 6.85–7; allies on Syracusan side 3.86 (against Leontini), 7.58 (against Athenians); troops requested/raised in rest of Sicily 7.7, 7.12, 7.21, 7.25, 7.32, 7.46; disorder of Syracusan troops/ships 6.72, 6.97, 6.98, 7.3, 7.23, 7.25

—(427) war with Leontini 3.86; (426/5) Sicels revolt from

subjection 3.103; (425) with Locrians, capture Messana 4.1, 4.24–5; (422) dispossess Leontinians, at war with them 5.4 (cf. 6.6, 6.8, 6.19, 6.86); (416/5) support Selinus against Egesta 6.6
—(415) assembly debates Athenian threat 6.32–41; preparations for war 6.45; Athenians sail into Great Harbour 6.50; (415/4) defeated by Athenians outside Syracuse 6.67–71, 6.79, 6.88, 6.91; assembly accepts structural reforms proposed by Hermocrates 6.72–3; envoys sent to Corinth and Sparta (6.34), 6.73, 6.80, 6.88, 6.93 (again in 414: 7.7, and in 413: 7.25); destroy (empty) Athenian camp at Catana 6.75, cf. 6.88; (414) fail to prevent capture of Epipolae 6.96–7; Athenians destroy counter-walls, defeat Syracusans in pitched battle 6.99–101; despair, approach Nicias, discuss ending the war 6.102–3, 7.2; meet and join with Gylippus' army 7.2–3; defeated by, then defeat Athenians on Epipolae, complete 3rd counter-wall 7.5–6, cf. 7.11 (Nicias); request troops from Corinth and Sparta 7.7, 7.12, 7.17, 7.18
—(413) man fleet of 80 triremes 7.21–2; lose 1st sea-battle, capture forts on Plemmyrium 7.22–4, 7.25, 7.31; reinforcing troops ambushed by Sicels 7.25, 7.32; reinforcements from Camarina and Gela 7.33; refine naval tactics and modify ships 7.36, 7.40–1; 2nd sea-battle, drawn 7.37–8; 3rd sea-battle, won and superiority assumed 7.40–1; dismay at arrival of Athenian reinforcements 7.42, 7.55; defeat Athenians in night-battle on Epipolae 7.43–6; attacks on Athenian wall 7.51–2, 7.54; 4th sea-battle, won 7.52–3; defeated on shore 7.53; block Great Harbour 7.59; 5th and final sea-battle won 7.69–72; measures to block Athenian retreat 7.73–4, 7.78, 7.79, 7.80; surrender of Demosthenes' division 7.80–2; surrender of Nicias' division 7.85; prisoners kept in quarries 7.86–7; execute Nicias and Demosthenes 7.86

—no involvement in war in Greece before 415: 3.86, 6.34; (412–411) Syracusan ships with Peloponnesian fleet in E. Aegean 8.26, 8.28, 8.35, 8.61, 8.78; at battle of Cynossema (411) 8.104–6; Syracusans an independent voice 8.29, 8.45, 8.84, 8.85
—Syracusan navy 4.24–5, 6.20, 6.34, 7.7, 7.12, 7.21–3, 7.36–41, 7.48, 7.51–3, 7.56, 7.70–2, 7.74, 8.2, 8.26; Syracusan cavalry 6.20–2, 6.37, 6.41, 6.52, 6.63–8 (total of 1,200: 6.67), 6.70–1, 6.98, 6.101, 7.4–6, 7.11, 7.13, 7.42, 7.44, 7.55, 7.78, 7.81, 7.84–5

Taenarum, promontory in Laconia: temple of Poseidon 1.128; 'curse of Taenarum' 1.128, 1.133; 7.19
Tamos, a Persian deputy governor of Ionia 8.31, 8.87
Tanagra, in Boeotia: (457) battle of Tanagra 1.107–8; walls demolished by Athenians 1.108; (426) defeated by Athenians 3.91; 4.76; (424/3) Boeotian base for battle of Delium 4.91, 4.97; Tanagraeans in battle of Delium 4.93; (413) raided by Thracian mercenaries under Diitrephes 7.29
Tantalus, Spartan governor of Thyrea 4.57
Taras, Greek city in S. Italy: (415) sympathetic to Syracusans 6.34, refuse access to Athenians 6.44; (414) Gylippus at Taras 6.104, 7.1; (411) ships in Peloponnesian fleet 8.91
Taulantians, barbarian people bordering Epidamnus 1.24
Tegea, city in Arcadia: disputes with Mantinea 4.134, 5.65; (430) Tegean ambassador to Persia executed by Athenians 2.67; (421) refuse to join Argive alliance against Sparta 5.32, 5.40 (cf. 5.62, 5.64); (418) in Peloponnesian expedition against Argos 5.57; Argive alliance prepares expedition against Tegea 5.62; ready to secede to Argive alliance, Spartans intervene 5.64; at battle of Mantinea 5.67, 5.71, 5.73; 5.74–6, 5.78, 5.82
Teichioussa, in Milesian territory 8.26, 8.28

Teichium, town in Aetolia 3.96

Teisamenus, Trachinian envoy
to Sparta (426) 3.92

Teisandrus, Aetolian envoy 3.100

Teisias, Athenian general at Melos
(416) 5.84

Tellias, Syracusan general: elected
(414) 6.103

Tellis, father of Brasidas (2.25 etc.):
(422/1) signatory of Peace of Nicias
and alliance 5.19, 5.24

Temenids, from Argos, ancestors of
Macedonian kings 2.99

Temenites, sanctuary outside
Syracuse 6.75, 6.99, 6.100

Temenitis, spur of Epipolae 7.3

Tenedos, NE Aegean island: Boeotian
colony, subject ally of Athens, with
Athenians in Sicily 7.57; (428) warn
Athenians of Lesbian revolt 3.2; (427)
Mytilenaean conspirators deposited in
Tenedos 3.28, 3.35

Tenos, Aegean island: subject ally of
Athens, with Athenians in Sicily 7.57;
(411) some Tenians support Four
Hundred 8.69 (cf. 8.65)

Teos, city in Ionia: 3.32; (412) secedes
from Athens 8.16; wall built by
Athenians demolished 8.16, 8.20;
refuge for Chian ships 8.19; agrees
equal access
for Athenians 8.20

Teres, father of Sitalces, king of
Odrysians 2.29

Tereus, legendary king of Daulia,
husband of Procne 2.29

Terias, river in Sicily 6.50, 6.94

Terina, gulf in S. Italy 6.104

Teutiaplus, Peloponnesian commander
from Elis 3.29–30

Teutloussa, small island S. of Syme 8.42

Thapsus, city in Sicily: founded from
Megara 6.4; (414) Athenian ships
anchored there 6.97, 6.99, sail from
there into Great Harbour 6.101–2;
(413) Demosthenes advocates moving
from Syracuse to Thapsus or
Catana 7.49

Tharyps, king of Molossians 2.80

Thasos, N. Aegean island: Parian
colony 4.104; colonized Galepsus
and Oesyme 4.107, 5.6;
(465/4–463/2) revolt, siege, and
capitulation to Athenians 1.100–1;

(424/3) Thucydides (1) at Thasos
4.104–5; (411) democracy put
down by Diitrephes 8.64

Theaenetus, seer, leader of Plataean
escape (428/7) 3.20

Theagenes, tyrant of Megara 1.126

THEBES, city in Boeotia: during
Persian War, government by
clique 3.62, medism 3.56, 3.62, 3.64–5,
Thebes a Persian base 1.90; (435)
help Corinth against Corcyra 1.27
—and Plataea 2.2–6, 2.71–2, 3.22,
3.54–68, 5.17, 7.18; (431) Theban
entry into Plataea and defeat 2.2–6,
2.19, 3.56, 3.65–6, 7.18; (427) speech
to Spartan judges at Plataea 3.61–7;
Spartan assault on Plataea to please the
Thebans 3.56–8, 3.68
—(426) support Tanagra against
Athenians 3.91; (424/3) Theban
troops at battle of Delium 4.93,
4.96; (423) demolish walls of
Thespiae 4.133; (422/1) object to
return of Plataea under Peace of
Nicias 5.17, cf. 3.52; (414) suppress
popular uprising in Thespiae
6.95; (413) send troops to Syracuse
7.19; come to rescue of
Mycalessus 7.30

THEMISTOCLES 1.90–3, 1.135–8;
persuades Athenians to build
ships 1.14, 1.93; (493/2) starts
fortification of Peiraeus 1.93; commands at battle of Salamis (480) 1.74,
honoured in Sparta 1.74, 1.91; (479/8)
rebuilds walls of Athens 1.90–3; in
Sparta 1.90–2; (c.470) ostracized,
living in Argos 1.135, 1.137; implicated in intrigues with Persia 1.135,
escapes arrest and flees to Persia
1.136–8; status as benefactor of
Corcyra 1.138; influence at Persian
court, governor of Magnesia, memorial
there 1.138; death and burial
1.138; Thucydides'
assessment of him 1.138

Theogenes, Athenian diplomat 4.27;
(422/1) signatory of Peace of Nicias
and alliance 5.19, 5.24

Theori, magistrates at Mantinea 5.47

Thera, Aegean island,
independent of Athens 2.9

Theramenes, son of Hagnon (8.68 etc.):
(411) a leader of the oligarchic

revolution at Athens 8.68; leader of moderate oligarchs opposed to extremists 8.89–92; suspects purpose of Eëtioneia and encourages demolition 8.90–2, 8.94

Therimenes, Spartan commander: (412/1) conveys reinforcing fleets to Astyochus 8.26, 8.29, 8.31; at conclusion of 2nd treaty between Sparta and Persia 8.36, 8.43, 8.52; lost at sea 8.38

Therme, in Macedonia 1.61, 2.29

Thermon, Spartan commander, sent to Speiraeum (412) 8.11

Thermopylae 2.101, 3.92; battle of Thermopylae (480) 4.36

Theseus, legendary king of Attica 2.15; sanctuary of Theseus (Theseium) in Athens 6.61

Thesmophylaces, magistrates at Elis 5.47

Thespiae, city in Boeotia: 4.76; (424/3) in battle of Delium, severe losses 4.93, 4.96, 4.133; (423) walls demolished by Thebans 4.133; (414) popular uprising suppressed by Thebans 6.95; (413) send troops to Sicily 7.19, 7.25

Thesprotia, in NW Greece 1.30, 1.46, 1.50, 2.80

Thessalus, son of Peisistratus (1) 1.20, 6.55

THESSALY: fertile 1.2; drove Boeotians out of Arne 1.12; political system 4.78; difficulty of transit 4.78, 4.108, 4.132, 5.13; Thessalian cavalry 1.107, 1.111, 2.22; largely friendly to Athens 4.78; (c.461) alliance with Athens and Argos 1.102, 1.107, 2.22; (457) Thessalian cavalry desert Athenians at Tanagra 1.107; (431) support Athens with cavalry 2.22; (429/8) fear of Thracian army 2.101; (426) opposition to colony of Heracleia (1) 3.93, 5.51; (424) Brasidas in and through Thessaly 4.78; (423) block reinforcing Spartan army 4.132; (422/1) refuse passage to Spartan army beyond Pierium 5.13; (413/2) protest at Agis' pressure on Achaea Phthiotis 8.3

Thoricus, on E. coast of Attica 8.95

THRACE: markets and mines 1.100–1, 4.105; Pausanias (1) touring Thrace 1.130; Heracleia (1) on route

to Thrace 3.92 (cf. 4.78); Sitalces king of Thrace 2.29, 2.67, 2.95–101; succeeded by Seuthes 4.101; (465/4) destroyed Athenian forces at Drabescus 1.100, 4.102; (429/8) Thracians levied by Sitalces for invasion of Macedonia 2.96; general fear of Thracian army 2.101; (414) join Athenians and Perdiccas in attack on Amphipolis 7.9
—Bithynian Thracians 4.75; Dians 2.96, 2.98, 7.27, 7.29–30; Thracian mercenaries 2.96, 4.129, 5.6, 7.27, 7.29–30; Thracian cavalry 2.29, 2.98

THRACEWARD region: tribute-paying region of Athenian empire 2.9; 1.56–60, 1.68 (Potidaea the key), 2.67; (432 on) in revolt from Athens 1.58–9, 2.29, 2.38, 2.79, 4.79–81, 4.84–8, 4.103–16, 5.12, 6.10; (425) Athenians driven out of Eïon (2) 4.7; (423) Athenian campaigns against Scione and Mende 4.122–3, 4.129–33; (422) against Torone 5.2–3, and Amphipolis 5.6–12; (422/1) refuse compliance with Peace of Nicias 5.21, 5.35; (421) Spartan troops withdrawn after Peace 5.34–5; (411) Diitrephes appointed to Athenian command in region 8.64

see also CHALCIDIANS

Thrasyboulus, Athenian trierarch: (411) with Thrasyllus, leader of counter-revolution against oligarchy in Samos 8.73, 8.75; elected general by Athenians in Samos 8.76; persuades assembly at Samos to recall Alcibiades 8.81; joins Thrasyllus in attack on Eresus 8.100, 8.103; at battle of Cynossema 8.104–5

Thrasycles, Athenian general: (422/1) signatory of Peace of Nicias and alliance 5.19, 5.24; (412) commands a fleet in E. Aegean 8.15, 8.17, 8.19

Thrasyllus, Athenian: (411) with Thrasyboulus, leader of counter-revolution against oligarchy in Samos 8.73, 8.75; elected general by Athenians in Samos 8.76; sails to Hellespont, failing to anticipate Mindarus' fleet 8.100–3; joined by Thrasyboulus in attack on Eresus

8.100, 8.103; at battle of
Cynossema 8.104–5
Thrasylus, Argive general 5.59, 5.60
(punished for agreeing
truce with Peloponnesians, 418)
Thrasymelidas, Spartan admiral at
Pylos 4.11
Thria/Thriasian plain,
in Attica 1.114, 2.19–21
Thronium, in Opuntian Locris 2.26
Thucles (1), father of
Eurymedon; 3.80 etc.
Thucles (2), leader of colonists to
Sicily from Chalcis 6.3
THUCYDIDES (1), son of Olorus
(4.104), Athenian general and
historian: goldmining rights, and
influence, in Thrace 4.105; caught
plague 2.48; (424/3) in Thasos, too
late to save Amphipolis from Brasidas,
but secures Eïon (1) 4.104–7; exiled
for 20 years 5.26
—as historian: method 1.1, 1.20–2,
2.48, 5.26, 5.68, 6.2, 6.55, 8.87;
chronology 1.97, 2.1, 2.2, 5.20,
5.26; exposure of false beliefs/
inadequate history 1.20, 1.21, 1.97,
6.54–9; use of Homer 1.3, 1.5,
1.9–10, 3.104; rationalistic explanations of natural phenomena 2.28,
3.89; 'second preface' 5.26
—assessments of/verdicts on:
Alcibiades 6.15, 8.48, 8.86;
Antiphon 8.68; Brasidas 4.81;
Cleon 3.36; government of Five
Thousand 8.97; Hermocrates 6.72;
Nicias 7.86; Pericles 2.65, 1.127,
1.139; Phrynichus 8.27; Sicilian
disaster 2.65, 7.87; Themistocles
1.138; Tissaphernes 8.87
Thucydides (2), Athenian general 1.117
Thucydides (3), consular representative
for Athens in Pharsalus: (411) helps
restore calm in Athens 8.92
Thuria, district of Messenia 1.101
Thurii, city in Italy: (415) Alcibiades
escapes escort at Thurii 6.61,
6.88; (414) dismissive of Gylippus 6.104; (413) anti-Athenian party
expelled 7.33; alliance with Athens
and troops provided 7.33, 7.35,
7.57; (412–411) Thurian ships in
Spartan service 8.35, 8.61, 8.84

Thyamis, river on border of
Thesprotia 1.46
Thyamus, mountain in Agraeis 3.106
Thymochares, Athenian general 8.95
Thyrea, in Cynouria (5.41): (431) offered
by Spartans as home for expelled
Aeginetans 2.27, 4.56–7; (424)
captured by Athenians 4.57; (414)
invaded by Argives 6.95
Thyssus, city on Acte peninsula
(Chalcidice) 4.109; (421)
Athenian ally, captured by
people of Dium (2) 5.35
Tilataeans, Thracian tribe 2.96
Timagoras (1), Tegean ambassador
to Persia, executed by Athenians
(430) 2.67
Timagoras (2), Cyzicene exile, agent of
Pharnabazus 8.6, 8.8, 8.39
Timanor, Corinthian commander 1.29
Timocrates (1), Spartan commissioner
sent to advise Cnemus (429) 2.85,
2.92 (suicide)
Timocrates (2), father of Timoxenus 2.33
Timocrates (3), father of Aristoteles 3.105
Timocrates (4), Athenian signatory
of peace of Nicias and alliance
(422/1) 5.19, 5.24
Timoxenus, Corinthian commander 2.33
TISSAPHERNES, Persian satrap:
appointed 'military governor of the
west' 8.5; (413/2) joins Chians in
request for Spartan help 8.5–6;
supported by Alcibiades 8.6;
instructed by King to deal with
Amorges 8.5, 8.28; (412) demolishes
landward wall at Teos 8.16,
8.20; negotiates 1st treaty between
Sparta and Persia 8.17–18, 8.36,
8.43; at battle of Miletus 8.25,
8.26; persuades Peloponnesians to
attack Iasus 8.28; (412/1) influences
revolt of Cnidus 8.35; 2nd treaty
between Sparta and Persia 8.36–7,
8.43, 8.52; meets Spartan
commissioners at Cnidus, leaves in
rage 8.43, 8.52; advised by
Alcibiades 8.45–7, 8.56; informed
of Phrynichus' letter to Astyochus
8.50; courted by Alcibiades for
alliance with Athenians 8.52;
negotiations with Peisander's
delegation fail 8.56; 3rd treaty

between Sparta and Persia 8.57–8;
promises Phoenician fleet 8.46,
('the King's fleet' in 8.58), 8.59,
8.78, 8.81, **8.87**, 8.88, 8.99,
8.109; (**411**) increasing disaffection
of Peloponnesians 8.78, 8.80, 8.83,
8.85; his fort in Miletus captured by
Milesians 8.84–5; sends Gaulites to
Sparta to represent him against
charges 8.85, cf. 8.87; motives in
not bringing up Phoenician fleet
8.87; Mindarus warned of his
duplicity 8.99; goes to meet
Peloponnesians at Hellespont for
complaint and exculpation 8.109;
sacrifices to Artemis at Ephesus 8.109
—rivalry with Pharnabazus 8.6, 8.8,
8.99, 8.109
—and Spartans/Peloponnesians
8.5–6, 8.28, 8.43 (cf. 8.52), 8.57, 8.58,
8.78, 8.83–5, 8.87–8, 8.99, 8.109
—and Alcibiades 8.6, 8.26, 8.45–7,
8.52, 8.56, 8.65, 8.81, 8.82, 8.85, 8.88
—pay for Peloponnesian fleet (412–
411): 8.5, 8.29, 8.36, 8.43–5, 8.50, 8.53,
8.57–8, 8.78, 8.80, 8.83, 8.85, 8.87, 8.99
—Athenian hopes of alliance with
Tissaphernes 8.47–8, 8.53–4, 8.56,
8.65, 8.76, 8.81, 8.88, 8.108
Tlepolemus, Athenian general 1.117
Tolmides, Athenian general 1.108, 1.113
Tolophon, in Ozolian Locris 3.101
Tolophus, Aetolian envoy 3.100
Tomeus, near Pylos 4.118
Torone, in Chalcidice: Still Harbour
5.2; temple of Dioscuri 4.110;
(424/3) captured by Brasidas
4.110–16; 4.120, 4.122, 4.129; (423)
Pasitelidas appointed Spartan
governor 4.132; (422) recaptured by
Cleon 5.2–3; (422/1) provision in
Peace of Nicias 5.18
Torymbas, Thessalian friend of
Brasidas 4.78
Trachis, region of Malis (3.92): (426)
Spartans found colony of Heracleia
(1) 3.92; 3.100, 4.78, 5.12, 5.51
trade 1.2, 1.7, 1.13, 1.37, 1.120, 2.38,
2.67, 3.74, 6.2, 6.31, 6.44, 7.13, 7.24,
7.50; merchant shipping 1.137, 2.67,
2.69, 3.3, 4.53, 6.44, 6.88, 8.35
Tragia, island off Samos 1.116
'Treasurers to the Greeks' 1.96

Treres, Thracian tribe 2.96
Triballians, Thracian tribe 2.96, 4.101
tribute paid to Athens 1.19, 1.56,
1.80, **1.96**, 1.99, 1.121, 2.13, 6.85,
6.91, **7.28**, 7.57; ships in place
of tribute 1.19, 6.85, 7.57;
tribute-paying regions 2.9;
tribute-paying subjects/independent
allies 6.85, 7.57: Persian
tribute 8.5–6; *see also* finance
trierarchs 2.24, **6.31**, 7.13, 7.24, 7.38,
7.69, 7.70, 8.45, 8.47, 8.73, 8.76
Trinacria, original name of Sicily 6.2
Triopium, promontory of Cnidian
peninsula, sanctuary of
Apollo 8.35, 8.60
Tripodiscus, village in Megarid 4.70
triremes: first built in Corinth 1.13;
increased use 1.14; Athenian
numbers at start of war 2.13;
Athenian state triremes 3.33, 3.77, 6.53,
6.61, 8.73–4, 8.86; speed 3.49
(2nd trireme to Mytilene), 8.101
(Mindarus from Chios to
Hellespont); portage 3.15, 3.81,
4.8; towed on ropes, 4.25;
marines on board 3.95, 6.21,
6.43, 7.1, 7.62, 7.70, 8.24;
mainsails, etc. stored when not
required 7.24, 8.28, 8.43
—the equipment of a sailor
2.93; sailors' pay 6.31, 8.45; petty
officers 6.31; coxswains 7.70;
upper-bench oarsmen 6.31;
lowest-tier oarsmen 4.32; need for
crews to train together 8.95;
outriggers 4.12, 7.34, 7.40;
catheads 7.34, 7.36, 7.62; modifications 7.34, 7.36, 7.40, 7.62, 7.65
—tactics: Athenian 2.84, 2.89,
3.77–8, **7.36**, 7.49, 7.62–3; Corinthian
7.34; Syracusan 7.36, 7.40–1
see also trierarchs
Tritaea, in Ozolian Locris 3.101
Troad, region of NW Asia Minor 1.131
Troezen, city in E. Peloponnese:
(446/5) returned to Peloponnesians
under Thirty Years Treaty 1.115,
4.21; (435) helps Corinth against
Corcyra 1.27; (430) ravaged by
Athenians 2.56; (425) raided from
fort at Methana 4.45; (423)
provision in one-year truce 4.118;

(413/2) required to build ships for
Peloponnesian League 8.3
Trogilus, inlet N. of Syracuse 6.99, 7.2
Trotilum, in Sicily 6.4
Troy/Trojan War 1.3, 1.8–12, 2.68,
4.120, 6.2; Trojans settled in
Sicily 6.2
tsunamis 3.89
Twelve Gods, altar in Athenian
agora 6.54
Tydeus, Chian, executed as
pro-Athenian agent (412/1) 8.38
Tyndareus, father of Helen 1.9
tyrants 1.17–18; Athenian tyrants:
Peisistratus 1.20, 3.104, 6.53–5,
Hippias 1.20, 6.54–9; deposed by
Spartans 1.18, 6.53, 6.59, 8.68;
Cylon's attempt at Athens 1.126;
Sicilian tyrants: 1.14, 1.17–18, 6.4–5,
6.38 (Gelo of Syracuse 6.4, 6.5,
Hippocrates of Gela 6.5); Anaxilas of
Rhegium 6.4; Evarchus of
Astacus 2.30, 2.33; Hippoclus of
Lampsacus 6.59; Polycrates of
Samos 1.13, 3.104; Theagenes of
Megara 1.126
—Athens the 'tyrant city' 1.122,
1.124, 2.63, 3.37, 6.85
Tyrrhenian Sea/Gulf 4.24, 6.62, 7.58

volcanoes 3.88, 3.116

weather: rain 2.5, 8.42; thunderstorm
and rain 6.70, 7.79; rain, wind, snow
assist Plataean escape (428/7)
3.22–3; snow 4.103; rigour of
winter in Potidaea 2.70; flash
flood 4.75; wind 2.84, 2.85,
8.31; storms at sea 2.25, 3.69, 4.3–4,
6.104, 8.31, 8.32, 8.34, 8.80, 8.99
White Castle, part of Memphis 1.104

Xanthippus, father of Pericles: 1.111 etc.
Xenares, Spartan ephor: (421) opposed

to peace treaty 5.36–8, 5.46; (420/19)
governor of Heracleia (1), killed in
local battle 5.51
Xenocleides, Corinthian
commander 1.46, 3.114
Xenon, Theban commander of Boeotians
sent to Sicily (413) 7.19
Xenophantidas, Laconian sent by
Pedaritus to Rhodes (412/1) 8.55
Xenophon, Athenian general 2.70, 2.79
Xerxes, King of Persia (486–465), father
of Artaxerxes: 1.14, 1.69, 1.73, 1.74,
1.118, 3.56, 4.50; and Pausanias
(1) 1.128–9; and Themistocles
1.137; canal dug across Acte
peninsula 4.109

Zacynthus, W. Greek island: colonized
from Achaea 2.66; independent ally
of Athens 2.9, 2.66, 3.94–5, 7.31,
7.57; (433) help Corcyra against
Corinthians 1.47; (431) envoys from
Athens at start of war 2.7; (430) failed
Peloponnesian attempt to win
Zacynthus 2.66; 2.80, 4.8, 4.13
Zancle, city in Sicily, later named
Messana (*q.v.*): foundation and early
history 6.4; colonized Himera 6.5
Zeus, god: Zeus of Ithome 1.103; god
of freedom, sacrificed to by Pausanias
(1) 2.71; festival of Zeus the Kindly at
Athens (Diasia) 1.126; 'greatest
festival of Zeus' in oracle to
Cylon 1.126; 'demigod son of Zeus'
(=Heracles) in suborned oracle 5.16
—temples/sanctuaries: Olympian
Zeus at Athens 2.15; Corcyra 3.70;
Nemean Zeus in Ozolian
Locris 3.96; Mt Lycaeum 5.16;
Mantinea 5.47; Olympia 3.14, 5.31,
5.50; Olympieium at Syracuse
6.64–5, 6.70, 6.75; Dios Hieron 8.19
Zeuxidamus, father of
Archidamus: 2.29 etc.

MAPS

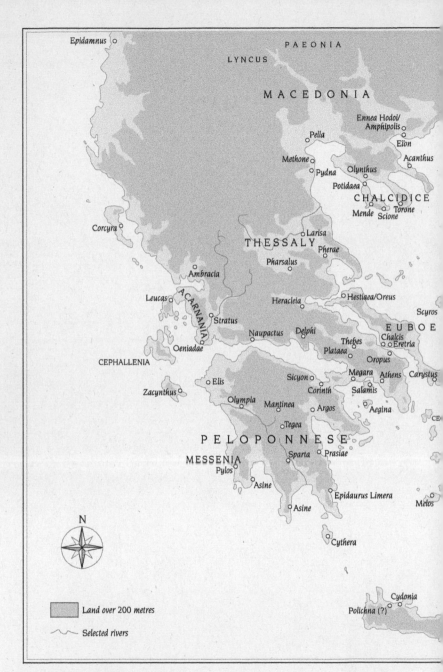

MAP I **Greece and the Aegean**

THRACE

Black Sea

Abdera
Thasos

Byzantium
Calchedon

Propontis

Imbros
CHERSONESE
Sestos Lampsacus
Abydos
Cyzicus

LEMNOS
Sigeium
Dascylium

Tenedos
AEOLIS
Antandrus
Atramyttium

Methymna

Eresus
Mytilene
LESBOS

egean

Sea

Cyme
Phocaea

Chios
Clazomenae
Sardis
Erythrae
Teos Colophon
Andros
Ephesus
IONIA
Magnesia

Samos Priene
Miletus

Delos
Naxos
Iasus
CARIA

Cos
Halicarnassus
Caunus
Cnidus

Thera

RHODES

CRETE

Gortyn

0   100   200 km
0   50   100 miles

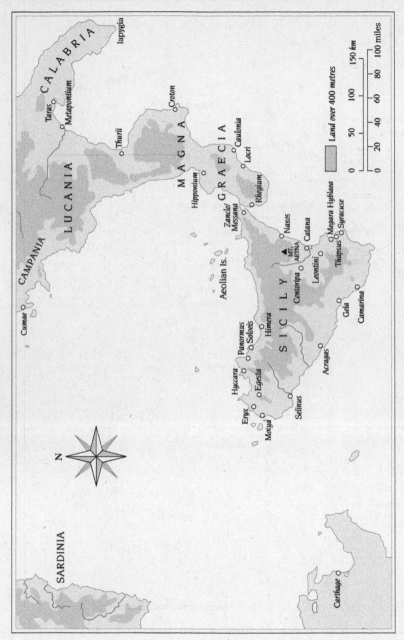

MAP 2 Carthage, Sicily, Southern Italy

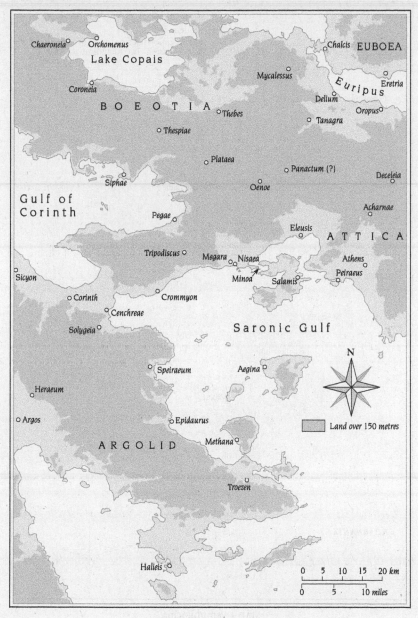

MAP 3 The Isthmus region

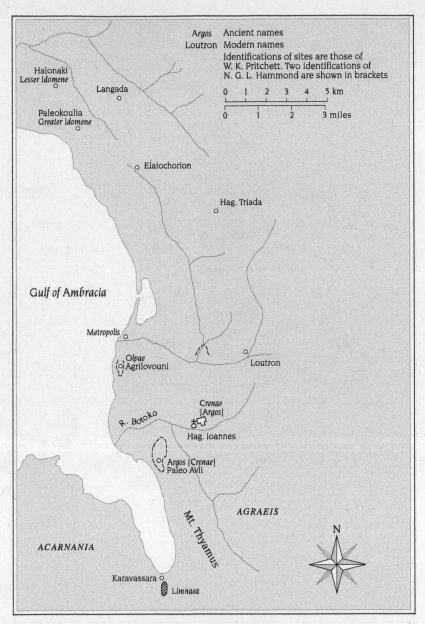

Argos   Ancient names
Loutron Modern names

Identifications of sites are those of
W. K. Pritchett. Two identifications of
N. G. L. Hammond are shown in brackets

0   1   2   3   4   5 km

0   1   2   3 miles

Halonaki
Lesser Idomene

Langada

Paleokoulia
Greater Idomene

Elaiochorion

Hag. Triada

Gulf of Ambracia

Metropolis

Olpae
Agrilovouni

Loutron

Crenae
[Argos]

R. Botoko

Hag. Ioannes

Argos [Crenae]
Paleo Avli

Mt. Thyamus

AGRAEIS

N

ACARNANIA

Karavassara

Limnaea

MAP 4 Amphilochia
(after Rhodes, *Thucydides, History, III* (Aris & Phillips, now Oxbow, 1994))

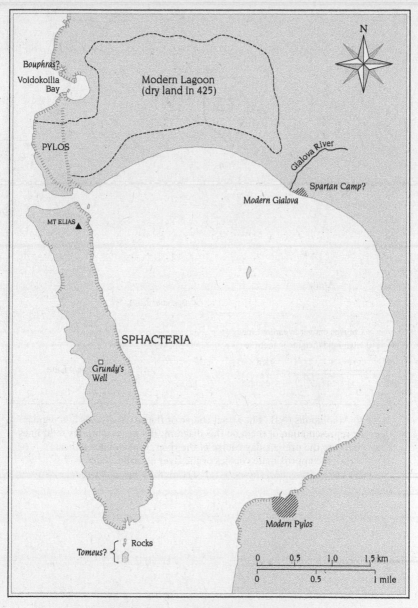

MAP 5 Pylos
(after Rhodes, *Thucydides, History, IV.I–V. 24* (Aris & Phillips, now Oxbow, 1998))

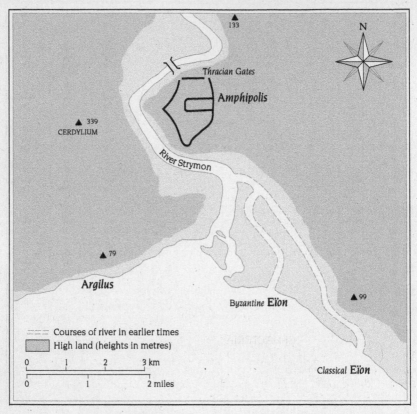

MAP 6 Amphipolis (NB. The actual course of the city walls was less regular than the representation of them on this diagram. Below Amphipolis solid lines indicate the present-day course of the river, broken lines indicate the approximate courses of the river at earlier dates.)

(after Rhodes, *Thucydides, History IV.I–V. 24* (Aris & Phillips, now Oxbow, 1998))

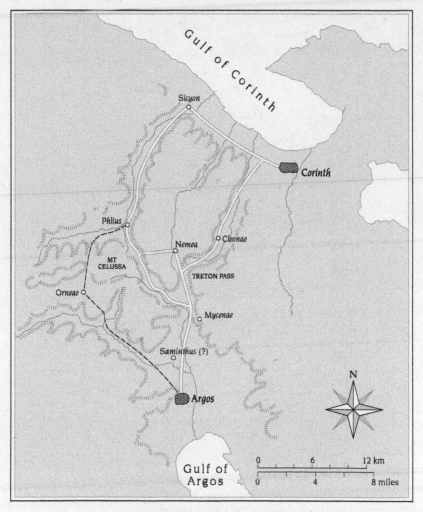

MAP 7 The vicinity of Argos
(after Rhodes, *A History of the Classical Greek World, 478–323 BC* (Blackwell, 2006) and
B. W. Henderson, *The Great War Between Athens and Sparta* (Macmillan, 1927))

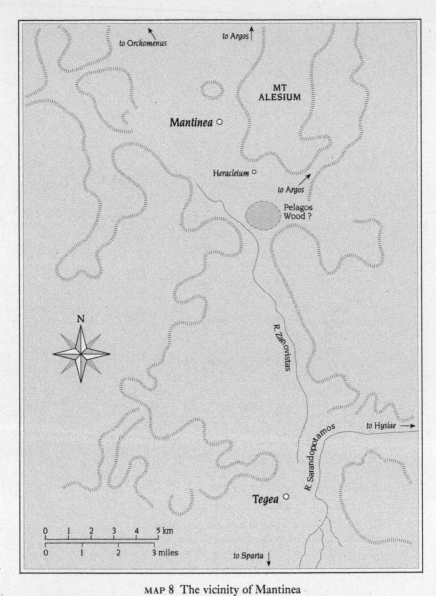

MAP 8 The vicinity of Mantinea
(after Rhodes, *A History of the Classical Greek World, 478–323 BC* (Blackwell, 2006) and
J. F. Lazenby, *The Peloponnesian War* (Routledge, 2004))

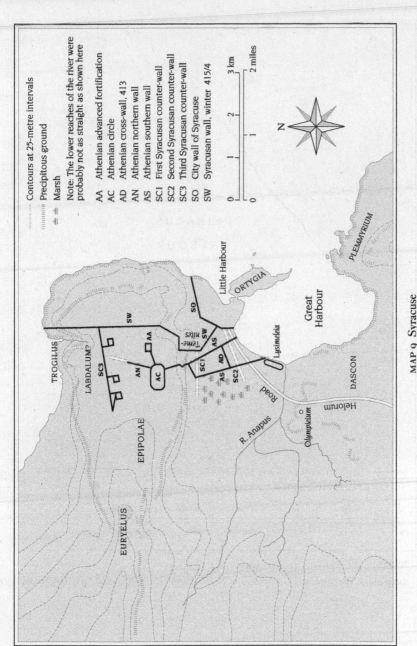

Contours at 25-metre intervals

Precipitous ground

Marsh

Note: The lower reaches of the river were
probably not as straight as shown here

AA   Athenian advanced fortification
AC   Athenian circle
AD   Athenian cross-wall, 413
AN   Athenian northern wall
AS   Athenian southern wall
SC1 First Syracusan counter-wall
SC2 Second Syracusan counter-wall
SC3 Third Syracusan counter-wall
SO   City wall of Syracuse
SW   Syracusan wall, winter 415/4

N

| 0 | 1 | 2 | 3 km |
| 0 | 1 | 2 miles |

TROGILUS

LABDALUM?

SW

SC3

AA

AN

AC

EPIPOLAE

EURYELUS

R. Anapus

Olympieium

Helorum Road

Lysimeleia

DASCON

SC1

AD

AS

SC2

Teme-
nites

SW

AS

SO

Little Harbour

ORTYGIA

Great
Harbour

PLEMMYRIUM

MAP 9 Syracuse

(after Rhodes, *A History of the Classical Greek World, 478–323 BC* (Blackwell, 2006) and K. J. Dover, *Thucydides Book VII* (OUP, 1965))

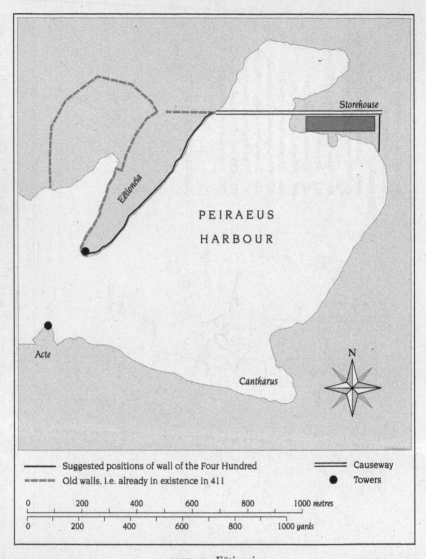

Storehouse

Eëtioneia

PEIRAEUS

HARBOUR

N

Acte

Cantharus

———— Suggested positions of wall of the Four Hundred
▬ ▬ ▬ Old walls, i.e. already in existence in 411

════ Causeway
● Towers

| 0 | 200 | 400 | 600 | 800 | 1000 *metres* |
| 0 | 200 | 400 | 600 | 800 | 1000 *yards* |

MAP 10 Eëtioneia
(after Simon Hornblower, *A Commentary on Thucydides*, vol. iii: *Books 5.25–8.109* (OUP, 2008))